Morality Matters

Race, Class, and Gender in Applied Ethics

Jeffrey R. Di Leo

University of Illinois, at Chicago

Boston   Burr Ridge, IL   Dubuque, IA   Madison, WI   New York
San Francisco   St. Louis   Bangkok   Bogotá   Caracas   Kuala Lumpur
Lisbon   London   Madrid   Mexico City   Milan   Montreal   New Delhi
Santiago   Seoul   Singapore   Sydney   Taipei   Toronto

McGraw-Hill Higher Education

*A Division of The **McGraw-Hill** Companies*

Library of Congress Cataloging-in-Publication Data
Morality matters : race, class, and gender in applied ethics / [edited by] Jeffrey R. Di Leo.
   p. cm.
  Includes bibliographical references and index.
  ISBN 0-7674-1236-2
  1. Applied ethics. I. Di Leo, Jeffrey R.
BJ1031 M667 2001
170—dc21   2001044899

1 2 3 4 5 6 7 8 9 0 DOC/DOC 0 9 8 7 6 5 4 3 2 1

Publisher, Kenneth King; production, Publishing Support Services; manuscript editor, Tom Briggs; design manager, Jean Mailander; text and cover designer, Linda Robertson; manufacturing manager, Randy Hurst. Cover image: Art Resource/ © Romare Beardon Foundation/Licensed by VAGA, New York, NY. The text was set in 9.5/11 New Baskerville by Carlisle Communications and printed on 45# Scholarly Matte by Quebecor/Fairfield.

mhhe.com

Brief Contents

Contents

◈ 2   Relativism and Human Rights   96

◈ 3   Abortion and Euthanasia   149

◈ 4   Punishment and the Death Penalty   220

◈ 5   Sexuality and Marriage   265

◈ 6   Racism and Affirmative Action   326

◈ 9   Poverty and Distributive Justice   513

◈ 10   Animal Rights and Environmental Ethics   587

Preface

ABOUT THIS BOOK

Over the past quarter-century, applied ethics not only has expanded its role in the philosophy curriculum but also has come to include a diverse range of new issues and approaches. Increased demand for courses on emerging topics such as business ethics, engineering ethics, environmental ethics, biomedical ethics, computer ethics, and legal ethics has been accompanied by a growing interest in exploring moral problems through a wider range of models and concepts. The shift from applied ethics courses primarily centered around teleological and deontological frameworks of moral evaluation to a broader mix of approaches is attributable to a number of factors. Among them is a growing dissatisfaction with using "views from nowhere" in the applied ethics classroom.

Today philosophers are much more concerned with the cultural and social situatedness of moral problems and are exploring ways to make their ethics courses reflect this change. Furthermore, there is greater consensus that theory and practice are interrelated. A growing number of philosophers believe that, while there is much to be learned by studying moral theory as something that is applied to "moral problems," it is also valuable to show students how moral problems are connected to the theoretical perspectives that one assumes. For example, because deontological frameworks tend to view gender as irrelevant to moral inquiry, problems associated with gender, such as the feminization of poverty, tend not to be identified as *moral* problems by deontologists. It has been argued that there are no moral problems unless there is a moral theory that identifies them, and vice versa.

Therefore, it is important to discuss with our students not only the strengths and weaknesses of the teleological and deontological frameworks of moral evaluation, but also the ways in which these moral theories have been challenged by alternative approaches. In some instances, as in the case of virtue theory, the emerging perspectives are merely updated versions of established moral traditions. However, these alternative approaches often call for us to evaluate moral problems in terms of underemphasized or neglected philosophical frameworks such as race, class, and gender.

To be sure, we are only beginning to understand how these emerging traditions will impact the history of moral philosophy. However, the major role that these emerging traditions play in contemporary moral philosophy is undeniable, both as theoretical challenges to traditional moral theories and as frameworks through which contemporary philosophers analyze current moral problems. As teachers, we aim to present the moral tradition and its critics as taking part in a *dialogue*—a dialogue that concerns not only the nature and consequences of our actions and moral deliberations, but also the issue of why and how morality matters to each of us. This textbook has been designed with these ideas in mind, striving for a balanced selection of readings from both the moral tradition and its challengers. In addition, the introductions and discussion questions for these readings are designed to facilitate a dialogue about the theories and to draw out their relevance to our students' moral lives.

The materials in this anthology include a number of literature and film summaries, as well as excerpts from court cases and descriptions of current events. These materials are included not only for their intrinsic merits as examples of moral arguments but also for the enjoyment they provide students in analyzing and discussing morality. Such materials are often more familiar to students and thus are less intimidating. Introducing a contemporary moral issue or a classical moral theory through a film, for example, can draw students into a dialogue on topics that may be difficult to discuss or inaccessible through abstract readings.

Stories, films, and the like are not without philosophical merit, for they play a significant role in the shaping of our moral framework. We use them as a basis for telling ourselves who we are and what we are doing, and as such, these works play a vital role in our moral understanding and education. Aside from the aforementioned considerations, these materials are presented in the belief that they can challenge, extend, and engage our moral understanding and imagination, as well as our capacities for practical judgment. They provide us with common ground with which to see and discuss morality in practice and to recognize the difference it makes in our own life and in the lives of other people.

This textbook contains ample materials to develop courses specifically suited to the needs of diverse student populations and differing instructional beliefs. For example, you might use this anthology to emphasize moral theory over moral problems by spending more time with the first two chapters. Or you can take the opposite approach, placing more emphasis on the moral problems in the later chapters to the exclusion of the moral theory at the beginning of the anthology. You may choose to use the films and stories as the starting point for discussing moral philosophy. There are also sufficient materials on feminism, race, and class to use these as the primary focus of the course. This textbook was designed to accommodate a number of instructional strategies without sacrificing philosophical rigor.

ON USING FILMS

While the summaries of the literature and the films are sufficient to foster class discussion, it is advisable that the students turn to the primary sources whenever possible. The literature summaries aim to capture the moral point of the story, thereby allowing your students to participate immediately in class discussions on the relevant moral issues. This also holds true for the films: while it would be ideal for the students to have seen the film before engaging in a class discussion of it, this is often not possible or feasible. Summaries allow for easy access to relevant discussion material.

Introducing films into your classroom has a number of benefits and drawbacks that you will need to take into account when designing your course. Most students enjoy watching films and sharing their views on what they have seen. However, some students regard films as little more than entertainment. Fortunately, convincing students of the relevance of films to morality matters is not very difficult. Films and fiction are a familiar way in which students have participated in moral thinking and will continue to be a major source of moral education for most of them beyond the classroom.

Modern culture has a number of important sites of moral deliberation that often go unnoticed by the average student. As ethics instructors, we can help our students to locate these potential sources of moral deliberation and encourage them to enter into personal dialogue with them. Literature, films, current events, and court cases often concern important moral issues. By identifying how morality matters are a constant part of our everyday lives, in activities that we generally enjoy, such as watching films, we can help our students to become more observant and reflective persons. Nevertheless, even if we assume that films can make an important contribution to our applied ethics courses, incorporating them into a teaching schedule is sometimes difficult.

While the film summaries provided in this book are adequate to capture the general shape of the moral controversies in the films, they are no substitute for viewing the film itself. However, an instructor who chooses to show all of the films summarized in this book during class will have little time left for lecture and discussion. Still, there are a number of good alternatives for incorporating film into your course without sacrificing class time to film viewings.

One option is to simply use the film summaries as the bases for class discussion. You might ask students to try to view the film on their own before class in order to be better prepared for discussion. While the summaries clearly are not as nuanced as the films themselves, they are a more than adequate basis for a lively discussion and debate.

Another option is to make the films available to the students for viewing on campus at their convenience. For example, many libraries have facilities for viewing films that are available to students. You can place on reserve the films to be discussed throughout the semester and ask that the students view them at their earliest convenience, but before class discussion of the film.

Still another option is to put the films on reserve and allow students to borrow them. Again, the students can select times that are convenient for them to view the films. Furthermore, since most of the films summarized in this book can be rented fairly easily, you might ask your students to do this on their own. You could also encourage them to form "viewing groups" to cut down on the expense of renting the films and to eliminate the problem of some students not having viewing equipment. Furthermore, students often find watching films with their peers to be quite enjoyable.

Yet another option is to schedule screenings of the films for your students outside of class. Establish one night a week in which your students can attend a screening of a film that you wish to discuss in class. You might even assign a student to manage the equipment.

Alternatively, you might show only key scenes from the films under consideration during class time. This will involve some additional preparation on your part. DVDs are recommended here because they include scene indexes that allow easy access to relevant parts of the film. If you are using VHS tapes, you might prepare a tape of the particular scenes that you want to view with your students. In any case, viewing scenes from films is a reasonable alternative to showing the entire film in class or requiring students to view the entire film as homework.

Of course, you can also incorporate films into your class on a more selective basis. For example, you might give students the option of writing papers on the films presented in this book. The discussion questions that follow the film summaries are many times rich enough to be the subject matter of papers. While it might take a semester or two for you to find the pedagogical strategy that works best for you, it will be well worth it. Few materials engage the imaginations and attention of students like film.

METHOD AND ORGANIZATION

Morality Matters contains an introduction and ten chapters. A number of readings in this anthology have been carefully edited to preserve the structure of the main argument(s) while omitting materials that are superfluous to the main lines of argumentation—including, at times, footnotes. Briefer entries not only help students with weaker reading/analysis skills to focus on arguments and positions but also allow for a greater diversity of materials to be anthologized.

The Introduction is designed to introduce your students to moral reasoning. To this end, fundamental logic and critical thinking materials are presented as are a few "moral scenarios" for contemplation and discussion. I recommend that you utilize these moral scenarios in the first week of the semester. They will help build student interest in the course and are excellent material for class debate.

Chapters 1 and 2 will introduce students to some of the main issues and positions in classical and contemporary ethical theory. Chapter 1 presents some classic responses to the question "What is morality?" Chapter 2 deals with moral and cultural relativism and includes an introduction to human rights due to its obvious link to the more general subject of cultural relativism. Given that many students have strong beliefs about relativism, you may want to discuss these topics early in the course.

The remaining eight chapters address the following moral problems: abortion and euthanasia (Chapter 3), punishment and the death penalty (Chapter 4), sexuality and marriage (Chapter 5), racism and affirmative action (Chapter 6), sexism and violence against women (Chapter 7), pornography and hate speech (Chapter 8), poverty and distributive justice (Chapter 9), and animal rights and the environment (Chapter 10). The chapter topics are paired to suggest that these issues might be related through some mutual concerns or concepts. The introductions to each chapter suggest ways in which these topics can be seen as interrelated. For example, pornography and hate speech are paired to suggest that they might be regarded as issues related to free speech and censorship. Animals and the environment are linked to suggest that they both concern our ethical obligations to nonhumans. Each chapter concludes with a "Media Gallery" containing summaries of literary works and films to help you animate these topics for the students, as well as suggestions for additional reading.

SPECIAL FEATURES

Morality Matters contains a number of features designed both to make ethical theory and moral problems accessible and relevant to students and to aide you in course development.

- *Supplementary readings.* Additional reading materials are suggested for each of the ten chapters. Here, you will find a wide-ranging selection of additional sources including, where applicable, a number of historical and multicultural selections as well as a listing of some of the omitted philosophical approaches to this material. These readings might also be used as the basis for student research or as assigned presentation/review topics.

- *Glossary.* Because some of the philosophical terminology will be new to students, *Morality Matters* contains a glossary of the philosophical terminology used in the readings. Also included in the glossary are some of the more difficult nonphilosophical terms found in the readings.

- *Arguments and fallacies.* Materials on arguments and fallacies are presented in the introductory chapter. These materials include definitions and examples of the more common informal fallacies, as well as a section explaining how to evaluate a moral argument.

- *Article introductions.* Each selection in this anthology is prefaced by a summary of the article that will prepare both student and instructor for what follows in the article. However, these synopses should not be regarded as a substitute for reading the article. Each article introduction also provides a biographical note about the author.

- *Chapter introductions.* Each chapter in this anthology is prefaced by an introduction that identifies for the student the main lines of argumentation on the moral issue and provides definitions of key terms associated with the chapter topic.

- *Discussion questions.* A list of discussion questions follows every selection, as do film, literature, and event summaries. You might assign these for homework, use them as essay topics, present them as discussion material, or simply give them as examination questions. In addition to providing you with course materials, they provide the diligent student with further points of entry into the material.

- *Media gallery including films and literature.* Each chapter concludes with selection of materials that you can use to stimulate discussion of the readings and main topics in the chapter. These include abstracts of controversial current events and summaries of films and literature that might be the focus of class discussions.

ACKNOWLEDGMENTS

I would like to thank my editor, Ken King, without whom this project would not have been possible. His unflagging encouragement and professional guidance are deeply appreciated, as are the patience and support of his assistants, Josh Tepfer and Georgia Gero-Chen. In addition, I would like to thank Thomas Briggs for the meticulous and caring attention he gave to copy-editing the manuscript; Marty Granahan for making the quest for permissions just a bit easier; and Vicki Moran for making sure that the production process ran smoothly and on schedule. I want to thank as well those who reviewed the manuscript, particularly David Corner of California State University at Sacramento, Kevin Graham of Creighton University, Robert L. Gibson of Community College of Denver and Metropolitan State College of Denver, Daniel Holbrook of Washington State University, Joan McGregor of Arizona State University, Marshall Missner of the University of Wisconsin at Oshkosh, Mario Morelli of Western Illinois University, Mechthild Nagel of State University of New York College at Cortland, Pam R. Sailors of Southwest Missouri State University, Thomas W. Simon of Illinois State University, and Julie C. Van Camp of California State University at Long Beach for their comments and suggestions. In addition, I extend thanks to the authors and publishers of the articles anthologized in this book for granting me permission to use their work. I also must extend my appreciation to the many students whom I have had the good fortune to teach at Indiana University at Bloomington, Indiana University/Purdue University at Indianapolis, the Georgia Institute of Technology, and the University of Illinois at Chicago. From them I learned what it takes to make a course successful for both student and teacher. A note of gratitude goes out to all of the students who helped me at various stages in the production of this book, particularly Sarah C. Dilworth, Andrea Graham, Jonathan Sanders, and Jill Ulasovich. My sincere appreciation goes out to Staci Liker, whose diligence and attention to detail have helped to bring this project to completion. In addition, I must thank Bruce Sielaff for sharing with me an earlier version of the wonderful moral scenarios found in the introduction, and Malcolm MacIver for assisting me many years ago in one of the first ethics courses I ever taught. My deepest debts of gratitude go out to my friend and colleague, Dr. Jack Green-Musselman of Southwestern University, for sharing his expertise in both contemporary applied ethics and pedagogy. I also deeply appreciate Indiana University's School of Continuing Studies for granting me permission to use selected materials from a course and learning guide designed by Dr. Green-Musselman and me, and for giving me the opportunity to work with diverse students as an instructor in their remarkable program over the past ten years. Finally, I thank my wife, Nina, for her patient support and guidance. This book is dedicated to those individuals and institutions that actively contend with contemporary moral problems, work for justice, and sincerely believe that morality matters.

Introduction

"The unexamined life is not worth living."

—Socrates

MORAL THEORIES AND MORAL REASONING

Answering questions about morality is a very difficult task. In realizing this, you are not alone: from the time of the Greek philosopher Socrates (470–399 B.C.) to today, philosophers have tried to answer questions about morality by developing moral theories. Their moral theories attempt to answer these questions by developing general frameworks, or approaches, to *normative* issues, or issues about what we should do.

Moral theories, like scientific theories, attempt to provide general principles or laws that can be applied to specific issues or events to help us understand them. For example, physicists often apply the law of gravity to explain how objects fall to the ground and use mathematical formulas to explain how certain objects fall in certain ways. If we can better understand how an object falls in certain circumstances—say, if thrown from a tall building—then we can use these principles or laws to build a more general, comprehensive theory about how objects fall. Similarly, philosophers often attempt to explain why a certain act is right (such as giving to the poor) by applying certain principles (such as that we have a duty to help others) and by defending those principles with arguments (such as that helping the poor will reduce human suffering). Philosophers often say that, if we can better understand why we should do certain things, such as why it is *right* to help the poor during a famine (see Chapter 9), we will learn how to lead good lives.

Moral theories are like scientific theories in that they both apply general principles to help us understand specific events. However, unlike scientific theories, which apply general but *impersonal* principles in an attempt to explain why events in the natural world happen in certain ways (e.g., scientific principles that explain why rocks fall faster than feathers), moral theories apply general *personal* principles to justify why *human* events *should* take place in certain ways (e.g., that we should provide famine relief because humans should not suffer needlessly). By focusing on how things *should* or *should not* happen, moral theorists develop general principles to help justify the normative dimension of the day-to-day lives of humans.

Chapter 1 will introduce you to a number of moral theories and traditions. Philosophers offer arguments about how their moral theories can show us how to lead good lives and why morality matters. Therefore, it is important that you become familiar with what constitutes a good argument before you begin to study specific moral theories. Consider the following statement: "If you work hard, you will be successful." This familiar phrase sounds plausible, but is it a sound argument? Can you identify the fallacy inherent in such a statement? What are the hidden premises and assumptions? What follows is a short introduction to help you build skills in the identification and creation of good arguments concerning morality.

ARGUMENTS

An *argument* is a collection of statements. One statement is the *conclusion* of the argument. The other statements, often called *premises* or *reasons*, serve to show that the conclusion is true or that it is reasonable to believe that the conclusion is true:

> *Example:* A dog was kept in the stable along with the horses. Sometimes a visitor came in to get a horse. When the dog did not know the visitor well, the dog barked. Last night a stranger entered the stable. Obviously, the dog barked.

> *Premise 1:* If the dog did not know the visitor well, then the dog barked.

> *Premise 2:* The dog did not know the visitor well.

> *Conclusion:* Therefore, the dog barked.

There are two types of arguments: *deductive* and *inductive*. A *valid* deductive argument is truth preserving: if the premises are true, then the conclusion must be true. A valid deductive argument guarantees this by following only truth-preserving forms, which are also called *valid forms*. Arguments that cannot offer this guarantee are *invalid*.

Think of a valid deductive argument as a box into which the premises are input and out of which the conclusion is output. If we input all true statements into the valid deductive box, then the box outputs a true conclusion. However, if we input any false statements into the box, then the box *could* output a false conclusion. That is, the valid deductive box guarantees a true conclusion only if it is given true premises.

Similarly, we can think of an invalid argument as a defective box. If we input true premises into this defective box, the conclusion can be either true or false. Again, if we input any false premises, the conclusion could be either true or false. That is, the invalid deductive box cannot guarantee anything about the truth or falsity of the conclusion.

Here is a brief summary:

- *Valid argument:* an argument whose conclusion must be true if its premises are true
- *Invalid argument:* an argument whose conclusion may be false when its premises are true
- *Sound argument:* a valid argument in which all the premises are true

The conclusion is guaranteed to be true only if the argument is *sound*—that is, only if two conditions are met: (1) the argument is valid, and (2) all the premises are true. If the argument is not valid, then—by definition—it cannot guarantee a true conclusion from true premises. If at least one premise is false, then the argument—even if it is valid—cannot guarantee the truth of the conclusion.

COMMON VALID FORMS OF ARGUMENT

Modus ponens, modus tollens, dilemma, hypothetical syllogism, and *disjunctive syllogism* are five of the more common valid argument forms. The following examples substitute verbal phrases for the P's and Q's.

- *Modus ponens:*   If P, then Q
                     P
                     Therefore, Q

    Example: If the dog hears a noise, then the dog barks.
                  The dog hears a noise.
                  Therefore, the dog barks.

- *Modus tollens:*   If P, then Q
                         Not Q
                         Therefore, not P

    Example: If the dog hears a noise, then the dog barks.
                 The dog does not bark.
                 Therefore, the dog does not hear a noise.

- *Hypothetical syllogism:*   If P, then Q
                             If Q, then R
                             Therefore, if P, then R

    Example: If the dog did not know the visitor well, then the dog
                 would have barked.
                 If the dog would have barked, then I would have been
                 awakened.
                 Therefore, if the dog did not know the visitor well, then
                 I would have been awakened.

- *Dilemma:*   Either P or Q
                  If P, then R
                  If Q, then S
                  Therefore, R or S

    Example: Either the dog is going to bite me, or the dog is going to
                 be friendly to me.
                 If the dog bites me, then I'll have to go to the hospital.
                 If the dog is friendly to me, then I'll be able to continue
                 walking home.
                 Therefore, either I'll have to go to the hospital or I'll be
                 able to continue walking home.

- *Disjunctive syllogism:*   Either P or Q
                            Not P
                            Therefore, Q

    Example: Either the dog bites me, or the dog licks me.
                 The dog does not bite me.
                 Therefore, the dog licks me.

Remember that even though the form of each of these arguments is *valid,* this does not mean that the argument is *sound.* If one premise is false, then the argument—even if it is valid—cannot guarantee the truth of the conclusion. For example, consider the case of the disjunctive syllogism. This argument would not be *sound* if premise/reason 1 (Either P or Q—*Either the dog bites me, or the dog licks me*) were not true. For example, the dog could have growled at me, in which case, he neither bit me nor licked me. Therefore, premise/reason 1 is untrue, making the argument as a whole *unsound.*

COMMON INVALID FORMS OF ARGUMENT

Denying the antecedent and *affirming the consequent* are two of the more common invalid argument forms. In both cases, the truth of the premises does not guarantee the truth of the conclusion.

- *Affirming the consequent:*   If P, then Q
                               Q
                               Therefore, P

Example:	If the dog hears a noise, then the dog barks. The dog barks. Therefore, the dog hears a noise.
Comment:	Something other than a noise, such as the presence of a stranger, could have also made the dog bark.

- *Denying the antecedent:*

	If P, then Q Not P Therefore, not Q
Example:	If the dog hears a noise, then the dog barks. The dog does not hear a noise. Therefore, the dog does not bark.
Comment:	The dog could have barked anyway.

Earlier we distinguished between *deductive* and *inductive* forms of argumentation. To this point, we have discussed only deductive forms of argumentation. As a general rule, a valid deductive argument with true premises is a good argument, whereas an invalid deductive argument with true premises is both a bad argument and invalid. In contrast, inductive forms of argumentation are neither valid nor invalid. This does not mean that all inductive arguments should be considered bad forms of argumentation. Think of *strong* inductive arguments as comparable or analogous to *valid* deductive arguments and *weak* inductive arguments as comparable or analogous to *invalid* deductive arguments.

The premises of an inductive argument do not guarantee the truth of the conclusion; rather, they establish its truth with varying degrees of probability. As a rule, inductive arguments should be regarded as establishing *probable* conclusions on the basis of their premises, whereas deductive arguments should be regarded as establishing *necessary* conclusions on the basis of their premises. Here is an example of an inductive argument:

These beans (an appropriately determined sample) are from this bag.

These beans are white.

Therefore, all the beans in this bag are white.

This is not a deductively valid argument because the truth of the premises does not guarantee the truth of the conclusion. However, as the sample of beans from the bag increases and continues to be only white beans, then the truth of the conclusion (all the beans in this bag are white) becomes more *probable*. *Weak* inductive arguments draw general conclusions from incomplete or small sets of facts, whereas *strong* inductive arguments draw general conclusions from more complete or larger sets of facts. Here is an example of a strong inductive argument:

The sun has always risen in the east.

Therefore, the sun will rise in the east tomorrow.

Compare this argument to a weak inductive argument:

I have never broken any bones in my body.

Therefore, I will never break any bones in my body.

The probability that the sun will rise in the east tomorrow is greater than the probability that I will never break any bones in my body. It is this greater probability which makes the first inductive argument stronger than the second one. While both arguments are invalid, the first is a good argument based on the probability of its conclusion being true, whereas the second is a bad argument based on the probability of its holding true for the rest of my life. Nevertheless, arguments in the form of the first one are always better than arguments in the form of denying the antecedent or affirming the consequent. Whereas arguments in the form of denying the antecedent or affirming the consequent are such that the truth of the premises *never* guarantees the truth of the conclusion, the truth of the premise in the first argument supports the truth of the conclusion with a high degree of certainty.

FALLACIES

Fallacies are mistakes in arguments and so should be avoided. We touched on one of the major fallacies previously: drawing conclusions from too little evidence. This is what distinguishes weak inductive arguments from strong ones. Denying the antecedent and affirming the consequent are also examples of fallacies. However, these are only a few of the many ways in which arguments can be in error. What follows is a listing of some of the more common fallacies in arguments. Understanding these fallacies will sharpen your critical thinking abilities and help you analyze the readings in this book.

- *Ad hominem:* attacking the character of an alleged authority, rather than his or her argument or qualifications. *Example:* "He's not from around here! How can he know what's going on?"
- *Appeal to authority:* seeking to persuade not by giving evidence, but merely by citing an authority. *Example:* "It's a strong argument because my teacher told us that it is a strong argument."
- *Appeal to fear:* seeking to persuade not by giving evidence, but merely by appealing to fear. *Example:* "Eat your carrots. If you don't, you'll go blind."
- *Appeal to ignorance* (ad ignorantiam): arguing that a claim is true simply because it has not been shown to be false. *Example:* "She's a witch! Nothing that has been said about her has disproven this!"
- *Appeal to pity* (ad misericordiam): seeking to persuade not through evidence, but by appealing to pity. *Example:* "Professor, you have to give me a passing grade in this course! If I don't pass it, I won't be able to graduate in June!"
- *Appealing to the crowd* (ad populum): seeking to persuade not through evidence, but by appealing to the masses. *Example:* "Cheating on exams is all right. Everybody does it!"
- *Begging the question:* assuming that which you want to prove, or, more formally, implicitly using your conclusion as a premise. *Example:* "God exists because it says so in the Bible, which I know is true because God wrote it!" (Or, more formally: "The Bible is true because God wrote it. The Bible says God exists. Therefore, God exists." The first premise assumes that God exists, for how could God write the Bible if God does not exist?)
- *Complex question:* asking a question in such a way that it is impossible for people to agree or disagree with it without committing themselves to the claim that the person who is asking the question seeks to promote. *Example:* "Do you still kick your dog?"
- *Composition:* assuming that the whole must have the properties of its parts. *Example:* "This must be a good school. All of the people I know who have gone to it are good students."
- *Division:* assuming that the parts must have the properties of the whole. *Example:* "He must be an excellent student. He goes to a very good school."
- *Equivocation:* using a single word in more than one sense. *Example:* "Men and women are physically different. Therefore, the sexes are not equal. The law should not treat men and women as though they are!" (The meaning of "equal" changes from "having the same physical attributes" to "having the same rights and opportunities.")

- *False analogy:* reaching a conclusion by comparing two significantly incomparable cases. *Example:* "You college professors have it easy! You only have to teach 30 weeks a year! At the factory, I only have 2 weeks a year off for vacation!"

- *False cause:* concluding that there is a causal link between two events when no such link has been established. *Example:* "We won every game that I wore these socks. These socks are the key to our success!"

- *False dilemma:* reducing the number of potential options to just two. These options are often sharply opposed and unfair to the person facing the dilemma. *Example:* "America. Love it or leave it!"

- *Genetic fallacy:* attacking a position, institution, or idea by condemning its background or origin. *Example:* "That company will never succeed. Its founder came from a highly unsuccessful family."

- *Hasty generalization:* using an isolated or exceptional case as the basis for an unwarranted general conclusion. *Example:* "I drove well over the speed limit the other time I took this road and didn't get a ticket. I won't get a speeding ticket this time either!"

- *Poisoning the well:* disparaging an argument before even mentioning it. *Example:* "No intelligent person would believe that . . ."

- *Provincialism:* mistaking a local fact for a universal one. *Example:* "Everybody eats their dinner around 5:30."

- *Red herring:* introducing irrelevant or secondary information into an argument, thereby diverting attention from the main subject of the argument. *Example:* During the course of a discussion of the morality of abortion, someone brings up the issue of how cute babies are.

- *Slippery slope:* unjustifiably assuming that a proposal or position that is not undesirable or dangerous will trigger a chain of events that will lead to another undesirable or dangerous proposal or position. *Example:* "Today he is the leader of a small country, with little outside influence. However, if we allow him to stay in power, one day he will control the world."

- *Straw man:* presenting a position in such a way that it is easy to refute. *Example:* "Why does God allow children to suffer? If he really is all-loving and all-caring, he would not do this. Therefore, God does not exist."

- *Sweeping generalization:* applying a general rule to a specific case to which the rule is not applicable because of special features of the case. *Example:* "If you work hard enough, you will get good grades." (There are people who work hard but still get poor grades. Other things can play a role in getting good grades, including intelligence.)

- *Weasel word:* changing the meaning of a word in the middle of an argument in order to bring about the desired conclusion. *Example:* Bill: "Philosophy is a very difficult subject." Sam: "Well, what about ethics? You said that's easy!" Bill: "Oh, but ethics is not really philosophy."

EVALUATING MORAL ARGUMENTS

The best way to evaluate moral theories is to examine the *arguments*, or reasons, that someone provides for choosing one moral theory over others. Learning how to critically examine these arguments—deciding if they are good arguments that will convince a reasonable person—is one of the most difficult tasks in studying moral philosophy. In learning to distinguish good arguments from bad ones, there is no substitute for practice. One of the best ways to do this is to talk to others, listen to what they have to say, and then write down your thoughts on the issue. Writing about and discussing moral issues will help you develop not only your understanding of matters concerning morality but also your argumentation and critical thinking skills in general.

To get an idea about how to make and evaluate good arguments in moral philosophy, first read the following passage. The author makes a point about the *good life*, or the most valuable thing in life that makes it worth living, and also suggests that the *right* way to pursue that life is to follow his advice. Decide if you agree or disagree, and give reasons for your views.

> The most important thing in life is to serve God on this earth. In particular, we should do whatever we can—no matter what the costs—to defend the innocent creatures created by God to serve him. In particular, this means that abortions are never permitted, for that is to kill an innocent creature created by God. Pro-choice advocates—who are really hysterical feminists who do not care about children—do not have any good arguments for permitting abortions. For example, if we kill fetuses, as they want us to do, the next thing you know, we will think it is moral to kill toddlers, or disabled adults, and where will we stop? Furthermore, all of the feminists also think that soldiers can kill in wartime—but this means that they support killing innocent creatures, which is wrong because, as I've said, God made these creatures and no one may kill them. As it says in Genesis, God made man in his own image, and this means if we kill fetuses, that is like killing God. This is clearly wrong! How could pro-choice advocates defend such a view? After all, most people in the world feel that serving God on this earth is the most important thing there is, and to pursue anything else is wrong.

Though he is convinced he is right, the author of this passage has not presented good arguments for his position. In fact, he has committed several of the fallacies mentioned previously, as well as other common argumentative mistakes. Can you identify them?

First, the author *asserts* that the most important thing to do is to serve God, but he does not tell us *why* this is so important or *why* God would want us to serve in this way. In fact, the author does not show us that God exists or even tell us what it means to serve God "no matter what the costs." To improve this argument, the author should define terms like "serve" and attempt to explain how he knows that God exists, what God wants, and so on. In short, good arguments do more than merely state or assert something ("God wants us to . . ."). They also suggest reasonable considerations related to *why* the statement is true ("God exists *because* . . ." and "God wants us to serve *because* . . .").

Second, authors should not make fun of anyone who disagrees with their assertions ("pro-choice advocates are . . . hysterical feminists"), but should address their arguments instead. This type of statement was defined previously as the *ad hominem fallacy.* Though this form of argumentation is popular, name-calling does not make for a good philosophical argument. In this example, we do not know what a "feminist" thinks because the author does not state his or her arguments.

Third, the author suggests that once we permit abortions, we will not know where to stop. This is a *slippery slope argument,* which asserts that one cannot draw a line or avoid certain consequences if a particular position is assumed. We can liken this form of argument to a rock on the top of a slippery slope: once the rock begins to slide down the hill (in this case, once we permit abortions), the rock will roll all the way to the bottom (the next thing you know, we will be killing children, the disabled, people we do not like, and so on). It is a fallacy because the author does not tell us *why* members of these other groups will be killed.

Fourth, the author says that those who support abortion also support killing in war. This would be a good argument if there were some pro-choice advocates who believed it and if there was some reason to think that killing in wartime meant killing innocent people. However, we are not told which pro-choice advocates hold this position, nor are we told why killing in times of war means killing innocent people. Given the lack of supporting reasons, the author has committed the *straw man fallacy*. Instead of attacking the pro-choice position, he claims that pro-choicers hold another view about war that he then easily knocks over (as one would knock over a person made of straw). Even though straw man arguments, like *ad hominem* arguments, are widely used, they are neither good nor fair forms of argumentation and should be avoided.

Fifth, the author cites Genesis as an authority to prove his point. While citing an authority may provide support to some point, it will not by itself *prove* the point. For example, if we cite the Congressional Budget Office to determine how much a government program costs, or Amnesty International to get estimates of human rights abuses, we can use this information as a way to begin supporting our argument. However, simply citing such sources will not *prove* our point. Just as we generally do not believe something merely because someone said it, so we should be wary when a so-called expert says something. "Experts" are just people. In evaluating a source, we should ask as many questions as possible. Is the person really an expert? What credentials does the person have? Is the person biased in any way? Does the person use the same material over and over to make a point? If so, does this suggest that there is little else to support his or her view? Does common sense suggest that the source is not trustworthy? If we apply all of these tests to the Bible's Book of Genesis, we see that there are reasons to be wary of this source. If we accept that humans had a hand in writing the Bible, then each person who helped to write the Bible may have been biased in writing it. Furthermore, not everyone believes that the Bible is God's word—in fact, not everyone believes in God. Assuming that everyone does believe in God is clearly to commit the *fallacy of provincialism*. Therefore, citing Genesis will not convince anyone about abortion if he or she does not believe in God.

Sixth, the author spends a lot of time repeating himself ("as I've said"), insisting that he is right ("This is clearly wrong!"), and asking how others could object ("How could pro-choice advocates defend such a view?"). Notice that he also adds that almost everyone feels the same way ("most people in the world feel . . ."). These are simply not good arguments, as we can easily see if we let someone *defend* abortion in the same way. For example, if we keep repeating that abortion is moral and ask how anyone could object, and if we then add that most everyone feels the same way, we have not said *why* we are right and our opponent is wrong. Imagine an entire discussion made up of such statements: it would never get anywhere! Everyone would merely yell (which does not make them right), repeat themselves (if they are wrong, repeating something does not make it right), and ask how others could object (which is not the same as *proving* that one is right). Finally, if someone insists that others all feel the same way, does that make him or her *right*? (What if everyone in your class cheated on exams?) This is called the *fallacy of appealing to the crowd*.

Again, making good arguments in moral philosophy is very difficult. It is especially hard because, as we saw in the abortion argument, discussing our ethical views often means discussing the very values by which we live. In short, it is hard to discuss such matters, so we should remember to be tolerant of, and patient with, those who hold different views.

RECONSTRUCTING ARGUMENTS AND EVALUATING PREMISES

In this book, however, we will not encounter arguments as flawed as the abortion one. Generally, we will deal with at least two arguments with conflicting conclusions. All of the conflicting conclusions cannot be true. To determine which conclusion to accept, we will follow these two steps: (1) reconstruct each argument as a valid argument, and (2) determine which argument has the true (or the more likely to be true) premises. This is, of course, sometimes easier said than done. Here are some general guidelines for reconstructing valid deductive moral arguments.

Guidelines for Reconstructing Valid Deductive Arguments

- Make sure that the argument is in the form of a deductively valid argument.
- Compose the premises so that they fit the pattern of valid deductive rules.
- Make sure that all of the premises required to make the argument valid are included.
- Avoid begging the question; that is, make sure that the premises do not assume the conclusion.
- Make sure that the premises are general enough to avoid looking like prejudices. If a premise focuses on a specific group, it might come across as a prejudice against that group.
- Avoid straw man arguments; that is, make sure that all the arguments are plausible and faithful to the proponents of that argument.
- Avoid equivocation; that is, make sure that the argument does not turn on different meanings of the same word.

Guidelines for Evaluating Premises

- Challenge premises by formulating counterexamples to the premises.
- Look for irrelevant premises such as those that appeal to our emotions or that unfairly represent the opposing position.
- Question the foundations or basis of premises that are causal claims.
- Look for premises that are based on moral intuitions, and challenge these intuitions by examining cases that go counter to the intuition.
- Don't dismiss arguments on the basis of one faulty premise, but rather try alternative premises to give the argument its strongest defense. The aim is to solve moral problems, not to summarily dismiss arguments.

It is easy to become offended or angered by moral judgments that do not match our own. Rather than quickly dismissing such arguments, we should try to analyze and reconstruct them. By examining the reasoning of people with opposing views, we can better understand *why* they may hold moral values different from our own. Good critical thinking skills and the ability to discern good moral reasoning from bad are fundamentally interrelated. Your own ability to get to the heart of moral controversies will improve as you work through the materials in this book.

MORAL SCENARIOS FOR OPENING DISCUSSION

Read each of the following and decide how you would act in each case. Be ready to defend your decision with some arguments. Think of the strongest reasons that you can for holding the position that you do in each case. Try to avoid the fallacies discussed previously. Also, if possible, put your argument into a deductively valid form. Remember that anticipating counterarguments can strengthen your position.

- *Scenario I: The Executioner's Choice.* One day you find yourself in a foreign land ruled by a cruel dictator. Strolling about, you suddenly come upon 20 people who have been rounded up *at random* to be executed momentarily. Quite unexpectedly, the captain in charge of the execution walks up to you and tells you that he will not execute 19 of the 20 people if you kill the twentieth. What do you do? What if the killing spares 49 people? What about 149 people?
- *Scenario II: False Testimony and the Old Pawnbroker.* Riots have broken out in your town over the killing of a young man, and people are being hurt and even killed.

The riots will stop if someone is charged and convicted for the killing. The police have reason to believe that you know who killed the young man and will take your testimony as conclusive proof. Yet you really don't know who the killer is. If the police ask you who killed the young man, do you tell them the truth and do nothing to stop the riots? Or do you lie to the police and tell them that a mean old pawnbroker whom no one likes did it and thereby stop the riots? No one will ever find out that you lied, and everyone will congratulate you on doing a good deed in turning in the pawnbroker.

- *Scenario III: The One-Night Stand.* Your favorite team has just won a championship, and you are celebrating at a large party. The next day, you reflect on the one-night stand you had with someone you met at the party. Do you tell your significant other, with whom you are very much in love and with whom you have agreed to have a monogamous relationship, about your one-night stand? Assume that the story of the interlude is known only by you and the person you met at the party, and that he or she will not say anything about it.

- *Scenario IV: Mother's Money.* You have the opportunity to embezzle hundreds of thousands of dollars of charity money meant for disabled and starving orphans around the world in order to save your mother from dying of lung cancer. This is the only way that you can afford to save your mother's life. If you embezzle, then she lives (and orphans die). If you do not embezzle, then she dies soon thereafter (and the orphans live). What should you do?

C H A P T E R
1

What Is Morality? Traditions and Theories

"We are discussing no small matter, but how we ought to live."

—Socrates in Plato's *Republic*

Socrates said that moral philosophy involves nothing less than a discussion of *how* we should live and *why* we should live this way. These are difficult and complex issues, and beginning students in moral philosophy are often discouraged by the lack of definite answers. Instead of answers, the study of moral philosophy seems only to beget more questions. What is morality? What is immorality? Why should we be moral? What does morality require from us? And so on. The readings in this chapter explore some of these questions. They are topics to which moral philosophers and others concerned with morality return time after time.

There are many different ways to respond to these questions. Some of the responses will be close to your own beliefs, and others will challenge your ideas about morality. Regardless, you should give each careful, critical attention no matter how the view corresponds with your own. Understanding morality involves examining and articulating your own positions, as well as those of others. In reading the selections in this chapter, continually ask yourself how and why acting according to these differing conceptions of morality can make a difference in your life and in the lives of others. Try not to reach a conclusion on any position before critically examining all of the arguments and the evidence provided by the author. Use the argumentative tools found in the Introduction to outline the strengths and weaknesses of the arguments. The readings in this book can help you to understand better how and why morality and moral philosophy do indeed matter. However, they can do this only if you approach them fairly and objectively.

Morality and moral philosophy are two different things. *Morality* refers to the particular practices, precepts, and customs of people and cultures, whereas *moral philosophy* refers to theoretical or philosophical reflection on morality in itself. A general definition of moral philosophy is the systematic study of morality. *Nonmoral* designates issues that lie outside the sphere of moral concern. Moral philosophy aims at helping us better understand the meaning and implications of moral concepts such as right and wrong, and good and bad, both in themselves and as they take part in moral practices. It also strives to justify moral principles and theories while always looking out for principles of right behavior that might serve as guides for those who want to do the right thing. Finally, moral philosophy examines values and virtues with an eye toward those that are potentially the most beneficial to individuals and to societies. *Ethics* is said by some to be synonymous with moral philosophy, whereas for others, it comprises the domains of both morality and moral philosophy.

In general, ethics may be divided into two branches: nonnormative and normative. *Nonnormative ethics* consists of the scientific or descriptive study of ethics and metaethics.

Scientific or descriptive study involves the factual investigation of moral behavior—for example, the research conducted by anthropologists. Cross-cultural studies by anthropologists reveal a wide array of moral codes and behaviors. *Metaethics* investigates the meaning of ethical terms such as "right" and "wrong," and "good" and "bad," as well as the procedures by which ethical claims are verified. Thus, rather than being concerned with what is actually right or wrong, metaethics is concerned with the meaning or significance of calling something "right" or "wrong" and with whether moral claims are objectively or subjectively verifiable.

Normative ethics is the branch of ethics that makes judgments about obligation and value. Thus, unlike nonnormative ethics, which is concerned only with issues such as the meaning of the terminology of ethics or the descriptive study of ethics, normative ethics is concerned with what is actually right or wrong. *General normative ethics* is the reasoned search for general moral principles of human conduct, including a critical study of the major theories about what things are good or bad and what acts are right or blameworthy. *Applied normative ethics* is the attempt to explain and justify positions on specific moral issues such as abortion or capital punishment. According to this definition, then, the majority of the readings in this book are applied normative ethics because they attempt to explain and justify positions on specific moral issues.

General moral principles are broad standards used to guide the two types of morality: individual and social. *Individual morality* deals with how individuals should act in particular situations. *Social morality* refers to how society ought to deal with morally important social issues. These two types of morality are related: societies use laws to deter or punish individuals who would or actually do perpetrate harmful immoral acts. However, not all immoral acts are illegal, and not all laws are concerned with immoral acts. For example, driving on the left side of the street is illegal, not because it is immoral, but because our traffic system is designed in such a way that driving in this manner would cause accidents. Similarly, it might be immoral to call into work sick when you are actually healthy, but it is not illegal.

General moral principles guide our individual morality by determining what we do and what kind of person we are. This chapter gives examples of four broad types of moral principles that guide individual morality. First, there are *proper human virtues*—virtues or excellences, such as loyalty, generosity, and honesty, that we as humans are obligated to develop. Second, according to the *principle of utility*, or the *greatest happiness principle*, we should attempt to produce the greatest balance of happiness over unhappiness. Third, we have two well-known views of *fairness:* the *golden rule* ("we should do unto others as we would have them do unto us") and *respect for persons* ("we should never use people merely as a means to our own ends"). Fourth, according to the *will of God*, religious belief is the ultimate source of morality. These general moral principles are often key features of more general normative theories. In addition, general normative theories, like the ones presented in this chapter, are representative of three major moral traditions: the consequentialist, the nonconsequentialist, and the aretaic.

One major difference between the aretaic and the consequentialist and nonconsequentialist moral traditions is that the latter begin from the question "What should I *do?*" whereas the former tradition begins from the question "What should I *be?*" The aretaic moral tradition is often classified as part of the "ethics of being or character," whereas the consequentialist and nonconsequentialist moral theory traditions are often placed in the "ethics of doing."

Consequentialist (or teleological) moral traditions locate the morality of actions in their nonmoral consequences. Examples of consequentialist general normative theories presented in this chapter include egoism and utilitarianism. *Nonconsequentialist* (or deontological) moral theories maintain that the morality of an action depends on factors other than consequences. Examples presented in this chapter include the divine command theory and the categorical imperative (or deontological ethics). *Aretaic* (or virtue) moral traditions are less concerned with the morality of particular actions than with issues concerning the kind of person we should become.

The first type of consequentialist theory presented in this chapter, *egoism,* claims that moral actions are ones that promote our long-term interests. Egoism is often closely associated with *hedonism,* the view that pleasure is the only intrinsic value. Egoists may be hedonists but may also identify with other values. Even hedonists differ with regard to the nature of pleasure. Common difficulties with hedonism include its inability to resolve conflicts of interest and to provide consistent moral counsel. Egoism also generally undermines the moral point of view, that is, the impartial attitude of one who attempts to see all sides of an issue without being committed to the interests of a particular individual or group.

The second type of consequentialist theory presented in this chapter is *utilitarianism.* According to this theory, moral actions are those that produce the best ratio of happiness to misery within the group at large. Proponents include the British philosophers Jeremy Bentham (1748–1832) and John Stuart Mill (1806–1873). Two major types of utilitarianism are act and rule utilitarianism. *Act utilitarianism* judges the rightness or wrongness of an action on a case-by-case basis according to the utilitarian principle. *Rule utilitarianism* uses the utilitarian principle to judge moral rules, not individual actions, by examining the effects of rules on overall happiness. There are some problems with rule utilitarianism, not only because it is far from clear how to apply the principle to rules but also because rules that allow for exceptions seem better than those that do not. For example, the rule "murder is wrong except in cases in which one's life or the lives of others are in danger" seems better than the rule "murder is wrong" because the former rule allows for a range of reasonable exceptions not permissible by the latter. However, critics of rule utilitarianism respond that such exceptions threaten to reduce rule utilitarianism to act utilitarianism.

One of the major differences between Bentham's utilitarianism and Mill's is that Bentham focused on considerations regarding the *quantity* of pleasure or pain (intensity, duration, certainty, proximity, fecundity, purity, and extent), whereas Mill focused on the *quality* of pleasure or pain, distinguishing the higher human pleasures from the lower ones. Whereas Bentham's utilitarianism made the criterion of ethics the production of the greatest amount of pleasure and the least amount of pain, Mill distinguishes between "higher pleasures," which are of more value, and "lower pleasures," which are of lesser value. "It is better to be a human being dissatisfied than a pig satisfied," said Mill, "better to be Socrates dissatisfied than a fool satisfied." Whereas Benthan tells us to maximize the sum of pleasure, Mill tells us to maximize the sum of higher pleasure. The differences between these two versions of utilitarianism are often foregrounded by terming Bentham's view *hedonistic utilitarianism* and Mill's view *eudaimonistic utilitarianism.*

Unlike the consequentialists, Aristotle is interested in what kind of person we should be. According to the aretaic moral tradition, morality is about becoming a good person and cultivating character. A good moral theory needs to identify good moral traits and explain how they can be developed or acquired. The aretaic moral tradition focuses on this aspect of ethics—it identifies the character traits or virtues of the morally good person and explains how these traits can be developed or acquired.

The *virtue theory* of the ancient Greek philosopher Aristotle (384–322 B.C.) holds that the goal of life is *eudaimonia* (happiness or well-being) and that virtue is arrived at through the exercise of moderation, or the Golden Mean. Unlike Bentham, who equates happiness solely with "pleasure and the absence of pain," Aristotle regards *eudaimonia* as having more to do with the quality of our lives as a whole. Consequently, *eudaimonia* refers to the objective character of our lives rather than to a particular psychological state. For Aristotle, *virtue* is the ability to be reasonable in our actions, desires, and emotions. He believes that we are happy if we perform our human "function" well and that the function of human beings is to act in accordance with reason. Furthermore, it is reason that controls our emotions and other nonrational indicators such as the desire for pleasure, so that we avoid both excess and deficiency and thus act virtuously. For Aristotle, training produces the habit of acting virtuously and thus a virtuous character.

One of the main reasons that some believe virtue ethics is important is that it emphasizes character and its development, something that moral theories and traditions often neglect. In her book *In a Different Voice*, Carol Gilligan argues that women's moral development and their mature approach to moral questions can at times be quite different from those of men. Gilligan criticizes Lawrence Kohlberg's theory of moral development. According to Kohlberg, people's moral abilities develop in stages. In the first stage, the *preconventional*, we follow authority to avoid punishment. In the second stage, the *conventional*, we desire acceptance by a group and follow conventional moral standards. In the third and final stage, the *postconventional*, we question conventional standards and base our ideas of morality on universal moral principles of human welfare, justice, and rights. When Kohlberg's theory is applied to women, it turns out that women are, on average, less morally developed than men. While many men continue to move up to the postconventional level of impartial principles, women are more likely to stay at the lower conventional level of personal attachments and loyalties.

Gilligan proposes an alternative model of moral development that reflects women's distinctive moral perspective. According to Gilligan, women also develop in three stages. The first stage involves caring for oneself only, the second involves caring for others only, and the third is a balance between caring for self and others—the recognition that caring for others depends on caring for oneself. Women develop by discovering better ways of caring for themselves and others. Women faced with moral decisions focus on relationships and view morality as taking care of these relationships, whereas men focus on following moral rules and principles. According to Gilligan, women's morality is not inferior to that of men. The virtues of caring and responsibility are needed to ensure that society does not become a collection of isolated individuals who guard their individual rights and justice but who are lonely, unattached, and uncaring.

Virtue ethics emphasizes the whole person rather than individual actions. Critics of virtue ethics argue that people turn to ethics to answer questions about the morality of action. When people are faced with a concrete moral problem, they want to know what to do, not what kind of character they should cultivate over a lifetime. Virtue ethics does not answer common moral questions such as "What should I do now in this situation?" One might respond to this criticism of virtue ethics by saying that this is the wrong question to ask. Rather, if we ask, "What would a virtuous or decent person do now in this situation?" virtue ethics would be able to provide a response.

The readings in this chapter also take up two types of nonconsequentialist theories: divine command theory and the categorical imperative, both of which are considered single-rule nonconsequentialist theories. According to *divine command theory*, we should always do the will of God. Two apparent weaknesses of the theory are its epistemic and justificatory difficulties. Epistemic questions concern the nature and limits of our knowledge. Adherents of the divine command theory state that we are to follow God's will, but how are we to *know* God's will so that we may follow it? From this epistemic issue comes the justificatory problem: Why does God command this rather than that?

For Kant, the *categorical imperative* is singular—that is, it is one and only one imperative—but is formulated or expressed in several different ways. One version states that "I am never to act unless I am acting on a maxim that I can will to become a universal law." Another states that "I will act as if the maxims I choose to follow always become universal laws of nature." Yet another one states that "I should act so as to treat humanity always as an end and never merely as a means." The idea is that acting in accordance with each of these formulations will result in the same action.

Kant also distinguishes a number of different types of duties. *Perfect duties* consist of actions whose maxims can consistently neither be conceived nor be willed by us to be universal laws of nature. *Imperfect duties* consist of actions whose maxims could become universal laws of nature, but it is impossible for us to will that their maxims should be universal laws of nature since such a will would be in conflict with itself. This, together with a distinction between duties to oneself and those to others, yields four fundamental duties. The first is perfect duty to oneself, which precludes suicide. The second is perfect duty to others, which precludes insincere promises. The third is imperfect duty to oneself, which precludes not developing one's natural potential. The fourth is imperfect duty to others, which precludes refusing to help those in need. One of the major flaws in Kant's ethical theory is that it fails to provide guidance when duties conflict. Another is that acts which Kant condemns as universally wrong, such as lying, seem sometimes justified—and perhaps even morally required—in some situations (e.g., lying to protect someone from capture by evil people who will hurt or even kill him or her).

In conclusion, open discussion of how we should live and why we should live this way can take us in many different directions. As students of moral philosophy, it is our responsibility to identify relevant questions and concerns and to do our best to address them fairly and knowledgeably. Understanding matters concerning both individual and social morality should be grounded in a knowledge of general moral theories and traditions. While the readings in this chapter aim to give you this background, they are admittedly only a small piece of a much greater and growing body of perspectives. Consider these readings as a foundation to enable you to formulate knowledgeable responses to the individual and social moral problems presented in the ensuing chapters.

JONATHAN BENNETT

The Conscience of Huckleberry Finn

In this article, Jonathan Bennett uses Nazi Gestapo leader Heinrich Himmler, American theologian Jonathan Edwards, and the fictional character Huckleberry Finn to examine the relationship between what he calls "sympathy" and "bad morality." Bennett is concerned with the role of feelings in moral deliberation and with how Himmler, Edwards, and Finn each resolves the conflict between what they believe to be their moral duty and their sympathies for those who may be hurt by their doing their moral duty. Bennett concludes that Edwards' resolution of this conflict is no better, and may be worse, than Himmler's.

Jonathan Bennett is widely known for his work in the history of philosophy, the philosophy of language, and metaphysics. Among his many books are *Rationality* (1964) and *Events and Their Names* (1988).

I

In this paper, I shall present not just the conscience of Huckleberry Finn but two others as well. One of them is the conscience of Heinrich Himmler. He became a Nazi in 1923; he served drably and quietly, but well, and was rewarded with increasing responsibility and power. At the peak of his career he held many offices and commands, of which the most powerful was that of leader of the SS—the principal police force of the Nazi regime. In this capacity, Himmler commanded the whole concentration-camp system, and was responsible for the execution of the so-called "final solution of the Jewish problem." It is important for my purposes that this piece of social engineering should be thought of not abstractly but in concrete terms of Jewish families being marched to what they think are bathhouses, to the accompaniment of loud-speaker renditions of extracts from *The Merry Widow* and *Tales of Hoffmann*, there to be choked to death by poisonous gases. Altogether, Himmler succeeded in murdering about four and a half million of them, as well as several million gentiles, mainly Poles and Russians.

The other conscience to be discussed is that of the Calvinist theologian and philosopher Jonathan Edwards. He lived in the first half of the eighteenth century, and has a good claim to be considered

America's first serious and considerable philosophical thinker. He was for many years a widely renowned preacher and Congregationalist minister in New England; in 1748 a dispute with his congregation led him to resign (he couldn't accept their view that unbelievers should be admitted to the Lord's Supper in the hope that it would convert them); for some years after that he worked as a missionary, preaching to Indians through an interpreter; then in 1758 he accepted the presidency of what is now Princeton University, and within two months died from a small-pox inoculation. Along the way he wrote some first-rate philosophy; his book attacking the notion of free will is still sometimes read. Why I should be interested in Edwards's *conscience* will be explained in due course.

I shall use Heinrich Himmler, Jonathan Edwards, and Huckleberry Finn to illustrate different aspects of a single theme, namely the relationship between *sympathy* on the one hand and *bad morality* on the other.

II

All that I can mean by a "bad morality" is a morality whose principles I deeply disapprove of. When I call a morality bad, I cannot prove that mine is better; but when I here call any morality bad, I think you will agree with me that it is bad; and that is all I need.

There could be dispute as to whether the springs of someone's actions constitute a *morality*. I think, though, that we must admit that someone who acts in ways which conflict grossly with our morality may nevertheless have a morality of his own—a set of principles of action which he sincerely assents to, so that for him the problem of acting well or rightly or in obedience to conscience is the problem of conforming to *those* principles. The problem of conscientiousness can arise as acutely for a bad morality as for any other: Rotten principles may be as difficult to keep as decent ones.

As for "sympathy" I use this term to cover every sort of fellow-feeling, as when one feels pity over someone's loneliness, or horrified compassion over his pain, or when one feels a shrinking reluctance to act in a way which will bring misfortune to someone else. These *feelings* must not be confused with *moral judgments*. My sympathy for someone in distress may lead me to help him, or even to think that I ought to help him; but in itself it is not a judgment about what I ought to do but just a *feeling* for him in his plight. We shall get some light on the difference between feelings and moral judgments when we consider Huckleberry Finn.

Obviously, feelings can impel one to action, and so can moral judgments; and in a particular case sympathy and morality may pull in opposite directions. This can happen not just with bad moralities, but also with good ones like yours and mine. For example, a small child, sick and miserable, clings tightly to his mother and screams in terror when she tries to pass him over to the doctor to be examined. If the mother gave way to her sympathy, that is to her feeling for the child's misery and fright, she would hold it close and not let the doctor come near; but don't we agree that it might be wrong for her to act on such a feeling? Quite generally, then, anyone's moral principles may apply to a particular situation in a way which runs contrary to the particular thrusts of fellow-feeling that he has in that situation. My immediate concern is with sympathy in relation to bad morality, but not because such conflicts occur only when the morality is bad.

Now, suppose that someone who accepts a bad morality is struggling to make himself act in accordance with it in a particular situation where his sympathies pull him another way. He sees the struggle as one between doing the right, conscientious thing, and acting wrongly and weakly, like the mother who won't let the doctor come near her sick, frightened baby. Since we don't accept this person's morality, we may see the situation very differently, thoroughly disapproving of the action he regards as the right one, and endorsing the action which from his point of view constitutes weakness and backsliding.

Conflicts between sympathy and bad morality won't always be like this, for we won't disagree with every single dictate of a bad morality. Still, it can happen in the way I have described, with the agent's right action being our wrong one, and vice versa. That is just what happens in a certain episode in Chapter 16 of *The Adventures of Huckleberry Finn*, an episode which brilliantly illustrates how fiction can be instructive about real life.

III

Huck Finn has been helping his slave friend Jim to run away from Miss Watson, who is Jim's owner. In their raft-journey down the Mississippi River, they are near to the place at which Jim will become legally free. Now let Huck take over the story:

> Jim said it made him all over trembly and feverish to be so close to freedom. Well I can tell you it made me all over trembly and feverish, too, to hear him, because I begun to get it through my head that he *was* most free—and who was to blame for it? Why, *me.* I couldn't get that out of my conscience, no how nor no way. . . . It hadn't ever come home to me, before, what this thing was that I was doing. But now it did; and it stayed with me, and scorched me more and more. I tried to make out to myself that *I* warn't to blame, because *I* didn't run Jim off from his rightful owner; but it warn't no use, conscience up and say, every time: "But you knowed he was running for his freedom, and you could a paddled ashore and told somebody." That was so—I couldn't get around that, no way. That was where it pinched. Conscience says to me: "What had poor Miss Watson done to you, that you could see her nigger go off right under your eyes and never say one single word? What did that poor old woman do to you, that you could treat her so mean? . . ." I got to feeling so mean and miserable I most wished I was dead.

Jim speaks his plan to save up to buy his wife, and then his children, out of slavery; and he adds that if the children cannot be bought he will arrange to steal them. Huck is horrified:

> Thinks I, this is what comes of my not thinking. Here was this nigger which I had as good as

helped to run away, coming right out flat-footed and saying he would steal his children—children that belonged to a man I didn't even know; a man that hadn't ever done me no harm.

I was sorry to hear Jim say that, it was such a lowering of him. My conscience got to stirring me up hotter than ever, until at last I says to it: "Let up on me—it ain't too late, yet—I'll paddle ashore at first light, and tell." I felt easy, and happy, and light as a feather, right off. All my troubles was gone.

This is bad morality all right. In his earliest years Huck wasn't taught any principles, and the only one he has encountered since then are those of rural Missouri, in which slave-owning is just one kind of ownership and is not subject to critical pressure. It hasn't occurred to Huck to question those principles. So the action, to us abhorrent, of turning Jim in to the authorities presents itself *clearly* to Huck as the right thing to do.

For us, morality and sympathy would both dictate helping Jim to escape. If we felt any conflict, it would have both these on one side and something else on the other—greed for a reward, or fear of punishment. But Huck's morality conflicts with his sympathy, that is, with his unargued, natural feeling for his friend. The conflict starts when Huck sets off in the canoe towards the shore, pretending that he is going to reconnoiter, but really planning to turn Jim in:

> As I shoved off, [Jim] says: "Pooty soon I'll be a-shout'n for joy, en I'll say, it's all on accounts o' Huck I's a free man . . . Jim won't ever forgit you, Huck; you's de bes' fren' Jim's ever had; en you's de *only* fren' old Jim's got now."
>
> I was paddling off, all in a sweat to tell on him; but when he says this, it seemed to kind of take the tuck all out of me. I went along slow then, and I warn't right down certain whether I was glad I started or whether I warn't. When I was fifty yards off, Jim says:
>
> "Dah you goes, de ole true Huck; de on'y white genlman dat ever kep' his promise to ole Jim." Well, I just felt sick. But I says, I *got* to do it—I can't get *out* of it.

In the upshot, sympathy wins over morality. Huck hasn't the strength of will to do what he sincerely thinks he ought to do. Two men hunting for runaway slaves ask him whether the man on his raft is black or white:

> I didn't answer up prompt. I tried to, but the words wouldn't come. I tried, for a second or two, to brace up and out with it, but I warn't man enough—hadn't the spunk of a rabbit. I see I was weakening; so I just give up trying, and up and says: "He's white."

So Huck enables Jim to escape, thus acting weakly and wickedly—he thinks. In this conflict between sympathy and morality, sympathy wins.

One critic has cited this episode in support of the statement that Huck suffers "excruciating moments of wavering between honesty and respectability." That is hopelessly wrong, and I agree with the perceptive comment on it by another critic, who says:

> The conflict waged in Huck is much more serious: He scarcely cares for respectability and never hesitates to relinquish it, but he does care for honesty and gratitude—and both honesty and gratitude require that he should give Jim up. It is not, in Huck, honesty at war with respectability but love and compassion for Jim struggling against his conscience. His decision is for Jim and hell: a right decision made in the mental chains that Huck never breaks. His concern for Jim is and remains *irrational.* Huck finds many reasons for giving Jim up and none for stealing him. To the end Huck sees his compassion for Jim as a weak, ignorant, and wicked felony.[1]

That is precisely correct—and it can have that virtue only because Mark Twain wrote the episode with such unerring precision. The crucial point concerns *reasons*, which all occur on one side of the conflict. On the side of conscience we have principles, arguments, considerations, ways of looking at things:

> "It hadn't ever come home to me before what I was doing"
>
> "I tried to make out that I warn't to blame"
>
> "Conscience said 'But you knowed . . .'—I couldn't get around that"
>
> "What had poor Miss Watson done to you?"
>
> "This is what comes of my not thinking"
>
> ". . . children that belonged to a man I didn't even know."

On the other side, the side of feeling, we get nothing like that. When Jim rejoices in Huck, as his only friend, Huck doesn't consider the claims of friendship or have the situation "come home" to him in a different light. All that happens is: "When he says this, it seemed to kind of take the tuck all out of me. I went along slow then, and I warn't right down certain whether I was glad I started or whether I warn't." Again, Jim's words about Huck's "promise" to him don't give Huck any *reason* for changing his plan: In his morality, promises to slaves probably don't count. Their effect on him is of a different kind: "Well, I just felt sick." And when the moment for final decision comes, Huck doesn't weigh up pros and cons: he simply *fails* to do what he believes to be right—he isn't strong enough, hasn't "the spunk of a rabbit." This passage in the novel is notable not just for its finely wrought irony, with Huck's weakness of will leading him to do the right thing, but also for its masterly handling of the difference between general moral principles and particular unreasoned emotional pulls.

IV

Consider now another case of bad morality in conflict with human sympathy: the case of the odious Himmler. Here, from a speech he made to some SS generals, is an indication of the content of his morality:

> What happens to a Russian, to a Czech, does not interest me in the slightest. What the nations can offer in the way of good blood of our type, we will take, if necessary by kidnapping their children and raising them here with us. Whether nations live in prosperity or starve to death like cattle interests me only in so far as we need them as slaves to our *Kultur*; otherwise it is of no interest to me. Whether 10,000 Russian females fall down from exhaustion while digging an antitank ditch interests me only in so far as the antitank ditch for Germany is finished.[2]

But has this a moral basis at all? And if it has, was there in Himmler's own mind any conflict between morality and sympathy? Yes there was. Here is more from the same speech:

> I also want to talk to you quite frankly on a very grave matter . . . I mean . . . the extermination of the Jewish race. . . . Most of you must know what it means when 100 corpses are lying side by side, or 500, or 1,000. To have stuck it out and at the same time—apart from exceptions caused by human weakness—to have remained decent fellows, that is what has made us hard. This is a page of glory in our history which has never been written and is never to be written.

Himmler saw his policies as being hard to implement while still retaining one's human sympathies—while still remaining a "decent fellow." He is saying that only the weak take the easy way out and just squelch their sympathies, and is praising the stronger and more glorious course of retaining one's sympathies while acting in violation of them. In the same spirit, he ordered that when executions were carried out in concentration camps, those responsible "are to be influenced in such a way as to suffer no ill effect in their character and mental attitude." A year later he boasted that the SS had wiped out the Jews

> without our leaders and their men suffering any damage in their minds and souls. The danger was considerable, for there was only a narrow path between the Scylla of their becoming heartless ruffians unable any longer to treasure life, and the Charybdis of their becoming soft and suffering nervous breakdowns.

And there really can't be any doubt that the basis of Himmler's policies was a set of principles which constituted his morality—a sick, bad, wicked *morality*. He described himself as caught in "the old tragic conflict between will and obligation." And when his physician Kersten protested at the intention to destroy the Jews, saying that the suffering involved was "not to be contemplated," Kersten reports that Himmler replied:

> He knew that it would mean much suffering for the Jews. . . . "It is the curse of greatness that it must step over dead bodies to create new life. Yet we must . . . cleanse the soil or it will never bear fruit. It will be a great burden for me to bear."

This, I submit, is the language of morality.

So in this case, tragically, bad morality won out over sympathy. I am sure that many of Himmler's killers did extinguish their sympathies, becoming "heartless ruffians" rather than "decent fellows"; but not Himmler himself. Although his policies ran against the human grain to a horrible degree, he did not sandpaper down his emotional surfaces so that there was no grain there, allowing his actions to slide along smoothly and easily. He did, after all, bear his hideous burden, and even paid a price for it. He suffered a variety of nervous and physical disabilities, including nausea and stomach-convulsions, and Kersten was doubtless right in saying that these were "the expression of a psychic division which extended over his whole life."

This same division must have been present in some of those officials of the Church who ordered heretics to be tortured so as to change their theological opinions. Along with the brutes and the cold careerists, there must have been some who cared, and who suffered from the conflict between their sympathies and their bad morality.

V

In the conflict between sympathy and bad morality, then, the victory may go to sympathy as in the case of Huck Finn, or to morality as in the case of Himmler.

Another possibility is that the conflict may be avoided by giving up, or not ever having, those sympathies which might interfere with one's principles. That seems to have been the case with Jonathan Edwards. I am afraid that I shall be doing an injustice to Edwards's many virtues, and to his great intellectual energy and inventiveness; for my concern is only with the worst thing about him—namely his morality, which was worse than Himmler's.

According to Edwards, God condemns some men to an eternity of unimaginably awful pain, though he arbitrarily spares others—"arbitrarily" because none deserve to be spared:

> Natural men are held in the hand of God over the pit of hell; they have deserved the fiery pit, and are already sentenced to it; and God is dreadfully provoked, his anger is as great toward them as to those that are actually suffering the executions of the fierceness of his wrath in hell . . . ; the devil is waiting for them, hell is gaping for them, the flames gather and flash about them, and would fain lay hold on them . . . ; and . . . there are no means within reach that can be any security to them. . . . All that preserves them is the mere arbitrary will, and unconvenanted unobliged forebearance of an incensed God.[3]

Notice that he says "they have deserved the fiery pit." Edwards insists that men *ought* to be condemned to eternal pain; and his position isn't that this is right because God wants it, but rather that God wants it because it is right. For him, moral standards exist independently of God, and God can be assessed in the light of them (and of course found to be perfect). For example, he says:

> They deserve to be cast into hell; so that . . . justice never stands in the way, it makes no objection against God's using his power at any moment to destroy them. Yea, on the contrary, justice calls aloud for an infinite punishment of their sins.

Elsewhere, he gives elaborate arguments to show that God is acting justly in damning sinners. For example, he argues that a punishment should be exactly as bad as the crime being punished; God is infinitely excellent; so any crime against him is infinitely bad; and so eternal damnation is exactly right as a punishment—it is infinite, but, as Edwards is careful also to say, it is "no more than infinite."

Of course, Edwards himself didn't torment the damned; but the question still arises of whether his sympathies didn't conflict with his *approval* of eternal torment. Didn't he find it painful to contemplate any fellow-human's being tortured for ever? Apparently not:

> The God that holds you over the pit of hell, much as one holds a spider or some loathsome insect over the fire, abhors you, and is dreadfully provoked . . . he is of purer eyes than to bear to have you in his sight; you are ten thousand times so abominable in his eyes as the most hateful venomous serpent is in ours.

When God is presented as being as misanthropic as that, one suspects misanthropy in the theologian. This suspicion is increased when Edwards claims that "the saints in glory will . . . understand how terrible the sufferings of the damned are; yet . . . will not be sorry for [them]."[4] He bases this partly on a view of human nature whose ugliness he seems not to notice:

> The seeing of the calamities of others tends to heighten the sense of our own enjoyments. When the saints in glory, therefore, shall see the doleful state of the damned, how will this heighten their sense of the blessedness of their own state. . . . When they shall see how miserable others of their fellow-creatures are . . . when they shall see the smoke of their torment . . . and hear their dolorous shrieks and cries, and consider that they in the mean time are in the most blissful state, and shall surely be in it to all eternity; how they will rejoice!

I hope this is less than the whole truth! His other main point about why the saints will rejoice to see the torments of the damned is that it is *right* that they should do so:

> The heavenly inhabitants . . . will have no love nor pity to the damned. . . . [This will not show] a want of spirit of love in them . . . for the heavenly inhabitants will know that it is not fit that they should love [the damned] because

they will know then, that God has no love to them, nor pity for them.

The implication that *of course* one can adjust one's feelings of pity so that they conform to the dictates of some authority—doesn't this suggest that ordinary human sympathies played only a small part in Edwards's life?

VI

Huck Finn, whose sympathies are wide and deep, could never avoid the conflict in that way; but he is determined to avoid it, and so he opts for the only other alternative he can see—to give up morality altogether. After he has tricked the slave-hunters, he returns to the raft and undergoes a peculiar crisis:

> I got aboard the raft, feeling bad and low, because I knowed very well I had done wrong, and I see it warn't no use for me to try to learn to do right; a body that don't get *started* right when he's little, ain't got no show—when the pinch comes there ain't nothing to back him up and keep him to his work, and so he gets beat. Then I thought a minute, and says to myself, hold on—s'pose you'd a done right and give Jim up; would you feel better than what you do now? No, says I, I'd feel bad—I'd feel just the same way I do now. Well, then, says I, what's the use you learning to do right, when it's troublesome to do right and ain't no trouble to do wrong, and the wages is just the same? I was stuck. I couldn't answer that. So I reckoned I wouldn't bother no more about it, but after this always do whichever come handiest at the time.

Huck clearly cannot conceive of having any morality except the one he has learned—too late, he thinks—from his society. He is not entirely a prisoner of that morality, because he does after all reject it; but for him that is a decision to relinquish morality as such; he cannot envisage revising his morality, altering its content in face of the various pressures to which it is subject, including pressures from his sympathies. For example, he does not begin to approach the thought that slavery should be rejected on moral grounds, or the thought that what he is doing is not theft because a person cannot be owned and therefore cannot be stolen.

The basic trouble is that he cannot or will not engage in abstract intellectual operations of any sort. In Chapter 33 he finds himself "feeling to blame, somehow" for something he knows he had no hand in; he assumes that this feeling is a deliverance of conscience; and this confirms him in his belief that conscience shouldn't be listened to:

> It don't make no difference whether you do right or wrong, a person's conscience ain't got no sense, and just goes for him *anyway*. If I had a yaller dog that didn't know no more than a person's conscience does, I would poison him. It takes up more than all of a person's insides, and yet ain't no good, nohow.

That brisk, incurious dismissiveness fits well with the comprehensive rejection of morality back on the raft. But this is a digression.

On the raft, Huck decides not to live by principles, but just to do whatever "comes handiest at the time" —always acting according to the mood of the moment. Since the morality he is rejecting is narrow and cruel, and his sympathies are broad and kind, the results will be good. But moral principles are good to have, because they help to protect one from acting badly at moments when one's sympathies happen to be in abeyance. On the highest possible estimate of the role one's sympathies should have, one can still allow for principles as embodiments of one's best feelings, one's broadest and keenest sympathies. On that view, principles can help one across intervals when one's feelings are at less than their best, i.e. through periods of misanthropy or meanness or self-centeredness or depression or anger.

What Huck didn't see is that one can live by principles and yet have ultimate control over their content. And one way such control can be exercised is by checking one's principles in the light of one's sympathies. This is sometimes a pretty straightforward matter. It can happen that a certain moral principle becomes untenable—meaning literally that one cannot hold it any longer—because it conflicts intolerably with the pity or revulsion or whatever that one feels when one sees what the principle leads to. One's experience may play a large part here: Experiences evoke feelings, and feelings force one to modify principles. Something like this happened to the English poet Wilfred Owen, whose experiences in the First World War transformed him from an enthusiastic soldier into a virtual pacifist. I can't document his change of conscience in detail; but I want to present something which he wrote about the way experience can put pressure on morality.

The Latin poet Horace wrote that it is sweet and fitting (or right) to die for one's country—*dulce et decorum est pro patria mori*—and Owen wrote a fine

poem about how experience could lead one to relinquish that particular moral principle.[5] He describes a man who is too slow donning his gas mask
during a gas attack—"As under a green sea I saw him
drowning," Owen says. The poem ends like this:

> In all my dreams before my helpless sight
> He plunges at me, guttering, choking,
>   drowning.
> If in some smothering dreams, you too could
>   pace
> Behind the wagon that we flung him in,
> And watch the white eyes writhing in his face,
> His hanging face, like a devil's sick of sin;
> If you could hear, at every jolt, the blood
> Come gargling from the froth-corrupted lungs,
> Bitter as the cud
> Of vile, incurable sores on innocent tongues,—
> My friend, you would not tell with such high zest
> To children ardent for some desperate glory,
> The old Lie: Dulce et decorum est
> Pro patria mori.

There is a difficulty about drawing from all this a
moral for ourselves. I imagine that we agree in our
rejection of slavery, eternal damnation, genocide,
and uncritical patriotic self-abnegation; so we shall
agree that Huck Finn, Jonathan Edwards, Heinrich
Himmler, and the poet Horace would all have done
well to bring certain of their principles under severe pressure from ordinary human sympathies.
But then we can say this because we can say that all
those are bad moralities, whereas we cannot look at
our own moralities and declare them bad. This is
not arrogance: It is obviously incoherent for someone to declare the system of moral principles that
he *accepts* to be *bad*, just as one cannot coherently
say of anything that one *believes* it but it is *false*.

Still, although I can't point to any of my beliefs
and say "That is false," I don't doubt that some of
my beliefs *are* false; and so I should try to remain
open to correction. Similarly, I accept every single
item in my morality—that is inevitable—but I am
sure that my morality could be improved, which is
to say that it could undergo changes which I should
be glad of once I had made them. So I must try to
keep my morality open to revision, exposing it to
whatever valid pressures there are—including pressures from my sympathies.

I don't give my sympathies a blank check in advance. In a conflict between principle and sympathy,
principles ought sometimes to win. For example, I
think it was right to take part in the Second World
War on the allied side; there were many ghastly indi-

vidual incidents which might have led someone to
doubt the rightness of his participation in that war;
and I think it would have been right for such a person
to keep his sympathies in a subordinate place on
those occasions, not allowing them to modify his principles in such a way as to make a pacifist of him.

Still, one's sympathies should be kept as sharp and
sensitive and aware as possible, and not only because
they can sometimes affect one's principles or one's
conduct or both. Owen, at any rate, says that feelings
and sympathies are vital even when they can do nothing but bring pain and distress. In another poem he
speaks of the blessings of being numb in one's feelings: "Happy are the men who yet before they are
killed/Can let their veins run cold," he says. These
are the ones who do not suffer from any compassion
which, as Owen puts it, "makes their feet/Sore on the
alleys cobbled with their brothers." He contrasts
these "happy" ones, who "lose all imagination," with
himself and others "who with a thought be-
smirch/Blood over all our soul." Yet the poem's verdict goes against the "happy" ones. Owen does not
say that they will act worse than the others whose
souls are besmirched with blood because of their
keen awareness of human suffering. He merely says
that they are the losers because they have cut themselves off from the human condition:

> By choice they made themselves immune
> To pity and whatever moans in man
> Before the last sea and the hapless stars;
> Whatever mourns when many leave these
>   shores;
> Whatever shares
> The eternal reciprocity of tears.

NOTES

1. M. J. Sidnell, "Huck Finn and Jim," *The Cambridge
   Quarterly*, 2: 205–206.
2. Quoted in William L. Shirer, *The Rise and Fall of the
   Third Reich* (New York, 1960), pp. 937–938. Next
   quotation: ibid., p. 966. All further quotations relating to Himmler are from Roger Manwell and
   Heinrich Fraenkel, *Heinrich Himmler* (London,
   1965), pp. 132, 197, 184 (twice), 187.
3. Vergilius Ferm, ed., *Puritan Sage: Collected
   Writings of Jonathan Edwards* (New York, 1953),
   p. 370. Next three quotations: ibid., p. 366,
   p. 294 ("no more than infinite"), p. 372.
4. This and the next two quotations are from "The
   End of the Wicked Contemplated by the
   Righteous: Or, The Torments of the Wicked in

Hell, No Occasion of Grief to the Saints in Heaven," from *The Works of President Edwards*, vol. 4 (London, 1817), pp. 507–508, 511–512, and 509 respectively.

5. We are grateful to the Executors of the Estate of Harold Owen, and to Chatto and Windus Ltd. for permission to quote from Wilfred Owen's "Dulce et Decorum Est" and "Insensibility."

DISCUSSION QUESTIONS

1. Why does Bennett believe that Jonathan Edwards' morality was no better than, if not worse than, the morality of Heinrich Himmler? Do you agree? Explain why or why not.
2. What does Bennett mean by "bad morality"? Do you agree with this definition? Why or why not?
3. What is "sympathy"? What role do you think it should play in our moral deliberations? Compare your view to Bennett's.
4. What examples can you suggest in which our sense of moral duty and principle should overrule our sympathies? Defend your view.

PHILIP HALLIE

The Evil That Men Think—And Do

In "The Consciousness of Huckleberry Finn," Jonathan Bennett argues that Jonathan Edwards is morally worse than Heinrich Himmler. Philip Hallie objects to Bennett's argument in this article on the grounds that it places far too much emphasis on the psychology of the evildoer and far too little emphasis on the fate of the victim. Hallie also offers summaries and evaluations of a number of contemporary theories of evil.

Philip Hallie taught philosophy at Wesleyan University and is the author of *The Paradox of Cruelty* (1969) and *Lest Innocent Blood Be Shed* (1979).

In a cartoon by Edward Kliban, a mechanic is waving his tools and pointing at what he has discovered under the hood of his customer's car. There, where the motor should be, squats a massive monster, a wicked grin revealing his terrible teeth. The mechanic is triumphantly proclaiming to his customer: "Well, *there's* your problem."

In her book *Wickedness*, Mary Midgley writes that evil must not be seen as "something positive" or demonic like Kliban's monster. If evil were a demon we could only exorcise it, not understand it. To do so, she writes, one must see the various types of wickedness as *mixtures* of motives, some of which can be life-enhancing in themselves but are destructive in certain combinations. For instance, a rapist-murderer can be motivated by power and sex, but his way of combining these often healthy drives is destructive. For Midgley wickedness is "essentially destructive," not the way a terrible-toothed monster can be destructive but the way a person acting under various motives can fail to care about the feelings or even the

Philip Hallie, *Hastings Center Report* (December 1985). Copyright © 1985 The Hastings Center. Reprinted by permission of the publisher.

lives of others. For her, evil is an absence of such caring, "an emptiness at the core of the individual. . . ." It is a negative, not a positive, demon.

This is a sensitive analysis, but the demon Wickedness is a straw demon: very few, if any, modern thinkers on the subject believe in the demonic. For most of them another cartoon would be more apt. A mechanic is waving his tools triumphantly before a customer and is pointing to what he has found under the hood of the car. There, where Kliban's demon was, is a mass of intricately intertwined pipes, and the mechanic is pointing to *this* and announcing, "Well, *there's* your problem." And the customer is as bewildered by this phenomenon as Kliban's customer was.

Many of the people who are writing about wickedness (or immorality or evil, call it what you will) are making it a very complicated matter, like those twisted pipes. Judith Shklar in her quite often brilliant book *Ordinary Vices* is more concerned with various ethical and political puzzles than she is with the ordinary vices she promises to talk about in her introduction and in her title. Usually the unique perplexities of unique people like Robert E. Lee, Richard II, Socrates, and Colonel Count Claus von Stauffenberg interest her more than any single idea of vice does. Her skeptical, energetic mind seeks out mine-fields, not highways: contradictions, not a monster.

My version of Kliban's cartoon applies also to the lucid, careful book *Immorality* by the philosopher Ronald D. Milo. Milo takes Aristotle's all-too-pat distinction between moral weakness and moral baseness, and refines it into a range of kinds and degrees of blameworthiness. In the seventh book of his *Nichomachean Ethics*, Aristotle said that the weak (or "incontinent") person is like a city that has good laws, but that does not live by them; the vicious (or "base") person is like a city that has bad laws by which it *does* live. The zealous mass murderer is vicious without remorse; while the weak, penitent adulterer or drunkard knows he is doing wrong, but does nothing about it. Milo refines and develops this rather crude distinction, so that Aristotle's baseness is no longer a simple contrast between two kinds of cities. Like Shklar, Milo is too perceptive and too circumspect to join the simplifiers that Midgley deplores.

And yet, despite their perceptiveness and circumspection, many of our analyzers of evil have grossly simplified the idea of immorality. In their scrupulous examinations of complexities they have left out much of the ferocious ugliness of Kliban's monster. They too are negligent simplifiers.

For instance, Jonathan Bennett has written an essay entitled "The Conscience of Huckleberry Finn," in which he proves to his satisfaction that the morality of the eighteenth-century American theologian Jonathan Edwards was "worse than Himmler's." He insists that Heinrich Himmler, head of the SS and of all the police systems of Nazi Germany, and responsible for all of the tortures and the deaths perpetrated upon noncombatants by Nazi Germany, was not as wicked as Jonathan Edwards, who never killed or meant to kill anyone.

Why? Because Jonathan Edwards had no pity for the damned, and Himmler did have sympathy for the millions of people he tortured and destroyed. Bennett contends that there are two forces at work in the consciences of human beings: general moral principles and unreasoned "emotional pulls." One such "pull" is sympathy, and Jonathan Edwards's sermons showed no sympathy for the sinners who were in the hands of an angry God, while Himmler's speeches to his Nazi subordinates did express the emotional pull of sympathy. In the mind, the only place where "morality" dwells for Bennett, Himmler is no heartless ruffian, but a decent fellow who had a wrong-headed set of principles and who felt the pangs of sympathy for human beings he was crushing and grinding into death and worse.

THE CENTRAL ROLE OF THE VICTIM

In Lewis Carroll's *Alice's Adventures in Wonderland* Tweedledee recites to Alice "The Walrus and the Carpenter." In the poem, the Walrus and the Carpenter come across some oysters while they are strolling on the beach. They manage to persuade the younger oysters to join them in

A pleasant walk, a pleasant talk
   Along the briny beach

After a while they rest on a rock that is "conveniently low," so that the two of them can keep an eye on the oysters and can reach them easily. After a little chat, the Carpenter and the Walrus start eating the oysters.

The Walrus is a sympathetic creature, given to crying readily, who thanks the oysters for joining them, while the Carpenter is interested only in eating:

"It seems a shame," the Walrus said
   "To play them such a trick.
After we've brought them out so far
   And made them trot so quick!"

The Carpenter said nothing but
    "The butter's spread too thick."

Then the Walrus, out of the goodness of his heart, bursts forth:

"I weep for you," the Walrus said:
    "I deeply sympathize."
With sobs and tears he sorted out
    Those of the largest size,
Holding his pocket-handkerchief
    Before his streaming eyes.

And they finish off all the oysters.

Bennett, with his concern for the saving grace of sympathy, might find the "morality" of the Walrus better than the morality of the cold-blooded Carpenter, but Lewis Carroll, or rather Tweedledee and Tweedledum, are not so simple-minded:

"I like the Walrus best," said Alice: "because he was a *little* sorry for the poor oysters."

"He ate more than the Carpenter, though," said Tweedledee. "You see he held his handkerchief in front, so that the Carpenter couldn't count how many he took: contrariwise."

"That was mean!" Alice said indignantly. "Then I like the Carpenter best—if he didn't eat so many as the Walrus."

"But he ate as many as he could get," said Tweedledum.

Then Alice gives up trying to rank the Walrus and the Carpenter and gives voice to a wisdom that is as sound as it is obvious:

"Well! They were both very unpleasant characters. . . ."

What Lewis Carroll saw, and what Bennett apparently does not, is that the victims are as essential in morality as the presence or absence of sympathy inside the head of the moral agent. And he also sees that sympathy, or rather expressions of sympathy, can be a device for eating more oysters by hiding your mouth behind a handkerchief—it certainly needn't slow your eating down.

Milo never violates the morally obvious as boldly as Bennett does, but when he ranks immoralities he too disregards the essential role of the victim in evil. His conclusions contradict Bennett's. For Milo, apparently, Himmler's would be "the most evil" kind of wrongdoing, just because of his scruples:

. . . we think that the most evil or reprehensible kind of wrongdoing consists in willingly and intentionally doing something that one believes

to be morally wrong, either because one simply does not care that it is morally wrong or because one prefers the pursuit of some other end to the avoidance of moral wrongdoing. . . .

This is a more subtle analysis of evil than Bennett's, but it too ranks evils without the wisdom of Tweedledum and Tweedledee. It too flattens out or ignores the central role of victims in the dance of evil.

WHERE EICHMANN'S EVIL LAY

The most distinguished modern philosophic treatment of evil is Hannah Arendt's *Eichmann in Jerusalem, A Report on the Banality of Evil.* Like most of the philosophers who came after her she believed that the evil person is not necessarily a monster. In her report on the Eichmann trial as she witnessed it in Jerusalem in 1961 she shows us a man who did not act out of evil motives. She shows us a man, Adolf Eichmann, whose main trait was to have no interesting traits, except perhaps his "remoteness from reality." His banality resides in his never having *realized* what he was doing to particular human beings. Hannah Arendt tells us that, except for personal advancement, "He had no motives at all." He was an unimaginative bureaucrat who lived in the clichés of his office. He was no Iago, no Richard III, no person who wished "to prove a villain."

There is truth in this position. Eichmann was a commonplace, trite man if you look at him only in the dock and if you do not see that his boring clichés are directly linked with millions of tortures and murders. If you see the victims of Eichmann and of the office he held, then—and only then—do you see the evil of this man. Evil does not happen only in people's heads. Eichmann's evil happened in his head (and here Arendt is not only right but brilliantly perceptive) *and* (and the "and" makes a tight, essential linkage) in the freight cars and in the camps of Central Europe. His evil is the sum-total of his unimaginative head and his unimaginable tortures and murders. And this sum-total is not banal, not flat, not common-place. It is horrific.

As one of the most powerful philosophers of our time, Arendt was conscious of leaving something out by concentrating her attention upon the internal workings of the mind of a bureaucrat. Early in her book she wrote: "On trial are his deeds, not the sufferings of the Jews."

As if "his deeds" could be neatly peeled away from what he did to the Jews! *Her separation* of the mental activity of Eichmann from the pain-racked deaths of millions that this mental activity brought about made Eichmann's evil banal. Without these actual murders and tortures Eichmann was not evil; his maunderings were those of a pitiable, not a culpable man. His evil lay in his deeds, as Arendt says, but not only in his mental "deeds": it lay in all that he intended and all that he carried out, in his mind and in the world around him.

THE MORALITY OF SEEING

In Saul Bellow's novel *The Dean's December*, the narrator, Dean Albert Corde, makes a plea for seeing what there is to be seen:

> In the American moral crisis, the first requirement was to experience what was happening and to see what must be seen. The facts were covered from our perception. . . . The increase of theories and discourse, itself a cause of new, strange forms of blindness, the false representations of "communication," led to horrible distortions of public consciousness. Therefore the first act of morality was to disinter the reality, retrieve reality, dig it out from the trash, represent it anew as art would represent it. . . .
>
> We were no longer talking about anything. The language of discourse had shut out experience altogether. . . . I tried to make myself the moralist of seeing. . . .

The dynamic of passions, moral principles, and perceptions within the heads of moral agents is a dynamic that is part of evil, but those of us who want to face and to understand evil as best we can must, it seems to me, try to live up to Corde's "morality of seeing." We must do our best to see not only what is happening in the inward polities of the doers of evil but *also* what is happening in the lives of the sufferers of evil.

For instance, to write about Himmler requires not only the reading of a few carefully crafted speeches; it also demands learning about the context of these speeches. It is true that at least once Himmler looked as if he felt queasy at an execution, and it is also true that he wrote about this queasiness in terms not entirely unlike those of the Walrus. But even a superficial study of what was actually happening within Fortress Europe in those days makes quite clear that he was coping with a particular problem by talking about "damage in . . . minds and souls" and "human weakness."

Look at almost any volume of the record of the 1947 Nuremberg Trials—for example Volume IV, especially pages 311–355—and it will become plain that the efficient murdering of children as well as other defenseless human beings was being hindered by the depression and even the nervous breakdowns of the people who were herding together and executing these people. Himmler, in order to minimize inefficiency, needed to prepare his followers to deal with such scruples. At least he needed to do this to carry out the project of exterminating the Jews of Europe as well as the majority of the Slavs.

Talking about these scruples was not a *cri du coeur*. He was not opening his heart to his subordinates, as Bennett suggests: he was preparing them for dealing with the psychological problems of the executioners. He was holding up a handkerchief before his eyes, to go back to the imagery of Tweedledee's poem, so that he and his followers could murder more and more helpless human beings.

A MONSTER IN ACTION

Even such vigorously human books as *Ordinary Vices* by Judith Shklar and *Wickedness* by Mary Midgley do not meet the obligations laid upon us by a morality of seeing. Shklar provides lurid and deep insights into the implications of making cruelty *summum malum*, the most indefensible and unforgivable evil, and into many other subjects, but she hastens into perplexities and puzzles before she carefully observes the factual contexts of her examples.

Midgley is memorably illuminating in her efforts to clear away the obstacles that keep us from taking wickedness seriously. For instance, very few readers of her book, if they are attentive, will ever describe a mass-murderer and a mass-rapist as "sick" after reading her truly remarkable analysis in the chapter entitled "The Elusiveness of Responsibility." One of her key arguments against replacing the words "wicked" and "evil" by the words "sick" and "ill" is that doing so *distances* us from the destruction that has been done. It removes the "sick" destroyers from blame and from anger (how dare you blame a person for being ill?). It "flattens out," to use her powerful phrase, the distinctions between murderers and kleptomaniacs, between those who make us defensibly angry, when we see what they have *done*, and those who engage only our compassion and help.

Still, so scrupulous is she in removing the obstacles to an awareness of wickedness that she does not reveal much about what evil is. Her description of wickedness as "negative" like darkness and cold (an absence of caring being like an absence of light or heat) is useful but difficult to understand in terms of examples, especially when she tells us that "evil in the quiet supporters [of, for example, a Hitler] is negative," and then tells us that what they do is "positive action." This is a confusing use of metaphysical terms that do not have a plain cash value in relation to observable facts. These terms bring us close to the medieval soup and its casuistical arguments about whether evil is a "privation of good" or something "positive."

Milo's *Immorality* offers a scrupulously lucid and sustained argument about the types and blameworthiness of immorality. It is especially adroit at understanding the relationships between moral weakness and deep wickedness. But he, like these other recent writers on evil, is reluctant to face the full force of evil. He, like them, does not look deeply and carefully at examples, at the terrible details in history and the arts.

These writers are, perhaps, too timid to look hard at Kliban's monster and say, "Well, *there's* your problem." Evil is thick with fact and as ugly as that grinning monster. It is no worse to see it this way than it is to see it as an internal dynamic in a moral agent's head, or a set of carefully honed distinctions, or an array of puzzles and perplexities (as Shklar seems to see it). Many of the insights of these writers are useful for understanding the monster, or rather the many monsters that embody evil, but there is no substitute for seeing the harshness and ugliness of fact.

Here is a monster in action: He is Otto Ohlendorf, who was, among other roles, head of Group D of the Action Groups assigned to exterminate Jews and Soviet political leaders in parts of Eastern Europe. To learn more about him, read pages 311–355 of Volume IV of the transcript of the Nuremberg trials of the major war criminals. Here is part of his testimony:

COLONEL POKROVSKY (for the Tribunal): Why did they (the execution squads) prefer execution by shooting to killing in the gas vans?

OHLENDORF: Because . . . in the opinion of the leader of the Einsatzkommandos [Action Groups], the unloading of the corpses was an unnecessary mental strain.

COL. POKROVSKY: What do you mean by "an unnecessary mental strain"?

OHLENDORF: As far as I can remember the conditions at the time—the picture presented by the corpses and probably because certain functions of the body had taken place, leaving the corpses lying in filth.

COL. POKROVSKY: You mean to say that the sufferings endured prior to death were clearly visible on the victims? Did I understand you correctly?

OHLENDORF: I don't understand the question; do you mean during the killing in the van?

COL. POKROVSKY: Yes.

OHLENDORF: I can only repeat what the doctor told me, that the victims were not conscious of their death in the van.

COL. POKROVSKY: In that case your reply to my previous question, that the unloading of the bodies made a very terrible impression on the members of the execution squad, becomes entirely incomprehensible.

OHLENDORF: And, as I said, the terrible impression created by the position of the corpses themselves, and by the state of the vans which had probably been dirtied and so on.

COL. POKROVSKY: I have no further questions to put to this witness at the present stage of the Trial (p. 334).

COLONEL AMEN (for the Tribunal): Referring to the gas vans which you said you received in the spring of 1942, what order did you receive with respect to the use of these vans?

OHLENDORF: These gas vans were in future to be used for the killing of women and children.

COL. AMEN: Will you explain to the Tribunal the construction of these vans and their appearance?

OHLENDORF: The actual purpose of these vans could not be seen from the outside. They looked like closed trucks, and were so constructed that at the start of the motor, gas was conducted into the van, causing death in 10 to 15 minutes.

COL. AMEN: Explain in detail just how one of these vans was used for an execution.

OHLENDORF: The vans were loaded with the victims and driven to the place of burial, which was usually the same as that used for the mass executions. The time needed for transportation was sufficient to insure the death of the victims.

COL. AMEN: How were the victims induced to enter the vans?

OHLENDORF: They were told that they were to be transported to another locality.

COL. AMEN: How was the gas turned on?

OHLENDORF: I am not familiar with the technical details.

COL. AMEN: How long did it take to kill the victims ordinarily?

OHLENDORF: About 10 to 15 minutes; the victims were not conscious of what was happening to them (p. 322).

OHLENDORF: I led the Einsatzgruppe, and therefore I had the task of seeing how the Einsatzkommandos executed the orders received.

HERR BABEL (for the Tribunal): But did you have no scruples in regard to the execution of these orders?

OHLENDORF: Yes, of course.

HERR BABEL: And how is it that they were carried out regardless of these scruples?

OHLENDORF: Because to me it is inconceivable that a subordinate leader should not carry out orders given by the leaders of the state (pp. 353–354).

I urge you to read the above extracts more than once. The wholeness of evil is there, and if Ohlendorf is not monstrous to you, you are the problem.

DISCUSSION QUESTIONS

1. Do you agree with Hallie that "victims are as essential in morality as the presence or absence of sympathy inside the head of the moral agent"? Defend your position.
2. What does Hannah Arendt mean by "the banality of evil"? Do you agree with Hallie's criticism of Arendt? Defend your position.
3. How might Jonathan Bennett regard Eichmann's morality in comparison to that of Himmler, Edwards, and Finn? Explain your view.
4. Why does Hallie believe that Judith Shklar and Mary Midgley "do not meet the obligations laid upon us by a morality of seeing"? Do you agree with him? Explain.
5. Which criticism by Hallie of a contemporary theory of morality do you agree with the most? Which the least? Explain and defend your position.

 JAMES RACHELS

Egoism and Moral Skepticism

James Rachels distinguishes between two types of egoism: psychological and ethical. Psychological egoism is the view that all people are selfish in everything they do. According to the psychological egoist, the only motive from which anyone ever acts is self-interest. Ethical egoism, unlike psychological egoism, is a normative view about how people *ought* to act. The ethical egoist believes that we have no obligation to do anything except what is in our own self-interest. According to the ethical egoist, whatever we do in our own self-interest, regardless of its effect on others, is morally justified. Rachels lays out a number of difficulties in both types of egoism.

James Rachels has been a member of the philosophy faculty at University of Alabama since 1977. He is the author of *The End of Life* (1986), *Created from Animals* (1991), *Can Ethics Provide Answers? And Other Essays in Moral Philosophy* (1997), and *The Elements of Moral Philosophy* (3rd ed., 1998).

James Rachels, *A New Introduction to Philosophy*. Edited by Steven M. Cahn. Harper & Row, 1971. Reprinted by permission of Steven M. Cahn.

I

Our ordinary thinking about morality is full of assumptions that we almost never question. We assume, for example, that we have an obligation to consider the welfare of other people when we decide what actions to perform or what rules to obey; we think that we must refrain from acting in ways harmful to others, and that we must respect their rights and interests as well as our own. We also assume that people are in fact capable of being motivated by such considerations, that is, that people are not wholly selfish and that they do sometimes act in the interests of others.

Both of these assumptions have come under attack by moral skeptics, as long ago as by Glaucon in Book II of Plato's *Republic.* Glaucon recalls the legend of Gyges, a shepherd who was said to have found a magic ring in a fissure opened by an earthquake. The ring would make its wearer invisible and thus would enable him to go anywhere and do anything undetected. Gyges used the power of the ring to gain entry to the Royal Palace where he seduced the Queen, murdered the King, and subsequently seized the throne. Now Glaucon asks us to imagine that there are two such rings, one given to a man of virtue and one given to a rogue. The rogue, of course, will use his ring unscrupulously and do anything necessary to increase his own wealth and power. He will recognize no moral constraints on his conduct, and, since the cloak of invisibility will protect him from discovery, he can do anything he pleases without fear of reprisal. So there will be no end to the mischief he will do. But how will the so-called virtuous man behave? Glaucon suggests that he will behave no better than the rogue: "No one, it is commonly believed, would have such iron strength of mind as to stand fast in doing right or keep his hands off other men's goods, when he could go to the market-place and fearlessly help himself to anything he wanted, enter houses and sleep with any woman he chose, set prisoners free and kill men at his pleasure, and in a word go about among men with the powers of a god. He would behave no better than the other; both would take the same course."[1] Moreover, why shouldn't he? Once he is freed from the fear of reprisal, why shouldn't a man simply do what he pleases, or what he thinks is best for himself? What reason is there for him to continue being "moral" when it is clearly not to his own advantage to do so?

These skeptical views suggested by Glaucon have come to be known as *psychological egoism* and *ethical egoism* respectively. Psychological egoism is the view that all men are selfish in everything that they do, that is, that the only motive from which anyone ever acts is self-interest. On this view, even when men are acting in ways apparently calculated to benefit others, they are actually motivated by the belief that acting in this way is to their own advantage, and if they did not believe this, they would not be doing that action. Ethical egoism is, by contrast, a normative view about how men *ought* to act. It is the view that, regardless of how men do in fact behave, they have no obligation to do anything except what is in their own interests. According to the ethical egoist, a person is always justified in doing whatever is in his own interest, regardless of the effect on others.

Clearly, if either of these views is correct, then "the moral institution of life" (to use Butler's well-turned phrase) is very different than what we normally think. The majority of mankind is grossly deceived about what is, or ought to be, the case, where morals are concerned.

II

Psychological egoism seems to fly in the face of the facts. We are tempted to say, "Of course people act unselfishly all the time. For example, Smith gives up a trip to the country, which he would have enjoyed very much, in order to stay behind and help a friend with his studies, which is a miserable way to pass the time. This is a perfectly clear case of unselfish behavior, and if the psychological egoist thinks that such cases do not occur, then he is just mistaken." Given such obvious instances of "unselfish behavior," what reply can the egoist make? There are two general arguments by which he might try to show that all actions, including those such as the one just outlined, are in fact motivated by self-interest. Let us examine these in turn:

A. The first argument goes as follows. If we describe one person's action as selfish, and another person's action as unselfish, we are overlooking the crucial fact that in both cases, assuming that the action is done voluntarily, *the agent is merely doing what he most wants to do.* If Smith stays behind to help his friend, that only shows that he wanted to help his friend more than he wanted to go to the country. And why should he be praised for his "unselfishness" when he is only doing what he most wants to do? So, since Smith is only doing what he wants to do, he cannot be said to be acting unselfishly.

This argument is so bad that it would not deserve to be taken seriously except for the fact that so many otherwise intelligent people have been taken in by it. First, the argument rests on the premise that people never voluntarily do anything except what they want to do. But this is patently false; there are at least two classes of actions that are exceptions to this generalization. One is the set of actions which we may not want to do, but which we do anyway as a means to an end which we want to achieve; for example, going to the dentist in order to stop a toothache, or going to work every day in order to be able to draw our pay at the end of the month. These cases may be regarded as consistent with the spirit of the egoist argument, however, since the ends mentioned are wanted by the agent. But the other set of actions are those which we do, not because we want to, nor even because there is an end which we want to achieve, but because we feel ourselves *under an obligation* to do them. For example, someone may do something because he has promised to do it, and thus feels obligated, even though he does not want to do it. It is sometimes suggested that in such cases we do the action because, after all, we want to keep our promises; so, even here, we are doing what we want. However, this dodge will not work: If I have promised to do something, and if I do not want to do it, then it is simply false to say that I want to keep my promise. In such cases we feel a conflict precisely because we do *not* want to do what we feel obligated to do. It is reasonable to think that Smith's action falls roughly into this second category: He might stay behind, not because he wants to, but because he feels that his friend needs help.

But suppose we were to concede, for the sake of the argument, that all voluntary action is motivated by the agent's wants, or at least that Smith is so motivated. Even if these were granted, it would not follow that Smith is acting selfishly or from self-interest. For if Smith wants to do something that will help his friend, even when it means forgoing his own enjoyments, that is precisely what makes him *un*selfish. What else could unselfishness be, if not wanting to help others? Another way to put the same point is to say that it is the *object* of a want that determines whether it is selfish or not. The mere fact that I am acting on *my* wants does not mean that I am acting selfishly; that depends on *what it is* that I want. If I want only my own good, and care nothing for others, then I am selfish; but if I also want other people to be well-off and happy, and if I act on *that* desire, then my action is not selfish. So much for this argument.

B. The second argument for psychological egoism is this. Since so-called unselfish actions always produce a sense of self-satisfaction in the agent,[2] and since this sense of satisfaction is a pleasant state

of consciousness, it follows that the point of the action is really to achieve a pleasant state of consciousness, rather than to bring about any good for others. Therefore, the action is "unselfish" only at a superficial level of analysis. Smith will feel much better with himself for having stayed to help his friend—if he had gone to the country, he would have felt terrible about it—and that is the real point of the action. According to a well-known story, this argument was once expressed by Abraham Lincoln:

> Mr. Lincoln once remarked to a fellow-passenger on an old-time mud-coach that all men were prompted by selfishness in doing good. His fellow-passenger was antagonizing this position when they were passing over a corduroy bridge that spanned a slough. As they crossed this bridge they espied an old razor-backed sow on the bank making a terrible noise because her pigs had got into the slough and were in danger of drowning. As the old coach began to climb the hill, Mr. Lincoln called out, "Driver, can't you stop just a moment?" Then Mr. Lincoln jumped out, ran back, and lifted the little pigs out of the mud and water and placed them on the bank. When he returned, his companion remarked: "Now Abe, where does selfishness come in on this little episode?" "Why, bless your soul, Ed, that was the very essence of selfishness. I should have had no peace of mind all day had I gone on and left that suffering old sow worrying over those pigs. I did it to get peace of mind, don't you see?"[3]

This argument suffers from defects similar to the previous one. Why should we think that merely because someone derives satisfaction from helping others this makes him selfish? Isn't the unselfish man precisely the one who *does* derive satisfaction from helping others, while the selfish man does not? If Lincoln "got peace of mind" from rescuing the piglets, does this show him to be selfish, or, on the contrary, doesn't it show him to be compassionate and good-hearted? (If a man were truly selfish, why should it bother his conscience that *others* suffer—much less pigs?) Similarly, it is nothing more than shabby sophistry to say, because Smith takes satisfaction in helping his friend, that he is behaving selfishly. If we say this rapidly, while thinking about something else, perhaps it will sound all right; but if we speak slowly, and pay attention to what we are saying, it sounds plain silly.

Moreover, suppose we ask *why* Smith derives satisfaction from helping his friend. The answer will be, it is because Smith cares for him and wants him to succeed. If Smith did not have these concerns, then he would take no pleasure in assisting him; and these concerns, as we have already seen, are the marks of unselfishness, not selfishness. To put the point more generally: If we have a positive attitude toward the attainment of some goal, then we may derive satisfaction from attaining that goal. But the *object* of our attitude is *the attainment of that goal*; and we must want to attain the goal *before* we can find any satisfaction in it. We do not, in other words, desire some sort of "pleasurable consciousness" and then try to figure out how to achieve it; rather, we desire all sorts of different things—money, a new fishing-boat, to be a better chess-player, to get a promotion in our work, etc.—and because we desire these things, we derive satisfaction from attaining them. And so, if someone desires the welfare and happiness of another person, he will derive satisfaction from that; but this does not mean that this satisfaction is the object of his desire, or that he is in any way selfish on account of it.

It is a measure of the weakness of psychological egoism that these insupportable arguments are the ones most often advanced in its favor. Why, then, should anyone ever have thought it a true view? Perhaps because of a desire for theoretical simplicity: In thinking about human conduct, it would be nice if there were some simple formula that would unite the diverse phenomena of human behavior under a single explanatory principle, just as simple formulae in physics bring together a great many apparently different phenomena. And since it is obvious that self-regard is an overwhelmingly important factor in motivation, it is only natural to wonder whether all motivation might not be explained in these terms. But the answer is clearly No; while a great many human actions are motivated entirely or in part by self-interest, only by a deliberate distortion of the facts can we say that all conduct is so motivated. This will be clear, I think, if we correct three confusions which are commonplace. The exposure of these confusions will remove the last traces of plausibility from the psychological egoist thesis.

The first is the confusion of selfishness with self-interest. The two are clearly not the same. If I see a physician when I am feeling poorly, I am acting in my own interest but no one would think of calling me "selfish" on account of it. Similarly, brushing my teeth, working hard at my job, and obeying the law are all in my self-interest but none of these are examples of selfish conduct. This is because selfish behavior is behavior that ignores the interests of others, in circumstances in which their interests ought not to be ignored. This concept has a definite evaluative flavor; to call someone "selfish" is not just to describe his action but to condemn it. Thus, you would not call me selfish for eating a normal meal in normal circumstances (although it may surely be in my self-interest); but you would call me selfish for hoarding food while others about are starving.

The second confusion is the assumption that every action is done *either* from self-interest or from other-regarding motives. Thus, the egoist concludes that if there is no such thing as genuine altruism then all actions must be done from self-interest. But this is certainly a false dichotomy. The man who continues to smoke cigarettes, even after learning about the connection between smoking and cancer, is surely not acting from self-interest, not even by his own standards—self-interest would dictate that he quit smoking at once—and he is not acting altruistically either. He *is*, no doubt, smoking for the pleasure of it, but all that this shows is that undisciplined pleasure-seeking and acting from self-interest are very different. This is what led Butler to remark that "The thing to be lamented is, not that men have so great regard to their own good or interest in the present world, for they have not enough."[4]

The last two paragraphs show (*a*) that it is false that all actions are selfish, and (*b*) that it is false that all actions are done out of self-interest. And it should be noted that these two points can be made, and were, without any appeal to putative examples of altruism.

The third confusion is the common but false assumption that a concern for one's own welfare is incompatible with any genuine concern for the welfare of others. Thus, it is obvious that everyone (or very nearly everyone) does desire his own well-being, it might be thought that no one can really be concerned with others. But again, this is false. There is no inconsistency in desiring that everyone, including oneself *and* others, be well-off and happy. To be sure, it may happen on occasion that our own interests conflict with the interests of others, and in these cases we will have to make hard choices. But even in these cases we might sometimes opt for the interests of others, especially when the others involved are our family or friends. But more importantly, not all cases are like this: Sometimes we are able to promote the welfare of others when our own interests are not involved at all. In these cases not even the strongest self-regard need prevent us from acting considerately toward others.

Once these confusions are cleared away, it seems to me obvious enough that there is no reason whatever to accept psychological egoism. On the contrary, if we simply observe people's behavior with an open mind, we may find that a great deal of it is motivated by self-regard, but by no means all of it; and that there is no reason to deny that "the moral institution of life" can include a place for the virtue of beneficence.[5]

III

The ethical egoist would say at this point, "Of course it is possible for people to act altruistically, and perhaps many people do act that way—but there is no reason why they *should* do so. A person is under no obligation to do anything except what is in his own interests."[6] This is really quite a radical doctrine. Suppose I have an urge to set fire to some public building (say, a department store) just for the fascination of watching the spectacular blaze: According to this view, the fact that several people might be burned to death provides no reason whatever why I should not do it. After all, this only concerns *their* welfare, not my own, and according to the ethical egoist the only person I need think of is myself.

Some might deny that ethical egoism has any such monstrous consequences. They would point out that it is really to my own advantage not to set the fire— for, if I do that I may be caught and put into prison (unlike Gyges, I have no magic ring for protection). Moreover, even if I could avoid being caught it is still to my advantage to respect the rights and interests of others, for it is to my advantage to live in a society in which people's rights and interests are respected. Only in such a society can I live a happy and secure life; so, in acting kindly toward others, I would merely be doing my part to create and maintain the sort of society which it is to my advantage to have.[7] Therefore, it is said, the egoist would not be such a bad man; he would be as kindly and considerate as anyone else, because he would see that it is to his own advantage to be kindly and considerate.

This is a seductive line of thought, but it seems to me mistaken. Certainly it is to everyone's advantage (including the egoist's) to preserve a stable society where people's interests are generally protected. But there is no reason for the egoist to think that merely because *he* will not honor the rules of the social game, decent society will collapse. For the vast majority of people are not egoists, and there is no reason to think that they will be converted by his example—especially if he is discreet and does not unduly flaunt his style of life. What this line of rea-

soning shows is not that the egoist himself must act benevolently, but that he must encourage *others* to do so. He must take care to conceal from public view his own self-centered method of decision-making, and urge others to act on precepts very different from those on which he is willing to act.

The rational egoist, then, cannot advocate that egoism be universally adopted by everyone. For he wants a world in which his own interests are maximized; and if other people adopted the egoistic policy of pursuing their own interests to the exclusion of his interest, as he pursues his interests to the exclusion of theirs, then such a world would be impossible. So he himself will be an egoist, but he will want others to be altruists.

This brings us to what is perhaps the most popular "refutation" of ethical egoism current among philosophical writers—the argument that ethical egoism is at bottom inconsistent because it cannot be universalized.[8] The argument goes like this:

To say that any action or policy of action is *right* (or that it *ought* to be adopted) entails that it is right for *anyone* in the same sort of circumstances. I cannot, for example, say that it is right for me to lie to you, and yet object when you lie to me (provided, of course, that the circumstances are the same). I cannot hold that it is all right for me to drink your beer and then complain when you drink mine. This is just the requirement that we be consistent in our evaluations; it is a requirement of logic. Now it is said that ethical egoism cannot meet this requirement because, as we have already seen, the egoist would not want others to act in the same way that he acts. Moreover, suppose he *did* advocate the universal adoption of egoistic policies: he would be saying to Peter, "You ought to pursue your own interests even if it means destroying Paul"; and he would be saying to Paul, "You ought to pursue your own interests even if it means destroying Peter." The attitudes expressed in these two recommendations seem clearly inconsistent—he is urging the advancement of Peter's interest at one moment, and countenancing their defeat at the next. Therefore, the argument goes, there is no way to maintain the doctrine of ethical egoism as a consistent view about how we ought to act. We will fall into inconsistency whenever we try.

What are we to make of this argument? Are we to conclude that ethical egoism has been refuted? Such a conclusion, I think, would be unwarranted; for I think that we can show, contrary to this argument, how ethical egoism can be maintained consistently. We need only to interpret the egoist's position in a

sympathetic way: We should say that he has in mind a certain kind of world which he would prefer over all others; it would be a world in which his own interests were maximized, regardless of the effects on other people. The egoist's primary policy of action, then, would be to act in such a way as to bring about, as nearly as possible, this sort of world. Regardless of however morally reprehensible we might find it, there is nothing *inconsistent* in someone's adopting this as his ideal and acting in a way calculated to bring it about. And if someone did adopt this as his ideal, then he would not advocate universal egoism; as we have already seen, he would want other people to be altruists. So if he advocates any principles of conduct for the general public, they will be altruistic principles. This would not be inconsistent; on the contrary, it would be perfectly consistent with his goal of creating a world in which his own interests are maximized. To be sure, he would have to be deceitful; in order to secure the good will of others, and a favorable hearing for his exhortations to altruism, he would have to pretend that he was himself prepared to accept altruistic principles. But again, that would be all right; from the egoist's point of view, this would merely be a matter of adopting the necessary means to the achievement of his goal—and while we might not approve of this, there is nothing inconsistent about it. Again, it might be said, "He advocates one thing, but does another. Surely *that's* inconsistent." But it is not; for what he advocates and what he does are both calculated as means to an end (the *same* end, we might note); and as such, he is doing what is rationally required in each case. Therefore, contrary to the previous argument, there is nothing inconsistent in the ethical egoist's view. He cannot be refuted by the claim that he contradicts himself.

Is there, then, no way to refute the ethical egoist? If by "refute" we mean show that he has made some *logical* error, the answer is that there is not. However, there is something more that can be said. The egoist challenge to our ordinary moral convictions amounts to a demand for an explanation of why we should adopt certain policies of action, namely, policies in which the good of others is given importance. We can give an answer to this demand, albeit an indirect one. The reason one ought not to do actions that would hurt other people is: Other people would be hurt. The reason one ought to do actions that would benefit other people is: Other people would be benefited. This may at first seem like a piece of philosophical sleight-of-hand, but it is not. The point is that the welfare of human beings is something that most of us value *for its own sake*, and not merely for the sake of

something else. Therefore, when *further* reasons are demanded for valuing the welfare of human beings, we cannot point to anything further to satisfy this demand. It is not that we have no reason for pursuing these policies, but that our reason *is* that these policies are for the good of human beings.

So if we are asked, "Why shouldn't I set fire to this department store?" one answer would be, "Because if you do, people may be burned to death." This is a complete, sufficient reason which does not require qualification or supplementation of any sort. If someone seriously wants to know why this action shouldn't be done, that's the reason. If we are pressed further and asked the skeptical question, "But why shouldn't I do actions that will harm others?" we may not know what to say—but this is because the questioner has included in his question the very answer we would like to give: "Why shouldn't you do actions that will harm others? Because doing those actions would harm others."

The egoist, no doubt, will not be happy with this. He will protest that *we* may accept this as a reason, but *he* does not. And here the argument stops: There are limits to what can be accomplished by argument, and if the egoist really doesn't care about other people—if he honestly doesn't care whether they are helped or hurt by his actions—then we have reached those limits. If we want to persuade him to act decently toward his fellow humans, we will have to make our appeal to such other attitudes as he does possess, by threats, bribes, or other cajolery. That is all that we can do.

Though some may find this situation distressing (we would like to be able to show that the egoist is just *wrong*), it holds no embarrassment for common morality. What we have come up against is simply a fundamental requirement of rational action, namely, that the existence of reasons for action always depends on the prior existence of certain attitudes in the agent. For example, the fact that a certain course of action would make the agent a lot of money is a reason for doing it only if the agent wants to make money; the fact that practicing at chess makes one a better player is a reason for practicing only if one wants to be a better player; and so on. Similarly, the fact that a certain action would help the agent is a reason for doing the action only if the agent cares about his own welfare, and the fact that an action would help others is a reason for doing it only if the agent cares about others. In this respect ethical egoism and what we might call ethical altruism are in exactly the same fix: Both require that the agent *care* about himself, or about other people, before they can get started.

So a nonegoist will accept "It would harm another person" as a reason not to do an action simply because he cares about what happens to that other person. When the egoist says that he does *not* accept that as a reason, he is saying something quite extraordinary. He is saying that he has no affection for friends or family, that he never feels pity or compassion, that he is the sort of person who can look on scenes of human misery with complete indifference, so long as he is not the one suffering. Genuine egoists, people who really don't care at all about anyone [other] than themselves, are rare. It is important to keep this in mind when thinking about ethical egoism; it is easy to forget just how fundamental to human psychological makeup the feeling of sympathy is. Indeed, a man without any sympathy at all would scarcely be recognizable as a man; and that is what makes ethical egoism such a disturbing doctrine in the first place.

IV

There are, of course, many different ways in which the skeptic might challenge the assumptions underlying our moral practice. In this essay I have discussed only two of them, the two put forward by Glaucon in the passage that I cited from Plato's *Republic*. It is important that the assumptions underlying our moral practice should not be confused with particular judgments made within that practice. To defend one is not to defend the other. We may assume—quite properly, if my analysis has been correct—that the virtue of beneficence does, and indeed should, occupy an important place in "the moral institution of life"; and yet we may make constant and miserable errors when it comes to

judging when and in what ways this virtue is to be exercised. Even worse, we may often be able to make accurate moral judgments, and know what we ought to do, but not do it. For these ills, philosophy alone is not the cure.

NOTES

1. *The Republic of Plato*, trans. F. M. Cornford (Oxford, 1941), p. 45.
2. Or, as it is sometimes said, "It gives him a clear conscience," or "He couldn't sleep at night if he had done otherwise," or "He would have been ashamed of himself for not doing it," and so on.
3. Frank C. Sharp, *Ethics* (New York, 1928), pp. 74–75. Quoted from the Springfield (Ill.) *Monitor* in *Outlook*, 56: 1059.
4. *The Works of Joseph Butler*, vol. 2, ed. W. E. Gladstone (Oxford, 1896), p. 26.
5. The capacity for altruistic behavior is not unique to human beings. Some interesting experiments with rhesus monkeys have shown that these animals will refrain from operating a device for securing food if this causes other animals to suffer pain. See Masserman, Wechkin, and Terris, "'Altruistic' Behavior in Rhesus Monkeys," *American Journal of Psychiatry*, 121 (1964): 584–585.
6. I take this to be the view of Ayn Rand, insofar as I understand her confusing doctrine.
7. Cf. Thomas Hobbes, *Leviathan* (London, 1651), chap. 17.
8. See, for example, Brian Medlin, "Ultimate Principles and Ethical Egoism," *Australasian Journal of Philosophy*, 35 (1957): 111–118; and D. H. Monro, *Empiricism and Ethics* (Cambridge, 1967), chap. 16.

DISCUSSION QUESTIONS

1. What exactly is the difference between ethical egoism and psychological egoism? Why is this distinction important?
2. Why does Rachels believe that "selfishness" is not the same as "self-interest"? How does he use this distinction to refute psychological egoism?
3. How convinced were you of Rachels' argument against the notion that every action is done either from self-interest or from other-regarding motives? Can you think of a counterargument?
4. What is Rachels' best argument against ethical egoism? Do you agree with it? Defend your position.
5. Rachels offers a number of arguments against egoism. In your opinion, which is the best general argument? Is it strong enough to convince you to reject egoism? Explain.

J O H N   A R T H U R

Morality, Religion, and Conscience

In this article, John Arthur takes up what is called "Euthyphro's problem" ("Is the pious loved by the gods because it is pious, or is it pious because they love it?"), in addition to other issues related to whether morality needs religion at its foundation. Arthur lays out three views in which morality depends on religious beliefs and then criticizes each. The first claims that without religious motivation people could not be expected to do the right thing. The second says that religion is necessary to provide guidance to people in their search for the correct course of action. The third claims that religion is essential for there even to be a right and wrong, since without a lawgiver there could be no law. Arthur concludes that "religion is not necessary in providing moral motivation or guidance." He then considers the ways in which religion and morality *do* influence each other.

John Arthur is a professor of philosophy at the State University of New York at Binghamton.

The question I discuss in this paper was famously captured by a character in Dostoyevsky's novel *The Brothers Karamazov.* "Without God" said Ivan, "everything is permitted." I want to argue that this is wrong: there is in fact no important sense in which morality depends on religion. Yet, I will also argue, there do remain important other respects in which the two *are* related. In the concluding section I extend the discussion of the origins of morality beyond religion by considering the nature of conscience, the ways morality is "social," and the implications of these ideas for moral education. First, however, I want to say something about the subjects: just what are we referring to when we speak of morality and of religion?

1. MORALITY AND RELIGION

A useful way to approach the first question—the nature of morality—is to ask what it would mean for a society to exist without a social moral code. How would such people think and behave? What would that society look like? First, it seems clear that such people would never feel guilt or resentment. For example, the notions that I ought to remember my parents' anniversary, that he has a moral responsibil-

ity to help care for his children after the divorce, that she has a right to equal pay for equal work, and that discrimination on the basis of race is unfair would be absent in such a society. Notions of duty, rights, and obligations would not be present, except perhaps in the legal sense; concepts of justice and fairness would also be foreign to these people. In short, people would have no tendency to evaluate or criticize the behavior of others, nor to feel remorse about their own behavior. Children would not be taught to be ashamed when they steal or hurt others, nor would they be allowed to complain when others treat them badly. (People might, however, feel regret at a decision that didn't turn out as they had hoped; but that would only be because their expectations were frustrated, not because they feel guilty.)

Such a society lacks a moral code. What, then, of religion? Is it possible that people lacking a morality would nonetheless have religious beliefs? It seems clear that it is possible. Suppose every day these same people file into their place of worship to pay homage to God (they may believe in many gods or in one all-powerful creator of heaven and earth). Often they can be heard praying to God for help in dealing with their problems and thanking Him for their good fortune. Frequently they give sacrifices to God, sometimes in the form of money spent to build beautiful temples and churches, other times by performing actions they believe God would approve such as helping those in need. These practices might also be institutionalized, in the sense that certain people are assigned important leadership roles. Specific texts might also be taken as authoritative, indicating the ways God has acted in history and His role in their lives or the lives of their ancestors.

To have a moral code, then, is to tend to evaluate (perhaps without even expressing it) the behavior of others and to feel guilt at certain actions when we perform them. Religion, on the other hand, involves beliefs in supernatural power(s) that created and perhaps also control nature, the tendency to worship and pray to those supernatural forces or beings, and the presence of organizational structures and authoritative texts. The practices of morality and religion are thus importantly different. One involves our attitudes toward various forms of behavior (lying and killing, for example), typically expressed using the notions of rules, rights, and obligations. The other, religion, typically involves prayer, worship, beliefs about the supernatural, institutional forms, and authoritative texts.

We come, then, to the central question: What is the connection, if any, between a society's moral code and its religious practices and beliefs? Many people have felt that morality is in some way dependent on religion or religious truths. But what sort of "dependence" might there be? In what follows I distinguish various ways in which one might claim that religion is necessary for morality, arguing against those who claim morality depends in some way on religion. I will also suggest, however, some other important ways in which the two are related, concluding with a brief discussion of conscience and moral education.

2. RELIGIOUS MOTIVATION AND GUIDANCE

One possible role which religion might play in morality relates to motives people have. Religion, it is often said, is necessary so that people will *do* right. Typically, the argument begins with the important point that doing what is right often has costs: refusing to shoplift or cheat can mean people go without some good or fail a test; returning a billfold means they don't get the contents. Religion is therefore said to be necessary in that it provides motivation to do the right thing. God rewards those who follow His commands by providing for them a place in heaven or by insuring that they prosper and are happy on earth. He also punishes those who violate the moral law. Others emphasize less self-interested ways in which religious motives may encourage people to act rightly. Since God is the creator of the universe and has ordained that His plan should be followed, they point out, it is important to live one's life in accord with this divinely ordained plan. Only by living a moral life, it is said, can people live in harmony with the larger, divinely created order.

The first claim, then, is that religion is necessary to provide moral motivation. The problem with that argument, however, is that religious motives are far from the only ones people have. For most of us, a decision to do the right thing (if that is our decision) is made for a variety of reasons: "What if I get caught? What if somebody sees me—what will he or she think? How will I feel afterwards? Will I regret it?" Or maybe the thought of cheating just doesn't arise. We were raised to be a decent person, and that's what we are—period. Behaving fairly and treating others well is more important than whatever we might gain from stealing or cheating, let alone seriously harming another person. So it seems clear that many motives for doing the right thing have nothing whatsoever to do with religion. Most of us, in fact, do worry about getting caught, being blamed, and being looked down on by others. We also may do what is right just because it's right, or because we don't want to hurt others or embarrass family and friends. To say that we need religion to act morally is mistaken; indeed it seems to me that many of us, when it really gets down to it, don't give much of a thought to religion when making moral decisions. All those other reasons are the ones which we tend to consider, or else we just don't consider cheating and stealing at all. So far, then, there seems to be no reason to suppose that people can't be moral yet irreligious at the same time.

A second argument that is available for those who think religion is necessary to morality, however, focuses on moral guidance and knowledge rather than on people's motives. However much people may want to do the right thing, according to this view, we cannot ever know for certain what is right without the guidance of religious teaching. Human understanding is simply inadequate to this difficult and controversial task; morality involves immensely complex problems, and so we must consult religious revelation for help.

Again, however, this argument fails. First, consider how much we would need to know about religion and revelation in order for religion to provide moral guidance. Besides being sure that there is a God, we'd also have to think about which of the many religions is true. How can anybody be sure his or her religion is the right one? But even if we assume the Judeo-Christian God is the real one, we still need to find out just what it is He wants us to do, which means we must think about revelation.

Revelation comes in at least two forms, and not even all Christians agree on which is the best way to understand revelation. Some hold that revelation occurs when God tells us what he wants by providing us with His words: The Ten Commandments are an example. Many even believe, as evangelist Billy Graham once said, that the entire Bible was written by God using thirty-nine secretaries. Others, however, doubt that the "word of God" refers literally to the words God has spoken, but believe instead that the Bible is a historical document, written by human beings, of the events or occasions in which God revealed Himself. It is an especially important document, of course, but nothing more than that. So on this second view revelation is not understood as *statements* made by God but rather as His *acts*, such as leading His people from Egypt, testing Job, and sending His son as an example of the ideal life. The Bible is not itself revelation; it's the historical account of revelatory actions.

If we are to use revelation as a moral guide, then, we must first know what is to count as revelation—words given us by God, historical events, or both? But even supposing that we could somehow answer those questions, the problems of relying on revelation are still not over since we still must interpret that revelation. Some feel, for example, that the Bible justifies various forms of killing, including war and capital punishment, on the basis of such statements as "An eye for an eye." Others, emphasizing such sayings as "Judge not lest ye be judged" and "Thou shalt not kill," believe the Bible demands absolute pacifism. How are we to know which interpretation is correct? It is likely, of course, that the answer people give to such religious questions will be influenced in part at least by their own moral beliefs: if capital punishment is thought to be unjust, for example, then an interpreter will seek to read the Bible in a way that is consistent with that moral truth. That is not, however, a happy conclusion for those wishing to rest morality on revelation, for it means that their understanding of what God has revealed is itself dependent on their prior moral views. Rather than revelation serving as a guide for morality, morality is serving as a guide for how we interpret revelation.

So my general conclusion is that far from providing a short-cut to moral understanding, looking to revelation for guidance often creates more questions and problems. It seems wiser under the circumstances to address complex moral problems like abortion, capital punishment, and affirmative action directly, considering the pros and cons of each side, rather than to seek answers through the much more controversial and difficult route of revelation.

3. THE DIVINE COMMAND THEORY

It may seem, however, that we have still not really gotten to the heart of the matter. Even if religion is not necessary for moral motivation or guidance, it is often claimed, religion is necessary in another more fundamental sense. According to this view, religion is necessary for morality because without God there could be no right or wrong. God, in other words, provides the foundation or bedrock on which morality is grounded. This idea was expressed by Bishop R. C. Mortimer:

> God made us and all the world. Because of that He has an absolute claim on our obedience. . . . From [this] it follows that a thing is not right simply because we think it is. It is right because God commands it.[1]

What Bishop Mortimer has in mind can be seen by comparing moral rules with legal ones. Legal statutes, we know, are created by legislatures; if the state assembly of New York had not passed a law limiting the speed people can travel, then there would be no such legal obligation. Without the statutory enactments, such a law simply would not exist. Mortimer's view, *the divine command theory*, would mean that God has the same sort of relation to moral law as the legislature has to statutes it enacts: without God's commands there would be no moral rules, just as without a legislature there would be no statutes.

Defenders of the divine command theory often add to this a further claim, that only by assuming God sits at the foundation of morality can we explain the objective difference between right and wrong. This point was forcefully argued by F. C. Copleston in a 1948 British Broadcasting Corporation radio debate with Bertrand Russell.

COPLESTON: . . . The validity of such an interpretation of man's conduct depends on the recognition of God's existence, obviously. . . . Let's take a look at the Commandant of the [Nazi] concentration camp at Belsen. That appears to you as undesirable and evil and to me too. To Adolf Hitler we suppose it appeared as something good and desirable. I suppose you'd have to admit that for Hitler it was good and for you it is evil.

RUSSELL: No, I shouldn't go so far as that. I mean, I think people can make mistakes in that as they can in other things. If you have jaundice you see things yellow that are not yellow. You're making a mistake.

COPLESTON: Yes, one can make mistakes, but can you make a mistake if it's simply a question of reference to a feeling or emotion? Surely Hitler would be the only possible judge of what appealed to his emotions.

RUSSELL: . . . You can say various things about that; among others, that if that sort of thing makes that sort of appeal to Hitler's emotions, then Hitler makes quite a different appeal to my emotions.

COPLESTON: Granted. But there's no objective criterion outside feeling then for condemning the conduct of the Commandant of Belsen, in your view. . . . The human being's idea of the content of the moral law depends certainly to a large extent on education and environment, and a man has to use his reason in assessing the validity of the actual moral ideas of his social group. But the possibility of criticizing the accepted moral code presupposes that there is an objective standard, that there is an ideal moral order, which imposes itself. . . . It implies the existence of a real foundation of God.[2]

Against those who, like Bertrand Russell, seek to ground morality in feelings and attitudes, Copleston argues that there must be a more solid foundation if we are to be able to claim truly that the Nazis were evil. God, according to Copleston, is able to provide the objective basis for the distinction, which we all know to exist, between right and wrong. Without divine commands at the root of human obligations, we would have no real reason for condemning the behavior of anybody, even Nazis. Morality, Copleston thinks, would then be nothing more than an expression of personal feeling.

To begin assessing the divine command theory, let's first consider this last point. Is it really true that only the commands of God can provide an objective basis for moral judgments? Certainly many philosophers have felt that morality rests on its own perfectly sound footing, be it reason, human nature, or natural sentiments. It seems wrong to conclude, automatically, that morality cannot rest on anything but religion. And it is also possible that

morality doesn't have any foundation or basis at all, so that its claims should be ignored in favor of whatever serves our own self-interest.

In addition to these problems with Copleston's argument, the divine command theory faces other problems as well. First, we would need to say much more about the relationship between morality and divine commands. Certainly the expressions "is commanded by God" and "is morally required" do not *mean* the same thing. People and even whole societies can use moral concepts without understanding them to make any reference to God. And while it is true that God (or any other moral being for that matter) would tend to want others to do the right thing, this hardly shows that being right and being commanded by God are the same thing. Parents want their children to do the right thing, too, but that doesn't mean parents, or anybody else, can make a thing right just by commanding it!

I think that, in fact, theists should reject the divine command theory. One reason is what it implies. Suppose we were to grant (just for the sake of argument) that the divine command theory is correct, so that actions are right just because they are commanded by God. The same, of course, can be said about those deeds that we believe are wrong. If God hadn't commanded us not to do them, they would not be wrong.

But now notice this consequence of the divine command theory. Since God is all-powerful, and since right is determined solely by His commands, is it not possible that He might change the rules and make what we now think of as wrong into right? It would seem that according to the divine command theory the answer is "yes": it is theoretically possible that tomorrow God would decree that virtues such as kindness and courage have become vices while actions that show cruelty and cowardice will henceforth be the right actions. (Recall the analogy with a legislature and the power it has to change law.) So now rather than it being right for people to help each other out and prevent innocent people from suffering unnecessarily, it would be right (God having changed His mind) to create as much pain among innocent children as we possibly can! To adopt the divine command theory therefore commits its advocate to the seemingly absurd position that even the greatest atrocities might be not only acceptable but morally required if God were to command them.

Plato made a similar point in the dialogue *Euthyphro*. Socrates is asking Euthyphro what it is that makes the virtue of holiness a virtue, just as we have been asking what makes kindness and courage virtues. Euthyphro has suggested that holiness is just whatever all the gods love.

SOCRATES: Well, then, Euthyphro, what do we say about holiness? Is it not loved by all the gods, according to your definition?

EUTHYPHRO: Yes.

SOCRATES: Because it is holy, or for some other reason?

EUTHYPHRO: No, because it is holy.

SOCRATES: Then it is loved by the gods because it is holy: it is not holy because it is loved by them?

EUTHYPHRO: It seems so.

SOCRATES: . . . Then holiness is not what is pleasing to the gods, and what is pleasing to the gods is not holy as you say, Euthyphro. They are different things.

EUTHYPHRO: And why, Socrates?

SOCRATES: Because we are agreed that the gods love holiness because it is holy: and that it is not holy because they love it.[3]

This raises an interesting question: Why, having claimed at first that virtues are merely what is loved (or commanded) by the gods, would Euthyphro so quickly contradict this and agree that the gods love holiness *because* it's holy, rather than the reverse? One likely possibility is that Euthyphro believes that whenever the gods love something they do so with good reason, not without justification and arbitrarily. To deny this, and say that it is merely the gods' love that makes holiness a virtue, would mean that the gods have no basis for their attitudes, that they are arbitrary in what they love. Yet—and this is the crucial point—it's far from clear that a religious person would want to say that God is arbitrary in that way. If we say that it is simply God's loving something that makes it right, then what sense would it make to say God wants us to do right? All that could mean, it seems, is that God wants us to do what He wants us to do; He would have no reason for wanting it. Similarly "God is good" would mean little more than "God does what He pleases." The divine command theory therefore leads us to the results that God is morally arbitrary, and that His wishing us to do good or even God's being just mean nothing more than that God does what He does and wants whatever He wants. Religious people who reject that consequence would also, I am suggesting, have reason to reject the divine command theory itself, seeking a different understanding of morality.

This now raises another problem, however. If God approves kindness because it is a virtue and hates the Nazis because they were evil, then it seems that God discovers morality rather than inventing it. So haven't we then identified a limitation on God's power, since He now, being a good God, must love kindness and command us not to be cruel? Without the divine command theory, in other words, what is left of God's omnipotence?

But why, we may ask, is such a limitation on God unacceptable? It is not at all clear that God really can do anything at all. Can God, for example, destroy Himself? Or make a rock so heavy that He cannot lift it? Or create a universe which was never created by Him? Many have thought that God cannot do these things, but also that His inability to do them does not constitute a serious limitation on His power since these are things that cannot be done at all: to do them would violate the laws of logic. Christianity's most influential theologian, Thomas Aquinas, wrote in this regard that "whatever implies contradiction does not come within the scope of divine omnipotence, because it cannot have the aspect of possibility. Hence it is more appropriate to say that such things cannot be done than that God cannot do them."[4]

How, then, ought we to understand God's relationship to morality if we reject the divine command theory? Can religious people consistently maintain their faith in God the Creator and yet deny that what is right is right because He commands it? I think the answer to this is "yes." Making cruelty good is not like making a universe that wasn't made, of course. It's a moral limit on God rather than a logical one. But why suppose that God's limits are only logical?

One final point about this. Even if we agree that God loves justice or kindness because of their nature, not arbitrarily, there still remains a sense in which God could change morality even having rejected the divine command theory. That's because if we assume, plausibly I think, that morality depends in part on how we reason, what we desire and need, and the circumstances in which we find ourselves, then morality will still be under God's control since God could have constructed us or our environment very differently. Suppose, for instance, that he created us so that we couldn't be hurt by others or didn't care about freedom. Or perhaps our natural environment were created differently, so that all we have to do is ask and anything we want is given to us. If God had created either nature or us that way, then it seems likely our morality might also be different in important ways from the one we now think correct. In that sense, then, morality depends on God whether or not one supports the divine command theory.

4. ON DEWEY'S THOUGHT THAT "MORALITY IS SOCIAL"

I have argued here that religion is not necessary in providing moral motivation or guidance, and against the divine command theory's claim that God is necessary for there to be morality at all. In this last section, I want first to look briefly at how religion and morality sometimes *do* influence each other. Then I will consider the development of moral conscience and the important ways in which morality might correctly be thought to be "social."

Nothing I have said so far means that morality and religion are independent of each other. But in what ways are they related, assuming I am correct in claiming morality does not *depend* on religion? First, of course, we should note the historical influence religions have had on the development of morality, as well as on politics and law. Many of the important leaders of the abolitionist and civil rights movements were religious leaders, as are many current members of the pro-life movement. The relationship is not, however, one-sided: morality has also influenced religion, as the current debate within the Catholic church over the role of women, abortion, and other social issues shows. In reality, then, it seems clear that the practices of morality and religion have historically each exerted an influence on the other.

But just as the two have shaped each other historically, so, too, do they interact at the personal level. I have already suggested how people's understanding of revelation, for instance, is often shaped by morality as they seek the best interpretations of revealed texts. Whether trying to understand a work of art, a legal statute, or a religious text, interpreters regularly seek to understand them in the best light—to make them as good as they can be, which requires that they bring moral judgment to the task of religious interpretation and understanding.

The relationship can go the other direction as well, however, as people's moral views are shaped by their religious training and beliefs. These relationships between morality and religion are often complex, hidden even from ourselves, but it does seem clear that our views on important moral issues, from sexual morality and war to welfare and capital punishment, are often influenced by our religious outlook. So not only are religious and moral practices and understandings historically linked, but for many religious people the relationship extends to the personal level—to their understanding of moral obligations as well as their sense of who they are and their vision of who they wish to be.

Morality, then, is influenced by religion (as is religion by morality), but morality's social character extends deeper even than that, I want to argue. First, of course, we possess a socially acquired language within which we think about our various choices and the alternatives we ought to follow, including whether a possible course of action is the right thing to do. Second, morality is social in that it governs relationships among people, defining our responsibilities to others and theirs to us. Morality provides the standards we rely on in gauging our interactions with family, lovers, friends, fellow citizens, and even strangers. Third, morality is social in the sense that we are, in fact, subject to criticism by others for our actions. We discuss with others what we should do, and often hear from them concerning whether our decisions were acceptable. Blame and praise are a central feature of morality.

While not disputing any of this, John Dewey has stressed another, less obvious aspect of morality's social character. Consider then the following comments regarding the origins of morality and conscience in an article he titled "Morality Is Social":

> In language and imagination we rehearse the responses of others just as we dramatically enact other consequences. We foreknow how others will act, and the foreknowledge is the beginning of judgment passed on action. We know *with* them; there is conscience. An assembly is formed within our breast which discusses and appraises proposed and performed acts. The community without becomes a forum and tribunal within, a judgment-seat of charges, assessments and exculpations. Our thoughts of our own actions are saturated with the ideas that others entertain about them. . . . Explicit recognition of this fact is a prerequisite of improvement in moral education. . . . Reflection is morally indispensable.[5]

So Dewey's thought is that to consider matters from the moral point of view means we must think beyond ourselves, by which he means imagining how we as well as others might respond to various choices now being contemplated. To consider a decision from the *moral* perspective, says Dewey, requires that we envision an "assembly of others" that is "formed within our breast." That means, in turn, that morality and conscience cannot be sharply distinguished from our nature as social beings since conscience invariably brings with it, or constitutes, the perspective of the other. "Is this right?" and

"What would this look like were I to have to defend it to others?" are not separable questions.[6]

It is important not to confuse Dewey's point here, however. He is *not* saying that what is right is finally to be determined by the reactions of actually existing other people, or even by the reaction of society as a whole. What is right or fair can never be finally decided by a vote, but instead might not meet the approval of any specific others. But what then might Dewey mean in speaking of such an "assembly of others" as the basis of morality? The answer is that rather than actual people or groups, the assembly Dewey envisions is hypothetical or "ideal." The "community without" is thus transformed into a "forum and tribunal within, a judgment seat of charges, assessments and exculpations." So it is through the powers of our imagination that we can meet our moral responsibilities and exercise moral judgment, using these powers to determine what morality requires by imagining the reaction of Dewey's "assembly of others."

Morality is therefore *inherently* social, in a variety of ways. It depends on socially learned language, is learned from interactions with others, and governs our interactions with others in society. But it also demands, as Dewey put it, that we know "with" others, envisioning for ourselves what their points of view would require along with our own. Conscience demands we occupy the positions of others.

Viewed in this light, God would play a role in a religious person's moral reflection and conscience since it is unlikely a religious person would wish to exclude God from the "forum and tribunal" that constitutes conscience. Rather, for the religious person conscience would almost certainly include the imagined reaction of God along with the reactions of others who might be affected by the action. Other people are also important, however, since it is often an open question just what God's reaction would be; revelation's meaning, as I have argued, is subject to interpretation. So it seems that for a religious person morality and God's will cannot be separated, though the connection between them is not the one envisioned by defenders of the divine command theory.

Which leads to my final point, about moral education. If Dewey is correct, then it seems clear there is an important sense in which morality not only can be taught but must be. Besides early moral training,

moral thinking depends on our ability to imagine others' reactions and to imaginatively put ourselves into their shoes. "What would somebody (including, perhaps, God) think if this got out?" expresses more than a concern with being embarrassed or punished; it is also the voice of conscience and indeed of morality itself. But that would mean, thinking of education, that listening to others, reading about what others think and do, and reflecting within ourselves about our actions and whether we could defend them to others are part of the practice of morality itself. Morality cannot exist without the broader, social perspective introduced by others, and this social nature ties it, in that way, with education and with public discussion, both actual and imagined. "Private" moral reflection taking place independent of the social world would be no moral reflection at all. It follows that moral *education*, in the form of both studying others' moral ideas and subjecting our own to discussion and criticism, is not only possible, but essential.

NOTES

1. R. C. Mortimer, *Christian Ethics* (London: Hutchinson's University Library, 1950), pp. 7–8.

2. This debate was broadcast on the "Third Program" of the British Broadcasting Corporation in 1948.

3. Plato, *Euthyphro*, trans. H. N. Fowler (Cambridge, MA: Harvard University Press, 1947).

4. Thomas Aquinas, *Summa Theologica*, Part I, Q. 25, Art. 3.

5. John Dewey, "Morality Is Social" in *The Moral Writings of John Dewey*, rev. ed., ed. James Gouinlock (Amherst, NY: Prometheus Books, 1994), pp. 182–184.

6. Obligations to animals raise an interesting problem for this conception of morality. Is it wrong to torture animals only because other *people* could be expected to disapprove? Or is it that the animal itself would disapprove? Or, perhaps, duties to animals rest on sympathy and compassion while human moral relations are more like Dewey describes, resting on morality's inherently social nature and on the dictates of conscience viewed as an assembly of others?

DISCUSSION QUESTIONS

1. What is "divine command theory"? Why does Arthur reject it? Do you agree with him? Why or why not?

2. What are the possible roles that religion might play in morality? Which is the strongest role? How would you defend it? Why might Arthur reject it? How would you respond to him?
3. What is the difference between something that is good because God says it is good, and something that God says is good because it is good?
4. Which of Arthur's arguments is the weakest? Why? Can you think of a solid counter-argument?
5. What does it mean to say that morality "cannot exist without the broader, social perspective introduced by others"? Do you agree? Why or why not?

 JEREMY BENTHAM

Classical Hedonism

In this selection, Jeremy Bentham argues that it is a fact of nature that the goal of individual lives is the pursuit of pleasure and the avoidance of pain. This position is known as "hedonism" (*hedone* is Greek for "pleasure"). For Bentham, good is only another word for "pleasure and the absences of pain." In terms of social morality, what is the right thing to do is whatever produces "the greatest good for the greatest number." We should strive in our lives to maximize pleasure and to minimize pain for as many people as possible. Actions that produce the greatest amounts of pleasure are to be valued morally over actions that produce lesser amounts of pleasure. His "hedonic" or utilitarian calculus asks us to consider the quantity of pleasure or pain resulting from our behavior in a number of respects including its intensity, duration, and certainty. Bentham believes that this is the most rational way to settle all moral controversies.

Jeremy Bentham (1748–1832) was the "father" of utilitarianism and the leader of a reform group based on utilitarian principles called the Philosophical Radicals. This reading is from *Introduction to the Principles of Morals and Legislation* (1789).

OF THE PRINCIPLE OF UTILITY

I. Nature has placed mankind under the governance of two sovereign masters, *pain* and *pleasure*. It is for them alone to point out what we ought to do, as well as to determine what we shall do. On the one hand the standard of right and wrong, on the other the chain of causes and effects, are fastened to their throne. They govern us in all we do, in all we say, in all we think: every effort we can make to throw off our subjection, will serve but to demonstrate and confirm it. In words a man may pretend to abjure their empire: but in reality he will remain subject to it all the while. The *principle of utility* recognizes this subjection, and assumes it for the foundation of that system, the object of which is to rear the fabric of felicity by the hands of reason and of law. Systems which attempt to question it, deal in sounds instead of sense, in caprice instead of reason, in darkness instead of light.

Jeremy Bentham, *Introduction to the Principles of Morals and Legislation* (1789).

But enough of metaphor and declamation: it is not by such means that moral science is to be improved.

II. The principle of utility is the foundation of the present work: it will be proper therefore at the outset to give an explicit and determinate account of what is meant by it. By the principle of utility is meant that principle which approves or disapproves of every action whatsoever, according to the tendency which it appears to have to augment or diminish the happiness of the party whose interest is in question: or, what is the same thing in other words, to promote or to oppose that happiness. I say of every action whatsoever; and therefore not only of every action of a private individual, but of every measure of government.

III. By utility is meant that property in any object, whereby it tends to produce benefit, advantage, pleasure, good, or happiness, (all this in the present case comes to the same thing) or (what comes again to the same thing) to prevent the happening of mischief, pain, evil, or unhappiness to the party whose interest is considered: if that party be the community in general, then the happiness of the community: if a particular individual, then the happiness of that individual.

VALUE OF A LOT OF PLEASURE OR PAIN, HOW TO BE MEASURED

I. Pleasures then, and the avoidance of pains, are the *ends* which the legislator has in view: it behoves him therefore to understand their *value*. Pleasures and pains are the *instruments* he has to work with: it behoves him therefore to understand their force, which is again, in other words, their value.

II. To a person considered *by himself*, the value of a pleasure or pain considered *by itself*, will be greater or less, according to the four following circumstances:

1. Its *intensity*.
2. Its *duration*.
3. Its *certainty* or *uncertainty*.
4. Its *propinquity* or *remoteness*.

III. These are the circumstances which are to be considered in estimating a pleasure or a pain considered each of them by itself. But when the value of any pleasure or pain is considered for the purpose of estimating the tendency of any *act* by which it is produced, there are two other circumstances to be taken into the account; these are,

5. Its *fecundity*, or the chance it has of being followed by sensations of the *same* kind: that is, pleasures, if it be a pleasure: pains, if it be a pain.
6. Its *purity*, or the chance it has of *not* being followed by sensations of the *opposite* kind: that is, pains, if it be a pleasure: pleasures, if it be a pain.

These two last, however, are in strictness scarcely to be deemed properties of the pleasure or the pain itself; they are not, therefore, in strictness to be taken into the account of the value of that pleasure or that pain. They are in strictness to be deemed properties only of the act, or other event, by which such pleasure or pain has been produced; and accordingly are only to be taken into the account of the tendency of such act or such event.

IV. To a *number* of persons, with reference to each of whom the value of a pleasure or a pain is considered, it will be greater or less, according to seven circumstances: to wit, the six preceding ones; *viz.*

1. Its *intensity*.
2. Its *duration*.
3. Its *certainty* or *uncertainty*.
4. Its *propinquity* or *remoteness*.
5. Its *fecundity*.
6. Its *purity*.

And one other; to wit:

7. Its *extent*; that is, the number of persons to whom it *extends*; or (in other words) who are affected by it.

V. To take an exact account then of the general tendency of any act, by which the interests of a community are affected, proceed as follows. Begin with any one person of those whose interests seem most immediately to be affected by it and take an account,

1. Of the value of each distinguishable *pleasure* which appears to be produced by it in the *first* instance.
2. Of the value of each *pain* which appears to be produced by it in the *first* instance.
3. Of the value of each pleasure which appears to be produced by it *after* the first. This constitutes the *fecundity* of the first *pleasure* and the *impurity* of the first *pain*.
4. Of the value of each *pain* which appears to be produced by it after the first. This constitutes

the *fecundity* of the first *pain*, and the *impurity* of the first pleasure.

5. Sum up all the values of all the *pleasures* on the one side, and those of all the pains on the other. The balance, if it be on the side of pleasure, will give the *good* tendency of the act upon the whole, with respect to the interests of that *individual* person; if on the side of pain, the *bad* tendency of it upon the whole.

6. Take an account of the *number* of persons whose interests appear to be concerned; and repeat the above process with respect to each. *Sum up* the numbers expressive of the degrees of *good* tendency, which the act has, with respect to each individual, in regard to whom the tendency of it is *good* upon the whole: do this again with respect to each individual, in regard to whom the tendency of it is *good* upon the whole: do this again with respect to each individual, in regard to whom the tendency of it is *bad* upon the whole. Take the *balance*; which, if on the side of *pleasure*, will give the general *good tendency* of the act, with respect to the total number or community of individuals concerned; if on the side of pain, the general *evil tendency*, with respect to the same community.

VI. It is not to be expected that this process should be strictly pursued previously to every moral judgment, or to every legislative or judicial operation. It may, however, be always kept in view: and as near as the process actually pursued on these occasions approaches to it, so near will such process approach to the character of an exact one.

VII. The same process is alike applicable to pleasure and pain, in whatever shape they appear: and by whatever denomination they are distinguished: to pleasure, whether it be called *good* (which is properly the cause or instrument of pleasure) or *profit* (which is distant pleasure, or the cause or instrument of distant pleasure,) or *convenience*, or *advantage, benefit, emolument, happiness*, and so forth: to pain, whether it be called *evil*, (which corresponds to *good*) or *mischief*, or *inconvenience*, or *disadvantage*, or *loss*, or *unhappiness*, and so forth.

VIII. Nor is this a novel and unwarranted, any more than it is a useless theory. In all this there is nothing but what the practice of mankind, wheresoever they have a clear view of their own interest, is perfectly conformable to. An article of property, an estate in land, for instance, is valuable, on what account? On account of the pleasures of all kinds which it enables a man to produce, and what comes to the same thing the pains of all kinds which it enables him to avert. But the value of such an article of property is universally understood to rise or fall according to the length or shortness of the time which a man had in it: the certainty or uncertainty of its coming into possession: and the nearness or remoteness of the time at which, if at all, it is to come into possession. As to the *intensity* of the pleasures which a man may derive from it, this is never thought of, because it depends upon the use which each particular person may come to make of it; which cannot be estimated till the particular pleasures he may come to derive from it, or the particular pains he may come to exclude by means of it, are brought to view. For the same reason, neither does he think of the *fecundity* or *purity* of those pleasures.

Thus much for pleasure and pain, happiness and unhappiness, in *general*.

DISCUSSION QUESTIONS

1. Do you agree with Bentham that "nature has placed mankind under the governance of two sovereign masters, *pain* and *pleasure*"? Is it possible to confirm or deny this claim? If so, how? If not, why not?

2. What is "utility"? Do you think that it can be quantified?

3. Is it possible to precisely measure degrees of pleasure and pain? Do you think that Bentham thought that the precise measurement of pain and pleasure was possible? To what extent does his moral theory depend on our ability to precisely measure pain and pleasure?

4. To what extent does morality depend on "happiness"? What are some problems with basing morality on happiness? What are some benefits of doing this? To what extent should morality depend on conscious deliberation about "happiness"? Explain.

R O B E R T   N O Z I C K

The Experience Machine

Robert Nozick argues against hedonism by asking us to conduct a "thought experiment." If the pursuit of pleasure and the avoidance of pain were really the ends of life, then we would all want to be hooked up to a machine that would allow us to experience whatever we wanted to experience. Nozick thinks that we would reject the "experience machine" and, with it, hedonism.

Robert Nozick is a philosophy professor at Harvard University and the author of *Anarchy, State and Utopia* (1973), *Philosophical Explanations* (1981), *The Examined Life* (1989), *The Nature of Rationality* (1993), and *Socratic Puzzles* (1997). The following selection is from *Anarchy, State and Utopia*.

There are also substantial puzzles when we ask what matters other than how *people's* experiences feel "from the inside." Suppose there were an experience machine that would give you any experience you desired. Superduper neuropsychologists could stimulate your brain so that you would think and feel you were writing a great novel, or making a friend, or reading an interesting book. All the time you would be floating in a tank, with electrodes attached to your brain. Should you plug into this machine for life, preprogramming your life's experiences? If you are worried about missing out on desirable experiences, we can suppose that business enterprises have researched thoroughly the lives of many others. You can pick and choose from their large library or smorgasbord of such experiences, selecting your life's experiences for, say, the next two years. After two years have passed, you will have ten minutes or ten hours out of the tank to select the experiences of your *next* two years. Of course, while in the tank you won't know that you're there; you'll think it's all actually happening. Others can also plug in to have the experiences they want, so there's no need to stay unplugged to serve them. (Ignore problems such as who will service the machines if everyone plugs in.) Would you plug in? *What else can matter to us, other than how our lives feel from the inside?* Nor should you refrain because of the few moments of distress between the moment you've decided and the moment you're plugged. What's a few moments of distress compared to a lifetime of bliss (if that's

what you choose), and why feel any distress at all if your decision *is* the best one?

What does matter to us in addition to our experiences? First, we want to do certain things, and not just have the experience of doing them. In the case of certain experiences, it is only because first we want to do the actions that we want the experiences of doing them or thinking we've done them. (But *why* do we want to do the activities rather than merely to experience them?) A second reason for not plugging in is that we want to be a certain way, to be a certain sort of person. Someone floating in a tank is an indeterminate blob. There is no answer to the question of what a person is like who has long been in the tank. Is he courageous, kind, intelligent, witty, loving? It's not merely that it's difficult to tell; there's no way he is. Plugging into the machine is a kind of suicide. It will seem to some, trapped by a picture, that nothing about what we are like can matter except as it gets reflected in our experiences. But should it be surprising that what *we are* is important to us? Why should we be concerned only with how our time is filled, but not with what we are?

Thirdly, plugging into an experience machine limits us to a man-made reality, to a world no deeper or more important than that which people can construct. There is no *actual* contact with any deeper reality, though the experience of it can be simulated. Many persons desire to leave themselves open to such contact and to a plumbing of deeper significance.[1] This clarifies the intensity of the conflict over psychoactive drugs, which some view as mere local experience machines, and others view as avenues to a deeper reality; what some view as equivalent to surrender to the experience machine, others view as following one of the reasons *not* to surrender!

We learn that something matters to us in addition to experience by imagining an experience machine and then realizing that we would not use it. We can continue to imagine a sequence of machines each designed to fill lacks suggested for the earlier machines. For example, since the experience machine doesn't meet our desire to *be* a certain way, imagine a transformation machine which transforms us into whatever sort of person we'd like to be (compatible with our staying us). Surely one would not use the transformation machine to become as one would wish, and thereupon plug into the experience machine![2] So something matters in addition to one's experiences *and* what one is like. Nor is the reason merely that one's experiences are unconnected with what one is like. For the experience machine might be limited to provide only experiences possible to the sort of person plugged in. Is it that we want to make a difference in the world? Consider then the result machine, which produces in the world any result you would produce and injects your vector input into any joint activity. We shall not pursue here the fascinating details of these or other machines. What is most disturbing about them is their living of our lives for us. Is it misguided to search for *particular* additional functions beyond the competence of machines to do for us? Perhaps what we desire is to live (an active verb) ourselves, in contact with reality. (And this, machines cannot do *for* us.) Without elaborating on the implications of this, which I believe connect surprisingly with issues about free will and causal accounts of knowledge, we need merely note the intricacy of the question of what matters *for people* other than their experiences. Until one finds a satisfactory answer, and determines that this answer does not *also* apply to animals, one cannot reasonably claim that only the felt experiences of animals limit what we may do to them.

NOTES

1. Traditional religious views differ on the *point* of contact with a transcendent reality. Some say that contact yields eternal bliss or Nirvana, but they have not distinguished this sufficiently from merely a *very* long run on the experience machine. Others think it is intrinsically desirable to do the will of a higher being which created us all, though presumably no one would think this if we discovered we had been created as an object of amusement by some superpowerful child from another galaxy or dimension. Still others imagine an eventual merging with a higher reality, leaving unclear its desirability, or where that merging leaves *us*.

2. Some wouldn't use the transformation machine at all; it seems like *cheating*. But the one-time use of the transformation machine would not remove all challenges; there would still be obstacles for the new us to overcome, a new plateau from which to strive even higher. And is this plateau any the less earned or deserved than that provided by genetic endowment and early childhood environment? But if the transformation machine could be used indefinitely often, so that we could accomplish anything by pushing a button to transform ourselves into someone who could do it easily, there would remain no limits we *need* to strain against or try to transcend. Would there be anything left *to do?* Do some theological views place God outside of time because an omniscient omnipotent being couldn't fill up his days?

DISCUSSION QUESTIONS

1. Do only our internal feelings matter to us? Nozick thinks not. Do you agree with him? Why or why not?
2. If someone told you today that there was an experience machine and that you could be hooked up to it, would you do it? Why or why not?
3. Nozick argues that "we want to *do* certain things, and not just have the experience of doing them." What is the difference? Do you agree with it?
4. Nozick says that "plugging into the machine is a kind of suicide." Why does he say this? Is he right?
5. Compare the experience machine in the 1999 movie *The Matrix* with Nozick's experience machine. How are they similar and/or different? Should the movie also be regarded as an argument against hedonism? Discuss.

 JOHN STUART MILL

Utilitarianism

Following Jeremy Bentham, John Stuart Mill explains human behavior in terms of the principle of greatest happiness. But Mill offers an important and significant qualification to Bentham's criterion of ethics. Whereas Bentham's utilitarianism makes the criterion of ethics the production of the greatest amount of pleasure and the least amount of pain, Mill distinguishes between "higher pleasures," which are of greater value, and "lower pleasures," which are of lesser value. Mill, unlike Bentham, also distinguishes between happiness and mere sensual pleasure. "It is better to be a human being dissatisfied than a pig satisfied," says Mill, "better to be Socrates dissatisfied than a fool satisfied." Whereas Bentham tells us to maximize the sum of pleasure, Mill tells us to maximize the sum of *higher* pleasure. Consequently, Mill's utilitarianism is sometimes called *eudaimonistic utilitarianism* (*eudaimonia* is Greek for "happiness") to distinguish it from Bentham's *hedonistic utilitarianism*.

John Stuart Mill (1806–1873) was one of the most important British philosophers of the nineteenth century. In addition to ethics, he made significant contributions to logic, the philosophy of science, and social and political theory. His *Utilitarianism* was published in 1861.

. . . The creed which accepts as the foundation of morals, Utility, or the Greatest Happiness Principle, holds that actions are right in proportion as they tend to promote happiness, wrong as they tend to produce the reverse of happiness. By happiness is intended pleasure, and the absence of pain; by unhappiness, pain, and the privation of pleasure. To give a clear view of the moral standard set up by the theory, much more requires to be said; in particular, what things it includes: in the ideas of pain and pleasure; and to what extent this is left an open question. But these supplementary explanations do not affect the theory of life on which this theory of morality is grounded—namely, that pleasure, and freedom from pain, are the only things desirable as ends; and that all desirable things (which are as numerous in the utilitarian as in any other scheme) are desirable either for the pleasure inherent in themselves, or as a means to the promotion of pleasure and the prevention of pain.

Now, such a theory of life excites in many minds, and among them in some of the most estimable in feeling and purpose, inveterate dislike. To suppose that life has (as they express it) no higher end than pleasure—no better and nobler object of desire and pursuit—they designate as utterly mean and groveling; as a doctrine worthy only of swine, to whom the followers of Epicurus were, at a very early period, contemptuously likened; and modern holders of the doctrine are occasionally made the subject of equally polite comparisons by its German, French, and English assailants.

When thus attacked, the Epicureans have always answered, that it is not they, but their accusers, who represent human nature in a degrading light; since the accusation supposes human beings to be capable of no pleasures except those of which swine are capable. If this supposition were true, the charge could not be gainsaid, but would then be no longer an imputation; for if the sources of pleasure were precisely the same to human beings and to swine, the rule of life which is good enough for the one would be good enough for the other. The comparison of the Epicurean life to that of beasts is felt as degrading, precisely because a beast's pleasures do not satisfy a human being's conception of happiness. Human beings have faculties more elevated than the animal

John Stuart Mill, *Utilitarianism* (1861).

appetites, and when once made conscious of them, do not regard anything as happiness which does not include their gratification. I do not, indeed, consider the Epicureans to have been by any means faultless in drawing out their scheme of consequences from the utilitarian principle. To do this in any sufficient manner, many Stoic, as well as Christian elements require to be included. But there is no known Epicurean theory of life which does not assign to the pleasures of the intellect, of the feelings and imagination, and of the moral sentiments, a much higher value as pleasures than to those of mere sensation. It must be admitted, however, that utilitarian writers in general have placed the superiority of mental over bodily pleasures chiefly in the greater permanency, safety, uncostliness, etc., of the former—that is, in their circumstantial advantages rather than in their intrinsic nature. And on all these points utilitarians have fully proved their case; but they might have taken the other, and, as it may be called, higher ground, with entire consistency. It is quite compatible with the principle of utility to recognize the fact, that some *kinds* of pleasure are more desirable and more valuable than others. It would be absurd that while, in estimating all other things, quality is considered as well as quantity, the estimation of pleasures should be supposed to depend on quantity alone.

If I am asked, what I mean by difference of quality in pleasures, or what makes one pleasure more valuable than another, merely as a pleasure, except its being greater in amount, there is but one possible answer. Of two pleasures, if there be one which all or almost all who have experience of both give a decided preference, irrespective of any feeling of moral obligation to prefer it, that is the more desirable pleasure. If one of the two is, by those who are competently acquainted with both, placed so far above the other that they prefer it, even though knowing it to be attended with a great amount of discontent, and would not resign it for any quantity of the other pleasure which their nature is capable of, we are justified in ascribing to the preferred enjoyment a superiority in quantity, so far out-weighing quantity as to render it, in comparison, of small account.

Now it is an unquestionable fact that those who are equally acquainted with, and equally capable of appreciating and enjoying, both, do give a most marked preference to the manner of existence which employs their higher faculties. Few human creatures would consent to be changed into any of the lower animals, for a promise of the fullest allowance of a beast's pleasures; no intelligent human being would consent to be a fool, no instructed person would be an ignoramus, no person of feeling and conscience would be selfish and base, even though they should be persuaded that the fool, the dunce, or the rascal is better satisfied with his lot than they are with theirs. They would not resign what they possess more than he for the most complete satisfaction of all the desires which they have in common with him. If they ever fancy they would, it is only in cases of unhappiness so extreme, that to escape from it they would exchange their lot for almost any other, however undesirable in their own eyes. A being of higher faculties requires more to make him happy, is capable probably of more acute suffering, and certainly accessible to it at more points, than one of an inferior type; but in spite of these liabilities, he can never really wish to sink into what he feels to be a lower grade of existence. We may give what explanation we please of this unwillingness; we may attribute it to pride, a name which is given indiscriminately to some of the most and to some of the least estimable feelings of which mankind are capable; we may refer it to the love of liberty and personal independence, an appeal to which was with the Stoics one of the most effective means for the inculcation of it; to the love of power, or to the love of excitement, both of which do really enter into and contribute to it: but its most appropriate appellation is a sense of dignity, which all human beings possess in one form or another, and in some, though by no means in exact, proportion to their higher faculties, and which is so essential a part of the happiness of those in whom it is strong, that nothing which conflicts with it could be, otherwise than momentarily, an object of desire to them. Whoever supposes that this preference takes place at a sacrifice of happiness—that the superior being, in anything like equal circumstances, is not happier than the inferior—confounds the two very different ideas, of happiness, and content. It is indisputable that the being whose capacities of enjoyment are low, has the greatest chance of having them fully satisfied; and a highly endowed being will always feel that any happiness which he can look for, as the world is constituted, is imperfect. But he can learn to bear its imperfections, if they are at all bearable; and they will not make him envy the being who is indeed unconscious of the imperfections, but only because he feels not at all the good which those imperfections qualify. It is better to be a human being dissatisfied than a pig satisfied; better to be Socrates dissatisfied than a fool satisfied. And if the fool, or the pig, are of a different opinion, it is because they only know their own side of the question. The other party to the comparison knows both sides.

It may be objected, that many who are capable of the higher pleasures, occasionally, under the influence of temptation, postpone them to the lower. But this is quite compatible with a full appreciation of the intrinsic superiority of the higher. Men often, from infirmity of character, make their election for the nearer good, though they know it to be the less valuable; and this no less when the choice is between two bodily pleasures, than when it is between bodily and mental. They pursue sensual indulgences to the injury of health, though perfectly aware that health is the greater good. It may be further objected, that many who begin with youthful enthusiasm for everything noble, as they advance in years sink into indolence and selfishness. But I do not believe that those who undergo this very common change, voluntarily choose the lower description of pleasures in preference to the higher. I believe that before they devote themselves exclusively to the one, they have already become incapable of the other. Capacity for the nobler feelings is in most natures a very tender plant, easily killed, not only by hostile influences, but by mere want of sustenance; and in the majority of young persons it speedily dies away if the occupations to which their position in life has devoted them, and the society into which it has thrown them, are not favorable to keeping that higher capacity in exercise. Men lose their high aspirations as they lose their intellectual tastes, because they have not time or opportunity for indulging them; and they addict themselves to inferior pleasures, not because they deliberately prefer them, but because they are either the only ones to which they have access, or the only ones which they are any longer capable of enjoying. It may be questioned whether any one who has remained equally susceptible to both classes of pleasures, ever knowingly and calmly preferred the lower; though many, in all ages, have broken down in an ineffectual attempt to combine both.

From this verdict of the only competent judges, I apprehend there can be no appeal. On a question which is the best worth having of two pleasures, or which of two modes of existence is the most grateful to the feelings, apart from its moral attributes and from its consequences, the judgment of those who are qualified by knowledge of both, or, if they differ, that of the majority among them, must be admitted as final. And there needs to be the less hesitation to accept this judgment respecting the quality of pleasures, since there is no other tribunal to be referred to even on the question of quantity. What means are there of determining which is the acutest of two pains, or the intensest of two pleasurable sensations, except the general suffrage of those who are familiar with both? Neither pains nor pleasures are homogeneous, and pain is always heterogeneous with pleasure. What is there to decide whether a particular pleasure is worth purchasing at the cost of a particular pain, except the feelings and judgment of the experienced? When, therefore, those feelings and judgment declare the pleasures derived from the higher faculties to be preferable *in kind*, apart from the question of intensity, to those of which the animal nature, disjoined from the higher faculties, is susceptible, they are entitled on this subject to the same regard.

I have dwelt on this point, as being a necessary part of a perfectly just conception of Utility or Happiness, considered as the directive rule of human conduct. But it is by no means an indispensable condition to the acceptance of the utilitarian standard; for that standard is not the agent's own greatest happiness, but the greatest amount of happiness altogether; and if it may possibly be doubted whether a noble character is always the happier for its nobleness, there can be no doubt that it makes other people happier, and that the world in general is immensely a gainer by it. Utilitarianism, therefore, could only attain its end by the general cultivation of nobleness of character, even if each individual were only benefited by the nobleness of others, and his own, so far as happiness is concerned, were a sheer deduction from the benefit. But the bare enunciation of such an absurdity as this last, renders refutation superfluous.

According to the Greatest Happiness Principle, as above explained, the ultimate end, with reference to and for the sake of which all other things are desirable (whether we are considering our own good or that of other people), is an existence exempt as far as possible from pain, and as rich as possible in enjoyments, both in point of quantity and quality; the test of quality, and the rule for measuring it against quantity, being the preference felt by those who in their opportunities of experience, to which must be added their habits of self-consciousness and self-observation, are best furnished with the means of comparison. This, being, according to the utilitarian opinion, the end of human action, is necessarily also the standard of morality; which may accordingly be defined, the rules and precepts for human conduct, by the observance of which an existence such as has been described might be, to the greatest extent possible, secured to all mankind; and not to them only, but, so far as the nature of things admits, to the whole sentient creation. . . .

The objectors to utilitarianism cannot always be charged with representing it in a discreditable light.

On the contrary, those among them who entertain anything like a just idea of its disinterested character, sometimes find fault with its standard as being too high for humanity. They say it is exacting too much to require that people shall always act from the inducement of promoting the general interests of society. But this is to mistake the very meaning of a standard of morals, and confound the rule of action with the motive of it. It is the business of ethics to tell us what are our duties, or by what test we may know them; but no system of ethics requires that the sole motive of all we do shall be a feeling of duty; on the contrary, ninety-nine hundredths of all our actions are done from other motives, and rightly so done, if the rule of duty does not condemn them. It is the more unjust to utilitarianism that this particular misapprehension should be made a ground of objection to it, inasmuch as utilitarian moralists have gone beyond almost all others in affirming that the motive has nothing to do with the morality of the action, though much with the worth of the agent. He who saves a fellow-creature from drowning does what is morally right, whether his motive be duty, or the hope of being paid for his trouble; he who betrays the friend that trusts him, is guilty of a crime, even if his object be to serve another friend to whom he is under greater obligation. But to speak only of actions done from the motive of duty, and in direct obedience to principle: it is a misapprehension of the utilitarian mode of thought, to conceive it as implying that people should fix their minds upon so wide a generality as the world, or society at large. The great majority of good actions are intended not for the benefit of the world, but for that of individuals, of which the good of the world is made up; and the thoughts of the most virtuous man need not on these occasions travel beyond the particular persons concerned, except so far as is necessary to assure himself that in benefiting them he is not violating the rights, that is, the legitimate and authorised expectations, of anyone else. The multiplication of happiness is, according to the utilitarian ethics, the object of virtue: the occasions on which any person (except one in a thousand) has it in his power to do this on an extended scale, in other words to be a public benefactor, are but exceptional; and on these occasions alone is he called on to consider public utility; in every other case, private utility, the interest or happiness of some few persons, is all he has to attend to. Those alone the influence of whose actions extends to society in general, need concern themselves habitually about so large an object. In the case of abstinences indeed—of things which people forbear to do from moral considerations, though the consequences in the particular case might be beneficial—it would be unworthy of an intelligent agent not to be consciously aware that the action is of a class which, if practiced generally, would be generally injurious, and that this is the ground of the obligation to abstain from it. The amount of regard for the public interest implied in this recognition, is no greater than is demanded by every system of morals, for they all enjoin to abstain from whatever is manifestly pernicious to society. . . .

CHAPTER IV: OF WHAT SORT OF PROOF THE PRINCIPLE OF UTILITY IS SUSCEPTIBLE

It has already been remarked, that questions of ultimate ends do not admit of proof, in the ordinary acceptation of the term. To be incapable of proof by reasoning is common to all first principles; to the first premises of our knowledge, as well as to those of our conduct. But the former, being matters of fact, may be the subject of a direct appeal to the faculties which judge of fact—namely, our senses, and our internal consciousness. Can an appeal be made to the same faculties on questions of practical ends? Or by what other faculty is cognizance taken of them?

Questions about ends are, in other words, questions about what things are desirable. The utilitarian doctrine is, that happiness is desirable, and the only thing desirable, as an end; all other things being only desirable as means to that end. What ought to be required of this doctrine—what conditions is it to requisite that the doctrine should fulfil—to make good its claim to be believed?

The only proof capable of being given that an object is visible, is that people actually see it. The only proof that a sound is audible, is that people hear it: and so of the other sources of our experience. In like manner, I apprehend, the sole evidence it is possible to produce that anything is desirable, is that people do actually desire it. If the end which the utilitarian doctrine proposes to itself were not, in theory and in practice, acknowledged to be an end, nothing could ever convince any person that it was so. No reason can be given why the general happiness is desirable, except that each person, so far as he believes it to be attainable, desires his own happiness. This, however, being a fact, we have not only all the proof which the case admits of, but all which it is possible to require, that happiness is a good: that each person's happiness is a good to that person, and the general happiness, therefore, a good to the aggregate of all persons.

Happiness has made out its title as *one* of the ends of conduct, and consequently one of the criteria of morality.

But it has not, by this alone, proved itself to be the sole criterion. To do that, it would seem, by the same rule, necessary to show, not only that people desire happiness, but that they never desire anything else. . . .

We have now, then, an answer to the question, of what sort of proof the principle of utility is susceptible. If the opinion which I have now stated is psychologically true—if human nature is so constituted as to desire nothing which is not either a part of happiness or a means of happiness, we can have no other proof, and we require no other, that these are the only things desirable. If so, happiness is the sole end of human action, and the promotion of it the test by which to judge of all human conduct; from whence it necessarily follows that it must be the criterion of morality, since a part is included in the whole.

And now to decide whether this is really so; whether mankind do desire nothing for itself but that which is a pleasure to them, or of which the absence is a pain; we have evidently arrived at a question of fact and experience, dependent, like all similar questions, upon evidence. It can only be determined by practised self-consciousness and self-observation, assisted by observation of others. I believe that these sources of evidence, impartially consulted, will declare that desiring a thing and finding it pleasant, aversion to it and thinking of it as painful, are phenomena entirely inseparable, or rather two parts of the same phenomenon; in strictness of language, two different modes of naming the same psychological fact: that to think of an object as desirable (unless for the sake of its consequences), and to think of it as pleasant, are one and the same thing; and that to desire anything, except in proportion as the idea of it is pleasant, is a physical and metaphysical impossibility.

DISCUSSION QUESTIONS

1. What is Mill's principle of utility? What does he mean by "utility"? Does he mean the same thing as Jeremy Bentham? Explain.
2. How does Mill explain the fact that some people choose lower pleasures over higher pleasures? Do you agree with his assessment?
3. How does Mill prove the principle of utility? Do you agree with his proof? Explain.
4. What are some objections that might be raised against Mill's eudaimonistic utilitarianism? How might he respond to them? Do Robert Nozick's criticisms hold for Mill as well as for Bentham? Why or why not?
5. In what sense is Mill's position an improvement over Bentham's? Which do you prefer, and why?

 IMMANUEL KANT

The Categorical Imperative

For Immanuel Kant, a human will governed by reason is a good will, and the good will is the only thing that is good without qualification. The human will experiences the laws of reason as commands issued by reason to act in various ways. Kant calls these commands

Immanuel Kant, *Fundamental Principles of the Metaphysics of Morals.* Translated by T. K. Abbott (1898).

"imperatives." There are two general kinds of imperatives: hypothetical and categorical. If an action is commanded as being necessary for bringing about some further end, the imperative is *hypothetical.* If an action is commanded as being good without qualification, the imperative is *categorical.* Because categorical imperatives are unconditional, our obedience to them is unqualified. Kant formulates the categorical imperative as follows: Act only according to that rule by which you can at the same time will that it should become a universal law. So, for Kant, you should do only those actions that conform to rules that you could will to be adopted universally. If you were to lie, for example, you would be following the rule "It is permissible to lie." This rule could not be adopted universally because it would be self-defeating: people would stop believing one another, and then it would do no good to lie. Therefore, you should not lie.

At its core, Kant's moral theory contains three basic ideas: (1) humans are rational, capable of thinking about the choices they face and selecting among them on the basis of reasons; (2) humans have an infinite worth or dignity—that is, humans are "ends-in-themselves"—and this sets them above all merely conditionally valuable things in the world; and (3) humans, as rational ends-in-themselves, are the authors of the moral law, so that their obedience to duty is an act, not of submission, but of *autonomy.* These three ideas are more apparent in another of Kant's formulations of the categorical imperative: act so that you treat humanity, whether in your own person or in that of another, always as an end and never as a means only.

Few philosophers have had more of an impact on the history of philosophy than Immanuel Kant (1724–1804). He spent his entire life in Königsberg, Prussia, where he was a professor of philosophy. His life is said to have been so orderly that the people of his town set their clocks according to the time Kant passed their houses on his daily walk. Among his many highly influential writings are his three "critiques": *Critique of Pure Reason* (1781), *Critique of Practical Reason* (1788), and *Critique of Judgment* (1790). The work from which this selection is taken, *Fundamental Principles of the Metaphysics of Morals,* was first published in 1785.

Nothing can possibly be conceived in the world, or even out of it, which can be called good, without qualification, except a Good Will. Intelligence, wit, judgment, and the other *talents* of the mind, however they may be named, or courage, resolution, perseverance, as qualities of temperament, are undoubtedly good and desirable in many respects; but these gifts of nature may also become extremely bad and mischievous if the will which is to make use of them, and which, therefore, constitutes what is called *character,* is not good. It is the same with the *gifts of fortune.* Power, riches, honour, even health, and the general well-being and contentment with one's condition which is called *happiness,* inspire pride, and often presumption, if there is not a good will to correct the influence of these on the mind, and with this also to rectify the whole principle of acting, and adapt it to its end. The sight of a being who is not adorned with a single feature of a pure and good will, enjoying unbroken prosperity, can never give pleasure to an impartial rational spectator. Thus a good will appears to constitute the indispensable condition even of being worthy of happiness.

There are even some qualities which are of service to this good will itself, and may facilitate its action, yet which have no intrinsic unconditional value, but always presuppose a good will, and this qualifies the esteem that we justly have for them, and does not permit us to regard them as absolutely good. Moderation in the affections and passions, self-control, and calm deliberation are not only good in many respects, but even seem to constitute part of the intrinsic worth of the person; but they are far from deserving to be called good without qualification, although they have been so unconditionally praised by the ancients. For without the principles of a good will, they may become extremely bad; and the coolness of a villain not only makes him far more dangerous, but also directly makes him more abominable in our eyes than he would have been without it.

A good will is good not because of what it performs or effects, not by its aptness for the attainment of some proposed end, but simply by virtue of the volition, that is, it is good in itself, and considered by itself is to be esteemed much higher than all that can be brought about by it in favour of any inclination, nay, even of the sum-total of all inclinations. Even if it should happen that, owing to special disfavour of fortune, or the niggardly provision of a step-motherly nature, this will should wholly lack power to accomplish its purpose, if with its greatest efforts it should yet achieve nothing, and there should remain only the good will (not, to be sure, a mere wish, but the summoning of all means in our power), then, like a jewel, it would still shine by its own light, as a thing which has its whole value in itself. Its usefulness or fruitlessness can neither add to nor take away anything from this value.

Thus the moral worth of an action does not lie in the effect expected from it, nor in any principle of action which requires to borrow its motive from this expected effect. For all these effects—agreeableness of one's condition, and even the promotion of the happiness of others—could have been also brought about by other causes, so that for this there would have been no need of the will of a rational being; whereas it is in this alone that the supreme and unconditional good can be found. The pre-eminent good which we call moral can therefore consist in nothing else than *the conception of law* in itself, *which certainly is only possible in a rational being,* in so far as this conception, and not the expected effect, determines the will. This is a good which is already present in the person who acts accordingly, and we have not to wait for it to appear first in the result.

But what sort of law can that be, the conception of which must determine the will, even without paying any regard to the effect expected from it, in order that this will may be called good absolutely and without qualification? As I have deprived the will of every impulse which could arise to it from obedience to any law, there remains nothing but the universal conformity of its actions to law in general, which alone is to serve the will as a principle, i.e. I am never to act otherwise than *so that I could also will that my maxim should become a universal law.* Here, now, it is the simple conformity to law in general, without assuming any particular law applicable to certain actions, that serves the will as its principle, and must so serve it, if duty is not to be a vain delusion and a chimerical notion. The common reason of men in its practical judgments perfectly coincides with this and always has in view the principle here suggested. Let the question be, for example: May I when in distress make a promise with the intention not to keep it? I

readily distinguish here between the two significations which the question may have: Whether it is prudent, or whether it is right, to make a false promise? The former may undoubtedly often be the case. I see clearly indeed that it is not enough to extricate myself from a present difficulty by means of this subterfuge, but it must be well considered whether there may not hereafter spring from this lie much greater inconvenience than that from which I now free myself, and as, with all my supposed *cunning,* the consequences cannot be so easily foreseen but that credit once lost may be much more injurious to me than any mischief which I seek to avoid at present, it should be considered whether it would not be more *prudent* to act herein according to a universal maxim, and to make it a habit to promise nothing except with the intention of keeping it. But it is soon clear to me that such a maxim will still only be based on the fear of consequences. Now it is a wholly different thing to be truthful from duty, and to be so from apprehension of injurious consequences. In the first case, the very notion of the action already implies a law for me; in the second case, I must first look about elsewhere to see what results may be combined with it which would affect myself. For to deviate from the principle of duty is beyond all doubt wicked; but to be unfaithful to my maxim of prudence may often be very advantageous to me, although to abide by it is certainly safer. The shortest way, however, and an unerring one, to discover the answer to this question whether a lying promise is consistent with duty, is to ask myself, Should I be content that my maxim (to extricate myself from difficulty by a false promise) should hold good as a universal law, for myself as well as for others? And should I be able to say to myself, "Everyone may make a deceitful promise when he finds himself in a difficulty from which he cannot otherwise extricate himself"? Then I presently become aware that while I can will the lie, I can by no means will that lying should be a universal law. For with such a law there would be no promises at all, since it would be in vain to allege my intention in regard to my future actions to those who would not believe this allegation, or if they over-hastily did so, would pay me back in my own coin. Hence my maxim, as soon as it should be made a universal law, would necessarily destroy itself.

I do not, therefore, need any far-reaching penetration to discern what I have to do in order that my will be morally good. Inexperienced in the course of the world, incapable of being prepared for all its contingencies, I only ask myself: Canst thou also will that thy maxim should be a universal law? If not, then it must be rejected, and that not because of a disadvantage accruing from it to myself or even to others, but because it cannot enter as a principle into a possible universal legislation, and reason extorts from me immediate respect for such legislation. I do not indeed as yet *discern* on what this respect is based (this the philosopher may inquire), but at least I understand this, that it is an estimation of the worth which far outweighs all worth of what is recommended by inclination, and that the necessity of acting from *pure* respect for the practical law is what constitutes duty, to which every other motive must give place, because it is the condition of a will being good *in itself*, and the worth of such a will is above everything. . . .

. . . Everything in nature works according to laws. Rational beings alone have the faculty of acting according *to the conception* of laws, that is according to principles, i.e. have a *will*. Since the deduction of actions from principles requires *reason*, the will is nothing but practical reason. If reason infallibly determines the will, then the actions of such a being which are recognized as objectively necessary are subjectively necessary also, i.e. the will is a faculty to choose *that only* which reason independent on inclination recognizes as practically necessary, i.e. as good. But if reason of itself does not sufficiently determine the will, if the latter is subject also to subjective conditions (particular impulses) which do not always coincide with the objective conditions; in a word, if the will does not *in itself* completely accord with reason (which is actually the case with men), then the actions which objectively are recognized as necessary are subjectively contingent, and the determination of such a will according to objective laws is *obligation*, that is to say, the relation of the objective laws to a will that is not thoroughly good is conceived as the determination of the will of a rational being by principles of reason, but which the will from its nature does not of necessity follow.

The conception of an objective principle, in so far as it is obligatory for a will, is called a command (of reason), and the formula of the command is called an Imperative. . . .

Now all *imperatives* command either *hypothetically* or *categorically*. The former represent the practical necessity of a possible action as means to something else that is willed (or at least which one might possibly will). The categorical imperative would be that which represented an action as necessary of itself without reference to another end, i.e. as objectively necessary.

Since every practical law represents a possible action as good, and on this account, for a subject who is practically determinable by reason, neces-

sary, all imperatives are formulae determining an action which is necessary according to the principle of a will good in some respects. If now the action is good only as a means *to something else*, then the imperative is *hypothetical*; if it is conceived as good *in itself* and consequently as being necessarily the principle of a will which of itself conforms to reason, then it is *categorical*. . . .

When I conceive a hypothetical imperative, in general I do not know beforehand what it will contain until I am given the condition. But when I conceive a categorical imperative, I know at once what it contains. For as the imperative contains besides the law only the necessity that the maxims shall conform to this law, while the law contains no conditions restricting it, there remains nothing but the general statement that the maxim of the action should conform to a universal law, and it is this conformity alone that the imperative properly represents as necessary.

There is . . . but one categorical imperative, namely, this: *Act only on that maxim whereby thou canst at the same time will that it should become a universal law.*

Now if all imperatives of duty can be deduced from this one imperative as from their principle, then, although it should remain undecided whether what is called duty is not merely a vain notion, yet at least we shall be able to show what we understand by it and what this notion means.

Since the universality of the law according to which effects are produced constitutes what is properly called *nature* in the most general sense (as to form), that is the existence of things so far as it is determined by general laws, the imperative of duty may be expressed thus: *Act as if the maxim of thy action were to become by thy will a universal law of nature.*

We will now enumerate a few duties, adopting the usual division of them into duties to ourselves and to others, and into perfect and imperfect duties.

1. A man reduced to despair by a series of misfortunes feels wearied of life, but is still so far in possession of his reason that he can ask himself whether it would not be contrary to his duty to himself to take his own life. Now he inquires whether the maxim of his action could become a universal law of nature. His maxim is: From self-love I adopt it as a principle to shorten my life when its longer duration is likely to bring more evil than satisfaction. It is asked then simply whether this principle founded on self-love can become a universal law of nature. Now we see at once that a system of nature of which it should be a law to destroy life by means of the very feeling whose special nature it is to impel to the improvement of

life would contradict itself, and therefore could not exist as a system of nature; hence that maxim cannot possibly exist as a universal law of nature, and consequently would be wholly inconsistent with the supreme principle of all duty.

2. Another finds himself forced by necessity to borrow money. He knows that he will not be able to repay it, but sees also that nothing will be lent to him, unless he promises stoutly to repay it in a definite time. He desires to make this promise, but he has still so much conscience as to ask himself: Is it not unlawful and inconsistent with duty to get out of a difficulty in this way? Suppose, however, that he resolves to do so, then the maxim of his action would be expressed thus: When I think myself in want of money, I will borrow money and promise to repay it, although I know that I never can do so. Now this principle of self-love or of one's own advantage may perhaps be consistent with my whole future welfare; but the question now is: Is it right? I change then the suggestion of self-love into a universal law, and state the question thus: How would it be if my maxim were a universal law? Then I see at once that it could never hold as a universal law of nature, but would necessarily contradict itself. For supposing it to be a universal law that everyone when he thinks himself in a difficulty should be able to promise whatever he pleases, with the purpose of not keeping his promise, the promise itself would become impossible, as well as the end that one might have in view in it, since no one would consider that anything was promised to him, but would ridicule all such statements as vain pretences.

3. A third finds in himself a talent which with the help of some culture might make him a useful man in many respects. But he finds himself in comfortable circumstances, and prefers to indulge in pleasure rather than to take pains in enlarging and improving his happy natural capacities. He asks, however, whether his maxim of neglect of his natural gifts, besides agreeing with his inclination to indulgence, agrees also with what is called duty. He sees then that a system of nature could indeed subsist with such a universal law although men (like the South Sea islanders) should let their talents rest, and resolve to devote their lives merely to idleness, amusement, and propagation of their species—in a word, to enjoyment; but he cannot possibly *will* that this should be a universal law of nature, or be implanted in us as such by a natural instinct. For, as a rational being, he necessarily wills that his faculties be developed, since they

serve him, and have been given him, for all sorts of possible purposes.

4. A fourth, who is in prosperity, while he sees that others have to contend with great wretchedness and that he could help them, thinks: What concern is it of mine? Let everyone be as happy as Heaven pleases, or as he can make himself; I will take nothing from him nor even envy him, only I do not wish to contribute anything to his welfare or to his assistance in distress! Now no doubt if such a mode of thinking were a universal law, the human race might very well subsist, and doubtless even better than in a state in which everyone talks of sympathy and good-will, or even takes care occasionally to put it into practice, but, on the other side, also cheats when he can, betrays the rights of men, or otherwise violates them. But although it is possible that a universal law of nature might exist in accordance with that maxim, it is impossible to *will* that such a principle should have the universal validity of a law of nature. For a will which resolved this would contradict itself, inasmuch as many cases might occur in which one would have need of the love and sympathy of others, and in which, by such a law of nature, sprung from his own will, he would deprive himself of all hope of the aid he desires. . . .

We have thus established at least this much, that if duty is a conception which is to have any import and real legislative authority for our actions, it can only be expressed in categorical, and not at all in hypothetical, imperatives. We have also, which is of great importance, exhibited clearly and definitely for every practical application the content of the categorical imperative, which must contain the principle of all duty if there is such a thing at all. We have not yet, however, advanced so far as to prove *à priori* that there actually is such an imperative, that there is a practical law which commands absolutely of itself, and without any other impulse, and that the following of this law is duty. . . .

Now I say: man and generally any rational being *exists* as an end in himself, *not merely as a means* to be arbitrarily used by this or that will, but in all his actions, whether they concern himself or other rational beings, must be always regarded at the same time as an end. All objects of the inclinations have only a conditional worth; for if the inclinations and the wants founded on them did not exist, then their object would be without value. But the inclinations themselves being sources of want are so far from having an absolute worth for which they should be desired, that, on the contrary, it must be the universal wish of every rational being to be wholly free from them. Thus the worth of any object which is *to be acquired* by our action is always conditional. Beings whose existence depends not on our will but on nature's, have nevertheless, if they are non-rational beings, only a relative value as means, and are therefore called *things*; rational beings, on the contrary, are called *persons*, because their very nature points them out as ends in themselves, that is as something which must not be used merely as means, and so far therefore restricts freedom of action (and is an object of respect). These, therefore, are not merely subjective ends whose existence has a worth *for us* as an effort of our action, but *objective ends*, that is things whose existence is an end in itself: an end moreover for which no other can be substituted, which they should subserve *merely* as means, for otherwise nothing whatever would possess *absolute worth*; but if all worth were conditioned and therefore contingent, then there would be no supreme practical principle of reason whatever.

If then there is a supreme practical principle or, in respect of the human will, a categorical imperative, it must be one which, being drawn from the conception of that which is necessarily an end for everyone because it is an *an end in itself*, constitutes an *objective* principle of will, and can therefore serve as a universal practical law. The foundation of this principle is: *rational nature exists as an end in itself.* Man necessarily conceives his own existence as being so: So far then this is a *subjective* principle of human actions. But every other rational being regards its existence similarly, just on the same rational principle, that holds for me: so that it is at the same time an objective principle, from which as a supreme practical law all laws of the will must be capable of being deduced. Accordingly the practical imperative will be as follows: *So act as to treat humanity, whether in thine own person or in that of any other, in every case as an end withal, never as means only.* . . .

The conception of every rational being as one which must consider itself as giving all the maxims of its will universal laws, so as to judge itself and its actions from this point of view—this conception leads to another which depends on it and is very fruitful, namely, that of a *kingdom of ends*.

By a *kingdom* I understand the union of different rational beings in a system by common laws. Now since it is by laws that ends are determined as regards their universal validity, hence, if we abstract from the personal differences of rational beings, and likewise from all the content of their private ends, we shall be able to conceive all ends combined in a systematic whole (including both rational beings as ends in themselves, and also the special ends which each may propose of himself), that is to say, we can conceive a kingdom of ends, which on the preceding principles is possible.

For all rational beings come under the *law* that each of them must treat itself and all others *never merely as means*, but in every case *at the same time as ends in themselves*. Hence results a systematic union of rational beings by common objective laws, i.e. a kingdom which may be called a kingdom of ends. . . .

DISCUSSION QUESTIONS

1. What does it mean to treat people as "ends-in-themselves"? What does it mean to treat others "merely as a means"? Explain the difference.
2. Why does Kant believe that the good will is the only thing that is good without qualification? Do you agree with him? Would John Stuart Mill or Jeremy Bentham agree with him? Can you think of anything else that might be good without qualification? How might Kant respond to your choice?
3. Kant believes that animals have no moral rights because they are not ends-in-themselves. Why aren't animals ends-in-themselves? Do you agree with Kant's position? Discuss.
4. The Golden Rule says that you should do unto others as you would have them do unto you. What do you think is the difference between the Golden Rule and the categorical imperative? Explain.
5. What is the major benefit of Kant's moral theory? What is its major weakness? In what sense would you call your own moral beliefs Kantian? Where do your views differ from Kant's?

A Critique of Kantianism

The philosopher Richard Taylor finds Kant's moral theory to be too abstract and too intellectual. Kant's moral philosophy, according to Taylor, at some point ceases to have much, if anything, to do with the morality that matters the most to us and becomes a "purely intellectual thing." For example, we ordinarily think of a person of good will to be a person that is kind and sympathetic. Kant's person of good will, as we have seen, is far from this type of person. A good will is a human will governed by reason, not sympathy and kindness. Consequently, for Kant, only acts done out of respect for the moral law have moral worth; acts done only out of kindness and sympathy have no moral worth. Taylor finds this approach to ethics "essentially wrong" and recommends a less abstract moral system, one that is more compatible with human nature.

Richard Taylor is the author of many books including *Good and Evil* (1973), *With Heart and Mind* (1973), and *Ethics, Faith and Reason* (1985).

It is not my intention to give any detailed exposition of Kant's ethical system. I propose instead to discuss certain of Kant's basic ideas in order to illustrate a certain approach to ethics that I think is essentially wrong. For this I could have chosen the ideas of some other modern moralist, but I prefer to illustrate my points by Kant's thought. I am doing this first because of his great fame and the reverence with which many philosophers still regard him, and secondly because it would be difficult to find any modern thinker who has carried to such an extreme the philosophical presuppositions that I am eager to repudiate. I shall, thus, use some of Kant's ideas to show how the basic ideas of morality, born originally of men's practical needs as social beings and having to do originally with men's practical relations with each other, can, under the influence of philosophy, become so detached from the world that they become pure abstractions, having no longer anything to do with morality insofar as this is a practical concern of men. Philosophical or metaphysical morals thereby ceases to have much connection with the morality that is the abiding practical concern of men and becomes, instead, a purely intellectual thing, something to contemplate and appreciate, much as one would appreciate a geometrical demonstration. Its vocabulary, which is the very vocabulary of everyday morals, no longer has the same meaning, but instead represents a realm of pure abstractions. Intellectually satisfying as this might be, it is nevertheless highly dangerous, for it leads men to suppose that the problems of ethics are essentially intellectual problems, that they are simply philosophical questions in need of philosophical answers. The result is that the eyes of the moralist are directed away from the world, in which moral problems are the most important problems there are, and toward a really nonexistent realm, a realm of ideas rather than things. The image of the philosophical and metaphysical moralist, who is quite lacking in any knowledge of the world and whose ideas about it are of the childish sort learned in a Sunday school, is a familiar one. He is a moralist whose dialectic is penetrating and whose reasoning is clear—he grapples with many philosophical problems of morality and has many subtle answers to philosophical difficulties—but who has little appreciation of the pain and sorrow of the world beyond the knowledge that it is there.

Richard Taylor, *Good and Evil,* Prometheus Books, 1999, 148–156. Reprinted with permission from the publisher.

DUTY AND LAW

Laws, as practical rules of human invention, find no place in Kant's metaphysical morals. The Moral Law that replaces them is sundered from any practical human concerns, for it seemed to Kant that men's practical ends and their moral obligations were not only quite different things but, more often than not, were actually opposed to each other. Obligations, which were originally only relations between men arising from mutual undertakings for mutual advantage, similarly disappear from the Kantian morality, to be replaced by an abstract sort of *moral* obligation that has no connection whatsoever with any earthly good. Duties—which were originally and are still imposed by rulers on subjects, masters on servants, employers on workmen, and so on, in return for certain compensations, privileges, and rights—are replaced by Kant with Duty in the abstract. This abstract Duty is deemed by him to be the sole proper motive of moral conduct; yet, it is not a duty *to* anyone, or a duty to do any particular thing. Men have always understood the notion of one's duty to sovereign or master, and Christians well understood the idea of duty toward God. In such cases, one's duty consisted simply of compliance with commands. But in Kant's system, duties are sundered from particular commands, and Duty becomes something singular and metaphysical. We are, according to this system, to do always what Duty requires, for no other reason than that Duty does require it. Beyond a few heterogeneous examples for illustration, we never learn from Kant just what this is, save only that it is the obligation to act from respect for the Moral Law. A man must cling to life, for example, and give no thought to suicide—not because any lawgiver or God has commanded it, not because things might work out all right for him if he sticks it out a little longer, but just because Duty requires it. A man must also help others in distress; not, again, because any man or God has admonished him to, not just because they need him, or because he cares for them, or because he wants to see their baneful condition improved—indeed, it is best that he have no such feelings at all—but just because it is his Duty.

THE GOOD WILL

It is in such terms that Kant defined the *good will*, declaring it to be the only thing in the universe that is unqualifiedly good. Now we normally think of a man of good will as one who loves his fellow men, as one

whose happiness is sympathetically bound up with that of others, and as one who has a keen and constant desire to abolish the suffering around him and make the lot of his neighbor more tolerable than it might be without his helping hand. Not so for Kant. Indeed, he dismisses the actions of such persons, "so sympathetically constituted that . . . they find an inner satisfaction in spreading joy, and rejoice in the contentment of others which they have made possible," as devoid of any moral worth. Human conduct, to have any genuine moral worth, must not spring from any such amiable feelings as these; these are, after all, nothing but human feelings; they are not *moral* incentives. To have genuine moral worth, according to this moralist, our actions must spring from the sense of Duty and nothing else. And one acts dutifully if he acts, not from love or concern for his fellows, but from respect for the Moral Law.

THE CATEGORICAL IMPERATIVE

The Moral Law assumed, in Kant's thought, the form of an imperative, or command. But unlike any command that was ever before heard by any man, this one issues from no commander! Like a question that no one ever asks, or an assertion that no one ever affirms, it is a command that no God or man ever promulgates. It is promulgated by Reason. Nor is this the humble rationality of living, mortal men; it is Reason itself, again in the abstract. And unlike what one would ordinarily think of as a command, this one has no definite content. It is simply the form, Kant says, not of any actual laws, but of The Law, which is again, of course, something abstract. It has, unlike any other imperative of which one has ever heard, no purpose or end. It is not the means to the achievement of anything; and it has no relation to what anyone wants. For this reason Kant called it the Categorical Imperative, a command that is supposed to command absolutely and for its own sake. The Categorical Imperative does not bid us to act in a manner calculated to advance human well-being, for the weal and woe of men has for Kant no necessary connection with morality. It does not bid us to act as we would want others to act, for what any men want has no more bearing on morals than what they happen to feel. This Imperative does not, in fact, bid us to do anything at all, nor, indeed, even to have any generous or sympathetic motive, but only to honor some maxim or rational principle of conduct. We are, whatever we do, to act in such a manner that we could, consistently with reason, will this maxim to be a universal Law, even a Law of Nature, binding on all rational beings. Kant does not ask us to consider how other rational beings, thus bound, might feel about our maxims, for again, how anyone happens to feel about anything has no bearing on morality anyway. It is Reason that counts. It is not the living and suffering human beings who manage sometimes to be reasonable but most of the time are not. It is not men's needs and wants, or any human desires, or any practical human goods. To act immorally is to act contrary to Reason; it is to commit a sort of metaphysical blunder in the relationship between one's behavior and his generalized motive. Human needs and feelings have so little to do with this that they are not even allowed into the picture. If a man reaches forth to help the sick, the troubled, or the dying, this must not be done from any motive of compassion or sentiment of love. Such love, as a feeling, is dismissed by Kant as "pathological," because it is not prompted by that rational respect for Duty that filled Kant with such awe. Indeed, Kant thought that such human feelings as love and compassion should not even be allowed to cooperate in the performance of Duty, for we must act solely *from* Duty, and not merely *in accordance* with it. Such feelings as love, sympathy, and friendship are therefore regarded by Kant as positively dangerous. They incline men to do from sheer goodness of heart what should be done only from Reason and respect for the Moral Law. To be genuinely moral, a man must tear himself away from his inclinations as a loving human being, drown the sympathetic promptings of his heart, scorn any fruits of his efforts, think last of all of the feelings, needs, desires, and inclinations either of himself or of his fellows and, perhaps detesting what he has to do, do it anyway—solely from respect for the Law.

RATIONAL NATURE AS AN END

This Moral Law is otherwise represented by Kant as respect for Rational Nature, something that again, of course, exists only in the abstract but is, presumably, somehow exemplified in men and, Kant thought, in God. Indeed, it is the only thing in men that Kant considered worthy of a philosopher's attention. Because men are deemed to embody this Rational Nature, human nature is declared to be an End in Itself, to possess an absolute Worth, or Dignity. This kind of absolute End is not like ordinary ends or goals, something relative to the aims or purposes of any creature. It is not anything anyone wants or would be moved to try to achieve. It is, like so many of Kant's abstractions, an absolute end. And the Worth that he supposes Rational Nature to possess is no worth *for* or *to* anything; it, too, is an abstract or absolute Worth. Kant peoples a veritable utopia, which he of course does not imagine as existing, with these Ends in Themselves, and calls it the Kingdom of Ends. Ends in Themselves are, thus, not to be thought of as those men that live and toil on earth; they are not suffering, rejoicing, fumbling, living, and dying human beings; they are not men that anyone has ever seen, or would be apt to recognize as men if he did see them, or apt to like very much if he did recognize them. They are abstract things, reifications of Rational Nature, fabricated by Kant and now called Rational Beings or Ends in Themselves. Their purpose, unlike that of any creature under the sun, is not to sorrow and rejoice, not to love and hate, not to beget offspring, not to grow old and die, and not to get on as best they can to such destinies as the world has allotted them. Their purpose is just to *legislate*—to legislate morally and rationally for this rational Kingdom of Ends.

THE SIGNIFICANCE OF KANT

Kant's system thus represents the rational, logical conclusion of the natural or true morality that was begotten by the Greeks, of the absolute distinction that they drew, and that men still want to draw. This is the distinction between what *is*, or the realm of observation and science, and what *ought* to be, or the realm of obligation and morals. No one has ever suggested that Kant was irrational, and although it is doubtful that his ideas have ever had much impact on human behavior, they have had a profound impact on philosophy, which has always prized reason and abstraction and tended to scorn fact. Kant's metaphysical system of morals rests on notions that are still a part of the fabric of our intellectual culture and inheritance. His greatest merit is that he was consistent. He showed men what sort of metaphysic of morals they must have—if they suppose that morality has any metaphysic, or any logic and method of its own. He showed what morality must be if we suppose it to be something rational and at the same time nonempirical or divorced from psychology, anthropology, or any science of man. That general conception of morals is, of course, still common in philosophy, and still permeates judicial thought, where it expresses itself in the ideas of guilt and desert. A man is thought to be "deserving" of punishment if he did, and could have avoided doing, something "wrong." Our basic moral pre-suppositions, in short, are still very much the same as Kant's, and Kant shows where they lead. We still assume, as he did, a basic dichotomy between what in fact *is* and what morally *ought* to be, between what the Greeks called convention and nature. Like the Greeks, and like Kant, we still feel a desperate need to *know* what, by nature or by some natural or rational moral principle, *ought* to be. Kant was entirely right in insisting that no knowledge of what in fact is—no knowledge of human nature, of history, of anthropology, or psychology—can yield this knowledge. But Kant did not consider, and many philosophical minds still think it somehow perverse to consider, that there may be no such knowledge—and not merely because no man has managed to attain it, but because there may really be nothing there to know in the first place. There may be no such thing as a true morality. Perhaps the basic facts of morality are, as Protagoras thought, conventions; that is, the practical formulas, some workable and some not, for enabling men to achieve whatever ideals and aspirations happen to move them. In the Kantian scheme, such considerations have nothing to do with morality which is concerned, not with what is, but with what morally ought to be, with what is in his strange sense commanded. According to the Protagorean scheme, on the other hand, such considerations exhaust the whole subject of morals. Here we are, human beings, possessed of needs, feelings, capacities, and aims that are for the most part not of our creation but are simply part of our endowment as human beings. These are the grist, the data, and the subject matter of morals. The problem is how we get from where we are to where we want to go. It is on our answer to this question that our whole happiness and our worth as human beings depends. Our problem is not whether our answers accord with nature or even with truth. Our problem is to find those answers that do in fact work, whose fruits are sunlight, warmth, and satisfaction in our lives as we live them.

DISCUSSION QUESTIONS

1. Should sympathy and kindness play a role in morality? If so, what role? Do you think that Immanuel Kant does not pay enough attention to sympathy and kindness in his moral theory? Why?
2. By most accounts, Kant's moral philosophy is highly abstract and very complex. Taylor finds this to be a fault, whereas many philosophers find it to be a virtue. What do you think? Is this a valid criticism of Kant? Discuss.
3. Taylor criticizes Kant's moral theory because it is not compatible with human nature. What do you think he would say about Jeremy Bentham's moral theory, which is based on human nature? In general, should moral theory be more in line with what human nature *is,* or with how humans *should be?* Why? Explain.
4. Taylor notes that for Kant to "act immorally is to act contrary to reason." Does Taylor believe that one may act immorally without acting contrary to reason? If so, when? Does he believe that one may act morally but contrary to reason? If so, when? What role should reason play in morality?

 ARISTOTLE

Virtue Ethics

Aristotle claims that the virtues are those characteristics that enable humans to live well in communities. Anyone who manages their skills and their opportunities well is considered virtuous. According to Aristotle, we all seek happiness, and being virtuous makes us happy—it enables us to achieve a state of well-being (*eudaimonia*). In addition, individual *eudaimonia* requires proper social institutions, as well as a good character. Consequently, ethics, for Aristotle, is taken to be a branch of politics. However, unlike Bentham, Aristotle does not believe that happiness is pleasure, nor is it honor or wealth. Rather, happiness is an activity of the soul in accordance with virtue. Right habits are acquired by living well, and these habits are in fact the virtues. These virtues are the best path to the happy life.

Aristotle distinguishes between two types of virtues: moral and intellectual. The *intellectual* virtues may be taught, whereas the *moral* virtues must be lived in order to be learned. Moral virtue comes from habit and is generally a state of character that is a mean between the vices of excess and deficiency. This concept of moderation or the Golden Mean is at the heart of Aristotle's virtue theory. Courage, for example, is presented as a virtue that is a mean between the extremes of rashness (an excess) and cowardice (a deficiency). While the moral virtues play an important role in the achievement of a state of well-being, it is the intellectual virtues found in the activity of contemplation or reason that produce the most perfect happiness. Nevertheless, while the contemplative life is the ultimate happy life, Aristotle says that it does not hurt to have friends, money, and good looks.

Aristotle (384–322 B.C.) is one of the most influential philosophers from Greek antiquity. He was the tutor of the young Alexander the Great, and his work has widely influenced Western thought. It is often said that Aristotle "knew everything," and the wide range of his writings seems to confirm this. His works investigate many topics, including logic, astronomy, biology, politics, ethics, rhetoric, drama, the soul, God, and physics.

Our discussion will be adequate if it has as much clearness as the subject-matter admits of, for precision is not to be sought for alike in all discussions, any more than in all the products of the crafts. Now fine and just actions, which political science investigates, admit of much variety and fluctuation of opinion, so that they may be thought to exist only by convention, and not by nature. And goods also give rise to a similar fluctuation because they bring harm to many people; for before now men have been undone by reason of their wealth, and others by reason of their courage. We must be content, then, in speaking of such subjects and with such premises to indicate the truth roughly and in outline, and in speaking about things which are only for the most part true and with premises of the same kind to reach conclusions that are no better. In the same spirit, therefore, should each type of statement be received; for it is the mark of an educated man to look for precision in each class of things just so far as the nature of the subject admits; it is evidently equally foolish to accept probable reasoning from a mathematician and to demand from a rhetorician scientific proofs.

Now each man judges well the things he knows, and of these he is a good judge. And so the man who has been educated in a subject is a good judge of that subject, and the man who has received an all-round education is a good judge in general. Hence a young man is not a proper hearer of lectures on political science; for he is inexperienced in the actions that occur in life, but its discussions start from these and are about these; and, further, since he tends to follow his passions, his study will be vain and unprofitable, because the end aimed at is not knowledge but action. And it makes no difference whether he is young in years or youthful in character; the defect does not depend on time, but on his living, and pursuing each successive object, as passion directs. For to such persons, as to the incontinent, knowledge brings no profit; but to those who desire and act in accordance with a rational principle knowledge about such matters will be of great benefit.

These remarks about the student, the sort of treatment to be expected, and the purpose of the inquiry, may be taken as our preface.

Let us resume our inquiry and state, in view of the fact that all knowledge and every pursuit aims at some good, what it is that we say political science aims at and what is the highest of all goods achievable by action. Verbally there is very general agreement; for

Aristotle, Happiness and Virtue, Books I: 3–5, 7–9, 13; II: 1, 6, 7, 9; X: 7, 8 from *Nichomachean Ethics*. Translated by W. D. Ross. *The Oxford Translation of Aristotle*, Vol. 9, Oxford University Press, 1925.

both the general run of men and people of superior refinement say that it is happiness, and identify living well and doing well with being happy; but with regard to what happiness is they differ, and the many do not give the same account as the wise. For the former think it is some plain and obvious thing, like pleasure, wealth, or honour; they differ, however, from one another—and often even the same man identifies it with different things, with health when he is ill, with wealth when he is poor; but, conscious of their ignorance, they admire those who proclaim some great ideal that is above their comprehension. Now some thought that apart from these many goods there is another which is self-subsistent and causes the goodness of all these as well. To examine all the opinions that have been held were perhaps somewhat fruitless; enough to examine those that are most prevalent or that seem to be arguable. . . .

Let us, however, resume our discussion from the point at which we digressed. To judge from the lives that men lead, most men, and men of the most vulgar type, seem (not without some ground) to identify the good, or happiness, with pleasure; which is the reason why they love the life of enjoyment. For there are, we may say, three prominent types of life—that just mentioned, the political, and thirdly the contemplative life. Now the mass of mankind are evidently quite slavish in their tastes, preferring a life suitable to beasts, but they get some ground for their view from the fact that many of those in high places share the tastes of Sardanapallus. A consideration of the prominent types of life shows that people of superior refinement and of active disposition identify happiness with honour; for this is, roughly speaking, the end of the political life. But it seems too superficial to be what we are looking for, since it is thought to depend on those who bestow honour rather than on him who receives it, but the good we divine to be something proper to a man and not easily taken from him. Further, men seem to pursue honour in order that they may be assured of their goodness; at least it is by men of practical wisdom that they seek to be honoured, and among those who know them, and on the ground of their virtue; clearly, then, according to them, at any rate, virtue is better. And perhaps one might even suppose this to be, rather than honour, the end of the political life. But even this appears somewhat incomplete; for possession of virtue seems actually compatible with being asleep, or with life-long inactivity, and, further, with the greatest sufferings and misfortunes; but a man who was living so no one would call happy, unless he were maintaining a

thesis at all costs. But enough of this; for the subject has been sufficiently treated even in the current discussions. Third comes the contemplative life, which we shall consider later.

The life of money-making is one undertaken under compulsion, and wealth is evidently not the good we are seeking; for it is merely useful and for the sake of something else. And so one might rather take the afore-named objects to be ends; for they are loved for themselves. But it is evident that not even these are ends; yet many arguments have been thrown away in support of them. . . .

Let us again return to the good we are seeking, and ask what it can be. It seems different in different actions and arts; it is different in medicine, in strategy, and in the other arts likewise. What then is the good of each? Surely that for whose sake everything else is done. In medicine this is health, in strategy victory, in architecture a house, in any other sphere something else, and in every action and pursuit the end; for it is for the sake of this that all men do whatever else they do. Therefore, if there is an end for all that we do, this will be the good achievable by action, and if there are more than one, these will be the goods achievable by action.

So the argument has by a different course reached the same point; but we must try to state this even more clearly. Since there are evidently more than one end, and we choose some of these (e.g. wealth, flutes, and in general instruments) for the sake of something else, clearly not all ends are final ends; but the chief good is evidently something final. Therefore, if there is only one final end, this will be what we are seeking, and if there are more than one, the most final of these will be what we are seeking. Now we call that which is in itself worthy of pursuit more final than that which is worthy of pursuit for the sake of something else, and that which is never desirable for the sake of something else more final than the things that are desirable both in themselves and for the sake of that other thing, and therefore we call final without qualification that which is always desirable in itself and never for the sake of something else.

Now such a thing happiness, above all else, is held to be; for this we choose always for itself and never for the sake of something else, but honour, pleasure, reason, and every virtue we choose indeed for themselves (for if nothing resulted from them we should still choose each of them), but we choose them also for the sake of happiness, judging that by means of them we shall be happy. Happiness, on the other hand, no one chooses for the sake of these, nor, in general, for anything other than itself. . . .

Presumably, however, to say that happiness is the chief good seems a platitude, and a clearer account of what it is, is still desired. This might perhaps be given, if we could first ascertain the function of man. For just as for a flute-player, a sculptor, or any artist, and, in general, for all things that have a function or activity, the good and the "well" is thought to reside in the function, so would it seem to be for man, if he has a function. Have the carpenter, then, and the tanner certain functions or activities, and has man none? Is he born without a function? Or as eye, hand, foot, and in general each of the parts evidently has a function, may one lay it down that man similarly has a function apart from all these? What then can this be? Life seems to be common even to plants, but we are seeking what is peculiar to man. Let us exclude, therefore, the life of nutrition and growth. Next there would be a life of perception, but *it* also seems to be common even to the horse, the ox, and every animal. There remains, then, an active life of the element that has a rational principle; of this, one part has such a principle in the sense of being obedient to one, the other in the sense of possessing one and exercising thought. And, as "life of the rational element" also has two meanings, we must state that life in the sense of activity is what we mean; for this seems to be the more proper sense of the term. Now if the function of man is an activity of soul which follows or implies a rational principle, and if we say "a so-and-so" and "a good so-and-so" have a function which is the same in kind, e.g. a lyre-player and a good lyre-player, and so without qualification in all cases, eminence in respect of goodness being added to the name of the function (for the function of a lyre-player is to play the lyre, and that of a good lyre-player is to do so well): if this is the case, [and we state the function of man to be a certain kind of life, and this to be an activity or actions of the soul implying a rational principle, and the function of a good man to be the good and noble performance of these, and if any action is well performed when it is performed in accordance with the appropriate excellence: if this is the case,] human good turns out to be activity of soul in accordance with virtue, and if there are more than one virtue, in accordance with the best and most complete.

But we must add "in a complete life." For one swallow does not make a summer, nor does one day; and so too one day, or a short time, does not make a man blessed and happy. . . .

We must consider it, however, in the light not only of our conclusion and our premises, but also of what is commonly said about it; for with a true view all the data harmonize, but with a false one the facts soon clash. Now goods have been divided into three classes, and some are described as external, others as relating to soul or to body; we call those that relate to soul most properly and truly goods, and psychical actions and activities we class as relating to soul. Therefore our account must be sound, at least according to this view, which is an old one and agreed on by philosophers. It is correct also in that we identify the end with certain actions and activities; for thus it falls among goods of the soul and not among external goods. Another belief which harmonizes with our account is that the happy man lives well and does well; for we have practically defined happiness as a sort of good life and good action. The characteristics that are looked for in happiness seem also, all of them, to belong to what we have defined happiness as being. For some identify happiness with virtue, some with practical wisdom, others with a kind of philosophic wisdom, others with these, or one of these, accompanied by pleasure or not without pleasure; while others include also external prosperity. Now some of these views have been held by many men and men of old, others by a few eminent persons; and it is not probable that either of these should be entirely mistaken, but rather that they should be right in at least some one respect or even in most respects.

With those who identify happiness with virtue or some one virtue our account is in harmony; for to virtue belongs virtuous activity. But it makes, perhaps, no small difference whether we place the chief good in possession or in use, in state of mind or in activity. For the state of mind may exist without producing any good result, as in a man who is asleep or in some other way quite inactive, but the activity cannot; for one who has the activity will of necessity be acting, and acting well. And as in the Olympic Games it is not the most beautiful and the strongest that are crowned but those who compete (for it is some of these that are victorious), so those who act win, and rightly win, the noble and good things in life.

Their life is also in itself pleasant. For pleasure is a state of *soul*, and to each man that which he is said to be a lover of is pleasant; e.g. not only is a horse pleasant to the lover of horses, and a spectacle to the lover of sights, but also in the same way just acts are pleasant to the lover of justice and in general virtuous acts to the lover of virtue. Now for most men their pleasures are in conflict with one another because these are not by nature pleasant, but the lovers of what is noble find pleasant the things that are by nature pleasant; and virtuous actions are such, so that these are pleasant for such men as well as in their own nature. Their life, therefore, has no further need of pleasure as a sort of adventitious charm, but has its pleasure in itself. For, besides what we have said, the man who does not rejoice in noble actions is not even good; since no one would call a man just who did not enjoy acting justly, nor any man liberal who did not enjoy liberal actions; and similarly in all other cases. If this is so, virtuous actions must be in themselves pleasant. But they are also *good* and *noble*, and have each of these attributes in the highest degree, since the good man judges well about these attributes; his judgment is such as we have described. Happiness then is the best, noblest, and most pleasant thing in the world. . . .

Yet evidently, as we said, it needs the external goods as well; for it is impossible, or not easy, to do noble acts without the proper equipment. In many actions we use friends and riches and political power as instruments; and there are some things the lack of which takes the lustre from happiness, as good birth, goodly children, beauty; for the man who is very ugly in appearance or ill-born or solitary and childless is not very likely to be happy, and perhaps a man would be still less likely if he had thoroughly bad children or friends or had lost good children or friends by death. As we said, then, happiness seems to need this sort of prosperity in addition; for which reason some identify happiness with good fortune, though others identify it with virtue.

For this reason also the question is asked, whether happiness is to be acquired by learning or by habituation or some other sort of training, or comes in virtue of some divine providence or again by chance. Now if there is *any* gift of the gods to men, it is reasonable that happiness should be god-given, and most surely god-given of all human things inasmuch as it is the best. But this question would perhaps be more appropriate to another inquiry; happiness seems, however, even if it is not god-sent but comes as a result of virtue and some process of learning or training, to be among the most god-like things; for that which is the prize and end of virtue seems to be the best thing in the world, and something godlike and blessed.

It will also on this view be very generally shared; for all who are not maimed as regards their potentiality for virtue may win it by a certain kind of study and care. But if it is better to be happy thus than by chance, it is reasonable that the facts should be so, since everything that depends on the action of nature is by nature as good as it can be, and similarly everything that depends on art or any rational

cause, and especially if it depends on the best of all causes. To entrust to chance what is greatest and most noble would be a very defective arrangement.

The answer to the question we are asking is plain also from the definition of happiness; for it has been said to be a virtuous activity of soul, of a certain kind. Of the remaining goods, some must necessarily pre-exist as conditions of happiness, and others are naturally co-operative and useful as instruments. And this will be found to agree with what we said at the outset; for we stated the end of political science to be the best end, and political science spends most of its pains on making the citizens to be of a certain character, viz. good and capable of noble acts.

It is natural, then, that we call neither ox nor horse nor any other of the animals happy; for none of them is capable of sharing in such activity. For this reason also a boy is not happy; for he is not yet capable of such acts, owing to his age; and boys who are called happy are being congratulated by reason of the hopes we have for them. For there is required, as we said, not only complete virtue but also a complete life, since many changes occur in life, and all manner of chances, and the most prosperous may fall into great misfortunes in old age, as is told of Priam in the Trojan Cycle; and one who has experienced such chances and has ended wretchedly no one calls happy. . . .

Since happiness is an activity of soul in accordance with perfect virtue, we must consider the nature of virtue; for perhaps we shall thus see better the nature of happiness. . . .

Virtue, then, being of two kinds, intellectual and moral, intellectual virtue in the main owes both its birth and its growth to teaching (for which reason it requires experience and time), while moral virtue comes about as a result of habit. . . . From this it is also plain that none of the moral virtues arises in us by nature; for nothing that exists by nature can form a habit contrary to its nature. For instance the stone which by nature moves downwards cannot be habituated to move upwards, not even if one tries to train it by throwing it up ten thousand times; nor can fire be habituated to move downwards, nor can anything else that by nature behaves in one way be trained to behave in another. Neither by nature, then, nor contrary to nature do the virtues arise in us; rather we are adapted by nature to receive them, and are made perfect by habit. . . .

We must, however, not only describe virtue as a state of character, but also say what sort of state it is. We may remark, then, that every virtue or excellence both brings into good condition the thing of which it is the excellence and makes the work of that thing be done well; e.g. the excellence of the eye makes both the eye and its work good; for it is by the excellence of the eye that we see well. Similarly the excellence of the horse makes a horse both good in itself and good at running and at carrying its rider and at awaiting the attack of the enemy. Therefore, if this is true in every case, the virtue of man also will be the state of character which makes a man good and which makes him do his own work well.

How this is to happen we have stated already, but it will be made plain also by the following consideration of the specific nature of virtue. In everything that is continuous and divisible it is possible to take more, less, or an equal amount, and that either in terms of the thing itself or relatively to us; and the equal is an intermediate between excess and defect. By the intermediate in the object I mean that which is equidistant from each of the extremes, which is one and the same for all men; by the intermediate relatively to us that which is neither too much nor too little—and this is not one, nor the same for all. For instance, if ten is many and two is few, six is the intermediate, taken in terms of the object; for it exceeds and is exceeded by an equal amount; this is intermediate according to arithmetical proportion. But the intermediate relatively to us is not to be taken so; if ten pounds are too much for a particular person to eat and two too little, it does not follow that the trainer will order six pounds; for this also is perhaps too much for the person who is to take it, or too little—too little for Milo, too much for the beginner in athletic exercises. The same is true of running and wrestling. Thus a master of any art avoids excess and defect, but seeks the intermediate and chooses this—the intermediate not in the object but relatively to us.

If it is thus, then, that every art does its work well—by looking to the intermediate and judging its works by this standard (so that we often say of good works of art that it is not possible either to take away or to add anything, implying that excess and defect destroy the goodness of the works of art, while the mean preserves it; and good artists, as we say, look to this in their work), and if, further, virtue is more exact and better than any art, as nature also is, then virtue must have the quality of aiming at the intermediate. I mean moral virtue; for it is this that is concerned with passions and actions, and in these there is excess, defect, and the intermediate. For instance, both fear and confidence and appetite and anger and pity and in general pleasure and pain may be felt both too much and too little, and in both cases not well; but to feel them at the right times, with reference to the right objects, towards the right people, with the right motive, and in the right way, is what is both intermediate and best, and this is characteristic of virtue. Similarly with regard to actions also there is excess, defect, and the intermediate. Now virtue is concerned with passions and actions, in which excess is a form of failure, and so is defect, while the intermediate is praised and is a form of success; and being praised and being successful are both characteristics of virtue. Therefore virtue is a kind of mean, since, as we have seen, it aims at what is intermediate.

Again, it is possible to fail in many ways (for evil belongs to the class of the unlimited, as the Pythagoreans conjectured, and good to that of the limited), while to succeed is possible only in one way (for which reason also one is easy and the other difficult—to miss the mark easy, to hit it difficult); for these reasons also, then, excess and defect are characteristic of vice, and the mean of virtue;

For men are good in but one way, but bad
in many.

Virtue, then, is a state of character concerned with choice, lying in a mean, i.e. the mean relative to us, this being determined by a rational principle, and by that principle by which the man of practical wisdom would determine it. Now it is a mean between two vices, that which depends on excess and that which depends on defect; and again it is a mean because the vices respectively fall short of or exceed what is right in both passions and actions, while virtue both finds and chooses that which is intermediate. Hence in respect of its substance and the definition which states its essence virtue is a mean, with regard to what is best and right an extreme.

But not every action nor every passion admits of a mean; for some have names that already imply badness, e.g. spite, shamelessness, envy, and in the case of actions adultery, theft, murder; for all of these and suchlike things imply by their names that they are themselves bad, and not the excesses or deficiencies of them. It is not possible, then, ever to be right with regard to them; one must always be wrong. Nor does goodness or badness with regard to such things depend on committing adultery with the right woman, at the right time, and in the right way, but simply to do any of them is to go wrong. It would be equally absurd, then, to expect that in unjust, cowardly, and voluptuous action there should be a mean, an excess, and a deficiency; for at that rate there would be a mean of excess and of deficiency, an excess of excess, and a deficiency of deficiency. But as there is no excess and deficiency of temperance and courage because what is intermediate is in a sense an extreme, so too of the actions we have mentioned there is no mean nor any excess and deficiency, but however they are done they are wrong; for in general there is neither a mean of excess and deficiency, nor excess and deficiency of a mean.

We must, however, not only make this general statement, but also apply it to the individual facts. For among statements about conduct those which are general apply more widely, but those which are particular are more genuine, since conduct has to do with individual cases, and our statements must harmonize with the facts in these cases. We may take these cases from our table. With regard to feelings of fear and confidence courage is the mean; of the people who exceed, he who exceeds in fearlessness has no name (many of the states have no name), while the man who exceeds in confidence is rash, and he who exceeds in fear and falls short in confidence is a coward. With regard to pleasures and pains—not all of them, and not so much with regard to the pains—the mean is temperance, the excess self-indulgence. Persons deficient with regard to the pleasures are not often found; hence such persons also have received no name. But let us call them "insensible."

With regard to giving and taking of money the mean is liberality, the excess and the defect prodigality and meanness. In these actions people exceed and fall short in contrary ways; the prodigal exceeds in spending and falls short in taking, while the mean man exceeds in taking and falls short in spending. (At present we are giving a mere outline or summary, and are satisfied with this; later these states will be more exactly determined.) With regard to money there are also other dispositions—a mean, magnificence (for the magnificent man differs from the liberal man; the former deals with large sums, the latter with small ones), and excess, tastelessness, and vulgarity, and a deficiency, niggardliness; these differ from the states opposed to liberality. . . .

That moral virtue is a mean, then, and in what sense it is so, and that it is a mean between two vices, the one involving excess, the other deficiency, and that it is such because its character is to aim at what is intermediate in passions and in actions, has been sufficiently stated. Hence also it is no easy task to be good. For in everything it is no easy task to find the middle, e.g. to find the middle of a circle is not for everyone but for him who knows; so, too, anyone can get angry—that is easy—or give or spend money; but to do this to the right person, to the right extent, at the right time, with the right motive,

and in the right way, *that* is not for everyone, nor is it easy; wherefore goodness is both rare and laudable and noble. . . .

If happiness is activity in accordance with virtue, it is reasonable that it should be in accordance with the highest virtue; and this will be that of the best thing in us. Whether it be reason or something else that is this element which is thought to be our natural ruler and guide and to take thought of things noble and divine, whether it be itself also divine or only the most divine element in us, the activity of this in accordance with its proper virtue will be perfect happiness. That this activity is contemplative we have already said.

Now this would seem to be in agreement both with what we said before and with the truth. For, firstly, this activity is the best (since not only is reason the best thing in us, but the objects of reason are the best of knowable objects); and, secondly, it is the most continuous, since we can contemplate truth more continuously than we can do anything. And we think happiness has pleasure mingled with it, but the activity of philosophic wisdom is admittedly the pleasantest of virtuous activities; at all events the pursuit of it is thought to offer pleasures marvellous for their purity and their enduringness, and it is to be expected that those who know will pass their time more pleasantly than those who inquire. And the self-sufficiency that is spoken of must belong most to the contemplative activity. For while a philosopher, as well as a just man or one possessing any other virtue, needs the necessaries of life, when they are sufficiently equipped with things of that sort the just man needs people towards whom and with whom he shall act justly, and the temperate man, the brave man, and each of the others is in the same case, but the philosopher, even when by himself, can contemplate truth, and the better the wiser he is; he can perhaps do so better if he has fellow-workers, but still he is the most self-sufficient. And this activity alone would seem to be loved for its own sake; for nothing arises from it apart from the contemplating, while from practical activities we gain more or less apart from the action. And happiness is thought to depend on leisure; for we are busy that we may have leisure, and make war that we may live in peace. Now the activity of the practical virtues is exhibited in political or military affairs, but the actions concerned with these seem to be unleisurely. Warlike actions are completely so (for no one chooses to be at war, or provokes war, for the sake of being at war; any one would seem absolutely murderous if he were to make enemies of his friends in order to bring about battle and slaughter); but the action of the statesman is also unleisurely, and—apart from the political action itself—aims at despotic power and honours, or at all events happiness, for him and his fellow citizens—a happiness different from political action, and evidently sought as being different. So if among virtuous actions political and military actions are distinguished by nobility and greatness, and these are unleisurely and aim at an end and are not desirable for their own sake, but the activity of reason, which is contemplative, seems both to be superior in serious worth and to aim at no end beyond itself, and to have its pleasure proper to itself (and this augments the activity), and the self-sufficiency, leisureliness, unweariedness (so far as this is possible for man), and all the other attributes ascribed to the supremely happy man are evidently those connected with this activity, it follows that this will be the complete happiness of man, if it be allowed a complete term of life (for none of the attributes of happiness is *in*complete).

But such a life would be too high for man; for it is not in so far as he is man that he will live so, but in so far as something divine is present in him; and by so much as this is superior to our composite nature is its activity superior to that which is the exercise of the other kind of virtue. If reason is divine, then in comparison with man, the life according to it is divine in comparison with human life. But we must not follow those who advise us, being men, to think of human things, and, being mortal, of mortal things, but must, so far as we can, make ourselves immortal, and strain every nerve to live in accordance with the best thing in us; for even if it be small in bulk, much more does it in power and worth surpass everything. This would seem, too, to be each man himself, since it is the authoritative and better part of him. It would be strange, then, if he were to choose not the life of his self but that of something else. And what we said before will apply now; that which is proper to each thing is by nature best and most pleasant for each thing; for man, therefore, the life according to reason is best and pleasantest, since reason more than anything else *is* man. This life therefore is also the happiest.

But in a secondary degree the life in accordance with the other kind of virtue is happy; for the activities in accordance with this befit our human estate. Just and brave acts, and other virtuous acts, we do in relation to each other, observing our respective duties with regard to contracts and services and all manner of actions and with regard to passions; and all of these seem to be typically human. Some of them seem even to arise from the body, and virtue of char-

acter to be in many ways bound up with the passions. Practical wisdom, too, is linked to virtue of character, and this to practical wisdom, since the principles of practical wisdom are in accordance with the moral virtues and rightness in morals is in accordance with practical wisdom. Being connected with the passions also, the moral virtues must belong to our composite nature; and the virtues of our composite nature are human; so, therefore, are the life and the happiness which correspond to these. The excellence of the reason is a thing apart; we must be content to say this much about it, for to describe it precisely is a task greater than our purpose requires. It would seem, however, also to need external equipment but little, or less than moral virtue does. Grant that both need the necessaries; and do so equally, even if the statesman's work is the more concerned with the body and things of that sort; for there will be little difference there; but in what they need for the exercise of their activities there will be much difference. The liberal man will need money for the doing of his liberal deeds, and the just man too will need it for the returning of services (for wishes are hard to discern, and even people who are not just pretend to wish to act justly); and the brave man will need power if he is to accomplish any of the acts that correspond to his virtue, and the temperate man will need opportunity; for how else is either he or any of the others to be recognized? It is debated, too, whether the will or the deed is more essential to virtue, which is assumed to involve both; it is surely clear that its perfection involves both; but for deeds many things are needed, and more, the greater and nobler the deeds are. But the man who is contemplating the truth needs no such thing, at least with a view to the exercise of his activity; indeed they are, one may say, even hindrances, at all events to his contemplation; but in so far as he is a man and lives with a number of people, he chooses to do virtuous acts; he will therefore need such aids to living a human life.

But that perfect happiness is a contemplative activity will appear from the following consideration as well. We assume the gods to be above all other beings blessed and happy; but what sort of actions must we assign to them? Acts of justice? Will not the gods seem absurd if they make contracts and return deposits, and so on? Acts of a brave man, then, confronting dangers and running risks because it is noble to do so? Or liberal acts? To whom will they give? It will be strange if they are really to have money or anything of the kind. And what would their temperate acts be? Is not such praise tasteless, since they have no bad appetites? If we were to run through them all, the circumstances of action would be found trivial and unworthy of gods. Still, everyone supposes that they *live* and therefore that they are active; we cannot suppose them to sleep like Endymion. Now if you take away from a living being action, and still more production, what is left but contemplation? Therefore the activity of God, which surpasses all others in blessedness, must be contemplative; and of human activities, therefore, that which is most akin to this must be most of the nature of happiness.

This is indicated, too, by the fact that the other animals have no share in happiness, being completely deprived of such activity. For while the whole life of the gods is blessed, and that of men too in so far as some likeness of such activity belongs to them, none of the other animals is happy, since they in no way share in contemplation. Happiness extends, then, just so far as contemplation does, and those to whom contemplation more fully belongs are more truly happy, not as a mere concomitant but in virtue of the contemplation; for this is in itself precious. Happiness, therefore, must be some form of contemplation.

But, being a man, one will also need external prosperity; for our nature is not self-sufficient for the purpose of contemplation, but our body also must be healthy and must have food and other attention. Still, we must not think that the man who is to be happy will need many things or great things, merely because he cannot be supremely happy without external goods; for self-sufficiency and action do not involve excess, and we can do noble acts without ruling earth and sea; for even with moderate advantages one can act virtuously (this is manifest enough; for private persons are thought to do worthy acts no less than despots—indeed even more); and it is enough that we should have so much as that; for the life of the man who is active in accordance with virtue will be happy. . . .

DISCUSSION QUESTIONS

1. According to Aristotle, what is happiness? Do you agree with him? Explain.
2. What is the connection between virtue and happiness according to Aristotle? Would Jeremy Bentham or John Stuart Mill agree with this? Why or why not? What is the difference between their views?
3. Aristotle says that a life of pleasure is suitable for beasts. Why does he believe this? What is wrong with a life of pleasure?
4. Aristotle believes that the philosopher will be happier than anyone else. Do you agree with him? Why or why not?
5. Richard Taylor criticizes Immanuel Kant's moral theory because it is not compatible with human nature. Is Aristotle's view subject to the same criticism? Explain.
6. In what sense does equality play a role in Aristotle's virtue ethics? Is it possible for everyone to be happy? Or only some people? Is this a strength or weakness of Aristotle's position? Compare Mill's and Aristotle's accounts of morality on the basis of the role of equality in their moral theory. Which do you prefer, and why?
7. Compare Mill, Kant, and Aristotle on the importance of individual happiness in moral theory. Whose position do you prefer, and why?

 CAROL GILLIGAN

In a Different Voice

Carol Gilligan argues that women have a moral voice or perspective that is distinct from that of men. A woman's moral perspective, she says, is by nature more personal and contextual than a man's. Whereas men are motivated more by impartial and abstract principles about duty, women are motivated more by emotions and a sense of care and responsibility.

Consequently, the ideals of caring and responsibility play a more central role in the moral orientations of women, and the "rights" perspective plays a more central role in the moral orientation of men. Gilligan concludes that existing moral theories embody a male bias and fail to account for women's moral orientation. It should be noted that Gilligan's article leads us into more general issues concerning the relationship of sex and gender to morality—issues that we will examine in the readings in Chapter 7.

Carol Gilligan is Patricia Albjerg Graham Professor of Gender Studies at Harvard University. She is the author of *In a Different Voice: Psychological Theory and Women's Development* (1982) and a founding member of the collaborative Harvard Project on Women's Psychology and Girls' Development.

In the second act of *The Cherry Orchard*, Lopahin, a young merchant, describes his life of hard work and success. Failing to convince Madame Ranevskaya to cut down the cherry orchard to save her estate, he will go on in the next act to buy it himself. He is the self-made man who, in purchasing the estate where his father and grandfather were slaves, seeks to eradicate the "awkward, unhappy life" of the past, replacing the cherry orchard with summer cottages where coming generations "will see a new life." In elaborating this developmental vision, he reveals the image of man that underlies and supports his activity: "At times when I can't go to sleep, I think: Lord, thou gavest us immense forests, unbounded fields and the widest horizons, and living in the midst of them we should indeed be giants"—at which point, Madame Ranevskaya interrupts him, saying, "You feel the need for giants—They are good only in fairy tales, anywhere else they only frighten us."

Conceptions of the human life cycle represent attempts to order and make coherent the unfolding experiences and perceptions, the changing wishes and realities of everyday life. But the nature of such conceptions depends in part on the position of the observer. The brief excerpt from Chekhov's play suggests that when the observer is a woman, the perspective may be of a different sort. Different judgments of the image of man as giant imply different ideas about human development, different ways of imagining the human condition, different notions of what is of value in life.

At a time when efforts are being made to eradicate discrimination between the sexes in the search for social equality and justice, the differences between the sexes are being rediscovered in the social sciences. This discovery occurs when theories formerly considered to be sexually neutral in their scientific objectivity are found instead to reflect a consistent observational and evaluative bias. Then the presumed neutrality of science, like that of language itself, gives way to the recognition that the categories of knowledge are human constructions. The fascination with point of view that has informed the fiction of the twentieth century and the corresponding recognition of the relativity of judgment infuse our scientific understanding as well when we begin to notice how accustomed we have become to seeing life through men's eyes.

A recent discovery of this sort pertains to the apparently innocent classic *The Elements of Style* by William Strunk and E. B. White. The Supreme Court ruling on the subject of discrimination in classroom texts led one teacher of English to notice that the elementary rules of English usage were being taught through examples which counterposed the birth of Napoleon, the writings of Coleridge, and statements such as "He was an interesting talker. A man who had traveled all over the world and lived in half a dozen countries," with "Well, Susan, this is a fine mess you are in" or, less drastically, "He saw a woman, accompanied by two children, walking slowly down the road."

Psychological theorists have fallen as innocently as Strunk and White into the same observational bias. Implicitly adopting the male life as the norm, they have tried to fashion women out of a masculine cloth. It all goes back, of course, to Adam and Eve—a story which shows, among other things, that if you make woman out of a man, you are bound to get into trouble. In the life cycle, as in the Garden of Eden, the woman has been the deviant.

The penchant of developmental theorists to project a masculine image, and one that appears frightening to women, goes back at least to Freud, who built his theory of psychosexual development around the experiences of the male child that culminate in the Oedipus complex. In the 1920s, Freud struggled to resolve the contradictions posed for his theory by the differences in female anatomy and the different configuration of the young girl's early family relationships. After trying to fit women into his masculine conception, seeing them as envying that which they missed, he came instead to acknowledge, in the strength and persistence of women's pre-Oedipal attachments to their mothers, a developmental difference. He considered this difference in women's development to be responsible for what he saw as women's developmental failure.

Having tied the formation of the superego or conscience to castration anxiety, Freud considered women to be deprived by nature of the impetus for a clear-cut Oedipal resolution. Consequently, women's superego—the heir to the Oedipus complex—was compromised: it was never "so inexorable, so impersonal, so independent of its emotional origins as we require it to be in men." From this observation of difference, that "for women the level of what is ethically normal is different from what it is in men," Freud concluded that women "show less sense of justice than men, that they are less ready to submit to the great exigencies of life, that they are more often influenced in their judgements by feelings of affection or hostility."

Thus a problem in theory became cast as a problem in women's development, and the problem in women's development was located in their experience of relationships. Nancy Chodorow, attempting to account for "the reproduction within each generation of certain general and nearly universal differences that characterize masculine and feminine personality and roles," attributes these differences between the sexes not to anatomy but rather to "the fact that women, universally, are largely responsible for early child care." Because this early social environment differs for and is experienced differently by male and female children, basic sex differences recur in personality development. As a result, "in any given society, feminine personality comes to define itself in relation and connection to other people more than masculine personality does."

In her analysis, Chodorow relies primarily on Robert Stoller's studies, which indicate that gender identity, the unchanging core of personality formation, is "with rare exception firmly and irreversibly established for both sexes by the time a child is around three." Given that for both sexes the primary caretaker in the first three years of life is typically female, the interpersonal dynamics of gender identity formation are different for boys and girls. Female identity formation takes place in a context of ongoing relationship since "mothers tend to experience their daughters as more like, and continuous with, themselves." Correspondingly, girls, in identifying themselves as female, experience themselves as like their mothers, thus fusing the experience of attachment with the process of identity formation. In contrast, "mothers experience their sons as a male opposite," and boys, in defining themselves as masculine, separate their mothers from themselves, thus curtailing "their primary love and sense of empathic tie." Consequently, male development entails a "more emphatic individuation and a more defensive firming of experienced ego boundaries." For boys, but not girls, "issues of differentiation have become intertwined with sexual issues."

Writing against the masculine bias of psychoanalytic theory, Chodorow argues that the existence of sex differences in the early experiences of individuation and relationship "does not mean that women have 'weaker' ego boundaries than men or are more prone to psychosis." It means instead that "girls emerge from this period with a basis for 'empathy' built into their primary definition of self in a way that boys do not." Chodorow thus replaces Freud's negative and derivative description of female psychology with a positive and direct account of her own: "Girls emerge with a stronger basis for experiencing another's needs or feelings as one's own (or of thinking that one is so experiencing another's needs and feelings). Furthermore, girls do not define themselves in terms of the denial of preoedipal relational modes to the same extent as do boys. Therefore, regression to these modes tends not to feel as much a basic threat to their ego. From very early, then, because they are parented by a person of the same gender . . . girls come to experience themselves as less differentiated than boys, as more continuous with and related to the external object-world, and as differently oriented to their inner object-world as well."

Consequently, relationships, and particularly issues of dependency, are experienced differently by women and men. For boys and men, separation and individuation are critically tied to gender identity since separation from the mother is essential for the development of masculinity. For girls and women, issues of femininity or feminine identity do not depend on the achievement of separation from the mother or on the progress of individuation. Since masculinity is defined through separation while femininity is defined through attachment, male gender identity is threatened by intimacy while female gender identity is threatened by separation. Thus males tend to have difficulty with relationships, while females tend to have problems with individuation. The quality of embeddedness in social interaction and personal relationships that characterizes women's lives in contrast to men's, however, becomes not only a descriptive difference but also a developmental liability when the milestones of childhood and adolescent development in the psychological literature are markers of increasing separation. Women's failure to separate then becomes by definition a failure to develop.

The sex differences in personality formation that Chodorow describes in early childhood appear during the middle childhood years in studies of children's games. Children's games are considered by George Herbert Mead and Jean Piaget as the crucible of social development during the school years. In games, children learn to take the role of the other and come to see themselves through another's eyes. In games, they learn respect for rules and come to understand the ways rules can be made and changed.

Janet Lever, considering the peer group to be the agent of socialization during the elementary school years and play to be a major activity of socialization at that time, set out to discover whether there are sex differences in the games that children play. Studying 181 fifth-grade, white, middle-class children, ages ten and eleven, she observed the organization and structure of their playtime activities. She watched the children as they played at school during recess and in physical education class, and in addition kept diaries of their accounts as to how they spent their out-of-school time. From this study, Lever reports sex differences: boys play out of doors more often than girls do; boys play more often in large and age-heterogeneous groups; they play competitive games more often, and their games last longer than girls' games. The last is in some ways the most interesting finding. Boys' games appeared to last longer not only because they required a higher level of skill and were thus less likely to become boring, but also because, when disputes arose in the course of a game, boys were able to resolve the disputes more effectively than girls: "During the course of this study, boys were seen quarrelling all the time, but not once was a game termi-

nated because of a quarrel and no game was interrupted for more than seven minutes. In the gravest debates, the final word was always, to 'repeat the play,' generally followed by a chorus of 'cheater's proof.'" In fact, it seemed that the boys enjoyed the legal debates as much as they did the game itself, and even marginal players of lesser size or skill participated equally in these recurrent squabbles. In contrast, the eruption of disputes among girls tended to end the game.

Thus Lever extends and corroborates the observations of Piaget in his study of the rules of the game, where he finds boys becoming through childhood increasingly fascinated with the legal elaboration of rules and the development of fair procedures for adjudicating conflicts, a fascination that, he notes, does not hold for girls. Girls, Piaget observes, have a more "pragmatic" attitude toward rules, "regarding a rule as good as long as the game repaid it."

Girls are more tolerant in their attitudes toward rules, more willing to make exceptions, and more easily reconciled to innovations. As a result, the legal sense, which Piaget considers essential to moral development, "is far less developed in little girls than in boys."

The bias that leads Piaget to equate male development with child development also colors Lever's work. The assumption that shapes her discussion of results is that the male model is the better one since it fits the requirements for modern corporate success. In contrast, the sensitivity and care for the feelings of others that girls develop through their play have little market value and can even impede professional success. Lever implies that, given the realities of adult life, if a girl does not want to be left dependent on men, she will have to learn to play like a boy.

To Piaget's argument that children learn the respect for rules necessary for moral development by playing rule-bound games, Lawrence Kohlberg adds that these lessons are most effectively learned through the opportunities for role-taking that arise in the course of resolving disputes. Consequently, the moral lessons inherent in girls' play appear to be fewer than in boys'. Traditional girls' games like jump rope and hopscotch are turn-taking games, where competition is indirect since one person's success does not necessarily signify another's failure. Consequently, disputes requiring adjudication are less likely to occur. In fact, most of the girls whom Lever interviewed claimed that when a quarrel broke out, they ended the game. Rather than elaborating a system of rules for resolving disputes, girls subordinated the continuation of the game to the continuation of relationships.

Lever concludes that from the games they play, boys learn both the independence and the organizational skills necessary for coordinating the activities of large and diverse groups of people. By participating in controlled and socially approved competitive situations, they learn to deal with competition in a relatively forthright manner—to play with their enemies and to compete with their friends—all in accordance with the rules of the game. In contrast, girls' play tends to occur in smaller, more intimate groups, often the best-friend dyad, and in private places. This play replicates the social pattern of primary human relationships in that its organization is more cooperative. Thus, it points less, in Mead's terms, toward learning to take the role of "the generalized other," less toward the abstraction of human relationships. But it fosters the development of the empathy and sensitivity necessary for taking the role of "the particular other" and points more toward knowing the other as different from the self.

The sex differences in personality formation in early childhood that Chodorow derives from her analysis of the mother-child relationship are thus extended by Lever's observations of sex differences in the play activities of middle childhood. Together these accounts suggest that boys and girls arrive at puberty with a different interpersonal orientation and a different range of social experiences.

. . .

"It is obvious," Virginia Woolf says, "that the values of women differ very often from the values which have been made by the other sex." Yet, she adds, "it is the masculine values that prevail." As a result, women come to question the normality of their feelings and to alter their judgments in deference to the opinion of others. In the nineteenth-century novels written by women, Woolf sees at work "a mind which was slightly pulled from the straight and made to alter its clear vision in deference to external authority." The same deference to the values and opinions of others can be seen in the judgments of twentieth-century women. The difficulty women experience in finding or speaking publicly in their own voices emerges repeatedly in the form of qualification and self-doubt, but also in intimations of a divided judgment, a public assessment and private assessment which are fundamentally at odds.

Yet the deference and confusion that Woolf criticizes in women derive from the values she sees as their strength. Women's deference is rooted not only in their social subordination but also in the substance of their moral concern. Sensitivity to the needs of others and the assumption of responsibility for taking care lead women to attend to voices other than their own and to include in their judgment other points of view. Women's moral weakness, manifest in an apparent diffusion and confusion of judgment, is thus inseparable from women's moral strength, an overriding concern with relationships and responsibilities. The reluctance to judge may itself be indicative of the care and concern for others that infuse the psychology of women's development and are responsible for what is generally seen as problematic in its nature.

Thus women not only define themselves in a context of human relationship but also judge themselves in terms of their ability to care. Women's place in man's life cycle has been that of nurturer, caretaker, and helpmate, the weaver of those networks of relationships on which she in turn relies. But while women have thus taken care of men, men have, in their theories of psychological development, as in their economic arrangements, tended to assume or devalue that care. When the focus on individuation and individual achievement extends into adulthood and maturity is equated with personal autonomy, concern with relationships appears as a weakness of women rather than as a human strength.

The discrepancy between womanhood and adulthood is nowhere more evident than in the studies on sex-role stereotypes reported by Broverman, Vogel, Broverman, Clarkson, and Rosenkrantz. The repeated finding of these studies is that the qualities deemed necessary for adulthood—the capacity for autonomous thinking, clear decision-making, and responsible action—are those associated with masculinity and considered undesirable as attributes of the feminine self. The stereotypes suggest a splitting of love and work that relegates expressive capacities to women while placing instrumental abilities in the masculine domain. Yet looked at from a different perspective, these stereotypes reflect a conception of adulthood that is itself out of balance, favoring the separateness of the individual self over connection to others, and leaning more toward an autonomous life of work than toward the interdependence of love and care.

The discovery now being celebrated by men in mid-life of the importance of intimacy, relationships, and care is something that women have known from the beginning. However, because that knowledge in women has been considered "intuitive" or "instinctive," a function of anatomy coupled with destiny, psychologists have neglected to describe its development. In my research, I have found that women's moral development centers on the elaboration of that knowledge and thus delineates a critical line of psychological development in the lives of both of the sexes. The subject of moral development not only provides the final illustration of the reiterative pattern in the observation and assessment of sex differences in the literature on human development, but also indicates more particularly why the nature and significance of women's development has been for so long obscured and shrouded in mystery.

The criticism that Freud makes of women's sense of justice, seeing it as compromised in its refusal of blind impartiality, reappears not only in the work of Piaget but also in that of Kohlberg. While in Piaget's account of the moral judgment of the child, girls are an aside, a curiosity to whom he devotes four brief entries in an index that omits "boys" altogether because "the child" is assumed to be male, in the research from which Kohlberg derives his theory, females simply do not exist. Kohlberg's six stages that describe the development of moral judgment from childhood to adulthood are based empirically on a study of eighty-four boys whose development Kohlberg has followed for a period of over twenty years. Although Kohlberg claims universality for his stage sequence, those groups not included in his original sample rarely reach his higher stages.

Prominent among those who thus appear to be deficient in moral development when measured by Kohlberg's scale are women, whose judgments seem to exemplify the third stage of his six-stage sequence. At this stage morality is conceived in interpersonal terms and goodness is equated with helping and pleasing others. This conception of goodness is considered by Kohlberg and Kramer to be functional in the lives of mature women insofar as their lives take place in the home. Kohlberg and Kramer imply that only if women enter the traditional arena of male activity will they recognize the inadequacy of this moral perspective and progress like men toward higher stages where relationships are subordinated to rules (stage four) and rules to universal principles of justice (stages five and six).

Yet herein lies a paradox, for the very traits that traditionally have defined the "goodness" of women, their care for and sensitivity to the needs of others, are those that mark them as deficient in moral development. In this version of moral development, however, the conception of maturity is derived from the study of men's lives and reflects the importance of individuation in their development. Piaget, challenging the common impression that a developmental theory is built like a pyramid from its base in infancy, points out that a conception of development instead hangs from its vertex of maturity, the point toward which progress is traced. Thus, a change in the definition of maturity does not simply alter the description of the highest stage but recasts the understanding of development, changing the entire account.

When one begins with the study of women and derives developmental constructs from their lives, the outline of a moral conception different from that described by Freud, Piaget, or Kohlberg begins to emerge and informs a different description of development. In this conception, the moral problem arises from conflicting responsibilities rather than from competing rights and requires for its resolution a mode of thinking that is contextual and narrative rather than formal and abstract. This conception of morality as concerned with the activity of care centers moral development around the understanding of responsibility and relationships, just as the conception of morality as fairness ties moral development to the understanding of rights and rules.

This different construction of the moral problem by women may be seen as the critical reason for their failure to develop within the constraints of Kohlberg's system. Regarding all constructions of responsibility as evidence of a conventional moral understanding, Kohlberg defines the highest stages of moral development as deriving from a reflective understanding of human rights. That the morality of rights differs from the morality of responsibility in its emphasis on separation rather than connection, in its consideration of the individual rather than the relationship as primary, is illustrated by two responses to interview questions about the nature of morality. The first comes from a twenty-five-year-old man, one of the participants in Kohlberg's study:

[*What does the word morality mean to you?*]
Nobody in the world knows the answer. I think it is recognizing the right of the individual, the rights of other individuals, not interfering with those rights. Act as fairly as you would have them treat you. I think it is basically to preserve the human being's right to existence. I think that is the most important. Secondly, the human being's right to do as he pleases, again without interfering with somebody else's rights.

[*How have your views on morality changed since the last interview?*] I think I am more aware of an individual's rights now. I used to be looking at it strictly from my point of view, just for me. Now I think I am more aware of what the individual has a right to.

Kohlberg cites this man's response as illustrative of the principled conception of human rights that exemplifies his fifth and sixth stages. Commenting on the response, Kohlberg says, "Moving to a perspective outside of that of his society, he identifies morality with justice (fairness, rights, the Golden Rule), with recognition of the rights of others as these are defined naturally or intrinsically. The human being's right to do as he pleases without interfering with somebody else's rights is a formula defining rights prior to social legislation."

The second response comes from a woman who participated in the rights and responsibilities study. She also was twenty-five and, at the time, a third-year law student:

[*Is there really some correct solution to moral problems, or is everybody's opinion equally right?*] No, I don't think everybody's opinion is equally right. I think that in some situations there may be opinions that are equally valid, and one could conscientiously adopt one of several courses of action. But there are other situations in which I think there are right and wrong answers, that sort of inhere in the nature of existence, of all individuals here who need to live with each other to live. We need to depend on each other, and hopefully it is not only a physical need but a need of fulfillment in ourselves, that a person's life is enriched by cooperating with other people and striving to live in harmony with everybody else, and to that end, there are right and wrong, there are things which promote that end and that move away from it, and in that way it is possible to choose in certain cases among different courses of action that obviously promote or harm that goal.

[*Is there a time in the past when you would have thought about these things differently?*] Oh, yeah, I think that I went through a time when I thought that things were pretty relative, that I can't tell you what to do and you can't tell me what to do, because you've got your conscience and I've got mine.

[*When was that?*] When I was in high school. I guess that it just sort of dawned on me that my own ideas changed, and because my own judgment changed, I felt I couldn't judge another person's judgment. But now I think even when it is only the person himself who is going to be affected, I say it is wrong to the extent it doesn't cohere with what I know about human nature and what I know about you, and just from what I think is true about the operation of the universe, I could say I think you are making a mistake.

[*What led you to change, do you think?*] Just seeing more of life, just recognizing that there are an awful lot of things that are common among people. There are certain things that you come to learn promote a better life and better relationships and more personal fulfillment than other things that in general tend to do the opposite, and the things that promote these things, you would call morally right.

This response also represents a personal reconstruction of morality following a period of questioning and doubt, but the reconstruction of moral understanding is based not on the primacy and universality of individual rights, but rather on what she describes as a "very strong sense of being responsible to the world." Within this construction, the moral dilemma changes from how to exercise one's rights without interfering with the rights of others to how "to lead a moral life which includes obligations to myself and my family and people in general." The problem then becomes one of limiting responsibilities without abandoning moral concern. When asked to describe herself, this woman says that she values "having other people that I am tied to, and also having people that I am responsible to. I have a very strong sense of being responsible to the world, that I can't just live for my enjoyment, but just the fact of being in the world gives me an obligation to do what I can to make the world a better place to live in, no matter how small a scale that may be on." Thus while Kohlberg's subject worries about people interfering with each other's rights, this woman worries about "the possibility of omission, of your not helping others when you could help them."

The issue that this woman raises is addressed by Jane Loevinger's fifth "autonomous" stage of ego development, where autonomy, placed in the context of relationships, is defined as modulating an excessive sense of responsibility through the recognition that other people have responsibility for their own destiny. The autonomous stage in Loevinger's account witnesses a relinquishing of moral dichotomies and their replacement with "a feeling for the complexity and multifaceted character of real people and real situations." Whereas the rights conception of morality that informs Kohlberg's principled level (stages five and six) is geared to arriving at an objectively fair or just resolution to moral dilemmas upon which all rational persons could agree, the responsibility conception focuses instead on the limitations of any particular resolution and describes the conflicts that remain.

Thus it becomes clear why a morality of rights and noninterference may appear frightening to women in its potential justification of indifference and unconcern. At the same time, it becomes clear why, from a male perspective, a morality of responsibility appears inconclusive and diffuse, given its insistent contextual relativism. Women's moral judgments thus elucidate the pattern observed in the description of the developmental differences between the sexes, but they also provide an alternative conception of maturity by which these differences can be assessed and their implications traced. The psychology of women that has consistently been described as distinctive in its greater orientation toward relationships and interdependence implies a more contextual mode of judgment and a different moral understanding. Given the differences in women's conceptions of self and morality, women bring to the life cycle a different point of view and order human experience in terms of different priorities.

The myth of Demeter and Persephone, which McClelland cites as exemplifying the feminine attitude toward power, was associated with the Eleusinian Mysteries celebrated in ancient Greece for over two thousand years. As told in the Homeric *Hymn to Demeter*, the story of Persephone indicates the strengths of interdependence, building up resources and giving, that McClelland found in his research on power motivation to characterize the mature feminine style. Although, McClelland says, "it is fashionable to conclude that no one knows what went on in the Mysteries, it is known that they were probably the most important religious ceremonies, even partly on the historical record, which were organized by and for women, especially at the onset before men by means of the cult of Dionysus began to take them over." Thus McClelland regards the myth as "a special presentation of feminine psychology." It is, as well, a life-cycle story par excellence.

Persephone, the daughter of Demeter, while playing in a meadow with her girlfriends, sees a beautiful narcissus which she runs to pick. As she does so, the earth opens and she is snatched away by Hades, who takes her to his underworld kingdom. Demeter, goddess of the earth, so mourns the loss of her daughter that she refuses to allow anything to grow. The crops that sustain life on earth shrivel up, killing men and animals alike, until Zeus takes pity on man's suffering and persuades his brother to return Persephone to her mother. But before she leaves, Persephone eats some pomegranate seeds, which ensures that she will spend part of every year with Hades in the underworld.

The elusive mystery of women's development lies in its recognition of the continuing importance of attachment in the human life cycle. Woman's place in man's life cycle is to protect this recognition while the developmental litany intones the celebration of separation, autonomy, individuation, and natural rights. The myth of Persephone speaks directly to the distortion in this view by reminding us that narcissism leads to death, that the fertility of the earth is in some mysterious way tied to the continuation of the mother-daughter relationship, and that the life cycle itself arises from an alternation between the world of women and that of men. Only when life-cycle theorists divide their attention and begin to live with women as they have lived with men will their vision encompass the experience of both sexes and their theories become correspondingly more fertile.

DISCUSSION QUESTIONS

1. What is the difference between a "morality of rights" and a "morality of responsibility"? What is the significance of this distinction for Gilligan?
2. Why does Gilligan find the male ethic inadequate? Do you agree with her? Can the same inadequacies be found in the female ethic? Defend your view.
3. Gilligan discusses and compares the moral development of male and female children. What is her position? What difficulties does she have with Freud's notion of moral development? Why does she find Chodorow's view stronger? Do you agree?
4. To what extent should moral development play a role in moral theory? What role do you suppose moral development would have in the ethical positions of Aristotle, Immanuel Kant, and John Stuart Mill?

5. To what extent are the moral theories of Kant, Aristotle, and Mill moralities of "rights"? To what extent are they moralities of "responsibility"? What do you think Gilligan would say?
6. Is there a natural connection between one's moral outlook and one's sex? Defend your view. Respond to possible criticisms by Gilligan.

GEORGE SHER

Other Voices, Other Rooms?

George Sher is skeptical of Carol Gilligan's findings in her book *In a Different Voice.* According to Sher, Gilligan's findings "seem neither to undermine nor decisively to ad-judicate among the familiar options of moral theory." Gilligan has not discovered any-thing new about moral theory, nor has she offered a serious challenge to existing moral theories. While women might be more sensitive to certain aspects of oppositions—such as care versus duty, partiality versus impartiality, and abstract principle versus contextual reality—these oppositions are not new to moral theory. All of the standard moral theo-ries seek to balance considerations of care and mercy with considerations of justice and duty. Nevertheless, Gilligan's proposed balance between care and duty might be better than some of the preceding theories. Furthermore, Sher concedes that Gilligan might be right that women are generally more concerned with particular dimensions of these oppositions than men. "Women's moral judgments may be expressed in a different voice," says Sher, "but that voice echoes through some quite familiar rooms."

George Sher is a professor of philosophy at Rice University and the author of *Desert* (1987), *Approximate Justice* (1997), and *Beyond Neutrality* (1997).

WOMEN'S PSYCHOLOGY AND MORAL THEORY

Of all the reasons for the recent surge of interest in Carol Gilligan's work, not the least is the idea that her findings may have important implications for moral theory. Although this idea is not always made explicit, its overall thrust is clear enough. By showing that women and men construe moral problems dif-ferently, and by demonstrating that their moral de-velopment traverses different stages, Gilligan is thought to have uncovered an imbalance in existing moral theories. She is thought to have shown that their standard categories and questions embody a subtle bias—a male bias—and thus to have opened our eyes to alternative possibilities.[1] Here I want to register some skepticism about this idea. Despite their undeniable importance, I believe Gilligan's findings open few new doors for moral theory. Women's moral judgments may be expressed in a dif-ferent voice, but that voice echoes through some quite familiar rooms.

For an initial sense of what is at stake, let us briefly review Gilligan's reconstruction of women's moral thought. Her conception of the prevailing

George Sher, *Women and Moral Theory.* Edited by E. Kittay and Diana Meyers. Rowman and Littlefield. Reprinted with permission from the publisher.

paradigms, and her views about how women deviate from them, are interwoven with her discussion of the three empirical studies around which her book[2] is built. Thus, I shall begin by citing a few representative passages:

> Claire's inability to articulate her moral position stems in part from the fact that hers is a contextual judgment, bound to the particulars of time and place, contingent always on "that mother" and that "unborn child" and thus resisting a categorical formulation. To her the possibilities of imagination outstrip the capacity for generalization. (pp. 58–59)

> Hypothetical dilemmas, in the abstraction of their presentation, divest moral actors from the history and psychology of their individual lives and separate the moral problem from the social contingencies of its possible occurrence. In doing so, these dilemmas are useful for the distillation and refinement of objective principles of justice and for measuring the formal logic of equality and reciprocity. However, the reconstruction of the dilemma in its contextual particularity allows the understanding of cause and consequence which engages the compassion and tolerance repeatedly noted to distinguish the moral judgments of women. (p. 100)

> Seeing in the dilemma not a math problem with humans but a narrative of relationships that extends over time, Amy envisions the wife's continuing need for her husband and the husband's continuing concern for his wife and seeks to respond to the druggist's need in a way that would sustain rather than sever connection. Just as she ties the wife's survival to the preservation of relationships, so she considers the value of the wife's life in a context of relationships. (p. 28)

> Women's construction of the moral problem as a problem of care and responsibility in relationships rather than as one of rights and rules ties the development of their moral thinking to changes in their understanding of responsibility and relationships, just as the conception of morality as justice ties development to the logic of equality and reciprocity. (p. 73)

> Thus it becomes clear why a morality of rights and noninterference may appear frightening to women in its potential justification of indifference and unconcern. At the same time, it becomes clear why, from a male perspective, a morality of responsibility appears inconclusive and diffuse given its insistent contextual relativism. (p. 22)

In these and many similar passages, Gilligan elaborates her conception of women's distinctive moral "voice" through a series of oppositions. She can be read as saying that women's morality is concrete and contextual rather than abstract; that it is non-principled rather than principled; that it is personal rather than impersonal; that it motivates through care rather than through awareness of duty; and that it is structured around responsibilities rather than rights. There is room for debate over which of these claims Gilligan regards as fundamental, and, indeed, over which she is committed to at all. But if our question is whether any aspect (or plausible extension) of Gilligan's findings can lead to a recasting of moral theory, then we will do well to examine each opposition.

Thus, consider first the suggestion that women's moral decisions are concrete and contextual rather than abstract. Taken literally, the opposition here seems spurious, for at least *prima facie*, it is hard to see either how all contextual features could ever be *irrelevant* to a moral decision, or how they all could be *relevant* to it. Even the most unbending absolutist, who believes that (say) no promises should ever be broken, must allow moral agents to pay enough attention to context to ascertain whether a particular act *would* break a promise; and additional attention to context is required by the notorious problem of conflict of duty. Yet, on the other hand, even the most ardent proponent of "situation ethics" must acknowledge that moral decision-making requires some selectivity of attention, and thus too, some abstraction from total context. The woman who agonizes over an abortion may be influenced by a myriad of "particulars of time and place"; but given the uncountable number of such particulars, she plainly cannot consider them all. *A fortiori*, she cannot assign them all weight. Thus, the proper question is not so much *whether* context is relevant, but rather how many, and which aspects of it are pertinent to our moral decisions, and how these interact to generate moral duties. But when the role of context is thus tamed,[3] it no longer represents a new discovery for moral theory. Instead, the questions it raises are the very stuff of orthodox normative ethics.[4]

Not surprisingly, these *a priori* remarks are borne out by the reports of Gilligan's own subjects. Despite

Gilligan's claim that these women make moral decisions contextually and concretely, their words often evidence a well developed sense of differential relevance. Moreover, this sense emerges not only in their responses to Kohlberg's hypothetical dilemmas, but also in their formulations of dilemmas from their actual lives. Thus, for example, Claire, whose doubts about her activities as an abortion counselor were the occasion for the first passage quoted, remarks that "yes, life is sacred, but the quality of life is also important, and it has to be the determining thing in this particular case" (p. 58). One might quarrel with Claire's characterization of life as "sacred" when she takes its value to be overridden by other considerations; but she is undeniably trying both to isolate the relevant features of her situation and to impose an order upon them.

This is, of course, not to deny that women may in general be more attuned than men to context; nor is it to deny that such receptivity may be extremely important in shaping women's moral assessments. Certainly genetic or environmental factors may have conspired to make women especially sensitive to what their acts really mean to the persons they affect. It is also conceivable that women may care more than men about this. Indeed, given Gilligan's data, such differences seem far more than mere possibilities. Furthermore, any reasonable theory will acknowledge that both the rightness of one's acts and one's moral goodness are heavily influenced by how accurately and fully one assesses one's situation and the possibilities for action within it. For a deontologist, one's attentiveness to context determines how well one appreciates the nature, and so too the right-making characteristics, of the available acts; for a consequentialist, it determines how well one appreciates those acts' potential consequences. Yet even taken together, these concessions imply at most that women may be better than men at one aspect of a multifaceted common enterprise. They surely do not imply that women operate within a "morality of context" while men do not. If Kohlberg's "masculine" stage-sequence construes moral development only as movement toward greater abstraction, and ignores the possibility that persons may also develop in sensitivity to context, then so much the worse for its pretensions to measure all aspects of moral progress. So much the worse, too, for its claim to capture all that is importantly common among traditional competing theories.

This way of dismissing the contextual/abstract distinction may seem too quick. Even if we agree that every moral decision requires both sensitivity to context and abstraction from it, we need not agree about the form such abstraction must take. More specifically, even if persons cannot make moral decisions without selectively focusing on some features of their situations, there remains a question about whether the selected features can license decisions all by themselves, or whether they can do so only in concert with more general moral principles. It is a commonplace of most moral theories that if a given constellation of facts is to be a good reason for a person X to do A, then a similar constellation must be equally good reason for another person Y, or for the same person X at a different time.[5] Putting the point slightly differently, most theories agree that all moral justification involves at least tacit appeal to principle. Yet Gilligan can be read as taking her findings to show that women's decisions are often *not* backed by universal principles.[6] Hence, her results may seem to point the way to a new view of what constitutes a moral reason.

With this, we have shifted from the first to the second of our contrasts. Underlying the opposition between the contextual and the abstract, we have found a further opposition between the principled and the nonprincipled. This second opposition is, for us, the more interesting; for the role of principle in moral thought is far less clear than the mere need for abstraction. There have, of course, been many attempts to show that nonprincipled decisions are irrational, or in other ways deficient. But when pitted against these, Gilligan's findings may seem to carry considerable weight. For if women commonly do make nonprincipled decisions, then to reject such decisions as unacceptable would be to dismiss the standard moral *modus operandi* of half the world's population.

It is, in fact, a nice question of metatheory how heavily such empirical findings should weigh against other, more nearly *a priori* arguments about standards of rationality. To philosophers sympathetic to naturalism, who operate in the spirit of Nelson Goodman's suggestion that "[t]he process of justification is the delicate one of making mutual adjustments between rules and accepted inferences,"[7] the empirical findings will presumably matter a lot. To others, more a prioristically inclined, they will presumably matter less. But in fact, and fortunately, we need not resolve the general problem of method here. For, despite appearances to the contrary, Gilligan's results show very little about the role of principle in women's decisions.

To see why, we must keep our attention firmly fixed on what acting on principle is. As we saw, to act on principle is just to act for reasons that one takes (or perhaps: would take) to apply with similar force to any others who were similarly situated. But, given the counterfactual element of this formulation, the mere fact that women's responses are rarely *couched* in terms of principle provides little evidence about the underlying structure of their decisions. Even persons who fail to mention principles in reconstructing their deliberations, and indeed even persons who explicitly disavow them, may well have decided on principled grounds. Their omissions or disavowals may reflect, not a lack of commitment to principles, but rather an imperfect appreciation of what such commitment amounts to. Whether one acts on principle depends not just on what one says about principles, but rather on what one does or would say (or do) about a variety of other matters. There are, of course, difficult problems here—problems about which questions would best elicit a person's considered views, about what distinguishes deviations from principles from lack of commitment to them, and about which acts or assertions would best show that persons regard their reasons as fully general. However, given our purposes, we need not resolve these problems. Instead, we need only note that *whatever* resolution one adopts, no one can establish the role of principle in a subject's deliberations without some focused and directive counterfactual inquiry. Since Gilligan's questions do not take this form, the responses she elicits do not show that women's decisions are generally nonprincipled (or even that they are less often principled than men's).

This is, I think, not quite to say that Gilligan's data provide *no* evidence for such a conclusion. Since that conclusion is one possible explanation of women's reluctance to appeal explicitly to principles, it does draw some confirmation from Gilligan's data. But because the same data can be explained in many other ways, the degree of confirmation is minimal. Of the plausible competing explanations, one—that Gilligan's subjects lack the somewhat recondite understanding of principled action that figures in philosophical debates—has already been noted. But there are also others. Women's principles may be hedged with more qualifications than men's, and so may be more difficult to articulate, and thus less ready at hand. Women, being more attuned to the need for qualification, may be more aware of the inadequacies of the principles that first come to mind, and so more hesitant to assert them. Women may attach comparatively less importance to the generality of their reasons, and comparatively more to the reasons' complete specification. Given these and other

possibilities, the fact that women seldom explicitly invoke moral principles implies little about whether their actual decisions are principled.

This is still not the end of the story. A further aspect of Gilligan's account is that women's moral decisions tend in two ways to be more personal than men's. For one thing, her female subjects often represent moral dilemmas as problems in balancing the needs of specific individuals (who sometimes, but not always, include themselves). For another, they often represent the proper resolutions to these dilemmas as stemming not from impersonal duty, but rather from personal sympathy and care. Since there is at least a *prima facie* tension between the duty to implement an impersonal principle and the concern that stems from a personal relationship, these findings may seem to lend further (if indirect) support to the view that women's decisions are nonprincipled. In addition, they may seem to add further dimension to the claim that women approach problems of conflicting interests differently than men. If these things are true, then our earlier question of how heavily to count actual practice in establishing standards of moral reasonableness will return with a vengeance.

Yet before concluding this, we must look more closely at the tension between personal relationship and impersonal principle, and at the prospects for resolving it within something like the traditional framework. Let us begin by asking why that tension should be thought to exist at all. Although there are surely many contributing factors, one obvious reason is the unique and unrepeatable nature of personal relationships. Because such relationships are rooted in particular histories of transactions between particular persons, any demands they impose must apply to those persons alone. Even if other persons are similarly situated, their different histories will insure that they are not subject to similar demands. Moreover, if personal relationships do impose demands, then those demands must apparently not just differ from, but also sometimes conflict with, the demands of impersonal principle. In particular, such conflict must arise whenever relationship and principle call for incompatible acts.

Thus interpreted, the opposition between the personal and the impersonal is at least *prima facie* plausible. Yet on this account, its challenge to the familiar body of theory invites at least two objections. Most obviously, even if historically rooted relationships do raise questions about the hegemony of a morality of principle, they cannot possibly provide a comprehensive alternative to it; for many pressing moral choices affect only persons with whom the agent *has* no personal relationship. This may be obscured by the prominence of parents, husbands, and lovers in the reports of Gilligan's subjects; but it emerges as soon as we scrutinize the "relationships" between newly pregnant women and the fetuses they carry. It emerges yet more clearly when we consider such cases as that of Hilary, who as a trial lawyer has discovered that the opposing counsel has

> overlooked a document that provided critical support for his client's "meritorious claim." Deliberating whether or not to tell her opponent . . . Hilary realized that the adversary system of justice impedes not only "the supposed search for truth" but also the expression of concern for the person on the other side. Choosing in the end to adhere to the system, in part because of the vulnerability of her own professional position, she sees herself as having failed to live up to her standard of personal integrity as well as to her moral ideal of self-sacrifice. (p. 135)

Whatever Hilary's compromised ideal amounts to, it is plainly *not* an ideal of responsiveness to personal relationships; for no such relationships here exist.[8]

Of course, even if decisions like Hilary's cannot be guided by the demands of personal relationships, they may still be motivated and guided by care and sympathy for all the affected parties. That this is part of what Gilligan takes Hilary to have sacrificed is suggested by her observation that the adversary system impedes "the expression of concern for the person on the other side." Yet as soon as care and concern are detached from the demands of unique and historically rooted relationships—as soon as they are said to be elicited merely by the affected parties' common humanity, or by the fact that those parties all have interests, or all can suffer—the care and concern are once again viewed as appropriate responses to shared and repeatable characteristics. By so regarding them, we completely lose the contrast between the particularity of relationship and the generality of principle. Having lost it, we seem to be left with an approach that seeks to resolve moral dilemmas through sympathetic identification with all the affected parties. Yet far from being novel, this approach—which is at least closely related to that of the familiar impartial and benevolent observer—is central to the existing tradition.[9]

There is also a deeper difficulty with the suggestion that a morality that is sensitive to the demands of relationship must be incompatible with a moral-

ity of duty and principle. As I have reconstructed it, the incompatibility arises when the demands of relationship and principle conflict. Yet the assumption that such conflict is inevitable should itself not go unquestioned. Even if we concede that relationships impose demands which *differ* from the demands of moral principles—and I think we ought to concede this—it remains possible that each set of demands might be adjusted to, and might be bounded by, the other. It is, on the one hand, not at all far-fetched that friendship might never demand that one betray the trust of another, or that one do anything else that is seriously wrong. It is also not far-fetched that the demands of some impersonal moral principles might be contingent on the prior demands of personal relationships. For one thing, we may sometimes be morally permitted, or even required, to give our friends and loved ones preference over others. For another, even where we are not forced to choose whom to help, we may be morally required to produce just the responses that our relationships demand. Such a convergence of demands upon a single action would be no more anomalous than the convergence that occurs when a given act is demanded both by (say) an obligation one has incurred by undertaking a public position and one's natural duty to support just institutions. In general, the demands of relationship and principle may be so interwoven that there is no theoretical bar to our being fully responsive to both.

Needless to say, there are many questions here. It is one thing to suggest that the demands of relationship and impersonal principle might be reconciled, and quite another to tell a plausible detailed story about how this would work. Of all the problems facing such an account, perhaps the most familiar is the objection that the motive of duty is in some sense alienating, and that persons who act merely on principle are *ipso facto* not displaying the affection and care appropriate to personal relationships. Bernard Williams has put this worry well in his influential discussion of the suggestion that a moral principle might license a decision to save one's wife rather than a stranger when only one can be saved. Williams remarks that "this construction provides the agent with one thought too many: it might have been hoped by some (for instance, by his wife) that his motivating thought, fully spelled out, would be the thought that it was his wife, not that it was his wife and, that in situations of this kind, it is permissible to save one's wife."[10] Yet Williams' worry, though provocative, is far from decisive. In an interesting recent essay, Marcia Baron has argued that the worry draws its apparent force partly from our tendency to associate acting from duty with motives that really are inimical to care and affection, but that have no intrinsic connection with duty, and partly from a failure to see that moral principles may operate not as independent sources of motivating force, but rather as filters through which other motives must pass.[11] Since I find Baron's diagnosis convincing, I shall not discuss this problem further. Instead, I shall briefly take up another, less familiar problem that the reconciliationist project faces.

In a nutshell, the further problem is that of justification. It is the problem of finding, within the standard repertoire of justificatory approaches, resources sufficient to ground not merely principles of impartial morality, but also principles licensing the sort of partiality that reconciliationism requires. Put (too) briefly, the difficulty here is that both deontologists and consequentialists have standardly tried to justify their favored principles from some abstract and general perspective. For this reason, the impersonality of their starting points may itself seem to guarantee the rejection of any principles which acknowledge the demands of personal relationships. As Williams notes, this point seems to obtain

> even when the moral point of view is itself explained under conditions of ignorance of some abstractly conceived contracting parties. . . . For while the contracting parties are pictured as making some kind of self-interested or prudential choice of a set of rules, they are entirely abstract persons making this choice in ignorance of their own particular properties, tastes, and so forth.[12]

If this is right, and if Gilligan is right to say that women often resolve dilemmas precisely by responding to the demands of personal relationships, then we will indeed be forced to choose between denying that women's decisions are made on moral grounds and radically altering our conceptions of what counts as well grounded morality.

But *does* the impersonality of the familiar justificatory approaches rule out the justification of principles that accommodate the demands of personal relationships? Although we obviously cannot examine all the possibilities, it will be worth our while to look more closely at one familiar strategy. Since the Rawlsian approach has already been mentioned, I shall stick with it. In this approach, a principle is justified if it would be chosen by rational and self-interested persons who were ignorant of the particulars of their situations, and thus were prevented from making biased choices. Although I am no particular friend of hypothetical contractarianism, I cannot see that its difficulties lie where Williams says they do. It is true that Rawls himself says little about personal relationships, and true also that Richards' adaptation of his framework leads to such "righteous absurdities" as that persons should not base their relationships on "arbitrary physical characteristics alone."[13] But none of this implies that Rawlsian contractors could not, in fact, agree on more sensible principles concerning relationships. It does not imply that they could not agree on principles that prescribe compliance with the demands of personal relationships under certain conditions, or that permit or require some partiality to friends and loved ones. In particular, the choice of such principles seems plainly *not* to be ruled out merely by the ignorance of the contracting parties. The contractors' ignorance does rule out the choice of principles that name either specific agents who are allowed or required to be partial or the specific recipients of their partiality. However, this is irrelevant; for the question is not whether any *given* person may or should display partiality to any other, but rather whether *all* persons may or should be partial to their wives, husbands, or friends. The relevant principles, even if licensing or dictating partiality, must do so impartially. Hence, there is no obvious reason why such principles could not be chosen even by contractors ignorant of the particulars of their lives.

Can we go further? Is there any positive reason for rational, self-interested, but ignorant Rawlsian contractors to opt for principles that adjust duties and obligations to the demands of personal relationships? To answer this question fully, we would have to say far more about the demands of relationships than can be said here. But given present purposes, which are merely dialectical, there is indeed something to be said. Our question about the Rawlsian contractors has arisen because their failure to choose principles adjusted to the demands of relationships would support the broader claim that *all* impersonal justificatory strategies yield principles that sometimes conflict with the demands of relationships. This, in turn, would combine with Gilligan's findings to suggest a reconceptualization of the moral point of view in more personal and relationship-oriented terms. But this last move will only be plausible if the demands of personal relationships are in themselves sufficiently compelling to warrant description as moral demands. Hence, for us, the question is not what the Rawlsian contractors would choose *simpliciter*, but rather what they would choose *on the assumption that the demands of relationships are this compelling.*

When the issue is framed in these terms, I think the Rawlsian contractors might well have good reason to choose principles that conflicted as little as possible with the demands of personal relationships. To see why, consider what the demands of relationships would have to be like to be compelling enough to qualify as moral demands. At a minimum, they would have to be so urgent that persons could not violate them without at the same time violating their own integrity. The demands would have to grow out of the kind of deep personal commitment that, as Williams put it, "compels . . . allegiance to life itself."[14] In addition, when viewed from the perspective of the other parties to relationships, the demands would have to dictate responses that were not merely optional, but were in some sense owed. The demands' nonfulfillment would have to be real grounds for complaint. Just how relationships can generate such demands is of course a large part of the mystery about them. But if they can—and I believe they not only can but often do—then the satisfaction of those demands, when they arise, must itself be a good that transcends mere personal preference. Like liberty and other Rawlsian primary goods, a general ability both to give and to receive such satisfaction must be something it is rational to want whatever else one wants. But if so, then rational contractors endowed with full general information about human psychology could hardly avoid wanting to protect this ability. Since protecting it requires choosing principles whose prescriptions are adjusted to the demands of important relationships, I conclude that they would indeed be motivated to choose such principles.

This conclusion might be challenged through appeal to the last of Gilligan's oppositions. As derived, the conclusion rests on the premise that morality is fundamentally a matter of what persons owe to others. It thus appears to presuppose that any genuinely moral principle must specify people's *rights*. Yet one of Gilligan's most persistent themes is that a preoccupation with rights rather than responsibilities is itself a typically male construction. As she often notes, her female subjects think less about what they are entitled to than about what they are responsible for providing. Thus, it may seem illegitimate for us to say that only demands that specify responses that are owed can qualify as moral. For, if we do say this, we may seem to beg the question against those who see Gilligan's work as prefiguring a new vision of morality.

Yet, here again, the worry is overdrawn. Let us simply grant that women, at least in the earlier stages of their development, think more readily of what they are responsible for providing than of what they are entitled to receive. Even so, nothing follows about the status of the responsibilities they acknowledge. Indeed, one very reasonable suggestion is that they regard themselves as responsible for providing sympathy, care, and help to others precisely *because* they regard themselves as owing these things. Putting the point in terms of rights, and ignoring the complexities and differing interpretations of that notion, we can say that nothing rules out the possibility that women regard others as having a *right* to their sympathy, care, and help. To suppose otherwise would be to conflate the well supported claim that women are less concerned than men with the protection of *their* rights with the quite different claim that women are less inclined than men to think that people *have* rights (or to hold views functionally equivalent to this).

All things considered, Gilligan's findings seem neither to undermine nor decisively to adjudicate among the familiar options of moral theory. They may edge us in certain theoretical directions, but the movement they compel takes us nowhere near the boundaries of the known territories. This is not to deny that the findings suggest that women are, in some respects, better equipped than men to reach morally adequate decisions; but it is to deny that that result requires any exotic recasting of our familiar understanding of "morally adequate." To all of this, the still-hopeful revisionist might finally complain that I have interpreted the received body of theory so broadly that it is not clear what *could* show that it needs radical revision. But this, though true, is precisely the point I want to make. The oppositions of concrete and abstract, personal and impersonal, duty and care are not recent empirical discoveries, but generic determinants of the moral problematic. We have always known that an adequate theory must assign each its proper place. What we have not known, and what Gilligan's findings bring us little closer to knowing, is what those places are.

NOTES

1. Thus, for example, Linda J. Nicholson writes, in an issue of *Social Research* devoted to Gilligan's work, that "many feminists have responded that the masculinity of the authors has affected the very content of the theory itself. . . .

I agree with the feminist argument" (Linda J. Nicholson, "Women, Morality and History," *Social Research*, 50, 3 [Autumn 1983]: 514). I do not mean to imply that either Nicholson or the other contributors to that issue subscribe to the specific views I criticize below.

2. Carol Gilligan, *In a Different Voice* (Cambridge, MA: Harvard University Press, 1982). All page references in the text are to this volume.

3. That it must be so tamed is one of the few points of agreement between Owen Flanagan and Lawrence Kohlberg in their interchange on moral development. See Owen J. Flanagan, "Virtue, Sex, and Gender: Some Philosophical Reflections on the Moral Psychology Debate," *Ethics*, 92 (April 1982): 499–512; and Lawrence Kohlberg, "A Reply to Owen Flanagan and Some Comments on the Puka-Goodpaster Exchange," *Ethics*, 92 (April 1982): 513–528.

4. Moral philosophers have proposed a variety of approaches to the question of which aspects of one's context are morally relevant. Some focus exclusively on a single factor, such as the happiness or preference-satisfaction that available acts would produce. See, for instance, John Stuart Mill, *Utilitarianism* (Indianapolis: Hackett, 1979). Others hold that more than one factor is relevant, but that some factors take priority over others. This approach is exemplified by John Rawls' "lexical ordering" of his principles of justice; see his *A Theory of Justice* (Cambridge, MA: Harvard University Press, 1971). Still others say that more than one factor is relevant, and that there are no priority rules to adjudicate conflicts. See, for example, W. D. Ross, *The Right and the Good* (Oxford: Oxford University Press, 1973); and William Frankena, *Ethics*, 2nd ed. (Englewood Cliffs, NJ: Prentice-Hall, 1973). Again, R. M. Hare has argued that a factor's moral relevance for an agent depends on his willingness to universalize a principle in which it appears; see his *Freedom and Reason* (Oxford: Oxford University Press, 1963).

5. For two of the many statements of this view, see Henry Sidgwick, *Methods of Ethics*, 7th ed. (London: Macmillan, 1922), bk. III, chap. 1, and J. L. Mackie, *Ethics: Inventing Right and Wrong* (Harmondsworth, England: Penguin Books, 1977), chap. 4.

6. As the editors of this volume have suggested to me, Gilligan's point may be not that women's decisions are nonprincipled, but only that their principles tend not to be couched in such terms as fairness and justice. I agree that this interpretation is available, but continue to regard the stronger interpretation as at least as plausible. More importantly, even if Gilligan herself does not hold the stronger view, the questions of its tenability and relation to her data remain worth discussing.

7. Nelson Goodman, *Fact, Fiction, and Forecast* (Indianapolis: Bobbs-Merrill, 1965), p. 64.

8. In a recent public presentation, Gilligan has distinguished between the view that care rests on attachment, and the view that care rests on knowledge gained through attachment. If she holds that personal relationships are important primarily because they provide a sort of knowledge that can guide and inform our dealings even with strangers, her view is of course not vulnerable to the objections just mounted. It is, however, then vulnerable to the objection to follow.

9. Two classical representatives of this approach are: David Hume, *Treatise of Human Nature*, ed. L. A. Selby-Bigge (Oxford: Oxford University Press, 1960), bk. III, pt. III, sec. 1; and Adam Smith, *The Theory of Moral Sentiments*, in L.A. Selby-Bigge, *The British Moralists*, vol. 1 (Oxford: Oxford University Press, 1897), pp. 257–277. For a more recent treatment, see R. M. Hare, *Moral Thinking* (Oxford: Oxford University Press, 1981), pt. II.

10. Bernard Williams, "Persons, Character, and Morality," in *The Identities of Persons*, ed. Amelie Rorty (Berkeley: University of California Press, 1976), pp. 214–215.

11. Marcia Baron, "The Alleged Moral Repugnance of Acting from Duty," *The Journal of Philosophy*, 81, 4 (April 1984): 197–220. For related discussion, see Peter Railton, "Alienation, Consequentialism, and the Demands of Morality," *Philosophy and Public Affairs*, 13, 2 (Spring 1984): 134–171.

12. Williams, "Persons, Character, and Morality," pp. 198–199. The approach to which Williams alludes is of course that developed by Rawls in *A Theory of Justice*.

13. David A. J. Richards, *A Theory of Reasons for Action* (Oxford: Oxford University Press, 1971), p. 94. The apt phrase "righteous absurdity" is used by Williams in "Persons, Character, and Morality," p. 212.

14. Williams, "Persons, Character, and Morality," p. 215.

DISCUSSION QUESTIONS

1. How does Sher argue against Carol Gilligan's claim that women's moral decisions are personal rather than impersonal? Do you agree with Sher's criticisms? Or do you agree with Gilligan on this point? Explain.

2. What does it mean to say that women's moral decisions are more contextual and concrete than abstract? Do you agree with Sher's criticisms of Gilligan's position on this issue? What is your own view?

3. Are women's moral judgments really more nonprincipled than principled? How might you prove such a point? What is Sher's position on this issue? Do you agree with him?

4. Sher does not think that Gilligan has discovered anything new about moral theory. Others strongly disagree with this. What do you think? Do you agree with Sher's overall evaluation of Gilligan's contribution to moral theory? Defend your view.

5. Can you think of any instances from literature or film in which an ethic of abstract principle comes into conflict with an ethic of care and compassion? Is this conflict presented in a "genderless" way? Or is the ethic of abstract principle associated more with the male characters, and the ethic of care and compassion more with the female characters? Does *Les Miserables* or *Huckleberry Finn* raise such a conflict? Use your example to support the views of either Sher or Gilligan.

R O N A L D   D U S K A

What Is Literature to Ethics?

In this article, Ronald Duska explores some of the ways in which literature helps us to deal with moral matters. Duska criticizes contemporary moral philosophy for being too formal and argues that "in many ways literature contributes more to the clarification of values and the development of morals than ethical theory as it is done today." Duska argues that "contemporary ethical theory is inadequate because it rests on an unrealistic picture of human life which largely ignores or misconstrues the role of the passions in constituting a meaningful human life." Literature shows us how the lives of humans are bound up with our passions and helps us to develop a sense of empathy for others. Literature, unlike contemporary ethical theory, helps us to become more caring and open human beings.

Ronald Duska is the Charles Lamont Post Chair of Ethics and the Professions at The American College and is the author of *Moral Development* (1973).

Quarry the granite rock with razors, or moor the vessel with a thread of silk; then may you hope with such keen and delicate instruments as human knowledge and human reason to contend against those giants, the passion and pride of man.

—John Henry Newman

Ronald Duska, *Listening: Journal of Religion and Culture* (winter 1982). Copyright © 1982 Ronald Duska. Used by permission of the author.

One can always learn from literature.[1] That statement might offend some purists among contemporary aestheticians who would want to claim that the function of literature as art is to delight and that to use literature for didactic purposes is to abuse it. But the fact remains that literature, good literature, has always been a marvelous teacher. It humanizes us as perhaps nothing else can. Hence the topic of this paper. I want to examine a few ways in which literature aids us in dealing with ethical matters. My conviction, which may appear perverse to some, is that in many ways literature contributes more to the clarification of values and the development of morals than ethical theory as it is done today.

I will claim that contemporary ethical theory is inadequate because it rests on an unrealistic picture of human life which largely ignores or misconstrues the role of the passions[2] in constituting a meaningful human life. Literature, however, expresses or represents in a unique way the passionate sources of human action and consequently shows us what a meaningful human life is in a way that ethics does not. In short, it provides us with what ethical theory does not, content for what has become the formally stringent but largely vacuous enterprise of contemporary ethical theory. I begin with a defense of that claim.

A generation ago, G. E. M. Anscombe requested a moratorium on ethical theory. Since then, Philippa Foot expressed a desire to quit talking about "morality." Rather than acceding to the wishes of these two esteemed philosophers, ethicists have talked and written even more about ethical issues. However, rather than dry as dust discussions of ethical theory or meta-ethics, the talk now revolves around pertinent and substantive ethical issues, often under the name of applied ethics. For my part, instead of teaching about naturalistic fallacies, I now find myself engaged in medical and business ethics, talking about abortion, genetic engineering, corporate responsibility, preferential hiring and a host of other topics. Nevertheless, periodically I ask myself "Why?" Is the kind of discussion carried on about these issues relevant? The topics certainly are relevant, but can this be said of our treatment of them?

The standard move of most "applied ethicists" is to take one of the two canonized ethical theories, either the deontological principles of Kant or Ross, possibly updated by his contemporary disciples and apply them/it to either a class of actions like suicide and abortion or to a particular ethical dilemma. For example, if we address euthanasia or suicide, two problems of the same stripe: either we begin by talking about the duty to oneself or others and the con-

tradictoriness of the taking of a human life to preserve the values of life; or we begin by talking of the rationality of euthanasia or suicide in terms of the consequences of this type of action, and determine whether it is right by deciding whether it will maximize happiness.

One must grant that both of these methods have something to be said in their favor, for they do show that if certain principles are accepted, certain actions logically follow as appropriate or inappropriate. Nevertheless, for anyone who has ever taught courses in applied ethics, this procedure leaves much to be desired.

What is the problem? First, it seems to be that the application of formal rules to materially concrete problems never leads to definitive solutions. For every answer there is a counter objection and a kind of skepticism is encouraged. Second, even if a definitive solution would be arrived at, a highly unlikely possibility, the question, why do what is prescribed would still remain, i.e., we could still ask, "Why be moral?" "Why do what we have determined that we should?"

There are defenses of these procedures. In a remarkably well written textbook called *Moral Reasoning*, Victor Grassian offers a defense of the study of ethics. According to Grassian, even though the study of ethics will not make us into a good person, it can serve to help us better understand and classify our own moral principles, even refine and change them (one hesitates to ask whether for the better or worse); and it can lead us to a consistent set of principles. Grassian states, at the end of the defense:

> By studying the arguments that philosophers give for their ethical positions and the objections they pose to the view of others, a person's ability to defend his own positions and recognize their shortcomings will itself be sharpened. This is by far the *most important* thing that the study of ethics has to offer.[3]

Marvelous! But with all the sharpening, changing and elimination of shortcomings, something is still missing. What is the good of all this eristic ability if it leads to the sharpening of misguided principles which can be used by a despot or tyrant to justify his behavior? Further, what is the good if it cannot lead to a good person behaving well? What Grassian offers is vaguely reminiscent of what the Sophists offered, is it not?

To give my point more substance let us examine a dilemma found in Grassian's text and demonstrate what ethical theorists are likely to do with it.

A POISONOUS CUP OF COFFEE

Tom hates his wife and, wanting her dead, puts poison in her coffee, thereby killing her. Joe also hates his wife and would like her dead. One day, Joe's wife accidentally puts poison in her coffee, thinking it's cream. Joe, who happens to be a chemist, has the antidote, but he does not give it to her. Knowing that he is the only one who can save her, he lets her die. Is Joe's failure to act as bad as Tom's action? Why or why not?

It seems fairly obvious that Grassian is using this dilemma to provoke a discussion of the difference (if there is any) between killing and letting die (a distinction that is quite useful in contrasting active and passive euthanasia, among other issues). For that, the dilemma might be pertinent. However, when we look at the questions asked, we cannot help but be frustrated. "Is Joe's failure to act *as bad as* Tom's action?" How would students, confronted with this question, answer it? It requires some sort of calculus to determine quantitatively the relative merits of two reprehensible actions. Presumably the answer would look something like this: From a utilitarian perspective the consequences for the woman are the same. However, Tom is liable to prosecution for homicide whereas it is unlikely that Joe is, and thus it would seem that Tom's action is worse than Joe's because it brings worse consequences. A possible answer from a deontological perspective might be that both actions are equally wrong because they use another person as a means, except that if one distinguishes between killing and letting die, one might say that Joe did not *use* his wife, if using must be an act of commission rather than an omission.

Note what happens. We begin with two obviously immoral acts and then are asked for reasons why one is worse than the other. The reasons are expected to be based on a very general principle, either deontological or consequentialist. The principles quite often conflict, as in cases where good consequences are brought about by immoral means. In that case neither set of reasons is persuasive.

Surely this sort of intellectual rumination is sterile. How, though, did this sort of procedure become so predominant? I suspect that ethicists, under the influence of or in response to positivism, got locked into a quasi-scientific mode of proceeding, or perhaps more accurately into using an engineering model. If I want to achieve a certain end, I need to perform certain appropriate operations. Given an end, my only problem is to discover acceptable means. Acceptable paths are those which fall within permissible procedures—in ethics the deontological requirements of justice and fairness determine what is acceptable. Thus, we have a goal, find acceptable means, and "Voila!" arrive rigorously at an answer. Unfortunately, deontology does not tell us what to do, only to do it with equity and fairness, while utilitarianism has yet to get clear about what the appropriate ends of man are. However, wouldn't the engineering model work if we could get clear about the ends of man?

If we could find the ends of man and get agreement on them, wouldn't my objections lose their force? It is quite fashionable in searching for an end to appeal to a picture or way of life which is held forth as an ideal. In appealing to such an ideal, one attempts to show how one's position on a certain moral issue can be understood in the light of that picture of the ideal life. This sort of appeal is supposed to serve as a justification of one's ethical judgments. We see this in the theory of R. M. Hare when he says, "If pressed to justify a decision completely, we have to give a complete specification of the way of life of which it is a part."[4] Or it can be seen in the theory of P. H. Nowell-Smith, when he says, "Moral philosophy is a practical science; its aim is to answer questions in the form, 'What shall I do?'" But no general answer can be given to this type of question. The most a moral philosopher can do is to paint a picture of various types of life in the manner of Plato and ask which type of life you really want to lead."[5]

It would make the task of this paper quite easy if I were to settle for either of these approaches and say, "Yes. Quite right. Except literature, or fiction if you prefer, is much better at painting pictures than philosophy. Thus, rather than depending on philosophers, let us go to novels and plays and perhaps biographies where we get presentations of specific lives and choose the ones that appeal to us." But there is something amiss. Hare speaks of deciding on a type of life that is completely specified. Who makes choices in that way? That is simply not what we do.[6] Nowell-Smith speaks of asking what type of life we want, but that is probably not what we do either.[7] Hare and Nowell-Smith attack the problem from the engineer's model. Give me a picture of your goal (chosen with Hare, and wanted with Nowell-Smith), and then we will figure out what needs to be done to get there. Hare and Nowell-Smith are not the only people who approach ethics in this way. It is a common way of proceeding in ethics. Generally, though, the goal was given the name "Happiness." Suppose, however, we raise some seemingly outrageous questions. Is happiness really the ultimate end of life? Or, if there is an ultimate end, is it the kind philosophers look for?

Happiness is quite often construed as some goal to be pursued or some state to be accomplished, as in "the pursuit of happiness." Often, too, it is thought to be reducible to pleasure or at least the avoidance of pain. It is seen as the goal, the *terminus ad quem* of life. This, however, is precisely the engineering view of life we discussed above.

However, happiness, thus construed, rarely serves as a real goal in life, except according to the anemic views of our engineering friends, the utilitarians. Aristotle's view of happiness, although quite vague and empty in terms of content, seems correct to the extent that he asserts that it is not an end in the sense of a product or a *terminus ad quem* of an activity. Rather, it is something that accompanies activity.

Anyone who has been disappointed when he has gone out for a good time ought to recognize that one does not seem to be able to "pursue" happiness successfully. This is the hedonistic paradox: those who strive for happiness rarely achieve it, whereas those who pursue other things might find it. Happiness accompanies a life process, but it is not the goal of life in the engineering sense of a goal.

If, however, life is not to be construed as the pursuit of a predetermined goal, how is it to be construed? R. G. Collingwood[8] in writing on art makes a distinction between art and craft that may be helpful. A craft for him is an enterprise where we have a clear goal in mind and where specific steps can be taken to achieve that goal. Collingwood's notion of a craftsman parallels our notion of an engineer. But art is not craft. The true artist does not know his end: he discovers it as he works it out. He works it out through the expressing of his emotions. I would like to suggest that human life is also the working out of our emotions or passions, without a clear notion of where the end is. Thus if ethics or morality concerns itself with the art of living, it should do this viewing life as art in Collingwood's sense and not in the sense of art as a craft.

But let us see if the living out of life is really like the working out of an art piece as Collingwood describes it. When a painter puts a line on the canvas he thereby limits the next line. It can be an indefinite number of lines, but it cannot be just any old line and be appropriate. When an author sketches his character, the character can develop in any number of ways but not just willy-nilly. By page two of *Catcher in the Rye* there are things that Salinger can do with Holden Caulfield, but there are also things he cannot do. To complete the work he must be creative, but creative within the limits set by the opening lines. Just as Salinger creates Caulfield without fully foreseeing possible outcomes, we create our lives without fully foreseeing possible outcomes. In sum, we do not know where we will end up, but a large part of the working out will depend on where we are. We need to creatively respond to where we are to make our life a finished whole.

There is a contemporary song, "The Gambler," which can also be seen as analogous to human life. One of the verses runs, "No hand's a winner and no hand's a loser" while another runs, "You never count your money while you're sittin at the table. There'll be plenty time for countin, when the dealin's done." In the game of life, the cards one is dealt and the attitudes one has dictate what one does to be successful. One can fold with bad cards, or one can bluff. One can lose with good cards or see it through and perhaps win. It depends on what one does with what one gets, and yet there are no guarantees. The point is that in most people's lived existence, the best laid plans go astray. Thus, to view the living of a human life as analogous to the process of an engineer building a bridge or a craftsman making a product is to misconstrue what is involved.

Very well, then, what is involved? To get at that I would like to turn to Camus' treatment of a classical literary figure, Sisyphus. Let us examine the closing lines of Camus' *Myth of Sisyphus*.

> I leave Sisyphus at the foot of the mountain! One always finds one's burden again. But Sisyphus teaches the higher fidelity that negates the gods and raises rocks. He too concludes that *all is well*. This universe henceforth without a master seems to him neither sterile nor futile. Each atom of that stone, each mineral flake of that night filled mountain, in itself form a world. The struggle itself toward the heights is enough to fill a man's heart. One must imagine Sisyphus happy.[9]

Incredible as it sounds, Camus suggests that Sisyphus is happy. This however is in no way the happiness associated with pleasure, but rather a happiness coming from a life that is full. Note that Camus asserts, "The struggle . . . is enough to *fill* a man's heart." Obviously, if we wish to call Sisyphus "happy" in Camus' sense we need to revise our meaning of the concept, since it does not accord with our common understanding of happiness. But let us leave that and recognize that what Camus is doing is approving of Sisyphus because he has made his life *full*. Could we not say that in the midst of a meaningless existence Sisyphus has carved out a meaningful life?

Note further that Sisyphus does not choose his life. His lot is given. "One always finds one's burden again." Further Sisyphus does not get what he wants. He, like the gambler, makes the best of what he gets. Nowell-Smith's "wants" and Hare's "choice" are wrong because life does not proceed the way they imagine. Their quasi-scientific engineering model has led them astray, and to the extent that happiness is construed as an end to be pursued it can serve as a goal for only the most shallow kinds of lives.

But if the craft-engineering model won't do, what will? The clue to this can be found in Sisyphus. Making one's life full seems to be the answer. But if we look at what makes Sisyphus' life full, it seems to be his determination and disposition, those things I would wish to include under the rubric of the passions.

If then the meaningful life is the passionate life, where do we go to find out about it? The best portraits of human passion are found in literature. They are not found in Ethics and some would argue that they are not found in Psychology either. Be that as it may, literature is surely a primary source. Let us claim then that passions are a necessary condition for a full human life. . . .

But will just any passions do? Passions may be a necessary condition for a full life, but are they sufficient? Is not something else necessary?

To examine that question I wish to cite some lines from *Othello*. Note his final speech:

> Soft you; a word or two before you go.
> I have done the state some service, and they
>   know't.
> No more of that. I pray you, in your letters,
> When you shall these unlucky deeds relate,
> Speak of me as I am; nothing extenuate,
> Nor set down aught in malice: then must you
>   speak
> Of one that loved not wisely but too well;
> Of one not easily jealous, but being wrought
> Perplex'd in the extreme; of one whose hand,
> Like the base Indian, threw a pearl away
> Richer than all his tribe; one of whose
>   subdued eyes
> Albeit unused to the melting mood,
> Drops tears as fast as the Arabian trees
> Their medicinal gum. Set you down this;
> And say besides, that in Aleppo once,
> Where a malignant and a turban'd Turk
> Beat a Venetian and traduced the state,
> I took by the throat the circumcised dog,
> And smote him, thus. (Stabs himself.)[10]

Here is without doubt a man living out his passions. Here is a life certainly not seeking happiness. But it is a tragic life. Consequently it is apparent that passions, though they make life full, do not necessarily make for the best life. The passions must be evaluated.

But the evaluation of passions is by no means impossible. Certain passions are appropriate, others not. For example, there are times my anger is inappropriate. There are passions that are destructive. . . . Othello's life is tragic. Why? Because jealousy is a destructive passion, just as is hate. One could even argue that Sisyphus' obstinacy is not the best of passions. Even though it gets him through his burdens it does not allow a life to flower as it might.

We make value judgments about passions easily. . . . Othello . . . does not need more passion; he needs better ones. In some situations passion itself is required and in others some passion *should* have been checked.

The surprising thing is that literature seems to have the ability to show the deficiencies and strengths of the passions. I am not sure I can solve the epistemological question of how this is possible, but it does seem to be a fact. One thought comes to mind though as worth pursuing. If living human life is like doing art in Collingwood's sense, and if there are ways of evaluating art, perhaps we can find some clues for evaluating life in aesthetics. This is not a new suggestion. It was made by Wittgenstein when he said that ethical reasons may well be like aesthetic reasons. Unfortunately, we are not able to develop this theme at this time, not so much for lack of space as for lack of knowing how. Consequently, I leave that as a topic to be pursued at a later time and make some final comments about what I have tried to show.

First, if ethics is irrelevant it is irrelevant because it misconstrues what life is really like, and its procedures for determining what to do fail to take into account the psychology of the passions and the passions' role in making life meaningful. To the extent that literature portrays, imitates or represents human life it shows us that most lives are problematic and, rather than being lives in pursuit of happiness, they are attempts to live out life, perhaps with a hope that we can eke out a bit of happiness along the way, but more importantly in a meaningful way. And, literature shows clearly that the meaning most often comes from the passions.

It should be noted that the encounter with literature can have other benefits. Literature, in allowing us to identify with others, allows us to develop empathy, a requisite for developing our ability to care. It also *shows* us ways of coping *with certain problems* and perhaps even *shows* the shortcomings and flaws of certain lives. All of these contributions are important. Still, the main point of this paper was to claim that literature is relevant to moral considerations because it deals with human beings' inner lives as they are, even if the characters are fictional, whereas ethics deals mainly with rules and maxims that seem so formal that they hardly touch human lives.

If this is so, it is clear that a task needs to be done by ethicists or at least philosophers. We need to begin[11] to deal with the psychology of the passions. Literature, to the extent that it portrays them faithfully, can teach us a great deal about them. Next we need to begin to evaluate them in terms of their potential for making a life good or bad. Literature again provides models. If we do this, we might begin to give our ethical considerations a content they desperately need, and talk about good men in a way that has force.

Let me conclude with a short comment on a few lines written by Stephen King: "If we say that morality proceeds simply from a good heart—which has little to do with ridiculous posturings and happily-ever-afterings—and immorality proceeds from a lack of care, from shoddy observation . . . we may realize we have arrived at a critical stance, one both workable and humane. Fiction is the truth inside the lie."[12]

If morality has to do with the heart, the passionate side of man, and immorality with a lack of care, then is it not obvious that we ethicists need to investigate these areas with much more concern? And is it not also obvious that one of the best places to start to understand and experience the passionate human being is in literature?

NOTES

1. Under the word "literature" I mean to include for the most part, novels, poems, stories and dramas. I also have in mind good literature, classics if you will, and not things like drugstore novels. I am of course assuming there is a difference between run of the mill literature and good or significant literature.

2. In this paper I am using the word "passions" rather indiscriminately in a generic sense to include a whole host of areas which would be placed under what psychologists call the affective side of man, i.e., feelings, emotions, attitudes, dispositions, etc. Much of the sorting out of what I have in mind can be found in Robert Solomon's excellent book, *The Passions* (Doubleday, 1973). The book is partly responsible for some of the directions of this paper, although I would not claim that the paper intentionally follows it, nor would I hold the book responsible for the shortcomings of my thoughts.

3. Victor Grassian, *Moral Reasoning* (Englewood Cliffs, NJ: Prentice-Hall, 1981), p. 5.

4. R. M. Hare, *The Language of Morals* (Cambridge, MA: Oxford University Press, 1960), p. 79.

5. P. H. Nowell-Smith, *Ethics* (Middlesex, England: Penguin Books, 1954), p. 319.

6. I am well aware of the dogmatic appearance of this remark. However, even though the point of this section is critical, I am more concerned with presenting an alternative view to this type of approach which Hare and Nowell-Smith offer, than with getting bogged down in what would be important, but nonetheless tedious refutations of their approach. If I would develop an argument, though, it would be to the effect that Hare forgets that human beings make decisions in a historical environmental context and that they have been conditioned by that environment. This results in our having habits and dispositions which partly constitute what we are and limit what we decide upon. We simply do not stand back from our context and make decisions without factors influencing us. . . .

7. As with the claim against Hare, I will not interrupt the presentation of the main point of the paper to develop a sustained argument against Nowell-Smith. However, he ought to recognize that we do not always know what we want and that occurs because our imagination is needed to intend new goals. Sartre makes an argument to this effect in his defense of freedom in *Being and Nothingness*. Note that literature, by giving us imaginative views of new possibilities of living, can furnish many new options. It seems it was this sort of thing that Oscar Wilde had in mind when he asserted that "Nature imitates Art."

8. Robin G. Collingwood, *Principles of Art* (London: Oxford University Press, 1938), esp. pp. 128–135.

9. Albert Camus, *The Myth of Sisyphus*, trans. Justin O'Brien (New York: Knopf, 1955).

10. *Othello*, Act V, Scene 2.

11. "Begin" may not be the correct word. As I have indicated, Robert Solomon has begun the type of enterprise I have in mind. What we need to do is expand on such work.

12. Stephen King, "Notes on Horror," *Quest*, 5, 5 (June 1981): 31.

DISCUSSION QUESTIONS

1. According to Duska, what is happiness? Compare his view with the views of John Stuart Mill and Aristotle. Which do you agree with most, and why?
2. What is Duska's criticism of utilitarianism? Evaluate his criticisms. How might a utilitarian respond to them?
3. According to Duska, what is passion, and what role does it play in morality? Do you agree with him? How would Immanuel Kant respond to Duska's claims about the role of passion in morality? Explain.
4. In this article, Duska discusses literature, but not film. Do you think that his theses hold as well for film? Why? Are there other mediums to which we might want to extend moral education as well?
5. Is it better to teach applied ethics through literature or through articles on contemporary moral theory? Would you rather study applied ethics through literature or through articles on contemporary moral theory? What are the differences? Should a work of literature be regarded as a work of ethics? Why or why not?
6. In a footnote to his essay, Duska wrote the following: "Under the word 'literature' I mean to include for the most part, novels, poems, stories and dramas. I also have in mind good literature, classics if you will, and not things like drugstore novels. I am of course assuming that there is a difference between run of the mill literature and good or significant literature." What is the difference? Do you think that it matters? One often finds Star Trek and Star Wars novels in drugstores. Are these poor sources of moral education? Why? Evaluate Duska's claims in detail.

MEDIA GALLERY

THE SHOP ON MAIN STREET (OBCHOD NA KORZE)

(Czechoslovakia, 1965) 2 hours 8 minutes
Directed by Ján Kadár

Film summary: The setting is a small town in Slovakia during the Second World War. Tono Brtko (Jozef Kroner) is an amiable carpenter. His nagging wife (Hana Slivková) thinks they should be improving their position, and her fascist brother (František Zvarík) agrees, telling Tono to join forces with the occupying Nazi forces. To appease his wife and brother-in-law, Tono takes a job as the "Aryan comptroller" for a Jewish-owned button shop on Main Street. To his dismay, he finds that the owner, Rosalie Lautmann (Ida Kaminská), an elderly deaf woman, has gone bankrupt. Tono's dreams of prestige are quickly dashed, and his frustration is compounded by Rosalie's deafness. Communicating with her is virtually impossible, and Rosalie remains in a dream world, unaware of the gravity of the war. Her Jewish friends bribe Tono into posing as her new assistant instead of her boss. Tono agrees, and slowly the two build a close friendship. Rosalie treats the carpenter with the kindness and respect he does not find in his own family. But troubles arise when an edict is passed demanding the deportation of the town's Jewish citizens. As the names are called off in the town square, Rosalie's name is mysteriously absent. Tono faces a moral dilemma. He must decide whether to protect his friend and risk arrest for harboring a Jew or to obey the law and report her. As the Jews gather for deportation in front of the shop, Tono panics. He tries to force Rosalie to join them, but she realizes what is happening and tries to escape. In a moment of panic, Tono shoves his friend into a cupboard and locks it, waiting until the troops have passed. When he opens the cupboard to release her, he finds that Rosalie has died. Tono takes his own life.

The Shop on Main Street was first shown in the United States at the New York Film Festival, where it received a standing ovation. It won an Oscar for Best Foreign Film in 1965. The film is based on the novel by Ladislav Grosman, *The Shop on Main Street*, trans. Iris Urwin (Garden City, NY: Doubleday, 1970).

1. Did Tono do the right thing? Should he have obeyed the law and reported Rosalie Lautmann to the authorities? Defend your response.
2. Compare and contrast what a Kantian, a utilitarian, and a virtue theorist would do in Tono's situation. Which response do you prefer? Why? How do their responses compare to your own?
3. Carol Gilligan presented us with a male ethic of duty and rights and contrasted it with a female ethic of care and responsibility. Is Tono's situation one in which an ethic of abstract principles comes into conflict with an ethic of care and compassion? Is the conflict presented as "genderless" in this movie? If so, could it be used as a criticism of Gilligan's position?
4. Why do you think Tono killed himself? Out of guilt? Out of frustration with issues of morality? What, if anything, do we learn about morality through his suicide?
5. How do we balance our desire for care and compassion for others in immediate peril with our obligations as citizens of a state? Can you think of other stories or films that raise similar situations as those of Tono? How do they compare?

 WALL STREET

(USA, 1987) 2 hours
Directed by Oliver Stone

Film summary: Gordon Gekko (Michael Douglas) is a Wall Street businessman with great wealth and power. He spends his days bending and breaking the law in order to increase his holdings. Gekko manipulates small investors in order to make a financial profit. He thinks little about taking companies away from their stockholders through ruthless and sometimes illegal means. Much of the film's action revolves around his relationship with a young broker, Bud Fox (Charlie Sheen), who is hungry for success. In order to impress Gekko, Fox passes along some insider information from his father, which puts his father's company in jeopardy. Eventually, Fox comes to believe that Gekko's trading techniques are both immoral and illegal.

While Oliver Stone clearly believes that Gekko's actions and much of the capitalist trading mentality of Wall Street are immoral, Gekko justifies his actions in the film with statements like "Nobody gets hurt," "Everybody's doing it," "Who knows except us?" and "There's something in this deal for everybody." Gekko's credo is "Greed is good," and he builds an entire value system around it. Stone's target in *Wall Street* is less the breaking of laws by Wall Street insiders than a value system based on greed. Michael Douglas won an Oscar for his portrayal of Gordon Gekko.

1. Gekko morally justifies his actions in the film by saying things like "Nobody gets hurt," "Everybody's doing it," "Who knows except us?" and "There's something in this deal for everybody." Are any of these good reasons to do what he does?
2. What's wrong with using "Nobody will know except us" as a justification for immoral activities? Explain.
3. Can greed ever be good, as Gordon Gekko claims? Can it be the center of a theory of morality? Or is greed always immoral? Defend your view.
4. Could a utilitarian justify Gekko's actions? A Kantian? Explain your view.
5. Is *Wall Street* a criticism or a defense of egoism? Defend your view.

"THE ONES WHO WALK AWAY FROM OMELAS"

By Ursula K. Le Guin

Story summary: Omelas, a mythical realm whose inhabitants bask in their seemingly perfect lives, has a dark secret lurking beneath its utopian facade. The happiness of the inhabitants of Omelas relies upon the misery and anguish of a single child. The narrator explains: "They all understand that their happiness, the beauty of their city, the tenderness of their friendships, the health of their children, the wisdom of their scholars, the skill of their makers, even the abundance of their harvest and the kindly weathers of their skies, depend wholly on this child's abominable misery." While many citizens of Omelas visit the "being" in its small, damp cellar and appreciate its suffering, others are horrified that a single person must suffer—even if this suffering is for the sake of an entire civilization. Moreover, those who sympathize with the child realize that, even if it were allowed to leave the cellar, any attempts to reintroduce it into society would be unsuccessful. The narrator elaborates: "Even if the child were released, it would not get much good out of its freedom: a little vague pleasure of warmth and food, no doubt, but little more. It is too degraded and imbecile to know any real joy." Nevertheless, there are a few citizens who remain deeply disturbed by the misery that this individual must suffer. Those people choose to leave the city and never return. The narrator explains: "At times, one of the adolescent girls or boys who go to see the child does not go home to weep or rage, does not, in fact, go home at all. Sometimes also a man or woman much older falls silent for a day or two, and then leaves home. . . . The place they go towards is a place even less imaginable to most of us than the city of happiness. . . . But they seem to know where they are going, the ones who walk away from Omelas."

Ursula Le Guin (b. 1929) is best known for her science fiction and fantasy tales, including *The Left Hand of Darkness* (1969). Le Guin has also contributed important essays on fantasy fiction, feminist issues, and other topics, some of which can be found in *Dancing at the Edge of the World* (1989). "The Ones Who Walk Away from Omelas" was published in 1976.

1. If you were a citizen of Omelas, would you stay or walk? Explain and justify your decision.
2. Can the suffering of one child to ensure the happiness of an entire society be morally justified by a utilitarian? A Kantian? If so, how? If not, why not?
3. Does it make a moral difference that the child lives in the society that benefits from its suffering? What if the child lived halfway around the world? Do you think that the same number of people would walk away from Omelas? Would you feel the same about the conditions on which this society's happiness is founded if the child lived halfway around the world? Explain.
4. Why do you think that Le Guin adds the following to her story? "Even if the child were released, it would not get much good out of its freedom: a little vague pleasure of warmth and food, no doubt, but little more. It is too degraded and imbecile to know any real joy." How does this affect the way you feel about Omelas? Explain.
5. Le Guin tells us that the children of Omelas are fully aware of the suffering of the child, but she makes a point of saying that those who stay in Omelas do not feel guilty. Is it possible to constantly feel guilty about the misery of others? Explain and give examples.

 BILLY BUDD

By Herman Melville

Novel summary: Billy Budd is a sailor on the British warship *Bellipotent.* The year is 1797, and there have been a number of mutinies as of late. Billy is a gentle, trusting soul and is well liked by his crewmates, but his superior officer, John Claggart, resents Billy's popularity. Claggart maliciously makes the false accusation that Billy is plotting a mutiny. Billy is shocked by Claggart's charges and is unable to speak out against his lies. The sailor strikes

Claggart and accidentally kills him. Although the crew sympathizes with Billy, he must go on trial. At his trial, Billy says of Claggart, "I never bore malice against the master-at-arms. I am sorry that he is dead. I did not mean to kill him. Could I have used my tongue I would not have struck him. But he foully lied to my face and in presence of my captain, and I had to say something, and I could only say it with a blow, God help me!" Captain Vere responds to Billy by saying, "I believe you, my man," but still testifies against Billy before the tribunal. This comes as a surprise to everyone as Captain Vere is widely regarded as a good man. While Captain Vere acknowledges that Claggart's accusation was malicious, he reminds the tribunal that they must judge Billy's deeds, not his motives. "To steady us a bit," says Captain Vere, "let us recur to the facts.—In wartime at sea a man-of-war's man strikes his superior in grade, and the blow kills. Apart from its effect the blow itself is, according to the Articles of War, a capital crime." The punishment for striking a senior officer according to military law is death by hanging. Captain Vere points out that the tribunal has a duty to obey the law just as sailors like Billy must obey their superiors and not take the law into their own hands. The recent mutinies only reinforce the need to abide by the letter of the law. To the suggestion that Billy be convicted of striking a superior officer but that the penalty be lessened, Captain Vere asks everyone to consider the consequences of such clemency. The ship's company would think that the captain lacked courage. "They would think that we flinch, that we are afraid of them—afraid of practicing a lawful rigor singularly demanded at this juncture, lest it should provoke new troubles." Clemency is not an option. Billy is convicted and hanged.

Herman Melville (1819–1891) is considered one of the great American authors and is best known for his novels about the sea, including his masterpiece, *Moby Dick*. *Billy Budd*, Melville's last work, was first published posthumously in 1924.

1. Captain Vere argues that clemency is not a possibility in this case because of its potentially bad consequences: other sailors will think that military discipline is soft and so be more inclined to commit crimes without the fear of punishment. Do you agree with this argument? Did Captain Vere do the right thing?
2. While Captain Vere clearly sympathizes with Billy, he says that he must do his duty. What might Jonathan Bennett say about Captain Vere's decision? Do you think that he would agree with the way in which Captain Vere weighs sympathy against duty? How about Carol Gilligan? What might she say about this?
3. Billy only wanted to tell Claggart that he disagreed with him. He could not speak, so he struck Claggart to tell him this. This blow killed Claggart. Should people be held accountable for the unforeseen bad consequences of their actions? Should people be held accountable for the bad consequences of good intentions? How would a utilitarian respond to this? A Kantian?
4. Is military duty different from moral duty? Should military duty always take precedence over moral duty? Defend your view.
5. How might Captain Vere's actions be regarded as a criticism of Kantian moral theory? How might they be regarded as a defense of Kantianism? Which do you think they reveal?
6. Does it seem to you that Captain Vere is doing his duty as a military officer for no other end than duty's sake, or because of the potential bad consequences of not doing his duty (e.g., a weakening of the power of military law)? Defend your view.

SUPPLEMENTARY READINGS

MORALITY: ITS NATURE AND JUSTIFICATION

Baier, Kurt. *The Moral Point of View.* Ithaca, NY: Cornell University Press, 1958.
Brandt, Richard. *A Theory of the Good and the Right.* Oxford: Oxford University Press, 1979.
Frankena, William. *Ethics.* Englewood Cliffs, NJ: Prentice-Hall, 1973.

Gert, Bernard. *Morality*. New York: Oxford University Press, 1998.

Harman, Gilbert. *The Nature of Morality: An Introduction to Ethics*. New York: Oxford University Press, 1977.

Hudson, W. D. *A Century of Moral Philosophy*. New York: St. Martin's Press, 1983.

MacIntyre, Alasdair. *Whose Justice? Which Rationality?* Notre Dame, IN: University of Notre Dame Press, 1988.

Nagel, Thomas. *The View from Nowhere*. New York: Oxford University Press, 1986.

Rachels, James. *The Elements of Moral Philosophy*, 3rd ed. New York: Random House, 1998.

Stace, W. T. *The Concept of Morals*. New York: Macmillan, 1937.

Wallace, Gerald, and A. D. M. Walker, eds. *The Definition of Morality*. London: Methuen, 1970.

Warnock, Mary. *Ethics Since 1900*. London: Oxford University Press, 1966.

Williams, Bernard. *Ethics and the Limits of Philosophy*. Cambridge, MA: Harvard University Press, 1985.

CONSEQUENTIALISM

Brandt, Richard. *Morality, Utilitarianism, and Rights*. New York: Cambridge University Press, 1992.

Hare, R. M. *Moral Thinking: Its Levels, Method and Point*. New York: Oxford University Press, 1981.

Lyons, David. *The Forms and Limits of Utilitarianism*. Oxford: Clarendon Press, 1965.

Miller, Harlan B., and William Williams, eds. *The Limits of Utilitarianism*. Minneapolis: University of Minnesota Press, 1982.

Quinton, Anthony. *Utilitarian Ethics*. New York: St. Martin's Press, 1973.

Scheffler, Samuel, ed. *Consequentialism and Its Critics*. Oxford: Oxford University Press, 1988.

———. *The Rejection of Consequentialism*. Oxford: Clarendon Press, 1982.

Sen, Amartya, and Bernard Williams, eds. *Utilitarianism and Beyond*. Cambridge: Cambridge University Press, 1982.

Smart, J. J. C., and Bernard Williams. *Utilitarianism: For and Against*. Cambridge: Cambridge University Press, 1973.

DEONTOLOGY

Acton, Harold. *Kant's Moral Philosophy*. New York: St. Martin's Press, 1970.

Baron, Marcia. *Kantian Ethics, Almost Without Apology*. Ithaca, NY: Cornell University Press, 1995.

Blum, Lawrence A. "Kant's and Hegel's Moral Rationalism: A Feminist Perspective." *Canadian Journal of Philosophy*, 12, 2 (1982): 287–302.

O'Neill, Onora. *Acting on Principle: An Essay on Kantian Ethics*. New York: Columbia University Press, 1975.

Paton, H. J. *The Categorical Imperative*. London: Hutchinson, 1947.

Schneewind, J. B. "Autonomy, Obligation and Virtue: An Overview of Kant's Moral Philosophy." Pp. 309–341 in *The Cambridge Companion to Kant*, ed. Paul Guyer. Cambridge: Cambridge University Press, 1992.

EGOISM

Butler, Joseph. *Five Sermons*. Ed. Stephen Darwall. Indianapolis: Hackett, 1983.

Machan, Tibor. "Recent Work on Ethical Egoism." *American Philosophical Quarterly*, 16 (1979): 1–15.

Milo, Ronald, ed. *Egoism and Altruism*. Belmont, CA: Wadsworth, 1973.

Nozick, Robert. "On the Randian Argument." *Personalist*, 52 (1971): 282–304.

Rand, Ayn. *The Virtue of Selfishness*. New York: New American Library, 1964.

Regis, Edward, Jr. "What Is Ethical Egoism?" *Ethics*, 91 (1980): 50–62.

VIRTUE ETHICS

Blum, Lawrence A. *Friendship, Altruism and Morality*. New York: Routledge & Kegan Paul, 1980.

Broadie, Sarah. *Ethics with Aristotle*. Oxford: Oxford University Press, 1991.

Dent, N. J. H. *The Moral Psychology of the Virtues*. Cambridge: Cambridge University Press, 1984.

Foot, Philippa. *Vices and Virtues*. Berkeley: University of California Press, 1978.

French, Peter, et al. *Ethical Theory, Character and Virtue*. Midwest Studies in Philosophy, vol. 13. Notre Dame, IN: University of Notre Dame Press, 1988.

Geach, P. T. *The Virtues*. Cambridge: Cambridge University Press, 1977.

Kekes, John. *Moral Tradition and Individuality*. Princeton, NJ: Princeton University Press, 1989.

Kruschwitz, Robert, and Robert Roberts. *The Virtues*. Belmont, CA: Wadsworth, 1987.

MacIntyre, Alasdair. *After Virtue*, 2nd ed. Notre Dame, IN: University of Notre Dame Press, 1984.

Mayo, Bernard. *Ethics and the Moral Life*. New York: Macmillan, 1958.

Murdoch, Iris. *The Sovereignty of Good*. New York: Schocken Books, 1971.

Rorty, Amelie. *Essays on Aristotle's Ethics*. Berkeley: University of California Press, 1980.

Sherman, Nancy. *The Fabric of Character: Aristotle's Theory of Virtue*. Oxford: Clarendon Press, 1985.

Wallace, James. *Virtues and Vices*. Ithaca, NY: Cornell University Press, 1978.

RELIGION AND MORALITY

Helm, Paul, ed. *Divine Commands and Morality*. Oxford: Oxford University Press, 1979.

Kant, Immanuel. *Religion Within the Limits of Reason Alone*, trans. T. M. Greene and H. H. Hudson. New York: Harper & Row, 1960.

Kierkegaard, Søren. *Fear and Trembling*, trans. Howard Hong and Edna Hong. Princeton, NJ: Princeton University Press, 1983.

Mitchell, Basil. *Morality: Religious and Secular*. Oxford: Oxford University Press, 1980.

Nielsen, Kai. *Ethics Without God*, rev. ed. Buffalo: Prometheus Books, 1990.

Outka, Gene, and J. P. Reeder, eds. *Religion and Morality: A Collection of Essays*. New York: Anchor Books, 1973.

FEMINISM AND MORALITY

Baier, Annette. "What Do Women Want in a Moral Theory?" *Noûs* (1985): 53–63.

Bar On, Bat-Ami, and Ann Ferguson, eds. *Daring to Be Good: Essays in Feminist Ethico-Politics*. New York: Routledge, 1998.

Card, Claudia. *Feminist Ethics*. Lawrence: University of Kansas Press, 1991.

Code, Loraine; Sheila Mullet; and Christine Overall, eds. *Feminist Perspectives: Philosophical Essays on Method and Morals*. Toronto: University of Toronto Press, 1988.

Gilligan, Carol. *In a Different Voice: Psychological Theory and Women's Development*. Cambridge, MA: Harvard University Press, 1982.

Held, Virginia. *Feminist Morality*. Chicago: University of Chicago Press, 1993.

Kittay, Eva Feder, and Diana T. Meyers, eds. *Women and Moral Theory*. Totowa, NJ: Littlefield, Adams, 1987.

Noddings, Nel. *Caring: A Feminine Approach to Ethics and Moral Education*. Berkeley: University of California Press, 1984.

Okin, Susan. *Justice, Gender and the Family*. New York: Basic Books, 1989.

Tong, Rosemarie. *Feminist Thought*, 2nd ed. Boulder, CO: Westview Press, 1998.

Young, Iris. *Justice and the Politics of Difference*. Princeton, NJ: Princeton University Press, 1990.

2

Relativism and Human Rights

Every day millions of people are denied what many consider to be their human rights. Some are imprisoned without being charged with a crime. Others are charged but are not given fair trials. Many are tortured or detained because of their political beliefs. Leaders of religious groups are murdered and their followers persecuted. Women are raped in acts of war. Children are forced to work in dangerous conditions for long hours at low wages. Ethnic groups are driven from their homes and countries, and some members are executed. And while the news media may report on selected human rights violations in places such as China, Burma, Tibet, and the former Yugoslavia, we can be sure that these are but a small percentage of the human rights atrocities committed worldwide.

Some people believe that all human beings, regardless of their racial/ethnic, sexual, economic, and cultural backgrounds, are guaranteed certain freedoms or rights. These *human rights* are *natural rights,* that is, rights with which all of us are born. The seventeenth-century British philosopher Thomas Hobbes, for example, said that every person has a right to life and that no society can arbitrarily abridge that right. John Locke, another seventeenth-century British philosopher, said that all humans have the right to life, property, and liberty. And Thomas Jefferson said in the Declaration of Independence that all people have the right to life, liberty, and the pursuit of happiness. In contrast, the eighteenth-century French philosopher Jean-Jacques Rousseau said that people give up their natural right to act impulsively and instinctively when they become members of the state and receive mere *civil rights* in return. The United Nations Declaration of Human Rights, adopted by the UN General Assembly in December 1948, is the central document in modern human rights policy.

Human rights, for many, belong to us by virtue of the fact that we are human beings. Some human rights theorists argue that no one and nothing have the right to interfere with the exercise of our natural rights. This includes governments and other sociocultural institutions. People have the right to protect their human rights, and governments have the right to protect individuals' human rights as well. Conversely, no individual and no government have the right to interfere with the human rights of others. In the United States, for example, the Bill of Rights guarantees our human rights, and the legal system enforces and sets the limits on human rights in order to resolve conflicts.

Many people believe that certain general *moral principles* cross racial/ethnic, sexual, economic, and cultural lines. These moral principles are absolute; that is, they hold for all people at all times and in all situations. Incest and slavery are, for the *moral absolutist,* as morally wrong today as they were 2500 years ago in ancient Greece. Furthermore, the moral absolutist contends that incest and slavery are wrong under any and all conditions. It is irrelevant, for example, that slavery was part of the American social, economic, and political condition prior to the mid-nineteenth century. Slavery is *always* morally wrong according to the moral absolutist.

The *moral relativist,* in contrast, contends that there are no absolute moral principles. What is morally the right or wrong thing to do depends on the time and place in which people live. Different societies, different people, and different historical periods can, and many times do, result in different moral principles according to the moral relativist. While moral relativism might sound similar to utilitarianism, it is fundamentally different.

Utilitarians believe that what will maximize happiness may differ from context to context, but they still contend that the principle of greatest utility should be the criterion in all moral matters. Even if moral relativists agree with utilitarians that what will maximize happiness may differ from context to context, they disagree with utilitarians that the principle of greatest utility should be applied in all situations. Moral relativists reject the utilitarian position that the principle of greatest utility is an absolute moral principle.

With regard to slavery, the moral relativist would argue that it can sometimes be morally right and other times be morally wrong. It all depends on the time and place in which people live. If people morally justify slavery, then it is morally right, says the moral relativist, regardless of the moral principle or principles used to justify it. The same holds for the opposite position: if people contend that slavery is morally unjustified, then it is morally wrong, says the moral relativist, regardless of the moral principle or principles used to show that slavery is morally unjustified. This leads many moral relativists to the conclusion that slavery in many parts of mid-nineteenth-century America was morally right because people in these parts of the country morally justified it, whereas in the twenty-first century it would be wrong because most people find it to be morally unjustifiable. There is disagreement as to whether relative moral principles should override human rights or whether human rights should override relative moral principles.

Others argue that human rights and moral principles depend on the time and place in which people live and that universal human rights are not possible. Furthermore, many contend that the dominant discourses on universal rights are founded upon Western notions of rights to the exclusion of non-Western notions. Others charge that the dominant discourse on universal rights excludes the interests of women and the poor. There have been many calls for a transformation of the concept of universal human rights, as well as criticism of Westerners for imposing their own concept of universal human rights on the rest of humanity.

Moral relativists have a variety of ways of defending their positions. The *cultural moral relativist* strategy is one of the more common ones. Cultural moral relativists argue, based on the belief that different societies or cultures have different moral principles, that there are no absolute moral principles. But others counter that, even if different societies or cultures do have different moral principles, it does not necessarily follow that there is no absolute moral truth.

According to one variation of the cultural moral relativist argument, if moral absolutism were true, then absolute moral principles would be familiar to everyone. However, they are not, and what people do know are their cultural or societal moral principles. Therefore, moral principles are not absolute. Moral absolutists disagree with this line of reasoning, arguing that absolute moral principles are available to everyone, regardless of place and time. According to another version of cultural moral relativism, moral principles are comprehensible only from within a culture or society. Consequently, those who are not a part of the culture *cannot* understand the moral principles of the culture. Furthermore, people should not criticize that which they do not understand—in this case, moral principles of other cultures, even if they go against what some regard as universal human rights. Proponents of this version of cultural relativism maintains that it is not fair to judge the moral beliefs of others as wrong if they simply accept and follow their societal or cultural moral principles. Critics of this version maintain that its inability to call any other culture's moral principles inferior is a major weakness. Also, not only is it impossible to criticize another culture on this view, it is also impossible to criticize one's own moral position.

In addition, cultural relativism is often presented as the belief that each person should live in accordance with the moral principles of his or her society or culture but that each person should also *respect* the moral principles of other cultures. For example, proponents of *cultural diversity* argue that people should respect the moral principles of other cultures even if they come into conflict with their own beliefs. They show respect for other cultures and societies by presenting their own moral principles as no better, and no worse, than any others. Also, proponents of cultural diversity believe that the fairness and legitimacy of an account of morality is directly proportional to the number of alternate moral principles that one takes into consideration in one's account of morality: the greater the diversity of moral principles accounted for, the greater the fairness and legitimacy of the account of morality.

The difficulties with this form of cultural relativism are well known. Some argue that it is impossible to respect another culture's moral principles if they conflict with one's own moral principles. For example, it is impossible to respect a culture that allows members of its population to be executed by the government for their political or religious beliefs. Others say that cultures often have sets of conflicting moral principles, and it is unclear which set one should respect. Still others charge that societies and cultures are not fixed entities but are continuously in flux, thereby making it difficult to locate with any precision the moral principles of the culture.

Yet another version of cultural relativism focuses on *tolerance* rather than respect and understanding. People should live in accordance with the moral principles of their society or culture only insofar as the moral principles of their culture are tolerant of the moral principles of other cultures. Some add as well that people should respect the moral principles of other cultures only insofar as members of that culture are tolerant of the moral principles of still other cultures. The weakness of this argument is that tolerance itself becomes an absolute moral value. Therefore, we have a version of cultural relativism in which all moral values are relative except tolerance. The idea of tolerance is also at the center of a version of moral relativism that advocates tolerance of the moral principles of each *person* in the world independently of her or his culture. Again, the difficulty with this view is that it makes tolerance into an absolute moral principle, one that may be difficult to follow. For example, if one person is beating another person up, it may be difficult for us to tolerate this action. Our moral principles may lead us to assist the injured party.

In addition to the many versions of cultural moral relativism, there are also versions of relativism in ethics that locate the source of morality in personal opinion and emotional response. *Ethical subjectivism* is the view that moral judgments are simply assertions of opinion on the part of the person making the moral judgment. *Emotivism* is the view that moral judgments express the emotional or affective state of the person making the moral judgment. Accordingly, for both emotivists and subjectivists, no two people mean the same thing in making the same moral judgment. Furthermore, according to most emotivists and subjectivists, moral judgments are neither statements of truth nor statements of falsehood.

The nature of human rights itself is a controversial topic for both moral absolutists and moral relativists. On the one hand, if we assume a form of relativism, it is entirely possible that the very idea of universal human rights becomes problematic. Consequently, for the moral relativist, it is difficult to clearly delineate human rights that cross *all* cultural boundaries and that do not interfere with, for example, indigenous cultural practices. For example, some argue that women's right to control their bodies in reproduction is a universal human right, and others contend that it is not because it conflicts with specific religious or cultural practices. On the other hand, if we assume a form of moral absolutism and develop a notion of human rights on the basis of moral absolutism, then we risk postulating universal human rights that are at odds with alternative perspectives on the nature of morality. For example, there is no reason to believe that a notion of human rights based on a Buddhist conception of morality would be the same as one based on a Western conception.

There has been an increasing demand in our society for the inclusion of the perspectives of women, minorities, and members of non-Western cultures. Consequently, for many people, *multiculturalism* has come to be a general term embracing these perspectives. Multicultural education gives us the opportunity to explore how and why a resolution of these disagreements over the nature of human rights can and will affect the lives of many people both in our own society and around the world. In any case, the increased awareness and consideration of human rights issues provides hope that some type of resolution to disagreements concerning human rights is possible.

RUTH BENEDICT

A Defense of Moral Relativism

Ruth Benedict (1887–1948) says that morality is culturally relative. "'Morality' is just another word for socially approved customs. While we prefer to say 'It is morally good' rather than 'It is habitual,'" says Benedict, the two phrases mean the same thing. For Benedict, morality, the habitual, the good, and the normal are all synonymous. Normality is, according to Benedict, defined by our culture. Furthermore, our moral system is not necessarily the inevitable consequence of reason or some rational decision-making process omitting inferior moral systems, but rather the product of mere historical chance. Society shapes our moral beliefs, and most people, Benedict argues, "are plastic to the moulding force of the society into which they are born."

Ruth Benedict, one of the foremost anthropologists of the twentieth century, is the author of *Patterns of Culture* (1934), *General Anthropology* (1938), and *Race and Racism* (1942).

Modern social anthropology has become more and more a study of the varieties and common elements of cultural environment and the consequences of these in human behavior. For such a study of diverse social orders, primitive peoples fortunately provide a laboratory not yet entirely vitiated by the spread of a standardized worldwide civilization. Dyaks and Hopis, Fijians and Yakuts are significant for psychological and sociological study because only among these simpler peoples has there been sufficient isolation to give opportunity for the development of localized social forms. In the higher cultures the standardization of custom and belief over a couple of continents has given a false sense of the inevitability of the particular forms that have gained currency, and we need to turn to a wider survey in order to check the conclusions we hastily base upon this near-universality of familiar customs. Most of the simpler cultures did not gain the wide currency of the one which, out of our experience, we identify with human nature, but this was for various historical reasons, and certainly not for any that gives us as its carriers a monopoly of social good or of social sanity. Modern civilization, from this point of view, becomes not a necessary pinnacle of human achievement but one entry in a long series of possible adjustments.

These adjustments, whether they are in mannerisms like the ways of showing anger, or joy, or grief in any society, or in major human drives like those of sex, prove to be far more variable than experience in any one culture would suggest. In certain fields, such as that of religion or of formal marriage arrangements, these wide limits of variability are well known and can be fairly described. In others it is not yet possible to give a generalized account, but that does not absolve us of the task of indicating the significance of the work that has been done and of the problems that have arisen.

One of these problems relates to the customary modern normal-abnormal categories and our conclusions regarding them. In how far are such categories culturally determined, or in how far can we with assurance regard them as absolute? In how far can we regard inability to function socially as diagnostic of abnormality, or in how far is it necessary to regard this as a function of the culture? . . .

The most spectacular illustrations of the extent to which normality may be culturally defined are those cultures where an abnormality of our culture is the cornerstone of their social structure. It is not possible to do justice to these possibilities in a short discussion. A recent study of an island of northwest Melanesia by Fortune describes a society built upon traits which we regard as beyond the border of paranoia. In this tribe the exogamic groups look upon each other as prime manipulators of black magic, so that one marries

Ruth Benedict, *Journal of General Psychology* 10 (1934): 55–82. Reprinted with permission of the Helen Dwight-Reid Educational Foundation. Published by Heldref Publications, 1319 Eighteenth St., N.W., Washington, D.C. 20036-1802.

always into an enemy group which remains for life one's deadly and unappeasable foes. They look upon a good garden crop as a confession of theft, for everyone is engaged in making magic to induce into his garden the productiveness of his neighbors'; therefore no secrecy in the island is so rigidly insisted upon as the secrecy of a man's harvesting of his yams. Their polite phrase at the acceptance of a gift is, "And if you now poison me, how shall I repay you this present?" Their preoccupation with poisoning is constant; no woman ever leaves her cooking pot for a moment untended. Even the great affinal economic exchanges that are characteristic of this Melanesian culture area are quite altered in Dobu since they are incompatible with this fear and distrust that pervades the culture. . . . They go farther and people the whole world outside their own quarters with such malignant spirits that all-night feasts and ceremonials simply do not occur here. They have even rigorous, religiously enforced customs that forbid the sharing of seed even in one family group. Anyone else's food is deadly poison to you, so that communality of stores is out of the question. For some months before harvest the whole society is on the verge of starvation, but if one falls to the temptation and eats up one's seed yams, one is an outcast and a beachcomber for life. There is no coming back. It involves, as a matter of course, divorce and the breaking of all social ties.

Now in this society where no one may work with another and no one may share with another, Fortune describes the individual who was regarded by all his fellows as crazy. He was not one of those who periodically ran amok and, beside himself and frothing at the mouth, fell with a knife upon anyone he could reach. Such behavior they did not regard as putting anyone outside the pale. They did not even put the individuals who were known to be liable to these attacks under any kind of control. They merely fled when they saw the attack coming on and kept out of the way. "He would be all right tomorrow." But there was one man of sunny, kindly disposition who liked work and liked to be helpful. The compulsion was too strong for him to repress it in favor of the opposite tendencies of his culture. Men and women never spoke of him without laughing; he was silly and simple and definitely crazy. Nevertheless, to the ethnologist used to a culture that has, in Christianity, made his type the model of all virtue, he seemed a pleasant fellow.

An even more extreme example, because it is of a culture that has built itself upon a more complex abnormality, is that of the North Pacific Coast of North America. The civilization of the Kwakiutl, at the time when it was first recorded in the last decades of the nineteenth century, was one of the most vigorous in North America. It was built up on an ample economic supply of goods, the fish which furnished their food staple being practically inexhaustible and obtainable with comparatively small labor, and the wood which furnished the material for their houses, their furnishings, and their arts being, with however much labor, always procurable. They lived in coastal villages that compared favorably in size with those of any other American Indians, and they kept up constant communication by means of sea-going dug-out canoes.

It was one of the most vigorous and zestful of the aboriginal cultures of North America, with complex crafts and ceremonials, and elaborate and striking arts. It certainly had none of the earmarks of a sick civilization. The tribes of the Northwest Coast had wealth, and exactly in our terms. That is, they had not only a surplus of economic goods, but they made a game of manipulation of wealth. It was by no means a mere direct transcription of economic needs and the filling of those needs. It involved the idea of capital, of interest, and of conspicuous waste. It was a game with all the binding rules of a game, and a person entered it as a child. His father distributed wealth for him, according to his ability, at a small feast or potlatch, and each gift the receiver was obliged to accept and to return after short interval with interest that ran to about 100 percent a year. By the time the child was grown, therefore, he was well launched, a larger potlatch had been given for him on various occasions of exploit or initiation, and he had wealth either out at usury or in his own possession. Nothing in the civilization could be enjoyed without validating it by the distribution of this wealth. Everything that was valued, names and songs as well as material objects, were passed down in family lines, but they were always publicly assumed with accompanying sufficient distributions of property. It was the game of validating and exercising all the privileges one could accumulate from one's various forebears, or by gift, or by marriage, that made the chief interest of the culture. Everyone in his degree took part in it, but many, of course, mainly as spectators. In its highest form it was played out between rival chiefs representing not only themselves and their family lines but their communities, and the object of the contest was to glorify oneself and to humiliate one's opponent. On this level of greatness the property involved was no longer represented by blankets, so many thousand of them to a potlatch, but by higher units of value. These higher units were like our bank notes. They were incised copper tablets, each of them named, and having a value that depended upon their illustrious history. This was as high as ten thousand blankets, and to possess one of them, still more to enhance its value at a great potlatch, was one of the greatest glories within the compass of the chiefs of the Northwest Coast. . . .

Every contingency of life was dealt with in . . . two traditional ways. To them the two were equivalent. Whether one fought with weapons or "fought with property," as they say, the same idea was at the bottom of both. In the olden times, they say, they fought with spears, but now they fight with property. One overcomes one's opponents in equivalent fashion in both, matching forces and seeing that one comes out ahead, and one can thumb one's nose at the vanquished rather more satisfactorily at a potlatch than on a battlefield. Every occasion in life was noticed, not in its own terms, as a stage in the sex life of the individual or as a climax of joy or grief, but as furthering this drama of consolidating one's own prestige and bringing shame to one's guests. Whether it was the occasion of the birth of a child, or a daughter's adolescence, or of the marriage of one's son, they were all equivalent raw material for the culture to use for this one traditionally selected end. They were all to raise one's own personal status and to entrench oneself by the humiliation of one's fellows. A girl's adolescence among the Nootka was an event for which her father gathered property from the time she was first able to run about. When she was adolescent he would demonstrate his greatness by an unheard-of distribution of these goods, and put down all his rivals. It was not as a fact of the girl's sex life that it figured in their culture, but as the occasion for a major move in the great game of vindicating one's own greatness and humiliating one's associates.

In their behavior at great bereavements this set of the culture comes out most strongly. Among the Kwakiutl it did not matter whether a relative had died in bed of disease, or by the hand of an enemy; in either case death was an affront to be wiped out by the death of another person. The fact that one had been caused to mourn was proof that one had been put upon. A chief's sister and her daughter had gone up to Victoria, and either because they drank bad whiskey or because their boat capsized they never came back. The chief called together his warriors. "Now, I ask you, tribes, who shall wail? Shall I do it or shall another?" The spokesman answered of course, "Not you, Chief. Let some other of the tribes." Immediately they set up the war pole to announce their intention of wiping out the injury, and gathered a war party. They set out, and found seven men and two children asleep and killed them. "Then they felt good when they arrived at Sebaa in the evening."

The point which is of interest to us is that in our society those who on that occasion would feel good, when they arrived at Sebaa that evening would be the definitely abnormal. There would be some, even in our society, but it is not a recognized and approved mood under the circumstances. On the Northwest Coast those are favored and fortunate to whom that mood under those circumstances is congenial, and those to whom it is repugnant are unlucky. This latter minority can register in their own culture only by doing violence to their congenial responses and acquiring others that are difficult for them. The person, for instance, who, like a Plains Indian whose wife has been taken from him, is too proud to fight, can deal with the Northwest Coast civilization only by ignoring its strongest bents. If he cannot achieve it, he is the deviant in that culture, their instance of abnormality.

This head-hunting that takes place on the Northwest Coast after a death is no matter of blood revenge or of organized vengeance. There is no effort to tie up the subsequent killing with any responsibility on the part of the victim for the death of the person who is being mourned. A chief whose son has died goes visiting wherever his fancy dictates, and he says to his host, "My prince has died today, and you go with him." Then he kills him. In this, according to their interpretation, he acts nobly because he has not been downed. He has thrust back in return. The whole procedure is meaningless without the fundamental paranoid reading of bereavement. Death, like all the other untoward accidents of existence, confounds man's pride and can only be handled in the category of insults. . . .

These illustrations, which it has been possible to indicate only in the briefest manner, force upon us the fact that normality is culturally defined. An adult shaped to the drives and standards of either of these cultures, if he were transported into our civilization, would fall into our categories of abnormality. He would be faced with the psychic dilemmas of the socially unavailable. In his own culture, however, he is the pillar of society, the end result of socially inculcated mores, and the problem of personal instability in his case simply does not arise.

No one civilization can possibly utilize in its mores the whole potential range of human behavior. Just as there are great numbers of possible phonetic articulations, and the possibility of language depends on a selection and standardization of a few of these in order that speech communication may be possible at all, so the possibility of organized behavior of every sort, from the fashions of local dress and houses to the dicta of a people's ethics and religion, depends upon a similar selection among the possible behavior traits. In the field of recognized economic obligations or sex tabus this selection is as non-rational and subconscious a process as it is in the field of phonetics. It is a process which goes on in the group for long periods of time and is historically conditioned by innumerable accidents of isolation or of contact of peoples. In any comprehensive study of psychology, the selection that different cultures have made in the course of history within the great circumference of potential behavior is of great significance.

Every society, beginning with some slight inclination in one direction or another, carries its preference farther and farther, integrating itself more and more completely upon its chosen basis, and discarding those types of behavior that are uncongenial. Most of those organizations of personality that seem to us most incontrovertibly abnormal have been used by different civilizations in the very foundations of their institutional life. Conversely the most valued traits of our normal individuals have been looked on in differently organized cultures as aberrant. Normality, in short, within a very wide range, is culturally defined. It is primarily a term for the socially elaborated segment of human behavior in any culture; and abnormality, a term for the segment that that particular civilization does not use. The very eyes with which we see the problem are conditioned by the long traditional habits of our own society.

It is a point that has been made more often in relation to ethics than in relation to psychiatry. We do not any longer make the mistake of deriving the morality of our own locality and decade directly from the inevitable constitution of human nature. We do not elevate it to the dignity of the first principle. We recognize that morality differs in every society and is a convenient term for socially approved habits. Mankind has always preferred to say, "It is a morally good," rather than "It is habitual," and the fact of this preference is matter enough for a critical science of ethics. But historically the two phrases are synonymous.

The concept of the normal is properly a variant of the concept of the good. It is that which society has approved. A normal action is one which falls well within the limits of expected behavior for a particular society. Its variability among different peoples is essentially a function of the variability of the behavior patterns that different societies have created for themselves, and

can never be wholly divorced from a consideration of culturally institutionalized types of behavior.

Each culture is a more or less elaborate working-out of the potentialities of the segment it has chosen. In so far as a civilization is well integrated and consistent within itself, it will tend to carry farther and farther, according to its nature, its initial impulse toward a particular type of action, and from the point of view of any other culture those elaborations will include more and more extreme and aberrant traits.

Each of these traits, in proportion as it reinforces the chosen behavior patterns of that culture, is for that culture normal. Those individuals to whom it is congenial either congenitally, or as the result of childhood sets, are accorded prestige in that culture, and are not visited with the social contempt or disapproval which their traits would call down upon them in a society that was differently organized. On the other hand, those individuals whose characteristics are not congenial to the selected type of human behavior in that community are the deviants, no matter how valued their personality traits may be in a contrasted civilization. . . .

The problem of understanding abnormal human behavior in any absolute sense independent of cultural factors is still far in the future. The categories of borderline behavior which we derive from the study of the neuroses and psychoses of our civilization are categories of prevailing local types of instability. They give much information about the stresses and strains of Western civilization, but no final picture of inevitable human behavior. Any conclusions about such behavior must await the collection by trained observers of psychiatric data from other cultures. Since no adequate work of the kind has been done at the present time, it is impossible to say what core of definition of abnormality may be found valid from the comparative material. It is as it is in ethics; all our local conventions of moral behavior and of immoral are without absolute validity, and yet it is quite possible that a modicum of what is considered right and what wrong could be disentangled that is shared by the whole human race. When data are available in psychiatry, this minimum definition of abnormal human tendencies will be probably quite unlike our culturally conditioned, highly elaborated psychoses such as those that are described, for instance, under the terms of schizophrenia and manic-depressive.

DISCUSSION QUESTIONS

1. Benedict argues against moral progress. What is her argument? Do you agree with her? Why or why not?

2. Do you agree with Benedict that "morality is just another word for socially approved customs"? Explain.

3. Many people believe that there are basic human rights that cross societal barriers. What would Benedict say about such human rights? Do you agree with her response? Defend your view.

4. It is a fact of the world that there are many different cultures with many different and sometimes conflicting moral beliefs. For example, some cultures have praised homosexual love whereas others have considered it immoral. Does the fact of cultural diversity give us suffient grounds for endorsing moral relativism? Present your case.

5. How might we resolve moral dilemmas in Benedict's model of morality? For example, some say that the death penalty is moral, and others say that it is immoral. How would Benedict resolve this moral dilemma? What do you think about this way of resolving moral dilemmas? How similar to or different from other ways of resolving moral dilemmas, such as utilitarianism or Kantianism, is it?

W. T. STACE

A Critique of Moral Relativism

W. T. Stace argues against moral relativism and defends moral absolutism. Stace finds moral relativism to be incoherent and unacceptable. First, moral relativism makes it impossible to say whether the moral standards of one culture are better or worse than those of another culture. Second, it is unclear precisely what counts as a "culture" for moral relativists. Moral absolutists say that the same moral standards apply to all people regardless of their culture. The fact that not everyone has the same moral beliefs is not evidence for moral relativism, says Stace, but rather is evidence of moral ignorance. While it is difficult to determine the grounds for moral absolutism, Stace believes that philosophers will ultimately provide a basis for a universal morality.

Walter Terence Stace (1886–1967) was a philosophy professor at Princeton University and is the author of many books including *The Meaning of Beauty* (1929), *The Concept of Morals* (1937), *The Destiny of Western Man* (1942), *Mysticism and Philosophy* (1960), and *Religion and the Modern Mind* (1960).

I

Any ethical position which denies that there is a single moral standard which is equally applicable to all men at all times may fairly be called a species of ethical relativity. There is not, the relativist asserts, merely one moral law, one code, one standard. There are many moral laws, codes, standards. What morality ordains in one place or age may be quite different from what morality ordains in another place or age. The moral code of Chinamen is quite different from that of Europeans, that of African savages quite different from both. Any morality, therefore, is relative to the age, the place, and the

Walter T. Stace, *The Concept of Morals*, Macmillan, 1937. Copyright © 1937 by Macmillan Publishing Company, renewed 1965 by Walter T. Stace. Reprinted by permission of Sribner, a Division of Simon & Schuster.

circumstances in which it is found. It is in no sense absolute.

This does not mean merely—as one might at first sight be inclined to suppose—that the very same kind of action which is *thought* right in one country and period may be *thought* wrong in another. This would be a mere platitude, the truth of which everyone would have to admit. Even the absolutist would admit this—would even wish to emphasize it—since he is well aware that different people have different sets of moral ideas, and his whole point is that some of these sets of ideas are false. What the relativist means to assert is, not this platitude, but that the very same kind of action which *is* right in one country and period may *be* wrong in another. And this, far from being a platitude, is a very startling assertion.

It is very important to grasp thoroughly the difference between the two ideas. For there is reason to think that many minds tend to find ethical relativity attractive because they fail to keep them clearly apart. It is so very obvious that moral ideas differ from country to country and from age to age. And it is so very easy, if you are mentally lazy, to suppose that to say this means the same as to say that no universal moral standard exists—or in other words that it implies ethical relativity. We fail to see that the word "standard" is used in two different senses. It is perfectly true that, in one sense, there are many variable moral standards. We speak of judging a man by the standard of his time. And this implies that different times have different standards. And this, of course, is quite true. But when the word "standard" is used in this sense it means simply the set of moral ideas current during the period in question. It means what people *think* right, whether as a matter of fact it *is* right or not. On the other hand, when the absolutist asserts that there exists a single universal moral "standard," he is not using the word in this sense at all. He means by "standard" what *is* right as distinct from what people merely think right. His point is that although what people think right varies in different countries and periods, yet what actually is right is everywhere and always the same. And it follows that when the ethical relativist disputes the position of the absolutist and denies that any universal moral standard exists, he too means by "standard" what actually is right. But it is exceedingly easy, if we are not careful, to slip loosely from using the word in the first sense to using it in the second sense, and to suppose that the variability of moral beliefs is the same thing as the variability of what really is moral. And unless we keep the two senses of the word "standard" distinct,

we are likely to think the creed of ethical relativity much more plausible than it actually is.

The genuine relativist, then, does not merely mean that Chinamen may think right what Frenchmen think wrong. He means that what *is* wrong for the Frenchman may *be* right for the Chinaman. And if one inquires how, in those circumstances, one is to know what actually is right in China or in France, the answer comes quite glibly. What is right in China is the same as what people think right in China; and what is right in France is the same as what people think right in France. So that if you want to know what is moral in any particular country or age, all you have to do is to ascertain what are the moral ideas current in that age or country. Those ideas are, *for that age or country,* right. Thus what is morally right is identified with what is thought to be morally right, and the distinction which we made above between these two is simply denied. To put the same thing in another way, it is denied that there can be or ought to be any distinction between the two senses of the word "standard." There is only one kind of standard of right and wrong, namely, the moral ideas current in any particular age or country.

Moral right *means* what people think morally right. It has no other meaning. What Frenchmen think right is, therefore, right *for Frenchmen.* And evidently one must conclude—though I am not aware that relativists are anxious to draw one's attention to such unsavory but yet absolutely necessary conclusions from their creed—that cannibalism is right for people who believe in it, that human sacrifice is right for those races which practice it, and that burning widows alive was right for Hindus until the British stepped in and compelled the Hindus to behave immorally by allowing their widows to remain alive.

When it is said that, according to the ethical relativist, what is thought right in any social group is right for that group, one must be careful not to misinterpret this. The relativist does not, of course, mean that there actually is an objective moral standard in France and a different objective standard in England, and that French and British opinions respectively give us correct information about these different standards. His point is rather that there are not objectively true moral standards at all. There is no single universal objective standard. Nor are there a variety of local objective standards. All standards are subjective. People's subjective feelings about morality are the only standards which exist.

To sum up: The ethical relativist consistently denies, it would seem, whatever the ethical absolutist asserts. For the absolutist there is a single universal moral standard. For the relativist there is no such standard. There are only local, ephemeral, and variable standards. For the absolutist there are two senses of the word "standard." Standards in the sense of sets of current moral ideas are relative and changeable. But the standard in the sense of what is actually morally right is absolute and unchanging. For the relativist no such distinction can be made. There is only one meaning of the word standard, namely, that which refers to local and variable sets of moral ideas. Or if it is insisted that the word must be allowed two meanings, then the relativist will say that there is at any rate no actual example of a standard in the absolute sense, and that the word as thus used is an empty name to which nothing in reality corresponds; so that the distinction between the two meanings becomes empty and useless. Finally—though this is merely saying the same thing in another way—the absolutist makes a distinction between what actually is right and what is thought right. The relativist rejects this distinction and identifies what is moral with what is thought moral by certain human beings or groups of human beings. . . .

II

I shall now proceed to consider, first, the main arguments which can be urged in favor of ethical relativity; and secondly, the arguments which can be urged against it. . . . The first [in favor] is that which relies upon the actual varieties of moral "standards" found in the world. It was easy enough to believe in a single absolute morality in older times when there was no anthropology, when all humanity was divided clearly into two groups, Christian peoples and the "heathen." Christian peoples knew and possessed the one true morality. The rest were savages whose moral ideas could be ignored. But all this is changed. Greater knowledge has brought greater tolerance. We can no longer exalt our own morality as alone true, while dismissing all other moralities as false or inferior. The investigations of anthropologists have shown that there exists side by side in the world a bewildering variety of moral codes. On this topic endless volumes have been written, masses of evidence piled up. Anthropologists have ransacked the Melanesian Islands, the jungles of New Guinea, the steppes of Siberia, the deserts of Australia, the forests of central Africa, and have brought back with them countless examples of weird, extravagant, and fantastic "moral" customs with which to confound us. We learn that all kinds of horrible practices are, in this, that, or the other place, regarded

as essential to virtue. We find that there is nothing, or next to nothing, which has always and everywhere been regarded as morally good by all men. Where, then, is our universal morality? Can we, in face of all this evidence, deny that it is nothing but an empty dream?

This argument, taken by itself, is a very weak one. It relies upon a single set of facts—the variable moral customs of the world. But this variability of moral ideas is admitted by both parties to the dispute, and is capable of ready explanation upon the hypothesis of either party. The relativist says that the facts are to be explained by the nonexistence of any absolute moral standard. The absolutist says that they are to be explained by human ignorance of what the absolute moral standard is. And he can truly point out that men have differed widely in their opinions about all manner of topics—including the subject-matters of the physical sciences—just as much as they differ about morals. And if the various different opinions which men have held about the shape of the earth do not prove that it has no one real shape, neither do the various opinions which they have held about morality prove that there is no one true morality.

Thus the facts can be explained equally plausibly on either hypothesis. There is nothing in the facts themselves which compels us to prefer the relativistic hypothesis to that of the absolutist. And therefore the argument fails to prove the relativist conclusion. If that conclusion is to be established, it must be by means of other considerations.

This is the essential point. But I will add some supplementary remarks. The work of the anthropologists, upon which ethical relativists seem to rely so heavily, has as a matter of fact added absolutely nothing *in principle* to what has always been known about the variability of moral ideas. Educated people have known all along that the Greeks tolerated sodomy, which in modern times has been regarded in some countries as an abominable crime; that the Hindus thought it a sacred duty to burn their widows; that trickery, now thought despicable, was once believed to be a virtue; that terrible torture was thought by our own ancestors only a few centuries ago to be a justifiable weapon of justice; that it was only yesterday that western peoples came to believe that slavery is immoral. Even the ancients knew very well that moral customs and ideas vary—witness the writings of Herodotus. Thus the principle of the variability of moral ideas was well understood long before modern anthropology was ever heard of. Anthropology has added nothing to the knowledge of this principle except a mass of new and extreme examples of it drawn from very remote sources. But to multiply examples of a principle already well known and universally admitted adds nothing to the argument which is built upon that principle. The discoveries of the anthropologists have no doubt been of the highest importance in their own sphere. But in any considered opinion they have thrown no new light upon the special problems of the moral philosopher.

Although the multiplication of examples has no logical bearing on the argument, it does have an immense *psychological* effect upon people's minds. These masses of anthropological learning are impressive. They are propounded in the sacred name of "science." If they are quoted in support of ethical relativity—as they often are—people *think* that they must prove something important. They bewilder and over-awe the simple-minded, batter down their resistance, make them ready to receive humbly the doctrine of ethical relativity from those who have acquired a reputation by their immense learning and their claims to be "scientific." Perhaps this is why so much ado is made by ethical relativists regarding the anthropological evidence. But we must refuse to be impressed. We must discount all this mass of evidence about the extraordinary moral customs of remote peoples. Once we have admitted—as everyone who is instructed must have admitted these last two thousand years without any anthropology at all—the principle that moral ideas vary, all this new evidence adds nothing to the argument. And the argument itself proves nothing for the reasons already given. . . .

The second argument in favor of ethical relativity . . . does not suffer from the disadvantage that it is dependent upon the acceptance of any particular philosophy such as radical empiricism. It makes its appeal to considerations of a quite general character. It consists in alleging that no one has ever been able to discover upon what foundation an absolute morality could rest, or from what source a universally binding moral code could derive its authority.

If, for example, it is an absolute and unalterable moral rule that all men ought to be unselfish, from whence does this *command* issue? For a command it certainly is, phrase it how you please. There is no difference in meaning between the sentence "You ought to be unselfish" and the sentence "Be unselfish." Now a command implies a commander. An obligation implies some authority which obliges. Who is this commander, what this authority? Thus the vastly difficult question is raised of *the basis of moral obligation*. Now the argument of the relativist would be that it is impossible to find any basis for a universally binding moral law; but that it is quite easy to discover a basis for morality if moral codes are admitted to be variable, ephemeral, and relative to time, place, and circumstance.

In this paper I am assuming that it is no longer possible to solve this difficulty by saying naively that the universal moral law is based upon the uniform commands of God to all men. There will be many, no doubt, who will dispute this. But I am not writing for them. I am writing for those who feel the necessity of finding for morality a basis independent of particular religious dogmas. And I shall therefore make no attempt to argue the matter.

The problem which the absolutist has to face, then, is this. The religious basis of the one absolute morality having disappeared, can there be found for it any other, any secular, basis? If not, then it would seem that we cannot any longer believe in absolutism. We shall have to fall back upon belief in a variety of perhaps mutually inconsistent moral codes operating over restricted areas and limited periods. No one of these will be better, or more true, than any other. Each will be good and true for those living in those areas and periods. We shall have to fall back, in a word, on ethical relativity.

For there is no great difficulty in discovering the foundations of morality, or rather of moralities, if we adopt the relativistic hypothesis. Even if we cannot be quite certain *precisely* what these foundations are—and relativists themselves are not entirely agreed about them—we can at least see in a general way the *sort* of foundations they must have. We can see that the question on this basis is not in principle impossible of answer—although the details may be obscure; while, if we adopt the absolutist hypothesis—so the argument runs—no kind of answer is conceivable at all. . . .

This argument is undoubtedly very strong. It *is* absolutely essential to solve the problem of the basis of moral obligation if we are to believe in any kind of moral standards other than those provided by mere custom or by irrational emotions. It is idle to talk about a universal morality unless we can point to the source of its authority—or at least to do so is to indulge in a faith which is without rational ground. To cherish a blind faith in morality may be, for the average man whose business is primarily to live right and not to theorize, sufficient. Perhaps it is his wisest course. But it will not do for the philosopher. His function, or at least one of his functions, is precisely to discover the rational grounds of our everyday beliefs—if they have any. Philosophically and intellectually, then, we cannot accept belief in a universally binding morality unless we can discover upon what foundation its obligatory character rests.

But in spite of the strength of the argument thus posed in favor of ethical relativity, it is not impregnable. For it leaves open one loophole. It is always possible that some theory, not yet examined, may provide a basis for a universal moral obligation. The argument rests upon the [universal] negative proposition that *there is no theory which can provide a basis for a universal morality.* But it is notoriously difficult to prove a negative. How can you prove that there are no green swans? All you can show is that none have been found so far. And then it is always possible that one will be found tomorrow. . . .

III

It is time that we turn our attention from the case in favor of ethical relativity to the case against it. Now the case against it consists, to a very large extent, in urging that, if taken seriously and pressed to its logical conclusion, ethical relativity can only end in destroying the conception of morality altogether, in undermining its practical efficacy, in rendering meaningless many almost universally accepted truths about human affairs, in robbing human beings of any incentive to strive for a better world, in taking the life-blood out of every ideal and every aspiration which has ever ennobled the life of man. . . .

First of all, then, ethical relativity, in asserting that the moral standards of particular social groups are the only standards which exist, renders meaningless all propositions which attempt to compare these standards with one another in respect of their moral worth. And this is a very serious matter indeed. We are accustomed to think that the moral ideas of one nation or social group may be "higher" or "lower" than those of another. We believe, for example, that Christian ethical ideals are nobler than those of the savage races of central Africa. Probably most of us would think that the Chinese moral standards are higher than those of the inhabitants of New Guinea. In short we habitually compare one civilization with another and judge the sets of ethical ideas to be found in them to be some better, some worse. The fact that such judgments are very difficult to make with any justice, and that they are frequently made on very superficial and prejudiced grounds, has no bearing on the question now at issue. The question is whether such judgments have any *meaning*. We habitually assume that they have.

But on the basis of ethical relativity they can have none whatever. For the relativist must hold that there is no *common* standard which can be applied to the various civilizations judged. Any such comparison of moral standards implies the existence of some superior standard which is applicable to both. And the existence of any such standard is precisely what the relativist denies. According to him the Christian standard is applicable only to Christians, the Chinese standard only to Chinese, the New Guinea standard only to the inhabitants of New Guinea.

What is true of comparisons between the moral standards of different races will also be true of comparisons between those of different ages. It is not unusual to ask such questions as whether the standard of our own day is superior to that which existed among our ancestors five hundred years ago. And when we remember that our ancestors employed slaves, practiced barbaric physical tortures, and burned people alive, we may be inclined to think that it is. At any rate we assume that the question is one which has meaning and is capable of rational discussion. But if the ethical relativist is right, whatever we assert on this subject must be totally meaningless. For here again there is no common standard which could form the basis of any such judgments.

This in its turn implies that the whole notion of moral *progress* is a sheer delusion. Progress means an advance from lower to higher, from worse to better. But on the basis of ethical relativity it has no meaning to say that the standards of this age are better (or worse) than those of a previous age. For there is no common standard by which both can be measured. Thus it is nonsense to say that the morality of the New Testament is higher than that of the Old. And Jesus Christ, if he imagined that he was introducing into the world a higher ethical standard than existed before his time, was merely deluded. . . .

I come now to a second point. Up to the present I have allowed it to be taken tacitly for granted that, though judgments comparing different races and ages in respect of the worth of their moral codes are impossible for the ethical relativist, yet judgments of comparison between individuals living within the same social group would be quite possible. For individuals living within the same social group would presumably be subject to the same moral code, that of their group, and this would therefore constitute, as between these individuals, a common standard by which they could both be measured. We have not here, as we had in the other case, the difficulty of the absence of any common standard of comparison. It should therefore be possible for the ethical relativist to say quite meaningfully that President Lincoln was a better man than some criminal or moral imbecile of his own time and country, or that Jesus was a better man than Judas Iscariot.

But is even this minimum of moral judgment really possible on relativist grounds? It seems to me that it is not. For when once the whole of humanity is abandoned as the area covered by a single moral standard, what smaller areas are to be adopted as the *loci* of different standards? Where are we to draw the lines of demarcation? We can split up humanity, perhaps—though the procedure will be very arbitrary—into races, races into nations, nations into tribes, tribes into families, families into individuals. Where are we going to draw the *moral* boundaries? Does the *locus* of a particular moral standard reside in a race, a nation, a tribe, a family, or an individual? Perhaps the blessed phrase "social group" will be dragged in to save the situation. Each such group, we shall be told, has its own moral code which is, for it, right. But what *is* a "group"? Can anyone define it or give its boundaries? This is the seat of that ambiguity in the theory of ethical relativity to which reference was made on an earlier page.

The difficulty is not, as might be thought, merely an academic difficulty of logical definition. If that were all, I should not press the point. But the ambiguity has practical consequences which are disastrous for morality. No one is likely to say that moral codes are confined within the arbitrary limits of the geographical divisions of countries. Nor are the notions of race, nation, or political state likely to help us. To bring out the essentially practical character of the difficulty let us put it in the form of concrete questions. Does the American nation constitute a "group" having a single moral standard? Or does the standard of what I ought to do change continuously as I cross the continent in a railway train? Do different States of the Union have different moral codes? Perhaps every town and village has its own peculiar standard. This may at first sight seem reasonable enough. "In Rome do as Rome does" may seem as good a rule in morals as it is in etiquette. But can we stop there? Within the village are numerous cliques each having its own set of ideas. Why should not each of these claim to be bound only by its own special and peculiar moral standards? And if it comes to that, why should not the gangsters of Chicago claim to constitute a group having its own morality, so that its murders and debaucheries must be viewed as "right" by the only standard which can legitimately be applied to it? And if it be answered that the nation will not tolerate this, that may be so. But this is to put the foundation of right simply in the superior force of the majority. In that case whoever is stronger will be right, however

monstrous his ideas and actions. And if we cannot deny to any set of people the right to have its own morality, is it not clear that, in the end, we cannot even deny this right to the individual? Every individual man and woman can put up, on this view, an irrefutable claim to be judged by no standard except his or her own.

If these arguments are valid, the ethical relativist cannot really maintain that there is anywhere to be found a moral standard binding upon anybody against his will. And he cannot maintain that, even within the social group, there is a common standard as between individuals. And if that is so, then even judgments to the effect that one man is morally better than another become meaningless. All moral valuation thus vanishes. There is nothing to prevent each man from being a rule unto himself. The result will be moral chaos and the collapse of all effective standards. . . .

But even if we assume that the difficulty about defining moral groups has been surmounted, a further difficulty presents itself. Suppose that we have now definitely decided what are the exact boundaries of the social group within which a moral standard is to be operative. And we will assume—as is invariably done by relativists themselves—that this group is to be some actually existing social community such as a tribe or nation. How are we to know, even then, what actually is the moral standard within that group? How is anyone to know? How is even a member of the group to know? For there are certain to be within the group—at least this will be true among advanced peoples—wide differences of opinion as to what is right, what wrong. Whose opinion, then, is to be taken as representing *the* moral standard of the group? Either we must take the opinion of the majority within the group, or the opinion of some minority. If we rely upon the ideas of the majority, the results will be disastrous. Wherever there is found among a people a small band of select spirits, or perhaps one man, working for the establishment of higher and nobler ideas than those commonly accepted by the group, we shall be compelled to hold that, for that people at that time, the majority are right, and that the reformers are wrong and are preaching what is immoral. We shall have to maintain, for example, that Jesus was preaching immoral doctrines to the Jews. Moral goodness will have to be equated always with the mediocre and sometimes with the definitely base and ignoble. If on the other hand we said that the moral standard of the group is to be identified with the moral opinions of some minority, then what minority is this to be? We cannot answer that it is to be the minority composed of the best and the most enlightened individuals of the group. This would involve us in a palpably vicious circle. For by what standard are these individuals to be judged the best and the most enlightened? There is no principle by which we could select the right minority. And therefore we should have to consider every minority as good as every other. And this means that we should have no logical right whatever to resist the claim of the gangsters of Chicago—if such a claim were made—that their practices represent the highest standards of American morality. It means in the end that every individual is to be bound by no standard save his own.

The ethical relativists are great empiricists. *What* is the actual moral standard of any group can only be discovered, they tell us, by an examination on the ground of the moral opinions and customs of that group. But will they tell us how they propose to decide, when they get to the ground, which of the many moral opinions they are sure to find there is *the* right one in that group? To some extent they will be able to do this for the Melanesian Islanders—from whom apparently all lessons in the nature of morality are in future to be taken. But it is certain that they cannot do

it for advanced peoples whose members have learned to think for themselves and to entertain among themselves a wide variety of opinions. They cannot do it unless they accept the calamitous view that the ethical opinion of the majority is always right. We are left therefore once more with the conclusion that, even within a particular social group, anybody's moral opinion is as good as anybody's else's, and that every man is entitled to be judged by his own standards.

Finally, not only is ethical relativity disastrous in its consequences for moral theory. It cannot be doubted that it must tend to be equally disastrous in its impact upon practical conduct. If men come really to believe that one moral standard is as good as another, they would conclude that their own moral standard has nothing special to recommend it. They might as well then slip down to some lower and easier standard. It is true that, for a time, it may be possible to hold one view in theory and to act practically upon another. But ideas, even philosophical ideas, are not so ineffectual that they can remain forever idle in the upper chambers of the intellect. In the end they seep down to the level of practice. They get themselves acted on.

DISCUSSION QUESTIONS

1. What is the best objection that Stace raises against moral relativism? Why do you think that it is a good objection? How do you imagine that Ruth Benedict might respond to Stace's objection?
2. How important is it to be able to say that the moral standards of one society are better than those of another? Should we object to moral theories that do not view one moral system as better than another? Defend your view.
3. What is moral absolutism? What is gained and what is lost with moral absolutism? How important is it for philosophers to provide a basis for a universal morality?
4. How do you think Benedict would respond to Stace's objections? Do you think that she was aware of them? What, if anything, would get her to change her position?
5. Can one support cultural diversity and support moral absolutism? Or is a defense of moral absolutism also an argument against cultural diversity? Explain your view.

 MARY MIDGLEY

Trying Out One's New Sword

Mary Midgley argues that moral isolationism is impossible and inconsistent. Moral isolationists, she says, claim that cultures are sealed units. But American culture, for example, is a mixture of many different influences: Greek, Jewish, Indian, Japanese, African, and so on. Therefore, concludes Midgley, the moral isolationist doctrine of sealed units is false. The moral isolationist also argues that we should not judge other cultures because we do not understand them. However, a typical response of the moral isolationist to non-tolerance of aberrant practices in other cultures is to justify the moral judgments of other cultures by trying to explain the reasons for those judgments. In doing so, the moral isolationist implies that it *is* possible to understand customs other than our own. Therefore, it is in fact possible to understand other cultures, and if we can understand them, we can judge them. Midgley introduces a number of other equally interesting and compelling arguments against moral isolationism.

Mary Midgley teaches at the University of Newcastle-upon-Tyne, England, and is the author of several books, including *Beast and Man* (1978), *Heart and Mind* (1981), *Animals and Why They Matter* (1984), *Evolution as a Religion* (1986), *Wisdom, Information and Wonder* (1991), and *The Ethical Primate* (1994).

A CRITIQUE OF MORAL ISOLATIONISM

All of us are, more or less, in trouble today about trying to understand cultures strange to us. We hear constantly of alien customs. We see changes in our lifetime which would have astonished our parents. I want to discuss here one very short way of dealing with this difficulty, a drastic way which many people now theoretically favour. It consists in simply denying that we can ever understand any culture except our own well enough to make judgments about it. Those who recommend this hold that the world is sharply divided into separate societies, sealed units, each with its own system of thought. They feel that the respect and tolerance due from one system to another forbids us ever to take up a critical position to any other culture. Moral judgment, they suggest, is a kind of coinage valid only in its country of origin.

I shall call this position "moral isolationism." I shall suggest that it is certainly not forced upon us, and indeed that it makes no sense at all. People usually take it up because they think it is a respectful attitude to other cultures. In fact, however, it is not respectful. Nobody can respect what is entirely unintelligible to them. To respect someone, we have to know enough about him to make a *favorable* judgment, however general and tentative. And we do understand people in other cultures to this extent. Otherwise, a great mass of our most valuable thinking would be paralysed.

To show this, I shall take a remote example, because we shall probably find it easier to think calmly about it than we should with a contemporary one, such as female circumcision in Africa or the Chinese Cultural Revolution. The principles involved will still be the same. My example is this. There is, it seems, a verb in classical Japanese which means "to try out one's new sword on a chance wayfarer." (The word is *tsujigiri*, literally "crossroads-cut.") A Samurai sword had to be tried out because, if it was to work properly, it had to slice through someone at a single blow, from the shoulder to the opposite flank. Otherwise, the warrior bungled his stroke. This could injure his honour, offend his ancestors, and even let down his emperor. So tests were needed, and wayfarers had to be expended. Any wayfarer would do—provided, of course, that he was not another Samurai. Scientists will recognize a familiar problem about the rights of experimental subjects.

Now when we hear of a custom like this, we may well reflect that we simply do not understand it; and therefore are not qualified to criticize it at all, because we are not members of that culture. But we are not members of any other culture either, except our own. So we extend the principle to cover all extraneous cultures, and we seem therefore to be moral isolationists. But this is, as we shall see, an impossible position. Let us ask what it would involve.

We must ask first: Does the isolating barrier work both ways? Are people in other cultures equally unable to criticize *us*? This question struck me sharply when I read a remark in *The Guardian* by an anthropologist about a South American Indian who had been taken into a Brazilian town for an operation, which saved his life. When he came back to his village, he made several highly critical remarks about the white Brazilians' way of life. They may very well have been justified. But the interesting point was that the anthropologist called these remarks "a damning indictment of Western civilization." Now the Indian had been in that town about two weeks. Was he in a position to deliver a damning indictment? Would we ourselves be qualified to deliver such an indictment on the Samurai, provided we could spend two weeks in ancient Japan? What do we really think about this?

My own impression is that we believe that outsiders can, in principle, deliver perfectly good indictments—only, it usually takes more than two weeks to make them damning. Understanding has degrees. It is not a slapdash yes-or-no matter. Intelligent outsiders can progress in it, and in some ways will be at an advantage over the locals. But if this is so, it must clearly apply to ourselves as much as anybody else.

Our next question is this: Does the isolating barrier between cultures block praise as well as blame? If I want to say that the Samurai culture has many virtues, or to praise the South American Indians, am I prevented from doing *that* by my outside status? Now, we certainly do need to praise other societies in this way. But it is hardly possible that we could praise them effectively if we could not, in principle, criticize them. Our praise would be worthless if it rested on definite grounds, if it did not flow from some understanding. Certainly we may need to praise things which we do not *fully* understand. We say "there's something very good here, but I can't quite make out what it is yet." This happens when we want to learn from strangers. And we can learn from strangers. But to do this we have to distinguish between those strangers who are worth learning from and those who are not. Can we then judge which is which?

This brings us to our third question: What is involved in judging? Now plainly there is no question here of sitting on a bench in a red robe and sentencing people. Judging simply means forming an opinion, and expressing it if it is called for. Is there anything wrong about this? Naturally, we ought to avoid forming—and expressing—*crude* opinions, like that of a simple-minded missionary, who might dismiss the whole Samurai culture as entirely bad, because non-Christian. But this is a different objection.

The trouble with crude opinions is that they are crude, whoever forms them, not that they are formed by the wrong people. Anthropologists, after all, are outsiders quite as much as missionaries. Moral isolationism forbids us to form *any* opinions on these matters. Its ground for doing so is that we don't understand them. But there is much that we don't understand in our own culture too. This brings us to our last question: If we can't judge other cultures, can we really judge our own? Our efforts to do so will be much damaged if we are really deprived of our opinions about other societies, because these provide the range of comparison, the spectrum of alternatives against which we set what we want to understand. We would have to stop using the mirror which anthropology so helpfully holds up to us.

In short, moral isolationism would lay down a general ban on moral reasoning. Essentially, this is the programme of immoralism, and it carries a distressing logical difficulty. Immoralists like Nietzsche are actually just a rather specialized sect of moralists. They can no more afford to put moralizing out of business than smugglers can afford to abolish customs regulations. The power of moral judgment is, in fact, not a luxury, not a perverse indulgence of the self-righteous. It is a necessity. When we judge something to be bad or good, better or worse than something else, we are taking it as an example to aim at or avoid. Without opinions of this sort, we would have no framework of comparison for our own policy, no chance of profiting by other people's insights or mistakes. In this vacuum, we could form no judgments on our own actions.

Now it would be odd if Homo sapiens had really got himself into a position as bad as this—a position where his main evolutionary asset, his brain, was so little use to him. None of us is going to accept this sceptical diagnosis. We cannot do so, because our involvement in moral isolationism does not flow from apathy, but from a rather acute concern about human hypocrisy and other forms of wickedness. But we polarize that concern around a few selected moral truths. We are rightly angry with those who despise, oppress or steamroll other cultures. We think that doing these things is actually *wrong*. But this is itself a moral judgment. We could not condemn oppression and insolence if we thought that all our condemnations were just a trivial local quirk of our own culture. We could still less do it if we tried to stop judging altogether.

Real moral scepticism, in fact, could lead only to inaction, to our losing all interest in moral questions, most of all in those which concern other societies. When we discuss these things, it becomes instantly clear how far we are from doing this. Suppose, for instance, that I criticize the bisecting Samurai, that I say his behavior is brutal. What will usually happen next is that someone will protest, will say that I have no right to make criticisms like that of another culture. But it is most unlikely that he will use this move to end the discussion of the subject. Instead, he will justify the Samurai. He will try to fill in the background, to make me understand the custom, by explaining the exalted ideals of discipline and devotion which produced it. He will probably talk of the lower value which the ancient Japanese placed on individual life generally. He may well suggest that this is a healthier attitude than our own obsession with security. He may add, too, that the wayfarers did not seriously mind being bisected, that in principle they accepted the whole arrangement.

Now an objector who talks like this is implying that it *is* possible to understand alien customs. That is just what he is trying to make me do. And he implies, too, that if I do succeed in understanding them, I shall do something better than giving up judging them. He expects me to change my present judgment to a truer one—namely, one that is favourable. And the standards I must use to do this cannot just be Samurai standards. They have to be ones current in my own culture. Ideals like discipline and devotion will not move anybody unless he himself accepts them. As it happens, neither discipline nor devotion is very popular in the West at present. Anyone who appeals to them may well have to do some more arguing to make *them* acceptable, before he can use them to explain the Samurai. But if he does succeed here, he will have persuaded us, not just that there was something to be said for them in ancient Japan, but that there would be here as well.

Isolating barriers simply cannot arise here. If we accept something as a serious moral truth about one culture, we can't refuse to apply it—in however different an outward form—to other cultures as well, wherever circumstance admit it. If we refuse to do this, we just are not taking the other culture seriously. This becomes clear if we look at the last argument used by my objector—that of justification by consent of the victim. It is suggested that sudden bisection is quite in order, *provided* that it takes place between consenting adults. I cannot now discuss how conclusive this justification is. What I am pointing out is simply that it can only work if we believe that *consent* can make such a transaction respectable—and this is a thoroughly modern and Western idea. It would prob-

ably never occur to a Samurai; if it did, it would surprise him very much. It is *our* standard. In applying it, too, we are likely to make another typically Western demand. We shall ask for good factual evidence that the wayfarers actually do have this rather surprising taste—that they are really willing to be bisected. In applying Western standards in this way, we are not being confused or irrelevant. We are asking the questions which arise *from where we stand,* questions which we can see the sense of. We do this because asking questions which you can't see the sense of is humbug. Certainly we can extend our questioning by imaginative effort. We can come to understand other societies better. By doing so, we may make their questions our own, or we may see that they are really forms of the questions which we are asking already. This is not impossible. It is just very hard work. The obstacles which often prevent it are simply those of ordinary ignorance, laziness, and prejudice.

If there were really an isolating barrier, of course, our own culture could never have been formed. It is no sealed box, but a fertile jungle of different influences—Greek, Jewish, Roman, Norse, Celtic and so forth—into which further influences are still pouring—American, Indian, Japanese, Jamaican, you name it. The moral isolationist's picture of separate, unmixable cultures is quite unreal. People who talk about British history usually stress the value of this fertilizing mix, no doubt rightly. But this is not just an odd fact about Britain. Except for the very smallest and most remote, all cultures are formed out of many streams. All have the problem of digesting and assimilating things which, at the start, they do not understand. All have the choice of learning something from this challenge, or, alternatively, of refusing to learn, and fighting it mindlessly instead.

This universal predicament has been obscured by the fact that anthropologists used to concentrate largely on very small and remote cultures, which did not seem to have this problem. These tiny societies, which had often forgotten their own history, made neat, self-contained subjects for study. No doubt it was valuable to emphasize their remoteness, their extreme strangeness, their independence of our cultural tradition. This emphasis was, I think, the root of moral isolationism. But, as the tribal studies themselves showed, even there the anthropologists were able to interpret what they saw and make judgments—often favourable—about the tribesmen. And the tribesmen, too, were quite equal to making judgments about the anthropologists—and about the tourists and Coca-Cola salesmen who followed them. Both sets of judgments, no doubt, were somewhat hasty, both have been refined in the light of further experience. A similar transaction between us and the Samurai might take even longer. But that is no reason at all for deeming it impossible. Morally as well as physically, there is only one world, and we all have to live in it.

DISCUSSION QUESTIONS

1. Moral isolationists say that we should *not* form opinions of other cultures' moral practices because we do not understand them. Do you agree with this? Defend your view.
2. What is the best defense of moral isolationism? How might Midgley react to your defense? Respond to her proposed objections.
3. What does it mean to say that the United States is morally isolationist? Is it? Explain.
4. Both W. T. Stace and Midgley say that there is difficulty with the notion of culture in cultural relativism. How should the cultural relativist define "culture"? Is your definition immune to the kind of criticisms raised by Stace and Midgley?
5. Is it possible to respect something that you do not or cannot understand? What does Midgley say about this? Do you agree with her position? Explain.

 M A R T H A   N U S S B A U M

Imagination and the Perspectives of Others

Whereas moral isolationists would contend that it is not possible to enter imaginatively into the lives of people from other cultures, Martha Nussbaum argues that it is possible to do so and that this is an important part of sound moral reasoning. Nussbaum, like Ronald Duska in the previous chapter, puts storytelling and literature at the heart of moral philosophy. "Literary works," says Nussbaum, "typically invite their readers to put themselves in the place of people of many different kinds and to take on their experiences." This kind of activity ultimately strengthens our capacity to make good ethical judgments. For Nussbaum, "an ethics of impartial respect for human dignity will fail to engage real human beings unless they are capable of entering imaginatively into the lives of distant others and to have emotions related to that participation."

Martha Nussbaum is a professor of law and ethics at the University of Chicago. She is the author of many books including *Women and Human Development* (2000), *Cultivating Humanity* (1997), *Poetic Justice* (1995), *Love's Knowledge* (1990), and *The Fragility of Goodness* (1986).

. . . Very often in today's political life we lack the capacity to see one another as fully human, as more than "dreams or dots." Often, too, those refusals of sympathy are aided and abetted by an excessive reliance on technical ways of modeling human behavior, especially those that derive from economic utilitarianism. These models can be very valuable in their place, but they frequently prove incomplete as a guide to political relations among citizens. Without the participation of the literary imagination, said [the poet Walt] Whitman, "things are grotesque, eccentric, fail of their full returns." We see much political argument today that is grotesque and eccentric in this way. The purpose of this book is to describe the ingredient of public discourse that Whitman found missing from his America and to show some roles it still might play in our own. It grows out of the conviction, which I share with Whitman, that storytelling and literary imagining are not opposed to rational argument, but can provide essential ingredients in a rational argument.

During the lifetimes of William James and John Dewey, it was taken for granted that academic philosophy, including philosophical discussion of literature and art, was part of public discourse. But during much of the present century, academic philosophy in the United States has had relatively few links with practical choice and public life. Recently, however, philosophers have once again become involved in public debate, not only about the basic issues of ethical and political theory, but also about more concrete issues in medicine, business, and law. During the past five years I, like numerous philosophical colleagues, have spent more and more time in professional schools—law schools in my case—giving visiting lectures and talking about issues with professional theorists and practitioners. In the spring of 1994, I taught law students for the first time, as a visiting professor in the law school at the University of Chicago. . . .

The subject of my legal teaching was, in fact, storytelling, for the course I was asked to teach was Law and Literature. The law students and I read Sophocles, and Plato, and Seneca, and Dickens. In connection with the literary works, we discussed compassion and mercy, the role of the emotions in public judgment, what is involved in imagining the situation of someone different from oneself. We talked about ways in which texts of different types present human beings—seeing them, in some cases, as ends in themselves, endowed with dignity and individuality, in others as abstract undistinguishable units or as mere means to the ends of others. . . .

We talked, as well, about more concrete social issues, including gender, homosexuality, and race. In a lecture hall less than fifty yards away from the black metal fence in the law school parking lot that marks the "line" between the world of the university and the world of the inner-city Chicago slums, in a class with only one African-American member in seventy, we

read Richard Wright's *Native Son*. Every Chicago place name marked a location we knew—though with respect to some of those locations almost all of us were in the position of Wright's Mary Dalton, when she says to Bigger Thomas that she has no idea how people live ten blocks away from her. "He knew as he stood there," says Wright of Bigger, "that he could never tell why he had killed. It was not that he did not really want to tell, but the telling of it would have involved an explanation of his entire life." We talked about the relevance of that passage to disputes about discretion and mercy in criminal sentencing—about a Supreme Court decision that instructs courts to treat defendants not "as members of a faceless, undifferentiated mass" but "as uniquely individual human beings." What might the role of a novel such as Wright's be, in conveying to future judges and lawyers an understanding of that requirement? I did not invent the course Law and Literature; in fact, it had been for some years a regular part of the law school's curriculum. The legal profession's interest in the relationship between philosophy and literature had at first surprised me. Gradually I had come to see that what was being sought from such teaching was the investigation and principled defense of a humanistic and multivalued conception of public rationality that is powerfully exemplified in the common-law tradition. This conception needs defending, since it has for some time been under attack from the more "scientific" conceptions offered by the law-and-economics movement. I had for some time been working on related philosophical ideas and had already begun to connect them to issues in the law. But the Chicago course marked the first time that I had tried to work out some of these ideas in the classroom, interacting with students who would shortly be lawyers and clerks for judges. Although I remain a legal amateur, and although I make this suggestion from the outside, still in considerable ignorance of the more technical and formal side of the law, which I am not proposing to demote and for which I have great respect, I believe more strongly than ever that thinking about narrative literature does have the potential to make a contribution to the law in particular, to public reasoning generally. . . .

The literary imagination is a part of public rationality, and not the whole. I believe that it would be extremely dangerous to suggest substituting empathetic imagining for rule-governed moral reasoning, and I am not making that suggestion. In fact, I defend the literary imagination precisely because it seems to me an essential ingredient of an ethical stance that asks us to concern ourselves with the good of other people whose lives are distant from our own. Such an ethical stance will have a large place for rules and formal decision procedures, including procedures inspired by economics. . . .

On the other hand, an ethics of impartial respect for human dignity will fail to engage real human beings unless they are made capable of entering imaginatively into the lives of distant others and to have emotions related to that participation. The emotions of the reader or spectator have been defended as essential to good ethical judgment by quite a few ethical theorists deeply concerned about impartiality—perhaps most notably by Adam Smith, whose *Theory of Moral Sentiments* is a central inspiration. . . . Although these emotions have limitations and dangers, . . . and although their function in ethical reasoning must be carefully circumscribed, they also contain a powerful, if partial, vision of social justice and provide powerful motives for just conduct. . . .

My central subject is the ability to imagine what it is like to live the life of another person who might, given changes in circumstance, be oneself or one of one's loved ones. . . . Literature focuses on the possible, inviting its readers to wonder about themselves. . . . Unlike most historical works, literary works typically invite their readers to put themselves in the place of people of many different kinds and to take on their experiences. In their very mode of address to their imagined reader, they convey the sense that there are links of possibility, at least on a very general level, between the characters and the reader. The reader's emotions and imagination are highly active as a result, and it is the nature of this activity, and its relevance for public thinking, that interests me.

Historical and biographical works do provide us with empirical information that is essential to good choice. They may in fact also arouse the relevant forms of imaginative activity, if they are written in an inviting narrative style. But to the extent that they promote identification and sympathy in the reader, they resemble literary works. This is especially so if they show the effect of circumstances on the emotions and the inner world—a salient part of the contribution of the literary, ...

Another way of putting this point is that good literature is disturbing in a way that history and social science writing frequently are not. Because it summons powerful emotions, it disconcerts and puzzles. It inspires distrust of conventional pieties and exacts a frequently painful confrontation with one's own thoughts and intentions. One may be told many things about people in one's own society and yet keep that knowledge at a distance. Literary

works that promote identification and emotional reaction cut through those self-protective stratagems, requiring us to see and to respond to many things that may be difficult to confront—and they make this process palatable by giving us pleasure in the very act of confrontation. . . .

In its engagement with a general notion of the human being, [Dickens's *Hard Times*] (like many novels) is, I think, while particularistic, not relativistic. That is, it recognizes human needs that transcend boundaries of time, place, class, religion, and ethnicity, and it makes the focus of its moral deliberation the question of their adequate fulfillment. Its criticism of concrete political and social situations relies on a notion of what it is for a human being to flourish, and this notion itself, while extremely general and in need of further specification, is neither local nor sectarian. On the other hand, part of the idea of flourishing is a deep respect for qualitative difference—so the norm enjoins that governments, wherever they are, should attend to citizens in all their concreteness and variety, responding in a sensitive way to historical and personal contingencies. But that is itself a universal injunction and part of a universal picture of humanness. And it is by relying on this universal ideal that the novel, so different from a guidebook or even an anthropological field report, makes readers participants in the lives of people very different from themselves and also critics of the class distinctions that give people similarly constructed an unequal access to flourishing. Once again, these insights need corroboration from theoretical arguments; they are not complete in themselves. . . .

[The] literary judge . . . is committed to neutrality, properly understood. That is, she will not tailor her principles to the demands of political or religious pressure groups and will give no group or individual special indulgence or favor on account of their relation to her or her affiliations. She is a judicious spectator and does not gush with irrelevant or ungrounded sentiment. On the other hand, as I have argued here, her neutrality does not require a lofty distance from the social realities of the cases before her; indeed, she is enjoined to examine those realities searchingly, with imaginative concreteness and the emotional responses that are proper to the judicious spectator—or to his surrogate, the novel-reader. . . .

. . . [The] literary judge would look in particular for evidence that certain groups have suffered unequal disadvantages and therefore need more attention if they are to be shown a truly equal concern.

This concern for the disadvantaged is built into the structure of the literary experience, which was, as we saw. Adam Smith's model for the experience of the judicious spectator. The reader participates vicariously in numerous different lives, some more advantaged and some less. In realist social novels, which are my focus, these lives are self-consciously drawn from different social strata, and the extent to which these varied circumstances allow for flourishing is made part of the reader's experience. The reader enters each of these lives not knowing, so to speak, which one of them is hers—she identifies first with [one] and then with [another], living each of those lives in turn and becoming aware that her actual place is in many respects an accident of fortune. She has empathetic emotions appropriate to the living of the life and, more important, spectatorial emotions in which she evaluates the way fortune has made this life conducive or not conducive to flourishing. This means that she will notice especially vividly the disadvantages faced by the least well off. . . . Why should the literary imagination be any more connected with equality than with inequality, or with democratic rather than aristocratic ideals? Why is the sunlight of judicial vision specially concerned with the "helpless things"?

When we read *Hard Times* as sympathetic participants, our attention has a special focus. Since the sufferings and anxieties of the characters are among the central bonds between reader and work, our attention is drawn in particular to those characters who suffer and fear. Characters who are not facing any adversity simply do not hook us in as readers; there is no drama in a life in which things are going smoothly. This tragic sensibility leads the reader to investigate with a particularly keen combination of identification and sympathy lives in which circumstance has played an impeding role. Sometimes, of course, the baneful circumstances are necessary and inevitable. Loved ones die; natural disasters destroy property and cities. Frequently, however, the tragedy that moves us is not necessary. Not all wars are inevitable; hunger and poverty and miserably unequal conditions of labor are not inevitable. Since we read a novel like *Hard Times* with the thought that we ourselves might be in a character's position—since our emotion is based in part on this sort of empathetic identification—we will naturally be most concerned with the lot of those whose position is worst, and we will begin to think

of ways in which that position might have been other than it is, might be made better than it is.

One way in which the situation of the poor or oppressed is especially bad is that it might have been otherwise. We see this especially clearly when we see their situation side by side with the situation of the rich and prosperous. In this way our thought will naturally turn in the direction of making the lot of the worst off more similar to the lot of the rich and powerful: since we ourselves might be, or become, either of those two people, we want to raise the floor. This may not get all the way to complete equality (whether of resources or of welfare or of capability to function), but it does at least lead political thought in the direction of ameliorating persistent inequalities and providing all with a decent minimum. One might of course have these thoughts without being a "poet." But . . . the ability to imagine vividly, and then to assess judicially, another person's pain, to participate in it and then to ask about its significance, is a powerful way of learning what the human facts are and of acquiring a motivation to alter them. . . .

Literary understanding, I would therefore argue, promotes habits of mind that lead toward social equality in that they contribute to the dismantling of the stereotypes that support group hatred. For this purpose, in principle any literary work that has the characteristics I have discussed . . . would be valuable: in reading . . . we learn habits of "fancying" that we can then apply to other groups that come before us, whether or not those groups are depicted in the novels we have read. But it is also very valuable to extend this literary understanding by seeking out literary experiences in which we do identify sympathetically with individual members of marginalized or oppressed groups within our own society, learning both to see the world, for a time, through their eyes and then reflecting as spectators on the meaning of what we have seen. If one of the significant contributions of the novel to public rationality is its depiction of the interaction between shared human aspirations and concrete social circumstances, it seems reasonable that we should seek novels that depict the special circumstances of groups with whom we live and whom we want to understand, cultivating the habit of seeing the fulfillment or frustration of their aspirations and desires within a social world that may be characterized by institutional inequalities. . . .

DISCUSSION QUESTIONS

1. Nussbaum says that "an ethics of impartial respect for human dignity will fail to engage real human beings unless they are capable of entering imaginatively into the

lives of distant others and to have emotions related to that participation." What might she say about Kantian ethics?

2. Compare Ronald Duska and Nussbaum on the role of literature in moral philosophy. Whose view do you think is stronger, and why? Are you convinced by their arguments that moral philosophy must involve a consideration of literature? Explain your view.

3. Is it possible to "enter imaginatively into the lives of distant others and to have emotions related to that participation" as Nussbaum suggests? Defend your view.

4. How might a moral isolationist respond to Nussbaum's claim that we can understand the perspectives of others? Who has the stronger argument? Why?

5. Are storytelling and literary imagining opposed to rational argument? Nussbaum thinks that they are not. What do you think? Defend your view.

CLAUDE AKE

The African Context of Human Rights

Claude Ake argues that the Western notion of human rights is not very interesting in the context of African realities. The Western notion of rights, such as that found in the U.S. Bill of Rights (see p. 140), lacks concreteness. "It ascribes abstract rights to abstract beings," says Ake. Nevertheless, Ake argues that more emphasis is needed on human rights in Africa. These rights will be collective rights grounded in socialism, rather than individual rights grounded in "procedural liberalism" like those found in the U.S. Bill of Rights. Collective rights are more useful to the hungry and the powerless than the "unrealizable rights" of westerners. What good is the right of free speech when one is being oppressed by a fascist government and suffering from hunger and poverty? (For more readings on hunger, poverty, and distributive justice see Chapter 9.)

Claude Ake was a professor of political science at the University of Port Harcourt in Nigeria and is the author of *Democracy and Development in Africa* (1996), *Is Africa Democratizing?* (1996), *The Democratization of Disempowerment in Africa* (1994), *The Feasibility of Democracy in Africa* (1992), and *A Political Economy of Africa* (1981).

Nobody can accuse Africa of taking human rights seriously. In a world which sees concern for human rights as a mark of civilized sensitivity, this indifference has given Africa a bad name. It is not unlikely that many consider it symptomatic of the rawness of life which has always been associated with Africa. I am in no position to say with any confidence why Africa has not taken much interest in human rights but I see good reasons why she should not have done so.

Before going into these reasons let us be clear what we are talking about. The idea of human rights is quite simple. It is that human beings have certain rights simply by virtue of being human. These rights are a necessary condition for the good life. Because of their singular importance, individuals are entitled

Claude Ake, *Africa Today*, vol. 34, nos. 1–2: 5–13. Copyright © 1987 Africa Today Associates. Reprinted with permission.

to, indeed, required to claim them and society is enjoined to allow them. Otherwise, the quality of life is seriously compromised.

The idea of human rights, or legal rights in general, presupposes a society which is atomized and individualistic, a society of endemic conflict. It presupposes a society of people conscious of their separateness and their particular interests and anxious to realize them. The legal right is a claim which the individual may make against other members of society, and simultaneously an obligation on the part of society to uphold this claim.

The values implicit in all this are clearly alien to those of our traditional societies. We put less emphasis on the individual and more on the collectivity, we do not allow that the individual has any claims which may override that of the society. We assume harmony, not divergence of interests, competition and conflict; we are more inclined to think of our obligations to other members of our society rather than our claims against them.

The Western notion of human rights stresses rights which are not very interesting in the context of African realities. There is much concern with the right to peaceful assembly, free speech and thought, fair trial, etc. The appeal of these rights is sociologically specific. They appeal to people with a full stomach who can now afford to pursue the more esoteric aspects of self-fulfillment. The vast majority of our people are not in this position. They are facing the struggle for existence in its brutal immediacy. Theirs is a totally consuming struggle. They have little or no time for reflection and hardly any use for free speech. They have little interest in choice for there is no choice in ignorance. There is no freedom for hungry people, or those eternally oppressed by disease. It is no wonder that the idea of human rights has tended to sound hollow in the African context.

The Western notion of human rights lacks concreteness. It ascribes abstract rights to abstract beings. There is not enough concern for the historical conditions in which human rights can actually be realized. As it turns out, only a few people are in a position to exercise the rights which society allows. The few who have the resources to exercise these rights do not need a bill of rights. Their power secures them. The many who do not have the resources to exercise their rights are not helped any by the existence of these rights. Their powerlessness dooms them.

The idea of human rights really came into its own as a tool for opposing democracy. The French Revolution had brought home forcefully to everyone the paradox of democracy, namely, that its two central values, liberty and equality, come into conflict at critical points. There is no democracy where there is no liberty for self-expression or choice. At the same time there is no democracy where there is no equality, for inequality reduces human relations to subordination and domination. The French Revolution and Jean-Jacques Rousseau revealed rather dramatically the paradoxical relation between these two central values of democracy by leaning heavily towards equality. They gave Europe a taste of what it would be like to take the idea of equality and the correlative idea of popular sovereignty seriously.

Bourgeois Europe was horrified. The idea of a popular sovereign insisting on equality and having unlimited power over every aspect of social life was unacceptable. For such power was a threat to the institution of private property as well as the conditions of accumulation. So they began to emphasize liberty rather than the collectivity. This emphasis was also a way of rejecting democracy in its pure form as popular sovereignty. That was the point of stressing the individual and his rights and holding that certain rights are inalienable. That was the point of holding that the individual could successfully sustain certain claims and certain immunities against the wishes of the sovereign or even the rest of society. It is ironical that all this is conveniently forgotten today and liberal democrats can pass as the veritable defenders of democracy.

CHANGING STATUS OF HUMAN RIGHTS IN AFRICA

Africa is at last beginning to take interest in human rights. For one thing, the Western conception of human rights has evolved in ways which have made it more relevant to the African experience, although its relevance still remains ambiguous. Because human rights is such an important part of the political ideology of the West, it was bound to register in Africa eventually. Human rights record is beginning to feature in Western decisions of how to relate to the countries and leaders of Africa. Western decisions on this score have been made with such cynical inconsistency that one wonders whether human rights record really matters to them at all. However, our leaders ever so eager to please are obliged to assume that it matters and to adjust their behavior accordingly. Also the authoritarian capitalism of Africa is under some pressure to be more liberal and thereby create political conditions more conducive to capitalist efficiency.

If these are the reasons why Africa is beginning to take more interest in human rights, they are by no means the reason why she ought to do so. The way I see it is that we ought to be interested in human rights because it will help us to combat social forces which threaten to send us back to barbarism. Because it will aid our struggle for the social transformation which we need to survive and to flourish. To appreciate this let us look at the historical conditions of contemporary Africa.

I hope we can all agree that for now, the most salient aspect of these conditions is the crisis. It has been with us for so long we might well talk of the permanent crisis. No one seems to know for sure what its character is but we know its devastating effects only too well. We Africans have never had it so bad. The tragic consequences of our development strategies have finally come home to us. Always oppressed by poverty and deprivation, our lives become harsher still with each passing day as real incomes continue to decline. We watch helplessly while millions of our people are threatened by famine and look pitifully to the rest of the world to feed us. Our social and political institutions are disintegrating under pressure from our flagging morale, our dwindling resources and the intense struggle to control them. What is the problem? I am not sure. But I am convinced that we are not dealing simply or even primarily with an economic phenomenon. There is a political dimension to it which is so critical, it may well be the most decisive factor.

This is the problem of democracy or the problem of political repression. A long time ago our leaders opted for political repression. Having abandoned democracy for repression, our leaders are delinked from our people. Operating in a vacuum, they proclaim their incarnation of the popular will, hear echoes of their own voices, and reassured, pursue with zeal, policies which have nothing to do with the aspirations of our people and which cannot, therefore, mobilize them. As their alienation from the people increases, they rely more and more on force and become even more alienated.

CONSEQUENCES OF THE PROBLEM OF DEMOCRACY

The consequences of this are disastrous. In the first place it means that there is no development. Political repression ensures that the ordinary people of Africa who are the object of development remain silent, so that in the end nobody really speaks for development and it never comes alive in practice. Development cannot be achieved by proxy. A people develops itself or not at all. And it can develop itself only through its commitment and its energy. That is where democracy comes in. Self-reliance is not possible unless the society is thoroughly democratic, unless the people are the end and not just the means of development. Development occurs, in so far as it amounts to the pursuit of objectives set by the people themselves in their own interest and pursued by means of their own resources.

Another consequence of repression is the brutalization of our people. Look around you. The willful brutalization of people occurring among us is appalling. Human life is taken lightly, especially if it is that of the underprivileged. All manner of inhuman treatment is meted out for minor offenses and sometimes for no offenses at all. Ordinary people are terrorized daily by wanton display of state power and its instruments of violence. Our prison conditions are guaranteed to traumatize. The only consensus we can mobilize is passive conformity arising from fear and resignation. As we continue to stagnate this gets worse.

Yet another disaster threatens us. I am referring to fascism. In all probability this is something which nobody wants. But we might get it anyway because circumstances are moving steadily in that direction. All the ingredients of fascism are present now in most parts of Africa: a political class which has failed even by its own standards, and which is now acutely conscious of its humiliation and baffled by a world it cannot control; a people who have little if any hope or sense of self-worth yearning for redeemers; a milieu of anomie; a conservative leadership pitted against a rising popular radicalism and poised to take cover in defensive radicalism. That is what it takes and it is there in plenty. If Africa succumbs it will be terrible—fascism has always been in all its historical manifestations.

It seems to me that for many African countries the specter of fascism is the most urgent and the most serious danger today. Unless we contain it effectively and within a very short time, then we are in a great deal of trouble.

If this analysis is correct, then our present agenda must be the task of preventing the rise of fascism. To have a chance of succeeding, this task requires a broad coalition of radicals, populists, liberals and even humane conservatives. That is, a coalition of all those who value democracy not in the procedural liberal sense but in the concrete socialist sense. This is where the idea of human rights comes in. It is easily the best ideological framework for such a coalition.

AN AFRICAN CONCEPTION OF HUMAN RIGHTS

We have now seen the relevance of human rights in the African context. But on a level of generality which does not tell us very much and so does not really settle the question of the applicability of the Western concept of human rights. I do not see how we can mobilize the African masses or the intelligentsia against fascism or whatever by accepting uncritically the Western notion of human rights. We have to domesticate it, re-create it in the light of African conditions. Let me indicate very briefly how these conditions redefine the idea of human rights.

First, we have to understand that the idea of legal rights presupposes social atomization and individualism, and a conflict model of society for which legal rights are the necessary mediation. However, in most of Africa, the extent of social atomization is very limited mainly because of the limited penetration of capitalism and commodity relations. Many people are still locked into natural economies and have a sense of belonging to an organic whole, be it a family, a clan, a lineage or an ethnic group. The phenomenon of the legal subject, the largely autonomous individual conceived as a bundle of rights which are asserted against all comers, has not really developed much especially outside the urban areas.

These are the conditions which explain the forms of consciousness which we insist on misunderstanding. For instance, ethnic consciousness and ethnic identity. It is the necessary consciousness associated with non-atomized social structures and mechanical solidarity. Ethnic consciousness will be with us as long as these structural features remain, no matter how we condemn it or try to engineer it out of existence.

All this means that abstract legal rights attributed to individuals will not make much sense for most of our people; neither will they be relevant to their consciousness and living conditions. It is necessary to extend the idea of human rights to include collective human rights for corporate social groups such as the family, the lineage, the ethnic group. Our people still think largely in terms of collective rights and express their commitment to it constantly in their behavior. This disposition underlies the zeal for community development and the enormous sacrifices which poor people readily make for it. It underlies the so-called tribalist voting pattern of our people, the willingness of the poor villager to believe that the minister from his village somehow represents his share of the national cake, our traditional land tenure systems, the high incidence of cooperative labor and relations of production in the rural areas. These forms of consciousness remain very important features of our lives. If the idea of human rights is to make any sense at all in the African context, it has to incorporate them in a concept of communal human rights.

For reasons which need not detain us here, some of the rights important in the West are of no interest and no value to most Africans. For instance, freedom of speech and freedom of the press do not mean much for a largely illiterate rural community completely absorbed in the daily rigors of the struggle for survival.

African conditions shift the emphasis to a different kind of rights. Rights which can mean something for poor people fighting to survive and burdened by ignorance, poverty and disease, rights which can mean something for women who are cruelly used. Rights which can mean something for the youth whose future we render more improbable every day. If a bill of rights is to make any sense, it must include among others, a right to work and to a living wage, a right to shelter, to health, to education. That is the least we can strive for if we are ever going to have a society which realizes basic human needs.

Finally, in the African context, human rights have to be much more than the political correlate of commodity fetishism which is what they are in the Western tradition. In that tradition the rights are not only abstract, they are also ascribed to abstract persons. The rights are ascribed to the human being from whom all specific determinations have been abstracted: the rights have no content just as individuals who enjoy them have no determination and so do not really exist.

All these problems which usually lurk beneath the surface appear in clear relief when we confront them with empirical reality. Granted, I have the freedom of speech. But where is this freedom, this right? I cannot read, I cannot write. I am too busy trying to survive I have no time to reflect. I am so poor I am constantly at the mercy of others. So where is this right and what is it really? Granted, I have the right to seek public office. That is all very well. But how do I realize this right? I am a full-time public servant who cannot find the time or the necessary resources to put up the organization required to win office. If I take leave from my work, I cannot hold out for more than one month without a salary. I have no money to travel about and meet the voters, even to pay the registration fees for my candidature. If I am not in a position to realize this right, then what is the point of saying that I have it? Do I really have it?

In Africa liberal rights make less sense even as ideological representations. If rights are to be meaningful in the context of a people struggling to stay afloat under very adverse economic and political conditions, they have to be concrete. Concrete in the sense that their practical import is visible and relevant to the conditions of existence of the people to whom they apply. And most importantly, concrete in the sense that they can be realized by their beneficiaries.

To be sure, there are rights which are realizable and there are people in Africa who effectively realize their rights. However, the people who are in a position to realize their rights are very few. They are able to realize their rights by virtue of their wealth and power. The litmus test for rights is those who need protection. Unfortunately these are precisely the people who are in no position to enjoy rights. Clearly, that will not do in African conditions. People are not going to struggle for formalities and esoteric ideas which will not change their lives.

Therefore, a real need arises, namely, to put more emphasis on the realization of human rights. How is this to be? Not in the way we usually approach such matters: by giving more unrealizable rights to the powerless and by begging the powerful to make concessions to them in the name of enlightened self-interest, justice and humanity. That approach will fail us always. Rights, especially those that have any real significance for our lives, are usually taken, not given—with the cooperation of those in power if possible, but without it if necessary. That is the way it was for other peoples and that is the way it is going to be in Africa.

The realization of rights is best guaranteed by the power of those who enjoy the rights. Following this, what is needed is the empowerment by whatever means, of the common people. This is not a matter of legislation, although legislation could help a little. It is rather a matter of redistributing economic and political power across the board. That means that it is in the final analysis a matter of political mobilization and struggle. And it will be a protracted and bitter struggle because those who are favored by the existing distribution of power will resist heartily.

CONCLUSION: HUMAN RIGHTS AND SOCIAL TRANSFORMATION

It is at this point that the ideal of human rights is fully articulated for it is now that we see its critical dialectical moment. Initially part of the ideological prop of liberal capitalism, the idea of human rights was a conservative force. It was meant to safeguard the interests of the men of property especially against the threatening egalitarianism of popular sovereignty. It was not of course presented as a tool of special interests but a universal value good for humanity. That went down well and it has been able to serve those who propagated it behind this mystification.

But ideas have their own dynamics which cannot easily be controlled by the people who brought them into being. In the case of human rights, its dynamics soon trapped it in a contradiction somewhat to the dismay of its protagonists. Fashioned as a tool against democracy, the idea became an important source of legitimation for those seeking the expansion of democracy. But in Europe, this contradiction never fully matured. An agile and accommodating political class and unprecedented affluence saw to that.

In Africa, prevailing objective conditions will press matters much further, particularly the question of empowerment. In all probability, the empowerment of people will become the primary issue. Once this happens, the social contradictions will be immensely sharpened and the idea of human rights will become an asset of great value to radical social transformation. I cannot help thinking that Africa is where the critical issues in human rights will be fought out and where the idea will finally be consummated or betrayed.

DISCUSSION QUESTIONS

1. Why does Ake think that rights such as those found in the U.S. Bill of Rights would be useless to the disadvantaged people of Africa? Do you agree with him? Take a look at the U.S. Bill of Rights (see p. 140), and identify the potentially useful and useless rights to Africans.
2. What is the difference between individual rights and collective rights? Give examples of each.
3. Do you think that collective rights can be grounded in what Ake calls "procedural liberalism"?

4. Ake says that the Western notion of human rights is not very interesting in the context of African realities. Does the U.S. Bill of Rights reflect the realities of America today? Explain
5. What is the connection between human rights and social transformation for Ake? Do you agree with him? Defend your view.

JANE PERLEZ

Uganda's Women: Children, Drudgery, and Pain

Jane Perlez reports on the life of a woman in rural Africa. Perlez's account of the life of Safuyati Kawuda is included here to put another face to Claude Ake's argument about human rights in Africa. It also raises more general issues about women's rights and our willingness to make judgments about other cultures.

Jane Perlez is a reporter for *The New York Times*.

NAMUTUMBA, Uganda—When 28-year-old Safuyati Kawuda married the man she remembers as "handsome and elegant," her husband scraped together the bride price: five goats and three chickens. The animals represented a centuries-old custom intended to compensate Mrs. Kawuda's father for losing the labor of his daughter.

In the decade since, Mrs. Kawuda has rarely seen her husband, who long ago left this hot and dusty village for a town 70 miles away. She has accepted her husband's acquisition of two other wives and has given birth to five of his 13 children.

Instead of laboring for her father she has toiled for her husband hauling firewood, fetching water, digging in the fields, producing the food the family eats, and bearing and caring for the children.

Like Mrs. Kawuda, women in rural Africa are the subsistence farmers. They produce, without tractors, oxen, or even plows, more than 70 percent of the continent's food, according to the World Bank. Back-breaking hand cultivation is a job that African men consider to be demeaning "women's work." The male responsibility is generally to sell the food the women produce. But as urbanization has stepped up, men have gone to the cities in search of other jobs, leaving women like Mrs. Kawuda alone.

MANY INEQUALITIES

The discrepancy between the physical labor of women and men is accompanied by other pervasive inequalities. In the vast majority of African countries, women do not own or inherit land. Within families, boys are encouraged to go to school, girls are not. In many places, women treat wife-beating as an accepted practice. The Uganda Women's Lawyers Association recently embarked on a campaign to convince women that wife-battering is not a sign of a man's love.

Recent surveys in Africa show other significant disparities between men and women. In ten

African countries, according to the United Nations Children's Fund, women and children together make up 77 percent of the population. Yet in only 16 percent of the households in those countries do the women have the legal right to own property.

Despite calls by the United Nations for the improvement of the lives of African women and efforts by the World Bank to finance projects focused on women, little has been done to improve the dismal status of rural women, African and Western experts say. With the continent's worsening economics in the 1980s, women suffered even more.

"The poor, the majority of whom are women, have had to take on additional work burdens in order to cope with cutbacks in social services and the increasing cost of living," the *Weekly Review,* a magazine in Kenya, reported last year.

NO EXPECTATIONS

Mrs. Kawuda has never attended school. She cannot read or write, although her husband can. She has no radio. The farthest she has been from home is Jinja, 70 miles away. She has no expectations of a better life because she has known nothing else. But her ignorance of the outside world does not stop her from knowing her life is unrelentingly tough. She knows that in her bones.

"Everything is difficult," Mrs. Kawuda said, as she bent over to hoe cassava, her bare, rough feet splattered with dark dirt, "It's more of a problem than it used to be to find firewood. If you can't find wood on the ground, you have to cut it and there is no one to help you. Digging in the fields is the most difficult, I don't like it."

Mrs. Kawuda shares her world of perpetual fatigue with her five children; her husband's second wife, Zainabu Kasoga, 27, and her four children. Her husband's third wife—"the town wife"—lives in Jinja, where the husband, 31-year-old Kadiri Mpyanku, a tea packer, spends most of his time.

When the husband visited Mrs. Kawuda on a recent weekend, he brought enough sugar for three days and a packet of beans. Mrs. Kawuda said she was dependent on him for clothes and other essentials, and money that she said he did not always have. In most households in the area, the men also live most of the time in either Jinja or Kampala, the capital.

Here in the village, 120 miles northeast of Kampala, Mrs. Kawuda and Mrs. Kasoga run a household with another woman, the wife of their husband's brother, Sayeda Naigaga, 20, and her three children.

VILLAGE LIFE

The women live without running water or electricity in three small, mud-wall structures. In the outdoor courtyard, life grinds on: the peeling and chopping of food, eating by adults and feeding of infants, washing, bathing, weaving and the receiving of guests all take place on the orange clay ground, packed smooth by the passage of bare feet.

In the old days, Ugandan men built separate houses for each wife, but such luxuries disappeared with the collapse of the economy. Mrs. Kawuda and her five children sleep in one room of the main shelter and Mrs. Kasoga and her four children in another. When their husband is around, he shuttles between the two bedrooms.

Mrs. Kawuda is of the Bisoga tribe, the second largest in Uganda and one where polygamy is common. Sexual and marriage mores differ in various parts of Africa. The Uganda Women's Lawyers Association estimates that 50 percent of marriages in Uganda are polygamous and, according to United Nations figures, a similar percentage exists in West Africa.

In Kenya, the Government's Women's Bureau estimates that about 30 percent of the marriages are polygamous. However, because of the economic burden of keeping several wives and families, the practice is declining, the bureau says.

WIVES OFTEN HOSTILE

Often the wives in a polygamous marriage are hostile toward each other. But perhaps as a survival instinct, Mrs. Kawuda and Mrs. Kasoga are friendly, taking turns with Mrs. Naigaga to cook for the 15-member household.

Days start with the morning ritual of collecting water. For these Ugandan women, the journey to the nearest pond takes half an hour. The six-gallon cans, when full of water, are heavy on the trip home.

Digging in the fields is the most loathed of the chores, but also the one the women feel most obliged to do since the family's food supply comes from what they grow. As they work under the sun, the women drape old pieces of clothing on their heads for protection. The youngest child, two-year-old Suniya, clings to her mother's back while Mrs. Kawuda hunches over, swinging a hoe, a sight as pervasive in rural Africa as an American mother gliding a cart along the aisles of a supermarket. "Having a baby on your back is easy," Mrs. Kawuda said. "When you are eight months pregnant and digging, it is more difficult."

There was no possibility the husband would help in the fields. It was his job to "supervise," said Mrs. Kawuda, ridiculing a suggestion that he might pitch in.

When he arrived late on a recent Saturday night, Mr. Mpyanku was treated as the imperious ruler by the children, some of whom tentatively came to greet him. He was barely acknowledged by the women, who seemed a little fearful and immediately served tea.

By early Sunday morning, he had disappeared to the nearby trading post to be with his male friends. "He has gone to discuss business with his friends," Mrs. Kawuda said. "What business can I discuss with him? Will we talk to him about digging cassava?"

Mrs. Kawuda said her husband had promised not to take any more wives. "But you never know what he thinks," she said. "I can't interfere in his affairs. If I did, he would say: 'Why is she poking her nose into my affairs?'"

Fertility and children remain at the center of rural marriage in Africa. Large numbers of children improve a household's labor pool and provide built-in security for parents in old age.

Mrs. Kawuda said she wanted one more child, in the hopes of its being another boy. After that, she said, she would use an injectible form of contraceptive. It is a method popular among African rural women because it can be used without their husband's knowledge. But in reality, contraception was an abstraction to Mrs. Kawuda since she had no idea where to get it. She has never heard of condoms.

A recent concern for African women is AIDS, which like much else in their lives they seem powerless to control. Unconvinced by her husband's assurances that he is faithful to his town wife, Mrs. Kawuda said: "He can say it's all right, we need not worry. But you never know what he does in town. He fears AIDS, too. But he messes around too much."

A worldly person compared to his wives, Mr. Mpyanku speaks reasonable English and has traveled to Kenya.

He described himself as the provider of cash for the rural family. But Mr. Mpyanku's emphasis is on his own livelihood and his urban life.

He rode the most comfortable form of transportation home, a nonstop mini bus from Jinja that cost about $1.50, instead of the cheaper taxi at $1. He would do the same on his return.

Yet his oldest child, a daughter, Maliyamu, ten, missed much of her schooling last year. Her report card said the $7 in school fees had not been paid. It was a cheerless sign that Mrs. Kawuda's daughter would, like her mother, remain uneducated and repeat for another generation the cycle of female poverty and punishing physical labor.

DISCUSSION QUESTIONS

1. Cultural relativists say that we should not judge other cultures because we cannot understand them. Can you read this article without judging the treatment of women in Uganda? If you cannot, try to articulate the assumptions that form the basis of your judgment. What are they? If you can read this article without forming a judgment, explain how this is possible.

2. What do you think Claude Ake would say about the plight of women in rural Uganda? Should he alter his views given what we now know about the conditions for women in Africa?

3. What, if any, human rights is Safuyati Kawuda being denied? Explain.

4. Is Safuyati Kawuda being treated immorally? If so, how?

5. What should we, as citizens of a foreign nation, do about the conditions for women in Uganda?

6. Is it possible to enter imaginatively—as Martha Nussbaum would say—into the perspective of Safuyati Kawuda? Do you think that this strengthens your capacity to make good ethical judgments? Defend your view.

KENNETH K. INADA

A Buddhist Response to the Nature of Human Rights

Kenneth K. Inada argues that the Buddhist view of human rights is based on a "soft relationship," whereas the Western view is based on a "hard relationship." On the Western view, says Inada, "persons are treated as separate and independent entities or even bodies, each having its own assumed identity or self-identity." On the Buddhist view, persons are treated with openness, expansiveness, depth, flexibility, absorptiveness, freshness, and creativity. Nevertheless, the soft relationship is not in contention with the hard relationship. Inada notes: "If anything, it has an inclusive nature that 'softens,' if you will, all contacts and allows for the binding of any element that comes along, even incorporating the entities of hard-relationships." A Buddhist view of human rights will be less concerned with legal formalities and more interested in the feelings that constitute the "saving truth of humanistic existence."

Kenneth K. Inada is the author of *Nagarjuna* (1970), *Buddhism and American Thinkers* (coeditor, 1984), and *Guide to Buddhist Philosophy* (1985).

It is incorrect to assume that the concept of human rights is readily identifiable in all societies of the world. The concept may perhaps be clear and distinct in legal quarters, but in actual practice suffers greatly from lack of clarity and gray areas due to impositions by different cultures. This is especially true in Asia, where the two great civilizations of India and China have spawned such outstanding systems as Hinduism, Buddhism, Jainism, Yoga, Confucianism, Taoism and Chinese Buddhism. These systems, together with other indigenous folk beliefs, attest to the cultural diversity at play that characterizes Asia proper. In focusing on the concept of human rights, however, we shall concentrate on Buddhism to bring out the common grounds of discourse.

Alone among the great systems of Asia, Buddhism has successfully crossed geographical and ideological borders and spread in time throughout the whole length and breadth of known Asia. Its doctrines are so universal and profound that they captured the imagination of all the peoples they touched and thereby established a subtle bond with all. What then is this bond? It must be something common to all systems of thought which opens up and allows spiritual discourse among them.

In examining the metaphysical ground of all systems, one finds that there is a basic feeling for a larger reality in one's own experience, a kind of reaching out for a greater cosmic dimension of being, as it were. It is a deep sense for the total nature of things. All this may seem so simple and hardly merits elaborating, but it is a genuine feeling common among Asians in their quest for ultimate knowledge based on the proper relationship of one's self in the world. It is an affirmation of a reality that includes but at once goes beyond the confines of sense faculties.

A good illustration of this metaphysical grounding is seen in the Brahmanic world of Hinduism. In it, the occluded nature of the self (*atman*) constantly works to cleanse itself of defilements by yogic discipline in the hope of ultimately identifying with the larger reality which is Brahman. In the process, the grounding in the larger reality is always kept intact, regardless of whether the self is impure or not. In other words, in the quest for the purity of things a larger framework of experience is involved from the beginning such that the ordinary self (*atman*) transforms into the larger Self (*Atman*) and finally merges into the ultimate ontological Brahman.

A similar metaphysical grounding is found in Chinese thought. Confucianism, for example, with its great doctrine of humanity (*jen*), involves the ever-widening and ever-deepening human relationship that issues forth in the famous statement, "All men are brothers." In this sense, humanity is not a mere abstract concept but one that extends concretely throughout the whole of sentient existence. Confucius once said that when he searched for *jen*, it is always close at hand.[1] It means that humanity is not something external to a person but that it is constitutive of the person's experience, regardless of whether there is consciousness of it or not. It means moreover that in the relational nature of society, individual existence is always more than that which one assumes it to be. In this vein, all experiences must fit into the larger cosmological scheme normally spoken of in terms of heaven, earth and mankind. This triadic relationship is ever-present and ever-in-force, despite one's ignorance, negligence or outright intention to deny it. The concept that permeates and enlivens the triadic relationship is the *Tao*. The *Tao* is a seemingly catchall term, perhaps best translated as the natural way of life and the world. In its naturalness, it manifests all of existence; indeed, it is here, there and everywhere since it remains aloof from human contrivance and manipulation. In a paradoxical sense, it depicts action based on non-action (*wu-wei*), the deepest state of being achievable. The following story illustrates this point.

A cook named Ting is alleged to have used the same carving knife for some 19 years without sharpening it at all. When asked how that is possible, he simply replied:

What I care about is the way (*Tao*), which goes beyond skill. When I first began cutting up oxen, all I could see was the ox itself. After three years I no longer saw the whole ox. And now—now I go at it by spirit and don't look with my eyes. Perception and understanding have come to a stop and spirit moves where it wants. I go along with the natural makeup, strike in the big hollows, guide the knife through the big openings, and follow things as they are. So I never touch the smallest ligament or tendon, much less a main joint. . . . I've had this knife of mine for nineteen years and I've cut up thousands of oxen with it, and yet the blade is as good as though it had just come from the grindstone.[2]

Such then is the master craftsman at work, a master in harmonious triadic relationship based on the capture of the spirit of *Tao* where the function is not limited to a person and his or her use of a tool. And it is clear that such a spirit of *Tao* in craftsmanship is germane to all disciplined experiences we are capable of achieving in our daily activities.

Buddhism, too, has always directed our attention to the larger reality of existence. The original enlightenment of the historical Buddha told of a pure unencumbered experience which opened up all experiential doors in such a way that they touched everything sentient as well as insentient. A Zen story graphically illustrates this point.

Once a master and a disciple were walking through a dense forest. Suddenly, they heard the clean chopping strokes of the woodcutter's axe. The disciple was elated and remarked, "What beautiful sounds in the quiet of the forest!" To which the master immediately responded, "You have got it all upside down. The sounds only make obvious the deep silence of the forest!" The response by the Zen master sets in bold relief the Buddhist perception of reality. Although existential reality refers to the perception of the world as a singular unified whole, we ordinarily perceive it in fragmented ways because of our heavy reliance on the perceptual apparatus and its consequent understanding. That is to say, we perceive by a divisive and selective method which however glosses over much of reality and indeed misses its holistic nature. Certainly, the hewing sounds of the woodcutter's axe are clearly audible and delightful to the ears, but they are so at the expense of the basic silence of the forest (i.e., total reality). Or, the forest in its silence constitutes the necessary background, indeed the basic source, from which all sounds (and all activities for that matter) originate. Put another way, sounds arising from the silence of the forest should in no way deprive nor intrude upon the very source of their own being. Only human beings make such intrusions by their crude discriminate habits of perception and, consequently, suffer a truncated form of existence, unknowingly for the most part.

Now that we have seen Asian lives in general grounded in a holistic cosmological framework, we would have to raise the following question: How does this framework appear in the presence of human rights? Or, contrarily, how does human rights function within this framework?

Admittedly, the concept of human rights is relatively new to Asians. From the very beginning, it did not sit well with their basic cosmological outlook. Indeed, the existence of such an outlook has pre-

vented in profound ways a ready acceptance of foreign elements and has created tension and struggle
between tradition and modernity. Yet, the key concept in the tension is that of human relationship.
This is especially true in Buddhism, where the emphasis is not so much on the performative acts and
individual rights as it is on the matter of manifesta-
tion of human nature itself. The Buddhist always
takes human nature as the basic context in which all
ancillary concepts, such as human rights, are understood and take on any value. Moreover, the context
itself is in harmony with the extended experiential
nature of things. And thus, where the Westerner is
much more at home in treating legal matters detached from human nature as such and quite confident in forging ahead to establish human rights with
a distinct emphasis on certain "rights," the Buddhist
is much more reserved but open and seeks to understand the implications of human behavior, based
on the fundamental nature of human beings, before
turning his or her attention to the so-called "rights"
of individuals.

An apparent sharp rift seems to exist between the
Western and Buddhist views, but this is not really so.
Actually, it is a matter of perspectives and calls for a
more comprehensive understanding of what takes
place in ordinary human relationships. For the basic
premise is still one that is focused on human beings
intimately living together in the selfsame world. A
difference in perspectives does not mean noncom-
munication or a simple rejection of another's view, as
there is still much more substance in the nature of
conciliation, accommodation and absorption than
what is initially thought of. Here we propose two contrasting but interlocking and complementary terms,
namely, "hard relationship" and "soft relationship."

The Western view on human rights is generally
based on a hard relationship. Persons are treated as
separate and independent entities or even bodies,
each having its own assumed identity or self-identity.
It is a sheer "elemental" way of perceiving things due
mainly to the strong influence by science and its
methodology. As scientific methodology thrives on
the dissective and analytic incursion into reality as
such, this in turn has resulted in our perceiving and
understanding things in terms of disparate realities.
Although it makes way for easy understanding, the
question still remains: Do we really understand what
these realities are in their own respective fullness of
existence? Apparently not. And to make matters
worse, the methodology unfortunately has been uncritically extended over to the human realm, into human nature and human relations. Witness its ready

acceptance by the various descriptive and behavioral
sciences, such as sociology, psychology and anthropology. On this matter, Cartesian dualism of mind
and body has undoubtedly influenced our ordinary
ways of thinking in such a manner that in our casual
perception of things we habitually subscribe to the
clear-cut subject-object dichotomy. This dualistic perspective has naturally filtered down into human relationships and has eventually crystallized into what we
refer to as the nature of a hard relationship. Thus, a
hard relationship is a mechanistic treatment of human beings where the emphasis is on beings as such
regardless of their inner nature and function in the
fullest sense; it is an atomistic analysis of beings where
the premium is placed on what is relatable and ma-
nipulable without regard for their true potentials for
becoming. In a way it is externalization in the extreme, since the emphasis is heavily weighted on seiz-
ing the external character of beings themselves. Very
little attention, if any, is given to the total ambience,
inclusive of inner contents and values, in which the
beings are at full play. In this regard, it can be said that
postmodern thought is now attempting to correct
this seemingly lopsided dichotomous view created by
our inattention to the total experiential nature of
things. We believe this is a great step in the right direction. Meanwhile, we trudge along with a heavy burden on our backs, though unaware of it for the most
part, by associating with people on the basis of hard
relationships.

To amplify on the nature of hard relationships, let
us turn to a few modern examples. First, Thomas
Hobbes, in his great work, *Leviathan*,[3] showed remarkable grasp of human psychology when he asserted that people are constantly at war with each
other. Left in this "state of nature," people will never
be able to live in peace and security. The only way out
of this conundrum is for all to establish a reciprocal
relationship of mutual trust that would work, i.e., to
strike up a covenant by selfish beings that guarantees
mutual benefits and gains, one in which each relin-
quishes certain rights in order to gain or realize a
personal as well as an overall state of peace and security. This was undoubtedly a brilliant scheme. But
the scheme is weak in that it treats human beings by
and large mechanically, albeit psychologically too, as
entities in a give-and-take affair, and thus perpetuates
the condition of hard relationships.

Another example can be offered by way of the
British utilitarian movement which later was consummated in American pragmatism. Jeremy Bentham's
hedonic calculus[4] (e.g., intensity of pleasure or pain,
duration of pleasure or pain, certainty or uncertainty

of pleasure or pain, purity or impurity of pleasure or pain, etc.) is a classic example of quantification of human experience. Although this is a most expedient or utilitarian way to treat and legislate behavior, we must remind ourselves that we are by no means mere quantifiable entities. John Stuart Mill introduced the element of quality in order to curb and tone down the excesses of the quantification process,[5] but, in the final analysis, human nature and relationships are still set in hard relations. American pragmatism fares no better since actions by and large take place in a pluralistic world of realities and are framed within the scientific mode and therefore it is unable to relinquish the nature of hard relationships.

In contemporary times, the great work of John Rawls, *A Theory of Justice,*[6] has given us yet another twist in pragmatic and social contract theories. His basic concept of justice as fairness is an example of the reciprocal principle in action, i.e., in terms of realizing mutual advantage and benefit for the strongest to the weakest or the most favored to the least favored in a society. Each person exercises basic liberty with offices for its implementation always open and access available. It is moreover a highly intellectual or rational theory. It thus works extremely well on the theoretical level but, in actual situations, it is not as practical and applicable as it seems since it still retains hard relationships on mutual bases. Such being the case, feelings and consciousness relative to injustice and inequality are not so readily sported and corrected. That is to say, lacunae exist as a result of hard relationships and they keep on appearing until they are detected and finally remedied, but then the corrective process is painfully slow. Thus the theory's strongest point is its perpetually self-corrective nature which is so vital to the democratic process. Despite its shortcomings, however, Rawls' theory of justice is a singular contribution to contemporary legal and ethical thought.

By contrast, the Buddhist view of human rights is based on the assumption that human beings are primarily oriented in soft relationships; this relationship governs the understanding of the nature of human rights. Problems arise, on the other hand, when a hard relationship becomes the basis for treating human nature because it cannot delve deeply into that nature itself and functions purely on the peripheral aspects of things. It is another way of saying that a hard relationship causes rigid and stifling empirical conditions to arise and to which we become invariably attached.

A soft relationship has many facets. It is the Buddhist way to disclose a new dimension to human nature and behavior. It actually amounts to a novel perception or vision of reality. Though contrasted with a hard relationship, it is not in contention with it. If anything, it has an inclusive nature that "softens," if you will, all contacts and allows for the blending of any element that comes along, even incorporating the entities of hard relationships. This is not to say, however, that soft and hard relationships are equal or ultimately identical. For although the former could easily accommodate and absorb the latter, the reverse is not the case. Still, it must be noted that both belong to the same realm of experiential reality and in consequence ought to be conversive with each other. The non-conversive aspect arises on the part of the "hard" side and is attributable to the locked-in character of empirical elements which are considered to be hard stubborn facts worth perpetuating. But at some point, there must be a break in the lock, as it were, and this is made possible by knowledge of and intimacy with the "soft" side of human endeavors. For the "soft" side has a passive nature characterized by openness, extensiveness, depth, flexibility, absorptiveness, freshness and creativity simply because it remains unencumbered by "hardened" empirical conditions.

What has been discussed so far can be seen in modern Thailand where tradition and change are in dynamic tension. Due to the onslaught of elements of modernity, Buddhism is being questioned and challenged. Buddhist Thailand, however, has taken up the challenge in the person of a leading monk named Buddhadasa who has led the country to keep a steady course on traditional values.[7]

> The heart of Buddhadasa's teaching is that the Dhamma (Sanskrit, Dharma) or the truth of Buddhism is a universal truth. Dhamma is equated by Buddhadasa to the true nature of things. It is everything and everywhere. The most appropriate term to denote the nature of Dhamma is *sunnata* (Sanskrit, *sunyata*) or the void. The ordinary man considers the void to mean nothing when, in reality, it means everything—everything, that is, without reference to the self.

We will return to the discussion of the nature of the void or *sunnata* later, but suffice it to say here that what constitutes the heart of Buddhist truth of existence is based on soft relationships where all forms and symbols are accommodated and allows for their universal usage.

Robert N. Bellah has defined religion as a set of normative symbols institutionalized in a society or internalized in a personality.[8] It is a rather good definition but does not go far enough when it comes to describing Buddhism, or Asian religions in general for that matter. To speak of symbols being institutionalized or internalized without the proper existential or ontological context seems to be a bit artificial and has strains of meanings oriented toward hard relationships. Bellah, being a social scientist, probably could not go beyond the strains of a hard relationship, for, otherwise, he would have ended in a nondescriptive realm. The only way out is to give more substance to the nature of religious doctrines themselves, as is the case in Buddhism. The Buddhist Dharma is one such doctrine which, if symbolized, must take on a wider and deeper meaning that strikes at the very heart of existence of the individual. In this respect, Donald Swearer is on the right track when he says:

> the adaptation of symbols of Theravada Buddhism presupposes an underlying ontological structure. The symbol system of Buddhism, then, is not to be seen only in relationship to its wider empirical context, but also in relationship to its ontological structure. This structure is denoted by such terms as Dhamma or absolute Truth, emptiness and non-attachment. These terms are denotative of what Dhiravamsa calls "dynamic being." They are symbolic, but in a universalistic rather than a particularistic sense.[9]

Swearer's reference to an underlying ontological structure is in complete harmony with our use of the term "soft relationship." And only when this ontological structure or soft relationship is brought into the dynamic tension between tradition and modernity can we give full accounting to the nature of human experience and the attendant creativity and change within a society.

Let us return to a fuller treatment of soft relationships. In human experience, they manifest themselves in terms of the intangible human traits that we live by, such as patience, humility, tolerance, deference, nonaction, humaneness, concern, pity, sympathy, altruism, sincerity, honesty, faith, responsibility, trust, respectfulness, reverence, love and compassion. Though potentially and pervasively present in any human relationship, they remain for the most part as silent but vibrant components in all experiences. Without them, human intercourse would be sapped of the human element and reduced to perfunctory activities. Indeed, this fact seems to constitute much of the order of the day where our passions are mainly directed to physical and materialistic matters.

The actualization and sustenance of these intangible human traits are basic to the Buddhist quest for an understanding of human nature and, by extension, the so-called rights of human beings. In order to derive a closer look at the nature of soft relationships, we shall focus on three characteristics, namely, mutuality, holism, and emptiness or void.

MUTUALITY

Our understanding of mutuality is generally limited to its abstract or theoretical nature. For example, it is defined in terms of a two-way action between two parties and where the action is invariably described with reference to elements of hard relationships. Except secondarily or deviously, nothing positive is mentioned about the substance of mutuality, such as the feelings of humility, trust and tolerance that transpire between the parties concerned. Although these feelings are present, unfortunately, they hardly ever surface in the relationship and almost always are overwhelmed by the physical aspect of things.

What is to be done? One must simply break away from the merely conceptual or theoretical understanding and fully engage oneself in the discipline that will bring the feelings of both parties to become vital components in the relationship. That is, both parties must equally sense the presence and value of these feelings and thus give substance and teeth to their actions.

Pursuing the notion of mutuality further, the Buddhist understands human experience as a totally open phenomenon, that persons should always be wide open in the living process. The phrase "an open ontology" is used to describe the unclouded state of existence. An illustration of this is the newborn child. The child is completely an open organism at birth. The senses are wide open and will absorb practically anything without prejudice. At this stage, also, the child will begin to imitate because its absorptive power is at the highest level. This open textured nature should continue on and on. In other words, if we are free and open, there should be no persistence in attaching ourselves to hard elements within the underlying context of a dynamic world of experience. The unfortunate thing, however, is that the open texture of our existence begins to blemish and fade away in time, being obstructed and overwhelmed by self-imposed fragmentation, narrowness and restriction, which gradually develop into a closed nature of existence. In this way, the hard relationship rules. But the nature of an open ontology leads us on to the next characteristic.

HOLISM

Holism of course refers to the whole, the total nature of individual existence and thus describes the unrestrictive nature of one's experience. Yet, the dualistic relationship we maintain by our crude habits of perception remains a stumbling block. This stunted form of perception is not conducive to holistic understanding and instead fosters nothing but fractured types of ontological knowledge taking. Unconscious for the most part, an individual narrows his or her vision by indulging in dualism of all kinds, both mental and physical, and in so doing isolates the objects of perception from the total process to which they belong. In consequence, the singular unified reality of each perceptual moment is fragmented and, what is more, fragmentation once settled breeds further fragmentation.

The Buddhist will appeal to the fact that one's experience must always be open to the total ambience of any momentary situation. But here we must be exposed to a unique, if not paradoxical, insight of the Buddhist. It is that the nature of totality is not a clearly defined phenomenon. In a cryptic sense, however, it means that the totality of experience has no borders to speak of. It is an open border totality, which is the very nature of the earlier mentioned "open ontology." It is a noncircumscribable totality, like a circle sensed which does not have a rounded line, a seamless circle, if you will. A strange phenomenon, indeed, but that is how the Buddhist sees the nature of individual existence as such. For the mystery of existence that haunts us is really the nature of one's own fullest momentary existence. Nothing else compares in profundity to this nature, so the Buddhist believes.

Now, the open framework in which experience takes place reveals that there is depth and substance in experience. But so long as one is caught up with the peripheral elements, so called, of hard relationships one will be ensnared by them and will generate limitations on one's understanding accordingly. On the other hand, if openness is acknowledged as a fact of existence, then the way out of one's limitations will present itself. All sufferings (*duhkha*), from the Buddhist standpoint, are cases of limited ontological vision (*avidya*, ignorance) hindered by the attachment to all sorts of elements that obsess a person.

Holism is conversant with openness since an open experience means that all elements are fully and extensively involved. In many respects, holistic existence exhibits the fact that mutuality thrives only in unhindered openness. But there is still another vital characteristic to round out or complete momentary experience. For this we turn to the last characteristic.

EMPTINESS

Emptiness in Sanskrit is *sunyata*.[10] Strictly speaking, the Sanskrit term, depicting zero or nothing, had been around prior to Buddhism, but it took the historical Buddha's supreme enlightenment (nirvana) to reveal an incomparable qualitative nature inherent to experience. Thus emptiness is not sheer voidness or nothingness in the nihilistic sense.

We ordinarily find it difficult to comprehend emptiness, much less to live a life grounded in it. Why? Again, we return to the nature of our crude habits of perception, which is laden with unwarranted forms. That is, our whole perpetual process is caught up in attachment to certain forms or elements which foster and turn into so-called empirical and cognitive biases. All of this is taking place in such minute and unknowing ways that we hardly, if ever, take notice of it until a crisis situation arises, such as the presence of certain obviously damaging prejudice or discrimination. Then and only then do we seriously wonder and search for the forms or elements that initially gave rise to those prejudicial or discriminatory forces.

Emptiness has two aspects. The first aspect alerts our perceptions to be always open and fluid, and to desist from attaching to any form or element. In this respect, emptiness technically functions as a force of "epistemic nullity,"[11] in the sense that it nullifies any reference to a form or element as preexisting perception or even postexisting for that matter. Second and more importantly, emptiness points at a positive content of our experience. It underscores the possibility of total experience in any given moment because there is now nothing attached to or persisted in. This latter point brings us right back to the other characteristics of holism and mutuality. Now, we must note that emptiness is that dimension of experience which makes it possible for the function of mutuality and holism in each experience, since there is absolutely nothing that binds, hinders or wants in our experience. Everything is as it is (*tathata*), under the aegis of emptiness; emptiness enables one to spread out one's experience at will in all directions, so to speak, in terms of "vertical" and "horizontal" dimensions of being. As it is the key principle of enlightened existence, it makes everything both possible and impossible. Possible in the sense that all experiences function within the total empty nature, just as all writings are possible on a clean slate or, back to the zen story, where the sounds are possible in the silence (emptiness) of the forest. At the same time, impossible in the sense that all attachments to forms and elements are categorically denied in the ultimate fullness of experience. In this way, emptiness completes our experience of reality and, at the same time, provides the grounds for the function of all human traits to become manifest in soft relationships.

It can now be seen that all three characteristics involve each other in the self-same momentary existence. Granted this, it should not be too difficult to accept the fact that the leading moral concept in Buddhism is compassion (*karuna*). Compassion literally means "passion for all" in an ontologically extensive sense. It covers the realm of all sentient beings, inclusive of non-sentients, for the doors of perception to total reality are always open. From the Buddhist viewpoint, then, all human beings are open entities with open feelings expressive of the highest form of humanity. This is well expressed in the famous concept of *bodhisattva* (enlightened being) in Mahayana Buddhism who has deepest concern for all beings and sympathetically delays his entrance to nirvana as long as there is suffering (ignorant existence) among sentient creatures. It depicts the coterminous nature of all creatures and may be taken as a philosophic myth in that it underscores the ideality of existence which promotes the greatest unified form of humankind based on compassion. This ideal form of existence, needless to say, is the aim and goal of all Buddhists.

As human beings we need to keep the channels of existential dialogue open at all times. When an act of violence is in progress, for example, we need to constantly nourish the silent and passive nature of nonviolence inherent in all human relations. Though nonviolence cannot counter violence on the latter's terms, still, its nourished presence serves as a reminder of the brighter side of existence and may even open the violator's mind to common or normal human traits such as tolerance, kindness and noninjury (*ahimsa*). Paradoxically and most unfortunately, acts of violence only emphasize the fact that peace and tranquillity are the normal course of human existence.

It can now be seen that the Buddhist view on human rights is dedicated to the understanding of persons in a parameter-free ambience, so to speak, where feelings that are extremely soft and tender, but nevertheless present and translated into human traits or virtues that we uphold, make up the very fiber of human relations. These relations, though their contents are largely intangible, precede any legal rights or justification accorded to human beings. In brief, human rights for the Buddhist are not only matters for legal deliberation and understanding, but they must be complemented by and based on something deeper and written in the very feelings of all sentients. The unique coexistent nature of rights and feelings constitutes the saving truth of humanistic existence.

NOTES

1. *Lu Yu* (The Analects of Confucius): VII, 29.

2. *The Complete Works of Chuang Tzu,* trans. Burton Watson (New York: Columbia University Press, 1960), pp. 50–51.

3. Thomas Hobbes, *Leviathan* (New York: Hafner, 1926).

4. Jeremy Bentham, *An Introduction to the Principles of Morals and Legislation* (New York: Hafner, 1948).

5. John Stuart Mill observed, "It is better to be a human being dissatisfied than a pig satisfied; better to be a Socrates dissatisfied than a fool satisfied." *Utilitarianism,* cited in Louis P. Pojman, *Philosophy: The Quest for Truth* (Belmont, CA: Wadsworth, 1989), p. 357.

6. John Rawls, *A Theory of Justice* (Cambridge, MA: Harvard University Press, 1971). Rawls also has a chapter on civil disobedience but it too is treated under the same concept of justice as fairness and suffers accordingly from the elements of hard relationships.

7. Donald K. Swearer, "Thai Buddhism: Two Responses to Modernity," in Bardwell L. Smith, ed., *Contributions to Asian Studies,* vol. 4: *Tradition and Change in Theravada Buddhism* (Leiden: Brill, 1973), p. 80. "Without reference to the self" means to uphold the Buddhist doctrine of non-self (Sanskrit, *anatman*) which underlies all momentary existence and avoids any dependence on a dichotomous self-oriented subject-object relationship. For an updated and comprehensive view of Buddhadasa's reformist's philosophy, see Donald K. Swearer, ed., *Me and Mine: Selected Essays on Bhikkhu Buddhadasa* (Albany: State University of New York Press, 1989).

8. Robert N. Bellah, "Epilogue" in Bellah, ed., *Religion and Progress in Modern Asia* (New York: Free Press, 1965), p. 173.

9. Swearer, "Thai Buddhism," p. 92.

10. Etymologically *sunyata* (in Pali, *sunnata*) means the state of being swollen, as in pregnancy, or the state of fullness of being. Thus, from the outset the term depicted the pure, open and full-textured nature of experiential reality.

11. See Kenneth Inada, "Nagarjuna and Beyond," *Journal of Buddhist Philosophy,* 2 (1984): 65–76, for development of this concept.

DISCUSSION QUESTIONS

1. What is the difference between human rights based on a "soft relationship" and human rights based on a "hard relationship"? Which do you prefer? Why?

2. Examine the case of Safuyati Kawuda (discussed in the reading by Jane Perlez) from the Buddhist perspective on human rights.

3. Do you agree with Inada that the rift between Western and Buddhist views of human rights is only an "apparent" one, not a real one? Defend your view.

4. Inada argues that we must get away from approaches to human rights that are mostly theoretical and conceptual. Do you agree? How does Inada's position on human rights compare with Claude Ake's? Explain.

5. Evaluate the U.S. Bill of Rights and the UN Universal Declaration of Human Rights (see p. 140) from the Buddhist human rights perspective. Are they satisfactory from this perspective? Why or why not?

 CHARLOTTE BUNCH

Women's Rights as Human Rights

Charlotte Bunch argues that the human rights community should incorporate gender perspectives. Like Claude Ake and Kenneth Inada, Bunch maintains that the Western conception of human rights is deeply flawed. For Bunch, the Western conception fails to take sufficient account of women's rights. Women around the world are subject to political oppression and various forms of violence based on their sex, and human rights policies marginalize these problems. Bunch argues that Western conceptions of human rights need to be transformed in order to recognize the particular rights of women. Women's rights, according to Bunch, tend to gravitate around socioeconomic rights, that is, rights centered around work, food, and shelter. She closes her article with some practical guidelines for transforming Western conceptions of human rights.

Charlotte Bunch is the author of many books including *Class and Feminism: A Collection of Essays from the Furies* (1974), *Passionate Politics* (1987), *Gender Violence* with Roxanna Carillo (1992), and *Demanding Accountability* with Niamh Reilly (1994).

Charlotte Bunch, *Human Rights Quarterly,* vol. 12, no. 4 (November 1990): 486–496. Copyright © 1990 The Johns Hopkins University Press. Reprinted with permission from the publisher.

Significant numbers of the world's population are routinely subject to torture, starvation, terrorism, humiliation, mutilation and even murder simply because they are female. Crimes such as these against any group other than women would be recognized as a civil and political emergency as well as a gross violation of the victims' humanity. Yet, despite a clear record of deaths and demonstrable abuse, women's rights are not commonly classified as human rights. This is problematic both theoretically and practically, because it has grave consequences for the way society views and treats the fundamental issues of women's lives. This paper questions why women's rights and human rights are viewed as distinct, looks at the policy implications of this schism, and discusses different approaches to changing it.

Women's human rights are violated in a variety of ways. Of course, women sometimes suffer abuses such as political repression that are similar to abuses suffered by men. In these situations, female victims are often invisible, because the dominant image of the political actor in our world is male. However, many violations of women's human rights are distinctly connected to being female—that is, women are discriminated against and abused on the basis of gender. Women also experience sexual abuse in situations where their other human rights are being violated, as political prisoners or members of persecuted ethnic groups, for example. In this paper I address those abuses in which gender is a primary or related factor because gender-related abuse has been most neglected and offers the greatest challenge to the field of human rights today.

The concept of human rights is one of the few moral visions ascribed to internationally. Although its scope is not universally agreed upon, it strikes deep chords of response among many. Promotion of human rights is a widely accepted goal and thus provides a useful framework for seeking redress of gender abuse. Further, it is one of the few concepts that speaks to the need for transnational activism and concern about the lives of people globally. The Universal Declaration of Human Rights,[1] adopted in 1948, symbolizes this world vision and defines human rights broadly. While not much is said about women, Article 2 entitles all to "the rights and freedoms set forth in this Declaration without distinction of any kind, such as race, colour, sex, language, religion, political or other opinion, national or social origin, property, birth or other status." Eleanor Roosevelt and the Latin American women who fought for the inclusion of sex in the Declaration

and for its passage clearly intended that it would address the problem of women's subordination.[2]

Since 1948 the world community has continuously debated varying interpretations of human rights in response to global developments. Little of this discussion, however, has addressed questions of gender, and only recently have significant challenges been made to a vision of human rights which excludes much of women's experiences. The concept of human rights, like all vibrant visions, is not static or the property of any one group; rather, its meaning expands as people reconceive of their needs and hopes in relation to it. In this spirit, feminists redefine human rights abuses to include the degradation and violation of women. The specific experiences of women must be added to traditional approaches to human rights in order to make women more visible and to transform the concept and practice of human rights in our culture so that it takes better account of women's lives.

In the next part of this article, I will explore both the importance and the difficulty of connecting women's rights to human rights, and then I will outline four basic approaches that have been used in the effort to make this connection.

BEYOND RHETORIC: POLITICAL IMPLICATIONS

Few governments exhibit more than token commitment to women's equality as a basic human right in domestic or foreign policy. No government determines its policies toward other countries on the basis of their treatment of women, even when some aid and trade decisions are said to be based on a country's human rights record. Among nongovernmental organizations, women are rarely a priority, and Human Rights Day programs on 10 December seldom include discussion of issues like violence against women or reproductive rights. When it is suggested that governments and human rights organizations should respond to women's rights as concerns that deserve such attention, a number of excuses are offered for why this cannot be done. The responses tend to follow one or more of these lines: (1) sex discrimination is too trivial, or not as important, or will come after larger issues of survival that require more serious attention; (2) abuse of women, while regrettable, is a cultural, private, or individual issue and not a political matter requiring state action; (3) while appropriate for other action, women's rights are not human rights per se;

or (4) when the abuse of women is recognized, it is considered inevitable or so pervasive that any consideration of it is futile or will overwhelm other human rights questions. It is important to challenge these responses.

The narrow definition of human rights, recognized by many in the West as solely a matter of state violation of civil and political liberties, impedes consideration of women's rights. In the United States the concept has been further limited by some who have used it as a weapon in the cold war almost exclusively to challenge human rights abuses perpetrated in communist countries. Even then, many abuses that affected women, such as forced pregnancy in Romania, were ignored.

Some important aspects of women's rights do fit into a civil liberties framework, but much of the abuse against women is part of a larger socioeconomic web that entraps women, making them vulnerable to abuses which cannot be delineated as exclusively political or solely caused by states. The inclusion of "second generation" or socioeconomic human rights to food, shelter, and work—which are clearly delineated as part of the Universal Declaration of Human Rights—is vital to addressing women's concerns fully. Further, the assumption that states are not responsible for most violations of women's rights ignores the fact that such abuses, although committed perhaps by private citizens, are often condoned or even sanctioned by states. I will return to the question of state responsibility after responding to other instances of resistance to women's rights as human rights.

The most insidious myth about women's rights is that they are trivial or secondary to the concerns of life and death. Nothing could be farther from the truth: sexism kills. There is increasing documentation of the many ways in which being female is life-threatening. The following are a few examples:

- Before birth: Amniocentesis is used for sex selection leading to the abortion of more female fetuses at rates as high as 99 percent in Bombay, India; in China and India, the two most populous nations, more males than females are born even though natural birth ratios would produce more females.[3]

- During childhood: The World Health Organization reports that in many countries, girls are fed less, breast fed for shorter periods of time, taken to doctors less frequently, and die or are physically and mentally maimed by malnutrition at higher rates than boys.[4]

- In adulthood: The denial of women's rights to control their bodies in reproduction threatens women's lives, especially where this is combined with poverty and poor health services. In Latin America, complications from illegal abortions are the leading cause of death for women between the ages of fifteen and thirty-nine.[5]

Sex discrimination kills women daily. When combined with race, class, and other forms of oppression, it constitutes a deadly denial of women's right to life and liberty on a large scale throughout the world. The most pervasive violation of females is violence against women in all its manifestations, from wife battery, incest, and rape, to dowry deaths,[6] genital mutilation,[7] and female sexual slavery. These abuses occur in every country and are found in the home and in the workplace, on streets, on campuses, and in prisons and refugee camps. They cross class, race, age, and national lines; and at the same time, the forms this violence takes often reinforce other oppressions such as racism, "able-bodyism," and imperialism. Case in point: in order to feed their families, poor women in brothels around U.S. military bases in places like the Philippines bear the burden of sexual, racial, and national imperialism in repeated and often brutal violation of their bodies.

Even a short review of random statistics reveals that the extent of violence against women globally is staggering:

- In the United States, battery is the leading cause of injury to adult women, and a rape is committed every six minutes.[8]

- In Peru, 70 percent of all crimes reported to police involve women who are beaten by their partners; and in Lima (a city of seven million people), 168,970 rapes were reported in 1987 alone.[9]

- In India, eight out of ten wives are victims of violence, either domestic battery, dowry-related abuse, or among the least fortunate, murder.[10]

- In France, 95 percent of the victims of violence are women; 51 percent at the hands of a spouse or lover. Similar statistics from places as diverse as Bangladesh, Canada, Kenya, and Thailand demonstrate that more than 50 percent of female homicides were committed by family members.[11]

Where recorded, domestic battery figures range from 40 percent to 80 percent of women beaten, usually repeatedly, indicating that the home is the most dangerous place for women and frequently the site of cruelty and torture. As the Carol Stuart murder in Boston demonstrated, sexist and racist attitudes in the United States often cover up the real threat to women; a woman is murdered in Massachusetts by a husband or lover every 22 days.[12]

Such numbers do not reflect the full extent of the problem of violence against women, much of which remains hidden. Yet rather than receiving recognition as a major world conflict, this violence is accepted as normal or even dismissed as an individual or cultural matter. Georgina Ashworth notes that

> the greatest restriction of liberty, dignity and movement and at the same time, direct violation of the person, is the threat and realization of violence. . . . However, violence against the female sex, on a scale which far exceeds the list of Amnesty International victims, is tolerated publicly; indeed some acts of violation are not crimes in law, others are legitimized in custom or court opinion, and most are blamed on the victims themselves.[13]

Violence against women is a touchstone that illustrates the limited concept of human rights and highlights the political nature of the abuse of women. As Lori Heise states: "This is not random violence. . . . [T]he risk factor is being female."[14] Victims are chosen because of their gender. The message is domination: stay in your place or be afraid. Contrary to the argument that such violence is only personal or cultural, it is profoundly political. It results from the structural relationships of power, domination, and privilege between men and women in society. Violence against women is central to maintaining those political relations at home, at work, and in all public spheres.

Failure to see the oppression of women as political also results in the exclusion of sex discrimination and violence against women from the human rights agenda. Female subordination runs so deep that it is still viewed as inevitable or natural, rather than seen as a politically constructed reality maintained by patriarchal interests, ideology, and institutions. But I do not believe that male violation of women is inevitable or natural. Such a belief requires a narrow and pessimistic view of men. If violence and domination are understood as a politically constructed reality, it is possible to imagine deconstructing that system and building more just interactions between the sexes.

The physical territory of this political struggle over what constitutes women's human rights is women's bodies. The importance of control over women can be seen in the intensity of resistance to laws and social changes that put control of women's bodies in women's hands: reproductive rights, freedom of sexuality whether heterosexual or lesbian, laws that criminalize rape in marriage, etc. Denial of reproductive rights and homophobia are also political means of maintaining control over women and perpetuating sex roles and thus have human rights implications. The physical abuse of women is a reminder of this territorial domination and is sometimes accompanied by other forms of human rights abuse such as slavery (forced prostitution), sexual terrorism (rape), imprisonment (confinement to the home), and torture (systematic battery). Some cases are extreme, such as the women in Thailand who died in a brothel fire because they were chained to their beds. Most situations are more ordinary like denying women decent educations or jobs, which leaves them prey to abusive marriages, exploitative work, and prostitution.

This raises once again the question of the state's responsibility for protecting women's human rights. Feminists have shown how the distinction between private and public abuse is a dichotomy often used to justify female subordination in the home. Governments regulate many matters in the family and individual spheres. For example, human rights activists pressure states to prevent slavery or racial discrimination and segregation even when these are conducted by nongovernmental forces in private or proclaimed as cultural traditions as they have been in both the southern United States and in South Africa. The real questions are: (1) who decides what are legitimate human rights? and (2) when should the state become involved and for what purposes? Riane Eisler argues that

> the issue is what types of private acts are and are not protected by the right to privacy and/or the principle of family autonomy. Even more specifically, the issue is whether violations of human rights within the family such as genital mutilation, wife beating, and other forms of violence designed to maintain patriarchal control should be within the purview of human rights theory and action. . . . [T]he underlying problem for human rights theory, as for most other fields of theory, is that the yardstick that has been developed for defining and measuring human rights has been based on the male as the norm.[15]

The human rights community must move beyond its male defined norms in order to respond to the brutal and systematic violation of women globally. This does not mean that every human rights group must alter the focus of its work. However, it does require examining patriarchal biases and acknowledging the rights of women as human rights. Governments must seek to end the politically and culturally constructed war on women rather than continue to perpetuate it. Every state has the responsibility to intervene in the abuse of women's rights within its borders and to end its collusion with the forces that perpetrate such violations in other countries.

TOWARD ACTION: PRACTICAL APPROACHES

The classification of human rights is more than just a semantics problem because it has practical policy consequences. Human rights are still considered to be more important than women's rights. The distinction perpetuates the idea that the rights of women are of a lesser order than the "rights of man," and, as Eisler describes it, "serves to justify practices that do not accord women full and equal status."[16] In the United Nations, the Human Rights Commission has more power to hear and investigate cases than the Commission on the Status of Women, more staff and budget, and better mechanisms for implementing its findings. Thus it makes a difference in what can be done if a case is deemed a violation of women's rights and not of human rights.[17]

The determination of refugee status illustrates how the definition of human rights affects people's lives. The Dutch Refugee Association, in its pioneering efforts to convince other nations to recognize sexual persecution and violence against women as justifications for granting refugee status, found that some European governments would take sexual persecution into account as an aspect of other forms of political repression, but none would make it the grounds for refugee status per se.[18] The implications of such a distinction are clear when examining a situation like that of the Bangladeshi women, who having been raped during the Pakistan-Bangladesh war, subsequently faced death at the hands of male relatives to preserve "family honor." Western powers professed outrage but did not offer asylum to these victims of human rights abuse.

I have observed four basic approaches to linking women's rights to human rights. These approaches are presented separately here in order to identify each more clearly. In practice, these approaches often overlap, and while each raises questions about the others, I see them as complementary. These approaches can be applied to many issues, but I will illustrate them primarily in terms of how they address violence against women in order to show the implications of their differences on a concrete issue.

1. Women's Rights as Political and Civil Rights

Taking women's specific needs into consideration as part of the already recognized "first generation" political and civil liberties is the first approach. This involves both raising the visibility of women who suffer general human rights violations as well as calling attention to particular abuses women encounter because they are female. Thus, issues of violence against women are raised when they connect to other forms of violation such as the sexual torture of women political prisoners in South America.[19] Groups like the Women's Task Force of Amnesty International have taken this approach in pushing for Amnesty to launch a campaign on behalf of women political prisoners which would address the sexual abuse and rape of women in custody, their lack of maternal care in detention, and the resulting human rights abuse of their children.

Documenting the problems of women refugees and developing responsive policies are other illustrations of this approach. Women and children make up more than 80 percent of those in refugee camps, yet few refugee policies are specifically shaped to meet the needs of those vulnerable populations who face considerable sexual abuse. For example, in one camp where men were allocated the community's rations, some gave food to women and their children in exchange for sex. Revealing this abuse led to new policies that allocated food directly to the women.[20]

The political and civil rights approach is a useful starting point for many human rights groups; by considering women's experiences, these groups can expand their efforts in areas where they are already working. This approach also raises contradictions that reveal the limits of a narrow civil liberties view. One contradiction is to define rape as a human rights abuse only when it occurs in state custody but not on the streets or in the home. Another is to say that a violation of the right to free speech occurs when someone is jailed for defending gay rights, but not when someone is jailed or even tortured and killed for homosexuality. Thus while this approach of adding women and stirring them into existing first generation human rights categories is useful, it is not enough by itself.

2. Women's Rights as Socioeconomic Rights

The second approach includes the particular plight of women with regard to "second generation" human rights such as the rights to food, shelter, health care, and employment. This is an approach favored by those who see the dominant Western human rights tradition and international law as too individualistic and identify women's oppression as primarily economic.

This tendency has its origins among socialists and labor activists who have long argued that political human rights are meaningless to many without economic rights as well. It focuses on the primacy of the need to end women's economic subordination as the key to other issues including women's vulnerability to violence. This particular focus has led to work on issues like women's right to organize as workers and opposition to violence in the workplace, especially in situations like the free trade zones which have targeted women as cheap, nonorganized labor. Another focus of this approach has been highlighting the feminization of poverty or what might better be called the increasing impoverishment of females. Poverty has not become strictly female, but females now comprise a higher percentage of the poor.

Looking at women's rights in the context of socioeconomic development is another example of this approach. Third world peoples have called for an understanding of socioeconomic development as a human rights issue. Within this demand, some have sought to integrate women's rights into development and have examined women's specific needs in relation to areas like land ownership or access to credit. Among those working on women in development, there is growing interest in violence against women as both a health and development issue. If violence is seen as having negative consequences for social productivity, it may get more attention. This type of narrow economic measure, however, should not determine whether such violence is seen as a human rights concern. Violence as a development issue is linked to the need to understand development not just as an economic issue but also as a question of empowerment and human growth.

One of the limitations of this second approach has been its tendency to reduce women's needs to the economic sphere which implies that women's rights will follow automatically with third world development, which may involve socialism. This has not proven to be the case. Many working from this approach are no longer trying to add women into either the Western capitalist or socialist development models, but rather seek a transformative development process that links women's political, economic, and cultural empowerment.

3. Women's Rights and the Law

The creation of new legal mechanisms to counter sex discrimination characterizes the third approach to women's rights as human rights. These efforts seek to make existing legal and political institutions work for women and to expand the state's responsibility for the violation of women's human rights. National and local laws which address sex discrimination and violence against women are examples of this approach. These measures allow women to fight for their rights within the legal system. The primary international illustration is the Convention on the Elimination of All Forms of Discrimination Against Women.[21]

The Convention has been described as "essentially an international bill of rights for women and a framework for women's participation in the development process . . . [which] spells out internationally accepted principles and standards for achieving equality between women and men."[22] Adopted by the UN General Assembly in 1979, the Convention has been ratified or acceded to by 104 countries as of January 1990. In theory these countries are obligated to pursue policies in accordance with it and to report on their compliance to the Committee on the Elimination of Discrimination Against Women (CEDAW).

While the Convention addresses many issues of sex discrimination, one of its shortcomings is failure to directly address the question of violence against women. CEDAW passed a resolution at its eighth session in Vienna in 1989 expressing concern that this issue be on its agenda and instructing states to include in their periodic reports information about statistics, legislation, and support services in this area.[23] The Commonwealth Secretariat in its manual on the reporting process for the Convention also interprets the issue of violence against women as "clearly fundamental to the spirit of the Convention," especially in Article 5 which calls for the modification of social and cultural patterns, sex roles, and stereotyping that are based on the idea of the inferiority or the superiority of either sex.[24]

The Convention outlines a clear human rights agenda for women which, if accepted by governments, would mark an enormous step forward. It also carries the limitations of all such international documents in that there is little power to demand its implementation. Within the United Nations, it is not generally regarded as a convention with teeth, as illustrated by the difficulty that CEDAW has had in getting countries to report on compliance with its provisions. Further, it is still treated by governments and most nongovernmental organizations as a document dealing with women's (read "secondary") rights, not human rights. Nevertheless, it is a useful statement of principles endorsed by the United Nations around which women can organize to achieve legal and political change in their regions.

4. Feminist Transformation of Human Rights

Transforming the human rights concept from a feminist perspective, so that it will take greater account of women's lives, is the fourth approach. This approach relates women's rights and human rights, looking first at the violations of women's lives and then asking how the human rights concept can change to be more responsive to women. For example, the GABRIELA women's coalition in the Philippines simply stated that "Women's Rights are Human Rights" in launching a campaign last year. As Ninotchka Rosca explained, coalition members saw that "human rights are not reducible to a question of legal and due process. . . . In the case of women, human rights are affected by the entire society's traditional perception of what is proper or not proper for women."[25] Similarly, a panel at the 1990 International Women's Rights Action Watch conference asserted that "Violence Against Women Is a Human Rights Issue." While work in the three previous approaches is often done from a feminist perspective, this last view is the most distinctly feminist with its woman-centered stance and its refusal to wait for permission from some authority to determine what is or is not a human rights issue.

This transformative approach can be taken toward any issue, but those working from this approach have tended to focus most on abuses that arise specifically out of gender, such as reproductive rights, female sexual slavery, violence against women, and "family crimes" like forced marriage, compulsory heterosexuality, and female mutilation. These are also the issues most often dismissed as not really human rights questions. This is therefore the most hotly contested area and requires that barriers be broken down between public and private, state and nongovernmental responsibilities.

Those working to transform the human rights vision from this perspective can draw on the work of others who have expanded the understanding of human rights previously. For example, two decades ago there was no concept of "disappearances" as a human rights abuse. However, the women of the Plaza de Mayo in Argentina did not wait for an official declaration but stood up to demand state accountability for these crimes. In so doing, they helped to create a context for expanding the concept of responsibility for deaths at the hands of paramilitary or right-wing death squads which, even if not carried out by the state, were allowed by it to happen. Another example is the developing concept that civil rights violations include "hate crimes," violence that is racially motivated or directed against homosexuals, Jews or other minority groups. Many accept that states have an obligation to work to prevent such rights abuses, and getting violence against women seen as a hate crime is being pursued by some.

The practical applications of transforming the human rights concept from feminist perspectives need to be explored further. The danger in pursuing only this approach is the tendency to become isolated from and competitive with other human rights groups because they have been so reluctant to address gender violence and discrimination. Yet most women experience abuse on the grounds of sex, race, class, nation, age, sexual preference, and politics as interrelated, and little benefit comes from separating them as competing claims. The human rights community need not abandon other issues but should incorporate gender perspectives into them and see how these expand the terms of their work. By recognizing issues like violence against women as human rights concerns, human rights scholars and activists do not have to take these up as their primary tasks. However, they do have to stop gatekeeping and guarding their prerogative to determine what is considered a "legitimate" human rights issue.

As mentioned before, these four approaches are overlapping and many strategies for change involve elements of more than one. All of these approaches contain aspects of what is necessary to achieve women's rights. At a time when dualist ways of thinking and views of competing economic systems are in question, the creative task is to look for ways to connect these approaches and to see how we can go beyond exclusive views of what people need in their lives. In the words of an early feminist group, we need bread and roses, too. Women want food and liberty and the possibility of living lives of dignity free from domination and violence. In this struggle, the recognition of women's rights as human rights can play an important role.

NOTES

1. Universal Declaration of Human Rights, adopted 10 December 1948, G.A. Res. 217A(III), U.N. Doc. A/810 (1948).

2. Blanche Wiesen Cook, "Eleanor Roosevelt and Human Rights: The Battle for Peace and Planetary Decency," in *Women and American Foreign Policy: Lobbyists, Critics, and Insiders,* ed. Edward P. Crapol (New York: Greenwood Press, 1987), pp. 98–118; Georgina Ashworth, "Of Violence and Violation: Women and Human Rights," *Change Thinkbook* II (London, 1986).

3. Vibhuti Patel, *In Search of Our Bodies: A Feminist Look at Women, Health, and Reproduction in India* (Shakti, Bombay, 1987); Lori Heise, "International Dimensions of Violence Against Women," *Response,* 12, 1 (1989): 3.

4. Sundari Ravindran, *Health Implications of Sex Discrimination in Childhood* (Geneva: World Health Organization, 1986). These problems and proposed social programs to counter them in India are discussed in detail in "Gender Violence: Gender Discrimination Between Boy and Girl in Parental Family," paper published by CHETNA (Child Health Education Training and Nutrition Awareness), Ahmedabad, 1989.

5. Debbie Taylor, ed., *Women: A World Report, A New Internationalist Book* (Oxford: Oxford University Press, 1985), p. 10. See Joni Seager and Ann Olson, eds., *Women In the World: An International Atlas* (London: Pluto Press, 1986), for more statistics on the effects of sex discrimination.

6. Frequently a husband will disguise the death of a bride as suicide or an accident in order to collect the marriage settlement paid him by the bride's parents. Although dowry is now illegal in many countries, official records for 1987 showed 1,786 dowry deaths in India alone. See Heise, "International Dimensions," p. 5.

7. For an in-depth examination of the practice of female circumcision see Alison T. Slack, "Female Circumcision: A Critical Appraisal," *Human Rights Quarterly,* 10 (1988): 439.

8. C. Everett Koop, M.D., "Violence Against Women: A Global Problem," presentation by the Surgeon General of the U.S., Public Health Service, Washington, DC, 1989.

9. Ana Maria Portugal, "Cronica de Una Violacion Provocada?" *Fempress,* especial "Contraviolencia," Santiago, 1988; Seager and Olson, *Women in the World,* p. 37.

10. Ashworth, "Of Violence and Volition," p. 9.

11. "Violence Against Women in the Family," Centre for Social Development and Humanitarian Affairs, United Nations Office at Vienna, 1989.

12. Bella English, "Stereotypes Led Us Astray," *The Boston Globe* (5 Jan. 1990), p. 17. See also the statistics in *Women's International Network News,* 1989; United Nations Office, "Violence Against Women"; Ashworth, "Of Violence and Volition"; Heise, "International Dimensions"; Portugal, "Cronica."

13. Ashworth, "Of Violence and Volition," p. 8.

14. Heise, "International Dimensions," p. 3.

15. Riane Eisler, "Human Rights: Toward an Integrated Theory for Action," *Human Rights Quarterly,* 9 (1987): 297. See also Alida Brill, *Nobody's Business: The Paradoxes of Privacy* (New York: Addison-Wesley, 1990).

16. Eisler, "Human Rights," p. 291.

17. Sandra Coliver, "United Nations Machineries on Women's Rights: How Might They Better Help Women Whose Rights Are Being Violated?" in *New Directions in Human Rights,* ed. Ellen L. Lutz, Hurst Hannum, and Kathryn J. Burke (Philadelphia: University of Pennsylvania Press, 1989).

18. Marijke Meyer, "Oppression of Women and Refugee Status," unpublished report to NGO Forum, Nairobi, Kenya, 1985, and "Sexual Violence Against Women Refugees," Ministry of Social Affairs and Labour, The Netherlands, June 1984.

19. Ximena Bunster describes this in Chile and Argentina in "The Torture of Women Political Prisoners: A Case Study in Female Sexual Slavery," in *International Feminism: Networking Against Female Sexual Slavery,* ed. Kathleen Barry, Charlotte Bunch, and Shirley Castley (New York: IWTC, 1984).

20. Report given by Margaret Groarke at Women's Panel, Amnesty International New York Regional Meeting, 24 Feb. 1990.

21. Convention on the Elimination of All Forms of Discrimination Against Women, G.A. Res. 34/180 (1980).

22. International Women's Rights Action Watch, "The Convention on the Elimination of All Forms of Discrimination Against Women" (Minneapolis: Humphrey Institute of Public Affairs, 1988), p. 1.

23. CEDAW Newsletter, 3 (13 April 1989), p. 2 (summary of U.N. Report on the Eighth Session, U.N.Doc. A/44/38, 14 April 1989).

24. Commonwealth Secretariat, "The Convention on the Elimination of All Forms of Discrimination Against Women: The Reporting Process—A Manual for Commonwealth Jurisdictions," London, 1989.

25. Speech given by Ninotchka Rosca at Amnesty International New York Regional Conference, 24 Feb. 1990, p. 2.

DISCUSSION QUESTIONS

1. Bunch mentions a number of ways in which the rights of women have been violated around the world. Which of these human rights violations do you find in the case of Safuyati Kawuda (discussed in the reading by Jane Perlez)?
2. Bunch argues that conceptions of human rights need to be "gendered". Do you agree? Why or why not?
3. Is a Buddhist conception of human rights compatible with Bunch's notions of women's rights as human rights? Explain.
4. Like Claude Ake and Kenneth Inada, Bunch maintains that the Western conception of human rights is deeply flawed. How do their views differ? How are they similar?
5. Evaluate the U.S. Bill of Rights and the UN Universal Declaration of Human Rights (see below) from the women's human rights perspective. Are they satisfactory from this perspective? Why or why not?

◈ The U.S. Bill of Rights and the UN Universal Declaration of Human Rights

From May through September 1787, the Constitutional Convention convened and drafted the United States Constitution, establishing a strong federal government. On September 17, 1787, the U.S. Constitution was signed and sent to the states for ratification. The U.S. Constitution went into effect after it was ratified by the ninth state, New Hampshire, on June 21, 1788.

The U.S. Bill of Rights, the first ten amendments to the U.S. Constitution, guarantees fundamental liberties to all U.S. citizens. The U.S. Bill of Rights was passed by Congress on September 25, 1789, and was ratified on December 15, 1791.

The United Nations Universal Declaration of Human Rights was drafted over 150 years after the U.S. Bill of Rights. In the 1940s, a movement emerged to make human rights protections a condition of peace at the close of World War II. Early in the decade, President Franklin Roosevelt had called for the global protection of the freedoms of speech, expression, and worship as well as the freedom from fear and want in his 1941 State of the Union message. In 1947, former First Lady Eleanor Roosevelt was elected to the United Nations Commission on Human Rights. This commission produced the UN Universal Declaration of Human Rights, which was adopted by the United States General Assembly in December 1948.

THE U.S. BILL OF RIGHTS

Amendment I

Congress shall make no law respecting an establishment of religion, or prohibiting the free exercise thereof; or abridging the freedom of speech, or of the press; or the right of the people peaceably to assemble, and to petition the Government for a redress of grievances.

Amendment II

A well regulated Militia, being necessary to the security of a free State, the right of the people to keep and bear Arms, shall not be infringed.

Amendment III

No Soldier shall, in time of peace be quartered in any house, without the consent of the Owner, nor in time of war, but in a manner to be prescribed by law.

Amendment IV

The right of the people to be secure in their persons, houses, papers, and effects, against unreasonable searches and seizures, shall not be violated, and no Warrants shall issue, but upon probable cause, supported by Oath or affirmation, and particularly describing the place to be searched, and the persons or things to be seized.

Amendment V

No person shall be held to answer for a capital, or otherwise infamous crime, unless on a presentment or indictment of a Grand Jury, except in cases arising in the land or naval forces, or in the Militia, when in actual service in time of War or public danger; nor shall any person be subject for the same offence to be twice put in jeopardy of life or limb; nor shall be compelled in any criminal case to be a witness against himself, nor be deprived of life, liberty, or property, without due process of law; nor shall private property be taken for public use, without just compensation.

Amendment VI

In all criminal prosecutions, the accused shall enjoy the right to a speedy and public trial, by an impartial jury of the State and district wherein the crime shall have been committed, which district shall have been previously ascertained by law, and to be informed of the nature and cause of the accusation; to be confronted with the witnesses against him; to have compulsory process for obtaining witnesses in his favor, and to have the Assistance of Counsel for his defence.

Amendment VII

In suits at common law, where the value in controversy shall exceed twenty dollars, the right of trial by jury shall be preserved, and no fact tried by a jury, shall be otherwise reexamined in any Court of the United States, than according to the rules of the common law.

Amendment VIII

Excessive bail shall not be required, nor excessive fines imposed, nor cruel and unusual punishments inflicted.

Amendment IX

The enumeration in the Constitution, of certain rights, shall not be construed to deny or disparage others retained by the people.

Amendment X

The powers not delegated to the United States by the Constitution, nor prohibited by it to the States, are reserved to the States respectively, or to the people.

THE UN UNIVERSAL DECLARATION OF HUMAN RIGHTS

Whereas recognition of the inherent dignity and of the equal and inalienable rights of all members of the human family is the foundation of freedom, justice and peace in the world,

Whereas disregard and contempt for human rights have resulted in barbarous acts which have outraged the conscience of mankind, and the advent of a world in which human beings shall enjoy freedom of speech and belief and freedom from fear and want has been proclaimed as the highest aspiration of the common people,

Whereas it is essential, if man is not to be compelled to have recourse, as a last resort, to rebellion against tyranny and oppression, that human rights should be protected by the rule of law,

Whereas it is essential to promote the development of friendly relations between nations,

Whereas the peoples of the United Nations have in the Charter reaffirmed their faith in fundamental human rights, in the dignity and worth of the human person and in the equal rights of men and women and have determined to promote social progress and better standards of life in larger freedom,

Whereas Member States have pledged themselves to achieve, in co-operation with the United Nations, the promotion of universal respect for and observance of human rights and fundamental freedoms,

Whereas a common understanding of these rights and freedoms is of the greatest importance for the full realization of this pledge,

Now, therefore, the General Assembly *proclaims* this Universal Declaration of Human Rights as a common standard of achievement for all peoples and all nations, to the end that every individual and every organ of society, keeping this Declaration constantly in mind, shall strive by teaching and education to promote respect for these rights and freedoms and by progressive measures, national and international, to secure their universal and effective recognition and observance, both among the peoples of Member States themselves and among the peoples of territories under their jurisdiction.

Article 1

All human beings are born free and equal in dignity and rights. They are endowed with reason and conscience and should act towards one another in a spirit of brotherhood.

Article 2

Everyone is entitled to all the rights and freedoms set forth in this Declaration, without distinction of any kind, such as race, colour, sex, language, religion, political or other opinion, national or social origin, property, birth or other status.

Furthermore, no distinction shall be made on the basis of the political, jurisdictional or international status of the country or territory to which a person belongs, whether it be independent, trust, non-self-governing or under any other limitation of sovereignty.

Article 3

Everyone has the right to life, liberty and security of person.

Article 4

No one shall be held in slavery or servitude; slavery and the slave trade shall be prohibited in all their forms.

Article 5

No one shall be subjected to torture or to cruel, inhuman or degrading treatment or punishment.

Article 6

Everyone has the right to recognition everywhere as a person before the law.

Article 7

All are equal before the law and are entitled without any discrimination to equal protection of the law. All are entitled to equal protection against any discrimination in violation of this Declaration and against any incitement to such discrimination.

Article 8

Everyone has the right to an effective remedy by the competent national tribunals for acts violating the fundamental rights granted him by the constitution or by law.

Article 9

No one shall be subjected to arbitrary arrest, detention or exile.

Article 10

Everyone is entitled in full equality to a fair and public hearing by an independent and impartial tribunal, in the determination of his rights and obligations and of any criminal charge against him.

Article 11

(1) Everyone charged with a penal offence has the right to be presumed innocent until proved guilty according to law in a public trial at which he has had all the guarantees necessary for his defence.

(2) No one shall be held guilty of any penal offence on account of any act or omission which did not constitute a penal offence, under national or international law, at the time when it was committed. Nor shall a heavier penalty be imposed than the one that was applicable at the time the penal offence was committed.

Article 12

No one shall be subjected to arbitrary interference with his privacy, family, home or correspondence, nor to attacks upon his honour and reputation. Everyone has the right to the protection of the law against such interference or attacks.

Article 13

(1) Everyone has the right to freedom of movement and residence within the borders of each State.

(2) Everyone has the right to leave any country, including his own, and to return to his country.

Article 14

(1) Everyone has the right to seek and to enjoy in other countries asylum from persecution.

(2) This right may not be invoked in the case of prosecutions genuinely arising from non-political crimes or from acts contrary to the purposes and principles of the United Nations.

Article 15

(1) Everyone has the right to a nationality.

(2) No one shall be arbitrarily deprived of his nationality nor denied the right to change his nationality.

Article 16

(1) Men and women of full age, without any limitation due to race, nationality or religion, have the right to marry and to found a family. They are entitled to equal rights as to marriage, during marriage and at its dissolution.

(2) Marriage shall be entered into only with the free and full consent of the intending spouses.

(3) The family is the natural and fundamental group unit of society and is entitled to protection by society and the State.

Article 17

(1) Everyone has the right to own property alone as well as in association with others.

(2) No one shall be arbitrarily deprived of his property.

Article 18

Everyone has the right to freedom of thought, conscience and religion; this right includes freedom to change his religion or belief, and freedom, either alone or in community with others and in public or private, to manifest his religion or belief in teaching, practice, worship and observance.

Article 19

Everyone has the right to freedom of opinion and expression; this right includes freedom to hold opinions without interference and to seek, receive and impart information and ideas through any media and regardless of frontiers.

Article 20

(1) Everyone has the right to freedom of peaceful assembly and association.

(2) No one may be compelled to belong to an association.

Article 21

(1) Everyone has the right to take part in the government of his country, directly or through freely chosen representatives.

(2) Everyone has the right of equal access to public service in his country.

(3) The will of the people shall be the basis of the authority of government; this will shall be expressed in periodic and genuine elections which shall be by universal and equal suffrage and shall be held by secret vote or by equivalent free voting procedures.

Article 22

Everyone, as a member of society, has the right to social security and is entitled to realization, through national effort and international co-operation and in accordance with the organization and resources of each State, of the economic, social and cultural rights indispensable for his dignity and the free development of his personality.

Article 23

(1) Everyone has the right to work, to free choice of employment, to just and favourable conditions of work and to protection against unemployment.

(2) Everyone, without any discrimination, has the right to equal pay for equal work.

(3) Everyone has the right to just and favourable remuneration ensuring for himself and his family an existence worthy of human dignity, and supplemented, if necessary, by other means of social protection.

(4) Everyone has the right to form and to join trade unions for the protection of his interests.

Article 24

Everyone has the right to rest and leisure, including reasonable limitation of working hours and periodic holidays with pay.

Article 25

(1) Everyone has the right to a standard of living adequate for the health and well-being of himself and of his family, including food, clothing, housing and medical care and necessary social services, and the right to security in the event of unemployment, sickness, disability, widowhood, old age or other lack of livelihood in circumstances beyond his control.

(2) Motherhood and childhood are entitled to special care and assistance. All children, whether

born in or out of wedlock, shall enjoy the same social protection.

Article 26

(1) Everyone has the right to education. Education shall be free, at least in the elementary and fundamental stages. Elementary education shall be compulsory. Technical and professional education shall be made generally available and higher education shall be equally accessible to all on the basis of merit.

(2) Education shall be directed to the full development of the human personality and to the strengthening of respect for human rights and fundamental freedoms. It shall promote understanding, tolerance and friendship among all nations, racial or religious groups, and shall further the activities of the United Nations for the maintenance of peace.

(3) Parents have a prior right to choose the kind of education that shall be given to their children.

Article 27

(1) Everyone has the right to freely participate in the cultural life of the community, to enjoy the arts and to share in scientific advancement and its benefits.

(2) Everyone has the right to the protection of the moral and material interests resulting from any scientific, literary or artistic production of which he is the author.

Article 28

Everyone is entitled to a social and international order in which the rights and freedoms set forth in this Declaration can be fully realized.

Article 29

(1) Everyone has duties to the community in which alone the free and full development of his personality is possible.

(2) In the exercise of his rights and freedoms, everyone shall be subject only to such limitations as are determined by law solely for the purpose of securing due recognition and respect for the rights and freedoms of others and of meeting the just requirements of morality, public order and the general welfare in a democratic society.

(3) These rights and freedoms may in no case be exercised contrary to the purposes and principles of the United Nations.

Article 30

Nothing in this Declaration may be interpreted as implying for any State, group or person any right to engage in any activity or to perform any act aimed at the destruction of any of the rights and freedoms set forth herein.

DISCUSSION QUESTIONS

1. Claude Ake argues that the U.S. Bill of Rights ascribes "abstract rights to abstract beings." Do you agree with him? If so, is this a virtue of the document or a deficiency? Explain.
2. Does the UN Universal Declaration of Human Rights ascribe, in Ake's words, "abstract rights to abstract beings"? If so, is this a virtue of the document or a deficiency? Explain.
3. To what extent, if any, is the U.S. Bill of Rights useful to the disadvantaged people of America? Defend your view. If it is not useful, how might it be altered to address their needs?
4. Should the U.S. Bill of Rights be rewritten as gender-specific as opposed to gender-neutral? How about the UN Universal Declaration of Human Rights? How would gender considerations alter these documents?
5. Which of the amendments of the U.S. Bill of Rights is the least valuable? Which is the most valuable? If you could add one amendment, what would it say? Defend your views against objections.
6. Which of the articles of the UN Universal Declaration of Human Rights is the least valuable? Which is the most valuable? If you could add one article, what would it say? Defend your views against objections.
7. Consider everything that you have read and discussed about human rights. Now formulate your own Bill of Universal Human Rights. You may base it on the U.S. Bill of Rights, or on the UN Universal Declaration of Human Rights, or on a doctrine of your own design.
8. Some suggest that human rights documents need to be formulated to fit the specific needs of communities; otherwise, they will not be considered legitimate in these communities. Do you agree with this suggestion? Look at the UN Universal Declaration

of Human Rights. What, if anything, in this document can be changed and/or omitted without significant damage to international human rights?

MEDIA GALLERY

 ### "MORALITY AS CUSTOM"

By Herodotus

Summary: In his *Histories*, Herodotus (485–430 B.C.) presented an early version of moral relativism. Darius, king of Persia, once asked some Greeks what it would take for them to eat the bodies of their dead fathers. The Greeks responded that they would not do it for any amount of money. Later, with the Greeks present, Darius asked the Callatians what it would take for them to burn the bodies of their dead fathers. The Callatians screamed and told Darius not to speak of such things. Herodotus uses this example to illustrate his point that morality is determined by custom. If someone were asked to select the best set of beliefs from among all the beliefs in the world, that person would choose those of his or her own country (or region or community). For Herodotus, this is the most likely consequence of our careful and thoughtful attention to all the beliefs in the world. Says Herodotus, "It is unlikely that anyone but a madman would mock such things." He reports that this is a widely held belief among the peoples of the ancient world regarding the relationship between morality and custom. Herodotus was the first Western historian and the first writer on morals in the Western world to present a version of moral relativism. Much of what we know about the ancient Greek world is directly attributable to the writings of Herodotus.

1. What does Herodotus mean when he says that "it is unlikely that anyone but a madman would mock such things"? Do you agree with him? Explain.
2. Herodotus presents us with an example of cultures with different ways of honoring their dead fathers. Is this a good basis for moral relativism? Defend your view.
3. Herodotus says that if someone were asked to select the best set of beliefs from among all the beliefs in the world, that person would choose those of his or her own country. Would you do this? Do you think that this is the dominant view today?
4. How might Mary Midgley respond to Herodotus's remarks about morality and custom?

 ### *DO THE RIGHT THING*

(USA, 1989) 2 hours
Directed by Spike Lee

Film summary: The action takes place over the course of one long, hot summer day. Sal's Famous Pizzeria is owned and operated by an Italian-American family in the predominantly black neighborhood of Bedford-Stuyvesant in Brooklyn. Sal (Danny Aiello), the owner, has been selling pizzas on the same corner for many years and has seen numerous changes in the neighborhood. He employs Mookie (Spike Lee) to deliver pizzas, and the two have an amicable if distant relationship. The film presents the relations between different ethnic groups in the neighborhood as strained, and little by little, the tensions increase. Sal is criticized for his restaurant's "Wall of Fame," which displays pictures of famous Italians and Italian-Americans. Mookie's friends insist that Sal put some pictures of famous African-Americans on the wall since most of his customers are Black. When Radio Raheem (Bill Nunn) enters the pizzeria with his radio blasting, Sal refuses to serve him unless he turns off the music. Raheem does not comply, and Sal vents his rage and frustration by destroying the radio with a baseball bat. In retaliation, Mookie's friends boycott the pizzeria. During the protest, the police kill Radio Raheem in an alleged effort to restrain him. Mookie loses self-control and throws a trash can through the window of Sal's restaurant, inciting angry protesters to destroy the pizzeria.

The film's credits include both a quote from Martin Luther King concerning the importance of nonviolence when confronting racism and a quote from Malcolm X imploring viewers to fight racism by "any means necessary." The film does not condone violence, but it does not reject it. It is a portrait of multicultural life in the United States today—one that asks more questions than it answers.

1. Reread Ruth Benedict's and Mary Midgley's articles, and think about them in the context of Spike Lee's film. Should we regard *Do the Right Thing* as a defense of moral isolationism or a rejection of it? Defend your view.
2. Brooklyn is composed of people from many different nationalities, races, and religions, but all of these people are still considered Americans. Should we regard the people of this community as belonging to one culture or to many? What does the film suggest, if anything? What are the dangers and benefits associated with considering Brooklyn as one culture or many?
3. What is the right thing to do with regard to Sal's "Wall of Fame"? Should Sal put up pictures of famous Blacks or not? Defend your view. What would a utilitarian say? A Kantian?

 ### RED CORNER

(USA, 1997) 1 hour 59 minutes
Directed by Jon Avnet

Film summary: In this film, Jack Moore (Richard Gere) is arrested in China for a murder that he did not commit. Moore meets a Chinese woman in a bar and invites her back to his hotel room. He is awakened the next morning by the Chinese police; the woman is dead, and Moore is covered in her blood. Moore is unfamiliar with the Chinese criminal justice system, where the conviction rate is 99 percent, and pleas of "not guilty" are highly discouraged. His lawyer advises him to plead guilty so that he will not alienate the court. Upon conviction, Moore is placed in solitary confinement. He sleeps on the ground, has no running water, and lives in filthy quarters. His eyeglasses are broken and not replaced. He is beaten by prison guards for not obeying their orders. Moore eventually escapes and reaches the U.S. Embassy. However, he voluntarily returns to prison when he learns that his lawyer has given her personal guarantee of his return, on penalty of losing her license. While the accuracy of the portrayal of prison conditions in China is questionable, *Red Corner* raises important moral issues concerning the denial of human rights to prisoners.

1. Is it always wrong to deny prisoners basic human rights? Defend your view.
2. The U.S. legal system assumes that people are innocent until proven guilty. Do you think that we should judge a court system that assumes that people are guilty until they are proven innocent as immoral? What would a cultural relativist say?
3. Would you include prisoner's rights in drafting a document on human rights? Explain why or why not. What rights would you grant prisoners?
4. Do you feel any sympathy for the way prisoners are treated in *Red Corner?*
5. Jack Moore did not know that he was going to be treated this way in prison. Would you feel differently about his treatment if you knew that he had prior knowledge of how he would be treated? Explain.

 ### WELCOME TO SARAJEVO

(USA/Great Britain, 1998) 1 hour 42 minutes
Directed by Michael Winterbottom

Film summary: This documentary-style movie about a group of American and British journalists sent to report on the Bosnian war is partly based on the experiences of ITN TV journalist Michael Nicholson. Television footage of the war is intercut with the fictional presentation of a group of journalists who are covering the conflict. One of the journalists, Henderson (Stephen Dillane), begins to question his moral position on the war as he avoids bombs and sniper fire in an effort to get the best story. Is it possible to maintain a moral distance from the atrocities that are taking place? Can one stand by passively and watch people suffer? Henderson becomes increasingly disturbed by the ruthlessness of the Serbs toward the Muslims and by the reluctance of the West to help the growing population of orphans. His emotional turmoil results in a personal attempt to save orphans from mistreatment by the Serbs. In particular, Henderson promises a ten-year-old orphan girl that he will bring her back to London with him. After a terrifying bus journey, Henderson and the orphans are stopped by the Serbs when they try to leave Sarajevo. Ignoring a United Nations mandate allowing children to leave the country, armed Serbs forcibly remove the screaming Muslim children from the bus.

Welcome to Sarajevo questions the efficacy of international human rights laws that guarantee countries' protection from foreign aggression. It is insufficient to have strong international human rights laws on the books; laws are worthless if they are not actively enforced.

1. *Welcome to Sarajevo* raises questions about the enforcement of international human rights laws. Should foreign nations be considered morally responsible if they are aware of human rights violations in places such as Sarajevo but do not act to help those whose rights are being violated? Defend your view.

2. If you were in Henderson's position, would you help the orphans? In general, what are our moral obligations to help those in need who are directly before us? Defend your view.

3. As presented in the film, among other reasons, the United Nations did not come to the assistance of the Muslims in Sarajevo because the war was considered an internal affair of Serbia and because there were thirteen other areas worldwide with worse human rights violations than in Serbia. Do you think these are good reasons for not coming to the aid of the Muslims? Defend your view.

4. Are strong human rights laws important even if they are not enforced? What should the penalty for nonenforcement of these laws be? How should we enforce them? Discuss.

SUPPLEMENTARY READINGS

RELATIVISM

Benedict, Ruth. *Patterns of Culture.* Boston: Houghton Mifflin, 1934.

Cook, John W. *Morality and Cultural Differences.* New York: Oxford University Press, 1999.

Finnes, John. *Moral Absolutes: Tradition, Revision, and Truth.* New York: Cambridge University Press, 1991.

Fleischacker, Samuel. *The Ethics of Culture.* Ithaca, NY: Cornell University Press, 1994.

Harman, Gilbert. "Moral Relativism Defended." *Philosophical Review,* 84 (1975): 3–22.

Harman, Gilbert, and Judith J. Thomson. *Moral Relativism and Moral Objectivity.* New York: Basil Blackwell, 1996.

Hurd, Heidi M. *Moral Combat.* New York: Cambridge University Press, 1999.

Ladd, John, ed. *Ethical Relativism.* Belmont, CA: Wadsworth, 1973.

Macklin, Ruth. *Against Relativism: Cultural Diversity and the Search for Ethical Universals in Medicine.* New York: Oxford University Press, 1999.

Margolis, Joseph. *The Truth About Relativism.* Cambridge, MA: Blackwell, 1991.

Melchert, Norman. *Who's to Say?—A Dialogue on Relativism.* Indianapolis: Hackett, 1994.

Midgley, Mary. *Can't We Make Moral Judgments?* New York: St. Martin's Press, 1993.

Moody-Adams, Michele M. *Fieldwork in Familiar Places: Morality, Culture, and Philosophy.* Cambridge, MA: Harvard University Press, 1997.

Stewart, Robert M., and Lynn L. Thomas. "Recent Work on Ethical Relativism." *American Philosophical Quarterly,* 28 (1991): 85–100.

Stout, Jeffrey. *Ethics After Babel.* Boston: Beacon Press, 1988.

Sumner, W. G. *Folkways.* Boston: Ginn, 1907.

Williams, Bernard. *Ethics and the Limits of Philosophy.* Cambridge, MA: Harvard University Press, 1985.

Wong, David. *Moral Relativity.* Berkeley: University of California Press, 1985.

HUMAN RIGHTS

An-Na'im, Abdullahi Ahmed, ed. *Human Rights in Cross-Cultural Perspectives: A Quest for Consensus.* Philadelphia: University of Pennsylvania Press, 1992.

An-Na'im, Abdullahi A., et al., eds. *Human Rights and Religious Values: An Uneasy Relationship?* Grand Rapids, MI: Eerdmans, 1995.

Beyani, Chaloka. *Human Rights Standards and the Movement of People Within States.* Oxford: Oxford University Press, 2000.

Brown, Seyom. *Human Rights in World Politics.* New York: Longman, 2000.

Davenport, Christian, ed. *Paths to State Repression: Human Rights Violations and Contentious Politics.* Lanham, MD: Rowman & Littlefield, 2000.

de Bary, Wm. Theodore. *Asian Values and Human Rights: A Confucian Communitarian Perspective.* Cambridge, MA: Harvard University Press, 1998.

de Bary, Wm. Theodore, and Tu Weiming, eds. *Confucianism and Human Rights.* New York: Columbia University Press, 1998.

Donnelly, Jack. *Universal Human Rights in Theory and Practice.* Ithaca, NY: Cornell University Press, 1989.

Dundes Renteln, Alison. *International Human Rights: Universalism Versus Relativism.* Newbury Park, CA: Sage, 1990.

Dunne, Tim, and Nicholas J. Wheeler, eds. *Human Rights in Global Politics.* New York: Cambridge University Press, 1999.

Hilsdon, Anne-Marie, et al., eds. *Human Rights and Gender Politics in the Asia-Pacific.* New York: Routledge, 2000.

Keown, Damien V.; Charles S. Prebish; and Wayne R. Husted, eds. *Buddhism and Human Rights.* Richmond, Surrey: Curzon, 1998.

Mamdani, Mahmood, ed. *Beyond Culture Talk and Rights Talk: Comparative Essays on the Politics of Rights and Culture.* New York: St. Martin's Press, 2000.

Mayer, Ann Elizabeth. *Islam and Human Rights: Tradition and Politics,* 3rd ed. Boulder, CO: Westview Press, 1999.

Morsink, Johannes. *The Universal Declaration of Human Rights: Origins, Drafting, and Intent.* Philadelphia: University of Pennsylvania Press, 1999.

Perry, Michael J. *The Idea of Human Rights: Four Inquiries.* New York: Oxford University Press, 1998.

Peters, Julie, and Andrea Wolper, eds. *Women's Rights, Human Rights: International Feminist Perspectives.* New York: Routledge, 1995.

Rowan, John R. *Conflicts of Rights: Moral Theory and Social Policy Implications.* Boulder, CO: Westview Press, 1999.

Shepherd, George W., Jr., and Mark O. C. Anikpo, eds. *Emerging Human Rights: The African Political Economy Context.* New York: Greenwood Press, 1990.

Sterba, James. "Human Rights: A Social Contract Perspective." *American Catholic Philosophical Association Proceedings,* 55 (1981): 268–275.

Van Ness, Peter, ed. *Debating Human Rights: Critical Essays from the United States and Asia.* New York: Routledge, 1999.

Williams, Mary E., ed. *Human Rights: Opposing Viewpoints.* San Diego: Greenhaven Press, 1998.

Wilson, Richard, ed. *Human Rights, Culture and Context: Anthropological Perspectives.* Chicago: Pluto Press, 1997.

Zoelle, Diana. *Globalizing Concern for Women's Human Rights.* New York: St. Martin's Press, 2000.

3

Abortion and Euthanasia

"Well," the man said, "if you don't want to you don't have to. I wouldn't have you do it if you didn't want to. But I know it's perfectly simple."

—Ernest Hemingway, "Hills like White Elephants"

Abortion and euthanasia have been and continue to be hotly debated moral issues in the United States. One involves the ending of a pregnancy before live birth, and the other the ending of a life marked by suffering and pain. The question of whether such actions are morally justified has become one of the most divisive issues in American history. Americans have debated and discussed, publicly and privately, abortion and euthanasia in just about every imaginable way and from nearly every conceivable perspective.

Recent bombings of abortion clinics, murders of abortion doctors, and picketing of abortion clinics remind us of the strong beliefs and feelings people have about such life-and-death issues. As students of moral philosophy, we should try to approach these issues and the materials on them with an open, critical mind. Our aim is not only to understand *why* we and others believe the things we do about the morality of abortion and euthanasia but also to consider the differences these beliefs make in our own lives and the lives of others. We should remember that labeling people as "pro-choice" and "pro-life" does not tell us very much about *why* they believe the things they do. In many cases, labels do not even tell us very much about the beliefs of those so labeled. For example, it would not necessarily be contradictory for a "pro-life" person to support abortion in some cases or for a "pro-choice" person to argue for the immorality of abortion in some cases. What matters to us most are the reasons or arguments held by these people—not the labels we use to identify them.

Another thing to keep in mind when reading the articles that follow is the distinction between what is *morally* and what is *legally* justifiable. In this chapter, for example, some articles defend the view that abortion is often immoral, and others that abortion is often moral. Still others focus on the legality, and not necessarily the moral status, of abortion and euthanasia. You should try to keep the legal and moral issues separate. While laws may be based on moral reasoning, the morality of an action and its legality are separate issues. To say that an action is legal is not the same thing as saying it is moral.

Abortion is the termination of a pregnancy. There is much debate concerning the conditions, if any, under which abortion is morally justifiable. For example, is abortion morally justifiable when the mother's life is in danger? In cases of rape or incest? Is it permissible when there is deformity in or damage to the fetus? When the fetus poses a challenge to the parents' financial well-being? These are all reasons women have had abortions. They are also reasons abortion has been challenged.

American women's legal right to have an abortion stems from the constitutional protections of individual privacy. While the Bill of Rights (see Chapter 2) does not explicitly mention privacy, *Griswold v. Connecticut* (1965) set the precedent that privacy is one of the rights of the people protected by the Ninth Amendment. The Supreme Court in *Griswold* said that it was a constitutional violation of spouse's right to sexual privacy for Connecticut to withhold information about birth control from married couples. In 1973, *Roe v. Wade* guaranteed abortion as fundamental to an individual woman's right to privacy. The Supreme Court said in *Roe* that the right to decide whether to bear children is protected by the Ninth through the Fourteenth Amendments. However, the right to terminate a pregnancy is not absolute. The state may limit a woman's right to terminate if it has a legitimate interest in safeguarding her health, in maintaining medical standards, or in protecting human life.

Although abortion is legal in the United States, the moral debate over abortion persists: Under what conditions—if any—is abortion morally justified? There are three main responses to this question: (1) conservatives believe that abortion is immoral under any circumstance, (2) liberals argue that a woman may choose to have an abortion under any circumstance, and (3) moderates consider abortion to be morally justifiable under certain circumstances related to the development of the fetus and the reasons for having the abortion.

Many argue for their position—conservative, moderate, or liberal—in part on the basis of the moral status of the fetus. According to the conservative view, the fetus has full moral status from conception. This means that at any time following conception the fetus holds all the rights given to all humans. It follows that abortion is never morally justified unless there is a moral reason to kill another human being. Defenders of the conservative position often support their view of the moral status of the fetus by appealing to (1) the difficulty in drawing a line between a fetus and a person (the so-called slippery slope argument), (2) the religious argument that the fetus receives a "soul" at the moment of conception, (3) some sufficient condition of personhood such as having a genetic code ("if the fetus has a genetic code, then it is a person"), or (4) the uncertainty argument ("if we don't know whether it's a person, then it's safer to err on the side of caution and assume that it is a person").

Proponents of one version of the liberal view deny the fetus any moral status. Hence, having an abortion is not like killing an adult human and is morally permissible. Proponents of another version of the liberal view claim that the fetus is not human in any arguable moral sense and so has no significant rights. Hence, abortion is morally permissible.

Moderates assign full moral status to the fetus at some point between conception and birth. The proposed criteria for full moral status include brain activity and viability—that is, when the fetus has developed sufficiently within the uterus to be able to survive and continue normal development outside the uterus. Only abortions occurring after the fetus has achieved this status are morally questionable. Note, however, that using viability as part of the proposed criteria for full moral status makes this criterion a shifting one. As medical technology improves, the viability point comes to be increasingly earlier in the pregnancy. In 1950, viability was around 30 weeks, but by 1973, the year of *Roe*, medical technology put viability at 24 weeks. Today, a fetus can survive outside of the uterus as early as 20 weeks. The changing status of medical technology has moved some moderates to tack on an additional condition for viability: with only normal assistance. Whereas food is considered normal, an artificial womb that has been produced by medical technology is not.

Although it is typical in abortion debates to ask at what point in development a fetus becomes a person, *Roe v. Wade* never states that the fetus is a person. Justice Harry Blackmun wrote that any restriction on abortion in the first trimester unconstitutionally violated a woman's right to privacy. In the second trimester, abortion may be regulated for important medical reasons only. And in the last trimester, after the fetus is viable, states may prohibit abortion to protect the potentiality of life, as well as for medical reasons. Still, the issue of *why* questions about the moral status of the fetus are frequently raised in the debate is interesting in and of itself. The reliance on the issue of moral status indicates deep assumptions about the nature of morality. In Western philosophy, morality is often thought to apply only to human beings, or to *persons*. The concept of "person" is broader than that of "human being." For example, some people would argue that cyborgs and androids (if they actually existed) should be regarded as "persons" but not "humans." The point is that, in Western ethics, only humans, or persons, can properly be understood to have moral rights and duties. Therefore, the moral status of the fetus is important because it indicates whether the fetus shares the same moral rights and duties as humans.

Should humans or persons be considered unique in having moral duties and obligations? Why shouldn't nonhuman animals (e.g., cats), or nonhuman living things (e.g., trees), or even nonliving things (e.g., rocks) enjoy the same moral rights and duties as humans or persons? Responses to these questions range from arguments that these entities do not look or act like persons or humans to arguments that they do not understand their actions and cannot realize the difference between right and wrong. Although Chapter 10 takes up these issues in greater detail, the latter argument concerning responsibility for one's actions is relevant to our current discussion.

First, this argument has the advantage of not holding certain entities morally responsible for their actions if they are unable to understand why their actions were right or wrong. For example, children usually are not held to the same legal standard of guilt and innocence as adults. Clearly, many children, like most cats, trees, and rocks, do not know right from wrong and thus cannot judge their actions.

Second, this focus on humans or persons is shared by the readings in Chapter 1. Recall that Aristotle, Mill, and Kant all discuss the *good* life and the *right* thing to do, for human beings and for persons. Aristotle argues that humans should endeavor to engage in practices like being a good friend because this is what makes their lives good. Mill states that, when people try to maximize their happiness, they are living good lives and doing the right thing. Finally, Kant believes that humans, as persons, are primarily rational beings and so should treat others as ends-in-themselves, and not merely as means to an end. In short, these philosophers may have different views about morality, but they all think that morality primarily applies to human beings, or to people.

Third, as these philosophers argue, this focus on humans has the advantage of providing a foundation for building general, normative views about morality. In other words, when we want to know what is right and what is wrong, where do we begin? It is difficult to know how to make moral decisions, especially if we do not know where to begin. If we assume that morality mainly concerns humans or persons, this at least gives us a starting point for building our ethical theories and developing our moral traditions.

Broadly conceived, *euthanasia* is the act or practice of painlessly putting to death those who suffer from terminal conditions. Furthermore, since the advent of medical technology able to prolong the life of those without hope of recovery, euthanasia has also come to mean intentionally not preventing the death of those suffering from terminal conditions. Some choose as well to drop the requirement of a "terminal condition" when discussing euthanasia.

In recent years, euthanasia (from the Greek meaning "good death") has become a controversial issue in the United States. In the 1990s, a Michigan physician, Dr. Jack Kevorkian, helped people with terminal diseases to kill themselves. In England and in the United States, the Hemlock Society, a group that is attempting to legalize euthanasia, believes that humans suffering from incurable diseases who are in extreme pain should be allowed to end their own lives or to be assisted by others in order to have a "good death."

One of the reasons that euthanasia is so controversial is that medical advances enable us to live much longer than our ancestors. Due to these advances, those who fall ill or are victims of an accident can turn to advanced medical technology to save or prolong their lives. However, many question whether medical practitioners must *always* preserve human life at any cost. The moral dilemma of euthanasia, then, involves the balance of the patient's right to a dignified and peaceful death with concerns over the devaluation of life, which result in allowing doctors to make life-and-death decisions.

Legal issues involved in euthanasia were famously established in the case of Karen Ann Quinlan. In April 1975, twenty-one-year-old Quinlan had two inexplicable seizures that left her comatose and irreversibly brain-damaged, though not brain-dead. Doctors labeled her condition a "chronic persistent vegetative state" and judged that no form of treatment could restore her cognitive life. Nevertheless, she was kept breathing by means of a respirator that pumped air through a tube in her throat and was fed by means of a nasal-gastro tube. After a few months, her weight dropped to seventy pounds and her body was bent in a rigid fetal position. Her father petitioned the New Jersey courts for permission to turn off the respirator so that Quinlan could die naturally. Though now unable to communicate her preferences, Quinlan had stated on three earlier occasions that she never wanted her life to be prolonged by extraordinary means. The lower courts refused her father's petition on the grounds that there is no constitutional basis for a "right to die," but only a right to live that would be violated by an act of euthanasia such as taking her off of life support. The higher courts, though, reversed this decision.

In 1976, the New Jersey Supreme Court ruled that the question of euthanasia in cases in which patients are incompetent to make decisions for themselves regarding life support involves the right of privacy (Supreme Court of New Jersey 355 A.2d 647). Justice Hughes, the chief justice in this case, addressed the issues in terms of Quinlan's right not to be invaded physically by painful medical technology and her right to independent choice. When the patient is incompetent to choose independently, Hughes ruled, the patient must be known to have expressed his or her preference for euthanasia in the past. If this has not occurred, then the closest family member must judge whether the patient would have preferred death. According to Hughes, the preferences of the closest family members is consistent with the opinion of the overwhelming majority of people in society.

In the United States, then, letting a patient die by withholding or withdrawing all *extraordinary* equipment that may prolong life is legal. This is called *passive euthanasia*. The cause of death in this case is whatever ailment naturally afflicts the patient, not any artificially administered treatment. Examples of extraordinary means include a respirator, an iron lung, or radiation treatment. These means of prolonging life impose an undue burden both on those providing the means and on those suffering the undue burden. *Ordinary* means of prolonging life, in contrast, do not place an undue burden on those providing the means and on those suffering the undue burden. Examples of ordinary means of prolonging life include food, water, and common antibiotics. *Active euthanasia* is *killing* a patient, that is, causing death by administering a lethal (though humane) treatment such as a drug overdose. Active euthanasia involves a doctor actually taking steps to cause or assist in the death of a patient. This practice is rejected by the American Medical Association and is illegal in all fifty states. However, as we will see in the readings, some have argued that there is no moral difference between passive and active euthanasia.

It should also be noted that the distinction between ordinary treatment and extraordinary treatment is important in euthanasia debates. Some argue that doctors should provide ordinary treatment to patients but not extraordinary treatment. Others argue that doctors should provide all types of treatment. Still others argue that in some instances it is even acceptable to withhold ordinary treatment—that is, food and water—from terminal patients. If feeding tubes, for example, are of no benefit to the patient or if the benefit of the feeding tubes is outweighed by its cost to the patient, some say that it may be morally permissible to withhold feeding or to withdraw the tubes even if this type of action is for the most part illegal. In the case of Karen Ann Quinlan, she lived for ten years without extraordinary treatment (no respirator) but received ordinary treatment during this time, in the form of high-nutrient feedings and regular doses of antibiotics to prevent infections. She never regained consciousness, though she did sometimes have reflexive responses to touch and sound. The question of whether it would have been morally right during this long period of comatose existence to withhold antibiotics so that Quinlan would die of infections makes this line of argument all the more significant.

Another set of distinctions often utilized in moral deliberations about euthanasia is based on the degree of consent or agreement by the patient regarding euthanasia. *Voluntary euthanasia* occurs when a person who is severely suffering and faced with the prospect of a painful end consciously and clearly requests euthanasia. *Nonvoluntary euthanasia* occurs when a patient is incapable of requesting or indicating a desire for death or of forming judgments in the matter—for example, when patients are comatose or senile and have left no legal document like a *living will* in which they state their preferences regarding extraordinary medical treatment. *Involuntary euthanasia* occurs where a person, despite severe suffering and faced with the prospect of a painful end, expresses the desire *not* to die, but is killed or allowed to die anyway. Many regard this as murder.

Finally, it must be noted that euthanasia is not limited to adults. Many children are born anencephalic, that is, with partial or near-total absence of a brain. Children born with birth defects such as Tay-Sachs disease live for only a short time and in great pain. Euthanasia bears on their condition as much as it does on the condition of adults. What is the proper course of treatment for these children? Who should decide the treatment and on what basis? Should we "let them die"? Care for them? Subject them to "active euthanasia"? The issue of whether we should preserve life at all costs is a difficult and complex one if for no other reason than it covers many different situations and contexts.

JUDITH JARVIS THOMSON

A Defense of Abortion

Through a number of imaginative scenarios—the most memorable of which concerns being plugged into a famous violinist—Judith Jarvis Thomson argues that the mother's right to control her own body and her right of self-defense are strong enough to outweigh the fetus's right to life. For the sake of argument, Thomson assumes that the fetus is a person from conception. Abortion, argues Thomson, is morally justifiable in cases in which rape is involved, the mother's life is threatened, and/or reasonable precautions were taken to avoid pregnancy. This article, published two years before *Roe v. Wade,* has become a classic in the abortion debate.

Judith Jarvis Thomson is a philosophy professor at the Massachusetts Institute of Technology, and her books include *Acts and Other Events* (1977), *Rights, Restitution and Risk* (1986), *The Realm of Rights* (1990), and *Moral Relativism and Moral Objectivity* (with Gilbert Harman, 1996).

Most opposition to abortion relies on the premise that the fetus is a human being, a person, from the moment of conception. The premise is argued for, but, as I think, not well. Take, for example, the most common argument. We are asked to notice that the development of a human being from conception through birth into childhood is continuous; then it is said that to draw a line, to choose a point in this development and say "before this point the thing is not a person, after this point it is a person" is to make an arbitrary choice, a choice for which in the nature of things no good reason can be given. It is concluded that the fetus is, or anyway that we had better say it is, a person from the moment of conception. But this conclusion does not follow. Similar things might be said about the development of an acorn into an oak tree, and it does not follow that acorns are oak trees, or that we had better say they are. Arguments of this form are sometimes called "slippery slope arguments"—the phrase is perhaps self-explanatory—and it is dismaying that opponents of abortion rely on them so heavily and uncritically.

I am inclined to agree, however, that the prospects for "drawing a line" in the development of the fetus look dim. I am inclined to think also that we shall probably have to agree that the fetus has al-

ready become a human person well before birth. Indeed, it comes as a surprise when one first learns how early in its life it begins to acquire human characteristics. By the tenth week, for example, it already has a face, arms and legs, fingers and toes; it has internal organs, and brain activity is detectable. On the other hand, I think that the premise is false, that the fetus is not a person from the moment of conception. A newly fertilized ovum, a newly implanted clump of cells, is no more a person than an acorn is an oak tree. But I shall not discuss any of this. For it seems to me to be of great interest to ask what happens if, for the sake of argument, we allow the premise. How, precisely, are we supposed to get from there to the conclusion that abortion is morally impermissible? Opponents of abortion commonly spend most of their time establishing that the fetus is a person, and hardly any time explaining the step from there to the impermissibility of abortion. Perhaps they think the step too simple and obvious to require much comment. Or perhaps instead they are simply being economical in argument. Many of those who defend abortion rely on the premise that the fetus is not a person, but only a bit of tissue that will become a person at birth; and why pay out more arguments than you have to? Whatever the explanation, I suggest that the step they take is neither easy nor obvious, that it calls for closer examination than it is commonly given, and that when we do give it this closer examination we shall feel inclined to reject it.

I propose, then, that we grant that the fetus is a person from the moment of conception. How does the argument go from here? Something like this, I take it. Every person has a right to life. So the fetus has a right to life. No doubt the mother has a right to decide what shall happen in and to her body; everyone would grant that. But surely a person's right to life is stronger and more stringent than the mother's right to decide what happens in and to her body, and so outweighs it. So the fetus may not be killed; an abortion may not be performed.

It sounds plausible. But now let me ask you to imagine this. You wake up in the morning and find yourself back to back in bed with an unconscious violinist. A famous unconscious violinist. He has been found to have a fatal kidney ailment, and the Society of Music Lovers has canvassed all the available medical records and found that you alone have the right blood type to help. They have therefore kidnapped you, and last night the violinist's circulatory system was plugged into yours, so that your kidneys can be used to extract poisons from his blood as well as your own. The director of the hospital now tells you, "Look, we're sorry the Society of Music Lovers did this to you—we would never have permitted it if we had known. But still, they did it, and the violinist now is plugged into you. To unplug you would be to kill him. But never mind, it's only for nine months. By then he will have recovered from his ailment, and can safely be unplugged from you." Is it morally incumbent on you to accede to this situation? No doubt it would be very nice of you if you did, a great kindness. But do you *have* to accede to it? What if it were not nine months, but nine years? Or longer still? What if the director of the hospital says, "Tough luck, I agree, but you've now got to stay in bed, with the violinist plugged into you, for the rest of your life. Because remember this. All persons have a right to life, and violinists are persons. Granted you have a right to decide what happens in and to your body, but a person's right to life outweighs your right to decide what happens in and to your body. So you cannot ever be unplugged from him." I imagine you would regard this as outrageous, which suggests that something really is wrong with that plausible-sounding argument I mentioned a moment ago.

In this case, of course, you were kidnapped; you didn't volunteer for the operation that plugged the violinist into your kidneys. Can those who oppose abortion on the ground I mentioned make an exception for a pregnancy due to rape? Certainly. They can say that persons have a right to life only if they didn't come into existence because of rape; or they can say that all persons have a right to life, but that some have less of a right to life than others, in particular, that those who came into existence because of rape have less. But these statements have a rather unpleasant sound. Surely the question of whether you have a right to life at all, or how much of it you have, shouldn't turn on the question of whether or not you are the product of a rape. And in fact the people who oppose abortion on the ground I mentioned do not make this distinction, and hence do not make an exception in case of rape.

Nor do they make an exception for a case in which the mother has to spend the nine months of her pregnancy in bed. They would agree that would be a great pity, and hard on the mother; but all the same, all persons have a right to life, the fetus is a person, and so on. I suspect, in fact, that they would not make an exception for a case in which, miraculously enough, the pregnancy went on for nine years, or even the rest of the mother's life.

Some won't even make an exception for a case in which continuation of the pregnancy is likely to shorten the mother's life; they regard abortion as impermissible even to save the mother's life. Such cases are nowadays very rare, and many opponents of abortion do not accept this extreme view. All the same, it is a good place to begin: a number of points of interest come out in respect to it.

1. Let us call the view that abortion is impermissible even to save the mother's life "the extreme view." I want to suggest first that it does not issue from the argument I mentioned earlier without the addition of some fairly powerful premises. Suppose a woman has become pregnant, and now learns that she has a cardiac condition such that she will die if she carries the baby to term. What may be done for her? The fetus, being a person, has a right to life, but as the mother is a person too, so has she a right to life. Presumably they have an equal right to life. How is it supposed to come out that an abortion may not be performed? If mother and child have an equal right to life, shouldn't we perhaps flip a coin? Or should we add to the mother's right to life her right to decide what happens in and to her body, which everybody seems to be ready to grant—the sum of her rights now outweighing the fetus's right to life?

The most familiar argument here is the following. We are told that performing the abortion would be directly killing the child, whereas doing nothing would not be killing the mother, but only letting her die. Moreover, in killing the child, one would be killing an innocent person, for the child has committed no crime, and is not aiming at his mother's death. And then there are a variety of ways in which this might be continued. (1) But as directly killing an innocent person is always and absolutely impermissible, an abortion may not be performed. Or, (2) as directly killing an innocent person is murder, and murder is always and absolutely impermissible, an abortion may not be performed. Or, (3) as one's duty to refrain from directly killing an innocent person is more stringent than one's duty to keep a person from dying, an abortion may not be performed. Or, (4) if one's only options are directly killing an innocent person or letting a person die, one must prefer letting the person die, and thus an abortion may not be performed.

Some people seem to have thought that these are not further premises which must be added if the conclusion is to be reached, but that they follow from the very fact that an innocent person has a right to life. But this seems to me to be a mistake, and perhaps the simplest way to show this is to bring out that while we must certainly grant that innocent persons have a right to life, the theses in (1) through (4) are all false. Take (2), for example. If directly killing an innocent person is murder, and thus is impermissible, then the mother's directly killing the innocent person inside her is murder, and thus is impermissible. But it cannot seriously be thought to be murder if the mother performs an abortion on herself to save her life. It cannot seriously be said that she *must* refrain, that she *must* sit passively by and wait for her death. Let us look again at the case of you and the violinist. There you are, in bed with the violinist, and the director of the hospital says to you, "It's all most distressing, and I deeply sympathize, but you see this is putting an additional strain on your kidneys, and you'll be dead within the month. But you *have* to stay where you are all the same. Because unplugging you would be directly killing an innocent violinist, and that's murder, and that's impermissible." If anything in the world is true, it is that you do not commit murder, you do not do what is impermissible, if you reach around to your back and unplug yourself from that violinist to save your life.

The main focus of attention in writings on abortion has been on what a third party may or may not do in answer to a request from a woman for an abortion. This is in a way understandable. Things being as they are, there isn't much a woman can safely do to abort herself. So the question asked is what a third party may do, and what the mother may do, if it is mentioned at all, is deduced, almost as an afterthought, from what it is concluded that third parties may do. But it seems to me that to treat the matter in this way is to refuse to grant to the mother that very status of person which is so firmly insisted on for the fetus. For we cannot simply read off what a person may do from what a third party may do. Suppose you find yourself trapped in a tiny house with a growing child. I mean a very tiny house, and a rapidly growing child—you are already up against the wall of the house and in a few minutes you'll be crushed to death. The child on the other hand won't be crushed to death; if nothing is done to stop him from growing he'll be hurt, but in the end he'll simply burst open the house and walk out a free man. Now I could well understand it if a bystander were to say, "There's nothing we can do for you. We cannot choose between your life and his, we cannot be the ones to decide who is to live, we cannot intervene." But it cannot be concluded that you too can do nothing, that you cannot attack it to save your life. However innocent the child may be, you do not have to wait passively while it crushes you to death. Perhaps a pregnant woman is vaguely felt to have the status of house, to which we don't allow the right of self-defense. But if the woman houses the child, it should be remembered that she is a person who houses it.

I should perhaps stop to say explicitly that I am not claiming that people have a right to do anything whatever to save their lives. I think, rather, that there are drastic limits to the right of self-defense. If someone threatens you with death unless you torture someone else to death, I think you have not the right, even to save your life, to do so. But the case under consideration here is very different. In our case there are only two people involved, one whose life is threatened, and one who threatens it. Both are innocent: the one who is threatened is not threatened because of any fault, the one who threatens does not threaten because of any fault. For this reason we may feel that we bystanders cannot intervene. But the person threatened can.

In sum, a woman surely can defend her life against the threat to it posed by the unborn child, even if doing so involves its death. And this shows not merely that the theses in (1) through (4) are false; it shows also that the extreme view of abortion is false, and so we need not canvass any other possible ways of arriving at it from the argument I mentioned at the outset.

2. The extreme view could of course be weakened to say that while abortion is permissible to save the mother's life, it may not be performed by a third party, but only by the mother herself. But this cannot be right either. For what we have to keep in mind is that the mother and the unborn child are not like two tenants in a small house which has, by an unfortunate mistake, been rented to both: the mother *owns* the house. The fact that she does adds to the offensiveness of deducing that the mother can do nothing from the supposition that third parties can do nothing. But it does more than this: it casts a bright light on the supposition that third parties can do nothing. Certainly it lets us see that a third party who says "I cannot choose between you" is fooling himself if he thinks this is impartiality. If Jones has found and fastened on a certain coat, which he needs to keep him from freezing, but which Smith also needs to keep him from freezing, then it is not impartiality that says "I cannot choose between you" when Smith owns the coat. Women have said again and again "This body is *my* body!" and they have reason to feel angry, reason to feel that it has been like shouting into the wind. Smith, after all, is hardly likely to bless us if we say to him, "Of course it's your coat, anybody would grant that it is. But no one may choose between you and Jones who is to have it."

We should really ask what it is that says "no one may choose" in the face of the fact that the body that houses the child is the mother's body. It may be simply a failure to appreciate this fact. But it may be something more interesting, namely, the sense that one has a right to refuse to lay hands on people, even where it would be just and fair to do so, even where justice seems to require that somebody do so. This justice might call for somebody to get Smith's coat back from Jones and yet you have a right to refuse to be the one to lay hands on Jones, a right to refuse to do physical violence to him. This, I think, must be granted. But then what should be said is not "no one may choose," but only "*I* cannot choose," and indeed not even this, but "*I* will not *act*," leaving it open that somebody else can or should, and in particular that anyone in a position of authority, with the job of securing people's rights, both can and should. So this is no difficulty. I have not been arguing that any given third party must accede to the mother's request that he perform an abortion to save her life, but only that he may.

I suppose that in some views of human life the mother's body is only on loan to her, the loan not being one which gives her any prior claim to it. One who held this view might well think it impartiality to say "I cannot choose." But I shall simply ignore this possibility. My own view is that if a human being has any just, prior claim to anything at all, he has a just, prior claim to his own body. And perhaps this needn't be argued for here anyway, since, as I mentioned, the arguments against abortion we are looking at do grant that the woman has a right to decide what happens in and to her body.

But although they do grant it, I have tried to show that they do not take seriously what is done in granting it. I suggest the same thing will reappear even more clearly when we turn away from cases in which the mother's life is at stake, and attend, as I propose we now do, to the vastly more common cases in which a woman wants an abortion for some less weighty reason than preserving her own life.

3. Where the mother's life is not at stake, the argument I mentioned at the outset seems to have a much stronger pull. "Everyone has a right to life, so the unborn person has a right to life." And isn't the child's right to life weightier than anything other than the mother's own right to life, which she might put forward as ground for an abortion?

This argument treats the right to life as if it were unproblematic. It is not, and this seems to me to be precisely the source of the mistake.

For we should now, at long last, ask what it comes to, to have a right to life. In some views, having a right to life includes having a right to be given at least the bare minimum one needs for continued life. But suppose that what in fact *is* the bare minimum a man needs for continued life is something he has no right at all to be given? If I am sick unto death, and the only thing that will save my life is the touch of Henry Fonda's cool hand on my fevered brow, then all the same, I have no right to be given the touch of Henry Fonda's cool hand on my fevered brow. It would be frightfully nice of him to fly in from the West Coast to provide it. It would be less nice, though no doubt well meant, if my friends flew out to the West Coast and carried Henry Fonda back with them. But I have no right at all against anybody that he should do this for me. Or again, to return to the story I told earlier, the fact that for continued life that violinist needs the continued use of your kidneys does not establish that he has a right to be given the continued use of your kidneys. He certainly has no right against you that *you* should give him continued use of your kidneys. For nobody has any right to use your kidneys unless you give him such a right; and nobody has the right against you that you shall give him this right—if you do allow him to go on using your kidneys, this is a kindness on your part, and not something he can claim from you as his due. Nor has he any right against anybody else that *they* should give him continued use of your kidneys. Certainly he had no right against the Society of Music Lovers that they should plug him into you in the first place. And if you now start to unplug yourself, having learned that you will otherwise have to spend nine years in bed with him, there is nobody in the world who must try to prevent you, in order to see to it that he is given something he has a right to be given.

Some people are rather stricter about the right to life. In their view, it does not include the right to be given anything, but amounts to, and only to, the right not to be killed by anybody. But here a related difficulty arises. If everybody is to refrain from killing that violinist, then everybody must refrain from doing a great many different sorts of things. Everybody must refrain from slitting his throat, everybody must refrain from shooting him—and everybody must refrain from unplugging you from him. But does he have a right against everybody that they shall refrain from unplugging you from him? To refrain from doing this is to allow him to continue to use your kidneys. It could be argued that he has a right against us that *we* should allow him to continue to use your kidneys. That is, while he had no right against us that we should give him the use of your kidneys, it might be argued that he anyway has a right against us that we shall not now intervene and deprive him of the use of your kidneys. I shall come back to third-party interventions later. But certainly the violinist has no right against you that *you* shall allow him to continue to use your kidneys. As I said, if you do allow him to use them, it is a kindness on your part, and not something you owe him.

The difficulty I point to here is not peculiar to the right to life. It reappears in connection with all the other natural rights; and it is something which an adequate account of rights must deal with. For present purposes it is enough just to draw attention to it. But I would stress that I am not arguing that people do not have a right to life—quite to the contrary, it seems to me that the primary control we must place on the acceptability of an account of rights is that it should turn out in that account to be a truth that all persons have a right to life. I am arguing only that having a right to life does not guarantee having either a right to be given the use of or a right to be allowed continued use of another person's body—even if one needs it for life itself. So the right to life will not serve the opponents of abortion in the very simple and clear way in which they seem to have thought it would.

4. There is another way to bring out the difficulty. In the most ordinary sort of case, to deprive someone of what he has a right to is to treat him unjustly. Suppose a boy and his small brother are jointly given a box of chocolates for Christmas. If the older boy takes the box and refuses to give his brother any of the chocolates, he is unjust to him, for the brother has been given a right to half of them. But suppose that, having learned that otherwise it means nine years in bed with that violinist, you unplug yourself from him. You surely are not being unjust to him, for you gave him no right to use your kidneys, and no one else can have given him any such right. But we have to notice that in unplugging yourself, you are killing him; and violinists, like everybody else, have a right to life, and thus in the view we were considering just now, the right not to be killed. So here you do what he supposedly has a right you shall not do, but you do not act unjustly to him in doing it.

The emendation which may be made at this point is this: the right to life consists not in the right not to be killed, but rather in the right not to be killed unjustly. This runs a risk of circularity, but never mind: it would enable us to square the fact that the violinist has a right to life with the fact that you do not act unjustly toward him in unplugging yourself, thereby killing him. For if you do not kill him unjustly, you do not violate his right to life, and so it is no wonder you do him no injustice.

But if this emendation is accepted, the gap in the argument against abortion stares us plainly in the face: it is by no means enough to show that the fetus is a person, and to remind us that all persons have a right to life—we need to be shown also that killing the fetus violates its right to life, i.e., that abortion is unjust killing. And is it?

I suppose we may take it as a datum that in a case of pregnancy due to rape the mother has not given the unborn person a right to the use of her body for food and shelter. Indeed, in what pregnancy could it be supposed that the mother has given the unborn person such a right? It is not as if there were unborn persons drifting about the world, to whom a woman who wants a child says "I invite you in."

But it might be argued that there are other ways one can have acquired a right to the use of another person's body than by having been invited to use it by that person. Suppose a woman voluntarily indulges in intercourse, knowing of the chance it will issue in pregnancy, and then she does become pregnant; is she not in part responsible for the presence, in fact the very existence, of the unborn person inside her? No doubt she did not invite it in. But doesn't her partial responsibility for its being there itself give it a right to the use of her body? If so, then her aborting it would be more like the boy's taking away the chocolates, and less like your unplugging yourself from the violinist—doing so would be depriving it of what it does have a right to, and thus would be doing it an injustice.

And then, too, it might be asked whether or not she can kill it even to save her own life: If she voluntarily called it into existence, how can she now kill it, even in self-defense?

The first thing to be said about this is that it is something new. Opponents of abortion have been so concerned to make out the independence of the fetus, in order to establish that it has a right to life, just as its mother does, that they have tended to overlook the possible support they might gain from making out that the fetus is *dependent* on the mother, in order to establish that she has a special kind of responsibility for it, a responsibility that gives it rights against her which are not possessed by any independent person—such as an ailing violinist who is a stranger to her.

On the other hand, this argument would give the unborn person a right to its mother's body only if her pregnancy resulted from a voluntary act, undertaken in full knowledge of the chance a pregnancy might result from it. It would leave out entirely the unborn person whose existence is due to rape. Pending the availability of some further argument, then, we would be left with the conclusion that unborn persons whose existence is due to rape have no right to the use of their mothers' bodies, and thus that aborting them is not depriving them of anything they have a right to and hence is not unjust killing.

And we should also notice that it is not at all plain that this argument really does go even as far as it purports to. For there are cases and cases, and the details make a difference. If the room is stuffy, and I therefore open a window to air it, and a burglar climbs in, it would be absurd to say, "Ah, now he can stay, she's given him a right to the use of her house—for she is partially responsible for his presence there, having voluntarily done what enabled him to get in, in full knowledge that there are such

things as burglars, and that burglars burgle." It would be still more absurd to say this if I had had bars installed outside my windows, precisely to prevent burglars from getting in, and a burglar got in only because of a defect in the bars. It remains equally absurd if we imagine it is not a burglar who climbs in, but an innocent person who blunders or falls in. Again, suppose it were like this: peopleseeds drift about in the air like pollen, and if you open your windows, one may drift in and take root in your carpets or upholstery. You don't want children, so you fix up your windows with fine mesh screens, the very best you can buy. As can happen, however, and on very, very rare occasions does happen, one of the screens is defective; and a seed drifts in and takes root. Does the person-plant who now develops have a right to the use of your house? Surely not—despite the fact that you voluntarily opened your windows, you knowingly kept carpets and upholstered furniture, and you knew that screens were sometimes defective. Someone may argue that you are responsible for its rooting, that it does have a right to your house, because after all you *could* have lived out your life with bare floors and furniture, or with sealed windows and doors. But this won't do—for by the same token anyone can avoid a pregnancy due to rape by having a hysterectomy, or anyway by never leaving home without a (reliable!) army.

It seems to me that the argument we are looking at can establish at most that there are *some* cases in which the unborn person has a right to the use of its mother's body, and therefore *some* cases in which abortion is unjust killing. There is room for much discussion and argument as to precisely which, if any. But I think we should sidestep this issue and leave it open, for at any rate the argument certainly does not establish that all abortion is unjust killing.

5. There is room for yet another argument here, however. We surely must all grant that there may be cases in which it would be morally indecent to detach a person from your body at the cost of his life. Suppose you learn that what the violinist needs is not nine years of your life, but only one hour: all you need do to save his life is to spend one hour in that bed with him. Suppose also that letting him use your kidneys for that one hour would not affect your health in the slightest. Admittedly you were kidnapped. Admittedly you did not give anyone permission to plug him into you. Nevertheless it seems to me plain you ought to allow him to use your kidneys for that hour—it would be indecent to refuse.

Again, suppose pregnancy lasted only an hour, and constituted no threat to life or health. And suppose that a woman becomes pregnant as a result of rape. Admittedly she did not voluntarily do anything to bring about the existence of a child. Admittedly she did nothing at all which would give the unborn person a right to the use of her body. All the same it might well be said, as in the newly emended violinist story, that she *ought* to allow it to remain for that hour—that it would be indecent in her to refuse.

Now some people are inclined to use the term "right" in such a way that it follows from the fact that you ought to allow a person to use your body for the hour he needs, that he has a right to use your body for the hour he needs, even though he has not been given that right by any person or act. They may say that it follows also that if you refuse, you act unjustly toward him. This use of the term is perhaps so common that it cannot be called wrong; nevertheless it seems to me to be an unfortunate loosening of what we would do better to keep a tight rein on. Suppose that box of chocolates I mentioned earlier had not been given to both boys jointly, but was given only to the older boy. There he sits, stolidly eating his way through the box, his small brother watching enviously. Here we are likely to say "You ought not to be so mean. You ought to give your brother some of those chocolates." My own view is that it just does not follow from the truth of this that the brother has any right to any of the chocolates. If the boy refuses to give his brother any, he is greedy, stingy, callous—but not unjust. I suppose that the people I have in mind will say it does follow that the brother has a right to some of the chocolates, and thus that the boy does act unjustly if he refuses to give his brother any. But the effect of saying this is to obscure what we should keep distinct, namely, the difference between the boy's refusal in this case and the boy's refusal in the earlier case, in which the box was given to both boys jointly, and in which the small brother thus had what was from any point of view clear title to half.

A further objection to so using the term "right" that from the fact that A ought to do a thing for B, it follows that B has a right against A that A do it for him, is that it is going to make the question of whether or not a man has a right to a thing turn on how easy it is to provide him with it; and this seems not merely unfortunate, but morally unacceptable. Take the case of Henry Fonda again. I said earlier that I had no right to the touch of his cool hand on my fevered brow, even though I needed it to save my life. I said it would be frightfully nice of him to fly in from the West Coast

to provide me with it, but that I had no right against him that he should do so. But suppose he isn't on the West Coast. Suppose he has only to walk across the room, place a hand briefly on my brow—and lo, my life is saved. Then surely he ought to do it, it would be indecent to refuse. Is it to be said "Ah, well, it follows that in this case she has a right to the touch of his hand on her brow, and so it would be an injustice in him to refuse"? So that I have a right to it when it is easy for him to provide it, though no right when it's hard? It's rather a shocking idea that anyone's rights should fade away and disappear as it gets harder and harder to accord them to him.

So my own view is that even though you ought to let the violinist use your kidneys for the one hour he needs, we should not conclude that he has a right to do so—we should say that if you refuse, you are, like the boy who owns all the chocolates and will give none away, self-centered and callous, indecent in fact, but not unjust. And similarly, that even supposing a case in which a woman pregnant due to rape ought to allow the unborn person to use her body for the hour he needs, we should not conclude that he has a right to do so; we should conclude that she is self-centered, callous, indecent, but not unjust, if she refuses. The complaints are no less grave; they are just different. However, there is no need to insist on this point. If anyone does wish to deduce "he has a right" from "you ought," then all the same he must surely grant that there are cases in which it is not morally required of you that you allow that violinist to use your kidneys, and in which he does not have a right to use them, and in which you do not do him an injustice if you refuse. And so also for mother and unborn child. Except in such cases as the unborn person has a right to demand it—and we were leaving open the possibility that there may be such cases—nobody is morally *required* to make large sacrifices, of health, of all other interests and concerns, of all other duties and commitments, for nine years, or even for nine months, in order to keep another person alive.

6. We have in fact to distinguish between two kinds of Samaritan: the Good Samaritan and what we might call the Minimally Decent Samaritan. The story of the Good Samaritan, you will remember, goes like this:

A certain man went down from Jerusalem to Jericho, and fell among thieves, which stripped him of his raiment, and wounded him, and departed, leaving him half dead.

And by chance there came down a certain priest that way; and when he saw him, he passed by on the other side.

And likewise a Levite, when he was at the place, came and looked on him, and passed by on the other side.

But a certain Samaritan, as he journeyed, came where he was; and when he saw him he had compassion on him.

And went to him, and bound up his wounds, pouring in oil and wine, and set him on his own beast, and brought him to an inn, and took care of him.

And on the morrow, when he departed, he took out two pence, and gave them to the host, and said unto him, "Take care of him; and whatsoever thou spendest more, when I come again, I will repay thee." (Luke 10:30–35)

The Good Samaritan went out of his way, at some cost to himself, to help one in need of it. We are not told what the options were, that is, whether or not the priest and the Levite could have helped by doing less than the Good Samaritan did, but assuming they could have, then the fact they did nothing at all shows they were not even Minimally Decent Samaritans, not because they were not Samaritans, but because they were not even minimally decent.

These things are a matter of degree, of course, but there is a difference, and it comes out perhaps most clearly in the story of Kitty Genovese, who, as you will remember, was murdered while thirty-eight people watched or listened, and did nothing at all to help her. A Good Samaritan would have rushed out to give direct assistance against the murderer. Or perhaps we had better allow that it would have been a Splendid Samaritan who did this, on the ground that it would have involved a risk of death for himself. But the thirty-eight not only did not do this, they did not even trouble to pick up a phone to call the police. Minimally Decent Samaritanism would call for doing at least that, and their not having done it was monstrous.

After telling the story of the Good Samaritan, Jesus said "Go, and do thou likewise." Perhaps he meant that we are morally required to act as the Good Samaritan did. Perhaps he was urging people to do more than is morally required of them. At all events it seems plain that it was not morally required of any of the thirty-eight that he rush out to give direct assistance at the risk of his own life, and that it is not morally required of anyone that he give long stretches of his life—nine years or nine months—to sustaining the life of a person who has

no special right (we were leaving open the possibility of this) to demand it.

Indeed, with one rather striking class of exceptions, no one in any country in the world is *legally* required to do anywhere near as much as this for anyone else. The class of exceptions is obvious. My main concern here is not the state of the law in respect to abortion, but it is worth drawing attention to the fact that in no state in this country is any man compelled by law to be even a Minimally Decent Samaritan to any person; there is no law under which charges could be brought against the thirty-eight who stood by while Kitty Genovese died. By contrast, in most states in this country women are compelled by law to be not merely Minimally Decent Samaritans, but Good Samaritans to unborn persons inside them. This doesn't by itself settle anything one way or the other, because it may well be argued that there should be laws in this country—as there are in many European countries—compelling at least Minimally Decent Samaritanism. But it does show that there is a gross injustice in the existing state of the law. And it shows also that the groups currently working against liberalization of abortion laws, in fact working toward having it declared unconstitutional for a state to permit abortion, had better start working for the adoption of Good Samaritan laws generally, or earn the charge that they are acting in bad faith.

I should think, myself, that Minimally Decent Samaritan laws would be one thing, Good Samaritan laws quite another, and in fact highly improper. But we are not here concerned with the law. What we should ask is not whether anybody should be compelled by law to be a Good Samaritan, but whether we must accede to a situation in which somebody is being compelled—by nature, perhaps—to be a Good Samaritan. We have, in other words, to look now at third-party interventions. I have been arguing that no person is morally required to make large sacrifices to sustain the life of another who has no right to demand them, and this even where the sacrifices do not include life itself; we are not morally required to be Good Samaritans or anyway Very Good Samaritans to one another. But what if a man cannot extricate himself from such a situation? What if he appeals to us to extricate him? It seems to me plain that there are cases in which we can, cases in which a Good Samaritan would extricate him. There you are, you were kidnapped, and nine years in bed with that violinist lie ahead of you. You have your own life to lead. You are sorry, but you simply cannot see giving up so much of your life to the sustaining of his. You cannot extricate yourself, and ask us to do so. I should have thought that—in light of his having no right to the use of your body—it was obvious that we do not have to accede to your being forced to give up so much. We can do what you ask. There is no injustice to the violinist in our doing so.

7. Following the lead of the opponents of abortion, I have throughout been speaking of the fetus merely as a person, and what I have been asking is whether or not the argument we began with, which proceeds only from the fetus's being a person, really does establish its conclusion. I have argued that it does not.

But of course there are arguments and arguments, and it may be said that I have simply fastened on the wrong one. It may be said that what is important is not merely the fact that the fetus is a person, but that it is a person for whom the woman has a special kind of responsibility issuing from the fact that she is its mother. And it might be argued that all my analogies are therefore irrelevant—for you do not have that special kind of responsibility for that violinist, Henry Fonda does not have that special kind of responsibility for me. And our attention might be drawn to the fact that men and women both *are* compelled by law to provide support for their children.

I have in effect dealt (briefly) with this argument in section 4 above; but a (still briefer) recapitulation now may be in order. Surely we do not have any such "special responsibility" for a person unless we have assumed it, explicitly or implicitly. If a set of parents do not try to prevent pregnancy, do not obtain an abortion, and then at the time of birth of the child do not put it out for adoption, but rather take it home with them, then they have assumed responsibility for it, they have given it rights, and they cannot *now* withdraw support from it at the cost of its life because they now find it difficult to go on providing for it. But if they have taken all reasonable precautions against having a child, they do not simply by virtue of their biological relationship to the child who comes into existence have a special responsibility for it. They may wish to assume responsibility for it, or they may not wish to. And I am suggesting that if assuming responsibility for it would require large sacrifices, then they may refuse. A Good Samaritan would not refuse—or anyway, a Splendid Samaritan, if the sacrifices that had to be made were enormous. But then so would a Good Samaritan assume responsibility for that violinist; so would Henry Fonda, if he is a Good Samaritan, fly in from the West Coast and assume responsibility for me.

8. My argument will be found unsatisfactory on two counts by many of those who want to regard abortion as morally permissible. First, while I do argue that abortion is not impermissible, I do not argue that it is always permissible. There may well be cases in which carrying the child to term requires only Minimally Decent Samaritanism of the mother, and this is a standard we must not fall below. I am inclined to think it a merit of my account precisely that it does *not* give a general yes or a general no. It allows for and supports our sense that, for example, a sick and desperately frightened fourteen-year-old schoolgirl, pregnant due to rape, may *of course* choose abortion, and that any law which rules this out is an insane law. And it also allows for and supports our sense that in other cases resort to abortion is even positively indecent. It would be indecent in the woman to request an abortion, and indecent in a doctor to perform it, if she is in her seventh month, and wants the abortion just to avoid the nuisance of postponing a trip abroad. The very fact that the arguments I have been drawing attention to treat all cases of abortion, or even all cases of abortion in which the mother's life is not at stake, as morally on a par ought to have made them suspect at the outset.

Secondly, while I am arguing for the permissibility of abortion in some cases, I am not arguing for the right to secure the death of the unborn child. It is easy to confuse these two things in that up to a certain point in the life of the fetus it is not able to survive outside the mother's body; hence removing it from her body guarantees its death. But they are importantly different. I have argued that you are not morally required to spend nine months in bed, sustaining the life of that violinist; but to say this is by no means to say that if, when you unplug yourself, there is a miracle and he survives, you then have a right to turn round and slit his throat. You may detach yourself even if this costs him his life; you have no right to be guaranteed his death, by some other means, if unplugging yourself does not kill him. There are some people who will feel dissatisfied by this feature of my argument. A woman may be utterly devastated by the thought of a child, a bit of herself, put out for adoption and never seen or heard of again. She may therefore want not merely that the child be detached from her, but more, that it die. Some opponents of abortion are inclined to regard this as beneath contempt—thereby showing insensitivity to what is surely a powerful source of despair. All the same, I agree that the desire for the child's death is not one which anybody may gratify, should it turn out to be possible to detach the child alive.

At this place, however, it should be remembered that we have only been pretending throughout that the fetus is a human being from the moment of conception. A very early abortion is surely not the killing of a person, and so is not dealt with by anything I have said here.

DISCUSSION QUESTIONS

1. Is the fetus a person for Thomson? What is the difference for Thomson between the fetus and the mother in terms of personhood? Do you agree with her? Does she have a good argument? Defend your position.
2. What is the violinist analogy? How does Thomson use it in her defense of abortion? Do you think that it is a good analogy? Can you think of a better analogy to either defend abortion or argue against it? Explain.
3. According to Thomson, we are not responsible for other people unless we voluntarily assume that responsibility. Do you agree with her? What are some of the implications of her view?
4. What is the difference between a Minimally Decent Samaritan and a Good Samaritan? How does Thomson use this distinction in her argument? Explain.
5. Do you agree with Thomson that abortion is morally justifiable even if the fetus is a person? Why or why not? Do you feel the same way about abortion regardless of the trimester? What if the fetus is in the third trimester? What might Thomson say about the morality of third-trimester abortions? Would you agree with her? Defend your view in detail, responding to possible objections by Thomson.

 DON MARQUIS

Why Abortion Is Immoral

Don Marquis, in his article "Why Abortion is Immoral," argues that the fetus, as a human, has the same moral status, or value, as any other human being. According to Marquis, to abort the fetus is to "deny it a future," and since humans are entitled to a future, so is the human fetus. In short, Marquis offers arguments in defense of the view that abortion is almost always immoral, because it involves killing an innocent human, or person.

Donald B. Marquis is a philosophy professor at the University of Kansas.

The view that abortion is, with rare exceptions, seriously immoral has received little support in the recent philosophical literature. No doubt most philosophers affiliated with secular institutions of higher education believe that the anti-abortion position is either a symptom of irrational religious dogma or a conclusion generated by seriously confused philosophical argument. The purpose of this essay is to undermine this general belief. This essay sets out an argument that purports to show, as well

Don Marquis, *Journal of Philosophy* LXXXVI, 4 (April 1989): 183–202. Reprinted by permission of the author and the publisher. Some notes have been omitted.

as any argument in ethics can show, that abortion is, except possibly in rare cases, seriously immoral, that it is in the same moral category as killing an innocent adult human being.

The argument is based on a major assumption. Many of the most insightful and careful writers on the ethics of abortion—such as Joel Feinberg, Michael Tooley, Mary Anne Warren, H. Tristram Engelhardt, Jr., L. W. Sumner, John T. Noonan, Jr., and Philip Devine—believe that whether or not abortion is morally permissible stands or falls on whether or not a fetus is the sort of being whose life it is seriously wrong to end. The argument of this essay will assume, but not argue, that they are correct.[1]

Also, this essay will neglect issues of great importance to a complete ethics of abortion. Some anti-abortionists will allow that certain abortions, such as abortion before implantation or abortion when the life of a woman is threatened by a pregnancy or abortion after rape, may be morally permissible. This essay will not explore the casuistry of these hard cases. The purpose of this essay is to develop a general argument for the claim that the overwhelming majority of deliberate abortions are seriously immoral.

I

A sketch of standard anti-abortion and pro-choice arguments exhibits how those arguments possess certain symmetries that explain why partisans of those positions are so convinced of the correctness of their own positions, why they are not successful in convincing their opponents, and why, to others, this issue seems to be unresolvable. An analysis of the nature of this standoff suggests a strategy for surmounting it.

Consider the way a typical anti-abortionist argues. She will argue or assert that life is present from the moment of conception or that fetuses look like babies or that fetuses possess a characteristic such as a genetic code that is both necessary and sufficient for being human. Anti-abortionists seem to believe that (1) the truth of all of these claims is quite obvious, and (2) establishing any of these claims is sufficient to show that abortion is morally akin to murder.

A standard pro-choice strategy exhibits similarities. The pro-choicer will argue or assert that fetuses are not persons or that fetuses are not rational agents or that fetuses are not social beings. Pro-choicers seem to believe that (1) the truth of any of

these claims is quite obvious, and (2) establishing any of these claims is sufficient to show that an abortion is not a wrongful killing.

In fact, both the pro-choice and the anti-abortion claims do seem to be true, although the "it looks like a baby" claim is more difficult to establish the earlier the pregnancy. We seem to have a standoff. How can it be resolved?

As everyone who has taken a bit of logic knows, if any of these arguments concerning abortion is a good argument, it requires not only some claim characterizing fetuses, but also some general moral principle that ties a characteristic of fetuses to having or not having the right to life or to some other moral characteristic that will generate the obligation or the lack of obligation not to end the life of a fetus. Accordingly, the arguments of the anti-abortionist and the pro-choicer need a bit of filling in to be regarded as adequate.

Note what each partisan will say. The anti-abortionist will claim that her position is supported by such generally accepted moral principles as "It is always prima facie seriously wrong to take a human life" or "It is always prima facie seriously wrong to end the life of a baby." Since these are generally accepted moral principles, her position is certainly not obviously wrong. The pro-choicer will claim that her position is supported by such plausible moral principles as "Being a person is what gives an individual intrinsic moral worth" or "It is only seriously prima facie wrong to take the life of a member of the human community." Since these are generally accepted moral principles, the pro-choice position is certainly not obviously wrong. Unfortunately, we have again arrived at a standoff.

Now, how might one deal with this standoff? The standard approach is to try to show how the moral principles of one's opponent lose their plausibility under analysis. It is easy to see how this is possible. On the one hand, the anti-abortionist will defend a moral principle concerning the wrongness of killing which tends to be broad in scope in order that even fetuses at an early stage of pregnancy will fall under it. The problem with broad principles is that they often embrace too much. In this particular instance, the principle "It is always prima facie wrong to take a human life" seems to entail that it is wrong to end the existence of a living human cancer-cell culture, on the grounds that the culture is both living and human. Therefore, it seems that the anti-abortionist's favored principle is too broad.

On the other hand, the pro-choicer wants to find a moral principle concerning the wrongness of killing which tends to be narrow in scope in order that fetuses will *not* fall under it. The problem with narrow principles is that they often do not embrace enough. Hence, the needed principles such as "It is prima facie seriously wrong to kill only persons" or "It is prima facie wrong to kill only rational agents" do not explain why it is wrong to kill infants or young children or the severely retarded or even perhaps the severely mentally ill. Therefore, we seem again to have a standoff. The anti-abortionist charges, not unreasonably, that pro-choice principles concerning killing are too narrow to be acceptable; the pro-choicer charges, not unreasonably, that anti-abortionist principles concerning killing are too broad to be acceptable.

Attempts by both sides to patch up the difficulties in their positions run into further difficulties. The anti-abortionist will try to remove the problem in her position by reformulating her principle concerning killing in terms of human beings. Now we end up with "It is always prima facie seriously wrong to end the life of a human being." This principle has the advantage of avoiding the problem of the human cancer-cell culture counterexample. But this advantage is purchased at a high price. For although it is clear that a fetus is both human and alive, it is not at all clear that a fetus is a human *being*. There is at least something to be said for the view that something becomes a human being only after a process of development, and that therefore first trimester fetuses and perhaps all fetuses are not yet human beings. Hence, the anti-abortionist, by this move, has merely exchanged one problem for another.

The pro-choicer fares no better. She may attempt to find reasons why killing infants, young children, and the severely retarded is wrong which are independent of her major principle that is supposed to explain the wrongness of taking human life, but which will not also make abortion immoral. This is no easy task. Appeals to social utility will seem satisfactory only to those who resolve not to think of the enormous difficulties with a utilitarian account of the wrongness of killing and the significant social costs of preserving the lives of the unproductive. A pro-choice strategy that extends the definition of "person" to infants or even to young children seems just as arbitrary as an anti-abortion strategy that extends the definition of "human being" to fetuses. Again, we find symmetries in the two positions and we arrive at a standoff.

There are even further problems that reflect symmetries in the two positions. In addition to counterexample problems, or the arbitrary application

problems that can be exchanged for them, the standard anti-abortionist principle "It is prima facie seriously wrong to kill a human being," or one of its variants, can be objected to on the grounds of ambiguity. If "human being" is taken to be a *biological* category, then the anti-abortionist is left with the problem of explaining why a merely biological category should make a moral difference. Why, it is asked, is it any more reasonable to base a moral conclusion on the number of chromosomes in one's cells than on the color of one's skin? If "human being," on the other hand, is taken to be a *moral* category, then the claim that a fetus is a human being cannot be taken to be a premise in the anti-abortion argument, for it is precisely what needs to be established. Hence, either the anti-abortionist's main category is a morally irrelevant, merely biological category, or it is of no use to the anti-abortionist in establishing (noncircularly, of course) that abortion is wrong.

Although this problem with the anti-abortionist position is often noticed, it is less often noticed that the pro-choice position suffers from an analogous problem. The principle "Only persons have the right to life" also suffers from an ambiguity. The term "person" is typically defined in terms of psychological characteristics, although there will certainly be disagreement concerning which characteristics are most important. Supposing that this matter can be settled, the pro-choicer is left with the problem of explaining why *psychological* characteristics should make a *moral* difference. If the pro-choicer should attempt to deal with this problem by claiming that an explanation is not necessary, that in fact we do treat such a cluster of psychological properties as having moral significance, the sharp-witted anti-abortionist should have a ready response. We do treat being both living and human as having moral significance. If it is legitimate for the pro-choicer to demand that the anti-abortionist provide an explanation of the connection between the biological character of being a human being and the wrongness of being killed (even though people accept this connection), then it is legitimate for the anti-abortionist to demand that the pro-choicer provide an explanation of the connection between psychological criteria for being a person and the wrongness of being killed (even though that connection is accepted).

Feinberg has attempted to meet this objection (he calls psychological personhood "commonsense personhood"):

> The characteristics that confer commonsense personhood are not arbitrary bases for rights

and duties, such as race, sex or species membership; rather they are traits that make sense out of rights and duties and without which those moral attributes would have no point or function. It is because people are conscious; have a sense of their personal identities; have plans, goals, and projects; experience emotions; are liable to pains, anxieties, and frustrations; can reason and bargain, and so on—it is because of these attributes that people have values and interests, desires and expectations of their own, including a stake in their own futures, and a personal well-being of a sort we cannot ascribe to unconscious or nonrational beings. Because of their developed capacities they can assume duties and responsibilities and can have and make claims on one another. Only because of their sense of self, their life plans, their value hierarchies, and their stakes in their own futures can they be ascribed fundamental rights. There is nothing arbitrary about these linkages.[2]

The plausible aspects of this attempt should not be taken to obscure its implausible features. There is a great deal to be said for the view that being a psychological person under some description is a necessary condition for having duties. One cannot have a duty unless one is capable of behaving morally, and a being's capability of behaving morally will require having a certain psychology. It is far from obvious, however, that having rights entails consciousness or rationality, as Feinberg suggests. We speak of the rights of the severely retarded or the severely mentally ill, yet some of these persons are not rational. We speak of the rights of the temporarily unconscious. The New Jersey Supreme Court based their decision in the Quinlan case on Karen Ann Quinlan's right to privacy, and she was known to be permanently unconscious at that time. Hence, Feinberg's claim that having rights entails being conscious is, on its face, obviously false.

Of course, it might not make sense to attribute rights to a being that would never in its natural history have certain psychological traits. This modest connection between psychological personhood and moral personhood will create a place for Karen Ann Quinlan and the temporarily unconscious. But then it makes a place for fetuses also. Hence, it does not serve Feinberg's pro-choice purposes. Accordingly, it seems that the pro-choicer will have as much difficulty bridging the gap between psychological personhood and personhood in the moral sense as the anti-abortionist has bridging the gap between being

a biological human being and being a human being in the moral sense.

Furthermore, the pro-choicer cannot any more escape her problem by making person a purely moral category than the anti-abortionist could escape by the analogous move. For if person is a moral category, then the pro-choicer is left without the resources for establishing (noncircularly, of course) the claim that a fetus is not a person, which is an essential premise in her argument. Again, we have both a symmetry and a standoff between pro-choice and anti-abortion views.

Passions in the abortion debate run high. There are both plausibilities and difficulties with the standard positions. Accordingly, it is hardly surprising that partisans of either side embrace with fervor the moral generalizations that support the conclusions they preanalytically favor, and reject with disdain the moral generalizations of their opponents as being subject to inescapable difficulties. It is easy to believe that the counterexamples to one's own moral principles are merely temporary difficulties that will dissolve in the wake of further philosophical research, and that the counterexamples to the principles of one's opponents are as straightforward as the contradiction between *A* and *O* propositions in traditional logic. This might suggest to an impartial observer (if there are any) that the abortion issue is unresolvable.

There is a way out of this apparent dialectical quandary. The moral generalizations of both sides are not quite correct. The generalizations hold for the most part, for the usual cases. This suggests that they are all *accidental* generalizations, that the moral claims made by those on both sides of the dispute do not touch on the *essence* of the matter.

This use of the distinction between essence and accident is not meant to invoke obscure metaphysical categories. Rather, it is intended to reflect the rather atheoretical nature of the abortion discussion. If the generalization a partisan in the abortion dispute adopts were derived from the reason why ending the life of a human being is wrong, then there could not be exceptions to that generalization unless some special case obtains in which there are even more powerful countervailing reasons. Such generalizations would not be merely accidental generalizations; they would point to, or be based upon, the essence of the wrongness of killing, what it is that makes killing wrong. All this suggests that a necessary condition of resolving the abortion controversy is a more theoretical account of the wrongness of killing. After all, if we merely believe, but do not understand, why killing adult human beings such as ourselves is wrong, how could we conceivably show that abortion is either immoral or permissible?

II

In order to develop such an account, we can start from the following unproblematic assumption concerning our own case: it is wrong to kill us. Why is it wrong? Some answers can be easily eliminated. It might be said that what makes killing us wrong is that a killing brutalizes the one who kills. But the brutalization consists of being inured to the performance of an act that is hideously immoral; hence, the brutalization does not explain the immorality. It might be said that what makes killing us wrong is the great loss others would experience due to our absence. Although such hubris is understandable, such an explanation does not account for the wrongness of killing hermits, or those whose lives are relatively independent and whose friends find it easy to make new friends.

A more obvious answer is better. What primarily makes killing wrong is neither its effect on the murderer nor its effect on the victim's friends and relatives, but its effect on the victim. The loss of one's life is one of the greatest losses one can suffer. The loss of one's life deprives one of all the experiences, activities, projects, and enjoyments that would otherwise have constituted one's future. Therefore, killing someone is wrong, primarily because the killing inflicts (one of) the greatest possible losses on the victim. To describe this as the loss of life can be misleading, however. The change in my biological state does not by itself make killing me wrong. The effect of the loss of my biological life is the loss to me of all those activities, projects, experiences, and enjoyments which would otherwise have constituted my future personal life. These activities, projects, experiences, and enjoyments are either valuable for their own sakes or are means to something else that is valuable for its own sake. Some parts of my future are not valued by me now, but will come to be valued by me as I grow older and as my values and capacities change. When I am killed, I am deprived both of what I now value which would have been part of my future personal life, but also what I would come to value. Therefore, when I die, I am deprived of all of the value of my future. Inflicting this loss on me is ultimately what makes killing me wrong. This being the case, it would seem that what makes killing *any*

adult human being prima facie seriously wrong is the loss of his or her future.

How should this rudimentary theory of the wrongness of killing be evaluated? It cannot be faulted for deriving an "ought" from an "is," for it does not. The analysis assumes that killing me (or you, reader) is prima facie seriously wrong. The point of the analysis is to establish which natural property ultimately explains the wrongness of the killing, given that it is wrong. A natural property will ultimately explain the wrongness of killing, only if (1) the explanation fits with our intuitions about the matter and (2) there is no other natural property that provides the basis for a better explanation of the wrongness of killing. This analysis rests on the intuition that what makes killing a particular human or animal wrong is what it does to that particular human or animal. What makes killing wrong is some natural effect or other of the killing. Some would deny this. For instance, a divine-command theorist in ethics would deny it. Surely this denial is, however, one of those features of divine-command theory which renders it so implausible.

The claim that what makes killing wrong is the loss of the victim's future is directly supported by two considerations. In the first place, this theory explains why we regard killing as one of the worst of crimes. Killing is especially wrong, because it deprives the victim of more than perhaps any other crime. In the second place, people with AIDS or cancer who know they are dying believe, of course, that dying is a very bad thing for them. They believe that the loss of a future to them that they would otherwise have experienced is what makes their premature death a very bad thing for them. A better theory of the wrongness of killing would require a different natural property associated with killing which better fits with the attitudes of the dying. What could it be?

The view that what makes killing wrong is the loss to the victim of the value of the victim's future gains additional support when some of its implications are examined. In the first place, it is incompatible with the view that it is wrong to kill only beings who are biologically human. It is possible that there exists a different species from another planet whose members have a future like ours. Since having a future like that is what makes killing someone wrong, this theory entails that it would be wrong to kill members of such a species. Hence, this theory is opposed to the claim that only life that is biologically human has great moral worth, a claim which many anti-abortionists have seemed to adopt. This opposition, which this theory has in common with personhood theories, seems to be a merit of the theory.

In the second place, the claim that the loss of one's future is the wrong-making feature of one's being killed entails the possibility that the futures of some actual nonhuman mammals on our own planet are sufficiently like ours that it is seriously wrong to kill them also. Whether some animals do have the same right to life as human beings depends on adding to the account of the wrongness of killing some additional account of just what it is about my future or the futures of other adult human beings which makes it wrong to kill us. No such additional account will be offered in this essay. Undoubtedly, the provision of such an account would be a very difficult matter. Undoubtedly, any such account would be quite controversial. Hence, it surely should not reflect badly on this sketch of an elementary theory of the wrongness of killing that it is indeterminate with respect to some very difficult issues regarding animal rights.

In the third place, the claim that the loss of one's future is the wrong-making feature of one's being killed does not entail, as sanctity of human life theories do, that active euthanasia is wrong. Persons who are severely and incurably ill, who face a future of pain and despair, and who wish to die will not have suffered a loss if they are killed. It is, strictly speaking, the value of a human's future which makes killing wrong in this theory. This being so, killing does not necessarily wrong some persons who are sick and dying. Of course, there may be other reasons for a prohibition of active euthanasia, but that is another matter. Sanctity-of-human-life theories seem to hold that active euthanasia is seriously wrong even in an individual case where there seems to be good reason for it independently of public policy considerations. This consequence is most implausible, and it is a plus for the claim that the loss of a future of value is what makes killing wrong that it does not share this consequence.

In the fourth place, the account of the wrongness of killing defended in this essay does straightforwardly entail that it is prima facie seriously wrong to kill children and infants, for we do presume that they have futures of value. Since we do believe that it is wrong to kill defenseless little babies, it is important that a theory of the wrongness of killing easily account for this. Personhood theories of the wrongness of killing, on the other hand, cannot straightforwardly account for the wrongness of killing infants and young children. Hence, such theories must add special ad hoc accounts of the

wrongness of killing the young. The plausibility of such ad hoc theories seems to be a function of how desperately one wants such theories to work. The claim that the primary wrong-making feature of a killing is the loss to the victim of the value of its future accounts for the wrongness of killing young children and infants directly; it makes the wrongness of such acts as obvious as we actually think it is. This is a further merit of this theory. Accordingly, it seems that this value of a future-like-ours theory of the wrongness of killing shares strengths of both sanctity-of-life and personhood accounts while avoiding weaknesses of both. In addition, it meshes with a central intuition concerning what makes killing wrong.

The claim that the primary wrong-making feature of a killing is the loss to the victim of the value of its future has obvious consequences for the ethics of abortion. The future of a standard fetus includes a set of experiences, projects, activities, and such which are identical with the futures of adult human beings and are identical with the futures of young children. Since the reason that is sufficient to explain why it is wrong to kill human beings after the time of birth is a reason that also applies to fetuses, it follows that abortion is prima facie seriously morally wrong.

This argument does not rely on the invalid inference that, since it is wrong to kill persons, it is wrong to kill potential persons also. The category that is morally central to this analysis is the category of having a valuable future like ours; it is not the category of personhood. The argument to the conclusion that abortion is prima facie seriously morally wrong proceeded independently of the notion of person or potential person or any equivalent. Someone may wish to start with this analysis in terms of the value of a human future, conclude that abortion is, except perhaps in rare circumstances, seriously morally wrong, infer that fetuses have the right to life, and then call fetuses "persons" as a result of their having the right to life. Clearly, in this case, the category of person is being used to state the *conclusion* of the analysis rather than to generate the *argument* of the analysis.

The structure of this anti-abortion argument can be both illuminated and defended by comparing it to what appears to be the best argument for the wrongness of the wanton infliction of pain on animals. This latter argument is based on the assumption that it is prima facie wrong to inflict pain on me (or you, reader). What is the natural property associated with the infliction of pain which makes such infliction wrong? The obvious answer seems to be that the infliction of pain causes suffering and that suffering is a misfortune. The suffering caused by the infliction of pain is what makes the wanton infliction of pain on me wrong. The wanton infliction of pain on other adult humans causes suffering. The wanton infliction of pain on animals causes suffering. Since causing suffering is what makes the wanton infliction of pain wrong and since the wanton infliction of pain on animals causes suffering, it follows that the wanton infliction of pain on animals is wrong.

This argument for the wrongness of the wanton infliction of pain on animals shares a number of structural features with the argument for the serious prima facie wrongness of abortion. Both arguments start with an obvious assumption concerning what it is wrong to do to me (or you, reader). Both then look for the characteristic or the consequence of the wrong action which makes the action wrong. Both recognize that the wrong-making feature of these immoral actions is a property of actions sometimes directed at individuals other than postnatal human beings. If the structure of the argument for the wrongness of the wanton infliction of pain on animals is sound, then the structure of the argument for the prima facie serious wrongness of abortion is also sound, for the structure of the two arguments is the same. The structure common to both is the key to the explanation of how the wrongness of abortion can be demonstrated without recourse to the category of person. In neither argument is that category crucial.

This defense of an argument for the wrongness of abortion in terms of a structurally similar argument for the wrongness of the wanton infliction of pain on animals succeeds only if the account regarding animals is the correct account. Is it? In the first place, it seems plausible. In the second place, its major competition is Kant's account. Kant believed that we do not have direct duties to animals at all, because they are not persons. Hence, Kant had to explain and justify the wrongness of inflicting pain on animals on the grounds that "he who is hard in his dealings with animals becomes hard also in his dealing with men."[3] The problem with Kant's account is that there seems to be no reason for accepting this latter claim unless Kant's account is rejected. If the alternative to Kant's account is accepted, then it is easy to understand why someone who is indifferent to inflicting pain on animals is also indifferent to inflicting pain on humans, for one is indifferent to what makes inflicting pain wrong in both cases. But, if Kant's account is accepted, there is no intelligible reason why one who is hard in his dealings with animals (or crabgrass or stones) should also be hard in his dealings with men. After all, men are persons: animals are no more persons than crabgrass or stones. Persons are Kant's crucial moral category. Why, in short, should a Kantian accept the basic claim in Kant's argument?

Hence, Kant's argument for the wrongness of inflicting pain on animals rests on a claim that, in a world of Kantian moral agents, is demonstrably false. Therefore, the alternative analysis, being more plausible anyway, should be accepted. Since this alternative analysis has the same structure as the anti-abortion argument being defended here, we have further support for the argument for the immorality of abortion being defended in this essay.

Of course, this value of a future-like-ours argument, if sound, shows only that abortion is prima facie wrong, not that it is wrong in any and all circumstances. Since the loss of the future to a standard fetus, if killed, is, however, at least as great a loss as the loss of the future to a standard adult human being who is killed, abortion, like ordinary killing, could be justified only by the most compelling reasons. The loss of one's life is almost the greatest misfortune that can happen to one. Presumably abortion could be justified in some circumstances, only if the loss consequent on failing to abort would be at least as great. Accordingly, morally permissible abortions will be rare indeed unless, perhaps, they occur so early in pregnancy that a fetus is not yet definitely an individual. Hence, this argument should be taken as showing that abortion is presumptively very seriously wrong, where the presumption is very strong—as strong as the presumption that killing another adult human being is wrong.

III

How complete an account of the wrongness of killing does the value of a future-like-ours account have to be in order that the wrongness of abortion is a consequence? This account does not have to be an account of the necessary conditions for the wrongness of killing. Some persons in nursing homes may lack valuable human futures, yet it may be wrong to kill them for other reasons. Furthermore, this account does not obviously have to be the sole reason killing is wrong where the victim did have a valuable future. This analysis claims only that, for any killing where the victim did have a valuable future like ours, having that future by itself is sufficient to create the strong presumption that the killing is seriously wrong.

One way to overturn the value of a future-like-ours argument would be to find some account of the wrongness of killing which is at least as intelligible and which has different implications for the ethics of abortion. Two rival accounts possess at least some degree of plausibility. One account is based on the obvious fact that people value the experience of living and wish for that valuable experience to continue. Therefore, it might be said, what makes killing wrong is the discontinuation of that experience for the victim. Let us call this the *discontinuation account.* Another rival account is based upon the obvious fact that people strongly desire to continue to live. This suggests that what makes killing us so wrong is that it interferes with the fulfillment of a strong and fundamental desire, the fulfillment of which is necessary for the fulfillment of any other desires we might have. Let us call this the *desire account.*

Consider first the desire account as a rival account of the ethics of killing which would provide the basis for rejecting the anti-abortion position. Such an account will have to be stronger than the value of a future-like-ours account of the wrongness of abortion if it is to do the job expected of it. To entail the wrongness of abortion, the value of a future-like-ours account has only to provide a sufficient, but not a necessary, condition for the wrongness of killing. The desire account, on the other hand, must provide us also with a necessary condition for the wrongness of killing in order to generate a pro-choice conclusion on abortion. The reason for this is that presumably the argument from the desire account moves from the claim that what makes killing wrong is interference with a very strong desire to the claim that abortion is not wrong because the fetus lacks a strong desire to live. Obviously, this inference fails if someone's having the desire to live is not a necessary condition of its being wrong to kill that individual.

One problem with the desire account is that we do regard it as seriously wrong to kill persons who have little desire to live or who have no desire to live or, indeed, have a desire not to live. We believe it is seriously wrong to kill the unconscious, the sleeping, those who are tired of life, and those who are suicidal. The value-of-a-human-future account renders standard morality intelligible in these cases; these cases appear to be incompatible with the desire account.

The desire account is subject to a deeper difficulty. We desire life, because we value the goods of this life. The goodness of life is not secondary to our desire for it. If this were not so, the pain of one's own premature death could be done away with merely by an appropriate alteration in the configuration of one's desires. This is absurd. Hence, it would seem that it is the loss of the goods of one's future, not the interference with the fulfillment of a strong desire to live, which accounts ultimately for the wrongness of killing.

It is worth noting that, if the desire account is modified so that it does not provide a necessary, but only a sufficient, condition for the wrongness of killing, the desire account is compatible with the value of a future-like-ours account. The combined accounts will yield an anti-abortion ethic. This suggests that one can retain what is intuitively plausible about the desire account without a challenge to the basic argument of this paper.

It is also worth noting that, if future desires have moral force in a modified desire account of the wrongness of killing, one can find support for an anti-abortion ethic even in the absence of a value of a future-like-ours account. If one decides that a morally relevant property, the possession of which is sufficient to make it wrong to kill some individual, is the desire at some future time to live—one might decide to justify one's refusal to kill suicidal teenagers on these grounds, for example—then, since typical fetuses will have the desire in the future to live, it is wrong to kill typical fetuses. Accordingly, it does not seem that a desire account of the wrongness of killing can provide a justification of a pro-choice ethic of abortion which is nearly as adequate as the value of a human-future justification on an anti-abortion ethic.

The discontinuation account looks more promising as an account of the wrongness of killing. It seems just as intelligible as the value of a future-like-ours account, but it does not justify an anti-abortion position. Obviously, if it is the continuation of one's activities, experiences, and projects, the loss of which makes killing wrong, then it is not wrong to kill fetuses for that reason, for fetuses do not have experiences, activities, and projects to be continued or discontinued. Accordingly, the discontinuation account does not have the anti-abortion consequences that the value of a future-like-ours account has. Yet, it seems as intelligible as the value of a future-like-ours account, for when we think of what would be wrong with our being killed, it does seem as if it is the discontinuation of what makes our lives worthwhile which makes killing us wrong.

Is the discontinuation account just as good an account as the value of a future-like-ours account?

The discontinuation account will not be adequate at all, if it does not refer to the *value* of the experience that may be discontinued. One does not want the discontinuation account to make it wrong to kill a patient who begs for death and who is in severe pain that cannot be relieved short of killing. (I leave open the question of whether it is wrong for other reasons.) Accordingly, the discontinuation account must be more than a bare discontinuation account. It must make some reference to the positive value of the patient's experiences. But, by the same token, the value of a future-like-ours account cannot be a bare future account either. Just having a future surely does not itself rule out killing the above patient. This account must make some reference to the value of the patient's future experiences and projects also. Hence, both accounts involve the value of experiences, projects, and activities. So far we still have symmetry between the accounts.

The symmetry fades, however, when we focus on the time period of the value of the experiences, etc., which has moral consequences. Although both accounts leave open the possibility that the patient in our example may be killed, this possibility is left open only in virtue of the utterly bleak future for the patient. It makes no difference whether the patient's immediate past contains intolerable pain, or consists in being in a coma (which we can imagine is a situation of indifference), or consists in a life of value. If the patient's future is a future of value, we want our account to make it wrong to kill the patient. If the patient's future is intolerable, whatever his or her immediate past, we want our account to allow killing the patient. Obviously, then, it is the value of that patient's future which is doing the work in rendering the morality of killing the patient intelligible.

This being the case, it seems clear that whether one has immediate past experiences or not does no work in the explanation of what makes killing wrong. The addition the discontinuation account makes to the value of a human future account is otiose. Its addition to the value-of-a-future account plays no role at all in rendering intelligible the wrongness of killing. Therefore, it can be discarded with the discontinuation account of which it is a part.

IV

The analysis of the previous section suggests that alternative general accounts of the wrongness of killing are either inadequate or unsuccessful in getting around the anti-abortion consequences of the value of a future-like-ours argument. A different strategy for avoiding these anti-abortion consequences involves limiting the scope of the value of a future argument. More precisely, the strategy involves arguing that fetuses lack a property that is essential for the value-of-a-future argument (or for any anti-abortion argument) to apply to them.

One move of this sort is based upon the claim that a necessary condition of one's future being valuable is that one values it. Value implies a valuer. Given this one might argue that, since fetuses cannot value their futures, their futures are not valuable to them. Hence, it does not seriously wrong them deliberately to end their lives.

This move fails, however, because of some ambiguities. Let us assume that something cannot be of value unless it is valued by someone. This does not entail that my life is of no value unless it is valued by me. I may think, in a period of despair, that my future is of no worth whatsoever, but I may be wrong because others rightly see value—even great value—in it. Furthermore, my future can be valuable to me even if I do not value it. This is the case when a young person attempts suicide, but is rescued and goes on to significant human achievements. Such young people's futures are ultimately valuable to them, even though such futures do not seem to be valuable to them at the moment of attempted suicide. A fetus's future can be valuable to it in the same way. Accordingly, this attempt to limit the anti-abortion argument fails.

Another similar attempt to reject the anti-abortion position is based on Tooley's claim that an entity cannot possess the right to life unless it has the capacity to desire its continued existence. It follows that, since fetuses lack the conceptual capacity to desire to continue to live, they lack the right to life. Accordingly, Tooley concludes that abortion cannot be seriously prima facie wrong. . . .

What could be the evidence for Tooley's basic claim? Tooley once argued that individuals have a prima facie right to what they desire and that the lack of the capacity to desire something undercuts the basis of one's right to it. . . . This argument plainly will not succeed in the context of the analysis of this essay, however, since the point here is to establish the fetus's right to life on other grounds. Tooley's argument assumes that the right to life cannot be established in general on some basis other than the desire for life. This position was considered and rejected in the preceding section of this paper.

One might attempt to defend Tooley's basic claim on the grounds that, because a fetus cannot apprehend continued life as a benefit, its continued life cannot be a benefit or cannot be something it has a right to or cannot be something that is in its interest. This might be defended in terms of the general proposition that, if an individual is literally incapable of caring about or taking an interest in some *X*, then one does not have a right to *X* or *X* is not a benefit or *X* is not something that is in one's interest.

Each member of this family of claims seems to be open to objections. As John C. Stevens has pointed out, one may have a right to be treated with a certain medical procedure (because of a health insurance policy one has purchased), even though one cannot conceive of the nature of the procedure.[4] And, as Tooley himself has pointed out, persons who have been indoctrinated, or drugged, or rendered temporarily unconscious may be literally incapable of caring about or taking an interest in something that is in their interest or is something to which they have a right, or is something that benefits them. Hence, the Tooley claim that would restrict the scope of the value of a future-like-ours argument is undermined by counterexamples.[5]

Finally, Paul Bassen has argued that, even though the prospects of an embryo might seem to be a basis for the wrongness of abortion, an embryo cannot be a victim and therefore cannot be wronged. An embryo cannot be a victim, he says, because it lacks sentience.[6] His central argument for this seems to be that, even though plants and the permanently unconscious are alive, they clearly cannot be victims. What is the explanation of this? Bassen claims that the explanation is that their lives consist of mere metabolism and mere metabolism is not enough to ground victimizability. Mentation is required.

The problem with this attempt to establish the absence of victimizability is that both plants and the permanently unconscious clearly lack what Bassen calls "prospects" or what I have called "a future life like ours." Hence, it is surely open to one to argue that the real reason we believe plants and the permanently unconscious cannot be victims is that killing them cannot deprive them of a future life like ours; the real reason is not their absence of present mentation.

Bassen recognizes that his view is subject to this difficulty, and he recognizes that the case of children seems to support this difficulty, for "much of what we do for children is based on prospects." He argues, however, that, in the case of children and in other such cases, "potentiality comes into play only where victimizability has been secured on other grounds." . . .

Bassen's defense of his view is patently question-begging, since what is adequate to secure victimiz-ability is exactly what is at issue. His examples do not support his own view against the thesis of this essay. Of course, embryos can be victims: when their lives are deliberately terminated, they are deprived of their futures of value, their prospects. This makes them victims, for it directly wrongs them.

The seeming plausibility of Bassen's view stems from the fact that paradigmatic cases of imagining someone as a victim involve empathy, and empathy requires mentation of the victim. The victims of flood, famine, rape, or child abuse are all persons with whom we can empathize. That empathy seems to be part of seeing them as victims.

In spite of the strength of these examples, the attractive intuition that a situation in which there is victimization requires the possibility of empathy is subject to counterexamples. Consider a case that Bassen himself offers: "Posthumous obliteration of an author's work constitutes a misfortune for him only if he had wished his work to endure." . . . The conditions Bassen wishes to impose upon the possibility of being victimized here seem far too strong. Perhaps this author, due to his unrealistic standards of excellence and his low self-esteem, regarded his work as unworthy of survival, even though it possessed genuine literary merit. Destruction of such work would surely victimize its author. In such a case, empathy with the victim concerning the loss is clearly impossible.

Of course, Bassen does not make the possibility of empathy a necessary condition of victimizability; he requires only mentation. Hence, on Bassen's actual view, this author, as I have described him, can be a victim. The problem is that the basic intuition that renders Bassen's view plausible is missing in the author's case. In order to attempt to avoid counterexamples, Bassen has made his thesis too weak to be supported by the intuitions that suggested it.

Even so, the mentation requirement on victimizability is still subject to counterexamples. Suppose a severe accident renders me totally unconscious for a month, after which I recover. Surely killing me while I am unconscious victimizes me, even though I am incapable of mentation during that time. It follows that Bassen's thesis fails. Apparently, attempts to restrict the value of a future-like-ours argument so that fetuses do not fall within its scope do not succeed.

V

In this essay, it has been argued that the correct ethic of the wrongness of killing can be extended to fetal life and used to show that there is a strong presumption that any abortion is morally impermissible. If the ethic of killing adopted here entails, however, that contraception is also seriously immoral, then there would appear to be a difficulty with the analysis of this essay.

But this analysis does not entail that contraception is wrong. Of course, contraception prevents the actualization of a possible future of value. Hence, it follows from the claim that futures of value should be maximized that contraception is prima facie immoral. This obligation to maximize does not exist, however; furthermore, nothing in the ethics of killing in this paper entails that it does. The ethics of killing in this essay would entail that contraception is wrong only if something were denied a human future of value by contraception. Nothing at all is denied such a future by contraception, however.

Candidates for a subject of harm by contraception fall into four categories: (1) some sperm or other, (2) some ovum or other, (3) a sperm and an ovum separately, and (4) a sperm and an ovum together. Assigning the harm to some sperm is utterly arbitrary, for no reason can be given for making a sperm the subject of harm rather than an ovum. Assigning the harm to some ovum is utterly arbitrary, for no reason can be given for making an ovum the subject of harm rather than a sperm. One might attempt to avoid these problems by insisting that contraception deprives both the sperm and the ovum separately of a valuable future like ours. On this alternative, too many futures are lost. Contraception was supposed to be wrong, because it deprived us of one future of value, not two. One might attempt to avoid this problem by holding that contraception deprives the combination of sperm and ovum of a valuable future like ours. But here the definite article misleads. At the time of contraception, there are hundreds of millions of sperm, one (released) ovum and millions of possible combinations of all of these. There is no actual combination at all. Is the subject of the loss to be a merely possible combination? Which one? This alternative does not yield an actual subject of harm either. Accordingly, the immorality of contraception is not entailed by the loss of a future-like-ours argument simply because there is no nonarbitrarily identifiable subject of the loss in the case of contraception.

VI

The purpose of this essay has been to set out an argument for the serious presumptive wrongness of abortion subject to the assumption that the moral permissibility of abortion stands or falls on the moral status of the fetus. Since a fetus possesses a property, the possession of which in adult human beings is sufficient to make killing an adult human being wrong, abortion is wrong. This way of dealing with the problem of abortion seems superior to other approaches to the ethics of abortion, because it rests on an ethics of killing which is close to self-evident, because the crucial morally relevant property clearly applies to fetuses, and because the argument avoids the usual equivocations on "human life," "human being," or "person." The argument rests neither on religious claims nor on Papal dogma. It is not subject to the objection of "speciesism." Its soundness is compatible with the moral permissibility of euthanasia and contraception. It deals with our intuitions concerning young children.

Finally, this analysis can be viewed as resolving a standard problem—indeed, *the* standard problem—concerning the ethics of abortion. Clearly, it is wrong to kill adult human beings. Clearly, it is not wrong to end the life of some arbitrarily chosen single human cell. Fetuses seem to be like arbitrarily chosen human cells in some respects and like adult humans in other respects. The problem of the ethics of abortion is the problem of determining the fetal property that settles this moral controversy. The thesis of this essay is that the problem of the ethics of abortion, so understood, is solvable.

NOTES

1. Feinberg, "Abortion," in *Matters of Life and Death: New Introductory Essays in Moral Philosophy*, ed. Tom Regan (New York: Random House, 1986), pp. 256–293; Tooley, "Abortion and Infanticide," *Philosophy and Public Affairs*, 2, 1 (1972): 37–65; Tooley, *Abortion and Infanticide* (New York: Oxford University Press, 1984); Warren, "On the Moral and Legal Status of Abortion," *The Monist*, 57, 1 (1973): 43–61; Engelhardt, "The Ontology of Abortion," *Ethics*, 84, 3 (1974): 217–234; Sumner, *Abortion and Moral Theory* (Princeton, NJ: Princeton University Press, 1981); Noonan, "An Almost Absolute Value in History," in *The Morality of Abortion: Legal and Historical Perspectives*, ed. Noonan (Cambridge, MA: Harvard University Press, 1970); and Devine, *The Ethics of Homocide* (Ithaca, NY: Cornell University Press, 1978).

2. Feinberg, "Abortion," p. 270.

3. "Duties to Animals and Spirits," in *Lectures on Ethics*, trans. Louis Infeld (New York: Harper, 1963), p. 239.

4. "Must the Bearer of a Right Have the Concept of That to Which He Has a Right?" *Ethics,* 95, 1 (1984): 68–74.

5. See Tooley again in "Abortion and Infanticide," pp. 47–49.

6. "Present Sakes and Future Prospects: The Status of Early Abortion," *Philosophy and Public Affairs,* 11, 4 (1982): 322–326.

DISCUSSION QUESTIONS

1. Why, according to Marquis, is killing wrong? Do you agree with his argument? Why or why not?
2. What is Marquis' argument against abortion? Critically evaluate it by comparing it with Judith Jarvis Thomson's argument. What are the strengths and weaknesses of their respective arguments? Who provides the better argument? Why?
3. Is abortion immoral in all cases, according to Marquis? If not, in what cases is it not immoral? Why? Do you agree with him? Explain.
4. What does Marquis' moral principle imply about the killing of nonhuman animals? For Marquis, is it wrong to kill nonhuman animals? Do you agree with this line of argument? Explain.
5. What is Marquis' position on contraception? Does his argument convince you? Why or why not?

 S A L L Y   M A R K O W I T Z

Abortion and Feminism

In "Abortion and Feminism," Sally Markowitz offers a defense of abortion derived from an awareness of women's oppression and a commitment to a more egalitarian society. According to Markowitz, the way we respond to the problem of personhood will not necessarily settle the dispute over abortion once and for all. The crucial issue is when, if ever, can people be required to sacrifice for the sake of others. "When one social group in a society is systematically oppressed by another," says Markowitz, "it is impermissible to require the oppressed group to make sacrifices that will exacerbate or perpetuate this oppression."

Sally Markowitz is a philosophy professor at Willamette University in Salem, Oregon.

In the past few decades, the issue of abortion, long of concern to women, has gained a prominent place in the platforms of politicians and a respectable, if marginal, one in the writings of moral philosophers. It is natural to speculate that the rise of and reactions to the women's liberation movement explain the feverish pitch of the recent debate, and no doubt there is much to this

Sally Markowitz, *Social Theory and Practice* 16 (spring 1990): 1–17. Reprinted by permission of the publisher and the author.

speculation. And yet, philosophical analyses of abortion have had surprisingly little to say directly about either women or feminism. Instead, their primary concern has been to decide whether or not the fetus is a person, with a right to life like yours or mine. That this question deserves philosophical attention becomes especially clear when we consider the frightening (if fanciful) ways it is asked and answered by those in power. Nevertheless, as many feminists and some philosophers have recognized, the way we respond to the problem of personhood will not necessarily settle the dispute over abortion once and for all. On some views, a full account must deal with the rights of pregnant women as well.

In fact, one popular defense of abortion is based on the woman's right to autonomy and avoids the personhood issue altogether. The central claim of the autonomy defense is that anti-abortion policies simply interfere in an impermissible way with the pregnant woman's autonomy. In what has become the classic philosophical statement of this view, Judith Jarvis Thomson ingeniously argues that even if the fetus has a right to life, it need not also have the right to use its mother's body to stay alive. The woman's body is her own property, to dispose of as she wishes.[1] But autonomy theorists need not rest their case on the vaguely disturbing notion of the pregnant woman's property rights to her own body. For example, Jane English, in another version of the view, argues that a woman is justified in aborting if pregnancy and childbearing will prevent her from pursuing the life she wants to live, the expression of her own autonomy.[2]

Philosophers have come to call this strategy the "feminist" or "woman's liberation" approach, and indeed some version of it seems to be favored by many feminists.[3] This is no surprise since such a view may seem to be quite an improvement over accounts that regard personhood as the only essential issue. At least it recognizes women as bearers of rights as well as of babies. In what follows, however, I shall suggest that this defense may fall short of the feminist mark. Then I shall offer another defense, one derived not from the right to autonomy, but from an awareness of women's oppression and a commitment to a more egalitarian society.

I will assume throughout that the fetus has a serious right to life. I do so not because I believe this to be true, but rather because a feminist defense of abortion rights should be independent of the status of the fetus. For if, as many feminists believe, the move towards a sexually egalitarian society requires women's control of their reproductive lives, and if

the permissibility of this control depends ultimately upon the status of the fetus, then the future of feminism rests upon how we resolve the personhood issue. This is not acceptable to most feminists. No doubt many feminists are comforted by arguments against the fetus's personhood. But regardless of the fetus's status, more must be said.

1

What, then, from a feminist point of view, is wrong with an autonomy defense? Feminists should be wary on three counts. First, most feminists believe not only that women in our society are oppressed, but also that our failure to face the scope and depth of this oppression does much to maintain it. This makes feminists suspicious of perspectives, often called humanist or liberal ones, that focus only on the individual and de-emphasize the issue of gender by either refusing to acknowledge that women have less power than men or denying that this inequity is worth much attention. While liberals and humanists may try to discuss social issues, including abortion, with as little mention as possible of gender, feminists tend to search for the hidden, unexpected, and perhaps unwelcome ways in which gender is relevant. From this perspective, defenses of abortion which focus only on the personhood of the fetus are not essentially or even especially feminist ones since they completely avoid any mention of gender. Autonomy arguments, though, are not much of an improvement. They may take into account the well-being of individual women, but they manage to skirt the issue of women's status, as a group, in a sexist society.

Secondly, the autonomy defense incorporates a (supposedly) gender-neutral right, one that belongs to every citizen; there's nothing special about being a woman—except, of course, for the inescapable fact that only women find themselves pregnant against their wills. Some feminists have become disillusioned with this gender-neutral approach. They reject it both on principle, because it shifts attention away from gender inequality, and for practical reasons, because it often works against women in the courts.[4] Instead, feminists have come to realize that sometimes gender should be relevant in claiming rights. Some of these rights, like adequate gynecological care, may be based on women's special physiology; others may stem from the special needs experienced by female casualties of a sexist society: the impoverished, divorced, or unwed mother, the rape victim, the anorexic teen, the coed who has been convinced that she lacks (or had better lack) mathematical aptitude. A thoroughly feminist analysis, then, will not hesitate, when appropriate, to claim a right on the basis of gender, rather than in spite of it.[5] And to do otherwise in the case of abortion may be not only to deny the obvious, but also to obscure the relation of reproductive practices to women's oppression.

The third problem feminists might have with an autonomy defense involves the content of the human ideal on which the right to autonomy rests. Some feminists, influenced by Marxist and socialist traditions, may reject an ideal that seems to be so intimately connected with the individualistic ideology of capitalism. Others may suspect that this ideology is not just capitalist but male-biased. And if feminists hesitate to justify abortion by appeal to a gender-neutral right derived from a gender-neutral ideal, they are even more suspicious of an ideal that seems to be gender neutral when really it's not. Increasingly, feminists reject the ideals of older feminists, like Simone de Beauvoir, who, in promoting for women what appeared to be an androgynous human ideal, unwittingly adopted one that was androcentric, or male-centered. Instead, feminists seek to free themselves from the misogynist perspective that sees women as incomplete men and ignores, devalues, or denies the existence of particularly female psychologies, values and experiences. On this view, to fashion a feminist human ideal we must look to women's values and experiences—or, at least, we must not look only to men's.[6]

This reevaluation has important implications for the abortion issue, since many feminists consider an overriding right to autonomy to be a characteristically male ideal, while nurturance and responsibility for other (the paradigmatic case of which, of course, is motherhood) to be characteristically female ones. Indeed, in the name of such women's values, some women who call themselves feminists have actually joined the anti-abortionist camp.[7] Most feminists, of course, don't go this far. But, paradoxically, many seem to find the ideal of autonomy less acceptable than the right to abortion it is supposed to justify. Clearly, something is awry. (I shall have more to say in section 4 about how autonomy is important to feminists.)

Feminists, therefore, need another argument. Instead of resting on an ideal many feminists reject, a feminist defense of abortion should somehow reflect an awareness of women's oppression and a commitment to ending it.

2

Of all the philosophers, feminist and otherwise, who have discussed abortion, Alison Jaggar seems to be the only one to address the problem from this perspective. Jaggar argues that in societies where mothers bear the responsibility for pregnancy, birth and child-rearing, women should control abortion decisions. Women who live in other, more cooperative social communities (wherever they are), where members of both sexes share such responsibilities, cannot claim a right of the same force. The strength of a woman's say about whether or not to abort, then, should be relative to the amount of support (financial, emotional, physical, medical, and otherwise) she can expect from those around her.[8]

It is disheartening that the philosophical community has not paid Jaggar's paper the attention it merits in the [decades] since its publication, but this lapse is hardly surprising. The notion of the individual's right to autonomy is so firmly entrenched that we have difficulty even entertaining other approaches. We find ourselves invoking such rights perhaps without realizing it even when we neither want nor need to. And, indeed, Jaggar is no exception; despite the promising intuition with which she starts, Jaggar finally offers us another, albeit more sophisticated, version of the autonomy argument. Quite simply, her argument implies that if abortion ought to be permissible in some societies but not in others, this is only because pregnancy and motherhood create obstacles to personal autonomy in some societies but not in others.

Jaggar bases her argument for abortion rights in our society on two principles. The first, or Right to Life Principle, holds that

the right to life, when it is claimed for a human being, means the right to a full human life and to whatever means are necessary to achieve this. . . . To be born, then, is only one of the necessary conditions for a full human life. The others presumably include nutritious food, breathable air, warm human companionship, and so on. If anyone has a right to life, she or he must be entitled to all of these.[9]

According to the second, or Personal Control Principle, "Decisions should be made by those, and only by those, who are importantly affected by them."[10] In our society, then, the state cannot legitimately set itself up as the protector of the fetus's right to life (as Jaggar has characterized it) because the mother and not the state will be expected to provide for this right, both during pregnancy and afterwards. But since, by the Personal Control Principle, only those whose lives will be importantly affected have the right to make a decision, in our society the pregnant woman should determine whether to continue her pregnancy.

Jaggar's argument incorporates both liberal and feminist perspectives, and there is a tension between them. Her argument is feminist rather than merely liberal because it does not rest exclusively on a universal right to autonomy. Instead, it takes seriously the contingent and socially variable features of reproduction and parenting, their relationship to women's position in a society, and the effect of anti-abortion policy on this position. But her argument is also a liberal one. Consider, for example, the Personal Control Principle. While Jaggar doesn't explicitly spell out its motivation, she does state that the principle "provides the fundamental justification for democracy and is accepted by most shades of political opinion."[11] Surely this wide acceptance has something to do with the belief, equally widely held, that citizens should be able to decide for themselves what courses their lives should take, especially when some courses involve sacrifices or burdens. This becomes clear when Jaggar explains that an individual or organization has no moral claim as a protector of the right to life "that would justify its insistence on just one of the many conditions necessary to a full human life, in circumstances where this would place the burden of fulfilling all the other conditions squarely on the shoulders of some other individual or organization."[12] Once again we have an appeal to a universal right to personal autonomy, indeed a right based on an ideal which not only might be unacceptable to many feminists, but may cast the net too widely even for some liberals. For example, one might claim that taxation policies designed to finance social programs interfere with personal choices about how to spend earnings, a matter that will have important consequences for one's life. Such a view also permits a range of private actions which some liberals may believe are immoral: for example, an adult grandchild may decide to stop caring for a burdensome and senile grandparent if such care places a heavy burden on the grandchild.

I shall not attempt to pass judgment here on the desirability of either redistributing income through taxation or passing laws requiring us to be Good Samaritans in our private lives. Nor do I want to beg the question, which I shall discuss later, of whether reproductive autonomy is, in all circumstances, overridingly important in a way other sorts of autonomy may not be. I can leave these matters open because a feminist defense of abortion need not depend on how we settle them. For there is a significant difference between the sacrifices required by restrictive abortion policies and those required by enforcing other sorts of Good Samaritanism: taxes and laws against letting the aged or handicapped starve to death apply to everyone; those prohibiting abortion apply only to women. While anyone might end up with a helpless, cantankerous grandparent and most of us end up paying taxes, only women end up pregnant. So anti-abortion laws require sacrifice not of everyone, but only of women.

3

This brings us to what I regard as the crucial question: When, if ever, can people be required to sacrifice for the sake of others? And how can feminists answer this question in a way that rests not on the individual right to personal autonomy, but on a view of social reality that takes seriously power relations between genders? I suggest the following principle, which I shall call the Impermissible Sacrifice Principle: *When one social group in a society is systematically oppressed by another, it is impermissible to require the oppressed group to make sacrifices that will exacerbate or perpetuate this oppression.* (Note that this principle does not exempt the members of oppressed groups from *all* sorts of sacrifices just because they are oppressed; they may be as morally responsible as anyone for rendering aid in some circumstances. Only sacrifices that will clearly perpetuate their oppression are ruled out.)

The Impermissible Sacrifice Principle focuses on power relationships between groups rather than on the rights of individuals. This approach will suit not only feminists but all who recognize and deplore other sorts of systematic social oppression as well. Indeed, if we take our opposition to oppression seriously, this approach may be necessary. Otherwise, when policy decisions are made, competing goals and commitments may distract us from the conditions we claim to deplore and encourage decisions that allow such conditions to remain. Even worse, these other goals and commitments can be used as excuses for perpetuating oppression. Testing policies against the Impermissible Sacrifice Principle keeps this from happening.

Feminists should welcome the applicability of the Impermissible Sacrifice Principle to groups other than women. Radical feminists are sometimes accused of being blind to any sort of oppression but their own. The Impermissible Sacrifice Principle, however, enables feminists to demonstrate solidarity with other oppressed groups by resting the case for abortion on the same principle that might, for example, block a policy requiring the poor rather than the rich to bear the tax burden, or workers rather than management to take a pay cut. On the other hand, feminists may worry that the Impermissible Sacrifice Principle, taken by itself, may not yield the verdict on abortion feminists seek. For if some radical feminists err by recognizing only women's oppression, some men err by not recognizing it at all. So the Impermissible Sacrifice Principle must be supplemented by what I shall call the Feminist Proviso: *Women are, as a group, sexually oppressed by men; and this oppression can neither be completely understood in terms of, nor otherwise reduced to, oppressions of other sorts.*

Feminists often understand this oppression to involve men's treating women as breeding machines, sexual or aesthetic objects, nurturers who need no nurturance. Women become alienated from their bodies, their sexuality, their work, their intellect, their emotions, their moral agency. Of course, feminists disagree about exactly how to formulate this analysis, especially since women experience oppression differently depending on their class, race, and ethnicity. But however we decide to understand women's oppression, we can be sure an anti-abortion policy will make it worse.

Adding the Feminist Proviso, then, keeps (or makes) sexism visible, ensuring that women are one of the oppressed groups to which the Principle applies. This should hardly need saying. Yet by focusing on other sorts of oppression the principle might cover, men often trivialize or ignore feminists' demands and women's pain. For example, someone (perhaps a white male) who is more sympathetic to the claims of racial minorities or workers than to those of women might try to trivialize or deny the sexual oppression of a white, affluent woman (perhaps his wife) by reminding her that she's richer than an unemployed black male and so should not complain. The Feminist Proviso also prevents an affluent white woman who rejects the unwelcome sexual advances of a minority or working class male from being dismissed (or dismissing herself) as a racist or classist. She may well be both. But she also lives in a world where, all things being equal, she is fair sexual game, in one way or another, for any male. Finally, the Impermissible Sacrifice Principle in conjunction

with the Feminist Proviso might be used to block the view that a black or Third World woman's first obligation is to bear children to swell the ranks of the revolution, regardless of the consequences of maternity within her culture. Having children for this reason may be a legitimate choice; but she also may have independent grounds to refuse.

I have added the Feminist Proviso so that the Impermissible Sacrifice Principle cannot be used to frustrate a feminist analysis. But I must also emphasize that the point is not to pit one oppressed group against another, but to make sure that the men in otherwise progressive social movements do not ignore women's oppression or, worse, find "politically correct" justifications for it. Women refuse to wait until "after the revolution" not just because they are impatient, but also because they have learned that not all revolutions are feminist ones.

The Impermissible Sacrifice Principle and the Feminist Proviso together, then, justify abortion on demand for women *because they live in a sexist society.* This approach not only gives a more explicitly feminist justification of abortion than the autonomy defense; it also gives a stronger one. For autonomy defenses are open to objections and qualifications that a feminist one avoids. Consider the ways the feminist approach handles these four challenges to the autonomy defense.

First, some philosophers have dismissed autonomy defenses by suggesting blithely that we simply compensate the pregnant woman.[13] Of what, though, will such compensation consist? Maternity leave? Tax breaks? Prenatal health care? Twenty points added to her civil-service exam score? Such benefits lighten one's load, no doubt. But what women suffer by being forced to continue unwanted pregnancies is not merely a matter of finances or missed opportunities; in a sexist society, there is reason to expect that an anti-abortion policy will reinforce a specifically *sexual* oppression, whatever sorts of compensation are offered. Indeed, even talk of compensation may be misguided, since it implies a prior state when things were as they should be; compensation seeks to restore the balance after a temporary upset. But in a sexist society, there is no original balance; women's oppression is the status quo. Even if individual women are compensated by money, services, or opportunities, sexual oppression may remain.

Second, an autonomy defense may seem appropriate only in cases where a woman engages in "responsible" sex: it is one thing to be a victim of rape or even contraceptive failure, one might argue; it is quite another voluntarily to have unprotected intercourse. A feminist defense suggests another approach. First, we might question the double standard that requires that women pay for "irresponsible" sex while men don't have to, even though women are oppressed by men. More importantly, if we focus on the *way* women are oppressed, we may understand many unwanted pregnancies to result from fear and paralysis rather than irresponsibility. For in a sexist society, many women simply do not believe they can control the conditions under which they have sex. And, sad to say, often they may be right.[14]

Third, what about poor women's access to abortion? The sort of right the autonomy theorists invoke, after all, seems to be a right to noninterference by the state. But this negative right seems to be in tension with a demand for state-funded abortions, especially since not everyone supports abortion. At any rate, we will need another argument to justify the funding of abortion for poor women. The defense I suggest, however, is clearly committed to providing all women with access to abortion, since to allow abortions only for those who can afford them forces poor women, who are doubly oppressed, to make special sacrifices. An egalitarian society must liberate all women, not just the rich ones.

Finally, autonomy defenses allow, indeed invite, the charge that the choice to abort is selfish. Even Thomson finds abortion, while not unjust, often to be "selfish" or "indecent." Although she has deprived nothing of its rights, the woman who aborts has chosen self-interested autonomy over altruism in the same way one might choose to watch while a child starves. Of course, one is tempted to point out that the (largely male) world of commerce and politics thrives on such "morally indecent" but legal actions. But then feminists are reduced to claiming a right to be as selfish as men are. Moreover, once the specter of selfishness is raised, this defense does not allow feminists to make enough of male anti-abortionists' motives. On an autonomy defense, these motives are simply not relevant, let alone damning, and feminists who dwell on them seem to be resorting to *ad hominems*. From a feminist perspective, however, abortion is a political issue, one which essentially concerns the interests of and power relations between men and women. Thus, what women and men can expect to gain or lose from an abortion policy becomes the point rather than the subject of *ad hominem* arguments.[15]

The approach I propose does well on each of these important counts. But its real test comes when we weigh the demands of the Impermissible Sacrifice Principle against fetal rights; for we have required that a feminist analysis be independent of the status of the fetus. Indeed, we may even be tempted to regard fetuses as constituting just the sort of oppressed group to whom the principle applies, and surely a fetus about to be aborted is in worse shape than the woman who carries it.

However, it may not make sense to count fetuses as an oppressed group. A disadvantaged one, perhaps. But the Impermissible Sacrifice Principle does not prescribe that more disadvantaged groups have a right to aid from less disadvantaged ones; it focuses only on the particular disadvantage of social oppression. That the fetus has a serious right to life does not imply that it's the sort of being that can be oppressed, if it cannot yet enter into the sorts of social relationships that constitute oppression. I cannot argue for this here; in any case, I suspect my best argument will not convince everyone. But feminists have another, more pointed response.

Whether or not we can weigh the disadvantage of fetuses against the oppression of women, we must realize what insisting on such a comparison does to the debate. It narrows our focus, turning it back to the conflict between the rights of fetuses and of women (even if now this conflict is between the rights of groups rather than of individuals). This is certainly not to deny that fetal rights should be relevant to an abortion policy. But feminists must insist that the oppression of women should be relevant too. And it is also relevant that unless our society changes in deep and global ways, anti-abortion policies, intentionally or not, will perpetuate women's oppression by men. This, then, is where feminists must stand firm.

Does this mean that instead of overriding the fetus's right to life by women's right to autonomy, I am proposing that feminists override the fetus's right by the right of women to live in a sexually egalitarian society? This is a difficult position for feminists but not an impossible one, especially for feminists with utilitarian leanings. Many feminists, for example, see sexism as responsible for a culture of death: war, violence, child abuse, ecological disaster. Eradicate sexism, it might be argued, and we will save more lives than we will lose. Some feminists might even claim that an oppressed woman's fate can be worse than that of an aborted fetus. Although I will not argue for such claims, they may be less implausible than they seem. But feminists need not rest their case on them. Instead, they may simply insist that society must change so that women are no longer oppressed. Such changes, of course, may require of men sacrifices unwelcome beyond their wildest dreams. But that, according to a feminist analysis, is the point.

So we should not see the choice as between liberating women and saving fetuses, but between two ways of respecting the fetus's right to life. The first requires women to sacrifice while men benefit. The second requires deep social changes that will ensure that men no longer gain and women lose through our practices of sexuality, reproduction, and parenthood. To point out how men gain from women's compulsory pregnancy is to steal the misplaced moral thunder from those male authorities—fathers, husbands, judges, congressmen, priests, philosophers—who, exhorting women to do their duty, present themselves as the benevolent, disinterested protectors of fetuses against women's selfishness. Let feminists insist that the condition for refraining from having abortions is a sexually egalitarian society. If men do not respond, and quickly, they will have indicated that fetal life isn't so important to them after all, or at least not important enough to give up the privileges of being male in a sexist society. If this makes feminists look bad, it makes men look worse still.

4

My defense maintains what seems to me to be Jaggar's most important insight: the strength of a right to abortion depends on women's condition in a particular society. But where Jaggar's argument seems motivated by the goal of securing personal autonomy for women, mine is not. Instead, I tie the permissibility of abortion directly to the goal of ending sexism. As I have suggested, this is a strength from the feminist point of view, since many feminists are not completely sure about their attitudes towards the liberal ideal of autonomy. But it remains to be asked, then, why feminists so often invoke an autonomy right. Are most feminists really liberal individualists at heart? Not necessarily. For it is easy to conflate two motivations for insisting upon a right to autonomy. One is the liberal conviction that personal autonomy is overridingly and intrinsically valuable; the other is the feminist conviction that in our society such autonomy for women frustrates and represents freedom from male domination. This is especially true of reproductive autonomy, for obvious reasons. Feminists see men making decisions about women's reproductive lives and then benefitting by the resulting gaps in power.

This exploitation must be stopped if we are to achieve sexual equality, and the easiest way to stop it in a society like ours is to wrest this control from men and give it to individual women. So it's not necessarily that women work towards a sexually egalitarian society simply to secure for themselves the degree of personal autonomy now reserved for men. Instead, by frustrating male dominance, women's autonomy will promote a more sexually egalitarian society.

These considerations allow us more fully to understand why some feminists resist a human ideal based on nurturance rather than autonomy. Such resistance does not merely reflect an attachment to an individualistic and, some would claim, androcentric human ideal. Nor are these feminist critics, for the most part, claiming they simply don't want to be nurturers. Their skepticism seems to have a more pragmatic and political basis: nurturing is fine, but not if only women do it. As Simone de Beauvoir put it in 1982, motherhood, despite its new feminist glorification, "is still the most skillful way there is of turning women into slaves."[16] On top of the demands of motherhood, moreover, women are expected to nurture men as well, rather than be nurtured by them. This makes for a hard and often an unrewarding day's work. The ultimate goal for feminists, then, is not to cease to nurture, nor even to nurture less, but to resist or transform relationships where nurturance becomes an expression of powerlessness.

But if nurturance isn't something women should avoid, neither is the liberal ideal of autonomy necessarily something women should embrace, except, again, insofar as it frustrates exploitation by men. Indeed, in a truly egalitarian society, women might not even think in terms of this ideal.

Some feminists might concede this point for autonomy in general but insist that sexual and reproductive autonomy are another matter: surely any sexually egalitarian society must include the right to abortion. This objection might take various forms. One might claim, for example, that pregnancy involves a woman's relation to her own body, over which she needs control for her emotional health and sense of identity. Or one might emphasize the special vulnerability to male oppression, physical and psychological, an anti-abortion policy might be expected to encourage, whatever the society. Both objections, though, are inconclusive for the same reason: Neither takes seriously enough how deeply our natures are shaped by gender; and gender, according to most feminists, is socially constructed.

For example, one's relationship to one's body, according to feminist psychologist Nancy Chodorow, depends on one's socially constructed gender identity. "We cannot know," claims Chodorow, "what children would make of their bodies in a nonsexually organized social world."[17] The same, it would seem, goes for adult women. Similarly, the claim that any sexually egalitarian society requires that individual women have complete control over abortion decisions seems to reflect a biological determinism many feminists would reject. Need women's potential vulnerability in pregnancy inevitably be exploited by men? In a society like ours, no doubt it will be. But what do we know about the behavior of men in a truly sexually egalitarian society? True, such a society is difficult to imagine. But this suggests only that we avoid dogmatism in our view of what such a society requires, especially when our certainty rests on intuitions about a human nature that may be almost wholly shaped by the very social organization we wish to change.

Of course, a sexually egalitarian society may turn out to require abortion rights; human (or, at least, male) nature may be, sad to say, only so malleable. Feminists, though, should not be troubled by this possibility: we need not show that abortion rights are necessary in all societies to argue that they are necessary in ours. In any case, since the verdict is not in, it is a good thing that a feminist defense need not rely on it.

Finally, since my discussion unequivocally assumes a feminist perspective, the approach I suggest may seem far removed from the standard ones popular in legal and philosophical circles. This should come as no surprise, since most philosophers and judges are not feminists. While feminists might regret this, they forget it at their own risk. The standard defenses of abortion—those that focus on autonomy rights or the status of the fetus—simply do not reflect or even acknowledge feminist concerns, and so such defenses are bound to frustrate the feminists who rely on them. This is not to say that feminists cannot in good faith use standard autonomy and non-personhood defenses when it is pragmatic to do so, but only that such defenses do not tell the whole (or even the right) story.

In any case, I hope my discussion has brought to light for everyone a dimension of the abortion issue too often ignored by philosophers: the relationship between reproductive practices and the liberation (or oppression) of women. After all, many philosophers, feminist and otherwise, reject utilitarianism because it seems to allow, indeed to require, sacrifices from arbitrarily chosen individuals for the sake of the general good. If such a consequence strikes us as undesirable, how much more so is a policy that requires significant sacrifices not merely from random individuals, but from members of an oppressed group, a group whose oppression, in fact, arises from and will be made worse by these very sacrifices? At least until we have a sexually egalitarian society, it is impermissible to forbid women to have abortions. If we sincerely believe (as I see no reason to) that abortion is at least *prima facie* wrong because it violates an overriding right of the fetus, our view should provide all the more incentive to change society so that women are no longer oppressed. As long as anti-abortionists reject or ignore the necessity of such change, the burden of moral proof, if not the blame, surely rests on them.

NOTES

1. Judith Jarvis Thomson, "A Defense of Abortion," *Philosophy and Public Affairs,* 1 (1971): 47–66.

2. Jane English, "Abortion and the Concept of a Person," in *Today's Moral Problems,* ed. Richard A. Wasserstrom (New York: Macmillan, 1985), pp. 448–457.

3. Peter Singer, *Practical Ethics* (Cambridge: Cambridge University Press, 1979), p. 113.

4. Catharine A. MacKinnon, *Feminism Unmodified: Discourses on Life and Law* (Cambridge, MA: Harvard University Press, 1987), pp. 35–36.

5. See, for example, Alison Jaggar, *Feminism, Politics and Human Nature* (Totowa, NJ: Rowman & Allanheld, 1983), esp. pts. 1 and 2; and MacKinnon, *Feminism Unmodified.*

6. See Sara Ruddick, "Maternal Thinking," *Feminist Studies,* 6 (1980): 345–346; Nancy Chodorow, *The Reproduction of Mothering: Psychoanalysis and the Sociology of Gender* (Berkeley and Los Angeles: University of California Press, 1978); Carol Gilligan, *In a Different Voice: Psychological Theory and Women's Development* (Cambridge, MA: Harvard University Press, 1982).

7. Sidney Callahan, "A Pro-Life Feminist Makes Her Case," *Commonweal* (25 Apr. 1986), quoted in the *Utne Reader,* 20 (1987): 104–108.

8. Alison Jaggar, "Abortion and a Woman's Right to Decide," in *Philosophy and Sex,* ed. Robert Baker and Frank Elliston (Buffalo: Prometheus Books, 1975), pp. 324–337.

9. Ibid., p. 328.

10. Ibid., p. 328.

11. Ibid., p. 329.

12. For classic discussions of sexism in the civil rights movement, see Susan Brownmiller, *Against Our Will: Men, Women, and Rape* (New York: Simon & Schuster, 1975), esp. pp. 210–255; and Michelle Wallace, *Black Macho and the Myth of the Superwoman* (New York: Dial Press, 1978).

13. Michael Tooley, "Abortion and Infanticide," in *The Problem of Abortion,* ed. Joel Feinberg (Belmont, CA: Wadsworth, 1983).

14. MacKinnon, *Feminism Unmodified*, p. 95.

15. This approach also allows us to understand the deep divisions between women on this issue. For many women in traditional roles fear the immediate effects on their lives of women's liberation generally and a permissive abortion policy in particular. On this, see Kristen Luker, *Abortion and the Politics of Motherhood* (Berkeley: University of California Press, 1984), esp. pp. 158–215.

16. Alice Schwarzer, *After the Second Sex: Conversations with Simone de Beauvoir* (New York: Pantheon Books, 1984), p. 114.

17. Nancy Chodorow, "Feminism and Difference," *Socialist Review*, 46 (1979): 66.

DISCUSSION QUESTIONS

1. What role does personhood play in Markowitz's defense of abortion?
2. What is the "autonomy defense"? What, according to Markowitz, is wrong with it? Evaluate her arguments, and formulate a response to them.
3. What is Alison Jaggar's argument for abortion? How does it compare with Judith Jarvis Thomson's argument? What are the major similarities and differences in their respective arguments? Which do you think is the stronger argument, and why?
4. When, if ever, can people be required to sacrifice for the sake of others? Compare your view with that of Markowitz.
5. What role, according to Markowitz, should feminism play in considerations of the permissibility of abortion? Do you think that the feminist perspective should be given a more prominent place in legal and philosophical considerations of abortion? Discuss your position in detail.

 L O R E T T A   J .   R O S S

African-American Women and Abortion

In "African-American Women and Abortion," Loretta J. Ross situates the African-American women's struggle for abortion rights and reproductive freedom in the context of their struggle against racism, sexism, and poverty. Ross defines "pro-life" and "pro-choice" as "the right to have, or not have, children and the right to raise them free from racism, sexism and poverty." Her article focuses on the agency of African-American

Loretta J. Ross, *Theorizing Black Feminisms: A Visionary Pragmatism of Black Women.* Edited by Stanlie M. James and Albena P. A. Busia. Routledge, 1993, 141–159. Used by permission of Loretta J. Ross.

women in the struggle both to obtain abortions and to participate in the national debates on abortion. She also shares with the reader the reproductive crises she experienced that were "consistent with being Black, poor and female in America." Issues concerning abortion rights and reproductive freedom are not abstract intellectual exercises for Ross, but an integral part of her life.

Loretta J. Ross is the founder and executive director of the National Center for Human Rights Education. She has testified before the U.S. Congress, the United Nations, and the Food and Drug Administration on women's health and civil rights issues.

INTRODUCTION

My quest to understand the activism of African-American women seeking abortions and birth control stems from experiences shared with millions of women who want real choices as to when, and under what conditions, we will have children. Here is my definition of what it means to be "pro-life" *and* "pro-choice"—the right to have, or not to have, children and the right to raise them free from racism, sexism and poverty.

Many people mistakenly view the African-American women's struggle for abortion rights and reproductive freedom as a relatively recent phenomenon, rather than placing it in the context of our historical struggle against racism, sexism and poverty. Whether these assumptions come from population experts or the African-American community, they fail to credit us with the power to make responsible decisions for ourselves. To ask whether African-American women favor or oppose abortion is the wrong question. We obtain 24 percent of the abortions in the United States, more than 500,000 annually (Henshaw et al., 1991: 75–81). The question is not *if* we support abortion, but *how*, and when, and why.

African-American women have a long history in the struggle for reproductive freedom, but racist and sexist assumptions about us, our sexuality and our fertility have disguised our contributions to the birth control and abortion movements in the United States. Distilling facts from the myths is difficult because so many accounts of African-American history are written from perspectives that fail even to acknowledge our presence in the reproductive freedom movement.

Similarly, if a decline in African-American birth rates occurs, the population experts usually ascribe it to poverty, coercive family planning, or other external factors, ignoring the possibility that we Black women were in any way responsible for the change.

The absence of discussion about abortion rights activism by African-American women in most feminist literature is also disappointing, reflecting a commonly held view that African-American women either are too politically naive or have an underdeveloped consciousness on issues of gender equality and abortion rights.

While volumes could be written on this topic, this paper merely aspires to be one step in the process of recording our "herstory." It remains for others to cover comprehensively various aspects of abortion, such as its medical technology, and the judicial and legislative battles that determined the legality of abortion and contraception.

Instead, I have chosen to focus on the activism: the *agency* of African-American women in the struggle both to obtain abortions and to participate in the national debate. I have also chosen to tell my own story in this paper because, in the tradition of Paula Giddings and others, I believe it is the deliberate combination of the personal and the objective that creates the authority, authenticity and uniqueness of the African-American female experience.

Recording our history of activism is important because the voices heard in support of abortion are usually white. Even with the best intentions, white women cannot speak for us. They cannot see the world through our history or represent the authority of our lives. And, while volumes could also be written about the racism and elitism historically besetting the feminist movement, white women are not the focus of this paper.

African-American women have been reluctant to analyze our history regarding abortion and to speak out collectively and publicly in support of abortion. To do so once seemed to further arguments of Black genocide, a charge that was not necessarily paranoid in view of past attacks on African-Americans. To speak out also risked replicating the narrow focus of the white abortion rights movement, by engaging in "privileged bias," of isolating abortion from other forms of control imposed on African-American women, through racism and poverty (Joseph and Lewis, 1981: 50).

If we are to connect ourselves to our foremothers who preceded us, we must transcend the tensions between these two extremes. To paraphrase bell hooks, our struggle is not so much to move from silence into speech, but to change the nature and direction of our speech, to make a speech that is heard (hooks, 1989: 6).

I chose to write on abortion because reproductive health activism has been a part of my life for more than twenty years. I have been privileged to be a part of both the Black liberation and the women's movements and to meet many other African-American women who share a commitment to improving the quality of life for African-American women by ending racism and poverty, and by advancing gender equality.

Abortion rights and reproductive freedom are not intellectual abstractions for me, but have determined many aspects of my life. By the time I was in my twenties, I had experienced many of the reproductive crises consistent with being Black, poor and female in America. At age 15 I became a teen mother because of sexual activity coupled with sexual ignorance, not an unusual combination even today. I realized for the first time the lack of options available to pregnant teens in the 1960s. Because abortion was illegal and traveling anywhere else was not possible, I had my son in a very difficult pregnancy, after staying in a home for unwed mothers.

As a college student two years later, I became pregnant again, due to contraceptive failure. I had an abortion, which fortunately was legal in Washington, DC, at the time.

It is providential that I kept my child rather than giving him up for adoption, because I was permanently sterilized by the Dalkon Shield IUD at age 23. I sued A. H. Robins, the maker of the shield, and became one of the first Black women to prevail against this multinational corporation. The company was eventually bankrupted by thousands of other women who were also sterilized. Thus my reproductive career lasted a brief eight years and included a full-term pregnancy, an abortion and sterilization.

Although winning against A. H. Robins was a moral victory, it did not mitigate the burning anger I felt because my IUD was inserted years after its dangers had already been substantially documented. Why was a defective contraceptive recommended to me? Why did I nearly die from acute pelvic inflammatory disease that several doctors failed to link to the defective IUD, preferring to believe in bizarre theories of rare venereal diseases among Black women? Doctors' diagnoses of African-American women were distorted with theories of diseases brought back by soldiers returning from Vietnam. My pelvic infection from the IUD was treated as a mysterious venereal disease. I wondered who really controlled my body. It certainly didn't seem to be me.

In the process I learned that simply surviving against the odds was personally liberating. But I also learned that for African-American women to survive, we all need liberation from devices and doctors and politicians who control our bodies.

Abortion, in and of itself, does not automatically create freedom. But it does allow women to exert some control over our biology, freeing us from the inevitability of unwanted pregnancies, and is therefore indispensable to bodily and political self-determination.

There is much yet to be written about our activism. But it was not persuasive analysis, arguments, or ideology that influenced African-American women to support abortion. We did so because we *needed* to. Necessity was the midwife to our politics.

ABORTION IN THE 1800s

Prior to the Civil War, almost 20 percent of the total U.S. population consisted of African-American slaves. By 1900, African-Americans were 12 percent of the total population as the forced breeding of slavery came to an end (Littlewood, 1977: 18). However, even before the Civil War, African-American women sought to control their fertility.

Controlling women's reproduction was important to maintain the race, class and gender inequality of the slave economy. Plantation owners tried to keep knowledge of birth control and abortion away from both slaves and white women to maintain the caste system of white supremacy used to justify slavery (P. Collins, 1991: 50). Black women's fertility increased the owners' labor force and property value and "slave masters wanted adolescent girls to have children, and . . . they practiced a passive, though insidious kind of breeding" (D. White, 1985: 98). Techniques included giving pregnant women lighter workloads and more rations and bonuses to increase Black women's willingness to have children. Punitive measures were also used: infertile women were treated "like barren sows and . . . passed from one unsuspecting buyer to the next" (D. White, 1985: 101).

African-Americans used birth control and abortion as a form of resistance to slavery. Abortion and infanticide were acts of desperation, motivated not by a desire to avoid the biological birth process or the burdens of parenting, but, instead, by a commitment to resist the oppressive conditions of slavery. When Black women resorted to abortion, the stories they told were not so much about the desire to be free of pregnancy, but rather about the miserable social conditions which dissuaded them from bringing new lives into the world (Fried, 1990: 17).

Abortion as a means of controlling fertility has been a part of African culture since the time when Egypt was the cradle of civilization. Abortion-inducing herbs and methods have been discovered in ancient societies in Africa, China and the Middle East (Petchesky, 1990: 28; S. Davis, 1988: 17). African queen and pharaoh Hatshepsut, who reigned in Egypt between 1500 and 179 B.C., invented a method of birth control (E. White, 1990: 121). Most of these skills were lost during slavery, except the knowledge retained by midwives which spanned across time. This folk knowledge blurred the distinction between birth control and abortion.

Historians declare that it is almost impossible to determine whether slave women practiced birth control and abortion. However, careful readings of slave journals and narratives reveal that some southern whites were certain that slave women knew how to avoid pregnancy as well as how to deliberately abort their pregnancies. When Daph, a woman on the Ferry Hill plantation in Virginia, miscarried twins in 1838, the overseer reported that Daph took an abortifacient to bring about the miscarriage (D. White, 1985: 84).

Suspicions about slave abortions ran high enough to spur public comment. In an 1856 essay, Dr. E. M. Pendleton claimed that planters regularly complained of whole families of women who failed to have children. Pendleton believed that "blacks are possessed of a secret by which they destroy the foetus at an early age of gestation" (D. White, 1985: 85). A Tennessee physician, Dr. John H. Morgan, said that he was certain that slave women were aborting either by "medicine, violent exercise, or by external and internal manipulations" (Sterling, 1984: 40).

Toward the end of the nineteenth century, "alum water" was one of many birth control measures used in southern rural communities served by midwives. Women in urban areas used petroleum jelly and quinine. Widely available and purchased very cheaply in stores, it was placed over the mouth of the uterus. Some remedies served both purposes. For example, boiling rusty nails created a douche used as either an abortifacient or a contraceptive. Some women used quinine tablets or turpentine

(orally or as a douche) and laxatives. Such concoctions were reputed to bring about severe cramps and contractions which approximated giving birth. Plant compounds like pennyroyal and papaya seeds were also used (Sterling, 1984: 40).

Despite this knowledge, folk methods of birth control and abortion were usually regarded as a sin by those influenced by Christianity. For example, the secret techniques for abortion kept by a midwife named Mollie became too much for her to bear when she converted to Christianity. She begged for forgiveness for having assisted hundreds of women in obtaining birth control and abortions (D. White, 1985: 126).

Nevertheless, African-American women informally discussed abortion and birth control and passed along the knowledge (Ward, 1986: 13–14). In 1894, *The Women's Era,* an African-American women's newsletter, wrote that "not all women are intended for mothers. Some of us have not the temperament for family life" (Giddings, 1984: 108). By the 1900s, Black women were making gains in controlling their fertility. "Their grandmothers married at twelve and fifteen," W. E. B. DuBois, one of the founders of the National Association for the Advancement of Colored People (NAACP), observed in the *Souls of Black Folk.* In 1910, he found 27 percent of African-American women still single past the age of 15. They were also having fewer children. Half of all married, educated African-American women had no children at the turn of the century. Even more revealing, one-fourth of all Black women—the majority of them rural and uneducated—had no children at all (Giddings, 1984: 137).

BIRTH CONTROL AND ABORTION: 1915–50

One perception of the birth control movement is that it was thrust upon reluctant African-Americans by a population control establishment anxious to control Black fertility. While the population establishment may have had an agenda, African-Americans had their own view of the matter. Probably the best documented source of information about the use of birth control by African-Americans was written by Jessie M. Rodrique, who asserts that "Black women were interested in controlling their fertility and the low birth rates reflect in part a conscious use of birth control. . . . Blacks were active and effective participants in the establishment of local clinics and in the birth control debate"

(DuBois and Ruiz, 1990: 333). It is both wrong, and racist, to assume that African-American women had no interest in controlling the spacing of their children and were the passive victims of medical, commercial and state policies of reproductive control.

Black fertility declined toward the end of the nineteenth century, indicative of the growing social awareness among African-Americans that birth spacing was integral to economics, health, race relations and racial progress. In fact, between 1915 and 1920, Black infant mortality actually dropped from 181 per 1,000 births to 102 for states registering 2,000 or more Black births (Giddings, 1984: 149).

African-American women saw themselves not as breeders or matriarchs, but as builders and nurturers of a race, a nation. Sojourner Truth's statement, "I feel as if the power of a nation is within me!" (Bell et al., 1979: 117), affirmed the role of African-American women as "seminal forces of the endurance and creativity needed by future generations of Blacks not merely to survive, but to thrive, produce, and progress" (ibid.: 117).

W. E. B. DuBois wrote in 1919 that "the future [African-American] woman . . . must have the right of motherhood at her own discretion" (DuBois and Ruiz, 1990: 336). Joining him was historian J. A. Rogers who wrote, "I give the Negro woman credit if she endeavors to be something other than a mere breeding machine. Having children is by no means the sole reason for being" (DuBois and Ruiz, 1990: 336).

The Colored Women's Club Movement, the organized voice of African-American women during the late nineteenth and early twentieth centuries, directly addressed issues of Black women's sexuality. This movement sought to "confront and redefine morality and assess its relationship to 'true womanhood'" (Giddings, 1984: 85). Stereotypes about Black women's sexuality and alleged immorality prompted many African-American women to "make the virtues as well as the wants of the colored women known to the American people . . . to put a new social value on themselves" (Lerner, 1972: 576).

The Club Movement also denounced the rampant sterilization of Black women and supported the establishment of family planning clinics in Black communities. In 1918, the Women's Political Association of Harlem announced a scheduled lecture on birth control. The National Urban League requested of the Birth Control Federation of America (the forerunner to Planned Parenthood) that a clinic be opened in the Columbus Hill section of the Bronx. Several ministers held discus-

sions about birth control at their churches and Adam Clayton Powell, an influential congressional leader, spoke at public meetings in support of family planning (DuBois and Ruiz, 1990: 338).

African-American organizations including the NAACP, the National Urban League and leading Black newspapers like the *Pittsburgh Courier* and the *San Francisco Spokesman* promoted family planning. The African-American newspapers of the period reported the mortality rates of women who had septic abortions and also championed the causes of Black doctors who were arrested for performing illegal abortions (DuBois and Ruiz, 1990: 335).

The *Baltimore Afro-American* wrote that pencils, nails and hat pins were instruments commonly used for self-induced abortions and that abortions among Black women were deliberate, not the result of poor health or sexually transmitted diseases. This was clearly a "means of getting rid of unwanted children" (DuBois and Ruiz, 1990: 335). Many women died as well, a fact not lost on African-American women.

EUGENICS AND GENOCIDE

It is up to science to meet the demands of
humanity . . . that life shall be given . . .
"frankly, gaily," or—not at all. Which shall it be?
Stella Browne, 1922
(Petchesky, 1990: 92)

Although motherhood was a highly prized social status in Africa, fears of depopulation were not a tremendous concern before American slavery. Africa's population decreased because of the slave trade, exploitative colonial labor policies and the introduction of new diseases from Europe. In the eighteenth century, 20 percent of the world's population lived in Africa; by the year 2000, the figure [was] expected to be less than 13 percent.

In the USA, as racism, lynchings and poverty took their heavy toll on African-Americans, fears of depopulation produced among them toward the end of the nineteenth century a pronatalist trend that had not previously existed. This trend also built successfully on traditional Black values that conferred adult status on women who became biological mothers, the first significant step toward womanhood (P. Collins, 1991: 134). This shift in the critical thinking of African-Americans on population and motherhood presaged an inevitable conflict between the right of women to exercise bodily self-determination and the need of the African-American community for political and economic self-determination. In both schools of thought, wombs were to be the weapon against racism and oppression.

The opposition to fertility control for African-American women in the 1920s came primarily from the Catholic Church for religious and political reasons, from white conservatives who feared the availability of birth control for white women, and from Black nationalist leaders like Marcus Garvey who believed that the continuation of the Black race demanded increasing, rather than decreasing, the African population as a defense against racial oppression.

When the movement for birth control began, its proponents like Margaret Sanger advocated giving women control over their fertility as a means of social mobility. This argument persuaded middle-class women, both Black and white, to support birth control. However, the early feminism of the movement, which prioritized women's control over their own bodies, collapsed under the weight of support offered by the growing number of people who were concerned about the rising population of African-Americans, other people of color and immigrants. Birth control advocacy quickly became a tool of racists who argued in favor of eugenics, or other population control policies, based on fears of African-Americans and others thought to be "undesirable" to the politically powerful. The elite sought to improve their control of society through the control of breeding (Corea, 1985: 138).

The eugenics movement, begun in the late 1800s and based on pseudo-scientific theories of race and heredity, evolved into a movement of biological determinism. To promote the reproduction of self-defined "racially superior" people, its proponents argued for both "positive" methods, such as tax incentives and education for the desirable, and "negative" methods, such as sterilization, involuntary confinement and immigration restrictions for the undesirable (Petchesky, 1990: 86). It was assumed that Black and immigrant women had a "moral obligation to restrict the size of their families." While birth control was demanded as a right for privileged women, it became a duty for the poor (Fried, 1990: 20).

A leading eugenicist proposed sterilization, based on IQ tests, of at least 10 million Americans because they were mentally or physically disabled, criminal, or simply, "feeble-minded" (Hartmann, 1987: 96). By 1932, the Eugenics Society could boast that at least twenty-seven states had passed compulsory sterilization laws and that thousands of "unfit" persons had already been surgically prevented from reproducing (A. Davis, 1983: 214). Many birth control advocates believed it was important to "prevent the American people from being replaced by alien or negro stock, whether it be by immigration or by overly high birth rates among others in this country" (Hartmann, 1987: 97).

The eugenicists' view that social intervention should be used to manipulate biological reproduction echoed other white supremacist views of the day. The Ku-Klux-Klan had an estimated 5 million members at this time, including representatives in Congress (Blee, 1991: 20). It should not be difficult to understand why birth control (and abortion) came to be regarded as genocidal by some African-Americans. This view was exacerbated by the high incidence of involuntary sterilization of African-American women.

It was not helpful that Margaret Sanger, like others who followed her, opportunistically built alliances with the oftentimes racist population control establishment, thereby advancing her cause at the expense of people of color. Sanger's campaign succeeded and benefited middle-class women because it concentrated on legal rights, medical acceptance and public policy. The result was the enactment of policies that were racist enough to be supported by the population control establishment and weak enough so that control over the technology and techniques of birth control would remain in the hands of the professional medical community. The eugenics movement was broader and encompassed far more historical trends than just the feminist movement. It was international in scope and its roots were firmly established in the colonialism of the era. Feminism played its part, both wittingly and unwittingly, in the advancement of the eugenics movement in particular, and white racism in general (Petchesky, 1990: 93).

The Birth Control Federation designed a "Negro Project" in 1939 to hire several African-American ministers to travel through the South to enlist the support of African-American doctors for birth control (Gordon, 1990: 328). The project did not necessarily want strong involvement of other portions of the African-American community, especially women, and argued that "the mass of Negroes, particularly in the South, still breed carelessly and disastrously, with the result that the increase among Negroes, even more than among Whites, is from that portion of the population least intelligent and fit, and least able to rear children properly" (Gordon, 1990: 328).

Not all advocates of birth control and abortion were as insensitive as the eugenicists. The *Courier,* a Black newspaper whose editorial policy favored family planning, said in 1936 that African-Americans should oppose sterilization programs being advanced by eugenicists because the burden would "fall upon colored people and it behooves us to watch the law and stop the spread of [eugenic sterilization]" (DuBois and Ruiz, 1990: 338). A clear sense of dual or "paired" values also emerged among African-American women: to want individual control over their bodies while simultaneously resisting government and private depopulation policies that blurred the distinction between incentives and coercion (Petchesky, 1990: 130). African-American women supported birth control, but at the same time they offered a strong critique of the eugenicists.

Ironically, because of the unavailability of family planning services, sterilization through hysterectomies was frequently chosen by African-American women desperate to control their fertility. Often women pleaded for the operation, because of the absence of organized, alternative birth control services. As had been proven earlier, women adapted themselves to whatever limited choices were available to help them control their lives.

THE UNDERGROUND MOVEMENT: 1950–70

The majority of abortions provided to African-American women in the 1950s and early 1960s were provided by doctors and midwives operating illegally. For example, Dr. Edgar Keemer, a Black physician in Detroit, practiced outside the law for more than thirty years until his arrest in 1956. Women also traveled to Mexico to have abortions (E. White, 1990: 121).

Middle-class women could sometimes persuade doctors to arrange for a discreet abortion or to provide a referral. Poor women either had the unplanned children or went to "the lady down the street" or the "woman downstairs"—either midwives or partially trained medical personnel. Abortions from these illegal providers were usually very expensive, and many white women came to Black neighborhoods to obtain abortions this way (Ward, 1986: 15; Baehr, 1990: 13). Fees for abortions were between $50 and $75, which was expensive considering that a pregnant woman might earn $10 a day (Ward, 1986: 15).

Long after the majority of "granny" midwives in other ethnic groups had been replaced by medically based hospital practices, there were still hundreds of Black lay midwives practicing in the deep South, with midwifery lineages extending as far back as slavery. They provided most of the abortion and contraceptive services for Black southern women (E. White, 1990: 98). If complications developed, women visited physicians who operated in the poor sections of the city. Only as a last resort did they go to hospitals, fearing the legal consequences of having obtained an illegal abortion. Thus, the rate of septic abortions reported to hospitals was very low.

Dr. Dorothy Brown, the first Black female general surgeon in the United States, graduated from Meharry Medical College in 1948 and, while in the Tennessee State Legislature, became in the 1950s the first state legislator in the USA to introduce a bill to legalize abortion (E. White, 1990: 47). In an interview at the 1983 founding conference of the National Black Women's Health Project, Dr. Brown asserted, "We should dispense quickly the notion that abortion is genocide, because genocide in this country dates back to 1619" (Worcester and Whatley, 1988: 38).

The pseudo-science of eugenics had been largely discredited after the Second World War, when worldwide condemnation followed the Nazi extermination, not only of 6 million Jews, but of countless Germans with African, Indian, or Asian blood, as well as gypsies, gay men and lesbians, the disabled, the mentally ill. In the mid-1950s, population "time bomb" theories from demographers gave rise to a newer, more legitimate and "scientific" approach to eugenics. The proponents of time bomb theories sanctimoniously argued that they were simply saving the poor from themselves.

Brochures published by groups like the Draper Fund and the Population Council showed "hordes of black and brown faces spilling over a tiny earth" (Petchesky, 1990: 118). The fund dated from 1958, when President Eisenhower appointed General William Draper, a New York investment banker and a key figure in the post-war reconstruction of Europe, to study foreign aid. The committee eventually developed an ideological link between population growth in the Third World and the USA's ability to govern world affairs. Draper told the Senate Foreign Relations Committee in 1959 that "the population problem . . . is the greatest bar to our whole economic aid program and to the progress of the world" (Hartmann, 1987: 103). By the early 1960s, the U.S. government began supporting population control policies overseas, and linked foreign aid with depopulation policies.

The domestic side of this world-view coincided with the growth of the civil rights movement, perhaps in response to the militancy of the movement and its potential for sweeping social change. The "political instability" of the African-American population convinced many members of the white elite and middle class that Black population growth should be curbed. White Americans feared, out of proportion to reality, that a growing welfare class of African-Americans concentrated in the inner cities would not only cause rampant crime, but exacerbate the national debt, and eventually produce a political threat from majority-Black voting blocs in urban areas (Littlewood, 1977: 8).

The new "politics of population" that emerged in the mid-1960s gave rise to family planning programs in the South that were directed at predominantly Black urban areas. Family planning was designed to reduce the number of Black births to control the ever-expanding Black population. This occurred at the same time as African-American leaders were expressing interest in "taking over" the big cities and "holding them as enclaves against increasing repression" (Littlewood, 1977: 9–10). The U.S. Congress took note, and pressured the newly created Office of Economic Opportunity to wage its war on poverty by emphasizing family planning programs for African-Americans the year after passage of the 1965 Voting Rights Act. It is interesting to note that George Bush, a Texas congressional representative at the time, supported family planning, even though his father once lost a Senate election in Connecticut after columnist Drew Pearson "revealed" the candidate's "involvement" with Planned Parenthood on the weekend before the ballots were cast (Littlewood, 1977: 51). This support was affirmed by Richard Nixon when he took office in 1969.

Medicaid was established in the 1960s to cover medical costs for the poor. Family planning was included only after a series of fights with Catholics and conservatives at the state level. Publicly supported birth control developed in the 1960s, aided by the mass availability of the pill and the IUD. In 1967, Congress passed the Child Health Act which specified that at least 6 percent of all maternal-child health grants to public health agencies had to be spent on family planning. This law stated that federal funds could be used to pay for services to any woman who had in the past needed, or might in the future need, welfare. It allowed family planners to offer a wide range of maternal and child care services to poor women. Joan Smith, current head of Louisiana's statewide family planning program, said at the time, "What caught my fancy was the idea of offering services to indigent women the same as private doctors were giving. Nobody treated poor women with dignity. We said we'd do it and we did" (Ward, 1986: 42).

Some medical experts opposed family planning for African-Americans, convinced that African-American women "wanted to be pregnant and have all those children and that even if they did not want repeated pregnancies, they could not possibly understand the principles of birth control because they were not bright enough and lacked behavioral control" (Ward, 1986: 17).

Although abortion was still illegal, some public health agencies operated an "underground railroad" of referrals for women to have illegal abortions (Ward, 1986: 58). It is estimated that from 200,000 to 1 million illegal abortions occurred annually in the late 1960s (S. Davis, 1988: 12). A major strength was the informal networks of African-American women who spread the news about the availability of services and became activists in support of birth control and better health care, and for abortion rights. Underground abortions were facilitated by church- and community-based referral services and cooperative doctors' networks that emerged in cities and states in the 1960s (Petchesky, 1990: 113).

Because of the blatant racism of the population control establishment that promoted family planning, Black nationalist campaigns against family planning re-emerged. Several birth control clinics were invaded by Black Muslims associated with the Nation of Islam, who published cartoons in *Muhammed Speaks* that depicted bottles of birth control pills marked with a skull and crossbones, or graves of unborn Black infants. The Pittsburgh branch of the NAACP declared that the local family planning clinic was an instrument of genocide. William "Bouie" Haden, leader of the militant United Movement for Progress, went one step further and threatened to firebomb the Pittsburgh clinic (Littlewood, 1977: 69).

Whitney Young, leader of the Urban League, also reversed his organization's support for family planning in 1962. Marvin Davies, head of the Florida NAACP, said, "Our women need to produce more babies, not less . . . and until we comprise 30 to 35 percent of the population, we won't really be able to affect the power structure in this country" (Littlewood, 1977: 75). This was a major ideological shift away from the early days of the NAACP and the

Urban League; both organizations had formerly supported women's rights as a means of racial progress. The NAACP of the 1920s would have been horrified to find itself in the 1960s sounding more like Marcus Garvey and less like DuBois.

The Black Power conference held in Newark in 1967, organized by Amiri Baraka, passed an anti–birth control resolution. Two years later, the May 1969 issue of *The Liberator* warned, "For us to speak in favor of birth control for Afro-Americans would be comparable to speaking in favor of genocide" (Giddings, 1984: 318).

The Black Panther Party was the only nationalist group to support free abortions and contraceptives on demand (Ward, 1986: 92), although not without considerable controversy within its ranks. "Half of the women in the party used birth control and we supported it because of our free health care program. We understood the conditions of the Black community," remembers Nkenge Toure, a former member, who also recalls that there were no formal political education discussions around the issue, but there was support from many party women.[1] Kathleen Cleaver, the wife of Eldridge Cleaver, wrote that "in order for women to obtain liberation, the struggles [Black liberation and women's rights] are going to have to be united" (Giddings, 1984: 311).

This view of women's liberation within the Black Panther Party often collided with male opposition to abortion and birth control. Some male members tried to shut down family planning clinics in New Orleans and Pittsburgh (Littlewood, 1977: 97). As Angela Davis concluded, the late 1960s and early 1970s were "a period in which one of the unfortunate hallmarks of some nationalist groups was their determination to push women into the background. The brothers opposing us leaned heavily on the male supremacist trends which were winding their way through the movement" (Giddings, 1984: 317).

White conservatives saw family planning as an assault on traditional values of motherhood, while some Black radicals saw it as a race- and class-directed eugenics program; thus the assault on birth control and abortion came from both the left and the right. That such disparate forces aligned themselves against African-American women proved that both white bigots and Black leaders could find common cause in the assertion of male authority over women's decisions regarding reproduction. Both tendencies sought to reverse a trend that saw women becoming more autonomous and presenting greater social and economic threats.

In contrast, African-American women exerted a dynamic and aggressive influence on the family planning movement. They constituted the largest single bloc of support for family planning and were so visible that politicians in some states began to see them as a potential political force (Ward, 1986: 59). They were assisted in their efforts by coalitions of Presbyterian, Episcopal, Unitarian, Baptist, Lutheran and Jewish congregations, representatives of which signed a "freedom-of-conscience" statement supporting the women in Pittsburgh and other cities.

African-American women noticed that "most of the commotion about the clinics . . . seemed to be coming from men—men who do not have to bear children" (Littlewood, 1977: 72). Even when the Black men successfully shut down clinics, as in Cleveland and Pittsburgh, women organized to reopen them because they "did not appreciate being thought of as random reproduction machines that could be put to political use" (Littlewood, 1977: 79), reported William Austin, who reviewed the dispute for a study by the Urban League. African-American women fully understood that there were no Planned Parenthood clinics in poor white neighborhoods, but they still perceived the free services to be in their own best interests (Littlewood, 1977: 79). Quoting from DuBois, they declared, "We're not interested in the quantity of our race. We're interested in the quality of it" (Ward, 1986: 93).

In Pittsburgh, about seventy women members of the National Welfare Rights Organization rebuffed attempts by African-American men to close family planning clinics. In particular, they rejected the leadership of William "Bouie" Haden who, it was discovered, was on the payroll of the Catholic Church. "Who appointed him our leader anyhow?" inquired Georgiana Henderson. "He is only one person—and a man at that. He can't speak for the women of Homewood. . . . Why should I let one loudmouth tell me about having children?" (Littlewood, 1977: 72). Other African-American women around the country declared they would not tolerate male expressions of territorial rights over women's bodies.

Shirley Chisolm, a Black congresswoman from Brooklyn, dismissed the genocide argument when asked to discuss her views on abortion and birth control:

To label family planning and legal abortion programs "genocide" is male rhetoric, for male ears. It falls flat to female listeners and to thoughtful male ones. Women know, and so do many men, that two or three children who are wanted, prepared for, reared amid love and stability, and educated to the limit of their ability will mean more for the future of the black and brown races from which they come than any number of neglected, hungry, ill-housed and ill-clothed youngsters.

(Chisolm, 1970: 114–115)

African-American women were also profoundly committed to the clinics because they knew teen pregnancy and death from septic abortions were the leading causes of death for Black women. Before the legalization of abortion, 80 percent of deaths caused by illegal abortions involved Black and Puerto Rican women (A. Davis, 1983: 204). In Georgia between 1965 and 1967, the Black maternal death rate due to illegal abortion was 14 times that of white women (Worcester and Whatley, 1988: 136). Based on these grim statistics, programs to curb adolescent pregnancy and obtain contraceptives gained support in the African-American community. Emphasis was also placed on establishing programs for education, like Head Start, and homes for unwed mothers. Women were not blind to the incongruity of the government plan to make contraceptives free and extremely accessible to African-American communities that lacked basic health care. They used infant and maternal mortality figures to overcome resistance to family planning. "I showed them the maternal mortality statistics for the previous five years," said one birth control advocate. "Fifty-four women lost their lives during childbirth in the District of Columbia, two of them white. So if [the family planners] were really interested in something genocidal, I'd tell all the black women to go out and get pregnant, and they'll die at the rate of 25-to-1" (Littlewood, 1977: 77).

Black women succeeded in keeping family planning clinics open, and understood the essential difference between population control and birth control in their "paired values." They organized to remove Haden as a delegate from the Homewood-Brushton Citizens Renewal Council in a demonstration of political strength that frightened both Black and white men. They also learned a valuable lesson about sexist backlash that equated Black male domination with African-American progress.

A distinct Black feminist consciousness emerged to counter the reactionary views promulgated by African-American men. In 1969, Frances Beal, then head of the Black Women's Liberation Committee of the Student Nonviolent Coordinating Committee (SNCC), wrote, "Black women have the right and the responsibility to determine when it is in *the interest of the struggle to have children or not to have them and this right must not be relinquished to any* . . . to determine when it is in *her own best interests* to have children" (Morgan, 1970: 393; original emphases).

This sentiment was echoed by Toni Cade (Bambara) in 1970 when she wrote, "I've been made aware of the national call to Sisters to abandon birth control . . . to picket family planning centers and abortion-referral groups and to raise revolutionaries. What plans do you have for the care of me and the child?" (Petchesky, 1990: 137). Black feminists argued that birth control and abortion were, in themselves, revolutionary—and that African liberation in any sense could not be won without women controlling their lives. The birth control pill, in and of itself, could not liberate African-American women, but it "gives her the time to fight for liberation in those other areas" (Petchesky, 1990: 172).

By the late 1960s, family planning became "synonymous with the civil rights of poor women to medical care" (Ward, 1986: xiii). It was regarded as a key to the prevention of disease and death, and as a public health measure to address many of society's problems. However, African-American women warily watched state legislative proposals to sterilize poor women who had too many "illegitimate" children, which fueled the genocide debate. None of the proposals succeeded, largely because of the militance of women like Fannie Lou Hamer who said that "six out of every ten Negro women were . . . sterilized for no reason at all. Often the women were not told that they had been sterilized until they were released from the hospital" (Littlewood, 1977: 80). A national fertility study conducted by Princeton University found that 20 percent of all married African-American women had been sterilized by 1970 (Fried, 1990: 23).

To African-American women, it seemed absurd to coerce them to limit their family size through involuntary sterilization when they were willing to do so voluntarily if safe methods were accessible. This combined support for birth control and abortion and opposition to sterilization, a unique view among African-American women at the time, did much to inform both the feminist and the civil rights movement in later decades. African-American women rejected the single-issue focus of the women's movement on abortion, which excluded other issues of reproductive freedom. They also opposed the myopic focus on race of the male-dominated civil rights movement, which ignored concerns of gender equality.

CONCLUSION

> Historical patterns suggest that just as Black women are vital to Black movements, Black movements are vital to the progress of feminist movements. Feminism always had the greatest currency in times of Black militancy or immediately thereafter.
>
> (Giddings, 1984: 340)

African-American women have always been concerned about our fertility, despite the myths and assumptions of others. When birth control and abortion were available, African-American women used them. When they were not, women resorted to dangerous methods limited only by their imaginations and physiology.

It is critical that the civil rights and the feminist movements acknowledge this history. We understand that we are needed in both movements, but we refuse to be pawns in a population numbers game or tokens to colorize a white movement. As we deepen our understanding of our history, we will reconceptualize how our activism is recorded because male-dominated and/or Eurocentric views of the political process produce definitions of power, activism and resistance that fail to capture the meaning of these concepts in the lives of African-American women (Collins, 1991: 140).

The fast-paced growth and militancy of the African-American women's movement will probably produce, again, its own form of backlash from some African-American men, a reaction that I call "blacklash." As Paula Giddings has predicted, "We are entering, once more, an era of Black assertiveness, one which will trigger historical tensions over the relationship of race and sex" (Giddings, 1984: 349). These tensions, however, will not keep us from taking control over our lives. As the Black Women's Liberation Group of Mt. Vernon, New York, wrote in 1970, "Birth control [and abortion] is the *freedom to fight* genocide of black women and children" (Morgan, 1970: 393).

Winning reproductive freedom will reward African-American women with true choices in our lives. We may learn, along the journey, to trust in the words of Audre Lorde:

> For Black women, learning to consciously extend ourselves to each other and to call upon each other's strengths is a life-saving strategy. In the best of circumstances surrounding our lives, it requires an enormous amount of mutual, consistent support for us to be emotionally able to look straight into the face of the powers aligned against us and still do our work with joy. It takes determination and practice.
>
> (Lorde, 1988: 123)

NOTE

1. Telephone interview by the author with Nkenge Toure, former member of the Black Panther Party, March 8, 1992, Washington, DC.

REFERENCES

Baehr, Ninia. *Abortion Without Apology: A Radical History for the 1990s.* Boston: South End Press, 1990.

Bell, Roseann P.; Bettye J. Parker; and Beverly Guy-Sheftall, eds. *Sturdy Black Bridges: Visions of Black Women in Literature.* New York: Anchor Books, 1979.

Blee, Kathleen. *Women of the Klan: Racism and Gender in the 1920s.* Berkeley: University of California Press, 1991.

Burgher, Mary. "Images of Self and Race in the Autobiographies of Black Women." In Bell, Parker, and Guy-Sheftall, eds., *Sturdy Black Bridges,* pp. 107–122.

Chisolm, Shirley. *Unbought and Unbossed,* special limited ed. New York: Hodge Taylor, 1970.

Collins, Kimberly A. *Slightly Off Center.* Atlanta: Say It Loud Press, 1991.

Collins, Patricia Hill. *Black Feminist Thought: Knowledge, Consciousness, and the Politics of Empowerment.* London: Routledge, 1991.

Corea, Gena. *The Hidden Malpractice: How American Medicine Mistreats Women.* New York: Harper & Row, 1985.

Davis, Angela. *Women, Race and Class.* New York: Vintage Books, 1983.

———. "Racism, Birth Control and Reproductive Rights." Pp. 15–26 in Marlene Gerber Fried, ed., *Abortion to Reproductive Freedom: Transforming a Movement.* Boston: South End Press, 1990.

Davis, Susan E., ed. *Women Under Attack: Victories, Backlash and the Fight for Reproductive Freedom.*

Committee for Abortion Rights and Against Sterilization Abuse. Boston: South End Press, 1988.

DuBois, Ellen Carol, and Vicki L. Ruiz, eds. *Unequal Sisters: A. Multicultural Reader in U.S. Women's History.* London: Routledge, 1990.

Fried, Marlene Gerber, ed. *Abortion to Reproductive Freedom: Transforming a Movement.* Boston: South End Press, 1990.

Giddings, Paula. *When and Where I Enter . . . : The Impact of Black Women on Race and Sex in America.* New York: Morrow, 1984.

Gordon, Linda. *Woman's Body, Woman's Right: Birth Control in America,* rev. ed. New York: Penguin Books, 1990.

Hartmann, Betsy. *Reproductive Rights and Wrongs: The Global Politics of Population Control and Contraceptive Choice.* New York: Harper & Row, 1987.

Henshaw, Stanley K.; Lisa M. Koonin; and Jack C. Smith. "Characteristics of U.S. Women Having Abortions, 1987." *Family Planning Perspectives,* Alan Guttmacher Institute, 23, 2 (March/April 1991): 75–81.

hooks, bell. *Talking Back: Thinking Feminist, Thinking Black.* Boston: South End Press, 1989.

Joseph, Gloria I., and Jill Lewis. *Common Differences: Conflicts in Black and White Feminist Perspectives.* Boston: South End Press, 1981.

Lerner, Gerda. *Black Women in White America.* New York: Vintage Books, 1972.

Littlewood, Thomas B. *The Politics of Population Control.* Notre Dame, IN: University of Notre Dame Press, 1977.

Lorde, Audre. *A Burst of Light.* Ithaca, NY: Firebrand Books, 1988.

Morgan, Robin, ed. *Sisterhood Is Powerful.* New York: Random House, 1970.

Petchesky, Rosalind Pollack. *Abortion and Woman's Choice: The State, Sexuality and Reproductive Freedom,* rev. ed. Boston: Northeastern University Press, 1990.

Rodrigue, Jessie M. "The Black Community and the Birth Control Movement." Pp. 333–342 in DuBois and Ruiz, eds., *Unequal Sisters.*

Simmons, Judy D. "Abortion: A Matter of Choice." Pp. 120–127 in E. White, ed., *The Black Women's Health Book.*

Sterling, Dorothy, ed. *We Are Your Sisters: Black Women in the Nineteenth Century.* New York: Norton, 1984.

Ward, Martha C. *Poor Women, Powerful Men: America's Great Experiment in Family Planning.* Boulder, CO: Westview Press, 1986.

White, Deborah Gray. *Ar'n't I a Woman? Female Slaves in the Plantation South.* New York: Norton, 1985.

White, Evelyn C., ed. *The Black Women's Health Book: Speaking for Ourselves.* Seattle: Seal Press, 1990.

Worcester, Nancy, and Marianne H. Whatley, eds. *Women's Health: Readings on Social, Economic and Political Issues.* Dubuque, IA: Kendall/Hunt, 1988.

DISCUSSION QUESTIONS

1. Why does Ross believe that the history of abortion and birth control with regard to African-American women is critical to feminism and the civil rights movement?

2. Ross and Sally Markowitz both draw feminism into the controversy over abortion. What are the commonalities between their work, and what are the differences?

3. What role should *class* play in the abortion controversy? What does Ross say about the role of class and abortion? Does what she says change the abortion controversy in any way? Explain.

4. What role should *race* play in the abortion controversy? What does Ross say about the role of race and abortion? Does what she says change the abortion controversy in any way? Explain.

5. Ross says that "abortion, in and of itself, does not automatically create freedom. But it does allow women to exert some control over our biology, freeing us from the inevitability of unwanted pregnancies, and is therefore indispensable to bodily and political self-determination." Do you agree with her? How important is control over biology in what she calls "self-determination"?

6. Compare and contrast Judith Jarvis Thomson, Sally Markowitz, Don Marquis, and Ross on abortion. Whose arguments were the strongest? Whose were the weakest? Why? Try to do this exercise without letting your feelings about abortion affect your analysis of the arguments for and against abortion. Do you find this to be impossible? If so, try to explain why.

U.S. SUPREME COURT

Roe v. Wade

In 1973 in *Roe v. Wade,* the U.S. Supreme Court guaranteed abortion as fundamental to an individual woman's right to privacy. In the majority opinion, written by Justice Harry Blackmun, the Court held that the right to decide whether to bear children is protected by the Ninth through the Fourteenth Amendments. However, the right to terminate is not absolute. The state may limit a woman's right to terminate if it has a legitimate interest in safeguarding the woman's health, in maintaining medical standards, or in protecting human life. In the dissenting opinion, written by Justice Byron White, the minority argued that there is nothing in the Constitution to warrant the kind of protection claimed by the majority. The legality of abortion should be left to the individual states.

MAJORITY OPINION IN *ROE V. WADE*

Justice Harry A. Blackmun

. . . [A]t the time of the adoption of our Constitution, and throughout the major portion of the 19th century, abortion was viewed with less disfavor than under most American statutes currently in effect. Phrasing it another way, a woman enjoyed a substantially broader right to terminate a pregnancy than she does in most States today. At least with respect to the early stage of pregnancy, and very possibly without such a limitation, the opportunity to make this choice was present in this country well into the 19th century. . . .

Three reasons have been advanced to explain historically the enactment of criminal abortion laws in the 19th century and to justify their continued existence.

It has been argued occasionally that these laws were the product of a Victorian social concern to discourage illicit sexual conduct. . . .

A second reason is concerned with abortion as a medical procedure. When most criminal abortion laws were first enacted, the procedure was a hazardous one for the woman. This was particularly true prior to the development of antisepsis. Antiseptic techniques, of course, were based on discoveries by Lister, Pasteur, and others first announced in 1867, but were not generally accepted and employed until

about the turn of the century. Abortion mortality was high. Even after 1900, and perhaps until as late as the development of antibiotics in the 1940s, standard modern techniques such as dilatation and curettage were not nearly so safe as they are today. Thus it has been argued that a State's real concern in enacting a criminal abortion law was to protect the pregnant woman, that is, to restrain her from submitting to a procedure that placed her life in serious jeopardy.

Modern medical techniques have altered this situation. Appellants and various *amici* refer to medical data indicating that abortion in early pregnancy, that is, prior to the end of first trimester, although not without its risk, is now relatively safe. Mortality rates for women undergoing early abortions, where the procedure is legal, appear to be as low as or lower than the rates for normal childbirth. Consequently, any interest of the State in protecting the woman from an inherently hazardous procedure, except when it would be equally dangerous for her to forgo it, has largely disappeared. Of course, important state interests in the area of health and medical standards do remain. The State has a legitimate interest in seeing to it that abortion, like any other medical procedure, is performed under circumstances that insure maximum safety for the patient. This interest obviously extends at least to the performing physician and his staff, to the facilities involved, to the availability of after-care, and to adequate provision for any complication or emergency that might arise. The prevalence of high mortality rates at illegal "abortion mills" strengthens, rather than weakens, the State's interest in regulating the conditions under which abortions are performed. Moreover, the risk to the woman increases as her pregnancy continues. Thus the State retains a definite interest in protecting the woman's own health and safety when an abortion is performed at a late stage of pregnancy.

The third reason is the State's interest—some phrase it in terms of duty—in protecting prenatal life. Some of the argument for this justification rests on the theory that a new human life is present from the moment of conception. The State's interest and general obligation to protect life then extends, it is argued, to prenatal life. Only when the life of the pregnant mother herself is at stake, balanced against the life she carries within her, should the interest of the embryo or fetus not prevail. Logically, of course, a legitimate state interest in this area need not stand or fall on acceptance of the belief that life begins at conception or at some other point prior to live birth. In assessing the State's interest, recognition may be given to the less rigid claim that as long as at least *potential* life is involved, the State may assert interests beyond the protection of the pregnant woman alone.

Parties challenging state abortion laws have sharply disputed in some courts the contention that a purpose of these laws, when enacted, was to protect prenatal life. Pointing to the absence of legislative history to support the contention, they claim that most state laws were designed solely to protect the woman. Because medical advances have lessened this concern, at least with respect to abortion in early pregnancy, they argue that with respect to such abortions the laws can no longer be justified by any state interest. There is some scholarly support for this view of original purpose. The few state courts called upon to interpret their laws in the late 19th and early 20th centuries did focus on the State's interest in protecting the woman's health rather than in preserving the embryo and fetus. . . .

The Constitution does not explicitly mention any right of privacy. In a line of decisions, however, going back perhaps as far as *Union Pacific R. Co. v. Botsford* (1891), the Court has recognized that a right of personal privacy, or a guarantee of certain areas or zones of privacy, does exist under the Constitution. In varying contexts the Court or individual Justices have indeed found at least the roots of that right in the First Amendment, . . . in the Fourth and Fifth Amendments . . . in the penumbras of the Bill of Rights . . . in the Ninth Amendment . . . or in the concept of liberty guaranteed by the first section of the Fourteenth Amendment. . . . These decisions make it clear that only personal rights that can be deemed "fundamental" or "implicit in the concept of ordered liberty," . . . are included in this guarantee of personal privacy. They also make it clear that the right has some extension to activities relating to marriage, . . . procreation, . . . contraception, . . . family relationships, . . . and child rearing and education. . . .

This right of privacy, whether it be founded in the Fourteenth Amendment's concept of personal liberty and restrictions upon state action, as we feel it is, or, as the District Court determined, in the Ninth Amendment's reservation of rights to the people, is broad enough to encompass a woman's decision whether or not to terminate her pregnancy. . . .

[S]ome *amici* argue that the woman's right is absolute and that she is entitled to terminate her pregnancy at whatever time, in whatever way, and for whatever reason she alone chooses. With this we do not agree. Appellants' arguments that Texas either has no valid interest at all in regulating the abortion decision, or no interest strong enough to support any limitation upon the woman's sole determination, is unpersuasive. The Court's decisions recognizing a right of privacy also acknowledge that some state regulation in areas protected by that right is appropriate. As noted above, a state may properly assert important interests in safe-guarding health, in maintaining medical standards, and in protecting potential life. At some point in pregnancy, these respective interests become sufficiently compelling to sustain regulation of the factors that govern the abortion decision. . . .

We therefore conclude that the right of personal privacy includes the abortion decision, but that this right is not unqualified and must be considered against important state interests in regulation.

Although the results are divided most (federal and state) courts have agreed that the right of privacy, however based, is broad enough to cover the abortion decision; that the right, nonetheless, is not absolute and is subject to some limitations; and that at some point the state interests as to protection of health, medical standards, and prenatal life, become dominant. We agree. . . .

The appellee and certain *amici* argue that the fetus is a "person" within the language and meaning of the Fourteenth Amendment. In support of this they outline at length and in detail the well-known facts of fetal development. If this suggestion of personhood is established, the appellant's case, of course, collapses, for the fetus' right to life is then guaranteed specifically by the Amendment. The appellant conceded as much on reargument. On the other hand, the appellee conceded on reargument that no case could be cited that holds that a fetus is a person within the meaning of the Fourteenth Amendment. . . .

All this, together with our observation, *supra,* that throughout the major portion of the 19th century prevailing legal abortion practices were far freer than they are today, persuades us that the word "person," as used in the Fourteenth Amendment, does not include the unborn. . . . Indeed, our decision in *United States v. Vuitch* (1971) inferentially is to the same effect, for we there would not have indulged in statutory interpretation favorable to abortion in specified circumstances if the necessary consequence was the termination of life entitled to Fourteenth Amendment protection.

. . . As we have intimated above, it is reasonable and appropriate for a State to decide that at some point in time another interest, that of health of the mother or that of potential human life, becomes significantly involved. The woman's privacy is no longer sole and any right of privacy she possesses must be measured accordingly.

Texas urges that, apart from the Fourteenth Amendment, life begins at conception and is present throughout pregnancy, and that, therefore, the State has a compelling interest in protecting that life from and after conception. We need not resolve the difficult question of when life begins. When those trained in the respective disciplines of medicine, philosophy, and theology are unable to arrive at any consensus, the judiciary, at this point in the development of man's knowledge, is not in a position to speculate as to the answer.

It should be sufficient to note briefly the wide divergence of thinking on this most sensitive and difficult question. There has always been strong support for the view that life does not begin until live birth. This was the belief of the Stoics. It appears to be the predominant, though not the unanimous, attitude of the Jewish faith. It may be taken to represent also the position of a large segment of the Protestant community, insofar as that can be ascertained; organized groups that have taken a formal position on the abortion issue have generally regarded abortion as a matter for the conscience of the individual and her family. As we have noted, the common law found greater significance in quickening. Physicians and their scientific colleagues have regarded that event with less interest and have tended to focus either upon conception or upon live birth or upon the interim point at which the fetus becomes "viable," that is, potentially able to live outside the mother's womb, albeit with artificial aid. Viability is usually placed at about seven months (28 weeks) but may occur earlier.

In areas other than criminal abortion the law has been reluctant to endorse any theory that life, as we recognize it, begins before live birth or to accord legal rights to the unborn except in narrowly defined situations and except when the rights are contingent upon live birth. . . . In short, the unborn have never been recognized in the law as persons in the whole sense.

In view of all this, we do not agree that, by adopting one theory of life, Texas may override the rights of the pregnant woman that are at stake. We repeat, however, that the State does have an important and legitimate interest in preserving and protecting the health of the pregnant woman, whether she be a resident of the State or a nonresident who seeks medical consultation and treatment there, and that it has still *another* important and legitimate interest in protecting the potentiality of human life. These interests are separate and distinct. Each grows in substantiality as the woman approaches term and, at a point during pregnancy, each becomes "compelling."

With respect to the State's important and legitimate interest in the health of the mother, the "compelling" point, in the light of present medical knowledge, is at approximately the end of the first trimester. This is so because of the now established medical fact . . . that until the end of the first trimester mortality in abortion is less than mortality in normal childbirth. It follows that, from and after this point, a State may regulate the abortion procedure to the extent that the regulation reasonably relates to the preservation and protection of maternal health. Examples of permissible state regulation in this area are requirements as to the qualifications of the person who is to perform the abortion; as to licensure of that person; as to the facility in which the procedure is to be performed, that is, whether it must be a hospital or may be a clinic or some other place of less-than-hospital status; as to the licensing of the facility; and the like.

This means, on the other hand, that, for the period of pregnancy prior to this "compelling" point, the attending physician, in consultation with his patient, is free to determine, without regulation by the State, that in his medical judgment the patient's pregnancy should be terminated. If that decision is reached, the judgment may be effectuated by an abortion free of interference by the State.

With respect to the State's important and legitimate interest in potential life, the "compelling" point is at viability. This is so because the fetus then presumably has the capability of meaningful life outside the mother's womb. State regulation protective of fetal life after viability thus has both logical and biological justifications. If the State is interested in protecting fetal life after viability, it may go so far as to proscribe abortion during that period except when it is necessary to preserve the life or health of the mother. . . .

To summarize and repeat:

1. A state criminal abortion statute of the current Texas type, that excepts from criminality only a *life saving* procedure on behalf of the mother, without regard to pregnancy stage and without recognition of the other interests involved, is violative of the Due Process Clause of the Fourteenth Amendment.

(a) For the stage prior to approximately the end of the first trimester, the abortion decision and its effectuation must be left to the medical judgment of the pregnant woman's attending physician.

(b) For the stage subsequent to approximately the end of the first trimester, the State, in promoting its interest in the health of the mother, may, if it chooses, regulate the abortion procedure in ways that are reasonably related to maternal health.

(c) For the stage subsequent to viability the State, in promoting its interest in the potentiality of human life, may, if it chooses, regulate, and even proscribe, abortion except where it is necessary, in appropriate medical judgment, for the preservation of the life or health of the mother.

2. The State may define the term "physician," as it has been employed [here], to mean only a physician currently licensed by the State, and may proscribe any abortion by a person who is not a physician as so defined.

. . . The decision leaves the State free to place increasing restrictions on abortion as the period of pregnancy lengthens, so long as those restrictions are tailored to the recognized state interests. The decision vindicates the right of the physician to administer medical treatment according to his professional judgment up to the points where important state interests provide compelling justifications for intervention. Up to those points the abortion decision in all its aspects is inherently, and primarily, a medical decision, and basic responsibility for it must rest with the physician. . . .

DISSENTING OPINION IN *ROE* V. *WADE*

Justice Byron R. White

At the heart of the controversy are those recurring pregnancies that pose no danger whatsoever to the life or health of the mother but are nevertheless unwanted for any one or more of a variety of reasons—convenience, family planning, economics, dislike of children, the embarrassment of illegitimacy, etc. The common claim before us is that for any one of such reasons, or for no reason at all, and without asserting or claiming any threat to life or health, any woman is entitled to an abortion at her request if she is able to find a medical advisor willing to undertake the procedure.

The Court for the most part sustains this position: During the period prior to the time the fetus becomes viable, the Constitution of the United States values the convenience, whim or caprice of the putative mother more than the life or potential life of the fetus; the Constitution, therefore, guarantees the right to an abortion as against any state law or policy seeking to protect the fetus from an abortion not prompted by more compelling reasons of the mother.

With all due respect, I dissent. I find nothing in the language or history of the Constitution to support the Court's judgment. The Court simply fashions and announces a new constitutional right for pregnant mothers and, with scarcely any reason or authority for its action, invests that right with sufficient substance to override most existing state abortion statutes. The upshot is that the people and the legislatures of the 50 States are constitutionally disentitled to weigh the relative importance of the continued existence and development of the fetus on the one hand against a spectrum of possible impacts on the mother on the other hand. As an exercise of raw judicial power, the Court perhaps has authority to do what it does today; but in my view its judgment is an improvident and extravagant exercise of the power of judicial review which the Constitution extends to this Court.

The Court apparently values the convenience of the pregnant mother more than the continued existence and development of the life or potential life which she carries. Whether or not I might agree with that marshalling of values, I can in no event join the Court's judgment because I find no constitutional warrant for imposing such an order of priorities on the people and legislatures of the States. In a sensitive area such as this, involving as it does issues over which reasonable men may easily and heatedly differ, I cannot accept the Court's exercise of its clear power of choice by interposing a constitutional barrier to state efforts to protect human life and by investing mothers and doctors with the constitutionally protected right to exterminate it. This issue, for the most part, should be left with the people and to the political processes the people have devised to govern their affairs.

DISCUSSION QUESTIONS

1. Justice White says that abortion is a controversial and complicated issue. Since the Constitution is not explicit on the matter of abortion, he claims, the decision should not be placed in the control of the federal government. Do you agree with this? Is this a good argument? Defend your view.
2. Justice White places the abortion issue in the control of state governments. Do you agree with this? If this were the case now, what impact do you think it would have? How would the abortion controversy be different?
3. Go back to Chapter 2, and read over the Bill of Rights. Do you find anything to support a case for or against abortion? Do you agree with Justice Blackmun's decision *on a constitutional basis?* Explain.
4. Justice Blackmun writes, "We need not resolve the difficult question of when life begins. When those trained in the respective disciplines of medicine, philosophy, and theology are unable to arrive at any consensus, the judiciary, at this point in the development of man's knowledge, is not in a position to speculate as to the answer." Do you agree with this? Make your case to Justice Blackmun.

JAMES RACHELS

Active and Passive Euthanasia

In "Active and Passive Euthanasia," James Rachels challenges the supposed difference between active and passive euthanasia. According to Rachels, there is no necessary moral difference between "killing" someone and "letting someone die." Furthermore, killing someone (active euthanasia) is sometimes even more humane than letting someone die (passive euthanasia). According to Rachels, one learns to think of killing in a much worse light than letting die; however, this does not mean that there is something about killing that makes it in itself worse than letting die. Rachels concludes that active euthanasia can be morally preferable to passive euthanasia.

James Rachels has been a member of the philosophy faculty at University of Alabama since 1977. He is the author of *The End of Life* (1986), *Created from Animals* (1991), *Can Ethics Provide Answers? and Other Essays in Moral Philosophy* (1997), and *The Elements of Moral Philosophy,* 3rd ed. (1998).

James Rachels, *New England Journal of Medicine,* vol. 292 (1975): 78–80. Copyright © 1975 Massachusetts Medical Society. All rights reserved. Reprinted with permission.

The distinction between active and passive euthanasia is thought to be crucial for medical ethics. The idea is that it is permissible, at least in some cases, to withhold treatment and allow a patient to die, but it is never permissible to take any direct action designed to kill the patient. This doctrine seems to be accepted by most doctors, and it is endorsed in a statement adopted by the House of Delegates of the American Medical Association on December 4, 1973:

> The intentional termination of the life of one human being by another—mercy killing—is contrary to that for which the medical profession stands and is contrary to the policy of the American Medical Association.
>
> The cessation of the employment of extraordinary means to prolong the life of the body when there is irrefutable evidence that biological death is imminent is the decision of the patient and/or his immediate family. The advice and judgment of the physician should be freely available to the patient and/or his immediate family.

However, a strong case can be made against this doctrine. In what follows I will set out some of the relevant arguments and urge doctors to reconsider their views on this matter.

To begin with a familiar type of situation, a patient who is dying of incurable cancer of the throat is in terrible pain, which can no longer be satisfactorily alleviated. He is certain to die within a few days, even if present treatment is continued, but he does not want to go on living for those days since the pain is unbearable. So he asks the doctor for an end to it, and his family joins in the request.

Suppose the doctor agrees to withhold treatment, as the conventional doctrine says he may. The justification for his doing so is that the patient is in terrible agony, and since he is going to die anyway, it would be wrong to prolong his suffering needlessly. But now notice this. If one simply withholds treatment, it may take the patient longer to die, and so he may suffer more than he would if more direct action were taken and a lethal injection given. This fact provides strong reason for thinking that, once the initial decision not to prolong his agony has been made, active euthanasia is actually preferable to passive euthanasia, rather than the reverse. To say otherwise is to endorse the option that leads to more suffering rather than less, and is contrary to the humanitarian impulse that prompts the decision not to prolong his life in the first place.

Part of my point is that the process of being "allowed to die" can be relatively slow and painful, whereas being given a lethal injection is relatively quick and painless. Let me give a different sort of example. In the United States about one in 600 babies is born with Down's syndrome. Most of these babies are otherwise healthy—that is, with only the usual pediatric care, they will proceed to an otherwise normal infancy. Some, however, are born with congenital defects such as intestinal obstructions that require operations if they are to live. Sometimes, the parents and the doctor will decide not to operate, and let the infant die. Anthony Shaw describes what happens then:

> When surgery is denied [the doctor] must try to keep the infant from suffering while natural forces sap the baby's life away. As a surgeon whose natural inclination is to use the scalpel to fight off death, standing by and watching a salvageable baby die is the most emotionally exhausting experience I know.
>
> It is easy at a conference, in a theoretical discussion to decide that such infants should be allowed to die. It is altogether different to stand by in the nursery and watch as dehydration and infection wither a tiny being over hours and days. This is a terrible ordeal for me and the hospital staff—much more so than for the parents who never set foot in the nursery.

I can understand why some people are opposed to all euthanasia, and insist that such infants must be allowed to live. I think I can also understand why other people favor destroying these babies quickly and painlessly. But why should anyone favor letting "dehydration and infection wither a tiny being over hours and days"? The doctrine that says that a baby may be allowed to dehydrate and wither, but may not be given an injection that would end its life without suffering, seems so patently cruel as to require no further refutation. The strong language is not intended to offend, but only to put the point in the clearest possible way.

My second argument is that the conventional doctrine leads to decisions concerning life and death made on irrelevant grounds.

Consider again the case of the infants with Down's syndrome who need operations for congenital defects unrelated to the syndrome to live. Sometimes, there is no operation, and the baby dies, but when there is no such defect, the baby lives on. Now, an operation such as that to remove an intestinal obstruction is not prohibitively difficult. The reason why such operations are not performed in these cases is, clearly, that the child has Down's syndrome and the parents and the doctor judge that because of that fact it is better for the child to die.

But notice that this situation is absurd, no matter what view one takes of the lives and potentials of such babies. If the life of such an infant is worth preserving, what does it matter if it needs a simple operation? Or, if one thinks it better that such a baby should not live on, what difference does it make that it happens to have an unobstructed intestinal tract? In either case, the matter of life and death is being decided on irrelevant grounds. It is the Down's syndrome, and not the intestines, that is the issue. The matter should be decided, if at all, on that basis, and not be allowed to depend on that essentially irrelevant question of whether the intestinal tract is blocked.

What makes this situation possible, of course, is the idea that when there is an intestinal blockage, one can "let the baby die," but when there is no such defect there is nothing that can be done, for one must not "kill" it. The fact that this idea leads to such results as deciding life or death on irrelevant grounds is another good reason why the doctrine would be rejected.

One reason why so many people think that there is an important moral difference between active and passive euthanasia is that they think killing someone is morally worse than letting someone die. But is it? Is killing, in itself, worse than letting die? To investigate this issue, two cases may be considered that are exactly alike except that one involves killing whereas the other involves letting someone die. Then, it can be asked whether this difference makes any difference to the moral assessments. It is important that the cases be exactly alike, except for this one difference, since otherwise one cannot be confident that it is this difference and not some other that accounts for any variation in the assessments of the two cases. So, let us consider this pair of cases:

In the first, Smith stands to gain a large inheritance if anything should happen to his six-year-old cousin. One evening while the child is taking his bath, Smith sneaks into the bathroom and drowns the child, and then arranges things so that it will look like an accident.

In the second, Jones also stands to gain if anything should happen to his six-year-old cousin. Like Smith, Jones sneaks in planning to drown the child in his bath. However, just as he enters the bathroom Jones sees the child slip and hit his head, and fall face down in the water. Jones is delighted; he stands by, ready to push the child's head back under if it is necessary, but it is not necessary. With only a little thrashing about, the child drowns all by himself, "accidentally," as Jones watches and does nothing.

Now Smith killed the child, whereas Jones "merely" let the child die. That is the only difference between them. Did either man behave better, from a moral point of view? If the difference between killing and letting die were in itself a morally important matter, one should say that Jones's behavior was less reprehensible than Smith's. But does one really want to say that? I think not. In the first place, both men acted from the same motive, personal gain, and both had exactly the same end in view when they acted. It may be inferred from Smith's conduct that he is a bad man, although that judgment may be withdrawn or modified if certain further facts are learned about him—for example, that he is mentally deranged. But would not the very same thing be inferred about Jones from his conduct? And would not the same further considerations also be relevant to any modification of this judgment? Moreover, suppose Jones pleaded, in his own defense, "After all, I didn't do anything except just stand there and watch the child drown. I didn't kill him; I only let him die." Again, if letting die were in itself less bad than killing, this defense should have at least some weight. But it does not. Such a "defense" can only be regarded as a grotesque perversion of moral reasoning. Morally speaking, it is no defense at all.

Now, it may be pointed out, quite properly, that the cases of euthanasia with which doctors are concerned are not like this at all. They do not involve personal gain or the destruction of normal healthy children. Doctors are concerned only with cases in which the patient's life is of no further use to him, or in which the patient's life has become or will soon become a terrible burden. However, the point is the same in these cases: the bare difference between killing and letting die does not, in itself, make a moral difference. If a doctor lets a patient die, for humane reasons, he is in the same moral position as if he had given the patient a lethal injection for humane reasons. If his decision was wrong—if, for example, the patient's illness was in fact curable—the decision would be equally regrettable no matter which method was used to carry it out. And if the doctor's decision was the right one, the method used is not in itself important.

The AMA policy statement isolates the crucial issue very well; the crucial issue is "the intentional termination of the life of one human being by another." But after identifying this issue, and forbidding "mercy killing," the statement goes on to deny that the cessation of treatment is the intentional termination of a life. This is where the mistake comes in, for what is the cessation of treatment, in these circumstances, if it is not "the intentional termination of the life of one human being by another"? Of course it is exactly that, and if it were not, there would be no point to it.

Many people will find this judgment hard to accept. One reason, I think, is that it is very easy to conflate the question of whether killing is, in itself, worse than letting die, with the very different question of whether most actual cases of killing are more reprehensible than most actual cases of letting die. Most actual cases of killing are clearly terrible (think, for example, of all the murders reported in the newspapers), and one hears of such cases every day. On the other hand, one hardly ever hears of a case of letting die, except for the actions of doctors who are motivated by humanitarian reasons. So one learns to think of killing in a much worse light than of letting die. But this does not mean that there is something about killing that makes it in itself worse than letting die, for it is not the bare difference between killing and letting die that makes the difference in these cases. Rather, the other factors—the murderer's motive of personal gain, for example, contrasted with the doctor's humanitarian motivation—account for different reactions to the different cases.

I have argued that killing is not in itself any worse than letting die; if my contention is right, it follows that active euthanasia is not any worse than passive euthanasia. What arguments can be given on the other side? The most common, I believe, is the following:

> The important difference between active and passive euthanasia is that, in passive euthanasia, the doctor does not do anything to bring about the patient's death. The doctor does nothing, and the patient dies of whatever ills already afflict him. In active euthanasia, however, the doctor does something to bring about the patient's death: he kills him. The doctor who gives the patient with cancer a lethal injection has himself caused his patient's death; whereas if he merely ceases treatment, the cancer is the cause of the death.

A number of points need to be made here. The first is that it is not exactly correct to say that in passive euthanasia the doctor does nothing, for he does do one thing that is very important: he lets the patient die. "Letting someone die" is certainly different, in some respects, from other types of action—mainly in that it is a kind of action that one may perform by way of not performing certain other actions. For example, one may let a patient die by way of not giving medication, just as one may insult someone by way of not shaking his hand. But for any purpose of moral assessment, it is a type of action nonetheless. The decision to let a patient die is subject to moral appraisal in the same way that a decision to kill him would be subject to moral appraisal: it may be assessed as wise or unwise, compassionate or sadistic, right or wrong. If a doctor deliberately let a patient die who was suffering from a routinely curable illness, the doctor would certainly be to blame if he had needlessly killed the patient. Charges against him would be appropriate. If so, it would be no defense at all for him to insist that he didn't "do anything." He would have done something very serious indeed, for he let his patient die.

Fixing the cause of death may be very important from a legal point of view, for it may determine whether criminal charges are brought against the doctor. But I do not think that this notion can be used to show a moral difference between active and passive euthanasia. The reason why it is considered bad to be the cause of someone's death is that death is regarded as a great evil—and so it is. However, if it has been decided that euthanasia—even passive euthanasia—is desirable in a given case, it has also been decided that in this instance death is no greater an evil than the patient's continued existence. And if this is true, the usual reason for not wanting to be the cause of someone's death simply does not apply.

Finally, doctors may think that all of this is only of academic interest—the sort of thing that philosophers may worry about but that has no practical bearing on their own work. After all, doctors must be concerned about the legal consequences of what they do, and active euthanasia is clearly forbidden by the law. But even so, doctors should also be concerned with the fact that the law is forcing upon them a moral doctrine that may be indefensible, and has a considerable effect on their practices. Of course, most doctors are not now in the position of being coerced in this matter, for they do not regard themselves as merely going along with what the law requires. Rather, in statements such as the AMA policy statement that I have quoted they are endorsing this doctrine as a central point of medical ethics. In that statement, active euthanasia is condemned not merely as illegal but as "contrary to that for which the medical profession stands," whereas passive euthanasia is approved. However, the preceding considerations suggest that there is really no moral difference between the two, considered in themselves (there may be important moral differences in some cases in their *consequences,* but, as I pointed out, these differences may make active euthanasia, and not passive euthanasia, the morally preferable option). So, whereas doctors may have to discriminate between active and passive euthanasia to satisfy the law, they should not do any more than that. In particular, they should not give the distinction any added authority and weight by writing it into official statements of medical ethics.

NOTE

1. A. Shaw, "Doctor, Do We Have a Choice?" *The New York Times Magazine* (30 Jan. 1972), p. 54.

DISCUSSION QUESTIONS

1. What is the difference between active euthanasia and passive euthanasia? What do you believe is the moral difference between them? What does Rachels believe? Compare your views.
2. What is the American Medical Association's position on euthanasia? Do you think it is a humane one? Explain.
3. Rachels argues that withholding of treatment is morally equivalent to intentionally terminating a life. Do you agree with him? What is your own position? Can you think of an example to illustrate your position?
4. Is it immoral to allow infants with Down syndrome to die? What does Rachels think? Do you agree with him? Defend your view.
5. Suppose we are told that, if we give a modest sum of money to a well-known and trusted organization, we can save the lives of twenty starving people. If we choose not to give money to this charity but could afford to do so, should we be held morally responsible for the deaths of these twenty people? Remember, we know they will die if we do not help them. Defend your position in detail.

 B O N N I E   S T E I N B O C K

The Intentional Termination of Life

In response to James Rachels' argument, Bonnie Steinbock claims that the distinction between active and passive euthanasia *can* be supported in cases in which the patient refuses treatment and in which the purpose of failing to treat a patient is not the termination of life, but rather the reduction of pain. According to Steinbock, the mistake Rachels makes is identifying the cessation of life-prolonging treatment with passive euthanasia or intentionally letting die. Steinbock believes that the decision not to operate on a child need not mean a decision to neglect the child. "Waiting for them to die may be tough on parents, doctors and nurses," says Steinbock, "but it isn't necessarily tough on the child."

Bonnie Steinbock is a philosophy professor at the State University of New York at Albany and the author of *Life Before Birth* (1994). She has also coedited *Ethical Issues in Modern Medicine,* 4th ed. (with John D. Arras, 1995), *Killing and Letting Die,* 2nd ed. (with Alastair Norcross, 1994), and *New Ethics for the Public's Health* (with Dan E. Beauchamp, 1999).

Bonnie Steinbock, *Ethics in Science and Medicine* (now *Social Science and Medicine*), vol. 6 (1979): 624–628. With permission from Elsevier Science. Notes have been omitted.

According to James Rachels and Michael Tooley, a common mistake in medical ethics is the belief that there is a moral difference between active and passive euthanasia. This is a mistake, they argue, because the rationale underlying the distinction between active and passive euthanasia is the idea that there is a significant moral difference between intentionally killing and intentionally letting die. "This idea," Tooley says, "is admittedly very common. But I believe that it can be shown to reflect either confused thinking, or a moral point of view unrelated to the interests of individuals." Whether the belief that there is a significant moral difference (between intentionally killing and intentionally letting die) is mistaken is not my concern here. For it is far from clear that this distinction *is* the basis of the doctrine of the American Medical Association which Rachels attacks. And if the killing/letting die distinction is not the basis of the AMA doctrine, then arguments showing that the distinction has no moral force do not, in themselves, reveal in the doctrine's adherents either "confused thinking" or "a moral point of view unrelated to the interests of individuals." Indeed, as we examine the AMA doctrine, I think it will become clear that it appeals to and makes use of a number of overlapping distinctions, which may have moral significance in particular cases, such as the distinction between intending and foreseeing, or between ordinary and extraordinary care. Let us then turn to the statement, from the House of Delegates of the American Medical Association, which Rachels cites:

> The intentional termination of the life of one human being by another—mercy-killing—is contrary to that for which the medical profession stands and is contrary to the policy of the American Medical Association.
>
> The cessation of the employment of extraordinary means to prolong the life of the body when there is irrefutable evidence that biological death is imminent is the decision of the patient and/or his immediate family. The advice and judgment of the physician should be freely available to the patient and/or his immediate family.

Rachels attacks this statement because he believes that it contains a moral distinction between active and passive euthanasia. . . .

I intend to show that the AMA statement does not imply support of the active/passive euthanasia distinction. In forbidding the intentional termination of life, the statement rejects both active and passive euthanasia. It does allow for ". . . the cessation of the employment of extraordinary means . . ." to prolong life. The mistake Rachels and Tooley make is in identifying the cessation of life-prolonging treatment with passive euthanasia or intentionally letting die. If it were right to equate the two, then the AMA statement would be self-contradictory, for it would begin by condemning, and end by allowing the intentional termination of life. But if the cessation of life-prolonging treatment is not always or necessarily passive euthanasia, then there is no confusion and no contradiction.

Why does Rachels think that the cessation of life-prolonging treatment is the intentional termination of life? He says:

> The AMA policy statement isolates the crucial issue very well; the crucial issue is "the intentional termination of the life of one human being by another." But after identifying this issue, and forbidding "mercy-killing," the statement goes on to deny that the cessation of treatment is the intentional termination of a life. This is where the mistake comes in, for what is the cessation of treatment, in these circumstances, if it is not "the intentional termination of the life of one human being by another"? Of course it is exactly that, and if it were not, there would be no point to it.

However, there *can* be a point (to the cessation of life-prolonging treatment) other than an endeavor to bring about the patient's death, and so the blanket identification of cessation of treatment with the intentional termination of a life is inaccurate. There are at least two situations in which the termination of life-prolonging treatment cannot be identified with the intentional termination of the life of one human being by another.

The first situation concerns the patient's right to refuse treatment. Both Tooley and Rachels give the example of a patient dying of an incurable disease, accompanied by unrelievable pain, who wants to end the treatment which cannot cure him but can only prolong his miserable existence. Why, they ask, may a doctor accede to the patient's request to stop treatment, but not provide a patient in a similar situation with a lethal dose? The answer lies in the patient's right to refuse treatment. In general, a competent adult has the right to refuse treatment, even where such treatment is necessary to prolong life. Indeed, the right to refuse treatment has been upheld even when the patient's reason for refusing treatment is generally agreed to be inadequate.

This right can be overridden (if, for example, the patient has dependent children) but, in general, no one may legally compel you to undergo treatment to which you have not consented. "Historically, surgical intrusion has always been considered a technical battery upon the person and one to be excused or justified by consent of the patient or justified by necessity created by the circumstances of the moment. . . ."

At this point, it might be objected that if one has the right to refuse life-prolonging treatment, then consistency demands that one have the right to decide to end his life and to obtain help in doing so. The idea is that the right to refuse treatment somehow implies a right to voluntary euthanasia, and we need to see why someone might think this. The right to refuse treatment has been considered by legal writers as an example of the right to privacy or, better, the right to bodily self-determination. You have the right to decide what happens to your own body, and the right to refuse treatment in an instance of that more general right. But if you have the right to determine what happens to your body, then should you not have the right to choose to end your life, and even a right to get help in doing so?

However, it is important to see that the right to refuse treatment is not the same as, nor does it entail, a right to voluntary euthanasia, even if both can be derived from the right to bodily self-determination. The right to refuse treatment is not itself a "right to die"; that one may choose to exercise this right even at the risk of death, or even *in order to die*, is irrelevant. The purpose of the right to refuse medical treatment is not to give persons a right to decide whether to live or die, but to protect them from the unwanted interferences of others. Perhaps we ought to interpret the right to bodily self-determination more broadly so as to include a right to die: but this would be a substantial extension of our present understanding of the right to bodily self-determination, and not a consequence of it. Should we recognize a right to voluntary euthanasia, we would have to agree that people have the right not merely to be left alone, but also the right to be killed. I leave to one side that substantive moral issue. My claim is simply that there can be a reason for terminating life-prolonging treatment other than "to bring about the patient's death."

The second case in which termination of treatment cannot be identified with intentional termination of life is where continued treatment has little chance of improving the patient's condition and brings greater discomfort than relief.

The question here is what treatment is appropriate to the particular case. A cancer specialist describes it in this way:

> My general rule is to administer therapy as long as a patient responds well and has the potential for a reasonably good quality of life. But when all feasible therapies have been administered and a patient shows signs of rapid deterioration, the continuation of therapy can cause more discomfort than the cancer. From that time I recommend surgery, radiotherapy, or chemotherapy only as a means of relieving pain. But if a patient's condition should once again stabilize after the withdrawal of active therapy and if it should appear that he could still gain some good time, I would immediately reinstitute active therapy. The decision to cease anticancer treatment is never irrevocable, and often the desire to live will push a patient to try for another remission, or even a few more days of life.

The decision here to cease anticancer treatment cannot be construed as a decision that the patient die, or as the intentional termination of life. It is a decision to provide the most appropriate treatment for that patient at that time. Rachels suggests that the point of the cessation of treatment is the intentional termination of life. But here the point of discontinuing treatment is not to bring about the patient's death but to avoid treatment that will cause more discomfort than the cancer and has little hope of benefiting the patient. Treatment that meets this description is often called "extraordinary." The concept is flexible, and what might be considered "extraordinary" in one situation might be ordinary in another. The use of a respirator to sustain a patient through a severe bout of respiratory disease would be considered ordinary; its use to sustain the life of a severely brain damaged person in an irreversible coma would be considered extraordinary.

Contrasted with extraordinary treatment is ordinary treatment, the care a doctor would normally be expected to provide. Failure to provide ordinary care constitutes neglect, and can even be construed as the intentional infliction of harm, where there is a legal obligation to provide care. The importance of the ordinary/extraordinary care distinction lies partly in its connection to the doctor's intention. The withholding of extraordinary care should be seen as a decision not to inflict painful treatment on a patient without reasonable hope of success. The withholding of ordinary care, by contrast, must be seen as neglect. Thus, one doctor says, "We have to draw a distinction between ordinary and extraordinary means. We never withdraw what's needed to make a baby comfortable, we would never withdraw the care a parent would provide. We never kill a baby. . . . But we may decide certain heroic intervention is not worthwhile."

We should keep in mind the ordinary/extraordinary care distinction when considering an example given by both Tooley and Rachels to show the irrationality of the active/passive distinction with regard to infanticide. The example is this: a child is born with Down's syndrome and also has an intestinal obstruction which requires corrective surgery. If the surgery is not performed, the infant will starve to death, since it cannot take food orally. This may take days or even weeks, as dehydration and infection set in. Commenting on this situation, Rachels says:

> I can understand why some people are opposed to all euthanasia, and insist that such infants must be allowed to live. I think I can also understand why other people favor destroying these babies quickly and painlessly. But why should anyone favor letting "dehydration and infection wither a tiny being over hours and days"? The doctrine that says that a baby may be allowed to dehydrate and wither, but may not be given an injection that would end its life without suffering, seems so patently cruel as to require no further refutation.

Such a doctrine perhaps does not need further refutation; but this is not the AMA doctrine. For the AMA statement criticized by Rachels allows only for the cessation of extraordinary means to prolong life when death is imminent. Neither of these conditions is satisfied in this example. Death is not imminent in this situation, any more than it would be if a normal child had an attack of appendicitis. Neither the corrective surgery to remove the intestinal obstruction, nor the intravenous feeding required to keep the infant alive until such surgery is performed, can be regarded as extraordinary means, for neither is particularly expensive, nor does either place an overwhelming burden on the patient or others. (The continued existence of the child might be thought to place an overwhelming burden on its parents, but that has nothing to do with the characterization

of the means to prolong its life as extraordinary. If it had, then *feeding* a severely defective child who required a great deal of care could be regarded as extraordinary.) The chances of success if the operation is undertaken are quite good, though there is always a risk in operating on infants. Though the Down's syndrome will not be alleviated, the child will proceed to an otherwise normal infancy.

It cannot be argued that the treatment is withheld for the infant's sake, unless one is prepared to argue that all mentally retarded babies are better off dead. This is particularly implausible in the case of Down's syndrome babies, who generally do not suffer and are capable of giving and receiving love, of learning and playing, to varying degrees.

In a film on this subject entitled "Who Should Survive?" a doctor defended a decision not to operate, saying that since the parents did not consent to the operation, the doctors' hands were tied. As we have seen, surgical intrusion requires consent, and in the case of infants, consent would normally come from the parents. But, as their legal guardians, parents are required to provide medical care for their children, and failure to do so can constitute criminal neglect or even homicide. In general, courts have been understandably reluctant to recognize a parental right to terminate life-prolonging treatment. Although prosecution is unlikely, physicians who comply with invalid instructions from the parents and permit the infant's death could be liable for aiding and abetting, failure to report child neglect, or even homicide. So it is not true that, in this situation, doctors are legally bound to do as the parents wish.

To sum up, I think that Rachels is right to regard the decision not to operate in the Down's syndrome example as the intentional termination of life. But there is no reason to believe that either the law or the AMA would regard it otherwise. Certainly the decision to withhold treatment is not justified by the AMA statement. That such infants have been allowed to die cannot be denied; but this, I think, is the result of doctors misunderstanding the law and the AMA position.

Withholding treatment in this case is the intentional termination of life because the infant is deliberately allowed to die; that is the point of not operating. But there are other cases in which that is not the point. If the point is to avoid inflicting painful treatment on a patient with little or no reasonable hope of success, this is not the intentional termination of life. The permissibility of such withholding of treatment, then, would have no implications for the permissibility of euthanasia, active or passive. . . .

Someone might say: Even if the withholding of treatment is not the intentional termination of life, does that make a difference, morally speaking? If life-prolonging treatment may be withheld, for the sake of the child, may not an easy death be provided, for the sake of the child, as well? The unoperated child with spina bifida may take months or even years to die. Distressed by the spectacle of children "lying around, waiting to die," one doctor has written, "It is time that society and medicine stopped perpetuating the fiction that withholding treatment is ethically different from terminating a life. It is time that society began to discuss mechanisms by which we can alleviate the pain and suffering for those individuals whom we cannot help."

I do not deny that there may be cases in which death is in the best interests of the patient. In such cases, a quick and painless death may be the best thing. However, I do not think that, once active or vigorous treatment is stopped, a quick death is always preferable to a lingering one. We must be cautious about attributing to defective children *our* distress at seeing them linger. Waiting for them to die may be tough on parents, doctors and nurses—it isn't necessarily tough on the child. The decision not to operate need not mean a decision to neglect, and it may be possible to make the remaining months of the child's life comfortable, pleasant and filled with love. If this alternative is possible, surely it is more decent and humane than killing the child. In such a situation, withholding treatment, foreseeing the child's death, is not ethically equivalent to killing the child, and we cannot move from the permissibility of the former to that of the latter. I am worried that there will be a tendency to do precisely that if active euthanasia is regarded as morally equivalent to the withholding of life-prolonging treatment.

DISCUSSION QUESTIONS

1. Why does Steinbock believe that the American Medical Association's position on euthanasia does not imply support of the active/passive euthanasia distinction? Do you agree with her? Why or why not?
2. Why does Steinbock believe that the right to refuse treatment is not the same as, nor does it entail, a right to voluntary euthanasia? Do you agree with her? Why or why not?
3. "I do not think that, once active or vigorous treatment is stopped," says Steinbock, "a quick death is always preferable to a lingering one." Do you agree with her? Why or why not?
4. What is the major difference between James Rachels' position on the Down syndrome infant example and Steinbock's position? Which do you prefer, and why?
5. Compare and contrast Rachels' and Steinbock's positions on euthanasia. Overall, who has the stronger arguments, and why? Do their arguments change your view on euthanasia? If so, why? If not, why not?

 JOANNE LYNN AND JAMES F. CHILDRESS

Must Patients Always Be Given Food and Water?

According to Joanne Lynn and James F. Childress, it is never sufficient to rule out "starvation" categorically. They maintain that there is widespread consensus that sometimes a patient is best served by not undertaking or continuing certain treatments that would sustain life, especially if these entail substantial suffering. Patients who are competent to determine the course of their therapy may refuse any and all interventions proposed by others, as long as their refusals do not seriously harm or impose unfair burdens upon others. Lynn and Childress argue that none of the medical interventions that provide food and fluids to patients is ideal because each entails some distress, medical limitations, and/or costs. Moreover, in cases where a patient is in a persistent vegetative state, it is very difficult to discern how any medical intervention can benefit or harm the patient. Of the four considerations frequently proposed as moral constraints on forgoing medical feeding and hydration, Lynn and Childress find none of them to dictate that artificial nutrition and hydration must always be provided.

Joanne Lynn is professor of medicine and director of the Center to Improve Care of the Dying at the George Washington University Medical School. Her books include *By No Extraordinary Means: The Choice to Forgo Life-Sustaining Food and Water* (edited 1989), *Handbook for Mortals: Guidance for People Facing Serious Illness* (with Joan K. Harrold, 1999), and *Improving Care for the End of Life: A Sourcebook for Health Care Managers and Clinicians* (with Janice Lynch Schuster and Andrea Kabcenell, 2000). James F. Childress is Edwin B. Kyle Professor of Religious Studies and professor of medical education at the University of Virginia. His books include *Who Should Decide: Paternalism in Health Care* (1982), *Christian Ethics: Problems and Prospects* (edited with Lisa Sowle Cahill, 1996), *Practical Reasoning in Bioethics* (1997), and *Principles of Biomedical Ethics,* 5th ed. (with Tom L. Beauchamp, 2001).

Many people die from the lack of food or water. For some, this lack is the result of poverty or famine, but for others it is the result of disease or deliberate decision. In the past, malnutrition and dehydration must have accompanied nearly every death that followed an illness of more than a few days. Most dying patients do not eat much on their own, and nothing could be done for them until the first flexible tubing for instilling food or other liquid into the stomach was developed about a hundred years ago. Even then, the procedure was so scarce, so costly in physician and nursing time, and so poorly tolerated that it was used only for patients who clearly could benefit. With the advent of more reliable and efficient procedures in the past few decades, these conditions can be corrected or ameliorated in nearly every patient who would otherwise be malnourished or dehydrated. In fact, intravenous lines and nasogastric tubes have become common images of hospital care.

Providing adequate nutrition and fluids is a high priority for most patients, both because they suffer directly from inadequacies and because these deficiencies hinder their ability to overcome other diseases. But are there some patients who need not receive these treatments? This question has become a prominent public policy issue in a number of recent cases. In May 1981, in Danville, Illinois, the parents and the physician of newborn conjoined twins with shared abdominal organs decided not to feed these children. Feeding and other treatments were given after court intervention, though a grand jury refused to indict the parents.[1] Later that year, two physicians in Los Angeles discontinued intravenous nutrition to a patient who had severe brain damage after an episode involving loss of oxygen following routine surgery. Murder charges were brought, but the hearing judge dismissed the charges at a preliminary hearing. On appeal, the charges were reinstated and remanded for trial.[2]

In April 1982, a Bloomington, Indiana, infant who had tracheoesophageal fistula and Down syndrome was not treated or fed, and he died after two courts ruled that the decision was proper but before all appeals could be heard.[3] When the federal government then moved to ensure that such infants would be fed in the future,[4] the Surgeon General,

Joanne Lynn and James F. Childress, *Hastings Center Report* 13 (October 1983): 7–21. Copyright © 1983 The Hastings Center. Reprinted with permission from the publisher.

Dr. C. Everett Koop, initially stated that there is never adequate reason to deny nutrition and fluids to a newborn infant.

While these cases were before the public, the nephew of Claire Conroy, an elderly incompetent woman with several serious medical problems, petitioned a New Jersey court for authority to discontinue her nasogastric tube feedings. Although the intermediate appeals court has reversed the ruling,[5] the trial court held that he had this authority since the evidence indicated that the patient would not have wanted such treatment and that its value to her was doubtful.

In all these dramatic cases and in many more that go unnoticed, the decision is made to deliberately withhold food or fluid known to be necessary for the life of the patient. Such decisions are unsettling. There is now widespread consensus that sometimes a patient is best served by not undertaking or continuing certain treatments that would sustain life, especially if these entail substantial suffering.[6] But food and water are so central to an array of human emotions that it is almost impossible to consider them with the same emotional detachment that one might feel toward a respirator or a dialysis machine.

Nevertheless, the question remains: Should it ever be permissible to withhold or withdraw food and nutrition? The answer in any real case should acknowledge the psychological contiguity between feeding and loving and between nutritional satisfaction and emotional satisfaction. Yet this acknowledgment does not resolve the core question.

Some have held that it is intrinsically wrong not to feed another. The philosopher G. E. M. Anscombe contends: "For wilful starvation there can be no excuse. The same can't be said quite without qualification about failing to operate or to adopt some courses of treatment."[7] But the moral issues are more complex than Anscombe's comment suggests. Does correcting nutritional deficiencies always improve patients' well-being? What should be our reflective moral response to withholding or withdrawing nutrition? What moral principles are relevant to our reflections? What medical facts about ways of providing nutrition are relevant? And what policies should be adopted by the society, hospitals, and medical and other health care professionals?

In our effort to find answers to these questions, we will concentrate upon the care of patients who are incompetent to make choices for themselves. Patients who are competent to determine the course of their therapy may refuse any and all interventions proposed by others, as long as their refusals do not seriously harm or impose unfair burdens upon others.[8] A competent patient's decision regarding whether or not to accept the provision of food and water by medical means such as tube feeding or intravenous alimentation is unlikely to raise questions of harm or burden to others.

What then should guide those who must decide about nutrition for a patient who cannot decide? As a start, consider the standard by which other medical decisions are made: one should decide as the incompetent person would have if he or she were competent, when that is possible to determine, and advance that person's interests in a more generalized sense when individual preferences cannot be known.

THE MEDICAL PROCEDURES

There is no reason to apply a different standard to feeding and hydration. Surely, when one inserts a feeding tube, or creates a gastrostomy opening, or inserts a needle into a vein, one intends to benefit the patient. Ideally, one should provide what the patient believes to be of benefit, but at least the effect should be beneficial in the opinions of surrogates and caregivers.

Thus, the question becomes, is it ever in the patient's interest to become malnourished and dehydrated, rather than to receive treatment? Posing the question so starkly points to our need to know what is entailed in treating these conditions and what benefits the treatments offer.

The medical interventions that provide food and fluids are of two basic types. First, liquids can be delivered by a tube that is inserted into a functioning gastrointestinal tract, most commonly through the nose and esophagus into the stomach or through a surgical incision in the abdominal wall and directly into the stomach. The liquids used can be specially prepared solutions of nutrients or a blenderized version of an ordinary diet. The nasogastric tube is cheap; it may lead to pneumonia and often annoys the patient and family, sometimes even requiring that the patient be restrained to prevent its removal.

Creating a gastrostomy is usually a simple surgical procedure, and, once the wound is healed, care is very simple. Since it is out of sight, it is aesthetically more acceptable and restraints are needed less often. Also, the gastrostomy creates no additional risk of pneumonia. However, while elimination of a nasogastric tube requires only removing the tube, a gastrostomy is fairly permanent, and can be closed only by surgery.

The second type of medical intervention is intravenous feeding and hydration, which also has two major forms. The ordinary hospital or peripheral IV, in which fluid is delivered directly to the bloodstream through a small needle, is useful only for temporary efforts to improve hydration and electrolyte concentrations. One cannot provide a balanced diet through the veins in the limbs: to do that requires a central line, or a special catheter placed into one of the major veins in the chest. The latter procedure is much more risky and vulnerable to infections and technical errors, and it is much more costly than any of the other procedures. Both forms of intravenous nutrition and hydration commonly require restraining the patient, cause minor infections and other ill effects, and are costly, especially since they ordinarily require the patient to be in a hospital.

None of these procedures, then, is ideal; each entails some distress, some medical limitations, and some costs. When may a procedure be forgone that might improve nutrition and hydration for a given patient? Only when the procedure and the resulting improvement in nutrition and hydration do not offer the patient a net benefit over what he or she would otherwise have faced.

Are there such circumstances? We believe that there are; but they are few and limited to the following three kinds of situations: (1) the procedures that would be required are so unlikely to achieve improved nutritional and fluid levels that they could be correctly considered futile; (2) the improvement in nutritional and fluid balance, though achievable, could be of no benefit to the patient; (3) the burdens of receiving the treatment may outweigh the benefit.

WHEN FOOD AND WATER MAY BE WITHHELD

Futile Treatment

Sometimes even providing "food and water" to a patient becomes a monumental task. Consider a patient with a severe clotting deficiency and a nearly total body burn. Gaining access to the central veins is likely to cause hemorrhage or infection, nasogastric tube placement may be quite painful, and there may be no skin to which to suture the stomach for a gastrostomy tube. Or consider a patient with severe congestive heart failure who develops cancer of the stomach with a fistula that delivers food from the stomach to the colon without passing through the intestine and being absorbed. Feeding the patient may be possible, but little is absorbed. Intravenous feeding cannot be tolerated because the fluid would be too much for the weakened heart. Or consider the infant with infarction of all but a short segment of bowel. Again, the infant can be fed, but little if anything is absorbed. Intravenous methods can be used, but only for a short time (weeks or months) until their complications, including thrombosis, hemorrhage, infections, and malnutrition, cause death.

In these circumstances, the patient is going to die soon, no matter what is done. The ineffective efforts to provide nutrition and hydration may directly cause suffering that offers no counterbalancing benefit for the patient. Although the procedures might be tried, especially if the competent patient wanted them or the incompetent patient's surrogate had reason to believe that this incompetent patient would have wanted them, they cannot be considered obligatory. To hold that a patient must be subjected to this predictably futile sort of intervention just because protein balance is negative or the blood serum is concentrated is to lose sight of the moral warrant for medical care and to reduce the patient to an array of measurable variables.

No Possibility of Benefit

Some patients can be reliably diagnosed to have permanently lost consciousness. This unusual group of patients includes those with anencephaly, persistent vegetative state, and some preterminal comas. In these cases, it is very difficult to discern how any medical intervention can benefit or harm the patient. These patients cannot and never will be able to experience any of the events occurring in the world or in their bodies. When the diagnosis is exceedingly clear, we sustain their lives vigorously mainly for their loved ones and the community at large.

While these considerations probably indicate that continued artificial feeding is best in most cases, there may be some cases in which the family and the caregivers are convinced that artificial feeding is offensive and unreasonable. In such cases, there seems to be more adequate reason to claim that withholding food and water violates any obligations that these parties or the general society have with regard to permanently unconscious patients. Thus, if the parents of an anencephalic infant or of a patient like Karen Quinlan in a persistent vegetative state feel strongly that no medical procedures should be applied to provide nutrition and hydration, and the caregivers are willing to comply, there should be no barrier in law or public policy to thwart the plan.[9]

Disproportionate Burden

The most difficult cases are those in which normal nutritional status or fluid balance could be restored, but only with a severe burden for the patient. In these cases, the treatment is futile in a broader sense—the patient will not actually benefit from the improved nutrition and hydration. A patient who is competent can decide the relative merits of the treatment being provided, knowing the probable consequences, and weighing the merits of life under various sets of constrained circumstances. But a surrogate decision maker for a patient who is incompetent to decide will have a difficult task. When the situation is irremediably ambiguous, erring on the side of continued life and improved nutrition and hydration seems the less grievous error. But are there situations that would warrant a determination that this patient, whose nutrition and hydration could surely be improved, is not thereby well served?

Though they are rare, we believe there are such cases. The treatments entailed are not benign. Their effects are far short of ideal. Furthermore, many of the patients most likely to have inadequate food and fluid intake are also likely to suffer the most serious side effects of these therapies.

Patients who are allowed to die without artificial hydration and nutrition may well die more comfortably than patients who receive conventional amounts of intravenous hydration.[10] Terminal pulmonary edema, nausea, and mental confusion are more likely when patients have been treated to maintain fluid and nutrition until close to the time of death.

Thus, those patients whose "need" for artificial nutrition and hydration arises only near the time of death may be harmed by its provision. It is not at all clear that they receive any benefit in having a slightly prolonged life, and it does seem reasonable to allow a surrogate to decide that, for this patient at this time, slight prolongation of life is not warranted if it involves measures that will probably increase the patient's suffering as he or she dies.

Even patients who might live much longer might not be well served by artificial means to provide fluid and food. Such patients might include those with fairly severe dementia for whom the restraints required could be a constant source of fear, dis-

comfort, and struggle. For such a patient, sedation to tolerate the feeding mechanisms might preclude any of the pleasant experiences that might otherwise have been available. Thus, a decision not to intervene, except perhaps briefly to ascertain that there are no treatable causes, might allow such a patient to live out a shorter life with fair freedom of movement and freedom from fear, while a decision to maintain artificial nutrition and hydration might consign the patient to end his or her life in unremitting anguish. If this were the case, a surrogate decision-maker would seem to be well justified in refusing the treatment.

INAPPROPRIATE MORAL CONSTRAINTS

Four considerations are frequently proposed as moral constraints on forgoing medical feeding and hydration. We find none of these to dictate that artificial nutrition and hydration must always be provided.

The Obligation to Provide "Ordinary" Care

Debates about appropriate medical treatment are often couched in terms of "ordinary" and "extraordinary" means of treatment. Historically, this distinction emerged in the Roman Catholic tradition to differentiate optional treatment from treatment that was obligatory for medical professionals to offer and for patients to accept.[11] These terms also appear in many secular contexts, such as court decisions and medical codes. The recent debates about ordinary and extraordinary means of treatment have been interminable and often unfruitful, in part because of a lack of clarity about what the terms mean. Do they represent the premises of an argument or the conclusion, and what features of a situation are relevant to the categorization as "ordinary" or "extraordinary"?[12]

Several criteria have been implicit in debates about ordinary and extraordinary means of treatment; some of them may be relevant to determining whether and which treatments are obligatory and which are optional. Treatments have been distinguished according to their simplicity (simple/complex), their naturalness (natural/artificial), their customariness (usual/unusual), their invasiveness (noninvasive/invasive), their chance of success (reasonable chance/futile), their balance of benefits and burdens (proportionate/disproportionate), and their expense (inexpensive/costly). Each set of paired terms or phrases in the parentheses suggests a continuum: as the treatment moves from the first of the paired terms to the second, it is said to become less obligatory and more optional.

However, when these various criteria, widely used in discussions about medical treatment, are carefully examined, most of them are not morally relevant in distinguishing optional from obligatory medical treatments. For example, if a rare, complex, artificial, and invasive treatment offers a patient a reasonable chance of nearly painless cure, then one would have to offer a substantial justification not to provide that treatment to an incompetent patient.

What matters, then, in determining whether to provide a treatment to an incompetent patient is not a prior determination that this treatment is "ordinary" per se, but rather a determination that this treatment is likely to provide this patient benefits that are sufficient to make it worthwhile to endure the burdens that accompany the treatment. To this end, some of the considerations listed above are relevant: whether a treatment is likely to succeed is an obvious example. But such considerations taken in isolation are not conclusive. Rather, the surrogate decision-maker is obliged to assess the desirability to this patient of each of the options presented, including nontreatment. For most people at most times, this assessment would lead to a clear obligation to provide food and fluids.

But sometimes, as we have indicated, providing food and fluids through medical interventions may fail to benefit and may even harm some patients. Then the treatment cannot be said to be obligatory, no matter how usual and simple its provision may be. If "ordinary" and "extraordinary" are used to convey the conclusion about the obligation to treat, providing nutrition and fluids would have become, in these cases, "extraordinary." Since this phrasing is misleading, it is probably better to use "proportionate" and "disproportionate," as the Vatican now suggests,[13] or "obligatory" and "optional."

Obviously, providing nutrition and hydration may sometimes be necessary to keep patients comfortable while they are dying even though it may temporarily prolong their dying. In such cases, food and fluids constitute warranted palliative care. But in other cases, such as a patient in a deep and irreversible coma, nutrition and hydration do not appear to be needed or helpful, except perhaps to comfort the staff and family.[14] And sometimes the interventions needed for nutrition and hydration are so burdensome that they are harmful and best not utilized.

The Obligation to Continue Treatments Once Started

Once having started a mode of treatment, many caregivers find it very difficult to discontinue it. While this strongly felt difference between the ease of withholding a treatment and the difficulty of withdrawing it provides a psychological explanation of certain actions, it does not justify them. It sometimes even leads to a thoroughly irrational decision process. For example, in caring for a dying, comatose patient, many physicians apparently find it harder to stop a functioning peripheral IV than not to restart one that has infiltrated (that is, has broken through the blood vessel and is leaking fluid into surrounding tissue), especially if the only way to reestablish an IV would be to insert a central line into the heart or to do a cutdown (make an incision to gain access to the deep large blood vessels).[15]

What factors might make withdrawing medical treatment morally worse than withholding it? Withdrawing a treatment seems to be an action, which, when it is likely to end in death, initially seems more serious than an omission that ends in death. However, this view is fraught with errors. Withdrawing is not always an act: failing to put the next infusion into a tube could be correctly described as an omission, for example. Even when withdrawing is an act, it may well be morally correct and even morally obligatory. Discontinuing intravenous lines in a patient now permanently unconscious in accord with that patient's well-informed advance directive would certainly be such a case. Furthermore, the caregiver's obligation to serve the patient's interests through both acts and omissions rules out the exculpation that accompanies omissions in the usual course of social life. An omission that is not warranted by the patient's interests is culpable.

Sometimes initiating a treatment creates expectations in the minds of caregivers, patients, and family that the treatment will be continued indefinitely or until the patient is cured. Such expectations may provide a reason to continue the treatment as a way to keep a promise. However, as with all promises, caregivers could be very careful when initiating a treatment to explain the indications for its discontinuation, and they could modify preconceptions with continuing reevaluation and education during treatment. Though all patients are entitled to expect the continuation of care in the patient's best interests, they are not and should not be entitled to the continuation of a particular mode of care.

Accepting the distinction between withholding and withdrawing medical treatment as morally significant also has a very unfortunate implication: caregivers may become unduly reluctant to begin some treatments precisely because they fear that they will be locked into continuing treatments that are no longer of value to the patient. For example, the physician who had been unwilling to stop the respirator while the infant Andrew Stinson died over several months is reportedly "less eager to attach babies to respirators now."[16] But if it were easier to ignore malnutrition and dehydration and to withhold treatments for these problems than to discontinue the same treatments when they have become especially burdensome and insufficiently beneficial for the patient, then the incentives would be perverse. Once a treatment has been tried, it is often much clearer whether it is of value to the patient, and the decision to stop it can be made more reliably.

The same considerations should apply to starting as to stopping a treatment, and whatever assessment warrants withholding should also warrant withdrawing.

The Obligation to Avoid Being the Unambiguous Cause of Death

Many physicians will agree with all that we have said and still refuse to allow a choice to forgo food and fluid because such a course seems to be a "death sentence." In this view death seems to be more certain from malnutrition and dehydration than from forgoing other forms of medical therapy. This implies that it is acceptable to act in ways that are likely to cause death, as in not operating on a gangrenous leg, only if there remains a chance that the patient will survive. This is a comforting formulation for caregivers, to be sure, since they can thereby avoid feeling the full weight of the responsibility for the time and manner of a patient's death. However, it is not a persuasive moral argument.

First, in appropriate cases discontinuing certain medical treatments is generally accepted despite the fact that death is as certain as with nonfeeding. Dialysis in a patient without kidney function or transfusions in a patient with severe aplastic anemia are obvious examples. The dying that awaits such patients often is not greatly different from dying of dehydration and malnutrition.

Second, the certainty of a generally undesirable outcome such as death is always relevant to a decision, but it does not foreclose the possibility that this course is better than others available to this patient. Ambiguity and uncertainty are so common in medical decision-making that caregivers are tempted to use them in distancing themselves from direct responsibility. However, caregivers are in fact responsible for the time and manner of death for many patients. Their distaste for this fact should not constrain otherwise morally justified decisions.

The Obligation to Provide Symbolically Significant Treatment

One of the most common arguments for always providing nutrition and hydration is that it symbolizes, expresses, or conveys the essence of care and compassion. Some actions not only aim at goals, they also express values. Such expressive actions should not simply be viewed as means to ends; they should also be viewed in light of what they communicate. From this perspective food and water are not only goods that preserve life and provide comfort; they are also symbols of care and compassion. To withhold or withdraw them—to "starve" a patient—can never express or convey care.

Why is providing food and water a central symbol of care and compassion? Feeding is the first response of the community to the needs of newborns and remains a central mode of nurture and comfort. Eating is associated with social interchange and community, and providing food for someone else is a way to create and maintain bonds of sharing and expressing concern. Furthermore, even the relatively low levels of hunger and thirst that most people have experienced are decidedly uncomfortable, and the common image of severe malnutrition or dehydration is one of unremitting agony. Thus, people are rightly eager to provide food and water. Such provision is essential to minimally tolerable existence and a powerful symbol of our concern for each other.

However, *medical* nutrition and hydration, we have argued, may not always provide net benefits to patients. Medical procedures to provide nutrition and hydration are more similar to other medical procedures than to typical human ways of providing nutrition and hydration, for example, a sip of water. It should be possible to evaluate their benefits and burdens, as we evaluate any other medical procedure. Of course, if family, friends, and caregivers feel that such procedures affirm important values even when they do not benefit the patient, their feelings should not be ignored. We do not contend that there is an obligation to withhold or to withdraw such procedures (unless consideration of the patient's advance directives or current best interest unambiguously dictates that conclusion); we only contend that nutrition and hydration may be forgone in some cases.

The symbolic connection between care and nutrition or hydration adds useful caution to decision-making. If decision-makers worry over withholding or withdrawing medical nutrition and hydration, they may inquire more seriously into the circumstances that putatively justify their decisions. This is generally salutary for health care decision-making. The critical inquiry may well yield the sad but justified conclusion that the patient will be served best by not using medical procedures to provide food and fluids.

A LIMITED CONCLUSION

Our conclusion—that patients or their surrogates, in close collaboration with their physicians and other caregivers and with careful assessment of the relevant information, can correctly decide to forgo the provision of medical treatments intended to correct malnutrition and dehydration in some circumstances—is quite limited. Concentrating on incompetent patients, we have argued that in most cases such patients will be best served by providing nutrition and fluids. Thus, there should be a presumption in favor of providing nutrition and fluids as part of the broader presumption to provide means that prolong life. But this presumption may be rebutted in particular cases.

We do not have enough information to be able to determine with clarity and conviction whether withholding or withdrawing nutrition and hydration was justified in the cases that have occasioned public concern, though it seems likely that the Danville and Bloomington babies should have been fed and that Claire Conroy should not.

It is never sufficient to rule out "starvation" categorically. The question is whether the obligation to act in the patient's best interests was discharged by withholding or withdrawing particular medical treatments. All we have claimed is that nutrition and hydration by medical means need not always be provided. Sometimes they may not be in accord with the patient's wishes or interests. Medical nutrition and hydration do not appear to be distinguishable in any morally relevant way from other

life-sustaining medical treatments that may on occasion be withheld or withdrawn.

NOTES

1. John A. Robertson, "Dilemma in Danville," *Hastings Center Report,* 11 (Oct. 1981): 5–8.

2. T. Rohrlich, "2 Doctors Face Murder Charges in Patient's Death," *Los Angeles Times* (19 Aug. 1982), p. Al; Jonathan Kirsch, "A Death at Kaiser Hospital," *California Magazine* (1982), pp. 79ff; Magistrate's findings, California v. Barber and Nejdl, No. A 925586, Los Angeles Man. Ct. Cal. (9 Mar. 1983); Superior Court of California, County of Los Angeles, California v. Barber and Nejdl, No. A0 25586k, tentative decision, 5 May 1983.

3. *In re* Infant Doe, No. GU 8204-00 (Cir. Ct. Monroe County, IN, 12 April 1982), writ of mandamus dismissed sub nom. State ex. rel. Infant Doe v. Baker, No. 482 S140 (Indiana Supreme Ct., 27 May 1982).

4. Office of the Secretary, Department of Health and Human Services, "Nondiscrimination on the Basis of Handicap," *Federal Register,* 48 (1983): 9630–9632. (Interim final rule modifying 45 C.F.R. #84.61.) See Judge Gerhard Gesell's decision, American Academy of Pediatrics v. Heckler, No. 83-0774, U.S. District Court, DC, 24 April 1983; and also George J. Annas, "Disconnecting the Baby Doe Hotline," *Hastings Center Report,* 13 (June 1983): 14–16.

5. *In re* Conroy, 190 NJ Super. 453, 464 A.2d 303 (App. Div. 1983).

6. President's Commission for the Study of Ethical Problems in Medicine and Biomedical and Behavioral Research, *Deciding to Forego Life-Sustaining Treatment* (Washington, DC: U.S. Government Printing Office, 1982).

7. G. E. M. Anscombe, "Ethical Problems in the Management of Some Severely Handicapped Children: Commentary 2," *Journal of Medical Ethics,* 7 (1981): 117–124.

8. See, e.g., President's Commission for the Study of Ethical Problems in Medicine and Biomedical and Behavioral Research, *Making Health Care Decisions* (Washington, DC: U.S. Government Printing Office, 1982).

9. President's Commission, *Deciding to Forego,* pp. 171–196.

10. Joyce V. Zerwekh, "The Dehydration Question," *Nursing,* 83 (1983): 47–51, with comments by Judith R. Brown and Marion B. Dolan.

11. James J. McCartney, "The Development of the Doctrine of Ordinary and Extraordinary Means of Preserving Life in Catholic Moral Theology Before the Karen Quinlan Case," *Linacre Quarterly*, 47 (1980): 215.

12. President's Commission, *Deciding to Forego*, pp. 82–90. For an argument that fluids and electrolytes can be "extraordinary," see Carson Strong, "Can Fluids and Electrolytes be 'Extraordinary' Treatment?" *Journal of Medical Ethics*, 7 (1981): 83–85.

13. The Sacred Congregation for the Doctrine of the Faith, Declaration on Euthanasia, Vatican City, 5 May 1980.

14. Paul Ramsey, *The Patient as Person* (New Haven, CT: Yale University Press, 1970), pp. 128–129;

Paul Ramsey, *Ethics at the Edges of Life: Medical and Legal Intersections* (New Haven, CT: Yale University Press, 1978), p. 275; Bernard Towers, "Irreversible Coma and Withdrawal of Life Support: Is It Murder If the IV Line Is Disconnected?" *Journal of Medical Ethics*, 8 (1982): 205.

15. See Kenneth C. Micetich, Patricia H. Steinecker, and David C. Thomasma, "Are Intravenous Fluids Morally Required for a Dying Patient?" *Archives of Internal Medicine*, 143 (1983): 975–978.

16. Robert and Peggy Stinson, *The Long Dying of Baby Andrew* (Boston: Little, Brown, 1983), p. 355.

DISCUSSION QUESTIONS

1. Some people argue that we are obligated to continue treatment to patients once it is initiated. Do you agree? Defend your position against possible objections by Lynn and Childress.

2. It is said that doctors are obligated to avoid being the unambiguous cause of death. Do you agree with this? How would Lynn and Childress respond to the suggestion that they are suggesting that doctors should be the unambiguous cause of death (albeit only in special cases)?

3. G. E. M Anscombe wrote that "for willful starvation, there can be no excuse. The same can't be said quite without qualification about failing to operate or to adopt some course of treatment." How do Lynn and Childress respond to Anscombe? Evaluate their response.

4. Lynn and Childress note three situations in which food and water may be withheld for a patient. What are they? Do you disagree with any of them? Why? Are there any that you would like to add? What are they?

5. In the case of Karen Ann Quinlan, she lived for ten years without extraordinary treatment (no respirator) but continued to receive ordinary treatment during this time. She was kept alive with high-nutrient feedings and regular doses of antibiotics to prevent infections. She never regained consciousness, though she did sometimes have reflex responses to touch and sound. In this particular case, would it have been morally right during this long period of comatose existence to withhold the antibiotics so that Quinlan would die of infections? Defend your view considering possible objections from James Rachels, Bonnie Steinbock, and Lynn and Childress.

MEDIA GALLERY

 A PRIVATE MATTER

(USA, 1992) 1 hour 29 minutes
Directed by Joan Micklin Silver

Film summary: A Private Matter is based on the true story of Sherri Finkbine, the hostess of the children's television show *Romper Room*. The film examines the controversy surrounding Finkbine's decision to terminate her pregnancy in 1962, as well as the roots of the abortion movement in the United States. At that time, Finkbine was pregnant with her fifth child, which she and her husband eagerly awaited. During the pregnancy, she suffered from insomnia. Without consulting her doctor, she began taking a tranquilizer that her husband had brought back from Europe. Finkbine later read that a number of children with severe deformities had been born in Europe. Some were blind and deaf, others had malformed internal organs, and still others had limbs that failed to develop or developed abnormally. These deformities were linked back to the presence of thalidomide in the very tranquilizer she was taking. Her doctor confirmed that her child was likely to have severe birth defects and recommended that she have an abortion. Finkbine presented her case to the three-member medical board of Phoenix, Arizona, and they granted her an abortion even though it was illegal at the time. Her doctor agreed to perform the abortion. In the meantime, a strong sense of moral outrage prompted Finkbine to warn other women about the potential dangers of the drug. She told her story to a local newspaper, and it made headlines. Soon, reporters revealed Finkbine's identity and negative publicity ensued. Finkbine was condemned by the Vatican newspaper as a murderer and became the focal point of an intensive anti-abortion campaign. The result of this controversy was a reversal of the medical board's abortion approval. The board stated that her case would not make it through the Arizona courts because abortion was permissible only to save the life of the mother. These events forced Finkbine to go to Sweden for the abortion. After the abortion, she inquired if the fetus was a boy or a girl. The fetus was so badly deformed that the doctor could not say.

1. Was Sherri Finkbine's decision to have an abortion morally justifiable? How much of a role, if any, does the potential for deformity in the infant play in your decision? Explain.
2. What if Finkbine had had the child and, seeing its deformities, decided to "let it die"? Would passive euthanasia have been morally justifiable in this case? What would James Rachels say? Defend your view.
3. While Finkbine could afford to circumvent the decisions of the U.S. legal justice system by going to Sweden for an abortion, many women cannot afford to do this. Does this situation suggest a "class bias" in the abortion laws at the time? Explain.
4. Do you think that it was fair that the Phoenix medical board granted Finkbine an abortion but that the strong sense of moral outrage that prompted her to warn other women about the potential dangers of the drug brought about a reversal of the decision? Would you have reported the dangers of the drug to others? Would it make a difference if you knew that by reporting the dangers you would not be able to have an abortion in the United States? What, if anything, does this indicate about morality?

 ### *WHOSE LIFE IS IT ANYWAY?*

(USA, 1981) 1 hour 58 minutes
Directed by John Badham

Film summary: Ken Harrison (Richard Dreyfuss) is a creative, energetic and devoted thirty-two-year-old sculptor. On the eve of the triumphant unveiling of his latest work, Harrison is severely injured in an automobile crash. His mind is unaffected, but he is left paralyzed from the neck down. Initially, Harrison is optimistic about his recovery, and he charms the hospital staff with his quick wit and sly jokes. However, as he becomes aware that he will always remain a quadriplegic, his attitude changes. He realizes that without the use of his hands he has lost his means of artistic creation and his identity as an artist. The doctor in charge of his case (John Cassavetes) insists that Harrison could still teach or write through dictation, but the sculptor has lost his desire to live. He tells his devoted and loving girlfriend (Christine Lahti) not to visit him, and he demands that his doctors cease treating him with dialysis and medications. The hospital staff tries to convince him that his life is worth living. The turning point occurs when Harrison is mishandled by one of the staff and finds himself dangling helplessly from the bed, unable to right himself. He is rescued by nurses and placed safely back in bed, but he is infuriated by his total dependence on others. Harrison decides definitively that he no longer wants to live and so hires a lawyer to sue for his right to die. The case hinges on Harrison's ability to prove that he is mentally fit to make this choice. When he demonstrates that he is in fact of sound mind, the judge grants him the right to be taken off of dialysis, which will result in his death within a few days. The doctors promise to make his last days comfortable and to be available in the event that he should change his mind, but Harrison is determined to die. *Whose Life Is It Anyway?* is a film adaptation of the popular play by Brian Clark.

1. Harrison argues that his identity as a sculptor is his life. Without the ability to sculpt, he has no life; therefore, he should be allowed to die. If you were the judge, what would you say to Harrison?
2. Imagine that James Rachels, Bonnie Steinbock, and Lynn and Childress were the judges. What would each of them say to Harrison? Would they agree that he should be allowed to die? Or would they say that such a decision is immoral? (Each judge gets a single yes or no vote.)
3. It is important that Harrison show the judge that he is of sound mind and that his decision to be allowed to die is rational. Should a hospital ever allow a patient to die? Does it matter whether the patient wants to be allowed to die?
4. What if Harrison were not on dialysis and still wanted to die? Would the doctors be justified in killing him by lethal injection? What is the difference between denying him dialysis and killing him by lethal injection? Would the fact that he was not on dialysis change your decision to allow him to die if you were the judge in his case? What if he wanted to die by starvation? Explain.

 ### RACING WITH THE MOON

(USA, 1984) 1 hour 38 minutes
Directed by Richard Benjamin

Film summary: This film is set in Point Muir, California, during World War II. Henry Nash (Sean Penn) and Nicky (Nicolas Cage) are best friends. Henry and Nicky are a few weeks away from leaving for the war. Sally Kaiser (Suzanne Atkinson) becomes pregnant by Nicky, her boyfriend, and they decide to have an abortion. However, neither of them can afford the $150 necessary for the operation. Nicky and Henry try to hustle the money playing pool with some soldiers but ultimately lose the game and their meager funds. With nowhere else to turn, Henry asks his girlfriend, Caddie Winger (Elizabeth McGovern), for the money. Henry believes that Caddie is from a wealthy family and does not know that she only lives in the house of the wealthy Donelly family, where her mother is a maid. Caddie agrees to help and attempts to steal a pearl necklace from Alice Donelly (Julie Philips), the Donelly's daughter. When Alice catches her in the act, Caddie admits that stealing the necklace was the only way she could think of to get the money. Alice promises to give her the money she needs. Henry, Sally, Caddie, and Nicky drive out to a run-down trailer where Sally is going to have her abortion. After the abortion, Caddie becomes upset with Henry. Trying to calm her, Henry tells her that he "wouldn't take her to a place like that—I'd marry you." Caddie then tells him that she is not from a wealthy family.

1. Sally's abortion is performed in a run-down trailer. Should a woman have to go to a trailer to have an abortion? Does the fact that Sally is poor affect the kind of medical treatment that is available to her? Is this right? Do you think that Alice Donelly would go to a trailer to have an abortion? Why or why not?
2. Even though the abortion cost only $150, neither Sally nor Nicky had that kind of money. Should cost be a barrier to having an abortion? Do you think that wealthy

women are in a better financial position to have a safe abortion than poor women? Do you think that this is right?

3. Caddie is willing to steal in order to help Sally finance her abortion. Do you think that stealing in order to finance a friend's abortion is morally justifiable?

4. Is there a connection between class and abortion? Does the fact that Sally is poor influence her feelings about abortion? Why?

5. Henry tells Caddie that he "wouldn't take her to a place like that—I'd marry you." Would this be the right thing to do? Should Nicky have asked Sally to marry him? Why or why not?

 ## "HILLS LIKE WHITE ELEPHANTS"

By Ernest Hemingway

Story summary: In "Hills like White Elephants," a young couple faces the difficult decision of whether to abort. The story, set in a bar at a train station, revolves around their conversation as they attempt to justify their decision. Between drinks, the young man attempts to comfort his girlfriend, Jig, by explaining that the operation is simple and that their relationship will remain intact when it is over. "I'll go with you and I'll stay with you all the time," he says. "They just let air in and then it's all perfectly natural," he continues. "We'll be fine afterward. Just like we were before." He states, "It's the only thing that bothers us. It's the only thing that's made us unhappy." However, Jig still has reservations about the procedure, saying, "And once they take it away, you never get it back." The boyfriend persists in attempting to ease her misgivings, but Jig remains unsure. Although he makes it appear that the decision rests in her hands, she realizes that a child would be a burden and that he wishes for her not to have it. Finally, she agrees to go through with the abortion although she does not want to. She explains, "Oh, yes. But I don't care about me. And I'll do it and then everything will be fine."

1. Jig has a first-trimester abortion although she does not seem to want one. What convinces her that she should have one? Do you think that it is a good reason?

2. The conversation between the couple as to whether to have an abortion is quite elliptical and abstract. Many things are assumed but not stated outright. Even the words "abortion" and "child" are never used. How typical do you think this is of the kind of conversations that young, unmarried couples might have about abortion? Why do you think that Hemingway chooses to present abortion in this way?

3. What might Jig mean when she says, "I don't care about me"? Do you think that most women do not care about themselves when it comes to making decisions about abortion? What do they care about if not themselves? Is this right?

4. The couple discusses abortion in terms of how safe the procedure is and how having the abortion would affect their relationship. Should these be major considerations? How do the authors in this chapter deal with these considerations? Are they important to them?

5. Near the end of the story, Jig asks her boyfriend to do something for her. He replies that he'd do anything for her. Jig asks him to "please please please please please please please stop talking." What should be the role of the father in decisions regarding abortion? What do you think about the role of the father in Hemingway's story? Why does Jig ask him to stop talking?

 ## THE CASE OF DR. JACK KEVORKIAN

Event summary: Dr. Jack Kevorkian believes that even those afflicted with a disease that is not diagnosed as terminal have the right to a dignified death. Some of his patients are in great pain but are unable to take their own lives. Kevorkian raises the difficult question of whether it is morally acceptable for doctors to assist their patients in taking their own lives. This possibility raises further questions of whether this type of euthanasia is more like suicide or murder. Kevorkian, a retired Michigan pathologist, has become the most visible proponent of the right-to-die movement and has assisted many people in suicide. A number of them have killed themselves with a machine that he made and set up for them. This machine sends a lethal dose of potassium chloride into the body at the push of a button by the person wishing to bring about his or her own death. Kevorkian has assisted in the suicide of many, including people suffering from Alzheimer's disease and multiple sclerosis. Kevorkian also urges doctors to assist in the suicide of their patients.

1. Should doctors ever assist patients in bringing about an end to their lives? Why or why not?
2. Should physician-assisted suicide be considered murder? What might James Rachels say? What about Bonnie Steinbock? Compare your response with theirs.
3. In *Whose Life Is It Anyway?* Harrison does not have the physical ability to commit suicide even though he desires to end his life. In his particular case, would it have been morally justifiable for a doctor to assist him in his suicide? Is there any difference between a case in which a patient can acquire the means to bring about the end of his or her life and one in which the patient cannot? Explain.
4. *Final Exit* is a book by Derek Humphry, founder of the Hemlock Society, a group that is attempting to legalize euthanasia. It instructs people how to die or how to kill themselves. If someone reads this book and dies after following its guidelines, is Humphry responsible for the death? What is the moral difference between Humphry telling someone how to end her or his life (in a book on the subject), and Kervorkian placing someone in the position to bring about her or his own death?
5. Dr. Jack Kevorkian is highly vocal about the assistance he gives to people. What if he went about his practice of assisting people in suicide without making it a public event? Would this make any difference in the way you felt about the morality of his actions? Would this make the deaths more dignified? More acceptable? Explain.

SUPPLEMENTARY READINGS

ABORTION

Baird, Robert M., and Stuart E. Rosenbaum, eds. *The Ethics of Abortion: Pro-Life vs. Pro-Choice.* Buffalo: Prometheus Books, 1989.

Brody, Baruch. *Abortion and the Sanctity of Human Life.* Cambridge, MA: Harvard University Press, 1975.

Callahan, Daniel. *Abortion: Law, Choice, and Morality.* New York: Macmillan, 1970.

Cohen, Marshall; Thomas Nagel; and Thomas Scanlon, eds. *The Rights and Wrongs of Abortion.* Princeton, NJ: Princeton University Press, 1974.

Corea, Gena. *The Hidden Malpractice: How American Medicine Mistreats Women.* New York: Harper & Row, 1985.

Davis, Angela. "Racism, Birth Control and Reproductive Rights." Pp. 15–26 in *Abortion to Reproductive Freedom,* ed. Marlene Gerber Fried. Boston: South End Press, 1990.

Feinberg, Joel, ed. *The Problem of Abortion,* 2nd. ed. Belmont, CA: Wadsworth, 1984.

Goldstein, R. D. *Mother-Love and Abortion: A Legal Interpretation.* Berkeley: University of California Press, 1988.

Gordon, Linda. *Woman's Body, Woman's Right: Birth Control in America,* rev. ed. New York: Penguin Books, 1990.

Harrison, B. W. *Our Right to Choose: Toward a New Ethic of Abortion.* Boston: Beacon Press, 1983.

Hartmann, Betsy. *Reproductive Rights and Wrongs: The Global Politics of Population Control and Contraceptive Choice.* New York: Harper & Row, 1987.

Kamm, Francis Myrna. *Creation and Abortion: A Study in Moral and Legal Philosophy*. New York: Oxford University Press, 1992.

Mohr, J. C. *Abortion in America: The Origins and Evolution of National Policy, 1800–1900*. New York: Oxford University Press, 1978.

Nicholson, Susan. *Abortion and the Roman Catholic Church*. Missoula, MT: Scholars Press, 1977.

Noonan, John. *How to Argue About Abortion*. New York: Free Press, 1979.

Shrage, Laurie. *Moral Dilemmas of Feminism: Prostitution, Adultery, and Abortion*. New York: Routledge, 1994.

Soloway, R. A. *Birth Control and the Population Question in England, 1877–1930*. Chapel Hill: University of North Carolina Press, 1982.

Steinbock, Bonnie. *Life Before Birth: The Moral and Legal Status of Embryos and Fetuses*. New York: Oxford University Press, 1992.

Summer, L. W. *Abortion and Moral Theory*. Princeton, NJ: Princeton University Press, 1981.

Tooley, Michael. *Abortion and Infanticide*. New York: Oxford University Press, 1983.

EUTHANASIA

Baird, Robert M., and Stuart E. Rosenbaum, eds. *Euthanasia: The Moral Issues*. Buffalo: Prometheus Books, 1989.

Behnke, John A., and Sissela Bok. *The Dilemmas of Euthanasia*. New York: Doubleday, Anchor, 1975.

Brody, Baruch, ed. *Suicide and Euthanasia: Historical and Contemporary Themes*. Dordrecht, Netherlands: Reidel, 1989.

Caughill, R. E., ed. *The Dying Patient: A Supportive Approach*. Boston: Little, Brown, 1976.

Dworkin, Gerald; R. G. Frey; and Sissela Bok. *Euthanasia and Physician-Assisted Suicide*. New York: Cambridge University Press, 1998.

Filene, Peter G. *In the Arms of Others: A Cultural History of the Right-to-Die in America*. Chicago: Dee, 1998.

Glover, J. *Causing Death and Saving Lives*. Harmondsworth, England: Penguin Books, 1987.

Grisez, Germain, and Joseph Boyle. *Life and Death with Liberty and Justice*. Notre Dame, IN: University of Notre Dame Press, 1975.

Harrold, Joan K., and Joanne Lynn, eds. *A Good Dying: Shaping Health Care for the Last Months of Life*. New York: Haworth Press, 1998.

Humphry, D., and A. Wickett. *The Right to Die—Understanding Euthanasia*. New York: Harper & Row, 1986.

Kass, Leon R. "Neither for Love nor Money: Why Doctors Must Not Kill." *The Public Interest*, 94 (1989): 25–46.

Kevorkian, Jack. "The Last Fearsome Taboo: Medical Aspects of Planned Death." *Medicine and Law*, 7 (1988): 1–14.

Kluge, Eike-Henner. *The Practice of Death*. New Haven, CT: Yale University Press, 1975.

Kohl, Marvin, ed. *Beneficent Euthanasia*. Buffalo: Prometheus Press, 1975.

Kübler-Ross, Elisabeth. *On Death and Dying*. New York: Macmillan, 1969.

Kuhse, H. *The Sanctity-of-Life Doctrine in Medicine—A Critique*. Oxford: Oxford University Press, 1986.

Lynn, Joanne, ed. *By No Extraordinary Means: The Choice to Forgo Life-Sustaining Food and Water*. Bloomington: Indiana University Press, 1986.

Maguire, Daniel C. *Death by Choice*. Garden City, NY: Doubleday, 1974.

Rachels, James. *The End of Life: Euthanasia and Morality*. New York: Oxford University Press, 1987.

Russell, O. Ruth. *Freedom to Die: Moral and Legal Aspects of Euthanasia*. New York: Human Sciences Press, 1975.

Steinbock, Bonnie, ed. *Killing and Letting Die*. Englewood Cliffs, NJ: Prentice-Hall, 1980.

Thomasma, David C., and Glenn C. Graber. *Euthanasia: Toward an Ethical Social Policy*. New York: Continuum, 1990.

Torr, James, ed. *Euthanasia: Opposing Viewpoints*. San Diego: Greenhaven Press, 2000.

CHAPTER
4

Punishment and the Death Penalty

It is generally agreed that punishment is the appropriate response when people break the law. We might think of punishment as hardship inflicted by a rightful authority on a person judged to have violated some law or rule. If we deem liberty a basic value, then punishment depriving people of liberty imposes a hardship upon them. The most common types of punishment are public censure, fines, community service, physical suffering, and imprisonment. However, even if we assume all of the above to be true, a question remains: What justifies punishment as the appropriate response to a violation of a law or rule? There are two traditional answers to this question: the retributionist and the utilitarian.

According to the *retributionist,* a lawbreaker deserves to be punished, so punishment serves to give the lawbreaker what he or she has earned. The concept of retributive justice is very old, dating back in Western thought to the Old Testament. It is linked to the law of retribution (*lex taliones*), which asserts that criminals deserve a punishment *proportional* to the crime. For many crimes, such as brutal murders, death amounts to a fair punishment. There are three main retributionist views as to why the lawbreaker *deserves* to be punished. On the first view, the *revenge retributionist view,* the mere fact that a person has violated a law is sufficient justification for punishing that person. According to the second view, the *respect-for-persons retributionist view,* a lawbreaker deserves to be punished because he or she has disrupted the balance of freedoms in a society. Punishment attempts to reinstate justice as it existed before the crime took place. On the third view, the *respect-for-the-offender view,* the failure to punish denies the offenders accountability for their actions and thus treats them with disrespect.

According to utilitarianism, however, punishment cannot be justified unless it can be shown that some good can come from it; that is, the punishment must have good consequences for society. There are three utilitarian justifications for punishment: prevention, reform, and deterrence. On the *prevention view,* we should punish to ensure that the lawbreakers do not repeat their crimes. According to the *deterrent view,* the purpose of punishment is to deter people from committing crimes. On these two views, punishment is to prevent crimes from occurring, which benefits society. On the *reform view,* the purpose of punishment is to provide lawbreakers with socially desirable characteristics. The punishment improves the behavior or character of members of society, which benefits society as a whole.

An interesting consequence follows from these general positions on punishment. For utilitarians, it can be argued that guilt is neither a necessary nor a sufficient condition for punishment, whereas for retributionists, guilt is a necessary and a sufficient condition for punishment. Even if a person is *not* guilty of lawbreaking, it does *not* follow that he or she should *not* be punished (the necessary condition). For example, we can imagine (as well as find) cases in which punishing an innocent person alleviates fears that a murderer or rapist is on the loose. And even if a person is guilty of breaking the law, it does not follow that she or he should be punished (the sufficient condition). For example, we can imagine a case in which someone has lied under oath but the lie was so inconsequential that the person was not punished for it.

For retributionists, guilt means that if someone is guilty of breaking the law, then it follows that that person should be punished (the sufficient condition), even if the crime is mercy killing or jay walking. And if someone is *not* guilty of breaking the law, then that person should *not* be punished even if his or her not being punished results in more social disorder or criminal activity than if punishment were administered.

Capital punishment is a type of punishment that raises difficult questions not only about the nature of punishment in general but also about its justification and use. Debate continues as to whether capital punishment is a justifiable form of punishment for certain crimes or whether it is an inhumane and unnecessary practice. Is the death penalty a violation of the Eighth Amendment, which states: "Excessive bail shall not be required, nor excessive fines imposed, nor cruel and unusual punishments inflicted"? Or is it fitting retribution for inhumane and barbaric crimes against humanity?

Those who argue for capital punishment, the so-called *retentionists,* often use a retributionist line of argument. Capital punishment is an appropriate and just response to certain crimes, argues the retributionist, for society has the right to execute a person convicted of murder. Capital punishment is a morally proper and legally just form of retribution for the wrongful act of murder, for it reestablishes the social order that the murderer disrupted by killing an innocent person. But retributionists also often contend that the punishment must be proportional to the crime. Following this line of reasoning, they argue that no punishment fits the crime of, say, murder as well as death. However, this defense of capital punishment has at least one disturbing consequence: if, for example, your father murders someone else's child, then, strictly following the concept of *lex taliones,* the child of your father should be killed. This punishment would be strictly proportional to the crime committed by your father and, as such, the only fair punishment.

Retentionists also often cite utilitarian arguments to support capital punishment. For example, they argue that capital punishment *prevents* lawbreakers from repeating their crimes, in the sense that, say, executed murderers are unable to kill again. The deterrent view is also a popular line of argument with retentionists, who claim that a strongly enforced death penalty reduces the number of murders.

We might then ask whether capital punishment is really a deterrent. There are two considerations here. One involves the *type* of criminal who commits capital offenses. A large percentage of murders occur when the perpetrators are in a highly emotional state. These people commit serious crimes without thinking rationally about the consequences of their actions. Thus, the threat of the death penalty probably does not deter them. In contrast, professional criminals consciously plan their crimes. These people are aware of the consequences of their actions and yet commit their crimes anyway. But it is not clear that capital punishment serves as a deterrent for them either, because they believe that if they plan carefully enough they will not be caught. There are also people who find capital punishment to be an *incentive.* For example, some people who commit capital offenses do so because they lack the courage to kill themselves and want society to do it for them. Others are part of subcultures in which committing a capital crime confers prestige on them. Consequently, capital punishment will not deter these people but rather encourage them.

The second consideration is the conflict between the swift execution of capital offenders, which would serve as a more effective deterrent, and due process of the law, which secures fair treatment for all people. Presently, the U.S. legal system attempts to provide fair treatment to persons convicted of a capital offense. However, this fair treatment results in lengthy delays between conviction and execution, in a large percentage of people who are never executed, and in a large number of overturned convictions, which in turn weakens the deterrent effect of the death penalty. Hence, for capital punishment to become an efficient deterrent, the United States seemingly would have to do away with the fair treatment of people under the law.

Some retentionists believe that the U.S. legal system could prevent, or deter, murderers but that it often does not because the law is too lenient on convicted murderers. These supporters point out that many of those on death row have committed other serious crimes and that our legal system permits these convicted murderers to appeal their convictions too often. They argue that because of these appeals very few convicted murderers—perhaps as few as 5–10 percent—actually end up being put to death. They point out that this sends the message that the death penalty is not an effective punishment and thus fails to deter or prevent others from committing murder.

Finally, retentionists generally do not believe that everyone convicted of the crime of murder should be put to death. Murder may be committed under many circumstances: murder for hire, murder of a police officer, murder accompanied by rape, brutal murder, murder in self-defense, multiple murders, underage murderers, and so on. Under which circumstances do we impose capital punishment, and under which do we opt for a different punishment? On what grounds?

Many critics of the death penalty—the so-called *abolitionists*—point to the wide variation in the administration of the death penalty and argue that this should be grounds for its abolition. For example, indigent people of color disproportionately receive a death sentence because poor legal representation and a biased legal system make it difficult for them to get a fair trial. Their slogan is "those without the capital get the punishment." In *Furman v. Georgia* (1972), the Supreme Court seemed to support this contention in ruling that capital punishment in the state of Georgia had been administered in an arbitrary and capricious manner.

Abolitionists also argue that the death penalty does not effectively deter or prevent other people from murder. They point out that a person who is willing to commit murder, a serious crime, is hardly rational enough to be deterred by the prospect of a punishment. Moreover, they often point out that restricting death row appeals is unfair, for innocent people are sometimes convicted of a crime, and if they cannot appeal, they will be wrongly punished when the government carries out the sentence. Recent events in the state of Illinois support this contention: from 1987 to 1999, eleven inmates were released from death row in that state after being exonerated or after the courts determined that they had been wrongly convicted. Finally, critics of the death penalty often argue that social retribution, or reestablishing the just social order, is merely another way of stating that our society wants revenge—and this is not a morally proper or legally just motivation for the death penalty.

ALBERT CAMUS

Reflections on the Guillotine

Albert Camus argues against capital punishment. The execution of criminals does not deter crime, he says, and is merely an act of revenge or retaliation. Camus believes that the execution of criminals is nothing less than an act of murder on the part of the government—and sometimes even the murder of innocent people. Furthermore, capital punishment is also psychologically cruel. According to Camus, capital punishment "is a frightful torture, both psychological and moral. . . . It punishes, but it forestalls nothing; indeed it may even arouse the impulse to murder."

Albert Camus (1913–1960) won the Nobel Prize for Literature in 1957 and was the author of many plays, essays, and novels including *The Stranger* (1942), *The Myth of Sisyphus* (1942), *The Plague* (1947), and *The Fall* (1957).

We all know that the great argument of those who defend capital punishment is the exemplary value of the punishment. Heads are cut off not only to punish but to intimidate, by a frightening example, any who might be tempted to imitate the guilty. Society is not taking revenge; it merely wants to forestall. It waves the head in the air so that potential murderers will see their fate and recoil from it.

This argument would be impressive if we were not obliged to note

1. that society itself does not believe in the exemplary value it talks about;
2. that there is no proof that the death penalty ever made a single murderer recoil when he had made up his mind, whereas clearly it had no effect but one of fascination on thousands of criminals;
3. that in other regards, it constitutes a repulsive example, the consequences of which cannot be foreseen.

To begin with, society does not believe in what it says. If it really believed what it says, it would exhibit the heads. Society would give executions the benefit of the publicity it generally uses for national bond issues or new brands of drinks. But we know that executions in our country, instead of taking place publicly, are now perpetrated in prison courtyards before a limited number of specialists. . . .

How can a furtive assassination committed at night in a prison courtyard be exemplary? At most, it serves the purpose of periodically informing the citizens that they will die if they happen to kill—a future that can be promised even to those who do not kill. For the penalty to be truly exemplary it must be frightening. . . .

But, after all, why should society believe in that example when it does not stop crime, when its effects, if they exist, are invisible? To begin with, capital punishment could not intimidate the man who doesn't know that he is going to kill, who makes up his mind to do it in a flash and commits his crime in a state of frenzy or obsession, nor the man who, going to an appointment to have it out with someone, takes along a weapon to frighten the faithless one or the opponent and uses it although he didn't want to or didn't think he wanted to. In other words, it could not intimidate the man who is hurled into crime as if into a calamity. This is tantamount to saying that it is powerless in the majority of cases. It is only fair to point out that in our country capital punishment is rarely applied in such cases. But the word "rarely" itself makes one shudder.

Does it frighten at least that race of criminals on whom it claims to operate and who live off crime? Nothing is less certain. We can read in Koestler that at a time when pickpockets were executed in England, other pickpockets exercised their talents in the crowd surrounding the scaffold where their colleague was being hanged. Statistics drawn up at the beginning of the [twentieth] century in England show that out of 250 who were hanged, 170 had previously attended one or more executions. And in 1886, out of 167 condemned men who had gone through the Bristol prison, 164 had witnessed at least one execution. . . .

If fear of death is, indeed, a fact, another fact is that such fear, however great it may be, has never sufficed to quell human passions. Bacon is right in saying that there is no passion so weak that it cannot confront and overpower fear of death. Revenge, love, honor, pain, another fear manage to overcome it. How could cupidity, hatred, jealousy fail to do what love of a person or a country, what a passion for freedom manage to do? For centuries the death penalty, often accompanied by barbarous refinements, has been trying to hold crime in check; yet crime persists. Why? Because the instincts that are warring in man are not, as the law claims, constant forces in a state of equilibrium. They are variable forces constantly waxing and waning, and their repeated lapses from equilibrium nourish the life of the mind as electrical oscillations, when close enough, set up a current. . . . But it may happen that one of the soul's forces breaks loose until it fills the whole field of consciousness; at such a moment no instinct, not even that of life, can oppose the tyranny of that irresistible force. For capital punishment to be really intimidating, human nature would have to be different; it would have to be as stable and serene as the law itself. But then human nature would be dead.

It is not dead. This is why, however surprising this may seem to anyone who has never observed or directly experienced human complexity, the murderer, most of the time, feels innocent when he kills. Every criminal acquits himself before he is judged. He considers himself, if not within his right, at least excused by circumstances. He does not think or foresee; when he thinks, it is to foresee that he will be forgiven altogether or in part. How could he fear what he considers highly improbable? He will fear death after the verdict but not before the crime. Hence the law, to be intimidating, should leave the murderer no chance, should be implacable in advance and particularly admit no extenuat-

ing circumstance. But who among us would dare ask this?

If anyone did, it would still be necessary to take into account another paradox of human nature. If the instinct to live is fundamental, it is no more so than another instinct of which the academic psychologists do not speak: the death instinct, which at certain moments calls for the destruction of oneself and of others. It is probable that the desire to kill often coincides with the desire to die or to annihilate oneself. Thus, the instinct for self-preservation is matched, in variable proportions, by the instinct for destruction. The latter is the only way of explaining altogether the various perversions which, from alcoholism to drugs, lead an individual to his death while he knows full well what is happening. Man wants to live, but it is useless to hope that this desire will dictate all his actions. He also wants to be nothing; he wants the irreparable, and death for its own sake. So it happens that the criminal wants not only the crime but the suffering that goes with it, even (one might say, especially) if that suffering is exceptional. When that odd desire grows and becomes dominant, the prospect of being put to death not only fails to stop the criminal, but probably even adds to the vertigo in which he swoons. Thus, in a way, he kills in order to die.

Such peculiarities suffice to explain why a penalty that seems calculated to frighten normal minds is in reality altogether unrelated to ordinary psychology. All statistics without exception, those concerning countries that have abolished execution as well as the others, show that there is no connection between the abolition of the death penalty and criminality. Criminal statistics neither increase nor decrease. The guillotine exists, and so does crime; between the two there is no other apparent connection than that of the law. . . .

"Nothing proves, indeed," say the conservatives, "that the death penalty is exemplary; as a matter of fact, it is certain that thousands of murderers have not been intimidated by it. But there is no way of knowing those it has intimidated; consequently, nothing proves that it is not exemplary." Thus, the greatest of punishments, the one that involves the last dishonor for the condemned and grants the supreme privilege to society, rests on nothing but an unverifiable possibility. Death, on the other hand, does not involve degrees or probabilities. It solidifies all things, culpability and the body, in a definitive rigidity. Yet it is administered among us in the name of chance and a calculation. Even if that calculation were reasonable, should there not be a certainty to authorize the most certain of deaths? However, the condemned is cut in two, not so much for the crime he committed but by virtue of all the crimes that might have been and were not committed, that can be and will not be committed. The most sweeping uncertainty in this case authorizes the most implacable certainty. . . .

What will be left of that power of example if it is proved that capital punishment has another power, and a very real one, which degrades men to the point of shame, madness, and murder? . . .

What can we think of those officials who call the guillotine "the shunting engine," the condemned man "the client" or "the parcel"? The priest Bela Just, who accompanied more than thirty condemned men, writes: "The slang of the administrators of justice is quite as cynical and vulgar as that of the criminals." And here are the remarks of one of our assistant executioners on his journeys to the provinces: "When we would start on a trip, it was always a lark, with taxis and the best restaurants part of the spree!" The same one says, boasting of the executioner's skill in releasing the blade: "You could *allow yourself the fun* of pulling the client's hair." The dissoluteness expressed here has other, deeper aspects. The clothing of the condemned belongs in principle to the executioner. The elder Deibler used to hang all such articles of clothing in a shed and *now and then would go and look at them.* But there are more serious aspects. Here is what our assistant executioner declares: "The new executioner is batty about the guillotine. He sometimes spends days on end at home sitting on a chair, ready with hat and coat on, waiting for a summons from the Ministry." . . .

The fine and solemn example, thought up by our legislators, at least produces one sure effect—to depreciate or to destroy all humanity and reason in those who take part in it directly. But, it will be said, these are exceptional creatures who find a vocation in such dishonor. They seem less exceptional when we learn that hundreds of persons offer to serve as executioners without pay. The men of our generation, who have lived through the history of recent years, will not be astonished by this bit of information. They know that behind the most peaceful and familiar faces slumbers the impulse to torture and murder. The punishment that aims to intimidate an unknown murderer certainly confers a vocation of killer on many another monster about whom there is no doubt. And since we are busy justifying our cruelest laws with probable considerations, let there be no doubt that out of those hundreds of men whose services were declined, one at least must have satisfied otherwise the bloodthirsty instincts the guillotine excited in him.

If, therefore, there is a desire to maintain the death penalty, let us at least be spared the hypocrisy of a justification by example. Let us be frank about that penalty which can have no publicity, that intimidation which works only on respectable people, so long as they are respectable, which fascinates those who have ceased to be respectable and debases or deranges those who take part in it. It is a penalty, to be sure, a frightful torture, both physical and moral, but it provides no sure example except a demoralizing one. It punishes, but it forestalls nothing; indeed, it may even arouse the impulse to murder. It hardly seems to exist, except for the man who suffers it—in his soul for months and years, in his body during the desperate and violent hour when he is cut in two without suppressing his life. Let us call it by the name which, for lack of any other nobility, will at least give the nobility of truth, and let us recognize it for what it is essentially: a revenge. . . .

Many laws consider a premeditated crime more serious than a crime of pure violence. But what then is capital punishment but the most premeditated of murders, to which no criminal's deed, however calculated it may be, can be compared? For there to be equivalence, the death penalty would have to punish a criminal who had warned his victim of the date at which he would inflict a horrible death on him and who, from that moment onward, had confined him at his mercy for months. Such a monster is not encountered in private life.

DISCUSSION QUESTIONS

1. Camus says that if society really thought that capital punishment intimidated potential criminals by a "frightening example," it would "exhibit the heads" of those who are executed. Since executions are not held in public, society does not really think that execution deters crime. Do you agree with him? Defend your view.

2. Capital punishment, says Camus, "could not intimidate the man who doesn't know that he is going to kill, who makes up his mind in a flash and commits his crime in a state of frenzy or obsession." Therefore, capital punishment is powerless to deter

many murderers. How might a proponent of capital punishment respond to this claim? How would Camus respond in turn?

3. Why does Camus believe that "for capital punishment to be really intimidating, human nature would have to be different; it would have to be stable and serene as the law itself"? What does he mean by this? Do you agree with him? Explain.

4. What does Camus mean when he says that "the murderer, most of the time, feels innocent when he kills"? Does this make sense to you? Are you inclined to agree or disagree with Camus?

5. Does Camus convince you that capital punishment is wrong? Why or why not? Does it make any difference that he is talking about the "guillotine" rather than the electric chair or lethal injection? Explain.

IMMANUEL KANT

The Retributive Theory of Punishment

Immanuel Kant views the death penalty as moral if it serves a retributive goal and immoral if it serves the goals of deterrence. As noted in Chapter 1, Kant believes that it is wrong to treat persons *merely* as a means to our ends. Instead, persons must be treated, as Kant's categorical imperative requires, as rational beings who have their own projects and plans—in short, as ends-in-themselves. These views influence Kant's beliefs about the death penalty. For Kant, someone who has committed murder should not be punished to *deter* others from killing, since this would treat the convicted murderer as a mere object, or thing, serving to teach others a lesson. Instead, Kant argues, the convicted murderer is guilty of a crime and, for this reason alone, should be executed. Capital punishment is retribution for the wrong committed, which, as Kant says, places the "pointer of the scale of justice" back in proper balance. A biographical sketch of Immanuel Kant appears in Chapter 1.

Judicial or juridical punishment (*poena forensis*) is to be distinguished from natural punishment (*poena naturalis*), in which crime as vice punishes itself, and does not as such come within the cognizance of the legislator. Juridical punishment can never be administered merely as a means for promoting another good, either with regard to the criminal himself or to civil society, but must in all cases be imposed only because the individual on whom it is inflicted *has committed a crime*. For one man ought never to be dealt with merely as a means subservient to the purpose of another, nor be mixed up with the subjects of real right. Against such treatment his inborn personality has a right to protect him, even although he may be condemned to lose his civil personality. He must first be found guilty and *punishable*, before there can be any thought of drawing from his punishment any benefit for himself or his fellow-citizens. The penal law is a categorical imperative; and woe to him who creeps through the serpent-windings of utilitarianism to discover some advantage that

Immanuel Kant, *The Philosophy of Law*, Part II. Translated by W. Hastie (1887).

may discharge him from the justice of punishment, or even from the due measure of it, according to the pharisaic maxim: "It is better that *one* man should die than that the whole people should perish." For if justice and righteousness perish, human life would no longer have any value in the world. What, then, is to be said of such a proposal as to keep a criminal alive who has been condemned to death, on his being given to understand that if he agreed to certain dangerous experiments being performed upon him, he would be allowed to survive if he came happily through them? It is argued that physicians might thus obtain new information that would be of value to the commonweal. But a court of justice would repudiate with scorn any proposal of this kind if made to it by the medical faculty; for justice would cease to be justice, if it were bartered away for any consideration whatever.

But what is the mode and measure of punishment which public justice takes as its principle and standard? It is just the principle of equality, by which the pointer of the scale of justice is made to incline no more to the one side than the other. It may be rendered by saying that the undeserved evil which any one commits on another, is to be regarded as perpetrated on himself. Hence it may be said: "If you slander another, you slander yourself; if you steal from another, you steal from yourself; if you strike another, you strike yourself; if you kill another, you kill yourself." This is the right of retaliation (*jus talionis*); and properly understood, it is the only principle which in regulating a public court, as distinguished from mere private judgment, can definitely assign both the quality and the quantity of a just penalty. All other standards are wavering and uncertain; and on account of other considerations involved in them, they contain no principle comformable to the sentence of pure and strict justice. It may appear, however, that difference of social status would not admit the application of the principle of retaliation, which is that of "like with like." But although the application may not in all cases be possible according to the letter, yet as regards the effect it may always be attained in practice, by due regard being given to the disposition and sentiment of the parties in the higher social sphere. Thus a pecuniary penalty on account of a verbal injury, may have no direct proportion to the injustice of slander; for one who is wealthy may be able to indulge himself in this offense for his own gratification. Yet the attack committed on the honor of the party aggrieved may

have its equivalent in the pain inflicted upon the pride of the aggressor, especially if he is condemned by the judgment of the court, not only to retract and apologize, but to submit to some meaner ordeal, as kissing the hand of the injured person. In like manner, if a man of the highest rank has violently assaulted an innocent citizen of the lower orders, he may be condemned not only to apologize but to undergo a solitary and painful imprisonment, whereby, in addition to the discomfort endured, the vanity of the offender would be painfully affected, and the very shame of his position would constitute an adequate retaliation after the principle of like with like. But how then would we render the statement "If you *steal* from another, you steal from yourself"? In this way, that whoever steals anything makes the property of all insecure; he therefore robs himself of all security in property, according to the right of retaliation. Such a one has nothing, and can acquire nothing, but he has the will to live; and this is only possible by others supporting him. But as the state should not do this gratuitously, he must for this purpose yield his powers to the state to be used in penal labour; and thus he falls for a time, or it may be for life, into a condition of slavery. But whoever has committed murder, must *die*. There is, in this case, no juridical substitute or surrogate, that can be given or taken for the satisfaction of justice. There is no *likeness* or proportion between life, however painful, and death; and therefore there is no equality between the crime of murder and the retaliation of it but what is judicially accomplished by the execution of the criminal. His death, however, must be kept free from all maltreatment that would make the humanity suffering in his person loathsome or abominable. Even if a civil society resolved to dissolve itself with the consent of all its members—as might be supposed in the case of a people inhabiting an island resolving to separate and scatter themselves throughout the whole world—the last murderer lying in the prison ought to be executed before the resolution was carried out. This ought to be done in order that everyone may realize the desert of his deeds, and that blood-guiltiness may not remain upon the people; for otherwise they might all be regarded as participators in the murder as a public violation of justice.

The equalization of punishment with crime, is therefore only possible by the cognition of the judge extending even to the penalty of death, according to the right of retaliation.

DISCUSSION QUESTIONS

1. Do you agree with the maxim "It is better that *one* man should die than that the whole people should perish"? Why or why not? Does Kant agree with this maxim? Why or why not? Compare your view with Kant's view.
2. What is Kant's position on a utilitarian view of punishment? Do you agree with him?
3. What is your view of the principle of retaliation? Compare it with Kant's view.
4. Compare and contrast Albert Camus and Kant on capital punishment. Whose arguments are stronger, and why?
5. Kant says that "whoever has committed murder must die." Do you agree with him? Are there any exceptions? Discuss.

ERNEST VAN DEN HAAG

On Deterrence and the Death Penalty

In this article, Ernest Van Den Haag agrees with Kant that capital punishment is just. For Van Den Haag, the death penalty is just because "the criminal volunteered to assume the risk of receiving a legal punishment he could have avoided by not committing this crime." In other words, Van Den Haag argues that people who commit murder are free to not kill another person, and if they do, they voluntarily risk the death penalty. Van Den Haag offers several other arguments in defense of the death penalty, including the one, rejected by Kant, that the death penalty deters, or prevents, some people from committing murder; thus, it is moral.

Ernest Van Den Haag is a psychoanalyst who lives and practices in New York. His books include *Punishing Criminals* (1975) and *The Death Penalty: A Debate* (with John P. Conrad, 1983).

I

If rehabilitation and the protection of society from unrehabilitated offenders were the only purposes of legal punishment the death penalty could be abolished: it cannot attain the first end, and is not needed for the second. No case for the death penalty can be made unless "doing justice," or "deterring others," are among our penal aims. Each of these purposes can justify capital punishment by itself; opponents, therefore, must show that neither actually does, while proponents can rest their case on either.

Although the argument from justice is intellectually more interesting, and, in my view, decisive enough, utilitarian arguments have more appeal: the claim that capital punishment is useless because it does not deter others, is most persuasive. I shall, therefore, focus on this claim. Lest the argument be thought to be unduly narrow, I shall show, nonetheless, that some claims of injustice rest on premises which the claimants reject when

Ernest Van Den Haag, *Journal of Criminal Law and Criminology*, vol. 60. no. 2. Reprinted by special permission of Northwestern University School of Law, *Journal of Criminal Law and Criminology*.

arguments for capital punishment are derived therefrom; while other claims of injustice have no independent standing: their weight depends on the weight given to deterrence.

II

Capital punishment is regarded as unjust because it may lead to the execution of innocents, or because the guilty poor (or disadvantaged) are more likely to be executed than the guilty rich.

Regardless of merit, these claims are relevant only if "doing justice" is one purpose of punishment. Unless one regards it as good, or at least, better, that the guilty be punished rather than the innocent, and that the equally guilty be punished equally, unless, that is, one wants penalties to be just, one cannot object to them because they are not. However, if one does include justice among the purposes of punishment, it becomes possible to justify any one punishment—even death—on grounds of justice. Yet, those who object to the death penalty because of its alleged injustice, usually deny not only the merits, or the sufficiency, of specific arguments based on justice, but the propriety of justice as an argument: they exclude "doing justice" as a purpose of legal punishment. If justice is not a purpose of penalties, injustice cannot be an objection to the death penalty, or to any other; if it is, justice cannot be ruled out as an argument for any penalty.

Consider the claim of injustice on its merits now. A convicted man may be found to have been innocent; if he was executed, the penalty cannot be reversed. Except for fines, penalties never can be reversed. Time spent in prison cannot be returned. However, a prison sentence may be remitted once the prisoner serving it is found innocent; and he can be compensated for the time served (although compensation ordinarily cannot repair the harm). Thus, though (nearly) all penalties are irreversible, the death penalty, unlike others, is irrevocable as well.

Despite all precautions, errors will occur in judicial proceedings: the innocent may be found guilty; or the guilty rich may more easily escape conviction, or receive lesser penalties than the guilty poor. However, these injustices do not reside in the penalties inflicted but in their maldistribution. It is not the penalty—whether death or prison—which is unjust when inflicted on the innocent. Inequity between poor and rich also involves distribution, not the penalty distributed. Thus injustice is not an objection to the death penalty but to the distributive

process—the trial. Trials are more likely to be fair when life is at stake—the death penalty is probably less often unjustly inflicted than others. It requires special consideration not because it is more, or more often, unjust than other penalties, but because it is always irrevocable. . . .

In general, the possibility of injustice argues against penalization of any kind only if the suspected usefulness of penalization is less important than the probable harm (particularly to innocents) and the probable inequities. The possibility of injustice argues against the death penalty only inasmuch as the added usefulness (deterrence) expected from irrevocability is thought less important than the added harm. (Were my argument specifically concerned with justice, I could compare the injustice inflicted by the courts with the injustice—outside the courts—avoided by the judicial process. I.e., "important" here may be used to include everything to which importance is attached.)

We must briefly examine now the general use and effectiveness of deterrence to decide whether the death penalty could add enough deterrence to be warranted.

III

Does any punishment "deter others" at all? Doubts have been thrown on this effect because it is thought to depend on the incorrect rationalistic psychology of some of its 18th and 19th century proponents. Actually deterrence does not depend on rational calculation, on rationality or even on capacity for it; nor do arguments for it depend on rationalistic psychology. Deterrence depends on the likelihood and on the regularity—not on the rationality—of human responses to danger; and further on the possibility of reinforcing internal controls by vicarious external experiences.

. . .

Unlike natural dangers, legal threats are constructed deliberately by legislators to restrain actions which may impair the social order. Thus legislation transforms social into individual dangers. Most people further transform external into internal danger: they acquire a sense of moral obligation, a conscience, which threatens them, should they do what is wrong. Arising originally from the external authority of rulers and rules, conscience is internalized and becomes independent of external forces. However, conscience is constantly reinforced in those whom it controls by the coercive imposition of external authority on recalcitrants and on those who have not acquired it. Most people refrain from offenses because they feel an obligation to behave lawfully. But this obligation would scarcely be felt if those who do not feel or follow it were not to suffer punishment.

Although the legislators may calculate their threats and the responses to be produced, the effectiveness of the threats neither requires nor depends on calculations by those responding. The predictor (or producer) of effects must calculate; those whose responses are predicted (or produced) need not. Hence, although legislation (and legislators) should be rational, subjects, to be deterred as intended, need not be: they need only be responsive.

Punishments deter those who have not violated the law for the same reasons—and in the same degrees (apart from internalization: moral obligation) as do natural dangers. Often natural dangers—all dangers not deliberately created by legislation (e.g., injury of the criminal inflicted by the crime victim) are insufficient. Thus, the fear of injury (natural danger) does not suffice to control city traffic; it must be reinforced by the legal punishment meted out to those who violate the rules. These punishments keep most people observing the regulations. However, where (in the absence of natural danger) the threatened punishment is so light that the advantage of violating rules tends to exceed the disadvantage of being punished (divided by the risk), the rule is violated (i.e., parking fines are too light). In this case the feeling of obligation tends to vanish as well. Elsewhere punishment deters.

To be sure, not everybody responds to threatened punishment. Non-responsive persons may be a) self-destructive or b) incapable of responding to threats, or even of grasping them. Increases in the size, or certainty, of penalties would not affect these two groups. A third group c) might respond to more certain or more severe penalties. . . . There is no reason to believe that all present and future offenders belong to the *a priori* non-responsive groups, or that all penalties have reached the point of diminishing, let alone zero returns. . . .

IV

The foregoing suggests the question posed by the death penalty: is the deterrence added (return) sufficiently above zero to warrant irrevocability (or other, less clear, disadvantages)? The question is not only whether the penalty deters, but whether it deters more than alternatives and whether the difference exceeds the cost of irrevocability. (I shall assume that the alternative is actual life imprisonment so as to exclude the complication produced by the release of the unrehabilitated.)

In some fairly infrequent but important circumstances the death penalty is the only possible deterrent. Thus, in case of acute *coups d'état,* or of acute substantial attempts to overthrow the government, prospective rebels would altogether discount the threat of any prison sentence. They would not be deterred because they believe the swift victory of the revolution will invalidate a prison sentence and turn it into an advantage. Execution would be the only deterrent because, unlike prison sentences, it cannot be revoked by victorious rebels. The same reasoning applies to deterring spies or traitors in wartime. Finally, men who, by virtue of past acts, are already serving, or are threatened, by a life sentence, could be deterred from further offenses only by the threat of the death penalty.

What about criminals who do not fall into any of these (often ignored) classes? Prof. Thorsten Sellin has made a careful study of the available statistics: he concluded that they do not yield evidence for the deterring effect of the death penalty. Somewhat surprisingly, Prof. Sellin seems to think that this lack of evidence for deterrence is evidence for the lack of deterrence. It is not. It means that deterrence has not been demonstrated statistically—not that non-deterrence has been.

It is entirely possible, indeed likely (as Prof. Sellin appears willing to concede), that the statistics used, though the best available, are nonetheless too slender a reed to rest conclusions on. They indicate that the homicide rate does not vary greatly between similar areas with or without the death penalty, and in the same area before and after abolition. However, the similar areas are not similar enough; the periods are not long enough; many social differences and changes, other than the abolition of the death penalty, may account for the variation (or lack of) in homicide rates with and without, before and after abolition; some of these social differences and changes are likely to have affected homicide rates. I am unaware of any statistical analysis which adjusts for such changes and differences. And logically, it is quite consistent with the postulated deterrent effect of capital punishment that there be less homicide after abolition: with retention there might have been still less.

Homicide rates do not depend exclusively on penalties any more than do other crime rates. A number of conditions which influence the propensity to crime, demographic, economic or generally social, changes or differences—even such matters as changes of the divorce laws or of the cotton price—may influence the homicide rate. Therefore variation or constancy cannot be attributed to variations or constancy of the penalties, unless we know that no other factor influencing the homicide rate has changed. Usually we don't. To believe in the death penalty deterrent does not require one to believe that the death penalty, or any other, is the only, or the decisive causal variable; this would be as absurd as the converse mistake that "social causes" are the only, or always the decisive factor. To favor capital punishment, the efficacy of neither variable need be denied. It is enough to affirm that the severity of the penalty may influence some potential criminals, and that the added severity of the death penalty adds to deterrence, or may do so. It is quite possible that such a deterrent effect may be offset (or intensified) by non-penal factors which affect propensity; its presence or absence therefore may be hard, and perhaps impossible, to demonstrate.

Contrary to what Prof. Sellin et al. seem to presume, I doubt that offenders are aware of the absence or presence of the death penalty state by state or period by period. Such unawareness argues against the assumption of a calculating murderer. However, unawareness does not argue against the death penalty if by deterrence we mean a preconscious, general response to a severe, but not necessarily specifically and explicitly apprehended or calculated threat. A constant homicide rate, despite abolition, may occur because of unawareness and not because of lack of deterrence: people remain deterred for a lengthy interval by the severity of the penalty in the past, or by the severity of penalties used in similar circumstances nearby.

I do not argue for a version of deterrence which would require me to believe that an individual shuns murder while in North Dakota, because of the death penalty, and merrily goes to it in South Dakota since it has been abolished there; or that he will start the murderous career from which he had hitherto refrained, after abolition. I hold that the generalized threat of the death penalty may be a deterrent, and the more so, the more generally applied. Deterrence will not cease in the particular areas of abolition or at the particular times of abolition. Rather, general deterrence will be somewhat weakened, through local (partial) abolition. Even

such weakening will be hard to detect owing to changes in many offsetting, or reinforcing, factors.

For all of these reasons, I doubt that the presence or absence of a deterrent effect of the death penalty is likely to be demonstrable by statistical means. . . . It is on our uncertainty that the case for deterrence must rest.

V

If we do not know whether the death penalty will deter others, we are confronted with two uncertainties. If we impose the death penalty, and achieve no deterrent effect thereby, the life of a convicted murderer has been expended in vain (from a deterrent viewpoint). There is a net loss. If we impose the death sentence and thereby deter some future murderers, we spared the lives of some future victims (the prospective murderers gain too; they are spared punishment because they were deterred). In this case, the death penalty has led to a net gain, unless the life of a convicted murderer is valued more highly than that of the unknown victim, or victims (and the non-imprisonment of the deterred nonmurderer).

The calculation can be turned around, of course. The absence of the death penalty may harm no one and therefore produce a gain—the life of the convicted murderer. Or it may kill future victims of murderers who could have been deterred, and thus produce a loss—their life.

To be sure, we must risk something certain—the death (or life) of the convicted man, for something uncertain—the death (or life) of the victims of murderers who may be deterred. This is in the nature of uncertainty—when we invest, or gamble, we risk the money we have for an uncertain gain. Many human actions, most commitments—including marriage and crime—share this characteristic with the deterrent purpose of any penalization, and with its rehabilitative purpose (and even with the protective).

More proof is demanded for the deterrent effect of the death penalty than is demanded for the deterrent effect of other penalties. This is not justified by the absence of other utilitarian purposes such as protection and rehabilitation; they involve no less uncertainty than deterrence.

Irrevocability may support a demand for some reason to expect more deterrence than revocable penalties might produce, but not a demand for more proof of deterrence, as has been pointed out above. The reason for expecting more deterrence lies in the greater severity, the terrifying effect inherent in finality. Since it seems more important to spare victims than to spare murderers, the burden of proving that the greater severity inherent in irrevocability adds nothing to deterrence lies on those who oppose capital punishment. Proponents of the death penalty need show only that there is no more uncertainty about it than about greater severity in general.

The demand that the death penalty be proved more deterrent than alternatives cannot be satisfied any more than the demand that six years in prison be proved to be more deterrent than three. But the uncertainty which confronts us favors the death penalty as long as by imposing it we might save future victims of murder. This effect is as plausible as the general idea that penalties have deterrent effects which increase with their severity. Though we have no proof of the positive deterrence of the penalty, we also have no proof of zero, or negative effectiveness. I believe we have no right to risk additional future victims of murder for the sake of sparing convicted murderers; on the contrary, our moral obligation is to risk the possible ineffectiveness of executions. However rationalized, the opposite view appears to be motivated by the simple fact that executions are more subjected to social control than murder. However, this applies to all penalties and does not argue for the abolition of any.

DISCUSSION QUESTIONS

1. Do you agree with Van Den Haag's views? Why or why not?
2. Do you agree with Van Den Haag that murderers know the risks of their illegal activity? Explain.
3. For Van Den Haag, the death penalty is just because "the criminal volunteered to assume the risk of receiving a legal punishment he could have avoided by not committing this crime." How does the death penalty deter would-be murderers?
4. Compare and contrast Van Den Haag and Immanuel Kant on capital punishment. Whose arguments are stronger, and why?
5. Capital punishment, says Albert Camus, "could not intimidate the man who doesn't know that he is going to kill, who makes up his mind in a flash and commits his crime in a state of frenzy or obsession." How would Van Den Haag respond to Camus' claim? Whose view is stronger, and why?

 HUGO BEDAU

The Death Penalty as a Deterrent

In this article, Hugo Bedau provides arguments and evidence against a number of Ernest Van Den Haag's claims. Specifically, Bedau focuses on challenging the following five claims made by Van Den Haag: (1) utilitarian abolitionists "claim that capital punishment is useless because it does not deter others"; (2) there are some classes of criminals for which the death penalty is the only deterrent; (3) the deterrence of the death penalty has not been demonstrated statistically, but it is mistaken to think that "non-deterrence"

Hugo Bedau, *Ethics* 80 (1970): 205–217. Copyright © 1970 by The University of Chicago Press. Reprinted by permission of the publisher and the author. Notes have been omitted.

has been demonstrated statistically; (4) capital punishment is to be favored over life imprisonment because "the added severity of the death penalty adds to the deterrence, or may do so"; and (5) "since it seems more important to spare victims than to spare murderers, the burden of proving that the greater the severity inherent in irrevocability adds nothing to deterrence lies on those who oppose capital punishment." For Bedau, the first claim is not reasonably attributable to abolitionists and is false; the second claim is misleading and many times empirically insignificant; the third claim is correct in what it affirms but false in what it denies; the fourth claim is "unempirical and one-sided"; and the final claim is a "muddle and a dodge." Bedau's approach to refuting Van Den Haag's claims is rigorous and utilizes a method of analyzing issues in applied ethics that directly focuses on premises and arguments.

Hugo Bedau taught philosophy at Tufts University and is one of the leading opponents of the death penalty. His edited books include *Capital Punishment in the United States* (1976) and *The Death Penalty in America* (3rd ed., 1982).

Professor Van Den Haag's recent article, "On Deterrence and the Death Penalty," raises a number of points of that mixed (i.e., empirical-and-conceptual-and-normative) character which typifies most actual reasoning in social and political controversy but which (except when its purely formal aspects are in question) tends to be ignored by philosophers. I pass by any number of tempting points in his critique in order to focus in detail only on those which affect his account of what he says is the major topic, namely, the argument for retaining or abolishing the death penalty as that issue turns on the question of *deterrence*.

On this topic, Van Den Haag's main contentions seem to be these five: (I) Abolitionists of a utilitarian persuasion "claim that capital punishment is useless because it does not deter others." (II) There are some classes of criminals and some circumstances in which "the death penalty is the only possible deterrent." (III) As things currently stand, "deterrence [namely of criminal homicide by the death penalty] has not been demonstrated statistically"; but it is mistaken to think that "non-deterrence" has been demonstrated statistically. (IV) The death penalty is to be favored over imprisonment, because "the added severity of the death penalty adds to deterrence, or may do so." (V) "Since it seems more important to spare victims than to spare murderers, the burden of proving that the greater severity inherent in irrevocability adds nothing to deterrence lies on those who oppose capital punishment."

Succinctly, I shall argue as follows: (I) is not reasonably attributable to abolitionists, and in any case it is false; (II) is misleading and, in the interesting cases, is empirically insignificant; (III), which is the heart of the dispute, is correct in what it affirms but wrong and utterly misleading in what it denies; (IV) is unempirical and one-sided as well; and (V) is a muddle and a dodge.

The reasons for pursuing in some detail what at first might appear to be mere polemical controversy is not that Professor Van Den Haag's essay is so persuasive or likely to be of unusual influence. The reason is that the issues he raises, even though they are familiar, have not been nearly adequately discussed, despite a dozen state, congressional, and foreign government investigations into capital punishment in recent years. In Massachusetts, for example, several persons under sentence of death have been granted stays of execution pending the final report of a special legislative commission to investigate the death penalty. The exclusive mandate of this commission is to study the question of deterrence. Its provisional conclusions, published late in 1968, though not in the vein of Van Den Haag's views, are liable to the kind of criticism he makes. This suggests that his reasoning may be representative of many who have tried to understand the arguments and research studies brought forward by those who would abolish the death penalty, and therefore that his errors are worth exposure and correction once and for all.

I

The claim Van Den Haag professes to find "most persuasive," namely, "capital punishment is useless because it does not deter others," is strange, and it is strange that he finds it so persuasive. Anyone who would make this claim must assume that only deterrent efficacy is relevant to assessing the utility of a punishment. In a footnote, Van Den Haag implicitly concedes that deterrence may not be the only utilitarian consideration, when he asserts that whatever our penal "theory" may tell us, "deterrence is . . . the *main actual* function of legal punishment if we disregard non-utilitarian ones" (italics added). But he does not pursue this qualification. Now we may concede that if by "function" we mean intended or professed function, deterrence is the main function of punishment. But what is deterrence? Not what Van Den Haag says it is, namely, "a preconscious, general response to a severe but not necessarily specifically and explicitly apprehended or calculated threat." How can we count as evidence of deterrence, as we may under this rubric of "general response," the desire of persons to avoid capture and punishment for the crimes they commit? Some criminologists have thought this is precisely what severe punishments tend to accomplish; if so, then they accomplish this effect only if they have failed as a deterrent. Van Den Haag's conception of deterrence is too ill-formulated to be of any serious use, since it does not discriminate between fundamentally different types of "general response" to the threat of punishment.

Let us say (definition 1) that a given punishment (P) is a *deterrent* for a given person (A) with respect to a given crime (C) at a given time (*t*) if and only if A does not commit C at *t* because he believes he runs some risk of P if he commits C, and A prefers, *ceteris paribus,* not to suffer P for committing C. This definition does not presuppose that P really is the punishment for C (a person could be deterred through a mistaken belief); it does not presuppose that A runs a high risk of incurring P (the degree of risk could be zero); or that A consciously thinks of P prior to *t* (it is left open as to the sort of theory needed to account for the operation of A's beliefs and preferences on his conduct). Nor does it presuppose that anyone ever suffers P (P could be a "perfect" deterrent), or that only P could have deterred A from C (some sanction less severe than P might have worked as well); and, finally, it does not presuppose that because P deters A at *t* from C, therefore P would deter A at any other time or anyone else at *t*. The definition insures that we cannot argue from the absence of instances of C to the conclusion that P has succeeded as a deterrent: The definition contains conditions (and, moreover, contains them intentionally) which prevent this. But the definition does allow us to argue from occurrences of C to the conclusion that P has failed on each such occasion as a deterrent.

Definition 1 suggests a general functional analogue appropriate to express scientific measurements of *differential deterrent efficacy* of a given punishment for a given crime with respect to a given population (definition 2). Let us say that a given punishment, P, deters a given population, H, from a crime, C, to the degree, D, that the members of H do not commit C because they believe that they run some risk of P if they commit C and, *ceteris paribus,* they prefer not to suffer P for committing C. If D = 0, then P has completely failed as a deterrent, whereas if D = 1, P has proved to be a perfect deterrent. Given this definition and the appropriate empirical results for various values of P, C, and H, it should be possible to establish on inductive grounds the relative effectiveness of a given punishment as a deterrent.

Definition 2 in turn leads to the following corollary for assertions of relative superior deterrent efficacy of one punishment over another. A given punishment, P_1, is a superior deterrent to another punishment, P_2, with respect to some crime, C, and some population, H, if and only if: If the members of H, believing that they are liable to P_1 upon committing C, commit C to the degree D_1; whereas if the members of H believe that they are liable to P_2 upon committing C, they commit C to the degree D_2, and $D_1 > D_2$. This formulation plainly allows that P_1 may be a more effective deterrent than P_2 for C_1 and yet less effective as a deterrent than P_2 for a different crime C_2 (with H constant), and so forth, for other possibilities. When speaking about deterrence in the sections which follow, I shall presuppose these definitions and this corollary. For the present, it is sufficient to notice that they have, at least, the virtue of eliminating the vagueness in Van Den Haag's definition complained of earlier.

Even if we analyze the notion of deterrence to accommodate the above improvements, we are left with the central objection to Van Den Haag's claim. Neither classic nor contemporary utilitarians have argued for or against the death penalty *solely* on the ground of deterrence, nor would their ethical theory entitle them to do so. One measure of the non-deterrent utility of the death penalty derives from its elimination (through death of a known criminal) of future possible crimes from that source; another arises from the elimination of the criminal's probable adverse influence upon others to emulate his ways; another lies in the generally lower budgetary outlays of tax moneys needed to finance a system of capital punishment as opposed to long-term imprisonment. There are still further consequences apart from deterrence which the scrupulous utilitarian must weigh, along with the three I have mentioned. Therefore, it is incorrect, because insufficient, to think that if it could be demonstrated that the death penalty is not a deterrent then we would be entitled to infer, on utilitarian assumptions, that "the death penalty is useless" and therefore ought to be abolished. The problem for the utilitarian is to make commensurable such diverse social utilities as those measured by deterrent efficacy, administrative costs, etc., and then to determine which penal policy in fact maximizes utility. Finally, inspection of sample arguments actually used by abolitionists will show that Van Den Haag has attacked a straw man: There are few if any contemporary abolitionists (and Van Den Haag names none) who argue solely from professional utilitarian assumptions, and it is doubtful whether there are any nonutilitarians who would abolish the death penalty solely on grounds of its deterrent inefficacy.

II

Governments faced by incipient rebellion or threatened by a *coup détat* may well conclude, as Van Den Haag insists they should, that rebels (as well as traitors and spies) can be deterred, if at all, by the threat of death, since "swift victory" of the revolution "will invalidate [the deterrent efficacy] of a prison sentence." This does not yet tell us how important it is that such deterrence be provided, any more than the fact that a threat of expulsion is the severest deterrent available to university authorities tells them whether they ought to insist on expelling campus rebels. Also, such severe penalties might have the opposite effect of inducing martyrdom, of provoking attempts to overthrow the government to secure a kind of political sainthood. This possibility Van Den Haag recognizes, but claims in a footnote that it "hardly impair[s] the force of the argument." Well, from a logical point of view it impairs it considerably; from an empirical point of view, since we are wholly without any reliable facts or hypotheses on politics in such extreme situations, the entire controversy remains quite speculative.

The one important class of criminals deterrable, if at all, by the death penalty consists, according to Van Den Haag, of those already under "life" sentence or guilty of a crime punishable by "life." In a trivial sense, he is correct; a person already suffering a given punishment, P, for a given crime, C_1, could not be expected to be deterred by anticipating the rein-

fliction of P were he to commit C_2. For if the anticipation of P did not deter him from committing C_1, how could the anticipation of P deter him from committing C_2, given that he is already experiencing P? This generalization seems to apply whenever P = "life" imprisonment. Actually, the truth is a bit more complex, because in practice (as Van Den Haag concedes, again in a footnote) so-called "life" imprisonment always has its aggravations (e.g., solitary confinement) and its mitigations (parole eligibility). These make it logically possible to deter a person already convicted of criminal homicide and serving "life" imprisonment from committing another such crime. I admit that the aggravations available are not in practice likely to provide much added deterrent effect; but exactly how likely or unlikely this effect is remains a matter for empirical investigation, not idle guesswork. Van Den Haag's seeming truism, therefore, relies for its plausibility on the false assumption that "life" imprisonment is a uniform punishment not open to further deterrence-relevant aggravations and mitigations.

Empirically, the objection to his point is that persons already serving a "life" sentence do not in general constitute a source of genuine alarm to custodial personnel. Being already incarcerated and integrated into the reward structure of prison life, they do not seem to need the deterrent controls allegedly necessary for other prisoners and the general public. There are exceptions to this generalization, but there is no known way of identifying them in advance, their number has proved to be not large, and it would be irrational, therefore, to design a penal policy (as several states have) which invokes the death penalty in the professed hope of deterring such convicted offenders from further criminal homicide. Van Den Haag cites no evidence that such policies accomplish their alleged purpose, and I know of none. As for the real question which Van Den Haag's argument raises—is there any class of actual or potential criminals for which the death penalty exerts a marginally superior deterrent effect over every less severe alternative?— we have no evidence at all, one way or the other. Until this proposition, or some corollary, is actually tested and confirmed, there is no reason to indulge Van Den Haag in his speculations.

III

It is not clear why Van Den Haag is so anxious to discuss whether there is evidence that the death penalty is a deterrent, or whether—as he thinks—there is no evidence that it is not a deterrent. For the issue over abolishing the death penalty, as all serious students of the subject have known for decades, is not whether (1) *the death penalty is a deterrent,* but whether (2) *the death penalty is a superior deterrent to "life" imprisonment,* and consequently the evidential dispute is also not over (1) but only over (2). As I have argued elsewhere, abolitionists have reason to contest (1) only if they are against *all* punitive alternatives to the death penalty; since few abolitionists (and none cited by Van Den Haag) take this extreme view, it may be ignored here. We should notice in passing, however, that if it were demonstrated that (1) were false, there would be no need for abolitionists to go on to marshal evidence against (2), since the truth of (1) is a presupposition of the truth of (2). Now it is true that some abolitionists may be faulted for writing as if the falsity of (1) followed from the falsity of (2), but this is not a complaint Van Den Haag makes, nor is it an error vital to the abolitionist argument against the death penalty. Similar considerations inveigh against certain pro-death-penalty arguments. Proponents must do more than establish (1), they must also provide evidence in favor of (2); and they cannot infer from evidence which establishes (1) that (2) is true or even probable (unless, of course, that evidence would establish [2] independently). These considerations show us how important it is to distinguish (1) and (2) and the questions of evidence which each raises. Van Den Haag never directly discusses (2), except when he observes in passing that "the question is not only whether the death penalty deters but whether it deters more than alternatives." But since he explicitly argues only over the evidential status of (1), it is unclear whether he wishes to ignore (2) or whether he thinks that his arguments regarding (1) also have consequences for the evidential status of (2). Perhaps Van Den Haag thinks that if there is no evidence disconfirming (1), then there can be no evidence disconfirming (2); or perhaps he thinks that none of the evidence disconfirming (2) also disconfirms (1). (If he thinks either, he is wrong.) Or perhaps he is careless, conceding on the one hand that (2) is important to the issue of abolition of the death penalty, only to slide back into a discussion exclusively about (1).

He writes as if his chief contentions were these two: We must not confuse (*a*) the assertion that there is no evidence that not-(1) (i.e., evidence that [1] is false); and abolitionists have asserted (*b*) whereas all they are entitled to assert is (*a*). I wish to proceed on the assumption that since (1) is not chiefly at issue, neither is (*a*) nor (*b*) (though I grant, as anyone

must, that the distinction between [*a*] and [*b*] is legitimate and important). What is chiefly at issue, even though Van Den Haag's discussion obscures the point, is whether abolitionists must content themselves with asserting that there is no evidence against (2), or whether they may go further and assert that there is evidence that not-(2) (i.e., evidence that [2] is false). I shall argue that abolitionists may make the stronger (latter) assertion.

In order to see the issue fairly, it is necessary to see how (2) has so far been submitted to empirical tests. First of all, the issue has been confined to the death penalty for criminal homicide; consequently, it is not (2) but a subsidiary proposition which critics of the death penalty have tested, namely, (2*a*) *the death penalty is a superior deterrent to "life" imprisonment for the crime of criminal homicide.* The falsification of (2*a*) does not entail the falsity of (2); the death penalty could still be a superior deterrent to "life" imprisonment for the crime of burglary, etc. However, the disconfirmation of (2*a*) is obviously a partial disconfirmation of (2). Second, (2*a*) has not been tested directly but only indirectly. No one has devised a way to count or estimate directly the number of persons in a given population who have been deterred from criminal homicide by the fear of the penalty. The difficulties in doing so are plain enough. For instance, it would be possible to infer from the countable numbers who have not been deterred (because they did commit a given crime) that everyone else in the population was deterred, but only on the assumption that the only reason why a person did not commit a given crime is because he was deterred. Unfortunately for this argument (though happily enough otherwise) this assumption is almost certainly false. Other ways in which one might devise to test (2*a*) directly have proved equally unfeasible. Yet it would be absurd to insist that there can be no *evidence* for or against (2*a*) unless it is *direct* evidence for or against it. Because Van Den Haag nowhere indicated what he thinks would count as evidence, direct or indirect, for or against (1), much less (2), his insistence upon the distinction between (*a*) and (*b*) and his rebuke to abolitionists is in danger of implicitly relying upon just this absurdity.

How, then, has the indirect argument over (2*a*) proceeded? During the past generation, at least six different hypotheses have been formulated, as corollaries of (2*a*), as follows:

i. Death-penalty jurisdictions should have a lower annual rate of criminal homicide than abolition jurisdictions;

ii. Jurisdictions which abolished the death penalty should show an increased annual rate of criminal homicide after abolition;

iii. Jurisdictions which reintroduced the death penalty should show a decreased annual rate of criminal homicide after reintroduction;

iv. Given two contiguous jurisdictions differing chiefly in that one has the death penalty and the other does not, the latter should show a higher annual rate of criminal homicide;

v. Police officers on duty should suffer a higher annual rate of criminal assault and homicide in abolition jurisdictions than in death-penalty jurisdictions;

vi. Prisoners and prison personnel should suffer a higher annual rate of criminal assault and homicide from life-term prisoners in abolition jurisdictions than in death-penalty jurisdictions.

It could be objected to these six hypotheses that they are, as a set, insufficient to settle the question posed by (2a) no matter what the evidence for them may be (i.e., that falsity of [i]–[vi] does not entail the falsity of [2]). Or it could be argued that each of (i)–(vi) has been inadequately tested or insufficiently (dis)confirmed so as to establish any (dis)confirmation of (2a), even though it is conceded that if these hypotheses were highly (dis)confirmed they would (dis)confirm (2a). Van Den Haag's line of attack is not entirely clear as between these two alternatives. It looks as if he ought to take the former line of criticism in its most extreme version. How else could he argue his chief point, that the research used by abolitionists has so far failed to produce *any* evidence against (1)—we may take him to mean (2) or (2a). Only if (i)–(vi) were *irrelevant* to (2a) could it be fairly concluded from the evidential disconfirmation of (i)–(vi) that there is still no disconfirmation of (2a). And this is Van Den Haag's central contention. The other ways to construe Van Den Haag's reasoning are simply too preposterous to be considered: He cannot think that the evidence is indifferent to or *confirms* (i)–(vi); nor can he think that there has been no *attempt* at all to disconfirm (2a); nor can he think that the evidence which disconfirms (i)–(vi) is not therewith also evidence which confirms the negations of (i)–(vi). If any of these three was true, it would be a good reason for saying that there is "no evidence"

against (2a); but each is patently false. If one inspects (i)–(vi) and (2a), it is difficult to see how one could argue that (dis)confirmation of the former does not constitute (dis)confirmation of the latter, even if it might be argued that verification of the former does not constitute verification of the latter. I think, therefore, that there is nothing to be gained by pursuing further this first line of attack.

Elsewhere, it looks as though Van Den Haag takes the other alternative of criticism, albeit rather crudely, as when he argues (against [iv], I suppose, since he nowhere formulated [i]–[vi]) that "the similar areas are not similar enough." As to why, for example, the rates of criminal homicide in Michigan and in Illinois from 1920 to 1960 are not relevant because the states aren't "similar enough," he does not try to explain. But his criticism does strictly concede that if the jurisdictions *were* "similar enough," then it would be logically possible to argue from the evidence against (iv) to the disconfirmation of (2a). And this seems to be in keeping with the nature of the case; it is this second line of attack which needs closer examination.

Van Den Haag's own position and objections apart, what is likely to strike the neutral observer who studies the ways in which (i)–(vi) have been tested and declared disconfirmed is that their disconfirmation of (2a), is imperfect for two related reasons. First, all the tests rely upon *unproved empirical assumptions;* second, it is not known whether there is any *statistical significance* to the results of the tests. It is important to make these concessions, and abolitionists and other disbelievers in the deterrent efficacy of the death penalty have not always done so.

It is not possible here to review all the evidence and to reach a judgment on the empirical status of (i)–(vi). But it is possible and desirable to illustrate how the two qualifications cited above must be understood, and then to assess their effect on the empirical status of (2a). The absence of statistical significance may be illustrated by reference to hypothesis (v). According to the published studies, the annual rate of assaults upon on-duty policemen in abolition jurisdictions is lower than in death-penalty jurisdictions (i.e., a rate of 1.2 attacks per 100,000 population in the former as opposed to 1.3 per 100,000 in the latter). But is this difference statistically significant or not? The studies do not answer this question because the data were not submitted to tests of statistical significance. Nor is there any way, to my knowledge, that these data could be subjected to any such tests. This is, of course, no reason to suppose that the evidence is really not evidence after all, or that though it is evidence against (i) it is not evidence against (2a). Statistical significance is, after all, only a measure of the strength of evidence, not a *sine qua non* of evidential status.

The qualification concerning unproved assumptions is more important, and is worth examining somewhat more fully (though, again, only illustratively). Consider hypothesis (i). Are we entitled to infer that (i) is disconfirmed because in fact a study of the annual homicide rates (as measured by vital statistics showing cause of death) unquestionably indicates that the rate in all abolition states is consistently lower than in all death-penalty states? To make this inference we must assume that (A_1) homicides as measured by vital statistics are in a generally constant ratio to criminal homicides, (A_2) the years for which the evidence has been gathered are representative and not atypical, (A_3) however much fluctuations in the homicide rate owe to other factors, there is a nonnegligible proportion which is a function of the penalty, and (A_4) the deterrent effect of a penalty is not significantly weakened by its infrequent imposition. (There are, of course, other assumptions, but these are central and sufficiently representative here.) Assumption A_1 is effectively unmeasurable because the concept of a criminal homicide is the concept of a homicide which *deserves* to be criminally prosecuted. Nevertheless, A_1 has been accepted by criminologists for over a generation. A_2 is confirmable, on the other hand, and bit by bit, a year at a time, seems to be being confirmed. Assumption A_3 is rather more interesting. To the degree to which it is admitted or insisted that other factors than the severity of the penalty affect the volume of homicide, to that degree A_3 becomes increasingly dubious; but at the same time testing (2a) by (i) becomes increasingly unimportant. The urgency of testing (2a) rests upon the assumption that it is the deterrent efficacy of penalties which is the chief factor in the volume of crimes, and it is absurd to hold that assumption and at the same time doubt A_3. On the other hand, A_4 is almost certainly false (and has been believed so by Bentham and other social theorists for nearly two hundred years). The falsity of A_4, however, is not of fatal harm to the disconfirmation of (i) because it is not known how frequently or infrequently a severe penalty such as death or life imprisonment needs to be imposed in order to maximize its deterrent efficacy. Such information as we do have on this point leads one to doubt that for the general population the frequency

with which the death sentence is imposed makes any significant difference to the volume of criminal homicide.

I suggest that these four assumptions and the way in which they bear upon interpretation and evaluation of the evidence against (i), and therefore the disconfirmation of (2a), are typical of what one finds as one examines the work of criminologists as it relates to the rest of these corollaries of (2a). Is it reasonable, in the light of these considerations, to infer that we have no evidence against (i)–(vi), or that although we do have evidence against (i)–(vi), we have none against (2a)? I do not think so. Short of unidentified and probably unobtainable "crucial experiments," we shall never be able to marshal evidence for (2a) or for (i)–(vi) except by means of certain additional assumptions such as A_1–A_4. To reason otherwise is to rely on nothing more than the fact that it is logically possible to grant the evidence against (i)–(vi) and yet deny that (2a) is false; or it is to insist that the assumptions which the inference relies upon are not plausible assumptions at all (or though plausible are themselves false or disconfirmed) and that no other assumptions can be brought forward which will both be immune to objections and still preserve the linkage between the evidence and the corollaries and (2a). The danger now is that one will repudiate assumptions such as A_1–A_4 in order to guarantee the failure of efforts to disconfirm (2a) via disconfirmation of (i)–(vi); or else that one will place the standards of evidence too high before one accepts the disconfirmation. In either case one has begun to engage in the familiar but discreditable practice of "protecting the hypothesis" by making it, in effect, immune to any kind of disconfirmation.

On my view things stand in this way. An empirical proposition not directly testable, (2), has a significant corollary, (2a), which in turn suggests a number of corollaries, (i)–(vi), each of which is testable with varying degrees of indirectness. Each of (i)–(vi) has been tested. To accept the results as evidence disconfirming (i)–(vi) and as therefore disconfirming (2a), it is necessary to make certain assumptions, of which A_1–A_4 are typical. These assumptions in turn are not all testable, much less directly tested; some of them, in their most plausible formulation, may even be false (but not in that formulation necessary to the inference, however). Since this structure of indirect testing, corollary hypotheses, unproved assumptions, is typical of the circumstances which face us when we wish to consider the evidence for or against any complex empirical hypothesis such as (2), I conclude that while (2) has by no means been disproved (whatever that might mean), it is equally clear that (2) has been disconfirmed, rather than confirmed or left untouched by the inductive arguments we have surveyed.

I have attempted to review and appraise the chief "statistical" arguments (as Van Den Haag calls them) marshaled during the past fifteen years or so in this country by those critical of the death penalty. But in order to assess these arguments more adequately, it is helpful to keep in mind two other considerations. First, most of the criminologists skeptical of (1) are led to this attitude not by the route we have examined—the argument against (2)—but by a general theory of the causation of crimes of personal violence. Given their confidence in that theory, and the evidence for it, they tend not to credit seriously the idea that the death penalty deters (very much), much less the idea that it is a superior deterrent to a severe alternative such as "life" imprisonment (which may not deter very much, either). . . . Second, very little of the empirical research purporting to establish the presence or absence of deterrent efficacy of a given punishment is entirely reliable because almost no effort has been made to isolate the relevant variables. Surely, it is platitudinously true that *some* persons in *some* situations considering *some* crimes can be deterred from committing them by *some* penalties. To go beyond this, however, and supplant these variables with a series of well-confirmed functional hypotheses about the deterrent effect of current legal sanctions is not possible today.

Even if one cannot argue, as Van Den Haag does, that there is no evidence against the claim that the death penalty is a better deterrent than life imprisonment, this does not yet tell us how good this evidence is, how reliable it is, how extensive, and how probative. Van Den Haag could, after all, give up his extreme initial position and retreat to the concession that although there is evidence against the superior deterrent efficacy of the death penalty, still, the evidence is not very good, indeed, not good enough to make reasonable the policy of abolishing the death penalty. Again, it is not possible to undertake to settle this question short of a close examination of each of the empirical studies which confirm (i)–(vi). The reply, so far as there is one, short of further empirical studies (which undoubtedly are desirable—I should not want to obscure that), is twofold: The evidence, such as it is, for (i)–(vi) is uniformly confirmatory in all cases; and the argument of section IV which follows.

IV

Van Den Haag's "argument" rests considerable weight on the claims that "the added severity of the death penalty adds to deterrence, or may do so," and that "the generalized threat of the death penalty may be a deterrent, and the more so, the more generally applied." These claims are open to criticism on at least three grounds.

First, as the modal auxiliaries signal, Van Den Haag has not really committed himself to any affirmative empirical claim, but only to a truism. It is always logically possible, no matter what the evidence, that a given penalty which is *ex hypothesi* more severe than an alternative, may be a better deterrent under some conditions not often realized, and be proven so by evidence not ever detectable. For this reason, there is no possible way to prove that Van Den Haag's claims are false, no possible preponderance of evidence against his conclusions which must, logically, force him to give them up. One would have hoped those who believe in the deterrent superiority of the death penalty could, at this late date, offer their critics something more persuasive than logical possibilities. As it is, Van Den Haag's appeal to possible evidence comes perilously close to an argument from ignorance: The possible evidence we might gather is used to offset the actual evidence we have gathered.

Second, Van Den Haag rightly regards his conclusion above as merely an instance of the general principle that, *ceteris paribus,* "the Greater the Severity the Greater the Deterrence," a "plausible" idea, as he says. Yet the advantage on behalf of the death penalty produced by this principle is a function entirely of the evidence for the principle itself. But we are offered no evidence at all to make this plausible principle into a confirmed hypothesis of contemporary criminological theory of special relevance to crimes of personal violence. Until we see evidence concerning specific crimes, specific penalties, specific criminal populations, which show that in general the Greater the Severity the Greater the Deterrence, we run the risk of stupefying ourselves by the merely plausible. Besides, without any evidence for this principle we will find ourselves at a complete standoff with the abolitionist (who, of course, can play the same game), because he has his own equally plausible first principle: The Greater the Severity of Punishment the Greater the Brutality Provoked throughout Society. When at last, exhausted and frustrated by mere plausibilities, we once again turn to study the evidence, we will find that the current literature on deterrence in criminology does not encourage us to believe in Van Den Haag's principle.

Third, Van Den Haag has not given any reason why, in the quest for deterrent efficacy, one should fasten (as he does) on the severity of the punishments in question, rather than (as Bentham long ago counseled) on the relevant factors, notably the ease and speed and reliability with which the punishment can be inflicted. Van Den Haag cannot hope to convince anyone who has studied the matter that the death penalty and "life" imprisonment differ only in their severity, and that in all other respects affecting deterrent efficacy they are equivalent; and if he believes this himself it would be interesting to have seen his evidence for it. The only thing to be said in favor of fastening exclusively upon the question of severity in the appraisal of punishments for their relative deterrent efficacy is that augmenting the severity of a punishment in and of itself usually imposes little if any added direct cost to operate the penal system; it even may be cheaper. This is bound to please the harried taxpayer, and at the same time gratify the demand on government to "do something" about crime. Beyond that, emphasizing the severity of punishments as the main (or indeed the sole) variable relevant to deterrent efficacy is unbelievably superficial.

V

Van Den Haag's final point concerning where the burden of proof lies is based, he admits, on playing off a certainty (the death of the persons executed) against a risk (that innocent persons, otherwise the would-be victims of those deterrable only by the death penalty, would be killed). This is not as analogous as he seems to think it is to the general nature of gambling, investment, and other risk-taking enterprises. In none of them do we deliberately cause anything to be killed, as we do, for instance, when we weed out carrot seedlings to enable those remaining to grow larger (a eugenic analogy, by the way, which might be more useful to Van Den Haag's purpose). In none, that is, do we venture a sacrifice in the hope of a future net gain; we only *risk* a present loss in that hope. Moreover, in gambling ventures we recoup what we risked if we win, whereas in executions we must lose something (the lives of persons executed) no matter if we lose or win (the lives of innocents protected). Van Den Haag's attempt to

locate the burden of proof by appeal to principles of gambling is a failure.

Far more significantly, Van Den Haag frames the issue in such a way that the abolitionist has no chance of discharging the burden of proof once he accepts it. For what evidence could be marshaled to prove what Van Den Haag wants proved, namely, that "the greater severity inherent in irrevocability [of the death penalty] . . . adds nothing to deterrence"? The evidence alluded to at the end of section IV does tend to show that this generalization (the negation of Van Den Haag's own principle) is indeed true, but it does not prove it. I conclude, therefore, that either Van Den Haag is wrong in his argument which shows the locus of burden of proof to lie on the abolitionist, or one must accept less than proof in order to discharge this burden (in which case, the very argument Van Den Haag advances shows that the burden of proof now lies on those who would retain the death penalty).

"Burden of proof" in areas outside judicial precincts where evidentiary questions are at stake tends to be a rhetorical phrase and nothing more. Anyone interested in the truth of a matter will not defer gathering evidence pending a determination of where the burden of proof lies. For those who do think there is a question of burden of proof, as Van Den Haag does, they should consider this: Advocacy of the death penalty is advocacy of a rule of penal law which empowers the state to deliberately take human life and in general to threaten the public with the taking of life. *Ceteris paribus,* one would think anyone favoring such a rule would be ready to offer considerable evidence for its necessity and efficacy. Surely, some showing of necessity, some evidentiary proof, is to be expected to satisfy the skeptical. Exactly when and in what circumstances have the apologists for capital punishment offered evidence to support their contentions? Where is that evidence recorded for us to inspect, comparable to the evidence cited in section III against the superior deterrent efficacy of the death penalty? Van Den Haag conspicuously cited no such evidence and so it is with all other proponents of the death penalty. The insistence that the burden of proof lies on abolitionists, therefore, is nothing but the rhetorical demand of every defender of the status quo who insists upon evidence from those who would effect change, while reserving throughout the right to dictate criteria and standards of proof and refusing to offer evidence for his own view.

I should have thought that the death penalty was a sufficiently momentous matter and of sufficient controversy that the admittedly imperfect evidence assembled over the past generation by those friendly to abolition would have been countered by evidence tending to support the opposite, retentionist, position. It remains a somewhat sad curiosity that nothing of the sort has happened; no one has ever published research tending to show, however inconclusively, that the death penalty after all is a deterrent, and a superior deterrent to "life" imprisonment. Among scholars at least, if not among legislators and other politicians, the perennial appeal to burden of proof really ought to give way to offering of proof by those interested enough to argue the issue.

DISCUSSION QUESTIONS

1. Ernest Van Den Haag says that "since it seems more important to spare victims than to spare murderers, the burden of proving that the greater the severity inherent in irrevocability adds nothing to deterrence lies on those who oppose capital punishment." Why does Bedau believe that this claim is a "muddle and a dodge"? Do you agree with him? Explain.
2. Why does Bedau believe that it is false to claim that capital punishment is useless for utilitarian abolitionists because it does not deter others? Is his argument sound? Why or why not?
3. Why does Bedau distinguish between "the death penalty as a deterrent" and the "death penalty as a superior deterrent to life imprisonment"? Do you find his use of this distinction convincing? Why or why not?
4. Van Den Haag claims that the deterrence of the death penalty has not been demonstrated statistically but that it would be a mistake to think that "non-deterrence" has been demonstrated statistically. Why does Bedau claim that this is correct in what it affirms but false in what it denies? Is this a good argument? Why or why not?
5. Consider Van Den Haag's arguments for capital punishment and Bedau's arguments against capital punishment. Which point in particular is the strongest on each side? Which argument is the strongest overall? How do their arguments influence your own views on capital punishment? Have these men failed to consider some argument that you think is important? Explain.

ANTHONY AMSTERDAM

Race and the Death Penalty

Anthony Amsterdam does not doubt that Warren McCleskey was guilty of murder under Georgia law. However, he disagrees with the U.S. Supreme Court decision in *McKleskey v. Georgia* (1987). In this case, the Court held that Warren McCleskey can be constitutionally put to death despite overwhelming and unexplained statistical evidence that the death penalty is being imposed by Georgia juries in a pattern which reflects the race of convicted murderers and their victims, and cannot be accounted for by any factor other than race.

Anthony Amsterdam, *Criminal Justice Ethics*, vol. 7, no. 1, (winter/spring 1988): 84-86. Reprinted by permission of the Institute for Criminal Justice Ethics, 555 West 57th Street, Suite 601, New York, NY 10019-1029.

For Anthony Amsterdam, the Supreme Court's decision in this case amounts to an open license to discriminate against people of color in capital sentencing. He charges that it reveals a majority of the Supreme Court to be tolerant of racism. Black defendants convicted of murder or rape, reports Amsterdam, have been sentenced to death and executed far out of proportion to their numbers. "[T]here can be no justice in a system which treats people of color differently than white people," writes Amsterdam, "or treats crimes against people of color differently from crimes against white people."

Anthony Amsterdam is a law professor at the New York University School of Law, Clinical Law Center.

There are times when even truths we hold self-evident require affirmation. For those who have invested our careers and our hopes in the criminal justice system, this is one of those times. Insofar as the basic principles that give value to our lives are in the keeping of the law and can be vindicated or betrayed by the decisions of any court, they have been sold down the river by a decision of the Supreme Court of the United States less than a year old [in 1988].

I do not choose by accident a metaphor of slavery. For the decision I am referring to is the criminal justice system's *Dred Scott* case. It is the case of Warren McCleskey, a black man sentenced to die for the murder of a white man in Georgia. The Supreme Court held that McCleskey can be constitutionally put to death despite overwhelming unrebutted and unexplained statistical evidence that the death penalty is being imposed by Georgia juries in a pattern which reflects the race of convicted murderers and their victims and cannot be accounted for by any factor other than race.

This is not just a case about capital punishment. The Supreme Court's decision, which amounts to an open license to discriminate against people of color in capital sentencing, was placed upon grounds that implicate the entire criminal justice system. Worse still, the Court's reasoning makes us all accomplices in its toleration of a racially discriminatory administration of criminal justice.

Let us look at the *McCleskey* case. His crime was an ugly one. He robbed a furniture store at gunpoint, and he or one of his accomplices killed a police officer who responded to the scene. McCleskey may have been the triggerman. Whether or not he was, he was guilty of murder under Georgia law.

But his case in the Supreme Court was not concerned with guilt. It was concerned with why McCleskey had been sentenced to death instead of life imprisonment for his crime. It was concerned with why, out of seventeen defendants charged with the killings of police officers in Fulton County, Georgia, between 1973 and 1980, only Warren McCleskey—a black defendant charged with killing a white officer— had been chosen for a death sentence. In the only other one of these seventeen cases in which the predominantly white prosecutor's office in Atlanta had pushed for the death penalty, a black defendant convicted of killing a black police officer had been sentenced to life instead.

It was facts of that sort that led the NAACP Legal Defense Fund to become involved in McCleskey's case. They were not unfamiliar facts to any of the lawyers who, like myself, had worked for the Legal Defense Fund for many years, defending Blacks charged with serious crimes throughout the South. We knew that in the United States black defendants convicted of murder or rape in cases involving white victims have always been sentenced to death and executed far out of proportion to their numbers, and under factual circumstances that would have produced a sentence of imprisonment—often a relatively light sentence of imprisonment—in identical cases with black victims or white defendants or both.

Back in the mid-sixties the Legal Defense Fund had presented to courts evidence of extensive statistical studies conducted by Dr. Marvin Wolfgang, one of the deans of American criminology, showing that the grossly disproportionate number of death sentences which were then being handed out to black defendants convicted of the rape of white victims could not be explained by any factor other than race. Prosecutors took the position then that these studies were insufficiently detailed to rule out the influence of every possible non-racial factor, and it was largely for that reason that the courts rejected our claims that our black death-sentenced clients had been denied the Equal Protection of the Laws. Fortunately, in 1972 we had won a Supreme Court decision that saved the lives of all those clients and outlawed virtually every death penalty statute in the United States on procedural grounds; and when the States enacted new death-penalty laws between 1973 and 1976, only three of them reinstated capital punishment for rape. Now that it no longer mattered much, the prosecutors could afford to take another tack. When we argued against the new capital murder statutes on the ground that the Wolfgang studies had shown the susceptibility of capital sentencing laws to racially discriminatory application, the Government of the United States came into the Supreme Court against us saying, Oh, yes, Wolfgang was "a careful and comprehensive study, and we do not question its conclusion that during the twenty years between [1945 and 1965] . . . , in southern states, there was discrimination in rape cases." However, said the Government, this "research does not provide support for a conclusion that racial discrimination continues, . . . or that it applies to murder cases."

So we were well prepared for this sort of selective agnosticism when we went to court in the *McCleskey* case. The evidence that we presented in support of McCleskey's claim of racial discrimination left nothing out. Our centerpiece was a pair of studies conducted by Professor David Baldus, of the University of Iowa, and his colleagues, which examined 2,484 cases of murder and nonnegligent manslaughter that occurred in Georgia between 1973, the date when its present capital murder statute was enacted, and 1979, the year after McCleskey's own death sentence was imposed. The Baldus team got its data on these cases principally from official state records, supplied by the Georgia Supreme Court and the Georgia Board of Pardons and Paroles.

Through a highly refined protocol, the team collected information regarding more than five hundred factors in each case—information relating to the demographic and individual characteristics of the defendant and the victim, the circumstances of the crime and the strength of the evidence of guilt, and the aggravating and mitigating features of each case: both the features specified by Georgia law to be considered in capital sentencing and every factor recognized in the legal and criminological literature as theoretically or actually likely to affect the choice of life or death. Using the most reliable and advanced techniques of social-science research, Baldus processed the data through a wide array of sophisticated statistical procedures, including multiple-regression analyses based upon alternative

models that considered and controlled for as few as 10 or as many as 230 sentencing factors in each analysis. When our evidentiary case was presented in court, Baldus reanalyzed the data several more times to take account of every additional factor, combination of factors, or model for analysis of factors suggested by the State of Georgia's expert witnesses, its lawyers, and the federal trial judge. The Baldus study has since been uniformly praised by social scientists as the best study of any aspect of criminal sentencing ever conducted.

What did it show? That death sentences were being imposed in Georgia murder cases in a clear, consistent pattern that reflected the race of the victim and the race of the defendant and could not be explained by any non-racial factor. For example:

1. Although less than 40 percent of Georgia homicide cases involve white victims, in 87 percent of the cases in which a death sentence is imposed, the victim is white. White-victim cases are almost eleven times more likely to produce a death sentence than are black-victim cases.

2. When the race of the defendant is considered too, the following figures emerge: 22 percent of black defendants who kill white victims are sentenced to death; 8 percent of white defendants who kill white victims are sentenced to death; 1 percent of black defendants who kill black victims are sentenced to death; 3 percent of white defendants who kill black victims are sentenced to death. It should be noted that out of the roughly 2,500 Georgia homicide cases found, only 64 involved killings of black victims by white defendants, so the 3 percent death-sentencing rate in this category represents a total of two death sentences over a six-year period. Plainly, the reason why racial discrimination against black defendants does not appear even more glaringly evident is that most black murderers kill black victims; almost no identified white murderers kill black victims; and virtually nobody is sentenced to death for killing a mere black victim.

3. No non-racial factor explains these racial patterns. Under multiple-regression analysis, the model with the maximum explanatory power shows that after controlling for

legitimate non-racial factors, murderers of white victims are still being sentenced to death 4.3 times more often than murderers of black victims. Multiple-regression analysis also shows that the race of the victim is as good a basis for predicting whether or not a murderer will be sentenced to death as are the aggravating circumstances which the Georgia statute explicitly says should be considered in favor of a death sentence, such as whether the defendant has a prior murder conviction, or whether he is the primary actor in the present murder.

4. Across the whole universe of cases, approximately 5 percent of Georgia killings result in a death sentence. Yet when more than 230 non-racial variables are controlled for, the death-sentencing rate is 6 percentage points higher in white-victim cases than in black-victim cases. What this means is that in predicting whether any particular person will get the death penalty in Georgia, it is less important to know whether or not he committed a homicide in the first place than to know whether, if he did, he killed a white victim or a black one.

5. However, the effects of race are not uniform across the entire range of homicide cases. As might be expected, in the least aggravated sorts of cases, almost no one gets a death sentence; in the really gruesome cases, a high percentage of both black and white murderers get death sentences; so it is in the mid-range of cases—cases like McCleskey's—that race has its greatest impact. The Baldus study found that in these mid-range cases the death-sentencing rate for killers of white victims is 34 percent as compared to 14 percent for killers of black victims. In other words, out of every thirty-four murderers sentenced to death for killing a white victim, twenty of them would not have gotten death sentences if their victims had been black.

The bottom line is this: Georgia has executed eleven murderers since it passed its present statute in 1973. Nine of the eleven were black. Ten of the eleven had white victims. Can there be the slightest doubt that this revolting record is the product of some sort of racial bias rather than a pure fluke?

A narrow majority of the Supreme Court pretended to have such doubts and rejected McCleskey's Equal Protection challenge to his death sentence. It did not question the quality or the validity of the Baldus study, or any of the findings that have been described here. It admitted that the manifest racial discrepancies in death sentencing were unexplained by any non-racial variable, and that Baldus's data pointed to a "likelihood" or a "risk" that race was at work in the capital sentencing process. It essentially conceded that if a similar statistical showing of racial bias had been made in an employment-discrimination case or in a jury-selection case, the courts would have been required to find a violation of the Equal Protection Clause of the Fourteenth Amendment. But, the Court said, racial discrimination in capital sentencing cannot be proved by a pattern of sentencing results: a death-sentenced defendant like McCleskey must present proof that the particular jury or the individual prosecutor, or some other decision-maker in his own case, was personally motivated by racial considerations to bring about his death. Since such proof is never possible to obtain, racial discrimination in capital sentencing is never possible to prove.

The Court gave four basic reasons for this result. First, since capital sentencing decisions are made by a host of different juries and prosecutors, and are supposed to be based upon "innumerable factors that vary according to the characteristics of the individual defendant and the facts of the particular capital offense," even sentencing patterns that are explicable by race and inexplicable except by race do not necessarily show that any single decision-maker in the system is acting out of a subjective purpose to discriminate. Second, capital punishment laws are important for the protection of society; the "[i]mplementation of these laws necessarily requires discretionary judgments"; and, "[b]ecause discretion is essential to the criminal justice process, we [sh]ould demand exceptionally clear proof before we . . . infer that the discretion has been abused." Third, this same respect for discretionary judgments makes it imprudent to require juries and prosecutors to explain their decisions, so it is better to ignore the inference of racial discrimination that flows logically from their behavior than to call upon them to justify such behavior upon non-racial grounds.

Fourth, more is involved than capital punishment. "McCleskey's claim . . . throws into serious question the principles that underlie our entire criminal justice system." This is so because "the Baldus study indicates a discrepancy that appears to correlate with race," and "[a]pparent disparities in sentencing are an inevitable part of our criminal justice system." "Thus," says the Court, "if we accepted McCleskey's claim that racial bias has impermissibly tainted the capital sentencing decision, we could soon be faced with similar claims as to other types of penalty. Moreover, the claim that . . . sentence rests on the irrelevant factor of race easily could be extended to apply to claims based on unexplained discrepancies that correlate to membership in other minority groups, and even to gender"—and even to claims based upon "the defendant's facial characteristics, or the physical attractiveness of the . . . victim." In other words, if we forbid racial discrimination in meting out sentences of life or death, we may have to face claims of discrimination against Blacks, or against women, or perhaps against ugly people, wherever the facts warrant such claims, in the length of prison sentences, in the length of jail sentences, in the giving of suspended sentences, in the making of pretrial release decisions, in the invocation of recidivist sentencing enhancements, in the prosecutor's decisions whether to file charges, and how heavily to load up the charges, against black defendants as compared with white defendants or against ugly defendants as compared with ravishingly beautiful defendants; and of course the whole criminal justice system will then fall down flat and leave us in a state of anarchy. In thirty years of reading purportedly serious judicial opinions, I have never seen one that came so close to Thomas De Quincy's famous justification for punishing the crime of murder: "If once a man indulges himself in murder, very soon he comes to think little of robbing; and from robbing he next comes to drinking and Sabbath-breaking, and from that to incivility and procrastination."

Notice that the Court's version of this slippery-slope argument merely makes explicit what is implied throughout its opinion in the *McCleskey* case. Its decision is not limited to capital sentencing but purports to rest on principles which apply to the whole criminal justice system. Every part of that system from arrest to sentencing and parole, in relation to every crime from murder to Sabbath-breaking, involves a multitude of separate decision-makers making individualized decisions based upon "innumerable [case-specific] factors." All of these decisions are important for the protection of society from crime. All are conceived as

"necessarily requir[ing] discretionary judgments." In making these discretionary judgments, prosecutors and judges as well as jurors have traditionally been immunized from inquiry into their motives. If this kind of discretion implies the power to treat black people differently from white people and to escape the responsibility for explaining why one is making life-and-death decisions in an apparently discriminatory manner, it implies a tolerance for racial discrimination throughout the length and breadth of the administration of criminal justice. What the Supreme Court has held, plainly, is that the very nature of the criminal justice system requires that its workings be excluded from the ordinary rules of law and even logic that guarantee equal protection to racial minorities in our society.

And it is here, I suggest, that any self-respecting criminal justice professional is obliged to speak out against this Supreme Court's conception of the criminal justice system. We must reaffirm that there can be no justice in a system which treats people of color differently from white people, or treats crimes against people of color differently from crimes against white people.

We must reaffirm that racism is itself a crime, and that the toleration of racism cannot be justified by the supposed interest of society in fighting crime. We must pledge that when anyone—even a majority of the Supreme Court—tells us that a power to discriminate on grounds of race is necessary to protect society from crime, we will recognize that we are probably being sold another shipment of propaganda to justify repression. Let us therefore never fail to ask the question whether righteous rhetoric about protecting society from crime really refers to protecting only white people. And when the answer, as in the McCleskey case, is that protecting only white people is being described as "protecting society from crime," let us say that we are not so stupid as to buy this version of the Big Lie, nor so uncaring as to let it go unchallenged.

Let us reaffirm that neither the toleration of racism by the Supreme Court nor the pervasiveness of racism in the criminal justice system can make it right, and that these things only make it worse. Let us reaffirm that racism exists, and is against the fundamental law of this Nation, whenever people of different races are treated differently by any public agency or institution as a consequence of their race and with no legitimate non-racial reason for the different treatment. Let us dedicate ourselves to eradicating racism, and declaring it unlawful, not simply in the superficial, short-lived situation where we can point to one or another specific decision-maker and show that his decisions were the product of conscious bigotry, but also in the far more basic, more intractable, and more destructive situations where hundreds upon hundreds of different public decision-makers, acting like Georgia's prosecutors and judges and juries—without collusion and in many cases without consciousness of their own racial biases—combine to produce a pattern that bespeaks the profound prejudice of an entire population.

Also, let us vow that we will never claim—or stand by unprotestingly while others claim for us—that, because our work is righteous and important, it should be above the law. Of course, controlling crime is vital work; that is why we give the agencies of criminal justice drastic and unique coercive powers, including the powers of imprisonment and death. And of course discretion in the execution of such powers is essential. But it is precisely because the powers that the system regulates are so awesome, and because the discretion of its actors is so broad, that it cannot be relieved of accountability for the exercise of that discretion. Nor can it be ex-empted from the scrutiny that courts of law are bound to give to documented charges of discrimination on the ground of race by any agency of government. Let us declare flatly that we neither seek nor will accept any such exemption, and that we find it demeaning to be told by the Supreme Court that the system of justice to which we have devoted our professional lives cannot do its job without a special dispensation from the safeguards that assure to people of every race the equal protection of the law.

This is a stigma criminal justice practitioners do not deserve. Service in the criminal justice system should be a cause not for shame but for pride. Nowhere is it possible to dedicate one's labors to the welfare of one's fellow human beings with a greater sense that one is needed and that the quality of what one does can make a difference. But to feel this pride, and to deserve it, we must consecrate ourselves to the protection of all people, not a privileged few. We must be servants of humanity, not of caste. Whether or not the Supreme Court demands this of us, we must demand it of ourselves and of our coworkers in the system. For this is the faith to which we are sworn by our common calling: that doing justice is never simply someone else's job; correcting injustice is never simply someone else's responsibility.

DISCUSSION QUESTIONS

1. What did the Baldus study show? Why didn't the Supreme Court think that the results of this study should be used as grounds for overturning Warren McKleskey's sentence? Do you agree with the Court's decision? Why or why not?

2. Formulate Amsterdam's claims into a general argument against capital punishment. How does it compare with the arguments of Hugo Bedau and Albert Camus against this form of punishment? Whose view is stronger, and why?

3. Amsterdam's article raises serious issues about the role of race and racism in the sentencing of criminals. Do these questions of institutionalized racism within the criminal justice system lead you to question the principles that underlie this system? Why? Compare your view with Amsterdam's.

4. What factors other than race might influence the application of the death penalty? Do you think that they are strong enough grounds to argue against the death penalty? What about the charge that "those without the capital get the punishment"? Do you think that the financial or social status of defendants affects the way in which they are sentenced? Reflect on specific cases with which you are familiar (e.g., O. J. Simpson or the Menendez brothers).

5. Think about Bedau's and Amsterdam's use of empirical evidence against the death penalty. In general, to what extent do you believe that contemporary moral controversies like capital punishment can be resolved by appeals to empirical evidence? Explain.

◆ U.S. SUPREME COURT

Furman v. Georgia

In this case, a narrow majority of the U.S. Supreme Court ruled in 1972 that the death penalty, as instituted by many states at the time, was unconstitutional. Two of the five justices making up the majority considered capital punishment to be inherently cruel and excessive. The remaining three ruled that it was unconstitutional only as the various states had implemented it at the time. Justice William Brennan, writing for the majority, states that for a punishment not to be cruel and unusual it "must not by its severity be degrading to human dignity," must not have been "inflicted in a wholly arbitrary fashion," must not be "clearly and totally rejected by society," and must not be unnecessarily severe.

Mr. Justice *Brennan,* concurring.

. . . There are, then, four principles by which we may determine whether a particular punishment is "cruel and unusual." The primary principle, which I believe supplies the essential predicate for the application of the others, is that a punishment must not by its severity be degrading to human dignity. The paradigm violation of this principle would be the infliction of a torturous punishment of the type that the Clause has always prohibited. Yet "[i]t is unlikely that any State at this moment in history," *Robinson v. California,* 370 U.S., at 666, would pass a law providing for the infliction of such a punishment. Indeed, no such punishment has ever been before this Court. The same may be said of the other principles. It is unlikely that this Court will confront a severe punishment that is obviously inflicted in wholly arbitrary fashion; no State would engage in a reign of blind terror. Nor is it likely that this Court will be called upon to review a severe punishment that is clearly and totally rejected throughout society; no legislature would be able even to authorize the infliction of such a punishment. Nor, finally, is it likely that this Court will have to consider a severe punishment that is patently unnecessary; no State today would inflict a severe punishment knowing that there was no reason whatever for doing so. In short, we are unlikely to have occasion to determine that a punishment is fatally offensive under any one principle.

Since the Bill of Rights was adopted, this Court has adjudged only three punishments to be within the prohibition of the Clause. . . . Each punishment, of course, was degrading to human dignity, but of none could it be said conclusively that it was fatally offensive under one or the other of the principles. Rather, these "cruel and unusual punishments" seriously implicated several of the principles, and it was the application of the principles in combination that supported the judgment. That, indeed, is not surprising. The function of these principles, after all, is simply to provide means by which a court can determine whether a challenged punishment comports with human dignity. They are, therefore, interrelated, and in most cases it will be their convergence that will justify the conclusion that a punishment is "cruel and unusual." The test, then, will ordinarily be a cumulative one: If a punishment is unusually severe, if there is a strong probability that it is inflicted arbitrarily, if it is substantially rejected by contemporary society, and if there is no reason to believe that it serves any penal purpose more effectively than some less severe punishment, then the continued infliction of that punishment violates the command of the Clause that the State may not inflict inhuman and uncivilized punishments upon those convicted of crimes.

. . . The question, then, is whether the deliberate infliction of death is today consistent with the command of the Clause that the State may not inflict punishments that do not comport with human dignity. I will analyze the punishment of death in terms of the principles set out above and the cumulative test to which they lead: It is a denial of human dignity for the State arbitrarily to subject a person to an unusually severe punishment that society has indicated it does not regard as acceptable, and that cannot be shown to serve any penal purpose more effectively than a significantly less drastic punishment. Under these principles and this test, death is today a "cruel and unusual" punishment.

Death is a unique punishment in the United States. In a society that so strongly affirms the sanctity of life, not surprisingly the common view is that death is the ultimate sanction. This natural human feeling appears all about us. There has been no national debate about punishment, in general or by imprisonment, comparable to the debate about the punishment of death. No other punishment has been so continuously restricted, . . . nor has any State yet abolished prisons, as some have abolished this punishment. And those States that still inflict death reserve it for the most heinous crimes. Juries, of course, have always treated death cases differently, as have governors exercising their communication powers. Criminal defendants are of the same view. "As all practicing lawyers know, who have defended persons charged with capital offenses, often the only goal possible is to avoid the death penalty." *Griffin v. Illinois,* . . . . Some legislatures have required particular procedures, such as two-stage trials and automatic appeals, applicable only in death cases. "It is the universal experience in the administration of criminal justice that those charged with capital offenses are granted special considerations." . . . This Court, too, almost always treats death cases as a class apart. And the unfortunate effect of this punishment upon the functioning of the judicial process is well known; no other punishment has a similar effect.

The only explanation for the uniqueness of death is its extreme severity. Death is today an unusually severe punishment, unusual in its pain, in its finality, and in its enormity. No other existing punishment is comparable to death in terms of physical and mental suffering. Although our information is not conclusive, it appears that there is no method available that guarantees an immediate and painless death. Since the discontinuance of flogging as a constitutionally permissible punishment, . . . death remains as the only punishment that may involve the conscious infliction of physical pain. In addition, we know that mental pain is an inseparable part of our practice of punishing criminals by

death for the prospect of pending execution exacts a frightful toll during the inevitable long wait between the imposition of sentence and the actual infliction of death. . . . As the California Supreme Court pointed out, "the process of carrying out a verdict of death is often so degrading and brutalizing to the human spirit as to constitute psychological torture." *People v. Anderson,* . . . . Indeed, as Mr. Justice Frankfurter noted, "the onset of insanity while awaiting execution of a death sentence is not a rare phenomenon." *Solesbee v. Balkcom,* . . . . The "fate of ever-increasing fear and distress" to which the expatriate is subjected, *Trop v. Dulles,* . . . can only exist to a greater degree for a person confined in prison awaiting death.

The unusual severity of death is manifested most clearly in its finality and enormity. Death, in these respects, is in a class by itself. Expatriation, for example, is a punishment that "destroys for the individual the political existence that was centuries in the development," that "strips the citizen of his status in the national and international political community," and that puts "[h]is very existence" in jeopardy. Expatriation thus inherently entails "the total destruction of the individual's status in organized society. . . . In short, the expatriate has lost the right to have rights." . . . Yet, demonstrably, expatriation is not "a fate worse than death." . . . Although death, like expatriation, destroys the individual's "political existence" and his "status in organized society," it does more, for, unlike expatriation, death also destroys "[h]is very existence." There is, too, at least the possibility that the expatriate will in the future regain "the right to have rights." Death forecloses even that possibility.

Death is truly an awesome punishment. The calculated killing of a human being by the State involves, by its very nature, a denial of the executed person's humanity. The contrast with the plight of a person punished by imprisonment is evident. An individual in prison does not lose "the right to have rights." A prisoner retains, for example, the constitutional rights to the free exercise of religion, to be free of cruel and unusual punishments, and to treatment as a "person" for purposes of due process of law and the equal protection of the laws. A prisoner remains a member of the human family. Moreover, he retains the right of access to the courts. His punishment is not irrevocable. Apart from the common charge, grounded upon the recognition of human fallibility, that the punishment of death must inevitably be inflicted upon innocent men, we know that death has been the lot of men whose convictions were unconstitutionally secured in view of later, retroactively applied, holdings of this Court. The punishment itself may have been unconstitutionally inflicted, . . . yet the finality of death precludes relief. An executed person has indeed "lost the right to have rights." As one 19th-century proponent of punishing criminals by death declared, "When a man is hung, there is an end of our relations with him. His execution is a way of saying, 'You are not fit for this world, take your chance elsewhere.'"

In comparison to all other punishments today, then, the deliberate extinguishment of human life by the State is uniquely degrading to human dignity. I would not hesitate to hold, on that ground alone, that death is today a "cruel and unusual" punishment, were it not that death is a punishment of longstanding usage and acceptance in this country. I therefore turn to the second principle—that the State may not arbitrarily inflict an unusually severe punishment.

. . . When the punishment of death is inflicted in a trivial number of the cases in which it is legally available, the conclusion is virtually inescapable that it is being inflicted arbitrarily. Indeed, it smacks of little more than a lottery system. The States claim, however, that this rarity is evidence not of arbitrariness, but of informed selectivity: Death is inflicted, they say, only in "extreme" cases.

Informed selectivity, of course, is a value not to be denigrated. Yet presumably the States could make precisely the same claim if there were 10 executions per year, or five, or even if there were but one. That there may be as many as 50 per year does not strengthen the claim. When the rate of infliction is at this low level, it is highly implausible that only the worst criminals or the criminals who commit the worst crimes are selected for this punishment. No one has yet suggested a rational basis that could differentiate in those terms the few who die from the many who go to prison. Crimes and criminals simply do not admit of a distinction that can be drawn so finely as to explain, on that ground, the execution of such a tiny sample of those eligible. Certainly the laws that provide for this punishment do not attempt to draw that distinction; all cases to which the laws apply are necessarily "extreme." Nor is the distinction credible in fact. If, for example, petitioner Furman or his crime illustrates the "extreme," then nearly all murderers and their murders are also "extreme." Furthermore, our pro-

cedures in death cases, rather than resulting in the selection of "extreme" cases for this punishment, actually sanction an arbitrary selection. For this Court has held that juries may, as they do, make the decision whether to impose a death sentence wholly unguided by standards governing that decision. . . . In other words, our procedures are not constructed to guard against the totally capricious selection of criminals for the punishment of death.

Although it is difficult to imagine what further facts would be necessary in order to prove that death is, as my Brother [Justice Potter] Stewart puts it, "wantonly and . . . freakishly" inflicted, I need not conclude that arbitrary infliction is patently obvious. I am not considering this punishment by the isolated light of one principle. The probability of arbitrariness is sufficiently substantial that it can be relied upon, in combination with the other principles, in reaching a judgment on the constitutionality of this punishment.

When there is a strong probability that an unusually severe and degrading punishment is being inflicted arbitrarily, we may well expect that society will disapprove of its infliction. I turn, therefore, to the third principle. An examination of the history and present operation of the American practice of punishing criminals by death reveals that this punishment has been almost totally rejected by contemporary society.

. . . The progressive decline in, and the current rarity of, the infliction of death demonstrate that our society seriously questions the appropriateness of this punishment today. The States point out that many legislatures authorize death as the punishment for certain crimes and that substantial segments of the public, as reflected in opinion polls and referendum votes, continue to support it. Yet the availability of this punishment through statutory authorization, as well as the polls and referenda, which amount simply to approval of that authorization, simply underscores the extent to which our society has in fact rejected this punishment. When an unusually severe punishment is authorized for wide-scale application but not, because of society's refusal, inflicted save in a few instances, the inference is compelling that there is a deep-seated reluctance to inflict it. Indeed, the likelihood is great that the punishment is tolerated only because of its disuse. The objective indicator of society's view of an unusually severe punishment is what society does with it, and today society will inflict death upon only a small sample of the eligible criminals. Rejection could hardly be more complete without becoming absolute. At the very least, I must conclude that contemporary society views this punishment with substantial doubt.

The final principle to be considered is that an unusually severe and degrading punishment may not be excessive in view of the purposes for which it is inflicted. This principle, too, is related to the others. When there is a strong probability that the State is arbitrarily inflicting an unusually severe punishment that is subject to grave societal doubts, it is likely also that the punishment cannot be shown to be serving any penal purpose that could not be served equally well by some less severe punishment.

The States' primary claim is that death is a necessary punishment because it prevents the commission of capital crimes more effectively than any less severe punishment. The first part of this claim is that the infliction of death is necessary to stop the individuals executed from committing further crimes. The sufficient answer to this is that if a criminal convicted of a capital crime poses a danger to society, effective administration of the States' pardon and parole laws can delay or deny his release from prison, and techniques of isolation can eliminate or minimize the danger while he remains confined.

The more significant argument is that the threat of death prevents the commission of capital crimes because it deters potential criminals who would not be deterred by the threat of imprisonment. The argument is not based upon evidence that the threat of death is a superior deterrent. Indeed, as my Brother [Justice Thurgood] Marshall establishes, the available evidence uniformly indicates, although it does not conclusively prove, that the threat of death has no greater deterrent effect than the threat of imprisonment. The States argue, however, that they are entitled to rely upon common human experience, and that experience, they say, supports the conclusion that death must be a more effective deterrent than any less severe punishment. Because people fear death the most, the argument runs, the threat of death must be the greatest deterrent.

It is important to focus upon the precise import of this argument. It is not denied that many, and probably most, capital crimes cannot be deterred by the threat of punishment. Thus the argument can apply only to those who think rationally about the commission of capital crimes. Particularly is that true when the potential criminal, under this argument, must not only consider the risk of punishment, but also distinguish between two possible punishments. The concern, then, is with a particular type of potential criminal, the rational person who will commit a capital crime knowing that the punishment is long-term imprisonment, which may well be for the rest of his life, but will not commit the crime knowing that the punishment is death. On the face of it, the assumption that such persons exist is implausible.

In any event, this argument cannot be appraised in the abstract. We are not presented with the theoretical question whether under any imaginable circumstances the threat of death might be a greater deterrent to the commission of capital crimes than the threat of imprisonment. We are concerned with the practice of punishing criminals by death as it exists in the United States today. Proponents of this argument necessarily admit that its validity depends upon the existence of a system in which the punishment of death is invariably and swiftly imposed. Our system, of course, satisfies neither condition. A rational person contemplating a murder or rape is confronted, not with the certainty of a speedy death, but with the slightest possibility that he will be executed in the distant future. The risk of death is remote and improbable; in contrast, the risk of long-term imprisonment is near and great. In short, whatever the speculative validity of the assumption that the threat of death is a superior deterrent, there is no reason to believe that as currently administered the punishment of death is necessary to deter the commission of capital crimes. Whatever might be the case were all or substantially all eligible criminals quickly put to death, unverifiable possibilities are an insufficient basis upon which to conclude that the threat of death today has any greater deterrent efficacy than the threat of imprisonment.

There is, however, another aspect to the argument that the punishment of death is necessary for the protection of society. The infliction of death, the States urge, serves to manifest the community's outrage at the commission of the crime. It is, they say, a concrete public expression of moral indignation that inculcates respect for the law and helps assure a more peaceful community. Moreover, we are told, not only does the punishment of death exert this widespread moralizing influence upon community values, it also satisfies the popular demand for grievous condemnation of abhorrent crimes and thus prevents disorder, lynching, and attempts by private citizens to take the law into their own hands.

The question, however, is not whether death serves these supposed purposes of punishment, but whether death serves them more effectively than imprisonment. There is no evidence whatever that utilization of imprisonment rather than death encourages private blood feuds and other disorders. Surely if there were such a danger, the execution of a handful of criminals each year would not prevent it. The assertion that death alone is a sufficiently emphatic denunciation for capital crimes suffers from the same defect. If capital crimes require the punishment of death in order to provide moral reinforcement for the basic values of the community, those values can only be undermined when death is so rarely inflicted upon the criminals who commit the crimes. Furthermore, it is certainly doubtful that the infliction of death by the State does in fact strengthen the community's moral code; if the deliberate extinguishment of human life has any effect at all, it more likely tends to lower our respect for life and brutalize our values. That, after all, is why we no longer carry out public executions. In any event, this claim simply means that one purpose of punishment is to indicate social disapproval of crime. To serve that purpose our laws distribute punishments according to the gravity of crimes and punish more severely the crimes society regards as more serious. That purpose cannot justify any particular punishment as the upper limit of severity.

DISCUSSION QUESTIONS

1. How does Justice Brennan tell us to determine whether a punishment is unnecessarily severe? Do you agree with his opinion? What is the result of the application of these criteria to the death penalty? Is it an unnecessarily severe punishment? Why or why not? Do you agree? Explain.
2. Justice Brennan writes that "death is truly an awesome punishment." What does he mean by this? Critically evaluate his claim.
3. How, according to Justice Brennan, do we know whether a punishment has been arbitrarily inflicted?
4. Formulate a definition of cruel and unusual punishment. How would your formulation differ from Justice Brennan's? What are your necessary and sufficient conditions for a punishment to be cruel and unusual? Again, how do they compare to Brennan's? Discuss.
5. To what degree should the morality (or legality) of a punishment depend on society's view of that punishment? What is the position of Justice Brennan on this question? Of Immanuel Kant? Of Albert Camus? Compare and contrast your view with theirs.

U.S. SUPREME COURT

Gregg v. Georgia

In *Gregg v. Georgia* (1976), the majority of the Supreme Court agreed that the death penalty is not "cruel and unusual" because, in part, it is consistent with the "evolving standards of decency that mark the progress of a civilized society." In short, the majority held that the death penalty is not "cruel and unusual" because society, as it becomes more and more advanced, has decided that capital punishment is morally acceptable. The majority also concurred that the death penalty serves both a retributive and a deterrent purpose and, in the case under consideration, was not arbitrarily applied. In his dissent, Justice Thurgood Marshall argues that the death penalty is excessive (a lesser penalty such as life imprisonment would serve just as well), is not necessarily a deterrent, and is not retributive (the death penalty is not consistent with human dignity). Marshall was the first African-American to be appointed to the Supreme Court.

The issue in this case is whether the imposition of the sentence of death for the crime of murder under the law of Georgia violates the Eighth and Fourteenth Amendments.

I

The petitioner, Troy Gregg, was charged with committing armed robbery and murder. In accordance with Georgia procedure in capital cases, the trial was in two stages, a guilt stage and a sentencing stage. . . .
. . . The jury found the petitioner guilty of two counts of murder.

At the penalty stage, which took place before the same jury, . . . the trial judge instructed the jury that it could recommend either a death sentence or a life prison sentence on each count. . . . The jury returned verdicts of death on each count.

The Supreme Court of Georgia affirmed the convictions and the imposition of the death sentences for murder. . . . The death sentences imposed for armed robbery, however, were vacated on the grounds that the death penalty had rarely been imposed in Georgia for that offense. . . .

II

. . . The Georgia statute, as amended after our decision in *Furman v. Georgia* (1972), retains the death penalty for six categories of crime: murder, kidnapping for ransom or where the victim is harmed, armed robbery, rape, treason, and aircraft hijacking. . . .

III

We address initially the basic contention that the punishment of death for the crime of murder is, under all circumstances, "cruel and unusual" in violation of the Eighth and Fourteenth Amendments of the Constitution. In part IV of this opinion, we will consider the sentence of death imposed under the Georgia statutes at issue in this case.

The Court on a number of occasions has both assumed and asserted the constitutionality of capital punishment. In several cases that assumption provided a necessary foundation for the decision, as the Court was asked to decide whether a particular method of carrying out a capital sentence would be allowed to stand under the Eighth Amendment. But until *Furman v. Georgia* (1972), the Court never confronted squarely the fundamental claim that the punishment of death always, regardless of the enormity of the offense or the procedure followed in imposing the sentence, is cruel and unusual punishment in violation of the Constitution. Although this issue was presented and addressed in *Furman*, it was not resolved by the Court. Four Justices would have held that capital punishment is not unconstitutional *per se*; two Justices would have reached the opposite conclusion; and three Justices, while agreeing that the statutes then before the Court were invalid as applied, left open the question whether such punishment may ever be imposed. We now hold that the punishment of death does not invariably violate the Constitution.

A

The history of the prohibition of "cruel and unusual" punishment already has been reviewed at length. The phrase first appeared in the English Bill of Rights of 1689, which was drafted by Parliament at the accession of William and Mary. The English version appears to have been directed against punishments unauthorized by statute and beyond the jurisdiction of the sentencing court, as well as those disproportionate to the offense involved. The American draftsmen, who adopted the English phrasing in drafting the Eighth Amendment, were primarily concerned, however, with proscribing "tortures" and other "barbarous" methods of punishment.

In the earliest cases raising Eighth Amendment claims, the Court focused on particular methods of execution to determine whether they were too cruel to pass constitutional muster. The constitutionality of the sentence of death itself was not at issue, and the criterion used to evaluate the mode of execution was its similarity to "torture" and other "barbarous" methods. . . .

But the Court has not confined the prohibition embodied in the Eighth Amendment to "barbarous" methods that were generally outlawed in the 18th century. Instead, the Amendment has been interpreted in a flexible and dynamic manner. The Court early recognized that "a principle to be vital must be capable of wider application than the mischief which gave it birth." Thus the clause forbidding "cruel and unusual" punishments "is not fastened to the obsolete but may acquire meaning as public opinion becomes enlightened by a humane justice." . . .

It is clear from the foregoing precedents that the Eighth Amendment has not been regarded as a static concept. As Mr. Chief Justice Warren said, in an oftquoted phrase, "[t]he Amendment must draw its meaning from the evolving standards of decency that mark the progress of a maturing society." Thus, an assessment of contemporary values concerning the infliction of a challenged sanction is relevant to the application of the Eighth Amendment. As we develop below more fully, this assessment does not call for a subjective judgment. It requires, rather, that we look to objective indicia that reflect the public attitude toward a given sanction.

But our cases also make clear that public perceptions of standards of decency with respect to criminal sanctions are not conclusive. A penalty also must accord with "the dignity of man," which is the "basic concept underlying the Eighth Amendment." This means, at least, that the punishment not be "excessive." When a form of punishment in the abstract (in this case, whether capital punishment may ever be imposed as a sanction for murder) rather than in the particular (the propriety of death as a penalty to be applied to a specific defendant for a specific crime) is under consideration, the inquiry into "excessiveness" has two aspects. First, the punishment must not involve the unnecessary and wanton infliction of pain. Second, the punishment must not be grossly out of proportion to the severity of the crime.

B

Of course, the requirements of the Eighth Amendment must be applied with an awareness of the limited role to be played by the courts. This does not mean that judges have no role to play, for the Eighth Amendment is a restraint upon the exercise of legislative power. . . .

But, while we have an obligation to ensure that constitutional bounds are not over-reached, we may not act as judges as we might as legislators. . . .

Therefore, in assessing a punishment selected by a democratically elected legislature against the constitutional measure, we presume its validity. We may not require the legislature to select the least severe penalty possible so long as the penalty selected is not cruelly inhumane or disproportionate to the crime involved. And a heavy burden rests on those who would attack the judgment of the representatives of the people.

This is true in part because the constitutional test is intertwined with an assessment of contemporary standards and the legislative judgment weighs heavily in ascertaining such standards. "[I]n a democratic society legislatures, not courts, are constituted to respond to the will and consequently the moral values of the people."

The deference we owe to the decisions of the state legislatures under our federal system is enhanced where the specification of punishments is concerned, for "these are peculiarly questions of legislative policy." Caution is necessary lest this Court become, "under the aegis of the Cruel and Unusual Punishment Clause, the ultimate arbiter of the standards of criminal responsibility . . . throughout the country." A decision that a given punishment is impermissible under the Eighth Amendment cannot be reversed short of a constitutional amendment. The ability of the people to express their preference through the normal democratic processes, as well as through ballot referenda, is shut off. Revisions cannot be made in the light of further experience.

C

In the discussion to this point we have sought to identify the principles and considerations that guide a court in addressing an Eighth Amendment claim. We now consider specifically whether the sentence of death for the crime of murder is a *per se* violation of the Eighth and Fourteenth Amendments to the Constitution. We note first that history and precedent strongly support a negative answer to this question.

The imposition of the death penalty for the crime of murder has a long history of acceptance both in the United States and in England. . . .

It is apparent from the text of the Constitution itself that the existence of capital punishment was accepted by the Framers. At the time the Eighth Amendment was ratified, capital punishment was a common sanction in every State. Indeed, the First Congress of the United States enacted legislation providing death as the penalty for specified crimes. . . .

For nearly two centuries, this Court, repeatedly and often expressly, has recognized that capital punishment is not invalid *per se*. . . .

Four years ago, the petitioners in *Furman* and its companion cases predicated their argument primarily upon the asserted proposition that standards of decency had evolved to the point where capital punishment no longer could be tolerated. The petitioners in those cases said, in effect, that the evolutionary process had come to an end, and that standards of decency required that the Eighth Amendment be construed finally as prohibiting capital punishment for any crime regardless of its depravity and impact on society. This view was accepted by two Justices. Three other Justices were unwilling to go so far; focusing on the procedures by which convicted defendants were selected for the death penalty rather than on the actual punishment inflicted, they joined in the conclusion that the statutes before the Court were constitutionally invalid.

The petitioners in the capital cases before the Court today renew the "standards of decency" argument, but developments during the four years since *Furman* have undercut substantially the assumptions upon which their argument rested. Despite the continuing debate, dating back to the nineteenth century, over the morality and utility of capital punishment, it is now evident that a large proportion of American society continues to regard it as an appropriate and necessary criminal sanction.

The most marked indication of society's endorsement of the death penalty for murder is the legislative response to *Furman*. The legislatures of at least thirty-five States have enacted new statutes that provide for the death penalty for at least some crimes that result in the death of another person. And the Congress of the United States, in 1974, enacted a statute providing the death penalty for aircraft piracy that results in death. These recently adopted statutes have attempted to address the concerns expressed by the Court in *Furman* primarily (i) by specifying the factors to be weighed and the procedures to be followed in deciding when to impose a capital sentence, or (ii) by making the death penalty mandatory for specified crimes. But all of the post-*Furman* statutes make clear that capital

punishment itself has not been rejected by the elected representatives of the people. . . .

The jury also is a significant and reliable objective index of contemporary values because it is so directly involved. The Court has said that "one of the most important functions any jury can perform in making . . . a selection [between life imprisonment and death for a defendant convicted in a capital case] is to maintain a link between contemporary community values and the penal system." It may be true that evolving standards have influenced juries in recent decades to be more discriminating in imposing the sentence of death. But the relative infrequency of jury verdicts imposing death sentence does not indicate rejection of capital punishment *per se*. Rather, the reluctance of juries in many cases to impose the sentence may well reflect the humane feeling that this most irrevocable of sanctions should be reserved for a small number of extreme cases. Indeed, the actions of juries in many states since *Furman* are fully compatible with the legislative judgments, reflected in the new statutes, as to the continued utility and necessity of capital punishment in appropriate cases. At the close of 1974 at least 254 persons had been sentenced to death since *Furman*, and by the end of March 1976, more than 460 persons were subject to death sentences.

As we have seen, however, the Eighth Amendment demands more than that a challenged punishment be acceptable to contemporary society. The Court also must ask whether it comports with the basic concept of human dignity at the core of the amendment. Although we cannot "invalidate a category of penalties because we deem less severe penalties adequate to serve the ends of penology," the sanction imposed cannot be so totally without penological justification that it results in the gratuitous infliction of suffering.

The death penalty is said to serve two principal social purposes: retribution and deterrence of capital crimes by prospective offenders.

In part, capital punishment is an expression of society's moral outrage at particularly offensive conduct. This function may be unappealing to many, but it is essential in an ordered society that asks its citizens to rely on legal processes rather than self-help to vindicate their wrongs.

The instinct for retribution is part of the nature of man, and channeling that instinct in the administration of criminal justice serves an important purpose in promoting the stability of a society governed by law. When people begin to believe that organized society is unwilling or unable to impose upon criminal offenders the punishment they "deserve," then there are sown the seeds of anarchy—of self-help, vigilante justice, and lynch law. *Furman v. Georgia* (Stewart, J., concurring).

Retribution is no longer the dominant objective of the criminal law, but neither is it a forbidden objective nor one inconsistent with our respect for the dignity of men. Indeed, the decision that capital punishment may be the appropriate sanction in extreme cases is an expression of the community's belief that certain crimes are themselves so grievous an affront to humanity that the only adequate response may be the penalty of death.

Statistical attempts to evaluate the worth of the death penalty as a deterrent to crimes of potential offenders have occasioned a great deal of debate. The results simply have been inconclusive. . . .

Although some of the studies suggest that the death penalty may not function as a significantly greater deterrent than lesser penalties, there is no convincing empirical evidence either supporting or refuting this view. We may nevertheless assume safely that there are murderers, such as those who act in passion, for whom the threat of death has little or no deterrent effect. But for many others, the death penalty undoubtedly is a significant deterrent. There are carefully contemplated murders, such as murder for hire, where the possible penalty of death may well enter into the cold calculus that precedes the decision to act. And there are some categories of murder, such as murder by a life prisoner, where other sanctions may not be adequate.

The value of capital punishment as a deterrent of crime is a complex factual issue the resolution of which properly rests with the legislatures, which can evaluate the results of statistical studies in terms of their own local conditions and with a flexibility of approach that is not available to the courts. Indeed, many of the post-*Furman* statutes reflect just such a responsible effort to define those crimes and those criminals for which capital punishment is most probably an effective deterrent.

In sum, we cannot say that the judgment of the Georgia Legislature that capital punishment may be necessary in some cases is clearly wrong. Considerations of federalism, as well as respect for the ability of a legislature to evaluate, in terms of its particular State, the moral consensus concerning the death penalty and its social utility as a sanction, require us to conclude, in the absence of more convincing evidence, that the infliction of death as a punishment for murder is not without justification and thus is not constitutionally severe.

Finally, we must consider whether the punishment of death is disproportionate in relation to the crime for which it is imposed. There is no question that death as a punishment is unique in its severity and irrevocability. When a defendant's life is at stake, the Court has been particularly sensitive to insure that every safeguard is observed. But we are concerned here only with the imposition of capital punishment for the crime of murder, and when a life has been taken deliberately by the offender, we cannot say that the punishment is invariably disproportionate to the crime. It is an extreme sanction, suitable to the most extreme of crimes.

We hold that the death penalty is not a form of punishment that may never be imposed, regardless of the circumstances of the offense, regardless of the character of the offender, and regardless of the procedure followed in reaching the decision to impose it.

IV

We now consider whether Georgia may impose the death penalty on the petitioner in this case.

A

While *Furman* did not hold that the infliction of the death penalty *per se* violates the Constitution's ban on cruel and unusual punishments, it did recognize that the penalty of death is different in kind from any other punishment imposed under our system of criminal justice. Because of the uniqueness of the death penalty, *Furman* held that it could not be imposed under sentencing procedures that created a substantial risk that it would be inflicted in an arbitrary and capricious manner. . . .

Furman mandates that where discretion is afforded a sentencing body on a matter so grave as the determination of whether a human life should be taken or spared, that discretion must be suitably directed and limited so as to minimize the risk of wholly arbitrary and capricious action.

It is certainly not a novel proposition that discretion in the area of sentencing be exercised in an informed manner. We have long recognized that "[f]or the determination of sentences, justice generally requires . . . that there be taken into account the circumstances of the offense together with the character and propensities of the offender." . . .

Jury sentencing has been considered desirable in capital cases in order "to maintain a link between contemporary community values and the penal system—a link without which the determination of punishment could hardly reflect 'the evolving standards of decency that mark the progress of a maturing society.' " But it creates special problems. Much of the information that is relevant to the sentencing decision may have no relevance to the question of guilt, or may even be extremely prejudicial to a fair determination of that question. This problem, however, is scarcely insurmountable. Those who have studied the question suggest that a bifurcated procedure—one in which the question of sentence is not considered until the determination of guilt has been made—is the best answer. . . . When a human life is at stake and when the jury must have information prejudicial to the question of guilt but relevant to the question of penalty in order to impose a rational sentence, a bifurcated system is more likely to ensure elimination of the constitutional deficiencies identified in *Furman.*

But the provision of relevant information under fair procedural rules is not alone sufficient to guarantee that the information will be properly used in the imposition of punishment, especially if sentencing is performed by a jury. Since the members of a jury will have had little, if any, previous experience in sentencing, they are unlikely to be skilled in dealing with the information they are given. To the extent that this problem is inherent in jury sentencing, it may not be totally correctable. It seems clear, however, that the problem will be alleviated if the jury is given guidance regarding the factors about the crime and the defendant that the State, representing organized society, deems particularly relevant to the sentencing decision. . . .

While some have suggested that standards to guide a capital jury's sentencing deliberations are impossible to formulate, the fact is that such standards have been developed. When the drafters of the Model Penal Code faced this problem, they concluded "that it is within the realm of possibility to point to the main circumstances of aggravation and of mitigation that should be weighed *and weighed against each other* when they are presented in a concrete case." While such standards are by necessity somewhat general, they do provide guidance to the sentencing authority and thereby reduce the likelihood that it will impose a sentence that fairly can be called capricious or arbitrary. Where the sentencing authority is required to specify the factors it relied upon in reaching its decision, the further safeguard of meaningful appellate review is available to ensure that death sentences are not imposed capriciously or in a freakish manner.

In summary, the concerns expressed in *Furman* that the penalty of death not be imposed in an arbitrary or capricious manner can be met by a carefully drafted statute that ensures that the sentencing authority is given adequate information and guidance. As a general proposition these concerns are best met by a system that provides for a bifurcated proceeding at which the sentencing authority is apprised of the information relevant to the imposition of sentence and provided with standards to guide its use of the information.

We do not intend to suggest that only the above-described procedures would be permissible under *Furman* or that any sentencing system constructed along these general lines would inevitably satisfy the concerns of *Furman,* for each distinct system must be examined on an individual basis. Rather, we have embarked upon this general exposition to make clear that it is possible to construct capital-sentencing systems capable of meeting *Furman*'s constitutional concerns.

B

We now turn to consideration of the constitutionality of Georgia's capital-sentencing procedures. In the wake of *Furman,* Georgia amended its capital punishment statute, but chose not to narrow the scope of its murder provisions. Thus, now as before *Furman,* in Georgia "[a] person commits murder when he unlawfully and with malice aforethought, either express or implied, causes the death of another human being." All persons convicted of murder "shall be punished by death or by imprisonment for life."

Georgia did act, however, to narrow the class of murderers subject to capital punishment by specifying ten statutory aggravating circumstances, one of which must be found by the jury to exist beyond a reasonable doubt before a death sentence can ever be imposed. In addition, the jury is authorized to consider any other appropriate aggravating or mitigating circumstances. The jury is not required to find any mitigating circumstance in order to make a recommendation of mercy that is binding on the trial court, but it must find a *statutory* aggravating circumstance before recommending a sentence of death.

These procedures require the jury to consider the circumstances of the crime and the criminal before it recommends sentence. No longer can a Georgia jury do as *Furman*'s jury did: reach a finding of the defendant's guilt and then, without guidance or direction, decide whether he should live or die. Instead, the jury's attention is directed to the specific circumstances of the crime: Was it committed in the course of another capital felony? Was it committed for money? Was it committed on a peace officer or judicial officer? Was it committed in a particularly heinous way or in a manner that endangered the lives of many persons? In addition, the jury's attention is focused on the characteristics of the person who committed the crime: Does he have a record of prior convictions for capital offenses? Are there any special facts about this defendant that mitigate against imposing capital punishment (e.g., his youth, the extent of his cooperation with the police, his emotional state at the time of the crime)? As a result, while some jury discretion still exists, "the discretion to be exercised is controlled by clear and objective standards so as to produce nondiscriminatory application."

As an important additional safeguard against arbitrariness and caprice, the Georgia statutory scheme provides for automatic appeal of all death sentences to the State's Supreme Court. That court is required by statute to review each sentence of death and determine whether it was imposed under the influence of passion or prejudice, whether the evidence supports the jury's finding of statutory aggravating circumstance, and whether the sentence is disproportionate compared to those sentences imposed in similar cases.

In short, Georgia's new sentencing procedures require as a prerequisite to the imposition of the death penalty, specific jury findings as to the circumstances of the crime or the character of the defendant. Moreover, to guard further against a situation comparable to that presented in *Furman*, the Supreme Court of Georgia compares each death sentence with the sentences imposed on similarly situated defendants to ensure that the sentence of death in a particular case is not disproportionate. On their face these procedures seem to satisfy the concerns of *Furman*. No longer should there be "no meaningful basis for distinguishing the few cases in which [the death penalty] is imposed from the many cases in which it is not." . . .

V

The basic concern of *Furman* centered on those defendants who were being condemned to death capriciously and arbitrarily. Under the procedures before the Court in that case, sentencing authorities were not directed to give attention to the nature or circumstances of the crime committed or to the character or record of the defendant. Left unguided, juries imposed the death sentence in a way that could only be called freakish. The new Georgia sentencing procedures, by contrast, focus the jury's attention on the particularized nature of the crime and the particularized characteristics of the individual defendant. While the jury is permitted to consider any aggravating or mitigating circumstances, it must find and identify at least one statutory aggravating factor before it may impose a penalty of death. In this way the jury's discretion is channeled. No longer can a jury wantonly and freakishly impose the death sentence; it is always circumscribed by the legislative guidelines. In addition, the review function of the Supreme Court of Georgia affords additional assurance that the concerns that prompted our decision in *Furman* are not present to any significant degree in the Georgia procedure applied here.

For the reasons expressed in this opinion, we hold that the statutory system under which Gregg was sentenced to death does not violate the Constitution. Accordingly, the judgment of the Georgia Supreme Court is affirmed.

DISSENTING OPINION

In *Furman v. Georgia* (1972) (concurring opinion), I set forth at some length my views on the basic issue presented to the Court in [this case]. The death penalty, I concluded, is a cruel and unusual punishment prohibited by the Eighth and Fourteenth Amendments. That continues to be my view.

I have no intention of retracing the "long and tedious journey" that led to my conclusion in *Furman*. My sole purposes here are to consider the suggestion that my conclusion in *Furman* has been undercut by developments since then, and briefly to evaluate the basis for my Brethren's holding that the extinction of life is a permissible form of punishment under the Cruel and Unusual Punishments Clause.

In *Furman*, I concluded that the death penalty is constitutionally invalid for two reasons. First, the death penalty is excessive. And second, the American people, fully informed as to the purposes of the death penalty and its liabilities, would in my view reject it as morally unacceptable.

Since the decision in *Furman*, the legislatures of thirty-five States have enacted new statutes authorizing the imposition of the death sentence for certain crimes, and Congress has enacted a law providing the death penalty for air piracy resulting in death. I would be less than candid if I did not acknowledge that these developments have a significant bearing on a realistic assessment of the moral acceptability of the death penalty to the American people. But if the constitutionality of the death penalty turns, as I have urged, on the opinion of an *informed* citizenry, then even the enactment of new death statutes cannot be viewed as conclusive. In *Furman,* I observed that the American people are largely unaware of the information critical to a judgment on the morality of the death penalty, and concluded that if they were better informed they would consider it shocking, unjust, and unacceptable. A recent study, conducted after the enactment of the post-*Furman* statutes, has confirmed that the American people know little about the death penalty, and that the opinions of an informed public would differ significantly from those of a public unaware of the consequences and effects of the death penalty.

Even assuming, however, that the post-*Furman* enactment of statutes authorizing the death penalty renders the prediction of the views of an informed citizenry an uncertain basis for a constitutional decision, the enactment of those statutes has no bearing whatsoever on the conclusion that the death penalty is unconstitutional because it is excessive. An excessive penalty is invalid under the Cruel and Unusual Punishments Clause "even though popular sentiment may favor" it. The inquiry here, then, is simply whether the death penalty is necessary to accomplish the legitimate legislative purposes in punishment, or whether a less severe penalty—life imprisonment—would do as well.

The two purposes that sustain the death penalty as nonexcessive in the Court's view are general deterrence and retribution. In *Furman,* I canvassed the relevant data on the deterrent effect of capital punishment. The state of knowledge at that point, after literally centuries of debate, was summarized as follows by a United Nations Committee:

> It is generally agreed between the retentionists and abolitionists, whatever their opinions about the validity of comparative studies of deterrence, that the data which now exist show no correlation between the existence of capital punishment and lower rates of capital crime.

The available evidence, I concluded in *Furman,* was convincing that "capital punishment is not necessary as a deterrent to crime in our society." . . .

The evidence I reviewed in *Furman* remains convincing, in my view, that "capital punishment is not necessary as a deterrent to crime in our society." The justification for the death penalty must be found elsewhere.

The other principal purpose said to be served by the death penalty is retribution. The notion that retribution can serve as a moral justification for the sanction of death finds credence in the opinion of my Brothers [Justices Potter] Stewart, [Lewis] Powell, and [John Paul] Stevens. . . . It is this notion that I find to be the most disturbing aspect of today's unfortunate [decision].

The concept of retribution is a multifaceted one, and any discussion of its role in the criminal law must be undertaken with caution. On one level, it can be said that the notion of retribution or reprobation is the basis of our insistence that only those who have broken the law be punished, and in this sense the notion is quite obviously central to a just system of criminal sanctions. But our recognition that retribution plays a crucial role in determining who may be punished by no means requires approval of retribution as a general justification for punishment. It is the question whether retribution can provide a moral justification for punishment—in particular, capital punishment—that we must consider.

My Brothers Stewart, Powell, and Stevens offer the following explanation of the retributive justification for capital punishments:

> The instinct for retribution is part of the nature of man, and channeling that instinct in the administration of criminal justice serves an important purpose in promoting the stability of a society governed by law. When people begin to believe that organized society is unwilling or unable to impose upon criminal offenders the punishment they "deserve," then there are sown the seeds of anarchy—of self-help, vigilante justice, and lynch law.

This statement is wholly inadequate to justify the death penalty. As my Brother [Justice William] Brennan stated in *Furman,* "[t]here is no evidence whatever that utilization of imprisonment rather than death encourages private blood feuds and other disorders." It simply defies belief to suggest that the death penalty is necessary to prevent the American people from taking the law into their own hands.

In a related vein, it may be suggested that the expression of moral outrage through the imposition of the death penalty serves to reinforce basic moral values—that it marks some crimes as particularly offensive and therefore to be avoided. The argument is akin to a deterrence argument, but differs in that it contemplates the individual's shrinking from antisocial conduct, not because he fears punishment, but because he has been told in the strongest possible way that the conduct is wrong. This contention, like the previous one, provides no support for the death penalty. It is inconceivable that any individual concerned about conforming his conduct to what society says is "right" would fail to realize that murder is "wrong" if the penalty were simply life imprisonment.

The foregoing contentions—that society's expression of moral outrage through the imposition of the death penalty preempts the citizenry from taking the law into its own hands and reinforces moral values—are not retributive in the purest sense. They are essentially utilitarian in that they portray the death penalty as valuable because of its beneficial results. These justifications for the death penalty are inadequate because the penalty is, quite clearly I think, not necessary to the accomplishment of those results.

There remains for consideration, however, what might be termed the purely retributive justification for the death penalty—that the death penalty is appropriate, not because of its beneficial effect on society, but because the taking of the murderer's life is itself morally good. Some of the language of the opinion of my Brothers Stewart, Powell, and Stevens . . . appears positively to embrace this notion of retribution for its own sake as a justification for capital punishment. They state:

> [T]he decision that capital punishment may be the appropriate sanction in extreme cases is an expression of the community's belief that certain crimes are themselves so grievous an affront to humanity that the only adequate response may be the penalty of death.

They then quote with approval from Lord Justice Denning's remarks before the British Royal Commission on Capital Punishment:

> The truth is that some crimes are so outrageous that society insists on adequate punishment, because the wrong-doer deserves it, irrespective of whether it is a deterrent or not.

Of course, it may be that these statements are intended as no more than observations as to the popular demands that it is thought must be responded to in order to prevent anarchy. But the implication of the statements appears to me to be quite different—namely, that society's judgment that the murderer "deserves" death must be respected not simply because the preservation of order requires it, but because it is appropriate that society make the judgment and carry it out. It is the latter notion, in particular, that I consider to be fundamentally at odds with the Eighth Amendment. The mere fact that the community demands the murderer's life in return for the evil he has done cannot sustain the death penalty, for as Justices Stewart, Powell, and Stevens remind us, "the Eighth Amendment demands more than that a challenged punishment be acceptable to contemporary society." To be sustained under the Eighth Amendment, the death penalty must "compor[t] with the basic concept of human dignity at the core of the Amendment"; the objective in imposing it must be "[consistent] with our respect for the dignity of [other] men." Under these standards, the taking of life "because the wrongdoer deserves it" surely must fail, for such a punishment has as its very basis the total denial of the wrongdoer's dignity and worth.

The death penalty, unnecessary to promote the goal of deterrence or to further any legitimate notion of retribution, is an excessive penalty forbidden by the Eighth and Fourteenth Amendments. I respectfully dissent from the Court's judgment upholding the [sentence] of death imposed upon the [petitioner in this case].

DISCUSSION QUESTIONS

1. How might we determine conclusively that the death penalty deters criminals better than life imprisonment? Explain.
2. Compare and contrast the majority opinion with Justice Marshall's as to whether the death penalty is cruel and unusual punishment. Whose position do you favor, and why?
3. What protections against the arbitrary application of the death penalty do the justices suggest? Do you believe that they would work? Would Anthony Amsterdam believe that they would work? Defend your view.
4. What is an excessive punishment? What does the Supreme Court say? Compare your view with the majority and minority opinions of the Court.

5. Compare the majority opinions in *Furman v. Georgia* and *Gregg v. Georgia*. What are the similarities? The differences?
6. Critically examine Justice Marshall's dissenting opinion. What are the weaknesses of his opinion? What are its strengths? Be specific, and defend your view.

MEDIA GALLERY

 CRIME AND PUNISHMENT

By Fyodor Dostoyevsky

Scene summary: One of the major events in Dostoyevsky's novel *Crime and Punishment* involves Raskolnikov's murder of Alena Ivanovna. Raskolnikov is a reclusive student living in a garret in St. Petersburg and attempting to retain his dignity in the midst of poverty. He habitually visits Alena Ivanovna, a miserly pawnbroker who ruthlessly cheats poor people out of their money. After visiting Ivanovna one day to pawn a ring, Raskolnikov overhears some men talking about her. "I swear I could kill that damned old woman and rob her, without a single twinge of conscience," one man states. "Kill her, take her money, and with the help of it devote oneself to the service of humanity and the good of all. What do you think, would not one tiny crime be wiped out by thousands of good deeds?" Although Raskolnikov realizes that the speaker is not serious about committing murder, he finds the justifications he needs to plot the crime himself. He returns home and sleeps for hours in an illness-induced stupor. When he awakens, Raskolnikov decides that he will murder the old woman. He arrives at her apartment without anyone noticing. Although the elderly woman is skeptical of the reasons for his unannounced visit, she allows the young man to enter. While she examines a cigarette case that Raskolnikov has brought as a distraction, he hits her over the head repeatedly with the ax that he hid in his coat. He then steals her key and opens the chest containing her wealth. As he fills his pockets, he hears someone entering the apartment. It is Alena's sister, Lizaveta. To cover his tracks, Raskolnikov murders Lizaveta. He then evades suspicious clients of Alena and returns home.

Fyodor Dostoyevsky (1821–1881) was one of Russia's greatest writers. His novels and short stories are known for their penetrating examination of the human condition, particularly its darker aspects. *Crime and Punishment* (1866), generally considered to be his first major novel, has been adapted to film a number of times. Dostoyevsky's other works include *The House of the Dead* (1861–62), *Notes from Underground* (1864), *The Idiot* (1868–69), *The Possessed* (1872), and *The Brothers Karamozov* (1879–80).

1. How should Raskolnikov be punished for his actions? Is the death penalty the appropriate punishment for the murder of Alena? For the murder of Lizaveta? Why or why not?
2. Raskolnikov believes that, because Alena Ivanovna brings misery to many people, her murder is morally justifiable. Is Raskolnikov correct? What if Alena were a cruel dictator who made many people's lives miserable? Would this affect your position on the morality of Raskolnikov's actions?
3. Does the misery that Alena brought about affect your view of the punishment Raskolnikov should receive? What if Alena were the dictator described above? Would this alter your view of the appropriate punishment for the murderer? Discuss.
4. What do you think a Kantian would say is the just punishment for Raskolnikov? Compare the Kantian position with a utilitarian position. Which do you believe is the better position, and why?

SACCO AND VANZETTI

(France/Italy, 1971) 2 hours
Directed by Giuliano Montaldo

Film summary: This film is based on the true story of Nicola Sacco and Bartolomeo Vanzetti, two Italian immigrants and acknowledged anarchists who were tried and executed for murder in 1920s America. Some consider their case to be a flagrant miscarriage of justice and the two men to be political martyrs; others regard the case as simply the proper administration of justice. In April 1920, two men were shot and killed in South Braintree, Massachusetts. One was the paymaster for a shoe company in that city, and the other was his guard. The murderers escaped with $15,000. Witnesses claimed that the murderers were two Italian men, and police arrested Sacco and Vanzetti for the crime. Even though both were anarchists and draft dodgers who carried firearms and made false statements upon arrest, neither had a prior criminal record, nor was there any evidence that they had the $15,000 in their possession. Nevertheless, in July 1921, they were found guilty of the crimes and sentenced to death. Much of the evidence used against them in the trial was later discredited, as was Judge Webster Thayer's handling of their trial. Demonstrations were organized worldwide by people who regarded Sacco and Vanzetti as innocent, but they were denied their appeal for a retrial and were executed in August 1927. Their guilt or innocence has been the subject of many books. The general consensus now is that, while Sacco may have been guilty, Vanzetti was innocent. In 1961, ballistics tests showed that the gun found on Sacco was probably the one used to kill the guard. The folk-singer and social and political activist Joan Baez sings the title song for the movie version of their story.

1. Was the execution of Sacco and Vanzetti morally right? Defend your view.
2. Would a utilitarian justify the use of the death penalty in this case? Support your position.
3. Would a retributivist justify the use of the death penalty in this case? Support your position.
4. What is the strongest justification for the execution of Sacco and Vanzetti? Defend your view.

 DEAD MAN WALKING *

(USA, 1995) 2 hours 2 minutes
Directed by Tim Robbins

Film summary: This movie is based on a true story about the relationship between Sister Helen Prejean (Susan Sarandon), a nun who lives and works with low-income people in New Orleans, and Matthew Poncelet (Sean Penn), a man convicted of kidnapping, raping, and murdering a young couple. Poncelet sends Sister Helen letters from death row asking for assistance. The nun visits him in prison, where she learns over the course of a number of meetings with him the horrifying details of his crime. Poncelet and a friend were high on drugs and drunk when a young couple parked their car in a secluded area nearby. Poncelet claims that he didn't kill either victim and that his accomplice was the real killer. During the course of the film, we learn that, while he indeed did not kill them, Poncelet was responsible for their brutalization. He is in need of legal help and spiritual support, and he believes that Sister Helen is the only person to whom he can

---

*Another contemporary film on capital punishment that is comparable to this one, though a bit more difficult to find, is Krzysztof Kieslowski's *A Short Film About Killing* (1988).

turn. Sister Helen grapples with this situation as her anti–death penalty beliefs conflict with her feelings for the victims and those who grieve for them. We see Sister Helen develop an empathic relationship with Poncelet even though he shows little or no remorse for his crimes. In fact, a district attorney in the film calls Poncelet "an unfeeling, perverse misfit." He is from a working-class background and is presented as a racist, arrogant, and uneducated. As the time of Poncelet's execution nears, Sister Helen and lawyer Hilton Barber (Robert Prosky) work to save him from death. The movie, based on a book of the same title by Sister Helen Prejean, effectively presents both sides of the death penalty debate.

1. "Ain't nobody with money on death row," says Poncelet in *Dead Man Walking*. He claims that the reason he is going to be executed is because he was too poor to hire a lawyer who could have gotten him a lesser sentence. What role do you think that wealth and/or class plays in the application of the death penalty? Do you think that Poncelet should have received a lesser sentence? Critics of the death penalty have noted that it is applied in a racist and classist manner. Should we support the death penalty even though poor people and people of color tend to be disproportionately targeted by its application?
2. Sister Helen's actions suggest that for her there is no moral difference between the state executing a murderer and an individual committing a murder. Both actions involve the taking of a life and so are morally reprehensible. Do you agree with her? Why or why not?
3. Sister Helen has a difficult time reconciling her anti–death penalty belief with her feelings for the victims of the crime and those who grieve for them. But ultimately her anti–death penalty sentiments hold sway. Why do you think she comes to this conclusion? Would you come to the same conclusion? Should we, like Sister Helen, "turn the other cheek" and forgive, or should we pursue justice based on the principle of an "eye for an eye"? Discuss.
4. What might Justice Thurgood Marshall (see *Gregg v. Georgia*) say about the execution of Poncelet? Does the case of Poncelet strengthen or weaken Marshall's general position on the death penalty? How?
5. Is the execution of Poncelet "cruel and unusual" punishment according to Justice William Brennan's conception of "cruel and unusual" punishment? Why or why not? Do you agree?

 THE GREEN MILE

(USA, 1999) 3 hours
Directed by Frank Darabont

Film summary: The Green Mile is set in 1935 on death row at Cold Mountain Correctional Facility, a prison in the southern United States. The film's title refers to the prison's terminology for death row, because the trip to the electric chair is called "walking the mile" and the tile of the death row cell block is a dark green. The cell block's head guard, Paul Edgecombe (Tom Hanks), develops a relationship with one of the inmates, John Coffey (Michael Clarke Duncan), a black man convicted of the gruesome murder of two little girls. Coffey is physically imposing but gentle in nature. When the guards learn that Coffey is innocent, they are faced with a moral dilemma: Should they perform their duty and execute an innocent man, or should they refuse to carry out the execution? They decide to carry out the execution, and Edgecombe subsequently quits his job. The movie opens with a scene of a guard purposefully not preparing a man properly for his execution in the electric chair. As a result of the guard's actions, the prisoner dies a slow and painful death before the crowd gathered to witness the execution. This movie is based upon a story that Stephen King published in the form of six novellas.

1. John Coffey is an innocent man who is still executed by the state. Are cases like this reason enough to argue against the death penalty? In other words, given that innocent people are sometimes executed for crimes they did not commit, should we do away with the death penalty as a form of punishment? Explain and defend your position.
2. If you had been physically present at the prison and witnessed the mishandled execution shown at the beginning of this film, do you think that your views on capital punishment would have changed? Does the fact that most of us have never witnessed an execution affect our views about capital punishment? Should it?
3. Does the fact that innocent people could be executed make capital punishment "cruel and unusual" punishment?
4. Would you have done your duty as an officer of the law as Edgecombe did and carried out the execution of an innocent man? Explain.
5. In *Gregg v. Georgia*, Justice Potter Stewart argued that the death penalty does not amount to cruel and unusual punishment because, in part, it accords with "evolving standards of decency" and does not entail wanton pain and violence. Does the fact that executions *can* be mishandled (though they seldom are) challenge Stewart's argument that the death penalty is not cruel and unusual punishment? Defend your view.

 ILLINOIS DEATH ROW CONVICTIONS THROWN OUT*

Event summary: On 20 February 1999, the *Chicago Tribune* reported that the Illinois Supreme Court had vacated Steven Smith's conviction and barred Cook County from trying him again. Smith was the eleventh death row inmate in Illinois in twelve years to be released from death row. "With Smith's release," says the article, "Illinois will have freed as many condemned inmates as it has executed since reinstating the death penalty in 1977, a statistic certain to be recited by capital-punishment foes advocating a state moratorium on executions." Smith was accused of killing an off-duty prison official in 1985. The prosecution's case against him rested on a witness whose credibility was seriously undermined. This crime, however, was not Smith's only offense. "Smith had previously been found guilty as a juvenile for a 1964 holdup and murder and as an adult for a 1969 gang-related shotgun killing." The accompanying table lists the eleven men who have been released from death row in Illinois after having been exonerated or after the courts determined that they had been wrongly convicted.

Defendant	County	Initial Conviction	Release
Perry Cobb	Cook	1979	1987
Darby Tillis	Cook	1979	1987
Joseph Burrows	Iroquois	1989	1994
Rolando Cruz	DuPage	1985	1995
Alejandro Hernandez	DuPage	1985	1995
Verneal Jimerson	Cook	1985	1996
Dennis Williams	Cook	1978	1996
Gary Gauger	McHenry	1993	1996
Carl Lawson	St. Clair	1990	1996
Anthony Porter	Cook	1983	1999
Steven Smith	Cook	1986	1999

*Ken Armstrong and Todd Lighty, "Death Row Conviction Thrown Out: 11th Reversal in 12 Years Will Free Chicago Man," *Chicago Tribune*, 10 Feb. 1999, pp. 1, 16.

1. The article states that these facts are certain to be cited by capital punishment foes advocating a state moratorium on executions. Explain how abolitionists might use this information to support their case. Formulate a retentionist response. Whose case is stronger, and why?
2. Do you think that statistics like this suggest that wrongly convicted people are being executed in America today? What bearing does this have on your beliefs about the morality of the death penalty? Explain.
3. Can these statistics be used to support the claim that the death penalty is cruel and unusual punishment? Would Justice Brennan agree with you? Would Justice Marshall? Explain.

SUPPLEMENTARY READINGS

Bedau, Hugo, ed. *The Death Penalty in America,* 3rd ed. New York: Oxford University Press, 1982.

Bedau, Hugo, and C. M. Pierce, eds. *Capital Punishment in the United States.* New York: AMS Press, 1976.

Berger, Raoul. *Death Penalties.* Cambridge, MA: Harvard University Press, 1982.

Berns, Walter. *For Capital Punishment.* New York: Basic Books, 1979.

Black, Charles L., Jr. *Capital Punishment: The Inevitability of Caprice and Mistake.* New York: Norton, 1981.

Camus, Albert. *Reflections on the Guillotine: An Essay on Capital Punishment,* trans. Richard Howard. Michigan City, IN: Fridjof-Karla Press, 1959.

Duff, R. A. *Trials and Punishments.* Cambridge: Cambridge University Press, 1986.

Ezorsky, Gertrude, ed. *Philosophical Perspectives on Punishment.* Albany: State University of New York Press, 1972.

Hart, H. L. A. *Punishment and Responsibility.* Oxford: Clarendon Press, 1968.

Honderich, T. *Punishment: The Supposed Justifications.* Harmondsworth, England: Penguin Books, 1984.

Lacey, N. *State Punishment: Political Principles and Community Values.* London: Routledge, 1988.

Meltser, Michael. *Cruel and Unusual: The Supreme Court and Capital Punishment.* New York: Random House, 1973.

Murphey, Jeffrie B. *Retribution, Justice and Therapy.* Dordrecht, Netherlands: Reidel, 1979.

Murphey, Jeffrie B., ed. *Punishment and Rehabilitation,* 2nd ed. Belmont, CA: Wadsworth, 1985.

Nathanson, Stephen. *An Eye for an Eye? The Morality of Punishing by Death.* Totowa, NJ: Rowman & Littlefield, 1987.

Primoratz, I. *Justifying Legal Punishment.* Atlantic Highlands, NJ: Humanities Press, 1989.

Sorell, Tom. *Moral Theory and Capital Punishment.* New York: Basil Blackwell, 1988.

Ten, C. L. *Crime, Guilt and Punishment: A Philosophical Introduction.* Oxford: Clarendon Press, 1987.

Van Den Haag, Ernest. *Punishing Criminals.* New York: Basic Books, 1975.

Van Den Haag, Ernest, and John P. Conrad. *The Death Penalty: A Debate.* New York: Plenum, 1983.

White, Welsh. *The Death Penalty in the Nineties.* Ann Arbor: University of Michigan Press, 1991.

5

Sexuality and Marriage

Lesbians and gay men are people who prefer sexual and romantic relationships with people of the same sex. In the United States, these people are treated differently in many respects than those who prefer relationships with members of the opposite sex. Incidents of discrimination in the workplace, denial of the right to sexual privacy, and the inability to have their partner legally recognized or to adopt children are all examples of how lesbians and gay men are treated differently in our society. Is this different treatment morally justifiable? Should lesbians and gay men be allowed to marry? To adopt children? Should lesbians and gay men have the same fundamental rights to sexual privacy that are granted to both single and married heterosexuals?

Lesbians, gay men, and bisexuals argue that they have been and continue to be subject to sexuality discrimination and unfair treatment. Many argue that sexuality is no more reason to deny individuals certain legal and social benefits than is their sex or the color of their skin. They claim that homosexuality is no more "unnatural" than a Black person's skin color when compared to a White person's and no more "abnormal" than a female's reproductive system when compared to the biology of a male. Thus, as the argument goes, sexuality provides no legitimate moral or legal justification for discrimination. Lesbians and gay men, like Blacks in the 1960s and women in the 1970s, have argued that biological differences do not provide the moral or legal right for society to deny them the same benefits enjoyed by other citizens. But these arguments are highly controversial, rooted as they are in common stereotypes about homosexuals, legal precedents, and a moral tradition regarding sexuality that is widely supported in the United States.

The myths about homosexuality in our society take many forms and are perpetuated through a number of sources. For example, some people believe that gay men and lesbians are more promiscuous than heterosexuals, and others claim that homosexuals molest children. Both of these beliefs have no basis in fact. There is simply no evidence that homosexuals are any more inclined to these actions than heterosexuals. Nevertheless, such cultural myths persist and are often the source of harassment of and violence against homosexuals. Identifying these myths about homosexuality helps to illuminate some of the sources of our disagreements concerning sexuality. It also provides a serious challenge to those who believe that the sexuality of lesbians and gay men is more important to their self-identities than it is to heterosexuals.

Legal rulings in the United States represent another hurdle for lesbians and gay men to overcome. By criminalizing same-sex marriages, same-sex sexual practices, and the adoption of children by same-sex couples, the courts are, in effect, stating that heterosexuals have different rights than homosexuals. For example, while *Bowers v. Hardwick* (1988) established that homosexuals do *not* have a right to sexual privacy, *Griswold v. Connecticut* (1965) and *Eisenstadt v. Baird* (1972) established that heterosexuals—married or otherwise—do have a right to sexual privacy. Such laws provide obstacles for lesbians and gay men who wish to have their relationships legally recognized. Without legal recognition of same-sex marriages, same-sex couples have a much more difficult time obtaining benefits such as health and life insurance. And even though some cities have enacted domestic partner laws that entitle same-sex and live-in couples to spousal benefits, these are exceptions to the general rule.

Perhaps the greatest challenge for lesbians and gay men comes from the Western religious tradition. According to the Vatican, anything that fails to respect the "essential order" of human life—whether it be suicide or homosexual conduct—is immoral and violates natural law. This traditional view is based on the belief that the natural purpose of sex is reproduction. To engage in sex without the intent to procreate is immoral. On this traditional view, then, homosexual sex, as well as any acts of sodomy even between heterosexual married partners, is unnatural and immoral. Contraception is also immoral in this line of reasoning. Furthermore, on this view, human sexuality is distinguished from animal sexuality by the presence of human love, and sex must be engaged in with love in order to be morally justifiable. In addition, sex must be engaged in with guarantees of sincerity and fidelity, which only marriage can provide. Thus, only sex with the intent to procreate by married partners is morally justifiable.

While the traditional view of marriage and sexuality has many supporters, it also has many critics. As the readings in this chapter indicate, the challenges to the traditional view of sexuality and marriage do not come solely from those seeking to support the rights of homosexuals. The traditional view of sexuality and marriage raises more general concerns about our moral beliefs concerning our sexual behavior. While some critics question the very possibility of a "sexual morality," others have different ways of connecting sexual behavior to moral beliefs. Some argue that sex does not hold a special status above any other human activity. Thus, the same standards that are used to determine whether any act is moral should be used to determine whether any sexual act is moral. An act is not immoral if it does not violate the rights of others, does not take unfair advantage of anyone, occurs with the knowing consent of all parties, and involves no deception. This general position is often called the *libertarian* view. On this view, for example, adultery is not immoral so long as the extramarital sexual relations involve no deception, or coercion; do not impinge upon the rights of others; and occur with the knowledge of all involved. The same could be said to apply to same-sex sexual relations.

Critics of the libertarian view have attempted to show that the assumption that a sexual act is comparable to any other human activity is incorrect. Two differences cited by the traditionalists between sexual and other acts have already been mentioned: (1) the purpose of sex is to procreate and (2) love is a necessary part of human sexuality. Libertarians generally reject these differences, because they are based on a conception of sexuality that libertarians do not accept.

Critics also attack the libertarian view on the grounds that sexual activities can have more serious personal and social ramifications than other human activities. Therefore, sexual activities *should* be treated differently than other human activities. Serious personal and social ramifications cited by such critics range from venereal diseases and challenges to personal fulfillment to threats to the family and marriage.

Venereal diseases such as gonorrhea, syphilis, herpes, and AIDS can be serious, and even fatal, if left untreated. Of all venereal diseases, AIDS is the most dangerous. There is no known cure for this disease, nor is there a vaccine to combat it. Over the past twenty years, AIDS has spread through heterosexual, bisexual, and homosexual communities at an alarming rate, which raises concerns about sexual morality. Although sexual promiscuity increases the risk of AIDS, this does not necessarily provide support for the traditional view of sexual morality. Libertarians argue that sexual freedom does not mean sexual irresponsibility. Sexually active people have moral obligations to avoid spreading any venereal diseases. By engaging in safe sex, sexually active people can decrease their chance of contracting AIDS and other venereal diseases.

Others argue that a more liberal sexual morality poses a threat to family life and the institution of marriage. They claim that the sexual revolution is partly responsible for the sharp increase in single-parent households. This is regarded as a social concern because most of these households are poor, and these families represent the vast majority of residents of homeless shelters and welfare recipients. Critics of the libertarian view argue that a more traditional sexual morality would have helped to prevent this from occurring.

However, we must realize that sexual morality is not the only possible contributor to the increase of poor, single-parent households. Rising unemployment rates, decreases in the quality of and access to education, and economic downturns all contribute to poverty in general, which in turn increases the number of poor, single-parent families. Furthermore, the lack of adequate education in birth control methods and difficulties in obtaining an abortion contribute to the birth of unwanted children, which contributes to the increase in the number of single-parent households. Libertarians argue that the solution to such social problems lies in education, easy access to birth control, and programs to alleviate poverty, not in restrictions on sexual freedom.

Finally, instead of focusing on the alleged threats of sexual morality to society, some focus on its effects on the individual. According to these critics of the libertarian view, our sexual behavior and sexuality play an important role in our personal development. Therefore, sexual activity should not be treated like other human activities. We need to take into account the relation of the participants to their own desire and the desire of their partners. Because our sexual behavior is linked to our moral well-being, sexual behavior is not the same as other human activities.

THOMAS AQUINAS

The Purpose of Sex

Thomas Aquinas's (1225–1274) views of sexuality and marriage are based on his *natural law theory*. Briefly, the natural world has a rational order, with values and purposes built into it by God. Everything that exists serves some purpose, and understanding things involves asking what purpose they serve. Furthermore, things are as they *ought* to be when they are serving their natural purposes. According to Aquinas's natural law theory, then, the natural purpose of sex is procreation, and any sexual activity not aimed at making children is "contrary to nature." So, for Aquinas, masturbation, oral sex, sex with contraception, and gay sex are immoral. Aquinas's views are heavily indebted to Aristotle and are aimed at reconciling reason with Christian faith.

Thomas Aquinas was the greatest of the medieval philosopher-theologians and a prodigious writer who produced over 8 million words. For centuries, his work was neglected by thinkers outside of the Catholic Church. Today, his writings are more widely studied by philosophers and have played an important role in contemporary philosophical debates, including those in moral philosophy. His masterpiece is the *Summa Theologiae* (Summation of Theology), the English translation of which fills sixty volumes. It was written to be a systematic introduction to theology for Dominican novices. This reading is taken from his *Summa Contra Gentiles,* which he compiled in 1264.

THE REASON WHY SIMPLE FORNICATION IS A SIN ACCORDING TO DIVINE LAW, AND THAT MATRIMONY IS NATURAL

1. We can see the futility of the argument of certain people who say that simple fornication is not a sin. For they say: Suppose there is a woman who is not married, or under the control of any man, either her father or another man. Now, if a man performs the sexual act with her, and she is willing, he does not injure her, because she favors the action and she has control over her own body. Nor does he injure any other person, because she is understood to be under no other person's control. So, this does not seem to be a sin.

2. Now, to say that he injures God would not seem to be an adequate answer. For we do not offend God except by doing something contrary to our own good, as has been said. But this does not appear contrary to man's good. Hence, on this basis, no injury seems to be done to God.

3. Likewise, it also would seem an inadequate answer to say that some injury is done to one's neighbor by this action, inasmuch as he may be scandalized. Indeed, it is possible for him to be scandalized by something which is not in itself a sin. In this event, the act would be accidentally sinful. But our problem is not whether simple fornication is accidentally a sin, but whether it is so essentially.

4. Hence, we must look for a solution in our earlier considerations. We have said that God exercises care over every person on the basis of what is good for him. Now, it is good for each person to attain his end, whereas it is bad for him to swerve away from his proper end. Now, this should be considered applicable to the parts, just as it is to the whole being; for instance, each and every part of man, and every one of his acts, should attain the proper end. Now, though the male semen is superfluous in regard to the

preservation of the individual, it is nevertheless necessary in regard to the propagation of the species. Other superfluous things, such as excrement, urine, sweat, and such things, are not at all necessary; hence, their emission contributes to man's good. Now, this is not what is sought in the case of semen, but, rather, to emit it for the purpose of generation, to which purpose the sexual act is directed. But man's generative process would be frustrated unless it were followed by proper nutrition, because the offspring would not survive if proper nutrition were withheld. Therefore, the emission of semen ought to be so ordered that it will result in both the production of the proper offspring and in the upbringing of this offspring.

5. It is evident from this that every emission of semen, in such a way that generation cannot follow, is contrary to the good for man. And if this be done deliberately, it must be a sin. Now, I am speaking of a way from which, *in itself*, generation could not result: such would be any emission of semen apart from the natural union of male and female. For which reason, sins of this type are called *contrary to nature*. But, if by accident generation cannot result from the emission of semen, then this is not a reason for it being against nature, or a sin; as for instance, if the woman happens to be sterile.

6. Likewise, it must also be contrary to the good for man if the semen be emitted under conditions such that generation could result but the proper upbringing would be prevented. We should take into consideration the fact that, among some animals where the female is able to take care of the upbringing of offspring, male and female do not remain together for any time after the act of generation. This is obviously the case with dogs. But in the case of animals of which the female is not able to provide for the upbringing of offspring, the male and female do stay together after the act of generation as long as is necessary for the upbringing and instruction of the offspring. Examples are found among certain species of birds whose young are not able to seek out food for themselves immediately after hatching. In fact, since a bird does not nourish its young with milk, made available by nature as it were, as occurs in the case of quadrupeds, but the bird must look elsewhere for food for its young, and since besides this it must protect them by sitting on them, the female is not able to do this by herself. So, as a result of divine providence, there is naturally implanted in the male of these animals a tendency to remain with the female in order to bring up the young. Now, it is abundantly evident that the female in the human species is not at all able to take care of the upbringing of offspring by herself, since the needs of human life demand many things which cannot be provided by one person alone. Therefore, it is appropriate to human nature that a man remain together with a woman after the generative act, and not leave her immediately to have such relations with another woman, as is the practice with fornicators.

7. Nor, indeed, is the fact that a woman may be able by means of her own wealth to care for the child by herself an obstacle to this argument. For natural rectitude in human acts is not dependent on things accidentally possible in the case of one individual, but, rather, on those conditions which accompany the entire species.

8. Again, we must consider that in the human species offspring require not only nourishment for the body, as in the case of other animals, but also education for the soul. . . . children must be instructed by parents who are already experienced people. Nor are they able to receive such instruction as soon as they are born, but after a long time, and especially after they have reached the age of discretion. Moreover, a long time is needed for this instruction. Then, too, because of the impulsion of the passions, through which prudent judgment is vitiated, they require not merely instruction but correction. Now, a woman alone is not adequate to this task; rather, this demands the work of a husband, in whom reason is more developed for giving instruction and strength is more available for giving punishment. Therefore, in the human species, it is not enough, as in the case of birds, to devote a small amount of time to bringing up offspring, for a long period of life is required. Hence, since among all animals it is necessary for male and female to remain together as long as the work of the father is needed by the offspring, it is natural to the human being for the man to establish a lasting association with a designated woman, over no short period of time. Now, we call this society *matrimony*. Therefore, matrimony is natural for man, and promiscuous performance of the sexual act, outside matrimony, is contrary to man's good. For this reason, it must be a sin.

9. Nor, in fact, should it be deemed a slight sin for a man to arrange for the emission of semen apart from the proper purpose of generating and bringing up children, on the argument that it is either a slight sin, or none at all, for a person to use a

part of the body for a different use than that to which it is directed by nature (say, for instance, one chose to walk on his hands, or to use his feet for something usually done with the hands) because man's good is not much opposed by such inordinate use. However, the inordinate emission of semen is incompatible with the natural good; namely, the preservation of the species. Hence, after the sin of homicide whereby a human nature already in existence is destroyed, this type of sin appears to take next place, for by it the generation of human nature is precluded.

10. Moreover, these views which have just been given have a solid basis in divine authority. That the emission of semen under conditions in which offspring cannot follow is illicit is quite clear. There is the text of Leviticus (18:22–23): "thou shalt not lie with mankind as with womankind . . . and thou shalt not copulate with any beast." And in 1 Corinthians (6:10): "Nor the effeminate, nor liers with mankind . . . shall possess the kingdom of God."

11. Also, that fornication and every performance of the act of reproduction with a person other than one's wife are illicit is evident. For it is said: "There shall be no whore among the daughters of Israel, nor whoremonger among the sons of Israel" (Deut. 23:17); and in Tobias (4:13): "Take heed to keep thyself from all fornication, and beside thy wife never endure to know a crime"; and in 1 Corinthians (6:18): "Fly fornication."

12. By this conclusion we refute the error of those who say that there is no more sin in the emission of semen than in the emission of any other superfluous matter, and also of those who state that fornication is not a sin. . . .

THAT MATRIMONY SHOULD BE INDIVISIBLE

1. If one will make a proper consideration, the preceding reasoning will be seen to lead to the conclusion not only that the society of man and woman of the human species, which we call matrimony, should be long-lasting, but even that it should endure throughout an entire life.

2. Indeed, possessions are ordered to the preservation of natural life, and since natural life, which cannot be preserved perpetually in the father, is by a sort of succession preserved in the son

in its specific likeness, it is naturally fitting for the son to succeed also to the things which belong to the father. So, it is natural that the father's solicitude for his son should endure until the end of the father's life. Therefore, if even in the case of birds the solicitude of the father gives rise to the cohabitation of male and female, the natural order demands that father and mother in the human species remain together until the end of life.

3. It also seems to be against equity if the aforesaid society be dissolved. For the female needs the male, not merely for the sake of generation, as in the case of other animals, but also for the sake of government, since the male is both more perfect in reasoning and stronger in his powers. In fact, a woman is taken into man's society for the needs of generation; then, with the disappearance of a woman's fecundity and beauty, she is prevented from association with another man. So, if any man took a woman in the time of her youth, when beauty and fecundity were hers, and then sent her away after she had reached an advanced age, he would damage that woman contrary to natural equity.

4. Again, it seems obviously inappropriate for a woman to be able to put away her husband, because a wife is naturally subject to her husband as governor, and it is not within the power of a person subject to another to depart from his rule. So, it would be against the natural order if a wife were able to abandon her husband. Therefore, if a husband were permitted to abandon his wife, the society of husband and wife would not be an association of equals, but, instead, a sort of slavery on the part of the wife.

5. Besides, there is in men a certain natural solicitude to know their offspring. This is necessary for this reason: the child requires the father's direction for a long time. So, whenever there are obstacles to the ascertaining of offspring they are opposed to the natural instinct of the human species. But, if a husband could put away his wife, or a wife her husband, and have sexual relations with another person, certitude as to offspring would be precluded, for the wife would be united first with one man and later with another. So, it is contrary to the natural instinct of the human species for a wife to be separated from her husband. And thus, the union of male and female in the human species must be not only lasting, but also unbroken.

6. Furthermore, the greater that friendship is, the more solid and long-lasting will it be. Now, there seems to be the greatest friendship between husband and wife, for they are united not only in the act of fleshly union, which produces a certain gentle association even among beasts, but also in the partnership of the whole range of domestic activity. Consequently, as an indication of this, man must even "leave his father and mother" for the sake of his wife, as is said in Genesis (2:24). Therefore, it is fitting for matrimony to be completely indissoluble. . . .

DISCUSSION QUESTIONS

1. Why does Aquinas believe that marriage is natural? Do you agree with his argument? Defend your view.
2. Aquinas believes that we can derive what *ought* to be the case from what *is* the case. For example, because sex produces children, it follows from this that it *ought* to be engaged in only for the purpose of producing children. What do you think about this general line of argumentation?
3. What would Aquinas say about same-sex marriage? Do you agree with this position? Why or why not?
4. Why does Aquinas believe that marriage should endure throughout an entire life? Do you agree? Defend your view.
5. Why would Aquinas argue that homosexuality is immoral? Do you agree with his reasoning? Why or why not?

IMMANUEL KANT

On Sexuality and Marriage

Immanuel Kant argues that "matrimony is the only condition in which use can be made of one's sexuality." For Kant, "matrimony is an agreement between two persons by which they grant each other equal reciprocal rights, each of them undertaking to surrender the whole of their person to the other with a complete right of disposal over it." Therefore, in marriage, we give our spouse complete rights over our body and soul. In return, we receive complete rights over the body and soul of our spouse. The gratification of sexual desire under these conditions is possible without degrading humanity or breaking moral laws. Matrimony affords us the opportunity to gratify morally our sexual desires while treating our spouse as an end in him- or herself. Otherwise, says Kant, "as soon as a person becomes an Object of appetite for another, all motives for moral relationship cease to function, because as an Object of appetite for another a person becomes a thing and can be treated and used as such by everyone." The gratification of

Immanuel Kant, *Lectures on Ethics*. Translated by Louis Infield. London: Methuen, 1932.

sexual desire under these conditions is immoral because we would be using others simply as a means to the fulfillment of our own sexual desires, and would not be treating them as individuals and as ends-in-themselves. A biographical sketch of Immanuel Kant appears in Chapter 1.

Human love is good-will, affection, promoting the happiness of others and finding joy in their happiness. But it is clear that, when a person loves another purely from sexual desire, none of these factors enter into the love. Far from there being any concern for the happiness of the loved one, the lover, in order to satisfy his desire and quiet his appetite, may even plunge the loved one into the depths of misery. Sexual love makes of the loved person an Object of appetite; as soon as that appetite has been satisfied, the person is cast aside as one casts away a lemon which has been sucked dry. Sexual love can, of course, be combined with concern for the other's well-being and so carry with it the characteristics of this love, but taken by itself and for itself, it is nothing more than appetite. Taken by itself it is a degradation of human nature; for as soon as a person becomes an Object of appetite for another, all motives of moral relationship cease to function, because as an Object of appetite for another a person becomes a thing and can be treated and used as such by everyone. This is the only case in which a human being is designed by nature as the Object of another's enjoyment. Sexual desire is at the root of it; and that is why we are ashamed of it, and why all strict moralists, and those who had pretensions to be regarded as saints, sought to suppress and extirpate it. . . .

Because sexuality is not an inclination which one human being has for another as such, but is an inclination for the sex of another, it is a principle of the degradation of human nature, in that it gives rise to the preference of one sex to the other, and to the dishonoring of that sex through the satisfaction of desires. The desire which a man has for a woman is not directed towards her because she is a human being, but because she is a woman; that she is a human being is of no concern to the man; only her sex is the object of his desires. Human nature is thus subordinated. Hence it comes about that all men and women do their best to make not their human nature but their sex more alluring and direct their activities and lusts entirely towards sex. Human nature is thereby sacrificed to sex. If then a man wishes to satisfy his desire, and a woman hers, they stimulate each other's desire; their inclinations meet, but their object is not human nature but sex, and each of them dishonors the human nature of the other. They make of humanity an instrument for the satisfaction of their lusts and inclinations, and dishonor it by placing it on a level with animal nature. Sexuality, therefore, exposes mankind to the danger of equality with the beasts. But as man has this desire from nature the question arises how far he can properly make use of it without injury to his manhood. . . .

The sole condition on which we are free to make use of our sexual desire depends upon the right to dispose over the person as a whole—over the welfare and happiness and generally over all the circumstances of that person. If I have the right over the whole person, I have also [the] right over the part, and so I have the right to use that person's sexual organs for the satisfaction of sexual desire. But how am I to obtain these rights over the whole person? Only by giving that person the same rights over the whole of myself. This happens only in marriage. Matrimony is an agreement between two persons by which they grant each other equal reciprocal rights, each of them undertaking to surrender the whole of their person to the other with a complete right of disposal over it. We can now apprehend by reason how a *sexual transaction* is possible without degrading humanity and breaking the moral laws. Matrimony is the only condition in which use can be made of one's sexuality. If one devotes one's person to another, one devotes not only sex but the whole person; the two cannot be separated. If, then, one yields one's person, body and soul, for good and ill and in every respect, so that the other has complete rights over it, and if the other does not similarly yield himself in return and does not extend in return the same rights and privileges, the arrangement is one-sided. But if I yield myself completely to another and obtain the person of the other in return, I win myself back; I have given myself up as the property of another, but in turn I take that other as my property, and so win myself back again in winning the person whose property I have become. In this way the two persons become a unity of will. Whatever good or ill, joy or sorrow befall either of them, the other will share in it. Thus sexuality leads to a union of human beings, and in that union alone its exercise is permissible.

DISCUSSION QUESTIONS

1. Do you agree with Kant that marriage affords us rights over the whole person of our spouse? Why or why not?
2. Kant says that matrimony is the only condition in which use can be made of one's sexuality. Do you agree with his argument? Why or why not? What are some of the implications of Kant's position? Are you comfortable with them? Explain.
3. Based on the selections from Kant that you have read, what do you think he might say about same-sex marriage? Furthermore, what do you think he might say about sexual relations between members of the same sex who are married? Defend the views that you propose for him.
4. Kant says that sexuality "exposes mankind to the danger of equality with the beasts." What is his argument? How does Kant deal with this danger? Is his response effective?
5. Are sexual relations between unmarried persons immoral? Present an argument. Compare Kant's view with your own.

RICHARD MOHR

Gay Basics

Richard Mohr claims that homosexuality is neither unnatural nor immoral. According to his view, just because we might describe something as unnatural or immoral—whether by popular vote or due to religious convictions—does not make it so. He argues, among other things, that morality is determined by more than our "social custom, history, and taboo." In the last section of his article, he suggests that if homosexuals were not discriminated against by our society they would lead happier lives.

Richard Mohr teaches philosophy at the University of Illinois and is the author of *Gays/Justice: A Study of Ethics, Society and Law* (1988).

SOME QUESTIONS, FACTS, AND VALUES
Who Are Gays Anyway?

A recent Gallup poll found that only one in five Americans reports having a gay or lesbian acquaintance. This finding is extraordinary given the number of practicing homosexuals in America. Alfred Kinsey's 1948 study of the sex lives of 12,000 white males shocked the nation: 37 percent had at least one homosexual experience to orgasm in their adult lives; an additional 13 percent had homosexual fantasies to orgasm; 4 percent were exclusively homosexual in their practices; another 5 percent had virtually no heterosexual experience; and nearly 20 percent had at least as many homosexual as heterosexual experiences.

Two out of five men one passes on the street have had orgasmic sex with men. Every second family in the country has a member who is essentially homosexual, and many more people regularly have homosexual experiences. Who are homosexuals? They are your friends, your minister, your teacher, your bank teller, your doctor, your mail carrier, your officemate, your roommate, your congressional representative, your sibling, parent, and spouse. They are everywhere, virtually all ordinary, virtually all unknown.

Several important consequences follow. First, the country is profoundly ignorant of the actual experience of gay people. Second, social attitudes and practices that are harmful to gays have a much greater overall harmful impact on society than is usually realized. Third, most gay people live in hiding—in the closet—making the "coming out" experience the central fixture of gay consciousness and invisibility the chief characteristic of the gay community.

IGNORANCE, STEREOTYPE, AND MORALITY

Ignorance about gays, however, has not stopped people from having strong opinions about them. The void which ignorance leaves has been filled with stereotypes. Society holds chiefly two groups of anti-gay stereotypes; the two are an oddly contradictory lot. One set of stereotypes revolves around alleged mistakes in an individual's gender identity: lesbians are women that want to be, or at least look and act like, men—bull dykes, diesel dykes; while gay men are those who want to be, or at least look and act like, women—queens, fairies, limp-wrists, nellies. These stereotypes of mismatched genders provide the materials through which gays and lesbians become the butts of ethniclike jokes. These stereotypes and jokes, though derisive, basically view gays and lesbians as ridiculous.

Another set of stereotypes revolves around gays as a pervasive, sinister, conspiratorial threat. The core stereotype here is the gay person as child molester, and more generally as sex-crazed maniac. These stereotypes carry with them fears of the very destruction of family and civilization itself. Now, that which is essentially ridiculous can hardly have

such a staggering effect. Something must be afoot in this incoherent amalgam.

Sense can be made of this incoherence if the nature of stereotypes is clarified. Stereotypes are not *simply* false generalizations from a skewed sample of cases examined. Admittedly, false generalizing plays some part in the stereotypes a society holds. If, for instance, one takes as one's sample homosexuals who are in psychiatric hospitals or prisons, as was done in nearly all early investigations, not surprisingly one will probably find homosexuals to be of a crazed and criminal cast. Such false generalizations, though, simply confirm beliefs already held on independent grounds, ones that likely led the investigator to the prison and psychiatric ward to begin with. Evelyn Hooker, who in the late fifties carried out the first rigorous studies to use nonclinical gays, found that psychiatrists, when presented with case files including all the standard diagnostic psychological profiles—but omitting indications of sexual orientation—were unable to distinguish files of gays from those of straights, even though they believed gays to be crazy and supposed themselves to be experts in detecting craziness. These studies proved a profound embarrassment to the psychiatric establishment, the financial well-being of which has been substantially enhanced by "curing" allegedly insane gays. The studies led the way to the American Psychiatric Association finally in 1973 dropping homosexuality from its registry of mental illnesses. Nevertheless, the stereotype of gays as sick continues apace in the mind of America.

False generalizations *help maintain* stereotypes; they do not *form* them. As the history of Hooker's discoveries shows, stereotypes have a life beyond facts; their origin lies in a culture's ideology—the general system of beliefs by which it lives—and they are sustained across generations by diverse cultural transmissions, hardly any of which, including slang and jokes, even purport to have a scientific basis. Stereotypes, then, are not the products of bad science but are social constructions that perform central functions in maintaining society's conception of itself.

On this understanding, it is easy to see that the anti-gay stereotypes surrounding gender identification are chiefly [a] means of reinforcing still powerful gender roles in society. If, as this stereotype presumes and condemns, one is free to choose one's social roles independently of gender, many guiding social divisions, both domestic and commercial, might be threatened. The socially gender-linked distinctions between breadwinner and homemaker, boss and secretary, doctor and nurse, protector and protected would blur. The accusations "dyke" and "fag" exist in significant part to keep women in their place and to prevent men from breaking ranks and ceding away theirs.

The stereotypes of gays as child molesters, sex-crazed maniacs, and civilization destroyers function to displace (socially irresolvable) problems from their actual source to a foreign (and so, it is thought, manageable) one. Thus the stereotype of child molester functions to give the family unit a false sheen of absolute innocence. It keeps the unit from being examined too closely for incest, child abuse, wife-battering, and the terrorism of constant threats. The stereotype teaches that the problems of the family are not internal to it, but external.

One can see these cultural forces at work in society's and the media's treatment of current reports of violence, especially domestic violence. When a mother kills her child or a father rapes his daughter—regular Section B fare even in major urban papers—this is never taken by reporters, columnists, or pundits as evidence that there is something wrong with heterosexuality or with traditional families. These issues are not even raised. But when a homosexual child molestation is reported it is taken as confirming evidence of the way homosexuals are. One never hears of heterosexual murders, but one regularly hears of "homosexual" ones. Compare the social treatment of Richard Speck's sexually motivated mass murder of Chicago nurses with that of John Wayne Gacy's murders of Chicago youths. Gacy was in the culture's mind taken as symbolic of gay men in general. To prevent the possibility that The Family was viewed as anything but an innocent victim in this affair, the mainstream press knowingly failed to mention that most of Gacy's adolescent victims were homeless hustlers. That knowledge would be too much for the six o'clock news and for cherished beliefs.

Because "the facts" largely don't matter when it comes to the generation and maintenance of stereotypes, the effects of scientific and academic research and of enlightenment generally will be, at best, slight and gradual in the changing fortunes of lesbians and gay men. If this account of stereotypes holds, society has been profoundly immoral. For its treatment of gays is a grand scale rationalization, a moral sleight-of-hand. The problem is not that society's usual standards of evidence and procedure in coming to judgments of social policy have been misapplied to gays; rather, when it comes to gays, the standards themselves have simply been ruled out of court and disregarded in favor of mechanisms that encourage unexamined fear and hatred.

ARE GAYS DISCRIMINATED AGAINST? DOES IT MATTER?

Partly because lots of people suppose they don't know any gay people and partly through willful ignorance of its own workings, society at large is unaware of the many ways in which gays are subject to discrimination in consequence of widespread fear and hatred. Contributing to this social ignorance of discrimination is the difficulty for gay people, as an invisible minority, even to complain of discrimination. For if one is gay, to register a complaint would suddenly target one as a stigmatized person, and so in the absence of any protections against discrimination, would simply invite additional discrimination. Further, many people, especially those who are persistently downtrodden and so lack a firm sense of self to begin with, tend either to blame themselves for their troubles or to view injustice as a matter of bad luck rather than as indicating something wrong with society. The latter recognition would require doing something to rectify wrong and most people, especially the already beleaguered, simply aren't up to that: So for a number of reasons discrimination against gays, like rape, goes seriously underreported.

First, gays are subject to violence and harassment based simply on their perceived status rather than because of any actions they have performed. A recent extensive study by the National Gay Task Force found that over 90 percent of gays and lesbians had been victimized in some form on the basis of their sexual orientation. Greater than one in five gay men and nearly one in ten lesbians had been punched, hit, or kicked; a quarter of all gays had had objects thrown at them; a third had been chased; a third had been sexually harassed; and 14 percent had been spit on—all just for being perceived as gay.

The most extreme form of anti-gay violence is "queer-bashing"—where groups of young men target a person who they suppose is a gay man and beat and kick him unconscious and sometimes to death amid a torrent of taunts and slurs. Such seemingly random but in reality socially encouraged violence has the same social origin and function as lynchings of blacks—to keep a whole stigmatized group in line. As with lynchings of the recent past, the police and courts have routinely averted their eyes, giving their implicit approval to the practice.

Few such cases with gay victims reach the courts. Those that do are marked by inequitable procedures and results. Frequently judges will describe "queer-bashers" as "just all-American boys." Recently a District of Columbia judge handed suspended sentences to queer-bashers whose victim had been stalked, beaten, stripped at knife point, slashed, kicked, threatened with castration, and pissed on, because the judge thought the bashers were good boys at heart—after all, they went to a religious prep school.

Police and juries will simply discount testimony from gays; they typically construe assaults on and murders of gays as "justified" self-defense—the killer need only claim his act was a panicked response to a sexual overture. Alternatively, when guilt seems patent, juries will accept highly implausible "diminished capacity" defenses, as in the case of Dan White's 1978 assassination of openly gay San Francisco city [supervisor] Harvey Milk: Hostess Twinkies made him do it.

These inequitable procedures and results collectively show that the life and liberty of gays, like those of blacks, simply count for less than the life and liberty of members of the dominant culture.

The equitable rule of law is the heart of an orderly society. The collapse of the rule of law for gays shows that society is willing to perpetrate the worst possible injustices against them. Conceptually there is only a difference in degree between the collapse of the rule of law and systematic extermination of members of a population simply for having some group status independent of any act an individual has performed. In the Nazi concentration camps, gays were forced to wear pink triangles as identifying badges, just as Jews were forced to wear yellow stars. In remembrance of that collapse of the rule of law, the pink triangle has become the chief symbol of the gay rights movement.

Gays are subject to widespread discrimination in employment—the very means by which one puts bread on one's table and one of the chief means by which individuals identify themselves to themselves and achieve personal dignity. Governments are leading offenders here. They do a lot of discriminating themselves, require that others do it (e.g., government contractors), and set precedents favoring discrimination in the private sector. The federal government explicitly discriminates against gays in the armed forces, the CIA, FBI, National Security Agency, and the State Department. The federal government refuses to give security clearances to gays and so forces the country's considerable private sector military and aerospace contractors to fire known gay employees. State and local governments regularly fire gay teachers, policemen, firemen, social workers, and anyone who has contact with the public. Further, through licensing laws states officially bar gays from a vast array of occupations and professions—everything from doctors, lawyers, accountants, and nurses to hairdressers, morticians, and used-car dealers. The American Civil Liberties Union's handbook *The Rights of Gay People* lists 307 such prohibited occupations.

Gays are subject to discrimination in a wide variety of other ways, including private-sector employment, public accommodations, housing, immigration and naturalization, insurance of all types, custody and adoption, and zoning regulations that bar "singles" or "nonrelated" couples. All of these discriminations affect central components of a meaningful life; some even reach to the means by which life itself is sustained. In half the states, where gay sex is illegal, the central role of sex to meaningful life is officially denied to gays.

All these sorts of discriminations also affect the ability of people to have significant intimate relations. It is difficult for people to live together as couples without having their sexual orientation perceived in the public realm and so becoming targets for discrimination. Illegality, discrimination, and the absorption by gays of society's hatred of them all interact to impede or block altogether the ability of gays and lesbians to create and maintain significant personal relations with loved ones. So every facet of life is affected by discrimination. Only the most compelling reasons could justify it.

BUT AREN'T THEY IMMORAL?

Many people think society's treatment of gays is justified because they think gays are extremely immoral. To evaluate this claim, different senses of "moral" must be distinguished. Sometimes by "morality" is meant the overall beliefs affecting behavior in a society—its mores, norms, and customs. On this understanding, gays certainly are not moral: lots of people hate them, and social customs are designed to register widespread disapproval of gays. The problem here is that this sense of morality is merely a *descriptive* one. On this understanding *every* society has a morality—even Nazi society, which had racism and mob rule as central features of its "morality," understood in this sense. What is needed in order to use the notion of morality to praise or condemn behavior is a sense of morality that is *prescriptive* or *normative*—a sense of morality whereby, for instance, the descriptive morality of the Nazis is found wanting.

As the Nazi example makes clear, that something is descriptively moral is nowhere near enough to make it normatively moral. A lot of people in a society saying something is good, even over eons, does not make it so. Our rejection of the long history of socially approved and state-enforced slavery is another good example of this principle at work. Slavery would be wrong even if nearly everyone liked it. So consistency and fairness require that we abandon the belief that gays are immoral simply because most people dislike or disapprove of gays or gay acts, or even because gay sex acts are illegal.

Furthermore, recent historical and anthropological research has shown that opinion about gays has been by no means universally negative. Historically, it has varied widely even within the larger part of the Christian era and even within the church itself. There are even societies—current ones—where homosexuality is not only tolerated but a universal compulsory part of social maturation. Within the last thirty years, American society has undergone a grand turnabout from deeply ingrained, near total condemnation to near total acceptance on two emotionally charged "moral" or "family" issues: contraception and divorce. Society holds its current descriptive morality of gays not because it has to, but because it chooses to.

If popular opinion and custom are not enough to ground moral condemnation of homosexuality, perhaps religion can. Such argument proceeds along two lines. One claims that the condemnation is a direct revelation of God, usually through the Bible; the other claims to be able to detect condemnation in God's plan as manifested in nature.

One of the more remarkable discoveries of recent gay research is that the Bible may not be as univocal in its condemnation of homosexuality as has been usually believed. Christ never mentions homosexuality. Recent interpreters of the Old Testament have pointed out that the story of Lot at Sodom is probably intended to condemn inhospitality rather than homosexuality. Further, some of the Old Testament condemnations of homosexuality seem simply to be ways of tarring those of the Israelites' opponents who happened to accept homosexual practices when the Israelites themselves

did not. If so, the condemnation is merely a quirk of history and rhetoric rather than a moral precept.

What does seem clear is that those who regularly cite the Bible to condemn an activity like homosexuality do so by reading it selectively. Do ministers who cite what they take to be condemnations of homosexuality in Leviticus maintain in their lives all the hygienic and dietary laws of Leviticus? If they cite the story of Lot at Sodom to condemn homosexuality, do they also cite the story of Lot in the cave to praise incestuous rape? It seems then not that the Bible is being used to ground condemnations of homosexuality as much as society's dislike of homosexuality is being used to interpret the Bible.

Even if a consistent portrait of condemnation could be gleaned from the Bible, what social significance should it be given? One of the guiding principles of society, enshrined in the Constitution as a check against the government, is that decisions affecting social policy are not made on religious grounds. If the real ground of the alleged immorality invoked by governments to discriminate against gays is religious (as it has explicitly been even in some recent court cases involving teachers and guardians), then one of the major commitments of our nation is violated.

BUT AREN'T THEY UNNATURAL?

The most noteworthy feature of the accusation of something being unnatural (where a moral rather than an advertising point is being made) is that the plaint is so infrequently made. One used to hear the charge leveled against abortion, but that has pretty much faded as anti-abortionists have come to lay all their chips on the hope that people will come to view abortion as murder. Incest used to be considered unnatural, but discourse now usually assimilates it to the moral machinery of rape and violated trust. The charge comes up now in ordinary discourse only against homosexuality. This suggests that the charge is highly idiosyncratic and has little, if any, explanatory force. It fails to put homosexuality in a class with anything else so that one can learn by comparison with clear cases of the class just exactly what it is that is allegedly wrong with it.

Though the accusation of unnaturalness looks whimsical, in actual ordinary discourse when applied to homosexuality, it is usually delivered with venom aforethought. It carries a high emotional charge, usually expressing disgust and evincing queasiness. Probably it is nothing but an emotional charge. For people get equally disgusted and queasy at all sorts of things that are perfectly natural—to be expected in nature apart from artifice—and that could hardly be fit subjects for moral condemnation. Two typical examples in current American culture are some people's responses to mothers' suckling in public and to women who do not shave body hair. When people have strong emotional reactions, as they do in these cases, without being able to give good reasons for them, we think of them not as operating morally, but rather as being obsessed and manic. So the feelings of disgust that some people have to[ward] gays will hardly ground a charge of immorality. People fling the term "unnatural" against gays in the same breath and with the same force as they call gays "sick" and "gross." When they do this, they give every appearance of being neurotically fearful and incapable of reasoned discourse.

When "nature" is taken in *technical* rather than ordinary usages, it looks like the notion also will not ground a charge of homosexual immorality. When unnatural means "by artifice" or "made by humans," it need only be pointed out that virtually everything that is good about life is unnatural in this sense, that the chief feature that distinguishes people from other animals is their very ability to make over the world to meet their needs and desires, and that their well-being depends upon these departures from nature. On this understanding of human nature and the natural, homosexuality is perfectly unobjectionable.

Another technical sense of natural is that something is natural, and so good, if it fulfills some function in nature. Homosexuality on this view is unnatural because it allegedly violates the function of genitals, which is to produce babies. One problem with this view is that lots of bodily parts have lots of functions, and just because some one activity can be fulfilled by only one organ (say, the mouth for eating) this activity does not condemn other functions of the organ to immorality (say, the mouth for talking, licking stamps, blowing bubbles, or having sex). So the possible use of the genitals to produce children does not, without more [defense], condemn the use of the genitals for other purposes, say, achieving ecstasy and intimacy.

The functional view of nature will only provide a morally condemnatory sense to the unnatural if a thing which might have many uses has but one proper function to the exclusion of other possible functions. But whether this is so cannot be established simply by looking at the thing. For what is seen is all its possible functions. The notion of function seemed like it might ground moral authority,

but instead it turns out that moral authority is needed to define proper function. Some people try to fill in this moral authority by appeal to the "design" or "order" of an organ, saying, for instance, that the genitals are designed for the purpose of procreation. But these people cheat intellectually if they do not make explicit *who* the designer and orderer is. If it is God, we are back to square one—holding others accountable for religious beliefs.

Further, ordinary moral attitudes about childbearing will not provide the needed supplement which in conjunction with the natural function view of bodily parts would produce a positive obligation to use the genitals for procreation. Society's attitude toward a childless couple is that of pity not censure—even if the couple could have children. The pity may be an unsympathetic one, that is, not registering a course one would choose *for oneself*, but this does not make it a course one would *require* of others. The couple who discovers they cannot have children are viewed not as having thereby had a debt canceled, but rather as having to forgo some of the richness of life, just as a quadriplegic is viewed not as absolved from some moral obligation to hop, skip, and jump, but as missing some of the richness of life. Consistency requires then that, at most, gays who do not or cannot have children are to be pitied rather than condemned. What *is* immoral is the willful preventing of people from achieving the richness of life. Immorality in this regard lies with those social customs, regulations, and statutes that prevent lesbians and gay men from establishing blood or adoptive families, not with gays themselves.

Sometimes people attempt to establish authority for a moral obligation to use bodily parts in a certain fashion simply by claiming that moral laws are natural laws and vice versa. On this account, inanimate objects and plants are good in that they follow natural laws by necessity, animals by instinct, and persons by a rational will. People are special in that they must first discover the laws that govern them. Now, even if one believes the view—dubious in the post-Newtonian, post-Darwinian world—that natural laws in the usual sense ($E = mc^2$, for instance) have some moral content, it is not at all clear how one is to discover the laws in nature that apply to people.

On the one hand, if one looks to people themselves for a model—and looks hard enough—one finds amazing variety, including homosexuality as a social ideal (upper-class fifty-century Athens) and even as socially mandatory (Melanesia today). When one looks to people, one is simply unable to strip away the layers of social custom, history, and taboo in order to see what's really there to any degree more specific than that people are the creatures that make over their world and are capable of abstract thought. That this is so should raise doubts that neutral principles are to be found in human nature that will condemn homosexuality.

On the other hand, if one looks to nature apart from people for models, the possibilities are staggering. There are fish that change gender over their lifetimes: should we "follow nature" and be operative transsexuals? Orangutans, genetically our next of kin, live completely solitary lives without social organization of any kind: ought we to "follow nature" and be hermits? There are many species where only two members per generation reproduce: should we be bees? The search in nature for people's purpose, far from finding sure models for action, is likely to leave one morally rudderless.

BUT AREN'T GAYS WILLFULLY THE WAY THEY ARE?

It is generally conceded that if sexual orientation is something over which an individual—for whatever reason—has virtually no control, then discrimination against gays is especially deplorable, as it is against racial and ethnic classes, because it holds people accountable without regard for anything they themselves have done. And to hold a person accountable for that over which the person has no control is a central form of prejudice.

Attempts to answer the question whether or not sexual orientation is something that is reasonably thought to be within one's own control usually appeal simply to various claims of the biological or "mental" sciences. But the ensuing debate over genes, hormones, twins, early childhood development, and the like, is as unnecessary as it is currently inconclusive. All that is needed to answer the question is to look at the actual experience of gays in current society and it becomes fairly clear that sexual orientation is not likely a matter of choice. For coming to have a homosexual identity simply does not have the same sort of structure that decision making has.

On the one hand, the "choice" of the gender of a sexual partner does not seem to express a trivial desire that might be as easily well fulfilled by a simple substitution of the desired object. Picking the gender of a sex partner is decidedly dissimilar, that is, to such activities as picking a flavor of ice cream. If an ice-cream parlor is out of one's flavor, one simply picks another. And if people were persecuted [and] threatened with jail terms, shattered careers, loss of family and housing, and the like, for eating, say, rocky road ice cream, no one would ever eat it; everyone would pick another easily available flavor. That gay people abide in being gay even in the face of persecution shows that being gay is not a matter of easy choice.

On the other hand, even if establishing a sexual orientation is not like making a relatively trivial choice, perhaps it is nevertheless relevantly like making the central and serious life choices by which individuals try to establish themselves as being of some type. Again, if one examines gay experience, this seems not to be the case. For one never sees anyone setting out to become a homosexual, in the way one does see people setting out to become doctors, lawyers, and bricklayers. One does not find "gays-to-be" picking some end—"At some point in the future, I want to become a homosexual"—and then setting about planning and acquiring the ways and means to that end, in the way one does see people deciding that they want to become lawyers, and then sees them plan what courses to take and what sort of temperaments, habits, and skills to develop in order to become lawyers. Typically gays-to-be simply find themselves having homosexual encounters and yet at least initially resisting quite strongly the identification of being homosexual. Such a person even very likely resists having such encounters, but ends up having them anyway. Only with time, luck, and great personal effort, but sometimes never, does the person gradually come to accept her or his orientation, to view it as a given material condition of life, coming as materials do with certain capacities and limitations. The person begins to act in accordance with his or her orientation and its capacities, seeing its actualization as a requisite for an integrated personality and as a central component of personal well-being. As a result, the experience of coming out to oneself has for gays the basic structure of a discovery, not the structure of a choice. And far from signaling immorality, coming out to others affords one of the few remaining opportunities in ever more bureaucratic, mechanistic, and socialistic societies to manifest courage.

HOW WOULD SOCIETY AT LARGE BE CHANGED IF GAYS WERE SOCIALLY ACCEPTED?

Suggestions to change social policy with regard to gays are invariably met with claims that to do so would invite the destruction of civilization itself:

after all, isn't that what did Rome in? Actually Rome's decay paralleled not the flourishing of homosexuality but its repression under the later Christianized emperors. Predictions of American civilization's imminent demise have been as premature as they have been frequent. Civilization has shown itself rather resilient here, in large part because of the country's traditional commitments to a respect for privacy, to individual liberties, and especially to people minding their own business. These all give society an open texture and the flexibility to try out things to see what works. And because of this one now need not speculate about what changes reforms in gay social policy might bring to society at large. For many reforms have already been tried.

Half the states have decriminalized homosexual acts. Can you guess which of the following states still have sodomy laws: Wisconsin, Minnesota; New Mexico, Arizona; Vermont, New Hampshire; Nebraska, Kansas? One from each pair does and one does not have sodomy laws. And yet one would be hard-pressed to point out any substantial difference between the members of each pair. (If you're interested, it is the second of each pair with them.) Empirical studies have shown that there is no increase in other crimes in states that have decriminalized [homosexual acts]. Further, sodomy laws are virtually never enforced. They remain on the books not to "protect society" but to insult gays, and for that reason need to be removed.

Neither has the passage of legislation barring discrimination against gays ushered in the end of civilization. Some 50 counties and municipalities, including some of the country's largest cities (like Los Angeles and Boston), have passed such statutes, and among the states and colonies Wisconsin and the District of Columbia have model protective codes. Again, no more brimstone has fallen in these places than elsewhere. Staunchly anti-gay cities, like Miami and Houston, have not been spared the AIDS crisis.

Berkeley, California, has even passed domestic partner legislation giving gay couples the same rights to city benefits as married couples, and yet Berkeley has not become more weird than it already was.

Seemingly hysterical predictions that the American family would collapse if such reforms [were passed] proved false, just as the same dire predictions that the availability of divorce would lessen the ideal and desirability of marriage proved completely unfounded. Indeed, if current discriminations, which drive gays into hiding and into anonymous relations, were lifted, far from seeing gays raze American families, one would see gays forming them.

Virtually all gays express a desire to have a permanent lover. Many would like to raise or foster children—perhaps these alarming numbers of gay kids who have been beaten up and thrown out of their "families" for being gay. But currently society makes gay coupling very difficult. A life of hiding is a pressure-cooker existence not easily shared with another. Members of non-gay couples are here asked to imagine what it would take to erase every trace of their own sexual orientation for even just a week.

Even against oppressive odds, gays have shown an amazing tendency to nest. And those gay couples who have survived the odds show that the structure of more usual couplings is not a matter of destiny but of personal responsibility. The so-called basic unit of society turns out not to be a unique immutable atom, but can adopt different parts, be adapted to different needs, and even be improved. Gays might even have a thing or two to teach others about division of labor, the relation of sensuality and intimacy, and stages of development in such relations.

If discrimination ceased, gay men and lesbians would enter the mainstream of the human community openly and with self-respect. The energies that the typical gay person wastes in the anxiety of leading a day-to-day existence of systematic disguise would be released for use in personal flourishing. From this release would be generated the many spinoff benefits that accrue to a society when its individual members thrive.

Society would be richer for acknowledging another aspect of human richness and diversity. Families with gay members would develop relations based on truth and trust rather than lies and fear. And the heterosexual majority would be better off for knowing that they are no longer trampling their gay friends and neighbors.

Finally and perhaps paradoxically, in extending to gays the rights and benefits it has reserved for its dominant culture, America would confirm its deeply held vision of itself as a morally progressing nation, a nation itself advancing and serving as a beacon for others—especially with regard to human rights. The words with which our national pledge ends—"with liberty and justice for all"—are not a description of the present but a call for the future. Ours is a nation given to a prophetic political rhetoric which acknowledges that morality is not arbitrary and that justice is not merely the expression of the current collective will. It is this vision that led the black civil rights movement to its successes. Those congressmen who opposed that movement and its centerpiece, the 1964 Civil Rights Act, on obscurantist grounds, but who lived long enough and were noble enough, came in time to express their heartfelt regret and shame at what they had done. It is to be hoped and someday to be expected that those who now grasp at anything to oppose the extension of that which is best about America to gays will one day feel the same.

DISCUSSION QUESTIONS

1. Is it true that society's prejudice makes homosexuals, lesbians, and bisexuals unhappy? Defend your position.
2. Is homosexuality a matter of choice? Compare your view with Mohr's.
3. Should homosexuality be illegal? Defend your view.
4. Does the Bible condemn homosexuality? What is Mohr's view? If the Bible does condemn homosexuality, is this a good reason to say that homosexuality is immoral? What does your response say about your perception of the relationship between religion and morality? Compare your view with John Arthur's (see Chapter 1).
5. What do you think a utilitarian would say about the morality of homosexuality? Explain.

MICHAEL LEVIN

Why Homosexuality Is Abnormal

Michael Levin argues that homosexuality is undesirable because it is a misuse of bodily parts. His arguments are based on natural selection theory, and he is particularly critical of utilitarian defenses of homosexuality. Levin maintains that calling homosexuality involuntary places it outside the scope of moral evaluation, and goes on to argue that homosexuality is likely to lead to unhappiness. Legislation legalizing homosexuality cannot be neutral about its value, says Levin, and legislation that legitimates, endorses or protects homosexuality is found by him to be *prima facie* objectionable.

Michael Levin, who began teaching philosophy at City College of New York in 1969, has been widely criticized for his views on homosexuality and affirmative action and has even been the subject of campus protests.

This paper defends the view that homosexuality is abnormal and hence undesirable—not because it is immoral or sinful, or because it weakens society or hampers evolutionary development, but for a purely mechanical reason. It is a misuse of bodily parts. Clear empirical sense attaches to the idea of *the use* of such bodily parts as genitals, the idea that they are *for* something, and consequently to the idea of their misuse. I argue on grounds involving natural selection that misuse of bodily parts can with high probability be connected to unhappiness. I regard these matters as prolegomena to such policy issues as the rights of homosexuals, the rights of those desiring not to associate with homosexuals, and legislation concerning homosexuality, issues which I shall not discuss systematically here. However, I do in the last section draw a seemingly evident corollary from my view that homosexuality is abnormal and likely to lead to unhappiness.

I have confined myself to male homosexuality for brevity's sake, but I believe that much of what I say applies *mutatis mutandis* to lesbianism. There may well be significant differences between the two: the data of [2], for example, support the popular idea that sex *per se* is less important to women and in particular lesbians than it is to men. On the other hand, lesbians are generally denied motherhood, which seems more important to women than is fatherhood—normally denied homosexual males— to men. On this matter, [2] offers no data. Overall, it is reasonable to expect general innate gender differences to explain the major differences between male homosexuals and lesbians.

Despite the publicity currently enjoyed by the claim that one's "sexual preference" is nobody's business but one's own, the intuition that there is something unnatural about homosexuality remains vital. The erect penis fits the vagina, and fits it better than any other natural orifice; penis and vagina seem made for each other. This intuition ultimately derives from, or is another way of capturing, the idea that the penis is not *for* inserting into the anus of another man—that so using the penis is not the way it is *supposed*, even *intended*, to be used. Such intuitions may appear to rest on an outmoded teleological view of nature, but recent work in the logic of functional ascription shows how they may be explicated, and justified, in suitably naturalistic terms. Such is the burden of Section 2, the particular application to homosexuality coming in Section 3. Furthermore, when we understand the sense in which homosexual acts involve a misuse of genitalia, we will see why such misuse is bad and not to be encouraged. (The case for this constitutes the balance of Section 3.) . . .

But before turning to these issues, I want to make four preliminary remarks. The first concerns the explicitness of my language in the foregoing paragraph and the rest of this paper. Explicit mention of bodily parts and the frank description of sexual acts are necessary to keep the phenomenon under discussion in clear focus. Euphemistic vagary about "sexual orientation" or "the gay lifestyle" encourages one to slide over homosexuality without having to face or even acknowledge what it really is.

Such talk encourages one to treat "sexual preference" as if it were akin to preference among flavors of ice-cream. Since unusual taste in ice-cream is neither right nor wrong, this usage suggests, why should unusual taste in sex be regarded as objectionable? Opposed to this usage is the unblinkable fact that the sexual preferences in question are such acts as mutual fellation. Is one man's taste for pistachio ice-cream really just like another man's taste for fellation? Unwillingness to call this particular spade a spade allows delicacy to award the field by default to the view that homosexuality is normal. Anyway, such delicacy is misplaced in a day when "the love that dare not speak its name" is shouting its name from the rooftops.

My second, related, point concerns the length of the present paper. . . . [We have shortened Levin's paper considerably.—Eds.]

The third point is this. The chain of intuitions I discussed earlier has other links, links connected to the conclusion that homosexuality is bad. They go something like this: Homosexual acts involve the use of the genitals for what they aren't for, and it is a *bad* or at least *unwise* thing to use a part of your body for what it isn't for. Calling homosexual acts "unnatural" is intended to sum up this entire line of reasoning. "Unnatural" carries disapprobative connotations, and any explication of it should capture this. . . . To have anything to do with our intuitions—even if designed to demonstrate them groundless—an explication of "abnormal" must capture the analytic truth that the abnormality of a practice is a reason for avoiding it. If our ordinary concept of normality turns out to be ill-formed, so that various acts are at worst "abnormal" in some nonevaluative sense, this will simply mean that, as we ordinarily use the expression, *nothing is abnormal.* (Not that anyone really believes this—people who deny that cacophagia or necrophilia are abnormal do so only to maintain the appearance of consistency.)

Fourth, I should mention Steven Goldberg's defense of a position similar to mine ([3]). . . .

ON "FUNCTION" AND ITS COGNATES

To bring into relief the point of the idea that homosexuality involves a misuse of bodily parts, I will begin with an uncontroversial case of misuse, a case in which the clarity of our intuitions is not obscured by the conviction that they are untrustworthy. Mr.

Jones pulls all his teeth and strings them around his neck because he thinks his teeth look nice as a necklace. He takes puréed liquids supplemented by intravenous solutions for nourishment. It is surely natural to say that Jones is misusing his teeth, that he is not using them for what they are for, that indeed the way he is using them is incompatible with what they are for. Pedants might argue that Jones's teeth are no longer part of him and hence that he is not misusing any bodily parts. To them I offer Mr. Smith, who likes to play "Old MacDonald" on his teeth. So devoted is he to this amusement, in fact, that he never uses his teeth for chewing—like Jones, he takes nourishment intravenously. Now, not only do we find it perfectly plain that Smith and Jones are misusing their teeth, we predict a dim future for them on purely physiological grounds; we expect the muscles of Jones's jaw that are used for—that *are* for—chewing to lose their tone, and we expect this to affect Jones's gums. Those parts of Jones's digestive tract that are for processing solids will also suffer from disuse. The net result will be deteriorating health and perhaps a shortened life. Nor is this all. Human beings enjoy chewing. Not only has natural selection selected in muscles for chewing and favored creatures with such muscles, it has selected a tendency to find the use of those muscles reinforcing. Creatures who do not enjoy using such parts of their bodies as deteriorate with disuse, will tend to be selected out. Jones, product of natural selection that he is, descended from creatures who at least tended to enjoy the use of such parts. Competitors who didn't simply had fewer descendants. So we expect Jones sooner or later to experience vague yearnings to chew something, just as we find people who take no exercise to experience a general listlessness. Even waiving for now my apparent reification of the evolutionary process, let me emphasize how little anyone is tempted to say "each to his own" about Jones or to regard Jones's disposition of his teeth as simply a deviation from a statistical norm. This sort of case is my paradigm when discussing homosexuality.

The main obstacle to talk of what a process or organic structure is for is that, literally understood, such talk presupposes an agent who intends that structure or process to be used in a certain way. Talk of function derives its primitive meaning from the human use of artifacts, artifacts being for what purposive agents intend them for. Indeed, there is in this primitive context a natural reason for using something for what it is for: to use it otherwise would frustrate the intention of some purposeful agent. Since it now seems clear that our bodily parts were not emplaced by purposeful agency, it is easy to dismiss talk of what they are for as "theologically" based on a faulty theory of how we came to be built as we are:

> The idea that sex was designed for propagation is a theological argument, but not a scientific one. . . . To speak of the "fit" of penis and vagina as proof of nature's intention for their exclusive union is pure theological reasoning—imposing a meaning or purpose upon a simple, natural phenomenon. ([4], 63)

Barash—who elsewhere uses its cognates freely—dismisses "unnatural" as a mere term of abuse: "people with a social or political axe to grind will call what they don't like 'unnatural' and what they do, 'natural'" ([1], 237). Hume long ago put the philosopher's case against the term "natural" with characteristic succinctness: "'Tis founded on final Causes; which is a consideration, that appears to me pretty uncertain & unphilosophical. For pray, what is the End of Man? Is he created for Happiness or for Virtue? For this Life or the next? For himself or for his Maker?" ([5], 134) . . .

An organ is for a given activity if the organ's performing that activity helps its host or organisms suitably related to its host, *and* if this contribution is how the organ got and stays where it is. . . . This definition . . . distinguishes what something is for from what it may be *used* for on some occasion. Teeth are for chewing—we have teeth because their use in chewing favored the survival of organisms with teeth—whereas Jones is using his teeth for ornamentation.

[This account of what it is for an organ to be *for* a certain activity] explains our intuition that, since their efficacy in chewing got them selected in, teeth are for masticating and Jones is preventing his teeth from doing their proper job. . . . Nature is interested in making its creatures like what is (inclusively) good for them. A creature that does not enjoy using its teeth for chewing uses them less than does a toothed competitor who enjoys chewing. Since the use of teeth for chewing favors the survival of an individual with teeth, and, other things being equal, traits favorable to the survival of individuals favor survival of the relevant cohort, toothed creatures who do not enjoy chewing tend to get selected out. We today are the filtrate of this process, descendants of creatures who liked to chew. . . .

Jones's behavior is ill-advised not only because of the avertible objective consequences of his defanging himself, but because he will feel that something is missing. Similarly, this is why you should exercise. It is not just that muscles are for running. We have already heard the sceptic's reply to that: "So what? Suppose I don't mind being flabby? Suppose I don't give a hang about what will propagate my genetic cohort?" Rather, running is good because nature made sure people like to run. This is, of course, the prudential "good," not the moral "good"—but I disavowed at the outset the doctrine that misuse of bodily parts is *morally* bad, at least in any narrow sense. You ought to run because running was once necessary for catching food: creatures who did not enjoy running, if there ever were any, caught less food and reproduced less frequently than competitors who enjoyed running. These competitors passed on their appetites along with their muscles *to you*. This is not to say that those who suffer the affective consequences of laziness must recognize them as such, or even be able to identify them against their general background feeling-tone. They may not realize they would feel better if they exercised. They may even doubt it. They may have allowed their muscles to deteriorate beyond the point at which satisfying exercise is possible. For all that, evolution has decreed that a life involving regular exercise is on the whole more enjoyable than a life without. The same holds for every activity that is the purpose of an organ.

APPLICATIONS TO HOMOSEXUALITY

The application of this general picture to homosexuality should be obvious. There can be no reasonable doubt that one of the functions of the penis is to introduce semen into the vagina. It does this, and it has been selected in because it does this. . . . Nature has consequently made this use of the penis rewarding. It is clear enough that any proto-human males who found unrewarding the insertion of penis into vagina have left no descendants. In particular, proto-human males who enjoyed inserting their penises into each other's anuses have left no descendants. This is why homosexuality is abnormal, and why its abnormality counts prudentially against it. Homosexuality is likely to cause unhappiness because it leaves unfulfilled an innate and innately rewarding desire. And should the reader's environmentalism threaten to get the upper hand, let me remind him again of an unproblematic case. Lack of exercise is bad and even abnormal not only because it is unhealthy but also because one feels poorly without regular exercise.

Nature made exercise rewarding because, until recently, we had to exercise to survive. Creatures who found running after game unrewarding were eliminated. Laziness leaves unreaped the rewards nature has planted in exercise, even if the lazy man cannot tell this introspectively. If this is a correct description of the place of exercise in human life, it is by the same token a correct description of the place of heterosexuality.

It hardly needs saying, but perhaps I should say it anyway, that this argument concerns tendencies and probabilities. Generalizations about human affairs being notoriously "true by and large and for the most part" only, saying that homosexuals are bound to be less happy than heterosexuals must be understood as short for "Not coincidentally, a larger proportion of homosexuals will be unhappy than a corresponding selection of the heterosexual population." There are, after all, genuinely jolly fat men. To say that laziness leads to adverse affective consequences means that, because of our evolutionary history, the odds are relatively good that a man who takes no exercise will suffer adverse affective consequences. Obviously, some people will get away with misusing their bodily parts. Thus, when evaluating the empirical evidence that bears on this account, it will be pointless to cite cases of well-adjusted homosexuals. I do not say they are nonexistent; my claim is that, of biological necessity, they are rare. . . .

Talk of what is "in the genes" inevitably provokes the observation that we should not blame homosexuals for their homosexuality if it is "in their genes." True enough. Indeed, since nobody decides what he is going to find sexually arousing, the moral appraisal of sexual object "choice" is entirely absurd. However, so saying is quite consistent with regarding homosexuality as a misfortune, and taking steps—this being within the realm of the will—to minimize its incidence, especially among children. Calling homosexuality involuntary does not place it outside the scope of evaluation. Victims of sickle-cell anemia are not blameworthy, but it is absurd to pretend that there is nothing wrong with them. Homosexual activists are partial to genetic explanations and hostile to Freudian environmentalism in part because they see a genetic cause as exempting homosexuals from blame. But surely people are equally blameless for indelible traits acquired in early childhood. And anyway, a blameless condition may still be worth trying to prevent. . . .

Utilitarians must take the present evolutionary scenario seriously. The utilitarian attitude toward homosexuality usually runs something like this:

even if homosexuality is in some sense unnatural, as a matter of brute fact homosexuals take pleasure in sexual contact with members of the same sex. As long as they don't hurt anyone else, homosexuality is as great a good as heterosexuality. But the matter cannot end here. Not even a utilitarian doctor would have words of praise for a degenerative disease that happened to foster a certain kind of pleasure (as sore muscles uniquely conduce to the pleasure of stretching them). A utilitarian doctor would presumably try just as zealously to cure diseases that feel good as less pleasant degenerative diseases. A pleasure causally connected with great distress cannot be treated as just another pleasure to be toted up on the felicific scoreboard. Utilitarians have to reckon with the inevitable consequences of pain-causing pleasure. . . .

ON POLICY ISSUES

Homosexuality is intrinsically bad only in a prudential sense. It makes for unhappiness. However, this does not exempt homosexuality from the larger categories of ethics—rights, duties, liability. Deontic categories apply to acts which increase or decrease happiness or expose the helpless to the risk of unhappiness.

If homosexuality is unnatural, legislation which raises the odds that a given child will become homosexual raises the odds that he will be unhappy. The only gap in the syllogism is whether legislation which legitimates, endorses or protects homosexuality does increase the chances that a child will become homosexual. If so, such legislation is *prima facie* objectionable. The question is not whether homosexual elementary school teachers will molest their charges. Prohomosexual legislation might increase the incidence of homosexuality in subtler ways. If it does, and if the protection of children is a fundamental obligation of society, legislation which legitimates homosexuality is a dereliction of duty. I am reluctant to deploy the language of "children's rights," which usually serves as one more excuse to interfere with the prerogatives of parents. But we do have obligations to our children, and one of them is to protect them from harm. If, as some have suggested, children have a right to protection from a religious education, they surely have a right to protection from homosexuality. So protecting them limits somebody else's freedom, but we are often willing to protect quite obscure children's rights at the expense of the freedom of others. There is a movement to ban TV commercials for sugar-coated cereals, to protect children from the relatively trivial harm of tooth decay. Such a ban would restrict the freedom of advertisers, and restrict it even though the last clear chance of avoiding the harm, and thus the responsibility, lies with the parents who control the TV set. I cannot see how one can consistently support such legislation and also urge homosexual rights, which risk much graver danger to children in exchange for increased freedom for homosexuals. (If homosexual behavior is largely compulsive, it is falsifying the issue to present it as balancing risks to children against the freedom of homosexuals.) The right of a homosexual to work for the Fire Department is not a negligible good. Neither is fostering a legal atmosphere in which as many people as possible grow up heterosexual.

It is commonly asserted that legislation granting homosexuals the privilege or right to be firemen endorses not homosexuality, but an expanded conception of human liberation. It is conjectural how sincerely this can be said in a legal order that forbids employers to hire whom they please and demands hours of paperwork for an interstate shipment of hamburger. But in any case legislation "legalizing homosexuality" cannot be neutral because passing it would have an inexpungeable speech-act dimension. Society cannot grant unaccustomed rights and privileges to homosexuals while remaining neutral about the value of homosexuality. Working from the assumption that society rests on the family and its consequences, the Judaeo-Christian tradition has deemed homosexuality a sin and withheld many privileges from homosexuals. Whether or not such denial was right, for our society to grant these privileges to homosexuals *now* would amount to declaring that it has rethought the matter and decided that homosexuality is not as bad as it had previously supposed. . . .

Up to now, society has deemed homosexuality so harmful that restricting it outweighs putative homosexual rights. If society reverses itself, it will in effect be deciding that homosexuality is not as bad as it once thought.

NOTES

1. D. Barash, *The Whispering Within* (New York: Harper & Row, 1979).
2. A. Bell and M. Weinberg, *Homosexualities* (New York: Simon & Schuster, 1978).

3. S. Goldberg, "What Is 'Normal'? Logical Aspects of the Question of Homosexual Behavior," *Psychiatry* (1975).

4. R. Gould, "What We Don't Know About Homosexuality," *New York Times Magazine* (24 Feb. 1974).

5. R. Gary, "Sex and Sexual Perversion," *Journal of Philosophy*, 74 (1978): 189–199.

6. E. Mossner, *The Life of David Hume* (New York: Nelson, 1954).

DISCUSSION QUESTIONS

1. How would Levin respond to Richard Mohr's claim that nature gives us no guide to human purpose or action? Is Levin right?
2. Compare and contrast Mohr's and Thomas Aquinas's views on the purpose of sex. How are they similar and different?
3. Do you believe that it is possible to "misuse" body parts? Do you believe that this can lead to unhappiness? Give specific examples.
4. Levin says "homosexuality is intrinsically bad in a prudential sense." What does he mean by this? Do you agree?
5. What does Levin mean by "unhappiness"? Do you agree with his conclusions? Compare and contrast Levin's view of happiness with Aristotle's and Jeremy Bentham's views (see Chapter 1).

 U.S. SUPREME COURT

Bowers v. Hardwick

In *Bowers v. Hardwick* (1988), the Supreme Court ruled against the right to be a homosexual and join with a partner. Whereas *Griswold v. Connecticut* (1965) established that heterosexual married couples have the right to sexual privacy, and *Eisenstadt v. Baird* (1972) that single heterosexuals also have a right to sexual privacy, *Bowers v. Hardwick* established that homosexuals do *not* share this right with heterosexuals. In the majority opinion, Justice Byron White argues that the sodomy law in Georgia which makes anal sex, oral sex, and bestiality (sex with animals) illegal is constitutional. Gays do not have the same right to sexual privacy under the Constitution as do married and individual heterosexuals. In a dissenting opinion, Justice Harry Blackmun argues that prior rights to sexual privacy established for heterosexuals naturally extend to homosexuals. Blackmun writes that "the mere knowledge that other individuals do not adhere to one's value system cannot be a legally cognizable interest, let alone an interest that can justify invading the houses, hearts, and minds of citizens who choose to live their lives differently."

Justice *White* delivered the opinion of the Court.

In August 1982, respondent Hardwick (hereafter respondent) was charged with violating the Georgia statute criminalizing sodomy by committing that act with another adult male in the bedroom of respondent's home. After a preliminary hearing, the District Attorney decided not to present the matter to the grand jury unless further evidence developed.

Respondent then brought suit in the Federal District Court, challenging the constitutionality of the statute insofar as it criminalized consensual sodomy. He asserted that he was a practicing homosexual, that the Georgia sodomy statute, as administered by the defendants, placed him in imminent danger of arrest, and that the statute for several reasons violates the Federal Constitution. The District Court granted the defendants' motion to dismiss for failure to state a claim. . . .

A divided panel of the Court of Appeals for the Eleventh Circuit reversed. . . . The court went on to hold that the Georgia statute violated respondent's fundamental rights because his homosexual activity is a private and intimate association that is beyond the reach of state regulation by reason of the Ninth Amendment and the Due Process Clause of the Fourteenth Amendment. The case was remanded for trial, at which, to prevail, the State would have to prove that the statute is supported by a compelling interest and is the most narrowly drawn means of achieving that end.

. . . We agree with petitioner that the Court of Appeals erred, and hence reverse its judgment.

This case does not require a judgment on whether laws against sodomy between consenting adults in general, or between homosexuals in particular, are wise or desirable. It raises no question about the right or propriety of state legislative decisions to repeal their laws that criminalize homosexual sodomy, or of state-court decisions invalidating those laws on state constitutional grounds. The issue presented is whether the Federal Constitution confers a fundamental right upon homosexuals to engage in sodomy and hence invalidates the laws of the many States that still make such conduct illegal and have done so for a very long time. The case also calls for some judgment about the limits of the Court's role in carrying out its constitutional mandate.

We first register our disagreement with the Court of Appeals and with respondent that the Court's prior cases have construed the Constitution to confer a right of privacy that extends to homosexual sodomy and for all intents and purposes have decided this case. . . . [These cases have been] described as dealing with child rearing and education; with family relationships; with procreation; with marriage; with contraception; and with abortion. [The cases dealing with contraception and abortion] were interpreted as construing the Due Process Clause of the Fourteenth Amendment to confer a fundamental individual right to decide whether or not to beget or bear a child.

Accepting the decisions in these cases and the above description of them, we think it evident that none of the rights announced in those cases bears any resemblance to the claimed constitutional right of homosexuals to engage in acts of sodomy that is asserted in this case. No connection between family, marriage, or procreation on the one hand and homosexual activity on the other has been demonstrated, either by the Court of Appeals or by respondent. Moreover, any claim that these cases nevertheless stand for the proposition that any kind of private sexual conduct between consenting adults is constitutionally insulated from state proscription is unsupportable. . . .

Precedent aside, however, respondent would have us announce, as the Court of Appeals did, a fundamental right to engage in homosexual sodomy. This we are quite unwilling to do. It is true that despite the language of the Due Process Clauses of the Fifth and Fourteenth Amendments, which appears to focus only on the processes by which life, liberty, or property is taken, the cases are legion in which those Clauses have been interpreted to have substantive content, subsuming rights that to a great extent are immune from federal or state regulation or proscription. Among such cases are those recognizing rights that have little or no textual support in the constitutional language. . . .

Striving to assure itself and the public that announcing rights not readily identifiable in the Constitution's text involves much more than the imposition of the Justices' own choice of values on the States and the Federal Government, the Court has sought to identify the nature of the rights qualifying for heightened judicial protection. In *Palko v. Connecticut* (1937), it was said that this category includes those fundamental liberties that are "implicit in the concept of ordered liberty," such that "neither liberty nor justice would exist if [they] were sacrificed." A different description of fundamental liberties appeared in *Moore v. East Cleveland* (1977), where they are characterized as those liberties that are "deeply rooted in this Nation's history and tradition."

It is obvious to us that neither of these formulations would extend a fundamental right to homosexuals to engage in acts of consensual sodomy. Proscriptions against that conduct have ancient roots. Sodomy was a criminal offense at common law and was forbidden by the laws of the original 13 States when they ratified the Bill of Rights. In 1868, when the Fourteenth Amendment was ratified, all but 5 of the 37 States in the Union had criminal sodomy laws. In fact, until 1961, all 50 States outlawed sodomy, and today, 24 States and the District of Columbia continue to provide criminal penalties for sodomy performed in private and between consenting adults. Against this background, to claim that a right to engage in such conduct is "deeply rooted in this Nation's history and tradition" or "implicit in the concept of ordered liberty" is, at best, facetious.

Nor are we inclined to take a more expansive view of our authority to discover new fundamental rights imbedded in the Due Process Clause. The Court is most vulnerable and comes nearest to illegitimacy when it deals with judge-made constitutional law having little or no cognizable roots in the language or design of the Constitution. . . .

Respondent, however, asserts that the result should be different where the homosexual conduct occurs in the privacy of the home. He relies on *Stanley v. Georgia* (1969), where the Court held that the First Amendment prevents conviction for possessing and reading obscene material in the privacy of one's home: "If the First Amendment means anything, it means that a State has no business telling a man, sitting alone in his house, what books he may read or what films he may watch."

Stanley did protect conduct that would not have been protected outside the home, and it partially prevented the enforcement of state obscenity laws; but the decision was firmly grounded in the First Amendment. The right pressed upon us here has no similar support in the text of the Constitution, and it does not qualify for recognition under the prevailing principles for construing the Fourteenth Amendment. Its limits are also difficult to discern. Plainly enough, otherwise illegal conduct is not always immunized whenever it occurs in the home. Victimless crimes, such as the possession and use of illegal drugs, do not escape the law where they are committed at home. *Stanley* itself recognized that its holding offered no protection for the possession in the home of drugs, firearms, or stolen goods. And if respondent's submission is limited to the voluntary sexual conduct between consenting adults, it would be difficult, except by fiat, to limit the claimed right to homosexual conduct while leaving exposed to prosecution adultery, incest, and other sexual crimes even though they are committed in the home. We are unwilling to start down that road.

Even if the conduct at issue here is not a fundamental right, respondent asserts that there must be a rational basis for the law and that there is none in this case other than the presumed belief of a majority of the electorate in Georgia that homosexual sodomy is immoral and unacceptable. This is said to be an inadequate rationale to support the law. The law, however, is constantly based on notions of morality, and if all laws representing essentially moral choices are to be invalidated under the Due Process Clause, the courts will be very busy indeed. Even respondent makes no such claim, but insists that majority sentiments about the morality of homosexuality should be declared inadequate. We do not agree, and are unpersuaded that the sodomy laws of some 25 States should be invalidated on this basis.

Accordingly, the judgment of the Court of Appeals is *Reversed*.

Justice *Blackmun*, dissenting.

This case is no more about "a fundamental right to engage in homosexual sodomy," as the Court purports to declare, than *Stanley v. Georgia* (1969) was about a fundamental right to watch obscene movies, or *Katz v. United States* (1967) was about a fundamental right to place interstate bets from a telephone booth. Rather, this case is about "the most comprehensive of rights and the right most valued by civilized men," namely, "the right to be let alone."

The statute at issue, Ga. Code Ann. § 16-6-2 (1984), denies individuals the right to decide for themselves whether to engage in particular forms of private, consensual sexual activity. The Court concludes that § 16-6-2 is valid essentially because "the laws of . . . many States . . . still make such conduct illegal and have done so for a very long time." But the fact that the moral judgments expressed by statutes like § 16-6-2 may be " 'natural and familiar . . . ought not to conclude our judgment upon the question whether statutes embodying them conflict with the Constitution of the United States.' " Like Justice Holmes, I believe that "[i]t is revolting to have no better reason for a rule of law than that so it was laid down in the time of Henry IV. It is still more revolting if the grounds upon which it was laid down have vanished long since, and the rule simply persists from blind imitation of the past." I believe we must analyze respondent Hardwick's claim in the light of the values that underlie the constitutional right to privacy. If that right means anything, it means that, before Georgia can prosecute its citizens for making choices about the most intimate aspects of their lives, it must do more than assert that the choice they have made is an "'abominable crime not fit to be named among Christians.'"

I

. . . A fair reading of the statute and of the complaint clearly reveals that the majority has distorted the question this case presents.

. . . The Court's almost obsessive focus on homosexual activity is particularly hard to justify in light of the broad language Georgia has used. . . . Georgia has provided that "[a] person commits the offense of sodomy when he performs or submits to any sexual act involving the sex organs of one person and the mouth or anus of another." The sex or status of the persons who engage in the act is irrelevant as a matter of state law. . . . Michael Hardwick's standing may rest in significant part on Georgia's apparent willingness to enforce against homosexuals a law it seems not to have any desire to enforce against heterosexuals. But his claim that § 16-6-2 involves an unconstitutional intrusion into his privacy and his right of intimate association does not depend in any way on his sexual orientation. . . .

. . . I believe that Hardwick has stated a cognizable claim that § 16-6-2 interferes with constitutionally protected interests in privacy and freedom of intimate association. . . . The Court's cramped reading of the issue before it makes for a short opinion, but it does little to make for a persuasive one.

II

"Our cases long have recognized that the Constitution embodies a promise that a certain private sphere of individual liberty will be kept largely beyond the reach of government." In construing the right to privacy, the Court has proceeded along two somewhat distinct, albeit complementary, lines. First, it has recognized a privacy interest with reference to certain *decisions* that are properly for the individual to make. Second, it has recognized a privacy interest with reference to certain *places* without regard for the particular activities in which the individuals who occupy them are engaged. The case before us implicates both the decisional and the spatial aspects of the right to privacy.

A

The Court concludes today that none of our prior cases dealing with various decisions that individuals are entitled to make free of governmental interference "bears any resemblance to the claimed constitutional right of homosexuals to engage in acts of sodomy that is asserted in this case." While it is true that these cases may be characterized by their connection to protection of the family, the Court's conclusion that they extend no further than this boundary ignores the warning . . . against "clos[ing] our eyes to the basic reasons why certain rights associated with the family have been accorded shelter under the Fourteenth Amendment's Due Process Clause." We protect those rights not because they contribute, in some direct and material way, to the general public welfare, but because they form so central a part of an individual's life. "[T]he concept of privacy embodies the 'moral fact that a person belongs to himself and not others nor to society as a whole.'" And so we protect the decision whether to marry precisely because marriage "is an association that promotes a way of life, not causes; a harmony in living, not political faiths; a bilateral loyalty, not commercial or social projects." We protect the decision whether to have a child because parenthood alters so dramatically an individual's self-definition, not because of demographic considerations or the Bible's command to be fruitful and multiply. And we protect the family because it contributes so powerfully to the happiness of individuals, not because of a preference for stereotypical households. The Court [has] recognized . . . that the "ability independently to define one's identity that is central to any concept of liberty" cannot truly be exercised in a vacuum; we all depend on the "emotional enrichment from close ties with others."

Only the most willful blindness could obscure the fact that sexual intimacy is "a sensitive, key relationship of human existence, central to family life, community welfare, and the development of human personality." The fact that individuals define themselves in a significant way through their intimate sexual relationships with others suggests, in a Nation as diverse as ours, that there may be many "right" ways of conducting those relationships, and that much of the richness of a relationship will come from the freedom an individual has to *choose* the form and nature of these intensely personal bonds.

In a variety of circumstances we have recognized that a necessary corollary of giving individuals freedom to choose how to conduct their lives is acceptance of the fact that different individuals will make different choices. For example, in holding that the clearly important state interest in public education should give way to a competing claim by the Amish to the effect that extended formal schooling threatened their way of life, the Court declared: "There can be no assumption that today's majority is 'right' and the Amish and others like them are 'wrong.' A way of life that is odd or even erratic but interferes with no rights or interests of others is not to be condemned because it is different." The Court claims that its decision today merely refuses to recognize a fundamental right to engage in homosexual sodomy; what the Court really has refused to recognize is the fundamental interest all individuals have in controlling the nature of their intimate associations with others.

B

The behavior for which Hardwick faces prosecution occurred in his own home, a place to which the Fourth Amendment attaches special significance. The Court's treatment of this aspect of the case is symptomatic of its overall refusal to consider the broad principles that have informed our treatment of privacy in specific cases. Just as the right to privacy is more than the mere aggregation of a number of entitlements to engage in specific behavior, so too, protecting the physical integrity of the home is more than merely a means of protecting specific activities that often take place there. Even when our understanding of the contours of the right to privacy depends on "reference to a 'place,'" the essence of a Fourth Amendment violation is 'not the breaking of [a person's] doors, and the rummaging of his drawers,' but rather is 'the invasion of his indefeasible right of personal security, personal liberty and private property.'"

The Court's interpretation of the pivotal case of *Stanley v. Georgia* (1969) is entirely unconvincing. *Stanley* held that Georgia's undoubted power to punish the public distribution of constitutionally unprotected, obscene material did not permit the State to punish the private possession of such material. According to the majority here, *Stanley* relied entirely on the First Amendment, and thus, it is claimed, sheds no light on cases not involving printed materials. But that is not what *Stanley* said. Rather, the *Stanley* Court anchored its holding in the Fourth Amendment's special protection for the individual in his home. . . .

. . . *Stanley* rested as much on the Court's understanding of the Fourth Amendment as it did on the First. . . . "The right of the people to be secure in their

. . . houses," expressly guaranteed by the Fourth Amendment, is perhaps the most "textual" of the various constitutional provisions that inform our understanding of the right to privacy, and thus I cannot agree with the Court's statement that "[t]he right pressed upon us here has no . . . support in the text of the Constitution." Indeed, the right of an individual to conduct intimate relationships in the intimacy of his or her own home seems to me to be the heart of the Constitution's protection of privacy.

III

The Court's failure to comprehend the magnitude of the liberty interests at stake in this case leads it to slight the question whether petitioner, on behalf of the State, has justified Georgia's infringement on these interests. I believe that neither of the two general justifications for § 16-6-2 that petitioner has advanced warrants dismissing respondent's challenge for failure to state a claim.

First, petitioner asserts that the acts made criminal by the statute may have serious adverse consequences for "the general public health and welfare," such as spreading communicable diseases or fostering other criminal activity. Inasmuch as this case was dismissed by the District Court on the pleadings, it is not surprising that the record before us is barren of any evidence to support petitioner's claim. In light of the state of the record, I see no justification for the Court's attempt to equate the private, consensual sexual activity at issue here with the "possession in the home of drugs, firearms, or stolen goods," to which *Stanley* refused to extend its protection. None of the behavior so mentioned in *Stanley* can properly be viewed as "[v]ictimless": drugs and weapons are inherently dangerous, and for property to be "stolen," someone must have been wrongfully deprived of it. Nothing in the record before the Court provides any justification for finding the activity forbidden by § 16-6-2 to be physically dangerous, either to the persons engaged in it or to others.

The core of petitioner's defense of § 16-6-2, however, is that respondent and others who engage in the conduct prohibited by § 16-6-2 interfere with Georgia's exercise of the "'right of the Nation and of the States to maintain a decent society.'" Essentially, petitioner argues, and the Court agrees, that the fact that the acts described in § 16-6-2 "for hundreds of years, if not thousands, have been uniformly condemned as immoral" is a sufficient reason to permit a State to ban them today.

I cannot agree that either the length of time a majority has held its convictions or the passions with which it defends them can withdraw legislation from this Court's scrutiny. As Justice Jackson wrote so eloquently, . . . "we apply the limitations of the Constitution with no fear that freedom to be intellectually and spiritually diverse or even contrary will distintegrate the social organization. . . . [F]reedom to differ is not limited to things that do not matter much. That would be a mere shadow of freedom. The test of its substance is the right to differ as to things that touch the heart of the existing order." It is precisely because the issue raised by this case touches the heart of what makes individuals what they are that we should be especially sensitive to the rights of those whose choices upset the majority.

The assertion that "traditional Judeo-Christian values proscribe" the conduct involved cannot provide an adequate justification for § 16-6-2. That certain, but by no means all, religious groups condemn the behavior at issue gives the State no license to impose their judgments on the entire citizenry. The legitimacy of secular legislation depends instead on whether the State can advance some justification for its law beyond its conformity to religious doctrine. Thus, far from buttressing his case, petitioner's invocation of Leviticus, Romans, St. Thomas Aquinas, and sodomy's heretical status during the Middle Ages undermines his suggestion that § 16-6-2 represents a legitimate use of secular coercive power. A State can no more punish private behavior because of religious intolerance than it can punish such behavior because of racial animus. "The Constitution cannot control such prejudices, but neither can it tolerate them. Private biases may be outside the reach of the law, but the law cannot, directly or indirectly, give them effect." No matter how uncomfortable a certain group may make the majority of this Court, we have held that "[m]ere public intolerance or animosity cannot constitutionally justify the deprivation of a person's physical liberty."

Nor can § 16-6-2 be justified as a "morally neutral" exercise of Georgia's power to "protect the public environment." Certainly, some private behavior can affect the fabric of society as a whole. Reasonable people may differ about whether particular sexual acts are moral or immoral, but "we have ample evidence for believing that people will not abandon morality, will not think any better of murder, cruelty and dishonesty, merely because some private sexual practice which they abominate is not punished by the law." Petitioner and the Court fail to see the difference between laws that protect public sensibilities and those that enforce private morality. Statutes banning public sexual activity are entirely consistent with protecting the individual's liberty interest in decisions concerning sexual relations: the same recognition that those decisions are intensely private which justifies protecting them from governmental interference can justify protecting individuals from unwilling exposure to the sexual activities of others. But the mere fact that intimate behavior may be punished when it takes place in public cannot dictate how States can regulate intimate behavior that occurs in intimate places.

This case involves no real interference with the rights of others, for the mere knowledge that other individuals do not adhere to one's value system cannot be a legally cognizable interest, let alone an interest that can justify invading the houses, hearts, and minds of citizens who choose to live their lives differently.

IV

It took but three years for the Court to see the error in its analysis in *Minersville School District v. Gobitis* (1940) and to recognize that the threat to national cohesion posed by a refusal to salute the flag was vastly outweighed by the threat to those same values posed by compelling such a salute. I can only hope that here, too, the Court soon will reconsider its analysis and conclude that depriving individuals of the right to choose for themselves how to conduct their intimate relationships poses a far greater threat to the values most deeply rooted in our Nation's history than tolerance of nonconformity could ever do. Because I think the Court today betrays those values, I dissent.

DISCUSSION QUESTIONS

1. Is it possible to argue consistently that, on the one hand, heterosexuals have a right to sexual privacy and that, on the other, homosexuals do not? Defend your view, and compare it with the Supreme Court's decision.
2. Is there a *moral* difference between heterosexual sodomy and homosexual sodomy? Defend your view.

3. How might Thomas Aquinas respond to the claim that heterosexuals have a right to sexual privacy? Do you agree with this position?
4. Why does Justice Blackmun believe that this case is *not* about "a fundamental right to engage in homosexual sodomy"? Do you agree with him?
5. Do we have a fundamental right to be "let alone"? Compare and contrast the views of Justice White and Justice Blackmun on this question. Do you agree with either of them? Defend your position.

Is Adultery Immoral?

Richard Wasserstrom defines "adultery" as extramarital sex and evaluates a number of arguments concerning its immorality. He supports arguments that adultery is immoral in that it involves breaking promises, taking unfair advantage of another person, or deceiving him or her. Whether we assume that promise-breaking and deception are wrong in and of themselves or that they are wrong because they inflict harm on another person, Wasserstrom contends that we have strong grounds to argue for the immorality of adultery. Nonetheless, the argument that adultery is wrong because a prohibition on extramarital sex helps to maintain the institution of marriage is at best an incomplete argument. Wasserstrom contends that for this argument to be convincing we ought to have strong reasons for believing that marriage is a morally desirable and just social institution. But, because of the complicated and loose structure of the concept of marriage, such reasons are difficult to defend.

Richard Wasserstrom is Professor Emeritus of philosophy at the University of California at Santa Cruz and is widely published in ethics and legal philosophy. His books include *The Judicial Decision: Toward a Theory of Legal Justification* (1961), *War and Morality* (ed., 1970), *Morality and the Law* (ed., 1971), and *Philosophy and Social Issues: Five Studies* (1980).

Many discussions of the enforcement of morality by the law take as illustrative of the problem under consideration the regulation of various types of sexual behavior by the criminal law. It was, for example, the Wolfenden Report's recommendations concerning homosexuality and prostitution that led Lord Devlin to compose his now famous lecture, "The Enforcement of Morals." And that lecture in turn provoked important philosophical responses from H. L. A. Hart, Ronald Dworkin, and others.

Much, if not all, of the recent philosophical literature on the enforcement of morals appears to take for granted the immorality of the sexual behavior in question. The focus of discussion, at least, is whether such things as homosexuality, prostitution, and adultery ought to be made illegal even if they are immoral, and not whether they are immoral.

I propose in this paper to think about the latter, more neglected topic, that of sexual morality, and to do so in the following fashion. I shall consider just one kind of behavior that is often taken to be a case of sexual immorality—adultery. I am interested in pursuing at least two questions. First, I want to explore the question of in what respects adulterous behavior falls within the domain of morality at all. For this surely is one of the puzzles one encounters when considering the topic of sexual morality. It is often hard to see on what grounds much of the behavior is deemed to be either moral or immoral, for example, private homosexual behavior between consenting adults. I have purposely selected adultery because it seems a more plausible candidate for moral assessment than many other kinds of sexual behavior.

The second question I want to examine is that of what is to be said about adultery, without being especially concerned to stay within the area of morality. I shall endeavor, in other words, to identify and to assess a number of the major arguments that might be advanced against adultery. I believe that they are the chief arguments that would be given in support of the view that adultery is immoral, but I think they are worth considering even if some of them turn out to be nonmoral arguments and considerations.

A number of the issues involved seem to me to be complicated and difficult. In a number of places I have at best indicated where further philosophical exploration is required without having successfully conducted the exploration myself. The paper may very well be more useful as an illustration of how one might begin to think about the subject of sexual morality than as an elucidation of important truths about the topic.

Before I turn to the arguments themselves there are two preliminary points that require some clarification. Throughout the paper I shall refer to the immorality of such things as breaking a promise, deceiving someone, etc. In a very rough way, I mean by this that there is something morally wrong that is done in doing the action in question. I mean that the action is, in a strong sense of "*prima facie,*" *prima facie* wrong or unjustified. I do not mean that it may never be right or justifiable to do the action; just that the fact that it is an action of this description always does count against the rightness of the action. I leave entirely open the question of what it is that makes actions of this kind immoral in this sense of "immoral."

The second preliminary point concerns what is meant or implied by the concept of adultery. I mean by "adultery" any case of extramarital sex, and I want to explore the arguments for and against

extramarital sex, undertaken in a variety of morally relevant situations. Someone might claim that the concept of adultery is conceptually connected with the concept of immorality, and that to characterize behavior as adulterous is already to characterize it as immoral or unjustified in the sense described above. There may be something to this. Hence the importance of making it clear that I want to talk about extramarital sexual relations. If they are always immoral, this is something that must be shown by argument. If the concept of adultery does in some sense entail or imply immorality, I want to ask whether that connection is a rationally based one. If not all cases of extramarital sex are immoral (again, in the sense described above), then the concept of adultery should either be weakened accordingly or restricted to those classes of extramarital sex for which the predication of immorality is warranted.

One argument for the immorality of adultery might go something like this: what makes adultery immoral is that it involves the breaking of a promise, and what makes adultery seriously wrong is that it involves the breaking of an important promise. For, so the argument might continue, one of the things the two parties promise each other when they get married is that they will abstain from sexual relationships with third persons. Because of this promise both spouses quite reasonably entertain the expectation that the other will behave in conformity with it. Hence, when one of the parties has sexual intercourse with a third person he or she breaks that promise about sexual relationships which was made when the marriage was entered into, and defeats the reasonable expectations of exclusivity entertained by the spouse.

In many cases the immorality involved in breaching the promise relating to extramarital sex may be a good deal more serious than that involved in the breach of other promises. This is so because adherence to this promise may be of much greater importance to the parties than is adherence to many of the other promises given or received by them in their lifetime. The breaking of this promise may be much more hurtful and painful than is typically the case.

Why is this so? To begin with, it may have been difficult for the nonadulterous spouse to have kept the promise. Hence that spouse may feel the unfairness of having restrained himself or herself in the absence of reciprocal restraint having been exercised by the adulterous spouse. In addition, the spouse may perceive the breaking of the promise as an indication of a kind of indifference on the part of the adulterous spouse. If you really cared about me and my feelings—the spouse might say—you would not have done this to me. And third, and related to the above, the spouse may see the act of sexual intercourse with another as a sign of affection for the other person and as an additional rejection of the nonadulterous spouse as the one who is loved by the adulterous spouse. It is not just that the adulterous spouse does not take the feelings of the spouse sufficiently into account; the adulterous spouse also indicates through the act of adultery affection for someone other than the spouse. I will return to these points later. For the present, it is sufficient to note that a set of arguments can be developed in support of the proposition that certain kinds of adultery are wrong just because they involve the breach of a serious promise which, among other things, leads to the intentional infliction of substantial pain by one spouse upon the other.

Another argument for the immorality of adultery focuses not on the existence of a promise of sexual exclusivity but on the connection between adultery and deception. According to this argument, adultery involves deception. And because deception is wrong, so is adultery.

Although it is certainly not obviously so, I shall simply assume in this paper that deception is always immoral. Thus the crucial issue for my purposes is the asserted connection between extramarital sex and deception. Is it plausible to maintain, as this argument does, that adultery always does involve deception and is on that basis to be condemned?

The most obvious person on whom deceptions might be practiced is the nonparticipating spouse; and the most obvious thing about which the nonparticipating spouse can be deceived is the existence of the adulterous act. One clear case of deception is that of lying. Instead of saying that the afternoon was spent in bed with A, the adulterous spouse asserts that it was spent in the library with B, or on the golf course with C.

There can also be deception even when no lies are told. Suppose, for instance, that a person has sexual intercourse with someone other than his or her spouse and just does not tell the spouse about it. Is that deception? It may not be a case of lying if, for example, the spouse is never asked by the other about the situation. Still, we might say, it is surely deceptive because of the promises that were exchanged at marriage. As we saw earlier, these promises provide a foundation for the reasonable belief that neither spouse will engage in sexual relationships with any other persons. Hence the failure to bring the fact of extramarital sex to the attention of the other spouse deceives that spouse about the present state of the marital relationship.

Adultery, in other words, can involve both active and passive deception. An adulterous spouse may just keep silent or, as is often the fact, the spouse may engage in an increasingly complex way of life devoted to the concealment of the facts from the nonparticipating spouse. Lies, half-truths, clandestine meetings, and the like may become a central feature of the adulterous spouse's existence. These are things that can and do happen, and when they do they make the case against adultery an easy one. Still, neither active nor passive deception is inevitably a feature of an extramarital relationship.

It is possible, though, that a more subtle but pervasive kind of deceptiveness is a feature of adultery. It comes about because of the connection in our culture between sexual intimacy and certain feelings of love and affection. The point can be made indirectly at first by seeing that one way in which we can, in our culture, mark off our close friends from our mere acquaintances is through the kinds of intimacies that we are prepared to share with them. I may, for instance, be willing to reveal my very private thoughts and emotions to my closest friends or to my wife, but to no one else. My sharing of these intimate facts about myself is from one perspective a way of making a gift to those who mean the most to me. Revealing these things and sharing them with those who mean the most to me is one means by which I create, maintain, and confirm those interpersonal relationships that are of most importance to me.

Now in our culture, it might be claimed, sexual intimacy is one of the chief currencies through which gifts of this sort are exchanged. One way to tell someone—particularly someone of the opposite sex—that you have feelings of affection and love for them is by allowing to them or sharing with them sexual behaviors that one doesn't share with the rest of the world. This way of measuring affection was certainly very much a part of the culture in which I matured. It worked something like this. If you were a girl, you showed how much you liked someone by the degree of sexual intimacy you would allow. If you liked a boy only a little, you never did more than kiss—and even the kiss was not very passionate. If you liked the boy a lot and if your feeling was reciprocated, necking, and possibly petting, was permissible. If the attachment was still stronger and you thought it might even become a permanent relationship, the sexual activity was correspondingly more intense and more intimate, although whether it would ever lead to sexual intercourse depended on whether the parties (and particularly the girl) accepted fully the prohibition on nonmarital sex. The situation for the boy was related, but not exactly the same. The assumption was that males did not naturally link sex with affection in the way in which females did. However, since women did, males had to take this into account. That is to say, because a woman would permit sexual intimacies only if she had feelings of affection for the male and only if those feelings were reciprocated, the male had to have and express those feelings, too, before sexual intimacies of any sort would occur.

The result was that the importance of a correlation between sexual intimacy and feelings of love and affection was taught by the culture and assimilated by those growing up in the culture. The scale of possible positive feelings toward persons of the other sex ran from casual liking at the one end to the love that was deemed essential to and characteristic of marriage at the other. The scale of possible sexual behavior ran from brief, passionless kissing or hand-holding at the one end to sexual intercourse at the other. And the correlation between the two scales was quite precise. As a result, any act of sexual intimacy carried substantial meaning with it, and no act of sexual intimacy was simply a pleasurable set of bodily sensations. Many such acts were, of course, more pleasurable to the participants because they were a way of saying what the participants' feelings were. And sometimes they were less pleasurable for the same reason. The point is, however, that in any event sexual activity was much more than mere bodily enjoyment. It was not like eating a good meal, listening to good music, lying in the sun, or getting a pleasant back rub. It was behavior that meant a great deal concerning one's feelings for persons of the opposite sex in whom one was most interested and with whom one was most involved. It was among the most authoritative ways in which one could communicate to another the nature and degree of one's affection.

If this sketch is even roughly right, then several things become somewhat clearer. To begin with, a possible rationale for many of the rules of conventional sexual morality can be developed. If, for example, sexual intercourse is associated with the kind of affection and commitment to another that is regarded as characteristic of the marriage relationship, then it is natural that sexual intercourse should be thought properly to take place between persons who are married to each other. And if it is thought that this kind of affection and commitment is only

to be found within the marriage relationship, then it is not surprising that sexual intercourse should only be thought to be proper within marriage.

Related to what has just been said is the idea that sexual intercourse ought to be restricted to those who are married to each other as a means by which to confirm the very special feelings that spouses have for each other. Because the culture teaches that sexual intercourse means that the strongest of all feelings for each other are shared by the lovers, it is natural that persons who are married to each other should be able to say this to each other in this way. Revealing and confirming verbally that these feelings are present is one thing that helps to sustain the relationship; engaging in sexual intercourse is another.

In addition, this account would help to provide a framework within which to make sense of the notion that some sex is better than other sex. As I indicated earlier, the fact that sexual intimacy can be meaningful in the sense described tends to make it also the case that sexual intercourse can sometimes be more enjoyable than at other times. On this view, sexual intercourse will typically be more enjoyable where the strong feelings of affection are present than it will be where it is merely "mechanical." This is so in part because people enjoy being loved, especially by those whom they love. Just as we like to hear words of affection, so we like to receive affectionate behavior. And the meaning enhances the independently pleasurable behavior.

More to the point, moreover, an additional rationale for the prohibition on extramarital sex can now be developed. For given this way of viewing the sexual world, extramarital sex will almost always involve deception of a deeper sort. If the adulterous spouse does not in fact have the appropriate feelings of affection for the extramarital partner, then the adulterous spouse is deceiving that person about the presence of such feelings. If, on the other hand, the adulterous spouse does have the corresponding feelings for the extramarital partner but not toward the nonparticipating spouse, the adulterous spouse is very probably deceiving the nonparticipating spouse about the presence of such feelings toward that spouse. Indeed, it might be argued, whenever there is no longer love between the two persons who are married to each other, there is deception just because being married implies both to the participants and to the world that such a bond exists. Deception is inevitable, the argument might conclude, because the feelings of affection that ought to accompany any act of sexual intercourse can only be held toward one other person at any given time in one's life. And if this is so, then the adulterous spouse always deceives either the partner in adultery or the nonparticipating spouse about the existence of such feelings. Thus extramarital sex involves deception of this sort and is for this reason immoral even if no deception vis-à-vis the occurrence of the act of adultery takes place.

What might be said in response to the foregoing arguments? The first thing that might be said is that the account of the connection between sexual intimacy and feelings of affection is inaccurate. Not inaccurate in the sense that no one thinks of things that way, but in the sense that there is substantially more divergence of opinion than that account suggests. For example, the view I have delineated may describe reasonably accurately the concepts of the sexual world in which I grew up, but it does not capture the sexual *weltanschauung* [worldview] of today's youth at all. Thus, whether or not adultery implies deception in respect to feelings depends very much on the persons who are involved and the way they look at the "meaning" of sexual intimacy.

Second, the argument leaves to be answered the question of whether it is desirable for sexual intimacy to carry the sorts of messages described above. For those persons for whom sex does have these implications, there are special feelings and sensibilities that must be taken into account. But it is another question entirely whether any valuable end—moral or otherwise—is served by investing sexual behavior with such significance. That is something that must be shown and not just assumed. It might, for instance, be the case that substantially more good than harm would come from a kind of demystification of sexual behavior: one that would encourage the enjoyment of sex more for its own sake and one that would reject the centrality both of the association of sex with love and of love with only one other person.

I regard these as two of the more difficult, unresolved issues that our culture faces today in respect to thinking sensibly about the attitudes toward sex and love that we should try to develop in ourselves and in our children. Much of the contemporary literature that advocates sexual liberation of one sort or another embraces one or the other of two different views about the relationship between sex and love.

One view holds that sex should be separated from love and affection. To be sure, sex is probably better when the partners genuinely like and enjoy each other. But sex is basically an intensive, exciting sensuous activity that can be enjoyed in a variety of suitable settings with a variety of suitable partners. The situation in respect to sexual pleasure is no different from that of the person who knows and appreciates fine food and who can have a very satisfying meal in any number of good restaurants with any number of congenial companions. One question that must be settled here is whether sex can be so demystified; another, more important question is whether it would be desirable to do so. What would we gain and what might we lose if we all lived in a world in which an act of sexual intercourse was no more or less significant or enjoyable than having a delicious meal in a nice setting with a good friend? The answer to this question lies beyond the scope of this paper.

The second view seeks to drive the wedge in a different place. It is not the link between sex and love that needs to be broken; rather, on this view, it is the connection between love and exclusivity that ought to be severed. For a number of the reasons already given, it is desirable, so this argument goes, that sexual intimacy continue to be reserved to and shared with only those for whom one has very great affection. The mistake lies in thinking that any "normal" adult will only have those feelings toward one other adult during his or her lifetime—or even at any time in his or her life. It is the concept of adult love, not ideas about sex, that, on this view, needs demystification. What are thought to be both unrealistic and unfortunate are the notions of exclusivity and possessiveness that attach to the dominant conception of love between adults in our and other cultures. Parents of four, five, six, or even ten children can certainly claim and sometimes claim correctly that they love all of their children, that they love them all equally, and that it is simply untrue to their feelings to insist that the numbers involved diminish either the quantity or the quality of their love. If this is an idea that is readily understandable in the case of parents and children, there is no necessary reason why it is an impossible or undesirable ideal in the case of adults. To be sure, there is probably a limit to the number of intimate, "primary" relationships that any person can maintain at any given time without the quality of the relationship being affected. But one adult ought surely be able to love two, three, or even six other adults at any one time without that love being different in kind or degree from that of the traditional, monogamous, lifetime marriage. And as between the individuals in these relationships, whether within a marriage or without, sexual intimacy is fitting and good.

The issues raised by a position such as this one are also surely worth exploring in detail and with care. Is there something to be called "sexual love" which is different from parental love or the non-sexual love of close friends? Is there something about love in general that links it naturally and appropriately with feelings of exclusivity and possession? Or is there something about sexual love, whatever that may be, that makes these feelings especially fitting here? Once again the issues are conceptual, empirical, and normative all at once: What is love? How could it be different? Would it be a good thing or a bad thing if it were different?

Suppose, though, that having delineated these problems we were now to pass them by. Suppose, moreover, we were to be persuaded of the possibility and the desirability of weakening substantially either the links between sex and love or the links between sexual love and exclusivity. Would it not then be the case that adultery could be free from all of the morally objectionable features described so far? To be more specific, let us imagine that a husband and wife have what is today sometimes characterized as an "open marriage." Suppose, that is, that they have agreed in advance that extramarital sex is—under certain circumstances—acceptable behavior for each to engage in. Suppose, that as a result there is no impulse to deceive each other about the occurrence or nature of any such relationships, and that no deception in fact occurs. Suppose, too, that there is no deception in respect to the feelings involved between the adulterous spouse and the extramarital partner. And suppose, finally, that one or the other or both of the spouses then has sexual intercourse in circumstances consistent with these understandings. Under this description, so the agreement might conclude, adultery is simply not immoral. At a minimum, adultery cannot very plausibly be condemned either on the ground that it involves deception or on the ground that it requires the breaking of a promise.

At least two responses are worth considering. One calls attention to the connection between marriage and adultery; the other looks to more instrumental arguments for the immorality of adultery. Both issues deserve further exploration.

One way to deal with the case of the "open marriage" is to question whether the two persons involved are still properly to be described as being married to each other. Part of the meaning of what it is for two persons to be married to each other, so this argument would go, is to have committed oneself to have sexual relationships only with one's spouse. Of course, it would be added, we know that that commitment is not always honored. We know

that persons who are married to each other often do commit adultery. But there is a difference between being willing to make a commitment to marital fidelity, even though one may fail to honor that commitment, and not making the commitment at all. Whatever the relationship may be between the two individuals in the case described above, the absence of any commitment to sexual exclusivity requires the conclusion that their relationship is not a marital one. For a commitment to sexual exclusivity is a necessary although not a sufficient condition for the existence of a marriage.

Although there may be something to this suggestion, as it is stated it is too strong to be acceptable. To begin with, I think it is very doubtful that there are many, if any, *necessary* conditions for marriage; but even if there are, a commitment to sexual exclusivity is not such a condition.

To see that this is so, consider what might be taken to be some of the essential characteristics of a marriage. We might be tempted to propose that the concept of marriage requires the following: a formal ceremony of some sort in which mutual obligations are undertaken between two persons of the opposite sex; the capacity on the part of the persons involved to have sexual intercourse with each other; the willingness to have sexual intercourse only with each other; and feelings of love and affection between the two persons. The problem is that we can imagine relationships that are clearly marital and yet lack one or more of these features. For example, in our own society, it is possible for two persons to be married without going through a formal ceremony, as in the common-law marriages recognized in some jurisdictions. It is also possible for two persons to get married even though one or both lacks the capacity to engage in sexual intercourse. Thus, two very elderly persons who have neither the desire nor the ability to have intercourse can, nonetheless, get married, as can persons whose sexual organs have been injured so that intercourse is not possible. And we certainly know of marriages in which love was not present at the time of the marriage, as, for instance, in marriages of state and marriages of convenience.

Counterexamples not satisfying the condition relating to the abstention from extramarital sex are even more easily produced. We certainly know of societies and cultures in which polygamy and polyandry are practiced, and we have no difficulty in recognizing these relationships as cases of marriages. It might be objected, though, that these are not counterexamples because they are plural marriages rather than marriages in which sex is permitted with someone other than with one of the persons to whom one is married. But we also know of societies in which it is permissible for married persons to have sexual relationships with persons to whom they were not married, for example, temple prostitutes, concubines, and homosexual lovers. And even if we knew of no such societies, the conceptual claim would still, I submit, not be well taken. For suppose all of the other indicia of marriage were present: suppose the two persons were of the opposite sex. Suppose they had the capacity and desire to have intercourse with each other, suppose they participated in a formal ceremony in which they understood themselves voluntarily to be entering into a relationship with each other in which substantial mutual commitments were assumed. If all these conditions were satisfied, we would not be in any doubt about whether or not the two persons were married even though they had not taken on a commitment of sexual exclusivity and even though they had expressly agreed that extramarital sexual intercourse was a permissible behavior for each to engage in.

A commitment to sexual exclusivity is neither a necessary nor a sufficient condition for the existence of a marriage. It does, nonetheless, have this much to do with the nature of marriage: like the other indicia enumerated above, its presence tends to establish the existence of a marriage. Thus, in the absence of a formal ceremony of any sort, an explicit commitment to sexual exclusivity would count in favor of regarding the two persons as married. The conceptual role of the commitment to sexual exclusivity can, perhaps, be brought out through the following example. Suppose we found a tribe which had a practice in which all the other indicia of marriage were present but in which the two parties were *prohibited* ever from having sexual intercourse with each other. Moreover, suppose that sexual intercourse with others was clearly permitted. In such a case we would, I think, reject the idea that the two were married to each other and we would describe their relationship in other terms, for example, as some kind of formalized, special friendship relation—a kind of heterosexual "blood-brother" bond.

Compare that case with the following. Suppose again that the tribe had a practice in which all of the other indicia of marriage were present, but instead of a prohibition on sexual intercourse between the persons in the relationship there was no rule at all. Sexual intercourse was permissible with the person

with whom one had this ceremonial relationship, but it was no more or less permissible than with a number of other persons to whom one was not so related (for instance, all consenting adults of the opposite sex). Although we might be in doubt as to whether we ought to describe the persons as married to each other, we would probably conclude that they were married and that they simply were members of a tribe whose views about sex were quite different from our own.

What all of this shows is that a *prohibition* on sexual intercourse between the two persons involved in a relationship is conceptually incompatible with the claim that the two of them are married. The *permissibility* of intramarital sex is a necessary part of the idea of marriage. But no such incompatibility follows simply from the added permissibility of extramarital sex.

These arguments do not, of course, exhaust the arguments for the prohibition on extramarital sexual relations. The remaining argument that I wish to consider—as I indicated earlier—is a more instrumental one. It seeks to justify the prohibition by virtue of the role that it plays in the development and maintenance of nuclear families. The argument, or set of arguments, might, I believe, go something like this.

Consider first a far-fetched nonsexual example. Suppose a society were organized so that after some suitable age—say, 18, 19, or 20—persons were forbidden to eat anything but bread and water with anyone but their spouse. Persons might still choose in such a society not to get married. Good food just might not be very important to them because they have underdeveloped taste buds. Or good food might be bad for them because there is something wrong with their digestive system. Or good food might be important to them, but they might decide that the enjoyment of good food would get in the way of the attainment of other things that were more important. But most persons would, I think, be led to favor marriage in part because they preferred a richer, more varied, diet to one of bread and water. And they might remain married because the family was the only legitimate setting within which good food was obtainable. If it is important to have society organized so that persons will both get married and stay married, such an arrangement would be well suited to the preservation of the family, and the prohibitions relating to food consumption could be understood as fulfilling that function.

It is obvious that one of the more powerful human desires is the desire for sexual gratification.

The desire is a natural one, like hunger and thirst, in the sense that it need not be learned in order to be present within us and operative upon us. But there is in addition much that we do learn about what the act of sexual intercourse is like. Once we experience sexual intercourse ourselves—and in particular once we experience orgasm—we discover that it is among the most intensive, short-term pleasures of the body.

Because this is so, it is easy to see how the prohibition upon extramarital sex helps to hold marriage together. At least during that period of life when the enjoyment of sexual intercourse is one of the desirable bodily pleasures, persons will wish to enjoy those pleasures. If one consequence of being married is that one is prohibited from having sexual intercourse with anyone but one's spouse, then the spouses in a marriage are in a position to provide an important source of pleasure for each other that is unavailable to them elsewhere in the society.

The point emerges still more clearly if this rule of sexual morality is seen as of a piece with the other rules of sexual morality. When this prohibition is coupled, for example, with the prohibition on non-marital sexual intercourse, we are presented with the inducement both to get married and to stay married. For if sexual intercourse is only legitimate within marriage, then persons seeking that gratification which is a feature of sexual intercourse are furnished explicit social directions for its attainment, namely, marriage.

Nor, to continue the argument, is it necessary to focus exclusively on the bodily enjoyment that is involved. Orgasm may be a significant part of what there is to sexual intercourse, but it is not the whole of it. We need only recall the earlier discussion of the meaning that sexual intimacy has in our own culture to begin to see some of the more intricate ways in which sexual exclusivity may be connected with the establishment and maintenance of marriage as the primary heterosexual, love relationship. Adultery is wrong, in other words, because a prohibition on extramarital sex is a way to help maintain the institutions of marriage and the nuclear family.

Now I am frankly not sure what we are to say about an argument such as this one. What I am convinced of is that, like the arguments discussed earlier, this one also reveals something of the difficulty and complexity of the issues that are involved. So, what I want now to do—in the brief and final portion of this paper—is to try to delineate with reasonable precision what I take several of the fundamental, unresolved issues to be.

The first is whether this last argument is an argument for the *immorality* of extramarital sexual intercourse. What does seem clear is that there are differences between this argument and the ones considered earlier. The earlier arguments condemned adulterous behavior because it was behavior that involved breaking a promise, taking unfair advantage, or deceiving another. To the degree to which the prohibition on extramarital sex can be supported by arguments which invoke considerations such as these, there is little question but that violations of the prohibition are properly regarded as immoral. And such a claim could be defended on one or both of two distinct grounds. The first is that things like promise-breaking and deception are just wrong. The second is that adultery involving promise-breaking or deception is wrong because it involves the straightforward infliction of harm on another human being—typically the nonadulterous spouse—who has a strong claim not to have that harm so inflicted.

The argument that connects the prohibition on extramarital sex with the maintenance and preservation of the institution of marriage is an argument for the instrumental value of the prohibition. To some degree this counts, I think, against regarding all violations of the prohibition as obvious cases of immorality. This is so partly because hypothetical imperatives are less clearly within the domain of morality than are categorical ones, and even more because instrumental prohibitions are within the domain of morality only if the end they serve or the way they serve it is itself within the domain of morality.

What this should help us see, I think, is the fact that the argument that connects the prohibition on adultery with the preservation of marriage is at best seriously incomplete. Before we ought to be convinced by it, we ought to have reasons for believing that marriage is a morally desirable and just social institution. And this is not quite as easy or obvious a task as it may seem to be. For the concept of marriage is, as we have seen, both a loosely structured and complicated one. There may be all sorts of intimate, interpersonal relationships which will resemble but not be identical with the typical marriage relationship presupposed by the traditional sexual morality. There may be a number of distinguishable sexual and loving arrangements which can all legitimately claim to be called *marriages*. The prohibitions of the traditional sexual morality may be effective ways to maintain some marriages and ineffective ways to promote and preserve others. The prohibitions of the traditional sexual morality may make good psychological sense if certain psychological theories are true, and they may be purveyors of immense psychological mischief if other psychological theories are true. The prohibitions of the traditional sexual morality may seem obviously correct if sexual intimacy carries the meaning that the dominant culture has often ascribed to it, and they may seem equally bizarre when sex is viewed through the perspective of the counterculture. Irrespective of whether instrumental arguments of this sort are properly deemed moral arguments, they ought not to fully convince anyone until questions like these are answered.

DISCUSSION QUESTIONS

1. What are the "necessary" and "sufficient" conditions for marriage? Compare your conditions with Wasserstrom's.
2. Wasserstrom distinguishes between "moral" and "nonmoral" arguments against adultery. What is the difference? Give an example of each.
3. Wasserstrom distinguishes between "active" and "passive" deception. What is the distinction, and why is it important? Is this distinction similar to James Rachels' distinction between "active" and "passive" euthanasia (see Chapter 3)? If so, do Rachels' arguments against this distinction hold for Wasserstrom's "active" and "passive" deception as well?
4. Why does Wasserstrom believe that a commitment to sexual exclusivity is neither a necessary nor a sufficient condition for the existence of marriage? Do you agree with him?
5. Do you believe that marriage is a morally desirable and just social institution? Defend your view. Why does Wasserstrom think that defending the moral desirability of marriage is so difficult? Do you agree?

 LAURENCE HOULGATE

Is Divorce Immoral?

Laurence Houlgate argues that it is morally wrong for the parents of some young children to divorce. He reasons as follows: (1) parents have a duty to behave in ways that promote the best interests of their young children and should particularly refrain from behavior that causes or is likely to cause them harm; (2) divorce is a type of behavior that causes or is likely to cause young children harm; therefore, (3) it is morally wrong for the parents of some young children to divorce. According to Houlgate, parents with young children who divorce for reasons such as "we have grown apart" or "we have become different persons than we were when we first married" are violating their moral duty to their children.

Laurence Houlgate is a professor of philosophy at California Polytechnic State University at San Luis Obispo. He is the author of *Family and State: The Philosophy of Family Law* (1988) and *Morals, Marriage and Parenthood* (1998), as well as numerous articles on ethics, law, and the family.

I. INTRODUCTION

In 1929 Bertrand Russell published *Marriage and Morals*,[1] an extended critique of traditional sexual morality and prevailing moral views about marriage and divorce. The book caused quite a sensation in Britain and the United States, in part because of Russell's suggestion that adultery may not always be wrong and his recommendation that young people contemplating marriage might want to live together for one or two years before solemnizing their relationship. Russell referred to the latter as "trial marriage," and he argued that its encouragement might have the felicitous effect of reducing the chances of marital breakdown and divorce. For this and other mild suggestions Russell was vilified by much of the American press and public.[2]

Forgotten in the commotion surrounding publication of the book was Russell's recommendation regarding divorce between couples who have young children. Russell was concerned about the high rate of divorce in America, which he attributed primarily to "extremely weak" family feeling. He regarded easy divorce "as a transitional stage on the way from the bi-parental to the purely maternal family," and he observed that this is "a stage involving considerable hardship for children, since, in the world as it is, children expect to have two parents and may become attached to their father before divorce takes place." In characteristically strong language, Russell concluded that "parents who divorce each other, except for grave cause, appear to me to be failing in their parental duty."[3]

There have been significant changes in divorce law in the United States since Russell wrote these words. Every state but South Dakota has adopted some form of "no-fault" divorce rules, making it much easier for persons to divorce than it was when Russell wrote *Marriage and Morals*. Under no-fault laws there is no longer a need to establish grounds in order to obtain a divorce. For example, a woman who wishes to divorce her husband is not required to prove that he is guilty of adultery or cruelty or has committed some other marital fault. It is sufficient to assert that "irreconcilable differences" caused the breakup of the marriage. Second, in many states only *one* of the spouses needs to claim that his or her differences with the other are irreconcilable. Mutual consent is no longer a necessary condition to the granting of a divorce.

Philosophers writing since Russell have had little to say about either the recent changes in divorce law or about the ethics of divorce, neither commenting on whether the new regulations represent moral progress, nor on the question whether it would ever be wrong for someone to seek a divorce.[4] The silence of philosophers about this and other matters related to marriage and family is unfortunate. Divorce is an act that has devastating personal and social consequences[5] for millions of adults and children.[6] If ethics is at least in part about conduct that affects the interests of others, then certainly the impact of divorce on the lives of so many people should qualify it as an act as deserving of the careful attention of the moral philosopher as the acts of punishment, abortion, or euthanasia.

II. THE DIVORCE CHILD-HARM ARGUMENT

One year after the publication of *Marriage and Morals*, fiction writer and essayist Rebecca West echoed Russell's views about the divorce of couples with children in an article for *The London Daily Express*. West wrote that "the divorce of married people with children is nearly always an unspeakable calamity." She gave several reasons for this:

> It is only just being understood, in the light of modern psychological research, how much a child depends for its healthy growth on the presence in the home of both its parents. . . . if a child is deprived of either its father or its mother it feels that it has been cheated out of a right. It cannot be reasoned out of this attitude, for children are illogical, especially where their affections are concerned, to an even greater degree than ourselves. A child who suffers from this resentment suffers much more than grief: he is liable to an obscuring of his vision, to a warping of his character. He may turn against the parent to whom the courts have given him, and regard him or her as responsible for the expulsion of the other from the home. He may try to compensate himself for what he misses by snatching everything else he can get out of life, and become selfish, and even thievish. He may, through yearning for the unattainable parent, get himself into a permanent mood of discontent, which will last his life long and make him waste every opportunity of love and happiness that comes to him later.[7]

This is a large catalog of psychological and behavioral ills to attribute to a single phenomenon, but Rebecca West thought that there was adequate psychological research to support her claims.[8] Although there was a long period after World War II during which some psychologists argued that "children can survive any family crisis without permanent damage—and grow as human beings in the process,"[9] by the 1980s the earlier research referred to by West was being confirmed. In one recently concluded long-term study of 131 middle-class children from the San Francisco, California, area, interviews conducted by clinicians at eighteen months, five years, and ten years after their parents' divorce showed that many were doing worse at each of these periods than they were immediately after their parents' separation.[10]

The results of a much longer study of the effects of divorce on children in Great Britain and the United States were published in 1991.[11] Unlike the San Francisco research, this longitudinal study used a large control group. In the British part of the survey, for example, a subsample of children who were in two-parent families during an initial interview at age 7 were followed through the next interview at age 11. At both points in time, parents and teachers independently rated the children's behavior problems,[12] and the children were given reading and mathematics achievement tests. Two hundred thirty-nine children whose parents divorced between these two age intervals were compared to over eleven thousand children whose families remained intact. Although the results were not as dramatic as those reached in the San Francisco study, children whose parents divorced showed more behavior problems and scored lower on the achievement tests at age 11.

Let us assume that there are adequate empirical grounds for the claim that children whose parents divorce while they are young may suffer from either short-term or long-term psychological distress, lowered school achievement scores, and various behavior problems.[13] If this is true, then the following simple argument for the immorality of the divorce of parents with young children seems to apply: (a) Parents have a duty to behave in ways that promote the best interests of their young children. In particular, they ought to refrain from behavior that causes or is likely to cause them harm. (b) Divorce is a type of behavior that harms some young children. Therefore, (c) it is morally wrong for the parents of some young children to divorce.

I call this the Divorce Child-Harm Argument or DCH. DCH is similar in structure to moral arguments used to condemn child abandonment and

various forms of child abuse. When we think of child abuse, we usually think of cases in which children have suffered severe physical injury or death as a result of parental behavior. But some child abuse statutes recognize emotional or psychological harm. Thus, the New York Family Court Act defines "impairment of emotional health" as

> a state of substantially limited psychological or intellectual functioning in relation to, but not limited to such factors as failure to thrive, control of aggressiveness or self-destructive impulses, ability to think and reason, or acting out or misbehavior, including incorrigibility, ungovernability or habitual truancy. . . .[14]

If we think that parental behavior that causes or is likely to cause the kind of emotional or psychological harm specified in the preceding statute is morally wrong, and if we think that parents who divorce are likely to cause emotional harm to their children, then it would appear that divorce is wrong for the same reason that these parental behaviors are wrong.

Faced with the conclusion of DCH, there are a number of ways in which the divorced parents of young children might attempt to defend themselves against the charge that it was wrong for them to divorce.

1. First, it may be objected that the preceding analogy between divorce and child abuse is misplaced. Children of divorce may suffer, but their suffering never rises to the minimum level of suffering required by legal standards for determining emotional abuse.

The response to this objection is that DCH does not argue that divorce *is* child abuse. Legal definitions of child abuse and neglect are formulated solely to deal with the problem of the conditions under which the state may justifiably intervene in the family to protect the child. DCH says nothing about state intervention, nor does it recommend any change in the laws regulating divorce. Instead, DCH is an argument about the morality of divorce. It argues that some divorces are wrong *for the same kind of reason* that child abuse is wrong. The reason that some divorces are wrong is that they cause or are likely to cause emotional harm to the children of the divorcing parents. Whether the emotional harm suffered by children whose parents divorce rises to the level of severity required by the child abuse standards of some states is beside the point. The point is whether some children whose parents divorce suffer emotional harm, *not* whether they suffer the kind or amount required by the courts to recognize a child abuse petition for purposes of court-ordered intervention.

2. The second objection to DCH is that so long as parents aggressively treat any symptoms of emotional harm that their children may suffer post-divorce in order to minimize the deleterious effects of the divorce, then they have done nothing wrong by obtaining the divorce. What *would* be wrong would be to ignore the symptoms and to leave them untreated.

This argument has the following structure: It is not wrong to divorce; it is only wrong to divorce and do nothing to minimize its bad effects on children. But consider the following counter-example: so long as I secure medical treatment for my child after I have engaged in risky behavior that resulted in his leg getting broken, then I have done nothing wrong in putting my child at risk. The reason that we resist the conclusion "I have done nothing wrong in putting my child at risk" is that we do not think it justifiable to engage in behavior that puts the lives and health of our children at risk in the first place. This is why we think it morally incumbent on us not to smoke when children are in the house, to put them in restraining seats when we have them in the car with us, and do countless other things to minimize their chances of injury in and out of the home. It is simply not enough to announce that one is prepared to treat a child's injuries after they occur. We demand that parents take steps to prevent the harm *before* it occurs.[15]

3. The third objection to DCH takes advantage of Russell's "loophole," or exception to his general claim (quoted above) that parents who divorce violate their parental duty. Russell's loophole is that the divorce might be justified if it was done for "grave cause." A grave cause exists when it is established that (a) the children will suffer more emotional harm if the marriage of their parents remains intact than they will suffer as a result of their parents' divorce; and (b) during the marriage, the parents could not control those behaviors that caused their children emotional harm. For example, with reference to (b), Russell mentions insanity or alcoholism as possible candidates for grave cause justifications for divorce because the

insane or alcoholic parent may be unable to prevent himself from engaging in the abusive behavior toward his spouse that also adversely affects his child.[16]

"Grave cause" is probably the most common of the rationales that parents will offer to justify their divorce. Thus, with reference to condition (a), those who conducted the 1991 longitudinal study mentioned above found that when they took into account such preseparation characteristics as family dysfunction and marital conflict, the apparent effect of divorce in some cases fell by about half to levels that were no longer significantly different from zero.[17] The authors of the study concluded that "much of the effect of divorce on children can be predicted by conditions that existed well before the separation occurred."[18] One commentator has recently concluded from this that the transition, through divorce, from an intact two-parent family to a single-parent family can no longer be objected to on the grounds that divorce is bad for children.[19]

However, this conclusion follows only if divorce is the only alternative available to the parents. Although a hostile family environment may cause a child to suffer as much [as] or more than he or she would suffer from the divorce, this does not yet establish the existence of a grave cause justifying the divorce. The parents must also prove condition (b); that is, they must show that they could not control the hostile family environment that caused their children to suffer. Russell has the best rejoinder to parents who claim that they had no choice but to obtain a divorce for the sake of their children:

> The husband and wife, if they have any love for their children, will regulate their conduct so as to give their children the best chance of a happy and healthy development. . . .
>
> [T]o cooperate in rearing children, even after passionate love has decayed, is by no means a superhuman task for sensible people who are capable of natural affections. . . .
>
> [A]s soon as there are children it is the duty of both parties to a marriage to do everything that they can to preserve harmonious relations, even if this requires considerable self-control.[20]

In other words, to say that one had no choice but to obtain a divorce in order not to expose one's children to marital discord is to make the extraordinary assumption that one could not control one's behavior. It is analogous to the contention of a cigarette smoker that he had to abandon his child in order to save her from the physical effects of his second-hand smoke. The point is that we are as capable of controlling the behavior toward our spouse that causes distress in our young children as we are capable of not smoking in their presence. Parents who take seriously their duty to promote the best interests of their children, and who are capable of controlling those aspects of their marital behavior that is harmful to their children, will choose the least detrimental alternative. They will "preserve harmonious relations" during their children's minority.

4. Finally, it may be objected that DCH puts far too much stress on the rights and interests of children, ignoring the legitimate needs of the parents. Surely, it might be said, the desires, projects, and commitments of each parent that give them reasons to divorce in the pursuit of ends that are their own may sometimes outweigh those reasons not to divorce that stem from the special non-contractual obligations that they have to nurture their young children.

To this I can only reply that if it is permissible for parents to divorce for such reasons,[21] then I cannot imagine what it would mean to say that they have obligations to nurture their children. How can one be said to have an *obligation* to nurture her young child if it is permissible for her to perform an act that risks harming the child for no other reason than that she wants to pursue her own projects? This empties the concept of parental obligation of most of its content. Parents of young children who divorce for no other reason than that they find their marriage unfulfilling and believe that this is justifiable seem to me to be parents who lack an understanding of what it is to have an obligation to their children. They must believe that they can treat their own children as they would treat any other child. In the case of children other than our own, most of us would acknowledge that the effect on these children of what we do counts for something. But even if it is proved to me and my spouse that (e.g.) the children of our next-door neighbor will suffer emotionally as a result of our divorce, we would not think that this puts us under an obligation to cancel or delay our separation. If we did delay it, this would be an act of charity, not a perfect duty of obligation. But with our own children, things are otherwise. Our children exert an "ethical pull" on us that is much stronger than the pull on us of the claims of other children.[22] Making provision for our children's emotional needs becomes a perfect duty

within the context of the family, and as such it outweighs our desire to pursue our own projects when this comes into conflict. This is surely a large part of what it means to become a parent.

III. CONCLUSION

I conclude that Russell is right about the wrongness of many of the divorces of parents who have young children. Such divorces are not justifiable if the reason is similar to one or more of the reasons given by many people who divorce: e.g., "We have grown apart," "We have become different persons than we were when we first married," "We are profoundly unhappy with one another," "We want to pursue a single lifestyle once again," or "I found someone else with whom I would much rather live." For those parents capable of exercising self-control over their negative emotions (e.g., spite, anger, jealousy), none of these reasons rises to the level of a grave cause, and parents who divorce for such reasons are violating their moral duty to their children.

NOTES

1. Bertrand Russell, *Marriage and Morals* (Garden City, NY: Horace Liveright, 1929).

2. Nine years later, in 1938, Russell was denied a professorial appointment at the College of the City of New York for reasons remarkably similar to those used by the Athenians to justify their conviction of Socrates. In part because of the views expressed in *Marriage and Morals,* concerned New York citizens were afraid that Professor Russell would corrupt the morals of the young people who would attend his lectures.

3. Russell, *Marriage and Morals,* p. 238.

4. There are some notable exceptions to this generalization. See, for example, Brian T. Trainor, "The State, Marriage and Divorce," *Journal of Applied Philosophy,* 9, 2 (1992): 135–148, for a defense of the claim that no-fault divorce laws are unjust; Christina Hoff Sommers, "Philosophers Against the Family," in George Graham and Hugh LaFollette, *Person to Person* (Philadelphia: Temple University Press, 1989), pp. 99–103, for a brief argument suggesting that the divorce of couples with children is sometimes morally wrong; Iris Marion Young, "Mothers, Citizenship, and Independence: A Critique of Pure Family Values," *Ethics,* 105 (April 1995): 535–556, for a critical discussion of the claim that

stable marriages are morally superior to single-parent families that either arise out of divorce or from births to unmarried women.

5. The adverse psychological effects of divorce on children are described in part II. Another deleterious consequence of divorce that some attribute to no-fault divorce laws is economic. Divorced women, and the minor children in their households—90 percent of whom live with their mothers—experience a sharp decline in their standard of living after divorce. See Lenore Weitzman, *The Divorce Revolution: The Unexplored Consequences* (New York: Free Press, 1985). Although 61 percent of women who divorced in the 1980s worked full-time and another 17 percent worked part-time, "the husband's average postdivorce per capita income surpassed that of his wife and children overall and in every income group." McLindon, "Separate but Unequal: The Economic Disaster of Divorce for Women and Children," *Family Law Quarterly*, 21, 3 (1987).

6. In 1988, for example, there were 1,167,000 divorces in the United States, involving 1,044,000 children, at a rate of 16.4 children per 1,000 under the age of 18 years. U.S. Bureau of the Census, *Statistical Abstract of the United States, 1993* (113th ed.) (Washington, DC, 1993).

7. Rebecca West, "Divorce," *The London Daily Express* (1930).

8. West was probably referring to the research [cited] in A. Skolnick and J. Skolnick, eds., *Family in Transition* (Boston: Little, Brown, 1977). In one early study of children of divorced parents between the ages of 6 and 12, half of them showed evidence of a "consolidation into troubled and conflicted depressive behavior patterns." Their behavior pattern included "continuing depression and low self-esteem, combined with frequent school and peer difficulties" (p. 452).

9. Mel Krantzler, *Creative Divorce: A New Opportunity for Personal Growth* (New York: Evans, 1974), p. 191.

10. Judith Wallerstein and Sandra Blakeslee, *Second Chances: Men, Women and Children a Decade After Divorce* (New York: Ticknor & Fields, 1989). Only children who had no previous history of emotional problems were selected for the study. At eighteen months after their parents' divorce, "an unexpectedly large number of children were on a downward

course. Their symptoms were worse than before. Their behavior at school was worse. Their peer relationships were worse." At a five-year follow-up, "some were better off than they had been during the failing marriage" (p. xv). But over a third of the whole group of these children "were significantly worse off than before. Clinically depressed, they were not doing well in school or with friends. They had deteriorated to the point that some early disturbances, such as sleep problems, poor learning, or acting out, had become chronic" (p. xvii). At the tenth-year interview, clinicians were astounded to discover that ". . . almost half of the children entered adulthood as worried, underachieving, self-deprecating, and sometimes angry young men and women" (p. 299).

11. Andrew J. Cherlin, Frank F. Furstenberg, et al., "Longitudinal Studies of Effects of Divorce on Children in Great Britain and the United States," *Science*, 252 (7 June 1991): 1386–1389.

12. The behavior problems listed were "temper tantrums, reluctance to go to school, bad dreams, difficulty sleeping, food fads, poor appetite, difficulty concentrating, bullied by other children, destructive, miserable or tearful, squirmy or fidgety, continually worried, irritable, upset by new situations, twitches or other mannerisms, fights with other children, disobedient at home, and sleepwalking" (Ibid., p. 1397).

13. Children also suffer economic harm as a result of the divorce of their parents. See the data in note 5, above. However, economic loss is the type of post-divorce harm that can be mitigated by the conduct of the parents. For example, if the mother is awarded custody of the children, then the father can offset the economic loss experienced by his former spouse by contributing sufficient funds to insure that the children's physical circumstances are not changed by the divorce.

14. N.Y. Family Court. Act para. 1012 (McKinney Supp. 1974).

15. This does not mean that we should never engage in behavior that risks harm to our children. After all, there is some risk in taking a child out for a walk, a drive in the car, or helping her learn to ski. But we balance such risks against the probable benefit to the child when we make such decisions. When parents divorce for no good reason, there is no predictable benefit to the child that will balance the risk that he or she will suffer emotional harm.

16. Bertrand Russell, "My Own View of Marriage," in *Bertrand Russell: On Ethics, Sex and Marriage,* ed. A. Seckel (New York: Prometheus Books, 1987), p. 279.

17. For example, the boys whose parents divorced showed only 9 percent more behavior problems than the boys from intact families (Cherlin and Furstenberg, "Longitudinal Studies," p. 1388). From a quite different perspective, Wallerstein and Blakely wrote that in their study of the effects of divorce "only one in ten children in our study experienced relief when their parents divorced. These were mostly older children in families where there had been open violence and where the children had lived with the fear that the violence would hurt a parent or themselves" (*Second Chances,* p. 11).

18. Cherlin and Furstenberg, "Longitudinal Studies," p. 1388.

19. Young, "Mothers," pp. 536–538.

20. Russell, *Marriage and Morals,* pp. 236–237, 317.

21. Thomas Nagel refers to these as "reasons of autonomy." See *The View from Nowhere* (1986).

22. Cf. Robert Nozick, *Philosophical Explanations* (London: Methuen, 1971), p. 152.

DISCUSSION QUESTIONS

1. Houlgate cites evidence that divorce is harmful to children. Do you find this evidence compelling? Why or why not?

2. According to Houlgate, divorce is the moral thing to do when the potential harm of remaining married is greater than the harm that will be caused by divorcing. Do you think that this is a good way of considering the morality or immorality of divorce? Would you use the "Divorce Child-Harm Argument" to assess the morality of divorce? Why or why not?

3. To what extent should children affect our moral deliberations about divorce? Houlgate argues that even in a marriage with no children it is still immoral to divorce a nonconsenting spouse. Do you agree with him? Why or why not?

4. Bertrand Russell recommends that young people contemplating marriage live together for one or two years before getting married. This "trial marriage" might reduce the chances of marital breakdown and divorce. Do you agree with him? Do you think that trial marriage might help to reduce the divorce rate? Do you think that trial marriage is moral? Defend your view.

5. Rebecca West writes that "the divorce of married people with children is nearly always an unspeakable calamity." Do you agree? Defend your position.

◆ CHESIRE CALHOUN

Feminism, Lesbianism, and the Family

Chesire Calhoun tells us that gays and lesbians are commonly portrayed as "outlaws" to the family. This depiction of gays and lesbians as unfit for marriage, parenting, and family, says Calhoun, is historically linked to anxieties about the stability of heterosexual marriage and parenting, as well as the heterosexual family. Calhoun argues that lesbians

Feminism and Families. Edited by Hilde Lindemann Nelson. Routledge, 1997, 131–150. Copyright © Chesire Calhoun (1997). Reprinted by permission of the author.

need to reexamine marriage from their position as "family's outlaws" rather than from the gender structure of marriage and motherhood.

Chesire Calhoun teaches philosophy and is director of women's studies at Colby College in Maine. She writes on feminist ethics, and on gay and lesbian ethics.

How should we understand lesbians' relation to the family, marriage, and mothering? Part of what makes this a difficult question to answer from a feminist standpoint is that feminism has undertheorized lesbian and gay oppression as an axis of oppression distinct from gender oppression.[1] As a result, lesbians' *difference* from heterosexual women is often not visible—even, oddly enough, within explicitly lesbian-feminist thought. In Parts I, II, and III of this essay, I critically review feminist analyses—particularly lesbian-feminist ones—of lesbians' relation to the family, marriage, and mothering. In Part IV, I develop a historical account of the construction of lesbians (and gays) as outlaws to the family.

My aim is to suggest that lesbians' distinctive relation to the family, marriage, and mothering is better captured by attending to the social construction of lesbians as familial outlaws than by attending exclusively to the gender structure of family, marriage, and mothering.

I. FEMINISM AND THE FAMILY

Feminist depictions and analyses of the family, marriage, and mothering have been driven by a deep awareness that the family centered around marriage, procreation, and child-rearing has historically been and continues to be a primary site of women's subordination to and dependence on men, and by an awareness that the gender ideology that rationalizes women's subordinate status is heavily shaped by assumptions about women's natural place within the family as domestic caretakers, as reproductive beings, and as naturally fit for mothering. It has been the task and success of feminism to document the dangers posed to women by family, marriage, and mothering in both their lived and ideological forms.

The ideology of the loving family often masks gender injustice within the family, including battery, rape, and child abuse. Women continue to shoulder primary responsibility for both child-rearing and domestic labor; and they continue to choose occupations compatible with child care, occupations which are often less well paid, more replaceable, and less likely to offer benefits and career-track mobility. The

expectation that women within families are first and foremost wives and mothers continues to offer employers a rationale for paying women less. Women's lower wages in the public workforce in turn make it appear economically rational within marriages for women to invest in developing their husband's career assets. No-fault divorce laws, which operate on the assumption that men and women exiting marriage have equally developed career assets (or that those career assets could be developed with the aid of short-term alimony) and that fail to treat the husband's career assets as community property, result in women exiting marriage at a significant economic disadvantage.[2] Women's custody of children after divorce, their lower earning potential, the unavailability of low-cost child care, the absence of adequate social support for single mothers, and, often, fathers' failure to pay full child support combine to reduce divorced women's economic position even further, resulting in the feminization of poverty. The ideology of the normal family as the self-sufficient, two-earner, nuclear family is then mobilized to blame single mothers for their poverty, to justify supervisory and psychological intervention into those families, and to rationalize reducing social support for them.

This picture, although generally taken as a picture of women's relation to the family, marriage, and mothering, is not, in fact, a picture of *women's* relation to the family, but is more narrowly a picture of *heterosexual* women's relation to the family, marriage, and mothering. It is a picture whose contours are shaped by an eye on the lookout for the ways that marriage, family, and mothering subordinate heterosexual women to men in the private household, in the public economy, and in the welfare state. Thus it fails to grasp lesbians' relation to the family.[3]

It has instead been the task of lesbian feminism from the 1970s through the 1990s to develop an analysis of lesbians' distinctive relation to the family. However, although lesbian feminism has developed feminist arguments for rejecting lesbian motherhood, lesbian marriages, and lesbian families, it too has failed to make lesbian difference from heterosexual women central to its analyses. It is to the promise and, I will argue, the failure of lesbian feminism to grasp lesbians' distinctive relation to the family that I now turn.

II. LESBIAN FEMINISM, THE FAMILY, MOTHERING, AND MARRIAGE

In understanding what lesbians' relation to the family, motherhood, and marriage is and ought to be, lesbian feminists took as their point of departure feminist critiques of heterosexual women's experience of family, motherhood, and marriage. Lesbian feminists were particularly alive to the fact that lesbians are uniquely positioned to evade the ills of the heterosexual, male-dominated family. In particular, they are uniquely positioned to violate the conventional gender expectation that they, as women, would be dependent on men in their personal relations, would fulfill the maternal imperative, would service a husband and children, and would accept confinement to the private sphere of domesticity. Because of their unique position, lesbians could hope to be in the vanguard of the feminist rebellion against the patriarchal family, marriage, and institution of motherhood.

Family

In the 1970s and '80s, lesbian feminists used feminist critiques of heterosexual women's subordination to men within the family as a platform for valorizing lesbian existence. Lesbian feminists like Monique Wittig and Charlotte Bunch, for instance, argued that the nuclear family based on heterosexual marriage enables men to appropriate for themselves women's productive and reproductive labor.[4] Because lesbians do not enter into this heterosexual nuclear family, they can be read as refusing to allow their labor to be appropriated by men.

Lesbian feminists similarly made use of feminist critiques of heterosexual women's confinement to the private sphere of family and exclusion from the public sphere of politics and labor to argue for a new vision of lesbians' personal life. In that vision, passionate friendships, centered around a common life of work, could and should replace the depoliticized, isolated life within the nuclear family. Janice Raymond, for instance, argued for the feminist value of historical all-women's communities, such as the pre-enclosure nunneries and the nineteenth-century Chinese marriage resisters' houses where women combined intimate friendships, community, and work.[5]

Lesbian-feminist interpretation of lesbians' relation to the family as nonparticipation in *heterosexual*, male-dominated, private families is then translated into nonparticipation in *any* form of family, including lesbian families. In a 1994 essay, for instance, Ruthann Robson argues against recent liberal legal efforts to redefine the family to include lesbian and gay families that are functionally equivalent to heterosexual ones.[6] She argues that, in advocating legal recognition of lesbian families, "we have forgotten the lesbian generated critiques of family as oppressive and often deadly."[7] In particular we have forgotten the critiques of the family as an institution of the patriarchal state, of marriage as slavery,[8] and of wives as property within marriage.[9] In her view, the category "family" should be abolished.

Motherhood

Feminist critiques of heterosexual women's experience also supplied the point of departure for lesbian-feminist critiques of lesbian motherhood. Lesbian motherhood, on this view, represents a concession to a key element of women's subordination—compulsory motherhood. By refusing to have children, or by giving up custody of their children at divorce, lesbians can refuse to participate in compulsory motherhood. They can thus refuse to accept the myth "that only family and children provide [women] with a purpose and place, bestow upon us honor, respect, love, and comfort."[10] Purpose and place is better found in political activities in a more public community of women. Lesbian feminists thus challenge lesbians contemplating motherhood to reflect more critically on their reasons for doing so and on the political consequences of participating in the present lesbian baby boom.

Not only does resistance to motherhood signal a rejection of conventional understandings of womanhood and women's fulfillment, it also frees lesbians to devote their lives to public political work for lesbians and heterosexual women. Thus lesbian resistance to motherhood is seen as instrumental to effective political action. Nancy Polikoff, for instance, claims that "[t]o the extent that motherhood drains the available pool of lesbians engaging in ongoing political work, its long-term significance is overwhelming."[11]

Lesbian motherhood also facilitates the closeting of lesbian existence. Even when lesbian mothers are careful not to pass as heterosexual, their very motherhood works against their being publicly perceived as deviants to the category "woman." And in her study of lesbian mothers, Ellen Lewin argues that motherhood enables lesbians to claim a less stigmatized place in the gender system; in particular, it enables them to claim for themselves the conventional womanly attributes of being altruistic, nurturant, and responsible—attributes which lesbians typically are stereotyped as lacking.[12]

Marriage

Like lesbian motherhood, lesbian (and gay) marriage seems antithetical to the lesbian-feminist goal of radically challenging conventional gender, sexual, and familial arrangements. Historically, the institution of marriage has been oppressively gender-structured. And, as Polikoff points out in a recent essay, the historical and cross-cultural record of same-sex marriages does not support the claim that same-sex marriages will revolutionize the gender structure of marriage. On the contrary, same-sex marriages that have been legitimized in other cultures—for instance, African woman-marriage, Native American marriages between a berdache and a same-sex partner, and nineteenth-century Chinese marriages between women—have all been highly gender-structured. Thus there is no reason to believe that " 'gender dissent' is inherent in marriage between two men or two women."[13]

Moreover, the attempt to secure legal recognition for lesbian and gay marriages is highly likely to work against efforts to critique the institution of marriage. In particular, by attempting to have specifically *marital* relationships recognized, advocates of marriage rights help to reinforce the assumption that long-term, monogamous relationships are more valuable than any other kind of relationship. As a result, the marriage rights campaign, if successful, will end up privileging those lesbian and gay relationships that most closely approximate the heterosexual norm over more deviant relationships that require a radical rethinking of the nature of families.[14]

Finally, arguments for lesbian and gay marriage rights on the grounds that lesbians and gays lack privileges that heterosexual couples enjoy—such as access to a spouse's health insurance benefits—are insufficiently radical.[15] Distributing basic benefits like health insurance through the middle-class family neglects the interests of poor and some working-class families as well as single individuals in having access to basic social benefits. If access to such benefits is the issue, then universal health insurance, not marriage, is what we should be advocating.

III. LESBIAN DISAPPEARANCE

The difficulty with the lesbian-feminist viewpoint is that it is one from which lesbian difference from heterosexual women persistently disappears from view.

First, the value of the family and marriage for *lesbians* is judged largely by evaluating the *heterosexual* nuclear family's effects on *heterosexual* women. Lesbians are to resist family and marriage because the family centered around the heterosexual married couple has been gender structured in a way that made marriage a form of slavery where heterosexual women could be treated as property and their labor appropriated by men. But to make this a principal reason for lesbians' not forming families and marriages of their own is to lose sight of the difference between lesbians and heterosexual women. Lesbian families and marriages are not reasonably construed as sites where women can be treated as property and where their productive and reproductive labor can be appropriated by men. It thus does not follow from the fact that heterosexual marriage and family has been oppressive for heterosexual women and a primary structure of patriarchy that *any* form of marriage or family, including lesbian ones, is oppressive for women and a primary structure of patriarchy.

The alternative argument—that creating lesbian families and marriages will not remedy the gender structure in heterosexual marriages and families—drops lesbians from view in a different way. Here, heterosexual women's interests are substituted for those of lesbians as the touchstone for determining what normative conclusions about the family, marriage, and mothering lesbians should come to. Lesbians are to resist forming marriages and families of their own because heterosexual women's struggle against the institution of marriage and family will not be promoted and may in fact be hindered by lesbian endorsement of the value of marriage and family. This line of reasoning ignores the possibility that lesbians may have interests of their own in forming families and marriages, interests that may conflict with heterosexual women's political aims.

Second, resistance to the forms of gender oppression and gender ideology to which lesbians, *as women*, are subject is presented as a distinctively lesbian task (that is, as a distinctively lesbian version of feminist resistance), when in fact these are broadly feminist tasks whose burden should be equally shared by heterosexual women and lesbians. Both lesbians and heterosexual women have reason to resist the construction of mothering as an unpaid, socially unsupported task.

Both have reason to reject women's confinement to the domestic sphere and reason to value participation in politically oriented communities of women. Both have reason to resist their gender socialization into the myth of feminine fulfillment through mothering and to assert their deviance from the category "woman." Both can have justice interests in objecting to a social and legal system that privileges long-term, monogamous relationships over all other forms of relationship and that does not provide universal access to basic benefits like health insurance. All of these are broadly feminist concerns. As a result, the lesbian-feminist perspective does not articulate any distinctively *lesbian* political tasks in relation to the family, marriage, and mothering. Instead, lesbians are submerged in the larger category "feminist."

Finally, the political relation between heterosexuals and nonheterosexuals and the ideologies of sexuality that support the oppression of lesbians and gays simply do not inform the lesbian-feminist analysis of lesbians' relation to the family, marriage, or mothering. What governs the lesbian-feminist perspective is above all the political relations between men and women, and to a lesser extent class relations and the political relations between those in normative long-term, monogamous relations (whether heterosexual or nonheterosexual) and all other human relations. As a result, the radicalness of lesbian and gay family, marriage, and parenting is measured on a scale that looks only at their power (or impotence) to transform gender relations, the privileging of long-term, monogamous relations, and class privilege. Not surprisingly, lesbian and gay families, marriages, and parenting fail to measure up. But this ignores the historical construction of lesbians and gays as outlaws to the natural family, as constitutionally incapable of more than merely sexual relationships, and as dangerous to children.

Within gender ideology, for instance, lesbians have not been and are not constructed as beings whose natural place is within the family as domestic caretakers, as reproductive beings, and as naturally fit mothers. On the contrary, the gender ideology that rationalizes the oppression of both lesbians and gays consists in part precisely in the assumption that both are aliens to the natural family, nonprocreative, incapable of enduring intimate ties, dangerous to children, and ruled by sexual instincts to the exclusion of parenting ones. Moreover, unlike heterosexual women, it is not their subordination *within* the family that marks their oppression but rather their denial of access *to* a legitimated and socially instituted sphere of family, marriage, and parenting.

Lesbians and gays are, for instance, denied the legal privileges and protections that heterosexuals enjoy with respect to their marital and familial relations. Among the array of rights related to marriage that heterosexuals enjoy but gays and lesbians do not are the rights to legal marriage, to live with one's spouse in neighborhoods zoned "single-family only," and to secure U.S. residency through marriage to a U.S. citizen; the rights to Social Security survivor's benefits, to inherit a spouse's estate in the absence of a will, and to file a wrongful death suit; the rights to give proxy consent, to refuse to testify against one's spouse, and to file joint income taxes.

Lesbians and gays similarly lack access to the privileges and protections that heterosexuals enjoy with respect to biological, adoptive, and foster children. Sexual orientation continues to be an overriding reason for denying custody to lesbian and gay parents who exit a heterosexual marriage. Gays and lesbians fare equally poorly with respect to adoption and foster parenting. New Hampshire prohibits gay and lesbian adoption and foster parenting, while other states, like Massachusetts, have policies making a child's placement with lesbian or gay parents unlikely. Even while adoption is successful, joint adoption generally is not—nor is adoption of a partner's biological child.

What comes into view in this picture of the legal inequities that lesbians and gays confront is the fact that the family, marriage, and parenting are a primary site of heterosexual privilege. The family centered around marriage, procreation, and child-rearing has historically been and continues to be constructed and institutionalized as the natural domain of heterosexuals only, and thus as a domain from which lesbians and gays are outlawed. This distinctively lesbian and gay relation to family, marriage, and parenting is what fails to make its appearance within feminist analyses and critiques of the family. But so long as the political position of lesbians and gays in relation to heterosexual control of family, marriage, and parenting remains out of view, distinctively lesbian (and gay) interests in family, marriage, and parenting and distinctively lesbian (and gay) political goals in relation to the family cannot make their appearance. It is to the construction of lesbians and gays as outlaws to the family that I now turn.

IV. FAMILIAL OUTLAWS

A constitutive feature of lesbian and gay oppression since at least the late nineteenth century has been the reservation of the private sphere for heterosexuals only. Because lesbians and gays are ideologically constructed as beings incapable of genuine romance, marriage, or families of their own, and because those assumptions are institutionalized in the law and social practice, lesbians and gays are displaced from this private sphere.

In what follows, I want to suggest that the historical construction of gays and lesbians as familial outlaws is integrally connected to the history of social anxiety about the failure and potential collapse of the heterosexual nuclear family. In particular, I want to suggest that in periods where there was heightened anxiety about the stability of the heterosexual nuclear family because of changes in gender, sexual, and family composition norms within the family, this anxiety was resolved by targeting a group of persons who could be ideologically constructed as outsiders to the family, identifying the behaviors that most deeply threatened the family with those outsiders, and stigmatizing that group. In each of the periods of anxiety about the family that I intend to consider, lesbians and gays had achieved fairly high social visibility, making them natural candidates for the group to be constructed as outsiders to the family. The construction of gays and lesbians as highly stigmatized outsiders to the family and as displaying the most virulent forms of family-disrupting behavior allayed anxieties about the potential failure of the heterosexual nuclear family in three ways. First, it externalized the threat to the family. As a result, anxiety about the possibility that the family was disintegrating from *within* could be displaced onto the spectre of the hostile outsider to the family. Second, stigma threatening comparisons between misbehaving members of the heterosexual family and the dangerous behavior of gays and lesbians could be used to compel heterosexual family members' compliance with gender, sexual, and family composition norms. Third, by locating the genuinely deviant, abnormal, perverse behavior outside the family, members of heterosexual families were enabled to adjust to new, liberalized norms for acceptable gender roles and sexual behavior within families[16] as well as new, liberalized norms for acceptable family composition. They could, in essence, reassure themselves with the thought "At least we aren't like them!"

The coincidence of anxiety about the failure of the heterosexual nuclear family and the ideological construction of gays and lesbians as familial outlaws is particularly striking in three periods: the 1880s to 1920s, the 1930s to 1950s, and the 1980s to 1990s. Although a variety of factors threatened the family

in each of these periods, I want to suggest that the three periods differ with respect to the familial norms that were most seriously challenged. In the 1880s to 1920s it was especially norms governing (women's) gender behavior, in the 1930s to 1950s, it was most critically norms governing (male) sexuality, and in the 1980s and 1990s it has been, above all, norms governing acceptable family composition that have been most centrally challenged.

1880s to 1920s

The 1880s to 1920s witnessed significant challenges to the gender structure of marriage. By the mid-1800s, the first wave of the feminist movement was under way, pressing for changes in women's gender roles within the family. First-wave feminists pushed for legal reforms that would recognize women as separate individuals within marriage by, for example, securing women property rights within marriage, and that would give women access to divorce. (Between 1860 and 1920 the divorce rate increased over 600 percent.[17]) They also pushed for increased access to higher education and employment as well as for contraception, abortion, and (through the temperance movement) control of male sexuality, all of which would enable women to limit family size and free women from a life devoted exclusively to childbearing and child-rearing.

First-wave feminists' explicit critique of women's gender role within the family produced an anxiety about the family that focused on its gender structure. Because turn-of-the-century gender ideology tied gender tightly to biology, the violation of gender norms was interpreted as having significant biological repercussions. From the mid-1800s on, physicians argued that "unnatural" women—that is, "over" educated women, women who worked at gender-atypical occupations, and women who practiced birth control or had abortions—were likely to suffer a variety of physically based mental ailments including weakness, nervousness, hysteria, loss of memory, insanity, and nymphomania.[18] Worse yet, their gender-inappropriate behavior might result in sterility or inability to produce physically and mentally healthy offspring. In particular, they risked producing children who were themselves inappropriately gendered—effeminate sons and masculine daughters. Not only could departure from women's traditional gender role as wife and mother have dire physical and mental consequences for both herself and her offspring, she herself might be suspected of being at a deep level not really a woman. Indeed, she might be suspected of being one of the third sex.

Beginning roughly in 1869 with the publication of Carl von Westphal's essay on the congenital invert, medical theorists began developing a new gender category variously labelled the sexual invert, the intermediate sex, the third sex, the urning, the man-woman. The image of the sexual invert crystallized anxiety about women's, and to a lesser extent, men's gender-crossing and symbolized the dangers of deviance from conventional gender norms. Although the invert is the historical precursor to the contemporary categories "lesbian" and "homosexual," the turn-of-the-century sexual invert was not constructed primarily *sexually*. What distinguished the invert was her or his *gender* inversion. The sexually inverted woman, for example, was distinguished from noninverted women by her masculine traits: short hair, independent and aggressive manner, athleticism, male attire, drinking, cigarette and sometimes cigar smoking, masculine sense of honor, dislike of needlework and domestic activities, and preference for science and masculine sports. The sexually inverted woman's attraction to conventionally gendered women and to effeminate men was simply a natural result of her generally masculine genderization. In her sexual relations, whether with women or with a husband, she would wear the pants.

Medical theorists postulated that, at a biological level, sexually inverted women were not real women. Some imagined that inverts were really hermaphrodites. Others, like Havelock Ellis, imagined that they possessed an excess of male "germs."[19] Others, like Krafft-Ebing, imagined that the invert was a throwback to an earlier evolutionary stage of bisexuality (that is, bi-*genderization*) and that in spite of her female brain and body, the psychosexual center in her brain was masculine.[20]

Because the mark of the sexual invert was her lack of conformity with women's conventional gender role, the line between the nonconforming sexual invert and the nonconforming feminist was often blurred. Feminist views and feminist-inspired deviance from gender norms might be both symptom and cause of sexual inversion. Like sexual inverts, feminists threatened to disrespect appropriate gender relations between women and men in marriage. One author of a 1900 *New York Medical Journal* essay, for instance, "warned that feminists and sexual perverts alike, both of whom he classed as 'degenerates,' married only men whom they could rule, govern and cause to follow [them] in voice and action."[21]

In short, the sexually inverted woman, sometimes indistinguishable from the feminist, symbolized the dangers of departing from women's conventional gender role. The idea that this new medical category of sexual inversion was created in direct response to first-wave feminists' challenge to gender norms is not new. Both Lillian Faderman and George Chauncey, Jr., for instance, have argued that given both the influence of feminist ideas and the burgeoning of economic opportunities for women, there was a cultural fear that women would replace marriages to men with Boston marriages or romantic friendships.[22] One response to that fear was greater attention to the ideal of companionate marriage, and thus to making marriage more attractive to women.[23] A second response, however, was a cultural backlash—or as Chauncey describes it, a heterosexual counter-revolution—against Boston marriages, romantic friendships, schoolgirl "raves," and same-sex institutions. The pathologizing of both gender deviance and same-sex relationships brought what were formerly taken to be innocent and normal intimacies between women under suspicion of harboring degeneracy and abnormality.

The pathologizing of relations between women was not confined to medical literature. As Lisa Duggan has documented, newspapers sensationalized violent intimate relationships between women, such as the case of Alice Mitchell, a sexual invert, who intended to elope with and marry Freda Ward and to cross-dress as a man, adopting the name Alvin. When their plan was discovered and the engagement forcibly terminated, Alice Mitchell murdered Freda so that no one else could have her. Duggan argues that Alice's clear intent to forge a new way of life outside the heterosexual, gender-structured family marked her as dangerous. In sensationalizing cases like Alice's,

> [t]he late-nineteenth century newspaper narratives of lesbian love featured violence as a boundary marker; murders or suicides served to abort the forward progress of the tale, signaling that such erotic love between women was not only tragic but ultimately hopeless. . . . The stories were thus structured to emphasize, ultimately, that no real love story was possible.[24]

Not only was no real love story possible, no real family relation was possible either. And this is the point I want to underscore. Controlling challenges to the conventional gender structure within heterosexual marriages was accomplished by constructing the fully gender-deviant woman as someone who was not only pathological and doomed to tragedy, but who was constitutionally unfit for family life. Her masculinity unfitted her for the marital role of wife, unfitted her for the task of producing properly gendered children, and unfitted her for any stable, intimate relationships. The cultural construction of the lesbian was thus, from the outset, the construction of a kind of being who was, centrally, an outsider to marriage, family, and motherhood.

The image of the doomed, mannish lesbian could be used to compel heterosexual women's compliance with gender norms. In addition, by equating the worst forms of gender deviance with lesbians, heterosexual families were helped to adjust to new gender norms for women (which, by comparison to lesbians, seemed normal). Finally, attributing the worst forms of gender deviance to a third sex externalized the threat to the heterosexual family, suggesting that the heterosexual family was not in fact being challenged from within by *real* women.

1930s to 1950s

The Depression of the 1930s and World War II in the 1940s created a new set of threats to the stability of the heterosexual family.[25] During the Depression, many men lost their traditional gender position in the family as breadwinners as a result of both massive unemployment and a drop in marriage rates. The sense of a cultural crisis in masculinity was reflected in numerous sociological studies of "The Unemployed Man and His Family."[26] Men's traditional position in the family and family stability itself was additionally undermined during World War II, which brought a rise in the frequency of prolonged separations, divorce, and desertion.[27]

One response was the attempt to reposition men as primary income earners in their families by discouraging or prohibiting married women from working. A second response, however, appears to have been a shift in the cultural construction of masculinity from being gender-based to being sexuality-based. In his historical study of New York gay culture during the first third of the twentieth century, for instance, George Chauncey argues that sexual categories for men underwent a significant transformation during the '30s and '40s. The gender-behavior-based contrast between "fairies," that is, effeminate men, and "men" (who might be "queer," "trade," that is, heterosexual men who accepted advances from homosexual men, or strictly heterosexual) gave way to the contemporary binarism between homosexual and heterosexual. Real manhood

ceased to be secured by simply avoiding feminine behaviors, and instead came to rest on exclusive heterosexuality.[28] The depiction of gay men, during the sex crime panics of 1937 to 1940 and 1949 to 1955, as violent child molesters further solidified the boundary between real, heterosexual men and homosexuals, while depiction of the heterosexual sexual psychopath as hypermasculine underscored the centrality of (hetero)sexuality to manhood.[29]

Compounding the shifts in gender arrangements within the family brought on by the Depression and World War II were shifts in cultural understandings of women's and children's sexuality. The idea of female sexual satisfaction, the use of birth control, and sexuality outside of marriage all gained increased acceptance. And the publicization of Freudian ideas underscored not only the sexuality of women, but the sexuality of children as well. The sexualization of women and children meant that both might fail to be merely innocent victims of male sexual aggression; they might instead play a role in inviting it.[30] These factors contributed to a changed understanding of sexuality and sexual norms both outside and inside the family. They also contributed to cultural anxiety about the power of sexuality to destabilize and undermine the family.

Those anxieties were crystallized during the sex crime panics in the twin figures of the heterosexual psychopathic rapist and the homosexual psychopath who seduced youth and molested children. Both figures symbolized sexuality run dangerously amok. The image of the dangerously sexual homosexual received added reinforcement during the McCarthy era's purge of "sex perverts" from governmental service on the grounds that they threatened not only the nation's children but its national security and the heterosexuality of its adult population as well.[31]

The images of the sexual psychopath and the homosexual child molester helped to redefine the sexual norm, setting the outer limits of acceptable sexual behavior: violent sex, sex with men, and sex with children.[32] By constructing new understandings of sexual abnormality, the images of the sexual psychopath and the homosexual child molester also helped Americans adjust to new sexual norms, such as the acceptability of nonprocreative sex, as well as to new understandings of both women and children as "normally" sexual beings. The location of the sexual danger posed to women and children outside the family also allayed anxiety that the family risked disruption by the potentially violent sexuality of its own members.

Again, the point I want to underscore is that resolving cultural anxiety about shifting gender and sexual patterns within the family was integrally connected with the social construction of gay men as familial outlaws. The very nature of homosexuality unfitted gay men for family. Constitutionally prone to uncontrolled and insatiable sexuality, gay [men] (and lesbians) could not be trusted to respect prohibitions on adult-child sexual interactions.[33] Nor, given the compulsive quality of their sexual desire, could gay men or lesbians be expected to maintain stable relationships with each other.

1980s to 1990s

The 1980s and 1990s have posed a different challenge to the family. Technological, social, and economic factors have combined to produce an explosion of new family and household forms that undermine the nuclear, biology-based family's claim to be *the* natural, normative social unit.

Increasingly, sophisticated birth control methods and technologically assisted reproduction using in-vitro fertilization, artificial insemination, contract pregnancy, fertility therapies, and the like undermine cultural understandings of the marital couple as a naturally reproductive unit, introduce nonrelated others into the reproductive process, and make it possible for women and men to have children without a heterosexual partner. The institutionalization of child care, as mothers work to support families, involves nonfamily members in the familial task of raising children. Soaring divorce rates have made single-parent households a common family pattern—so common that Father's Day cards now include ones addressed to mothers, and others announcing their recipient is "like a dad." The high incidence of divorce has also meant an increase in divorce-extended families that incorporate children, grandparents, and other kin from former marriages as well as former spouses who may retain shared custody or visitation rights.[34] As a result of remarriage, semen donation, and contract pregnancy, the rule of one-mother, one-father per child (both of whom are expected to be biological parents) that has dominated legal reasoning about custody and visitation rights has ceased to be adequate to the reality of many families. Multiple women and/or multiple men become involved in children's lives through their biological, gestation, or parenting contributions.[35] The extended kinship networks of the Black urban poor, including "fictive kin," which enable extensive pooling of resources, have become increasingly common in the working class as the shift from goods to service production and the decline of industrial and unionized occupations has made working class persons' economic position increasingly fragile.[36] And the impoverishment of single-parent households has increasingly involved welfare agencies in family survival.

In short, as Judith Stacey observes,

> No longer is there a single culturally dominant family pattern to which the majority of Americans conform and most of the rest aspire. Instead, Americans today have crafted a multiplicity of family and household arrangements that we inhabit uneasily and reconstitute in response to changing personal and occupational circumstances.[37]

We now live, in her view, in the age of the postmodern family. It is an age where one marriage and its biological relations have ceased to determine family composition. Choice increasingly appears to be the principle determining family composition: choice to single-parent, choice of fictive kin, choice to combine nuclear families (in extended kin networks, in remarriage, or in divorce-extended families), choice of semen donors or contract birthgivers, choice to dissolve marital bonds, choice of who will function as a parent in children's lives (in spite of the law's failure to acknowledge the parental status of many functional parents.) That is, what Kath Weston describes as a distinctively gay and lesbian concept of "chosen families," contrasted to heterosexuals' biological families, in fact characterizes the reality of many heterosexual families who fail in various ways to construct a nuclear family around a procreative married couple.[38]

As family forms multiply, the traditional, heterosexual and procreative, nuclear family delimited by bonds of present marriage and blood relation and capable of sustaining itself rather than pooling resources across households has ceased to be the "natural" family form.[39] Not only has the pluralization of family forms undermined the credibility of the claim that the traditional family is the most natural family form, it has also highlighted the failure of the traditional family to satisfy individual needs better than other personal relationships or alternative family forms.[40]

Cultural anxiety about the future of the family crystallized in the 1980s and 1990s in at least two major images: those of the unwed welfare mother and of the lesbian or gay whose mere public visibility threatens to undermine family values and destroy the family. The depiction of lesbians and gays as be-ings whose "lifestyle" contradicts family values was preceded in the 1970s by the gay liberation move-ment, and with it, a rise in lesbian custody suits and in litigation contesting the denial of marriage li-censes to gays.[41] Both the sheer visibility of gays and lesbians as well as their specific bid for acknowledg-ment of gay and lesbian marriages and families made gays and lesbians natural targets for the expression of cultural anxieties about the family.

In the late 1980s, for instance, Britain passed Clause 28 of the Local Government Act that, in ad-dition to prohibiting the promotion of homosexual-ity, also forbade local authorities from promoting "the teaching in any maintained school of the ac-ceptability of homosexuality as a pretended family relationship."[42] The pretended nature of gays' and lesbians' family relationships has, in the United States, been repeatedly underscored in court rulings affirming that marriage requires one man and one woman. The pretend nature of lesbian motherhood has also been underscored in custody rulings that have assumed that being parented by a lesbian is not in a child's best interests—because the child may be molested, or may fail to be socialized into her or his appropriate gender or into heterosexuality, or may be harmed by the stigma of having a lesbian parent.[43]

Not only are gays and lesbians constructed as be-ings whose "marriages" and "families" fail to be the genuine article, they are also constructed as beings who, simply by being publicly visible or mention-able, assault family values. As a result, antidiscrimi-nation measures are equated with hostility to the family, even though ending workplace discrimina-tion or punishing hate crimes would appear to have little to do with advocating one family form rather than another. So, for instance, the author of a 1995 law journal article argues that gays and lesbians should not be protected against discrimination because gay sexuality is "deeply hostile to the self-understanding of those members of the community who are willing to commit themselves to real mar-riage."[44] He makes it clear that any policy protecting a "gay lifestyle" threatens the stability of the family, and for that reason should be rejected:

> A political community which judges that the stability and protective and educative generosity of family life is of fundamental importance to that community's present and future can rightly judge that it has a compelling interest in denying that homosexual conduct—a "gay lifestyle"—is a valid, humanly acceptable choice

and form of life, and in doing whatever it *properly* can, as a community with uniquely wide but still subsidiary functions, to discourage such conduct.[45]

So threatening to the family are gays and lesbians taken to be that even protecting them against hate crimes may be interpreted as dangerously close to at-tacking the family. Thus the Hate Crimes Act passed by Congress in 1990 (which covers sexual orienta-tion) includes the affirmation that "federal policy should encourage the well-being, financial security, and health of the American family," almost immedi-ately followed with the warning that "[n]othing in this Act shall be construed, nor shall any funds ap-propriated to carry out the purpose of the Act be used, to promote or encourage homosexuality."[46]

As in previous periods, constructing lesbians and gays as dangerous outlaws to the family serves several functions. First, it externalizes the threat to the het-erosexual, procreative, nuclear family, diverting at-tention from heterosexuals' own choices to create multiple, new family arrangements that undermine the hegemony of the traditional family. Second, de-picting gay and lesbian relationships as "pretended" families, by comparison to which even the most de-viant heterosexual families can appear normal, helps heterosexual families adjust to changing norms for family composition. Finally, the equation of heterosexuality with family values and homosexu-ality and lesbianism with hostility to the family serves to compel loyalty to the sexual norm prescribing heterosexuality. It also renders suspect some of the alternative family arrangements that heterosexuals might be inclined to choose, such as supportive, familylike relationships between women involved in single parenting.

V. NOT FOR HETEROSEXUALS ONLY

I have argued for the existence of a historical pattern in which anxiety about the stability of the family goes hand in hand with the ideological depiction of gays and lesbians as unfit for marriage, parenting, and family. The construction of lesbians and gays as natural outlaws to the family and the masking of heterosexuals' own family-disrupting behavior re-sults in the reservation of the private sphere for het-erosexuals only.[47]

It is because being an outlaw to the family has been so central to the social construction of lesbianism that I think lesbians' relation to the family is better captured by attention to their outlaw status than to the gender structure of marriage and motherhood (as is characteristic of lesbian feminism). Indeed, on the historical backdrop of the various images of family outlaws—the mannish lesbian, the homosexual child molester, and their pretended family relationships—lesbian-feminist resistance to lesbian and gay marriages, lesbian motherhood, and the formation of lesbian and gay families looks suspiciously like a concession to the view of lesbians and gays as family outlaws. Because being denied access to a legitimate and protected private sphere has been and continues to be central to lesbian and gay oppression, the most important scale on which to measure lesbian and gay political strategies is one that assesses their power (or impotence) to resist conceding the private sphere to heterosexuals only. On such a scale, the push for marriage rights, parental rights, and recognition as legitimate families measures up.

For similar reasons, it seems to me a mistake to make advocacy of "queer families" *the* political goal for lesbians and gays. By "queer families" I mean ones not centered around marriage or children, but composed instead of chosen, adult, supportive relationships (which would include lesbian-feminist political communities of women).

Equating gay families with queer, nonmarital, and nonparenting families concedes too much to the ideology of gays and lesbians as family outlaws, unfit for genuine marriage and dangerous to children. In addition, describing families that depart substantially from traditional family forms as distinctively gay conceals the queerness of many heterosexual families. I have tried to show that, historically, gays and lesbians have become family outlaws not because *their* relationships and families were distinctively queer, but because *heterosexuals'* relationships and families queered the gender, sexual, and family composition norms. The depiction of gays and lesbians as deviant with respect to family norms was a product of anxiety about that deviancy within heterosexual families. Thus claiming that gay and lesbian families are (or should be) distinctively queer and distinctively deviant helps conceal the deviancy in heterosexual families, and thereby helps to sustain the illusion that heterosexuals are specially entitled to access to a protected private sphere because they, unlike their gay and lesbian counterparts, are supporters of the family.

All this is not to say that there is no merit in lesbian feminists' concern that normalizing lesbian motherhood will reinforce the equation of "woman" with "mother." Overcoming the idea that lesbian motherhood is a contradiction in terms may very well result in lesbians' being expected to fulfill the maternal imperative just as heterosexual women are. But this is just to say that the oppression of lesbians and gays is structurally different from gender oppression. Thus, strategies designed to resist *lesbian* oppression (such as pushing for the legal right to coadopt) are not guaranteed to counter *gender* oppression (which might better be achieved by resisting motherhood altogether). In gaining access to a legitimate and protected private sphere of mothering, marriage, and family, lesbians will need to take care that it does not prove to be as constraining as the private sphere has been for heterosexual women.

Nor have I meant to claim that there is no merit in both lesbian feminists' and queer theorists' concern that normalizing lesbian and gay marriage will reinforce the distinction between good, assimilationist gays and bad gay and heterosexual others whose relationships violate familial norms (the permanently single, the polygamous, the sexually nonmonogamous, the member of a commune, and so on). Overcoming the idea that lesbian and gay marriages are merely pretended family relationships may very well result in married lesbians and gays being looked upon more favorably than those who remain outside accepted familial forms. But this is just to say that countering lesbians' and gays' family outlaw status is not the same thing as struggling to have a broad array of social relationships recognized as (equally) valuable ones. It is, however, important not to exaggerate the level of conformity involved in having familial status. I have argued that families often fail to conform to gender, sexual, and family composition norms. This has not prevented heterosexuals from claiming that, their deviancy notwithstanding, they still have real marriages and real families, and are themselves naturally suited for marriage, family, and parenting. Thus, lesbians and gays who resist their construction as family outlaws are not bidding for access to one, highly conventional family form (such as the nuclear, two-parent, self-sufficient, procreative family). They are instead bidding for access to the same privilege that heterosexuals now enjoy, namely, the privilege of claiming that *in spite of their multiple deviations* from norms governing the family, their families are nevertheless *real* ones and they are themselves naturally suited for marriage, family, and parenting *however* these may be defined and redefined.

NOTES

1. I have argued this claim in both "Separating Lesbian Theory from Feminist Theory," *Ethics*, 104 (1994): 558–581, and in "The Gender Closet: Lesbian Disappearance Under the Sign 'Women,'" *Feminist Studies*, 21 (Spring 1995): 7–34.

2. For discussion of women's vulnerability in marriage and after divorce, see Susan Moller Okin, *Justice, Gender and the Family* (New York: Basic Books, 1989), and Lenore J. Weitzman, *The Divorce Revolution: The Unexpected Social and Economic Consequences for Women and Children in America* (New York: Free Press, 1985).

3. This is not to say that lesbians are entirely left out of the picture. Although drawn from a heterosexual viewpoint, this picture of the family, marriage, and mothering as a primary site of women's subordination and dependence is one that lesbians do nevertheless fit into in many ways. Lesbians, too, can find themselves in heterosexual marriages, undergoing divorce, becoming single parents, disadvantaged in a sex-segregated workforce that pays women less, without adequate child care or child support, vulnerable to welfare bureaucracies, and so on.

4. Monique Wittig, *The Straight Mind and Other Essays* (Boston: Beacon Press, 1992); Charlotte Bunch, "Lesbians in Revolt," in *Passionate Politics, Essays 1968–1986* (New York: St. Martin's Press, 1987).

5. Janice G. Raymond, *A Passion for Friends* (Boston: Beacon Press, 1986).

6. Ruthann Robson, "Resisting the Family: Repositioning Lesbians in Legal Theory," *Signs*, 19 (1994): 975–996.

7. Ibid., p. 977.

8. Ibid., p. 976.

9. Ibid., pp. 986–987.

10. Irena Klepfisz, "Women Without Children/ Women Without Families/Women Alone," in *Politics of the Heart: A Lesbian Parenting Anthology*, ed. Sandra Pollack and Jeanne Vaughn (New York: Firebrand Books, 1987), p. 57.

11. Nancy D. Polikoff, "Lesbians Choosing Children: The Personal Is Political," in Pollack and Vaughn, *Politics of the Heart*, p. 51.

12. Ellen Lewin, *Lesbian Mothers: Accounts of Gender in American Culture* (Ithaca, NY: Cornell University Press, 1993), p. 16.

13. Nancy D. Polikoff, "We Will Get What We Ask For: Why Legalizing Gay and Lesbian Marriage Will Not 'Dismantle the Legal Structure of Gender in Every Marriage,'" *Virginia Law Review*, 79 (1993): 1535–1550, p. 1538.

14. Robson's objection to functionalist approaches to the family in legal thinking is precisely that functionalist approaches are inherently conservative and "guarantee exclusion of the very relationships that might transform the functions," such as sexual relationships among three lesbians (Robson, "Resisting the Family," p. 989).

15. Paula Ettelbrick, "Since When Is Marriage a Path to Liberation?" in *Lesbians, Gay Men, and the Law*, ed. William B. Rubenstein (New York: New Press, 1993); and Polikoff, "We Will Get What We Ask For."

16. Estelle B. Freedman develops this thesis in "'Uncontrolled Desires': The Response to the Sexual Psychopath 1920–1960," in *Passion and Power: Sexuality in History*, ed. Kathy Peiss and Christina Simmons with Robert A. Padgug (Philadelphia: Temple University Press, 1989).

17. Eli Zaretsky, "The Place of the Family in the Origins of the Welfare State," in *Rethinking the Family: Some Feminist Questions*, ed. Barrie Thorne with Marilyn Yalom (New York: Longman, 1982), p. 199.

18. Carroll Smith-Rosenberg and Charles Rosenberg, "The Female Animal: Medical and Biological Views of Woman and Her Role in Nineteenth-Century America," in *Concepts of Health and Disease: Interdisciplinary Perspectives*, ed. Arthur L. Caplan, H. Tristram Engelhardt, Jr., and James J. McCartney (Reading, MA: Addison-Wesley, 1981).

19. Havelock Ellis, *Studies in the Psychology of Sex*, vol. II: *Sexual Inversion* (Philadelphia: Davis, 1928).

20. Richard von Krafft-Ebing, *Psychopathia Sexualis: A Medico-Forensic Study* (New York: Pioneer Publications, Inc., 1947).

21. Quoted in George Chauncey, Jr., "From Sexual Inversion to Homosexuality: The Changing Medical Conceptualization of Female 'Deviance,'" in Peiss et al., *Passion and Power*, p. 92.

22. Chauncey, Jr., "From Sexual Inversion to Homosexuality"; Lillian Faderman, *Surpassing the Love of Men: Romantic Friendship and Love Between Women from the Renaissance to the Present* (New York: Morrow, 1981); Lillian Faderman, "Nineteenth-Century Boston Marriage as a

Possible Lesson for Today," in *Boston Marriages: Romantic but Asexual Relationships Among Contemporary Lesbians,* ed. Esther D. Rothblum and Kathleen A. Brehony (Amherst: University of Massachusetts Press, 1993).

23. Chauncey, Jr., "From Sexual Inversion to Homosexuality."

24. Lisa Duggan, "The Trials of Alice Mitchell: Sensationalism, Sexology, and the Lesbian Subject in Turn-of-the-Century America." *Signs,* 18 (1993): 791–814, p. 808.

25. See Freedman, " 'Uncontrolled Desires' "; John D'Emilio, "The Homosexual Menace: The Politics of Sexuality in Cold War America," in Peiss et al., *Passion and Power;* and George Chauncey, Jr., *Gay New York: Gender, Urban Culture, and the Making of the Gay Male World, 1890–1940* (New York: Basic Books, 1994).

26. Chauncey, Jr., *Gay New York,* pp. 353–354.

27. D'Emilio, "The Homosexual Menace," p. 233.

28. Chauncey, Jr., *Gay New York.* One of his central aims in this work is to argue that the hetero-homosexual binarism is of significantly more recent invention than generally acknowledged.

29. This point is made by Freedman in " 'Uncontrolled Desires.' "

30. Freedman, " 'Uncontrolled Desires.' "

31. John D'Emilio, in "The Homosexual Menace," points out that there was virtually no evidence supporting McCarthy-era allegations that lesbians and gays were vulnerable to blackmail and hence unsuitable for government employment. He suggests that the massive efforts to counter the "homosexual menace" can only be explained as a result of the Depression and World War II's disruption of family life, gender arrangements, and patterns of sexuality.

32. Freedman, " 'Uncontrolled Desires,' " and D'Emilio, "The Homosexual Menace."

33. Fear that the child will be sexually molested is one reason for denying *lesbians* custody of their children.

34. Judith Stacey cites one San Francisco study of divorced couples as revealing that one-third of them sustained kinship ties with former spouses and their relatives; *Brave New Families: Stories of Domestic Upheaval in Late Twentieth Century America* (New York: Basic Books, 1990), p. 254. "Divorce-extended" is her term.

35. For an exhaustive discussion of the inadequacies of the one-mother, one-father assumption to both heterosexual and gay/lesbian families see Nancy D. Polikoff, "This Child Does Have Two Mothers," *The Georgetown Law Journal,* 78 (1990): 459–575.

36. Stacey, *Brave New Families.*

37. Ibid., p. 17.

38. Kath Weston, *Families We Choose: Lesbians, Gays, Kinship* (New York: Columbia University Press, 1991).

39. Indeed, it has become doubly denaturalized. First, in failing to be repetitively enacted by individuals creating families, the heterosexual, procreative, nuclear family has lost its appearance of being the natural family form. That is, just as gender is "naturalized" through repeated performances (Judith Butler, *Gender Trouble: Feminism and the Subversion of Identity* [New York: Routledge, 1990]), so too one might imagine that the family itself is naturalized through being repetitively enacted. Second, family composition extends well beyond those "naturally" linked by blood and those whose marital coupling "naturally" issues in progeny.

40. Jeffrey Weeks, "Pretended Family Relationships," in *Against Nature: Essays on History, Sexuality, and Identity* (London: Rivers Oram Press, 1991), p. 143.

41. For 1970s marriage cases, see Rubenstein, *Lesbians, Gay Men, and the Law.*

42. Quoted in Weeks, "Pretended Family Relationships," p. 137.

43. Although courts are moving to the assumption that the mother's lesbianism per se is not a bar to her fitness as a parent, this did not prevent the Virginia Supreme Court in the recent case of *Bottoms v. Bottoms* from ruling that, even so, *active* lesbianism on the part of the mother could be a bar to her fitness.

44. John M. Finnis, "Law, Morality, and 'Sexual Orientation,' " *Notre Dame Journal of Law, Ethics, and Public Policy,* 9 (1995): 11–39, p. 32.

45. Ibid., pp. 32–33.

46. U.S.C. #534, quoted in Robson, "Resisting the Family," p. 981, ftn. 16.

47. Justice White, in *Bowers v. Hardwick,* argued that homosexual sodomy is not protected by the right to privacy because, in his view, the right to privacy protects the private sphere of family, marriage, and procreation, and he opined that there was no connection between family, marriage, and procreation on the one hand, and homosexuality on the other.

DISCUSSION QUESTIONS

1. Do you agree with Calhoun that gays and lesbians are "family's outlaws"? Do you agree with her that families with same-sex parents are "real" families? Defend your view.
2. Should society sanction same-sex marriages? If so, on what grounds? If not, on what grounds? Should society sanction the adoption of children by same-sex couples? Defend your view, and compare it with Calhoun's.
3. Must our moral beliefs about sexuality be consistent with our moral beliefs about marriage? Could someone argue, for example, that homosexuality is moral but that same-sex marriage is immoral? Defend your view. Compare it with what you take to be Richard Wasserstrom's, Thomas Aquinas's, and Calhoun's respective positions.
4. In part V of her article, Calhoun uses the phrase "the social construction of lesbianism." What does she mean by "social construction"? What does it mean to say that lesbianism is "socially constructed"? Would Thomas Aquinas agree that lesbianism (or homosexuality) is socially constructed? Why or why not?
5. What does Calhoun mean when she says that lesbians need to reexamine marriage from their position as "family's outlaws" rather than from the gender structure of marriage and motherhood? What difference does this make? Why does she think this is important? Defend and discuss your view.

MEDIA GALLERY

"BETWEEN MEN"

By Doris Lessing

Story summary: Doris Lessing's "Between Men" is the story of two women who have spent their lives catering to men in order to obtain financial stability and personal support. But whereas Maureen Jeffries has had numerous affairs, Peggy Bayley married her lover in order to achieve these goals. To the surprise of many, Peggy allows her husband, Professor Tom Bayley, to have an affair with Maureen, yet they remain best friends. And, although both women initially claim to be satisfied with the lives they have led, all their intimate relationships eventually fail. While meeting for drinks one evening, both women admit that they have compromised themselves by having sex too quickly in their relationships. Maureen had been a painter and believes that if she had not spent so much time helping some man achieve his ambition she could have developed her own skills and supported herself. She explains, "It's all so unfair, so unfair, so unfair . . . they were all like that. I'm not saying I'd have been a great painter, but I might have been something. Something of my own. . . . Not one of those men did anything but make fun, patronize me . . . all of them, in one way or another. And of course, one always gives in. . . ." Peggy suggests that the two women band together to open a dress shop and break the boundaries that men have imposed on them. Maureen agrees. At the end and in a drunken state, Peggy mumbles, "No giving it up the firsht time a m-m-man appearsh. . . . We musht we *musht* agree to that, work firsht, or elshe, or else you know where we're going to end up."

Doris Lessing (1919–) is a British writer whose novels and short stories are largely concerned with people caught in the social and political upheavals of the twentieth century. The most widely read of her novels is *The Golden Notebook* (1962), a complex story of a woman writer who attempts to come to terms with her life through her art.

1. How would Richard Wasserstrom evaluate the morality of Maureen's extramarital affair with Tom Bayley? Do you agree with Wasserstrom's analysis? Explain.

2. How does the fact that Maureen and Tom do not hide their affair from Peggy affect the morality of their actions? How would a libertarian respond?
3. What seems to be Lessing's position on the morality of adultery? Do you agree with her? Why or why not?
4. Why does Peggy marry Tom? Is it a good reason? What would Thomas Aquinas say about it? Do you believe that they should not have gotten married? Discuss.
5. Do the actions of Peggy, Maureen, and Tom serve to maintain or break down the institution of marriage? Provide an argument for your view. How might Lessing respond to your argument?

"THE ROAD FROM COLONUS"

By E. M. Forster

Story summary: E. M. Forster's "The Road from Colonus" is the story of Mr. Lucas, a man who feels isolated from and repressed by his family and society. On a trip to Greece, Lucas separates from the rest of the group and realizes that he no longer need suppress his sexual desire to be with another man. The narrator explains: "For the last month a strange desire had possessed him to die fighting," and he has never felt so free from the societal conventions that have oppressed him for so long. However, Lucas's family forces him to return with them to England, where he must once again confront his family and the facade he presents to appease them. Although Lucas vows to follow his true desires once he returns home, this task proves to be difficult. Consequently, he remains trapped in the same roles that he played before he left for Greece.

E. M. Forster (1879–1970) was a British novelist, essayist, and social and literary critic. He is the author of *Where Angels Fear to Tread* (1905), *A Room with a View* (1908), *Howard's End* (1910), and *A Passage to India* (1924), among many other works. *Maurice,* a novel with a homosexual theme, was published posthumously in 1971.

1. Many people find themselves in a position similar to that of Mr. Lucas. They have sexual desire for persons of the same sex but find that their feelings are not supported by their families. Should families be supportive of members who find themselves attracted to persons of the same sex? What would you do if a family member announced that he or she had such feelings? Discuss.
2. Like many stories about homosexuality, Forster's does not speak directly about it. Rather, the subject is presented through symbols and metaphors. Do you think that this is the best way to address this subject? Or would you rather have Mr. Lucas explicitly discuss his feeling?
3. Mr. Lucas comes to understand his sexuality better only after he leaves his familiar environment. However, he finds the road back from this discovery very difficult. He is tormented by reminders that his sexual desires are not supported in his society. Would it have been better for him never to have discovered his true desires? Discuss.
4. Forster seems to be saying that the prejudices of Mr. Lucas's family and his society are making him unhappy. Do you think that these prejudices are morally justifiable? Would he be happier if he were not confronted by them? Defend your view.

CRIMES AND MISDEMEANORS

(USA, 1989) 1 hour 34 minutes
Directed by Woody Allen

Film summary: Renowned optometrist and public figure Judah Rosenthal (Martin Landau) is about to speak at a banquet in his honor. Judah is anxious because he has recently discovered a letter addressed to his wife, Miriam (Claire Bloom), from his bois-

terous lover, Dolores Paley (Anjelica Huston). Dolores is trying to contact Miriam to reveal Judah's infidelity because he has decided to terminate the relationship. Elsewhere
in New York, Cliff Stern (Woody Allen), a documentary filmmaker, is struggling with his
work and his marriage to Wendy (Joanna Gleason). Wendy's brother Lester (Alan Alda)
is a rich and famous TV producer whom Cliff loathes for his arrogance and his success.
Lester offers Cliff a job filming a documentary about Lester's life, though he makes it
quite clear that he is doing so only as a favor to Wendy. As Judah struggles with the end
of his adulterous relationship, Cliff finds himself drawn into one when he meets attractive production assistant Halley Reed (Mia Farrow). Conflicts arise when unmarried
Lester also exhibits amorous intentions toward Halley. Meanwhile, Judah meets with his
brother Jack (Jerry Orbach) and discusses an extreme solution to his problem: killing
his mistress. Landau vividly portrays the conflict of conscience that threatens to overwhelm Judah after Jack has killed Dolores.

1. Consider the extramarital affairs in *Crimes and Misdemeanors* in terms of Richard
   Wasserstrom's discussion of the morality of adultery. Would Wasserstrom consider the
   extramarital affairs in *Crimes and Misdemeanors* to be immoral? Explain. Do you agree
   with him?
2. Do you think that the extramarital affairs in *Crimes and Misdemeanors* can be used as
   support for Wasserstrom's argument that sexual exclusivity is neither a necessary nor
   a sufficient condition for the existence of marriage?
3. Use this film as the basis for a general argument either for or against the moral desirability of marriage.
4. *Crimes and Misdemeanors* uses many unique characters and situations to develop a
   complex story about marriage and fidelity. It shows the effects of adultery on a marriage, as well as the conditions that lead people to commit adultery. Should we consider issues of marriage and fidelity on a case-by-case basis? Or should our view of the
   morality of extramarital affairs be considered independent of the factors that led to
   the infidelity? Defend your position, and compare it to the traditional and libertarian
   views of marital fidelity (see the introduction to this chapter).

 THE STORY OF US

(USA, 2000) 1 hour 36 minutes
Directed by Rob Reiner

Film summary: Ben Jordan (Bruce Willis) and Katie Jordan (Michelle Pfeiffer) have been
married for fifteen years and have a twelve-year-old boy and a ten-year-old girl. However,
there are problems with their marriage. They find that they have grown apart, and after
dropping their children off at camp for the summer, they decide to live apart. Eventually,
Ben gets his own apartment, and Katie begins to date another man. They decide that
they will tell their children about their impending divorce after they pick them up from
summer camp. However, by the time they reach the camp, Katie has had a change of
heart. Before they get in the truck to drive their children home from camp, Katie says
that they should not break up, and Ben agrees.

1. In her speech to Ben about why they should not break up, Katie says that "it's not for
   the sake of the children." Rather, she says, she and Ben have a history together, and
   "histories do not happen overnight." Therefore, they should stay together. Do you
   think that it is right for Ben and Katie to consider getting a divorce without thinking
   about the effect of their divorce on their children?
2. Clearly, Ben and Katie have changed over the course of the fifteen years they have
   been married. Katie accuses Ben of loving who they were, not who they are. She says,

"We can't stay together just because we get a glimpse of who we were." Do married couples have a moral obligation to stay together even if as individuals and/or a couple they change over the course of their marriage? Present your argument, and formulate the critical response that Laurence Houlgate might make.

3. Ben and Katie never speak directly to their children about the troubles that they are having in their marriage. However, the children can hear them arguing. Should Ben and Katie have spoken to their children about the troubles they were having? Why or why not? Do they have a moral obligation to speak to their children about their marriage?

4. After deciding to end their marriage, at the last moment Katie has a change of heart. The movie ends with Ben and Katie feeling good about their marriage and being committed to it. How do you feel about this as a conclusion to the movie? What moral message does it present about dealing with marital difficulties? Are you comfortable with this message?

 LOVE AND DEATH ON LONG ISLAND

(USA, 1997) 1 hour 34 minutes
Directed by Richard Kwietniowski

Film summary: Giles De'Ath (John Hurt) is a reclusive, middle-aged writer living in London. One day he ventures out to see the film adaptation of one of his favorite novels but inadvertently ends up in a theater screening a sophomoric comedy called *Hotpants College II*. He is about to leave when a young actor in the film grabs his attention. Several days later, Giles visits a museum where a painting of a young writer reminds him of the actor. He returns to the theater to see the movie in its entirety and becomes enthralled by the star, Ronnie Bostock (Jason Priestley). Giles begins scanning film magazines and teen idol magazines for articles about and photos of the actor, and he compiles an extensive dossier. He also purchases his first television and VCR so that he can watch all of Ronnie's films and complete his research. Giles tells his literary agent that he is exploring a new, revitalizing subject: finding beauty where no one has looked before. Giles travels to New York with the intention of tracking Ronnie down on Long Island. Taking a room at a cheap motel, he wanders the streets in hopes of a chance meeting. He sees the actor's fiancée, Audrey (Fiona Loewi), at a supermarket and engineers an "accidental" meeting with her. Audrey is charmed by Giles' enthusiasm for Ronnie and asks if Giles would consider writing a script for the young actor. Audrey later arranges a meeting between the two men, and Giles showers Ronnie with praise. Ronnie is impressed and intrigued by his fan, and they begin to spend time together. They read through the script of *Hotpants College III,* and Giles begins to rewrite the film adding tender, heroic scenes with literary allusions. Audrey senses the growing relationship between the two men and suddenly announces that she and Ronnie are leaving Long Island. Giles arranges a farewell meeting with Ronnie and proposes that he should leave America altogether and start over in Europe with his help. When Ronnie says that he must meet Audrey, Giles detains him, insisting that his relationship with Audrey will not last and confessing his own passionate love for the actor. Ronnie quietly exits, pausing to lay a sympathetic hand on Giles' shoulder. Giles, in shock, returns to his motel and writes the story of his infatuation, which he faxes to Ronnie. Ronnie is deeply moved by the story and wonders how his life might have changed had he been able to open his heart to Giles. The young man reflects for a moment and then rips the fax to shreds.

1. The movie tells us little about what Giles was like before he met Ronnie. While we know that he was married to an older woman who has recently died, we are told nothing about his past feelings about members of the same sex. In any case, Giles does not seem to be surprised that he is falling in love with Ronnie, and he does not fight his feelings. Do you think that Giles' growing love for Ronnie is immoral? Why or why not?

2. Giles is presented as being out of touch with contemporary Western culture and technology. Do you think that Giles would have pursued his love of Ronnie if he were more

in touch with contemporary Western culture and technology? What effect do you believe that contemporary Western culture has on our beliefs about sexuality?

3. While Ronnie recognizes that he has more to gain from being with Giles than with Audrey and gives every indication that he loves Giles as much as Giles loves him, he stays with Audrey. Why do you think he does this?

4. Traditionally, American cinema has seldom seriously and explicitly explored love between people of the same sex. Why do you think this is the case? Should this situation be changed? Why or why not?

THE WEDDING BANQUET [XIYAN]

(USA/Taiwan, 1993) 1 hour 51 minutes
Directed by Ang Lee

Film summary: Wai-Tung (Winston Chao) is a young, gay Chinese man from Taiwan who lives with his American boyfriend, Simon (Mitchell Lichtenstein), in a brownstone in New York. Wai-Tung has fashioned a comfortable life for himself managing loft properties that he purchased with the help of his father. All is well except for the pressure from his parents in Taiwan, who eagerly await the day when Wai-Tung will marry a nice Chinese girl and present them with a grandchild. Wai-Tung cannot bring himself to tell his parents that he is gay and continues to deceive them by completing the dating service forms they send. One day his partner, Simon, devises an ingenious plan to make everyone happy. One of Wai-Tung's tenants is a young Chinese woman, Wei-Wei (May Chin), an artist who does not have a green card and cannot afford her rent. In despair, she plans to return to China. Simon convinces his lover that a marriage to Wei-Wei will be beneficial for everyone, allowing Wei-Wei to stay in the United States while placating Wai-Tung's family in Taiwan. The plan seems perfect until Wai-Tung's father and mother (Sihung Lung and Ah-Leh Gua) suddenly announce that they will travel from Taiwan for the wedding. For Wei-Wei, the pretend marriage with Wai-Tung makes sense but is also painful, because she has a crush on him and wants to be married to him. For Wai-Tung, maintaining the deception is stressful and exhausting. Simon feels increasingly alienated as he participates in the family gatherings as an unrecognized outsider. Meanwhile, Wai-Tung's parents are disappointed with the couple's modest arrangements and insist that Wai-Tung and Wei-Wei have a proper Chinese wedding banquet. The wedding night marks the beginning of the plan's unraveling. Wai-Tung becomes drunk and has sex with Wei-Wei. When she becomes pregnant, Simon is outraged and threatens to leave Wai-Tung. Then, when Wai-Tung's father has a mild stroke, Wai-Tung confesses his deception to his mother. Wai-Tung's father in turn confesses to Simon that he has guessed the nature of their relationship but let the deception continue in order to get a grandchild. Wei-Wei considers having an abortion and returning to China but later changes her mind, asking Simon to be one of the fathers of her child.

The Wedding Banquet was nominated for an Oscar for Best Foreign Film.

1. When Wai-Tung confesses to his mother that he is gay, he emphasizes the strength of his love for Simon while his mother stresses her need for a grandchild. Use this situation to compare the strengths and weaknesses of traditional and libertarian positions on sexuality and marriage (see the introduction to this chapter).

2. Wei-Wei has a private moment with Wai-Tung's mother after the deception has been revealed. The older woman admits, "We old women sometimes envy young women like you. Independent, well educated, with your own life. You don't depend on men. You do as you choose." Later she seeks affirmation of her beliefs in traditional roles: "A woman is still a woman—husbands and children are still most important to us, right?" Wei-Wei responds, "Not really." How is Wei-Wei's situation similar to and different from

the situation of the women in Doris Lessing's "Between Men"? Do you think that Wei-Wei's position on marriage is stronger than theirs? Discuss.

3. *The Wedding Banquet* has been criticized by gays and lesbians for Wai-Tung's sexual relations with Wei-Wei. Although Wai-Tung was in a loving, committed partnership with Simon, he certainly had feelings for Wei-Wei, which may have included guilt, gratitude, friendship, and love. Why do you think that gay and lesbian audiences were critical of their sexual relations? Could this incident be construed as a critique of homosexuality? How would you describe Wai-Tung's feelings toward Wei-Wei? Do you think that he was bisexual?

4. Wai-Tung fills out a dating service quesionnaire early in the film although he is not interested in the "ideal woman" he describes. He admits, "It's stupid, all these lies, but I'm used to it." What pressures convince Wai-Tung to keep up the lie? What dangers does the film suggest may follow from lying about one's sexuality? Use these dangers as the basis of a commentary on the traditional and libertarian positions on sexuality.

5. The film ends with Wei-Wei deciding to keep the baby. Wai-Tung questions whether she can be an artist and a mother at the same time. Wei-Wei asks Simon if he will be "one of the fathers of her child." Should we consider this family to be an "outlaw" family in Chesire Calhoun's sense? Relate this family situation to Calhoun's discussion of family outlaws. Could it be used as evidence to support Calhoun's position? Why or why not?

6. While Wai-Tung's father seems to accept his son's homosexuality, his mother reverts to arguments that her son has been emotionally hurt by a woman and suffers from a "temporary psychological problem." She maintains the hope that Wai-Tung will "return to normal" when he sees his child. To what extent do you believe that our ideas of "normal sexuality" are determined by our culture? By our parents and family? Compare your view with the positions of Thomas Aquinas and Richard Mohr.

7. Initially, Wai-Tung clearly says "no" to Wei-Wei's sexual advances. Should this be considered rape? How do Wei-Wei's notions about sexuality affect her decision to pursue Wai-Tung despite his request that she stop? Would your views about the morality of Wei-Wei's actions be different if Wai-Tung were heterosexual? Explain.

THE 1996 DEFENSE OF MARRIAGE ACT

In September 1996, Congress passed the Defense of Marriage Act (DOMA). The House vote was 342–67; the Senate vote was 85–14.

PUBLIC LAW 104–199
DATE: 21 SEPTEMBER 1996
No State, territory, or possession of the United States, or Indian tribe, shall be required to give effect to any public act, record, or judicial proceeding of any other State, territory, possession, or tribe respecting a relationship between persons of the same sex that is treated as marriage under the laws of such other State, territory, possession, or tribe, or a right or claim arising from such relationship.

In determining the meaning of any Act of Congress, or of any ruling, regulation, or interpretation of the various administrative bureaus and agencies of the United States, the word "marriage" means only a legal union between one man and one woman as husband and wife, and the word "spouse" refers only to a person of the opposite sex who is a husband or a wife.

1. What legal difference does the Defense of Marriage Act make? What moral difference does it make? Which do you believe is more significant, and why?

2. Why do you think that this law was passed by both the House and Senate by such a large margin? If you were a member of Congress, would you have voted for or against it? Why?

3. How does this law affect the lives of same-sex couples? Do you think that it is fair, for example, that same-sex couples who would like to be married and who have been together for years are not entitled to the same social and economic benefits as opposite-sex, married couples who have been together for the same amount of time? Explain.

4. Do you think that Congress views same-sex couples as "family outlaws" (in Chesire Calhoun's sense)? Is this law proof of that belief? Why or why not?

SUPPLEMENTARY READINGS

Aquinas, Thomas. *On the Truth of the Catholic Faith*, trans. V. J. Bourke. New York: Doubleday, 1956.

Atkinson, Ronald. *Sexual Morality*. New York: Harcourt, Brace, 1965.

Augustine. *St. Augustine on Marriage and Sexuality*, ed. Elizabeth A. Clark. Washington, DC: Catholic University of America Press, 1996.

Baker, Robert, and Frederick Elliston, eds. *Philosophy and Sex*, 2nd ed. Buffalo: Prometheus Books, 1984.

Cohen, Cheryl H. "The Feminist Sexuality Debate: Ethics and Politics." *Hypatia*, 3 (1986): 71–86.

Cole, W. G. *Sex in Christianity and Psychoanalysis*. New York: Oxford University Press, 1955.

Foucault, Michel. *The History of Sexuality*, vol. 1: *An Introduction*. London: Allen Lane, 1979.

Gathorne-Hardy, Jonathan. *Marriage, Love, Sex and Divorce*. New York: Summit Books, 1981.

Houlgate, Laurence D. *Morals, Marriage, and Parenthood: An Introduction to Family Ethics*. Belmont, CA: Wadsworth, 1999.

———. *The Child and the State: A Normative Theory of Juvenile Rights*. Baltimore: Johns Hopkins University Press, 1980.

Hunter, J. F. M. *Thinking About Sex and Love: A Philosophical Inquiry*. New York: St. Martin's Press, 1980.

Jaggar, Alison M., and Paula Rotheberg Struhl, eds. *Feminist Frameworks*, 3rd ed. New York: McGraw-Hill, 1993.

Nussbaum, Martha C. *Sex and Social Justice*. New York: Oxford University Press, 1999.

Okin, Susan Moller. *Justice, gender and the family*. New York: Basic Books, 1989.

Person, Ethel Spector, and Catherine R. Simpson, eds. *Women: Sex and Sexuality*. Chicago: University of Chicago Press, 1980.

Punzo, V. C. *Reflective Naturalism*. New York: Macmillan, 1969.

Rich, Adrienne. "Compulsory Heterosexuality and Lesbian Existence." In *Women: Sex and Sexuality*, ed. Ethel Person and Catherine Simpson. Chicago: University of Chicago Press, 1980.

Rich, Ruby. "Review Essay: Feminism and Sexuality in the 1980s." *Feminist Studies*, 12 (1986): 525–561.

Russell, Bertrand. *Marriage and Morals*. New York: Liveright, 1970.

Sacred Congregation for the Doctrine of Faith. *Declaration of Sexual Ethics*. Vatican City, 1975.

Scruton, Roger. *Sexual Desire: A Moral Philosophy of the Erotic*. New York: Free Press, 1986.

Soble, Alan, ed. *Philosophy of Sex*, 2nd ed. Totowa, NJ: Littlefield, Adams, 1991.

Taylor, Richard. *Having Love Affairs*. Buffalo: Prometheus Books, 1982.

Vance, Carole, ed. *Pleasure and Danger: Exploring Female Sexuality*. London: Pandora Press, 1992.

Vannoy, Russell. *Sex Without Love: A Philosophical Investigation*. Buffalo: Prometheus Books, 1980.

Verene, D. P., ed. *Sexual Love and Western Morality*. New York: Harper & Row, 1972.

Whitely, C. H., and W. M. Whitely. *Sex and Morals*. New York: Basic Books, 1967.

Wilson, James Q. "Against Homosexual Marriage." *Commentary*, 101 (March 1996): 34–39.

Wilson, John. *Love, Sex and Feminism*. New York: Praeger, 1980.

6

Racism and Affirmative Action

Racism refers to the inability or refusal to recognize the rights, needs, dignity, or value of people of particular races or geographical origins. While philosophical justifications of racism can be traced back to at least the fifteenth century, the term "racism" did not come into prominence until the mid-nineteenth century. In the 1850s, people in Europe, particularly in France and Germany, were proposing pseudoscientific theories that "race" is a determinate biological category that can be used to establish a hierarchy among different ethnic groups. Most of these defenses of the division of people into groups based on shared, fundamental, biologically inheritable moral and intellectual characteristics were developed to justify preexisting prejudicial practices, actions, and beliefs. A practice, action, or belief is *racist* if it promotes, creates, constitutes, or takes unfair advantage of any irrelevant or impertinent differences between races.

In the United States, at least until 1954, racial discrimination was neither illegal nor widely regarded as immoral. Job discrimination, housing discrimination, judicial discrimination, and educational discrimination were a normal part of the Native American, Asian-American, Latino/a-American, Chicano/a-American, and African-American experience. Add to this list slavery, lynchings, unjust imprisonment, and assorted forms of public humiliation, and you get a fair sense of the range of America's racially discriminatory practices. Again, we must remember that the enslavement of African-Americans was merely one part of a larger set of racially discriminatory practices that included the exploitation of Asian-American labor by the American railroad and agricultural industries and the genocide of Native Americans and their forced expulsion from their homelands. But *Brown v. Board of Education* and the emergence of the American civil rights movement radically reshaped the character of racism in our country.

In 1954, the U.S. Supreme Court, in *Brown v. Board of Education of Topeka, Kansas,* reversed the long-standing "separate but equal" doctrine and began the desegregation of schools. By the next year, the civil rights movement in America was beginning to take shape. Events like Rosa Park's refusal in December 1955 to adhere to the policy of Blacks having to sit at the back of public buses spurred the formation of various civil rights groups. Groups like Reverend Martin Luther King's Southern Christian Leadership Conference began a nonviolent campaign against racial discrimination. One of the positive results of the efforts of the various civil rights groups was the passage of the Civil Rights Act of 1957, which established a commission to investigate infringements of the voting rights of Blacks. Also, in the same year, President Eisenhower sent troops to enforce a federal court order to desegregate the Little Rock, Arkansas, high schools. Five years later, President Kennedy would dispatch troops to enforce integration at the University of Mississippi.

By the 1960s, many organizations had focused attention on how society unfairly treated Blacks in America. One of the most visible displays of solidarity regarding civil rights in America was the 1962 march on Washington, DC, in support of the civil rights of Blacks. Many legal institutions and societal beliefs were shown to be racist and to prevent Blacks from achieving the full benefits of American citizenship. For example, until the 1960s, many states had customs, if not laws, that required Blacks to sit in the back of public buses, to use separate drinking fountains in public parks, and to attend different public schools than Whites. As a result of the efforts of thousands of Americans, both Black and White, many of these customs were challenged and laws were changed. And in 1964, the United States passed the Civil Rights Act to end all discrimination, including religious, racial, and sex discrimination.

The civil rights movement had a profound impact on American society. One result of this movement was that women, who believed that they had also traditionally been treated unfairly by society, began to organize. Through protests and organized campaigning, these women—many of whom were also supporters of the civil rights movement—brought about changes in American law and social life in the 1960s and 1970s. For example, the Civil Rights Act of 1964, which made it illegal to sexually harass women in the workplace, was at least in part a result of the efforts of women who wished to be treated better by society. The moral and political goals of feminists are also due largely to the efforts of women in the 1960s and 1970s to change what they viewed as sexist laws and practices in the United States. Consequently, many have argued that racial discrimination and sexual discrimination, or simply, racism and sexism, have some deep similarities.

It can be useful to draw a distinction between different types of racism. Some of the more common types are overt racism, covert racism, unintentional racism, and institutional racism (see Chapter 10 for a discussion of environmental racism). Overt and covert racism both result when race is seen as sufficient grounds for handling people differently. *Overt racism* occurs when people of other races are subjected to unprovoked violence, racial slurs, and unequal treatment. Examples of overt racism include the speech and action of members of groups like the Ku Klux Klan, neo-Nazis, and skinheads. These groups openly state their hatred for particular races of people and center their actions around their overtly stated racist beliefs. But overt racism is probably not the most common form of racism in the United States. Covert racism is much more common.

Covert racists seldom if ever openly state their disdain of or hatred for people of other races. The reason many people become covert racists is that overt racism is not socially accepted. Just think about the negative public response to the allegedly racist comments made by sports figures such as football player Reggie White and baseball player John Rocker. Some people argue that overt racism is much less dangerous than covert racism. We know what John Rocker believes because he tells us as much, and so we are free to openly challenge his beliefs. *Covert racism,* in contrast, is much less easy to identify because it is not openly stated. But other people argue that overt racism is much more dangerous than covert racism. Overt racism challenges the moral opinion of the public majority that racism and racist comments and actions are wrong, whereas covert racism tacitly acknowledges and respects the belief that racist comments and actions are wrong.

Unintentional racism occurs when an action, practice, or belief *has the effect* of either taking unfair advantage or asserting impertinent differences between the races. Whereas overt and covert racism are characterized by the motives and intentions of the racists, unintentional racism is defined by the harmful consequences of people's speech and actions. Many times, unintentional racists do not intend to cause harm on racial grounds. Nevertheless, the consequences of their speech and/or action are regarded by others as a form of racism. An example of unintentional racism is the denial of a qualified non-White person a job on the grounds that a person of that race has never held such a position. Another example is a police officer pulling over a Black motorist driving in a predominantly White neighborhood even if the driver has not committed any moving violations. These actions are viewed by many as racist because they would not have occurred had the person in question been White.

Many times, the cause of racism can be linked to generalizations and stereotypes about people of varying racial backgrounds. Usually, these generalizations and stereotypes are unsubstantiated and so need to be changed. The problem is that these unsubstantiated assumptions and stereotypes often are a basic part of our social, political, and economic institutions. Thus, changing these beliefs entails altering institutions that form the basis of our society, which can be very difficult. Racism of this kind is called *institutional racism* (or structural racism). It can be further classified as overt, covert, or unintentional. For example, segregated public schools are an example of overt institutional racism; neighborhoods with highways built to divide White from non-White populations are an example of covert institutional racism; and educational tests using questions that White students have a better chance of answering correctly than non-White students are an example of unintentional institutional racism.

Affirmative action programs are the best-known strategy to eliminate racism, particularly the kinds of racial prejudice and discrimination that occur in the workplace and in education. We can divide affirmative action programs into two broad types: those that use race as a factor in hiring and admissions procedures and those that do not.

Some proponents of affirmative action maintain that race should not be an explicit factor in hiring and admissions procedures. Such affirmative action programs aim to be color-blind in the sense that every possible effort is made to ensure that race plays no role in admissions and hiring procedures. These color-blind affirmative action programs—which are sometimes called *active nondiscrimination programs*—actively seek to identify and eliminate all forms of racism in business and education. These programs mandate harsh punishments for identifiably racist actions and speech and attempt to eliminate institutionalized forms of racism by altering the policies of institutions. Some critics, however, believe that these programs are too passive because they do not actively seek to hire or admit and include non-White people (as well as women). They argue that making sure that no one discriminates on the basis of race and devising color-blind admissions and hiring policies are much less effective in promoting equality in the workplace and in education than affirmative action programs that actively move to increase the number of non-Whites (and women) in business and education.

Other proponents of affirmative action maintain that race should be an explicit factor in hiring and admissions policies in an attempt to deal with past and current racism. One type of race-based affirmative action program actively encourages underrepresented groups to apply for admission to universities and for positions in businesses. This case-by-case approach to race-based affirmative action allows employers or schools to increase the racial (and gender) balance without mandating that a particular number of people be hired. While some institutions reach a more equitable balance through such policies, some argue that the case-by-case approach is ineffective in situations in which discrimination is firmly institutionalized. Another type of race-based affirmative action program neither discourages nor encourages anyone from applying for admission or employment but gives preferential treatment to underrepresented groups such as non-Whites and women. In still another form of race-based affirmative action, a predetermined number of admissions or slots or jobs are set aside for members of underrepresented groups. These quota goals typically are equivalent to population percentages. So, if 15 percent of the population is Latino/a, then the school or business with the quota goal will aim to have 15 percent of its students or employees be Latino/a.

While race-based affirmative action programs are instituted to ensure fair and equal treatment for all, some critics argue that to achieve fair treatment the programs must treat some people unfairly and in an unequal way. This is the principle objection to most race-based affirmative action programs. Critics maintain, for example, that by implementing procedures that give preferential treatment to people who are members of groups victimized by discrimination, these programs unfairly discriminate against people who are qualified for jobs or admission but who are not members of victimized groups. There are two main lines of response to this criticism of race-based affirmative action: the argument from compensation and the argument from social utility.

Proponents of the argument from social utility maintain that race-based affirmative action programs are the best way to achieve a color-blind society. In other words, the social utility of quota systems and preferential treatment programs outweighs the loss of utility incurred by denying qualified applicants from overrepresented groups admission or employment. Critics respond that the argument from social utility still does not address the issue of how such programs, which are instituted to ensure fair and equal treatment for all people, at the same time treat some people unfairly and in an unequal way. Others argue that merely changing racial and gender demographics in the workplace or classroom will not make society color- and gender-blind. People will be discriminated against regardless of demographics, and the problems of discrimination must be addressed by some other means. However, aside from affirmative action programs, it is not clear what those means would be.

Proponents of the argument from compensation maintain that White people owe direct compensation to Blacks and/or Native Americans for the wrongs they have done to those groups. Critics of this defense of race-based affirmative action programs maintain that it is a flawed argument because the Whites who wronged Blacks and/or Native Americans are not injured by these programs. Another version of the compensation argument for race-based affirmative action maintains that Whites owe Blacks and/or Native Americans compensation for the benefits from racism that Whites enjoy in the classroom and the workplace. Again, critics challenge this argument on the grounds that it says that we are treating some people unequally in order to treat all people equally.

Some critics of affirmative action go so far as to argue against race-based affirmative action on the grounds that discrimination itself does not exist. Supporters of affirmative action respond that there are two main types of evidence for discrimination: statistical evidence regarding the relationship between racial or gender group and job type and salary, and attitudes and policies that seem to account for these statistics. Statistical evidence indicates that women and minorities hold less desirable jobs and are paid less than their White male counterparts. In addition, a survey of business attitudes and practices revealed that males are favored in employment selection and promotion, in career development decisions, in promotion to managerial positions, and in some recruitment procedures. From this evidence, most conclude that discrimination against women and minorities in the workplace exists.

Legal precedents on affirmative action include the Supreme Court of the state of Washington ruling in *DeFunis v. Overgaard* (1973) that racial classifications are not unconstitutional if there is a compelling state interest in making such classifications. In this case, the University of Washington Law School was shown to have a compelling state interest in making such classifications because there was a need to increase the number of non-White judges, prosecutors, and lawyers in the state. In *Regents of the University of California v. Bakke* (1978), the U.S. Supreme Court ruled that quotas are acceptable only if there is evidence that an institution has illegally discriminated in the past; otherwise, quotas are unconstitutional. The Court held that a case-by-case method of affirmative action, which treats people as individuals and uses race as only one factor among many, is constitutionally acceptable. Since *Bakke*, the courts have further restricted affirmative action measures at universities, resulting in a decrease in race-based university admissions policies.

KWAME ANTHONY APPIAH

Racisms

In "Racisms," Kwame Anthony Appiah aims to clarify our ordinary ways of thinking about race and racism and to point out some of their presuppositions. Appiah claims that there are "at least three distinct doctrines that might be held to express the theoretical content of what we call 'racism.'" The first, *racialism,* is the proposition that "there are heritable characteristics, possessed by members of our species, that allow us to divide them into a small set of races, in such a way that all the members of these races share certain traits and tendencies with each other that they do not share with members of any other race." The second, *extrinsic racism,* is the proposition that races are morally significant because they are "contingently correlated with morally relevant properties." The third, *intrinsic racism,* is the proposition that races are morally significant because "they are intrinsically morally significant." For Appiah, *racial prejudice* is the tendency to assent to false propositions about races and "to do so even in the face of evidence and argument that should appropriately lead to giving those propositions up." Appiah believes that racialism is false. Furthermore, since both extrinsic and intrinsic racism presuppose racialism, Appiah says that he "could not logically support racism of either variety." Additionally, even if racialism were true, both forms of racism would be incorrect—extrinsic racism because the genes that underlie our standard racial categories do not determine the genes that determine our moral and intellectual categories, and intrinsic racism because "it breaches the Kantian imperative to make moral distinctions only on morally relevant grounds."

Kwame Anthony Appiah is a professor of Afro-American studies and philosophy at Harvard University. He is also the author and editor of many books including *Assertion and Conditionals* (1985), *In My Father's House: Africa in the Philosophy of Culture* (1992), *Identities* (coedited with Henry Louis Gates, Jr., 1995), *Color Conscious: The Political Morality of Race* (with Amy Gutmann, 1996), *The Dictionary of Global Culture* (coedited with Henry Louis Gates, Jr., 1997), and *Africana: The Encyclopedia of the African and African American Experience* (edited with Henry Louis Gates, Jr., 1999). He has also written a number of novels.

If the people I talk to and the newspapers I read are representative and reliable, there is a good deal of racism about. People and policies in the United States, in Eastern and Western Europe, in Asia and Africa and Latin America are regularly described as "racist." Australia had, until recently, a racist immigration policy; Britain still has one; racism is on the rise in France; many Israelis support Meir Kahane, an anti-Arab racist; many Arabs, according to a leading authority, are anti-Semitic racists,[1] and the movement to establish English as the "official language" of the United States is mo-

tivated by racism. Or, at least, so many of the people I talk to and many of the journalists with the newspapers I read believe.

But visitors from Mars—or from Malawi—unfamiliar with the Western concept of racism could be excused if they had some difficulty in identifying what exactly racism was. We see it everywhere, but rarely does anyone stop to say what it is, or to explain what is wrong with it. Our visitors from Mars would soon grasp that it had become at least conventional in recent years to express abhorrence for racism. They might even notice that those most of-

---

Anatomy of Racism. Edited by David Theo Goldberg. University of Minnesota Press, 1990, 3–17. Reprinted by permission of University of Minnesota Press.

ten accused of it—members of the South African Nationalist party, for example—may officially abhor it also. But if they sought in the popular media of our day—in newspapers and magazines, on television or radio, in novels or films—for an explicit definition of this thing "we" all abhor, they would very likely be disappointed.

Now, of course, this would be true of many of our most familiar concepts. *Sister, chair, tomato*—none of these gets defined in the course of our daily business. But the concept of racism is in worse shape than these. For much of what we say about it is, on the face of it, inconsistent.

It is, for example, held by many to be racist to refuse entry to a university to an otherwise qualified "Negro" candidate, but not to be so to refuse entry to an equally qualified "Caucasian" one. But "Negro" and "Caucasian" are both alleged to be names of races, and invidious discrimination on the basis of race is usually held to be a paradigm case of racism. Or, to take another example, it is widely believed to be evidence of an unacceptable racism to exclude people from clubs on the basis of race; yet most people, even those who think of "Jewish" as a racial term, seem to think that there is nothing wrong with Jewish clubs, whose members do not share any particular religious beliefs, or Afro-American societies, whose members share the juridical characteristic of American citizenship and the "racial" characteristic of being black.

I say that these are inconsistencies "on the face of it," because, for example, affirmative action in university admissions is importantly different from the earlier refusal to admit blacks or Jews (or other "Others") that it is meant, in part, to correct. Deep enough analysis may reveal it to be quite consistent with the abhorrence of racism; even a shallow analysis suggests that it is intended to be so. Similarly, justifications can be offered for "racial" associations in a plural society that are not available for the racial exclusivism of the country club. But if we take racism seriously we ought to be concerned about the adequacy of these justifications.

In this essay, then, I propose to take our ordinary ways of thinking about race and racism and point up some of their presuppositions. And since popular concepts are, of course, usually fairly fuzzily and untheoretically conceived, much of what I have to say will seem to be both more theoretically and more precisely committed than the talk of racism and racists in our newspapers and on television. My claim is that these theoretical claims are required to make sense of racism as the practice of reasoning human beings. If anyone were to suggest that much, perhaps most, of what goes under the name "racism" in our world cannot be given such a rationalized foundation, I should not disagree: but to the extent that a practice cannot be rationally reconstructed it ought, surely, to be given up by reasonable people. The right tactic with racism, if you really want to oppose it, is to object to it rationally in the form in which it stands the best chance of meeting objections. The doctrines I want to discuss can be rationally articulated: and they are worth articulating rationally in order that we can rationally say what we object to in them.

RACIST PROPOSITIONS

There are at least three distinct doctrines that might be held to express the theoretical content of what we call "racism." One is the view—which I shall call *racialism*[2]—that there are heritable characteristics, possessed by members of our species, that allow us to divide them into a small set of races, in such a way that all the members of these races share certain traits and tendencies with each other that they do not share with members of any other race. These traits and tendencies characteristic of a race constitute, on the racialist view, a sort of racial essence; and it is part of the content of racialism that the essential heritable characteristics of what the nineteenth century called the "Races of Man" account for more than the visible morphological characteristics—skin color, hair type, facial features—on the basis of which we make our informal classifications. Racialism is at the heart of nineteenth-century Western attempts to develop a science of racial difference; but it appears to have been believed by others—for example, Hegel, before then, and many in other parts of the non-Western world since—who have had no interest in developing scientific theories.

Racialism is not, in itself, a doctrine that must be dangerous, even if the racial essence is thought to entail moral and intellectual dispositions. Provided positive moral qualities are distributed across the races, each can be respected, can have its "separate but equal" place. Unlike most Western-educated people, I believe—and I have argued elsewhere[3]—that racialism is false; but by itself, it seems to be a cognitive rather than a moral problem. The issue is how the world is, not how we would want it to be.

Racialism is, however, a presupposition of other doctrines that have been called "racism," and these other doctrines have been, in the last few centuries, the basis of a great deal of human suffering and the source of a great deal of moral error.

One such doctrine we might call "extrinsic racism": extrinsic racists make moral distinctions between members of different races because they believe that the racial essence entails certain morally relevant qualities. The basis for the extrinsic racists' discrimination between people is their belief that members of different races differ in respects that *warrant* the differential treatment, respects—such as honesty or courage or intelligence—that are uncontroversially held (at least in most contemporary cultures) to be acceptable as a basis for treating people differently. Evidence that there are no such differences in morally relevant characteristics—that Negroes do not necessarily lack intellectual capacities, that Jews are not especially avaricious—should thus lead people out of their racism if it is purely extrinsic. As we know, such evidence often fails to change an extrinsic racist's attitudes substantially, for some of the extrinsic racist's best friends have always been Jewish. But at this point—if the racist is sincere—what we have is no longer a false doctrine but a cognitive incapacity, one whose significance I shall discuss later in this essay.

I say that the *sincere* extrinsic racist may suffer from a cognitive incapacity. But some who espouse extrinsic racist doctrines are simply insincere intrinsic racists. For *intrinsic racists,* on my definition, are people who differentiate morally between members of different races because they believe that each race has a different moral status, quite independent of the moral characteristics entailed by its racial essence. Just as, for example, many people assume that the fact that they are biologically related to another person—a brother, an aunt, a cousin—gives them a moral interest in that person,[4] so an intrinsic racist holds that the bare fact of being of the same race is a reason for preferring one person to another. (I shall return to this parallel later as well.)

For an intrinsic racist, no amount of evidence that a member of another race is capable of great moral, intellectual, or cultural achievements, or has characteristics that, in members of one's own race, would make them admirable or attractive, offers any ground for treating that person as he or she would treat similarly endowed members of his or her own race. Just so, some sexists are "intrinsic sexists," holding that the bare fact that someone is a woman (or man) is a reason for treating her (or him) in certain ways.

There are interesting possibilities for complicating these distinctions: some racists, for example,

claim, as the Mormons once did, that they discriminate between people because they believe that God requires them to do so. Is this an extrinsic racism, predicated on the combination of God's being an intrinsic racist and the belief that it is right to do what God wills? Or is it intrinsic racism because it is based on the belief that God requires these discriminations because they are right? (Is an act pious because the gods love it, or do they love it because it is pious?) Nevertheless, the distinctions between racialism and racism and between two potentially overlapping kinds of racism provide us with the skeleton of an anatomy of the propositional contents of racial attitudes.

RACIST DISPOSITIONS

Most people will want to object already that this discussion of the propositional content of racist moral and factual beliefs misses something absolutely crucial to the character of the psychological and sociological reality of racism, something I touched on when I mentioned that extrinsic racist utterances are often made by people who suffer from what I called a "cognitive incapacity." Part of the standard force of accusations of racism is that their objects are in some way *irrational*. The objection to Professor Shockley's claims about the intelligence of blacks is not just that they are false; it is rather that Professor Shockley seems, like many people we call "racist," to be unable to see that the evidence does not support his factual claims and that the connection between his factual claims and his policy prescriptions involves a series of non sequiturs.

What makes these cognitive incapacities especially troubling—something we should respond to with more than a recommendation that the individual, Professor Shockley, be offered psychotherapy—is that they conform to a certain pattern: namely, that it is especially where beliefs and policies that are to the disadvantage of nonwhite people that he shows the sorts of disturbing failure that have made his views both notorious and notoriously unreliable. Indeed, Professor Shockley's reasoning works extremely well in some other areas: that he is a Nobel Laureate in physics is part of what makes him so interesting an example.

This cognitive incapacity is not, of course, a rare one. Many of us are unable to give up beliefs that play a part in justifying the special advantages we gain (or hope to gain) from our positions in the social order—in particular, beliefs about the positive characters of the class of people who share that position. Many people who express extrinsic racist beliefs—many white South Africans, for example—are beneficiaries of social orders that deliver advantages to them by virtue of their "race," so that their disinclination to accept evidence that would deprive them of a justification for those advantages is just an instance of this general phenomenon.

So, too, evidence that access to higher education is as largely determined by the quality of our earlier educations as by our own innate talents, does not, on the whole, undermine the confidence of college entrants from private schools in England or the United States or Ghana. Many of them continue to believe in the face of this evidence that their acceptance at "good" universities shows them to be intellectually better endowed (and not just better prepared) than those who are rejected. It is facts such as these that give sense to the notion of false consciousness, the idea that an ideology can prevent us from acknowledging facts that would threaten our position.

The most interesting cases of this sort of ideological resistance to the truth are not, perhaps, the ones I have just mentioned. On the whole, it is less surprising, once we accept the admittedly problematic notion of self-deception, that people who think that certain attitudes or beliefs advantage them or those they care about should be able, as we say, to "persuade" themselves to ignore evidence that undermines those beliefs or attitudes. What is more interesting is the existence of people who resist the truth of a proposition while thinking that its wider acceptance would in no way disadvantage them or those individuals about whom they care—this might be thought to describe Professor Shockley; or who resist the truth when they recognize that its acceptance would actually advantage them—this might be the case with some black people who have internalized negative racist stereotypes; or who fail, by virtue of their ideological attachments, to recognize what is in their own best interests at all.

My business here is not with the psychological or social processes by which these forms of ideological resistance operate, but it is important, I think, to see the refusal on the part of some extrinsic racists to accept evidence against the beliefs as an instance of a widespread phenomenon in human affairs. It is a plain fact, to which theories of ideology must address themselves, that our species is prone both morally and intellectually to such distortions of judgment, in particular to distortions of judgment that reflect partiality. An inability to change your mind in the face of

appropriate[5] evidence is a cognitive incapacity; but it is one that all of us surely suffer from in some areas of belief; especially in areas where our own interests or self-images are (or seem to be) at stake.

It is not, however, as some have held, a tendency that we are powerless to resist. No one, no doubt, can be impartial about everything—even about everything to which the notion of partiality applies; but there is no subject matter about which most sane people cannot, in the end, be persuaded to avoid partiality in judgment. And it may help to shake the convictions of those whose incapacity derives from this sort of ideological defense if we show them how their reaction fits into this general pattern. It is, indeed, because it generally *does* fit this pattern that we call such views "racism"—the suffix "-ism" indicating that what we have in mind is not simply a theory but an ideology. It would be odd to call someone brought up in a remote corner of the world with false and demeaning views about white people a "racist" if that person gave up those beliefs quite easily in the face of appropriate evidence.

Real live racists, then, exhibit a systematically distorted rationality, the kind of systematically distorted rationality that we are likely to call "ideological." And it is a distortion that is especially striking in the cognitive domain: extrinsic racists, as I said earlier, however intelligent or otherwise well informed, often fail to treat evidence against the theoretical propositions of extrinsic racism dispassionately. Like extrinsic racism, intrinsic racism can also often be seen as ideological; but since scientific evidence is not going to settle the issue, a failure to see that it is wrong represents a cognitive incapacity only on controversially realist views about morality. What makes intrinsic racism similarly ideological is not so much the failure of inductive or deductive rationality that is so striking in someone like Professor Shockley but rather the connection that it, like extrinsic racism, has with the interests—real or perceived—of the dominant group.[6] Shockley's racism is in a certain sense directed *against* nonwhite people: many believe that his views would, if accepted, operate against their objective interests, and he certainly presents the black "race" in a less than flattering light.

I propose to use the old-fashioned term "racial prejudice" in the rest of this essay to refer to the deformation of rationality in judgment that characterizes those whose racism is more than a theoretical attachment to certain propositions about race.

RACIAL PREJUDICE

It is hardly necessary to raise objections to what I am calling "racial prejudice"; someone who exhibits such deformations of rationality is plainly in trouble. But it is important to remember that propositional racists in a racist culture have false moral beliefs but may not suffer from racial prejudice. Once we show them how society has enforced extrinsic racist stereotypes, once we ask them whether they really believe that race in itself, independently of those extrinsic racist beliefs, justifies differential treatment, many will come to give up racist propositions, although we must remember how powerful a weight of authority our arguments have to overcome. Reasonable people may insist on substantial evidence if they are to give up beliefs that are central to their cultures.

Still, in the end, many will resist such reasoning; and to the extent that their prejudices are really not subject to any kind of rational control, we may wonder whether it is right to treat such people as morally responsible for the acts their racial prejudice motivates, or morally reprehensible for holding the views to which their prejudice leads them. It is a bad thing that such people exist; they are, in a certain sense, bad people. But it is not clear to me that they are responsible for the fact that they are bad. Racial prejudice, like prejudice generally, may threaten an agent's autonomy, making it appropriate to treat or train rather than to reason with them.

But once someone has been offered evidence both (1) that their reasoning in a certain domain is distorted by prejudice, and (2) that the distortions conform to a pattern that suggests a lack of impartiality, they ought to take special care in articulating views and proposing policies in that domain. They ought to do so because, as I have already said, the phenomenon of partiality in judgment is well attested in human affairs. Even if you are not immediately persuaded that you are yourself a victim of such a distorted rationality in a certain domain, you should keep in mind always that this is the usual position of those who suffer from such prejudices. To the extent that this line of thought is not one that itself falls within the domain in question, one can be held responsible for not subjecting judgments that *are* within that domain to an especially extended scrutiny; and this is a fortiori true if the policies one is recommending are plainly of enormous consequence.

If it is clear that racial prejudice is regrettable, it is also clear in the nature of the case that providing even a superabundance of reasons and evidence will often not be a successful way of removing it. Nevertheless, the racist's prejudice will be articulated through the sorts of theoretical propositions I dubbed extrinsic and intrinsic racism. And we should certainly be able to say something reasonable about why these theoretical propositions should be rejected.

Part of the reason that this is worth doing is precisely the fact that many of those who assent to the propositional content of racism do not suffer from racial prejudice. In a country like the United States, where racist propositions were once part of the national ideology, there will be many who assent to racist propositions simply because they were raised to do so. Rational objection to racist propositions has a fair chance of changing such people's beliefs.

EXTRINSIC AND INTRINSIC RACISM

It is not always clear whether someone's theoretical racism is intrinsic or extrinsic, and there is certainly no reason why we should expect to be able to settle the question. Since the issue probably never occurs to most people in these terms, we cannot suppose that they must have an answer. In fact, given the definition of the terms I offered, there is nothing barring someone from being both an intrinsic and an extrinsic racist, holding both that the bare fact of race provides a basis for treating members of his or her own race differently from others and that there are morally relevant characteristics that are differentially distributed among the races. Indeed, for reasons I shall discuss in a moment, *most* intrinsic racists are likely to express extrinsic racist beliefs, so that we should not be surprised that many people seem, in fact, to be committed to both forms of racism.

The Holocaust made unreservedly clear the threat that racism poses to human decency. But it also blurred our thinking because in focusing our attention on the racist character of the Nazi atrocities, it obscured their character as atrocities. What is appalling about Nazi racism is not just that it presupposes, as all racism does, false (racialist) beliefs—not simply that it involves a moral incapacity (the inability to extend our moral sentiments to all our fellow creatures) and a moral failing (the making of moral distinctions without moral differences)—but that it leads, first, to oppression and then to mass slaughter. In recent years, South African racism has had a similar distorting effect. For although South African racism has not led to killings on the scale of the Holocaust—even if it has both left South Africa judicially executing more (mostly black) people per head of population than most other countries and led to massive differences between the life chances of white and nonwhite South Africans—it *has* led to the systematic oppression and economic exploitation of people who are not classified as "white," and to the infliction of suffering on citizens of all racial classifications, not least by the police state that is required to maintain that exploitation and oppression.

Part of our resistance, therefore, to calling the racial ideas of those, such as the Black Nationalists of the 1960s, who advocate racial solidarity, by the same term that we use to describe the attitudes of Nazis or of members of the South African Nationalist party, surely resides in the fact that they largely did not contemplate using race as a basis for inflicting harm. Indeed, it seems to me that there is a significant pattern in the modern rhetoric of race, such that the discourse of racial solidarity is usually expressed through the language of *intrinsic* racism, while those who have used race as the basis for oppression and hatred have appealed to *extrinsic* racist ideas. This point is important for understanding the character of contemporary racial attitudes.

The two major uses of race as a basis for moral solidarity that are most familiar in the West are varieties of Pan-Africanism and Zionism. In each case it is presupposed that a "people," Negroes or Jews, has the basis for shared political life in the fact of being of the same race. There are varieties of each form of "nationalism" that make the basis lie in shared traditions; but however plausible this may be in the case of Zionism, which has in Judaism, the religion, a realistic candidate for a common and nonracial focus for nationality, the peoples of Africa have a good deal less in common culturally than is usually assumed. I discuss this issue at length in *In My Father's House: Essays in the Philosophy of African Culture,* but let me say here that I believe the central fact is this: what blacks in the West, like secularized Jews, have mostly in common is that they are perceived—both by themselves and by others—as belonging to the same race, and that this common race is used by others as the basis for discriminating against them. "If you ever forget you're a Jew, a goy will remind you." The Black Nationalists, like some Zionists, responded to their experience of racial discrimination by accepting the racialism it presupposed.[7]

Although race is indeed at the heart of Black Nationalism, however, it seems that it is the fact of a shared race, not the fact of a shared racial character, that provides the basis for solidarity. Where racism is implicated in the basis for national solidarity, it is intrinsic, not (or not only) extrinsic. It is this that makes the idea of fraternity one that is naturally applied in nationalist discourse. For, as I have already observed, the moral status of close family members is not normally thought of in most cultures as depending on qualities of character; we are supposed to love our brothers and sisters in spite of their faults and not because of their virtues. Alexander Crummell, one of the founding fathers of Black Nationalism, literalizes the metaphor of family in these startling words:

> Races, like families, are the organisms and ordinances of God; and race feeling, like family feeling, is of divine origin. The extinction of race feeling is just as possible as the extinction of family feeling. Indeed, a race is a family.[8]

It is the assimilation of "race feeling" to "family feeling" that makes intrinsic racism seem so much less objectionable than extrinsic racism. For this metaphorical identification reflects the fact that, in the modern world (unlike the nineteenth century), intrinsic racism is acknowledged almost exclusively as the basis of feelings of community. We can surely, then, share a sense of what Crummell's friend and co-worker Edward Blyden called "the poetry of politics," that is, "the feeling of race," the feeling of "people with whom we are connected."[9] The racism here is the basis of acts of supererogation, the treatment of others better than we otherwise might, better than moral duty demands of us.

This is a contingent fact. There is no logical impossibility in the idea of racialists whose moral beliefs lead them to feelings of hatred for other races while leaving no room for love of members of their own. Nevertheless most racial hatred is in fact expressed through extrinsic racism: most people who have used race as the basis for causing harm to others have felt the need to see the other as independently morally flawed. It is one thing to espouse fraternity without claiming that your brothers and sisters have any special qualities that deserve recognition, and another to espouse hatred of others who have done nothing to deserve it.[10]

Many Afrikaners—like many in the American South until recently—have a long list of extrinsic racist answers to the question why blacks should not have full civil rights. Extrinsic racism has usually been the basis for treating people worse than we otherwise might, for giving them less than their humanity entitles them to. But this too is a contingent fact. Indeed, Crummell's guarded respect for white people derived from a belief in the superior moral qualities of the Anglo-Saxon race.

Intrinsic racism is, in my view, a moral error. Even if racialism were correct, the bare fact that someone was of another race would be no reason to treat them worse—or better—than someone of my race. In our public lives, people are owed treatment independently of their biological characters: if they are to be differently treated, there must be some morally relevant difference between them. In our private lives, we are morally free to have aesthetic preferences between people, but once our treatment of people raises moral issues, we may not make arbitrary distinctions. Using race in itself as a morally relevant distinction strikes most of us as obviously arbitrary. Without associated moral characteristics, why should race provide a better basis than hair color or height or timbre of voice? And if two people share all the properties morally relevant to some action we ought to do, it will be an error—a failure to apply the Kantian injunction to universalize our moral judgments—to use the bare facts of race as the basis for treating them differently. No one should deny that a common ancestry might, in particular cases, account for similarities in moral character. But then it would be the moral similarities that justified the different treatment.

It is presumably because most people—outside the South African Nationalist party and the Ku Klux Klan—share the sense that intrinsic racism requires arbitrary distinctions that they are largely unwilling to express in situations that invite moral criticism. But I do not know how I would argue with someone who was willing to announce an intrinsic racism as a basic moral idea; the best one can do, perhaps, is to provide objections to possible lines of defense of it.

DE GUSTIBUS

It might be thought that intrinsic racism should be regarded not so much as an adherence to a (moral) proposition as the expression of a taste, analogous, say, to the food prejudice that makes most English people unwilling to eat horse meat, and most Westerners unwilling to eat the insect grubs that the !Kung people find so appetizing. The analogy does at least this much for us, namely, to provide a model of the way that *extrinsic* racist propositions can be a reflection of an underlying prejudice. For, of course,

in most cultures food prejudices are rationalized: we say insects are unhygienic and cats taste horrible. Yet a cooked insect is no more health-threatening than a cooked carrot, and the unpleasant taste of cat meat, far from justifying our prejudice against it, probably derives from that prejudice.

But there the usefulness of the analogy ends. For intrinsic racism, as I have defined it, is not simply a taste for the company of one's "own kind," but a moral doctrine, one that is supposed to underlie differences in the treatment of people in contexts where moral evaluation is appropriate. And for moral distinctions we cannot accept that "de gustibus non est disputandum." We do not need the full apparatus of Kantian ethics to require that public morality be constrained by reason.

A proper analogy would be with someone who thought that we could continue to kill cattle for beef, even if cattle exercised all the complex cultural skills of human beings. I think it is obvious that creatures that shared our capacity for understanding as well as our capacity for pain should not be treated the way we actually treat cattle—that "intrinsic speciesism" would be as wrong as racism. And the fact that most people think it is worse to be cruel to chimpanzees than to frogs suggests that they may agree with me. The distinction in attitudes surely reflects a belief in the greater richness of the mental life of chimps. Still, I do not know how I would *argue* against someone who could not see this; someone who continued to act on the contrary belief might, in the end, simply have to be locked up.

THE FAMILY MODEL

I have suggested that intrinsic racism is, at least sometimes, a metaphorical extension of the moral priority of one's family; it might, therefore, be suggested that a defense of intrinsic racism could proceed along the same lines as a defense of the family as a center of moral interest. The possibility of a defense of family relations as morally relevant—or, more precisely, of the claim that one may be morally entitled (or even obliged) to make distinctions between two otherwise morally indistinguishable people because one is related to one and not to the other—is theoretically important for the prospects of a philosophical defense of intrinsic racism. This is because such a defense of the family involves—like intrinsic racism—a denial of the basic claim, expressed so clearly by Kant, that from the perspective of morality, it is as rational agents *simpliciter* that we are to assess and be assessed. For anyone who follows Kant in this, what matters, as we might say, is not who you are but how you try to live. Intrinsic racism denies this fundamental claim also. And, in so doing, as I have argued elsewhere, it runs against the mainstream of the history of Western moral theory.[11]

The importance of drawing attention to the similarities between the defense of the family and the defense of the race, then, is not merely that the metaphor of family is often invoked by racism; it is that each of them offers the same general challenge to the Kantian stream of our moral thought. And the parallel with the defense of the family should be especially appealing to an intrinsic racist, since many of us who have little time for racism would hope that the family is susceptible to some such defense.

The problem in generalizing the defense of the family, however, is that such defenses standardly begin at a point that makes the argument for intrinsic racism immediately implausible: namely, with the family as the unit through which we live what is most intimate, as the center of private life. If we distinguish, with Bernard Williams, between ethical thought, which takes seriously "the demands, needs, claims, desires, and generally, the lives of other people,"[12] and morality, which focuses more narrowly on obligation, it may well be that private life matters to us precisely because it is altogether unsuited to the universalizing tendencies of morality.

The functioning family unit has contracted substantially with industrialization, the disappearance of the family as the unit of production, and the increasing mobility of labor, but there remains that irreducible minimum: the parent or parents with the child or children. In this "nuclear" family, there is, of course, a substantial body of shared experience, shared attitudes, shared knowledge and beliefs; and the mutual psychological investment that exists within this group is, for most of us, one of the things that gives meaning to our lives. It is a natural enough confusion—which we find again and again in discussions of adoption in the popular media—that identifies the relevant group with the biological unit of *genitor, genetrix,* and *offspring* rather than with the social unit of those who share a common domestic life.

The relations of parents and their biological children are of moral importance, of course, in part because children are standardly the product of behavior voluntarily undertaken by their biological parents. But the moral relations between biological siblings and half-siblings cannot, as I have already pointed out, be accounted for in such terms. A rational defense of the family ought to appeal to the causal responsibility of the biological parent and the common life of the domestic unit, and not to the brute fact of biological relatedness, even if the former pair of considerations defines groups that are often coextensive with the groups generated by the latter. For brute biological relatedness bears no necessary connection to the sorts of human purposes that seem likely to be relevant at the most basic level of ethical thought.

An argument that such a central group is bound to be crucially important in the lives of most human beings in societies like ours is not, of course, an argument for any specific mode of organization of the "family": feminism and the gay liberation movement have offered candidate groups that could (and sometimes do) occupy the same sort of role in the lives of those whose sexualities or whose dispositions otherwise make the nuclear family uncongenial; and these candidates have been offered specifically in the course of defenses of a move toward societies that are agreeably beyond patriarchy and homophobia. The central thought of these feminist and gay critiques of the nuclear family is that we cannot continue to view any one organization of private life as "natural," once we have seen even the broadest outlines of the archaeology of the family concept.

If that is right, then the argument for the family must be an argument for a mode of organization of life and feeling that subserves certain positive functions; and however the details of such an argument would proceed it is highly unlikely that the same functions could be served by groups on the scale of races, simply because, as I say, the family is attractive in part exactly for reasons of its personal scale.

I need hardly say that rational defenses of intrinsic racism along the lines I have been considering are not easily found. In the absence of detailed defenses to consider, I can only offer these general reasons for doubting that they can succeed: the generally Kantian tenor of much of our moral thought threatens the project from the start; and the essentially unintimate nature of relations within "races" suggests that there is little prospect that the defense of the family—which seems an attractive and plausible project that extends ethical life beyond the narrow range of a universalizing morality—can be applied to a defense of races.

CONCLUSIONS

I have suggested that what we call "racism" involves both propositions and dispositions.

The propositions were, first, that there are races (this was *racialism*) and, second, that these races are morally significant either (a) because they are contingently correlated with morally relevant properties (this was *extrinsic racism*) or (b) because they are intrinsically morally significant (this was *intrinsic racism*).

The disposition was a tendency to assent to false propositions, both moral and theoretical, about races—propositions that support policies or beliefs that are to the disadvantage of some race (or races) as opposed to others, and to do so even in the face of evidence and argument that should appropriately lead to giving those propositions up. This disposition I called "racial prejudice."

I suggested that intrinsic racism had tended in our own time to be the natural expression of feelings of community, and this is, of course, one of the reasons why we are not inclined to call it racist. For, to the extent that a theoretical position is not associated with irrationally held beliefs that tend to the *dis*advantage of some group, it fails to display the *directedness* of the distortions of rationality characteristic of racial prejudice. Intrinsic racism may be as irrationally held as any other view, but it does not *have* to be directed *against* anyone.

So far as theory is concerned, I believe racialism to be false: since theoretical racism of both kinds presupposes racialism, I could not logically support racism of either variety. But even if racialism were true, both forms of theoretical racism would be incorrect. Extrinsic racism is false because the genes that account for the gross morphological differences that underlie our standard racial categories are not linked to those genes that determine, to whatever degree such matters are determined genetically, our moral and intellectual characters. Intrinsic racism is mistaken because it breaches the Kantian imperative to make moral distinctions only on morally relevant grounds—granted that there is no reason to believe that race, *in se*, is morally relevant, and also no reason to suppose that races are like families in providing a sphere of ethical life that legitimately escapes the demands of a universalizing morality.

NOTES

1. Bernard Lewis, *Semites and Anti-Semites* (New York: Norton, 1986).

2. I shall be using the words "racism" and "racialism" with the meanings I stipulate; in some dialects of English they are synonyms, and in most dialects their definition is less than precise. For discussion of recent biological evidence see M. Nei and A. K. Roychoudhury, "Genetic Relationship and Evolution of Human Races," *Evolutionary Biology,* vol. 14 (New York: Plenum, 1983), pp. 1–59; for useful background see also M. Nei and A. K. Roychoudhury, "Gene Differences Between Caucasian, Negro, and Japanese Populations," *Science,* 177 (Aug. 1972): 434–435.

3. See my "The Uncompleted Argument: Du Bois and the Illusion of Race," *Critical Inquiry,* 12 (Autumn 1985); reprinted in *"Race," Writing and Difference,* ed. Henry Louis Gates (Chicago: University of Chicago Press, 1986), pp. 21–37.

4. This fact shows up most obviously in the assumption that adopted children intelligibly make claims against their natural siblings: natural parents are, of course, causally responsible for their child's existence and that could be the basis of moral claims, without any sense that biological relatedness entailed rights or responsibilities. But no such basis exists for an interest in natural *siblings;* my sisters are not causally responsible for my existence. . . .

5. Obviously what evidence should *appropriately* change your beliefs is not independent of your social or historical situation. In mid-nineteenth-century America, in New England quite as much as in the heart of Dixie, the pervasiveness of the institutional support for the prevailing system of racist belief—the fact that it was reinforced by religion and state, and defended by people in the universities and colleges, who had the greatest cognitive authority—meant that it would have been appropriate to insist on a substantial body of evidence and argument before giving up assent to racist propositions. In California in the 1980s, of course, matters stand rather differently. To acknowledge this is not to admit to a cognitive relativism; rather, it is to hold that, at least in some domains, the fact that a belief is widely held—and especially by people in positions of cognitive authority—may be a good prima facie reason for believing it.

6. Ideologies, as most theorists of ideology have admitted, standardly outlive the period in which they conform to the objective interests of the dominant group in a society; so even some-

one who thinks that the dominant group in our society no longer needs racism to buttress its position can see racism as the persisting ideology of an earlier phase of society. (I say "group" to keep the claim appropriately general; it seems to me a substantial further claim that the dominant group whose interests an ideology serves is always a class.) I have argued, however, in "The Conservation of 'Race' " that racism continues to serve the interests of the ruling classes in the West; in *Black American Literature Forum*, 23 (Spring 1989): 37–60.

7. As I argued in "The Uncompleted Argument: Du Bois and the Illusion of Race." The reactive (or dialectical) character of this move explains why Sartre calls its manifestations in Négritude an "antiracist racism"; see "Orphée Noir," his preface to Senghor's *Anthologie de la nouvelle poésie nègre et malagache de langue française* (Paris: PUF, 1948). Sartre believed, of course, that the synthesis of this dialectic would be the transcendence of racism; and it was his view of it as a stage—the antithesis—in that process that allowed him to see it as a positive advance over the original "thesis" of European racism. I suspect that the reactive character of antiracist racism accounts for the tolerance that is regularly extended to it in liberal circles; but this tolerance is surely hard to justify unless one shares Sartre's optimistic interpretation of it as a stage in a process that leads to the end of all racisms. (And unless your view of this dialectic is deterministic you should in any case want to play an argumentative role in moving to this next stage.)

For a similar Zionist response see Horace Kallen's "The Ethics of Zionism," *Maccabaean* (Aug. 1906).

8. "The Race Problem in America," in Brotz's *Negro Social and Political Thought* (New York: Basic Books, 1966), p. 184.

9. *Christianity, Islam and the Negro Race* (1887; reprinted Edinburgh: Edinburgh University Press, 1967), p. 197.

10. This is in part a reflection of an important asymmetry: loathing, unlike love, needs justifying; and this, I would argue, is because loathing usually leads to acts that are *in se* undesirable, whereas love leads to acts that are large *in se* desirable—indeed, supererogatorily so.

11. See my "Racism and Moral Pollution," *Philosophical Forum*, 18 (Winter–Spring 1986–87): 185–202.

12. *Ethics and the Limits of Philosophy* (Cambridge, MA: Harvard University Press, 1985), p. 12. I do not, as is obvious, share Williams's skepticism about morality.

DISCUSSION QUESTIONS

1. Do you agree with Appiah that many people have a "cognitive incapacity" that does not allow them to give up beliefs that play a part in justifying special advantages they gain or hope to gain? Explain.
2. Assume that there are people who suffer from a cognitive incapacity to acknowledge evidence that would make members of a race other than their own admirable or attractive to them. What can we do, as a society, to help these people to overcome their cognitive incapacity?
3. Appiah argues that racialism is false. What is his argument? Do you agree with it? Why or why not?
4. How, according to Appiah, do intrinsic racism and extrinsic racism presuppose racialism?
5. Appiah argues that, even if racialism were true, intrinsic racism and extrinsic racism would still be incorrect. Critically examine his arguments.
6. Discuss the following claim from Appiah: "to the extent that a practice cannot be rationally reconstructed it ought, surely, to be given up by reasonable people." Can you think of any practices that both cannot be rationally reconstructed and should not be given up by reasonable people? Explain.

JEAN-PAUL SARTRE

Anti-Semite and Jew

Jean-Paul Sartre argues that an anti-Semite chooses to be a mediocre person out of "fear of being alone." Pride makes the anti-Semite's mediocrity "a rigid aristocracy." The anti-Semite finds "the existence of the Jew absolutely necessary," says Sartre, "[o]therwise to whom would he be superior?" Sartre explains that anti-Semitism organizes the anti-Semite's life and that the passionate hatred of Jews is used by the anti-Semite to enhance his or her own self-esteem.

Jean-Paul Sartre (1905–1980) is the major French existentialist philosopher, as well as a novelist and playwright. He was a prisoner of war in World War II. His philosophical works include *The Transcendence of the Ego* (1936), *Being and Nothingness* (1943), *Existentialism as Humanism* (1946), and *Critique of Dialectical Reason* (1960). His literary works include *Nausea* (novel, 1938), *The Flies* (play, 1943), and *No Exit* (play, 1945). He was awarded the Nobel Prize for literature in 1964 but declined the award. The following is a selection from *Anti-Semite and Jew* (1946).

If the Jew did not exist, the anti-Semite would invent him. . . .

Anti-Semitism is a free and total choice of oneself, a comprehensive attitude that one adopts not only toward Jews but toward men in general, toward history and society; it is at one and the same time a passion and a conception of the world. . . .

Ordinarily hate and anger have a *provocation:* I hate someone who has made me suffer, someone who condemns or insults me. . . .

Anti-Semitic passion could not have such a character. It precedes the facts that are supposed to call it forth: it seeks them out to nourish itself upon them; it must even interpret them in a special way so that they may become truly offensive. Indeed, if you so much as mention a Jew to an anti-Semite, he will show all the signs of a lively irritation. If we recall that we must always *consent* to anger before it can manifest itself and that, as is indicated so accurately by the French idiom, we "put ourselves" into anger, we shall have to agree that the anti-Semite has *chosen* to live on the plane of passion. It is not unusual for people to elect to live a life of passion rather than one of reason. But ordinarily they love the *objects* of passion: women, glory, power, money. Since the anti-Semite has chosen hate, we are forced to conclude that it is the *state* of passion that he loves. . . .

How can one choose to reason falsely? It is because of a longing for impenetrability. The rational man groans as he gropes for the truth; he knows that his reasoning is no more than tentative, that other considerations may supervene to cast doubt on it. He never sees very clearly where he is going; he is "open"; he may even appear to be hesitant. But there are people who are attracted by the durability of a stone. They wish to be massive and impenetrable; they wish not to change. Where, indeed, would change take them? We have here a basic fear of oneself and of truth. What frightens them is not the content of truth, of which they have no conception, but the form itself of truth, that thing of indefinite approximation. It is as if their own existence were in continual suspension. But they wish to exist all at once and right away. They do not want any acquired opinions: they want them to be innate. Since they are afraid of reasoning, they wish to lead the kind of life wherein reasoning and research play only a subordinate role, wherein one seeks only what he has already found, wherein one becomes only what he already was. This is nothing but passion. . . .

If then, as we have been able to observe, the anti-Semite is impervious to reason and to experience, it is not because his conviction is strong. Rather, his conviction is strong because he has chosen first of all to be impervious.

He has chosen also to be terrifying. People are afraid of irritating him. No one knows to what lengths the aberrations of his passion will carry him—but he knows, for this passion is not provoked by something external. He has it well in hand; it is obedient to his will: now he lets go the reins and now he pulls back on them. He is not afraid of himself, but he sees in the eyes of others a disquieting image—his own—and he makes his words and gestures conform to it. Having this external model, he is under no necessity to look for his personality within himself. He has chosen to find his being entirely outside himself, never to look within, to be nothing save the fear he inspires in others. What he flees even more than Reason is his intimate awareness of himself. . . .

The anti-Semite has no illusions about what he is. He considers himself an average man, modestly average, basically mediocre. There is no example of an anti-Semite's claiming individual superiority over the Jews. But you must not think that he is ashamed of his mediocrity; he takes pleasure in it; I will even assert that he has chosen it. This man fears every kind of solitariness, that of the genius as much as that of the murderer; he is the man of the crowd. However small his stature, he takes every precaution to make it smaller, lest he stand out from the herd and find himself face to face with himself. He has made himself an anti-Semite because that is something one cannot be alone. The phrase, "I hate the Jews," is one that is uttered in chorus; in pronouncing it, one attaches himself to a tradition and to a community—the tradition and community of the mediocre.

We must remember that a man is not necessarily humble or even modest because he has consented to mediocrity. On the contrary, there is a passionate pride among the mediocre, and anti-Semitism is an attempt to give value to mediocrity as such, to create an elite of the ordinary. To the anti-Semite, intelligence is Jewish; he can thus disdain it in all tranquility, like all the other virtues which the Jew possesses. They are so many ersatz attributes that the Jew cultivates in place of that balanced mediocrity which he will never have. . . .

Thus I would call anti-Semitism a poor man's snobbery. . . . Anti-Semitism is not merely the joy of hating; it brings positive pleasures too. By treating the Jew as an inferior and pernicious being, I affirm at the same time that I belong to the elite. This elite, in contrast to those of modern times which are based on merit or labor, closely resembles an aristocracy of birth. There is nothing I have to do to merit my superiority, and neither can I lose it. It is given once and for all. It is a *thing*. . . .

We begin to perceive the meaning of the anti-Semite's choice of himself. He chooses the irremediable out of fear of being free; he chooses mediocrity out of fear of being alone, and out of pride he makes of this irremediable mediocrity a rigid aristocracy. To this end he finds the existence of the Jew absolutely necessary. Otherwise, to whom would he be superior? Indeed, it is vis-à-vis the Jew and the Jew alone that the anti-Semite realizes that he has rights. If by some miracle all the Jews were exterminated as he wishes, he would find himself nothing but a concierge or a shopkeeper in a strongly hierarchical society in which the quality of "true Frenchman" would be at a low valuation, because everyone would possess it. He would lose his sense of rights over the country because no one would any longer contest them, and that profound equality which brings him close to the nobleman and the man of wealth would disappear all of a sudden, for it is primarily negative. His frustrations, which he has attributed to the disloyal competition of the Jew, would have to be imputed to some other cause, lest he be forced to look within himself. He would run the risk of falling into bitterness, into a melancholy hatred of the privileged classes. Thus the anti-Semite is in the unhappy position of having a vital need for the very enemy he wishes to destroy.

DISCUSSION QUESTIONS

1. Why, according to Sartre, is the anti-Semite in the position of vitally needing the very enemy he wishes to destroy?
2. Sartre says, "If the Jew did not exist, the anti-Semite would invent him." What does he mean by this? Do you agree with him?
3. Do you think that Sartre's critique of anti-Semitism is also a good general critique of racism? Defend your view in detail.

4. According to Sartre, an anti-Semite "has made himself an anti-Semite because that is something one cannot be alone." Why can't one be an anti-Semite alone? Evaluate Sartre's reasoning.
5. Sartre says that anti-Semitism is "an attempt to give value to mediocrity as such, to create an elite of the ordinary." What is Sartre's argument? Do you agree with it? Defend your view.
6. How would you convince an anti-Semite that he or she should not be anti-Semitic?

 RICHARD WASSERSTROM

Racism and Sexism

Richard Wasserstrom argues that a completely nonracist and nonsexist society would be one in which race or sex functions the way eye color does in our society. According to Wasserstrom's assimilationist ideal, while physiological differences in skin color or genitals would remain, they would have little or no significance in determining a person's political rights, institutional benefits, or sense of identity, or how others would regard him or her. The "assimilationist ideal would require the eradication of all sex-told differentiation," writes Wasserstrom. "It would never teach about the inevitable or essential attributes of masculinity or femininity. . . . It would never encourage or discourage the ideas of sisterhood or brotherhood; and it would be unintelligible to talk about the virtues as well as disabilities of being a woman or a man." Wasserstrom contrasts this ideal of assimilation with the ideals of tolerance and diversity and finds "a strong presumptive case for something very close to, if not identical with, the assimilationist ideal." He opens the essay with a description of the social realities of racism and sexism, examining its institutions, attitudes, and ideologies. In a longer version of this article, Wasserstrom also argues that much of opposition to affirmative action programs is not justifiable because they are founded "upon confusion in thinking about the relevant issues and upon a failure to perceive and appreciate some of the ways in which our society is racist and sexist." A biographical sketch of Richard Wasserstrom appears in Chapter 5.

INTRODUCTION

Racism and sexism are two central issues that engage the attention of many persons living within the United States today. But while there is relatively little disagreement about their importance as topics, there is substantial, vehement, and apparently intractable disagreement about what individuals, practices, ideas, and institutions are either racist or sexist—and for what reasons. In dispute are a number of related questions concerning how individuals and institutions ought to regard and respond to matters relating to race or sex.

One particularly contemporary example concerns those programs variously called programs of "affirmative action," "preferential treatment," or "reverse

Richard Wasserstrom, *Racism, Sexism, and Preferential Treatment. UCLA Law Review* (February 1977): 581–615. Copyright © 1977 by Richard Wasserstrom. Reprinted with the permission of the author. Notes and Section III have been omitted.

discrimination" that are a feature of much of our institutional life. Attitudes and beliefs about these programs are diverse. Some persons are convinced that all such programs in virtually all of their forms are themselves racist and sexist and are for these among other reasons indefensible. The programs are causally explicable, perhaps, but morally reprehensible. Other persons—a majority, I suspect—are sorely troubled by these programs. They are convinced that some features of some programs, e.g., quotas, are indefensible and wrong. Other features and programs are tolerated, but not with fervor or enthusiasm. They are seen as a kind of moral compromise, as, perhaps, a lesser evil among a set of unappealing options. They are reluctantly perceived and implemented as a covert, euphemistic way to do what would clearly be wrong—even racist or sexist—to do overtly and with candor. And still a third group has a very different view. They think these programs are important and appropriate. They do not see these programs, quotas included, as racist or sexist, and they see much about the dominant societal institutions that is. They regard the racism and sexism of the society as accounting in substantial measure for the failure or refusal to adopt such programs willingly and to press vigorously for their full implementation.

I think that much of the confusion in thinking and arguing about racism, sexism and affirmative action results from a failure to see that there are three different perspectives within which the topics of racism, sexism and affirmative action can most usefully be examined. The first of these perspectives concentrates on what in fact is true of the culture, on what can be called the social realities. Here the fundamental question concerns the way the culture is: What are its institutions, attitudes and ideologies in respect to matters of race and sex?

The second perspective is concerned with the way things ought to be. From this perspective, analysis focuses very largely on possible, desirable states of affairs. Here the fundamental question concerns ideals: What would the good society—in terms of its institutions, its attitudes, and its values—look like in respect to matters involving race and sex?

The third perspective looks forward to the means by which the ideal may be achieved. Its focus is on the question: What is the best or most appropriate way to move from the existing social realities, whatever they happen to be, to a closer approximation of the ideal society? This perspective is concerned with instrumentalities.

Many of the debates over affirmative action and over what things are racist and sexist are unillumi-nating because they neglect to take into account these three perspectives, which are important and must be considered separately. While I do not claim that all the significant normative and conceptual questions concerning race, sex, or affirmative action can be made to disappear, I do believe that an awareness and use of these perspectives can produce valuable insights that contribute to their resolution. In particular, it can almost immediately be seen that the question of whether something is racist or sexist is not as straightforward or unambiguous as may appear at first. The question may be about social realities, about how the categories of race or sex in fact function in the culture and to what effect. Or the question may be about ideals, about what the good society would make of race or sex. Or the question may be about instrumentalities, about how, given the social realities as to race and sex, to achieve a closer approximation of the ideal. It can also be seen, therefore, that what might be an impermissible way to take race or sex into account in the ideal society, may also be a desirable and appropriate way to take race or sex into account, given the social realities.

It is these three different perspectives and these underlying issues that I am interested in exploring. This framework is used to clarify a number of the central matters that are involved in thinking clearly about the topics of racism, sexism and affirmative action. Within this framework, some of the analogies and disanalogies between racism and sexism are explored—the ways they are and are not analytically interchangeable phenomena. I also provide an analytic scheme for distinguishing different respects in which a complex institution such as the legal system might plausibly be seen to be racist or sexist. And I examine some of the key arguments that most often arise whenever these topics are considered. In respect to programs of affirmative action, or preferential treatment [elsewhere], I argue specifically that much of the opposition to such programs is not justifiable. It rests upon confusion in thinking about the relevant issues and upon a failure to perceive and appreciate some of the ways in which our society is racist and sexist. I argue that there is much to be said for the view that such programs, even when they include quotas, are defensible and right. [Wasserstrom's analysis of programs of affirmative action—the final section of the original version of this paper—has been omitted.—Eds.]

I. SOCIAL REALITIES

One way to think and talk about racism and sexism is to concentrate upon the perspective of the social realities. Here one must begin by insisting that to talk about either is to talk about a particular social and cultural context. In this section I concentrate upon two questions that can be asked about the social realities of our culture. First, I consider the position of blacks and females in the culture vis-à-vis the position of those who are white, and those who are male. And second, I provide an analysis of the different ways in which a complex institution, such as our legal system, can be seen to be racist or sexist. The analysis is offered as a schematic account of the possible types of racism or sexism.

A. The Position of Blacks and Women

In our own culture the first thing to observe is that race and sex are socially important categories. They are so in virtue of the fact that we live in a culture which has, throughout its existence, made race and sex extremely important characteristics of and for all the people living in the culture.

It is surely possible to imagine a culture in which race would be an unimportant, insignificant characteristic of individuals. In such a culture, race would be largely if not exclusively a matter of superficial physiology; a matter, we might say, simply of the way one looked. And if it were, then any analysis of race and racism would necessarily assume very different dimensions from what they do in our society. In such a culture, the meaning of the term "race" would itself have to change substantially. This can be seen by the fact that in such a culture it would literally make no sense to say of a person that he or she was "passing." This is something that can be said and understood in our own culture and it shows at least that to talk of race is to talk of more than the way one looks.

Sometimes when people talk about what is wrong with affirmative action programs, or programs of preferential hiring, they say that what is wrong with such programs is that they take a thing as superficial as an individual's race and turn it into something important. They say that a person's race doesn't matter; other things do, such as qualifications. Whatever else may be said of statements such as these, as descriptions of the social realities they seem to be simply false. One complex but true empirical fact about our society is that the race of an individual is much more than a fact of superficial physiology. It is, instead, one of the dominant characteristics that affects both the way the individual looks at the world and the way the world looks at the individual. As I have said, that need not be the case. It may in fact be very important that we work toward a society in which that would not be the case, but it is the case now and it must be understood in any adequate and complete discussion of racism. That is why, too, it does not make much sense when people sometimes say, in talking about the fact that they are not racists, that they would not care if an individual were green and came from Mars, they would treat that individual the same way they treat people exactly like themselves. For part of *our* social and cultural history is to treat people of certain races in a certain way, and we do not have a social or cultural history of treating green people from Mars in any particular way. To put it simply, it is to misunderstand the social realities of race and racism to think of them simply as questions of how some people respond to other people whose skins are of different hues, irrespective of the social context.

I can put the point another way: Race does not function in our culture as does eye color. Eye color is an irrelevant category; nobody cares what color people's eyes are; it is not an important cultural fact; nothing turns on what eye color you have. It is important to see that race is not like that at all. And this truth affects what will and will not count as cases of racism. In our culture to be nonwhite—and especially to be black—is to be treated and seen to be a member of a group that is different from and inferior to the group of standard, fully developed persons, the adult white males. To be black is to be a member of what was a despised minority and what is still a disliked and oppressed one. That is simply part of the awful truth of our cultural and social history, and a significant feature of the social reality of our culture today.

We can see fairly easily that the two sexual categories, like the racial ones, are themselves in important respects products of the society. Like one's race, one's sex is not merely or even primarily a matter of physiology. To see this we need only realize that we can understand the idea of a transsexual. A transsexual is someone who would describe himself or herself either as a person who is essentially a female but through some accident of nature is trapped in a male body, or a person who is essentially a male but through some accident of nature is trapped in the body of a female. His (or her) description is some kind of a shorthand way of saying that he (or she) is more comfortable with the role allocated by the culture to people who are physiologically of the opposite sex. The fact that we regard this assertion of the transsexual as intelligible seems to me to show how deep the notion of sexual identity is in our culture and how little it has to do with physiological differences between males and females. Because people do pass in the context of race and because we can understand what passing means; because people are transsexuals and because we can understand what transsexuality means, we can see that the existing social categories of both race and sex are in this sense creations of the culture.

It is even clearer in the case of sex than in the case of race that one's sexual identity is a centrally important, crucially relevant category within our culture. I think, in fact, that it is more important and more fundamental than one's race. It is evident that there are substantially different role expectations and role assignments to persons in accordance with their sexual physiology, and that the positions of the two sexes in the culture are distinct. We do have a patriarchal society in which it matters enormously whether one is a male or a female. By almost all important measures it is more advantageous to be a male rather than a female.

Women and men are socialized differently. We learn very early and forcefully that we are either males or females and that much turns upon which sex we are. The evidence seems to be overwhelming and well-documented that sex roles play a fundamental role in the way persons think of themselves and the world—to say nothing of the way the world thinks of them. Men and women are taught to see men as independent, capable, and powerful; men and women are taught to see women as dependent, limited in abilities, and passive. A woman's success or failure in life is defined largely in terms of her activities within the family. It is important for her that she marry, and when she does she is expected to take responsibility for the wifely tasks: the housework, the child care, and the general emotional welfare of the husband and children. Her status in society is determined in substantial measure by the vocation and success of her husband. Economically, women are substantially worse off than men. They do not receive any pay for the work that is done in the home. As members of the labor force their wages are significantly lower than those paid to men, even when they are engaged in similar work and have similar educational backgrounds. The higher the prestige or the salary of the job, the less present women are in the labor force. And, of course, women are conspicuously absent from most positions of authority and power in the major economic and political institutions of our society.

As is true for race, it is also a significant social fact that to be a female is to be an entity or creature viewed as different from the standard, fully developed person who is male as well as white. But to be female, as opposed to being black, is not to be conceived of as simply a creature of less worth. That is one important thing that differentiates sexism from racism: The ideology of sex, as opposed to the ideology of race, is a good deal more complex and confusing. Women are both put on a pedestal and deemed not fully developed persons. They are idealized; their approval and admiration is sought; and they are at the same time regarded as less competent than men and less able to live fully developed, fully human lives—for that is what men do. At best, they are viewed and treated as having properties and attributes that are valuable and admirable for humans of this type. For example, they may be viewed as especially empathetic, intuitive, loving, and nurturing. At best, these qualities are viewed as good properties for women to have, and, provided they are properly muted, are sometimes valued within the more well-rounded male. Because the sexual ideology is complex, confusing, and variable, it does not unambiguously proclaim the lesser value attached to being female rather than being male, nor does it unambiguously correspond to the existing social realities. For these, among other reasons, sexism could plausibly be regarded as a deeper phenomenon than racism. It is more deeply embedded in the culture, and thus less visible. Being harder to detect, it is harder to eradicate. Moreover, it is less unequivocally regarded as unjust and unjustifiable. That is to say, there is less agreement within the dominant ideology that sexism even implies an unjustifiable practice or attitude. Hence, many persons announce, without regret or embarrassment, that they are sexists or male chauvinists; very few announce openly that they are racists. For all of these reasons sexism may be a more insidious evil than racism, but there is little merit in trying to decide between two seriously objectionable practices which one is worse.

While I do not think that I have made very controversial claims about either our cultural history or our present-day culture, I am aware of the fact that they have been stated very imprecisely and that I have offered little evidence to substantiate them. In a crude way we ought to be able both to understand the claims and to see that they are correct if we reflect seriously and critically upon our own cultural institutions, attitudes, and practices. But in a more refined, theoretical way, I am imagining that a more precise and correct description of the social reality in respect to race and sex would be derivable from a composite, descriptive account of our society which utilized the relevant social sciences to examine such things as the society's institutions, practices, attitudes and ideology—if the social sciences could be value-free and unaffected in outlook or approach by the fact that they, themselves, are largely composed of persons who are white and male.

Viewed from the perspective of social reality it should be clear, too, that racism and sexism should not be thought of as phenomena that consist simply in taking a person's race or sex into account, or even simply in taking a person's race or sex into account in an arbitrary way. Instead, racism and sexism consist in taking race and sex into account in a certain way, in the context of a specific set of institutional arrangements and a specific ideology which together create and maintain a *system* of unjust institutions and unwarranted beliefs and attitudes. That system is and has been one in which political, economic, and social power and advantage are concentrated in the hands of those who are white and male.

One way to bring this out, as well as to show another respect in which racism and sexism are different, concerns segregated bathrooms—a topic that may seem silly and trivial but which is certainly illuminating and probably important. We know, for instance, that it is wrong, clearly racist, to have racially segregated bathrooms. There is, however, no common conception that it is wrong, clearly sexist, to have sexually segregated ones. How is this to be accounted for? The answer to the question of why it was and is racist to have racially segregated bathrooms can be discovered through a consideration of the role that this practice played in that system of racial segregation we had in the United States—from, in other words, an examination of the social realities. For racially segregated bathrooms were an important part of that system. And that system had an ideology; it was complex and perhaps not even wholly internally consistent. A significant feature of the ideology was that blacks were not only less than fully developed humans, but that they were also dirty and impure. They were the sorts of creatures who could and would contaminate white persons if they came into certain kinds of contact with them—in the bathroom, at the dinner table, or in bed, although it was appropriate for

blacks to prepare and handle food, and even to nurse white infants. This ideology was intimately related to a set of institutional arrangements and power relationships in which whites were politically, economically, and socially dominant. The ideology supported the institutional arrangements, and the institutional arrangements reinforced the ideology. The net effect was that racially segregated bathrooms were both a part of the institutional mechanism of oppression and an instantiation of this ideology of racial taint. The point of maintaining racially segregated bathrooms was not in any simple or direct sense to keep both whites and blacks from using each other's bathrooms; it was to make sure that blacks would not contaminate bathrooms used by whites. The practice also taught both whites and blacks that certain kinds of contacts were forbidden because whites would be degraded by the contact with the blacks.

The failure to understand the character of these institutions of racial oppression is what makes some of the judicial reasoning about racial discrimination against blacks so confusing and unsatisfactory. At times when the courts have tried to explain what is constitutionally wrong with racial segregation, they have said that the problem is that race is an inherently suspect category. What they have meant by this, or have been thought to mean, is that any differentiation among human beings on the basis of racial identity is inherently unjust, because arbitrary, and therefore any particular case of racial differentiation must be shown to be fully rational and justifiable. But the primary evil of the various schemes of racial segregation against blacks that the courts were being called upon to assess was not that such schemes were a capricious and irrational way of allocating public benefits and burdens. That might well be the primary wrong with racial segregation if we lived in a society very different from the one we have. The primary evil of these schemes was instead that they designedly and effectively marked off all black persons as degraded, dirty, less than fully developed persons who were unfit for full membership in the political, social, and moral community.

It is worth observing that the social reality of sexually segregated bathrooms appears to be different. The idea behind such sexual segregation seems to have more to do with the mutual undesirability of the use by both sexes of the same bathroom at the same time. There is no notion of the possibility of contamination; or even directly of inferiority and superiority. What seems to be involved—at least in part—is the importance of inculcating and preserving a sense of secrecy concerning the genitalia of the opposite sex. What seems to be at stake is the maintenance of that same sense of mystery or forbiddenness about the other sex's sexuality which is fostered by the general prohibition upon public nudity and the unashamed viewing of genitalia.

Sexually segregated bathrooms simply play a different role in our culture than did racially segregated ones. But that is not to say that the role they play is either benign or unobjectionable—only that it is different. Sexually segregated bathrooms may well be objectionable, but here too, the objection is not on the ground that they are prima facie capricious or arbitrary. Rather, the case against them now would rest on the ground that they are, perhaps, one small part of that scheme of sex-role differentiation which uses the mystery of sexual anatomy, among other things, to maintain the primacy of heterosexual sexual attraction central to that version of the patriarchal system of power relationships we have today. Whether sexually segregated bathrooms would be objectionable, because irrational, in the good society depends once again upon what the good society would look like in respect to sexual differentiation.

B. Types of Racism or Sexism

Another recurring question that can profitably be examined within the perspective of social realities is whether the legal system is racist or sexist. Indeed, it seems to me essential that the social realities of the relationships and ideologies concerning race and sex be kept in mind whenever one is trying to assess claims that are made about the racism or sexism of important institutions such as the legal system. It is also of considerable importance in assessing such claims to understand that even within the perspective of social reality, racism or sexism can manifest itself, or be understood, in different ways. That these are both important points can be seen through a brief examination of the different, distinctive ways in which our own legal system might plausibly be understood to be racist. The mode of analysis I propose serves as well, I believe, for an analogous analysis of the sexism of the legal system, although I do not undertake the latter analysis in this paper.

The first type of racism is the simplest and the least controversial. It is the case of overt racism, in which a law or a legal institution expressly takes into account the race of individuals in order to assign benefits and burdens in such a way as to bestow an unjustified benefit upon a member or members of the racially dominant group or an unjustified burden upon members of the racial groups that are oppressed. We no longer have many, if any, cases of overt racism in our legal system today, although we certainly had a number in the past. Indeed, the historical system of formal, racial segregation was both buttressed by, and constituted of, a number of overtly racist laws and practices. At different times in our history, racism included laws and practices which dealt with such things as the exclusion of nonwhites from the franchise, from decent primary and secondary schools and most professional schools, and the prohibition against interracial marriages.

The second type of racism is very similar to overt racism. It is covert, but intentional, racism, in which a law or a legal institution has as its purpose the allocation of benefits and burdens in order to support the power of the dominant race, but does not use race specifically as a basis for allocating these benefits and burdens. One particularly good historical example involves the use of grandfather clauses which were inserted in statutes governing voter registration in a number of states after passage of the fifteenth amendment.

Covert racism within the law is not entirely a thing of the past. Many instances of de facto school segregation in the North and West are cases of covert racism. At times certain school boards—virtually all of which are overwhelmingly white in composition—quite consciously try to maintain exclusively or predominantly white schools within a school district. The classifications such school boards use are not ostensibly racial, but are based upon the places of residence of the affected students. These categories provide the opportunity for covert racism in engineering the racial composition of individual schools within the board's jurisdiction.

What has been said so far is surely neither novel nor controversial. What is interesting, however, is that a number of persons appear to believe that as long as the legal system is not overtly or covertly racist, there is nothing to the charge that it is racist. So, for example, Mr. Justice Powell said in a speech a few years ago:

It is of course true that we have witnessed racial injustice in the past, as has every other country with significant racial diversity. But no one can fairly question the present national commitment to full equality and justice. Racial discrimination, by state action, is now proscribed by laws and court decisions which protect civil liberties more broadly than in any other country. But laws alone are not enough. Racial prejudice in the hearts of men cannot be legislated out of existence; it will pass only in time, and as human beings of all races learn in humility to respect each other—a process not furthered by recrimination or undue self-accusation. (*New York Times* [31 Aug. 1972], sec. 1, p. 33)

I believe it is a mistake to think about the problem of racism in terms of overt or covert racial discrimination by state action, which is now banished, and racial prejudice, which still lingers, but only in the hearts of persons. For there is another, more subtle kind of racism—unintentional, perhaps, but effective—which is as much a part of the legal system as are overt and covert racist laws and practices. It is what some critics of the legal system probably mean when they talk about the "institutional racism" of the legal system.

There are at least two kinds of institutional racism. The first is the racism of sub-institutions within the legal system such as the jury, or the racism of practices built upon or countenanced by the law. These institutions and practices very often, if not always, reflect in important and serious ways a variety of dominant values in the operation of what is apparently a neutral legal mechanism. The result is the maintenance and reenforcement of a system in which whites dominate over nonwhites. One relatively uninteresting (because familiar) example is the case of de facto school segregation. As observed above, some cases of de facto segregation are examples of covert racism. But even in school districts where there is no intention to divide pupils on grounds of race so as to maintain existing power relationships along racial lines, school attendance zones are utilized which are based on the geographical location of the pupil. Because it is a fact in our culture that there is racial discrimination against black people in respect to housing, it is also a fact that any geographical allocation of pupils—unless one pays a lot of attention to housing patterns—will have the effect of continuing to segregate minority pupils very largely on grounds of race. It is perfectly appropriate to regard this effect as a case of racism in public education.

A less familiar, and hence perhaps more instructive, example concerns the question of the importance of having blacks on juries, especially in cases in which blacks are criminal defendants. The orthodox view within the law is that it is unfair to try a black defendant before an all-white jury if blacks were overtly or covertly excluded from the jury rolls used to provide the jury panel, but not otherwise. One reason that is often given is that the systematic exclusion of blacks increases too greatly the chance of racial prejudice operating against the black defendant. The problem with this way of thinking about things is that it does not make much sense. If whites are apt to be prejudiced against blacks, then an all-white jury is just as apt to be prejudiced against a black defendant, irrespective of whether blacks were systematically excluded from the jury rolls. I suspect that the rule has developed in the way it has because the courts think that many, if not most, whites are not prejudiced against blacks, unless, perhaps, they happen to live in an area where there is systematic exclusion of blacks from the jury rolls. Hence prejudice is the chief worry, and a sectional, if not historical, one at that.

White prejudice against blacks is, I think, a problem, and not just a sectional one. However, the existence or nonexistence of prejudice against blacks does not go to the heart of the matter. It is a worry, but it is not the chief worry. A black person may not be able to get a fair trial from an all-white jury even though the jurors are disposed to be fair and impartial, because the whites may unknowingly bring into the jury box a view about a variety of matters which affects in very fundamental respects the way they will look at and assess the facts. Thus, for example, it is not, I suspect, part of the experience of most white persons who serve on juries that police often lie in their dealings with people and the courts. Indeed, it is probably not part of their experience that persons lie about serious matters except on rare occasions. And they themselves tend to take truth telling very seriously. As a result, white persons for whom these facts about police and lying are a part of their social reality will have very great difficulty taking seriously the possibility that the inculpatory testimony of a police witness is a deliberate untruth. However, it may also be a part of the social reality that many black persons, just because they are black, have had encounters with the police in which the police were at best indifferent to whether they, the police, were speaking the truth. And even more black persons may have known a friend or a relative who has had such an experience. As a result, a black juror would be more likely than his or her white counterpart to approach skeptically the testimony of ostensibly neutral, reliable witnesses such as police officers. The point is not that all police officers lie; nor is the point that all whites always believe everything police say, and blacks never do.

The point is that because the world we live in is the way it is, it is likely that whites and blacks will on the whole be disposed to view the credibility of police officers very differently. If so, the legal system's election to ignore this reality, and to regard as fair and above reproach the common occurrence of all-white juries (and white judges) passing on the guilt or innocence of black defendants is a decision in fact to permit and to perpetuate a kind of institutional racism within the law.

The second type of institutional racism is what I will call "conceptual" institutional racism. We have a variety of ways of thinking about the legal system, and we have a variety of ways of thinking within the legal system about certain problems. We use concepts. Quite often without realizing it, the concepts used take for granted certain objectionable aspects of racist ideology without our being aware of it. The second *Brown* case (*Brown II*) (1955) provides an example. There was a second *Brown* case because, having decided that the existing system of racially segregated public education was unconstitutional (*Brown I*) (1954), the Supreme Court gave legitimacy to a second issue—the nature of the relief to be granted—by treating it as a distinct question to be considered and decided separately. That in itself was striking because in most cases, once the Supreme Court has found unconstitutionality, there has been no problem about relief (apart from questions of retroactivity): The unconstitutional practices and acts are to cease. As is well known, the Court in *Brown II* concluded that the desegregation of public education had to proceed "with all deliberate speed." The Court said that there were "complexities arising from the transition to a system of public education freed from racial discrimination." More specifically, time might be necessary to carry out the ruling because of

> problems related to administration, arising from the physical condition of the school plant, the school transportation system personnel, revision of school districts and attendance areas into compact units to achieve a system of determining admission to the public school on a non-racial basis, and revision of local laws and regulations which may be necessary in solving the foregoing problems. (*Brown v. Board of Education,* 349 U.S. at 300-01 [1955])

Now, I do not know whether the Court believed what it said in this passage, but it is a fantastic bit of nonsense that is, for my purposes, most instructive. Why? Because there was nothing complicated about most of the dual school systems of the south-

ern states. Many counties, especially the rural ones, had one high school, typically called either "Booker T. Washington High School" or "George Washington Carver High School," where all the black children in the county went; another school, often called "Sidney Lanier High School" or "Robert E. Lee High School," was attended by all the white children in the county. There was nothing difficult about deciding that—as of the day after the decision—half of the children in the county, say all those who lived in the southern part of the county, would go to Robert E. Lee High School, and all those who lived in the northern half would go to Booker T. Washington High School. *Brown I* could have been implemented the day after the Court reached its decision. But it was also true that the black schools throughout the South were utterly wretched when compared to the white schools. There never had been any system of separate but equal education. In almost every measurable respect, the black schools were inferior. One possibility is that, without being explicitly aware of it, the members of the Supreme Court made use of some assumptions that were a significant feature of the dominant racist ideology. If the assumptions had been made explicit, the reasoning would have gone something like this: Those black schools are wretched. We cannot order white children to go to those schools, especially when they have gone to better schools in the past. So while it is unfair to deprive blacks, to make them go to these awful, segregated schools, they will have to wait until the black schools either are eliminated or are sufficiently improved so that there are good schools for everybody to attend.

What seems to me to be most objectionable, and racist, about *Brown II* is the uncritical acceptance of the idea that during this process of change, black schoolchildren would have to suffer by continuing to attend inadequate schools. The Supreme Court's solution assumed that the correct way to deal with this problem was to continue to have the black children go to their schools until the black schools were brought up to par or eliminated. That is a kind of conceptual racism in which the legal system accepts the dominant racist ideology, which holds that the claims of black children are worth less than the claims of white children in those cases in which conflict is inevitable. It seems to me that any minimally fair solution would have required that during the interim process, if anybody had to go to an inadequate school, it would have been the white children, since they were the ones who had previously had the benefit of the good schools. But this is simply not the way racial matters are thought about within the dominant ideology.

A study of *Brown II* is instructive because it is a good illustration of conceptual racism within the legal system. It also reflects another kind of conceptual racism—conceptual racism about the system. *Brown I* and *II* typically are thought of by our culture, and especially by our educational institutions, as representing one of the high points in the legal system's fight against racism. The dominant way of thinking about the desegregation cases is that the legal system was functioning at its very best. Yet, as I have indicated, there are important respects in which the legal system's response to the then existing system of racially segregated education was defective and hence should hardly be taken as a model of the just, institutional way of dealing with this problem of racial oppression. But the fact that we have, as well as inculcate, these attitudes of effusive praise toward *Brown I* and *II* and its progeny reveals a kind of persistent conceptual racism in talk about the character of the legal system, and what constitutes the right way to have dealt with the social reality of American racial oppression of black people.

In theory, the foregoing analytic scheme can be applied as readily to the social realities of sexual oppression as to racism. Given an understanding of the social realities in respect to sex—the ways in which the system of patriarchy inequitably distributes important benefits and burdens for the benefit of males, and the ideology which is a part of that patriarchal system and supportive of it—one can examine the different types of sexism that exist within the legal system. In practice the task is more difficult because we are inclined to take as appropriate even overt instances of sexist laws, e.g., that it is appropriately a part of the definition of rape that a man cannot rape his wife. The task is also more difficult because sexism is, as I have suggested, a "deeper" phenomenon than racism. As a result, there is less awareness of the significance of much of the social reality, e.g., that the language we use to talk about the world and ourselves has embedded within it ideological assumptions and preferences that support the existing patriarchal system. Cases of institutional sexism will therefore be systematically harder to detect. But these difficulties to one side, the mode of analysis seems to me to be in principle equally applicable to sexism, although, as I indicate in the next section on ideals, a complete account of the sexism of the legal system necessarily awaits a determination of what is the correct picture of the good society in respect to sexual differences.

II. IDEALS

A second perspective is also important for an understanding and analysis of racism and sexism. It is the perspective of the ideal. Just as we can and must ask what is involved today in our culture in being of one race or of one sex rather than the other, and how individuals are in fact viewed and treated, we can also ask different questions: What would the good or just society make of race and sex, and to what degree, if at all, would racial and sexual distinctions ever be taken into account? Indeed, it could plausibly be argued that we could not have an adequate idea of whether a society was racist or sexist unless we had some conception of what a thoroughly nonracist or nonsexist society would look like. This perspective is an extremely instructive as well as an often neglected one. Comparatively little theoretical literature dealing with either racism or sexism has concerned itself in a systematic way with this perspective. Moreover, as I shall try to demonstrate, it is on occasion introduced in an inappropriate context, e.g., in discussions of the relevance of the biological differences between males and females.

To understand more precisely what some of the possible ideals are in respect to racial or sexual differentiation, it is necessary to distinguish in a crude way among three levels or areas of social and political arrangements and activities. First, there is the area of basic political rights and obligations, including the right to vote and to travel and the obligation to pay taxes. Second, there is the area of important, nongovernmental institutional benefits and burdens. Examples are access to and employment in the significant economic markets, the opportunity to acquire and enjoy housing in the setting of one's choice, the right of persons who want to marry each other to do so, and the duties (nonlegal as well as legal) that persons acquire in getting married. Third, there is the area of individual, social interaction, including such matters as whom one will have as friends, and what aesthetic preferences one will cultivate and enjoy.

As to each of these three areas we can ask whether in a nonracist society it would be thought appropriate ever to take the race of the individuals into account. Thus, one picture of a nonracist society is that which is captured by what I call the assimilationist ideal: A nonracist society would be one in which the race of an individual would be the functional equivalent of the eye color of individuals in our society today. In our society no basic political rights and obligations are determined on the basis of eye color. No important institutional benefits and burdens are connected with eye color. Indeed, except for the mildest sort of aesthetic preferences, a person would be thought odd who even made private, social decisions by taking eye color into account. And for reasons that we could fairly readily state, we could explain why it would be wrong to permit anything but the mildest, most trivial aesthetic preference to turn on eye color. The reasons would concern the irrelevance of eye color for any political or social institution, practice, or arrangement. It would, of course, be equally odd for a person to say that while he or she looked blue-eyed; he or she regarded himself or herself as really a brown-eyed person. That is, because eye color functions differently in our culture than does race or sex, there is no analogue in respect to eye color to passing or transsexuality. According to the assimilationist ideal, a nonracist society would be one in which an individual's race was of no more significance in any of these three areas than is eye color today.

The assimilationist ideal is not, however, the only possible, plausible ideal. There are two others that are closely related, but distinguishable. One is the ideal of diversity; the other, the ideal of tolerance. Both can be understood by considering how religion, rather than eye color, tends to be thought about in our culture. According to the ideal of diversity, heterodoxy in respect to religious belief and practice is regarded as a positive good. In this view there would be a loss—it would be a worse society—were everyone to be a member of the same religion. According to the other view, the ideal of tolerance, heterodoxy in respect to religious belief and practice would be seen more as a necessary, lesser evil. In this view there is nothing intrinsically better about diversity in respect to religion, but the evils of achieving anything like homogeneity far outweigh the possible benefits.

Now, whatever differences there might be between the ideals of diversity and tolerance, the similarities are more striking. Under neither ideal would it be thought that the allocation of basic political rights and duties should take an individual's religion into account. We would want equalitarianism or nondiscrimination even in respect to most important institutional benefits and burdens—for example, access to employment in the desirable vocations. Nonetheless, on both views it would be deemed appropriate to have some institutions (typically those which are connected in an intimate way with these religions) which do in a variety of ways take the religion of members of the society into account. For example, it might be thought permissible and appropriate for members of a religious group to join together in collective associations which have religious, educational and social dimensions. And on the individual, interpersonal level, it might be thought unobjectionable, or on the diversity view, even admirable, were persons to select their associates, friends, and mates on the basis of their religious orientation. So there are two possible and plausible ideals of what the good society would look like in respect to religion in which religious differences would be to some degree maintained because the variety of religions was seen either as a valuable feature of the society, or as one to be tolerated. The picture is a more complex, less easily describable one than that of the assimilationist ideal.

The point of all this is its relevance to the case of sexism. One central and difficult question is what the ideal society would look like in respect to sex. The assimilationist ideal does not seem to be as readily plausible and obviously attractive here as it is in the case of race. Many persons invoke the possible realization of the assimilationist ideal as a reason for rejecting the equal rights amendment and indeed the idea of women's liberation itself. My view is that the assimilationist ideal may be just as good and just as important an ideal in respect to sex as it is in respect to race. But many persons think there are good reasons why an assimilationist society in respect to sex would not be desirable. One reason for their view might be that to make the assimilationist ideal a reality in respect to sex would involve more profound and fundamental revisions of our institutions and our attitudes than would be the case in respect to race. It is certainly true that on the institutional level we would have to alter radically our practices concerning the family and marriage. If a nonsexist society is a society in which one's sex is no more significant than eye color in our society today, then laws which require the persons who are being married to be of different sexes would clearly be sexist laws. Insofar as they are based upon the desirability of unifying the distinctive features of one male and one female, laws and institutions which conceive of the nuclear family as ideally composed of two and only two adults should also be thought of as anachronistic as well as sexist laws and institutions.

On the attitudinal and conceptual level, the assimilationist ideal would require the eradication of all sex-role differentiation. It would never teach about the inevitable or essential attributes of masculinity or femininity; it would never encourage or discourage the ideas of sisterhood or brotherhood; and it would be unintelligible to talk about the virtues as well as disabilities of being a woman or a man. Were sex like eye color, these things would make no sense. A nonsexist world might conceivably tolerate both homosexuality and heterosexuality (as peculiar kinds of personal erotic preference), but any kind of sexually *exclusive* preference would be either as anomalous or as statistically fortuitous as is a sexual preference connected with eye color in our society today. Just as the normal, typical adult is virtually oblivious to the eye color of other persons for all major interpersonal relationships, so the normal, typical adult in this kind of nonsexist society would be indifferent to the sexual, physiological differences of other persons for all interpersonal relationships. Bisexuality, not heterosexuality or homosexuality, would be the norm for intimate, sexual relationships in the ideal society that was assimilationist in respect to sex.

All of this seems to me to be worth talking about because unless and until we are clear about issues such as these we cannot be wholly certain about whether, from the perspective of the ideal, some of the institutions in our own culture are or are not sexist. We know that racially segregated bathrooms are racist. We know that laws that prohibit persons of different races from marrying are racist. But throughout our society we have sexually segregated bathrooms, and we have laws which prohibit individuals of the same sex from marrying. As I have argued above, from the perspective of the existing social reality there are important ways to distinguish the racial from the sexual cases and to criticize both practices. But that still leaves open the question of whether in the good society these sexual distinctions, or others, would be thought worth preserving either because they were meritorious, or at least to be tolerated because they were necessary.

As I have indicated, it may be that the problem is with the assimilationist ideal. It may be that in respect to sex (and conceivably, even in respect to race) something more like either of the ideals in respect to religion—pluralistic ideals founded on diversity or tolerance—is the right one. But the problem then—and it is a very substantial one—is to specify with a good deal of precision and care what the ideal really comes to. Which legal, institutional and personal differentiations are permissible and which are not? Which attitudes and beliefs concerning sexual identification and difference are properly introduced and maintained and which are not? Part, but by no means all, of the attractiveness of the assimilationist ideal is its clarity and simplicity. In the good society of the assimilationist sort, we would be able to tell easily and unequivocally whether any law, practice or attitude was in any respect either racist or sexist. Part, but by no means all, of the unattractiveness of any pluralistic ideal is that it makes the question of what is racist or sexist a much more difficult and complicated one to answer. But although simplicity and lack of ambiguity may be virtues, they are not the only virtues to be taken into account in deciding among competing ideals. We quite appropriately take other considerations to be relevant to an assessment of the value and worth of alternative nonracist and nonsexist societies.

Nor do I even mean to suggest that all persons who reject the assimilationist ideal in respect to sex would necessarily embrace either something like the ideal of tolerance or the ideal of diversity. Some persons might think the right ideal was one in which substantially greater sexual differentiation and sex-role identification was retained than would be the case under either of these conceptions. Thus, someone might believe that the good society was, perhaps, essentially like the one they think we now have in respect to sex: equality of political rights, such as the right to vote, but all of the sexual differentiation in both legal and nonlegal institutions that is characteristic of the way in which our society has been and still is ordered. And someone might also believe that the usual ideological justifications for these arrangements are the correct and appropriate ones. This could, of course, be regarded as a version of the ideal of diversity, with the emphasis upon the extensive character of the institutional and personal difference connected with sexual identity. Whether it is a kind of ideal of diversity or a different ideal altogether turns, I think, upon two things: first, how pervasive the sexual differentiation is; second, whether the ideal contains a conception of the appropriateness of significant institutional and interpersonal inequality, e.g., that the woman's job is in large measure to serve and be dominated by the male. The more this latter feature is present, the clearer the case for regarding this as a distinctively different ideal.

The question of whether something is a plausible and attractive ideal turns in part on the nature of the empirical world. If it is true, for example, that race is not only a socially significant category in our culture but also largely a socially created one, then many ostensible objections to the assimilationist ideal appear to disappear immediately. What I mean is this: It is obvious that we could formulate and use some sort of a crude, incredibly imprecise physiological concept of race. In this sense we could even say that race is a naturally occurring rather than a socially created feature of the world. There are diverse skin colors and related physiological characteristics distributed among human beings. But the fact is that except for skin hue and the related physiological characteristics, race is a socially created category. And skin hue, as I have shown, is neither a necessary nor a sufficient condition for being classified as black in our culture. Race as a naturally occurring characteristic is also a socially irrelevant category. There do not in fact appear to be any characteristics that are part of this natural concept of race and that are in any plausible way even relevant to the appropriate distribution of any political, institutional, or interpersonal concerns in the good society. Because in this sense race is like eye color, there is no plausible case to be made on this ground against the assimilationist ideal.

There is, of course, the social reality of race. In creating and tolerating a society in which race matters, we must recognize that we have created a vastly more complex concept of race which includes what might be called the idea of ethnicity as well—a set of attitudes, traditions, beliefs, etc., which the society has made part of what it means to be of a race. It may be, therefore, that one could argue that a form of the pluralist ideal ought to be preserved in respect to race, in the socially created sense, for reasons similar to those that might be offered in support of the desirability of some version of the pluralist ideal in respect to religion. As I have indicated, I am skeptical, but for the purposes of this essay it can well be left an open question.

Despite appearances, the case of sex is more like that of race than is often thought. What opponents of assimilationism seize upon is that sexual difference appears to be a naturally occurring category of obvious and inevitable social relevance in a way, or to a degree, which race is not. The problems with this way of thinking are twofold. To begin with, an analysis of the social realities reveals that it is the socially created sexual differences which tend in fact to matter the most. It is sex-role differentiation, not gender per se, that makes men and women as different as they are from each other, and it is sex-role differences which are invoked to justify most sexual differentiation at any of the levels of society.

More importantly, even if naturally occurring sexual differences were of such a nature that they were of obvious prima facie social relevance, this would by no means settle the question of whether in the good society sex should or should not be as minimally significant as eye color. Even though there are biological differences between men and women in nature, this fact does not determine the question of what the good society can and should make of these differences. I have difficulty understanding why so many persons seem to think that it does settle the question adversely to anything like the assimilationist ideal. They might think it does settle the question for two different reasons. In the first place, they might think the differences are of such a character that they substantially affect what would be possible within a good society of human persons. Just as the fact that humans are mortal necessarily limits the features of any possible good society, so, they might argue, the fact that males and females are physiologically different limits the features of any possible good society.

In the second place, they might think the differences are of such a character that they are relevant to the question of what would be desirable in the good society. That is to say, they might not think that the differences *determine* to a substantial degree what is possible, but that the differences ought to be taken into account in any rational construction of an ideal social existence.

The second reason seems to me to be a good deal more plausible than the first. For there appear to be very few, if any, respects in which the ineradicable, naturally occurring differences between males and females *must* be taken into account. The industrial revolution has certainly made any of the general differences in strength between the sexes capable of being ignored by the good society in virtually all activities. And it is sex-role acculturation, not biology, that mistakenly leads many persons to the view that women are both naturally and necessarily better suited than men to be assigned the primary responsibilities of child rearing. Indeed, the only fact that seems required to be taken into account is the fact that reproduction of the human species requires that the fetus develop *in utero* for a period of months. Sexual intercourse is not necessary, for artificial insemination is available. Neither marriage nor the family is required for conception or child rearing. Given the present state of medical knowledge and the natural realities of female pregnancy, it is difficult to see why any important institutional or interpersonal arrangements *must* take the existing gender difference of *in utero* pregnancy into account.

But, as I have said, this is still to leave it a wholly open question to what degree the good society *ought* to build upon any ineradicable gender differences to construct institutions which would maintain a substantial degree of sexual differentiation. The arguments are typically far less persuasive for doing so than appears upon the initial statement of this possibility. Someone might argue that the fact of menstruation, for instance, could be used as a premise upon which to predicate different social roles for females than for males. But this could only plausibly be proposed if two things were true: first, that menstruation would be debilitating to women and hence relevant to social role even in a culture which did not teach women to view menstruation as a sign of uncleanliness or as a curse; and second, that the way in which menstruation necessarily affected some or all women was in fact related in an important way to the role in question. But even if both of these were true, it would still be an open question whether any sexual differentiation ought to be built upon these facts. The society could still elect to develop institutions that would nullify the effect of the natural differences. And suppose, for example, what seems implausible—that some or all women will not be able to perform a particular task while menstruating, e.g., guard a border. It would be easy enough, if the society wanted to, to arrange for substitute guards for the women who were incapacitated. We know that persons are not good guards when they are sleepy, and we make arrangements so that persons alternate guard duty to avoid fatigue. The same could be done for menstruating women, even given these implausibly strong assumptions about menstruation. At the risk of belaboring the obvious, what I think it important to see is that the case against the assimilationist ideal—if it is to be a good one—must rest on arguments concerned to show why some other ideal would be preferable; it cannot plausibly rest on the claim that it is either necessary or inevitable.

There is, however, at least one more argument based upon nature, or at least the "natural," that is worth mentioning. Someone might argue that significant sex-role differentiation is natural not in the sense that it is biologically determined but only in the sense that it is a virtually universal phenomenon in human culture. By itself, this claim of virtual universality, even if accurate, does not directly establish anything about the desirability or undesirability of

any particular ideal. But it can be made into an argument by the addition of the proposition that where there is a virtually universal social practice, there is probably some good or important purpose served by the practice. Hence, given the fact of sex-role differentiation in all, or almost all, cultures, we have some reason to think that substantial sex-role differentiation serves some important purpose for and in human society.

This is an argument, but I see no reason to be impressed by it. The premise which turns the fact of sex-role differentiation into any kind of a strong reason for sex-role differentiation is the premise of conservatism. And it is no more convincing here than elsewhere. There are any number of practices that are typical and yet upon reflection seem without significant social purpose. Slavery was once such a practice; war perhaps still is.

More to the point, perhaps, the concept of "purpose" is ambiguous. It can mean in a descriptive sense "plays some role" or "is causally relevant." Or it can mean in a prescriptive sense "does something desirable" or "has some useful function." If "purpose" is used prescriptively in the conservative premise, then there is no reason to think that premise is true.

To put it another way, the question is whether it is desirable to have a society in which sex-role differences are to be retained at all. The straightforward way to think about that question is to ask what would be good and what would be bad about a society in which sex functioned like eye color does in our society. We can imagine what such a society would look like and how it would work. It is hard to see how our thinking is substantially advanced by reference to what has typically or always been the case. If it is true, as I think it is, that the sex-role differentiated societies we have had so far have tended to concentrate power in the hands of males, have developed institutions and ideologies that have perpetuated that concentration and have restricted and prevented women from living the kinds of lives that persons ought to be able to live for themselves, then this says far more about what may be wrong with any nonassimilationist ideal than does the conservative premise say what may be right about any nonassimilationist ideal.

Nor is this all that can be said in favor of the assimilationist ideal. For it seems to me that the strongest affirmative moral argument on its behalf is that it provides for a kind of individual autonomy that a nonassimilationist society cannot attain. Any nonassimilationist society will have sex roles. Any nonassimilationist society will have some institutions that distinguish between individuals by virtue of their gender, and any such society will necessarily teach the desirability of doing so. Any substantially nonassimilationist society will make one's sexual identity an important characteristic, so that there are substantial psychological, role, and status differences between persons who are males and those who are females. Even if these could be attained without systemic dominance of one sex over the other, they would, I think, be objectionable on the ground that they necessarily impaired an individual's ability to develop his or her own characteristics, talents and capacities to the fullest extent to which he or she might desire. Sex roles, and all that accompany them, necessarily impose limits—restrictions on what one can do, be or become. As such, they are, I think, at least prima facie wrong.

To some degree, all role-differentiated living is restrictive in this sense. Perhaps, therefore, all role-differentiation in society is to some degree troublesome, and perhaps all strongly role-differentiated societies are objectionable. But the case against sexual differentiation need not rest upon this more controversial point. For one thing that distinguishes sex roles from many other roles is that they are wholly involuntarily assumed. One has no choice whatsoever about whether one shall be born a male or female. And if it is a consequence of one's being born a male or a female that one's subsequent emotional, intellectual, and material devel-opment will be substantially controlled by this fact, then substantial, permanent, and involuntarily assumed restraints have been imposed on the most central factors concerning the way one will shape and live one's life. The point to be emphasized is that this would necessarily be the case, even in the unlikely event that substantial sexual differentiation could be maintained without one sex or the other becoming dominant and developing institutions and an ideology to support that dominance.

I do not believe that all I have said in this section shows in any conclusive fashion the desirability of the assimilationist ideal in respect to sex. I have tried to show why some typical arguments against the assimilationist ideal are not persuasive, and why some of the central ones in support of that ideal are persuasive. But I have not provided a complete account, or a complete analysis. At a minimum, what I have shown is how thinking about this topic ought to proceed, and what kinds of arguments need to be marshalled and considered before a serious and informed discussion of alternative conceptions of a nonsexist society can even take place. Once assembled, these arguments need to be individually and carefully assessed before any final, reflective choice among the competing ideals can be made. There does, however, seem to me to be a strong presumptive case for something very close to, if not identical with, the assimilationist ideal.

. . .

DISCUSSION QUESTIONS

1. Wasserstrom postulates what an ideal nonracist and nonsexist society would be like. Do you agree with him, or would your nonracist and nonsexist society be different? Defend your view.
2. Wasserstrom argues that "race does not function in our society as does eye color." What is his argument? Critically analyze it.
3. Review the arguments Wasserstrom presents against the assimilationist ideal. Which argument do you believe to be the strongest one against the assimilationist ideal? Why? Is Wasserstrom's counterargument a convincing one?
4. What, according to Wasserstrom, are the "social realities" of racism and sexism? Do the social realities of 1977 (the original date of publication of his article) still hold today? What has changed in the intervening quarter century? What has stayed the same? Discuss why you believe these things to be the case.
5. In Chapter 5 of her book *Inessential Woman*, Elizabeth V. Spelman argues that Wasserstrom's position on racism and sexism "leaves no room for the Black woman. For a Black woman cannot be [as Wasserstrom says] 'female, as opposed to being black'; she is female *and* Black. Since Wasserstrom's argument proceeds from the assumption that one is either female or Black, it cannot be an argument that applies to Black women. Moreover, we cannot generate a composite image of Black women from Wasserstrom's argument, since the description of women as being put on a pedestal, or being dependent, never generally applied to Black women in the United States and

was never meant to apply to them. . . . If the terms of one's theory require that a person is either female or Black, clearly there is no room to describe someone who is both." Critically evaluate this criticism of Wasserstrom. Is there room for Black women in Wasserstrom's argument? How devastating is this charge to Wasserstrom's arguments on racism and sexism? How might Wasserstrom respond to it?

6. In *Justice and the Politics of Difference*, Iris Marion Young criticizes the assimilationist ideal proposed by Richard A. Wasserstrom and argues for a "politics of difference." Young says that recent social movements of oppressed groups show that "a positive self-definition of group difference is in fact more liberatory" than Wasserstrom's "ideal of justice that defines liberation as the transcendence of group difference." According to Young, Wasserstrom's "assimilationist ideal assumes that equal social status for all persons requires treating everyone according to the same principles, rules and standards." In contrast, according to a politics of difference, "equality as the participation and inclusion of all groups sometimes requires different treatment for oppressed or disadvantaged groups." Social policy, for Young, sometimes needs to accord certain groups special treatment in order to meet her standards of social justice. Young argues that the normative ideal of the homogeneous public is oppressive and, in some cases, amounts to genocide. Critically evaluate Young's criticism of Wasserstrom.

 BERNARD BOXILL

Blacks and Social Justice

Bernard Boxill argues for affirmative action. He claims that arguments for affirmative action/preferential treatment are straightforward, and fall into two classes of argumentation: backward-looking and forward-looking. "Backward-looking arguments justify preferential treatment considered as compensation for past wrongs," says Boxill, whereas "forward-looking arguments justify preferential treatment considered as a means to present or future goods, particularly equality." For Boxill, neither the forward-looking argument nor the backward-looking argument is in itself sufficient to justify affirmative action. "My argument," says Boxill, "is that qualified blacks deserve compensation for discrimination because even they have been wronged and probably harmed by it, and that preferential treatment is appropriate compensation for them because it suits their objectives and abilities." Boxill's argument for affirmative action is achieved by combining the forces of both the forward-looking and backward-looking arguments and by drawing on the way they complement and support each other.

Bernard Boxill is a professor of philosophy at the University of North Carolina at Chapel Hill and is the author of *Blacks and Social Justice* (1984, 1992). The following reading is from *Blacks and Social Justice*.

Bernard Boxill, *Blacks and Social Justice*, Rowman and Littlefield, 1992, 147–172. Reprinted with permission from the publisher. Notes have been omitted.

LIBERALS INTO FORMER LIBERALS

As Michael Kinsley has observed in *Harper's,* "No single development of the past fifteen years has turned more liberals into former liberals than affirmative action." This metamorphosis, if it is not merely an unmasking, is ostensibly due to the belief that affirmative action perverts the just goal of civil rights. That goal, protest the disillusioned liberals, is to guarantee that persons be treated as individuals and judged on their merits; but affirmative action, they complain, guarantees that individuals are treated as mere members of racial groups, and their merits disparaged and ignored.

These liberals are not appeased by Allan Bakke's victory in the Supreme Court in 1978. For although the court ruled that Bakke was wrongly denied admission to the medical school at the University of California at Davis, it allowed that race could be used as a factor in considering applicants. As *Time* announced on its cover: "What Bakke Means. Race: Yes. Quotas: No."

As with busing, the arguments for preferential treatment fell into two classes, backward-looking and forward-looking. Backward-looking arguments justify preferential treatment considered as compensation for past and present wrongs done to blacks and their effects. Forward-looking arguments justify preferential treatment considered as a means to present or future goods, particularly equality. Both the assumptions and the aims of these two kinds of argument must be carefully distinguished.

Backward-looking arguments assume that blacks have been, or are being, wronged. Forward-looking arguments assume that blacks are generally inferior to whites in status, education, and income. Backward-looking arguments aim at compensating blacks. Forward-looking arguments aim at improving the status, education, and income of blacks.

THE BACKWARD-LOOKING ARGUMENT

The fundamental backward-looking argument is simply stated: Black people have been and are being harmed by racist attitudes and practices. Those wronged deserve compensation. Therefore, black people deserve compensation. Preferential treatment is an appropriate form of compensation for black people. Therefore black people deserve preferential treatment.

Criticism of this argument falls into two main classes: on the one hand, critics charge that the claims to compensation of the black beneficiaries of preferential treatment are unfounded or vacuously satisfied; on the other hand, they charge that these claims are outweighed by other considerations.

The most common version of the first type always uttered by the critic with an air of having played a trump, is that, since those members of groups that have been discriminated against who benefit from preferential hiring must be minimally qualified, they are not the members of the group who deserve compensation. The philosopher Alan Goldman, for example, argues this way: "Since hiring within the preferred group still depends upon relative qualifications and hence upon past opportunities for acquiring qualifications, there is in fact a reverse ratio established between past discriminations and present benefits, so that those who most benefit from the program, those who actually get jobs, are those who least deserve to." But surely a conclusion that preferential hiring is unjustified based on the argument above is a non sequitur. Let us grant that qualified blacks are less deserving of compensation than unqualified blacks, that those who most deserve compensation should be compensated first, and finally that preferential hiring is a form of compensation. How does it follow that preferential hiring of qualified blacks is unjustified? Surely the assumption that unqualified blacks are more deserving of compensation than qualified blacks does not require us to conclude that qualified blacks deserve no compensation. Because I have lost only one leg, I may be less deserving of compensation than another who has lost two legs, but it does not follow that I deserve no compensation at all.

Even Thomas Nagel, one of the country's leading philosophers and a strong defender of preferential treatment on the basis of the forward-looking argument, resorts to this criticism of the backward-looking argument. Thus he labels a "bad" argument, one that maintains that the "beneficiaries of affirmative action deserve it as compensation for past discrimination," because, he says, "no effort is made to give preference to those who have suffered most from discrimination." Indeed, Nagel makes exactly the same point as Goldman: Because the blacks who benefit from preferential treatment are qualified, "they are not necessarily, or even probably the ones who especially deserve it. Women or blacks who don't have the qualifications even to be considered are likely to have been handicapped more by the effects of discrimination than those who receive preference." But for the reasons given, this criticism is bogus. Furthermore, since Nagel defends preferential treatment on forward-looking, egalitarian grounds, this puts him into deeper trouble than it does those who reject preferential treatment altogether.

For, if preferential treatment makes no effort to give preference to those who have suffered most, neither does it make an effort to give preference to those who are most unequal to whites. In other words, if the qualified have suffered least, they are also least unequal, and it seems a bad strategy, if one is aiming for equality, to prefer them. Nagel could object that preferring the qualified is a good egalitarian strategy because it will lead indirectly to equality. But a variant of the idea is open to the advocate of the backward-looking argument. He could argue that preferential treatment of the qualified also helps to compensate the unqualified insofar as it shows them that if one is qualified, being black is no longer a bar to promotion.

. . .

The argument I am proposing in support of preferential treatment should be distinguished from another argument which, I admit, has a certain superficial attractiveness. My argument is that qualified blacks deserve compensation for discrimination because even they have been wronged and probably harmed by it, and that preferential treatment is appropriate compensation for them because it suits their objectives and abilities. The other, superficially attractive, argument is that qualified blacks deserve compensation because they are probably the very blacks who would, in the absence of discrimination, have qualified without preferential treatment. But only a moment's reflection is needed to see that this argument is flawed. As James S. Fishkin points out in *Justice, Equal Opportunity and the Family,* "There is no reason to believe that those blacks who are presently 'best prepared' offer even a remote approximation to those blacks 'who in the absence of discrimination probably would have qualified.'"

But this eminently sound observation does not imply that the "best prepared" are not wronged or harmed by discrimination. That is an altogether distinct claim. The best prepared need not be the ones who would have qualified in the absence of discrimination, but they may nevertheless be disadvantaged by discrimination. Thus, I reject Fishkin's concomitant, completely unsupported, claim that "it is far from clear that the more advantaged members of a racial minority generally are worse off than they would otherwise have been, were it not for discrimination practiced against their forebears in previous generations." This assumes that discrimination does not generally disadvantage those who are discriminated against, and that is an outrageous and gratuitous conclusion.

But suppose I am wrong and many blacks have in fact escaped the effects of discrimination? This is the fundamental objection to preferential treatment, for, if so many blacks have escaped discrimination and its effects that it results in "compensation" being given large numbers of people who did not deserve it, then it would be unfair. However, even if some blacks escape discrimination altogether, it must be admitted that there is a pervasive prejudice against blacks as a group and a tendency to discriminate against them. Consequently, if . . . the realistic threat of transgression is itself transgression, even those who escape discrimination are wronged and possibly harmed by the discrimination against other blacks. This leads us to the argument proposed by Judith Jarvis Thomson that "even those who were not themselves down-graded for being black or female have suffered the consequences of the downgrading of other blacks and women: lack of self-confidence and lack of self-respect." Goldman has taken this argument as the basis for belief in the concept of a kind of "indirect," "vicarious" wrong. Thus he objects that we should reserve "vicarious compensation"—and what he means by this I do not know—"to those who suffer psychologically or vicariously from injustice toward others, and that we should draw the line [past which compensation is no longer called for] at indirect psychological pressures." But his objection misses the point about the harmfulness of discrimination.

Consider, for example, how Goldman illustrates his point: "A traumatized witness," he writes, "does not suffer the harm of the real victim. Similarly, a Jewish millionaire in Scarsdale, no matter how much he suffered vicariously or psychologically from hearing of the German concentration camps, is not owed the reparations due a former inmate." But Goldman fails to distinguish two kinds of witness to injustice. There is the witness who identifies with the victim, and there is the witness whom the transgressors identify with the victim. The first suffers vicariously. The second may not suffer vicariously. However, it does not follow that the latter does not suffer at all. He certainly might suffer at the realization that he too was under sentence and could be next. Therefore there are two completely different kinds of suffering that a witness to the persecution of others might endure. The first stems from sympathy for the victims; it is vicarious and could be called indirect. The second stems from the witness's self-interested realization that he may [be] under sentence too and could be the next to be harmed. But, though this suffering may be "psychological," it is not vicarious, and there is nothing indirect about it. The example of the Scarsdale Jew—the stipulation that he is a millionaire is irrelevant—obscures this. Safely ensconced in Scarsdale, any Jew, millionaire or not, was safe from Hitler. Goldman's example insinuates that the Jew who was not himself victimized could feel only vicarious suffering. To make the argument more balanced, I suggest pondering the plight of a Jewish multimillionaire in Berlin.

Failure to distinguish these two kinds of suffering is responsible for the idea that vicarious suffering is relevant to a consideration of the undermining of self-confidence and self-respect to which Judith Jarvis Thomson was presumably referring. For while the realization that, like the actual victim, the witness to discrimination is also under sentence and could be next, has everything to do with the undermining of his self-confidence and self-respect, vicarious suffering has nothing to do with it. Consequently, the vicarious suffering of middle-class blacks for lower-class blacks, if it exists to any appreciable degree, is completely irrelevant to the question of what undermines their self-confidence and self-respect. What does is the uncertainty and ambiguity of their own lives.

But the red herring of vicarious suffering is misleading in yet another way: It suggests that the undermining of self-confidence and self-respect is a consequence of "injustice toward others." Of course, one's vicarious suffering is no indication of injustice to oneself. Though a white person may suffer vicariously at the thought of discrimination against lower-class blacks, the injustice is to them and not to him. However, when black people feel threatened and insulted when other black people are discriminated against because of their color, the injustice is both to those actually discriminated against and to those who are spared. Because the blacks discriminated against are discriminated against because they are black, all black people receive a warning that they too may experience the same treatment. They are wronged, and liable to be wrongfully harmed, in two ways. First, they are wronged because the realistic threat under which they live transgresses their right to equal security.

Second, they are wronged by the judgmental injustice that assumes that because they are black they deserve less consideration than others. Justice Thurgood Marshall's comment in *Bakke* is apropos: "It is unnecessary in twentieth century America to have individual Negroes demonstrate that they have been victims of racial discrimination. [It] has been so pervasive that none, regardless of wealth or position, has managed to escape its impact."

To sum up to this point: The criticism of the backward-looking argument for preferential treatment under consideration is unsound in one of its forms, and irrelevant in the other. Insofar as it assumes that many blacks have escaped wrongful harm as a result of discrimination it is unsound. Even if some blacks have escaped harm this would not be sufficient to make preferential treatment unjustified, because the overwhelming majority it benefited would deserve compensation. Insofar as the criticism assumes the blacks preferred are less wronged or harmed than other blacks it is irrelevant. The backward-looking argument does not exclude compensating unqualified blacks, or deny that compensating unqualified blacks, or deny that they are more deserving of compensation. Neither does it say that qualified blacks must be compensated first. It asserts only that blacks deserve compensation for the wrongful harms of discrimination. Thus, it is unaffected by the claim that qualified blacks may be the least wronged and harmed of blacks. The fact that qualified blacks are wrongfully harmed at all, and that preferential treatment is appropriate compensation, is sufficient justification for it.

Now, I have admitted that it is a weak argument which tries to justify preferential treatment of qualified blacks applying for desirable places and positions on the grounds that, had there been no discrimination, these blacks would probably have qualified for such places and positions without preferential treatment. The key assumption in this argument is simply not plausible. But if we assume that compensation is owed to blacks as a group, then a stronger version of that argument can be advanced, which goes as follows: Blacks as a group have been wronged, and are disadvantaged, by slavery and discrimination. Consequently, blacks as a group deserve compensation. Furthermore, had it not been for slavery and discrimination, blacks as a group would be more nearly equal in income, education, and well-being to other groups who did not suffer from slavery or the extent and kind of discrimination from which blacks have suffered. Consequently, assuming that compensating a group for wrongful disadvantages requires bringing it to the condition it would have been in had it not been wrongfully disadvantaged, compensating blacks as a group requires making them, as a group, more nearly equal to those other groups. But if blacks as a group were more nearly equal in income, education, and well-being to such groups, some blacks would then fill desirable positions. Accordingly, compensating blacks as a group requires putting some blacks in desirable positions. However, only the blacks who are now most qualified can, fittingly, be placed in desirable positions. Hence, even if those blacks are *not* the very ones who would have filled such places and positions had there been no slavery and discrimination, compensating blacks as a group may specifically require preferential treatment of qualified blacks.

Many objections can be raised to this argument. Perhaps the most obvious is that its concept of compensation differs from the conception of compensation used in the argument that blacks, as individuals, deserve compensation. In that argument, I did not contend that compensating blacks requires placing them in positions they would have occupied had there been no slavery and discrimination. I contended that blacks deserve compensation because they are wronged by discrimination, and that places in universities and professional schools are appropriate compensation for qualified blacks because of their interests and objectives. However, in outlining the group compensation argument I am saying that compensating blacks as a group requires placing them in positions they would have occupied had there been no slavery and discrimination. Is this inconsistent? I think I can demonstrate that it isn't.

I endorse the view that, ideally, compensating either individuals or groups for wrongs requires placing them in positions they would have occupied had they not been wronged. The problem is that this ideal conception of compensation cannot be applied in the case of compensation for individual blacks for the wrongs of slavery and discrimination. To place a wronged individual in a position he would have occupied had he not been wronged depends on an estimate of how much the wrong has detracted from his assets, which in turn depends on an estimate of his assets. For an individual's assets—his capacities, abilities, goals, interests, and enjoyments—determine in large part the position he will come to occupy if he is not wronged. For example, if thugs break the basketball player Dr. J's legs, he will receive more compensation than I would if they broke my legs, because it is known

that his legs are a greater asset to him than are my legs to me. Similarly, some years ago the newspapers reported that a certain screen star had insured her legs with Lloyd's of London for several million pounds. Whether or not the story was true, it seemed good sense to many people because they thought the star's legs were such an enormous asset that it would take several million pounds to compensate her for them if they were flawed or lost. It should now be clear why the ideal conception of compensation cannot be used to support an argument in favor of compensating black individuals for the wrongs of slavery and discrimination. In most cases, it simply makes no sense to even try to estimate what any black individual's assets might have been before he was wronged by slavery and discrimination. For, from the very start of their lives—while they are yet in the womb—and of their parents' lives, and of the lives of their ancestors, all the way back to the first black slaves born in the New World, blacks have been wronged by slavery and discrimination. Yet the fact remains that because they have been wronged they deserve compensation. Accordingly, under the circumstances the ideal conception of compensation must be discarded. By way of compensating blacks all that can practically be done is to adopt my proposal and award them some benefit—such as preferential treatment—appropriate to their interests and objectives.

The argument for group compensation does not run into this sort of difficulty. We can form some estimate of the assets blacks as a group had before slavery and discrimination. Consequently, we can apply the ideal conception of compensation, and reasonably propose to place blacks as a group in the position they would have occupied had there been no slavery and discrimination.

It may be objected, however, that placing blacks in the position they would have occupied had there been no slavery and discrimination would not make blacks equal or nearly equal to other groups because blacks are inferior to other groups, especially white groups, in native talent. But this objection begs the question. The claim that blacks are inferior to whites in native talent is an inference based largely on the fact that the average black I.Q. is lower than the average white I.Q. But that inference is highly controversial. Another, possibly sounder inference is that black I.Q.s have been lowered as a result of slavery and discrimination. If this assumption is sound, and if I.Q.s are as important for determining people's lives as they are said to be, then blacks' lower average I.Q., far from supporting the case against compensation, very [much] supports the case for it.

A somewhat less radical objection is that the estimate we can form of the assets of blacks as a group before slavery and discrimination suggests that even without slavery and discrimination they would not have been nearly equal to other groups. Thomas Sowell, for example, suggests this. ". . . the wide diversity among American ethnic groups," he argues, "precludes any assumptions that any group—especially from a non-urban, non-industrial background— would earn the national average in income." But this is not only a weak argument in itself, it is also inconsistent with many other points Sowell himself has stressed as important and decisive in relation to the issue of discrimination.

It is a weak argument, first, because some groups from a "non-urban, non-industrial background," for example, the Irish Catholics, earn *above* the national average income. If Irish Catholics can, why not blacks? Sowell's assertion that such groups tend to earn considerably less than the national average income may be true if we look only at relatively recent immigrants such as the Puerto Ricans. But blacks have been in America for three hundred years. It is invidious to assume that, unlike other groups from non-urban, non-industrial backgrounds, they would not have bettered themselves had it not been for slavery and its aftermath. Finally, although blacks originally came from a non-urban, non-industrial background, it does not follow that they lacked economically valuable assets. . . . Sowell's master, Booker T. Washington, [boasted] that the policy of importing black slaves proved that blacks had economically valuable skills, and given the importance Sowell attributes to motives of economic self-interest, he is in no position to confound Washington's argument. Given that blacks did have economically valuable skills, surely, in the absence of slavery and discrimination, they would have realized their assets, parlayed their earnings in order to further improve their skills, and, with three hundred years in which to do it, would today be as urbanized and industrialized as anybody else.

. . .

But what if Sowell is right, and "culture—not discrimination—decides who gets ahead." Assuming that a group's culture is what determines the jobs and positions its members are interested in, certain philosophers seem to agree with him. Thus, Barry Gross implies that blacks may simply not be interested in desirable positions, and argues that black under-representation in desirable positions is no clear indication of discrimination: "The members of a group might simply lack interest in certain jobs (for example, Italians in the public school system are in short supply)." But this analogy fails, though Gross does not appear to notice it, when applied to the case of blacks. For it isn't as if blacks are under-represented in the public school system, or in law, or in banking, or in the professions. They are under-represented in all of these fields. Consequently, though Gross may be right that sociologically, certain groups are simply not represented in various jobs and at various levels in percentages closely approximating their percentage of the population, he fails to see that the case of blacks presents a matter of an altogether different order. Lack of interest presumably culturally determined—in this or in that area may explain away the under-representation of a cultural group in one or two specific areas. However, unless we assume that some cultural groups have no interest in *any* of the traditional professional areas, we cannot explain a group's under-representation in all desirable positions by citing cultural differences.

The deeper and more serious implication of the claim that blacks are disadvantaged by their culture, not by discrimination, is that blacks, because of their culture, lack the discipline necessary for becoming qualified for desirable positions. But whether or not this is true, it cannot weigh against the argument for group compensation for blacks. For even if the traits which inhibit the success of blacks—supposedly a lack of appropriate work habits and discipline—are cultural traits it does not follow that they are not the result of wrongful harm. In order to survive and retain their sanity and equilibrium in impossibly unjust situations, people may have to resort to patterns of behavior, and consequently may develop habits or traits, which are debilitating and unproductive in a more humane environment. I see no reason why these cultural traits—which may be deeply ingrained and extremely difficult to eradicate— should not be classed as unjust injuries. This being the case, we have discovered another inconsistency in Sowell's argument. The cultural characteristics he blames for holding back blacks he considers to be the result of slavery and its aftermath. The "legacy of slavery," he declares, is "foot-dragging, work avoiding patterns," "duplicity and theft," and a "tragic hostility to menial jobs." Consequently, if it is blacks' culture which holds them back, then blacks deserve compensation for the culture which slavery imposed on them. Yet Sowell affirms the premise and denies the conclusion.

It is admittedly unusual to think of cultural traits as wrongful harms because we think of culture as, in an important sense, self-imposed. This is true of most cultures in the traditional sense of ethnic and national cultures. Such cultures come with built-in philosophical self-justifications. In the sense that participants in them therefore have elaborate resources with which to justify themselves, they may be viewed as self-imposed. Consequently, though such cultures may encourage development of traits which inhibit advancement in modern society, it would be philosophically hazardous to call such traits wrongful harms. At most, they might be considered self-imposed harms. But not all cultures are self-imposed, and certain cultures contain no mechanism of philosophical self-justification and self-definition. Thus, in describing what he calls the "culture of poverty," Oscar Lewis notes that though it is a genuine culture in the traditional anthropological sense, in that it provides human beings with a "design for living," it "does not provide much support . . . poverty of culture is one of the crucial traits of the culture of poverty." Consequently, if we assume that the cultural legacy of slavery is of this nature and is harmful, inasmuch as it tends to block self-development, self-realization, and autonomy, as well as undermine self-respect and self-esteem, it follows that blacks have been wrongfully harmed, and therefore, according to the terms of the backward-looking argument, deserve compensation.

Moreover, there are other grounds on which the claim that blacks constitute a cultural group is not notably advantageous for the critics of preferential treatment. For, if it is true, it confounds the objection of some critics that blacks do not comprise a group in the sense required by the group compensation argument. For example, Goldman objects to treating blacks as a legitimate group eligible for compensatory treatment because they "do not qualify as genuine groups or social organizations in the sense in which sociologists generally use these terms." He goes on to point out that in genuine groups there is "actual interaction among members, each of whom occupies a certain position or plays a certain role in the group reciprocal to other roles, roles being reciprocal when their performances are mutually dependent." But by that very account cultural groups do qualify as genuine groups. There is "actual interaction" among the members of a cultural group. That interaction is, of course, not specifically economic or political. Members of a cultural group do not, for example, necessarily buy from each other or employ each other or rule each other. Still, they do interact and that interaction is just as important as economic or political interaction.

Members of a cultural group share basic values and ideals—that is what we mean by culture—and they interact intellectually by exchanging ideas about these values and ideals; by clarifying, criticizing, and extending them; and by severing and drawing connections between them. In this way they come better to understand themselves. All prosperous and progressive peoples engage in this bustling process of self-clarification. W. E. B. Du Bois thought that it was a condition of progress, and it was the basis of his theory of "the talented tenth." If a group is to progress, he argued, it must pay special attention to the cultural education of its talented tenth. If we make "technical skill the object of education," he observed, "we may possess artisans but not, in nature, men." Other writers, Booker T. Washington particularly, have believed that cultural activity is the reward of progress. In either case, it is obviously a great good. If, then, it is argued that blacks are underrepresented in positions of wealth and prestige because of culturally-induced differences, then they have been wronged as a group, and preferential hiring of qualified blacks is justified as a way of compensating the group. For, it needs no argument to show that the intellectually most active and advanced of a cultural group play a crucial role in the process of self-clarification. If, then, as seems likely, they will be among those qualified, and preferential hiring will give them the opportunity to play this crucial role, then preferential hiring is a way of compensating the group.

. . .

. . . it has seemed to many critics that preferential treatment, insofar as it involves preferential admissions and hiring, is unfair to young white males. For example, according to Robert K. Fullinwider, a research associate at the Center for Philosophy and Public Policy at the University of Maryland, the compensation argument for preferential treatment confuses the sound compensation principle—"he who wrongs another shall pay for the wrong"—with the "suspect" principle—"he who benefits from a wrong shall pay for the wrong." To clinch the point, Fullinwider asks us to consider the following ingenious example: A neighbor pays a construction company to pave his driveway, but someone maliciously directs the workmen to pave Fullinwider's driveway instead. Fullinwider admits that his neighbor has been "wronged and damaged" and that he himself has "benefited from the wrong." However, since he is not responsible for the wrong, he denies that he is "morally required to compensate" his neighbor by "paying" him for it.

This example makes us see that not all cases where compensation may be due are straightforward, though one kind of case clearly is. If John steals Jeff's bicycle and "gives" it to me, however innocent I may be, I have no right to it and must return it to Jeff as soon as I discover the theft. Given that this example is unproblematic, in what way does it differ from Fullinwider's, which is problematic?

One difference is that, whereas I can simply hand over Jeff's bicycle to him, Fullinwider cannot simply hand over the pavement in his driveway. It will be objected that the proposal was not that Fullinwider should hand over the pavement, but that he should pay his neighbor for it. But this is a different case. I did not say that I had a duty to pay Jeff for his bicycle. I said that I had a duty to return the bicycle to Jeff. If Jeff told me to keep the bicycle but pay him for it, I do not admit that I would have a duty to do so. I could object fairly that when I accepted the bicycle I did not believe that I would have to pay for it, and if I had thought that I would have to, I might have not accepted it. Paying for the bicycle now would impose on me, because I might have preferred to spend my money in a different way and, being innocent of any wrongdoing, I see no reason why I should be penalized. The point is that though the beneficiary of an injustice has no right to his advantage, if he is innocent of the injustice, he does not deserve to be penalized. Thus, where compensation is concerned, the obligations of the innocent beneficiary of injustice and of the person responsible for the injustice are quite different. Though the former has no right to his benefits, the process of compensation cannot impose any losses on him over and above the loss of his unfair benefits. If compensation is impossible without such loss, it is unjustified. On the other hand, in the case of the person responsible for injustice, even if compensation requires him to give up more than he has unfairly gained, it is still justified.

But, though Fullinwider's example is cogent as far as it goes, it is irrelevant as an argument against preferential hiring. It is cogent as far as it goes because, as the above analysis shows, requiring young white males to pay women and minorities for all the unfair advantages they have enjoyed would indeed be unfair. The advantages cannot, as in my example of the bicycle, simply be transferred from their hands into those of the preferred group. Compensation of this kind would impose on young white males time and effort over and above the cost of the unfair advantages they are required to return. They could justly protest that they are being penalized, because they might not have accepted the advantages had they known what they would cost them—now they are "out" both the advantages and their time and effort. But preferential hiring does not require young white males to pay, at an additional cost to themselves, the price of their advantages. It proposes instead to compensate the injured with goods no one has yet established a right to and therefore in a way that imposes no unfair losses on anyone. And these goods are, of course, jobs.

It may be objected that, although a white male applicant may not have established a right to this or that job, he has a right to fair competition for it, and preferential hiring violates that right. But, on the contrary, by refusing to allow him to get the job because of an unfair advantage, preferential hiring makes the competition fairer. The white male applicant can still complain, of course, that, had he known that preferential hiring would be instituted, he would not have accepted his advantages in the first place. Since, if he knew that preferential hiring would be instituted, he would necessarily also have known that his advantages were unfair, his complaint would amount to his saying that, had he known his advantages were unfair, he would not have accepted them. But then, if he is concerned with fairness, and if preferential hiring makes the competition fairer, he should have no objections to it. Or to state the proposition somewhat less contentiously, preferential hiring imposes no unfair losses on him.

Thus, a fairer application of Fullinwider's example about the driveway to the case of preferential hiring would be as follows: Suppose an "improve-your-neighborhood group" offered a valuable prize for the best driveway on the block. Would Fullinwider be justified in insisting that he deserves to get the prize over his neighbor who has, at further cost to himself, built another, somewhat inferior driveway?

To sum up my discussion of forms of the backward-looking argument for preferential treatment, while I have insisted that all, or nearly all, blacks are victims of racial injustice, I have conceded that it has handicapped some blacks more than others, and that other kinds of injustice have handicapped some whites more than racial injustice has handicapped blacks. Consequently, although the backward-looking argument is the bedrock of the case for preferential treatment, to complete that case we must look forward.

THE FORWARD-LOOKING ARGUMENT

Whereas the backward-looking argument tried to justify preferential treatment as compensation for past wrongful harms, the forward-looking argument tries to justify preferential treatment on the grounds that it may secure greater equality or increase total social utility. Moreover, the fact that blacks were slaves and the victims of discrimination is irrelevant to the forward-looking argument, which, its proponents imply, would not lose force even if blacks had never been slaves and never [been] discriminated against. All that is relevant to the argument is that blacks are often poor [and] generally less than equal to whites in education, influence, and income, and preferentially treating them will alleviate their poverty, reduce their inequality, and generally increase total utility.

The forward-looking argument has one very clear advantage over the backward-looking argument. As we have seen, a persistent criticism of the backward-looking argument is that, although some blacks deserve no compensation for discrimination because they have not been harmed by discrimination, they are precisely the ones benefiting from preferential treatment. I have tried to rebut this criticism, but this is unnecessary if the forward-looking argument is adopted. For that argument does not require the assumption that the beneficiaries of preferential treatment have been harmed by discrimination, or even that they have been harmed at all. Indeed, it does not require that they be less than equal to whites, and is consistent with their being relatively privileged. For it endorses a strategy of increasing the incomes and education even of blacks superior in those respects to most whites if, however indirectly, this will, in the long run, effectively increase blacks' equality and increase total social utility.

Now whether or not preferential treatment has such consequences is in the end an empirical question, but some critics, as I will show, insist on concocting specious *a priori* arguments to show that preferential treatment necessarily causes a loss in social utility.

Thus it has been argued that since, by definition, preferential treatment awards positions to the less qualified over the more qualified, and since the more qualified perform more efficiently than the less qualified, therefore preferential treatment causes a loss of utility. But suppose that less qualified blacks are admitted to medical school in preference to more qualified whites, and suppose the resulting black doctors practice in poor black neighborhoods treating serious illnesses, while if the whites they were preferred to had been admitted they would have practiced in affluent white neighborhoods, treating minor illnesses. In that sort of case, it is not at all necessarily true that preferential treatment causes a loss in utility. Some authors try to avoid the force of this argument by switching the basis of their criticism from the fact that preferential treatment may reward the less qualified to the false assertion that preferential treatment may reward the "unqualified." Thus, Goldman reminds us that "all will suffer when unqualified persons occupy many positions." This is criticism of a straw man.

It has also been claimed that the forward-looking argument that preferential treatment increases utility is open to a serious philosophical objection. Thus philosopher George Sher writes that the utilitarian, or forward-looking, defense of preferential treatment is "vulnerable" to the "simple but serious" objection that "if it is acceptable to discriminate in favor of minorities and women when doing so maximizes utility then it is hard to see why it should not also be acceptable to discriminate against minorities and women when that policy maximizes welfare." And against Thomas Nagel, who argues that racial discrimination, unlike reverse discrimination, "has no social advantages . . . and attaches a sense of reduced worth to a feature with which people are born," Sher makes a similar objection. He says that Nagel gives us no reason to believe that "there could never be alternative circumstances in which racial, ethnic, or sexual discrimination had social advantages which did outweigh the sense of reduced worth it produced," and maintains that Nagel still has not shown us that such discrimination is illegitimate under "any circumstances at all."

The serious utilitarian is likely to dismiss Sher's criticisms with the same impatience with which he dismisses the stock criticism that utilitarianism allows slavery. As R. M. Hare notes, it is the "strength" of the utilitarian doctrine that "the utilitarian cannot reason a priori that whatever the facts about the world and human nature, slavery is wrong. He has to show it is wrong by showing, through a study of history and other factual observation, that slavery does have the effects (namely the production of misery) that make it wrong." In particular, he is not undone by the arguments of the intuitionist who thinks up "fantastic" examples which show slavery to be right according to the principles of utilitarianism, because these show only that the intuitionist has "lost contact with the actual world." Much the same thing can be said about Sher's notion that there are circumstances in which racial discrimination would be legitimate according to utilitarian principles.

. . .

Sher also attacks the argument that preferential treatment is justified because it conduces to equality. He allows that preferential treatment may reduce inequality between the races but points out that it does not reduce inequalities between individuals. "To practice reverse discrimination," he says, is ". . . merely to rearrange the inequalities of distribution which now prevail." "What the defender [of reverse discrimination] needs to show," Sher declares, "is that it is consistent to denounce whichever inequalities follow racial, ethnic or sexual lines, while at the same time not denouncing those other inequalities which reverse discrimination inevitably perpetuates."

There is a well-recognized ambiguity in the term "equality" that it is relevant to consider here. "Equality" may mean equality of opportunity, or equality of result, or equality of wealth. By his championship of direct redistribution of wealth, Sher assumes that the notion of equality advanced by the forward-looking argument is equality of wealth. In this way he saves himself the trouble of considering the argument for reverse discrimination that maintains that, although it sins against a present equality of opportunity, [it] promotes a future equality of opportunity by providing blacks with their own successful "role models."

Sher's critique is made even weaker by the fact that he concedes to Nagel his point that racial inequalities are especially wrong because they are apt to "lead to further inequalities of self-respect." He thinks he can safely concede this because even if he does the egalitarian defense of reverse discrimination fails decisively. "At best," he writes, this concession allows only that racial "inequalities would have first claim on our attention if we were forced to choose among inequalities—which as we have seen, there is no reason to think we are. It does not show, and no further argument *could* show, that any consistent egalitarian could ignore the import of the other inequalities altogether."

But on what grounds has Sher managed to conclude that the advocates of reverse discrimination, presumably consistent egalitarians, "ignore the import of the other inequalities altogether"? By what bizarre train of reasoning does it follow from the fact that the advocate of reverse discrimination thinks racial inequalities particularly harmful, that he must therefore "ignore the import of the other inequalities altogether"? And granting that other inequalities have a claim on our attention, how does it follow, as Sher says, that a policy of reverse discrimination is "dubious"? Even if, *contra* our assumption, racial inequalities are *not* more harmful than others, since we are *not* forced to choose among inequalities, why can't we attack all inequalities at once, racial inequalities through reverse discrimination, and other inequalities through other policies?

The only argument against this would be that the other policies might make reverse discrimination superfluous. But there are obvious weaknesses in it. Stigmas are not likely to be erased just because *incomes* are equalized. Apart from the extraordinary difficulties of equalizing incomes in a capitalist context—if this is possible at all—stigmas are likely to remain attached to members of groups because of the menial work many of them do, however equal their incomes. Preferential treatment is aimed at removing such stigmas.

. . . I have used more space in rebutting criticisms than in arguing positively for conclusions. This is because the main arguments for affirmative action are straightforward, and yet philosophers persist in concocting ever more desperately ingenious objections to it. Not that I believe that any one of the various backward- and forward-looking arguments is by itself sufficient to justify affirmative action. Affirmative action is justified by the combined force of these arguments and by the way they complement and support each other. The weaknesses in some are made up [for] by the strengths of others. For example, the weakness in the case for compensation on an individual basis is made up for by the case for compensation on a group basis, and the weaknesses of both these cases are strengthened by considerations stemming from the forward-looking argument. A society which tries to be just tries to compensate the victims of its injustice, and when these victims are easily identified, either as individuals or as a group less than equal to others, the case for treating them preferentially is overwhelming.

DISCUSSION QUESTIONS

1. What is Boxill's forward-looking argument for affirmative action? How does it avoid the objections raised against forward-looking arguments for affirmative action? Does it successfully avoid them? Discuss.
2. What is Boxill's backward-looking argument for affirmative action? How does it avoid the objections raised against backward-looking arguments for affirmative action? Does it successfully avoid them? Discuss.
3. Do you agree with Boxill's argument that Blacks have been harmed by discrimination? Do you agree with him that Blacks deserve compensation for the harm that has been done to them by discrimination? Explain your view.
4. Some say that the social and economic position of Blacks is due more to culture than to discrimination. What do they mean by this? How does Boxill respond to this argument? How do you respond to it?

 LINO A. GRAGLIA

Affirmative Discrimination

Lino A. Graglia argues against affirmative action and quotas. He rejects both the "disadvantage/remedy" and the "diversity" arguments for affirmative action. The disadvantage/remedy argument, that "racial preferences can be justified as compensation for past unfair disadvantages, is obviously invalid," says Graglia, "because preferences truly meant to compensate for disadvantage would be applied on the basis of disadvantage, not on the basis of race." Graglia continues, "Persons who have been unfairly disadvantaged should undoubtedly be made whole to the extent feasible, but race is neither an accurate nor an appropriate proxy for such disadvantage." The diversity argument for affirmative action is flawed, he says, because, "just as the remedy argument uses race as a proxy for disadvantage, the diversity argument uses race as a proxy for unusual characteristics. . . . 'Affirmative action' enforcers do not check schools for diversity of views or experience in the student body; they check only for the presence of blacks." For Graglia, the terms "affirmative action" and "diversity" are simply buzzwords for "racial discrimination."

Lino A. Graglia is a professor of law at the University of Texas at Austin. He is the author of numerous articles on the law and *Disaster by Decree: The Supreme Court Decisions on Race and the Schools* (1976).

The *Brown* decision in 1954, and a companion case, *Bolling v. Sharpe,* prohibited legally required racial segregation in schools and, it quickly appeared, in any government-run facility—e.g., public beaches and bath-houses, municipal golf courses, city buses. The power and appeal of the *Brown* non-discrimination principle proved irresistible and led to the greatest civil-rights advance in our history,

Lino A. Graglia, *National Review* (5 July 1993): 26–31. Reprinted by permission of the author.

the enactment of the 1964 Civil Rights Act, soon supplemented by the 1965 Voting Rights Act and the 1968 Fair Housing Act. Racial discrimination was at last effectively prohibited.

It is not to be expected, however, that so great a moral crusade would be permitted to come to an end merely because its objective had been accomplished. On the contrary, total success more easily serves as a spur to still greater accomplishments.

Racial discrimination had been prohibited and largely ended, but equality of condition between blacks and whites obviously would not quickly be the result. The time had therefore come to move to equality of condition by fiat. The crucial move was made by the Supreme Court in *Green v. County School Board* in 1968, in which the Court changed the *Brown* prohibition of segregation and all racial discrimination by government into a requirement of integration and racial discrimination by government.

It was not politically feasible in 1968 for the Court candidly to state its new position. The Court avoided this by insisting that although assignment to schools by race was indeed now required, it was not required for its own sake, but only as a "remedy" for past unconstitutional segregation. As Justice Blackmun wrote, concurring in the *Bakke* case ten years later, "In order to get beyond racism, we must first take race into account. There is no other way." . . .

The term "affirmative action" had perhaps first been used in Executive Order 10925, issued by the Kennedy Administration in March 1961, directed at eliminating racial discrimination by government contractors. It originally meant the taking of positive steps—for example, the widespread advertising of job openings—to equalize opportunity. But with the passing of time its meaning changed. . . .

Title VI prohibits racial discrimination by institutions that receive federal funds. Yet in 1978, in *Regents of the University of California v. Bakke,* the Court held that Title VI also did not apply to discrimination against whites. There was no evidence in any of the cases that the preferred blacks had been discriminated against by the employer or educational institution or that the rejected whites had caused or benefited from any such discrimination. Despite the remedy rationale, the absence of a showing of actual racial injury and racial benefit was simply irrelevant.

GROUP BENEFITS, GROUP COSTS

The basis of the rationale is the assumption that members of all racial groups can be expected to ap-

pear in all institutions and activities more or less proportionately to their numbers in the general population. The "underrepresentation" of any racial group, it is therefore argued, can be taken as evidence of discrimination. The argument necessarily invites a search for alternative explanations, and alternative explanations are not difficult to find.

The fact is that there is a very large, long-standing, and apparently unyielding difference between blacks as a group and whites as a group—despite, of course, large areas of overlap—in academic ability as measured by standard aptitude and achievement tests, such as the Scholastic Aptitude Test (SAT), Law School Admissions Test (LSAT), Medical College Admission Test (MCAT), and Graduate Record Examination, Quantitative (GREQ). Robert Klitgaard, a former admissions officer at Harvard, reports that of those who took the GREQ in the 1978–79 school year, only 143 blacks had scores above 650, compared to 27,470 whites, and only 50 blacks had scores above 700, compared to 14,450 whites. Among law-school entrants in the fall of 1976, the total number of blacks with LSAT scores above 600 (old scale) and an undergraduate Grade Point Average (GPA) above 3.25 (B+) was 39; the number of whites with such scores was 13,151.

Any messenger who brings news this bad will, of course, have to be attacked. In the early days of "affirmative action" (the late 1960s and early 1970s) a principal claim of its proponents was that the standard tests were biased against members of racial minorities. If this were true, then the admission of members of such groups with lower scores than are required for whites would not constitute the use of racial preferences but merely an attempt to make prediction more accurate; no "affirmative action" is involved in adjusting measuring devices to measure more accurately.

The claim, however, is not true. By test bias is meant, presumably, that the test generally underpredicts the actual performance of members of some group. There is now general agreement that the ability and achievement tests are not biased by this standard. Indeed, investigations have shown that the tests very substantially *overpredict* the actual performance of blacks.

Even leaving overprediction out of account, the number of blacks meeting the ordinary admission criteria for even moderately selective institutions is extremely low. Most elite schools of all types, however, now strive to obtain an entering class that is at least 5 percent black. To obtain this percentage requires, not that blacks be preferred to whites when all other things are more or less equal—a common understanding of "affirmative action"—or even that the ordinary admission standards be bent or shaded; it requires that ordinary standards be largely abandoned.

A frequently noted effect is virtually to guarantee that the preferentially admitted students are placed in schools for which they are greatly underqualified. It is as if professional baseball decided to "advantage" an identifiable group of players at the beginning of their professional careers by placing them in a league at least one level above the one in which they could be expected to compete effectively.

EQUALITY BY STEALTH

The admission of an identifiable group of greatly underqualified students is a prescription for frustration, resentment, loss of self-esteem, and racial animosity. Forces powerful enough to institute so radical and unpromising a program will, however, be powerful enough to respond to its disastrous consequences with something other than a confession that they have made a terrible mistake. If the racially admitted prove unable to do the work, that will indicate that the curriculum has to be changed. If racial preferences generate racial resentments, that will indicate that whites require specialized instruction in the moral shortcomings of their race. If "affirmative action" is then even more strongly protested, that will indicate that protest must be disallowed.

Thus are born demands for black studies and multiculturalism, which perform the twin functions of reducing the need for ordinary academic work and providing support for the view that the academic difficulties of the black students are the result, not of substantially lower qualifications, but of racial antipathy.

And thus the current insistence on "political correctness," sanctioned by ostracism, vilification, or worse, and the suddenly discovered need for "anti-harassment" and "hate speech" codes. Nothing is more politically incorrect than to point out that a school's "affirmative action" policy is actually a policy of racially preferential admissions, unless it is to specify the actual disparity in the admissions standards being applied to persons from different racial groups. Proponents of anti-harassment codes are correct that it is extremely humiliating to racially preferred students to have a public discussion of the school's admission policy. Instead of concluding that the policy is, for this reason alone, very unlikely to prove beneficial, they conclude that such discussions must be banned.

"Affirmative action" is a fungus that can survive only underground in the dark. If "affirmative action" is a morally defensible policy, why are its proponents loath to have it known just how moral they have been? Because, of course, no one wants it known that he is, as black Yale law professor Stephen Carter puts it, "an affirmative action baby." Or as Thomas Sowell puts it: "What all the arguments and campaigns for quotas are really saying, loud and clear, is that *black people just don't have it,* and that they will have to be given something in order to have something. . . . Those black people who are already competent . . . will be completely undermined, as black becomes synonymous—in the minds of black and white alike—with incompetence, and black achievement becomes synonymous with charity or payoffs."

A recent typically ludicrous illustration of the deceit inherent in "affirmative action" was proved when Georgetown law student Timothy Maguire disclosed in a student newspaper his discovery that his black classmates were admitted with much lower LSAT scores and GPAs than those required of whites. The result was outraged protest by the black students and indignant disavowal, in effect, of "affirmative action" by those who were most responsible for its adoption. Although known as an ardent proponent of racially preferential admissions, Dean Judith Areen flatly denied that any racially preferential admissions took place at the school she led. Those who mistakenly thought otherwise failed to understand that many factors—e.g., a required essay—are considered in determining admission.

We are to understand, apparently, that there is an inverse correlation between high LSAT scores and GPAs [and] an ability to write an essay on why one wants to be a law student at Georgetown. This peculiarity also manifests itself disproportionately in the case of black applicants. This explanation made sense to the editorial writers of the *New York Times,* who repeated it in an editorial severely chastising Maguire for his "obsession with numbers" and total misunderstanding of the Georgetown admission process.

The American Association of Law Schools (AALS), the Law School Admission Council, and the American Bar Association (ABA), Section of Legal Education and Admission to the Bar, felt called upon to comment on the Georgetown incident. Like Dean Areen, the highest officials of the legal-education establishment asserted that the critics failed to understand the complexities of the law-school admission process. "Besides the LSAT and undergraduate GPA," a joint press release explained, "several other considerations are taken into account." These considerations include "personal statements from applicants, letters of recommendation, work experience, and the applicant's prior success in overcoming personal disadvantage." The list included no mention of race. Small wonder that innocent newspapers like the *New York Times* are bewildered as to how strange notions about the use of racial preferences in law-school admissions could possibly have arisen.

To law schools, however, the press release did more than provide a demonstration of lawyerly skill and example of lawyerly integrity. The AALS and ABA are accrediting institutions. Their stated accreditation standards make clear—and their visiting accreditation committees, usually nicely balanced by race and sex, make even clearer—that a substantial number of black students is an accreditation consideration.

DISADVANTAGE AND DIVERSITY

The various arguments offered for "affirmative action" have grown almost too threadbare with use to require further refutation. By far the most important, that racial preferences can be justified as compensation for past unfair disadvantages, is obviously invalid, because preferences truly meant to compensate for disadvantage would be applied on the basis of disadvantage, not on the basis of race. Persons who have been unfairly disadvantaged should undoubtedly be made whole to the extent feasible, but race is neither an accurate nor an appropriate proxy for such disadvantage. It is inaccurate because not all and only blacks have suffered from disadvantage. Indeed, racially preferential admissions to institutions of higher education ordinarily help, not those most in need of help, but middle-class and upper-middle-class blacks. The argument from disadvantage has potency only because, as Glenn Loury has put it, "The suffering of the poorest blacks creates, if you will, a fund of political capital upon which all members of the group can draw when pressing racially based claims."

Racially preferential admission is also an inappropriate means of compensation for several reasons. First, our historical assimilationist national policy has been to insist upon the general irrelevancy of one's membership in a particular racial group as a basis for government action. Second, lack of qualification for a course study can be rationally addressed only by taking steps to remove the lack, not by overlooking it and proceeding as if it did not exist. Finally, it is plainly unjust that the cost of racially preferential admissions should be largely borne by the particular individuals whom the racially preferred replace, even though they bear no particular responsibility for the disadvantage for which compensation is supposedly being made.

The newest buzzword for racial discrimination—which after more than two decades of official sanction still may not speak its proper name—is "diversity," a word that is largely replacing the term "affirmative action" (as it becomes less a euphemism than a pejorative) and providing an alternative to the remedy rationale. Just as the remedy argument uses race as a proxy for disadvantage, the diversity argument uses race as a proxy for unusual characteristics. But just as disadvantage, not race, would be the criterion if the objective were compensation, so unusual characteristics or experiences would be the criterion if the objective were educational diversity. In practice, the blacks who are preferentially admitted are frequently the children of teachers or other professionals and have a social, economic, and educational background virtually indistinguishable from that of the average middle-class white applicant. "Affirmative action" enforcers do not check schools for diversity of views or experience in the student body; they check only for the presence of blacks and—to a much lesser extent—members of other preferred groups.

The diversity argument was made popular by Justice Powell's opinion in the *Bakke* case, the Court's first decision upholding explicit discrimination against whites. Justice Powell was an inveterate seeker of the middle way, which usually meant, as in *Bakke,* evading the problem by attempting to have it both ways. For example, he found the use of racial quotas unconstitutional because it violates an excluded applicant's "right to individual consideration without regard to his race" and "involves the use of an explicit racial classification." He then, however, approved of the use of an applicant's ("minority") race as a "plus factor," even though it violates the same right and uses the same classification. Expressing views that were his alone, Powell announced that discrimination against whites is every bit as constitutionally disfavored as discrimination against blacks, to be subjected to the strictest judicial scrutiny and permitted only when found to serve a "compelling interest" that could not be served in any other way. He then held that discrimination against whites in admission to medical school is constitutionally permissible nonetheless, because it serves the school's interest—protected by the First Amendment, he said—in a student body with a diversity of views. Powell's attempt to find a middle way between protecting and not protecting whites equally with blacks failed, but it made "diversity" a term of art and rallying cry in the fight for racially preferential admissions.

PERVERSE INCENTIVES

Among the defects serious enough to be disqualifying of both the remedy and the diversity rationales is that they create perverse and destructive incentives. The remedy rationale requires insistence, not only upon America's racist past, but, even more important, upon the assumption that racism continues largely unabated, although, perhaps, in more subtle and less overt forms. If blacks disproportionately fail to obtain desirable positions because of a lack of the usual qualifications, then the appropriate remedy, even if the lack is due to past racial discrimination, is to attempt to upgrade their qualifications. If the failure is due to present discrimination, however, the only corrective may be racial preferences and quotas.

Proponents of "affirmative action" must, therefore, continually assert that white Americans are implacably opposed to black advance. Professor Derrick Bell of the Harvard Law School claims, for example, that if a magic pill were discovered to make blacks exceptionally law-abiding, whites would destroy it to prevent that from happening. Black crime, he tells us, is actually in the interest of whites because much of the country's economic activity—for example, the production of prison uniforms—is dependent upon it.

In fact, there is every indication that most whites are intensely interested in black progress and derive an extra measure of satisfaction from every example of black success. Basketball games and boxing matches seem only to have gained in appeal and marketability as they became increasingly dominated by blacks. The highest incomes in the entertainment industry in recent years have been earned by blacks. The only noticeable expressions of discontent with the fact that Colin Powell is the nation's highest [-ranking] national security officer have been by black proponents of "affirmative action."

The corollary to insistence that whites are opposed to black advance is the essential futility of hopes for progress by blacks through their own efforts. But the notion that academic success and hard work are pointless for blacks is debilitating, almost certainly the last message that it is in their interest to hear.

As the remedy rationale requires insistence on pervasive white racism, the diversity rationale requires insistence on the existence of important racial differences. Preference for blacks will not produce any significant benefits of diversity unless there are in fact important differences between blacks and whites, and unless the preferred blacks can be relied upon to manifest them. It is thus in the interest of blacks in general—and perhaps, indeed, the duty of the preferred black in particular—to "act black" as much as possible. In the school context this usually means, unfortunately, displaying an exceptional sensitivity to possible racial slights and an ability to see malignant racism as the explanation of most historical events and social phenomena.

OTHER AGENDAS

The drive for "affirmative action" is a phenomenon in need of further and more candid explanation than it has so far received. How can adoption of a policy that is virtually a formula for escalating racial consciousness and tension be thought a desirable course of action?

A more plausible explanation for at least some of the demand for "affirmative action" is that it supports an extensive "civil rights" bureaucracy that grew up in the long fight to end racial discrimination and that is now prospering and expanding in the movement to reinstate it. Every college and school, if not every department, must now have an "affirmative action" officer and specialists in racial- and ethnic-group liaison. The more racial tension increases on campus and generally, the greater will be the need for their services.

Further, it remains true that a large proportion of blacks live in the desperate social conditions of an "underclass." It is argued by many that improvement of these conditions requires that the issue of race not be permitted to recede from public attention. "Affirmative action" serves to keep the issue very much alive.

Racial issues seem also to be for some people part of a larger agenda. There are, particularly in our colleges and universities, earnest seekers for a more just and equal society who find themselves thoroughly alienated from their present society and its institutions. The worldwide waning of the appeal of socialism has reduced the potential of economic class differences as the basis of hope for "fundamental social change." Race and sex differences are the most likely substitutes. The pursuit of perfect economic equality, it has turned out, may not be such a good idea, but surely no one today can be so insensitive to the demands of justice as to oppose equality in terms of race and sex. Proponents of any proposal advanced in the name of increasing such equality will enjoy a huge advantage over opponents.

The most important basis for the continuing support of "affirmative action" is indicated perhaps by the arguments made for it by a law professor at a major public university in two debates held about ten years apart. In the first debate, ten or twelve years ago, he supported "affirmative action" with a long list of the then standard arguments: biased tests, compensation, role models, services to deprived groups, and so on. His enthusiasm for "affirmative action" because of the many good effects he expected it to have seemed unbounded. Indeed, "affirmative action" was working so well at his school that the school decided to drop Japanese-Americans as a specially preferred group because substantial numbers of Japanese-American applicants had been found to meet the ordinary standards. He confidently foresaw the day when the same would be true, first of Mexican-Americans and then of blacks.

In another debate about two years ago, this professor's enthusiasm was gone and his argument much changed. He still supported "affirmative action," but his reasons had been reduced to a single one: "We simply must have blacks in this institution." The problem is undoubtedly a severe one: if a stable multiracial society requires that all racial groups be more or less proportionately represented in all important institutions and activities, it requires what no multiracial society has ever achieved.

A more promising approach to social stability, surely, is to maintain a system of law, government, and public policy that uniformly insists on the total irrelevance, at least for official or public purposes, of claimed membership in any particular racial group. It may be naïve idealism to believe that racial peace can be achieved through official inculcation of the view that racial distinctions are odious and pointless, but it is at least an ideal worth pursuing. We can be certain, on the other hand, that racial peace will not be found through policies that enhance racial consciousness, presume the existence of widespread and near-ineradicable racial animosity, and insist that racial distinctions are of central importance.

DISCUSSION QUESTIONS

1. Why does Graglia always place "affirmative action" within quotation marks?
2. Why does Graglia believe that affirmative action is a "fungus that can survive only underground in the dark"? Do you agree with him? Why or why not?
3. Graglia rejects the diversity argument for affirmative action. What is his argument, and how might you respond to it?
4. Why does Graglia believe that racial preferences cannot be justified as compensation for past unfair disadvantages? Critique his argument.
5. Graglia says that "diversity" is the "newest buzzword for racial discrimination." Critically evaluate his argument.
6. Graglia says that admitting "an identifiable group of greatly underqualified students" into a college or university "is a prescription for frustration, resentment, loss of self-esteem, and racial animosity." Do you agree with his argument? Discuss.
7. What do you think "merit" really means?

Class, Not Race

Richard Kahlenberg argues in favor of affirmative action based on class, not race. He points out that for many years the political left argued that class was more important than race and that confusing race and class "was not only seen as wrong but as dangerous." Today, however, "both liberals and conservatives conflate race and class because it serves both of their purposes to do so." Conservatives see gaps between Whites and Blacks in SAT scores as "evidence of intractable racial differences," whereas liberals view these figures as indicating the need to do more about racism in America. "We rarely," says Kahlenberg, "see a breakdown of scores by class, which would show enormous gaps between rich and poor, gaps that would help explain the differences in scores by race." Kahlenberg argues that class-based affirmative action public policies would find more public support and would be more administrable than race-based affirmative action public policies. Therefore, proponents of affirmative action policy should turn their attention toward class-based criteria and away from race-based criteria.

Richard D. Kahlenberg is a senior fellow at the Century Foundation (formerly the Twentieth Century Fund), where he writes about education, equal opportunity, and civil rights. Previously, Kahlenberg was a fellow at the Center for National Policy, a visiting associate professor of constitutional law at George Washington University, and a legislative assistant to Senator Charles S. Robb (D-VA). His publications include *Broken Contract: A Memoir of Harvard Law School* (1992), *The Remedy: Class, Race, and Affirmative Action* (1996), and *All Together Now: Creating Middle Class Schools Through Public School Choice* (2000).

For many years, the left argued not only that class was important, but also that it was more important than race. This argument was practical, ideological and politic. An emphasis on class inequality meant Robert Kennedy riding in a motorcade through cheering white and black sections of racially torn Gary, Indiana, in 1968, with black Mayor Richard Hatcher on one side, and white working-class boxing hero Tony Zale on the other.

Ideologically, it was clear that with the passage of the Civil Rights Act of 1964, class replaced caste as the central impediment to equal opportunity. Martin Luther King Jr. moved from the Montgomery Boycott to the Poor People's Campaign, which he described as "his last, greatest dream," and "something bigger than just a civil rights movement for Negroes." RFK told David Halberstam that "it was pointless to talk about the real problem in America being black and white, it was really rich and poor, which was a much more complex subject."

Finally, the left emphasized class because to confuse class and race was seen not only as wrong but as dangerous. This notion was at the heart of the protest over Daniel Patrick Moynihan's 1965 report, *The Negro Family: The Case for National Action*, in which Moynihan depicted the rising rates of illegitimacy among poor blacks. While Moynihan's critics were wrong to silence discussion of illegitimacy among blacks, they rightly noted that the title of the report, which implicated all blacks, was misleading, and that fairly high rates of illegitimacy also were present among poor whites—a point which Moynihan readily endorses today. (In the wake of the second set of L.A. riots in 1992, Moynihan rose on the Senate floor to reaffirm that family structure "is not an issue of race but of class. . . . It is class behavior.")

Richard D. Kahlenberg, *New Republic* 3 (April 1995): 24–26. Reprinted by permission of the publisher.

The irony is that affirmative action based on race violates these three liberal insights. It provides the ultimate wedge to destroy Robert Kennedy's coalition. It says that despite civil rights protections, the wealthiest African American is more deserving of preference than the poorest white. It relentlessly focuses all attention on race.

In contrast, Lyndon Johnson's June 1965 address to Howard University, in which the concept of affirmative action was first unveiled, did not ignore class. In a speech drafted by Moynihan, Johnson spoke of the bifurcation of the black community, and, in his celebrated metaphor, said we needed to aid those "hobbled" in life's race by past discrimination. This suggested special help for disadvantaged blacks, not all blacks; for the young Clarence Thomas, but not for Clarence Thomas's son. Johnson balked at implementing the thematic language of his speech. His Executive Order 11246, calling for "affirmative action" among federal contractors, initially meant greater outreach and required hiring without respect to race. In fact, LBJ rescinded his Labor Department's proposal to provide for racial quotas in the construction industry in Philadelphia. It fell to Richard Nixon to implement the "Philadelphia Plan," in what Nixon's aides say was a conscious effort to drive a wedge between blacks and labor. (Once he placed racial preferences on the table, Nixon adroitly extricated himself, and by 1972 was campaigning against racial quotas.)

The ironies were compounded by the Supreme Court. In the 1974 case, *DeFunis v. Odegaard,* in which a system of racial preferences in law school admissions was at issue, it was the Court's liberal giant, William O. Douglas, who argued that racial preferences were unconstitutional, and suggested instead that preferences be based on disadvantage. Four years later, in the *Bakke* case, the great proponent of affirmative action as a means to achieve "diversity" was Nixon appointee Lewis F. Powell Jr. Somewhere along the line, the right wing embraced Douglas and Critical Race Theory embraced Powell.

Today, the left pushes racial preferences, even for the most advantaged minorities, in order to promote diversity and provide role models for disadvantaged blacks—an argument which, if it came from Ronald Reagan, the left would rightly dismiss as trickle-down social theory. Today, when William Julius Wilson argues the opposite of the Moynihan report—that the problems facing the black community are rooted more in class than race—it is Wilson who is excoriated by civil rights groups. The

left can barely utter the word "class," instead resorting to euphemisms such as "income groups," "wage earners," and "people who play by the rules."

For all of this, the left has paid a tremendous price. On a political level, with a few notable exceptions, the history of the past twenty-five years is a history of white, working-class Robert Kennedy Democrats turning first into Wallace Democrats, then into Nixon and Reagan Democrats and ultimately into today's Angry White Males. Time and again, the white working class votes its race rather than its class, and Republicans win. The failure of the left to embrace class also helps turn poor blacks, for whom racial preferences are, in Stephen Carter's words, "stunningly irrelevant," toward Louis Farrakhan.

On the merits, the left has committed itself to a goal—equality of group results—which seems highly radical, when it is in fact rather unambitious. To the extent that affirmative action, at its ultimate moment of success, merely creates a self-perpetuating black elite along with a white one, its goal is modest—certainly more conservative than real equality of opportunity, which gives blacks and whites and other Americans of all economic strata a fair chance at success.

The priority given to race over class has inevitably exacerbated white racism. Today, both liberals and conservatives conflate race and class because it serves both of their purposes to do so. Every year, when SAT scores are released, the breakdown by race shows enormous gaps between blacks on the one hand and whites and Asians on the other. The NAACP cites these figures as evidence that we need to do more. Charles Murray cites the same statistics as evidence of intractable racial differences. We rarely see a breakdown of scores by class, which would show enormous gaps between rich and poor, gaps that would help explain the differences in scores by race.

On the legal front, it once made some strategic sense to emphasize race over class. But when states moved to the remedial phase—and began trying to address past discrimination—the racial focus became a liability. The strict scrutiny that struck down Jim Crow is now used, to varying degrees, to curtail racial preferences. Class, on the other hand, is not one of the suspect categories under the Fourteenth Amendment, which leaves class-based remedies much less assailable.

If class-based affirmative action is a theory that liberals should take seriously, how would it work in practice? . . . Michael Kinsley has asked, "Does Clarence

Thomas, the sharecropper's kid, get more or fewer preference points than the unemployed miner's son from Appalachia?" Most conservative proponents of class-based affirmative action have failed to explain their idea with any degree of specificity. Either they're insincere—offering the alternative only for tactical reasons—or they're stumped.

The former is more likely. While the questions of implementation are serious and difficult, they are not impossible to answer. At the university level, admissions committees deal every day with precisely the type of apples-and-oranges question that Kinsley poses. Should a law school admit an applicant with a 3.2 GPA from Yale or a 3.3 from Georgetown? How do you compare those two if one applicant worked for the Peace Corps but the other had slightly higher LSATs?

In fact, a number of universities already give preferences for disadvantaged students in addition to racial minorities. Since 1989 Berkeley has granted special consideration to applicants "from socioeconomically disadvantaged backgrounds . . . regardless of race or ethnicity." Temple University Law School has, since the 1970s, given preference to "applicants who have overcome exceptional and continuous economic deprivation." And at Hastings College of Law, 20 percent of the class is set aside for disadvantaged students through the Legal Equal Opportunity Program. Even the U.C.-Davis medical program challenged by Allan Bakke was limited to "disadvantaged" minorities, a system which Davis apparently did not find impossible to administer.

Similar class-based preference programs could be provided by public employers and federal contractors for high school graduates not pursuing college, on the theory that at that age their class-based handicaps hide their true potential and are not at all of their own making. In public contracting, government agencies could follow the model of New York City's old class-based program, which provided preferences based not on the ethnicity or gender of the contractor, but to small firms located in New York City which did part of their business in depressed areas or employed economically disadvantaged workers.

The definition of class or disadvantage may vary according to context, but if, for example, the government chose to require class-based affirmative action from universities receiving federal funds, it is possible to devise an enforceable set of objective standards for deprivation. If the aim of class-based affirmative action is to provide a system of genuine equality of opportunity, a leg up to promising students who have done well despite the odds, we have a wealth of sociological data to devise an obstacles test. While some might balk at the very idea of reducing disadvantage to a number, we currently reduce intellectual promise to numbers—SATs and GPAs—and adding a number for disadvantage into the calculus just makes deciding who gets ahead and who does not a little fairer.

There are three basic ways to proceed: with a simple, moderate or complex definition. The simple method is to ask college applicants their family's income and measure disadvantage by that factor alone, on the theory that income is a good proxy for a whole host of economic disadvantages (such as bad schools or a difficult learning environment). This oversimplified approach is essentially the tack we've taken with respect to compensatory race-based affirmative action. For example, most affirmative action programs ask applicants to check a racial box and sweep all the ambiguities under the rug. Even though African Americans have, as Justice Thurgood Marshall said in *Bakke,* suffered a history "different in kind, not just degree, from that of other ethnic groups," universities don't calibrate preferences based on comparative group disadvantage (and, in the Davis system challenged by Bakke, two-thirds of the preferences went to Mexican-Americans and Asians, not blacks). We also ignore the question of when an individual's family immigrated in order to determine whether the family was even theoretically subject to the official discrimination in this country on which preferences are predicated.

"Diversity" was supposed to solve all this by saying we don't care about compensation, only viewpoint. But, again, if universities are genuinely seeking diversity of viewpoints, they should inquire whether a minority applicant really does have the "minority viewpoint" being sought. Derrick Bell's famous statement—"the ends of diversity are not served by people who look black and think white"—is at once repellent and a relevant critique of the assumption that all minority members think alike. In theory, we need some assurance from the applicant that he or she will in fact interact with students of different backgrounds, lest the cosmetic diversity of the freshman yearbook be lost to the reality of ethnic theme houses.

The second way to proceed, the moderately complicated calculus of class, would look at what sociologists believe to be the Big Three determinants of life chances: parental income, education and occupation. Parents' education, which is highly correlated with a child's academic achievement, can be measured in number of years. And while ranking occupations might seem hopelessly complex, various attempts to do so objectively have yielded remarkable consistent results—from the Barr Scale of the early 1920s to Alba Edwards' Census rankings of the 1940s to the Duncan Scores of the 1960s.

The third alternative, the complex calculus of disadvantage, would count all the factors mentioned, but might also look at net worth, the quality of secondary education, neighborhood influences and family structure. An applicant's family wealth is readily available from financial aid forms, and provides a long-term view of relative disadvantage, to supplement the "snapshot" picture that income provides. We also know that schooling opportunities are crucial to a student's life chances, even controlling for home environment. Some data suggest that a disadvantaged student at a middle-class school does better on average than a middle-class student at a school with high concentrations of poverty. Objective figures are available to measure secondary school quality—from per student expenditure, to the percentage of students receiving free or reduced-price lunches, to a school's median score on standardized achievement tests. Neighborhood influences, measured by the concentration of poverty within Census tracts or zip codes, could also be factored in, since numerous studies have found that living in a low-income community can adversely affect an individual's life chances above and beyond family income. Finally, everyone from Dan Quayle to Donna Shalala agrees that children growing up in single-parent homes have a tougher time. This factor could be taken into account as well.

The point is not that this list is the perfect one, but that it *is* possible to devise a series of fairly objective and verifiable factors that measure the degree to which a teenager's true potential has been hidden. (As it happens, the complex definition is the one that disproportionately benefits African Americans. Even among similar income groups, blacks are more likely than whites to live in concentrated poverty, go to bad schools and live in single-parent homes.) It's just not true that a system of class preferences is inherently harder to administer than a system based on race. Race only seems simpler because we have ignored the ambiguities. And racial preferences are just as easy to ridicule. To paraphrase Kinsley, does a new Indian immigrant get fewer or more points than a third-generation Latino whose mother is Anglo?

Who should benefit? Mickey Kaus, in "Class Is In," . . . argued that class preferences should be reserved for the underclass. But the injuries of class extend beyond the poorest. The offspring of the working poor and the working class lack advantages, too, and indeed SAT scores correlate lockstep with income at every increment. Unless you believe in genetic inferiority, these statistics suggest unfairness is not confined to the underclass. As a practical matter, a teenager who emerges from the underclass has little chance of surviving at an elite college. At Berkeley, administrators found that using a definition of disadvantaged, under which neither parent attended a four-year college and the family could not afford to pay $1,000 in education expenses, failed to bring in enough students who were likely to pass.

Still, there are several serious objections to class-based preferences that must be addressed.

1. *We're not ready to be color-blind because racial discrimination continues to afflict our society.* Ron Brown says affirmative action "continues to be needed not to redress grievances of the past, but the current discrimination that continues to exist." This is a relatively new theory, which conveniently elides the fact that preferences were supposed to be temporary. It also stands logic on its head. While racial discrimination undoubtedly still exists, the Civil Rights Act of 1964 was meant to address prospective discrimination. Affirmative action—discrimination in itself—makes sense only to the extent that there is a current-day legacy of *past* discrimination which new prospective laws cannot reach back and remedy.

In the contexts of education and employment, the Civil Rights Act already contains powerful tools to address intentional and unintentional discrimination. The Civil Rights Act of 1991 reaffirmed the need to address unintentional discrimination—by requiring employers to justify employment practices that are statistically more likely to hurt minorities—but it did so without crossing the line to required preferences. This principle also applies to Title VI of the Civil Rights Act, so that if, for example, it can be shown that the SAT produces an unjustified disparate impact, a university can be barred from using it. In addition, "soft" forms of affirmative action, which require employers and universities to broaden the net and interview people from all races, are good ways of ensuring positions are not filled by word of mouth, through wealthy white networks.

We have weaker tools to deal with discrimination in other areas of life—say, taxi drivers who refuse to pick up black businessmen—but how does a preference in education or employment remedy that wrong? By contrast, there is nothing illegal about bad schools, bad housing and grossly stunted opportunities for the poor. A class preference is perfectly appropriate.

2. *Class preferences will be just as stigmatizing as racial preferences.* Kinsley argues that "any debilitating self-doubt that exists because of affirmative action is not going to be mitigated by being told you got into Harvard because of your 'socioeconomic disadvantage' rather than your race."

But class preferences are different from racial preferences in at least two important respects. First, stigma—in one's own eyes and the eyes of others—is bound up with the question of whether an admissions criterion is accepted as legitimate. Students with good grades aren't seen as getting in "just because they're smart." And there appears to be a societal consensus—from Douglas to Scalia—that kids from poor backgrounds deserve a leg up. Such a consensus has never existed for class-blind racial preference.

Second, there is no myth of inferiority in this country about the abilities of poor people comparable to that about African Americans. Now, if racial preferences are purely a matter of compensatory justice, then the question of whether preferences exacerbate white racism is not relevant. But today racial preferences are often justified by social utility (bringing different racial groups together helps dispel stereotypes) in which case the social consequences are highly relevant. The general argument made by proponents of racial preferences—that policies need to be grounded in social reality, not ahistorical theory—cuts in favor of the class category. Why? Precisely because there is no stubborn myth for it to reinforce.

Kaus makes a related argument when he says that class preferences "will still reward those who play the victim." But if objective criteria are used to define the disadvantaged, there is no way to "play" the victim. Poor and working-class teenagers are the victims of class inequality not of their own making. Preferences, unlike, say, a welfare check, tell poor teenagers not that they are helpless victims, but that we think their long-run potential is great, and we're going to give them a chance—if they work their tails off—to prove themselves.

3. *Class preferences continue to treat people as members of groups as opposed to individuals.* Yes. But so do university admissions policies that summarily reject students below a certain SAT level. It's hard to know what treating people as individuals means. (Perhaps if university admissions committees interviewed the teachers of each applicant back to kindergarten to get a better picture of their academic potential, we'd be treating them more as individuals.) The question is not whether we treat people as members of groups—that's inevitable—but whether the group is a relevant one. And in measuring disadvantage (and hidden potential) class is surely a much better proxy than race.

4. *Class-based affirmative action will not yield a diverse student body in elite colleges.* Actually, there is reason to believe that class preferences will disproportionately benefit people of color in most contexts—since minorities are disproportionately poor. In the university context, however, class-based preferences were rejected during the 1970s in part because of fear that they would produce inadequate numbers of minority students. The problem is that when you control for income, African American students do worse than white and Asian students on the SAT—due in part to differences in culture and linguistic patterns, and in part to the way income alone as a measurement hides other class-based differences among ethnic groups.

The concern is a serious and complicated one. Briefly, there are four responses. First, even [Charles] Murray and Richard Herrnstein agree that the residual racial gap in scores has declined significantly in the past two decades, so the concern, though real, is not as great as it once was. Second, if we use the sophisticated definition of class discussed earlier—which reflects the relative disadvantage of blacks vis-à-vis whites of the same income level—the racial gap should close further. Third, we can improve racial diversity by getting rid of unjustified preferences—for alumni kids or students from underrepresented geographic regions—which disproportionately hurt people of color. Finally, if the goal is to provide genuine equal opportunity, not equality of group result, and if we are satisfied that a meritocratic system which corrects for class inequality is the best possible approximation of that equality, then we have achieved our goal.

5. *Class-based affirmative action will cause as much resentment among those left out as race-based affirmative action.* Kinsley argues that the rejected applicant in the infamous Jesse Helms commercial from 1990 would feel just as angry for losing out on a class-based as a race-based preference, since both involve "making up for past injustice." The difference, of course, is that class preferences go to the actual victims of class injury, mooting the whole question of intergenerational justice. In the racial context, this was called "victim specificity." Even the Reagan administration was in favor of compensating actual victims of racial discrimination.

The larger point implicit in Kinsley's question is a more serious one: that any preference system, whether race- or class-based, is "still a form of zero-sum social engineering." Why should liberals push for class preferences at all? Why not just provide more funding for education, safer schools, better nutrition? The answer is that liberals should do these things; but we cannot hold our breath for it to happen. . . . Cheaper alternatives, such as prefer-

ences, must supplement more expensive strategies of social spending. Besides, to the extent that class preferences help change the focus of public discourse from race to class, they help reforge the coalition needed to sustain the social programs liberals want.

Class preferences could restore the successful formula on which the early civil rights movement rested: morally unassailable underpinnings and a relatively inexpensive agenda. It's crucial to remember that Martin Luther King Jr. called for special consideration based on class, not race. After laying out a forceful argument for the special debt owed to blacks, King rejected the call for a Negro Bill of Rights in favor of a Bill of Rights for the Disadvantaged. It was King's insight that there were nonracial ways to remedy racial wrongs, and the injuries of class deserve attention along with the injuries of race.

None of this is to argue that King would have opposed affirmative action if the alternative were to do nothing. For Jesse Helms to invoke King's color-blind rhetoric now that it is in the interests of white people to do so is the worst kind of hypocrisy. Some form of compensation is necessary, and I think affirmative action, though deeply flawed, is better than nothing. . . .

DISCUSSION QUESTIONS

1. Kahlenberg contends that priority given to race over class has exacerbated White racism. What is his argument? Do you agree with him?
2. Derrick Bell says that "the ends of diversity are not served by people who look black and think white." Does Kahlenberg agree with Bell? Do you? What implications does Bell's statement have for race-based affirmative action policies?
3. Kahlenberg raises four serious objections to class-based preferences. What are they, and how does he respond to them? Critically discuss his response to each of them. What is the strongest criticism, and why?
4. Why does Kahlenberg believe that the opportunity to save affirmative action of any kind may soon pass? Do you agree with him that affirmative action should be saved? Why or why not?
5. Kahlenberg says that affirmative action based on race is flawed. What reasons does he give? Do you agree with him? How might a proponent of race-based preferences respond to these alleged flaws?
6. Is class a stronger foundation for affirmative action policies than race? Discuss.
7. Compare and contrast the strengths and weaknesses of Lino Graglia's, Richard Kahlenberg's, and Bernard Boxill's respective positions on affirmative action. Formulate and defend your own position on affirmative action based on your understanding of the strengths and weaknesses of their views.

◈ U.S. SUPREME COURT

Regents of the University of California v. Bakke

In *Regents of the University of California v. Bakke* (1978), the U.S. Supreme Court said "yes" to affirmative action based on race but "no" to quotas. Allan Bakke, a White male, was denied admission to the University of California, Davis, Medical School in the mid-1970s. At the time, UC-Davis admitted 100 students each year to its medical school, and reserved 16 of these admissions for minority students. While Bakke had higher undergraduate GPA and MCAT scores than any of the 16 minority students admitted to the medical school, he was still denied admission. Bakke was not considered for any of the 16 minority student places based on his race. He filed suit against the University of California, and both the trial court and the California Supreme Court ruled that he had been the victim of *invidious* racial discrimination. The University of California appealed to the U.S. Supreme Court. The Supreme Court ruled that the medical school's admissions policy was unconstitutional, but it did not rule that race could not be considered in university admissions programs. Thus, the Supreme Court's decision in part concurred with the lower court's rulings and in part reversed them. Justice Lewis E. Powell, Jr., writing for the majority, argued that, while the university's admissions policy violated Bakke's Fourteenth Amendment right to not be "totally excluded" on the basis of race, still the University of California had a legitimate interest in devising an admissions policy whereby race and ethnic origin could be considered along with other factors. What follows is Justice Powell's decision.

I

Over the past 30 years, this Court has embarked upon the crucial mission of interpreting the Equal Protection Clause with the view of assuring to all persons "the protection of equal laws," in a Nation confronting a legacy of slavery and racial discrimination. Because the landmark decisions in this area arose in response to the continued exclusion of Negroes from the mainstream of American society, they could be characterized as involving discrimination by the "majority" white race against the Negro minority. But they need not be read as depending upon that characterization for their results. It suffices to say that "[o]ver the years, this Court has consistently repudiated '[d]istinctions between citizens solely because of their ancestry' as being 'odious to a free people whose institutions are founded upon the doctrine of equality.'"

Petitioner [the University of California] urges us to adopt for the first time a more restrictive view of the Equal Protection Clause and hold that discrimination against members of the white "majority" cannot be suspect if its purpose can be characterized as "benign." The clock of our liberties, however, cannot be turned back to 1868. It is far too late to argue that the guarantee of equal protection to *all* persons permits the recognition of special wards entitled to a degree of protection greater than that accorded others. "The Fourteenth Amendment is not directed solely against discrimination due to a 'two-class theory'—that is, based upon differences between 'white' and Negro." . . .

II

We have held that in "order to justify the use of a suspect classification, a State must show that its purpose or interest is both constitutionally permissible and substantial and that its use of the classification is 'necessary . . . to the accomplishment' of its purpose or the safeguarding of its interest." The special admissions program purports to serve the purposes of: (i) "reducing the historic deficit of traditionally disfavored minorities in medical schools and in the medical profession"; (ii) countering the effects of societal discrimination; (iii) increasing the number of physicians who will practice in communities currently underserved; and (iv) obtaining the educational benefits that flow from an ethnically diverse student body. It is necessary to decide which, if any, of these purposes is substantial enough to support the use of a suspect classification.

A

If petitioner's purpose is to assure within its student body some specified percentage of a particular group merely because of its race or ethnic origin, such a preferential purpose must be rejected not as insubstantial but as facially invalid. Preferring members of any one group for no reason other than race or ethnic origin is discrimination for its own sake. This the Constitution forbids.

B

The State certainly has a legitimate and substantial interest in ameliorating, or eliminating where feasible, the disabling effects of identified discrimination. The line of school desegregation cases, commencing with *Brown v. Board of Education* (1954), attests to the importance of this state goal and the commitment of the judiciary to affirm all lawful means toward its attainment. In the school cases, the States were required by court order to redress the wrongs worked by specific instances of racial discrimination. That goal was far more focused than the remedying of the effects of "societal discrimination," an amorphous concept of injury that may be ageless in its reach into the past.

We have never approved a classification that aids persons perceived as members of relatively victimized groups at the expense of other innocent individuals in the absence of judicial, legislative, or administrative findings of constitutional or statutory violations. After such findings have been made, the governmental interest in preferring members of the injured groups at the expense of others is substantial, since the legal rights of the victims must

be vindicated. In such a case, the extent of the injury and the consequent remedy will have been judicially, legislatively, or administratively defined. Also, the remedial action usually remains subject to continuing oversight to assure that it will work the least harm possible to other innocent persons competing for the benefit. Without such findings of constitutional or statutory violations, it cannot be said that the government has any greater interest in helping one individual than in refraining from harming another. Thus, the government has no compelling justification for inflicting such harm.

Petitioner does not purport to have made, and is in no position to make, such findings. Its broad mission is education, not the formulation of any legislative policy or the adjudication of particular claims of illegality. . . . [I]solated segments of our vast governmental structures are not competent to make those decisions, at least in the absence of legislative mandates and legislatively determined criteria. Before relying upon these sorts of findings in establishing a racial classification, a governmental body must have the authority and capability to establish, in the record, that the classification is responsive to identified discrimination. Lacking this capability, petitioner has not carried its burden of justification on this issue.

Hence, the purpose of helping certain groups whom the faculty of the Davis Medical School perceived as victims of "societal discrimination" does not justify a classification that imposes disadvantages upon persons like respondent [Allan Bakke], who bear no responsibility for whatever harm the beneficiaries of the special admissions program are thought to have suffered. To hold otherwise would be to convert a remedy heretofore reserved for violations of legal rights into a privilege that all institutions throughout the Nation could grant at their pleasure to whatever groups are perceived as victims of societal discrimination. That is a step we have never approved.

C

Petitioner identifies, as another purpose of its program, improving the delivery of health-care services to communities currently underserved. It may be assumed that in some situations a State's interest in facilitating the health care of its citizens is sufficiently compelling to support the use of a suspect classification. But there is virtually no evidence in the record indicating that petitioner's special admissions program is either needed or geared to promote that goal. The court below addressed this failure of proof:

> The University concedes it cannot assure that minority doctors who entered under the program, all of whom expressed an "interest" in practicing in a disadvantaged community, will actually do so. It may be correct to assume that some of them will carry out this intention, and that it is more likely they will practice in minority communities than the average white doctor. Nevertheless, there are more precise and reliable ways to identify applicants who are genuinely interested in the medical problems of minorities than by race. An applicant of whatever race who has demonstrated his concern for disadvantaged minorities in the past and who declares that practice in such a community is his primary professional goal would be more likely to contribute to alleviation of the medical shortage than one who is chosen entirely on the basis of race and disadvantage. In short, there is no empirical data to demonstrate that any one race is more selflessly socially oriented or by contrast that another is more selfishly acquisitive.

Petitioner simply has not carried its burden of demonstrating that it must prefer members of particular ethnic groups over all other individuals in order to promote better health-care delivery to deprived citizens. Indeed, petitioner has not shown that its preferential classification is likely to have any significant effect on the problem.

D

The fourth goal asserted by petitioner is the attainment of a diverse student body. This clearly is a constitutionally permissible goal for an institution of higher education. Academic freedom, though not a specifically enumerated constitutional right, long has been viewed as a special concern of the First Amendment. The freedom of a university to make its own judgments as to education includes the selection of its student body.

Ethnic diversity, however, is only one element in a range of factors a university properly may consider in attaining the goal of a heterogeneous student body. Although a university must have wide discretion in making the sensitive judgments as to who should be admitted, constitutional limi-

tations protecting individual rights may not be disregarded. Respondent urges—and the courts below have held—that petitioner's dual admissions program is a racial classification that impermissibly infringes his rights under the Fourteenth Amendment. As the interest of diversity is compelling in the context of a university's admissions program, the question remains whether the program's racial classification is necessary to promote this interest.

III

A

It may be assumed that the reservation of a specified number of seats in each class for individuals from the preferred ethnic groups would contribute to the attainment of considerable ethnic diversity in the student body. But petitioner's argument that this is the only effective means of serving the interest of diversity is seriously flawed. In a most fundamental sense the argument misconceives the nature of the state interest that would justify consideration of race or ethnic background. It is not an interest in simple ethnic diversity, in which a specified percentage of the student body is in effect guaranteed to be members of selected ethnic groups, with the remaining percentage an undifferentiated aggregation of students. The diversity that furthers a compelling state interest encompasses a far broader array of qualifications and characteristics of which racial or ethnic origin is but a single though important element. Petitioner's special admissions program, focused *solely* on ethnic diversity, would hinder rather than further attainment of genuine diversity.

Nor would the state interest in genuine diversity be served by expanding petitioner's two-track system into a multitrack program with a prescribed number of seats set aside for each identifiable category of applicants. Indeed, it is inconceivable that a university would thus pursue the logic of petitioner's two-track program to the illogical end of insulating each category of applicants with certain desired qualifications from competition with all other applicants.

The experience of other university admissions programs, which take race into account in achieving the educational diversity valued by the First Amendment, demonstrates that the assignment of a fixed number of places to a minority group is not a necessary means toward that end. An illuminating example is found in the Harvard College program:

> In recent years Harvard College has expanded the concept of diversity to include students from disadvantaged economic, racial and ethnic groups. Harvard College now recruits not only Californians or Louisianans but also blacks and Chicanos and other minority students. . . .
>
>   In practice, this new definition of diversity has meant that race has been a factor in some admission decisions. When the Committee on Admissions reviews the large middle group of applicants who are "admissible" and deemed capable of doing good work in their courses, the race of an applicant may tip the balance in his favor just as geographic origin or a life spent on a farm may tip the balance in other candidates' cases. A farm boy from Idaho can bring something to Harvard College that a Bostonian cannot offer. Similarly, a black student can usually bring something that a white person cannot offer. . . .
>
>   In Harvard College admissions the Committee has not set target-quotas for the number of blacks, or of musicians, football players, physicists or Californians to be admitted in a given year. . . . But that awareness [of the necessity of including more than a token number of black students] does not mean that the Committee sets a minimum number of blacks or of people from west of the Mississippi who are to be admitted. It means only that in choosing among thousands of applicants who are not only "admissible" academically but have other strong qualities, the Committee, with a number of criteria in mind, pays some attention to distribution among many types and categories of students.

In such an admissions program, race or ethnic background may be deemed a "plus" in a particular applicant's file, yet it does not insulate the individual from comparison with all other candidates for the available seats. The file of a particular black applicant may be examined for his potential contribution to diversity without the factor of race being decisive when compared, for example, with that of an applicant identified as an Italian-American if the latter is thought to exhibit qualities more likely to promote beneficial educational pluralism. Such qualities could include exceptional personal talents, unique work or service experience, leadership potential, maturity, demonstrated compassion, a history of overcoming disadvantage, ability to communicate with the poor, or other qualifications deemed important. In short, an admissions program operated in this way is flexible enough to consider all pertinent elements of diversity in light of the particular qualifications of each applicant, and to place them on the same footing for consideration, although not necessarily according them the same weight. Indeed, the weight attributed to a particular quality may vary from year to year depending upon the "mix" both of the student body and the applicants for the incoming class.

This kind of program treats each applicant as an individual in the admissions process. The applicant who loses out on the last available seat to another candidate receiving a "plus" on the basis of ethnic background will not have been foreclosed from all consideration for that seat simply because he was not the right color or had the wrong surname. It would mean only that his combined qualifications, which may have included similar nonobjective factors, did not outweigh those of the other applicant. His qualifications would have been weighed fairly and competitively, and he would have no basis to complain of unequal treatment under the Fourteenth Amendment.

It has been suggested that an admissions program which considers race only as one factor is simply a subtle and more sophisticated—but no less effective—means of according racial preference than the Davis program. A facial intent to discriminate, however, is evident in petitioner's preference program and not denied in this case. No such facial infirmity exists in an admissions program where race or ethnic background is simply one element—to be weighed fairly against other elements—in the selection process. "A boundary line," as Mr. Justice Frankfurter remarked in another connection, "is none the worse for being narrow." And a court would not assume that a university, professing to employ a facially nondiscriminatory admissions policy, would operate it as a cover for the functional equivalent of a quota system. In short, good faith would be presumed in the absence of a showing to the contrary in the manner permitted by our cases.

B

In summary, it is evident that the Davis special admissions program involves the use of an explicit racial classification never before countenanced by this Court. It tells applicants who are not Negro,

Asian, or Chicano that they are totally excluded from a specific percentage of the seats in an entering class. No matter how strong their qualifications, quantitative and extracurricular, including their own potential for contribution to educational diversity, they are never afforded the chance to compete with applicants from the preferred groups for the special admissions seats. At the same time, the preferred applicants have the opportunity to compete for every seat in the class.

The fatal flaw in petitioner's preferential program is its disregard of individual rights as guaranteed by the Fourteenth Amendment. Such rights are not absolute. But when a State's distribution of benefits or imposition of burdens hinges on ancestry or the color of a person's skin or ancestry, that individual is entitled to a demonstration that the challenged classification is necessary to promote a substantial state interest. Petitioner has failed to carry this burden. For this reason, that portion of the California court's judgment holding petitioner's special admissions program invalid under the Fourteenth Amendment must be affirmed.

C

In enjoining petitioner from ever considering the race of any applicant, however, the courts below failed to recognize that the State has a substantial interest that legitimately may be served by a properly devised admissions program involving the competitive consideration of race and ethnic origin. For this reason, so much of the California court's judgment as enjoins petitioner from any consideration of the race of any applicant must be reversed.

DISCUSSION QUESTIONS

1. Justice Powell said that the flaw in the University of California's preferential program is "its disregard of individual rights as guaranteed by the Fourteenth Amendment." Look up the Fourteenth Amendment. Do you agree with the Supreme Court? Why or why not?
2. How would you rewrite the admissions policy to bring it in accordance with the Supreme Court's ruling?
3. In *Regents of the University of California v. Bakke* (1978), the U.S. Supreme Court said "yes" to affirmative action based on race but "no" to quotas. Do you agree with this decision? Why or why not?
4. How would Bernard Boxill and Lino Graglia respond to Justice Powell's decision? Compare and contrast their responses.
5. If you were in Allan Bakke's position, what would you have done, and how would you have justified your actions to yourself and others?
6. How important to our society are policies aimed at diversifying fields such as medicine? Explain.
7. How do you account for the fact that Bakke's scores on the GRE and MCAT were higher than those of all of the minority students who were admitted to the medical school? Is this an example of unintentional, institutional racism?

MEDIA GALLERY

"BATTLE ROYAL"
By Ralph Ellison

Story summary: Ralph Ellison's "Battle Royal," later the first chapter of his novel *Invisible Man* (1952), deals with a variety of issues confronting twentieth-century America, including racism, sexism, and classism. The narrator is a nameless young Black man who has just graduated from high school. Because he gives a speech on graduation day praising humility as central to progress, he is invited to deliver the speech again for "a gathering of the town's leading white citizens" at an expensive hotel. These leading citizens include "bankers, lawyers, judges, doctors, fire chiefs, teachers, merchants . . . [e]ven one of the more fashionable pastors." The narrator is looking forward to giving his speech and is the pride of his community. However, this is not a gathering to celebrate the narrator's accomplishments. Instead, the evening's entertainment includes a naked white woman dancing, the narrator and nine other Black youths fighting each other blindfolded, and these same adolescents being jolted repeatedly as they scramble for largely fake money on an electrified rug. When the narrator finally is allowed to give his speech, dripping with blood, with a black eye, and choking on his own blood and saliva, the White men hardly even listen to him. The only time he catches their attention is when he accidentally strays from his theme of cooperation with Whites to promote "[s]ocial . . . equality." After quickly assuring the men that he meant to say "social responsibility," the narrator is given a briefcase and a scholarship "to the state college for Negroes." With tears of joy, the narrator rushes home, only to dream that his grandfather "refused to laugh at the clowns no matter what they did" and that his new briefcase contained an almost endless series of envelopes, one within the other, until he gets to the final one. It reads, "Keep This Nigger-Boy Running." This line haunts the narrator throughout the rest of *Invisible Man.*

"Battle Royal" displays several aspects of the culture of the South in this period. While the narrator is an intelligent, well-spoken, and respectful human being, the rich White men are fat, ignorant, and rude. They denigrate the White woman and the Black boys alike: Both are mere pieces of entertainment, one representing the men's sexism and the other their racial bigotry. The narrator is praised only when he appears to be willing to lead fellow African-Americans in their continuing inferior status, in exchange for a chance to go to college and to become successful himself. Indeed, at this point, the narrator idolizes the conciliatory Booker T. Washington and wishes nothing more than to impress the White men with his speech. It takes a tragic accident to open his eyes to the hypocrisy of such a role, as the head of the college that he attends expels him for allowing a rich White man to see some of the darker elements of Southern Black society. The college head frequently calls the narrator "Nigger" and has been utterly co-opted by the White elites, internalizing their racist views and turning against the people he is supposed to be helping. Throughout all of this, the narrator remembers something else that his grandfather said, on his deathbed: " 'our life is a war and I have been a traitor all my days, a spy in the enemy's country. . . . I want you to overcome 'em with yeses, undermine 'em with grins . . . let 'em swallow you till they vomit or bust wide open.' " Even while following this advice and seemingly being rewarded by Blacks and Whites alike, however, the narrator discovers that his grandfather's plan is not sufficient to topple the racism and oppression that ultimately destroy his own life. The narrator realizes that he is invisible to Whites, just as he is invisible when he is part of their twisted entertainments in the battle royal. For the rest of the novel, the White men do indeed "Keep This Nigger-Boy Running," as he is exploited by people as diverse as businessmen, doctors, policemen, and communist leaders. Thus, even as the narrator continually believes that he is moving up in the White world, in actuality, he is simply being used for his abilities—specifically, his rhetorical skills, which have the potential for inspiring other Blacks to do what he advocates and thus to serve the interests of that White world. Only by totally breaking away from society can the narrator escape these forces that are trying to control him.

Ralph Ellison (1914–1994) was a teacher, writer, and lecturer. In 1936, he joined the Federal Writers' Project in New York City, and he served in the Merchant Marines during World War II. *Invisible Man,* which won the National Book Award for fiction in 1953, was his only published novel. However, it is one of the greatest novels of the twentieth century. His second novel, *Juneteenth,* was unfinished at his death and was published posthumously in 1999. He published two collections of essays during his lifetime: *Shadow and Act* (1964) and *Going to the Territory* (1986). *Flying Home and Other Stories* was published posthumously in 1996.

1. Why do you think that the evening's entertainment in "Battle Royal" included a naked White woman dancing, the narrator and nine other Black youths fighting each other blindfolded, and these same adolescents being jolted repeatedly as they scramble for largely fake money on an electrified rug? Why was this entertainment observed by "a gathering of the town's leading white citizens"? Can you identify any entertainment today that is similar in the sense that it makes an exotic/pathetic spectacle of African-Americans (or women)—for example, a contemporary TV show?

2. Why is it that the only time the narrator catches the attention of the town's leading White citizens is when he accidentally strays from his theme of cooperation with Whites to promote "[s]ocial . . . equality"? Why does the narrator quickly assure the men that he meant to say "social responsibility"?

3. The narrator's grandfather tells him that "'our life is a war and I have been a traitor all my days, a spy in the enemy's country. . . . I want you to overcome 'em with yeses, undermine 'em with grins . . . let 'em swallow you till they vomit or bust wide open.'" However, the narrator ultimately comes to a different conclusion than his grandfather as to its effectiveness as a means to battle racism and oppression. Why might some believe that this is not a sufficient strategy to topple racism and oppression? Why do you think that the narrator's grandfather believed this to be a sufficient strategy? Should people accept the consequences of racism (or sexism) with humility, or should they reject them? Why or why not?

4. In *Invisible Man,* the nameless young Black man believes that he is effectively invisible because the people he encounters "see only my surroundings, themselves, or figments of their imagination." What does he mean by this?

5. At the end of *Invisible Man,* the nameless young Black man retreats into a hole in the ground, which he furnishes and makes his home. Twentieth-century America—both the North and the South—disgusts him. Only by totally breaking away from society can he escape these forces that are trying to control him. What do you think about this general strategy for dealing with oppression and discrimination? Explain.

6. Does Ellison's "Battle Royal" speak to the state of racism, sexism, and classism in America today? Or have things changed so much over the past fifty years that Ellison could not write "Battle Royal" today? How might it be rewritten to address the current situation? Explain.

 "WHITE RAT"

By Gayl Jones

Story summary: "White Rat" (1975) is about a mulatto man and the challenges he faces in a society that judges people by the color of their skin. People call him "White Rat" because he looks White, and when he tells people that he is Black, they don't believe him. Instead, they respond, "I ain't never heard of a white man want to be a nigger." One day, White Rat is arrested for disorderly conduct while drunk and locked up with some Whites. He attempts to explain to the authorities that he is indeed Black, but they don't believe him. White Rat later tries to marry Maggie, but the court won't allow a White man to marry a Black woman. He is told, "Round here nigger don't marry white." He again tries to explain that he is Black and finally succeeds: "'I'm a nigger. Nigger marry nigger, don't they?' He just look at me like he think I'm crazy. I say, 'I got rel'tives blacker'n your shit. Ain't you never heard a niggers what look like they white.' He just look at me like I'm a nigger too, and tell me where to sign." White Rat and Maggie marry. White Rat explains how difficult it is to be so White and how "nowadays everybody want to be a nigger, or it getting that way. . . . I keep telling Maggie it get harder and harder to be a white nigger now specially since it don't count no more how much white blood you got in you, in fact, it make you worser for it." He tells Maggie that she is lucky for being Black because she will never be mistaken for a White woman. Maggie later has a child with White Rat, little Henry, who is born club-footed. White Rat blames Maggie out of superstition: "To tell the truth in the beginning I blamed Maggie, cause I herited all those hill man's superstitions and nigger superstitions too, and I said she didn't do something right when she was carrying him or she did something she shouldn't oughta did or looked at something she shouldn't oughta looked at like some crows fucking or something." White Rat ultimately ruins their relationship because of his alcoholism, and Maggie runs away with J. T. After Maggie becomes pregnant by J. T., he leaves her. White Rat tells Maggie that he will be a father to the child even though it is not his. Maggie reluctantly agrees, and they move back together.

Born in 1949 in Lexington, Kentucky, Gayl Jones attended Connecticut College and got a Ph.D. from Brown University. She taught at the University of Michigan in the mid-1970s before resigning following a dispute with the university concerning her husband. She is the author of *Corregidora* (1975), *Eva's Man* (1976), *The White Rat: Short Stories* (1977), *Song For Anninho* (1981), *Liberating Voices: Oral Tradition in African American Literature* (1991), *Healing* (1998), and *Mosquito* (1999). *Healing* (1998) marked a return to fiction writing after a nearly twenty-year break.

1. Skin color is often used as a determinant of race. How does the story of White Rat make this notion problematic? Does it provide you with strong enough grounds to reject the notion of race being based on skin color? Explain.
2. White Rat is told that "Round here nigger don't marry white." Does the marriage of Maggie and White Rat reveal a problem with upholding such a law? Furthermore, do you think that laws that prohibit marriage between people of differing races are morally objectionable? Defend your view.
3. White Rat is told, "I ain't never heard of a white man want to be a nigger." Why do you think people would say this?
4. Why do you think White Rat wants to be considered Black? Should society respect his decision?
5. How should race be determined in our society? Of what moral value is the differentiation of people by race? Of what social value? Defend your views.

 TO KILL A MOCKINGBIRD

(USA, 1962) 2 hours 9 minutes
Directed by Robert Mulligan

Film summary: Based on the novel by Harper Lee, *To Kill a Mockingbird* is a dramatic look at life in the South in the 1930s. The story is told from the point of view of two young children, Scout (Mary Badham) and Jem (Phillip Alford), whose lawyer father defends a Black man accused of beating and raping a White woman. Atticus Finch (Gregory Peck) endures verbal and physical threats against his family when he agrees to become Tom Robinson's lawyer. At the trial, Finch reveals that there was no medical examination of Mayella Ewell (Collin Wilcox) and no evidence that she was raped. Finch argues that the bruises on the right side of Mayella's face could not have been caused by Robinson, who had lost the use of his left hand in an accident. Robinson (Brock Peters) testifies that Mayella invited him into her home and made advances toward him but that he refused her and ran away. All evidence supports the argument that Mayella was covering up her solicitation of Robinson and that her drunken father, Bob Ewell (James Anderson), had beaten her after discovering her act. When the White jury members find Robinson guilty, Finch promises to file an appeal. However, as Robinson is being transported back to the jail, he breaks away from the guards and is shot and killed. When Finch brings the news to the Robinson family, he is confronted by Bob Ewell, who spits in his face. Later, Ewell attacks Scout and Jem. The children are saved through the intervention of Boo Radley (Robert Duvall), the reclusive neighbor who had been a source of mystery and terror for the children. When Sheriff Tate (Frank Overton) finds Ewell with a knife in his chest, he decides not to bring the matter to court and concludes that Ewell fell on his own knife.

To Kill a Mockingbird won three Oscars, including Best Actor for Gregory Peck.

1. In the next chapter, Angela Davis cites figures showing that "rape charges have been indiscriminately aimed at Black men, the guilty and the innocent alike." Davis argues that fraudulent rape charges against Blacks are a powerful invention of racism. Is the rape charge in this movie being used as a form of racism? Defend your view.

2. Atticus Finch endures verbal and physical threats against his family when he agrees to become Tom Robinson's lawyer. However, he reacts to those threats in a nonconfrontational manner. For example, when Bob Ewell spits in his face, Atticus calmly wipes it off and walks away. Should Atticus explain to those who disagree with his actions why he is acting this way, or should he confront the perpetrators in some other way? Or is his nonverbal and nonphysical reaction to racist verbal and physical actions an appropriate response? What would you do if you were in Atticus Finch's place? Explain.

3. Scout asks her father, "Atticus, do you defend niggers?" Atticus responds, "Don't say nigger Scout." Scout replies, "I didn't say it. Cecil Jacobs did. That's why I had to fight him." Why do you think Scout fought Cecil? Was it because he used a racial slur? Was it because he was being offensive with regard to her father? Explain. Also, why does Atticus tell Scout not to say "nigger"? What is the connection between such language and racism? Do you think that the connection means something different for children than it does for adults? If so, how?

4. Atticus tells Scout, "I'm simply defending a Negro. Tom Robinson. Scout, there are some things that you are not old enough to understand just yet. There's been some high talk around town to the effect that I should not do much about defending this man." Scout asks, "If you shouldn't be defending him then why are you doing it?" Atticus replies, "For a number of reasons. The main one is that if I didn't, then I could not hold my head up in town. I couldn't even tell you or Jem not to do something again." What do you think of Atticus's response to Scout's question? Why is he defending Tom? Why does he say, "if I didn't, then I could not hold my head up in town"? If you were in Atticus's position, would you defend Tom? What reason would you give your children? Would it be similar to Atticus's response?

5. When Sheriff Tate decides not to bring Ewell's death before the court, he argues, "There's a black man dead for no reason. Now the man responsible for it is dead. Let the dead bury the dead this time, Mr. Finch." Bob Ewell did not shoot Tom Robinson, so how is he responsible for Robinson's death? Can you morally justify Sheriff Tate's decision? Explain.

6. Sheriff Tate also argues in defense of Boo Radley: "I never heard tell it was against the law for any citizen to do his utmost to prevent a crime from being committed, which is exactly what he did. To my way of thinking, taking one man who's done you and this town a big service and dragging him—with his shy ways—into the limelight, to me, that's a sin." Is the sheriff's decision to hush up the Ewell death moral? Should the case be investigated and Boo Radley brought before a jury of his peers? Does the decision of the jury in the Robinson trial affect your opinion? Are you surprised that Atticus agrees to this, particularly after he said to Scout that he couldn't tell her and Jem not to do something again if he didn't defend Tom?

WHITE MAN'S BURDEN

(USA, 1995) 1 hour 38 minutes
Directed by Desmond Nakaro

Film summary: Whites are the minority population in the society depicted in *White Man's Burden*. White citizens are subject to racial profiling by the police, and the media is dominated by Black actors and commentators. Louis Pinnock (John Travolta) works in a factory owned by Thaddeus Thomas (Harry Belafonte). Pinnock is wrongly accused of violating Thomas's privacy by peeping in his windows and consequently loses his job. A string of misfortunes follow Pinnock's termination. He is unable to find work through social services and cannot pay his bills. When his car breaks down, two police officers wrongly profile him as a criminal and severely beat him. The Pinnocks owe rent to their landlord and are evicted from their home. Pinnock's wife Marsha (Kelly Lynch) moves to her mother's home, and Pinnock must part with his children. In desperation, he meets with Thomas and demands money in recompense for his lost employment. When Thomas is unable to withdraw funds from the bank, Pinnock kidnaps him. Several days later, the two men are found by the police. Though Pinnock surrenders, an officer spots a gun in his hand and shoots and kills him.

1. Does Thomas "owe" Pinnock anything? Is Thomas morally responsible for the downward spiral of Pinnock's life?
2. When Thomas attempts to give money to Marsha following her husband's death, she refuses it, asking, "How much do you think would be enough?" Did she do the right thing? Why or why not? What would Bernard Boxill say is "enough"? What do you think would be enough?
3. Is racial profiling morally unjustifiable? Is it racist? When, if ever, is it morally justifiable to profile someone as more of a threat to commit crime based on their race? Defend your position.
4. By reversing the social and economic positions of Whites and Blacks, is this film suggesting that our social and economic positions are due only to culture? Defend your view.
5. Thomas' attempt to give money to Marsha following her husband's death suggests that racial discrimination negatively affects both the discriminator and the discriminated. Do you agree with this? Why or why not?

 IN THE HEAT OF THE NIGHT

(USA, 1967) 1 hour 49 minutes
Directed by Norman Jewison

Film summary: A murder has been committed in Sparta, Mississippi, sometime in the 1960s. Sam Wood (Warren Oates), a police officer, discovers the body of Mr. Colbert, a northern entrepreneur who had been building a factory in town, in an alley during a routine patrol. Chief Gillespie (Rod Steiger) tells Wood to look around town for the murderer. Wood finds Virgil Tibbs (Sidney Poitier), alone at 3:00 A.M., in a nearby train station. Wood immediately arrests him and takes him to the station as the murder suspect. Gillespie asks Tibbs, "What did you hit him with?" Tibbs responds, "Hit whom?" Soon, Gillespie finds out that Tibbs is a homicide detective from Pennsylvania, on the way home after visiting his mother. He was simply waiting for a 4:05 A.M. train to Memphis when Wood picked him up, purely on the basis of the color of his skin. Somewhat embarrassed, Gillespie tells Tibbs to go home. Soon, it becomes apparent that the case cannot be solved without the help of Tibbs, and through a series of events, he becomes the primary detective in a highly racist and racially divided community. Mrs.

Colbert (Lee Grant) tells the Mayor that "the negro officer [should] not be taken off the case or she'll pack up her husband's engineers and leave town." Tibbs understands the difficult position in which he has been put. "They've got a murder they don't know what to do with," says Tibbs. "They need a whipping boy." A number of times, Gillespie is convinced that he has found the murderer, only to be proved wrong by Tibbs. Eventually, Tibbs identifies the murderer, and Gillespie comes to respect and admire his abilities.

1. Gillespie tells Tibbs that Mr. Colbert came down from Chicago to build a factory that would employ a thousand men, half of whom would be "colored." Mr. Colbert, says Gillespie, probably got killed for this reason. If the murderer is not found, Mrs. Colbert says that the factory will not go up. Gillespie says, "It's a lot of jobs for a lot of colored people. They're your people." Tibbs responds, "Not mine, yours." What does Tibbs mean that they are not "his" people?
2. Do you think that Tibbs would have been released if he were not a police officer? Why?
3. Throughout the film, Gillespie is shown as being quick to jump to erroneous conclusions about people. He also wrestles with the notion that Tibbs could actually be a very good detective—possibly even a better police officer than himself. Eventually, Gillespie comes to respect and admire Tibbs's abilities. Do you think that Gillespie was a racist in the beginning of the movie when he assumed that Tibbs was guilty? Or when he assumed that Tibbs could not be a good detective because he was Black? Do you think that Gillespie changes his mind about Blacks over the course of the movie— particularly when he breaks up an attempt by some racist Whites to beat up Tibbs? What, if anything, made Gillespie change his mind?
4. Tibbs does not say a word to Wood when Wood arrests him for no particular reason. If confronted by racists, how would you convince them that they should not be racist? Or, for that matter, would you even try to confront them about their racism? Do we have a moral obligation to confront racists about their beliefs?

SUPPLEMENTARY READINGS

RACISM

Adelman, Jeanne, and Gloria Enguídanos, eds. *Racism in the Lives of Women.* New York: Haworth, 1995.

Bell, Linda, and David Blumenfeld, eds. *Overcoming Sexism and Racism.* Lanham, MD: Rowman & Littlefield, 1994.

Benedict, Ruth. *Race: Science and Politics,* rev. ed. New York: Viking Press, 1945.

Davis, Angela. *Women, Race and Class.* New York: Vintage Books, 1983.

Day, Beth. *Sexual Life Between Blacks and Whites: The Roots of Racism.* New York: World Publishing/ Times Mirror, 1972.

Delgado, Richard. *Critical Race Theory: The Cutting Edge.* Philadelphia: Temple University Press, 1995.

Domínguez, Virginia. *White by Definition: Social Classification in Creole Louisiana.* New Brunswick, NJ: Rutgers University Press, 1986.

D'Souza, Dinesh. *The End of Racism.* New York: Free Press, 1995.

Fanon, Franz. *Black Skin, White Masks.* New York: Grove Press, 1967.

Funderberg, L. *Black, White, Other: Biracial Americans Talk About Race and Identity.* New York: Morrow, 1994.

Gates, Henry Louis. *Loose Canons: Notes on the Culture Wars.* New York: Oxford University Press, 1992.

Giddings, Paula. *When and Where I Enter . . . : The Impact of Black Women on Race and Sex in America.* New York: Morrow, 1984.

Goldberg, David Theo. *Racist Culture: Philosophy and the Politics of Meaning.* Cambridge, MA: Blackwell, 1993.

————, ed. *Anatomy of Racism.* Minneapolis: University of Minnesota Press, 1990.

Hernton, Calvin. *Sex and Racism in America.* New York: Grove Press, 1965.

Ignatiev, Noel. *How the Irish Became White: Irish-Americans and African-Americans in 19th Century Philadelphia.* New York: Verso, 1995.

Kuhl, Stefan. *The Nazi Connection: Eugenics, American Racism, and German National Socialism.* New York: Oxford University Press, 1994.

Outlaw, Lucius T. *On Race and Philosophy.* New York: Routledge, 1996.

Roediger, David R. *The Wages of Whiteness: Race and the Making of the American Working Class.* London: Verso, 1992.

Root, M. P. P., ed. *Racially Mixed People in America.* Newbury Park, CA: Sage, 1993.

Spelman, Elizabeth V. *Inessential Woman: Problems of Exclusion in Feminist Thought.* Boston: Beacon Press, 1988.

Spickard, Paul. *Mixed Blood: Intermarriage and Ethnic Identity in Twentieth Century America.* Madison: University of Wisconsin Press, 1989.

Thomas, Laurence. "Sexism and Racism: Some Conceptual Differences." *Ethics,* 90 (1980): 239–250.

Webster, Yehudi O. *The Racialization of America.* New York: St. Martin's Press, 1992.

West, Cornell. *Race Matters.* Boston: Beacon Press, 1993.

Williams, Patricia. *The Alchemy of Race and Rights.* Cambridge, MA: Harvard University Press, 1991.

Zack, Naomi. *Race and Mixed Race.* Philadelphia: Temple University Press, 1993.

————, ed. *RACE/SEX: Their Sameness, Difference and Interplay.* New York: Routledge, 1997.

AFFIRMATIVE ACTION

Alonso, William, and Paul Starr, eds. *The Politics of Numbers.* New York: Russell Sage Foundation, 1987.

Ball, Howard. *The Bakke Case: Race, Education, and Affirmative Action.* Lawrence: University Press of Kansas, 2000.

Beauchamp, Tom. "The Justification of Reverse Discrimination." In *Social Justice and Preferential Treatment,* ed. William Blackstone and Robert Heslep. Athens: University of Georgia Press, 1976.

Bell, Derrick. *And We Are Not Saved: The Elusive Quest for Racial Justice.* New York: Basic Books, 1987.

Blackstone, William. "Reverse Discrimination and Compensatory Justice." *Social Theory and Practice,* 3, 3 (Spring 1975): 253–288.

Blackstone, William, and Robert Heslep. *Social Justice and Preferential Treatment.* Athens: University of Georgia Press, 1976.

Bowen, William G., and Derek Bok. *The Shape of the River: Long-Term Consequences of Considering Race in College and University Admissions.* Princeton, NJ: Princeton University Press, 1998.

Bowie, Norman. *Equal Opportunity.* Boulder, CO: Westview Press, 1976.

Boxill, Bernard. "The Morality of Reparation." *Social Theory and Practice,* 2, 1 (1972): 113–122.

————. "Sexual Blindness and Sexual Equality." *Social Theory and Practice,* 6, 3 (Fall 1980): 281–298.

Carter, Stephen. *Reflections of an Affirmative Action Baby.* New York: Basic Books, 1991.

Chavez, Lydia. *The Color Bind: California's Battle to End Affirmative Action.* Berkeley: University of California Press, 1998.

Cohen, Marshall; Thomas Nagel; and Thomas Scanlon. *Equality and Preferential Treatment.* Princeton, NJ: Princeton University Press, 1977.

Cose, Ellis. *Color-Blind: Seeing Beyond Race in a Race-Obsessed World.* New York: HarperCollins, 1997.

Crosby, Faye J., and Cheryl VanDeVeer, eds. *Sex, Race, and Merit: Debating Affirmative Action in Education and Employment.* Ann Arbor: University of Michigan Press, 2000.

Dworkin, Ronald. "Why Bakke Has No Case." *The New York Review of Books,* 19 (Nov. 1977).

Ezorsky, Gertrude. *Racism and Justice.* Ithaca, NY: Cornell University Press, 1991.

Glazer, Nathan. "Individual Rights Against Group Rights." Pp. 123–138 in *The Rights of Minority Cultures,* ed. Will Kymlicka. Oxford: Oxford University Press, 1995.

Goldman, Alan. *Justice and Reverse Discrimination.* Princeton, NJ: Princeton University Press, 1979.

Gross, Barry. *Reverse Discrimination.* Buffalo: Prometheus Press, 1977.

Kellough, J. Edward. "Affirmative Action in Government Employment." *The Annals,* 523 (Sept. 1992): 117–130.

Murray, Charles. "Affirmative Racism." *New Republic,* 31 (Dec. 1984).

———. *The Bell Curve.* New York: Simon & Schuster, 1994.

Newton, Lisa H. "Reversed Discrimination as Unjustified." *Ethics,* 83 (1973): 308–312.

Rai, Kul B. *Affirmative Action and the University: Race, Ethnicity, and Gender in Higher Education Employment.* Lincoln: University of Nebraska Press, 2000.

Riccucci, Norma M. "Merit, Equity, and Test Validity." *Administration and Society,* 23, 1 (May 1991): 74–93.

Sher, George. "Justifying Reverse Discrimination in Employment." *Philosophy and Public Affairs,* 4, 2 (Winter 1975): 159–170.

———. "Reverse Discrimination, the Future, and the Past." *Ethics,* 90 (Oct. 1979): 81–87.

Sowell, Thomas. *The Economics and Politics of Race: An International Perspective.* New York: Morrow, 1983.

———. *Civil Rights: Rhetoric or Reality.* New York: Morrow, 1984.

Wasserstrom, Richard. *Philosophy and Social Issues: Five Studies.* Notre Dame, IN: University of Notre Dame Press, 1980.

West, Cornell. "Beyond Affirmative Action: Equality and Identity." In West, *Race Matters.* Boston: Beacon Press, 1993.

Williams, Patricia. *The Rooster's Egg: On the Persistence of Prejudice.* Cambridge, MA: Harvard University Press, 1995.

Wilson, William Julius. *The Truly Disadvantaged.* Chicago: University of Chicago Press, 1987.

Young, Iris Marion. *Justice and the Politics of Difference.* Princeton, NJ: Princeton University Press, 1990.

Sexism and Violence Against Women

For many years, members of the women's movement and feminist philosophers have been addressing two of the most unfortunate dimensions of contemporary American society: sexism and violence against women. Thanks in great part to the efforts of many activists—women and men alike—there is much hope that our society will continue to evolve into a safer, fairer, and generally better place for women to live. Yet, even though we are more aware today of the presence of sexism and violence against women in our society, both are still widespread and widely misunderstood. Furthermore, many forms of sexism and violence against women are still either overlooked or unacknowledged. One of the most controversial contemporary moral issues is whether sexism is linked to the various forms of violence against women including rape, domestic battery, and acquaintance rape. Some argue that, if our society did not tolerate as many of the nonviolent sexist acts, practices, and beliefs—or even institutions—as it does, there would be far less violence against women. Others argue that there is little or no connection between sexism and violence against women. Still others maintain that there is no such thing as nonviolent sexism: all sexism is a form of violence against women.

Sexism is anything which promotes, creates, constitutes or takes unfair advantage of any impertinent or irrelevant differences between the sexes. One of the major issues regarding sexism is simply whether particular acts, practices, and attitudes are sexist. While some practices, such as denying women the same opportunities in business and education or the rights to vote and own property, are widely acknowledged to be sexist, many other acts, practices, and beliefs are much less widely acknowledged as sexist. For example, is it sexist to encourage boys to wear pants and to discourage them from wearing dresses? Is it sexist to encourage girls to play with dolls and to discourage them from playing baseball? Is it sexist to deny women the same opportunities in athletics? Or are there pertinent and justifiable differences between males and females that can be used to support the different ways that women and men are treated?

The examples here are numerous. Many wonder why, for example, there are not more women in politics and public service, why there are far fewer female CEOs than male, why women are more frequently the victims of violence than men, why women on average make less money—often even for the same work—than men. Sexism has been one of the most powerful explanations provided for this list of inequities.

The general argument for equal treatment of the sexes is as follows: people ought to be treated the same unless there is a relevant difference between certain groups. There are no pertinent differences between men and women. Therefore, men and women ought to be treated equally. Some believe that this argument is flawed because in many contexts in our society there *are* relevant differences between the sexes. For example, some would argue that women should not be firefighters because most women do not have the strength required to carry a person out of a burning building. Therefore, being a man or a woman is a pertinent difference in considering who should be a firefighter.

Of course, the counterargument is that it is not the fault of potential women fire-fighters that men believe that women cannot carry people out of burning buildings. There is nothing *by nature* that prevents a woman from gaining the strength and knowledge needed to be as good a firefighter as a man. Rather, it is because of a set of *societal* beliefs and practices that sex becomes a relevant difference, and consequently the basis of an argument for sexual discrimination, in firefighter selection. Given these and other considerations, many believe that the stronger argument against sexism and for equal treatment of the sexes is as follows: people ought to be treated the same unless there is a *pertinent* natural difference between groups. There are no relevant natural differences between men and women. Therefore, men and women ought to be treated equally. According to this line of argumentation, *natural* differences are biological in origin, and *nonnatural* differences are nonbiological in origin. Most believe that the origin of those nonbiological differences is culture or society.

Consequently, most contemporary discussions of sexism and sexual inequality distinguish between sex and gender (or sex role). *Sex* refers to the differences between men and women that are biological in origin. *Gender* or *sex role* refers to the differences between men and women that are cultural or societal in origin. The words *male* and *female* generally refer to distinctions made on the basis of sex, and *masculine* and *feminine* refer to distinctions made on the basis of gender or sex role. One of the key questions of the debate over sexism is the extent to which sex determines gender. Traditionally, the response has been that gender is almost entirely determined by sex and that there is a natural connection between sex and gender, but this view has been widely challenged. One of the primary assumptions of most feminist thought is that there is not a natural or essential connection between sex and gender. Furthermore, if any connection between sex and gender does exist, then it is a culturally determined one.

In the debate over sexism, we can identify a number of distinct strands of argumentation, each of which takes a position as to whether there are natural and relevant differences between the sexes. Most of the positions that you will come across are variations on one of the following four.

One position that was famously advocated by John Stuart Mill, among others, is that there are no natural *and* relevant differences between the sexes. Proponents of this approach do not deny that there are many natural differences between men and women, but they also argue that these differences are not pertinent ones, particularly in a modern society. They believe that both men and women can raise children, and the fact that only women can bear children has no relevancy here. What makes a woman better suited to rock a baby to sleep? Or better suited to change a diaper? Furthermore, they believe that the social reinforcement of sex roles is superfluous if there actually are natural and pertinent differences between the sexes. There is no need to reinforce something that is a natural difference. If women are really better than men at raising children, then social reinforcement of sex roles cannot change this. Rather, what social reinforcement can do is make nonnatural differences between the sexes *appear* natural. And this, of course, is unfair. If a particular woman cannot raise her children better than her mate, she should not be told by society that she *should* be able to do it simply because she is a woman (or that women are naturally better at raising children than men).

Similarly, if a particular man cannot lift more weight than a particular woman, then he should not be told by society that he *should* be able to merely because he is a man (or that men are naturally stronger than women). While men and women might have certain natural tendencies, society should not reinforce them. We should strive toward a society that will embrace the natural differences between the sexes rather than use them to subordinate one sex to another. Furthermore, because there are no naturally relevant differences between the sexes, proponents of this line of argumentation tend to believe that people should be able to freely choose the life they wish to lead, without interference from others.

However, this approach to sex equality is not without its opponents. Some maintain that this approach cannot adequately show that there are no natural and pertinent differences between the sexes; others argue that it does nothing to eliminate the sex inequality that is already a part of our society. If we are free to choose the life we wish to lead, then we are free to choose to be sexist as well. For some, this position on sexual equality simply does not make sufficient provisions for ending the kind of beliefs and institutions that make it nearly impossible for a woman to become a firefighter. Nevertheless, despite these weaknesses—which many believe are more apparent than real—variations of this line of argumentation have been taken up by quite a number of feminists.

Many, however, disagree with the fundamental assumption that there are no natural and pertinent differences between the sexes and use this as the basis for reaching differing conclusions on sexism. Some, such as Carol Gilligan (who is anthologized in Chapter 1) maintain that there *are* natural differences between the sexes and that we should embrace these differences and strive toward a society that encourages sex differences. These natural differences, however, should never be used as grounds for subordinating one sex to the other. Rather, like the different voices in a chorus that blend to make beautiful music, we should strive to blend the natural differences between men and women to form the optimal society. A nonoppressive, sexually diverse society grounded in natural differences is the goal of proponents of this line of argumentation. Some who take up this position even maintain that, because women have a physical connection to another in childbirth, they place more value on nonphysical relationships with others than do men. One problem with these contentions on sex equality is that they might unwittingly lead us to mistake many nonnatural differences for natural ones. Critics of this position on sex equality often claim that in the long run it will only perpetuate the socially generated sex differences that it wishes to overcome and thereby reinforce sex inequality based on nonnatural differences.

The view that there are natural and relevant differences between the sexes but that we should seek to eliminate rather than embrace them is one way around the problems mentioned previously. Instead of striving for a society that encourages sexual differences, we should move to eliminate sex differences. Proponents of this position often support the development of technology that would remove natural differences between men and women—differences that often put women at a disadvantage in society. For example, if childbearing prevents women from being competitive in some professions with men, then we should support technologies that would eliminate this natural difference between men and women. Proponents of this approach frequently also argue for a sex-blind society wherein natural differences between men and women have been eliminated. They contend as well that even if the natural and pertinent sex differences were eliminated, it would still take a long time for socially determined sex roles based on the inequality of the sexes to disappear.

Objections to this position on sex equality come from a number of different directions. Some argue that eliminating natural and relevant differences between men and women also entails eliminating some things that give both men and women pleasure. For example, some women simply enjoy being pregnant. Denying them their capacity to do this is tantamount to denying them one of the most satisfying parts of their lives.

Others argue that eliminating natural and pertinent differences will not necessarily make people happier. People's happiness depends at least as much on the kind of society they live in as on the natural differences between the sexes. For example, it is entirely possible that in a sex-blind society not being able to be pregnant might make women unhappy. According to one modification of this position, rather than eliminate natural and relevant differences, we should strive toward sex roles that are the same for members of both sexes. Therefore, androgynous sex roles would be the ideal in a society marked by natural and pertinent differences between the sexes.

Proponents of a fourth position maintain that there are many natural differences between men and women and that these differences ought to be used as grounds for treating the sexes unequally in many situations. For example, obviously, men cannot bear children, but women can. On the grounds of differences like this, some argue that our roles in society should be determined strictly on the basis of sex. For society to work well, people should do what they are naturally best inclined to do. Consequently, because women bear children, they are better suited to be their primary caregivers. In other words, women are by nature better suited than men to stay at home and raise children. Therefore, they *should* stay home and raise children, and society should support and reinforce such roles for women. Furthermore, women should be subordinate to men because men are, on average, stronger than women.

Note that this argument makes quite a jump from "stronger" to "should subordinate others"—a conceptual gap that needs to be filled in to make these arguments work. Those who adhere to this line of argumentation also at times argue that a society in which men try to do things that women are more naturally inclined to do, or vice versa, is doomed to failure because both men and women will become frustrated by trying to do things that they cannot by nature do. Therefore, according to this strand of argumentation, sexism is morally justified. Even though this view has been the dominant one in the history of philosophy, defended by the likes of Aristotle and Kant, among others, it has been widely challenged. Many find these arguments weak and claim that, rather than leading to a better society, they lead to a worse one. For most, this line of argumentation is radically antifeminist.

It is one thing to speculate about what society would be like if the sexes were treated equally; it is altogether another to examine how the sexes are actually treated unequally today. One of the more disturbing dimensions of sexism in our society is that many people simply do not believe women who claim that they were forced to have sex with men. This holds true both when the woman knew the man beforehand and when she did not. Some say that if a woman, for example, goes up to a man's room after drinking with him at a party, then social norms indicate that she might want to have sex with him. If they do indeed have sex under these conditions, even if the woman says no to sex, some people believe that this is not a case of rape because the woman went up to the man's room, which is tantamount to saying yes to sex. Others charge that, even if the woman goes up to the room with the man, if she says no to sex and is then forced to have sex by the man, it is rape. It does not matter that she went up to the man's room. Feminists and others add still another dimension to the issue of consent: any act by the woman aside from explicitly consenting to sex is morally irrelevant. While it might be unwise for a woman to go up to a man's room late at night after drinking with him, if she protests to sex, there is no consent.

There are many myths about rape. One of the biggest is that women are primarily raped by men whom they do not know. In fact, less than one third of rapes involve an assault by a man unknown to the victim. Most women are raped by men with whom they are familiar, men they know from work, school, or even social circles. These assaults are sometimes called acquaintance rape, and rape that occurs on or after a date is sometimes called date rape.

Some people have argued that rape should not be considered primarily a sex act, but rather is a form of violence used to intimidate women and keep them in a state of fear. Under these conditions, the subordination of women to men is easier for men to maintain. This subordination, or *patriarchy*, tells women that they are less important than men and exist for the pleasure of men. Under conditions of patriarchal domination, it is understandable why many women who claim not to have consented to sex are not believed by authorities. Rape is a form of patriarchal domination, and institutional power structures, largely controlled by men, dismiss many cases of rape. This subordination is also useful in explaining why many rapes go unreported: many women fear that authorities in patriarchal power structures will not believe them.

Rape is not the only form of violence against women, nor is it the only form of patriarchal domination. In our society, domestic violence has been and continues to be a problem. Patriarchal systems of domination of women by men have instilled in many women the mistaken belief that the violence done to them by their spouse or partner is morally justifiable. Justifications for domestic violence like "He is under a lot of stress, and I got on his nerves—I deserved it" make sense to women in a society in which they feel that they are not equal to men and so must obey men or suffer violent consequences.

Finally, it must be noted that many contend that no discussion of sexism and violence against women is complete without a simultaneous consideration of issues of race and class or wealth. For many, a failure to take into account race and class is a failure to adequately account for the realities of sexism and violence against women in contemporary society. Myths and stereotypes about men and women of color often significantly alter the type of sexism with which they are confronted. To be sure, these considerations complicate any discussion of sexism and violence against women. At the same time, they compel us to provide accounts of sexism and violence against women that address the problems of people who actually live in our society.

MARILYN FRYE

Sexism

Marilyn Frye provides a definition of sexism and argues that sexism is not always apparent either to those who suffer from it or to those who inflict it upon others. It is the imperceptibility of sexism that enables it to flourish in our society. According to Frye, the "term *sexist* characterizes cultural and economic structures which create and enforce the elaborate and rigid patterns of sex-marking and sex-announcing which divide the species, along lines of sex, into dominators and subordinates." For Frye, acts that reinforce those cultural and economic structures are sexist acts, and acts that undermine those structures are acts of resistance to sexism. Consequently, for Frye, "the locus of sexism is primarily in the system or framework, not in the particular act." Her analysis of sexism aims to make the systemic structures of sex-marking and sex-announcing more visible by identifying some of the different ways in which sex differences are reinforced in our society. The continued cultural emphasis on sex differences for Frye only serves to reinforce and perpetuate acts of domination and subordination.

Marilyn Frye is a professor of philosophy at Michigan State University and is the author of *The Politics of Reality: Essays in Feminist Theory* (1983), *Willful Virgin: Essays in Feminism, 1976–1992* (1992), and *Feminist Interpretations of Mary Daly* (coedited with Sarah Lucia, 2000).

The first philosophical project I undertook as a feminist was that of trying to say carefully and persuasively what sexism is, and what it is for someone, some institution or some act to be sexist. This project was pressed on me with considerable urgency because, like most women coming to a feminist perception of themselves and the world, I was seeing sexism everywhere and trying to make it perceptible to others. I would point out, complain and criticize, but most frequently my friends and colleagues would not see that what I declared to be sexist was sexist, or at all objectionable.

As the critic and as the initiator of the topic, I was the one on whom the burden of proof fell—it was I who had to explain and convince. Teaching philosophy had already taught me that people cannot be persuaded of things they are not ready to be persuaded of; there are certain complexes of will and prior experience which will inevitably block persuasion, no matter the merits of the case presented. I knew that even if I could explain fully and clearly what I was saying when I called something sexist, I would not necessarily be able to convince various others of the correctness of this claim. But what troubled me enormously was that I could not explain it in any way which satisfied *me*. It is this sort of moral and intellectual frustration which, in my case at least, always generates philosophy.

The following was the product of my first attempt to state clearly and explicitly what sexism is:

> The term "sexist" in its core and perhaps
> most fundamental meaning is a term which
> characterizes anything whatever which
> creates, constitutes, promotes or exploits
> any irrelevant or impertinent marking of
> the distinction between the sexes.

When I composed this statement, I was thinking of the myriads of instances in which persons of the two sexes are treated differently, or behave differently, but where nothing in the real differences between females and males justifies or explains the differ-

---

Marilyn Frye, *The Politics of Reality: Essays in Feminist Theory*, The Crossing Press, 1983, 17–40. Reprinted by permission of the publisher.

ence of treatment or behavior. I was thinking, for instance, of the tracking of boys into Shop and girls into Home Ec, where one can see nothing about boys or girls considered in themselves which seems to connect essentially with the distinction between wrenches and eggbeaters. I was thinking also of sex discrimination in employment—cases where someone otherwise apparently qualified for a job is not hired because she is a woman. But when I tried to put this definition of "sexist" to use, it did not stand the test.

Consider this case: If a company is hiring a supervisor who will supervise a group of male workers who have always worked for male supervisors, it can scarcely be denied that the sex of a candidate for the job is relevant to the candidate's prospects of moving smoothly and successfully into an effective working relationship with the supervisees (though the point is usually exaggerated by those looking for excuses not to hire women). Relevance is an intrasystematic thing. The patterns of behavior, attitude and custom within which a process goes on determine what is relevant to what in matters of describing, predicting or evaluating. In the case at hand, the workers' attitudes and the surrounding customs of the culture make a difference to how they interact with their supervisor and, in particular, *make* the sex of the supervisor a relevant factor in predicting how things will work out. So then, if the company hires a man, in preference to a more experienced and knowledgeable woman, can we explain our objection to the decision by saying it involved distinguishing on the basis of sex when sex is irrelevant to the ability to do the job? No: sex is relevant here.

So, what did I mean to say about "sexist"? I was thinking that in a case of a candidate for a supervisory job, the reproductive capacity of the candidate has nothing to do with that person's knowing what needs to be done and being able to give properly timed, clear and correct directions. What I was picturing was a situation purified of all sexist perception and reaction. But, of course, *if* the whole context were not sexist, sex would not be an issue in such a job situation; indeed, it might go entirely unnoticed. It is precisely the fact that the sex of the candidate *is* relevant that is the salient symptom of the sexism of the situation.

I had failed, in that first essay, fully to grasp or understand that the locus of sexism is primarily in the system or framework, not in the particular act. It is not accurate to say that what is going on in cases of sexism is that distinctions are made on the basis of

sex when sex is irrelevant; what is wrong in cases of sexism is, in the first place, that sex *is* relevant; and then that the making of distinctions on the basis of sex reinforces the patterns which make it relevant.

In sexist cultural/economic systems, sex is always relevant. To understand what sexism is, then, we have to step back and take a larger view.

Sex-identification intrudes into every moment of our lives and discourse, no matter what the supposedly primary focus or topic of the moment is. Elaborate, systematic, ubiquitous and redundant marking of a distinction between the two sexes of humans and most animals is customary and obligatory. One *never* can ignore it.

Examples of sex-marking behavior patterns abound. A couple enters a restaurant; the headwaiter or hostess addresses the man and does not address the woman. The physician addresses the man by surname and honorific (Mr. Baxter, Rev. Jones) and addresses the woman by given name (Nancy, Gloria). You congratulate your friend—a hug, a slap on the back, shaking hands, kissing; one of the things which determines which of these you do is your friend's sex. In everything one does one has two complete repertoires of behavior, one for interactions with women and one for interactions with men. Greeting, storytelling, order-giving and order-receiving, negotiating, gesturing deference or dominance, encouraging, challenging, asking for information: one does all of these things differently depending upon whether the relevant others are male or female.

That this is so has been confirmed in sociological and socio-linguistic research, but it is just as easily confirmed in one's own experience. To discover the differences in how you greet a woman and how you greet a man, for instance, just observe yourself, paying attention to the following sorts of things: frequency and duration of eye contact, frequency and type of touch, tone and pitch of voice, physical distance maintained between bodies, how and whether you smile, use of slang or swear words, whether your body dips into a shadow curtsy or bow. That I have two repertoires for handling introductions to people was vividly confirmed for me when a student introduced me to his friend, Pat, and I really could not tell what sex Pat was. For a moment I was stopped cold, completely incapable of action. I felt myself helplessly caught between two paths—the one I would take if Pat were female and the one I would take if Pat were male. Of course the paralysis does not last. One is rescued by one's ingenuity and good will; one can invent a way to behave as one says "How do you do?" to a human being. But the habitual ways are not for humans: they are one way for women and another for men. . . .

In order to behave "appropriately" toward women and men, we have to know which of the people we encounter are women and which are men. But if you strip humans of most of their cultural trappings, it is not always that easy to tell without close inspection which are female, which are male. The tangible and visible physical differences between the sexes are not particularly sharp or numerous and in the physical dimensions we associate with "sex differences," the range of individual variation is very great. The differences between the sexes could easily be, and sometimes are, obscured by bodily decoration, hair removal and the like. So the requirement of knowing everyone's sex in every situation and under almost all observational conditions generates a requirement that we all let others know our sex in every situation. And we do. We announce our sexes in a thousand ways. We deck ourselves from head to toe with garments and decorations which serve like badges and buttons to announce our sexes. For every type of occasion there are distinct clothes, gear and accessories, hairdos, cosmetics and scents, labeled as "ladies" or "men's" and labeling us as females or males, and most of the time most of us choose, use, wear or bear the paraphernalia associated with our sex. It goes below the skin as well. There are different styles of gait, gesture, posture, speech, humor, taste and even of perception, interest and attention that we learn as we grow up to be women or to be men and that label and announce us as women or as men. It begins early in life: even infants in arms are color coded.

That we wear and bear signs of our sexes, and that this is absolutely compulsory, is made clearest in the relatively rare cases when we do not do so, or not enough. Responses ranging from critical to indignant to hostile meet mothers whose babies are not adequately coded; one of the most agitated criticisms of the sixties' hippies was that "you can't tell the boys from the girls." The requirement of sex-announcement is laden, indeed, with all the urgency of the taboo against homosexuality. One appears heterosexual by informing people of one's sex *very* emphatically and *very* unambiguously, and lesbians and homosexuals who wish *not* to pass as heterosexual generally can accomplish this just by cultivating ambiguous sex-indicators in clothes, behavior and style. The power of this ambiguity to generate unease and punitive responses in others mirrors and demonstrates the rigidity and urgency of this strange social rule that we all be and assertively act "feminine" or "masculine" (and not both)—that we flap a full array of sex-signals at all times.

The intense demand for marking and for asserting what sex each person is adds up to a strenuous requirement that there *be* two distinct and sharply dimorphic sexes. But, in reality, there are not. There are people who fit on a biological spectrum between two not-so-sharply defined poles. In about 5 percent of live births, possibly more, the babies are in some degree and way not perfect exemplars of male and female. There are individuals with chromosome patterns other than XX or YY and individuals whose external genitalia at birth exhibit some degree of ambiguity. There are people who are chromosomally "normal" who are at the far ends of the normal spectra of secondary sex characteristics—height, musculature, hairiness, body density, distribution of fat, breast size, etc.—whose overall appearance fits the norm of people whose chromosomal sex is the opposite of theirs.

These variations notwithstanding, persons (mainly men, of course) with the power to do so actually *construct* a world in which men are men and women are women and there is nothing in between and nothing ambiguous; they do it by chemically and/or surgically altering people whose bodies are indeterminate or ambiguous with respect to sex. Newborns with "imperfectly formed" genitals are immediately "corrected" by chemical or surgical means, children and adolescents are given hormone "therapies" if their bodies seem not to be developing according to what physicians and others declare to be the norm for what has been declared to be that individual's sex. Persons with authority recommend and supply cosmetics and cosmetic regimens, diets, exercises and all manner of clothing to revise or disguise the too-hairy lip, the too-large breast, the too-slender shoulders, the too-large feet, the too-great or too-slight stature. Individuals whose bodies do not fit the picture of exactly two sharply dimorphic sexes are often enough quite willing to be altered or veiled for the obvious reason that the world punishes them severely for their failure to be the "facts" which would verify the doctrine of two sexes. The demand that the world be a world in which there are exactly two sexes is inexorable, and we are all compelled to answer to it emphatically, unconditionally, repetitiously and unambiguously.

Even being physically "normal" for one's assigned sex is not enough. One must *be* female or male, actively. Again, the costumes and performances. Pressed to acting feminine or masculine, one colludes (co-lude: play along) with the doctors and counselors in the creation of a world in which the apparent dimorphism of the sexes is so extreme that one can only think there is a great gulf between female and male, that the two are, essentially and fundamentally and naturally, utterly different. One helps to create a world in which it seems to us that we *could* never mistake a woman for a man or a man for a woman. We never need worry.

Along with all the making, marking and announcing of sex-distinction goes a strong and visceral feeling or attitude to the effect that sex-distinction is the most important thing in the world: that it would be the end of the world if it were not maintained, clear and sharp and rigid; that a sex-dualism which is rooted in the nature of the beast is absolutely crucial and fundamental to all aspects of human life, human society and human economy. . . .

It is a general and obvious principle of information theory that when it is very, very important that certain information be conveyed, the suitable strategy is redundancy. If a message *must* get through, one sends it repeatedly and by as many means or media as one has at one's command. On the other end, as a receiver of information, if one receives the same information over and over, conveyed by every medium one knows, another message comes through as well, and implicitly: the message that this information is very, very important. The enormous frequency with which information about people's sexes is conveyed conveys implicitly the message that this topic is enormously important. I suspect that this is the single topic on which we most frequently receive information from others throughout our entire lives. If I am right, it would go partway to explaining why we end up with an almost irresistible impression, unarticulated, that the matter of people's sexes is the most important and most fundamental topic in the world.

We exchange sex-identification information, along with the implicit message that it is very important, in a variety of circumstances in which there really is no concrete or experientially obvious point in having the information. There are reasons, as this discussion has shown, why you should want to know whether the person filling your water glass or your tooth is male or female and why that person wants to know what you are, but those reasons are woven invisibly into the fabric of social structure and they do not have to do with the bare mechanics of things being filled. Furthermore, the same culture which drives us to this constant in-

formation exchange also simultaneously enforces a strong blanket rule requiring that the simplest and most nearly definitive physical manifestations of sex difference be hidden from view in all but the most private and intimate circumstances. The double message of sex-distinction and its preeminent importance is conveyed, in fact, in part *by* devices which systematically and deliberately cover up and hide from view the few physical things which do (to a fair extent) distinguish two sexes of humans. The messages are overwhelmingly dissociated from the concrete facts they supposedly pertain to, and from matrices of concrete and sensible reasons and consequences. . . .

If one is made to feel that a thing is of prime importance, but common sensory experience does not connect it with things of obvious concrete and practical importance, then there is mystery, and with that a strong tendency to the construction of mystical or metaphysical conceptions of its importance. If it is important, but not of mundane importance, it must be of transcendent importance. All the more so if it is *very* important.

This matter of our sexes must be very profound indeed if it must, on pain of shame and ostracism, be covered up and must, on pain of shame and ostracism, be boldly advertised by every means and medium one can devise.

There is one more point about redundancy that is worth making here. If there is one thing more effective in making one believe a thing than receiving the message repetitively, it is rehearsing it repetitively. Advertisers, preachers, teachers, all of us in the brainwashing professions, make use of this apparently physical fact of human psychology routinely. The redundancy of sex-marking and sex-announcing serves not only to make the topic seem transcendently important, but to make the sex-duality it advertises seem transcendently and unquestionably *true*. . . .

Sex-marking and sex-announcing are equally compulsory for males and females; but that is as far as equality goes in this matter. The meaning and import of this behavior is profoundly different for women and for men.

Whatever features an individual male person has which tend to his social and economic disadvantage (his age, race, class, height, etc.), one feature which never tends to his disadvantage in the society at large is his maleness. The case for females is the mirror image of this. Whatever features an individual female person has which tend to her social and economic advantage (her age, race, etc.), one feature which always tends to her disadvantage is her femaleness. Therefore, when a male's sex-category is the thing about him that gets first and most repeated notice, the thing about him that is being framed and emphasized and given primacy is a feature which in general is an asset to him. When a female's sex-category is the thing about her that gets first and most repeated notice, the thing about her that is being framed and emphasized and given primacy is a feature which in general is a liability to her. Manifestations of this divergence in the meaning and consequences of sex-announcement can be very concrete.

Walking down the street in the evening in a town or city exposes one to some risk of assault. For males the risk is less; for females the risk is greater. If one announces oneself male, one is presumed by potential assailants to be more rather than less likely to defend oneself or be able to evade the assault and, if the male-announcement is strong and unambiguous, to be a noncandidate for sexual assault. If one announces oneself female, one is presumed by potential assailants to be less rather than more likely to defend oneself or to evade the assault and, if the female-announcement is strong and unambiguous, to be a prime candidate for sexual assault. Both the man and the woman "announce" their sex through style of gait, clothing, hairstyle, etc., but they are not equally or identically affected by announcing their sex. The male's announcement tends toward his protection or safety, and the female's announcement tends toward her victimization. It could not be more immediate or concrete; the meaning of the sex-identification could not be more different.

The sex-marking behavioral repertoires are such that in the behavior of almost all people of both sexes addressing or responding to males (especially within their own culture/race) generally is done in a manner which suggests basic respect, while addressing or responding to females is done in a manner that suggests the females' inferiority (condescending tones, presumptions of ignorance, over-familiarity, sexual aggression, etc.). So, when one approaches an ordinary well-socialized person in such cultures, if one is male, one's own behavioral announcement of maleness tends to evoke supportive and beneficial response and if one is female, one's own behavioral announcement of femaleness tends to evoke degrading and detrimental response.

The details of the sex-announcing behaviors also contribute to the reduction of women and the elevation of men. The case is most obvious in the matter of clothing. As feminists have been saying for

two hundred years or so, ladies' clothing is generally restrictive, binding, burdening and frail; it threatens to fall apart and/or to uncover something that is supposed to be covered if you bend, reach, kick, punch or run. It typically does not protect effectively against hazards in the environment, nor permit the wearer to protect herself against the hazards of the human environment. Men's clothing is generally the opposite of all this—sturdy, suitably protective, permitting movement and locomotion. The details of feminine manners and postures also serve to bind and restrict. To be feminine is to take up little space, to defer to others, to be silent or affirming of others, etc. It is not necessary here to survey all this, for it has been done many times and in illuminating detail in feminist writings. My point here is that though both men and women must behave in sex-announcing ways, the behavior which announces femaleness is in itself both physically and socially binding and limiting as the behavior which announces maleness is not.

The sex-correlated variations in our behavior tend systematically to the benefit of males and the detriment of females. The male, announcing his sex in sex-identifying behavior and dress, is both announcing and acting on his membership in a dominant caste—dominant within his subculture and to a fair extent across subcultures as well. The female, announcing her sex, is both announcing and acting on her membership in the subordinated caste. She is obliged to inform others constantly and in every sort of situation that she is to be treated as inferior, without authority, assaultable. She cannot move or speak within the usual cultural norms without engaging in self-deprecation. The male cannot move or speak without engaging in self-aggrandizement. Constant sex-identification both defines and maintains the caste boundary without which there could not be a dominance–subordination structure. . . .

The cultural and economic structures which create and enforce elaborate and rigid patterns of sex-marking and sex-announcing behavior, that is, create gender as we know it, mold us as dominators and subordinates (I do not say "mold our minds" or "mold our personalities"). They construct two classes of animals, the masculine and the feminine, where another constellation of forces might have constructed three or five categories, and not necessarily hierarchically related. Or such a spectrum of sorts that we would not experience them as "sorts" at all.

The term "sexist" characterizes cultural and economic structures which create and enforce the elaborate and rigid patterns of sex-marking and sex-announcing which divide the species, along lines of sex, into dominators and subordinates. Individual acts and practices are sexist which reinforce and support those structures, either as culture or as shapes taken on by the enculturated animals. Resistance to sexism is that which undermines those structures by social and political action and by projects of reconstruction and revision of ourselves.

DISCUSSION QUESTIONS

1. Critically discuss Frye's final definition of "sexism." How is it different from her earlier definition? Why does she change her definition?
2. What does Fry mean by "sex-marking" and "sex-announcing"? Provide your own examples of these.
3. For Frye, "the locus of sexism is primarily in the system or framework, not in the particular act." What does she mean by this? What is her argument? Do you agree with her? Why or why not?
4. Sexism is not always apparent either to those who suffer from it or to those who inflict it upon others, argues Frye. What do you think about this claim? Does Frye convince you that this is the case? Discuss.
5. Frye writes that "people cannot be persuaded of things they are not ready to be persuaded of." What does she mean by this? Do you agree with her? How do people who do not find their society to be sexist come to be "ready to be persuaded" that it is?
6. Do you think that all sex-marking necessarily has to do with dominance and subordination? Is sex-marking and sex-announcing conceivable within the context of equality? Explain.

STEVEN GOLDBERG

The Inevitability of Patriarchy

Steven Goldberg disagrees with Marilyn Frye and others that sexism is the consequence of cultural and economic frameworks, arguing instead that sexism is inevitable because of certain biological factors. According to Goldberg, males have hormonal systems that generate a greater capacity for aggression than do females. Cultural and economic institutions conform to the reality of hormonal sexual differentiation and to the statistical reality of the "aggression advantage" that males derive from their hormonal systems. "Male roles are not given high status primarily *because* men fill these roles," says Goldberg. "Men fill these roles because of their biological aggression 'advantage.'" Sexism and sexual oppression are not the result of male aggressive energies directed toward females, argues Goldberg, nor are they the result of cultural and economic institutions directed toward oppressing women. "In reality," says Goldberg, "these male energies are directed toward attainment of desired positions and toward succeeding in whatever areas a particular society considers important. . . . The fact that women lose out in these competitions, so that the sex-role expectations of a society would have to become different for men and women even if they were not different for other reasons, is an inevitable byproduct of the reality of the male's aggression advantage and not the cause, purpose, or primary function of it."

Steven Goldberg is the author of *The Inevitability of Patriarchy* (1974), *When Wish Replaces Thought: Why So Much of What You Believe Is False* (1991), and *Why Men Rule: A Theory of Male Dominance* (1993).

THE FEMINIST ASSUMPTION

The view of man and woman in society that implicitly underlies all of the arguments of the feminists is this: there is nothing inherent in the nature of human beings or of society that necessitates that any role or task (save those requiring great strength or the ability to give birth) be associated with one sex or the other; there is no natural order of things decreeing that dyadic and social authority must be associated with men, nor is there any reason why it must be men who rule in every society. Patriarchy, matriarchy, and "equiarchy" are all equally possible and—while every society may invoke "the natural order of things" to justify its particular system—all the expectations we have of men and women are culturally determined and have nothing to do with any sort of basic male or female nature.

There is nothing internally contradictory in such a hypothesis; indeed, it is an ideal place from which to begin an empirical investigation into the nature of man, woman, and society. However, the feminist does not use this as a heuristic first step but unquestioningly accepts it as true. . . .

. . . The only biological hypothesis included [here] states that those individuals whose male anatomy leads to a social identification as "male" have hormonal systems which generate a greater capacity for "aggression" (or a lower threshold for the release of "aggression"—for our purposes this is the same thing) than those individuals whose female anatomy leads to a social identification as "female" and that socialization and institutions conform to the reality of hormonal sexual differentiation and to the statistical reality of the "aggression advantage" which males derive from their hormonal systems. . . .

AGGRESSION AND ATTAINMENT

In other words, I believe that in the past we have been looking in the wrong direction for the answer to the question of why every society rewards male roles with higher status than it does female roles (even when the male tasks in one society are the female tasks in another). While it is true that men are always in the positions of authority from which status tends to be defined, male roles are not given high status primarily *because* men fill these roles; men fill these roles because their biological aggression "advantage" can be manifested *in any non-child related area rewarded by high status in any society.* (Again: the line of reasoning used in this book demonstrates only that the biological factors we discuss would make the social institutions we discuss inevitable and does not preclude the existence of other forces also leading in the same direction; there may be a biologically based tendency for women to prefer male leadership, but there need not be for male attainment of leadership and high-status roles to be inevitable.) As we shall see, this aggression "advantage" can be most manifested and can most enable men to reap status rewards *not* in those relatively homogeneous, collectivist primitive societies in which both male and female must play similar economic roles if the society is to survive or in the monarchy (which guarantees an occasional female leader); this biological factor will be given freest play in the complex, relatively individualistic, bureaucratic, democratic society which, of necessity, must emphasize organizational authority and in which social mobility is relatively free of traditional barriers to advancement. There were more female heads of state in the first two-thirds of the sixteenth century than in the first two-thirds of the twentieth.

The mechanisms involved here are easily seen if we examine any roles that males have attained by channeling their aggression toward such attainment. We will assume for now that equivalent women could *perform* the tasks of roles as well as men if they could attain the roles. Here we can speak of the corporation president, the union leader, the governor, the chairman of an association, or any other role or position for which aggression is a precondition for attainment. Now the environmentalist and the feminist will say that the fact that all such roles are nearly always filled by men is attributable not to male aggression but to the fact that women have not been allowed to enter the competitive race to attain these positions, that they have been told that these positions are in male areas, and that girls are socialized away from competing with boys in general. Women *are* socialized in this way, but again we must ask why. If innate male aggression has nothing to do with male attainment of positions of authority and status in the political, academic, scientific, or financial spheres, if aggression has nothing to do with the reasons why *every* society socializes girls away from those areas which are given high status and away from competition in general, then why is it never the *girls* in any society who are socialized toward these areas, why is it never the nonbiological roles played by women that have high status, why is it always boys who are told to compete, and why do women never "force" men into the low-status, nonmaternal roles that women play in every society?

These questions pose no problem if we acknowledge a male aggression that enables men to attain any nonbiological role given high status by any society. For one need merely consider the result of a society's *not* socializing women away from competitions with men, from its *not* directing girls toward roles women are more capable of playing than are men or roles with status low enough that men will not strive for them. No doubt some women would be aggressive enough to succeed in competitions with men and there would be considerably more women in high-status positions than there are now. But most women would lose in such competitive struggles with men (because men have the aggression advantage) and so most women would be forced to live adult lives as failures in areas in which the society had *wanted them to succeed.* It is women, far more than men, who would never allow a situation in which girls were socialized in such a way that the vast majority of them were doomed to adult lifetimes of failure to live up to their own expectations. Now I have no doubt that there is a biological factor that gives women the desire to emphasize maternal and nurturance roles, but the point here is that we can accept the feminist assumption that there is no female propensity of this sort and still see that a society must socialize

women away from roles that men will attain through their aggression. For if women did not develop an alternative set of criteria for success, their sense of their own competence would suffer intolerably. It is undeniable that the resulting different values and expectations that are attached to men and women will tend to work against the aggressive woman while they work for the man who is no more aggressive. But this is the unavoidable result of the fact that most men are more aggressive than most women so that this woman, who is as aggressive as the average man, but more aggressive than most women, is an exception. Furthermore, even if the sense of competence of each sex did not necessitate society's attaching to each sex values and expectations based on those qualities possessed by each sex, observation of the majority of each sex by the population would "automatically" lead to these values and expectations being attached to men and women.

SOCIALIZATION'S CONFORMATION TO BIOLOGICAL REALITY

Socialization is the process by which society prepares children for adulthood. The way in which its goals conform to the reality of biology is seen quite clearly when we consider the method in which testosterone generates male aggression (testosterone's serially developing nature). Preadolescent boys and girls have roughly equal testosterone levels, yet young boys are far more aggressive than young girls. Eva Figes has used this observation to dismiss incorrectly the possibility of a hormone-aggression association.[1] Now it is quite probable that the boy is more aggressive than the girl for a purely biological reason. We have seen that it is simplistic to speak simply in terms of hormone levels and that there is evidence of male-female differences in the behavior of infants shortly after birth (when differential socialization is not a plausible explanation of such differences). The fetal alteration of the boy's brain by the testosterone that was generated by his testes has probably left him far more sensitive to the aggression-related properties of the testosterone that is present during boyhood than the girl, who did not receive such alteration. But let us for the moment assume that this is not the case. This does not at all reduce the importance of the hormonal factor. For even if the boy is more aggressive than the girl only because the society allows him to be, the boy's socialization still flows from society's acknowledging biological reality. Let us consider what would happen if girls had the same innate aggression as boys and if a society did not socialize girls away from aggressive competitions. Perhaps half of the third-grade baseball team would be female. As many girls as boys would frame their expectations in masculine values and girls would develop not their feminine abilities but their masculine ones. During adolescence, however, the same assertion of the male chromosomal program that causes the boys to grow beards raises their testosterone level, and their potential for aggression, to a level far above that of the adolescent woman. If society did not teach young girls that beating boys at competitions was unfeminine (behavior inappropriate for a woman), if it did not socialize them away from the political and economic areas in which aggression leads to attainment, these girls would grow into adulthood with self-images based not on succeeding in areas for which biology has left them better prepared than men, but on competitions that most women could not win. If women did not develop feminine qualities as girls (assuming that such qualities do not spring automatically from female biology), then they would be forced to deal with the world in the aggressive terms of men. They would lose every source of power their feminine abilities now give them and they would gain nothing. . . .

DISCRIMINATION OF A SORT

If one is convinced that sexual biology gives the male an advantage in aggression, competitiveness, and dominance, but he does not believe that it engenders in men and women different propensities, cognitive aptitudes, and modes of perception, and if he considers it discrimination when male aggression leads to attainment of position even when aggression is not relevant to the task to be performed, then the unavoidable conclusion is that discrimination so defined is unavoidable. Even if one is convinced . . . that the differing biological substrates that underlie the mental apparatus of men and women *do* engender different propensities, cognitive aptitudes, and modes of perception, he will probably agree that the relevance of this to male attainment of male roles is small when compared to the importance of male biological aggression to attainment. Innate tendencies to specific aptitudes *would* indicate that at any given level of competence there will be more men than women or vice versa (depending on the qualities relevant to the task) and that the very best will, in all probability, come from the sex whose potentials are relevant to the task. Nonetheless, drastic sexual differences in occupational and authority roles reflect male aggression and society's acknowledgment of it far more than they do differences in aptitudes, yet they are still inevitable.

In addition, even if artificial means were used to place large numbers of women in authority positions, it is doubtful that stability could be maintained. Even in our present male bureaucracies problems arise whenever a subordinate is more aggressive than his superior and, if the more aggressive executive is not allowed to rise in the bureaucracy, delicate psychological adjustments must be made. Such adjustments are also necessary when a male bureaucrat has a female superior. When such situations are rare exceptions adjustments can be made without any great instability occurring, particularly if the woman in the superior position complements her aggression with sensitivity and femininity. It would seem likely, however, that if women shared equally in power at each level of the bureaucracy, chaos would result for two reasons. Even if we consider the bureaucracy as a closed system, the excess of male aggression would soon manifest itself either in men moving quickly up the hierarchy or in a male refusal to acknowledge female authority. But a bureaucracy is not a closed system, and the discrepancy between male dominance in private life and bureaucratic female dominance (from the point of view of the male whose superior is a woman) would soon engender chaos. Consider that even the present minute minority of women in high authority positions expend enormous amounts of energy trying *not* to project the commanding authority that is seen as the mark of a good male executive. It is true that the manner in which aggression is manifested will be affected by the values of the society in general and the nature of the field of competition in particular; aggression in an academic environment is camouflaged far more than in the executive arena. While a desire for control and power and a single-mindedness of purpose are no doubt relevant, here aggression is not easily defined. One might inject the theoretical argument that women could attain positions of authority and leadership by countering the male's advantage in aggression with feminine abilities. Perhaps, but the equivalents of the executive positions in every area of suprafamilial life in every society have been attained by men, and there seems no reason to believe that, suddenly, feminine means will be capable of neutralizing male aggression in these areas. And, in any case, an emphasis on feminine abilities is hardly what the feminists desire. All of this can be seen in a considerably more optimistic light, from the point of view of most women, if one considers that the biological abilities possessed only by women are complemented by biologically generated propensities directing women to roles that can be filled only by women. But it is still the same picture. . . .

"OPPRESSION"

All of this indicates that the theoretical model that conceives of male success in attaining positions of status, authority, and leadership as *oppression* of the female is incorrect if only because it sees male aggressive energies as *directed toward* females and sees the institutional mechanisms that flow from the fact of male aggression as *directed toward* "oppressing" women. In reality these male energies are directed toward attainment of desired positions and toward succeeding in whatever areas a particular society considers important. The fact that women lose out in these competitions, so that the sex-role expectations of a society would have to become different for men and women even if they were not different for other reasons, is an inevitable byproduct of the reality of the male's aggression advantage and not the cause, purpose, or primary function of it. In other words, men who attain the more desired roles and positions do so because they channel their aggression advantage toward such attainment; whether the losers in such competitions are other men or women is important only in that—because so few women succeed in these competitions—the society will attach different expectations to men and women (making it more difficult for the exceptional, aggressive woman to attain such positions even when her aggression is equal to that of the average man).

NOTE

1. Eva Figes, *Patriarchal Attitudes* (Greenwich, CT: Fawcett World, 1971), p. 8.

DISCUSSION QUESTIONS

1. Why, according to Goldberg, is sexism morally justifiable? Critically analyze his argument.
2. Compare and contrast Goldberg and Marilyn Frye on the foundations of sexism. Who do you agree with? Is sexism the consequence of cultural and economic frameworks, as Frye contends, or the inevitable consequence of biological factors, as Goldberg contends?
3. For the sake of argument, assume that it *is* the case that males have hormonal systems that generate a greater capacity for aggression than females. Can we derive what *ought* to be the case from what *is* the case? Is this what Goldberg is doing? Is he saying that, because males' aggression advantage *is* the case, sexism *ought* to be the case? Is sexism morally justifiable on the basis of biology? How might Frye or John Stuart Mill (see p. 412) respond to this line of argument?
4. Is violence against women ever morally justifiable on the basis of biology? Why or why not? Defend your view.
5. Goldberg says that "if society did not teach young girls that beating boys at competitions was unfeminine . . . these girls would grow into adulthood with self-images based on succeeding in . . . competitions that most women could not win." Is it really true that "aggression" helps people land jobs and keep them? Does the type of job play a role? Does aggression help one to land a job as a mathematician? A chef? Defend your view against counterarguments.

 PLATO

On the Equality of Women

This reading is from the fifth book of Plato's *Republic*. In it, Socrates argues for the equality of the sexes. The first four books have Socrates discussing with his friends the definition of justice through, in part, the construction of an ideal city. If the city is to be just, it must be protected from unrest both within and without. The job of protecting the city falls upon a class of citizens called "guardians." According to Plato, these guardians must be trained carefully in order to ensure that they do their job reliably. Good guardians must be obedient, loyal, and courageous. In earlier books, Socrates said that both men and women could be guardians as long as they had a loyal and courageous character. He also said that private marriages among the guardians would destroy the camaraderie and trust of the guardians and suggested that wives be shared in common. In this, the fifth book of the *Republic*, Socrates' interlocutors, Polemarchus and Adeimantus, encourage him to discuss in more detail the role of women in the just city. In the following selection, Socrates argues that this ideal city will have arranged marriages and will educate men and women identically. He also suggests that modesty about our bodies is immature and keeps the city from functioning justly. Therefore, men and women, young and old, should exercise together naked. For Plato, the physical similarities and differences between men and women are not important. The virtuous life is achieved through the state of one's character, not one's physical characteristics. For example, in the passage about "bald men," Socrates argues that in most cases only one's character is relevant to one's job. Says Socrates, "We never meant when we constructed the State, that the opposition of natures should extend to every difference, but only to those differences which affected the pursuit in which the individual is engaged." Therefore, men and women of similar character should do similar jobs. Even though some physical qualities may be necessary for some jobs, for Socrates this is only rarely the case. The implications of Socrates' reflections on the equality of women in the city are that sexism is not in the best interests of the state. Nevertheless, even if "all the pursuits of men are the pursuits of women also," Socrates adds, "but in all of them a women is inferior to a man."

Plato (427–347 B.C., Socrates' (470–399 B.C.) student, wrote many dialogues like *The Republic* wherein Socrates appears as a main character. Socrates is widely considered to be the father of Western moral philosophy.

Well, I replied, I suppose that I must retrace my steps and say what I perhaps ought to have said before in the proper place. The part of the men has been played out, and now properly enough comes the turn of the women. Of them I will proceed to speak, and the more readily since I am invited by you.

For men born and educated like our citizens, the only way, in my opinion, of arriving at a right conclusion about the possession and use of women and children is to follow the path on which we originally started, when we said that the men were to be the guardians and watchdogs of the herd.

True.

Let us further suppose the birth and education of our women to be subject to similar or nearly similar regulations; then we shall see whether the result accords with our design.

What do you mean?

Plato, *The Republic*. Translated by Benjamin Jowett, 3rd edition. Oxford University Press, 1882.

What I mean may be put into the form of a question. I said: Are dogs divided into hes and shes, or do they both share equally in hunting and in keeping watch and in the other duties of dogs? or do we entrust to the males the entire and exclusive care of the flocks, while we leave the females at home, under the idea that the bearing and suckling their puppies is labour enough for them?

No, he said, they share alike; the only difference between them is that the males are stronger and the females weaker.

But can you use different animals for the same purpose, unless they are bred and fed in the same way?

You cannot.

Then, if women are to have the same duties as men, they must have the same nurture and education?

Yes.

The education which was assigned to the men was music and gymnastic.

Yes.

Then women must be taught music and gymnastic and also the art of war, which they must practice like the men?

That is the inference, I suppose.

I should rather expect, I said, that several of our proposals, if they are carried out, being unusual, may appear ridiculous.

No doubt of it.

Yes, and the most ridiculous thing of all will be the sight of women naked in the palaestra, exercising with the men, especially when they are no longer young; they certainly will not be a vision of beauty, any more than the enthusiastic old men who in spite of wrinkles and ugliness continue to frequent the gymnasia.

Yes, indeed, he said: according to present notions the proposal would be thought ridiculous.

But then, I said, as we have determined to speak our minds, we must not fear the jests of the wits which will be directed against this sort of innovation; how they will talk of women's attainments both in music and gymnastic, and above all about their wearing armour and riding upon horseback!

Very true, he replied.

Yet having begun we must go forward to the rough places of the law; at the same time begging of these gentlemen for once in their life to be serious. Not long ago, as we shall remind them, the Hellenes were of the opinion, which is still generally received among the barbarians, that the sight of a naked man was ridiculous and improper; and when first the

Cretans and then the Lacedaemonians introduced the custom, the wits of that day might equally have ridiculed the innovation.

No doubt.

But when experience showed that to let all things be uncovered was far better than to cover them up, and the ludicrous effect to the outward eye vanished before the better principle which reason asserted, then the man was perceived to be a fool who directs the shafts of his ridicule at any other sight but that of folly and vice, or seriously inclines to weigh the beautiful by any other standard but that of the good.

Very true, he replied.

First, then, whether the question is to be put in jest or in earnest, let us come to an understanding about the nature of woman: Is she capable of sharing either wholly or partially in the actions of men, or not at all? And is the art of war one of those arts in which she can or cannot share? That will be the best way of commencing the enquiry, and will probably lead to the fairest conclusion.

That will be much the best way.

Shall we take the other side first and begin by arguing against ourselves; in this manner the adversary's position will not be undefended.

Why not? he said.

Then let us put a speech into the mouths of our opponents. They will say: "Socrates and Glaucon, no adversary need convict you, for you yourselves, at the first foundation of the State, admitted the principle that everybody was to do the one work suited to his own nature." And certainly, if I am not mistaken, such an admission was made by us. "And do not the natures of men and women differ very much indeed?" And we shall reply: Of course they do. Then we shall be asked, "Whether the tasks assigned to men and to women should not be different, and such as are agreeable to their different natures?" Certainly they should. "But if so, have you not fallen into a serious inconsistency in saying that men and women, whose natures are so entirely different, ought to perform the same actions?"—What defense will you make for us, my good Sir, against any one who offers these objections?

That is not an easy question to answer when asked suddenly; and I shall and I do beg of you to draw out the case on our side.

These are the objections, Glaucon, and there are many others of a like kind, which I foresaw long ago; they made me afraid and reluctant to take in hand any law about the possession and nurture of women and children.

By Zeus, he said, the problem to be solved is anything but easy.

Why yes, I said, but the fact is that when a man is out of his depth, whether he has fallen into a little swimming bath or into mid ocean, he has to swim all the same.

Very true.

And must not we swim and try to reach the shore: we will hope that Arion's dolphin or some other miraculous help may save us?

I suppose so, he said.

Well then, let us see if any way of escape can be found. We acknowledged—did we not? that different natures ought to have different pursuits, and that men's and women's natures are different. And now what are we saying?—that different natures ought to have the same pursuits,—this is the inconsistency which is charged upon us.

Precisely.

Verily, Glaucon, I said, glorious is the power of the art of contradiction!

Why do you say so?

Because I think that many a man falls into the practice against his will. When he thinks that he is reasoning he is really disputing, just because he cannot define and divide, and so know that of which he is speaking; and he will pursue a merely verbal opposition in the spirit of contention and not of fair discussion.

Yes, he replied, such is very often the case; but what has that to do with us and our argument?

A great deal; for there is certainly a danger of our getting unintentionally into a verbal opposition.

In what way?

Why we valiantly and pugnaciously insist upon the verbal truth, that different natures ought to have different pursuits, but we never considered at all what was the meaning of sameness or difference of nature, or why we distinguished them when we assigned different pursuits to different natures and the same to the same natures.

Why, no, he said, that was never considered by us.

I said: Suppose that by way of illustration we were to ask the question whether there is not an opposition in nature between bald men and hairy men; and if this is admitted by us, then, if bald men are cobblers, we should forbid the hairy men to be cobblers, and conversely?

That would be a jest, he said.

Yes, I said, a jest; and why? because we never meant when we constructed the State, that the opposition of natures should extend to every difference, but only to those differences which affected the pursuit in which the individual is engaged; we should have argued, for example, that a physician and one who is in mind a physician may be said to have the same nature.

True.

Whereas the physician and the carpenter have different natures?

Certainly.

And if, I said, the male and female sex appear to differ in their fitness for any art or pursuit, we should say that such pursuit or art ought to be assigned to one or the other of them; but if the difference consists only in women bearing and men begetting children, this does not amount to a proof that a woman differs from a man in respect of the sort of education she should receive; and we shall therefore continue to maintain that our guardians and their wives ought to have the same pursuits.

Very true, he said.

Next, we shall ask our opponent how, in reference to any of the pursuits or arts of civic life, the nature of a woman differs from that of a man?

That will be quite fair.

And perhaps he, like yourself, will reply that to give a sufficient answer on the instant is not easy; but after a little reflection there is no difficulty.

Yes, perhaps.

Suppose then that we invite him to accompany us in the argument, and then we may hope to show him that there is nothing peculiar in the constitution of women which would affect them in the administration of the State.

By all means.

Let us say to him: Come now, and we will ask you a question:—when you spoke of a nature gifted or not gifted in any respect, did you mean to say that one man will acquire a thing easily, another with difficulty; a little learning will lead the one to discover a great deal; whereas the other, after much study and application, no sooner learns than he forgets; or again, did you mean, that the one has a body which is a good servant to his mind, while the body of the other is a hindrance to him?—would not these be the sort of differences which distinguish the man gifted by nature from the one who is ungifted?

No one will deny that.

And can you mention any pursuit of mankind in which the male sex has not all these gifts and qualities in a higher degree than the female? Need I waste time in speaking of the art of weaving, and the management of pancakes and preserves, in which womankind does really appear to be great, and in which for her to be beaten by a man is of all things the most absurd?

You are quite right, he replied, in maintaining the general inferiority of the female sex: although many women are in many things superior to many men, yet on the whole what you say is true.

And if so, my friend, I said, there is no special faculty of administration in a State which a woman has because she is a woman, or which a man has by virtue of his sex, but the gifts of nature are alike diffused in both; all the pursuits of men are the pursuits of women also, but in all of them a woman is inferior to a man.

Very true.

Then are we to impose all our enactments on men and none of them on women?

That will never do.

One woman has a gift of healing, another not; one is a musician, and another has no music in her nature?

Very true.

And one woman has a turn for gymnastic and military exercises, and another is unwarlike and hates gymnastics?

Certainly.

And one woman is a philosopher, and another is an enemy of philosophy; one has spirit, and another is without spirit?

That is also true.

Then one woman will have the temper of a guardian, and another not. Was not the selection of the male guardians determined by differences of this sort?

Yes.

Men and women alike possess the qualities which make a guardian; they differ only in their comparative strength or weakness.

Obviously.

And those women who have such qualities are to be selected as the companions and colleagues of men who have similar qualities and whom they resemble in capacity and in character?

Very true.

And ought not the same natures to have the same pursuits?

They ought.

Then, as we were saying before, there is nothing unnatural in assigning music and gymnastic to the wives of the guardians—to that point we come round again.

Certainly not.

The law which we then enacted was agreeable to nature, and therefore not an impossibility or mere aspiration; and the contrary practice, which prevails at present, is in reality a violation of nature.

That appears to be true.

We had to consider, first, whether our proposals were possible, and secondly whether they were the most beneficial?

Yes.

And the possibility has been acknowledged?

Yes.

The very great benefit has next to be established?

Quite so.

You will admit that the same education which makes a man a good guardian will make a woman a good guardian; for their original nature is the same?

Yes.

I should like to ask you a question.

What is it?

Would you say that all men are equal in excellence, or is one man better than another?

The latter.

And in the commonwealth which we were founding do you conceive the guardians who have been brought up on our model system to be more perfect men, or the cobblers whose education has been cobbling?

What a ridiculous question!

You have answered me, I replied: Well, and may we not further say that our guardians are the best of our citizens?

By far the best.

And will not their wives be the best women?

Yes, by far the best.

And can there be anything better for the interests of the State than that the men and women of a State should be as good as possible?

There can be nothing better.

And this is what the arts of music and gymnastic, when present in such manner as we have described, will accomplish?

Certainly.

Then we have made an enactment not only possible but in the highest degree beneficial to the State?

True.

Then let the wives of our guardians strip, for their virtue will be their robe, and let them share in the toils of war and the defence of their country; only in the distribution of labours the lighter are to be assigned to the women, who are the weaker natures, but in other respects their duties are to be the same. And as for the man who laughs at naked women exercising their bodies from the best of motives, in his laughter he is plucking

A fruit of unripe wisdom,

and he himself is ignorant of what he is laughing at, or what he is about;—for that is, and ever will be, the best of sayings, *That the useful is the noble and the hurtful is the base.*

Very true.

DISCUSSION QUESTIONS

1. What is Socrates' position on sexism? What is his position on sex roles? What are the major strengths and weaknesses of his views?
2. What does Socrates mean when he says that "all the pursuits of men are the pursuits of women also, but in all of them a women is inferior to a man"? Do you agree with him? Why or why not?
3. Socrates believes that both men and women should be entrusted with protecting the state. What is his argument?
4. Socrates says that "we never meant when we constructed the State, that the opposition of natures should extend to every difference, but only to those differences which affected the pursuit in which the individual is engaged." What does he mean by this?
5. Do you think that Socrates' observations on men and women hold in contemporary American society? Or are they the products of a different era? Defend your view.

 A R I S T O T L E

On the Inequality of Women

Aristotle disagrees with Socrates' position on the equality of women. Unlike Socrates, Aristotle maintains that men and women have different natural tendencies toward virtue. For example, the courage of a man is not the same as that of a woman—"the courage of a man is shown in commanding, of a woman in obeying." Consequently, women "would seem to be more useful," says Aristotle, "among the farmers rather than among the guardians" (*Politics* bk. II, chap. 4). Also, for Aristotle, there is no equality between the sexes in marriage. He writes that husbands rule over their wives and that this *constitutional* type of rule is possible only with the consent of the wives. The constitutional rule of husbands over their wives differs from the *royal rule* that fathers hold over children due to the superior position of fathers. For a household to function smoothly, it is necessary that either the husband or the wife rule consistently. Thus, given that men have a natural tendency toward the virtues necessary for rule, Aristotle argues that men are usually better suited to rule in the marriage relation and in the household than women. The following is from Book 1, Chapters 12 and 13, of Aristotle's *Politics*. A biographical sketch of Aristotle appears in Chapter 1.

Aristotle, *The Works of Aristotle.* Edited by W. David Ross. Translated by J. I. Beave. Vol. 10, Oxford University Press, 1921.

Of household management we have seen that there are three parts—one is the rule of a master over slaves, . . . another of a father, and the third of a husband. A husband and father . . . rules over wife and children, both free, but the rule differs, the rule over his children being a royal, over his wife a constitutional rule. For although there may be exceptions to the order of nature, the male is by nature fitter for command than the female, just as the elder and full-grown is superior to the younger and more immature. But in most constitutional states the citizens rule and are ruled by turns, for the idea of a constitutional state implies that the natures of the citizens are equal, and do not differ at all. Nevertheless, when one rules and the other is ruled we endeavour to create a difference of outward forms and names and titles of respect, . . . The relation of the male to the female is of this kind, but there the inequality is permanent. A question may indeed be raised, whether there is any excellence at all in a slave beyond and higher than merely instrumental and ministerial qualities—whether he can have the virtues of temperance, courage, justice, and the like; or whether slaves possess only bodily and ministerial qualities. And, whichever way we answer the question, a difficulty arises; for, if they have virtue, in what will they differ from freemen? On the other hand, since they are men and share in rational principle, it seems absurd to say that they have no virtue. A similar question may be raised about women and children, whether they too have virtues: ought a woman to be temperate and brave and just, and is a child to be called temperate, and intemperate, or not? So in general we may ask about the natural ruler, and the natural subject, whether they have the same or different virtues. For if a noble nature is equally required in both, why should one of them always rule, and the other always be ruled? Nor can we say that this is a question of degree, for the difference between ruler and subject is a difference of kind, which the difference of more and less never is. Yet how strange is the supposition that the one ought, and that the other ought not, to have virtue! For if the ruler is intemperate and unjust, how can he rule well? if the subject, how can he obey well? If he be licentious and cowardly, he will certainly not do his duty. It is evident, therefore, that both of them must have a share of virtue, but varying as natural subjects also vary among themselves. Here the very constitution of the soul has shown us the way; in it one part naturally rules, and the other is subject, and the virtue of the ruler we maintain to be different from that of the subject;—the one being the

virtue of the rational, and the other of the irrational part. Now, it is obvious that the same principle applies generally, and therefore almost all things rule and are ruled according to nature. But the kind of rule differs;—the freeman rules over the slave after another manner from that in which the male rules over the female, or the man over the child; although the parts of the soul are present in all of them, they are present in different degrees. For the slave has no deliberative faculty at all; the woman has, but it is without authority, and the child has, but it is immature. So it must necessarily be supposed to be with the moral virtues also; all should partake of them, but only in such manner and degree as is required by each for the fulfilment of his duty. Hence the ruler ought to have moral virtue in perfection, for his function, taken absolutely, demands a master artificer, and rational principle is such an artificer; the subjects, on the other hand, require only that measure of virtue which is proper to each of them. Clearly, then, moral virtue belongs to all of them; but the temperance of a man and of a woman, or the courage and justice of a man and of a woman, are not, as Socrates maintained, the same; the courage of a man is shown in commanding, of a woman in obeying. And this holds of all other virtues, as will be more clearly seen if we look at them in detail. . . . All classes must be deemed to have their special attributes; as the poet says of women,

Silence is a woman's glory,

but this is not equally the glory of man. The child is imperfect, and therefore obviously his virtue is not relative to himself alone, but to the perfect man and to his teacher, and in like manner the virtue of the slave is relative to a master. Now we determined that a slave is useful for the wants of life, and therefore he will obviously require only so much virtue as will prevent him from failing in his duty through cowardice or lack of self-control. . . . the slave shares in his master's life; the artisan is less closely connected with him, and only attains excellence in proportion as he becomes a slave. The meaner sort of mechanic has a special and separate slavery; and whereas the slave exists by nature, not so the shoemaker or other artisan. It is manifest, then, that the master ought to be the source of such excellence in the slave, and not a mere possessor of the art of mastership which trains the slave in his duties. Wherefore they are mistaken who forbid us to converse with slaves and say that we should employ command only, for slaves stand even more in need of admonition than children.

So much for this subject; the relations of husband and wife, parent and child, their several virtues, what in their intercourse with one another is good, and what is evil, will have to be discussed when we speak of the different forms of government. For, inasmuch as every family is a part of a state, and these relationships are the parts of a family, and the virtue of the part must have regard to the virtue of the whole, women and children must be trained by education with an eye to the constitution, if the virtues of either of them are supposed to make any difference in the virtues of the state. And they must make a difference: for the children grow up to be citizens, and half the free persons in a state are women.

DISCUSSION QUESTIONS

1. What is Aristotle's position on sexism? Compare his view with the position developed by Socrates. Whose view do you prefer, and why?
2. Do you believe that men and women have or tend to have different virtues? For example, do you agree with Aristotle that "the courage of a man is shown in commanding, of a woman in obeying"? Or do men and women share the same type of courage?
3. What is the difference between women and slaves according to Aristotle?
4. Aristotle argues that women are not as suited to be guardians of the city as men because women tend to lack the virtues necessary for good guardianship. Compare Aristotle's view on guardianship with Socrates'.
5. Aristotle says that "silence is a woman's glory" but that "this is not equally the glory of man." Do you agree with him? Why or why not? What percentage of the population in America today do you think would agree with Aristotle's claim about women's silence? Explain. How would these percentages break down according to sex?
6. Aristotle and Socrates lived in a different world than the one in which we live. Do you think that it is important for us to worry about the position of women in ancient Greece? Why or why not? What bearing do you think that the views of Socrates and Aristotle have on contemporary discussions of sexism? Explain.

JOHN STUART MILL

Sexism as Inequality

John Stuart Mill defends sexual equality and argues against all forms of legal discrimination against women. "All women are brought up from the earliest years in the belief that their ideal of character is the very opposite of that of men; not self-will, and government by self-control, but submission, and yielding to the control of others," writes Mill. "All the moralities tell them," he continues, "that it is the duty of women, and all the current sentimentalities that it is their nature, to live for others." While Mill is sympathetic to many traditional claims about the social roles of men and women, he nevertheless makes many controversial proposals, including the analogy between the subjugation of women and the possession of slaves. Mill believes that the enlightenment ideals

John Stuart Mill, *The Subjection of Women*, 1869, Chapter 1.

of individual freedom and autonomy have almost eradicated slavery despite its long tradition. These same ideals should, if followed, eradicate the subordination of women to men. Mill strongly advocates the freedom of choice and the equality of persons both in this work and in others, such as *On Liberty* and *Utilitarianism*. He also believes that moral progress is possible and does occur over history. Most of the civilized world has abandoned slavery, yet the oppression of women remains unrecognized by most men and is widely accepted. For Mill, men must recognize the slavery of women if reform is to happen. In the following selection, Mill responds to a number of objections raised by his predecessors to the equality of women, including the charge that women's subordination across history indicates their willingness to consent to it. It is widely held that Harriet Taylor Mill, John Stuart Mill's best friend and strongest intellectual influence before they married (she was married to someone else during much of their friendship), was an important inspiration for him. The compassion that Mill expresses in his presentation of women's position might be attributable to her strong influence. The following reading is from Chapter 1 of *The Subjection of Women* (1869). A biographical sketch of Mill appears in Chapter 1.

The object of this Essay is to explain as clearly as I am able, the grounds of an opinion which I have held from the very earliest period when I had formed any opinions at all on social or political matters . . . : That the principle which regulates the existing social relations between the two sexes—the legal subordination of one sex to the other—is wrong in itself, and now one of the chief hindrances to human improvement; and that it ought to be replaced by a principle of perfect equality, admitting no power or privilege on the one side, nor disability on the other. . . .

The generality of a practice is in some cases a strong presumption that it is, or at all events once was, conducive to laudable ends. This is the case, when the practice was first adopted, or afterwards kept up, as a means to such ends, and was grounded on experience of the mode in which they could be most effectually attained. If the authority of men over women, when first established, had been the result of a conscientious comparison between different modes of constituting the government of society; if, after trying various other modes of social organization—the government of women over men, equality between the two, and such mixed and divided modes of government as might be invented—it had been decided, on the testimony of experience, that the mode in which women are wholly under the rule of men, having no share at all in public concerns, and each in private being under the legal obligation of obedience to the man with whom she has associated her destiny, was the arrangement most conducive to the happiness and well being of both; its general adoption might then be fairly thought to be some evidence that, at the time when it was adopted, it was the best. . . . But the state of the case is in every respect the reverse of this. In the first place, the opinion in favour of the present system, which entirely subordinates the weaker sex to the stronger, rests upon theory only; for there never has been trial made of any other: so that experience, in the sense in which it is vulgarly opposed to theory, cannot be pretended to have pronounced any verdict. And in the second place, the adoption of this system of inequality never was the result of deliberation, or forethought, or any social ideas, or any notion whatever of what conduced to the benefit of humanity or the good order of society. It arose simply from the fact that from the very earliest twilight of human society, every woman (owing to the value attached to her by men, combined with her inferiority in muscular strength) was found in a state of bondage to some man. Laws and systems of polity always begin by recognizing the relations they find already existing between individuals. They convert what was a mere physical fact into a legal right, give it the sanction of society, and principally aim at the substitution of public and organized means of asserting and protecting these rights, instead of the irregular and lawless conflict of physical strength. Those who had already been compelled to obedience became in this manner legally bound to it. Slavery, from being a mere affair of force between the master and the slave, became regularized and a matter of compact among the masters, who, binding themselves to one another for common protection, guaranteed by their collective strength the private possessions of each, including his slaves. In early times, the great majority of the male sex were slaves, as well as the whole of the female. And many ages elapsed, some of them ages of high cultivation, before any thinker was bold enough to question the rightfulness, and the absolute social necessity, either of the one slavery or of the other. By degrees such thinkers did arise: and (the general progress of society assisting) the slavery of the male sex has, in all the countries of Christian Europe at least (though, in one of them, only within the last few years), been at length abolished, and that of the female sex has been gradually changed into a milder form of dependence. But this dependence, as it exists at present, is not an original institution, taking a fresh start from considerations of justice and social expediency—it is the primitive state of slavery lasting on, through successive mitigations and modifications occasioned by the same causes which have softened the general manners, and brought all human relations more under the control of justice and the influence of humanity. It has not lost the taint of its brutal origin. No presumption in its favour, therefore, can be drawn from the fact of its existence. . . .

Some will object, that a comparison cannot fairly be made between the government of the male sex and the forms of unjust power which I have adduced in illustration of it, since these are arbitrary, and the effect of mere usurpation, while it on the contrary is natural. But was there ever any domination which did not appear natural to those who possessed it? There was a time when the division of mankind into two classes, a small one of masters and a numerous one of slaves, appeared, even to the most cultivated minds, to be a natural, and the only natural, condition of the human race. No less an intellect, and one which contributed no less to the progress of human thought, than Aristotle, held this opinion without doubt or misgiving; and rested it on the same premises on which the same assertion in regard to the dominion of men over women is usually based, namely that there are different natures among mankind, free natures, and slave natures; that the Greeks were of a free nature, the barbarian races of Thracians and Asiatics of a slave nature. But why need I go back to Aristotle? Did not the slaveowners of the Southern United States maintain the same doctrine, with all the fanaticism with which men cling to the theories that justify their passions and legitimate their personal interests? Did they not call heaven and earth to witness that the dominion of the white man over the black is natural, that the black race is by nature incapable of freedom, and marked out for

slavery? some even going so far as to say that the freedom of manual labourers is an unnatural order of things anywhere. . . . So true is it that unnatural generally means only uncustomary, and that everything which is usual appears natural. The subjection of women to men being a universal custom, any departure from it quite naturally appears unnatural. But how entirely, even in this case, the feeling is dependent on custom, appears by ample experience. Nothing so much astonishes the people of distant parts of the world, when they first learn anything about England, as to be told that it is under a queen: the thing seems to them so unnatural as to be almost incredible. To Englishmen this does not seem in the least degree unnatural, because they are used to it; but they do feel it unnatural that women should be soldiers or members of Parliament. In the feudal ages, on the contrary, war and politics were not thought unnatural to women, because not unusual; it seemed natural that women of the privileged classes should be of manly character, inferior in nothing but bodily strength to their husbands and fathers. The independence of women seemed rather less unnatural to the Greeks than to other ancients, on account of the fabulous Amazons (whom they believed to be historical), and the partial example afforded by the Spartan women; who, though no less subordinate by law than in other Greek states, were more free in fact, and being trained to bodily exercises in the same manner with men, gave ample proof that they were not naturally disqualified for them. There can be little doubt that Spartan experience suggested to Plato, among many other of his doctrines, that of the social and political equality of the two sexes.

But, it will be said, the rule of men over women differs from all these others in not being a rule of force: it is accepted voluntarily; women make no complaint, and are consenting parties to it. In the first place, a great number of women do not accept it. Ever since there have been women able to make their sentiments known by their writings (the only mode of publicity which society permits to them), an increasing number of them have recorded protests against their present social condition: and recently many thousands of them, headed by the most eminent women known to the public, have petitioned Parliament for their admission to the Parliamentary Suffrage. The claim of women to be educated as solidly, and in the same branches of knowledge, as men, is urged with growing intensity, and with a great prospect of success; while the demand for their admission into professions and occupations hitherto closed against them, becomes every year more urgent. . . . it [is not] only in our own country and in America that women are beginning to protest, more or less collectively, against the disabilities under which they labour. France, and Italy, and Switzerland, and Russia now afford examples of the same thing. How many more women there are who silently cherish similar aspirations, no one can possibly know; but there are abundant tokens how many *would* cherish them, were they not so strenuously taught to repress them as contrary to the proprieties of their sex. It must be remembered, also, that no enslaved class ever asked for complete liberty at once. When Simon de Montfort called the deputies of the commons to sit for the first time in Parliament, did any of them dream of demanding that an assembly, elected by their constituents, should make and destroy ministries, and dictate to the king in affairs of state? No such thought entered into the imagination of the most ambitious of them. The nobility had already these pretensions; the commons pretended to nothing but to be exempt from arbitrary taxation, and from the gross individual oppression of the king's officers. It is a political law of nature that those who are under any power of ancient origin, never begin by complaining of the power itself, but only of its oppressive exercise. There is never any want of women who complain of ill usage by their husbands. There would be infinitely more, if complaint were not the greatest of all provocatives to a repetition and increase of the ill usage. It is this which frustrates all attempts to maintain the power but protect the woman against its abuses. In no other case (except that of a child) is the person who has been proved judicially to have suffered an injury, replaced under the physical power of the culprit who inflicted it. Accordingly wives, even in the most extreme and protracted cases of bodily ill usage, hardly ever dare avail themselves of the laws made for their protection: and if, in a moment of irrepressible indignation, or by the interference of neighbours, they are induced to do so, their whole effort afterwards is to disclose as little as they can, and to beg off their tyrant from his merited chastisement.

All causes, social and natural, combine to make it unlikely that women should be collectively rebellious to the power of men. They are so far in a position different from all other subject classes, that their masters require something more from them than actual service. Men do not want solely the obedience of women, they want their sentiments. All men, except the most brutish, desire to have, in the woman most nearly connected with them, not a forced slave but a willing one, not a slave merely, but a favourite. They have therefore put everything in practice to enslave their minds. The masters of all other slaves rely, for maintaining obedience, on fear; either fear of themselves, or religious fears. The masters of women wanted more than simple obedience, and they turned the whole force of education to effect their purpose. All women are brought up from the very earliest years in the belief that their ideal of character is the very opposite to that of men; not self-will, and government by self-control, but submission, and yielding to the control of others. All the moralities tell them that it is the duty of women, and all the current sentimentalities that it is their nature, to live for others; to make complete abnegation of themselves, and to have no life but in their affections. And by their affections are meant the only ones they are allowed to have—those to the men with whom they are connected, or to the children who constitute an additional and indefeasible tie between them and a man. When we put together three things—first, the natural attraction between opposite sexes; secondly, the wife's entire dependence on the husband, every privilege or pleasure she has being either his gift, or depending entirely on his will; and lastly, that the principal object of human pursuit, consideration, and all objects of social ambition, can in general be sought or obtained by her only through him, it would be a miracle if the object of being attractive to men had not become the polar star of feminine education and formation of character. And, this great means of influence over the minds of women having been acquired, an instinct of selfishness made men avail themselves of it to the utmost as a means of holding women in subjection, by representing to them meekness, submissiveness, and resignation of all individual will into the hands of a man, as an essential part of sexual attractiveness. Can it be doubted that any of the other yokes which mankind have succeeded in breaking, would have subsisted till now if the same means had existed, and had been as sedulously used, to bow down their minds to it? If it had been made the object of the life of every young plebeian to find personal favour in the eyes of some patrician, of every young serf with some seigneur; if domestication with him, and a share of his personal affections, had been held out as the prize which they all should look out for, the most gifted and aspiring being able to reckon on the most desirable prizes; and if, when this prize had been obtained, they had been shut out by a wall of brass from all interests not centering in him, all feelings and desires but those which he shared or inculcated; would not serfs and seigneurs, plebeians and patricians, have been as broadly distinguished at this day as men and women are? and would not all but a thinker here and there, have believed the distinction to be a fundamental and unalterable fact in human nature?

The preceding considerations are amply sufficient to show that custom, however universal it may be, affords in this case no presumption, and ought not to create any prejudice, in favour of the arrangements which place women in social and political subjection to men. But I may go farther, and maintain that the course of history, and the tendencies of progressive human society, afford not only no presumption in favour of this system of inequality of rights, but a strong one against it; and that, so far as the whole course of human improvement up to this time, the whole stream of modern tendencies, warrants any inference on the subject, it is, that this relic of the past is discordant with the future, and must necessarily disappear.

DISCUSSION QUESTIONS

1. What are Mill's counterarguments to the charge that women voluntarily consent to the rule of men over them? Critically analyze these counterarguments.
2. Mill draws an analogy between the subjugation of women and the possession of slaves. What is it? Do you think that it is a good analogy? Why or why not?
3. Why does Mill believe that the subordination of women is a cultural phenomenon, not a natural one? Does he have a good argument?
4. How do you think Mill would respond to Aristotle's claim that women's natural virtue is to obey, not to rule?
5. Mill believes that moral progress is possible and does occur over history. Do you agree with him? Give an argument in defense of your position.

SIMONE DE BEAUVOIR

The Second Sex

Simone de Beauvoir argues that "woman is the Other." She approaches the issue of "woman" from the point of view of the individual woman's consciousness of herself as such. "Otherness," for de Beauvoir, is a secondary status, one that the "Self" posits by negation and out of a sense of inadequacy. Consequently, women share the status of "Other" with any group that has been so negated. For de Beauvoir, there does not seem to be any natural sex difference. All differences that have been recognized throughout history are merely the creations of defensive self-consciousness. This includes the traditional view of women in the Western philosophical tradition as atypical and deviant. Without the creation of feminine consciousness by men, argues de Beauvoir, *there would be no such thing as woman at all.* For de Beauvoir, woman is seen by man, and by herself, as "the other," an atypical person. Woman helps man define himself through her alienness but can never become man. For de Beauvoir, just as for John Stuart Mill, these are cultural facts, not natural ones. The only way women can become authentic persons is to leave behind their role as "the second sex" by developing a consciousness that overcomes these distinctions: a consciousness that is neither Other nor Self and that is unbound by the dichotomous dictates of the master/slave relation. Education, for de Beauvoir, is one the most important means to the establishment of this "new woman." In *The Second Sex,* de Beauvoir writes, "The truth is that when a woman is engaged in an enterprise worthy of a human being, she is quite able to show herself as active, effective, taciturn—and as ascetic—as a man."

Simone de Beauvoir (1908–1986) was a French philosopher who, after the publication in 1949 of *The Second Sex,* became a heroine for women's movements around the world. She is widely regarded as one of the founding figures of classical feminism and is one of the most respected modern philosophers. She was the life-long companion of Jean-Paul Sartre. The following is from *The Second Sex.*

For a long time I have hesitated to write a book on woman. The subject is irritating, especially to women; and it is not new. Enough ink has been spilled in the quarreling over feminism, now practically over, and perhaps we should say no more about it. It is still talked about, however, for the voluminous nonsense uttered during the last century seems to have done little to illuminate the problem. After all, is there a problem? And if so, what is it? Are there women, really? Most assuredly the theory of the eternal feminine still has its adherents who will whisper in your ear: "Even in Russia women still are *women*"; and other erudite persons—sometimes the very same—say with a sigh: "Woman is losing her way, woman is lost." One wonders if women still exist, if they will always exist, whether or not it is desirable that they should, what place they occupy in this world, what their place should be. "What has become of women?" was asked recently in an ephemeral magazine.

But first we must ask: what is a woman? "*Tota mulier in utero,*" says one, "woman is a womb." But in speaking of certain women, connoisseurs declare that they are not women, although they are equipped with a uterus like the rest. All agree in recognizing the fact that females exist in the human species; today as always they make up about one half of humanity. And yet we are told that femininity is in danger; we are exhorted to be women, remain women, become women. It would appear, then, that every female human being is not necessarily a woman; to be so considered she must share in that mysterious and threatened reality known as femininity. Is this attribute something secreted by the ovaries? Or is it a Platonic essence, a product of the philosophic imagination? Is a rustling petticoat enough to bring it down to earth? Although some women try zealously to incarnate this essence, it is hardly patentable. It is frequently described in vague and dazzling terms that seem to have been borrowed from the vocabulary of the seers, and indeed in the times of St. Thomas [Aquinas] it was considered an essence as certainly defined as the somniferous virtue of the poppy.

But conceptualism has lost ground. The biological and social sciences no longer admit the existence of unchangeable fixed entities that determine given characteristics, such as those ascribed to woman, the Jew, or the Negro. Science regards any characteristic as a reaction dependent in part upon a *situation.* If today femininity no longer exists, then it never existed. But does the word *woman,* then, have no specific content? This is stoutly affirmed by those who hold to the philosophy of the enlightenment, of rationalism, of nominalism; women, to them, are merely the human beings arbitrarily designated by the word *woman.* Many American women particularly are prepared to think that there is no longer any place for woman as such; if a backward individual still takes herself for a woman, her friends advise her to be psychoanalyzed and thus get rid of this obsession. In regard to a work, *Modern Woman: The Lost Sex,* which in other respects has its irritating features, Dorothy Parker has written: "I cannot be just to books which treat of woman as woman. . . . My idea is that all of us, men as well as women, should be regarded as human beings." But nominalism is a rather inadequate doctrine, and the antifemininists have had no trouble in showing that woman simply *are not* men. Surely woman is, like man, a human being; but such a declaration is abstract. The fact is that every concrete human being is always a singular, separate individual. To decline to accept such notions as the eternal feminine, the black soul, the Jewish character, is not to deny that Jews, Negroes, women exist today—this denial does not represent a liberation for those concerned, but rather a flight from reality. Some years ago a well-known woman writer refused to permit her portrait to appear in a series of photographs especially devoted to women writers; she wished to be counted among the men. But in order to gain this privilege she made use of her husband's influence! Women who assert that they are men lay claim none the less to masculine consideration and respect. I recall also a young Trotskyite standing on a platform at a boisterous meeting and getting ready to use her fists, in spite of her evident fragility. She was denying her feminine weakness; but it was for love of a militant male whose equal she wished to be. The attitude of defiance of many American women proves that they are haunted by a sense of their femininity. In truth, to go for a walk with one's eyes open is enough to demonstrate that humanity is divided into two classes of individuals whose clothes, faces, bodies, smiles, gaits, interests, and occupations are manifestly different. Perhaps these differences are superficial, perhaps they are destined to disappear. What is certain is that right now they do most obviously exist.

If her functioning as a female is not enough to define woman, if we decline also to explain her through "the eternal feminine," and if nevertheless we admit, provisionally, that women do exist, then we must face the question: what is a woman?

To state the question is, to me, to suggest, at once, a preliminary answer. The fact that I ask it is in itself significant. A man would never get the notion of writing a book on the peculiar situation of the human male. But if I wish to define myself, I must first of all say: "I am a woman"; on this truth must be based all further discussion. A man never begins by presenting himself as an individual of a certain sex; it goes without saying that he is a man. The terms *masculine* and *feminine* are used symmetrically only as a matter of form, as on legal papers. In actuality the relation of the two sexes is not quite like that of two electrical poles, for man represents both the positive and the neutral, as is indicated by the common use of *man* to designate human beings in general; whereas woman represents only the negative, defined by limiting criteria, without reciprocity. In the midst of an abstract discussion it is vexing to hear a man say: "You think thus and so because you are a woman"; but I know that my only defense is to reply: "I think thus and so because it is true," thereby removing my subjective self from the argument. It would be out of the question to reply: "And you think the contrary because you are a man," for it is understood that the fact of being a man is no peculiarity. A man is in the right in being a man; it is the woman who is in the wrong. It amounts to this: just as for the ancients there was an absolute vertical with reference to which the oblique was defined, so there is an absolute human type, the masculine. Woman has ovaries, a uterus; these peculiarities imprison her in her subjectivity, circumscribe her within the limits of her own nature. It is often said that she thinks with her glands. Man superbly ignores the fact that his anatomy also includes glands, such as the testicles, and that they secrete hormones. He thinks of his body as a direct and normal connection with the world, which he believes he apprehends objectively, whereas he regards the body of woman as a hindrance, a prison, weighed down by everything peculiar to it. "The female is a female by virtue of a certain *lack* of qualities," said Aristotle; "we should regard the female nature as afflicted with a natural defectiveness." And St. Thomas [Aquinas] for his part pronounced woman to be an "imperfect man," an "incidental" being. This is symbolized in Genesis where Eve is depicted as made from what Bossuet called "a supernumerary bone" of Adam.

Thus humanity is male and man defines woman not in herself but as relative to him; she is not regarded as an autonomous being. Michelet writes: "Woman, the relative being. . . ." And Benda is most positive in his *Rapport d'Uriel:* "The body of man makes sense in itself quite apart from that of woman, whereas the latter seems wanting in significance by itself. . . . Man can think of himself without woman. She cannot think of herself without man." And she is simply what man decrees; thus she is called "the sex," by which is meant that she appears essentially to the male as a sexual being. For him she is sex—absolute sex, no less. She is defined and differentiated with reference to man and not he with reference to her; she is the incidental, the inessential as opposed to the essential. He is the Subject, he is the Absolute—she is the Other.

The category of the *Other* is as primordial as consciousness itself. In the most primitive societies, in the most ancient mythologies, one finds the expression of a duality—that of the Self and the Other. This duality was not originally attached to the division of the sexes; it was not dependent upon any empirical facts. It is revealed in such works as that of Granet on Chinese thought and those of Dumézil on the East Indies and Rome. The feminine element was at first no more involved in such pairs as Varuna-Mitra, Uranus-Zeus, Sun-Moon, and Day-Night than it was in the contrasts between Good and Evil, lucky and unlucky auspices, right and left, God and Lucifer. Otherness is a fundamental category of human thought.

Thus it is that no group ever sets itself up as the One without at once setting up the Other over against itself. If three travelers chance to occupy the same compartment, that is enough to make vaguely hostile "others" out of all the rest of the passengers on the train. In small-town eyes all persons not be-longing to the village are "strangers" and suspect; to the native of a country all who inhabit other countries are "foreigners"; Jews are "different" for the anti-Semite, Negroes are "inferior" for American racists, aborigines are "natives" for colonists, proletarians are the "lower class" for the privileged. . . .

The native traveling abroad is shocked to find himself in turn regarded as a "stranger" by the natives of neighboring countries. As a matter of fact, wars, festivals, trading, treaties, and contests among tribes, nations, and classes tend to deprive the concept *Other* of its absolute sense and to make manifest its relativity; willy-nilly, individuals and groups are forced to realize the reciprocity of their relations. How is it, then, that this reciprocity has not been recognized between the sexes, that one of the contrasting terms is set up as the sole essential, denying any relativity in regard to its correlative and defining the latter as pure otherness? Why is it that women do not dispute male sovereignty? No subject will readily volunteer to become the object, the inessential; it is not the Other who, in defining himself as the Other, establishes the One. The Other is posed as such by the One in defining himself as the One. But if the Other is not to regain the status of being the One, he must be submissive enough to accept this alien point of view. Whence comes this submission in the case of woman? . . .

History has shown us that men have always kept in their hands all concrete powers; since the earliest days of the patriarchate they have thought best to keep woman in a state of dependence; their codes of law have been set up against her; and thus she has been definitely established as the Other. This arrangement suited the economic interests of the males; but it conformed also to their ontological and moral pretensions. Once the subject seeks to assert himself, the Other, who limits and denies him, is nonetheless a necessity to him: he attains himself only through that reality which he is not, which is something other than himself. That is why man's life is never abundance and quietude; it is dearth and activity, it is struggle. Before him, man encounters Nature; he has some hold upon her, he endeavors to mold her to his desire. But she cannot fill his needs. Either she appears simply as a purely impersonal opposition, she is an obstacle and remains a stranger; or she submits passively to man's will and permits assimilation, so that he takes possession of her only through consuming her—that is, through destroying her. In both cases he remains alone; he is alone when he touches a stone, alone when he devours a fruit. There can be no presence

of an other unless the other is also present in and for himself: which is to say that true alterity—otherness—is that of a consciousness separate from mine and substantially identical with mine.

It is the existence of other men that tears each man out of his immanence and enables him to fulfill the truth of his being, to complete himself through transcendence, through escape toward some objective, through enterprise. But this liberty not my own, while assuring mine, also conflicts with it: there is the tragedy of the unfortunate human consciousness; each separate conscious being aspires to set himself up alone as sovereign subject. Each tries to fulfill himself by reducing the other to slavery. But the slave, though he works and fears, senses himself somehow as the essential; and, by a dialectical inversion, it is the master who seems to be the inessential. It is possible to rise above this conflict if each individual freely recognizes the other, each regarding himself and the other simultaneously as object and as subject in a reciprocal manner. But friendship and generosity, which alone permit in actuality this recognition of free beings, are not facile virtues; they are assuredly man's highest achievement, and through that achievement he is to be found in his true nature. But this true nature is that of a struggle unceasingly begun, unceasingly abolished; it requires man to outdo himself at every moment. We might put it in other words and say that man attains an authentically moral attitude when he renounces *mere being* to assume his position as an existent; through this transformation also he renounces all possession, for possession is one way of seeking mere being; but the transformation through which he attains true wisdom is never done, it is necessary to make it without ceasing, it demands a constant tension. And so, quite unable to fulfill himself in solitude, man is incessantly in danger in his relations with his fellows: his life is a difficult enterprise with success never assured.

But he does not like difficulty; he is afraid of danger. He aspires in contradictory fashion both to life and to repose, to existence and to merely being; he knows full well that "trouble of spirit" is the price of development, that his distance from the object is the price of his nearness to himself; but he dreams of quiet in disquiet and of an opaque plenitude that nevertheless would be endowed with consciousness. This dream incarnated is precisely woman; she is the wished-for intermediary between nature, the stranger to man, and the fellow being who is too closely identical. She opposes him with neither the hostile silence of nature nor the hard requirement of a reciprocal relation; through a unique privilege she is a conscious being and yet it seems possible to possess her in the flesh. Thanks to her, there is a means for escaping that implacable dialectic of master and slave which has its source in the reciprocity that exists between free beings. . . .

. . . There were not at first free women whom the males had enslaved nor were there even castes based on sex. To regard woman simply as a slave is a mistake; there were women among the slaves, to be sure, but there have always been free women—that is, women of religious and social dignity. They accepted man's sovereignty and he did not feel menaced by a revolt that could make of him in turn the object. Woman thus seems to be the inessential who never goes back to being the essential, to be the absolute Other, without reciprocity. This conviction is dear to the male, and every creation myth has expressed it, among others the legend of Genesis, which, through Christianity, has been kept alive in Western civilization. Eve was not fashioned at the same time as the man; she was not fabricated from a different substance, nor of the same clay as was used to model Adam: she was taken from the flank of the first male. Not even her birth was independent; God did not spontaneously choose to create her as an end in herself and in order to be worshipped directly by her in return for it. She was destined by Him for man; it was to rescue Adam from loneliness that He gave her to him, in her mate was her origin and her purpose; she was his complement on the order of the inessential. Thus she appeared in the guise of privileged prey. She was nature elevated to transparency of consciousness; she was a conscious being, but naturally submissive. And therein lies the wondrous hope that man has often put in woman: he hopes to fulfill himself as a being by carnally possessing a being, but at the same time confirming his sense of freedom through the docility of a free person. No man would consent to be a woman, but every man wants women to exist. "Thank God for having created woman." "Nature is good since she has given women to men." In such expressions man once more asserts with naïve arrogance that his presence in this world is an ineluctable fact and a right, that of woman a mere accident—but a very happy accident. Appearing as the Other, woman appears at the same time as an abundance of being in contrast to that existence the nothingness of which man senses in himself; the Other, being regarded as the object in the eyes of the subject, is regarded as *en soi;* therefore as a being. In woman is incarnated in positive form the lack that the existent carries in his heart, and it is in seeking to be made whole through her that man hopes to attain self-realization. . . .

Perhaps the myth of woman will some day be extinguished; the more women assert themselves as human beings, the more the marvelous quality of the Other will die out in them. But today it still exists in the heart of every man.

A myth always implies a subject who projects his hopes and his fears toward a sky of transcendence. Women do not set themselves up as Subject and hence have erected no virile myth in which their projects are reflected; they have no religion or poetry of their own: they still dream through the dreams of men. Gods made by males are the gods they worship. Men have shaped for their own exaltation great virile figures: Hercules, Prometheus, Parsifal; woman has only a secondary part to play in the destiny of these heroes. No doubt there are conventional figures of man caught in his relations to woman: the father, the seducer, the husband, the jealous lover, the good son, the wayward son; but they have all been established by men, and they lack the dignity of myth, being hardly more than clichés. Whereas woman is defined exclusively in her relation to man. The asymmetry of the categories—male and female—is made manifest in the unilateral form of sexual myths. We sometimes say "the sex" to designate woman; she is the flesh, its delights and dangers. The truth that for woman man is sex and carnality has never been proclaimed because there is no one to proclaim it. Representation of the world, like the world itself, is the work of men; they describe it from their own point of view, which they confuse with absolute truth.

It is always difficult to describe a myth; it cannot be grasped or encompassed; it haunts the human consciousness without ever appearing before it in fixed form. The myth is so various, so contradictory, that at first its unity is not discerned: Delilah and Judith, Aspasia and Lucretia, Pandora and Athena—woman is at once Eve and the Virgin Mary. She is an idol, a servant, the source of life, a power of darkness; she is the elemental silence of truth, she is artifice, gossip, and falsehood; she is healing presence and sorceress; she is man's prey, his downfall, she is everything that he is not and that he longs for, his negation and his *raison d'être.* . . .

Man seeks in woman the Other as Nature and as his fellow being. But we know what ambivalent feelings Nature inspires in man. He exploits her, but she crushes him, he is born of her and dies in her; she is the source of his being and the realm that he subjugates to his will; Nature is a vein of gross material in which the soul is imprisoned, and she is the supreme reality; she is contingence and Idea, the finite and the whole; she is what opposes the Spirit, and the Spirit itself. Now ally, now enemy, she appears as the dark chaos from whence life wells up, as this life itself, and as the over-yonder toward which life tends. Woman sums up nature as Mother, Wife, and Idea; these forms now mingle and now conflict, and each of them wears a double visage. . . .

This, then, is the reason why woman has a double and deceptive visage: she is all that man desires and all that he does not attain. She is the good mediatrix between propitious Nature and man; and she is the temptation of unconquered Nature, counter to all goodness. She incarnates all moral values, from good to evil, and their opposites; she is the substance of action and whatever is an obstacle to it, she is man's grasp on the world and his frustration; as such she is the source and origin of all man's reflection on his existence and of whatever expression he is able to give to it; and yet she works to divert him from himself, to make him sink down in silence and in death. She is servant and companion, but he expects her also to be his audience and critic and to confirm him in his sense of being; but she opposes him with her indifference, even with her mockery and laughter. He projects upon her what he desires and what he fears, what he loves and what he hates. And if it is so difficult to say anything specific about her, that is because man seeks the whole of himself in her and because she is All. She is All, that is, on the plane of the inessential; she is all the Other. And, as the other, she is other than herself, other than what is expected of her. Being all, she is never quite *this* which she should be; she is everlasting deception, the very deception of that existence which is never successfully attained nor fully reconciled with the totality of existents.

DISCUSSION QUESTIONS

1. Why does de Beauvoir believe that "woman is the Other"? What is her argument? Do you think that it is a good one?
2. What is the connection between sexism and racism for de Beauvoir? What is the connection between sexism and anti-Semitism for de Beauvoir?
3. De Beauvoir writes that "humanity is male and man defines woman not in herself but as relative to him; she is not regarded as an autonomous being." What does she mean by this?
4. "No subject will readily volunteer to become the object, the inessential; it is not the Other who, in defining himself as the Other, establishes the One," says de Beauvoir. What does she mean by this? Do you think that John Stuart Mill would agree with her? Why or why not?
5. Compare and contrast Plato, Aristotle, Mill, and de Beauvoir on the equality of the sexes. What are the strongest arguments for and against sexism that the philosophical tradition provides? Which do you ultimately side with, and why?

LOIS PINEAU

Date Rape

Lois Pineau identifies and argues against many of the myths surrounding date rape. One of those myths is the "belief that the natural aggression of men and the natural reluctance of women somehow makes date rape understandable." Another myth about date

Lois Pineau, *Law and Philosophy*, No. 8 (1989): 217–243. With kind permission from Kluwer Academic Publishers.

rape is that "a woman generates some sort of contractual obligation whenever her behaviour is interpreted as seductive"—what Pineau calls the "'she asked for it' contractual view." Still another is the myth that women like to be raped. Pineau says that the only way of refuting these myths about rape effectively "is to excavate the logical propositions involved, and to expose their misapplication to the situations to which they have been applied." Pineau believes that these myths concerning date rape undercut the legal actions available to victims of date rape. Moreover, she argues that these myths "often emerge in the arguments of judges who acquit date rapists, and policemen who refuse to lay charges." Pineau says that often myths about date rape lead the court to believe that "the very things that make it reasonable for *him* to believe that the defendant consented are often the very things that incline the court to believe that she consented." In order for victims of date rape to be adequately protected by the law, the law must recognize criteria of "what it would be reasonable for *her* to agree to"—not just the point of view of the "reasonable man" but the point of view of the "reasonable woman" as well.

Lois Pineau taught philosophy at Kansas State University in Manhattan, Kansas, and has since moved on to pursue a law degree at McMaster University in Canada.

A FEMINIST ANALYSIS

Date rape is nonaggravated sexual assault, nonconsensual sex that does not involve physical injury, or the explicit threat of physical injury. But because it does not involve physical injury, and because physical injury is often the only criterion that is accepted as evidence that *actus reas* is nonconsensual, what is really sexual assault is often mistaken for seduction. The replacement of the old rape laws with the new laws on sexual assault have done nothing to resolve this problem.

Rape, defined as nonconsensual sex, usually involving penetration by a man of a woman who is not his wife, has been replaced in some criminal codes with the charge of sexual assault. This has the advantage both of extending the range of possible victims of sexual assault, the manner in which people can be assaulted, and replacing a crime which is exclusive of consent, with one for which consent is a defence. But while the consent of a woman is now consistent with the conviction of her assailant in cases of aggravated assault, nonaggravated sexual assault is still distinguished from normal sex solely by the fact that it is not consented to. Thus the question of whether someone has consented to a sexual encounter is still important, and the criteria for consent continue to be the central concern of discourse on sexual assault.

However, if a man is to be convicted, it does not suffice to establish that the *actus reas* was nonconsensual. In order to be guilty of sexual assault a man must have the requisite *mens rea*, i.e., he must either

have believed that his victim did not consent or that she was probably not consenting. In many common law jurisdictions a man who sincerely believes that a woman consented to a sexual encounter is deemed to lack the required *mens rea*, even though the woman did not consent, and even though his belief is not reasonable. Recently, strong dissenting voices have been raised against the sincerity condition, and the argument made that *mens rea* be defeated only if the defendant has a reasonable belief that the plaintiff consented. The introduction of legislation which excludes "honest belief" (unreasonable sincere belief) as a defence, will certainly help to provide women with greater protection against violence. But while this will be an important step forward, the question of what constitutes a reasonable belief, the problem of evidence when rapists lie, and the problem of the entrenched attitudes of the predominantly male police, judges, lawyers, and jurists who handle sexual assault cases, remains.

The criteria for *mens rea*, for the reasonableness of belief, and for consent are closely related. For although a man's sincere belief in the consent of his victim may be sufficient to defeat *mens rea*, the court is less likely to believe his belief is sincere if his belief is unreasonable. If his belief is reasonable, they are more likely to believe in the sincerity of his belief. But evidence of the reasonableness of his belief is also evidence that consent really did take place. For the very things that make it reasonable for *him* to believe that the defendant consented are often the very things that incline the court to believe that she consented. What is often missing is the voice of the woman herself, an account of what it would be reasonable for *her* to agree to, that is to say, an account of what is reasonable from *her* standpoint.

Thus, what is presented as reasonable has repercussions for four separate but related concerns: (1) the question of whether a man's belief in a woman's consent was reasonable; (2) the problem of whether it is reasonable to attribute *mens rea* to him; (3) the question of what could count as reasonable from the woman's point of view; (4) the question of what is reasonable from the court's point of view. These repercussions are of the utmost practical concern. In a culture which contains an incidence of sexual assault verging on epidemic, a criterion of reasonableness which regards mere submission as consent fails to offer persons vulnerable to those assaults adequate protection.

The following statements by self-confessed date rapists reveal how our lack of a solution for dealing with date rape protects rapists by failing to provide their victims with legal recourse:

All of my rapes have been involved in a dating situation where I've been out with a woman I know. . . . I wouldn't take no for an answer. I think it had something to do with my acceptance of rejection. I had low self-esteem and not much self-confidence and when I was rejected for something which I considered to be rightly mine, I became angry and I went ahead anyway. And this was the same in any situation, whether it was rape or it was something else.

When I did date, when I was younger, I would pick up a girl and if she didn't come across I would threaten her or slap her face then tell her she was going to fuck—that was it. But that's because I didn't want to waste time with any come-ons. It took too much time. I wasn't interested because I didn't like them as people anyway, and I just went with them just to get laid. Just to say that I laid them.

There is, at this time, nothing to protect women from this kind of unscrupulous victimization. A woman on a casual date with a virtual stranger has almost no chance of bringing a complaint of sexual assault before the courts. One reason for this is the prevailing criterion for consent. According to this criterion, consent is implied unless some emphatic episodic sign of resistance occurred, and its occurrence can be established. But if no episodic act occurred, or if it did occur, and the defendant claims

that it didn't, or if the defendant threatened the plaintiff but won't admit it in court, it is almost impossible to find any evidence that would support the plaintiff's word against the defendant. This difficulty is exacerbated by suspicion on the part of the courts, police, and legal educators that even where an act of resistance occurs, this act should not be interpreted as a withholding of consent, and this suspicion is especially upheld where the accused is a man who is known to the female plaintiff.

In Glanville Williams' classic textbook on criminal law we are warned that where a man is unknown to a woman, she does not consent if she expresses her rejection in the form of an episodic and vigorous act at the "vital moment." But if the man is known to the woman she must, according to Williams, make use of "all means available to her to repel the man." Williams warns that women often welcome a "mastery advance" and present a token resistance. He quotes Byron's couplet,

A little still she strove, and much repented
And whispering "I will ne'er consent"—
consented

by way of alerting law students to the difficulty of distinguishing real protest from pretence. Thus, while in principle, a firm unambiguous stand, or a healthy show of temper ought to be sufficient, if established, to show nonconsent, in practice the forceful overriding of such a stance is apt to be taken as an indication that the resistance was not seriously intended, and that the seduction had succeeded. The consequence of this is that it is almost impossible to establish the defendant's guilt beyond a reasonable doubt.

Thus, on the one hand, we have a situation in which women are vulnerable to the most exploitive tactics at the hands of men who are known to them. On the other hand, almost nothing will count as evidence of their being assaulted, including their having taken an emphatic stance in withholding their consent. The new laws have done almost nothing to change this situation. Yet clearly, some solution must be sought. Moreover, the road to that solution presents itself clearly enough as a need for a reformulation of the criterion of consent. It is patent that a criterion that collapses whenever the crime itself succeeds will not suffice. . . .

The reasoning that underlies the present criterion of consent is entangled in a number of mutually supportive mythologies which see sexual assault as masterful seduction, and silent submission as sexual enjoyment. Because the prevailing ideology has so much informed our conceptualization of sexual interaction, it is extraordinarily difficult for us to distinguish between assault and seduction, submission and enjoyment, or so we imagine. At the same time, this failure to distinguish has given rise to a network of rationalizations that support the conflation of assault with seduction, submission and enjoyment. . . .

RAPE MYTHS

The belief that the natural aggression of men and the natural reluctance of women somehow make date rape understandable underlies a number of prevalent myths about rape and human sexuality. These beliefs maintain their force partly on account of a logical compulsion exercised by them at an unconscious level. The only way of refuting them effectively, is to excavate the logical propositions involved, and to expose their misapplication to the situations to which they have been applied. In what follows, I propose to excavate the logical support for popular attitudes that are tolerant of date rape. These myths are not just popular, however, but often emerge in the arguments of judges who acquit date rapists, and policemen who refuse to lay charges.

The claim that the victim provoked a sexual incident, that "she asked for it," is by far the most common defence given by men who are accused of sexual assault. Feminists, rightly incensed by this response, often treat it as beneath contempt, singling out the defence as an argument against it. On other fronts, sociologists have identified the response as part of an overall tendency of people to see the world as just, a tendency which disposes them to conclude that people for the most part deserve what they get. However, an inclination to see the world as just requires us to construct an account which yields this outcome, and it is just such an account that I wish to examine with regard to date rape.

The least sophisticated of the "she asked for it" rationales, and in a sense, the easiest to deal with, appeals to an injunction against sexually provocative behaviour on the part of women. If women should not be sexually provocative, then, from this standpoint, a woman who is sexually provocative deserves to suffer the consequences. Now it will not do to respond that women get raped even when they are not sexually provocative, or that it is men who get to interpret (unfairly) what counts as sexually provocative. The question should be: Why shouldn't a woman be sexually provocative? Why

should this behaviour warrant any kind of aggressive response whatsoever?

Attempts to explain that women have a right to behave in sexually provocative ways without suffering dire consequences still meet with surprisingly tough resistance. Even people who find nothing wrong or sinful with sex itself, in any of its forms, tend to suppose that women must not behave sexually unless they are prepared to carry through on some fuller course of sexual interaction. The logic of this response seems to be that at some point a woman's behaviour commits her to following through on the full course of a sexual encounter as it is defined by her assailant. At some point she has made an agreement, or formed a contract, and once that is done, her contractor is entitled to demand that she satisfy the terms of that contract. Thus, this view about sexual responsibility and desert is supported by other assumptions about contracts and agreement. But we do not normally suppose that casual nonverbal behaviour generates agreements. Nor do we normally grant private persons the right to enforce contracts. What rationale would support our conclusion in this case?

The rationale, I believe, comes in the form of a belief in the especially insistent nature of male sexuality, an insistence which lies at the foot of natural male aggression, and which is extremely difficult, perhaps impossible to contain. At a certain point in the arousal process, it is thought, a man's rational will gives way to the prerogatives of nature. His sexual need can and does reach a point where it is uncontrollable, and his natural masculine aggression kicks in to assure that this need is met. Women, however, are naturally more contained, and so it is their responsibility not to provoke the irrational in the male. If they do go so far as that, they have both failed in their responsibilities, and subjected themselves to the inevitable. One does not go into the lion's cage and expect not to be eaten. Natural feminine reluctance, it is thought, is no protection against a sexually aroused male.

This belief about the normal aggressiveness of male sexuality is complemented by common knowledge about female gender development. Once, women were taught to deny their sexuality and to aspire to ideals of chastity. Things have not changed so much. Women still tend to eschew conquest mentalities in favour of a combination of sex and affection. Insofar as this is thought to be merely a cultural requirement, however, there is an expectation that women will be coy about their sexual desire. The assumption that women both want to indulge sexually, and are inclined to sacrifice this desire for higher ends, gives rise to the myth that they want to be raped. After all, doesn't rape give them the sexual enjoyment they *really* want, at the same time that it relieves them of the responsibility for admitting to and acting upon what they want? And how then can we blame men, who have been socialized to be aggressively seductive precisely for the purpose of overriding female reserve? If we find fault at all, we are inclined to cast our suspicions on the motives of the woman. For it is on her that the contradictory roles of sexual desirer and sexual denier have been placed. Our awareness of the contradiction expected of her makes us suspect her honesty. In the past, she was expected to deny her complicity because of the shame and guilt she felt at having submitted. This expectation persists in many quarters today, and is carried over into a general suspicion about her character, and the fear that she might make a false accusation out of revenge, or some other low motive.

But if women really want sexual pleasure, what inclines us to think that they will get it through rape? This conclusion logically requires a theory about the dynamics of sexual pleasure that sees that pleasure as an emergent property of overwhelming male insistence. For the assumption that a raped female experiences sexual pleasure implies that the person who rapes her knows how to cause that pleasure independently of any information she might convey on that point. Since her ongoing protest is inconsistent with requests to be touched in particular ways in particular places, to have more of this and less of that, then we must believe that the person who touches her knows these particular ways and places instinctively, without any directives from her.

Thus, we find, underlying and reinforcing this belief in incommunicative male prowess, a conception of sexual pleasure that springs from wordless interchanges, and of sexual success that occurs in a place of meaningful silence. The language of seduction is accepted as a tacit language: eye contact, smiles, blushes, and faintly discernible gestures. It is, accordingly, imprecise and ambiguous. It would be easy for a man to make mistakes about the message conveyed, understandable that he should mistakenly think that a sexual invitation has been made, and a bargain struck. But honest mistakes, we think, must be excused.

In sum, the belief that women should not be sexually provocative is logically linked to several other beliefs, some normative, some empirical. The normative beliefs are that (1) people should keep the agreements they make, (2) that sexually provocative behaviour, taken beyond a certain point, generates agreements, (3) that the peculiar nature of male and female sexuality places such agreements in a special category, one in which the possibility of retracting an agreement is ruled out, or at least made highly unlikely, (4) that women are not to be trusted, in sexual matters at least. The empirical belief, which turns out to be false, is that male sexuality is not subject to rational and moral control.

DISPELLING THE MYTHS

The "she asked for" justification of sexual assault incorporates a conception of a contract that would be difficult to defend in any other context and the presumptions about human sexuality which function to reinforce sympathies rooted in the contractual notion of just deserts are not supported by empirical research.

The belief that a woman generates some sort of contractual obligation whenever her behaviour is interpreted as seductive is the most indefensible part of the mythology of rape. In law, contracts are not legitimate just because a promise has been made. In particular, the use of pressure tactics to extract agreement is frowned upon. Normally, an agreement is upheld only if the contractors were clear on what they were getting into, and had sufficient time to reflect on the wisdom of their doing so. Either there must be a clear tradition in which the expectations involved in the contract are fairly well known (marriage), or there must be an explicit written agreement concerning the exact terms of the contract and the expectations of the persons involved. But whatever the terms of a contract, there is no private right to enforce it. So that if I make a contract with you on which I renege, the only permissible recourse for you is through due legal process.

Now it is not clear whether sexual contracts can be made to begin with, or if so, what sort of sexual contracts would be legitimate. But assuming that they could be made, the terms of those contracts would not be enforceable. To allow public enforcement would be to grant the State the overt right to force people to have sex, and this would clearly be unacceptable. Granting that sexual contracts are legitimate, state enforcement of such contracts would have to be limited to ordering nonsexual compensation for breaches of contract. So it makes no difference whether a sexual contract is tacit or explicit.

There are no grounds whatsoever that would justify enforcement of its terms.

Thus, even if we assume that a woman has initially agreed to an encounter, her agreement does not automatically make all subsequent sexual activity to which she submits legitimate. If during coitus a woman should experience pain, be suddenly overcome with guilt or fear of pregnancy, or simply lose her initial desire, those are good reasons for her to change her mind. Having changed her mind, neither her partner nor the state has any right to force her to continue. But then if she is forced to continue she is assaulted. Thus, establishing that consent occurred at a particular point during a sexual encounter should not conclusively establish the legitimacy of the encounter. What is needed is a reading of whether she agreed throughout the encounter.

If the "she asked for it" contractual view of sexual interchange has any validity, it is because there is a point at which there is no stopping a sexual encounter, a point at which that encounter becomes the inexorable outcome of the unfolding of natural events. If a sexual encounter is like a slide on which I cannot stop halfway down, it will be relevant whether I enter the slide of my own free will, or am pushed.

But there is no evidence that the entire sexual act is like a slide. While there may be a few seconds in the "plateau" period just prior to orgasm in which people are "swept" away by sexual feelings to the point where we could justifiably understand their lack of heed for the comfort of their partner, the greater part of a sexual encounter comes well within the bounds of morally responsible control of our own actions. Indeed, the available evidence shows that most of the activity involved in sex has to do with building the requisite level of desire, a task that involves the proper use of foreplay, the possibility of which implies control over the form that foreplay will take. Modern sexual therapy assumes that such control is universally accessible, and so far there has been no reason to question that assumption. Sexologists are unanimous, moreover, in holding that mutual sexual enjoyment requires an atmosphere of comfort and communication, a minimum of pressure, and an ongoing check-up on one's partner's state. They maintain that different people have different predilections, and that what is pleasurable for one person is very often anathema to another. These findings show that the way to achieve sexual pleasure, at any time at all, let alone with a casual acquaintance, decidedly does not involve overriding the other person's express reserva-

tions and providing them with just any kind of sexual stimulus. And while we do not want to allow science and technology a voice in which the voices of particular women are drowned, in this case science seems to concur with women's perception that aggressive incommunicative sex is not what they want. But if science and the voice of women concur, if aggressive seduction does not lead to good sex, if women do not like it, or want it, then it is not rational to think that they would agree to it. Where such sex takes place, it is therefore rational to presume that the sex was not consensual.

The myth that women like to be raped is closely connected, as we have seen, to doubt about their honesty in sexual matters, and this suspicion is exploited by defence lawyers when sexual assault cases make it to the courtroom. It is an unfortunate consequence of the presumption of innocence that rape victims who end up in court frequently find that it is they who are on trial. For if the defendant is innocent, then either he did not intend to do what he was accused of, or the plaintiff is mistaken about his identity, or she is lying. Often the last alternative is the only plausible defence, and as a result, the plaintiff's word seldom goes unquestioned. Women are frequently accused of having made a false accusation, either as a defensive mechanism for dealing with guilt and shame, or out of a desire for revenge.

Now there is no point in denying the possibility of false accusation, though there are probably better ways of seeking revenge on a man than accusing him of rape. However, we can now establish a logical connection between the evidence that a woman was subjected to high-pressure, aggressive "seduction" tactics, and her claim that she did not consent to that encounter. Where the kind of encounter is not the sort to which it would be reasonable to consent, there is a logical presumption that a woman who claims that she did not consent is telling the truth. Where the kind of sex involved is not the sort of sex we would expect a woman to like, the burden of proof should not be on the woman to show that she did not consent, but on the defendant to show that contrary to every reasonable expectation she did consent. The defendant should be required to convince the court that the plaintiff persuaded him to have sex with her even though there are no visible reasons why she should.

In conclusion, there are no grounds for the "she asked for it" defence. Sexually provocative behaviour does not generate sexual contracts. Even where there are sexual agreements, they cannot be legitimately enforced either by the State, or by private right, or by natural prerogative. Secondly, all the evidence suggests that neither women nor men find sexual enjoyment in rape or in any form of noncommunicative sexuality. Thirdly, male sexual desire is containable, and can be subjected to moral and rational control. Fourthly, since there is no reason why women should not be sexually provocative, they do not "deserve" any sex they do not want. This last is a welcome discovery. The taboo on sexual provocativeness in women is a taboo both on sensuality and on teasing. But sensuality is a source of delight, and teasing is playful and inspires wit. What a relief to learn that it is not sexual provocativeness, but its enemies, that constitutes a danger to the world. . . .

In thinking about sex we must keep in mind its sensual ends, and the facts show that aggressive, high-pressure sex contradicts those ends. Consensual sex in dating situations is presumed to aim at mutual enjoyment. It may not always do this, and when it does, it might not always succeed. There is no logical incompatibility between wanting to continue a sexual encounter, and failing to derive sexual pleasure from it.

But it seems to me that there is a presumption in favour of the connection between sex and sexual enjoyment, and that if a man wants to be sure that he [is] not forcing himself on a woman, he has an obligation either to ensure that the encounter really is mutually enjoyable, or to know the reasons why she would want to continue the encounter in spite of her lack of enjoyment. A closer investigation of the nature of this obligation will enable us to construct a more rational and more plausible norm of sexual conduct.

Onara O'Neill has argued that in intimate situations we have an obligation to take the ends of others as our own, and to promote those ends in a non-manipulative and non-paternalistic manner. Now it seems that in honest sexual encounters just this is required. Assuming that each person enters the encounter in order to seek sexual satisfaction, each person engaging in the encounter has an obligation to help the other seek his or her ends. To do otherwise is to risk acting in opposition to what the other desires, and hence to risk acting without the other's consent.

But the obligation to promote the sexual ends of one's partner implies that obligation to know what those ends are, and also the obligation to know how those ends are attained. Thus, the problem comes down to a problem of epistemic responsibility, the responsibility to know. The solution, in my view, lies in the practice of a communicative sexuality, one which combines the appropriate knowledge of the other with respect for the dialectics of desire. . . .

CULTURAL PRESUMPTIONS

Now it may well be that we have no obligation to care for strangers, and I do not wish to claim that we do. Nonetheless, it seems that O'Neill's point about the special moral duties we have in certain intimate situations is supported by a conceptual relation between certain kinds of personal relationships and the expectation that it should be a communicative relation. Friendship is a case in point. It is a relation that is greatly underdetermined by what we usually include in our sets of rights and obligations. For the most part, rights and obligations disappear as terms by which friendship is guided. They are still there, to be called upon, in case the relationship breaks down, but insofar as the friendship is a friendship, it is concerned with fostering the quality of the interaction and not with standing on rights. Thus, because we are friends, we share our property, and property rights between us are not invoked. Because we are friends, privacy is not an issue. Because we are friends we may see to each other's needs as often as we see to our own. The same can be said for relations between lovers, parents and dependent children, and even between spouses, at least when interaction is functioning at an optimal level. When such relations break down to the point that people must stand on their rights, we can often say that the actors ought to make more of an effort, and in many instances fault them for their lack of charity, tolerance, or benevolence. Thus, although we have a right to end friendships, it may be a reflection on our lack of virtue that we do so, and while we cannot be criticized for violating other people's rights, we can be rightfully deprecated for lacking the virtue to sustain a friendship.

But is there a similar conceptual relation between the kind of activity that a date is, and the sort of moral practice that it requires? My claim is that there is, and that this connection is easily established once we recognize the cultural presumption that dating is a gesture of friendship and regard. Traditionally, the decision to date indicates that two people have an initial attraction to each other, that they are disposed to like each other, and look forward to enjoying each other's company. Dating derives its implicit meaning from this tradition. It retains this meaning unless other aims are explicitly stated, and even then it may not be possible to alienate this meaning. It is a rare woman who will not spurn a man who states explicitly, right at the onset, that he wants to go out with her solely on the condition that he have sexual intercourse with her at the end of the evening, and that he has no interest in her company apart from gaining that end, and no concern for mutual satisfaction.

Explicit protest to the contrary aside, the conventions of dating confer on it its social meaning, and this social meaning implies a relationship which is more like friendship than the cutthroat competition of opposing teams. As such, it requires that we do more than stand on our rights with regard to each other. As long as we are operating under the auspices of a dating relationship, it requires that we behave in the mode of friendship and trust. But if a date is more like a friendship than a business contract, then clearly respect for the dialectics of desire is incompatible with the sort of sexual pressure that is inclined to end in date rape. And clearly, also, a conquest mentality which exploits a situation of trust and respect for purely selfish ends is morally pernicious. Failure to respect the dialectics of desire when operating under the auspices of friendship and trust is to act in flagrant disregard of the moral requirement to avoid manipulative, coercive, and exploitive behaviour. Respect for the dialectics of desire is *prima facie* inconsistent with the satisfaction of one person at the expense of the other. The proper end of friendship relations is mutual satisfaction. But the requirement of mutuality means that we must take a communicative approach to discovering the ends of the other, and this entails that we respect the dialectics of desire.

But now that we know what communicative sexuality is, and that it is morally required, and that it is the only feasible means to mutual sexual enjoyment, why not take this model as the norm of what is reasonable in sexual interaction. The evidence of sexologists strongly indicates that women whose partners are aggressively uncommunicative have little chance of experiencing sexual pleasure. But it is not reasonable for women to consent to what they have little chance of enjoying. Hence it is not reasonable for women to consent to aggressive noncommunicative sex. Nor can we reasonably suppose that women have consented to sexual encounters which we know and they know they do not find enjoyable. With the communicative model as the norm, the aggressive contractual model should strike us as a model of deviant sexuality, and sexual encounters patterned on that model should strike us as encounters to which *prima facie* no one would reasonably agree. But if acquiescence to an encounter counts as consent only if the acquiescence is reasonable, something to which a reasonable person, in full possession of knowledge relevant to the encounter, would agree, then acquiescence to aggressive noncommunicative sex is not reasonable. Hence, acquiescence under such conditions should not count as consent.

Thus, where communicative sexuality does not occur, we lack the main ground for believing that the sex involved was consensual. Moreover, where a man does not engage in communicative sexuality, he acts either out of reckless disregard, or out of willful ignorance. For he cannot know, except through the practice of communicative sexuality, whether his partner has any sexual reason for continuing the encounter. And where she does not, he runs the risk of imposing on her what she is not willing to have. All that is needed then, in order to provide women with legal protection from "date rape" is to make both reckless indifference and willful ignorance a sufficient condition of *mens rea* and to make communicative sexuality the accepted norm of sex to which a reasonable woman would agree. Thus, the appeal to communicative sexuality as a norm for sexual encounters accomplishes two things. It brings the aggressive sex involved in "date rape" well within the realm of sexual assault, and it locates the guilt of date rapists in the failure to approach sexual relations on a communicative basis.

DISCUSSION QUESTIONS

1. Pineau argues that sexually provocative behavior does not generate sexual contracts. What is her argument? Do you agree with it? Why or why not?
2. According to Pineau, myths about rape "often emerge in the arguments of judges who acquit date rapists, and policemen who refuse to lay charges." What does she mean by this?
3. What is the difference between the point of view of a "reasonable man" and that of a "reasonable woman"? What does this have to do with adequate protection under the law for victims of date rape? Do you agree with Pineau that the reasonable woman's point of view needs to be recognized by the law?
4. One of the myths about rape discussed by Pineau is the "belief that the natural aggression of men and the natural reluctance of women somehow make date rape un-

derstandable." How does Pineau refute this myth? How might Steven Goldberg counter Pineau's argument?.

5. Do you think that there is a general connection between sexism and date rape? How would you respond to the following charge: sexism in American culture and society allows the myths about date rape discussed by Pineau to flourish and persist and, consequently, provides the grounds for the dismissal or disregard of acts of violence against women such as date rape?

PATRICIA YANCEY MARTIN AND ROBERT HUMMER

Fraternities and Rape on Campus

Patricia Yancey Martin and Robert A. Hummer present evidence showing that fraternities create attitudes, norms, and practices that predispose fraternity men, both individually and collectively, to coerce women sexually. According to Martin and Hummer, fraternity houses are "rape-prone contexts" that are in need of public scrutiny. Fraternities contribute heavily to coercive and often violent sex. "Practices associated with the social construction of fraternity brotherhood emphasize a macho conception of men and masculinity," argue Martin and Hummer, "a narrow, stereotyped conception of women and femininity, and the treatment of women as commodities." Fraternity norms and practices influence fraternity brothers "to view the sexual coercion of women, which is a felony crime, as sport, a contest or a game." Martin and Hummer argue that unless fraternities change their practices, goals, and structures, women on campus will continue to be subject to the violence.

Patricia Yancey Martin is professor of sociology and Daisy Parker Flory Alumni Professor at Florida State University at Tallahassee. She has written papers on organizations that process rape victims, rape crisis centers as "unobtrusive mobilizers," gender and sexuality at work, and group rape. She is completing books on the politics of rape processing work (using data from police, prosecutors, hospitals, and rape crisis centers) and on gender and sexuality in organizations. Robert A. Hummer is associate professor of sociology at the University of Texas at Austin and a research associate at UT's Population Research Center. He is the coauthor of *Living and Dying in the USA: Behavioral, Health, and Social Forces of Adult Mortality* (with Richard G. Rogers and Charles B. Nam, 1999).

Rapes are perpetrated on dates, at parties, in chance encounters, and in specially planned circumstances. That group structure and processes, rather than individual values or characteristics, are the impetus for many rape episodes was documented by Blanchard (1959) 30 years ago (also see Geis 1971), yet sociologists have failed to pursue this theme (for an exception, see Chancer 1987). A recent review of research (Muehlenhard and Linton 1987) on sexual violence, or rape, devotes only a few pages to the situational

Patricia Yancey Martin and Robert Hummer, *Gender & Society* 3 (December 1989): 457–473. Copyright © 1989 Sage Publications, Inc. Reprinted by permission of Sage Publications, Inc.

context of rape events, and these are conceptualized as potential risk factors for individuals rather than qualities of rape-prone social contexts.

Many rapes, far more than come to the public's attention, occur in fraternity houses on college and university campuses, yet little research has analyzed fraternities at American colleges and universities as rape-prone contexts (cf. Ehrhart and Sandler 1985). Most of the research on fraternities reports on samples of individual fraternity men. One group of studies compares the values, attitudes, perceptions, family socioeconomic status, psychological traits (aggressiveness, dependence), and so on, of fraternity and nonfraternity men (Bohrnstedt 1969; Fox, Hodge, and Ward 1987; Kanin 1967; Lemire 1979; Miller 1973). A second group attempts to identify the effects of fraternity membership over time on the values, attitudes, beliefs, or moral precepts of members (Hughes and Winston 1987; Marlowe and Auvenshine 1982; Miller 1973; Wilder, Hoyt, Doren, Hauck, and Zettle 1978; Wilder, Hoyt, Surbeck, Wilder, and Carney 1986). With minor exceptions, little research addresses the group and organizational context of fraternities or the social construction of fraternity life (for exceptions, see Letchworth 1969; Longino and Kart 1973; Smith 1964).

Gary Tash, writing as an alumnus and trial attorney in his fraternity's magazine, claims that over 90 percent of all gang rapes on college campuses involve fraternity men (1988, p. 2). Tash provides no evidence to substantiate this claim, but students of violence against women have been concerned with fraternity men's frequently reported involvement in rape episodes (Adams and Abarbanel 1988). Ehrhart and Sandler (1985) identify over 50 cases of gang rapes on campus perpetrated by fraternity men, and their analysis points to many of the conditions that we discuss here. Their analysis is unique in focusing on conditions in fraternities that make gang rapes of women by fraternity men both feasible and probable. They identify excessive alcohol use, isolation from external monitoring, treatment of women as prey, use of pornography, approval of violence, and excessive concern with competition as precipitating conditions to gang rape (also see Merton 1985; Roark 1987).

The study reported here confirmed and complemented these findings by focusing on both conditions and processes. We examined dynamics associated with the social construction of fraternity life, with a focus on processes that foster the use of coercion, including rape, in fraternity men's relations with women. Our examination of men's social fra-

ternities on college and university campuses as groups and organizations led us to conclude that fraternities are a physical and sociocultural context that encourages the sexual coercion of women. We make no claims that all fraternities are "bad" or that all fraternity men are rapists. Our observations indicated, however, that rape is especially probable in fraternities because of the kinds of organizations they are, the kinds of members they have, the practices their members engage in, and a virtual absence of university or community oversight. Analyses that lay blame for rapes by fraternity men on "peer pressure" are, we feel, overly simplistic (cf. Burkhart 1989; Walsh 1989). We suggest, rather, that fraternities create a sociocultural context in which the use of coercion in sexual relations with women is normative and in which the mechanisms to keep this pattern of behavior in check are minimal at best and absent at worst. We conclude that unless fraternities change in fundamental ways, little improvement can be expected.

METHODOLOGY

Our goal was to analyze the group and organizational practices and conditions that create in fraternities an abusive social context for women. We developed a conceptual framework from an initial case study of an alleged gang rape at Florida State University that involved four fraternity men and an 18-year-old coed. The group rape took place on the third floor of a fraternity house and ended with the "dumping" of the woman in the hallway of a neighboring fraternity house. According to newspaper accounts, the victim's blood-alcohol concentration, when she was discovered, was .349 percent, more than three times the legal limit for automobile driving and an almost lethal amount. One law enforcement officer reported that sexual intercourse occurred during the time the victim was unconscious: "She was in a life-threatening situation" (*Tallahassee Democrat*, 1988b). When the victim was found, she was comatose and had suffered multiple scratches and abrasions. Crude words and a fraternity symbol had been written on her thighs (*Tampa Tribune*, 1988). When law enforcement officials tried to investigate the case, fraternity members refused to cooperate. This led, eventually, to a five-year ban of the fraternity from campus by the university and by the fraternity's national organization.

In trying to understand how such an event could have occurred, and how a group of over 150 members (exact figures are unknown because the fraternity refused to provide a membership roster) could hold rank, deny knowledge of the event, and allegedly lie to a grand jury, we analyzed newspaper articles about the case and conducted open-ended interviews with a variety of respondents about the case and about fraternities, rapes, alcohol use, gender relations, and sexual activities on campus. Our data included over 100 newspaper articles on the initial gang rape case; open-ended interviews with Greek (social fraternity and sorority) and non-Greek (independent) students (N = 20); university administrators (N = 8, five men, three women); and alumni advisers to Greek organizations (N = 6). Open-ended interviews were held also with judges, public and private defense attorneys, victim advocates, and state prosecutors regarding the processing of sexual assault cases. Data were analyzed using the grounded theory method (Glaser 1978; Martin and Turner 1986). In the following analysis, concepts generated from the data analysis are integrated with the literature on men's social fraternities, sexual coercion, and related issues.

FRATERNITIES AND THE SOCIAL CONSTRUCTION OF MEN AND MASCULINITY

Our research indicated that fraternities are vitally concerned—more than with anything else—with masculinity (cf. Kanin 1967). They work hard to create a macho image and context and try to avoid any suggestion of "wimpishness," effeminacy, and homosexuality. Valued members display, or are willing to go along with, a narrow conception of masculinity that stresses competition, athleticism, dominance, winning, conflict, wealth, material possessions, willingness to drink alcohol, and sexual prowess vis-à-vis women.

Valued Qualities of Members

When fraternity members talked about the kind of pledges they prefer, a litany of stereotypical and narrowly masculine attributes and behaviors was recited and feminine or woman-associated qualities and behaviors were expressly denounced (cf. Merton 1985). Fraternities seek men who are "athletic," "big guys," good in intramural competition, "who can talk college sports." Males "who are willing to drink alcohol," "who drink socially," or "who can hold their liquor" are sought. Alcohol and ac-

tivities associated with the recreational use of alcohol are cornerstones of fraternity social life. Nondrinkers are viewed with skepticism and rarely selected for membership.[1]

Fraternities try to avoid "geeks," nerds, and men said to give the fraternity a "wimpy" or "gay" reputation. Art, music, and humanities majors, majors in traditional women's fields (nursing, home economics, social work, education), men with long hair, and those whose appearance or dress violate current norms are rejected. Clean-cut, handsome men who dress well (are clean, neat, conforming, fashionable) are preferred. One sorority woman commented that "the top ranking fraternities have the best looking guys."

One fraternity man, a senior, said his fraternity recruited "some big guys, very athletic" over a two-year period to help overcome its image of wimpiness. His fraternity had won the interfraternity competition for highest grade-point average several years running but was looked down on as "wimpy, dancy, even gay." With their bigger, more athletic recruits, "our reputation improved; we're a much more recognized fraternity now." Thus a fraternity's reputation and status depends on members' possession of stereotypically masculine qualities. Good grades, campus leadership, and community service are "nice" but masculinity dominance—for example, in athletic events, physical size of members, athleticism of members—counts most.

Certain social skills are valued. Men are sought who "have good personalities," are friendly, and "have the ability to relate to girls" (cf. Longino and Kart 1973). One fraternity man, a junior, said: "We watch a guy [a potential pledge] talk to women . . . we want guys who can relate to girls." Assessing a pledge's ability to talk to women is, in part, a preoccupation with homosexuality and a conscious avoidance of men who seem to have effeminate manners or qualities. If a member is suspected of being gay, he is ostracized and informally drummed out of the fraternity. A fraternity with a reputation as wimpy or tolerant of gays is ridiculed and shunned by other fraternities. Militant heterosexuality is frequently used by men as a strategy to keep each other in line (Kimmel 1987).

Financial affluence or wealth, a male-associated value in American culture, is highly valued by fraternities. In accounting for why the fraternity involved in the gang rape that precipitated our research project had been recognized recently as "the best fraternity chapter in the United States," a university official said: "They were good-looking, a big fraternity, had lots of BMWs [expensive, German-made automobiles]." After the rape, newspaper stories described the fraternity members' affluence, noting the high number of members who owned expensive cars (*St. Petersburg Times*, 1988).

The Status and Norms of Pledgeship

A pledge (sometimes called an associate member) is a new recruit who occupies a trial membership status for a specific period of time. The pledge period (typically ranging from 10 to 15 weeks) gives fraternity brothers an opportunity to assess and socialize new recruits. Pledges evaluate the fraternity also and decide if they want to become brothers. The socialization experience is structured partly through assignment of a Big Brother to each pledge. Big Brothers are expected to teach pledges how to become a brother and to support them as they progress through the trial membership period. Some pledges are repelled by the pledging experience, which can entail physical abuse; harsh discipline; and demands to be subordinate, follow orders, and engage in demeaning routines and activities, similar to those used by the military to "make men out of boys" during boot camp.

Characteristics of the pledge experience are rationalized by fraternity members as necessary to help pledges unite into a group, rely on each other, and join together against outsiders. The process is highly masculinist in execution as well as conception. A willingness to submit to authority, follow orders, and do as one is told is viewed as a sign of loyalty, togetherness, and unity. Fraternity pledges who find the pledge process offensive often drop out. Some do this by openly quitting, which can subject them to ridicule by brothers and other pledges, or they may deliberately fail to make the grades necessary for initiation or transfer schools and decline to reaffiliate with the fraternity on the new campus. One fraternity pledge who quit the fraternity he had pledged described an experience during pledgeship as follows:

> This one guy was always picking on me. No matter what I did, I was wrong. One night after dinner, he and two other guys called me and two other pledges into the chapter room. He said, "Here, X, hold this 25 pound bag of ice at arms' length 'til I tell you to stop." I did it even though my arms and hands were killing me. When I asked if I could stop, he grabbed me around the throat and lifted me off the floor. I thought he would choke me to death. He

cussed me and called me all kinds of names. He took one of my fingers and twisted it until it nearly broke. . . . I stayed in the fraternity for a few more days, but then I decided to quit. I hated it. Those guys are sick. They like seeing you suffer.

Fraternities' emphasis on toughness, withstanding pain and humiliation, obedience to superiors, and using physical force to obtain compliance contributes to an interpersonal style that de-emphasizes caring and sensitivity but fosters intragroup trust and loyalty. If the least macho or most critical pledges drop out, those who remain may be more receptive to, and influenced by, masculinist values and practices that encourage the use of force in sexual relations with women and the covering up of such behavior (cf. Kanin 1967).

Norms and Dynamics of Brotherhood

Brother is the status occupied by fraternity men to indicate their relations to each other and their membership in a particular fraternity organization or group. Brother is a male-specific status; only males can become brothers, although women can become "Little Sisters," a form of pseudomembership. "Becoming a brother" is a rite of passage that follows the consistent and often lengthy display by pledges of appropriately masculine qualities and behaviors. Brothers have a quasi-familial relationship with each other, are normatively said to share bonds of closeness and support, and are sharply set off from nonmembers. Brotherhood is a loosely defined term used to represent the bonds that develop among fraternity members and the obligations and expectations incumbent upon them (cf. Marlowe and Auvenshine [1982] on fraternities' failure to encourage "moral development" in freshman pledges).

Some of our respondents talked about brotherhood in almost reverential terms, viewing it as the most valuable benefit of fraternity membership. One senior, a business-school major who had been affiliated with a fairly high-status fraternity throughout four years on campus, said:

> Brotherhood spurs friendship for life, which I consider its best aspect, although I didn't see it that way when I joined. Brotherhood bonds and unites. It instills values of caring about one another, caring about community, caring about ourselves. The values and bonds [of brotherhood] continually develop over the

four years [in college] while normal friendships come and go.

Despite this idealization, most aspects of fraternity practice and conception are more mundane. Brotherhood often plays itself out as an overriding concern with masculinity and, by extension, femininity. As a consequence, fraternities comprise collectivities of highly masculinized men with attitudinal qualities and behavioral norms that predispose them to sexual coercion of women (cf. Kanin 1967; Merton 1985; Rapaport and Burkhart 1984). The norms of masculinity are complemented by conceptions of women and femininity that are equally distorted and stereotyped and that may enhance the probability of women's exploitation (cf. Ehrhart and Sandler 1985; Sanday 1981, 1986).

Practices of Brotherhood

Practices associated with fraternity brotherhood that contribute to the sexual coercion of women include a preoccupation with loyalty, group protection and secrecy, use of alcohol as a weapon, involvement in violence and physical force, and an emphasis on competition and superiority.

Loyalty, Group Protection, and Secrecy   Loyalty is a fraternity preoccupation. Members are reminded constantly to be loyal to the fraternity and to their brothers. Among other ways, loyalty is played out in the practices of group protection and secrecy. The fraternity must be shielded from criticism. Members are admonished to avoid getting the fraternity in trouble and to bring all problems "to the chapter" (local branch of a national social fraternity) rather than to outsiders. Fraternities try to protect themselves from close scrutiny and criticism by the Interfraternity Council (a quasi-governing body composed of representatives from all social fraternities on campus), their fraternity's national office, university officials, law enforcement, the media, and the public. Protection of the fraternity often takes precedence over what is procedurally, ethically, or legally correct. Numerous examples were related to us of fraternity brothers' lying to outsiders to "protect the fraternity."

Group protection was observed in the alleged gang rape case with which we began our study. Except for one brother, a rapist who turned state's evidence, the entire remaining fraternity membership was accused by the university and criminal justice officials of lying to protect the fraternity. Members consistently failed to cooperate even

though the alleged crimes were felonies, involved only four men (two of whom were not even members of the local chapter), and the victim of the crime nearly died. According to a grand jury's findings, fraternity officers repeatedly broke appointments with law enforcement officials, refused to provide police with a list of members, and refused to cooperate with police and prosecutors investigating the case (*Florida Flambeau,* 1988).

Secrecy is a priority value and practice in fraternities, partly because full-fledged membership is premised on it (for confirmation, see Ehrhart and Sandler 1985; Longino and Kart 1973; Roark 1987). Secrecy is also a boundary-maintaining mechanism, demarcating in-group from out-group, us from them. Secret rituals, handshakes, and mottoes are revealed to pledge brothers as they are initiated into full brotherhood. Since only brothers are supposed to know a fraternity's secrets, such knowledge affirms membership in the fraternity and separates a brother from others. Extending secrecy tactics from protection of private knowledge to protection of the fraternity from criticism is a predictable development. Our interviews indicated that individual members knew the difference between right and wrong, but fraternity norms that emphasize loyalty, group protection, and secrecy often overrode standards of ethical correctness.

Alcohol as Weapon   Alcohol use by fraternity men is normative. They use it on weekdays to relax after class and on weekends to "get drunk," "get crazy," and "get laid." The use of alcohol to obtain sex from women is pervasive—in other words, it is used as a weapon against sexual reluctance. According to several fraternity men whom we interviewed, alcohol is the major tool used to gain sexual mastery over women (cf. Adams and Abarbanel 1988; Ehrhart and Sandler 1985). One fraternity man, a 21-year-old senior, described alcohol use to gain sex as follows: "There are girls that you know will fuck, then some you have to put some effort into it. . . . You have to buy them drinks or find out if she's drunk enough. . . ."

A similar strategy is used collectively. A fraternity man said that at parties with Little Sisters: "We provide them with 'hunch punch' and things get wild. We get them drunk and most of the guys end up with one." "'Hunch punch,'" he said, "is a girls' drink made up of overproof alcohol and powdered Kool-Aid, no water or anything, just ice. It's very strong. Two cups will do a number on a female." He had plans in the next academic term to surreptitiously give hunch punch to women in a "prim and proper" sorority because "having sex with prim and proper sorority girls is definitely a goal." These women are a challenge because they "won't openly consume alcohol and won't get openly drunk as hell." Their sororities have "standards committees" that forbid heavy drinking and easy sex.

In the gang rape case, our sources said that many fraternity men on campus believed the victim had a drinking problem and was thus an "easy make." According to newspaper accounts, she had been drinking alcohol on the evening she was raped; the lead assailant is alleged to have given her a bottle of wine after she arrived at his fraternity house. Portions of the rape occurred in a shower, and the victim was reportedly so drunk that her assailants had difficulty holding her in a standing position (*Tallahassee Democrat*, 1988a). While raping her, her assailants repeatedly told her they were members of another fraternity under the apparent belief that she was too drunk to know the difference. Of course, if she was too drunk to know who they were, she was too drunk to consent to sex (cf. Allgeier 1986; Tash 1988).

One respondent told us that gang rapes are wrong and can get one expelled, but he seemed to see nothing wrong in sexual coercion one-on-one. He seemed unaware that the use of alcohol to obtain sex from a woman is grounds for a claim that a rape occurred (cf. Tash 1988). Few women on campus (who also may not know these grounds) report date rapes, however; so the odds of detection and punishment are slim for fraternity men who use alcohol for "seduction" purposes (cf. Byington and Keeter 1988; Merton 1985).

Violence and Physical Force Fraternity men have a history of violence (Ehrhart and Sandler 1985; Roark 1987). Their record of hazing, fighting, property destruction, and rape has caused them problems with insurance companies (Bradford 1986; Pressley 1987). Two university officials told us that fraternities "are the third riskiest property to insure behind toxic waste dumps and amusement parks." Fraternities are increasingly defendants in legal actions brought by pledges subjected to hazing (Meyer 1986; Pressley 1987) and by women who were raped by one or more members. In a recent alleged gang rape incident at another Florida university, prosecutors failed to file charges but the victim filed a civil suit against the fraternity nevertheless (*Tallahassee Democrat,* 1989).

Competition and Superiority Interfraternity rivalry fosters in-group identification and out-group hostility. Fraternities stress pride of membership and superiority over other fraternities as major goals. Interfraternity rivalries take many forms, including competition for desirable pledges, size of pledge class, size of membership, size and appearance of fraternity house, superiority in intramural sports, highest grade-point averages, giving the best parties, gaining the best or most campus leadership roles, and, of great importance, attracting and displaying "good looking women." Rivalry is particularly intense over members, intramural sports, and women (cf. Messner 1989).

FRATERNITIES' COMMODIFICATION OF WOMEN

In claiming that women are treated by fraternities as commodities, we mean that fraternities knowingly, and intentionally, *use* women for their benefit. Fraternities use women as bait for new members, as servers of brothers' needs, and as sexual prey.

Women as Bait Fashionably attractive women help a fraternity attract new members. As one fraternity man, a junior, said, "They are good bait." Beautiful, sociable women are believed to impress the right kind of pledges and give the impression that the fraternity can deliver this type of woman to its members. Photographs of shapely, attractive coeds are printed in fraternity brochures and videotapes that are distributed and shown to potential pledges. The women pictured are often dressed in bikinis, at the beach, and are pictured hugging the brothers of the fraternity. One university official says such recruitment materials give the message: "Hey, they're here for you, you can have whatever you want," and, "we have the best looking women. Join us and you can have them too." Another commented: "Something's wrong when males join an all-male organization as the best place to meet women. It's so illogical."

Fraternities compete in promising access to beautiful women. One fraternity man, a senior, commented that "the attraction of girls [i.e., a fraternity's success in attracting women] is a big status symbol for fraternities." One university official commented that the use of women as a recruiting tool is so well entrenched that fraternities that might be willing to forgo it say they cannot afford to unless other fraternities do so as well. One fraternity man said, "Look, if we don't have Little Sisters, the fraternities that do will get all the good pledges." Another said, "We won't have as good a rush [the period during which new members are assessed and selected] if we don't have these women around."

In displaying good-looking, attractive, skimpily dressed, nubile women to potential members, fraternities implicitly, and sometimes explicitly, promise sexual access to women. One fraternity man commented that "part of what being in a fraternity is all about is the sex" and explained how his fraternity uses Little Sisters to recruit new members:

> We'll tell the sweetheart [the fraternity's term for Little Sister], "You're gorgeous; you can get him." We'll tell her to fake a scam and she'll go hang all over him during a rush party, kiss him, and he thinks he's done wonderful and wants to join. The girls think it's great too. It's flattering for them.

Women as Servers   The use of women as servers is exemplified in the Little Sister program. Little Sisters are undergraduate women who are rushed and selected in a manner parallel to the recruitment of fraternity men. They are affiliated with the fraternity in a formal but unofficial way and are able, indeed required, to wear the fraternity's Greek letters. Little Sisters are not full-fledged fraternity members, however; and fraternity national offices and most universities do not register or regulate them. Each fraternity has an officer called Little Sister Chairman who oversees their organization and activities. The Little Sisters elect officers among themselves, pay monthly dues to the fraternity, and have well-defined roles. Their dues are used to pay for the fraternity's social events, and Little Sisters are expected to attend and hostess fraternity parties and hang around the house to make it a "nice place to be." One fraternity man, a senior, described Little Sisters this way: "They are very social girls, willing to join in, be affiliated with the group, devoted to the fraternity." Another member, a sophomore, said: "Their sole purpose is social—attend parties, attract new members, and 'take care' of the guys."

Our observations and interviews suggested that women selected by fraternities as Little Sisters are physically attractive, possess good social skills, and are willing to devote time and energy to the fraternity and its members. One undergraduate woman gave the following job description for Little Sisters to a campus newspaper:

> It's not just making appearances at all the parties but entails many more responsibilities. You're going to be expected to go to all the intramural games to cheer the brothers on, support and encourage the pledges, and just be around to bring some extra life to the house. [As a Little Sister] you have to agree to take on a new responsibility other than studying to maintain your grades and managing to keep your checkbook from bouncing. You have to make time to be a part of the fraternity and support the brothers in all they do. (*The Tomahawk*, 1988)

The title of Little Sister reflects women's subordinate status; fraternity men in a parallel role are called Big Brothers. Big Brothers assist a sorority primarily with the physical work of sorority rushes, which, compared to fraternity rushes, are more formal, structured, and intensive. Sorority rushes take place in the daytime and fraternity rushes at night so fraternity men are free to help. According to one fraternity member, Little Sister status is a benefit to women because it gives them a social outlet and "the protection of the brothers." The gender-stereotypic conceptions and obligations of these Little Sister and Big Brother statuses indicate that fraternities and sororities promote a gender hierarchy on campus that fosters subordination and dependence in women, thus encouraging sexual exploitation and the belief that it is acceptable.

Women as Sexual Prey   Little Sisters are a sexual utility. Many Little Sisters do not belong to sororities and lack peer support for refraining from unwanted sexual relations. One fraternity man (whose fraternity has 65 members and 85 Little Sisters) told us they had recruited "wholesale" in the prior year to "get lots of new women." The structural access to women that the Little Sister program provides and the absence of normative supports for refusing fraternity members' sexual advances may make women in this program particularly susceptible to coerced sexual encounters with fraternity men.

Access to women for sexual gratification is a presumed benefit of fraternity membership, promised in recruitment materials and strategies and through brothers' conversations with new recruits. One fraternity man said: "We always tell the guys that you get sex all the time, there's always new girls. . . . After I became a Greek, I found out I could be with females at will." A university official told us that, based on his observations, "no one [i.e., fraternity men] on this campus wants to have 'relationships.' They just want to have fun [i.e., sex]." Fraternity men plan and execute strategies aimed at obtaining sexual gratification, and this occurs at both individual and collective levels.

Individual strategies include getting a woman drunk and spending a great deal of money on her. As for collective strategies, most of our undergraduate interviewees agreed that fraternity parties often culminate in sex and that this outcome is planned. One fraternity man said fraternity parties often involve sex and nudity and can "turn into orgies." Orgies may be planned in advance, such as the Bowery Ball party held by one fraternity. A former fraternity member said of this party:

> The entire idea behind this is sex. Both men and women come to the party wearing little or nothing. There are pornographic pinups on the walls and usually porno movies playing on the TV. The music carries sexual overtones. . . . They just get schnockered [drunk] and, in most cases, they also get laid.

When asked about the women who come to such a party, he said: "Some Little Sisters just won't go. . . . The girls who do are looking for a good time, girls who don't know what it is, things like that."

Other respondents denied that fraternity parties are orgies but said that sex is always talked about among the brothers and they all know "who each other is doing it with." One member said that most of the time, guys have sex with their girlfriends "but with socials, girlfriends aren't allowed to come and it's their [members'] big chance [to have sex with other women]." The use of alcohol to help them get women into bed is a routine strategy at fraternity parties.

CONCLUSIONS

In general, our research indicated that the organization and membership of fraternities contribute heavily to coercive and often violent sex. Fraternity houses are occupied by same-sex (all men) and same-age (late teens, early twenties) peers whose maturity and judgment is often less than ideal. Yet fraternity houses are private dwellings that are mostly off-limits to, and away from scrutiny of, university and community representatives, with the result that fraternity house events seldom come to the attention of outsiders. Practices associated with the social construction of fraternity brotherhood emphasize a macho conception of men and masculinity, a narrow, stereotyped conception of women and femininity, and the treatment of women as commodities. Other practices contributing to coercive sexual relations and the cover-up of rapes include excessive alcohol use, competitiveness, and norma-

tive support for deviance and secrecy (cf. Bogal-Allbritten and Allbritten 1985; Kanin 1967).

Some fraternity practices exacerbate others. Brotherhood norms require "sticking together" regardless of right or wrong; thus rape episodes are unlikely to be stopped or reported to outsiders, even when witnesses disapprove. The ability to use alcohol without scrutiny by authorities and alcohol's frequent association with violence, including sexual coercion, facilitates rape in fraternity houses. Fraternity norms that emphasize the value of maleness and masculinity over femaleness and femininity and that elevate the status of men and lower the status of women in members' eyes undermine perceptions and treatment of women as persons who deserve consideration and care (cf. Ehrhart and Sandler 1985; Merton 1985).

Androgynous men and men with a broad range of interests and attributes are lost to fraternities through their recruitment practices. Masculinity of a narrow and stereotypical type helps create attitudes, norms, and practices that predispose fraternity men to coerce women sexually, both individually and collectively (Allgeier 1986; Hood 1989; Sanday 1981, 1986). Male athletes on campus may be similarly disposed for the same reasons (Kirshenbaum 1989; Telander and Sullivan 1989).

Research into the social contexts in which rape crimes occur and the social constructions associated with these contexts illuminate rape dynamics on campus. Blanchard (1959) found that group rapes almost always have a leader who pushes others into the crime. He also found that the leader's latent homosexuality, desire to show off to his peers, or fear of failing to prove himself a man are frequently an impetus. Fraternity norms and practices contribute to the approval and use of sexual coercion as an accepted tactic in relations with women. Alcohol-induced compliance is normative, whereas, presumably, use of a knife, gun, or threat of bodily harm would not be because the woman who "drinks too much" is viewed as "causing her own rape" (cf. Ehrhart and Sandler 1985).

Our research led us to conclude that fraternity norms and practices influence members to view the sexual coercion of women, which is a felony crime, as sport, a contest, or a game (cf. Sato 1988). This sport is played not between men and women but between men and men. Women are the pawns or prey in the interfraternity rivalry game; they prove that a fraternity is successful or prestigious. The use of women in this way encourages fraternity men to see women as objects and sexual coercion as sport. Today's societal norms support young women's right to engage in sex at their discretion, and coercion is unnecessary in a mutually desired encounter. However, nubile young women say they prefer to be "in a relationship" to have sex while young men say they prefer to "get laid" without a commitment (Muehlenhard and Linton 1987). These differences may reflect, in part, American puritanism and men's fears of sexual intimacy or perhaps intimacy of any kind. In a fraternity context, getting sex without giving emotionally demonstrates "cool" masculinity. More important, it poses no threat to the bonding and loyalty of the fraternity brotherhood (cf. Farr 1988). Drinking large quantities of alcohol before having sex suggests that "scoring" rather than intrinsic sexual pleasure is a primary concern of fraternity men.

Unless fraternities' composition, goals, structures, and practices change in fundamental ways, women on campus will continue to be sexual prey for fraternity men. As all-male enclaves dedicated to opposing faculty and administration and to cementing in-group ties, fraternity members eschew any hint of homosexuality. Their version of masculinity transforms women, and men with womanly characteristics, into the out-group. "Womanly men" are ostracized; feminine women are used to demonstrate members' masculinity. Encouraging renewed emphasis on their founding values (Longino and Kart 1973), service orientation and activities (Lemire 1979), or members' moral development (Marlowe and Auvenshine 1982) will have little effect on fraternities' treatment of women. A case for or against fraternities cannot be made by studying individual members. The fraternity qua group and organization is at issue. Located on campus along with many vulnerable women, embedded in a sexist society, and caught up in masculinist goals, practices, and values, fraternities' violation of women—including forcible rape—should come as no surprise.

NOTE

1. Recent bans by some universities on open-keg parties at fraternity houses have resulted in heavy drinking before coming to a party and an increase in drunkenness among those who attend. This may aggravate, rather than improve, the treatment of women by fraternity men at parties.

REFERENCES

Adams, Aileen, and Gail Abarbanel. *Sexual Assault on Campus: What Colleges Can Do.* Santa Monica, CA: Rape Treatment Center, 1988.

Allgeier, Elizabeth. 1986. "Coercive Versus Consensual Sexual Interactions." G. Stanley Hall Lecture to American Psychological Association Annual Meeting, Washington, DC, August.

Blanchard, W. H. "The Group Process in Gang Rape." *Journal of Social Psychology,* 49 (1959): 259–266.

Bogal-Allbritten, Rosemarie B., and William L. Allbritten. "The Hidden Victims: Courtship Violence Among College Students." *Journal of College Student Personnel,* 43 (1985): 201–204.

Bohrnstedt, George W. "Conservatism, Authoritarianism and Religiosity of Fraternity Pledges." *Journal of College Student Personnel,* 27 (1969): 36–43.

Bradford, Michael. "Tight Market Dries Up Nightlife at University." *Business Insurance* (2 March 1986): 2, 6.

Burkhart, Barry. Comments in Seminar on Acquaintance/Date Rape Prevention: A National Video Teleconference, 2 Feb. 1989.

Burkhart, Barry R., and Annette L. Stanton. "Sexual Aggression in Acquaintance Relationships." Pp. 43–65 in *Violence in Intimate Relationships,* ed. G. Russell. Englewood Cliffs, NJ: Spectrum, 1985.

Byington, Diane B., and Karen W. Keeter. "Assessing Needs of Sexual Assault Victims on a University Campus." Pp. 23–31 in *Student Services: Responding to Issues and Challenges.* Chapel Hill: University of North Carolina Press, 1988.

Chancer, Lynn S. "New Bedford, Massachusetts, March 6, 1983–March 22, 1984: The 'Before and After' of a Group Rape." *Gender & Society,* 1 (1987): 239–260.

Ehrhart, Julie K., and Bernice R. Sandler. *Campus Gang Rape: Party Games?* Washington, DC: Association of American Colleges, 1985.

Farr, K. A. "Dominance Bonding Through the Good Old Boys Sociability Network." *Sex Roles,* 18 (1988): 259–277.

Florida Flambeau. "Pike Members Indicted in Rape" (19 May 1988), pp. 1, 5.

Fox, Elaine; Charles Hodge; and Walter Ward. "A Comparison of Attitudes Held by Black and White Fraternity Members." *Journal of Negro Education,* 56 (1987): 521–534.

Geis, Gilbert. "Group Sexual Assaults." *Medical Aspects of Human Sexuality,* 5 (1971): 101–113.

Glaser, Barney G. *Theoretical Sensitivity: Advances in the Methodology of Grounded Theory.* Mill Valley, CA: Sociology Press, 1978.

Hood, Jane. "Why Our Society Is Rape-Prone." *New York Times* (16 May 1989).

Hughes, Michael J., and Roger B. Winston, Jr. "Effects of Fraternity Membership on Interpersonal Values." *Journal of College Student Personnel,* 45 (1987): 405–411.

Kanin, Eugene J. "Reference Groups and Sex Conduct Norm Violations." *The Sociological Quarterly,* 8 (1967): 495–504.

Kimmel, Michael, ed. *Changing Men: New Directions in Research on Men and Masculinity.* Newbury Park, CA: Sage, 1987.

Kirshenbaum, Jerry. "Special Report, An American Disgrace: A Violent and Unprecedented Lawlessness Has Arisen Among College Athletes in all Parts of the Country." *Sports Illustrated* (27 Feb. 1989), pp. 16–19.

Lemire, David. "One Investigation of the Stereotypes Associated with Fraternities and Sororities." *Journal of College Student Personnel,* 37 (1979): 54–57.

Letchworth, G. E. "Fraternities Now and in the Future." *Journal of College Student Personnel,* 10 (1969): 118–122.

Longino, Charles F., Jr., and Cary S. Kart. "The College Fraternity: An Assessment of Theory and Research." *Journal of College Student Personnel,* 31 (1973): 118–125.

Marlowe, Anne F., and Dwight C. Auvenshine. "Greek Membership: Its Impact on the Moral Development of College Freshmen." *Journal of College Student Personnel,* 40 (1982): 53–57.

Martin, Patricia Yancey, and Barry A. Turner. "Grounded Theory and Organizational Research." *Journal of Applied Behavioral Science,* 22 (1986): 141–157.

Merton, Andrew. "On Competition and Class: Return to Brotherhood." *Ms.* (Sept. 1985), pp. 60–65, 121–122.

Messner, Michael. "Masculinities and Athletic Careers." *Gender & Society,* 3 (1989): 71–88.

Meyer, T. J. "Fight Against Hazing Rituals Rages on Campuses." *Chronicle of Higher Education* (12 March 1986): 34–36.

Miller, Leonard D. "Distinctive Characteristics of Fraternity Members." *Journal of College Student Personnel,* 31 (1973): 126–128.

Muehlenhard, Charlene L., and Melaney A. Linton. "Date Rape and Sexual Aggression in Dating Situations: Incidence and Risk Factors." *Journal of Counseling Psychology,* 34 (1987): 186–196.

Pressley, Sue Anne. "Fraternity Hell Night Still Endures." *Washington Post* (11 Aug. 1987), p. B1.

Rapaport, Karen, and Barry R. Burkhart. "Personality and Attitudinal Characteristics of Sexually Coercive College Males." *Journal of Abnormal Psychology,* 93 (1984): 216–221.

Roark, Mary L. "Preventing Violence on College Campuses." *Journal of Counseling and Development,* 65 (1987): 367–370.

St. Petersburg Times. "A Greek Tragedy" (29 May 1988), pp. 1F, 6F.

Sanday, Peggy Reeves. "The Socio-Cultural Context of Rape: A Cross-Cultural Study." *Journal of Social Issues,* 37 (1981): 5–27.

———."Rape and the Silencing of the Feminine." Pp. 84–101 in *Rape,* ed. S. Tomaselli and R. Porter. Oxford: Basil Blackwell, 1986.

Sato, Ikuya. "Play Theory of Delinquency: Toward a General Theory of 'Action.'" *Symbolic Interaction,* 11 (1988): 191–212.

Smith, T. "Emergence and Maintenance of Fraternal Solidarity." *Pacific Sociological Review,* 7 (1964): 29–37.

Tallahasee Democrat. "FSU Fraternity Brothers Charged" (27 April 1988a), pp. 1A, 12A.

———. "FSU Interviewing Students About Alleged Rape" (24 April 1988b), p. 1D.

———. "Woman Sues Stetson in Alleged Rape" (19 Mar. 1989), p. 3B.

Tampa Tribune. "Fraternity Brothers Charged in Sexual Assault of FSU Coed" (27 April 1988), p. 6B.

Tash, Gary B. "Date Rape." *The Emerald of Sigma Pi Fraternity,* 75, 4 (1988): 1–2.

Telander, Rick, and Robert Sullivan. "Special Report, You Reap What You Sow." *Sports Illustrated* (27 Feb. 1989), pp. 20–34.

The Tomahawk. "A Look Back at Rush, A Mixture of Hard Work and Fun" (April/May 1988), p. 3D.

Walsh, Claire. Comments in Seminar on Acquaintance/ Date Rape Prevention: A National Video Teleconference, 2 Feb. 1989.

Wilder, David H.; Arlyne E. Hoyt; Dennis M. Doren; William E. Hauck; and Robert D. Zettle. "The Impact of Fraternity and Sorority Membership on Values and Attitudes." *Journal of College Student Personnel,* 36 (1978): 445–449.

Wilder, David H.; Arlyne E. Hoyt; Beth Shuster Surbeck; Janet C. Wilder; and Patricia Imperatrice Carney. "Greek Affiliation and Attitude Change in College Students." *Journal of College Student Personnel,* 44 (1986): 510–519.

DISCUSSION QUESTIONS

1. The "practices associated with the social construction of fraternity brotherhood," argue Martin and Hummer, "emphasize a macho conception of men and masculinity, a narrow, stereotyped conception of women and femininity, and the treatment of

women as commodities." What do they mean by this? And what is wrong with it? Do you agree with their argument?

2. According to Martin and Hummer, fraternity norms and practices influence fraternity brothers "to view the sexual coercion of women, which is a felony crime, as sport, a contest or a game." What, according to Martin and Hummer, is wrong with this? Analyze their argument.

3. Fraternity brotherhood norms require "sticking together," point out Martin and Hummer, regardless of right or wrong. "Thus, rape episodes are unlikely to be stopped or reported to outsiders, even when the witnesses are wrong." If you were the member of a fraternity and witnessed a rape, would you report it to outsiders even if it violated the fraternity brotherhood norms requiring "sticking together" regardless of right or wrong? How would you morally justify your decision?

4. Martin and Hummer argue that unless fraternities change their practices, goals, and structures women on campus will continue to be subject to sexual violence. Do you agree with them? Why or why not? Would you be willing to take your arguments as far as the student senate of your college or university? Explain.

5. Given that fraternities are embedded in a sexist society, say Martin and Hummer, it should not be a surprise that they are often the sites of violence against women. Do you agree with them? Explain your view.

 S U Z A N N E   P H A R R

Hate Violence Against Women

Suzanne Pharr argues that hate violence against women is morally the same as hate crimes against people of color, Jews, and gay men and lesbians. "This country minimizes hate violence against women," says Pharr, "because women's lives are not valued, because the violence is so commonplace that people become numb to it, because people do not want to look at the institutions and systems that support it, and because people do not want to recognize how widespread the hatred is and how many perpetrators there are among us on every level of society." Pharr argues that sexist violence must be monitored in the same way that racist, anti-Semitic, and homophobic violence is monitored. "Men beat, rape and kill women because they *can*," says Pharr, "because they live in a society that gives permission to the hatred of women." Pharr's article suggests that monitoring the scope and nature of hate violence against women will work to bring about a society that values women and does not permit violence of this type to persist.

Suzanne Pharr, activist and founder of the Women's Project out of Little Rock, Arkansas, is the author of *Homophobia: A Weapon of Sexism* (2nd expanded ed., 1997), *In the Time of the Right: Reflections on Liberation* (1996), and *Exile and Pride: Disability, Queerness and Liberation* (with Eli Clare, 1999).

Suzanne Pharr, *Transformation: A Quarterly Journal of Political Analysis*, vol. 5, no. 1 (January 1990): 1–3. Published by the Woman's Project, 2224 Main St., Little Rock, AR 72206. Reprinted with permission.

Women and men in Canada, the U.S., and world-wide were stunned and appalled by the massacre of 14 women in the University of Montreal engineering school. There has been outrage, grief and intense questioning in the aftermath of this murder. People have wanted to know what could be the motivation for such an outrageous act, and there has been some relief drawn from the suicide note that many read as a statement of a deranged mind, suggesting that these killings were an isolated incident.

However, those of us who are longtime workers in the women's anti-violence movement know that these killings, while seeming to contain elements of madness, are simply one more piece of the more routine, less sensational hate murders of women that we deal with every day. According to the FBI, there are several thousand women killed by their husbands and boyfriends each year. This number does not include the great numbers of women killed by rapists on the street and in their homes. Almost all of these are women who die horrible deaths of brutality and terror with no public outcry and outrage for the waste of their lives.

There is media and public response when the murder is sensational either in numbers, in the esteemed worth of the victim, or when it is cross-race and the perpetrator is a man of color. Hence, the extensive coverage of the Montreal massacre, the rape of the white female investment banker in Central Park, and the Republicans' use of Willie Horton as the rapist most to be feared. Otherwise, when murders and rapes of women are briefly reported daily in our papers and on television, the public, accustomed to the ordinariness of rape and murder of women and desensitized to it, simply see it as one more trivial incident in the expected way of life for women. It's just one more woman violated or dead; turn the page; flip the channel.

To see how staggering these numbers are, let's look just at one state, the small (pop. 2.3 million), mostly rural state of Arkansas. At the Women's Project, for almost a year now we've been monitoring hate violence in Arkansas, and unlike other monitoring groups, we include sexist violence along with racist, anti-Semitic and homophobic violence. During the first six months of the year, we were putting the project in place and quite possibly missed some of the murders of women; nevertheless, our records show 37 women and girls murdered in 1989. Their killers were husbands, boyfriends, acquaintances, strangers. Most of the women were killed in their homes and all were murders in which robbery was not the motive. Their ages ranged from 5 years old to 88. Some were raped and killed; all were brutal murders. Some were urban, some rural; some rich, some poor; some white, some women of color.

A few examples will be enough to show the level of hatred and violence that was present in all the murders. A 67-year-old woman was shot twice with a crossbow and dumped into a farm pond, her head covered with plastic and her body weighted down with six concrete blocks; a 22-year-old woman was abducted from her home by three armed men while her small children watched, taken to an abandoned house, raped, sodomized and killed; a 30-year-old teacher was slashed and stabbed dozens of times; a 19-year-old woman was beaten to death and buried in a shallow grave; a 5-year-old girl was raped, strangled and stuffed into a tree; a 32-year-old paraplegic was killed, a 35-lb. weight tied to her, and dropped into the Ouachita River; an 86-year-old woman was suffocated in her home.

Added to these brutal murders are the statistics from Arkansas Children and Family Services that indicate 1353 girls were sexually assaulted in 1988, and from the Arkansas Crime Information Center that 656 rapes were reported in 1988. In November the Arkansas *Gazette* reported that in the first six months of 1989, Little Rock had more rapes—119—than Washington, D.C.—90—a city three times its size. When we understand that only about 10% of all rapes are reported, these numbers become significantly larger. All in all, when the numbers of murders, rapes, and sexual assaults of girls are put together there emerges a grim picture of the brutal hate violence launched against women and girls.

I don't believe Arkansas is an exception in this violence. From battered women's programs, from rape crisis programs, from crime statistics, we know that women are beaten, raped and killed in every state of this country, every day. Because so many women are viciously beaten and their lives placed in jeopardy, this country has over 1100 battered women's programs, all filled to overflowing, and more being developed every day.

Wherever we live in the U.S., women live in a war zone where we may be attacked, terrorized, or abducted at any moment. Women are not safe in the home, on the street, or at the workplace. Or, as in Montreal, in a school setting on the eve of final exams for 14 women about to enter engineering jobs that only recently became accessible to them in a world that considers engineering "men's work." There is no safe place, no "proper" kind of woman whose behavior exempts her, no fully protected woman.

While we recognize the absence of safety in all women's lives, no matter what class or race, we also are aware that women of color have even less safety than white women. Women of color are the targets of the combined hatred of racism and sexism, and as such, they experience both racist and sexist violence against their lives from white people as well as sexist violence from men of color, and often racist responses and services when they seek help.

Recently, the writers of a hate crime bill that went before Congress could not agree to put women alongside people of color, Jews, gay men and lesbians as targets of hate crimes. This seems to me a critical error in moral and political judgment, one reminiscent of the immoral decision the white women of the 19th century women's movement made when they decided to turn their backs on black women in order to secure the participation of white Southern women. There is never a "more politically appropriate" time to bring in a group of people—in this case, 52% of the population—that is this country's largest target of hate crimes. When hate crimes are limited to anti-Semitic, racist, and homophobic violence, there is inherent confusion: when Jewish women are killed, when women of color are killed, when lesbians are raped or killed, it is often impossible to determine if they were attacked because of their religion, race, sexual identity, or their *gender.*

The U.S. Justice Department's guidelines to determine bias motivation for a crime include common sense (i.e., cross burning or offensive graffiti), language used by the assailant, the severity of the attack, a lack of provocation, previous history of similar incidents in the same area, and an absence of any other apparent motive. Under this definition, rape would be an apparent hate crime, often severe—including armed assault, beating and killing—often repeated in the same neighborhood or area, no other apparent motive, and almost always abusive woman-hating language.

The same would be true with our monitored cases of battering that ends in murder. In the majority of the cases, the woman was beaten (sometimes there was a long history of battering) and then killed. Rather than cross burnings or offensive graffiti, the hate material is pornography. Most telling is the absence of any other apparent motive. And then there are the countless beatings and acts of terrorism that don't end in murder but do lasting physical and psychological damage to women. An example from Arkansas:

(A woman) reported battery and terroristic threatening. She said her neighbor/ex-boyfriend threatened her with a handgun, and beat her, knocking her down a flight of stairs where she landed on a rock terrace.

(She) sustained permanent damage to her eardrum, two black eyes and extensive bruises and lacerations. She stated her assailant was not intoxicated; that he bragged of having been a Golden Gloves boxer; and he allegedly told her he could not be arrested for beating her since he struck her with his hands open. (Washington County *Observer* 8/17/89)

Men beat, rape and kill women because they *can;* that is, because they live in a society that gives permission to the hatred of women.

This country minimizes hate violence against women because women's lives are not valued, because the violence is so commonplace that people become numb to it, because people do not want to look at the institutions and systems that support it, and because people do not want to recognize how widespread the hatred is and how many perpetrators there are among us on every level of society.

It is only when women's lives are valued that this violence will be ended. If 37 African Americans were killed by whites in Arkansas, our organization would be leading the organizing to investigate and end the murders; or if 37 Jews were killed by gentiles; or if 37 gay men or lesbians were murdered by heterosexuals—for all of these other groups we monitor violence against, we would be in the forefront of organizing on their behalf. But why not on behalf of women? We talk about violence against women and help develop organizations that provide safety and support for victims, but even we sometimes get numbed to its immensity, to its everydayness, to the loss of freedom it brings with it.

All of us must stop minimizing this violence against women. We must bring it to the forefront of our social consciousness and name it for what it is: not the gentler, less descriptive words such as family violence, or domestic violence, or wife or spouse abuse, or sexual assault, but *hate violence against women.* It does not erupt naturally or by chance from the domesticity of our lives; it comes from a climate of woman hating.

For too long when women have named this violence as what it is, we have been called man-haters by people who want the truth kept quiet. "Man-hater" is a common expression but "woman-hater" is not, despite the brutal evidence of woman-hating that surrounds us: murder, rape, battering, incest. The common use of the word "man-hater" is a diversionary tactic that keeps us from looking at the hard reality of the source of violence in our lives. The threat of the label "man-hater" threatens women with loss of privilege and controls our behavior, but more importantly, it keeps us from working honestly and forcefully on our own behalf to end the violence that destroys us.

Social change occurs when those who experience injustice organize to improve or save their lives. Women must overcome the fear of organizing on behalf of women, no matter what the threat. We must organize together to eliminate the root causes of violence against us.

We must make sure that hate violence against women is monitored and documented separate from general homicides so that we can be clear about the extent of it, the tactics, the institutions and systems that allow it to continue. We must hold our institutions accountable. In December 1989, the Arkansas *Gazette* ran a series of articles about local hospitals "dumping" rape victims, that is, refusing to give rape examinations because they did not want to get involved in legal cases. Such inhumane practices are dehumanizing to women and lead to public indifference to rape and its terrible consequences.

We must create a society that does not give men permission to rape and kill women. We all must believe that women's lives are as important as the lives of men. If we created a memorial to the women dead from this war against them—just over the past decade—our memorial would rest next to the Vietnam Memorial in Washington in numbers and human loss to this nation. The massacre must end.

DISCUSSION QUESTIONS

1. Pharr says that we "live in a society that gives permission to the hatred of women." What is her argument? Do you agree with her? What is your evidence?
2. Should hate violence against women be considered as morally equivalent to hate crimes against people of color, Jews, and gay men and lesbians? Why or why not? Why might someone disagree with your position?
3. Pharr says that we should not use phrases such as "family violence," "domestic violence," "spouse abuse" or "sexual assault." Why? What is wrong with these phrases? Do you agree with her?
4. Why does Pharr argue for the monitoring of hate violence against women? What difference does she think that such monitoring will make? Do you agree with her argument? Why or why not?
5. Pharr argues that "women of color have even less safety than white women." What is her argument? Is it a good one?

bell hooks

Violence in Intimate Relationships

If Suzanne Pharr is correct that "women live in a war zone," then bell hooks wants us to take its *injuries* just as seriously as its *casualties*. "Feminist work calling attention to male violence against women has helped create a climate where the issues of physical abuse by loved ones can be freely addressed," says hooks, "especially sexual abuse within families."

bell hooks, *Talking Back: Thinking Feminist, Thinking Black.* South End Press, 1989. Used by permission of the publisher.

However, "overemphasis on extreme cases of violent abuse may lead us to ignore the problem of occasional hitting, and it may make it difficult for women to talk about this problem." All forms of violence against women, and not just the extreme cases such as murders, need to be confronted and acknowledged as serious problems. For hooks, "these lesser forms of physical abuse damage individuals psychologically and, if not properly addressed and recovered from, can set the stage for more extreme incidents." Feminists need to pay more attention to these lesser acts of violence, if their aim of eliminating violence against women is to be achieved.

bell hooks is a professor of English at City College in New York and is the author of many books, including *Ain't I a Woman: Black Women and Feminism* (1981), *Feminist Theory: From Margin to Center* (1984), *Talking Back: Thinking Feminist, Thinking Black* (1989), *Black Looks: Race and Representation* (1992), *Sisters of the Yam: Black Women and Self-Recovery* (1993), *Outlaw Culture: Resisting Representations* (1994), *Teaching to Transgress: Education as the Practice of Freedom* (1994), *Art on My Mind: Visual Politics* (1995), *Killing Rage: Ending Racism* (1995), *Bone Black: Memories of Girlhood* (1996), *Reel to Real* (1996), *Feminism Is for Everybody: Passionate Politics* (2000), and *All About Love: New Visions* (2000).

We were on the freeway, going home from San Francisco. He was driving. We were arguing. He had told me repeatedly to shut up. I kept talking. He took his hand from the steering wheel and threw it back, hitting my mouth—my open mouth, blood gushed, and I felt an intense pain. I was no longer able to say any words, only to make whimpering, sobbing sounds as the blood dripped on my hands, on the handkerchief I held too tightly. He did not stop the car. He drove home. I watched him pack his suitcase. It was a holiday. He was going away to have fun. When he left I washed my mouth. My jaw was swollen and it was difficult for me to open it.

I called the dentist the next day and made an appointment. When the female voice asked what I needed to see the doctor about, I told her I had been hit in the mouth. Conscious of race, sex, and class issues, I wondered how I would be treated in this white doctor's office. My face was no longer swollen so there was nothing to identify me as a woman who had been hit, as a black woman with a bruised and swollen jaw. When the dentist asked me what had happened to my mouth, I described it calmly and succinctly. He made little jokes about "How we can't have someone doing this to us now, can we?" I said nothing. The damage was repaired. Through it all, he talked to me as if I were a child, someone he had to handle gingerly or otherwise I might become hysterical.

This is one way women who are hit by men and seek medical care are seen. People within patriarchal society imagine that women are hit because we are hysterical, because we are beyond reason. It is most often the person who is hitting that is beyond reason, who is hysterical, who has lost complete control over responses and actions.

Growing up, I had always thought that I would never allow any man to hit me and live. I would kill him. I had seen my father hit my mother once and I wanted to kill him. My mother said to me then, "You are too young to know, too young to understand." Being a mother in a culture that supports and promotes domination, a patriarchal, white-supremacist culture, she did not discuss how she felt or what she meant. Perhaps it would have been too difficult for her to speak about the confusion of being hit by someone you are intimate with, someone you love. In my case, I was hit by my companion at a time in life when a number of forces in the world outside our home had already "hit" me, so to speak, made me painfully aware of my powerlessness, my marginality. It seemed then that I was confronting being black and female and without money in the worst possible ways. My world was spinning. I had already lost a sense of grounding and security. The memory of this experience has stayed with me as I have grown as a feminist, as I have thought deeply and read much on male violence against women, on adult violence against children.

In this essay, I do not intend to concentrate attention solely on male physical abuse of females. It is crucial that feminists call attention to physical abuse in all its forms. In particular, I want to discuss being physically abused in singular incidents by someone you love. Few people who are hit once by someone they love respond in the way they might to a singular physical assault by a stranger. Many children raised in households where hitting has been a normal response by primary caretakers react ambivalently to physical assaults as adults, especially if they are being hit by someone who cares for them and whom they care for. Often female parents use physical abuse as a means of control. There is continued need for feminist research that examines such violence. Alice Miller has done insightful work on the impact of hitting even though she is at times antifeminist in her perspective. (Often in her work, mothers are blamed, as if their responsibility in parenting is greater than that of fathers.) Feminist discussions of violence against women should be expanded to include a recognition of the ways in which women use abusive physical force toward children not only to challenge the assumptions that women are likely to be nonviolent, but also to add to our understanding of why children who were hit growing up are often hit as adults or hit others.

Recently, I began a conversation with a group of black adults about hitting children. They all agreed that hitting was sometimes necessary. A professional black male in a southern family setting with two children commented on the way he punished his daughters. Sitting them down, he would first interrogate them about the situation or circumstance for which they were being punished. He said with great pride, "I want them to be able to understand fully why they are being punished." I responded by saying that "they will likely become women whom a lover will attack using the same procedure you who have loved them so well used and they will not know how to respond." He resisted the idea that his behavior would have any impact on their responses to violence as adult women. I pointed to case after case of women in intimate relationships with men (and sometimes women) who are subjected to the same form of interrogation and punishment they experienced as children, who accept their lover assuming an abusive, authoritarian role. Children who are the victims of physical abuse—whether one beating or repeated beatings, one violent push or several—whose wounds are inflicted by a loved one, experience an extreme sense of dislocation. The world one has most intimately known, in which one felt relatively safe and secure, has collapsed. Another world has come into being, one filled with terrors, where it is difficult to distinguish between a safe situation and a dangerous one, a gesture of love and a violent, uncaring gesture. There is a feeling of vulnerability, exposure, that never goes away, that lurks beneath the surface. I know. I was one of those children. Adults hit by loved ones usually experience similar sensations of dislocation, of loss, of newfound terrors.

Many children who are hit have never known what it feels like to be cared for, loved without physical aggression or abusive pain. Hitting is such a widespread practice that any of us are lucky if we can go through life without having this experience. One undiscussed aspect of the reality of children who are hit finding themselves as adults in similar circumstances is that we often share with friends and lovers the framework of our childhood pains and this may determine how they respond to us in difficult situations. We share the ways we are wounded and expose vulnerable areas. Often, these revelations provide a detailed model for anyone who wishes to wound or hurt us. While the literature about physical abuse often points to the fact that children who are abused are likely to become abusers or be abused, there is no attention given to sharing woundedness in such a way that we let intimate others know exactly what can be done to hurt us, to make us feel as though we are caught in the destructive patterns we have struggled to break. When partners create scenarios of abuse similar, if not exactly the same, to those we have experienced in childhood, the wounded person is hurt not only by the physical pain but by the feeling of calculated betrayal. Betrayal. When we are physically hurt by loved ones, we feel betrayed. We can no longer trust that care can be sustained. We are wounded, damaged—hurt to our hearts.

Feminist work calling attention to male violence against women has helped create a climate where the issues of physical abuse by loved ones can be freely addressed, especially sexual abuse within families. Exploration of male violence against women by feminists and non-feminists shows a connection between childhood experience of being hit by loved ones and the later occurrence of violence in adult relationships. While there is much material available discussing physical abuse of women by men, usually extreme physical abuse, there is not much discussion of the impact that one incident of hitting may have on a person in an intimate relationship, or how the person who is hit recovers from that experience. Increasingly, in discussion with women about physical abuse in relationships, irrespective of sexual preference, I find that most of us have had the experience of being violently hit at least once. There is little discussion of how we are damaged by such experiences (especially if we have been hit as children), of the ways we cope and recover from this wounding. This is an important area for feminist research precisely because many cases of extreme physical abuse begin with an isolated incident of hitting. Attention must be given to understanding and stopping these isolated incidents if we are to eliminate the possibility that women will be at risk in intimate relationships.

Critically thinking about issues of physical abuse has led me to question the way our culture, the way we as feminist advocates focus on the issue of violence and physical abuse by loved ones. The focus has been on male violence against women and, in particular, male sexual abuse of children. Given the nature of patriarchy, it has been necessary for feminists to focus on extreme cases to make people confront the issue, and acknowledge it to be serious and relevant. Unfortunately, an exclusive focus on extreme cases can and does lead us to ignore the more frequent, more common, yet less extreme case of occasional hitting. Women are also less likely to acknowledge occasional hitting for fear that they will then be seen as someone who is in a bad relationship or someone whose life is out of control. Currently, the literature about male violence against women identifies the physically abused woman as a "battered woman." While it has been important to have an accessible terminology to draw attention to the issue of male violence against women, the terms used reflect biases because they call attention to only one type of violence in intimate relationships. The term "battered woman" is problematical. It is not a term that emerged from feminist work on male violence against women; it was already used by psychologists and sociologists in the literature on domestic violence. This label "battered woman" places primary emphasis on physical assaults that are continuous, repeated, and unrelenting. The focus is on extreme violence, with little effort to link these cases with the everyday acceptance within intimate relationships of physical abuse that is not extreme, that may not be repeated. Yet these lesser forms of physical abuse damage individuals psychologically and, if not properly addressed and recovered from, can set the stage for more extreme incidents.

Most importantly, the term "battered woman" is used as though it constitutes a separate and unique category of womanness, as though it is an identity, a mark that sets one apart rather than being simply a descriptive term. It is as though the experience of being repeatedly violently hit is the sole defining characteristic of a woman's identity and all other aspects of who she is and what her experience has been are submerged. When I was hit, I too used the popular phrases "batterer," "battered woman," "battering" even though I did not feel that these words adequately described being hit once. However, these were the terms that people would listen to, would see as important, significant (as if it is not really significant for an individual, and more importantly for a woman, to be hit once). My partner was angry to be labelled a batterer by me. He was reluctant to talk about the experience of hitting me precisely because he did not want to be labelled a batterer. I had hit him once (not as badly as he had hit me) and I did not think of myself as a batterer. For both of us, these terms were inadequate. Rather than enabling us to cope effectively and positively with a negative situation, they were part of all the mechanisms of denial; they made us want to avoid confronting what had happened. This is the case for many people who are hit and those who hit.

Women who are hit once by men in their lives, and women who are hit repeatedly, do not want to be placed in the category of "battered woman" because it is a label that appears to strip us of dignity, to deny that there has been any integrity in the relationships we are in. A person physically assaulted by a stranger or a casual friend with whom they are not intimate may be hit once or repeatedly but they do not have to be placed into a category before doctors, lawyers, family, counselors, etc. take their problem seriously. Again, it must be stated that establishing categories and terminology has been part of the effort to draw public attention to the seriousness of male violence against women in intimate relationships. Even though the use of convenient labels and categories has made it easier to identify problems of physical abuse, it does not mean the terminology should not be critiqued from a feminist perspective and changed if necessary.

Recently, I had an experience assisting a woman who had been brutally attacked by her husband (she never commented on whether this was the first incident or not), which caused me to reflect anew on the use of the term "battered woman." This young woman was not engaged in feminist thinking or aware that "battered woman" was a category. Her husband had tried to choke her to death. She managed to escape from him with only the clothes she was wearing. After she recovered from the trauma, she considered going back to this relationship. As a church-going woman, she believed that her marriage vows were sacred and that she should try to make the relationship work. In an effort to share my feeling that this could place her at great risk, I brought her Lenore Walker's *The Battered Woman* because it seemed to me that there was much that she was not revealing, that she felt alone, and that the experiences she would read about in the book would give her a sense that other women had experienced what she was going through. I hoped reading the book would give her the courage to confront the reality of her situation. Yet I found it difficult to share because I could see that her self-esteem had already been greatly attacked, that she had lost a sense of her worth and value, and that possibly this categorizing of her identity would add to the feeling that she should just forget, be silent (and certainly returning to a situation where one is likely to be abused is one way to mask the severity of the problem). Still I had to try. When I first gave her the book, it disappeared. An unidentified family member had thrown it away. They felt that she would be making a serious mistake if she began to see herself as an absolute victim, which they felt the label "battered woman" implied. I stressed that she should ignore the labels and read the content. I believed the experience shared in this book helped give her the courage to be critical of her situation, to take constructive action.

Her response to the label "battered woman," as well as the responses of other women who have been victims of violence in intimate relationships, compelled me to critically explore further the use of this term. In conversation with many women, I found that it was seen as a stigmatizing label, one which victimized women seeking help felt themselves in no condition to critique. As in "who cares what anybody is calling it—I just want to stop this pain." Within patriarchal society, women who are victimized by male violence have had to pay a price for breaking the silence and naming the problem. They have had to be seen as fallen women, who have failed in their "feminine" role to sensitize and civilize the beast in the man. A category like "battered woman" risks reinforcing this notion that the hurt woman, not only the rape victim, becomes a social pariah, set apart, marked forever by this experience.

A distinction must be made between having a terminology that enables women, and all victims of violent acts, to name the problem and categories of labeling that may inhibit that naming. When individuals are wounded, we are indeed often scarred, often damaged in ways that do set us apart from those who have not experienced a similar wounding, but an essential aspect of the recovery process is the healing of the wound, the removal of the scar. This is an empowering process that should not be diminished by labels that imply this wounding experience is the most significant aspect of identity.

As I have already stated, overemphasis on extreme cases of violent abuse may lead us to ignore the problem of occasional hitting, and it may make it difficult for women to talk about this problem. A critical issue that is not fully examined and written about in great detail by researchers who study and work with victims is the recovery process. There is a dearth of material discussing the recovery process of individuals who have been physically abused. In those cases where an individual is hit only once in an intimate relationship, however violently, there may be no recognition at all of the negative impact of this experience. There may be no conscious attempt by the victimized person to work at restoring her or his well-being, even if the person seeks therapeutic help, because the one incident may not be seen as serious or damaging. Alone and in isolation, the person who has been hit must struggle to regain broken trust—to forge some strategy of recovery. Individuals are often able to process an experience of being hit mentally that may not be processed emotionally. Many women I talked with felt that even after the incident was long forgotten, their bodies remain troubled. Instinctively, the person who has been hit may respond fearfully to any body movement on the part of a loved one that is similar to the posture used when pain was inflicted.

Being hit once by a partner can forever diminish sexual relationships if there has been no recovery process. Again there is little written about ways folks recover physically in their sexualities as loved ones who continue to be sexual with those who have hurt them. In most cases, sexual relationships are dramatically altered when hitting has occurred. The sexual realm may be the one space where the person who has been hit experiences again the sense of vulnerability, which may also arouse fear. This can lead either to an attempt to avoid sex or to unacknowledged sexual withdrawal wherein the person participates but is passive. I talked with women who had been hit by lovers who described sex as an ordeal, the one space where they confront their inability to trust a partner who has broken trust. One woman emphasized that to her, being hit was a "violation of her body space" and that she felt from then on she had to protect that space. This response, though a survival strategy, does not lead to healthy recovery.

Often, women who are hit in intimate relationships with male or female lovers feel as though we have lost an innocence that cannot be regained. Yet this very notion of innocence is connected to passive acceptance of concepts of romantic love under patriarchy which have served to mask problematic realities in relationships. The process of recovery must include a critique of this notion of innocence which is often linked to an unrealistic and fantastic vision of love and romance. It is only in letting go of the perfect, no-work, happily-ever-after union idea, that we can rid our psyches of the sense that we have failed in some way by not having such relationships. Those of us who never focussed on the negative impact of being hit as children find it necessary to re-examine the past in a therapeutic manner as part of our recovery process. Strategies that helped us survive as children may be detrimental for us to use in adult relationships.

Talking about being hit by loved ones with other women, both as children and as adults, I found that many of us had never really thought very much about our own relationship to violence. Many of us took pride in never feeling violent, never hitting. We had not thought deeply about our relationship to inflicting physical pain. Some of us expressed terror and awe when confronted with physical strength on the part of others. For us, the healing process included the need to learn how to use physical force constructively, to remove the terror—the dread. Despite the research that suggests children who are hit may become adults who hit—women hitting children, men hitting women and children—most of the women I talked with not only did not hit but were compulsive about not using physical force.

Overall the process by which women recover from the experience of being hit by loved ones is a complicated and multi-faceted one, an area where there must be much more feminist study and research. To many of us, feminists calling attention to the reality of violence in intimate relationships has not in and of itself compelled most people to take the issue seriously, and such violence seems to be daily on the increase. In this essay, I have raised issues that are not commonly talked about, even among folks who are particularly concerned about violence against women. I hope it will serve as a catalyst for further thought, that it will strengthen our efforts as feminist activists to create a world where domination and coercive abuse are never aspects of intimate relationships.

DISCUSSION QUESTIONS

1. hooks says, "People within patriarchal society imagine that women are hit because we are hysterical, because we are beyond reason." Why does she believe that this is not the case? Why are women hit? Do you agree with her? Explain.

2. According to hooks, there might be a connection between the form of interrogation and punishment we learned as children and the behavior of the lover who assumes an abusive, authoritarian role. What is her argument connecting the corporal punishment of children with violence against women? Is it a good argument? Evaluate it.

3. Why does hooks object to the term "battered woman"? Do you agree with her argument? Why or why not?

4. Should the hitting of children as punishment be considered violence against children? How is the hitting of children for doing something wrong morally different from one partner in an intimate relationship hitting the other for doing something wrong? Defend your view.

5. What impact does patriarchal society have on the reality of physical abuse against women? Do you believe that the more sexism there is in society, the more violence there will be against women? Argue your case.

ANGELA DAVIS

Rape, Racism and the Myth of the Black Rapist

Angela Davis argues that sexism, racism, and the class structure of American society combine to make rape one of the fastest-growing crimes in our country. According to Davis, the class structure of capitalist society encourages men to "become routine agents of sexual exploitation" and "also harbors an incentive to rape." Rape laws in the United States, says Davis, "as a rule were framed originally to protect men of the upper classes, whose daughters and wives might be assaulted." What happens to working-class women has usually been of little concern to the courts, and few White men have been prosecuted for sexual violence against women. Davis cites figures showing that "rape charges have been indiscriminately aimed at Black men, the guilty and the innocent alike." The fraudulent rape charge against Blacks is a powerful invention of racism. Moreover, Davis thinks that capitalist and middle-class men probably account for a significant proportion of unreported rapes. Given that most women have been the victim of either attempted or accomplished sexual attacks, and that rape is closely associated with racism, sexism, and class structure, Davis argues that the anti-rape movement in America must aim for more than just the eradication of rape. It must also seek the eradication of sexism, racism, and monopoly capitalism.

Angela Davis is a professor in the History of Consciousness program at the University of California at Santa Cruz. Her books include *Women, Race and Class* (1981), *Angela Davis: An Autobiography* (1988), *Women, Culture and Politics* (1989), and *Blues Legacies and Black Feminism: Gertrude "Ma" Rainey, Bessie Smith, and Billie Holiday* (1998).

Some of the most flagrant symptoms of social deterioration are acknowledged as serious problems only when they have assumed such epidemic proportions that they appear to defy solution. Rape is a case in point. In the United States today, it is one of the fastest-growing violent crimes.[1] After ages of silence, suffering and misplaced guilt, sexual assault is explosively emerging as one of the telling dysfunctions of present-day capitalist society. The rising public concern about rape in the United States has inspired countless numbers of women to divulge their past encounters with actual or would-be assailants. As a result, an awesome fact has come to light: appallingly few women can claim that they have not been victims, at one time in their lives, of either attempted or accomplished sexual attacks.

In the United States and other capitalist countries, rape laws as a rule were framed originally for the protection of men of the upper classes, whose daughters and wives might be assaulted. What happens to working-class women has usually been of little concern to the courts; as a result, remarkably few white men have been prosecuted for the sexual violence they have inflicted on these women. While the rapists have seldom been brought to justice, the rape charge has been indiscriminately aimed at Black men, the guilty and innocent alike. Thus, of the 455 men executed between 1930 and 1967 on the basis of rape convictions, 405 of them were Black.[2]

In the history of the United States, the fraudulent rape charge stands out as one of the most formidable artifices invented by racism. The myth of the Black rapist has been methodically conjured up whenever recurrent waves of violence and terror against the Black community have required convincing justifications. If Black women have been conspicuously absent from the ranks of the contemporary anti-rape movement, it may be due, in part, to that movement's indifferent posture toward the frame-up rape charge as an incitement to racist aggression. Too many innocents have been offered sacrificially to gas chambers and lifer's cells for Black women to join those who often seek relief from policemen and judges. Moreover, as rape victims themselves, they have found little if any sympathy from these men in uniforms and robes. And stories about police assaults on Black women—rape victims sometimes suffering a second rape—are heard too frequently to be dismissed as aberrations. "Even at the strongest time of the civil rights movement in Birmingham," for example,

> Young activists often stated that nothing could protect Black women from being raped by Birmingham police. As recently as December, 1974, in Chicago, a 17-year-old Black woman reported that she was gang-raped by 10 policemen. Some of the men were suspended, but ultimately the whole thing was swept under the rug.[3]

During the early stages of the contemporary anti-rape movement, few feminist theorists seriously analyzed the special circumstances surrounding the Black woman as rape victim. The historical knot binding Black women—systematically abused and violated by white men—to Black men—maimed and murdered because of the racist manipulation of the rape charge—has just begun to be acknowledged to any significant extent. Whenever Black women have challenged rape, they usually and simultaneously expose the use of the frame-up rape charge as a deadly racist weapon against their men. As one extremely perceptive writer put it:

> The myth of the black rapist of white women is the twin of the myth of the bad black woman—both designed to apologize for and facilitate the continued exploitation of black men and women. Black women perceived this connection very clearly and were early in the forefront of the fight against lynching.[4]

. . . Racism has always drawn strength from its ability to encourage sexual coercion. While Black women and their sisters of color have been the main targets of these racist-inspired attacks, white women have suffered as well. For once white men were persuaded that they could commit sexual assaults against Black women with impunity, their conduct toward women of their own race could not have remained unmarred. Racism has always served as a provocation to rape, and white women in the United States have necessarily suffered the ricochet fire of these attacks. This is one of the many ways in which racism nourishes sexism, causing white women to be indirectly victimized by the special oppression aimed at their sisters of color.

The experience of the Vietnam War furnished a further example of the extent to which racism could function as a provocation to rape. Because it was drummed into the heads of U.S. soldiers that they were fighting an inferior race, they could be taught that raping Vietnamese women was a necessary military duty. They could even be instructed to "search" the women with their penises.[5] It was the unwritten policy of the U.S. Military Command to systematically encourage rape, since it was an extremely effective weapon of mass terrorism. Where are the thousands upon thousands of Vietnam veterans who witnessed and participated in these horrors? To what extent did those brutal experiences affect their attitudes toward women in general? While it would be quite erroneous to single out Vietnam veterans as the main perpetrators of sexual crimes, there can be little doubt that the horrendous repercussions of the Vietnam experience are still being felt by all women in the United States today.

It is a painful irony that some anti-rape theorists, who ignore the part played by racism in instigating rape, do not hesitate to argue that men of color are especially prone to commit sexual violence against women. . . .

The myth of the Black rapist continues to carry out the insidious work of racist ideology. It must bear a good portion of the responsibility for the failure of most anti-rape theorists to seek the identity of the enormous numbers of anonymous rapists who remain unreported, untried and unconvicted. As long as their analyses focus on accused rapists who are reported and arrested, thus on only a fraction of the rapes actually committed, Black men—and other men of color—will inevitably be viewed as the villains responsible for the current epidemic of sexual violence. The anonymity surrounding the vast majority of rapes is consequently treated as a statistical detail—or else as a mystery whose meaning is inaccessible.

But why are there so many anonymous rapists in the first place? Might not this anonymity be a privilege enjoyed by men whose status protects them from prosecution? Although white men who are employers, executives, politicians, doctors, professors, etc., have been known to "take advantage" of women they consider their social inferiors, their sexual misdeeds seldom come to light in court. Is it not therefore quite probable that these men of the capitalist and middle classes account for a significant proportion of the unreported rapes? Many of these unreported rapes undoubtedly involve Black women as victims: their historical experience proves that racist ideology implies an open invitation to rape. As the basis of the license to rape Black women during slavery was the slaveholders' economic power, so the class structure of capitalist society also harbors an incentive to rape. It seems, in fact, that men of the capitalist class and their middle-class partners are immune to prosecution because they commit their sexual assaults with the same unchallenged authority that legitimizes their daily assaults on the labor and dignity of working people.

The existence of widespread sexual harassment on the job has never been much of a secret. It is precisely on the job, indeed, that women—especially when they are not unionized—are most vulnerable. Having already established their economic domination over their female subordinates, employers, managers and foremen may attempt to assert this authority in sexual terms. That working-class women are more intensely exploited than their men adds to their vulnerability to sexual abuse, while sexual coercion simultaneously reinforces their vulnerability to economic exploitation.

Working-class men, whatever their color, can be motivated to rape by the belief that their maleness accords them the privilege to dominate women. Yet since they do not possess the social or economic authority—unless it is a white man raping a woman of color—guaranteeing them immunity from prosecution, the incentive is not nearly as powerful as it is for the men of the capitalist class. When working-class men accept the invitation to rape extended by the ideology of male supremacy, they are accepting a bribe, an illusory compensation for their powerlessness.

The class structure of capitalism encourages men who wield power in the economic and political realm to become routine agents of sexual exploitation. The present rape epidemic occurs at a time when the capitalist class is furiously reasserting its authority in face of global and internal challenges. Both racism and sexism, central to its domestic strategy of increased economic exploitation, are receiving unprecedented encouragement. It is not a mere coincidence that as the incidence of rape has arisen, the position of women workers has visibly worsened. So severe are women's economic losses that their wages in relationship to men are lower than they were a decade ago. The proliferation of sexual violence is the brutal face of a generalized intensification of the sexism which necessarily accompanies this economic assault.

Following a pattern established by racism, the attack on women mirrors the deteriorating situation of workers of color and the rising influence of racism in the judicial system, the educational institutions and in the government's posture of studied neglect toward Black people and other people of color. The most dramatic sign of the dangerous resurgence of racism is the new visibility of the Ku Klux Klan and the related epidemic of violent assaults on Blacks, Chicanos, Puerto Ricans and Native Americans. The present rape epidemic bears an extraordinary likeness to this violence kindled by racism.

Given the complexity of the social context of rape today, any attempt to treat it as an isolated phenomenon is bound to founder. An effective strategy against rape must aim for more than the eradication of rape—or even of sexism—alone. The struggle against racism must be an ongoing theme of the anti-rape movement, which must not only defend women of color, but the many victims of the racist manipulation of the rape charge as well. The crisis dimensions of sexual violence constitute one of the facets of a deep and ongoing crisis of capitalism. As the violent fact of sexism, the threat of rape will continue to exist as long as the overall oppression of women remains an essential crutch for capitalism. The anti-rape movement and its important current activities—ranging from emotional and legal aid to self-defense and educational campaigns—must be situated in a strategic context which envisages the ultimate defeat of monopoly capitalism.

NOTES

1. Nancy Gager and Cathleen Schurr, *Sexual Assault: Confronting Rape in America* (New York: Grosset & Dunlap, 1976), p. 1.

2. Michael Meltsner, *Cruel and Unusual: The Supreme Court and Capital Punishment* (New York: Random House, 1973), p. 75.

3. "The Racist Use of Rape and the Rape Charge." A Statement to the Women's Movement from a Group of Socialist Women (Louisville, KY: Socialist Women's Caucus, 1974), pp. 5–6.

4. Gerda Lerner, ed., *Black Women in White America: A Documentary History* (New York: Pantheon Books, 1972), p. 193.

5. Arlene Eisen-Bergman, *Women in Vietnam* (San Francisco: People's Press, 1975), chap. 5.

DISCUSSION QUESTIONS

1. What is the "myth of the Black rapist"? What evidence does Davis present to show the presence of this myth in American society? Do you agree with her argument? Defend your view.
2. What, according to Davis, is the connection between the high rates of rape in the United States and the class structure of society? Does her view imply that non-monopoly-capitalist societies should have lower numbers of rapes? Analyze her argument.
3. What is the "historical knot" binding Black women to Black men concerning rape?
4. Davis argues that racism nourishes sexism. What does she mean by this? Do you agree with her argument?
5. Davis argues that the anti-rape movement in America must aim for more than merely the eradication of rape. It must also aim for the eradication of sexism, racism, and monopoly capitalism. What is her argument? Do you think that it is a strong argument? Why or why not?
6. The boxer Mike Tyson was convicted of rape and sentenced to prison in Indiana. He served his sentence and was released. The media relentlessly reported every aspect of this event. Do you think that the reporting would have been different had Tyson not been Black? Does the media contribute to the perpetuation of the myth of the Black rapist? Is the media disproportionately fascinated with violent crimes by Black men against women (e.g., the O. J. Simpson trial)? Defend your views.

MEDIA GALLERY

"RAPE FANTASIES"

By Margaret Atwood

Story summary: In "Rape Fantasies" (1977), Margaret Atwood explores the subject of rape through satire. The story is set within the context of a conversation among five women on lunch break. One of the women, reading from a magazine, ignites the conversation by saying, "How about it girls, do you have rape fantasies? It says here all women have rape fantasies." Estelle, the narrator, notes to herself that rape is the "hot topic" in the magazines and other media: "The way they're going on about it in magazines you'd think it was just invented, and not only that but it's something terrific, like a vaccine for cancer. They put it in capital letters on the front cover, and inside they have these questionnaires like the ones they used to have about whether you were a good enough wife or an endomorph or an ectomorph, remember that? with the scoring upside down on page 73, and then these numbered do-it-yourself dealies, you know? RAPE, TEN THINGS TO DO ABOUT IT, like it was ten new hairdos or something." The women proceed to question one another as to whether they have rape fantasies. And, while the question shocks some of them initially, some admit to having such fantasies and go on to explain them in detail to the others. Ironically, each "rape fantasy" proves to be nothing more than an unusual sexual encounter. For example, one woman characterizes her "rape fantasy" as involving a man who indulges in a bubble bath with her before sexually assaulting her. She says that she wouldn't scream because no one would hear her. "Besides, all the articles say it's better not to resist, that way you don't get hurt." Estelle responds that such "rape fantasies" are not rape fantasies at all: "I mean, you aren't getting *raped*, it's just some guy you haven't met formally who happens to be more attractive than Derek Cummins, and you have a good time. Rape is when they've got a knife or something and you don't want to." Estelle explains, "In a real rape fantasy, what you should feel is this anxiety, like when you think about your apartment building catching on fire." However, while Estelle attributes rape with fear and uneasiness, her own rape fantasies demonstrate a naivete with regard to the matter as well. Estelle's rape fantasies are marked by men with whom she willingly has sex out of a sense of pity or obligation. She neither distinguishes sex from rape nor perceives herself to be a victim of forced intercourse. At the end of the story, however, Estelle reaches a new level of understanding when she confronts the inhumanity and degradation of rape. She says, "How could a fellow do that to a person . . . once you let him know you're human, you have a life too, I don't see how they could go ahead with it, right?" Ultimately, Estelle comes to understand the victimization of women in rape, and its ultimate inhumanity.

Margaret Atwood, who was born in 1939, is a noted Canadian poet, novelist, critic, and feminist. She published her first poem at age 19 and her first book of poetry, *Double Persephone,* in 1961. Atwood has taught literature at several Canadian universities. Her novels include *The Edible Woman* (1969), *Surfacing* (1972), *Lady Oracle* (1976), *Life Before Man* (1979), *Bodily Harm* (1981), *The Handmaid's Tale* (1985), *Cat's Eye* (1988), and the *Robber Bride* (1993).

1. Estelle concludes that rape is an inhumane act that victimizes women, whereas the other women do not seem to come to this conclusion. What is the danger of thinking of rape as anything less than a dehumanizing and inhumane act?
2. Atwood makes a point throughout the story of showing how the women's fantasies about rape are connected to media representations of rape. Are feature stories about rape like the ones described by Atwood (e.g., "Rape: Ten Things to Do About It") helpful to women? What does Atwood seem to be saying? Do you agree with her conclusion? What is the moral status of these stories?
3. Suzanne Pharr says that we "live in a society that gives permission to the hatred of women." Are magazines and other media that promote rape as a "hot topic" giving permission to the hatred of women? What would Pharr say? What do you think?
4. Lois Pineau argues against the myth that women like to be raped. What are the sources of this myth according to Atwood? Compare Atwood's argument against this myth with Pineau's. Whose argument do you prefer, and why?
5. The rape fantasies reported by the women in Atwood's story involve consensual sexual relations with men. Why do these women confuse consensual sexual relations with nonconsensual sexual relations? What dangers do they face by doing this?

"THE GIRLS IN THEIR SUMMER DRESSES"

By Irwin Shaw

Story summary: Irwin Shaw's "The Girls in Their Summer Dresses" is a story about a failing marriage. While walking down Fifth Avenue on a sunny afternoon, Michael gawks at the beautiful women passing him. His wife, Frances, is noticeably perturbed by Michael's behavior, stating "You always look at other women. Everywhere. Every damned place we go." Frances, however, does not proceed to complain about Michael's behavior anymore. Instead, she suggests that they spend the entire day alone together as husband and wife, since they rarely have such an opportunity. She explains, "We only see each other in bed. I want to go out with my husband all day long. I want him to talk only to me and listen only to me." Michael agrees, and they plan out the rest of the afternoon together. As they continue walking down the street, Michael explains to Frances that he has never had an affair during their five years of marriage. Frances responds by telling him how it upsets her when he looks at other women on the street, but Michael does not want to hear this. Frances, upset, suggests that they have a drink. While at the bar, Frances and Michael continue their conversation about his interest in other women. Even though Frances believes that he has not pursued any of them as of yet, she knows that eventually he will. The issue is quickly put under wraps when they decide to spend the rest of the afternoon with another couple, perhaps to alleviate the intensity of their conversation. As Frances gets up to use the telephone, Michael stares at her, just as he does to other women, suggesting that she, too, is nothing more than a body to him. The narrator explains, "Michael watched her walk, thinking what a pretty girl, what nice legs."

Irwin Shaw (1913–1984) was born in Brooklyn, and educated at Brooklyn College. He was a prolific playwright, screenwriter, and author of critically acclaimed short stories and best-selling novels. His most popular novel was *Rich Man, Poor Man* (1970). His stories began appearing in magazines like *The New Yorker* and *Esquire* in the late 1930s. "The Girls in Their Summer Dresses" was first published in 1939.

1. Michael gawks at beautiful women. Are his actions sexist? What might Marilyn Frye say? Defend your view.
2. Some would argue that men who stare at women are "objectifying" them—that is, treating them as though they were objects, not persons. Do you agree with this general position? Explain.
3. Is the act of gawking at women a form of violence against women? Why might some people feel that it is? Why might others disagree? What do you think?
4. At the end of the story, Michael looks at his wife as he would look at a beautiful woman who passed him on the street. The narrator says, "Michael watched her walk, thinking what a pretty girl, what nice legs." Why do you think that Shaw wrote this into the story? Is he saying that Michael cannot pay attention to his wife unless he regards her merely as a beautiful body? If not, what is he saying? Do you think that Michael should be treating his wife this way?
5. In general, is it morally objectionable to gawk at people? What, if anything, is morally wrong with this type of action? Defend your view.

 THELMA AND LOUISE
(USA, 1991) 2 hours 8 minutes
Directed by Ridley Scott

Film summary: Thelma and Louise is the story of two best friends whose simple weekend getaway turns into a flight from the law. Louise (Susan Sarandon) works as a waitress. Her boyfriend, Jimmy (Michael Madson), is reluctant to propose marriage to her. Thelma (Geena Davis) is married to Darryl (Christopher McDonald), a man who has very little respect for the needs of his wife. On their way to their weekend getaway cabin, Thelma and Louise stop off at a bar for a drink and bite to eat. Harlan (Timothy Carhart) begins to hit on Thelma and, after a dance with her in which she becomes dizzy and heated, suggests that they go outside the bar for some fresh air. Harlan proceeds to push Thelma to have sex with him despite her protestations. He becomes infuriated with her and, after hitting her, attempts to rape her. When Louise points a gun to Harlan's head and orders him to let Thelma go, he says, "Calm down, we're just having a little fun. That's all." Louise angrily responds, "In the future, when a woman is crying like that, she's not having fun!" When Harlan mocks Louise's remarks, she shoots and kills him. When Thelma suggests that they turn themselves in to the police and explain how Harlan was attempting to rape her, Louise says, "One hundred people saw you dancing cheek to cheek with him. Who is gonna believe you? We don't live in that kind of world, Thelma!" As they attempt to ellude the authorities, Thelma and Louise find themselves committing more illegal acts, including robbing a convenience store and destroying a tanker truck. Their escape to Mexico is thwarted when the police corner them at the edge of the Grand Canyon. Refusing to give up or give in, Thelma and Louise drive off the cliff to their deaths.

1. When Louise tells Harlan to let Thelma go, he says, "Calm down, we're just having a little fun. That's all." Louise responds, "In the future, when a woman is crying like that, she's not having fun!" Why do you think Harlan believes that he and Thelma were merely having fun? Is Harlan's comment in any way defensible? How representative of patriarchal society are Harlan's actions? What do you think of Louise's verbal response to them? What would you have said to Harlan, and why? Defend your view.

2. Thelma and Louise begin the film paying close attention to how they are dressed and made up. By the end of the film, they have discarded their jewelry and makeup, and their clothing is generally untidy. Why do you think that they make these changes? Is there a connection between our ideas about beauty and the moral structure of society? Defend your position. What do you think Marilyn Frye would say about this? Consider her comments about sex-marking and sex-announcing.

3. A trucker (Marco St. John) passing Thelma and Louise on the highway made some lewd gestures toward them. Thelma and Louise signal him to pull over to the side of the road and ask him if he would make such gestures to his mother. When he refuses to apologize for making the lewd gestures, they shoot at his truck and blow it up. Why do you think that Thelma and Louise were so offended by the trucker's actions? Was their response to him—blowing up his truck—morally justifiable? Defend your view.

4. At the end of the movie, the police have cornered Thelma and Louise at the edge of a cliff. They order the women to "raise their hands in plain view" and say that "any failure to obey that command will be considered an act of aggression against us." Thelma and Louise decide to drive off of the edge of the cliff rather than surrender to the police. Why do they do this? Do you think that they believe that death is the only escape from male domination, sexism, and violence against women? What would you have done if you were in Thelma and Louise's position? Explain.

5. During the course of the film, we find out that Louise once was raped in Texas. This contributed to her odd request that they drive to Mexico without passing through Texas. What effect do you think that Louise's past experiences had on her argument to Thelma that they should not turn themselves in? Recall that Louise tells Thelma that the police would not believe her rape claim because everyone had seen her dancing with Harlan just moments before. Do you think that they did the right thing by not turning themselves in? Do you think that the police would have believed them? What would you have done if you were in their position? What do you think Lois Pineau would say about Louise's reactions to the attempted rape of Thelma?

6. Suzanne Pharr says, "This country minimizes hate violence against women, because women's lives are not valued, because the violence is so commonplace that people become numb to it, because people do not want to look at the institutions and systems that support it, and because people do not want to recognize how widespread the hatred is and how many perpetrators there are among us on every level of society." Is this comment by Pharr supported by the film *Thelma and Louise?* Why or why not?

 ### *THE COLOR PURPLE*

(USA, 1985) 2 hours 32 minutes
Directed by Steven Spielberg

Based on the novel by Alice Walker, *The Color Purple* portrays a young Black woman's struggle to control her life in a small southern town in the early twentieth century. By the age of fourteen, Celie (Whoopi Goldberg) has had a son and a daughter by her father. The children of this incestuous relationship are taken from Celie and adopted by Reverend Samuel (Carl Anderson) and his wife. Celie is married off to Albert Johnston (Danny Glover), a widower who beats her and forces her to serve him and care for his children. Celie's only consolation is her proximity to her beloved sister Nettie (Akosua Busia), who comes to live in the household. Albert makes advances toward Nettie, and when she refuses him, he banishes her from the farm, and the sisters part in tears. Albert's son Harpo (Willard Pugh) marries Sophia (Oprah Winfrey), a strong-willed woman who leaves him when he beats her. Albert is madly in love with singer and performer Shug Avery (Margaret Avery), and he takes her into the household. After some initial jealousies, Shug and Celie develop a close relationship, and Celie also falls in love with Shug. Meanwhile, Sophia gets into an argument with a White man and is sent to prison for eight years. When she is released, she is forced to serve as a maid for Miss Millie, the White man's wife. Celie and Shug discover the letters from Nettie that Albert has been hiding for years. Nettie has moved to Africa with Reverend Samuel's family and is caring for Celie's children while the Samuels do missionary work. When Shug marries and decides to move to Memphis, Celie finally breaks from Albert and goes with her. Celie returns years later to claim her inheritance when her father dies. She learns that the man who fathered her children was her stepfather and that she will inherit the family farm. When Albert receives a letter from the immigration office, he makes the arrangements for Nettie and the children to return from Africa, and Celie is reunited with her family.

The Color Purple received eleven Oscar nominations yet won none.

1. When Nettie encourages Celie to stand up to Albert early in the marriage, Celie responds, "I don't know how to fight. All I know is how to stay alive." Why do you think that Celie does not know how to fight? What role do you think sexism plays in her inability to fight? Do Celie's actions confirm Aristotle's claim that "silence is a woman's glory"? Explain.
2. Harpo is discouraged when Sophia speaks her mind and gives him orders. His father recommends that he beat her. Why does Celie also tell Harpo to beat Sophia? What might bell hooks say about an abused woman (Celie) encouraging the abuse of another woman (Sophia)?
3. When Miss Millie wrongly accuses Sophia's relatives of attacking her, she claims, "I've always been good to you people. I've always been good to coloreds." Does our charity to others give us the right to treat them as less than equals? Why do you think some people feel that it does? Evaluate their reasoning, and generally reflect on the connection between charity and prejudice.
4. When Celie finally leaves Albert, he insults her and insists she won't make it in the world. "Look at you," Albert tells her, "You're black, you're poor, you're ugly and you're a woman. You're nothing at all." Do you think that verbal abuse is just as serious a form of violence against women as is physical abuse? Defend your view.
5. To what extent do you believe that the violence in the intimate relationships in *The Color Purple* is representative of the actual violence that goes on in intimate relationships?
6. What is the connection between sexism and violence against women in *The Color Purple*? Defend your reading of the movie.
7. Quite a few Black men protested publicly after this film came out that it "fed into" stereotypes of Black men as "shiftless, violent rapists." Do you think that this film unfairly depicts Black men? Why or why not?

 IN THE COMPANY OF MEN

(Canada, 1997) 1 hour 37 minutes
Directed and written by Neil Labute

Film summary: In an airport, about to embark on a six-week business trip, Chad (Aaron Eckhart) and Howard (Matt Malloy) complain about the women in their lives. They have been friends since college and work for the same company. Chad tells Howard how Suzanne (Emily Cline) left him without so much as a note, and Howard tells Chad how his fiancée told him she wanted to see other men. They agree that women and work are getting out of balance and that women can reject men at a moment's notice. Chad says, "We cannot even tell a joke in the workplace, yet a woman can change her mind. We need to put our foot down." Chad proposes that they find a vulnerable woman, one who is "disfigured in some way" and believes that romance and a sexual life are lost to her. He suggests that they both pursue her and one day abruptly dump her, just as the women in their lives did to them. Chad says that they'll be able to laugh about this until they are very old men. Furthermore, it will "restore a little dignity to their lives" and will be payback for the messy relationships they've been going through. Howard hesitatingly agrees, and soon Chad has located a suitable victim: a deaf woman who works in the office where their business trip has taken them. Christine (Stacy Edwards) soon falls in love with Chad and has sex with him. Chad continues to despise Christine but keeps his feelings to himself. In the meantime, Howard truly falls in love with Christine, but she does not have the same feelings for Howard. Christine does not tell Chad about her relationship with Howard, nor does she tell Howard about her relationship with Chad until Howard confronts her with the game that is being played on her. Christine is unwilling to believe that Chad does not love her, but soon she finds out the truth. Howard remains in love with Christine weeks after the business trip and confronts Chad at his home about it. Chad tells Howard that Suzanne never left him and that he played both Christine and Howard. Howard asks why, and Chad responds, "Because I could. So, how's it feel to really hurt someone? See you [at work] on Monday." Howard, crushed, seeks out Christine, who will not so much as even listen to him.

1. Roger Ebert wrote in the *Chicago Sun-Times* that this is "the kind of bold, uncompromising film that insists on being thought about afterward." What do think about this film? Is it a critique of sexism or an homage to sexism? Defend your view.
2. In the workplace as depicted in this film, men are continuously making cruel, sexist jokes about women. To what extent do you believe that this reflects the workplace in America today? Would you be surprised to hear cruel, sexist jokes around the water cooler? How would you respond to them? How should you respond to them? Would you feel that responding negatively to them would affect your position in the company?
3. Chad "plays" both Howard and Christine for the simple reason that he has the power to do so. How do you think that he is morally able to justify his actions? Is this ethic similar to the one in which he engages in the workplace? Why or why not?
4. Christine does not tell either man about her relationship with the other. Should she have? Did this in any way contribute to the situation in which she finds herself? Is her lack of forthrightness in any way to blame for the wretched condition in which she finds herself? If you were Christine, would you have spoken sooner to Chad about Howard and to Howard about Chad?
5. Howard seems to sense from the beginning that there is something wrong with the "game" that Chad is setting up. However, he ultimately goes along with it. Why? Why does he put his moral intuitions to the side and play along with Chad?
6. Howard and Christine find themselves in the same place at the end of the film: they are both the victims of Chad's cruel game. Or are they? To what extent do you believe that Howard and Christine are victims? To what extent did they contribute to their own victimization? Explain.

 THE GENERAL'S DAUGHTER

(USA, 1999) 1 hour 55 minutes
Directed by Simon West

Film summary: Captain Elisabeth Campbell (Leslie Stefanson), the daughter of General Joe Campbell (James Cromwell), has been murdered. Her naked corpse is found staked spread-eagle to the ground; she has been strangled. Paul Brenner (John Travolta) and Sarah Sunhill (Madeleine Stowe) investigate this bizarre murder. They find a secret room in Captain Campbell's basement with S & M props and equipment, along with a video recording system. They also learn that she apparently slept with most of her father's staff. A flashback sequence shows her being violently gang-raped by Army cadets when she was in her third year at West Point. Apparently, some of the male cadets resented her stellar performance at West Point and carried out the rape to demoralize her. In the process, they almost killed her. When her father found out about the rape, he instructed her to forget that it had ever occurred. The entire incident at West Point was covered up. However, this violent event altered the course of Elisabeth Campbell's life and apparently was the main cause of her sexual promiscuity. The film suggests as well that it led to the bizarre situation of her wanting to reenact the rape scene in order to exorcise the traumatic memory of the event. While the details of the solving of her crime are interesting, they are overshadowed by the detailed portrayal of the gang rape of Elisabeth Campbell at West Point. In his review of this film for the *Chicago Sun-Times*, Roger Ebert wrote, "I . . . admired the darkly atmospheric look of the film, and the way it sustains its creepy mood. But I cringed when the death of the general's daughter was played out. Did the details have to be so graphic? Did we need to linger on the sight of a terrified woman? Did the filmmakers hesitate before supplying actual shots of her being strangled? Can anything be left to the imagination? I believe that any subject matter is legitimate for artistic purposes, but this isn't art. It's a thriller that could have spared us the details of that woman's horrible death." These and similar questions make this otherwise pedestrian Hollywood film morally intriguing—or, morally revolting, depending on how you look at it.

This film is based on the novel by Nelson DeMille. The screenplay was written by William Goldman and Christopher Bertolini.

1. Some might argue that *The General's Daughter* is an antisexism, profeminist, proequality film because of its portrayal of sexism in the military and because of the way in which a victim of sexism and sexual violence fought back. Others might argue that the graphic depiction of violence to a woman in this film is nothing short of sexist and misogynistic: any redeeming value that this film might have had is lost in the prolonged rape and strangulation shots. What do you think? Defend your view.

2. Roger Ebert asks, "Did we need to linger on the sight of a terrified woman?" What do you think? Why did Simon West, the director, choose to linger on these scenes? Why didn't he simply hint at the violence that was taking place, as many other filmmakers do, rather than graphically portraying it?

3. Roger Ebert comments that "the death of Elisabeth Campbell is so unnecessarily graphic and gruesome that by the end I felt sort of unclean. If this had been a documentary, or even a fiction film with serious intentions, I would have accepted it. But does entertainment have to go this far just to shake us up?" What do you think?

4. Consider the following claim: *The General's Daughter* is a film that condemns violence against women. Argue pro or con for this claim.

5. Consider two other famous films about military men and rape: Otto Preminger's *Anatomy of a Murder* (1959) and Gottfried Reinhardt's *Town Without Pity* (1961). View one of these films, and compare it to *The General's Daughter*. What are their similarities and differences? Which do you prefer, and why? Compare how you think Marilyn Frye and Steven Goldberg would respond to them.

6. Many people are tired of violence against women being presented as entertainment in films like *The General's Daughter*. Write an essay on a film that you have seen that does not portray women as victims. If you are stuck for examples, you might view any film starring Mae West or Katherine Hepburn. Compare the effect of viewing a film like this with a film that portrays women as victims.

THE UNITED NATIONS DECLARATION ON THE RIGHTS OF WOMEN

The United Nations Declaration on the Rights of Women was adopted November 7, 1967. What follows are excerpts from that declaration.

Article 1—Discrimination against women, denying or limiting as it does their equality of rights with men, is fundamentally unjust and constitutes an offence against human dignity.

Article 2—All appropriate measures shall be taken to abolish existing laws, customs, regulations and practices which are discriminatory against women, and to establish adequate legal protection for equal rights of men and women. . . .

Article 3—All appropriate measures shall be taken to educate public opinion and to direct national aspirations towards the eradication of prejudice and the abolition of customary and all other practices which are based on the idea of the inferiority of women.

Article 4—All appropriate measures shall be taken to ensure to women on equal terms with men, without any discrimination:
(a) The right to vote in all elections and be eligible for election to all publicly elected bodies;
(b) The right to vote in all public referenda;
(c) The right to hold public office and to exercise all public functions. Such rights shall be guaranteed by legislation.

Article 5—Women shall have the same rights as men to acquire, change or retain their nationality. Marriage to an alien shall not automatically affect the nationality of the wife either by rendering her stateless or by forcing upon her the nationality of her husband.

Article 6—1. Without prejudice to the safeguarding of the unity and the harmony of the family, which remains the basic unit of any society, all appropriate measures, particularly legislative measures, shall be taken to ensure to women, married or unmarried, equal rights with men in the field of civil law. . . .
2. All appropriate measures shall be taken to ensure the principle of equality of status of the husband and wife, and in particular:
(a) Women shall have the same right as men as to free choice of a spouse and to enter into marriage rights with men during marriage and at its dissolution. In all cases the interest of the children shall be paramount. . . .
(c) Parents shall have equal rights and duties in matters relating to their children. In all cases the interest of the children shall be paramount.
3. Child marriage and the betrothal of young girls before puberty shall be prohibited, and effective action, including legislation, shall be taken to specify a minimum age for marriage and to make the registration of marriages in an official registry compulsory.

Article 7—All provisions of penal codes which constitute discrimination against women shall be repealed.

Article 8—All appropriate measures, including legislation, shall be taken to combat all forms of traffic in women and exploitation of prostitution of women.

Article 9—All appropriate measures shall be taken to ensure to girls and women, married or unmarried, equal rights with men in education at all levels. . . .

Article 10—1. All appropriate measures shall be taken to ensure to women, married or unmarried, equal rights with men in the field of economic and social life. . . .

2. In order to prevent discrimination against women on account of marriage or maternity and to ensure their effective right to work, measures shall be taken to prevent their dismissal in the event of marriage or maternity and to provide paid maternity leave, with the guarantee of returning to former employment, and to provide the necessary social services, including child-care facilities.

3. Measures taken to protect women in certain types of work, for reasons inherent in their physical nature, shall not be regarded as discriminatory.

Article 11—1. The principle of equality of rights of men and women demands implementation in all States in accordance with the principles of the Charter of the United Nations and of the Universal Declaration of Human Rights.

2. Governments, non-governmental organizations and individuals are urged, therefore, to do all in their power to promote the implementation of the principles contained in this Declaration.

1. Article 3 of the United Nations Declaration on the Rights of Women states, "All appropriate measures shall be taken to educate public opinion and to direct national aspirations towards the eradication of prejudice and the abolition of customary and all other practices which are based on the idea of the inferiority of women." How important is this article relative to the others? What is the best way to satisfy Article 3? Do you think that our national aspirations are directed toward the eradication of prejudice against women? Explain.
2. What items in the excerpts from The United Nations Declaration on the Rights of Women protect women from violence in intimate relationships? What items might be added to the excerpted selections to provide (further) protection for women from violence in intimate relationships?
3. Critically comment on Article 10, item 3: "Measures taken to protect women in certain types of work, for reasons inherent in their physical nature, shall not be regarded as discriminatory."
4. How might Plato, Aristotle, John Stuart Mill, and Simone de Beauvoir respectively respond to Article 1? Compare your own view with theirs.
5. Many cultures have customs that are regarded by some as discriminatory against women. Article 2 states, "All appropriate measures should be taken to abolish these customs." Would a cultural relativist agree with this? Do you? Why or why not?
6. Is the United Nations Declaration on the Rights of Women respectful to the rights of men? Does it conflict with the rights of men in any way?
7. Imagine that you are Steven Goldberg and have just read the United Nations Declaration on the Rights of Women. What is your response to it? Which items do you find agreeable? Which, if any, do you find objectionable? Explain, and respond to Goldberg's objections.

SUPPLEMENTARY READINGS

SEXISM AND SEXUAL EQUALITY

Bartky, Sandra. *Femininity and Domination: Studies in the Phenomenology of Oppression.* New York: Routledge, 1990.

Brod, Harry. *The Making of Masculinities: The New Men's Studies.* Boston: Unwin Hyman, 1987.

Burke, Phyllis. *Gender Shock: Exploding the Myths of Male and Female.* New York: Anchor Books, 1996.

de Beauvoir, Simone. *The Second Sex,* trans. H. M. Parshley. New York: Vintage Books, 1974.

Dines, Gial, and Jean Humez, eds. *Gender, Race and Class in the Media.* Thousand Oaks, CA: Sage, 1995.

Eisenstein, Zillah. *Feminism and Sexual Equality.* New York: Monthly Review Press, 1984.

English, Jane. *Sex Equality.* Englewood Cliffs, NJ: Prentice-Hall, 1978.

Faludi, Susan. *Backlash: The Undeclared War Against American Women.* New York: Crown, 1991.

Faustino-Sterling, Anne. *Myths of Gender: Biological Theories of Women and Men.* New York: Basic Books, 1992.

Friedan, Betty. *The Feminine Mystique.* New York: Dell, 1970.

Frye, Marilyn. *The Politics of Reality.* Trumansburg, NY: Crossing Press, 1983.

Gilligan, Carol. *In a Different Voice.* Cambridge, MA: Harvard University Press, 1982.

Gornick, Vivian, and Barbara K. Moran, eds. *Women in Sexist Society.* New York: Signet, 1972.

Haskell, Molly. *From Reverence to Rape: The Treatment of Women in the Movies.* Chicago: University of Chicago Press, 1987.

Henley, Nancy. *Body Politics: Power, Sex and Non-Verbal Communication.* Englewood Cliffs, NJ: Prentice-Hall, 1977.

Henley, Nancy, and Clara Mayo. *Gender and Non-Verbal Behavior.* New York: Springer, 1981.

hooks, bell. *Talking Back: Thinking Feminist, Thinking Black.* Boston: South End Press, 1989.

Jaggar, Alison M. *Feminist Politics and Human Nature.* Totowa, NJ: Rowman & Allanheld, 1983.

McDonald, Myra. *Representing Women: Myths of Femininity in the Popular Media.* New York: St. Martin's Press, 1995.

Mill, John Stuart, and Harriet Taylor Mill. *Essays on Sex Equality,* ed. Alice S. Rossi. Chicago: University of Chicago Press, 1970.

Millett, Kate. *Sexual Politics.* New York: Avon Books, 1971.

Sadker, Myra, and David Sadker. *Failing at Fairness: How America's Schools Cheat Girls.* New York: Scribner, 1994.

Spelman, Elizabeth V. *Inessential Woman: Problems of Exclusion in Feminist Thought.* Boston: Beacon Press, 1988.

Wolgast, Elizabeth. *Equality and the Rights of Women.* Ithaca, NY: Cornell University Press, 1980.

Wolf, Naomi. *The Beauty Myth: How Images of Beauty Are Used Against Women.* New York: Morrow, 1991.

Wollstonecraft, Mary. *A Vindication of the Rights of Women.* New York: Norton, 1967 (1792).

Wood, Julia. *Gendered Lives: Communication, Gender and Culture.* Belmont, CA: Wadsworth, 1994.

VIOLENCE AGAINST WOMEN

Bohmer, Carol, and Andrea Parrot. *Sexual Assault on Campus: The Problem and Its Solution.* New York: Lexington, 1993.

Brandwein, Ruth A., ed. *Battered Women, Children, and Welfare Reform: The Ties That Bind.* Thousand Oaks, CA: Sage, 1999.

Brownmiller, Susan. *Against Our Will: Men, Women and Rape.* New York: Simon & Schuster, 1975.

Buchwald, Emelie; Pamela Fletcher; and Martha Roth, eds. *Transforming a Rape Culture.* Minneapolis: Milkweed, 1993.

Felder, Raoul, and Barbara Victor. *Getting Away with Murder: Weapons for the War Against Domestic Violence.* New York: Simon & Schuster, 1996.

Gordon, Linda. *Heroes of Their Own Lives: The Politics and History of Family Violence, Boston, 1880–1960.* New York: Viking Press, 1988.

Koss, Mary. *No Safe Haven: Male Violence Against Women at Home, at Work, and in the Community.* Washington, DC: American Psychological Association, 1994.

Martin, Del. *Battered Wives.* San Francisco: Glide, 1976.

NiCarthy, Ginny. *Getting Free: A Handbook for Women in Abusive Relationships.* Seattle: Seal Press, 1986.

Parrot, Andrea, and Laurie Bechhofer. *Acquaintance Rape: The Hidden Crime.* New York: Wiley, 1991.

Roleff, Tamara L., ed. *Domestic Violence: Opposing Viewpoints.* San Diego: Greenhaven Press, 2000.

Sanday, Peggy. *Fraternity Gang Rape.* New York: New York University Press, 1990.

———. *A Woman Scorned: Acquaintance Rape on Trial.* New York: Doubleday, 1996.

Schechter, Susan. *Women and Male Violence: The Visions and Struggles of the Battered Women's Movement.* Boston: South End Press, 1982.

Stark, Evan, and Anne Flitcraft. *Women at Risk: Domestic Violence and Women's Health.* Thousand Oaks, CA: Sage, 1996.

Walker, Alice, and Pratibha Parmar. *Warrior Marks: Female Genital Mutilation and the Sexual Blinding of Women.* New York: Harcourt Brace, 1993.

Warshaw, Robin, and Mary P. Koss. *I Never Called It Rape.* New York: Harper & Row, 1988.

White, Evelyn C. *Chain, Chain, Change: For Black Women Dealing with Physical and Emotional Abuse.* Seattle: Seal Press, 1985.

Zambrano, Myrna. *For the Latina in an Abusive Relationship.* Seattle: Seal Press, 1983.

Zillman, Dolph, and Jennings Bryant. "Pornography, Sexual Callousness, and the Trivialization of Rape." *Journal of Communication,* 32 (1982): 10–21.

8

Pornography and Hate Speech

The prohibition on pornography and hate speech is an extremely controversial issue today. Both pornography and hate speech raise issues concerning our freedom of expression, as well as questions about the harm that they can cause to others. With pornography, there is much debate as to whether sexually explicit works cause sexual violence, degrade women, and endanger public morality, or whether they are simply a form of harmless free expression with important social functions. With hate speech, there is much debate as to whether hate speech is a form of verbal and symbolic harassment, or whether tolerance of hate speech is necessary in a society that values freedom of speech and thought. While the debate is not likely to be resolved any time soon, it has brought about a deeper understanding of the nature of pornography and hate speech and of the pros and cons of regulating them in an open society.

One key to understanding the debate over pornography involves gaining a sense of the specific way in which the courts define pornography as opposed to the way the term is used in everyday speech. While many would agree that pornography is simply written or pictorial matter intended to arouse sexual feelings, the courts define it much differently. *Pornography,* according to the legal definition, is sexually explicit material that is obscene. But here, again, the common use of "obscene" is much different from how the courts define it.

While "obscene" is commonly used to refer to anything that is especially offensive, indecent, or repulsive, the legal definition of obscenity is much different. In *Miller v. California* (1973), the Supreme Court held that a work is *obscene* when "(a) the average person, applying contemporary community standards, would find that the work, taken as a whole, appeals to the prurient interest and; (b) the work depicts or describes, in a patently offensive way, sexual conduct that is specifically defined by the applicable state law and; (c) the work, taken as a whole, lacks serious literary, artistic, political or scientific value" (415 U.S. 15, p. 25). Consequently, for the courts, all obscenity necessarily involves sexual conduct, whereas in everyday usage it does not. We say, for example, that the amount of money a person makes is obscene. According to the courts, the amount of money that a person makes could never be considered obscene because it does not involve the depiction or description of sexual conduct.

Furthermore, according to the legal definition of obscenity, the mere fact that a work depicts or describes sexual conduct does not make it pornographic. *Erotica* refers to sexually explicit, but not obscene, pictures or descriptions that are sexually interesting. Feminists often further distinguish between erotica and pornography by defining pornography as sexually explicit material that is degrading to women and erotica as sexually explicit material that depicts sexuality in a mutually empowering manner.

Censorship is the prohibition on the dissemination of words or pictures. In *Roth v. United States* (1957), the Supreme Court ruled that obscene works are not constitutionally protected speech and so may be legally censored by individual states. The Court ruled that since no constitutional right is violated legislators need only show a "rational relation to a legitimate state end" as opposed to a "necessary means to a compelling state interest" when a constitutional right is violated. Despite the Court's ruling, many feel that censorship reduces their liberty.

Traditionally, government restrictions on liberty have been justified on four major grounds: (1) the *harm principle*, whereby governments may prohibit acts in which one person harms another; (2) the *offense principle*, whereby governments may prohibit acts in which one person offends another; (3) *legal moralism*, whereby governments may prohibit acts that are immoral even if they do not harm or offend anyone; and (4) *legal paternalism*, whereby governments may prohibit acts in which a person may harm her- or himself. However, these four ways of ethically justifying government restrictions are not equally accepted by the American judicial system. The first two are much more commonly accepted.

Clearly, the harm principle is the most common position used to argue for and against the censorship of pornography. In 1985, Edwin Meese, President Ronald Reagan's attorney general, formed a commission to study the effects of pornography. The Meese Commission claimed that both violent and nonviolent but degrading pornography relate significantly to sexual violence and antisocial attitudes and that child pornography relates directly to child abuse. The Meese Commission and others concur that there is a definite link between pornography and harm to others. Many people also allege that men are more inclined to rape, assault, sexually harass, and generally act violent toward women after watching or reading pornographic materials. Others, particularly feminists, argue that pornography harms women by producing degrading images of them. Thus, if it is true that pornography causes harm to people other than those who read or watch it, then on the grounds of the harm principle, the government is justified in prohibiting its dissemination.

The Meese Commission report notwithstanding, it is very difficult to determine whether there is a connection between pornography and harm to others. And, even if we could establish a connection, this would not show that the pornography itself is the cause of the harm. Advertisements, television shows, and movies also commonly depict women in degrading and dehumanizing ways. Thus, to be consistent, the government would have to consider censoring these constitutionally protected materials. Some would argue that those who are inclined to harm others simply desire to watch or read pornographic materials. According to this slippery slope type of argument, if we allow the censorship of pornography on the grounds that it is demeaning to women, then we will have to censor everything that is demeaning to women—pornographic *and* nonpornographic. Others argue that the harm principle in itself is not enough to support the censoring of pornography. We must also show that the harm from pornography outweighs the benefits and that the costs of enforcing a prohibition on pornography are not too high.

The alleged benefits of pornography to society include invigorating sexual relations, aiding in the sexual development of sexually repressed people, and causing a decrease in sexual tension that might otherwise lead to sexual violence. Moreover, some people in the gay community argue that pornography is one of the few avenues for exploring gay sexuality and thus is an important part of the lives of many gays. Similarly, some argue that pornography plays an important role in the lives of disabled individuals who cannot have full sexual lives. But this utilitarian approach to pornography is widely debated.

According to arguments against pornography on the grounds of legal paternalism, pornography is harmful to those who read or watch it. This harm can come in the form of the false images of male and female sexuality that it produces or in the degrading and dehumanizing view of women that it promotes. Thus, the government is justified in prohibiting pornography because doing so alleviates potential harm that people might incur by reading or viewing pornography.

Still, many people believe that the government has no business telling them what is in their own best interest. Regardless of the constitutional status of obscene materials, censorship in an open society is simply wrong. Proponents of this view cite Justice William Brennan's dissenting opinion in *Paris Adult Theatre I v. Slaton* (1973), wherein he argues that the concept of "obscenity" is so vague that any widespread attempt to censor pornography will necessarily tread on constitutionally protected material.

Legal moralists put the debate over pornography on a different level. If pornography is immoral, they argue, then the government is justified in prohibiting its use regardless of whether it causes harm or is offensive to others. Censorship is simply an issue of morality versus immorality. Still, the question remains as to the grounds on which we are to deem pornography moral or immoral. In any case, legal paternalism, like legal moralism, is not commonly supported by the courts.

The arguments from legal moralism, legal paternalism, the harm principle, and offense to others are equally applicable to the issue of hate speech and speech codes on campus. Like arguments concerning the prohibition of pornography, arguments concerning the prohibition of hate speech balance concerns about the importance of freedom of speech and expression with concerns about the alleged harm or offense that words can do. The issue is further complicated when we consider whether a college campus is a special type of community and what role its special nature should play in the prohibition of speech. Some argue that colleges and universities must ensure the open exchange of ideas, no matter how offensive or harmful the ideas may be to others. The reason for this is that the free flow of ideas is essential in a community dedicated to the pursuit of truth. Others argue that without speech codes some students will not be allowed to pursue higher education because of the verbal and symbolic harassment that they might face from other students. Verbal discrimination and bigotry prohibit the targets of such behavior from openly pursuing their education. As you read the articles in this chapter, try to make connections between the arguments relating to hate speech and speech codes and the arguments relating to pornography.

CATHARINE MACKINNON

Pornography, Civil Rights and Speech

Catharine MacKinnon, with her colleague Andrea Dworkin, argues that pornography, as defined in their proposed civil rights laws, is a practice of sex discrimination that should be actionable in civil court by people who can prove pornography harmed them. The laws include claims for coercion into pornography, forcing pornography on a person, committing assault due to specific pornography, and trafficking in pornography. The goal is to stop the violence against women and children that their hearings documented is endemic to pornography's making and use. Key to part of MacKinnon's argument is her analysis of the concrete role of pornography in constructing and institutionalizing a sexuality of male dominance over women and children. She also analyzes evidence that pornography is predicated upon and promotes the social and economic inequality of the sexes.

Catharine MacKinnon is a professor of law at the University of Michigan, and a visiting professor of law at the University of Chicago (on a long-term arrangement). She is the author of many books and articles including *Sexual Harassment of Working Women* (1979), *Feminism Unmodified* (1987), *Toward a Feminist Theory of the State* (1989), and *Only Words* (1993). She has also coedited, with Andrea Dworkin, *In Harm's Way: The Pornography Civil Rights Hearings* (1997).

There is a belief that this is a society in which women and men are basically equals. Room for marginal corrections is conceded, flaws are known to exist, attempts are made to correct what are conceived as occasional lapses from the basic condition of sex equality. Sex discrimination law has concentrated most of its focus on these occasional lapses. It is difficult to overestimate the extent to which this belief in equality is an article of faith for most people, including most women, who wish to live in self-respect in an internal universe, even (perhaps especially) if not in the world. It is also partly an expression of natural law thinking: if we are inalienably equal, we can't "really" be degraded.

This is a world in which it is worth trying. In this world of presumptive equality, people make money based on their training or abilities or diligence or qualifications. They are employed and advanced on the basis of merit. In this world of just deserts, if someone is abused, it is thought to violate the basic rules of the community. If it doesn't, victims are seen to have done something they could have cho-

sen to do differently, by exercise of will or better judgment. Maybe such people have placed themselves in a situation of vulnerability to physical abuse. Maybe they have done something provocative. Or maybe they were just unusually unlucky. In such a world, if such a person has an experience, there are words for it. When they speak and say it, they are listened to. If they write about it, they will be published. If certain experiences are never spoken about, if certain people or issues are seldom heard from, it is supposed that silence has been chosen. The law, including much of the law of sex discrimination and the First Amendment, operates largely within the realm of these beliefs.

Feminism is the discovery that women do not live in this world, that the person occupying this realm is a man, so much more a man if he is white and wealthy. This world of potential credibility, authority, security, and just rewards, recognition of one's identity and capacity, is a world that some people do inhabit as a condition of birth, with variations among them. It is not a basic condition accorded humanity in this society, but a prerogative of status, a privilege, among other things, of gender.

I call this a discovery because it has not been an assumption. Feminism is the first theory, the first practice, the first movement, to take seriously the situation of all women from the point of view of all women, both on our situation and on social life as a whole. The discovery has therefore been made that the implicit social content of humanism, as well as the standpoint from which legal method has been designed and injuries have been defined, has not been women's standpoint. Defining feminism in a way that connects epistemology with power as the politics of women's point of view, this discovery can be summed up by saying that women live in another world: specifically, a world of *not* equality, a world of inequality.

Looking at the world from this point of view, a whole shadow world of previously invisible silent abuse has been discerned. Rape, battery, sexual harassment, forced prostitution, and the sexual abuse of children emerge as common and systematic. We find that rape happens to women in all contexts, from the family, including rape of girls and babies, to students and women in the workplace, on the streets, at home, in their own bedrooms by men they do not know and by men they do know, by men they are married to, men they have had a social conversation with, and, least often, men they have never seen before. Overwhelmingly, rape is something that men do or attempt to do to women (44 percent of American women according to a recent study) at some point in our lives. Sexual harassment of women by men is common in workplaces and educational institutions. Based on reports in one study of the federal workforce, up to 85 percent of women will experience it, many in physical forms. Between a quarter and a third of women are battered in their homes by men. Thirty-eight percent of little girls are sexually molested inside or outside the family. Until women listened to women, this world of sexual abuse was *not spoken* of. It was the unspeakable. What I am saying is, if you *are* the tree falling in the epistemological forest, your demise doesn't make a sound if no one is listening. Women did not "report" these events, and overwhelmingly do not today, because no one is listening, because no one believes us. This silence does not mean nothing happened, and it does not mean consent. It is the silence of women of which Adrienne Rich has written, "Do not confuse it with any kind of absence."[1]

Believing women who say we are sexually violated has been a radical departure, both methodologically and legally. The extent and nature of rape, marital rape, and sexual harassment itself, were discovered in this way. Domestic battery as a syndrome, almost a habit, was discovered through refusing to believe that when a woman is assaulted by a man to whom she is connected, it is not an assault. The sexual abuse of children was uncovered, Freud notwithstanding, by believing that children were not making up all this sexual abuse. Now what is striking is that when each discovery is made, and somehow made real in the world, the response has been: it happens to men too. If women are hurt, men are hurt. If women are raped, men are raped. If women are sexually harassed, men are sexually harassed. If women are battered, men are battered. Symmetry must be reasserted. Neutrality must be reclaimed. Equality must be reestablished.

The only areas where the available evidence supports this, where anything like what happens to women also happens to men, involve children— little boys are sexually abused—and prison. The liberty of prisoners is restricted, their freedom restrained, their humanity systematically diminished, their bodies and emotions confined, defined, and regulated. If paid at all, they are paid starvation wages. They can be tortured at will, and it is passed off as discipline or as means to a just end. They become compliant. They can be raped at will, at any moment, and nothing will be done about it. When they scream, nobody hears. To be a prisoner means to be defined as a member of a group for whom the rules of what can be done to you, of what is seen as abuse of you, are reduced as part of the definition of your status. To be a woman is that kind of definition and has that kind of meaning. . . .

What women do is seen as not worth much, or what is not worth much is seen as something for women to do. *Women* are seen as not worth much, is the thing. Now why are these basic realities of the subordination of women to men, for example, that only 7.8 percent of women have never been sexually assaulted, not effectively believed, not perceived as real in the face of all this evidence? Why don't *women* believe our own experiences? In the face of all this evidence, especially of systematic sexual abuse—subjection to violence with impunity is one extreme expression, although not the only expression, of a degraded status—the view that basically the sexes are equal in this society remains unchallenged and unchanged. The day I got this was the day I understood its real message, its real coherence: *This is equality for us.*

I could describe this, but I couldn't explain it until I started studying a lot of pornography. In pornography, there it is, in one place, all of the abuses that women had to struggle so long even to begin to articulate, all the *unspeakable* abuse: the rape, the battery, the sexual harassment, the prostitution, and the sexual abuse of children. Only in the pornography it is called something else: sex, sex, sex, sex, and sex, respectively. Pornography sexualizes rape, battery, sexual harassment, prostitution, and child sexual abuse; it thereby celebrates, promotes, authorizes, and legitimizes them. More generally, it eroticizes the dominance and submission that is the dynamic common to them all. It makes hierarchy sexy and calls that "the truth about sex" or just a mirror of reality. Through this process, pornography constructs what a woman is as what men want from sex. This is what the pornography means.

Pornography constructs what a woman is in terms of its view of what men want sexually, such that acts of rape, battery, sexual harassment, prostitution, and sexual abuse of children become acts of sexual equality. Pornography's world of equality is a harmonious and balanced place. Men and women are perfectly complementary and perfectly bipolar. Women's desire to be fucked by men is equal to men's desire to fuck women. All the ways men love to take and violate women, women love to be taken and violated. The women who most love this are most men's equals, the most liberated; the most participatory child is the most grown-up, the most equal to an adult. Their consent merely expresses or ratifies these preexisting facts.

The content of pornography is one thing. There, women substantively desire dispossession and cruelty. We desperately want to be bound, battered, tortured, humiliated, and killed. Or, to be fair to the soft core, merely taken and used. This is erotic to the male point of view. Subjection itself, with self-determination ecstatically relinquished, is the content of women's sexual desire and desirability. Women are there to be violated and possessed, men to violate and possess us, either on screen or by camera or pen on behalf of the consumer. On a simple descriptive level, the inequality of hierarchy, of which gender is the primary one, seems necessary for sexual arousal to work. Other added inequalities identify various pornographic genres or subthemes, although they are always added through gender: age, disability, homosexuality, animals, objects, race (including anti-Semitism), and so on. Gender is never irrelevant.

What pornography *does* goes beyond its content: it eroticizes hierarchy, it sexualizes inequality. It makes dominance and submission into sex. Inequality is its central dynamic; the illusion of freedom coming together with the reality of force is central to its working. Perhaps because this is a bourgeois culture, the victim must look free, appear to be freely acting. Choice is how she got there. Willing is what she is when she is being equal. It seems equally important that then and there she actually be forced and that forcing be communicated on some level, even if only through still photos of her in postures of receptivity and access, available for penetration. Pornography in this view is a form of forced sex, a practice of sexual politics, an institution of gender inequality.

From this perspective, pornography is neither harmless fantasy nor a corrupt and confused misrepresentation of an otherwise natural and healthy sexual situation. It institutionalizes the sexuality of male supremacy, fusing the eroticization of dominance and submission with the social construction of male and female. To the extent that gender is sexual, pornography is part of constituting the meaning of that sexuality. Men treat women as who they see women as being. Pornography constructs who that is. Men's power over women means that the way men see women defines who women can be. Pornography is that way. Pornography is not imagery in some relation to a reality elsewhere constructed. It is not a distortion, reflection, projection, expression, fantasy, representation, or symbol either. It is a sexual reality.

In Andrea Dworkin's definitive work, *Pornography: Men Possessing Women,* sexuality itself is a social construct gendered to the ground. Male dominance here is not an artificial overlay upon an underlying inalterable substratum of uncorrupted essential sexual being. Dworkin presents a sexual theory of gender inequality of which pornography is a constitutive practice. The way pornography produces its meaning constructs and defines men and women as such. Gender has no basis in anything other than the social reality its hegemony constructs. Gender is what gender means. The process that gives sexuality its male supremacist meaning is the same process through which gender inequality becomes socially real.

In this approach, the experience of the (overwhelmingly) male audiences who consume pornography is therefore not fantasy or simulation or catharsis but sexual reality, the level of reality on which sex itself largely operates. Understanding this dimension of the problem does not require noticing that pornography models are real women to whom, in most cases, something real is being done; nor does it even require inquiring into the systematic infliction of pornography and its sexuality upon women, although it helps. What matters is the way in which the pornography itself provides what those who consume it want. Pornography *participates* in its audience's eroticism through creating an accessible sexual object, the possession and consumption of which *is* male sexuality, as socially constructed; to be consumed and possessed as which, *is* female sexuality, as socially constructed; pornography is a process that constructs it that way.

The object world is constructed according to how it looks with respect to its possible uses. Pornography defines women by how we look according to how we can be sexually used. Pornography codes how to look at women, so you know what you can do with one when you see one. Gender is an assignment made visually, both originally and in everyday life. A sex object is defined on the basis of its looks, in terms of its usability for sexual pleasure, such that both the looking—the quality of the gaze, including its point of view—and the definition according to use become eroticized as part of the sex itself. This is what the feminist concept "sex object" means. In this sense, sex in life is no less mediated than it is in art. Men have sex with their image of a woman. It is not that life and art imitate each other; in this sexuality, they *are* each other. . . .

To defend pornography as consistent with the equality of the sexes is to defend the subordination of women to men as sexual equality. What in the pornographic view is love and romance looks a great deal like hatred and torture to the feminist. Pleasure and eroticism become violation. Desire appears as lust for dominance and submission. The vulnerability of women's projected sexual availability, that acting we are allowed (that is, asking to be acted upon), is victimization. Play conforms to scripted roles. Fantasy expresses ideology, is not exempt from it. Admiration of natural physical beauty becomes objectification. Harmlessness becomes harm. Pornography is a harm of male supremacy made difficult to see because of its pervasiveness, potency, and, principally, because of its success in making the world a pornographic place. Specifically, its harm cannot be discerned, and will not be addressed, if viewed and approached neutrally, because it *is* so much of "what is." In other words, to the extent pornography succeeds in constructing social reality, it becomes invisible as harm. If we live in a world that pornography creates through the power of men in a male-dominated situation, the issue is not what the harm of pornography is, but how that harm is to become visible.

Obscenity law provides a very different analysis and conception of the problem of pornography. In 1973 the legal definition of obscenity became that which the average person, applying contemporary community standards, would find that, taken as a whole, appeals to the prurient interest; that which depicts or describes in a patently offensive way— you feel like you're a cop reading someone's *Miranda* rights—sexual conduct specifically defined by the applicable state law; and that which, taken as a whole, lacks serious literary, artistic, political or scientific value. Feminism doubts whether the average person gender-neutral exists; has more questions about the content and process of defining what community standards are than it does about deviations from them; wonders why prurience counts but powerlessness does not and why sensibilities are better protected from offense than women are from exploitation; defines sexuality, and thus its violation and expropriation, more broadly than does state law; and questions why a body of law that has not in practice been able to tell rape from intercourse should, without further guidance, be entrusted with telling pornography from anything less. Taking the work "as a whole" ignores that which the victims of pornography have long known: legitimate settings diminish the perception of injury done to those whose trivialization and objectification they contextualize. Besides, and this is a heavy one, if a woman is subjected, why should it matter that the work has other value? Maybe what redeems the work's value is what enhances its injury to women, not to mention that existing standards of literature, art, science, and politics, examined in a feminist light, are remarkably consonant with pornography's mode, meaning, and message. And finally—first and foremost, actually—although the subject of these materials is overwhelmingly women, their contents almost entirely made up of women's bodies, our invisibility has been such, our equation as a sex *with* sex has been such, that the law of obscenity has never even considered pornography a women's issue.

Obscenity, in this light, is a moral idea, an idea about judgments of good and bad. Pornography, by contrast, is a political practice, a practice of power and powerlessness. Obscenity is ideational and abstract; pornography is concrete and substantive. The two concepts represent two entirely different things. Nudity, excess of candor, arousal or excitement, prurient appeal, illegality of the acts depicted, unnaturalness or perversion are all qualities that bother obscenity law when sex is depicted or portrayed. Sex forced on real women so that it can be sold at a profit and forced on other real women; women's bodies trussed and maimed and raped and made into things to be hurt and obtained and accessed, and this presented as the nature of women in a way that is acted out, over and over; the coercion that is visible and the coercion that has become invisible—this and more bothers feminists about pornography. Obscenity as such probably does little harm. Pornography is integral to attitudes and behaviors of violence and discrimination that define the treatment and status of half the population.

At the request of the city of Minneapolis, Andrea Dworkin and I conceived and designed a local human rights ordinance in accordance with our approach to the pornography issue. We define pornography as a practice of sex discrimination, violation of women's civil rights, the opposite of sexual equality. Its point is to hold those who profit from and benefit from that injury accountable to those who are injured. It means that women's injury—our damage, our pain, our enforced inferiority—should outweigh their pleasure and their profits, or sex equality is meaningless.

We define pornography as the graphic sexually explicit subordination of women through pictures or words that also includes women dehumanized as sexual objects, things, or commodities; enjoying pain or humiliation or rape; being tied up, cut up, mutilated, bruised, or physically hurt; in postures of sexual submission or servility or display; reduced to body parts, penetrated by objects or animals, or presented in scenarios of degradation, injury, torture; shown as filthy or inferior; bleeding, bruised, or hurt in a context that makes these conditions sexual. Erotica, defined by distinction as not this, might be sexually explicit materials premised on equality. We also provide that the use of men, children, or transsexuals in the place of women is pornography. The definition is substantive in that it is sex-specific, but it covers everyone in a sex-specific way, so is gender neutral in overall design. . . .

To define pornography as a practice of sex discrimination combines a mode of portrayal that has a legal history—the sexually explicit—with an active term that is central to the inequality of the sexes—subordination. Among other things, subordination means to be in a position of inferiority or loss of power, or to be demeaned or denigrated. To be someone's subordinate is the opposite of being their equal. The definition does not include all sexually explicit depictions *of* the subordination of women. That is not what it says. It says, this which *does* that: the sexually explicit that subordinates women. To these active terms to capture what the pornography *does*, the definition adds a list of what it must also

contain. This list, from our analysis, is an exhaustive description of what must be in the pornography for it to do what it does behaviorally. Each item in the definition is supported by experimental, testimonial, social, and clinical evidence. We made a legislative choice to be exhaustive and specific and concrete rather than conceptual and general, to minimize problems of chilling effect, making it hard to guess wrong, thus making self-censorship less likely, but encouraging (to use a phrase from discrimination law) voluntary compliance, knowing that if something turns up that is not on the list, the law will not be expansively interpreted.

The list in the definition, by itself, would be a content regulation. But together with the first part, the definition is not simply a content regulation. It is a medium-message combination that resembles many other such exceptions to First Amendment guarantees. . . .

This law aspires to guarantee women's rights consistent with the First Amendment by making visible a conflict of rights between the equality guaranteed to all women and what, in some legal sense, is now the freedom of the pornographers to make and sell, and their consumers to have access to, the materials this ordinance defines. Judicial resolution of this conflict, if the judges do for women what they have done for others, is likely to entail a balancing of the rights of women arguing that our lives and opportunities, including our freedom of speech and action, are constrained by—and in many cases flatly precluded by, in, and through—pornography, against those who argue that the pornography is harmless, or harmful only in part but not in the whole of the definition; or that it is more important to preserve the pornography than it is to prevent or remedy whatever harm it does. . . .

The harm of pornography, broadly speaking, is the harm of the civil inequality of the sexes made invisible as harm because it has become accepted as the sex difference. Consider this analogy with race: if you see Black people as different, there is no harm to segregation; it is merely a recognition of that difference. To neutral principles, separate but equal was equal. The injury of racial separation to Blacks arises "solely because [they] choose to put that construction upon it." Epistemologically translated: how you see it is not the way it is. Similarly, if you see women as just different, even or especially if you don't know that you do, subordination will not look like subordination at all, much less like harm. It will merely look like an appropriate recognition of the sex difference.

Pornography does treat the sexes differently, so the case for sex differentiation can be made here. But men as a group do not tend to be (although some individuals may be) treated the way women are treated in pornography. As a social group, men are not hurt by pornography the way women as a social group are. Their social status is not defined as *less* by it. So the major argument does not turn on mistaken differentiation, particularly since the treatment of women according to pornography's dictates makes it all too often accurate. The salient quality of a distinction between the top and the bottom in a hierarchy is not difference, although top is certainly different. . . .

Free speech only enhances the power of the pornographers while doing nothing substantively to guarantee the free speech of women, for which we need civil equality. The situation in which women presently find ourselves with respect to the pornography is one in which more *pornography* is inconsistent with rectifying or even counterbalancing its damage through speech, because so long as the pornography exists in the way it does there *will not be more speech by women.* Pornography strips and devastates women of credibility, from our accounts of sexual assault to our everyday reality of sexual subordination. We are stripped of authority and reduced and devalidated and silenced. Silenced here means that the purposes of the First Amendment, premised upon conditions presumed and promoted by protecting free speech, do not pertain to women because they are not our conditions. Consider them: individual self-fulfillment—how does pornography promote our individual self-fulfillment? How does sexual inequality even permit it? Even if she can form words, who listens to a woman with a penis in her mouth? Facilitating consensus—to the extent pornography does so, it does so one-sidedly by silencing protest over the injustice of sexual subordination. Participation in civic life—central to Professor Meiklejohn's theory—how does pornography enhance women's participation in civic life? Anyone who cannot walk down the street or even lie down in her own bed without keeping her eyes cast down and her body clenched against assault is unlikely to have much to say about the issues of the day, still less will she become Tolstoy. Facilitating change—*this law* facilitates the change that existing First Amendment theory had been used to throttle. Any system of freedom of expression that does not address a problem where the free speech of men silences the free speech of women, a real conflict between speech interests as

well as between people, is not serious about securing freedom of expression in this country.

For those of you who still think pornography is only an idea, consider the possibility that obscenity law got one thing right. Pornography is more act-like than thoughtlike. The fact that pornography, in a feminist view, furthers the idea of the sexual inferiority of women, which is a political idea, doesn't make the pornography itself into a political idea. One can express the idea a practice embodies. That does not make that practice into an idea. Segregation expresses the idea of the inferiority of one group to another on the basis of race. That does not make segregation an idea. A sign that says "Whites Only" is only words. Is it therefore protected by the First Amendment? Is it not an act, a practice, of segregation because what it means is inseparable from what it does? *Law* is only words.

The issue here is whether the fact that words and pictures are the central link in the cycle of abuse will immunize that entire cycle, about which we cannot do anything without doing something about the pornography. As Justice Stewart said in *Ginsburg,* "When expression occurs in a setting where the capacity to make a choice is absent, government regulation of that expression may coexist with and *even implement* First Amendment guarantees."[2] I would even go so far as to say that the pattern of evidence we have closely approaches Justice Douglas' requirement that "freedom of expression can be suppressed if, and to the extent that, it is so closely brigaded with illegal action as to be an inseparable part of it."[3] Those of you who have been trying to separate the acts from the speech—that's an act, that's an act, there's a law against that act, regulate that act, don't touch the speech—notice here that the illegality of the acts involved doesn't mean that the speech that is "brigaded with" it *cannot* be regulated. This is when it *can* be.

I take one of two penultimate points from Andrea Dworkin, who has often said that pornography is not speech for women, it is the silence of women. Remember the mouth taped, the woman gagged, "Smile, I can get a lot of money for that." The smile is not her expression, it is her silence. . . .

Classically, opposition to censorship has involved keeping government off the backs of people. Our law is about getting some people off the backs of other people. The risks that it will be misused have to be measured against the risks of the status quo. Women will never have that dignity, security, compensation that is the promise of equality so long as the pornography exists as it does now. The situation of women suggests that the urgent issue of our freedom of speech is not primarily the avoidance of state intervention as such, but getting affirmative access to speech for those to whom it has been denied.

NOTES

1. Adrienne Rich, "Cartographies of Silence," *The Dream of a Common Language*, 16, 17 (1978).
2. Ginsburg v. New York, 390 U.S. 629, 649 (1968) (Stewart, J., concurring in result) (emphasis added).
3. Roth v. United States, 354 U.S. 476, 514 (Douglas, J., dissenting) (citing Giboney v. Empire Storage & Ice Co., 336 U.S. 490, 498 [1949]); Labor Board v. Virginia Power Co., 314 U.S. 469, 477–78 (1941). See also Memoirs v. Massachusetts, 383 U.S. 413, 426 (1966) (Douglas, J., concurring) (First Amendment does not permit the censorship of expression not brigaded with illegal action); Pittsburgh Press Co. v. Human Relations Comm'n, 413 U.S. 376, 398 (1973) (Douglas, J., dissenting) (speech and action not so closely brigaded as to be one).

DISCUSSION QUESTIONS

1. What is the difference between "erotica" and "pornography" according to MacKinnon? Do you agree with this distinction? Why or why not?
2. What does MacKinnon mean when she says, "Feminism is the discovery that women do not live in this [equal] world, that the person occupying this realm [of equality] is a man, so much more a man if he is white and wealthy"? Critically discuss her position.
3. On what basis does MacKinnon argue that antipornography laws do not violate, but rather promote, freedom of speech? Do you agree with her? Defend your position.
4. What does MacKinnon mean when she calls gender and sexuality "social constructs"? What role does this analysis play in her overall argument? Can she reach her conclusions about pornography and censorship without analyzing gender and sexuality as social constructs? Do you think that gender and sexuality are socially shaped or biologically determined?
5. What is MacKinnon's argument that pornography is a type of sex discrimination that violates the guarantee of equal rights? Do you agree with her argument? Defend your position in detail.

 LISA DUGGAN, NAN D. HUNTER, AND CAROLE S. VANCE

False Promises

Lisa Duggan, Nan D. Hunter, and Carole S. Vance oppose the views of Catharine MacKinnon. For them, pornography is not sex discrimination that should be actionable in civil court by people who can prove pornography harmed them. There are many other forms of sexist material not prohibited by ordinances that are just as harmful to women. In

Lisa Duggan, Nan D. Hunter, and Carole S. Vance, *Women Against Censorship*. Edited by V. Burstyn. Douglas and McIntyre, 1985, 130–151. Copyright © 1985 Lisa Duggan, Nan D. Hunter and Carol S. Vance. Reprinted with permission from the authors.

addition, because these ordinances are so broadly conceived, they potentially could be used to ban any sexually explicit material. "Far-right elements recognize the possibility of using the full potential of the ordinances to enforce their sexually conservative world view," write Duggan, Hunter, and Vance, "and have supported them for that reason." As a result, these ordinances might even hinder, rather than further, the feminist movement.

Lisa Duggan is a professor of history and American studies at New York University, and Nan D. Hunter is a professor of law at Brooklyn Law School. Hunter and Duggan coedited *Sex Wars: Essays in Sexual Dissent and American Politics* (1995). Carole S. Vance is an anthropologist in Columbia University's School of Public Health. Columbia University's Program for the Study of Sexuality, Gender, Health, and Human Rights is the brainchild of Vance.

FEMINIST ANTIPORNOGRAPHY LEGISLATION

On February 24, 1986, the U.S. Supreme Court ruled that the Indianapolis version of the antipornography ordinance was unconstitutional. Although this ruling settles the legal question of the ordinance's validity, the political debate on the wisdom of invoking state power to suppress sexual materials continues. That debate, which will be with us for many years to come, encompasses many of the same points of disagreement—over the social meanings of language and imagery and the political risks to women of protectionist strategy—which we analyze in this article.

In the United States, after two decades of increasing community tolerance for dissenting or disturbing sexual or political materials, there is now growing momentum for retrenchment. In an atmosphere of increased conservatism, evidenced by a wave of book banning and anti-gay harassment, support for new repressive legislation of various kinds—from an Oklahoma law forbidding schoolteachers from advocating homosexuality to new antipornography laws passed in Minneapolis and Indianapolis—is growing.

The antipornography laws have mixed roots of support, however. Though they are popular with the conservative constituencies that traditionally favor legal restrictions on sexual expression of all kinds, they were drafted and are endorsed by antipornography feminists who oppose traditional obscenity and censorship laws. The model law of this type, which is now being widely copied, was drawn up in the politically progressive city of Minneapolis by two radical feminists, author Andrea Dworkin and attorney Catharine MacKinnon. It was passed by the city council there, but vetoed by the mayor. A similar law was passed in Indianapolis, but later declared unconstitutional in federal court. The city is appealing that ruling to the Supreme Court. Other versions of the legislation have been considered, and either discarded or defeated, in several other places including Suffolk County, New York, Madison, Wisconsin, Los Angeles County, California, and Cambridge, Massachusetts. Pennsylvania Senator Arlen Specter has introduced legislation modeled on parts of the Dworkin-MacKinnon bill in Congress, and the Reagan-initiated Attorney General's Commission on Pornography is weighing its merits as a censorship strategy.

Dworkin, MacKinnon and their feminist supporters believe that the new antipornography laws are not censorship laws. They also claim that the legislative effort behind them is based on feminist support. Both of these claims are dubious at best. Though the new laws are civil laws that allow individuals to sue the makers, sellers, distributors, or exhibitors of pornography, and not criminal laws leading to arrest and imprisonment, their censoring impact would be substantially as severe as criminal obscenity laws. Materials could be removed from public availability by court injunction, and publishers and booksellers could be subject to potentially endless legal harassment. Passage of the laws was therefore achieved with the support of right-wing elements who expect the new laws to accomplish what censorship efforts are meant to accomplish. Ironically, many antifeminist conservatives backed these laws, while many feminists opposed them. In Indianapolis, the law was supported by extreme right-wing religious fundamentalists, including members of the Moral Majority, while there was *no* local feminist support. In other cities, traditional procensorship forces have expressed interest in the new approach to banning sexually explicit materials. Meanwhile, anticensorship feminists have become alarmed at these new developments and are seeking to galvanize feminist opposition to the new antipornography legislative strategy pioneered in Minneapolis.

One is tempted to ask in astonishment, how can this be happening? How can feminists be entrusting the patriarchal state with the task of legally distinguishing between permissible and impermissible sexual images? But in fact this new development is not as surprising as it at first seems. For the reasons explored by Ann Snitow, pornography has come to be seen as a central cause of women's oppression by a significant number of feminists. Some even argue that pornography is the root of virtually all forms of exploitation and discrimination against women. It is a short step from such a belief to the conviction that laws against pornography can end the inequality of the sexes. But this analysis takes feminists very close—indeed far too close—to measures that will ultimately support conservative, antisex, procensorship forces in American society, for it is with these forces that women have forged alliances in passing such legislation.

The first feminist-inspired antipornography law was passed in Minneapolis in 1983. Local legislators had been frustrated when their zoning restrictions on porn shops were struck down in the courts. Public hearings were held to discuss a new zoning ordinance. The Neighborhood Pornography Task Force of South and South Central Minneapolis invited Andrea Dworkin and Catharine MacKinnon, who were teaching a course on pornography at the University of Minnesota, to testify. They proposed an alternative that, they claimed, would completely eliminate, rather than merely regulate, pornography. They suggested that pornography be defined as a form of sex discrimination, and that an amendment to the city's civil rights law be passed to proscribe it. City officials hired Dworkin and MacKinnon to develop their new approach and to organize another series of public hearings.

The initial debate over the legislation in Minneapolis was intense, and opinion was divided within nearly every political grouping. In contrast, the public hearings held before the city council were tightly controlled and carefully orchestrated; speakers invited by Dworkin and MacKinnon—sexual abuse victims, counselors, educators and social scientists—testified about the harm pornography does women. (Dworkin and MacKinnon's agenda was the compilation of a legislative record that would help the law stand up to its inevitable court challenges.) The legislation passed, supported by antipornography feminists, neighborhood groups concerned about the effects of porn shops on residential areas, and conservatives opposed to the availability of sexually explicit materials for "moral" reasons.

In Indianapolis, the alignment of forces was different. For the previous two years, conservative antipornography groups had grown in strength and public visibility, but they had been frustrated in their efforts. The police department could not convert its obscenity arrests into convictions; the city's zoning law was also tied up in court challenges. Then Mayor William Hudnut III, a Republican and a Presbyterian minister, learned of the Minneapolis law. Mayor Hudnut thought Minneapolis's approach to restricting pornography might be the solution to the Indianapolis problems. Beulah Coughenour, a conservative Republican stop-ERA activist, was recruited to sponsor the legislation in the city-county council.

Coughenour engaged MacKinnon as consultant to the city—Dworkin was not hired, but then, Dworkin's passionate radical feminist rhetoric would not have gone over well in Indianapolis. MacKinnon worked with the Indianapolis city prosecutor (a well-known antivice zealot), the city's legal department and Coughenour on the legislation. The law received the support of neighborhood groups, the Citizens for Decency and the Coalition for a Clean Community. There were no crowds of feminist supporters—in fact, there were no feminist supporters at all. The only feminists to make public statements opposed the legislation, which was nevertheless passed in a council meeting packed with 300 religious fundamentalists. All 24 Republicans voted for its passage; all five Democrats opposed it to no avail.

A group of publishers and booksellers challenged the law in Federal District Court, where they won the first round. This initial decision was then upheld by the Federal Appeals Court. The city is appealing again to the Supreme Court, though it may take a year or two for a final decision to be reached.

In the meantime, other versions of the Dworkin-MacKinnon bill have appeared. A version of the law introduced in Suffolk County on Long Island in New York emphasized its conservative potential—pornography was said to cause "sodomy" and "disruption" of the family unit, in addition to rape, incest, exploitation and other acts "inimical to the public good." In Suffolk, the law was put forward by a conservative, anti-ERA male legislator who wishes to "restore ladies to what they used to be." The Suffolk County bill clearly illustrates the repressive antifeminist potential of the new antipornography legislation.

Versions of the bill, nearer to the original intent of the authors, have been considered in Madison, Los Angeles and Cambridge. In these cities, feminist opposition to antipornography ordinances was organized, and Feminist Anti-Censorship Taskforce groups helped to defeat the idea. In Madison, the measure was not introduced after a FACT press conference wiped out support for an ordinance on the Dane County Board of Supervisors. In Los Angeles, FACT efforts helped defeat a measure before the County Board of Supervisors, though the vote was close and individual supervisors responded little to feminist opinion on either side. In Cambridge, voters defeated the measure after a heated referendum campaign in which feminists dominated both sides of the debate.

At present, Edwin Meese's Commission on Pornography is preparing a report on new ways to control pornography. The Commission is controlled by moral conservatives, and it is expected to issue repressive recommendations designed to help legislators and courts suppress sexual images. The Commission is considering the "feminist" antipornography arguments and legislation. It is likely to try to use what it can, while discarding those aspects of the feminist approach which conflict with a conservative outlook. The Meese Commission's report may very well show how far the right-wing will go in co-opting feminist language and laws in the service of its own repressive agenda.

Yet it is true that some of the laws have been proposed and supported by antipornography feminists. This is therefore a critical moment in the feminist debate over sexual politics. As anticensorship feminists work to develop alternatives to antipornography campaigns, we also need to examine carefully the new laws and expose their underlying assumptions. We need to know why these laws, for all their apparent feminist rhetoric, actually appeal to conservative antifeminist forces, and why feminists should be preparing to move in a different direction.

DEFINITIONS: THE CENTRAL FLAW

The antipornography ordinances passed in Minneapolis and Indianapolis were framed as amendments to municipal civil rights laws. They provide for complaints to be filed against pornography in the same manner that complaints are filed against employment discrimination. If enforced, the laws would make illegal public or private availability (except in libraries) of any materials deemed pornographic.

Such material could be the object of a lawsuit on several grounds. The ordinance would penalize four kinds of behavior associated with pornography: its production, sale, exhibition or distribution ("trafficking"); coercion into pornographic performance; forcing pornography on a person; and assault or physical attack due to pornography.

Under this law, a woman "acting as a woman against the subordination of women" could file a complaint; men could also file complaints if they could "prove injury in the same way that a woman is injured." The procedural steps in the various versions differ, but they generally allow the complainant either to file an administrative complaint with the city's equal opportunity commission, or to file a lawsuit directly in court. If the local commission found the law had been violated, it would file a lawsuit. By either procedure, the court—not "women"—would have the final say on whether the materials fit the definition of pornography, and would have the authority to award monetary damages and issue an injunction (or court order) preventing further distribution of the material in question.

The Minneapolis ordinance defines pornography as "the sexually explicit subordination of women, graphically depicted, whether in pictures or words." To be actionable, materials would also have to fall within one of a number of categories: nine in the Minneapolis ordinance, six in the Indianapolis version.

Although proponents claim that these ordinances represent a new way to regulate pornography, the strategy is still laden with our culture's old, repressive approach to sexuality. The implementation of such laws hinges on the definition of pornography as interpreted by the court. The definition provided in the Minneapolis legislation is vague, leaving critical phrases such as "the explicit subordination of women," "postures of sexual submission" and "whores by nature" to the interpretation of the citizen who files a complaint and to the civil court judge who hears the case. The legislation does not prohibit just the images of gross sexual violence that most supporters claim to be its target, but instead drifts toward covering an increasingly wide range of sexually explicit material.

The most problematic feature of this approach, then, is a conceptual flaw embedded in the law itself. Supporters of this type of legislation say that the target of their efforts is misogynist, sexually explicit and violent representation, whether in pictures or words. Indeed, the feminist antipornography movement is fueled by women's anger at the most repugnant examples of pornography. But a close examination of the wording of the model legislative text, and examples of purportedly actionable material offered by proponents of the legislation in court briefs suggest that the law is actually aimed at a range of material considerably broader than what proponents claim is their target. The discrepancies between the law's explicit and implicit aims have been almost invisible to us, because these distortions are very similar to distortions about sexuality in the culture as a whole. The legislation and supporting texts deserve close reading. Hidden beneath illogical transformations, nonsequiturs, and highly permeable definitions are familiar sexual scripts drawn from mainstream, sexist culture that potentially could have very negative consequences for women.

The Venn diagram illustrates the three areas targeted by the law, and represents a scheme that classifies words or images that have any of three characteristics: violence, sexual explicitness or sexism.

Clearly, a text or an image might have only one characteristic. Material can be violent but not sexually explicit or sexist: for example, a war movie in which both men and women suffer injury or death without regard to or because of their gender. Material can be sexist but not sexually explicit and violent. A vast number of materials from mainstream media—television, popular novels, magazines, newspapers—come to mind, all of which depict either distraught housewives or the "happy sexism" of the idealized family, with mom self-sacrificing, other-directed and content. Finally, material can be sexually explicit but not violent or sexist: for example, the freely chosen sexual behavior depicted in sex education films or women's own explicit writing about sexuality.

As the diagram illustrates, areas can also intersect, reflecting a range of combinations of the three characteristics. Images can be violent and sexually explicit without being sexist—for example, a narrative about a rape in a men's prison, or a documentary about the effect of a rape on a woman. The latter example illustrates the importance of context in evaluating whether material that is sexually ex-

plicit and violent is also sexist. The intent of the maker, the context of the film and the perception of the viewer together render a depiction of a rape sympathetic, harrowing, even educational, rather than sensational, victim-blaming and laudatory.

Another possible overlap is between material that is violent and sexist but not sexually explicit. Films or books that describe violence directed against women by men in a way that clearly shows gender antagonism and inequality, and sometimes strong sexual tension, but no sexual explicitness fall into this category—for example, the popular genre of slasher films in which women are stalked, terrified and killed by men, or accounts of mass murder of women, fueled by male rage. Finally, a third point of overlap arises when material is sexually explicit and sexist without being violent—that is, when sex is consensual but still reflects themes of male superiority and female abjectness. Some sex education materials could be included in this category, as well as a great deal of regular pornography.

The remaining domain, the inner core, is one in which the material is simultaneously violent, sexually explicit and sexist—for example, an image of a naked woman being slashed by a knife-wielding rapist. The Minneapolis law, however, does not by any means confine itself to this material.

To be actionable under the law as pornography, material must be judged by the courts to be "the sexually explicit subordination of women, graphically depicted whether in pictures or in words that also includes at least one or more" of nine criteria. Of these, only four involve the intersection of violence, sexual explicitness and sexism, and then only arguably. Even in these cases, many questions remain about whether images with all three characteristics do in fact cause violence against women. And the task of evaluating material that is ostensibly the target of these criteria becomes complicated—indeed, hopeless—because most of the clauses that contain these criteria mix actions or qualities of violence with those that are not particularly associated with violence.

The section that comes closest to the stated purpose of the legislation is clause (iii): "women are presented as sexual objects who experience sexual pleasure in being raped." This clause is intended to cover depictions of rape that are sexually explicit and sexist; the act of rape itself signifies the violence. But other clauses are not so clearcut, because the list of characteristics often mixes signs or byproducts of violence with phenomena that are unrelated or irrelevant to judging violence.

For example, clause (iv) [states]: "women are presented as sexual objects tied up or cut up or mutilated or bruised or physically hurt." All these except the first, "tied up," generally occur as a result of violence. "Tied up," if part of consensual sex, is not violent and, for some practitioners, not particularly sexist. Women who are tied up may be participants in nonviolent sex play involving bondage, a theme in both heterosexual and lesbian pornography. (See, for example, *The Joy of Sex* and *Coming to Power.*) Clause (ix) contains another mixed list, in which "injury," "torture," "bleeding," "bruised" and "hurt" are combined with words such as "degradation" and "shown as filthy and inferior," neither of which is violent. Depending on the presentation, "filthy" and "inferior" may constitute sexually explicit sexism, although not violence. "Degradation" is a sufficiently inclusive term to cover most acts of which a viewer disapproves.

Several other clauses have little to do with violence at all; they refer to material that is sexually explicit and sexist, thus falling outside the triad of characteristics at which the legislation is supposedly aimed. For example, movies in which "women are presented as dehumanized sexual objects, things, or commodities" may be infuriating and offensive to feminists, but they are not violent.

Finally, some clauses describe material that is neither violent nor necessarily sexist. Clause (v), "women . . . in postures of sexual submission or sexual servility, including by inviting penetration," and clause (viii), "women . . . being penetrated by objects or animals," are sexually explicit, but not violent and not obviously sexist unless one believes that penetration—whether heterosexual, lesbian, or autoerotic masturbation—is indicative of gender inequality and female oppression. Similarly problematic are clauses that invoke representations of "women . . . as whores by nature" and "women's body parts . . . such that women are reduced to those parts."

Briefs filed in support of the Indianapolis law show how broadly it could be applied. In the amicus brief filed on behalf of Linda Marchiano ("Linda Lovelace," the female lead in *Deep Throat*) in Indianapolis, Catharine MacKinnon offered *Deep Throat* as an example of the kind of pornography covered by the law. *Deep Throat* served a complicated function in this brief, because the movie, supporters of the ordinance argue, would be actionable on two counts: coercion into pornographic performance, because Marchiano alleges that she was coerced into making the movie; and trafficking in pornography, because the content of the film falls within one of the categories in the Indianapolis ordinance's definition—that which prohibits presenting women as sexual objects "through postures or positions of servility or submission or display." Proponents of the law have counted on women's repugnance at allegations of coerced sexual acts to spill over and discredit the sexual acts themselves in this movie.

The aspects of *Deep Throat* that MacKinnon considered to be indicative of "sexual subordination" are of particular interest, since any movie that depicted similar acts could be banned under the law. MacKinnon explained in her brief that the film "subordinates women by using women . . . sexually, specifically as eager servicing receptacles for male genitalia and ejaculate. The majority of the film represents 'Linda Lovelace' in, minimally, postures of sexual submission and/or servility." In its brief, the City of Indianapolis concurred: "In the film *Deep Throat* a woman is being shown as being ever eager for oral penetration by a series of men's penises, often on her hands and knees. There are repeated scenes in which her genitalia are graphically displayed and she is shown as enjoying men ejaculating on her face."

These descriptions are very revealing, since they suggest that multiple partners, group sex and oral sex subordinate women and hence are sexist. The notion that the female character is "used" by men suggests that it is improbable that a woman would engage in fellatio of her own accord. *Deep Throat* does draw on several sexist conventions common in the entire visual culture—the woman as object of the male gaze, and the assumption of heterosexuality, for example. But it is hardly an unending paean to male dominance, since the movie contains many contrary themes. In it, the main female character is shown as both actively seeking her own pleasure and as trying to please men; a secondary female character is shown as actually directing encounters with multiple male partners. Both briefs described a movie quite different from the one viewers see.

As its heart, this analysis implies that heterosexual sex itself is sexist; that women do not engage in it of their own volition; and that behavior pleasurable to men is necessarily repugnant to women. In some contexts, for example, the representation of fellatio and multiple partners can be sexist, but are we willing to concede that they always are? If not, then what is proposed as actionable under the Indianapolis law includes merely sexually explicit representation (the traditional target of obscenity laws), which proponents of the legislation vociferously insist they are not interested in attacking.

Some other examples offered through exhibits submitted with the City of Indianapolis brief and also introduced in the public hearing further illustrate this point. Many of the exhibits are depictions of sadomasochism. The court briefs treat SM material as depicting violence and aggression, not consensual sex, in spite of avowals to the contrary by many SM practitioners. With this legislation, then, a major question for feminists that has only begun to develop would be closed for discussion. Instead, a simplistic reduction has been advanced as the definitive feminist position. The description of the material in the briefs focused on submissive women and implied male domination, highlighting the similarity proponents would like to find between all SM narratives and male/female inequality. The actual exhibits, however, illustrated plots and power relations far more diverse than the descriptions provided by MacKinnon and the City of Indianapolis would suggest, including SM between women and female dominant/male submissive SM. For example, the Indianapolis brief stated that in the magazine *The Bitch Goddesses,* "women are shown in torture chambers with their nude body parts being tortured by their 'master' for 'even the slightest offense.' . . . The magazine shows a woman in a scenario of torture." But the brief failed to mention that the dominants in this magazine are all female, with one exception. This kind of discrepancy characterized many examples offered in the briefs.

This is not to say that such representations do not raise questions for feminists. The current lively discussion about lesbian SM clearly demonstrates that the issue is still unresolved. But in the Indianapolis briefs all SM material was assumed to be male dominant/female submissive, thereby squeezing a nonconforming reality into prepackaged, inadequate— and therefore dangerous—categories. This legislation would virtually eliminate all SM pornography by recasting it as violent, thereby attacking a sexual minority while masquerading as an attempt to end violence against women.

Analysis of clauses in the Minneapolis ordinance and several examples offered in court briefs filed in connection with the Indianapolis ordinance show that the law targets material that is sexually explicit and sexist, but ignores material that is violent and sexist, violent and sexually explicit, only violent or only sexist.

Certain troubling questions arise here, for if one claims, as some antipornography activists do, that there is a direct relationship between images and behavior, why should images of violence against women or scenarios of sexism in general not be similarly proscribed? Why is sexual explicitness singled out as the cause of women's oppression? For proponents to exempt violent and sexist images, or even sexist images, from regulation is inconsistent, especially since they are so pervasive.

Even more difficulties arise from the vagueness of certain terms crucial in interpreting the ordinances. The term "subordination" is especially important, since pornography is defined as the "sexually explicit subordination of women." The authors of this legislation intend it to modify each of the clauses, and they appear to believe that it provides a definition of sexism that each example must meet. The term is never defined in the legislation, yet the Indianapolis brief, for example, suggests that the average viewer, on the basis of "his or her common understanding of what it means for one person to subordinate another," should be able to decide what is pornographic. But what kind of sexually explicit acts place a woman in an inferior status? To some, *any* graphic sexual act violates women's dignity and therefore subordinates them. To others, consensual heterosexual lovemaking within the boundaries of procreation and marriage is acceptable, but heterosexual acts that do not have reproduction as their aim lower women's status and hence subordinate them. Still others accept a wide range of nonprocreative, perhaps even nonmarital, heterosexuality but draw the line at lesbian sex, which they view as degrading.

The term "sex object" is also problematic. The City of Indianapolis's brief maintains that "the term sexual object, often shortened to sex object, has enjoyed a wide popularity in mainstream American culture in the past fifteen years, and is used to denote the objectification of a person on the basis of their sex or sex appeal. . . . People know what it means to disregard all aspects of personhood but sex, to reduce a person to a thing used for sex." But, indeed, people do not agree on this point. The definition of "sex object" is far from clear or uniform. For example, some feminist and liberal cultural critics have used the term to mean sex that occurs without strong emotional ties and experience. More conservative critics maintain that any detachment of women's sexuality from procreation, marriage and family objectifies it, removing it from its "natural" web of associations and context. Unredeemed and unprotected by domesticity and family, women—and their sexuality—become things used by men. In both these views, women are never sexually autonomous agents who direct and enjoy their sexuality for their own purposes, but rather are victims. In the same vein, other problematic terms include "inviting penetration," "whores by nature" and "positions of display."

Through close analysis of the proposed legislation, one sees how vague the boundaries of the definitions that contain the inner core of the Venn diagram really are. Their dissolution does not happen equally at all points, but only at some: the inner core begins to include sexually explicit and sexist material, and finally expands to include purely sexually explicit material. Thus "sexually explicit" becomes identified and equated with "violent" with no further definition or explanation.

It is also striking that so many feminists have failed to notice that the laws (as well as examples of actionable material) cover so much diverse work, not just that small and symbolic epicenter where many forms of opposition to women converge. It suggests that for us, as well as for others, sexuality remains a difficult area. We have no clearly developed framework in which to think about sex equivalent to the frameworks that are available for thinking about race, gender and class issues. Consequently, in sex, as in few other areas of human behavior, unexamined and unjustifiable prejudice passes itself off as considered opinion about what is desirable and normal. And finally, sex arouses considerable anxiety, stemming from both the meeting with individual difference and from the prospect—suggested by feminists themselves—that sexual behavior is constructed socially and is not simply natural.

The law takes advantage of everyone's relative ignorance and anxious ambivalence about sex, distorting and oversimplifying what confronts us in building a sexual politic. For example, antipornography feminists draw on several feminist theories about the role of violent, aggressive or sexist representations. The first is relatively straightforward: that these images trigger men into action. The second suggests that violent images act more subtly, to socialize men to act in sexist or violent ways by making this behavior seem commonplace and more acceptable, if not expected. The third assumption is that violent, sexually explicit or even sexist images are offensive to women, assaulting their sensibilities and sense of self. Although we have all used metaphor to exhort women to action or illustrate a point, antipornography proponents have frequently used these conventions of speech as if they were literal statements of fact. But these metaphors have gotten out of hand, as Julie Abraham has noted, for they fail to recognize that the assault

committed by a wife beater is quite different from the visual "assault" of a sexist ad on TV. The nature of that difference is still being clarified in a complex debate within feminism that must continue; this law cuts off speculation, settling on a causal relationship between image and action that is starkly simple, if unpersuasive.

This metaphor also paves the way for reclassifying images that are merely sexist as also violent and aggressive. Thus, it is no accident that the briefs supporting the legislation first invoke violent images and rapidly move to include sexist and sexually explicit images without noting that they are different. The equation is made easier by the constant shifts back to examples of depictions of real violence, almost to draw attention away from the sexually explicit or sexist material that in fact would be affected by the laws.

Most important, what underlies this legislation and the success of its analysis in blurring and exceeding boundaries is an appeal to a very traditional view of sex: sex is degrading to women. By this logic, any illustrations or descriptions of sexually explicit acts that involve women are in themselves affronts to women's dignity. In its brief, the City of Indianapolis was quite specific about this point: "The harms caused by pornography are by no means limited to acts of physical aggression. The mere existence of pornography in society degrades and demeans all women." Embedded in this view are several other familiar themes: that sex is degrading to women, but not to men; that men are raving beasts; that sex is dangerous for women; that sexuality is male, not female; that women are victims, not sexual actors; that men inflict "it" on women; that penetration is submission; that heterosexual sexuality, rather than the institution of heterosexuality, is sexist.

These assumptions, in part intended, in part unintended, lead us back to the traditional target of obscenity law: sexually explicit material. What initially appeared novel, then, is really the reappearance of a traditional theme. It's ironic that a feminist position on pornography incorporates most of the myths about sexuality that feminism has struggled to displace.

THE DANGERS OF APPLICATION

The Minneapolis-style ordinances embody a political view that holds pornography to be a central force in "creating and maintaining" the oppression of women. This view appears in summary form in the legislative findings section at the beginning of the Minneapolis bill, which describes a chain reaction of misogynistic acts generated by pornography. The legislation is based on the interweaving of several themes: that pornography constructs the meaning of sexuality for women and, as well, leads to discrete acts of violence against women; that sexuality is the primary cause of women's oppression; that explicitly sexual images, even if not violent or coerced, have the power to subordinate women; and that women's own accounts of force have been silenced because, as a universal and timeless rule, society credits pornographic constructions rather than women's experiences. Taking the silencing contention a step further, advocates of the ordinance effectively assume that women have been so conditioned by the pornographic world view that if their own experiences of the sexual acts identified in the definition are not subordinating, then they must simply be victims of false consciousness.

The heart of the ordinance is the "trafficking" section, which would allow almost anyone to seek the removal of any materials falling within the law's definition of pornography. Ordinance defenders strenuously protest that the issue is not censorship because the state, as such, is not authorized to initiate criminal prosecutions. But the prospect of having to defend a potentially infinite number of privately filed complaints creates at least as much of a chilling effect against sexual speech as does a criminal law. And as long as representatives of the state—in this case, judges—have ultimate say over the interpretation, the distinction between this ordinance and "real" censorship will not hold.

In addition, three major problems should dissuade feminists from supporting this kind of law: first, the sexual images in question do not cause more harm than other aspects of misogynist culture; second, sexually explicit speech, even in male-dominated society, serves positive social functions for women; and third, the passage and enforcement of antipornography laws such as those supported in Minneapolis and Indianapolis are more likely to impede, rather than advance, feminist goals.

Ordinance proponents contend that pornography does cause violence because it conditions male sexual response to images of violence and thus provokes violence against women. The strongest research they offer is based on psychology experiments that employ films depicting a rape scene, toward the end of which the woman is shown to be enjoying the attack. The ordinances, by contrast, cover a much broader range of materials than this

one specific heterosexual rape scenario. Further, the studies ordinance-supporters cite do not support the theory that pornography causes violence against women. Taken at their strongest, some studies indicate that exposure to some pornography promotes sexist attitudes and beliefs in some subjects. Interestingly, researchers have found that subjects exposed to "debriefing" sessions at the end of the experiments, in which rape myths are identified and dispelled, are found to have fewer sexist attitudes when tested months later than the "controls" who were not exposed to any pornography. This indicates that education efforts can indeed be effective in countering the sexist messages of pornography.

In addition, the argument that pornography itself plays a major role in the general oppression of women contradicts the evidence of history. It need hardly be said that pornography did not lead to the burning of witches or the English common law treatment of women as chattel property. If anything functioned then as the prime communication medium for woman-hating, it was probably religion. Nor can pornography be blamed for the enactment of laws from at least the eighteenth century that allowed a husband to rape or beat his wife with impunity. In any period, the causes of women's oppression have been many and complex, drawing on the fundamental social and economic structures of society. Ordinance proponents offer little evidence to explain how the mass production of pornography—a relatively recent phenomenon—could have become so potent a causative agent so quickly.

The silencing of women is another example of the harm attributed to pornography. Yet if this argument were correct, one would expect that as the social visibility of pornography has increased, the tendency to credit women's accounts of rape would have decreased. In fact, although the treatment of women complainants in rape cases is far from perfect, the last 15 years of work by the women's movement has resulted in marked improvements. In many places, the corroboration requirement has now been abolished; cross-examination of victims as to past sexual experiences has been prohibited; and a number of police forces have developed specially trained units and procedures to improve the handling of sexual assault cases. The presence of rape fantasies in pornography may in part reflect a backlash against these women's movement advances, but to argue that most people routinely disbelieve women who file charges of rape belittles the real improvements made in social consciousness and law.

The third type of harm suggested by the ordinance backers is a kind of libel: the maliciously false characterization of women as a group of sexual masochists. The City of Indianapolis brief argues that pornography, like libel, is "a lie [which] once loosed" cannot be effectively rebutted by debate and further speech.

To claim that all pornography as defined by the ordinance is a lie is a false analogy. If truth is a defense to charges of libel, then surely depictions of consensual sex cannot be thought of as equivalent to a falsehood. For example, some women (and men) do enjoy bondage or display. The declaration by fiat that sadomasochism is a "lie" about sexuality reflects an arrogance and moralism that feminists should combat, not engage in. When mutually desired sexual experiences are depicted, pornography is not "libelous."

Not only does pornography not cause the kind and degree of harm that can justify the restraint of speech, but its existence serves some social functions which benefit women. Pornographic speech has many, often anomalous, characteristics. One is certainly that it magnifies the misogyny present in the culture and exaggerates the fantasy of male power. Another, however, is that the existence of pornography has served to flout conventional sexual mores, to ridicule sexual hypocrisy and to underscore the importance of sexual needs. Pornography carries many messages other than woman-hating: it advocates sexual adventure, sex outside of marriage, sex for no reason other than pleasure, casual sex, anonymous sex, group sex, voyeuristic sex, illegal sex, public sex. Some of these ideas appeal to women reading or seeing pornography, who may interpret some images as legitimating their own sense of sexual urgency or desire to be sexually aggressive. Women's experience of pornography is not as universally victimizing as the ordinance would have it.

The new antipornography laws, as restrictions on sexual speech, in many ways echo and expand upon the traditional legal analysis of sexually explicit speech under the rubric of obscenity. The U.S. Supreme Court has consistently ruled that sexual speech defined as "obscenity" does not belong in the system of public discourse, and is therefore an exception to the First Amendment and hence not entitled to protection under the free speech guarantee. (The definition of obscenity has shifted over the years and remains imprecise.) In 1957 the Supreme Court ruled that obscenity could be suppressed regardless of whether it presented an imminent threat of illegal activity. In the opinion of the Supreme Court, graphic sexual images do not communicate "real" ideas. These, it would seem, are only found in the traditionally defined public arena. Sexual themes can qualify as ideas if they use sexuality for argument's sake, but not if they speak in the words and images of "private" life—that is, if they graphically depict sex itself. At least theoretically, and insofar as the law functions as a pronouncement of moral judgment, sex is consigned to remain unexpressed and in the private realm.

The fallacies in this distinction are obvious. Under the U.S. Constitution, for example, it is acceptable to write "I am a sadomasochist" or even "Everyone should experiment with sadomasochism in order to increase sexual pleasure." But to write a graphic fantasy about sadomasochism that arouses and excites readers is not protected unless a court finds it to have serious literary, artistic or political value, despite the expressive nature of the content. Indeed, the fantasy depiction may communicate identity in a more compelling way than the "I am" statement. For sexual minorities, sexual acts can be self-identifying and affirming statements in a hostile world. Images of those acts should be protected for that reason, for they do have political content. Just as the personal can be political, so can the specifically and graphically sexual.

Supporters of the antipornography ordinances both endorse the concept that pornographic speech contains no ideas or expressive interest, and at the same time attribute to pornography the capacity to trigger violent acts by the power of its misogyny. The city's brief in defense of the Indianapolis ordinance expanded this point by arguing that all sexually explicit speech is entitled to less constitutional protection than other speech. The antipornography groups have cleverly capitalized on this approach—a product of a totally nonfeminist legal system—and are now attempting, through the mechanism of the ordinances, to legitimate a new crusade for protectionism and sexual conservatism.

The consequences of enforcing such a law, however, are much more likely to obstruct than advance feminist political goals. On the level of ideas, further narrowing of the public realm of sexual speech coincides all too well with the privatization of sexual, reproductive and family issues sought by the far right—an agenda described very well, for example, by Rosalind Petchesky in "The Rise of the New Right," in *Abortion and Woman's Choice*. Practically speaking, the ordinances could result in attempts to eliminate the images associated with homosexuality. Doubtless there are heterosexual women who believe that lesbianism is a "degrading" form of "subordination." Since the ordinances allow for suits against materials in which men appear "in place of women," far-right antipornography crusaders could use these laws to suppress gay male pornography. Imagine a Jerry Falwell–style conservative filing a complaint against a gay bookstore for selling sexually explicit materials showing men with other men in "degrading" or "submissive" or "objectified" postures—all in the name of protecting women.

And most ironically, while the ordinances would do nothing to improve the material conditions of most women's lives, their high visibility might well divert energy from the drive to enact other, less popular laws that would genuinely empower women—comparable worth legislation, for example, or affirmative action requirements or fairer property and support principles in divorce laws.

Other provisions of the ordinances concern coercive behavior: physical assault which is imitative of pornographic images, coercion into pornographic performance and forcing pornography on others. On close examination, however, even most of these provisions are problematic.

Existing law already penalizes physical assault, including when it is associated with pornography. Defenders of the laws often cite the example of models who have been raped or otherwise harmed while in the process of making pornographic images. But victims of this type of attack can already sue or prosecute those responsible. (Linda Marchiano, the actress who appeared in the film *Deep Throat,* has not recovered damages for the physical assaults she describes in her book *Ordeal* because the events happened several years before she decided to try to file a suit. A lawsuit was thus precluded by the statute of limitations.) Indeed, the ordinances do not cover assault or other harm incurred while producing pornography, presumably because other laws already achieve that end.

The ordinances do penalize coercing, intimidating or fraudulently inducing anyone into performing for pornography. Although existing U.S. law already provides remedies for fraud or contracts of duress, this section of the ordinance seeks to facilitate recovery of damages by, for example, pornography models who might otherwise encounter substantial prejudice against their claims. Supporters of this section have suggested that it is comparable to the Supreme Court's ban on child pornography. The analogy has been stretched to the point where the City of Indianapolis brief argued that women, like children, need "special protection." "Children are incapable of consenting to

engage in pornographic conduct, even absent physical coercion and therefore require special protection," the brief stated. "By the same token, the physical and psychological well-being of women ought to be afforded comparable protection, for the coercive environment in which most pornographic models work vitiates any notion that they consent or 'choose' to perform in pornography."

The reality of women's lives is far more complicated. Women do not become pornography models because society is egalitarian and they exercise a "free choice," but neither do they "choose" this work because they have lost all power for deliberate, volitional behavior. Modeling or acting for pornography, like prostitution, can be a means of survival for those with limited options. For some women, at some points in their lives, it is a rational economic decision. Not every woman regrets having made it, although no woman should have to settle for it. The fight should be to expand the options and to insure job safety for women who do become porn models. By contrast, the impact of the ordinance as a whole would be either to eliminate jobs or drive the pornography industry further underground.

One of the vaguest provisions in the ordinance prohibits "forcing" pornography on a person. "Forcing" is not defined in the law, and one is left to speculate whether it means forced to respond to pornography, forced to read it or forced to glance at it before turning away. Also unclear is whether the perpetrator must in fact have some superior power over the person being forced—that is, is there a meaningful threat that makes the concept of force real.

Again, widely varying situations are muddled and a consideration of context is absent. "Forcing" pornography on a person "in any public space" is treated identically to using it as a method of sexual harassment in the workplace. The scope of "forcing" could include walking past a newsstand or browsing in a bookstore that had pornography on display. The force involved in such a situation seems mild when compared, for example, to the incessant sexist advertising on television.

The concept behind the "forcing" provision is appropriate, however, in the case of workplace harassment. A worker should not have to endure, especially on pain of losing her job, harassment based on sex, race, religion, nationality or any other factor. But this general policy was established by the U.S. courts as part of the guarantees of Title VII of the 1964 Civil Rights Act. Pornography used as a means of harassing women workers is already legally actionable, just as harassment by racial slurs is actionable. Any literature endorsing the oppression of women—whether pornography or the Bible—could be employed as a harassment device to impede a woman's access to a job, or to education, public accommodations or other social benefits. It is the usage of pornography in this situation, not the image itself, that is discriminatory. Appropriately, this section of the ordinances provides that only perpetrators of the forcing, not makers and distributors of the images, could be held liable.

Forcing of pornography on a person is also specifically forbidden "in the home." In her testimony before the Indianapolis City Council, Catharine MacKinnon referred to the problem of pornography being "forced on wives in preparation for later sexual scenes." Since only the person who forces the pornography on another can be sued, this provision becomes a kind of protection against domestic harassment. It would allow wives to sue husbands for court orders or damages for some usages of pornography. Although a fascinating attempt to subvert male power in the domestic realm, it nonetheless has problems. "Forcing" is not an easy concept to define in this context. It is hard to know what degree of intrusion would amount to forcing images onto a person who shares the same private space.

More important, the focus on pornography seems a displacement of the more fundamental issues involved in the conflicts that occur between husbands and wives or lovers over sex. Some men may invoke images that reflect their greater power to pressure women into performing the supposedly traditional role of acceding to male desires. Pornography may facilitate or enhance this dynamic of male dominance, but it is hardly the causative agent. Nor would removing the pornography do much to solve the problem. If the man invokes instead his friends' stories about sexual encounters or his experiences with other women, is the resulting interaction with his wife substantially different? Focusing on the pornography rather than on the relationship and its social context may serve only to channel heterosexual women's recognition of their own intimate oppression toward a movement hailed by the far right as being antiperversion rather than toward a feminist analysis of sexual politics.

The last of the sections that deals with actual coercive conduct is one that attempts to deal with the assault, physical injury or attack of any person in a way that is directly caused by specific pornography. The ordinances would allow a lawsuit against the makers and distributors of pornographic materials that were imitated by an attacker—the only provision of the ordinance that requires proof of causation. Presenting such proof would be extremely difficult. If the viewer's wilful decision to imitate the image were found to be an intervening, superceding cause of the harm, the plaintiff would not recover damages.

The policy issues here are no different from those concerning violent media images that are nonsexual: Is showing an image sufficient to cause an act of violence? Even if an image could be found to cause a viewer's behavior, was that behavior reasonably foreseeable? So far, those who have produced violent films have not been found blameworthy when third persons acted out the violence depicted. If this were to change, it would mean, for example, that the producer of the TV movie *The Burning Bed,* which told the true story of a battered wife who set fire to her sleeping husband, could be sued if a woman who saw the film killed her husband in a similar way. The result, of course, would be the end of films depicting real violence in the lives of women.

The ordinances' supporters offer no justification for singling out sexual assault from other kinds of violence. Certainly the experience of sexual assault is not always worse than that of being shot or stabbed or suffering other kinds of nonsexual assault. Nor is sexual assault the only form of violence that is fueled by sexism. If there were evidence that sexual images are more likely to be imitated, there might be some justification for treating them differently. But there is no support for this contention.

These laws, which would increase the state's regulation of sexual images, present many dangers for women. Although the ordinances draw much of their feminist support from women's anger at the market for images of sexual violence, they are aimed not at violence, but at sexual explicitness. Far-right elements recognize the possibility of using the full potential of the ordinances to enforce their sexually conservative world view, and have supported them for that reason. Feminists should therefore look carefully at the text of these "model" laws in order to understand why many believe them to be a useful tool in *anti*feminist moral crusades.

The proposed ordinances are also dangerous because they seek to embody in law an analysis of the role of sexuality and sexual images in the oppression of women with which all feminists do not agree. Underlying virtually every section of the proposed laws there is an assumption that sexuality is a realm of unremitting, unequaled victimization for women. Pornography appears as the monster that made this so. The ordinances' authors seek to impose their analysis by putting state power behind it. But this analysis is not the only feminist perspective on sexuality. Feminist theorists have also argued that the sexual terrain, however power-laden, is actively contested. Women are agents, and not merely victims, who make decisions and act on them, and who desire, seek out and enjoy sexuality.

The key provisions of the original Minneapolis ordinance are reprinted below:

(1) *Special Findings on Pornography:* The council finds that pornography is central in creating and maintaining the civil inequality of the sexes. Pornography is a systematic practice of exploitation and subordination based on sex which differentially harms women. The bigotry and contempt it promotes, with the acts of aggression it fosters, harm women's opportunities for equality of rights in employment, education, property rights, public accommodations and public services; create public harassment and private denigration; promote injury and degradation such as rape, battery and prostitution and inhibit just enforcement of laws against these acts; contribute significantly to restricting women from full exercise of citizenship and participation in public life, including in neighborhoods; damage relations between the sexes; and undermine women's equal exercise of rights to speech and action guaranteed to all citizens under the constitutions and laws of the United States and the State of Minnesota.
(gg) *Pornography.* Pornography is a form of discrimination on the basis of sex.

(1) Pornography is the sexually explicit subordination of women, graphically depicted, whether in pictures or in words, that also includes one or more of the following:

(i) women are presented as dehumanized sexual objects, things or commodities; or

(ii) women are presented as sexual objects who enjoy pain or humiliation; or

(iii) women are presented as sexual objects who experience sexual pleasure in being raped; or

(iv) women are presented as sexual objects tied up or cut up or mutilated or bruised or physically hurt; or

(v) women are presented in postures of sexual submission; [or sexual servility, including by inviting penetration;]* or

(vi) women's body parts—including but not limited to vaginas, breasts, and buttocks—are exhibited, such that women are reduced to those parts; or

(vii) women are presented as whores by nature; or

(viii) women are presented being penetrated by objects or animals; or

(ix) women are presented in scenarios of degradation, injury, abasement, torture, shown as filthy or inferior, bleeding, bruised, or hurt in a context that makes these conditions sexual.

(2) The use of men, children, or trans sexuals in the place of women . . . is pornography for purposes of . . . this statute.

(l) *Discrimination by trafficking in pornography.* The production, sale, exhibition, or distribution of pornography is discrimination against women by means of trafficking in pornography:

(1) City, state, and federally funded public libraries or private and public university and college libraries in which pornography is available for study, including on open shelves shall not be construed to be trafficking in pornography but special display presentations of pornography in said places is sex discrimination.

(2) The formation of private clubs or associations for purposes of trafficking in pornography is illegal and shall be considered a conspiracy to violate the civil rights of women.

(3) Any woman has a cause of action hereunder as a woman acting against the subordination of women. Any man or transsexual who alleges injury by pornography in the way women are injured by it shall also have a cause of action.

(m) *Coercion into pornographic performances.* Any person, including a transsexual, who is coerced, intimidated, or fraudulently induced (hereafter, "coerced") into performing for pornography shall have a cause of action against the maker(s), seller(s), exhibitor(s) or distributor(s) of said pornography for damages and for the elimination of the products of the performance(s) from the public view.

(1) *Limitation of action.* This claim shall not expire before five years have elapsed from

---

*The bracketed phrase appears in an early version of the Minneapolis ordinance but may have been removed before the bill was formally introduced in the city council. It has reappeared, however, in subsequent defenses of the ordinance by its supporters.

the date of the coerced performance(s) or from the last appearance or sale of any product of the performance(s); whichever date is later;

(2) Proof of one or more of the following facts or conditions shall not, without more, negate a finding of coercion:

(aa) that the person is a woman; or

(bb) that the person is or has been a prostitute; or

(cc) that the person has attained the age of majority; or

(dd) that the person is connected by blood or marriage to anyone involved in or related to the making of the pornography; or

(ee) that the person has previously had, or been thought to have had, sexual relations with anyone including anyone involved in or related to the making of the pornography; or

(ff) that the person has previously posed for sexually explicit pictures for or with anyone, including anyone involved in or related to the making of the pornography at issue; or

(gg) that anyone else, including a spouse or other relative, has given permission on the person's behalf; or

(hh) that the person actually consented to a use of the performance that is changed into pornography; or

(ii) that the person knew that the purpose of the acts or events in question was to make pornography; or

(jj) that the person showed no resistance or appeared to cooperate actively in the photographic sessions or in the sexual events that produced the pornography; or

(kk) that the person signed a contract, or made statements affirming a willingness to cooperate; or

(ll) that no physical force, threats, or weapons were used in the making of the pornography; or

(mm) that the person was paid or otherwise compensated.

(n) *Forcing pornography on a person.* Any woman, man, child, or transsexual who has pornography forced on them in any place of employment, in education, in a home, or in any public place has a cause of action against the perpetrator and/or institution.

(o) *Assault or physical attack due to pornography.* Any woman, man, child, or transsexual who is assaulted, physically attacked or injured in a way that is directly caused by specific pornography has a claim for damages against the perpetrator, the maker(s), distributor(s), seller(s), and/or exhibitor(s), and for an injunction against the specific pornography's further exhibition, distribution, or sale. No damages shall be assessed (A) against maker(s) for pornography made, (B) against distributor(s) for pornography distributed, (C) against seller(s) for pornography sold, or (D) against exhibitor(s) for pornography exhibited prior to the effective date of this act.

(p) *Defenses.* Where the materials which are the subject matter of a cause of action under subsections (l), (m), (n), or (o) of this section are pornography, it shall not be a defense that the defendant did not know or intend that the materials are pornography or sex discrimination.

DISCUSSION QUESTIONS

1. Why do Duggan, Hunter, and Vance believe that these laws, which would increase the state's regulation of sexual images, present many dangers to women? What are the dangers? How would Catherine MacKinnon respond to this claim? Who has the better arguments, and why?

2. According to Duggan, Hunter, and Vance, "Dworkin, MacKinnon and their feminist supporters believe that the new antipornography laws are not censorship laws." Why do Duggan, Hunter, and Vance challenge this belief? What are their arguments? How would MacKinnon respond to them? Do you believe that these antipornography laws are not censorship laws? Discuss.

3. Should feminists entrust the patriarchal state with the task of legally distinguishing between permissible and impermissible sexual images? Why or why not? Compare your arguments with those of Duggan, Hunter, and Vance.

4. Is pornography a form of sex discrimination? Present an argument, and respond to possible challenges by MacKinnon and by Duggan, Hunter, and Vance.

5. Discuss the relationship between sex discrimination and race discrimination. Is racist literature a form of race discrimination? If we agree that pornography should be prohibited, should we also agree to a parallel set of arguments that racist literature should be prohibited?

6. Is there a direct relationship between images and behavior? To what extent should our beliefs about the relationship between images and behavior be the basis for antipornography laws? To what extent should they be the basis for censorship? Should images of violence against women or scenarios of sexism in general be prohibited by law? Defend your views.

GERALD GUNTHER

Good Speech, Bad Speech—No

Gerald Gunther argues against prohibiting campus hate speech. For Gunther, campus speech codes are incompatible with the mission and meaning of universities and send the wrong message from academia to society as a whole. "University campuses," says Gunther, "should exhibit greater, not less, freedom of expression than prevails in society at large." While there is a need for universities to combat racial and other forms of discrimination, Gunther believes that campus speech codes are not the way to do it. Drawing from his own experiences as a student in Nazi Germany who was the object of anti-Semitic speech, Gunther says that his position on campus speech in no way advocates hateful ideas and is sensitive to the hurt that they can cause. Gunther says that he finds himself in the position of "denouncing the bigots' hateful ideas with all my power, yet at the same time challenging any community's attempt to suppress hateful ideas by force of law."

Gerald Gunther is William Nelson Cromwell Professor of Law (Emeritus) at Stanford University and is the author of *John Marshall's Defense of McCulloch v. Maryland* (1969), *Individual Rights in Constitutional Law* (5th ed., 1992), *Learned Hand: The Man and the Judge* (1994), and *Constitutional Law* (with Kathleen Sullivan, 13th ed., 1997), among other works.

I am deeply troubled by current efforts—however well-intentioned—to place new limits on freedom of expression at this and other campuses. Such limits are not only incompatible with the mission and meaning of a university; they also send exactly the wrong message from academia to society as a whole. University campuses should exhibit greater, not less, freedom of expression than prevails in society at large.

Proponents of new limits argue that historic First Amendment rights must be balanced against "Stanford's commitment to the diversity of ideas and persons." Clearly, there is ample room and need for vigorous University action to combat racial and other discrimination. But curbing freedom of speech is the wrong way to do so. The proper answer to bad speech is usually more and better speech—not new laws, litigation, and repression.

Lest it be thought that I am insensitive to the pain imposed by expressions of racial or religious hatred, let me say that I have suffered that pain and

Gerald Gunther, *Stanford Lawyer* 42 (spring 1990): 7, 9, 41. Reprinted with permission from the author.

empathize with others under similar verbal assault. My deep belief in the principles of the First Amendment arises from my own experiences.

I received my elementary education in a public school in a very small town in Nazi Germany. There I was subjected to vehement anti-Semitic remarks from my teacher, classmates and others—"Judensau" (Jew pig) was far from the harshest. I can assure you that they hurt. More generally, I lived in a country where ideological orthodoxy reigned and where the opportunity for dissent was severely limited.

The lesson I have drawn from my childhood in Nazi Germany and my happier adult life in this country is the need to walk the sometimes difficult path of denouncing the bigots' hateful ideas with all my power, yet at the same time challenging any community's attempt to suppress hateful ideas by force of law.

Obviously, given my own experience, I do *not* quarrel with the claim that words *can* do harm. But I firmly deny that a showing of harm suffices to deny First Amendment protection, and I insist on the elementary First Amendment principle that our Constitution usually protects even offensive, harmful expression.

That is why—at the risk of being thought callous or doctrinaire—I feel compelled to speak out against the attempt by some members of the Stanford community to enlarge the area of forbidden speech under the Fundamental Standard. Such proposals, in my view, seriously undervalue the First Amendment and far too readily endanger its precious content. Limitations on free expression beyond those established by law should be eschewed in an institution committed to diversity and the First Amendment.

In explaining my position, I will avoid extensive legal arguments. Instead, I want to speak from the heart, on the basis of my own background and of my understanding of First Amendment principles—principles supported by an even larger number of scholars and Supreme Court justices, especially since the days of the Warren Court.

Among the core principles is that any official effort to suppress expression must be viewed with the greatest skepticism and suspicion. Only in very narrow, urgent circumstances should government or similar institutions be permitted to inhibit speech. True, there are certain categories of speech that may be prohibited; but the number and scope of these categories has steadily shrunk over the last fifty years. Face-to-face insults are one such category; incitement to immediate illegal action is another. But opinions expressed in debates and arguments about a wide range of political and social issues should not be suppressed simply because of disagreement with those views, with the content of the expression.

Similarly, speech should not and cannot be banned simply because it is "offensive" to substantial parts or a majority of a community. The refusal to suppress offensive speech is one of the most difficult obligations the free speech principle imposes upon all of us; yet it is also one of the First Amendment's greatest glories—indeed it is a central test of a community's commitment to free speech.

The Supreme Court's 1989 decision to allow flag-burning as a form of political protest, in *Texas v. Johnson,* warrants careful pondering by all those who continue to advocate campus restraints on "racist speech." As Justice Brennan's majority opinion in *Johnson* reminded, "If there is a bedrock principle underlying the First Amendment, it is that the Government may not prohibit the expression of an idea simply because society finds the idea itself offensive or disagreeable." In refusing to place flag-burning outside the First Amendment, moreover, the *Johnson* majority insisted (in words especially apt for the "racist speech" debate): "The First Amendment does not guarantee that other concepts virtually sacred to our Nation as a whole—*such as the principle that discrimination on the basis of race is odious and destructive*—will go unquestioned in the marketplace of ideas. We decline, therefore, to create for the flag an exception to the joust of principles protected by the First Amendment." (Italics added.)

Campus proponents of restricting offensive speech are currently relying for justification on the Supreme Court's allegedly repeated reiteration that "fighting words" constitute an exception to the First Amendment. Such an exception has indeed been recognized in a number of lower court cases. However, there has only been *one* case in the history of the Supreme Court in which a majority of the Justices has ever found a statement to be a punishable resort to "fighting words." That was *Chaplinsky v. New Hampshire,* a nearly fifty-year-old case involving words which would very likely not be found punishable today.

More significant is what has happened in the nearly half-century since: Despite repeated appeals to the Supreme Court to recognize the applicability of the "fighting words" exception by affirming challenged convictions, the Court has in every instance refused. One must wonder about the strength of an exception that, while theoretically recognized, has for so long not been found apt in practice. (Moreover, the proposed Stanford rules are *not* limited to face-to-face insults to an addressee, and thus go well beyond the traditional, albeit fragile, "fighting words" exception.)

The phenomenon of racist and other offensive speech that Stanford now faces is not a new one in the history of the First Amendment. In recent decades, for example, well-meaning but in my view misguided majorities have sought to suppress not only racist speech but also antiwar and antidraft speech, civil rights demonstrators, the Nazis and the Ku Klux Klan, and left-wing groups.

Typically, it is people on the extremes of the political spectrum (including those who advocate overthrow of our constitutional system and those who would not protect their opponents' right to dissent were they the majority) who feel the brunt of repression and have found protection in the First Amendment; typically, it is well-meaning people in the majority who believe that their "community standards," their sensibilities, their sense of outrage, justify restraints.

Those in power in a community recurrently seek to repress speech they find abhorrent; and their efforts are understandable human impulses. Yet freedom of expression—and especially the protection of dissident speech, the most important function of the First Amendment—is an anti-majoritarian principle. Is it too much to hope that, especially on a university campus, a majority can be persuaded of the value of freedom of expression and of the resultant need to curb our impulses to repress dissident views?

The principles to which I appeal are not new. They have been expressed, for example, by the most distinguished Supreme Court justices ever since the beginning of the Court's confrontations with First Amendment issues nearly seventy years ago. These principles are reflected in the words of so imperfect a First Amendment defender as Justice Oliver Wendell Holmes: "If there is any principle of the Constitution that more imperatively calls for attachment than any other it is the principle of free thought—not free thought for those who agree with us but freedom for the thought that we hate."

This is the principle most elaborately and eloquently addressed by Justice Louis D. Brandeis, who reminded us that the First Amendment rests on a belief "in the power of reason as applied through public discussion" and therefore bars "silence coerced by law—the argument of force in its worst form."

This theme, first articulated in dissents, has repeatedly been voiced in majority opinions in more recent decades. It underlies Justice Douglas's remark in striking down a conviction under a law banning speech that "stirs the public to anger"; "[a] function of free speech [is] to invite dispute. . . . Speech is often provocative and challenging. That is why freedom of speech [is ordinarily] protected against censorship or punishment."

It underlies Justice William J. Brennan's comment about our "profound national commitment to the principle that debate on public issues should be uninhibited, robust and wide-open, and that it may well include vehement, caustic and sometimes unpleasantly sharp attacks"—a comment he followed with a reminder that constitutional protection "does not turn upon the trust, popularity or social utility of the ideas and beliefs which are offered."

These principles underlie as well the repeated insistence by Justice John Marshall Harlan, again in majority opinions, that the mere "inutility or immortality" of a message cannot justify its repression, and that the state may not punish because of "underlying content of the message." Moreover, Justice Harlan, in one of the finest First Amendment opinions on the books, noted, in words that Stanford would ignore at its peril at this time:

> The constitutional right of free expression is powerful medicine in a society as diverse and populous as ours. . . . To many, the immediate consequence of this freedom may often appear to be only verbal tumult, discord and even offensive utterance. These are, however, within established limits, in trust necessary side effects of the broader enduring values which the process of open debate permits us to achieve. That the air may at times seem filled with verbal cacophony is, in this sense, not a sign of weakness but of strength.

In this same passage, Justice Harlan warned that a power to ban speech merely because it is offensive is an "inherently boundless" notion, and added that "we think it is largely because governmental officials cannot make principled distinctions in this area that the Constitution leaves matters of taste and style so largely to the individual." (The Justice made these comments while overturning the conviction of an antiwar protestor for "offensive conduct." The defendant had worn, in a courthouse corridor, a jacket bearing the words "Fuck the Draft." It bears noting, in light of the ongoing campus debate, that Justice Harlan's majority opinion also warned that "we cannot indulge in the facile assumption that one can forbid particular words without also running the substantial risk of suppressing ideas in the process.")

I restate these principles and repeat these words for reasons going far beyond the fact that they are familiar to me as a First Amendment scholar. I believe—in my heart as well as my mind—that these principles and ideals are not only established but right. I hope that the entire Stanford community will seriously reflect upon the risks to free expression, lest we weaken hard-won liberties at Stanford and, by example, in this nation.

DISCUSSION QUESTIONS

1. Why does Gunther believe that we should not support codes to prohibit speech on campus? What is his argument? Do you agree with it?
2. How do you think that Gunther's experiences as a youth in Nazi Germany (he was the object of anti-Semitic speech) affect his position on campus speech? Do you think that your position on campus speech codes is affected by your experiences as the object of hate speech on campus or in society? Explain your view.
3. "University campuses," says Gunther, "should exhibit greater, not less, freedom of expression than prevails in society at large." What is Gunther's argument? Do you agree with him? Present an argument for your position.
4. Gunther says that "speech should not and cannot be banned because it is 'offensive' to substantial parts or a majority of a community." What is Gunther's argument? Do you agree with him? Present an argument for your position.
5. Gunther discusses the Supreme Court's 1989 decision to allow flag-burning as a form of political protest. Do you agree with the Court's decision? Why or why not?
6. What are "fighting words"? Do you think that "fighting words" should be an exception to the First Amendment? Explain your position.
7. Gunther admits that "hate speech" may do harm, yet he does not see this as grounds for regulating it. Yet other actions *are* prohibited on the grounds that they cause harm to others. What is the difference? Do you agree with Gunther's argument? Why or why not?

 A N D R E W   A L T M A N

Liberalism and Campus Hate Speech

Andrew Altman disagrees with Gerald Gunther about rules prohibiting campus hate speech. Nevertheless, Altman argues that his position is a middle ground between those who, like Gunther, reject all forms of campus hate speech regulation and those who favor broadly drawn rules prohibiting hate speech. Even though he believes that campus hate speech can cause serious psychological harm, Altman does not favor sweeping regulation. Rather, Altman argues that "some forms of hate speech inflict on their victims a certain kind of wrong, and it is on the basis of this wrong that regulation can be justified." Altman says that the "kind of wrong in question is one that is inflicted in virtue of the performance of a certain kind of speech-act characteristic of some forms of hate

Andrew Altman, *Ethics* 103 (1993): 302–317. Reprinted by permission from University of Chicago Press.

speech." This certain kind of speech act is described as one that treats one person as subordinate to another. Hate speech that treats its targets as moral subordinates is wrong according to Altman and should be restricted by campus hate speech regulations.

Andrew Altman is professor of philosophy at George Washington University. He is the author of *Critical Legal Studies: A Liberal Critique* (1990) and *Arguing About Law: An Introduction to Legal Philosophy* (1996).

In this article, I develop a liberal argument in favor of certain narrowly drawn rules prohibiting hate speech. The argument steers a middle course between those who reject all forms of campus hate-speech regulation and those who favor relatively sweeping forms of regulation. Like those who reject all regulation, I argue that rules against hate speech are not viewpoint-neutral. Like those who favor sweeping regulation, I accept the claim that hate speech can cause serious psychological harm to those at whom it is directed. However, I do not believe that such harm can justify regulation, sweeping or otherwise. Instead, I argue that some forms of hate speech inflict on their victims a certain kind of wrong, and it is on the basis of this wrong that regulation can be justified. The kind of wrong in question is one that is inflicted in virtue of the performance of a certain kind of speech-act characteristic of some forms of hate speech, and I argue that rules targeting this speech-act wrong will be relatively narrow in scope.[1]

HATE SPEECH, HARASSMENT, AND NEUTRALITY

Hate-speech regulations typically provide for disciplinary action against students for making racist, sexist, or homophobic utterances or for engaging in behavior that expresses the same kinds of discriminatory attitudes.[2] The stimulus for the regulations has been an apparent upsurge in racist, sexist, and homophobic incidents on college campuses over the past decade. The regulations that have actually been proposed or enacted vary widely in the scope of what they prohibit.

The rules at Stanford University are narrow in scope. They require that speech meet three conditions before it falls into the proscribed zone: the speaker must intend to insult or stigmatize another on the basis of certain characteristics such as race, gender, or sexual orientation; the speech must be addressed directly to those whom it is intended to stigmatize; and the speech must employ epithets or terms that similarly convey "visceral hate or contempt" for the people at whom it is directed.[3]

On the other hand, the rules of the University of Connecticut, in their original form, were relatively sweeping in scope. According to these rules, "Every member of the University is obligated to refrain from actions that intimidate, humiliate or demean persons or groups or that undermine their security or self-esteem." Explicitly mentioned as examples of proscribed speech were "making inconsiderate jokes . . . stereotyping the experiences, background, and skills of individuals, . . . imitating stereotypes in speech or mannerisms [and] attributing objections to any of the above actions to 'hypersensitivity' of the targeted individual or group."

Even the narrower forms of hate-speech regulation, such as we find at Stanford, must be distinguished from a simple prohibition of verbal harassment. As commonly understood, harassment involves a pattern of conduct that is intended to annoy a person so much as to disrupt substantially her activities. No one questions the authority of universities to enact regulations that prohibit such conduct, whether the conduct be verbal or not. There are three principal differences between hate-speech rules and rules against harassment. First, hate-speech rules do not require a pattern of conduct: a single incident is sufficient to incur liability. Second, hate-speech rules describe the offending conduct in ways that refer to the moral and political viewpoint it expresses. The conduct is not simply annoying or disturbing; it is racist, sexist, or homophobic.

The third difference is tied closely to the second and is the most important one: rules against hate speech are not viewpoint-neutral. Such rules rest on the view that racism, sexism, and homophobia are morally wrong. The liberal principle of viewpoint-neutrality holds that those in authority should not be permitted to limit speech on the ground that it expresses a viewpoint that is wrong, evil, or otherwise deficient. Yet, hate-speech rules rest on precisely such a basis. Rules against harassment, on the other hand, are not viewpoint-biased. Anyone in our society could accept the prohibition of harassment because it would not violate their normative political or moral beliefs to do so. The same cannot be said for hate-speech rules because they embody a view of race, gender, and homosexuality contrary to the normative viewpoints held by some people.

If I am correct in claiming that hate-speech regulations are not viewpoint-neutral, this will raise a strong prima facie case against them from a liberal perspective. . . .

Viewpoint-neutrality is not simply a matter of the effects of speech regulation on the liberty of various groups to express their views in the language they prefer. It is also concerned with the kinds of justification that must be offered for speech regulation. The fact is that any plausible justification of hate-speech regulation hinges on the premise that racism, sexism, and homophobia are wrong. Without that premise there would be no basis for arguing that the viewpoint-neutral proscription of verbal harassment is insufficient to protect the rights of minorities and women. The liberal who favors hate-speech regulations, no matter how narrowly drawn, must therefore be prepared to carve out an exception to the principle of viewpoint-neutrality.

THE HARMS OF HATE SPEECH

Many of the proponents of campus hate-speech regulation defend their position by arguing that hate speech causes serious harm to those who are the targets of such speech. Among the most basic of these harms are psychological ones. Even when it involves no direct threat of violence, hate speech can cause abiding feelings of fear, anxiety, and insecurity in those at whom it is targeted. As Mari Matsuda has argued, this is in part because many forms of such speech tacitly draw on a history of violence against certain groups.[4] The symbols and language of hate speech call up historical memories of violent persecution and may encourage fears of current violence. Moreover, hate speech can cause a variety of other harms, from feelings of isolation, to a loss of self-confidence, to physical problems associated with serious psychological disturbance.[5]

The question is whether or not the potential for inflicting these harms is sufficient ground for some sort of hate-speech regulation. As powerful as these appeals to the harms of hate speech are, there is a fundamental sticking point in accepting them as justification for regulation, from a liberal point of view. The basic problem is that the proposed justification sweeps too broadly for a liberal to counte-

nance it. Forms of racist, sexist, or homophobic speech that the liberal is committed to protecting may cause precisely the kinds of harm that the proposed justification invokes.

The liberal will not accept the regulation of racist, sexist, or homophobic speech couched in a scientific, religious, philosophical, or political mode of discourse. The regulation of such speech would not merely carve out a minor exception to the principle of viewpoint-neutrality but would, rather, eviscerate it in a way unacceptable to any liberal. Yet, those forms of hate speech can surely cause in minorities the harms that are invoked to justify regulation: insecurity, anxiety, isolation, loss of self-confidence, and so on. Thus, the liberal must invoke something beyond these kinds of harm in order to justify any hate-speech regulation.

Liberals who favor regulation typically add to their argument the contention that the value to society of the hate speech they would proscribe is virtually nil, while scientific, religious, philosophical, and political forms of hate speech have at least some significant value. Thus, Mary Ellen Gale says that the forms she would prohibit "neither advance knowledge, seek truth, expose government abuses, initiate dialogue, encourage participation, further tolerance of divergent views, nor enhance the victim's individual dignity or self respect."[6] As an example of such worthless hate speech, Gale cites an incident of white students writing a message on the mirror in the dorm room of blacks: "African monkeys, why don't you go back to the jungle."[7] But she would protect a great deal of racist or sexist speech, such as a meeting of neo-Nazi students at which swastikas are publicly displayed and speeches made that condemn the presence of Jews and blacks on campus.[8]

Although Gale ends up defending relatively narrow regulations, I believe liberals should be very hesitant to accept her argument for distinguishing regulable from nonregulable hate speech. One problem is that she omits from her list of the values that valuable speech serves one which liberals have long considered important, especially for speech that upsets and disturbs others. Such speech, it is argued, enables the speaker to "blow off steam" in a relatively nondestructive and nonviolent way. Calling particular blacks "African monkeys" might serve as a psychological substitute for harming them in a much more serious way, for example, by lynchings or beatings.

Gale could respond that slurring blacks might just as well serve as an encouragement and prelude to the more serious harms. But the same can be said of forms of hate speech that Gale would protect from regulation, for example, the speech at the neo-Nazi student meeting. Moreover, liberals should argue that it is the job of legal rules against assault, battery, conspiracy, rape, and so on to protect people from violence. It is, at best, highly speculative that hate speech on campus contributes to violence against minorities or women. And while the claim about blowing off steam is also a highly speculative one, the liberal tradition clearly puts a substantial burden of proof on those who would silence speech.

There is a more basic problem with any effort to draw the line between regulable and nonregulable hate speech by appealing to the value of speech. Such appeals invariably involve substantial departures from the principle of viewpoint-neutrality. There is no way to make differential judgments about the value of different types of hate speech without taking one or another moral and political viewpoint. Gale's criteria clearly illustrate this as they are heavily tilted against the values of racists and sexists, and yet she does not adequately address the question of how a liberal position can accommodate such substantial departures from viewpoint-neutrality. . . .

I do not assume that the principle of viewpoint-neutrality is an absolute or ultimate one within the liberal framework. Liberals do defend some types of speech regulation that seem to rely on viewpoint-based claims. For example, they would not reject copyright laws, even if it could be shown—as seems plausible—that those laws are biased against the views of people who regard private property as theft.[9] Moreover, the viewpoint-neutrality principle itself rests on deeper liberal concerns which it is thought to serve. Ideally, a liberal argument for the regulation of hate speech would show that regulations can be developed that accommodate these deeper concerns and that simultaneously serve important liberal values. I believe that there is such a liberal argument. In order to show this, however, it is necessary to examine a kind of wrong committed by hate speakers that is quite different from the harmful psychological effects of their speech.

SUBORDINATION AND SPEECH ACTS

Some proponents of regulation claim that there is an especially close connection between hate speech and the subordination of minorities. Thus, Charles Lawrence contends, "all racist speech constructs the social reality that constrains the liberty of non-whites because of their race."[10] Along the same lines, Mari Matsuda claims, "racist speech is particularly harmful because it is a mechanism of subordination."[11]

The position of Lawrence and Matsuda can be clarified and elaborated using J. L. Austin's distinction between perlocutionary effects and illocutionary force.[12] The perlocutionary effects of an utterance consist of its causal effects on the hearer: infuriating her, persuading her, frightening her, and so on. The illocutionary force of an utterance consists of the kind of speech act one is performing in making the utterance: advising, warning, stating, claiming, arguing, and so on. Lawrence and Matsuda are not simply suggesting that the direct perlocutionary effects of racist speech constitute harm. Nor are they simply suggesting that hate speech can persuade listeners to accept beliefs that then motivate them to commit acts of harm against racial minorities. That again is a matter of the perlocutionary effects of hate speech. Rather, I believe that they are suggesting that hate speech can inflict a wrong in virtue of its illocutionary acts, the very speech acts performed in the utterances of such speech.[13]

What exactly does this speech-act wrong amount to? My suggestion is that it is the wrong of treating a person as having inferior moral standing. In other words, hate speech involves the performance of a certain kind of illocutionary act, namely, the act of treating someone as a moral subordinate.[14]

Treating persons as moral subordinates means treating them in a way that takes their interests to be intrinsically less important, and their lives inherently less valuable, than the interests and lives of those who belong to some reference group. There are many ways of treating people as moral subordinates that are natural as opposed to conventional: the status of these acts as acts of subordination depend solely on universal principles of morality and not on the conventions of a given society. Slavery and genocide, for example, treat people as having inferior moral standing simply in virtue of the affront of such practices to universal moral principles.

Other ways of treating people as moral subordinates have both natural and conventional elements. The practice of racial segregation is an example. It is subordinating because the conditions imposed on blacks by such treatment violate moral principles but also because the act of separation is a convention for putting the minority group in its (supposedly) proper, subordinate place.

I believe that the language of racist, sexist, and homophobic slurs and epithets provides wholly conventional ways of treating people as moral subordinates. Terms such as "kike," "faggot," "spic," and "nigger" are verbal instruments of subordination. They are used not only to express hatred or contempt for people but also to "put them in their place," that is, to treat them as having inferior moral standing.

It is commonly recognized that through language we can "put people down," to use the vernacular expression. There are many different modes of putting people down: putting them down as less intelligent or less clever or less articulate or less skillful. Putting people down in these ways is not identical to treating them as moral subordinates, and the ordinary put-down does not involve regarding someone as having inferior moral standing. The put-downs that are accomplished with the slurs and epithets of hate speech are different from the ordinary verbal put-down in that respect, even though both sorts of put-down are done through language.

I have contended that the primary verbal instruments for treating people as moral subordinates are the slurs and epithets of hate speech. In order to see this more clearly, consider the difference between derisively calling someone a "faggot" and saying to that person, with equal derision, "You are contemptible for being homosexual." Both utterances can treat the homosexual as a moral subordinate, but the former accomplishes it much more powerfully than the latter. This is, I believe, because the conventional rules of language make the epithet "faggot" a term whose principal purpose is precisely to treat homosexuals as having inferior moral standing.

I do not believe that a clean and neat line can be drawn around those forms of hate speech that treat their targets as moral subordinates. Slurs and epithets are certainly used that way often, but not always, as is evidenced by the fact that sometimes victimized groups seize on the slurs that historically have subordinated them and seek to "transvalue" the terms. For example, homosexuals have done this with the term "queer," seeking to turn it into a term of pride rather than one of subordination. . . .

The absence of a neat and clean line around those forms of hate speech that subordinate through speech acts does not entail that it is futile to attempt to formulate regulations that target such hate speech. Rules and regulations rarely have an exact fit with what they aim to prevent: over- and underinclusiveness are pervasive in any system of rules that seeks to regulate conduct. The problem is to develop rules that have a reasonably good fit. Later I argue that there are hate-speech regulations that target subordinating hate speech reasonably well. But first I must argue that such speech commits a wrong that may be legitimately targeted by regulation.

SPEECH-ACT WRONG

I have argued that some forms of hate speech treat their targets as moral subordinates on account of race, gender, or sexual preference. Such treatment runs counter to the central liberal idea of persons as free and equal. To that extent, it constitutes a wrong, a speech-act wrong inflicted on those whom it addresses. However, it does not follow that it is a wrong that may be legitimately targeted by regulation. A liberal republic is not a republic of virtue in which the authorities prohibit every conceivable wrong. The liberal republic protects a substantial zone of liberty around the individual in which she is free from authoritative intrusion even to do some things that are wrong.

Yet, the wrongs of subordination based on such characteristics as race, gender, and sexual preference are not just any old wrongs. Historically, they are among the principal wrongs that have prevented— and continue to prevent—Western liberal democracies from living up to their ideals and principles. As such, these wrongs are especially appropriate targets of regulation in our liberal republic. Liberals recognize the special importance of combating such wrongs in their strong support for laws prohibiting discrimination in employment, housing, and public accommodations. And even if the regulation of speech-act subordination on campus is not regarded as mandatory for universities, it does seem that the choice of an institution to regulate that type of subordination on campus is at least justifiable within a liberal framework.

In opposition, it may be argued that subordination is a serious wrong that should be targeted but that the line should be drawn when it comes to subordination through speech. There, viewpoint-neutrality must govern. But I believe that the principle of viewpoint-neutrality must be understood as resting on deeper liberal concerns. Other things being equal, a departure from viewpoint-neutrality will be justified if it can accommodate these deeper concerns while at the same time serving the liberal principle of the equality of persons.

The concerns fall into three basic categories. First is the Millian idea that speech can promote individual development and contribute to the public political dialogue, even when it is wrong, misguided, or otherwise deficient. Second is the Madisonian reason that the authorities cannot be trusted with formulating and enforcing rules that silence certain views: they will be too tempted to abuse such rules in order to promote their own advantage or their own sectarian viewpoint.[15] Third is the idea that any departures from viewpoint-neutrality might serve as precedents that could be seized upon by would-be censors with antiliberal agendas to further their broad efforts to silence speech and expression.[16]

These concerns that underlie viewpoint-neutrality must be accommodated for hate-speech regulation to be justifiable from a liberal perspective. But that cannot be done in the abstract. It needs to be done in the context of a particular set of regulations. In the next section, I argue that there are regulations that target reasonably well those forms of hate speech that subordinate, and in the following section I argue that such regulations accommodate the concerns that underlie the liberal endorsement of the viewpoint-neutrality principle.

TARGETING SPEECH-ACT WRONG

If I am right in thinking that the slurs and epithets of hate speech are the principal instruments of the speech-act wrong of treating someone as a moral subordinate and that such a wrong is a legitimate target of regulation, then it will not be difficult to formulate rules that have a reasonably good fit with the wrong they legitimately seek to regulate. In general, what are needed are rules that prohibit speech that *(a)* employs slurs and epithets conventionally used to subordinate persons on account of their race, gender, religion, ethnicity, or sexual preference, *(b)* is addressed to particular persons, and *(c)* is expressed with the intention of degrading such persons on account of their race, gender, religion, ethnicity, or sexual preference. With some modification, this is essentially what one finds in the regulations drafted by Grey for Stanford.[17]

Restricting the prohibition to slurs and epithets addressed to specific persons will capture many speech-act wrongs of subordination. But it will not capture them all. Slurs and epithets are not necessary for such speech acts, as I conceded earlier. In addition, it may be possible to treat someone as a moral subordinate through a speech act, even though the utterance is not addressing that person. However, prohibiting more than slurs and epithets would run a high risk of serious overinclusiveness, capturing much speech that performs legitimate speech acts such as stating and arguing. And prohibiting all use of slurs and epithets, whatever the context, would mandate a degree of intrusiveness into the private lives of students that would be difficult for liberals to license.

The regulations should identify examples of the kinds of terms that count as epithets or slurs conventionally used to perform speech acts of subordination. This is required in order to give people sufficient fair warning. But because the terms of natural languages are not precise, univocal, and unchanging, it is not possible to give an exhaustive list, nor is it mandatory to try. Individuals who innocently use an epithet that conventionally subordinates can plead lack of the requisite intent. . . .

ACCOMMODATING LIBERAL CONCERNS

I have argued that regulations should target those forms of hate speech that inflict the speech-act wrong of subordination on their victims. This wrong is distinct from the psychological harm that hate speech causes. In targeting speech-act subordination, the aim of regulation is not to prohibit speech that has undesirable psychological effects on individuals but, rather, to prohibit speech that treats people as moral subordinates. To target speech that has undesirable psychological effects is invariably to target certain ideas, since it is through the communication of ideas that the psychological harm occurs. In contrast, targeting speech-act subordination does not target ideas. Any idea would be free from regulation as long as it was expressed through a speech-act other than one which subordinates: stating, arguing, claiming, defending, and so on would all be free of regulation.[18]

Because of these differences, regulations that target speech-act subordination can accommodate the liberal concerns underlying viewpoint-neutrality, while regulations that sweep more broadly cannot. Consider the important Millian idea that individual development requires that people be left free to say things that are wrong and to learn from their mistakes. Under the sort of regulation I endorse, people would be perfectly free to make racist, sexist, and homophobic assertions and arguments and to learn of the deficiencies of their views from the counterassertions and counterarguments of others. And the equally important Millian point that public dialogue gains even through the expression of false ideas is accommodated in a similar way. Whatever contribution a racist viewpoint can bring to public discussion can be made under regulations that only target speech-act subordination.

The liberal fear of trusting the authorities is somewhat more worrisome. Some liberals have argued that the authorities cannot be trusted with impartial enforcement of hate-speech regulations. Nadine Strossen, for example, claims that the hate-speech regulations at the University of Michigan have been applied in a biased manner, punishing the racist and homophobic speech of blacks but not of whites.[19] Still, it is not at all clear that the biased application of rules is any more of a problem with rules that are not viewpoint-neutral than with those that are. A neutral rule against harassment can also be enforced in a racially discriminatory manner. There is no reason to think *a priori* that narrowly drawn hate-speech rules would be any more liable to such abuse. Of course, if it did turn out that there was a pervasive problem with the biased enforcement of hate-speech rules, any sensible liberal would advocate rescinding them. But absent a good reason for thinking that this is likely to happen—not just that it could conceivably happen—the potential for abusive enforcement is no basis for rejecting the kind of regulation I have defended.

Still remaining is the problem of precedent: even narrowly drawn regulations targeting only speech-act subordination could be cited as precedent for more sweeping, antiliberal restrictions by those at other universities or in the community at large who are not committed to liberal values.[20] In response to this concern, it should be argued that narrowly drawn rules will not serve well as precedents for would-be censors with antiliberal agendas. Those who wish to silence socialists, for example, on the ground that socialism is as discredited as racism will find scant precedential support from regulations that allow the expression of racist opinions as long as they are not couched in slurs and epithets directed at specific individuals.

There may be some precedent-setting risk in such narrow regulations. Those who wish to censor the arts, for example, might draw an analogy between the epithets that narrow hate-speech regulations proscribe and the "trash" they would proscribe: both forms of expression are indecent, ugly, and repulsive to the average American, or so the argument might go.

Yet, would-be art censors already have precedents at their disposal providing much closer analogies in antiobscenity laws. Hate-speech regulations are not likely to give would-be censors of the arts any additional ammunition. To this, a liberal opponent of any hate-speech regulation might reply that there is no reason to take the risk. But the response will be that there is a good reason, namely, to prevent the wrong of speech-act subordination that is inflicted by certain forms of hate speech.

CONCLUSION

There is a defensible liberal middle ground between those who oppose all campus hate-speech regulation and those who favor the sweeping regulation of such speech. But the best defense of this middle ground requires the recognition that speech acts of subordination are at the heart of the hate-speech issue. Some forms of hate speech do wrong to people by treating them as moral subordinates. This is the wrong that can and should be the target of campus hate-speech regulations.

NOTES

1. In a discussion of the strictly legal issues surrounding the regulation of campus hate speech, the distinction between private and public universities would be an important one. The philosophical considerations on which this article focuses, however, apply both to public and private institutions.

2. In this article, I will focus on the restruction of racist (understood broadly to include anti-Semitic), sexist, and homophobic expression. In addition to such expression, regulations typically prohibit discriminatory utterances based on ethnicity, religion, and physical appearance. The argument I develop in favor of regulation applies noncontroversially to ethnicity and religion, as well as to race, gender, and sexual preference. But in a later section I argue against the prohibition of discriminatory remarks based on appearance. I understand "speech" as whatever has nonnatural meaning according to Grice's account, i.e., any utterances or actions having the following nested intentions behind them: the intention to produce a certain effect in the audience, to have the audience recognize that intention, and to have that recognition be the reason for the production of the effect. See Paul Grice, "Meaning," in his *Studies in the Way of Words* (Cambridge, MA: Harvard University Press, 1989), pp. 220–221. On this Gricean account, not only verbal utterances but also the display of symbols or flags, gestures, drawings, and more will count as speech. Although some commentators have produced counterexamples to this account of speaker's meaning, I do not believe that they pose insurmountable problems. See Robert Fogelin, "Review of Grice, *Studies in the Way of Words,*" *Journal of Philosophy,* 88 (1991): 217.

3. The full text of the Stanford regulations is in Thomas Grey, "Civil Rights v. Civil Liberties: The Case of Discriminatory Verbal Harassment," *Social Philosophy and Policy,* 8 (1991): 106–107.

4. Mari Matsuda, "Legal Storytelling: Public Response to Racist Speech: Considering the Victim's Story," *Michigan Law Review,* 87 (1989): 2329–2334, 2352.

5. See Richard Delgado, "Words That Wound: A Tort Action for Racial Insults, Epithets and Name-Calling," *Harvard Civil Rights—Civil Liberties Law Review,* 17 (1982): 137, 146.

6. Mary Ellen Gale, "Reimagining the First Amendment: Racist Speech and Equal Liberty," *St. John's Law Review,* 65 (1991): 179–180.

7. Ibid., p. 176.

8. Ibid.

9. I think liberals could argue that the deviation of copyright laws from viewpoint-neutrality is both minor and reasonable, given the extreme rarity of the antiproperty view in our society and given the great social value that such laws are seen as serving.

10. Charles Lawrence, "If He Hollers Let Him Go: Regulating Racist Speech on Campus," *Duke Law Journal* (1990): 444.

11. Matsuda, *Legal Storytelling,* p. 2357.

12. J. L. Austin, *How to Do Things with Words* (New York: Oxford University Press, 1962), pp. 98 ff. The concept of an illocutionary act has been refined and elaborated by John Searle in a series of works starting with "Austin on Locutionary and Illocutionary Acts," *Philosophical Review,* 77 (1968): 420–421. Also see his *Speech Acts* (New York: Cambridge University Press, 1969), p. 31, and *Expression and Meaning* (New York: Cambridge University Press, 1979); and John Searle and D. Vanderveken, *Foundations of Illocutionary Logic* (New York: Cambridge University Press, 1985).

13. Both Lawrence and Matsuda describe racist speech as a unique form of speech in its internal relation to subordination. See Lawrence, "If He Hollers," p. 440, n. 42; and Matsuda, *Legal Storytelling,* p. 2356. I do not think that their view is correct. Homophobic and sexist speech, e.g., can also be subordinating. In fact, Lawrence and Matsuda are applying to racist speech essentially the same idea that several feminist writers have applied to pornography. These feminists argue that pornography does not simply depict the subordination of women; it actually subordinates them. See Melinda Vadas, "A First Look at the Pornography/Civil Rights Ordinance: Could Pornography Be the Subordination of Women?" *Journal of Philosophy,* 84 (1987): 487–511.

14. Lawrence and Matsuda argue that all racist speech is subordinating. I reject their argument below and claim that the speech act of treating someone as a moral subordinate is not characteristic of all forms of racist speech. They also describe the wrong of speech-act subordination as a "harm." But the wrong does not in itself interfere with a person's formulation and pursuit of her plans and purposes. On that basis, I have been persuaded by my colleague Peter Caws that it is better to avoid the term "harm" when describing speech-act subordination. Why such speech acts are, from a liberal perspective, wrongs is explained below.

15. See Frederick Schauer, "The Second-Best First Amendment," *William and Mary Law Review,* 31 (1989): 1–2.

16. Peter Linzer, "White Liberal Looks at Racist Speech," *St. John's Law Review,* 65 (1991): 219.

17. Stanford describes the intent that is needed for a hate speaker to be liable as the intent to insult or stigmatize. My reservations about formulating the requisite intent in terms of "insult" are given below.

18. A similar argument was made by some supporters of a legal ban on desecrating the American flag through such acts as burning it: to the extent that the ban would prohibit some people from expressing their political viewpoints, it was only a minor departure from viewpoint-neutrality, since those people had an array of other ways to express their views. But the critical difference between the flag-burning case and the hate-speech case is that flag burning is not an act that treats anyone as a moral subordinate.

19. Nadine Strossen, "Regulating Racist Speech on Campus: A Modest Proposal?" *Duke Law Journal* (1990): 557–558. Eric Barendt argues that the British criminal law against racist speech "has often been used to convict militant black spokesmen" (Barendt, *Freedom of Speech* [Oxford: Clarendon Press, 1985], p. 163).

20. This concern should be distinguished from the idea that any hate-speech regulation is a step down the slippery slope to the totalitarian control of ideas. That idea is difficult to take seriously.

Even for nations that have gone much farther in regulating hate speech than anything envisioned by liberal proponents of regulation in the United States, countries such as England, France, and Germany, the idea that they are on the road to totalitarianism is preposterous.

DISCUSSION QUESTIONS

1. Should public universities and colleges have different campus speech codes than private universities and colleges? Is it important to distinguish between public and private academic institutions when discussing campus speech codes? Why or why not?
2. What does Altman mean by "speech acts of subordination"? Give an example. Why does Altman believe that such speech acts should be prohibited on campus? Do you agree with him?
3. Altman says that the "rules against hate speech are not viewpoint-neutral." What does he mean by this? What is his argument? Evaluate it.
4. What are the three basic liberal concerns for persons? Do you agree with them? Why or why not?
5. Charles Lawrence says that "all racist speech constructs the social reality that constrains the liberty of non-whites because of their race." What does this mean? Do you agree with him? Why or why not? Defend your view.
6. Suppose your college or university is planning to make a public statement regarding its policy on campus hate speech. There have been a couple of incidents of hate speech on campus, and students and faculty want to know what is going to be done and why. How would you advise your administration as to how it should deal with campus hate speech? What policy would you advise them to adopt?

 R I C H A R D   D E L G A D O   A N D   J E A N   S T E F A N C I C

Dealing with Words That Wound

Richard Delgado and Jean Stefancic argue that hate speech is the source of subordination. For Delgado and Stefancic, people who argue that hate speech is a symptom of subordination are wrong. Hate speech directed toward people of color, women, and gays and lesbians "constructs a social reality" in which these people are always at risk. The repetition of hateful words and images causes and reinforces the discrimination of people of color, women, and gays and lesbians. They also argue that the harm done by pornography is akin to the harm done through hate speech. Consequently, those interested in restricting pornography should join forces with those interested in restricting hate speech. "With the help of sympathetic scholars committed to equality and fair treatment for all, legal barriers to the regulation of hate speech and hard-core pornography will one day appear," charge Delgado and Stefancic, "anachronistic and inhumane."

Richard Delgado is Jean N. Lindsley Professor of Law at the University of Colorado, and Jean Stefancic is a research associate in law at the University of Colorado. They have coauthored a number of books including *Failed Revolutions: Social Reform and the Limits of Legal Imagination* (1994), *No Mercy: How Conservative Think Tanks and Foundations Changed America's Social Agenda* (1996), and *Must We Defend Nazis?: Hate Speech, Pornography, and the New First Amendment* (1997).

In recent years, some legal scholars and social activists have been seeking ways to combat the harm done to members of minority groups by hateful speech. Other scholars and activists have been focusing on the harm done to women by hard-core pornography. Today, the two groups of reformers are joining to formulate legal theories and approaches that draw on scholarly research concerning the way that the roles and identities of women, people of color, and gays and lesbians are constructed in society.

A conference held at the University of Chicago Law School in the spring was the first to bring together legal scholars, feminists, and community organizers to address hate speech and pornography in tandem.

It was just the beginning of the collaboration that will be needed, but it came at a critical time. A few years ago, when feminists in Indianapolis and Minneapolis succeeded in enacting antipornography ordinances (drafted by the writer-activist Andrea Dworkin and the University of Michigan law professor Catharine MacKinnon), courts and mayors struck them down. Later, two federal courts struck down hate-speech codes at the Universities of Wisconsin and Michigan.

When the United States Supreme Court handed down its decision in June 1992 in *R.A.V. v. St. Paul, Minn.*, prohibiting the city from banning cross burning, momentum slowed even further. Most cities and universities considering hate-speech codes put them on hold.

A possible turning point came in June, however, when the Supreme Court upheld enhanced sentences for hate-motivated crimes in a case known as *Wisconsin v. Mitchell.* That ruling, together with two Canadian Supreme Court decisions in 1990 and 1992 upholding prohibitions on pornography and hate crimes, suggests that narrowly drawn restraints may one day be possible in the United States. (Canada has a constitutional system much like ours and shares a similar English-common-law heritage.)

A great deal of work remains to be done, however. The judiciary remains conservative, and much of the public harbors little sympathy for feminist or minority-group causes. But the emerging cooperation between two groups of reformers who previously had worked separately is notable. Those interested in restricting pornography and hate speech often have regarded each other warily, as though gains for one group could come only at the expense of the other, or as if one group's success in pricking America's conscience might cause the public to ignore the equally pressing claims of the other.

But now both groups of scholars and activists are realizing that dealing with stigmatizing expression—words that wound or degrading depictions of women—requires a fuller understanding of how subordination occurs in the first place. Unless those in the forefront of social change and legal reform understand how and why certain words acquire the power to wound, our efforts are likely to prove unsuccessful.

We are beginning to recognize that hateful speech is not the symptom of subordination (as it is often thought to be), but its very source. When a woman, black, gay, or lesbian is unfairly refused a job, that refusal hurts both the individual and society; that is why we have civil-rights laws and affirmative action. But the reason that certain people are refused jobs—as well as why the refusal hurts them and creates more than a momentary setback—stems from a background of cultural and ethnic imagery. Repetition of certain words and images recalls and reinforces that imagery.

From an early age, all of us are exposed to a host of stereotypes, stock characters, narratives, stories, and plots in which women are ornaments and people of color are stupid, happy-go-lucky, or licentious. We are beginning to understand how society uses such images to construct a social reality in which women and blacks are always at risk, one in which each new slight or injury reverberates against a history of similar ones. After years of repetition, offenses are targeted as much at groups as at individuals. Some actions, such as burning a cross or painting a swastika on a synagogue, gain a power that most insults directed at individuals lack—the power to demoralize.

Words can create categories, expectations, and subconscious assumptions so deep-seated that only troublesome mechanisms such as affirmative action can make headway against the system of subordination that they support. Unless we name and challenge this root cause of subordination, the progress of women and minorities in gaining equal access to jobs, credit, or education will be slow and limited. Indeed, gains for one group may well come at the expense of another, particularly in hard times when sympathy and money are limited.

The emerging insight into the roots and pervasiveness of subordination through symbolic depiction provides a framework that both groups of reformers can accept wholeheartedly, one that places the highest priority on exposing the harm of injurious words and images. This task will entail defining a radically new understanding of a First Amendment that protects equality as much as it has liberty; it will entail understanding the Constitution as a document that embraces not just one value, but many. Speech has never been protected absolutely—witness the dozens of "exceptions" that we have created or tolerated when free speech conflicts with other important social values, such as national security, intellectual property, the right to privacy, and the right to protect one's reputation, to name a few.

Further, it is not necessary to hold that words are actions, as some argue, to subject them to regulation. An important social interest, comparable to the interests undergirding the doctrines of libel, defamation, intentional infliction of emotional distress, or deceptive advertising, should suffice. Equality and everyone's right to be treated as a person worthy of respect represent, we believe, a comparable interest.

Earlier scholarship has already moved in this direction. Legal theorists such as Mari Matsuda of the University of California at Los Angeles and Charles Lawrence of Stanford University have urged that hate speech that takes the form of face-to-face taunts and revilement has no place in a system of protected expression. It wounds the victim while conveying no valid information; it is less akin to a political speech than to a slap in the face. In our own previous work, we have demonstrated that invective aimed at aspects of a person's core identity can seriously wound and damage, particularly young people. Some U.S. courts already afford individuals redress—through private actions for libel, assault, and intentional infliction of emotional distress—when they experience particularly vicious racial slurs, finding that the First Amendment interest of the speaker was weak or nonexistent in comparison with the seriousness of the harm done.

The federal-court decisions concerning university speech codes indicate that such codes must be carefully tailored if they are to pass judicial muster, since they are broadly regulatory in impact, unlike the private tort actions mentioned above. Still, we do not believe that college administrators must sit idly by while many young minority students become embittered or leave the university because of repeated verbal abuse directed against their races or identities.

For example, although the Supreme Court ruled in last year's cross-burning case that regulations aimed at curbing insult and invective must be race-neutral—that is, apply equally to all—the Court's decision in June in *Wisconsin v. Mitchell* upheld statutes that impose extra penalties if conduct that is otherwise prohibited is directed at victims because of their race or on some other discriminatory basis.

As a short-term solution, then, it would seem that a university's conduct code could be amended to include two separate provisions. One could penalize severe, disruptive, face-to-face insults (for example, a professor saying to a student in the professor's office, "You incompetent, illiterate fool"). A separate provision could stipulate that punishment for a campus offense would be increased for any behavior already prohibited in the code if that behavior was motivated by bias. The offenses designated in the first provision would be race-neutral (that is the lesson we should draw from the cross-burning case). Punishment could be tailored to motivation and seriousness (the lesson of the recent hate-crimes case). The combination of the two provisions might provide campus administrators with the tool that they need to deal with insults and hate speech, while remaining within Constitutional bounds.

Longer-term solutions and broader remedies will entail at least the following tasks:

- Lawyers and social scientists must be prepared to demonstrate through research the harm done by racial insults and pornography and to show how the law's conception of harm can be reasonably expanded to include notions of damaged identity.

- Lawyers and legal scholars must be ready to draw courts' attention to the experience of many other Western industrialized countries in successfully regulating pornography and hate speech. A growing literature on this topic is available.

- Scholars also need to find ways to demonstrate how "more speech"—the usual argument used by those opposed to curbing racist speech—is not a viable solution, and how talking back to the aggressor in most cases is either dangerous or futile.

- University officials must be prepared to show how institutions' interests are implicated when members of minority groups on campus must live with the fear of insult or assault, leading to demoralization and heavy dropout rates.
- We must drive home to all participants in the debate about hate speech the idea that speech without equality is a hollow illusion, and that true dialogue presupposes something like rough equality between the speakers—dialogue that cannot take place unless the most vicious forms of hate speech are curbed.

Above all, we need to explain how the old adage about "sticks and stones" may be misleading in one highly significant respect: The broken bone will heal. But the harm of being identified as a "nigger" or "fag" or "broad" will not fade—at least not without a concerted effort to challenge those pernicious categories. With the help of sympathetic scholars committed to equality and fair treatment for all, legal barriers to the regulation of hate speech and hard-core pornography will one day appear as anachronistic and inhumane as the 1896 doctrine upheld by the Supreme Court in *Plessy v. Ferguson*—that facilities could be separate but equal.

DISCUSSION QUESTIONS

1. Delgado and Stefancic claim that it is not necessary to hold that words are actions to subject them to regulation. Why do they believe this? Do you believe this? Go back to Andrew Altman's article, and determine whether he treats words as actions in his defense of campus speech codes.
2. Delgado and Stefancic say that the harm done by pornography is akin to the harm done through hate speech. Do you agree with them? Should the groups opposed to pornography and to hate speech join forces? Why might someone think that they shouldn't? Why do you think the two groups have often avoided joining forces?
3. What are the major barriers to the regulation of hate speech? Do you think that they should be overcome? What do Delgado and Stefancic think? Compare your views.
4. Compare and contrast the approaches to campus speech codes presented by Gerald Gunther, Altman, and Delgado and Stefancic. Who presents the better arguments, and why?
5. Delgado and Stefancic claim that hate speech directed toward people of color, women, and gays and lesbians is the *source* of discrimination against them, rather than a *symptom* of discrimination against them. What is their argument? Is it a good one? Why or why not? Do you think it is possible to either prove or disprove this claim? How would you do it? Discuss.

U.S. DISTRICT COURT

Doe v. University of Michigan

In *Doe v. University of Michigan* (1989), the court found the university's hate speech and harassment policy to be unconstitutional because it was overbroad and vague. The speech code at the University of Michigan prohibited individuals, under penalty of sanctions, from "stigmatizing or victimizing" individuals or groups on the basis of race, ethnicity, religion, sex, sexual orientation, creed, national origin, ancestry, age, marital status, handicap, or Vietnam-era veteran status. Depending on the intent of the accused student, the effect of the conduct, and the accused student's status as a repeat offender, one or more of the following sanctions could be imposed: formal reprimand, community service, class attendance, restitution, removal from student housing, suspension, suspension from specific courses and activities, or expulsion. Doe, a psychology graduate student who wished his legal name to be withheld, brought the suit against the university because he believed that the policy might sanction classroom discussions of some of his work in biopsychology. Doe feared that certain controversial theories positing biologically based differences between the sexes and races that were part of his work might be perceived as sexist and racist by some students, and he feared that discussion of these theories in the classroom might be sanctionable under the policy.

---

1. INTRODUCTION

It is an unfortunate fact of our constitutional system that the ideals of freedom and equality are often in conflict. The difficult and sometimes painful task of our political and legal institutions is to mediate the appropriate balance between these two competing values. Recently, the University of Michigan at Ann Arbor (the University), a state-chartered university, . . . adopted a Policy . . . in an attempt to curb what the University's governing Board of Regents (Regents) viewed as a rising tide of racial intolerance and harassment on campus. The Policy prohibited individuals, under the penalty of sanctions, from "stigmatizing or victimizing" individuals or groups on the basis of race, ethnicity, religion, sex, sexual orientation, creed, national origin, ancestry, age, marital status, handicap or Vietnam-era veteran status. . . .

2. FACTS GENERALLY

According to the University, in the last three years incidents of racism and racial harassment appeared to become increasingly frequent at the University. For example, on January 27, 1987, unknown persons distributed a flier declaring "open season" on blacks, which it referred to as "saucer lips, porch monkeys, and jigaboos." On February 4, 1987, a student disc jockey at an on-campus radio station allowed racist jokes to be broadcast. At a demonstration protesting these incidents, a Ku Klux Klan uniform was displayed from a dormitory window. . . .

On December 14, 1987, the Acting President circulated a confidential memorandum to the University's executive officers detailing a proposal for an anti-discrimination disciplinary policy. The proposed policy prohibited "[h]arassment of anyone through word or deed or any other behavior which discriminates on the basis of inappropriate criteria." The Acting President recognized at the time that the proposed policy would engender serious First Amendment problems, but reasoned that

> just as an individual cannot shout "Fire!" in a crowded theater and then claim immunity from prosecution for causing a riot on the basis of exercising his rights of free speech, so a great many American universities have taken the position that students at a university cannot by speaking or writing discriminatory remarks which seriously offend many individuals beyond the immediate victim, and which, therefore detract from the necessary educational climate of a campus, claim immunity from a campus disciplinary proceeding. I believe that position to be valid.

The other "American universities" to which the President referred . . . were not identified at any time. Nor was any document presented to the Court in any form which "valid[ates]" this "position." . . .

3. THE UNIVERSITY OF MICHIGAN POLICY ON DISCRIMINATION AND DISCRIMINATORY HARASSMENT

A. The Terms of the Policy

The Policy established a three-tiered system whereby the degree of regulation was dependent on the location of the conduct at issue. The broadest range of speech and dialogue was "tolerated" in variously described public parts of the campus. Only an act of physical violence or destruction of property was considered sanctionable in these settings. Publications sponsored by the University such as the *Michigan Daily* and the *Michigan Review* were not subject to regulation. The conduct of students living in University housing is primarily governed by the standard provisions of individual leases, however the Policy appeared to apply in this setting as well. The Policy by its terms applied specifically to "[e]ducational and academic centers, such as classroom buildings, libraries, research laboratories, recreation and study centers[.]" In these areas, persons were subject to discipline for:

1. Any behavior, verbal or physical, that stigmatizes or victimizes an individual on the basis of race, ethnicity, religion, sex, sexual orientation, creed, national origin, ancestry, age, marital status, handicap or Vietnam-era veteran status, and that
   a. Involves an express or implied threat to an individual's academic efforts, employment, participation in University sponsored extra-curricular activities or personal safety; or
   b. Has the purpose or reasonably foreseeable effect of interfering with an individual's academic efforts, employment, participation in University sponsored extra-curricular activities or personal safety; or
   c. Creates an intimidating, hostile, or demeaning environment for educational pursuits, employment or participation in University sponsored extra-curricular activities.
2. Sexual advances, requests for sexual favors, and verbal or physical conduct that stigmatizes or victimizes an individual on the basis of sex or sexual orientation where such behavior:
   a. Involves an express or implied threat to an individual's academic efforts, employment, participation in University sponsored extra-curricular activities or personal safety; or
   b. Has the purpose or reasonably foreseeable effect of interfering with an individual's academic efforts, employment, participation in University sponsored extra-curricular activities or personal safety; or

   c. Creates an intimidating, hostile, or demeaning environment for educational pursuits, employment or participation in University sponsored extra-curricular activities. . . .

B. Hearing Procedures

Any member of the University community could initiate the process leading to sanctions by either filing a formal complaint with an appropriate University office or by seeking informal counseling with described University officials and support centers. . . .

C. Sanctions

The Policy provided for progressive discipline based on the severity of the violation. It stated that the University encouraged hearing panels to impose sanctions that include an educational element in order to sensitize the perpetrator to the harmfulness of his or her conduct. The Policy provided, however, that compulsory class attendance should not be imposed "in an attempt to change deeply held religious or moral convictions." Depending on the intent of the accused student, the effect of the conduct, and whether the accused student is a repeat offender, one or more of the following sanctions may be imposed: (1) formal reprimand; (2) community service; (3) class attendance; (4) restitution; (5) removal from University housing; (6) suspension from specific courses and activities; (7) suspension; (8) expulsion. The sanctions of suspension and expulsion could only be imposed for violent or dangerous acts, repeated offenses, or a willful failure to comply with a lesser sanction. The University President could set aside or lessen any sanction.

D. Interpretive Guide

Shortly after the promulgation of the policy in the fall of 1988, the University Office of Affirmative Action issued an interpretive guide (Guide) entitled *What Students Should Know About Discrimination and Discriminatory Harassment by Students in the University Environment*. The Guide purported to be an authoritative interpretation of the Policy and provided examples of sanctionable conduct. These included:

A flyer containing racist threats distributed in a residence hall.

Racist graffiti written on the door of an Asian student's study carrel.

A male student makes remarks in class like "Women just aren't as good in this field as men," thus creating a hostile learning atmosphere for female classmates.

Students in a residence hall have a floor-party and invite everyone on their floor except one person because they think she might be a lesbian.

A black student is confronted and racially insulted by two white students in a cafeteria.

Male students leave pornographic pictures and jokes on the desk of a female graduate student.

Two men demand that their roommate in the residence hall move out and be tested for AIDS.

In addition, the Guide contained a separate section entitled "You are a harasser when . . ." which contains the following examples of discriminatory conduct:

You exclude someone from a study group because that person is of a different race, sex, or ethnic origin than you are.

You tell jokes about gay men and lesbians.

Your student organization sponsors entertainment that includes a comedian who slurs Hispanics.

You display a confederate flag on the door of your room in the residence hall.

You laugh at a joke about someone in your class who stutters.

You make obscene telephone calls or send racist notes or computer messages.

You comment in a derogatory way about a particular person or group's physical appearance or sexual orientation, or their cultural origins, or religious beliefs.

It is not clear whether each of these actions would subject a student to sanctions, although the title of the section suggests that they would. . . .

4. STANDING

Doe is a psychology graduate student. His specialty is the field of biopsychology, which he describes as the interdisciplinary study of the biological bases of individual differences in personality traits and mental abilities. Doe said that certain controversial theories positing biologically-based differences between sexes and races might be perceived as "sexist" and "racist" by some students, and he feared that discussion of such theories might be sanctionable under the Policy. He asserted that his right to freely and openly discuss these theories was impermissibly chilled, and he requested that the Policy be declared unconstitutional and enjoined on the grounds of vagueness and overbreadth. . . .

. . . The Policy prohibited conduct which "stigmatizes or victimizes" students on the basis of "race, ethnicity, religion, sex, sexual orientation" and other invidious factors. However, the terms "stigmatize" and "victimize" are not self defining. These words can only be understood with reference to some exogenous value system. What one individual might find victimizing or stigmatizing, another individual might not.

. . . The record clearly shows that there existed a realistic and credible threat that Doe could be sanctioned were he to discuss certain biopsychological theories.

. . . [T]he University attorney who researched the law and assisted in the drafting of the Policy, wrote a memorandum in which he conceded that merely offensive speech was constitutionally protected, but declared that

[w]e cannot be frustrated by the reluctance of the courts and the common law to recognize the personal damage that is caused by discriminatory speech, nor should our policy attempt to conform to traditional methods of identifying harmful speech. Rather the University should identify and prohibit that speech that causes damage to individuals within the community.

The record before the Court thus indicated that the drafters of the policy intended that speech need only be offensive to be sanctionable.

The Guide also suggested that the kinds of ideas Doe wished to discuss would be sanctionable. The Guide was the University's authoritative interpretation of the Policy. It explicitly stated that an example of sanctionable conduct would include:

A male student makes remarks in class like "Women just aren't as good in this field as men," thus creating a hostile learning atmosphere for female classmates.

Doe said in an affidavit that he would like to discuss questions relating to sex and race differences in his capacity as a teaching assistant in Psychology 430, Comparative Animal Behavior. He went on to say:

> An appropriate topic for discussion in the discussion groups is sexual differences between male and female mammals, including humans. [One] . . . hypothesis regarding sex differences in mental abilities is that men as a group do better than women in some spatially related mental tasks partly because of a biological difference. This may partly explain, for example, why many more men than women choose to enter the engineering profession.

Doe also said that some students and teachers regarded such theories as "sexist" and he feared that he might be charged with a violation of the Policy if he were to discuss them. In light of the statements in the Guide, such fears could not be dismissed as speculative and conjectural. The ideas discussed in Doe's field of study bear sufficient similarity to ideas denounced as "harassing" in the Guide to constitute a realistic and specific threat of prosecution.

. . . A review of the University's discriminatory harassment complaint files suggested that on at least three separate occasions, students were disciplined or threatened with discipline for comments made in a classroom setting. These are . . . discussed *infra.* At least one student was subject to a formal hearing because he stated in the context of a social work research class that he believed that homosexuality was a disease that could be psychologically treated. As will be discussed below, the Policy was enforced so broadly and indiscriminately, that plaintiff's fears of prosecution were entirely reasonable. Accordingly, the Court found that Doe had standing to challenge the policy.

5. VAGUENESS AND OVERBREADTH

. . . While the University's power to regulate so-called pure speech is . . . limited, . . . certain categories can be generally described as unprotected by the First Amendment. It is clear that so-called "fighting words" are not entitled to First Amendment protection. *Chaplinsky v. New Hampshire*, 315 U.S. 568 (1942). These would include "the lewd and obscene, the profane, the libelous, and the insulting or 'fighting words'—those which by their very utterance inflict injury or tend to incite an immediate breach of

the peace." . . . Under certain circumstances racial and ethnic epithets, slurs, and insults might fall within this description and could constitutionally be prohibited by the University. In addition, such speech may also be sufficient to state a claim for common law intentional infliction of emotional distress. Credible threats of violence or property damage made with the specific intent to harass or intimidate the victim because of his race, sex, religion, or national origin is punishable both criminally and civilly under state law. Similarly, speech which has the effect of inciting imminent lawless action and which is likely to incite such action may also be lawfully punished. . . .

What the University could not do, however, was establish an antidiscrimination policy which had the effect of prohibiting certain speech because it disagreed with ideas or messages sought to be conveyed. *Texas v. Johnson* [holding that laws punishing flag burning are unconstitutional]. As the Supreme Court stated in *West Virginia State Board of Education v. Barnette*, 319 U.S. 624 (1943):

> If there is any star fixed in our constitutional constellation, it is that no official, high or petty, can prescribe what shall be orthodox in politics, nationalism, religion, or other matters of opinion or force citizens to confess by word or act their faith therein.

Nor could the University proscribe speech simply because it was found to be offensive, even gravely so, by large numbers of people. *Texas v. Johnson, supra.* . . . These principles acquire a special significance in the university setting, where the free and unfettered interplay of competing views is essential to the institution's educational mission. . . .

Overbreadth

Doe claimed that the Policy was invalid because it was facially overbroad. It is fundamental that statutes regulating First Amendment activities must be narrowly drawn to address only the specific evil at hand. . . .

The Supreme Court has consistently held that statutes punishing speech or conduct solely on the grounds that they are unseemly or offensive are unconstitutionally overbroad. In *Houston v. Hill*, the Supreme Court struck down a City of Houston ordinance which provided that "[i]t shall be unlawful for any person to assault or strike or in any manner oppose, molest, and abuse or interrupt any policeman in the execution of his duty." . . . In *Paplish v. University of Missouri,* (1973), the Supreme Court ordered the reinstatement of a university student expelled for distributing an underground newspaper sporting the headline "Motherfucker acquitted" on the grounds that "the mere dissemination of ideas—no matter how offensive to good taste—on a state university campus may not be shut off in the name alone of conventions of decency." . . . Although the Supreme Court acknowledged that reasonable restrictions on the time, place, and manner of distribution might have been permissible, "the opinions below show clearly that [plaintiff] was dismissed because of the disapproved *content* of the newspaper." *Id.* Most recently, in *Texas v. Johnson, supra,* the Supreme Court invalidated a Texas statute prohibiting burning of the American flag on the grounds that there was no showing that the prohibited conduct was likely to incite a breach of the peace. These cases stand generally for the proposition that the state may not prohibit broad classes of speech, some of which may indeed be legitimately regulable, if in so doing a substantial amount of constitutionally protected conduct is also prohibited. This was the fundamental infirmity of the Policy. . . .

Vagueness

Doe also urges that the Policy be struck down on the grounds that it is impermissibly vague. A statute is unconstitutionally vague when "men of common intelligence must necessarily guess at its meaning." A statute must give adequate warning of the conduct which is to be prohibited and must set out explicit standards for those who apply it. . . .

Looking at the plain language of the Policy, it was simply impossible to discern any limitation on its scope or any conceptual distinction between protected and unprotected conduct. . . . The operative words in the cause section required that language must "stigmatize" or "victimize" an individual. However, both of these terms are general and elude precise definition. Moreover, it is clear that the fact that a statement may victimize or stigmatize an individual does not, in and of itself, strip it of protection under the accepted First Amendment tests. . . .

. . . Students of common understanding were necessarily forced to guess at whether a comment about a controversial issue would later be found to be sanctionable under the Policy. The terms of the Policy were so vague that its enforcement would violate the due process clause.

DISCUSSION QUESTIONS

1. The University of Michigan's hate speech and harassment policy prohibited individuals from "stigmatizing or victimizing" on the basis of race, ethnicity, religion, sex, sexual orientation, creed, national origin, ancestry, age, marital status, handicap, or Vietnam-era veteran status. What does it mean to "stigmatize or victimize" someone? Should universities protect students against "stigmatization" and "victimization"? Why or why not?

2. Why did Doe believe that the University of Michigan hate speech and harassment policy was "overbroad"? Do you agree with him and the court that it was overbroad? Explain.

3. Why did Doe believe that the University of Michigan hate speech and harassment policy was "vague"? Do you agree with him and the court that it was vague? Explain.

4. Do you think that "overbroad" and "vague" are sufficient grounds for dismissing the University of Michigan's hate speech and harassment policy? Why or why not?

5. How would Gerald Gunther, Andrew Altman, and Richard Delgado and Jean Stefancic respond to the court's ruling in *Doe v. University of Michigan?* What objections might they raise to the ruling? What praise might they give to the ruling?

6. *Doe v. University of Michigan* raises the question as to what can be presented in the classroom without sanction. Should the classroom be a place where any (moral) theory can be presented and discussed, or are there some things that simply should not be discussed? Are there some things that you have read in this book or that have come up in classroom discussion that you think should not have been read or discussed without sanction? Provide an argument for your position.

MEDIA GALLERY

 THE PEOPLE OF THE STATE OF CALIFORNIA V. LAWRENCE FERLINGHETTI

Case summary: On March 25, 1957, Chester MacPhee, then U.S. collector of customs for the Port of San Francisco, impounded a shipment of 125 copies of Allen Ginsberg's book *Howl and Other Poems* on the San Francisco docks. The books were on their way to Lawrence Ferlinghetti's City Lights bookstore from Villier Publishers in England. "The words and the sense of the writing is obscene," MacPhee declared, adding, "you wouldn't want your children to come across it." MacPhee's attempt to ban the book immediately created a demand for it. Foreseeing potential obscenity issues, Ferlinghetti had submitted the original manuscript to the American Civil Liberties Union before sending it to the printer. The ACLU advised Ferlinghetti that, as far as they were concerned, it was not an obscene document and they would probably defend him should he be prosecuted. The ACLU also informed MacPhee that they disagreed with him, as did the U.S. attorney in San Francisco, who refused to pursue legal action. When the attorney general in Washington, DC, advised MacPhee to release the books, he did so. However, a week later, Ferlinghetti and bookstore manager Shigeyoshi Murao were arrested by an officer from the city's Juvenile Bureau. The commander of the Juvenile Bureau, Captain William A. Hanrahan, signed complaints against Ferlinghetti and Murao, charging them with publishing or selling obscene literature in violation of the California Penal Code. The trial was held before municipal court Judge Clayton Horn. For the defense, testimony came from nine expert witnesses, including writer Kenneth Rexroth, University of California faculty members Mark Schorer and Leo Lowenthal, San Francisco State College professors Walter Van Tilburg Clark and Herbert Blau, and *San Francisco Examiner* book editor Luther Nichols, all of whom reiterated that *Howl* was a serious work of art. In addition to the expert witnesses, Ferlinghetti had expert legal help, including ACLU attorney Albert Pendich and trial lawyer J. W. Ehrlich. Ginsberg was traveling in Europe during the trial and never took the stand. Neither did Ferlinghetti.

On October 3, 1957, Judge Horn found Ferlinghetti and Murao not guilty and ruled that the book was not obscene. *"Honi soit qui mal y pense"* (Evil to him who thinks evil), wrote Horn. "I do not believe that *Howl* is without even 'the slightest redeeming social importance.' The first part of *Howl* presents a picture of a nightmare world; the second part is an indictment of those elements in modern society destructive of the best qualities of human nature; such elements are predominantly identified as materialism, conformity, and mechanization leading toward war. The third part presents a picture of an individual who is a specific representation of what the author conceives as a general condition . . . 'Footnote to Howl' seems to be a declamation that everything in the world is holy, including parts of the body by name. It ends in a plea for holy living." The judge also set forth certain rules for the guidance of authorities in the future, establishing the legal precedent of "redeeming social importance" that in the next decade would allow Grove Press to publish D. H. Lawrence's *Lady Chatterley's Lover* and Henry Miller's *Tropic of Cancer,* among other books:

1. If the material has the slightest redeeming social importance it is not obscene because it is protected by the First and Fourteenth Amendments of the United States Constitution, and the California Constitution.
2. If it does not have the slightest redeeming social importance it may be obscene.
3. The test of obscenity in California is that the material must have a tendency to deprave or corrupt readers by exciting lascivious thoughts or arousing lustful desire to the point that it presents a clear and present danger of inciting to anti-social or immoral action.

4. The book or material must be judged as a whole by its effect on the *average adult* in the community.
5. If the material is objectionable only because of coarse and vulgar language which is not erotic or aphrodisiac in character it is not obscene.
6. Scienter must be proved.
7. Book reviews may be received in evidence if properly authenticated.
8. Evidence of expert witnesses in the literary field is proper.
9. Comparison of the material with other similar material previously adjudicated is proper.
10. The people owe a duty to themselves and to each other to preserve and protect their constitutional freedoms from any encroachment by government unless it appears that the allowable limits of such protection have been breached, and then to take only such action as will heal the breach.
11. I agree with Mr. Justice Douglas: I have the same confidence in the ability of our people to reject noxious literature as I have in their capacity to sort out the true from the false in theology, economics, politics, or any other field.
12. In considering material claimed to be obscene it is well to remember the motto: "*Honi soit qui mal y pense.*" (Evil to him who thinks evil.)

Commenting on the "obscene" language of *Howl,* Horn said, "The author has used these words because he believed that his portrayal required them. The people state that it is not necessary to use such words and that others would be more palatable to good taste. The answer is that life is not encased in one formula whereby everyone acts the same or conforms to a particular pattern. Would there be any freedom of speech or press if one must reduce his vocabulary to vapid innocuous euphemism? An author should be real in treating his subject and be allowed to express his thoughts and ideas in his own words."

1. Do you agree with Judge Horn that the "social importance" of a work is sufficient grounds not to deem it obscene?
2. Judge Horn wrote that "the publishing of 'smut' or 'hard core pornography' is without any social importance, and obscene by present-day standards, and should be punished for the good of the community." Comment on this statement.
3. Judge Horn set forth certain rules for the guidance of authorities in the future regarding obscenity. Do you agree with them? Would you add or delete any? Why?
4. MacPhee declared that he wouldn't want his children to come across *Howl and Other Poems.* Would you let your children read books such as D. H. Lawrence's *Lady Chatterley's Lover,* Henry Miller's *Tropic of Cancer,* or Allen Ginsberg's *Howl and Other Poems*? Why or why not? Furthermore, is whether you would let your children read a book a good way to determine whether it is obscene? Why or why not?
5. Many publishers are now putting parts of their novels and poems on the Web. Should there be restrictions on what can be excerpted from novels and poems onto the Web? What if the passages in question were those considered by some to be "coarse and vulgar"? Propose a set of guidelines, and defend them.
6. The controversy over *Howl and Other Poems* occurred in 1957. If the poem were published today, do you think that the same type of controversy would occur? Why or why not?

 BLACKBOARD JUNGLE
(USA, 1955) 1 hour 50 minutes
Directed by Richard Brooks

Film summary: In this film, Richard Dadier (Glenn Ford) takes a job in an inner-city high school. He endures physical and verbal abuse from his students and threats to his pregnant wife. In one key scene, Dadier brings a voice machine to his class and asks the students to speak into it. Initially, Dadier refuses to let Pete Morales (Rafael Campos), a Puerto Rican student, speak into the machine, but the other students insist that Morales be allowed to speak. After Morales is finished speaking, the students accuse Dadier of not calling on Morales because he does not like him. One student says, "Morales is a spic—maybe you [Dadier] don't like spics!" The students begin to use some other racial epithets, and Dadier tells them to stop. When one student says that he was only kidding when he used the racial epithet, Dadier says, "That's how things always get started, like a street fight, someone pushes someone in fun, and soon a fight breaks out." Dadier explains that using a racial epithet is just like the push that starts a street fight—the action will inevitably turn violent. While Dadier says that it is okay to call a member of one's own racial or religious group by that group's epithet, it is not okay to call a member of another racial or religious group by an epithet.

1. Do you think that racial and religious epithets are a form of hate speech? What is their connection with hate speech? Should schools prohibit the use of racial and religious epithets? Why or why not?
2. Dadier says that, while it is okay to call a member of one's own racial or religious group by that group's epithet, it is not okay to call a member of another racial or religious group by an epithet. Do you agree with him? Is there a right way and a wrong way to use racial and religious epithets? Explain.
3. Dadier seems to assume that the violence in his school is in part connected to students' use (or misuse) of racial and religious epithets. Do you think this is true? Is there a connection between violence and the use of racial and religious epithets? Are they like the little shove in the playground that leads to a brawl?
4. The principal, Mr. Wameke (John Hoyt), calls Dadier into his office and tells him that some students have accused him of maligning various religious and racial groups. Dadier defends himself by saying that he did indeed use the expressions "spic" and "nigger," but he used them as examples of what should not be said. He tells the principal that they were part of a "lesson on democracy." What do you think he meant by this? How is instructing students when to use and when not to use racial and religious epithets a lesson in democracy?
5. Suppose you were in Dadier's shoes. What would you have said to your students if racial and/or religious epithets had been used in your classroom? How might Richard Delgado and Jean Stefancic have responded?
6. Dadier believes that his student Gregory Miller (Sidney Poitier) has falsely reported to the principal that he has been maligning racial and religious groups in his classroom. When he confronts Miller about it, he gets very angry and says, "Why you black . . ." And then, realizing what he said and almost said, he quickly apologizes to Miller, saying that he lost his head. Should Miller have reported Dadier to the principal? Defend your view.

 AMERICAN HISTORY X

(USA, 1999) 2 hours
Directed by Tony Kaye

Film summary: The film is set in Venice Beach, California, a community with increasing amounts of gang activity, racial tension, and violence. Derek Vinyard (Edward Norton) had been an excellent student in high school. However, the murder of his father by a gang member while fighting a fire marks a turning point in Derek's life. His racial prejudices, which he learned in part from his father, become more pronounced. Eventually, he joins a loosely organized local group of neo-Nazi skinheads. Their leader, Cameron (Stacy Keach), keeps a low profile, directing the younger neo-Nazis to commit acts of violence, both verbal and physical. Soon Derek is leading groups of skinheads in committing acts of violence. In one of their more violent actions, on a local supermarket run by a Korean man, Derek incites his fellow skinheads by feeding them hate speech about the Mexican workers employed at the supermarket. Even as his power within the group grows, Derek's relationship with his mother and his sister deteriorates to the point at which he verbally and physically assaults them over dinner one night. Davina Vinyard (Jennifer Lien), his sister, and Doris Vinyard (Beverly D'Angelo), his mother, refuse to accept his racist views of the world and are willing to stand up to him. After the assault, his mother tells him that he must move out of the house, and he agrees to do so the next morning. However, that night, three African American youths break into Derek's car, which is parked in front of the home. The youths want to get back at Derek (and his fellow skinheads) for beating and verbally abusing them during a basketball game. Derek's younger brother, Danny (Edward Furlong), informs him of the break-in, and Derek immediately goes for his gun. One of the youths manages to escape, but Derek shoots and kills the other two. He is sentenced to three years in prison. While in prison, Derek comes to renounce his neo-Nazi beliefs, even as Danny becomes increasingly involved with the local neo-Nazis, all of whom idolize Derek. After his release from prison, Derek attempts to convince his younger brother that he, too, should reject the racial prejudices and violent ways of the neo-Nazis. However, just after Derek seems to have convinced Danny, the younger Vinyard is shot to death in his high school.

1. In school, Danny is asked to write a paper about why Derek is a neo-Nazi and why he is so hateful. Why do you think people become members of hate-based groupes like the neo-Nazis? Do you believe such groups should be tolerated in the United States?
2. Imagine that you are given the task of convincing a neo-Nazi that he or she should not be one. What argument or arguments would you offer?
3. Derek incited the neo-Nazis to commit violent acts against the Korean owner of a supermarket and his Hispanic employees through hate speech. Is the fact that such speech often leads to acts of physical violence a sufficient ground for prohibiting all hate speech? Defend your view, and anticipate possible criticisms.
4. In school, Danny is asked to write a paper on a civil rights leader of his choice. When he chooses to write one on Adolf Hitler, his teacher sends him to the principal's office. What would you do if you were Danny's teacher? How would you defend your actions to your colleagues? To your other students? To Danny?
5. When Derek tries to distance himself from the other neo-Nazis in prison because he does not think they are true enough to the principles of the group, he is raped and violently beaten. Immediately after this incident, he renounces his neo-Nazi beliefs, commenting that they have never brought him any happiness. If you were the filmmaker, would you have chosen to portray Derek's shift from neo-Nazism in this way? If so, why? If not, why not, and how would you have done it?
6. *American History X* contains many instances of hate speech and scenes of violence against Hispanic Americans, Korean Americans, and African Americans by neo-Nazis. However, the moral of the movie seems to be that hate speech and hate violence are wrong. Do you think that this is an effective way to send a message about hate speech and hate groups? What criteria would you use to determine whether a film has effectively combated hate speech and hate violence as opposed to glorifying it? Explain.
7. Cameron, the leader of the neo-Nazis, brags to Derek that, while Derek was in prison, the organization attracted new members and became much better organized primarily through the use of the Internet. Says Cameron, "We're on the Web, we're organized." Should hate speech and/or organizations that disseminate hate speech be banned from the Web? Defend your position, and respond to possible objections.

THE PEOPLE VS. LARRY FLYNT

(USA, 1996) 2 hours 10 minutes
Directed by Milos Forman

Film summary: Is Larry Flynt, the founder of *Hustler* magazine, a First Amendment hero or a misogynist pornographer? Flynt would argue that he has the right to be both. *The People vs. Larry Flynt* follows Flynt's career from his early years as owner of a Cincinnati strip club to his subsequent success as a multimillion-dollar pornography publisher. Flynt (Woody Harrelson) is sentenced to twenty-five years in jail for pandering obscenities and engaging in organized crime. After serving five months, Flynt is cleared by an appellate court. Under the spiritual guidance of Ruth Carter Stapleton (Donna Hanover), sister of former President Jimmy Carter, Flynt converts to Christianity. He loses faith after he is shot and paralyzed by a sniper in Georgia. Confined to a wheelchair, Flynt lives in seclusion with his wife Althea (Courtney Love) in his Hollywood mansion. He runs a satirical advertisement in his magazine that makes untrue claims about the sexual practices of religious leader Jerry Falwell (Richard Paul). Falwell sues Flynt, and the case eventually reaches the Supreme Court, which rules in Flynt's favor.

1. Flynt insists that all he is guilty of is bad taste. *Hustler* has published articles advising men to find "easy" sexual partners such as mentally handicapped women and minors. Do you consider this advice merely to be in "bad taste," or is Flynt guilty of something more serious?
2. Should communities be allowed to set their own standards? What limits, if any, should be put on these standards? Defend your position.
3. The Supreme Court's ruling reads, "In the world of debate about public affairs, many things with motives that are less than admirable are nonetheless protected by the First Amendment." Comment on this ruling.
4. Formulate a debate between Catharine MacKinnon and Lisa Duggan, Nan Hunter, and Carole Vance over the publication of *Hustler* magazine.
5. Do you think that Milos Forman's portrayal of Larry Flynt is "biased"? Explain. If you were going to set the life of Larry Flynt to film, would you do it in the same way as Forman? Why or why not?

 SKOKIE RESIDENTS COMBAT HATRED*

Event summary: The racial and ethnic diversity of Skokie, Illinois is a source of pride in the community. However, this diversity also makes the village a target for anti-ethnic groups. In November 2000, the Ku Klux Klan successfully applied for a permit to hold a rally in Skokie, on the steps of the Cook County Courthouse. On 16 December 2000, about 20 Klansmen demonstrated at a rally attended by 250 people. Clashes broke out, and about 20 people were arrested. According to the *Tribune,* "Police confiscated baseball bats, knives and crowbars from members of the crowd" (p. 2). One man was charged with unlawful use of a weapon when police found a semiautomatic handgun in his car, and police were searching for skinheads who attacked a black couple leaving the rally. On 17 December 2000, 1400 people turned out in Skokie for a Peace and Harmony "counter-rally." The *Tribune* quoted the mayor of Skokie: "When a group promotes hatred and bigotry, we must let it be known that when one of us is attacked, as a group or an individual, we consider it an attack on all of us" (p. 2). This, however, is not the first time that Skokie has had to deal with rallies by hate groups. In 1978, neo-Nazis attempted to march on the village.

---

*Source: Vanesa Gezari, "Rally Strengthens Fight Against Klan: Skokie Residents Combat Hatred," *Chicago Tribune* (18 Dec. 2000), sect. 2, pp. 1–2.

1. Do you believe that hate groups should be allowed to hold rallies in communities like Skokie? What is to be gained by such rallies? What can be lost in such rallies? Is your view in any way affected by the fact that most rallies like this involve violence?
2. According to the mayor of Skokie, "When a group promotes hatred and bigotry, we must let it be known that when one of us is attacked, as a group or an individual, we consider it an attack on all of us." Do you agree with the mayor? Why or why not?
3. Ricky Birdsong, former coach of the Northwestern University basketball team, lived in Skokie. In 1999, he was shot and killed by the White supremacist Benjamin Smith. Birdsong's wife continues to live in Skokie. Benjamin Smith's White supremacist views were well documented before he killed Birdsong, a Black man. Should individuals like Benjamin Smith be prevented from publicly expressing their beliefs? When, if ever, should hate speech be prohibited? Why?
4. The residents of Skokie responded to the Klan rally with a counter-rally. Do you think that this was an appropriate response? Or do you think that they should have done something else? Explain.

2 LIVE CREW

Event summary: In 1990, Charles Freeman, a record store owner in Ft. Lauderdale, Florida, was convicted for selling a copy of 2 Live Crew's *As Nasty As They Wanna Be* to an undercover police officer. An all-White Florida jury agreed that the album was "obscene," and Freeman was sentenced to a year in jail and a $1000 fine. Freeman responded to the sentencing by saying "They don't know nothing about the goddam ghetto. They don't know where my store is. The verdict does not reflect my community standards as a black man in Broward County" (*Newsweek*, 15 Oct. 1990, p. 74).

1. How would Ruth Benedict or another of the cultural relativists respond to the jury's verdict? Should the jury have taken into account *where* the record was sold? Why should this matter?
2. Is obscenity wrong no matter what the context? Defend your position.
3. How might Catharine MacKinnon respond to the jury's decision in the Freeman case?
4. Compare the case of Charles Freeman with that of Allen Ginsberg. Do you think that Judge Horn would have found the music of 2 Live Crew to be obscene? Why or why not? (Or, if you are not familiar with 2 Live Crew's music but are familiar with other contemporary music that might be or has been labeled obscene, use it instead.)
5. Under what conditions, if any, do you think that the sale of musical recordings or the performance of music should be prohibited? Defend your view. Anticipate possible objections and respond to them.

SUPPLEMENTARY READINGS

PORNOGRAPHY

Assister, Alison. *Pornography, Feminism and the Individual.* London: Pluto Press, 1989.
Assister, Alison, and Carol Avedon, eds. *Bad Girls and Naughty Pictures.* London: Pluto Press, 1993.
Baird, Robert M., and Stuart E. Rosenbaum, eds. *Pornography: Private Right or Public Menace?* Buffalo: Prometheus Books, 1991.
Berger, Ronald J. *Feminism and Pornography.* New York: Praeger, 1992.
Brod, Harry. "Pornography and the Alienation of Male Sexuality." *Social Theory and Practice,* 14 (1988): 265–284.

Burstyn, Varda, ed. *Women Against Censorship.* Toronto: Douglas & McIntyre, 1985.

Christianson, F. M. *Pornography: The Other Side.* New York: Praeger, 1990.

Cole, Susan. *Pornography and the Sex Crisis.* Toronto: Amanita, 1989.

Copp, David, and Susan Wendell, eds. *Pornography and Censorship.* Buffalo: Prometheus Books, 1983.

Cornell, Drucilla. *The Imaginary Domain: Abortion, Pornography and Sexual Harassment.* New York: Routledge, 1995.

————, ed. *Feminism and Pornography.* New York: Oxford University Press, 2000.

Delacoste, Frederique, and Priscilla Alexander, eds. *Sex Work: Writings by Women in the Sex Industry.* Pittsburgh: Cleis Press, 1987.

Downs, Donald A. *The New Politics of Pornography.* Chicago: University of Chicago Press, 1989.

Dworkin, Andrea. *Pornography: Men Possessing Women.* New York: Plume, 1989.

————. *Intercourse.* New York: Free Press, 1987.

Dworkin, Ronald. "Women and Pornography." Review of Catharine MacKinnon's *Only Words. The New York Review of Books* (21 Oct. 1993), pp. 36, 37, 40–42.

Ellis, Kate; Beth Jaker; Nan D. Hunter; Barbara O'Dair; and Abby Tallmer, eds. *Caught Looking: Feminism, Pornography and Censorship,* 3rd ed. East Haven, CT: Long River Books, 1992.

Feinberg, Joel. *Offense to Others.* New York: Oxford University Press, 1985.

Griffin, Susan. *Pornography and Silence: Culture's Revenge Against Nature.* New York: Harper & Row, 1981.

Holbrook, David. *The Case Against Pornography.* New York: Library Press, 1973.

Hunt, Lynn, ed. *The Invention of Pornography: Obscenity and the Origins of Modernity, 1500–1800.* New York: Zone Books, 1993.

Itzen, Catherine, ed. *Pornography: Women, Violence and Civil Liberties, a Radical View.* Oxford: Oxford University Press, 1992.

Kimmel, Michael S., ed. *Men Confront Pornography.* New York: Penguin USA/Meridian, 1991.

Lederer, Laura. *Take Back the Night: Women on Pornography.* New York: Morrow, 1980.

MacKinnon, Catharine. *Feminism Unmodified: Discourses on Life and Law.* Cambridge, MA: Harvard University Press, 1987.

————. "Pornography: Not a Moral Issue." *Women's Studies International Forum,* 9 (1986): 63–78.

MacKinnon, Catharine A., and Andrea Dworkin, eds. *Harm's Way: The Pornography Civil Rights Hearings.* Cambridge, MA: Harvard University Press, 1998.

Malamuth, Neil M., and Edward Donnerstein. Orlando, FL: Academic Press, 1984.

Parent, W. A. "A Second Look at Pornography and the Subordination of Women." *Journal of Philosophy,* 87 (1990): 202–211.

Pornography and Sexual Violence: Evidence of the Links. London: Everywoman, 1988; being "The Complete Transcript of the Public Hearings on Ordinances to Add Pornography as Discrimination Against Women: Minneapolis City Council, Government Operations Committee, December 12/13, 1983."

Russell, Diana E. H. *Dangerous Relationships: Pornography, Misogyny, and Rape.* Thousand Oaks, CA: Sage, 1998.

Soble, Alan. *Pornography: Marxism, Feminism and the Future of Sexuality.* New Haven, CT: Yale University Press, 1986.

Stoltenberg, John. "Gays and the Pro-Pornography Movement: Having the Hots for Sex Discrimination." In *Men Confront Pornography,* ed. Michael Kimmel. New York: Meridian, 1991.

————. *Refusing to Be a Man: Essays on Sex and Justice.* Portland, OR: Breitenbush Books, 1989.

Strossen, Nadine. *Defending Pornography: Free Speech, Sex, and the Fight for Women's Rights.* New York: New York University Press, 2000.

Tate, Tim. *Child Pornography: An Investigation.* London: Methuen, 1990.

HATE SPEECH

Abel, Richard L. *Speaking Respect, Respecting Speech.* Chicago: University of Chicago Press, 1998.

Anastaplo, George. *Campus Hate-Speech Codes and Twentieth Century Atrocities.* Lewiston, ME: Edward Mellen Press, 1997.

Butler, Judith. *Excitable Speech: A Politics of the Performative.* New York: Routledge, 1997.

Cleary, Edward J. *Beyond the Burning Cross: The First Amendment and the Landmark R.A.V. Case.* New York: Random House, 1994.

Coliver, Sandra, ed. *Striking a Balance: Hate Speech, Freedom of Expression, and Non-Discrimination.* London: Article 19, International Centre Against Censorship, Human Rights Centre, University of Essex, 1992.

Delgado, Richard, and Jean Stefancic. *Must We Defend Nazis?: Hate Speech, Pornography, and the New First Amendment.* New York: New York University Press, 1997.

Fiss, Owen M. *The Irony of Free Speech.* Cambridge, MA: Harvard University Press, 1996.

Gates, Henry Louis, Jr., et al. *Speaking of Race, Speaking of Sex: Hate Speech, Civil Rights, and Civil Liberties.* New York: New York University Press, 1994.

Greenawalt, Kent. *Fighting Words: Individuals, Communities, and Liberties of Speech.* Princeton, NJ: Princeton University Press, 1995.

Hauell, Timothy C. *Campus Hate Speech on Trial.* Lawrence: University Press of Kansas, 1998.

Heumann, Milton, and Thomas W. Church, eds. *Hate Speech on Campus: Cases, Case Studies and Commentary.* Boston: Northeastern University Press, 1997.

Heyman, Steven J., ed. *Hate Speech and the Constitution.* New York: Garland, 1996.

Jones, Thomas David. *Human Rights: Group Defamation, Freedom of Expression, and the Law of Nations.* The Hague: M. Nijhoff, 1998.

MacKinnon, Catharine. *Only Words.* Cambridge, MA: Harvard University Press, 1993.

Marcus, Laurence R. *Fighting Words: The Politics of Hateful Speech.* Westport, CT: Praeger, 1996.

Maschke, Karen J., ed. *Pornography, Sex Work, and Hate Speech.* New York: Garland, 1997.

Matsuda, Mari; Charles Lawrence; and Kimberle Williams Crenshaw. *Words That Wound: Critical Race Theory, Assaultive Speech, and the First Amendment.* Boulder, CO: Westview Press, 1993.

Nelson, Cary. "Hate Speech and Political Correctness." In *Manifesto of a Tenured Radical.* New York: New York University Press, 1997.

Shiell, Timothy C. *Campus Hate Speech on Trial.* Lawrence: University Press of Kansas, 1998.

Shiffrin, Steven H. *Dissent, Injustice, and the Meanings of America.* Princeton, NJ: Princeton University Press, 1999.

Strum, Philippa. *When the Nazis Came to Skokie: Freedom for Speech We Hate.* Lawrence: University Press of Kansas, 1999.

Sunstein, Cass R. *Democracy and the Problem of Free Speech.* New York: Free Press, 1993.

Tribe, Lawrence H. "Speech as Power, Spending and the Mask of Neutral Principles." In *Constitutional Choices.* Cambridge, MA: Harvard University Press, 1985.

Walker, Samuel. *Hate Speech: The History of an American Controversy.* Lincoln: University of Nebraska Press, 1994.

Weinstein, James. *Hate Speech, Pornography, and the Radical Attack on Free Speech Doctrine.* Boulder, CO: Westview Press, 1999.

Williams, Patricia J. *The Rooster's Egg.* Cambridge, MA: Harvard University Press, 1995.

Winters, Paul A., ed. *Hate Crimes.* San Diego: Greenhaven Press, 1996.

Wolfson, Nicholas. *Hate Speech, Sex Speech, Free Speech.* Westport, CT: Praeger, 1997.

Zingo, Martha T. *Sex/Gender Outsiders, Hate Speech, and Freedom of Expression: Can They Say That About Me?* Westport, CT: Praeger, 1998.

CHAPTER

9

Poverty and Distributive Justice

Many people live in a condition of inadequate food, shelter, and clothing. Some reside in our communities; others live halfway across the world. Some become extremely ill because their basic needs are unmet; others die. Each of their lives, as well as the lives of their families and their community members, is deeply affected by poverty. Are we obligated to help these people in need? Does it make a difference whether they live in our community or country or live across the ocean? What is the scope of our moral obligation to others? What is the moral difference between providing unemployment benefits to people in our own country and providing famine relief to people in other countries? Some believe that spending money to alleviate the suffering caused by famines in Bangladesh or Somalia is not our responsibility, and others argue that the affluent are morally obligated to help the needy. Others disagree as to what extent affluent Americans are morally obligated to help out their less affluent fellow citizens. These are all issues of *distributive justice*.

On the issue of world hunger and famine relief, two positions have been widely debated: the developmentalist and the neo-Malthusian. *Developmentalists* believe that affluent countries such as the United States have a moral obligation to assist poorer countries stricken by famine and other life-threatening situations. Probably the strongest general argument in support of this view is that "we are all in this together." World hunger and poverty are not isolated events, but rather are connected to the well-being of everyone and everything. The planet succeeds or fails as a unit. Therefore, rich countries such as the United States will actually benefit by helping poorer countries improve their conditions.

A classic formulation of the developmentalist argument is to be found in Peter Singer's "Famine, Affluence and Morality." His general claim is that, if we can help prevent something bad, such as death from starvation or disease, from happening to others without sacrificing anything of comparable moral importance, then we have a moral obligation to do so. Singer does not believe that it is important whether the extreme poverty exists in our own community or halfway around the globe. It is also not important whether others could help them as well. What is important is that we have a moral obligation to make sacrifices to help the poor.

It follows from this argument that the existence of poverty and world hunger will probably result in a need for us to change our lifestyles. There will be much less indulgence in things like concerts, movies, and dining out if there are people in the world who might benefit from our sacrifices. For Singer, we have not only *negative duties* (e.g., to refrain from harming other people) but also *positive duties* (e.g., to help those in harm's way). One criticism of Singer's position is that, even if we agree that suffering from, say, extreme poverty is bad, it does not follow that we ought to give to the poor and to prevent the poor from suffering until we give up something of "comparable moral importance."

One of the strengths of developmentalist arguments such as Singer's for helping those in poverty is that they leave the meaning of the phrase "comparable moral importance" deliberately vague. For example, it assumes neither a utilitarian meaning (happiness determines moral importance) nor a Kantian meaning (acts that have moral importance preserve our autonomy). Consequently, proponents of the developmentalist argument argue that it works for a broad range of meanings of "comparable moral importance" and so holds for a wide range of positions on morality. Utilitarians and Kantians alike are morally obligated to help the poor. Detractors counter that the developmentalist argument is weak because we do not know exactly what developmentalists mean by "comparable moral importance."

The neo-Malthusian position on world hunger and famine relief derives from the population growth theory of Thomas Malthus (1766–1834). In his *Essay on the Principles of Population* (six editions, 1797–1826), Malthus wrote that checks in the rate of population growth are desirable. He argued that food production could only be increased in an arithmetic ratio, whereas population increase was potentially greater, in a geometric ratio. The laws of nature demand that a balance be maintained between resources and population. Malthus therefore advocated strong checks on population: *positive checks* such as famine, disease, and war, and *preventative checks* such as premarital chastity, celibacy, and late marriage. While Malthus saw the importance of preventative checks, he is commonly associated with positive checks. One of the more discussed and controversial contemporary preventative checks is China's one family/one child policy. In order to slow down population growth in China, the Chinese government has instituted a law prohibiting families from having more than one child. This policy indicates very clearly how Malthusian principles used in the service of the state can override the interests of families and individuals.

We now know that population growth, at least in the short run, does not necessarily outrun resources. Nevertheless, many still cling to Malthusian beliefs, contending that overpopulation is the cause of world hunger. These *neo-Malthusians* reject the developmentalist argument for helping the poor on the grounds that it only will lead to more extreme poverty and, ultimately, more deaths. As the argument goes, if we are successful in helping the poor, then their numbers will increase. More people means more mouths to feed, backs to clothe, and shelters to construct. Hence, a population increase will result in a strain on the resources of the once poverty-stricken country and in more poverty and death. Therefore, the neo-Malthusians conclude that it is better not to help the poor and to allow some extreme poverty and death now in order to avoid more extreme poverty and death later. According to the neo-Malthusian line of argumentation, we are under no moral obligation to help the poor.

One common version of the neo-Malthusian argument uses a lifeboat analogy. Garrett Hardin, for example, asks us to imagine that each country in the world is a lifeboat at sea, each with a certain amount of supplies and a certain number of passengers. He then asks if it is a good idea for each lifeboat to rescue swimmers from the dangerous waters. For Hardin, the swimmers are just like citizens in other countries who need food, and we in our lifeboat, with few people and lots of supplies, are just like the citizens of the United States who can help out. However, Hardin believes that if we help out our lifeboat eventually will become overloaded and sink.

Developmentalists respond to the neo-Malthusian arguments against helping the poor in a number of ways. Some developmentalists dispute the charge that population growth causes extreme poverty, claiming just the opposite: that extreme poverty causes population growth. Other developmentalists argue that, even if population growth causes poverty, this is still not a good general argument against helping the poor. While it might show that giving them food is wrong, it does not show that we are not morally obligated to helping them out with population control. Still others claim that assistance to poor countries does not make them poorer, but rather gives them an opportunity to rise above their current economic conditions. Developmentalists argue that helping poor countries is the only way that those countries can break the downward cycle of poverty wherein the poor countries get poorer (and the rich countries get richer). Eventually, poor countries will become self-sufficient due to the assistance of rich countries and will themselves be able to help out other less fortunate countries. Finally, developmentalists point to the many instances in our history in which we have allowed people to come to the United States because their home countries experienced terrible famines or severe economic hardships. For instance, many of the Irish immigrants who came to this country beginning in 1845 were fleeing Ireland's terrible potato famines. Without the assistance of the United States, this famine would have killed more Irish citizens than it did. Many developmentalists argue that we have gained from these humanitarian policies, which contribute to our rich cultural diversity.

So far, we have discussed distributive justice at the international level. However, there are just as many controversies concerning distributive justice at the national level. Some believe that wealthy individuals have a moral and legal duty to help out poor citizens who cannot work or who cannot find work that pays enough to feed and clothe their families and keep roofs over their heads. Some believe that not helping poor families in this country is much like not helping famine victims in other countries: that it is cruel and inhumane, particularly if we can afford to help the poor. Others believe that the wealthy are under no personal moral obligation to help the poor. Arguments here include the following: the wealthy do not intend to harm the poor by not assisting them; the wealthy are not responsible for the conditions of the poor; and the wealthy are only morally obligated to assist their families and maybe their friends. Others argue that it is the role of governments, and not individuals, to assist the poor.

Three of the major notions of distributive justice are egalitarianism, libertarianism, and liberalism. *Egalitarians* tend to believe that the state is a more important moral unit than the individuals of which it is comprised. The equal distribution of goods is of the highest value for egalitarians. Moreover, this value justifies strong state mechanisms for the redistribution of goods and resources, as well as the curtailing of liberty if necessary. Still, the biggest difference among libertarianism, liberalism, and egalitarianism is that egalitarians reject the right of individuals to hold productive property privately, whereas libertarians and liberals do not. For egalitarians, the products of people's labor are owned collectively and are distributed to each individual according to his or her need and from each according to his or her ability. The emphasis here is on positive rights, not negative rights. Egalitarians argue that justice requires providing all individuals with whatever is necessary for them to live their lives. They contend that negative rights are of little value to someone who does not have food, shelter, and proper health care. Egalitarian notions of distributive justice can be practiced in a variety of political systems, including democracies. An egalitarian-based system of distributive justice can support all of the same political rights as a democratic system, including freedom of speech, freedom of religion, and due process of the law.

Historically, liberalism has been closely associated with capitalism. Some even contend that liberalism was developed as a justification for the rise of capitalism. Most contemporary liberals, however, distance themselves from this position by arguing that markets must be regulated if for no other reason than to ensure equal opportunity. Liberals who defend free markets are called libertarians (or classical liberals), whereas those who do not are called welfare liberals, or liberal egalitarians, or simply liberals. The historical figure most closely associated with liberalism is John Stuart Mill; John Locke (1632–1704) and Immanuel Kant (1724–1804) are also important figures in the development of liberalism.

Liberals generally agree with libertarians that individuals have the right to protection from harm by others and the right to private property. They disagree, however, with the libertarians on the notion of positive rights. Liberals argue that the least advantaged individuals have some positive right to some of the basic necessities of life, though they do not go so far as to allow these positive rights to interfere greatly with the structure of the underlying capitalist economy. Liberals tolerate a degree of economic and social inequality, whereas libertarians tolerate all economic and social inequality so long as every individual has the opportunity to freely compete for the goods of life. The liberal social and political philosopher John Rawls argues that a given level of inequality is justified only when such inequality in provision of goods and services will be to the benefit of the representative least advantaged of that society. But libertarians would generally rather see people starve than support an unequal distribution of goods and services to benefit the representative least advantaged of society. Inequality is justified for the liberals only if it benefits the least advantaged members of society and if the positions that led to the inequality (e.g., employment) were open to everyone in the first place.

Libertarians (or *classical liberals*) trace the roots of their ideas to the social and political writings of the British philosopher John Locke, rather than John Stuart Mill. Libertarians believe that individuals have a fundamental right to liberty, that is, to be left alone. However, libertarians believe that individuals have only negative rights (rights of noninterference), not positive rights. Libertarians believe that we have the right to life in the negative sense that others have a duty not to interfere in our right to live our lives. They do not believe that we have the right to life in the positive sense that others have a duty to provide us with goods to help us live or even live well. Consequently, individuals have a right not to be harmed and not to have the products of their labor taken from them. Libertarians contend as well that there is not a strong bond between the state and its citizens. The state exists mainly to protect individuals from harming one another, to enforce contracts, and to ensure a common marketplace for the free exchange of goods. If the state does this, then it is just. Accordingly, government programs to assist those without adequate food, shelter, or health care are generally not supported by libertarians. They view government welfare programs as based on positive rights and, as such, as being outside the bounds of their concept of distributive justice. In the big picture, however, libertarianism is a relatively minor school of distributive justice as compared to liberalism, which is one of the dominant schools of distributive justice in the modern world.

PETER SINGER

Famine, Affluence and Morality

Peter Singer argues that, if we can prevent something bad from happening without sacrificing anything of comparable moral importance, then we ought to do it. Suffering from extreme poverty is bad, says Singer, and there is some extreme poverty we can prevent without sacrificing anything of comparable moral importance. Therefore, he concludes, we ought to prevent some extreme poverty. Singer contends that his argument in this article upsets the traditional distinction between duty and charity.

Peter Singer was educated at the University of Melbourne (Australia) and Oxford University. In 1977, he was appointed to a chair of philosophy at Monash University in Melbourne and subsequently served as founding director of that university's Centre for Human Bioethics. In 1999, he became Ira W. DeCamp Professor of Bioethics in the University Center for Human Values at Princeton University. He was the founding president of the International Association of Bioethics and, with Helga Kuhse, founding coeditor of the journal *Bioethics*. His books include *Democracy and Disobedience* (1973), *Practical Ethics* (1979; 2nd ed., 1993), *Marx* (1980), *Hegel* (1983), *Animal Factories* (with Jim Mason, 1980), *Should the Baby Live?* (with Helga Kuhse, 1985), *How Are We to Live?* (1995), and *Ethics into Action: Henry Spira and the Animal Rights Movement* (1998). His works have been translated into nineteen languages.

As I write this, in November 1971, people are dying in East Bengal from lack of food, shelter, and medical care. The suffering and death that are occurring there now are not inevitable, not unavoidable in any fatalistic sense of the term. Constant poverty, a cyclone, and a civil war have turned at least nine million people into destitute refugees; nevertheless, it is not beyond the capacity of the richer nations to give enough assistance to reduce any further suffering to very small proportions. The decisions and actions of human beings can prevent this kind of suffering. Unfortunately, human beings have not made the necessary decisions. At the individual level, people have, with very few exceptions, not responded to the situation in any significant way. Generally speaking, people have not given large sums to relief funds; they have not written to their parliamentary representatives demanding increased government assistance; they have not demonstrated in the streets, held symbolic fasts, or done anything else directed toward providing the refugees with the means to satisfy their essential needs. At the government level, no government has given the sort of massive aid that would enable the refugees to survive for more than a few days. Britain, for instance, has given rather more than most countries. It has, to date, given £14,750,000. For comparative purposes, Britain's share of the nonrecoverable development costs of the Anglo-French Concorde project is already in excess of £275,000,000, and on present estimates will reach £440,000,000. The implication is that the British government values a supersonic transport more than thirty times as highly as it values the lives of the nine million refugees. Australia is another country which, on a per capita basis, is well up in the "aid to Bengal" table. Australia's aid, however, amounts to less than one-twelfth of the cost of Sydney's new opera house. The total amount given, from all sources, now stands at about £65,000,000. The estimated cost of keeping the refugees alive for one year is £464,000,000. Most of the refugees have now been in the camps for more than six months. The World Bank has said that India needs a minimum of £300,000,000 in assistance from other countries before the end of the year. It seems obvious that assistance on this scale will not be forthcoming. India will be forced to choose between letting the refugees starve or diverting funds from her own development program, which will mean that more of her own people will starve in the future.[1]

These are the essential facts about the present situation in Bengal. So far as it concerns us here, there is nothing unique about this situation except its magnitude. The Bengal emergency is just the latest and most acute of a series of major emergencies in various parts of the world, arising both from natural and from man-made causes. There are also many parts of the world in which people die from malnutrition and lack of food independent of any special emergency. I take Bengal as my example only because it is the present concern, and because the size of the problem has ensured that it has been given adequate publicity. Neither individuals nor governments can claim to be unaware of what is happening there.

What are the moral implications of a situation like this? In what follows, I shall argue that the way people in relatively affluent countries react to a situation like that in Bengal cannot be justified; indeed, the whole way we look at moral issues—our moral conceptual scheme—needs to be altered, and with it, the way of life that has come to be taken for granted in our society.

In arguing for this conclusion I will not, of course, claim to be morally neutral. I shall, however, try to argue for the moral position that I take, so that anyone who accepts certain assumptions, to be made explicit, will, I hope, accept my conclusion.

I begin with the assumption that suffering and death from lack of food, shelter, and medical care are bad. I think most people will agree about this, although one may reach the same view by different routes. I shall not argue for this view. People can hold all sorts of eccentric positions, and perhaps for some of them it would not follow that death by starvation is in itself bad. It is difficult, perhaps impossible, to refute such positions, and so for brevity I will henceforth take this assumption as accepted. Those who disagree need read no further.

My next point is this: if it is in our power to prevent something bad from happening, without thereby sacrificing anything of comparable moral importance, we ought, morally, to do it. By "without sacrificing anything of comparable moral importance" I mean without causing anything else comparably bad to happen, or doing something that is wrong in itself, or failing to promote some moral good, comparable in significance to the bad thing that we can prevent. This principle seems almost as uncontroversial as the last one. It requires us only to prevent what is bad, and not to promote what is good, and it requires this of us only when we can do it without sacrificing anything that is, from the moral point of view, comparably important. I could even, as far as the application of my argument to the Bengal emergency is concerned, qualify the point so as to make it: if it is in our power to prevent something very bad from happening, without thereby sacrificing anything morally significant, we ought, morally, to do it. An application of this principle would be as follows: if I am walking past a shallow pond and see a child drowning in it, I ought to wade in and pull the child out. This will mean getting my clothes muddy, but this is insignificant, while the death of the child would presumably be a very bad thing.

The uncontroversial appearance of the principle just stated is deceptive. If it were acted upon, even in its qualified form, our lives, our society, and our world would be fundamentally changed. For the principle takes, firstly, no account of proximity or distance. It makes no moral difference whether the person I can help is a neighbor's child ten yards from me or a Bengali whose name I shall never know, ten thousand miles away. Secondly, the principle makes no distinction between cases in which I am the only person who could possibly do anything and cases in which I am just one among millions in the same position.

I do not think I need to say much in defense of the refusal to take proximity and distance into account. The fact that a person is physically near to us, so that we have personal contact with him, may make it more likely that we *shall* assist him, but this does not show that we *ought* to help him rather than another who happens to be further away. If we accept any principle of impartiality, universalizability, equality, or whatever, we cannot discriminate against someone merely because he is far away from us (or we are far away from him). Admittedly, it is possible that we are in a better position to judge what needs to be done to help a person near to us than one far away, and perhaps also to provide the assistance we judge to be necessary. If this were the case, it would be a reason for helping those near to us first. This may once have been a justification for being more concerned with the poor in one's own town than with famine victims in India.

Unfortunately for those who like to keep their moral responsibilities limited, instant communication and swift transportation have changed the situation. From the moral point of view, the development of the world into a "global village" has made an important, though still unrecognized, difference to our moral situation. Expert observers and supervisors, sent out by famine relief organizations or permanently stationed in famine-prone areas, can direct our aid to a refugee in Bengal almost as effectively as we could get it to someone in our own block. There would seem, therefore, to be no possible justification for discriminating on geographical grounds.

There may be greater need to defend the second implication of my principle—that the fact that there are millions of other people in the same position, in respect to the Bengali refugees, as I am, does not make the situation significantly different from a situation in which I am the only person who can prevent something very bad from occurring. Again, of course, I admit that there is a psychological difference between the cases: one feels less guilty about doing nothing if one can point to others, similarly placed, who have also done nothing. Yet this can make no real difference to our moral obligations.[2] Should I consider that I am less obliged to pull the drowning child out of the pond if on looking around I see other people, no further away than I am, who have also noticed the child but are doing nothing? One has only to ask this question to see the absurdity of the view that numbers lessen obligation. It is a view that is an ideal excuse for inactivity; unfortunately most of the major evils—poverty, overpopulation, pollution—are problems in which everyone is almost equally involved.

The view that numbers do make a difference can be made plausible if stated in this way: if everyone in circumstances like mine gave £5 to the Bengal Relief Fund, there would be enough to provide food, shelter, and medical care for the refugees; there is no reason why I should give more than anyone else in the same circumstances as I am; therefore I have no obligation to give more than £5. Each premise in this argument is true, and the argument looks sound. It may convince us, unless we notice that it is based on a hypothetical premise, although the conclusion is not stated hypothetically. The argument would be sound if the conclusion were: if everyone in circumstances like mine were to give £5, I would have no obligation to give more than £5. If the conclusion were so stated, however, it would be obvious that the argument has no bearing on a situation in which it is not the case that everyone else gives £5. This, of course,

is the actual situation. It is more or less certain that not everyone in circumstances like mine will give £5. So there will not be enough to provide the needed food, shelter, and medical care. Therefore by giving more than £5 I will prevent more suffering than I would if I gave just £5.

It might be thought that this argument has an absurd consequence. Since the situation appears to be that very few people are likely to give substantial amounts, it follows that I and everyone else in similar circumstances ought to give as much as possible, that is, at least up to the point at which by giving more one would begin to cause serious suffering for oneself and one's dependents—perhaps even beyond this point to the point of marginal utility, at which by giving more one would cause oneself and one's dependents as much suffering as one would prevent in Bengal. If everyone does this, however, there will be more than can be used for the benefit of the refugees, and some of the sacrifice will have been unnecessary. Thus, if everyone does what he ought to do, the result will not be as good as it would be if everyone did a little less than he ought to do, or if only some do all that they ought to do.

The paradox here arises only if we assume that the actions in question—sending money to the relief funds—are performed more or less simultaneously, and are also unexpected. For if it is to be expected that everyone is going to contribute something, then clearly each is not obliged to give as much as he would have been obliged to had others not been giving too. And if everyone is not acting more or less simultaneously, then those giving later will know how much more is needed, and will have no obligation to give more than is necessary to reach this amount. To say this is not to deny the principle that people in the same circumstances have the same obligations, but to point out that the fact that others have given or may be expected to give, is a relevant circumstance: those giving after it has become known that many others are giving and those giving before are not in the same circumstances. So the seemingly absurd consequence of the principle I have put forward can occur only if people are in error about the actual circumstances—that is, if they think they are giving when others are not, but in fact they are giving when others are. The result of everyone doing what he really ought to do cannot be worse than the result of everyone doing less than he ought to do, although the result of everyone doing what he reasonably believes he ought to do could be.

If my argument so far has been sound, neither our distance from a preventable evil nor the number of other people who, in respect to that evil, are in the same situation as we are, lessens our obligation to mitigate or prevent that evil. I shall therefore take as established the principle I asserted earlier. As I have already said, I need to assert it only in its qualified form: if it is in our power to prevent something very bad from happening, without thereby sacrificing anything else morally significant, we ought, morally, to do it.

The outcome of this argument is that our traditional moral categories are upset. The traditional distinction between duty and charity cannot be drawn, or at least, not in the place we normally draw it. Giving money to the Bengal Relief Fund is regarded as an act of charity in our society. The bodies which collect money are known as "charities." These organizations see themselves in this way—if you send them a check, you will be thanked for your "generosity." Because giving money is regarded as an act of charity, it is not thought that there is anything wrong with not giving. The charitable man may be praised, but the man who is not charitable is not condemned. People do not feel in any way ashamed or guilty about spending money on new clothes or a new car instead of giving it to famine relief. (Indeed, the alternative does not occur to them.) This way of looking at the matter cannot be justified. When we buy new clothes not to keep ourselves warm but to look "well-dressed" we are not providing for any important need. We would not be sacrificing anything significant if we were to continue to wear our old clothes, and give the money to famine relief. By doing so, we would be preventing another person from starving. It follows from what I have said earlier that we ought to give money away, rather than spend it on clothes which we do not need to keep us warm. To do so is not charitable, or generous. Nor is it the kind of act which philosophers and theologians have called "supererogatory"—an act which it would be good to do, but not wrong not to do. On the contrary, we ought to give the money away, and it is wrong not to do so.

I am not maintaining that there are no acts which are charitable, or that there are no acts which it would be good to do but not wrong not to do. It may be possible to redraw the distinction between duty and charity in some other place. All I am arguing here is that the present way of drawing the distinction, which makes it an act of charity for a man living at the level of affluence which most people in the "developed nations" enjoy to give money to save someone else from starvation, cannot be supported. It is beyond the scope of my argument to consider whether the distinction should be redrawn or abolished altogether. There would be many other possible ways of drawing the distinction—for instance, one might decide that it is good to make other people as happy as possible, but not wrong not to do so.

Despite the limited nature of the revision in our moral conceptual scheme which I am proposing, the revision would, given the extent of both affluence and famine in the world today, have radical implications. These implications may lead to further objections, distinct from those I have already considered. I shall discuss two of these.

One objection to the position I have taken might be simply that it is too drastic a revision of our moral scheme. People do not ordinarily judge in the way I have suggested they should. Most people reserve their moral condemnation for those who violate some moral norm, such as the norm against taking another person's property. They do not condemn those who indulge in luxury instead of giving to famine relief. But given that I did not set out to present a morally neutral description of the way people make moral judgments, the way people do in fact judge has nothing to do with the validity of my conclusion. My conclusion follows from the principle which I advanced earlier, and unless that principle is rejected, or the arguments shown to be unsound, I think the conclusion must stand, however strange it appears.

It might, nevertheless, be interesting to consider why our society, and most other societies, do judge differently from the way I have suggested they should. In a well-known article, J. O. Urmson suggests that the imperatives of duty, which tell us what we must do, as distinct from what it would be good to do but not wrong not to do, function so as to prohibit behavior that is intolerable if men are to live together in society.[3] This may explain the origin and continued existence of the present division between acts of duty and acts of charity. Moral attitudes are shaped by the needs of society, and no doubt society needs people who will observe the rules that make social existence tolerable. From the point of view of a particular society, it is essential to prevent violations of norms against killing, stealing, and so on. It is quite inessential, however, to help people outside one's own society.

If this is an explanation of our common distinction between duty and supererogation, however, it is not a justification of it. The moral point of view requires us to look beyond the interests of our own society. Previously, as I have already mentioned, this may hardly have been feasible, but it is quite feasible now. From the moral point of view, the prevention of the starvation of millions of people outside our society must be considered at least as pressing as the upholding of property norms within our society.

It has been argued by some writers, among them Sidgwick and Urmson, that we need to have a basic moral code which is not too far beyond the capacities of the ordinary man, for otherwise there will be a general breakdown of compliance with the moral code. Crudely stated, this argument suggests that if we tell people that they ought to refrain from murder and give everything they do not really need to famine relief, they will do neither, whereas if we tell them that they ought to refrain from murder and that it is good to give to famine relief but not wrong not to do so, they will at least refrain from murder. The issue here is: Where should we draw the line between conduct that is required and conduct that is good although not required, so as to get the best possible result? This would seem to be an empirical question, although a very difficult one. One objection to the Sidgwick-Urmson line of argument is that it takes insufficient account of the effect that moral standards can have on the decisions we make. Given a society in which a wealthy man who gives five percent of his income to famine relief is regarded as most generous, it is not surprising that a proposal that we all ought to give away half our incomes will be thought to be absurdly unrealistic. In a society which held that no man should have more than enough while others have less than they need, such a proposal might seem narrow-minded. What it is possible for a man to do and what he is likely to do are both, I think, very greatly influenced by what people around him are doing and expecting him to do. In any case, the possibility that by spreading the idea that we ought to be doing very much more than we are to relieve famine we shall bring about a general breakdown of moral behavior seems remote. If the stakes are an end to widespread starvation, it is worth the risk. Finally, it should be emphasized that these considerations are relevant only to the issue of what we should require from others, and not to what we ourselves ought to do.

The second objection to my attack on the present distinction between duty and charity is one which has from time to time been made against utilitarianism. It follows from some forms of utilitarian theory that we all ought, morally, to be working full time to increase the balance of happiness over misery. The position I have taken here would not lead to this conclusion in all circumstances, for if there were no bad occurrences that we could prevent without sacrificing something of comparable moral importance, my argument would have no application. Given the present conditions in many parts of the world, however, it does follow from my argument that we ought, morally, to be working full time to relieve great suffering of the sort that occurs as a result of famine or other disasters. Of course, mitigating circumstances can be adduced—for instance, that if we wear ourselves out through overwork, we shall be less effective than we would otherwise have been. Nevertheless, when all considerations of this sort have been taken into account, the conclusion remains: we ought to be preventing as much suffering as we can without sacrificing something else of comparable moral importance. This conclusion is one which we may be reluctant to face. I cannot see, though, why it should be regarded as a criticism of the position for which I have argued, rather than a criticism of our ordinary standards of behavior. Since most people are self-interested to some degree, very few of us are likely to do everything that we ought to do. It would, however, hardly be honest to take this as evidence that it is not the case that we ought to do it.

It may still be thought that my conclusions are so wildly out of line with what everyone else thinks and has always thought that there must be something wrong with the argument somewhere. In order to show that my conclusions, while certainly contrary to contemporary Western moral standards, would not have seemed so extraordinary at other times and in other places, I would like to quote a passage from a writer not normally thought of as a way-out radical, Thomas Aquinas.

> Now, according to the natural order instituted by divine providence, material goods are provided for the satisfaction of human needs. Therefore the division and appropriation of property, which proceeds from human law, must not hinder the satisfaction of man's necessity from such goods. Equally, whatever a man has in superabundance is owed, of natural right, to the poor for their sustenance. So Ambrosius says, and it is also to be found in the *Decretum Gratiani*: "The bread which you withhold belongs to the hungry; the clothing you shut away, to the naked; and the money you bury in the earth is the redemption and freedom of the penniless."[4]

I now want to consider a number of points, more practical than philosophical, which are relevant to the application of the moral conclusion we have reached. These points challenge not the idea that we ought to be doing all we can to prevent starvation, but the idea that giving away a great deal of money is the best means to this end.

It is sometimes said that overseas aid should be a government responsibility, and that therefore one ought not to give to privately run charities. Giving privately, it is said, allows the government and the noncontributing members of society to escape their responsibilities.

This argument seems to assume that the more people there are who give to privately organized famine relief funds, the less likely it is that the government will take over full responsibility for such aid. This assumption is unsupported, and does not strike me as at all plausible. The opposite view—that if no one gives voluntarily, a government will assume that its citizens are uninterested in famine relief and would not wish to be forced into giving aid—seems more plausible. In any case, unless there were a definite probability that by refusing to give one would be helping to bring about massive government assistance, people who do refuse to make voluntary contributions are refusing to prevent a certain amount of suffering without being able to point to any tangible beneficial consequence of their refusal. So the onus of showing how their refusal will bring about government action is on those who refuse to give.

I do not, of course, want to dispute the contention that governments of affluent nations should be giving many times the amount of genuine, no-strings-attached aid that they are giving now. I agree, too, that giving privately is not enough, and that we ought to be campaigning actively for entirely new standards for both public and private contributions to famine relief. Indeed, I would sympathize with someone who thought that campaigning was more important than giving oneself, although I doubt whether preaching what one does not practice would be very effective. Unfortunately, for many people the idea that "it's the government's responsibility" is a reason for not giving which does not appear to entail any political action either.

Another, more serious reason for not giving to famine relief funds is that until there is effective population control, relieving famine merely postpones starvation. If we save the Bengal refugees now, others, perhaps the children of these refugees, will face starvation in a few years' time. In support of this, one may cite the now well-known facts about the population explosion and the relatively limited scope for expanded production.

This point, like the previous one, is an argument against relieving suffering that is happening now, because of a belief about what might happen in the future; it is unlike the previous point in that very good evidence can be adduced in support of this belief about the future. I will not go into the evidence here. I accept that the earth cannot support indefinitely a population rising at the present rate. This certainly poses a problem for anyone who thinks it important to prevent famine. Again, however, one could accept the argument without drawing the conclusion that it absolves one from any obligation to do anything to prevent famine. The conclusion that should be drawn is that the best means of preventing famine, in the long run, is population control. It would then follow from the position reached earlier that one ought to be doing all one can to promote population control (unless one held that all forms of population control were wrong in themselves, or would have significantly bad consequences). Since there are organizations working specifically for population control, one would then support them rather than more orthodox methods of preventing famine.

A third point raised by the conclusion reached earlier relates to the question of just how much we all ought to be giving away. One possibility, which has already been mentioned, is that we ought to give until we reach the level of marginal utility—that is, the level at which, by giving more, I would cause as much suffering to myself or my dependents as I would relieve by my gift. This would mean, of course, that one would reduce oneself to very near the material circumstances of a Bengali refugee. It will be recalled that earlier I put forward both a strong and a moderate version of the principle of preventing bad occurrences. The strong version, which required us to prevent bad things from happening unless in doing so we would be sacrificing something of comparable moral significance, does seem to require reducing ourselves to the level of marginal utility. I should also say that the strong version seems to me to be the correct one. I proposed the more moderate version—that we should prevent bad occurrences unless to do so, we had to sacrifice something morally significant—only in order to show that even on this surely undeniable principle a great change in our way of life is required. On the more moderate principle, it may not follow that we ought to reduce ourselves to the level of marginal utility, for one might hold that to reduce oneself and one's family to this level is to cause something significantly bad to happen. Whether this is so I shall not discuss, since, as I have said, I can see no good reason for holding the moderate version of the principle rather than the strong version. Even if we accepted the principle only in its moderate form, however, it should be clear that we would have to give away enough to ensure that the consumer society, dependent as it is on people spending on trivia rather than giving famine relief, would slow down and perhaps disappear entirely. There are several reasons why this would be desirable in itself. The value and necessity of economic growth are now being questioned not only by conservationists, but by economists as well.[5] There is no doubt, too, that the consumer society has had a distorting effect on the goals and purposes of its members. Yet looking at the matter purely from the point of view of overseas aid, there must be a limit to the extent to which we should deliberately slow down our economy; for it might be the case that if we gave away, say, forty percent of our Gross National Product, we would slow down the economy so much that in absolute terms we would be giving less than if we gave twenty-five percent of the much larger GNP that we would have if we limited our contribution to this smaller percentage.

I mention this only as an indication of the sort of factor that one would have to take into account in working out an ideal. Since Western societies generally consider one percent of the GNP an acceptable level for overseas aid, the matter is entirely academic. Nor does it affect the question of how much an individual should give in a society in which very few are giving substantial amounts.

It is sometimes said, though less often now than it used to be, that philosophers have no special role to play in public affairs, since most public issues depend primarily on an assessment of facts. On questions of fact, it is said, philosophers as such have no special expertise, and so it has been possible to engage in philosophy without committing oneself to any position on major public issues. No doubt there are some issues of social policy and foreign policy about which it can truly be said that a really expert assessment of the facts is required before taking sides or acting, but the issue of famine is surely not one of these. The facts about the existence of suffering are beyond dispute. Nor, I think, is it disputed that we can do something about it, either through orthodox methods of famine relief or through population control or both. This is there-

fore an issue on which philosophers are competent to take a position. The issue is one which faces everyone who has more money than he needs to support himself and his dependents, or who is in a position to take some sort of political action. These categories must include practically every teacher and student of philosophy in the universities of the Western world. If philosophy is to deal with matters that are relevant to both teachers and students, this is an issue that philosophers should discuss.

Discussion, though, is not enough. What is the point of relating philosophy to public (and personal) affairs if we do not take our conclusions seriously? In this instance, taking our conclusion seriously means acting upon it. The philosopher will not find it any easier than anyone else to alter his attitudes and way of life to the extent that, if I am right, is involved in doing everything that we ought to be doing. At the very least, though, one can make a start. The philosopher who does so will have to sacrifice some of the benefits of the consumer society, but he can find compensation in the satisfaction of a way of life in which theory and practice, if not yet in harmony, are at least coming together.

NOTES

1. There was also a third possibility: that India would go to war to enable the refugees to return to their lands. Since I wrote this paper, India has taken this way out. The situation is no longer that described above, but this does not affect my argument, as the next paragraph indicates.

2. In view of the special sense philosophers often give to the term, I should say that I use "obligation" simply as the abstract noun derived from "ought," so that "I have an obligation to" means no more, and no less, than "I ought to." This usage is in accordance with the definition of "ought" given by the *Shorter Oxford English Dictionary:* "the general verb to express duty or obligation." I do not think any issue of substance hangs on the way the term is used; sentences in which I use "obligation" could all be rewritten, although somewhat clumsily, as sentences in which a clause containing "ought" replaces the term "obligation."

3. J. O. Urmson, "Saints and Heroes," in *Essays in Moral Philosophy,* ed. Abraham I. Melden (Seattle and London, 1958), p. 214. For a related but significantly different view see also Henry Sidgwick, *The Methods of Ethics,* 7th ed. (London, 1907), pp. 220–221, 492–493.

4. *Summa Theologica*, II–II, Question 66, Article 7, in *Aquinas, Selected Political Writings*, ed. A. P. d'Entreves, trans J. G. Dawson (Oxford, 1948), p. 171.

5. See, for instance, John Kenneth Galbraith, *The New Industrial State* (Boston, 1967); and E. J. Mishan, *The Costs of Economic Growth* (London, 1967).

DISCUSSION QUESTIONS

1. Singer assumes that "suffering and death from lack of food, shelter and medical care are bad" and says he will not argue for this. Do you agree with him? Does his refusal to argue for this point weaken his argument in any way? Explain.
2. What does Singer mean by "comparable moral importance"? What role does this play in his general argument?
3. Critically comment on the following quote from Singer: "If we accept any principle of impartiality, universalizability, equality, or whatever, we cannot discriminate against someone merely because he is far away from us (or we are far away from him)."
4. Is Singer's argument sound? Raise one objection to it. How might Singer respond to this objection?
5. Is Singer's argument based on utilitarian moral principles or Kantian moral principles? Explain.
6. Singer says that his argument upsets the traditional distinction between "duty" and "charity." What is this distinction, and how does Singer upset it? Is he successful? Why or why not?

 GARRETT HARDIN

Lifeboat Ethics

Garrett Hardin thinks that Peter Singer goes too far, and he uses utilitarian grounds to counter Singer's view. According to Hardin, rich countries like the United States do not have a moral obligation to help out poor countries. Moreover, aid in the form of famine relief may even make matters worse by causing more population growth and by putting rich countries at risk. Hardin asks us to imagine that each rich country is a lifeboat at sea, each with a certain amount of supplies and a certain number of people. He then asks if it is a good idea for each lifeboat to help swimmers who need food, a seat in the boat, and so on. For Hardin, the swimmers are just like citizens from poor countries, and we in our lifeboats are like the citizens of the United States. However, Hardin thinks that if we help we may cause our lifeboats to sink, or—as his "thought experiment" goes—we may use up the food supplies of our own country.

Garrett Hardin is professor emeritus of biology at the University of California at Santa Barbara and the author of many books, including *Nature and Man's Fate* (1959), *Stalking the Wild Taboo* (1973), *Exploring New Ethics for Survival* (1973), *The Limits of Altruism: An Ecologist's View of Survival* (1977), and *Naked Emperors* (1982).

Environmentalists use the metaphor of the earth as a "spaceship" in trying to persuade countries, industries and people to stop wasting and polluting our natural resources. Since we all share life on this planet, they argue, no single person or institution has the right to destroy, waste, or use more than a fair share of its resources.

But does everyone on earth have an equal right to an equal share of its resources? The spaceship metaphor can be dangerous when used by misguided idealists to justify suicidal policies for sharing our resources through uncontrolled immigration and foreign aid. In their enthusiastic but unrealistic generosity, they confuse the ethics of a spaceship with those of a lifeboat.

A true spaceship would have to be under the control of a captain, since no ship could possibly survive if its course were determined by committee. Spaceship Earth certainly has no captain; the United Nations is merely a toothless tiger, with little power to enforce any policy upon its bickering members.

If we divide the world crudely into rich nations and poor nations, two thirds of them are desperately poor, and only one third comparatively rich, with the United States the wealthiest of all. Metaphorically each rich nation can be seen as a lifeboat full of comparatively rich people. In the ocean outside each lifeboat swim the poor of the world, who would like to get in, or at least to share some of the wealth. What should the lifeboat passengers do?

First, we must recognize the limited capacity of any lifeboat. For example, a nation's land has a limited capacity to support a population and as the current energy crisis has shown us, in some ways we have already exceeded the carrying capacity of our land.

ADRIFT IN A MORAL SEA

So here we sit, say, 50 people in our lifeboat. To be generous, let us assume it has room for 10 more, making a total capacity of 60. Suppose the 50 of us in the lifeboat see 100 others swimming in the water outside, begging for admission to our boat or for handouts. We have several options: we may be tempted to try to live by the Christian ideal of being "our brother's keeper," or by the Marxist ideal of "to each according to his needs." Since the needs of all in the water are the same, and since they can all be seen as "our brothers," we could take them all into our boat, making a total of 150 in a boat designed for 60. The boat swamps, everyone drowns. Complete justice, complete catastrophe.

Since the boat has an unused excess capacity of 10 more passengers, we could admit just 10 more to it. But which 10 do we let in? How do we choose? Do we pick the best 10, the neediest 10, "first come, first served"? And what do we say to the 90 we exclude? If we do let an extra 10 into our lifeboat, we will have lost our "safety factor," an engineering principle of critical importance. For example, if we don't leave room for excess capacity as a safety factor in our country's agriculture, a new plant disease or a bad change in the weather could have disastrous consequences.

Suppose we decide to preserve our small safety factor and admit no more to the lifeboat. Our survival is then possible, although we shall have to be constantly on guard against boarding parties.

While this last solution clearly offers the only means of our survival, it is morally abhorrent to many people. Some say they feel guilty about their good luck. My reply is simple: "Get out and yield your place to others." This may solve the problem of the guilt-ridden person's conscience, but it does not change the ethics of the lifeboat. The needy person to whom the guilt-ridden person yields his place will not himself feel guilty about his good luck. If he did, he would not climb aboard. The net result of conscience-stricken people giving up their unjustly held seats is the elimination of that sort of conscience from the lifeboat.

This is the basic metaphor within which we must work out our solutions. Let us now enrich the image, step by step, with substantive additions from the real world, a world that must solve real and pressing problems of overpopulation and hunger.

The harsh ethics of the lifeboat become even harsher when we consider the reproductive differences between the rich nations and the poor nations. The people inside the lifeboats are doubling in numbers every 87 years; those swimming around outside are doubling, on the average, every 35 years, more than twice as fast as the rich. And since the world's resources are dwindling, the difference in prosperity between the rich and the poor can only increase.

As of 1973, the U.S. had a population of 210 million people, who were increasing by 0.8 percent per year. Outside our lifeboat, let us imagine another 210 million people (say, the combined populations of Colombia, Ecuador, Venezuela, Morocco, Pakistan, Thailand and the Philippines), who are increasing at a rate of 3.3 percent per year. Put differently, the doubling time for this aggregate population is 21 years, compared to 87 years for the U.S. . . .

In sharing with "each according to his needs," we must recognize that needs are determined by population size, which is determined by the rate of reproduction, which at present is regarded as a sovereign right of every nation, poor or not. This being so, the philanthropic load created by the sharing ethic of the spaceship can only increase.

THE TRAGEDY OF THE COMMONS

The fundamental error of spaceship ethics, and the sharing it requires, is that it leads to what I call "the tragedy of the commons." Under a system of private property, the men who own property recognize their responsibility to care for it, for if they don't they will eventually suffer. A farmer, for instance, will allow no more cattle in a pasture than its carrying capacity justifies. If he overloads it, erosion sets in, weeds take over, and he loses the use of the pasture.

If a pasture becomes a commons open to all, the right of each to use it may not be matched by a corresponding responsibility to protect it. Asking everyone to use it with discretion will hardly do, for the considerate herdsman who refrains from overloading the commons suffers more than a selfish one who says his needs are greater. If everyone would restrain himself, all would be well; but it takes only one less than everyone to ruin a system of voluntary restraint. In a crowded world of less than perfect human beings, mutual ruin is inevitable if there are no controls. This is the tragedy of the commons.

One of the major tasks of education today should be the creation of such an acute awareness of the dangers of the commons that people will recognize its many varieties. For example, the air and water have become polluted because they are treated as commons. Further growth in the population or percapita conversion of natural resources into pollutants will only make the problem worse. The same holds true for the fish of the oceans. Fishing fleets have nearly disappeared in many parts of the world, [and] technological improvements in the art of fishing are hastening the day of complete ruin. Only the replacement of the system of the commons with a responsible system of control will save the land, air, water and oceanic fisheries. . . .

LEARNING THE HARD WAY

What happens if some organizations or countries budget for accidents and others do not? If each country is solely responsible for its own well-being, poorly managed ones will suffer. But they can learn from experience. They may mend their ways, and learn to budget for infrequent but certain emergencies. For example, the weather varies from year to year, and periodic crop failures are certain. A wise and competent government saves out of the production of the good years in anticipation of bad years to come. Joseph taught this policy to Pharaoh in Egypt more than 2,000 years ago. Yet the great majority of the governments in the world today do not follow such a policy. They lack either the wisdom or the competence, or both. Should those nations that do manage to put something aside be forced to come to the rescue each time an emergency occurs among the poor nations?

"But it isn't their fault!" Some kind-hearted liberals argue. "How can we blame the poor people who are caught in an emergency? Why must they suffer for the sins of their governments?" The concept of blame is simply not relevant here. The real question is, what are the operational consequences of establishing a world food bank? If it is open to every country every time a need develops, slovenly rulers will not be motivated to take Joseph's advice. Someone will always come to their aid. Some countries will deposit food in the world food bank, and others will withdraw it. There will be almost no overlap. As a result of such solutions to food shortage emergencies, the poor countries will not learn to mend their ways, and will suffer progressively greater emergencies as their populations grow.

POPULATION CONTROL THE CRUDE WAY

On the average, poor countries undergo a 2.5 percent increase in population each year; rich countries, about 0.8 percent. Only rich countries have anything in the way of food reserves set aside, and even they do not have as much as they should. Poor countries have none. If poor countries received no food from the outside, the rate of their population growth would be periodically checked by crop failures and famines. But if they can always draw on a world food bank in time of need, their population can continue to grow unchecked, and so will their "need" for aid. In the short run, a world food bank may diminish that need, but in the long run it actually increases the need without limit.

Without some system of worldwide food sharing, the proportion of people in the rich and poor nations might eventually stabilize. The overpopulated poor countries would decrease in numbers, while the rich countries that had room for more people would increase. But with a well-meaning system of sharing, such as a world food bank, the growth differential between the rich and the poor countries will not only persist, it will increase. Because of the higher rate of population growth in the poor countries of the world, 88 percent of today's children are born poor, and only 12 percent rich. Year by year the ratio becomes worse, as the fast-reproducing poor outnumber the slow-reproducing rich.

A world food bank is thus a commons in disguise. People will have more motivation to draw from it than to add to any common store. The less provident and less able will multiply at the expense of the abler and more provident, bringing eventual ruin upon all who share in the commons. Besides, any system of "sharing" that amounts to foreign aid from the rich nations to the poor nations will carry the taint of charity, which will contribute little to the world peace so devoutly desired by those who support the idea of a world food bank. . . .

OVERLOADING THE ENVIRONMENT

Every human born constitutes a draft on all aspects of the environment: food, air, water, forests, beaches, wildlife, scenery and solitude. Food can, perhaps, be significantly increased to meet a growing demand. But what about clean beaches, unspoiled forests, and solitude? If we satisfy a growing population's need for food, we necessarily decrease its per capita supply of the other resources needed by men.

India, for example, now has a population of 600 million, which increases by 15 million each year. This population already puts a huge load on a relatively impoverished environment. The country's forests are now only a small fraction of what they were three centuries ago, and floods and erosion continually destroy the insufficient farmland that remains. Every one of the 15 million new lives added to India's population puts an additional burden on the environment, and increases the economic and social costs of crowding. However humanitarian our intent, every Indian life saved through medical or nutritional assistance from abroad diminishes the quality of life for those who remain, and for subsequent generations. If rich countries make it possible, through foreign aid, for 600 million Indians to swell to 1.2 billion in a mere

28 years, as their current growth rate threatens, will future generations of Indians thank us for hastening the destruction of their environment? Will our good intentions be sufficient excuse for the consequences of our actions?. . .

IMMIGRATION VS. FOOD SUPPLY

World food banks *move food to the people,* hastening the exhaustion of the environment of the poor countries. Unrestricted immigration, on the other hand, *moves people to the food,* thus speeding up the destruction of the environment of the rich countries. We can easily understand why poor people should want to make this latter transfer, but why should rich hosts encourage it?. . .

I can hear U.S. liberals asking: "How can you justify slamming the door once you're inside? You say that immigrants should be kept out. But aren't we all immigrants, or the descendants of immigrants? If we insist on staying, must we not admit all others?" Our craving for intellectual order leads us to seek and prefer symmetrical rules and morals: a single rule for me and everybody else; the same rule yesterday, today and tomorrow. Justice, we feel, should not change with time and place.

We Americans of non-Indian ancestry can look upon ourselves as the descendants of thieves who are guilty morally, if not legally, of stealing this land from its Indian owners. Should we then give back the land to the now living American descendants of those Indians? However morally or logically sound this proposal may be, I, for one, am unwilling to live by it and I know no one else who is. Besides, the logical consequence would be absurd. Suppose that, intoxicated with a sense of pure justice, we should decide to turn our land over to the Indians. Since all our other wealth has also been derived from the land, wouldn't we be morally obliged to give that back to the Indians too?

PURE JUSTICE VS. REALITY

Clearly, the concept of pure justice produces an infinite regression to absurdity. Centuries ago, wise men invented statutes of limitations to justify the rejection of such pure justice, in the interest of preventing continual disorder. The law zealously defends property rights, but only relatively recent property rights. Drawing a line after an arbitrary time has elapsed may be unjust, but the alternatives are worse.

We are all the descendants of thieves, and the world's resources are inequitably distributed. But we must begin the journey to tomorrow from the point where we are today. We cannot remake the past. We cannot safely divide the wealth equitably among all peoples so long as people reproduce at different rates. To do so would guarantee that our grandchildren, and everyone else's grandchildren, would have only a ruined world to inhabit.

To be generous with one's own possessions is quite different from being generous with those of posterity. We should call this point to the attention of those who, from a commendable love of justice and equality, would institute a system of the commons, either in the form of a world food bank, or of unrestricted immigration. We must convince them if we wish to save at least some parts of the world from environmental ruin.

Without a true world government to control reproduction and the use of available resources, the sharing ethic of the spaceship is impossible. For the foreseeable future, our survival demands that we govern our actions by the ethics of a lifeboat, harsh though they may be. Posterity will be satisfied with nothing less.

DISCUSSION QUESTIONS

1. What is the "spaceship metaphor"? According to Hardin, why is it wrong? Do you agree with him? Explain.
2. What is the "lifeboat metaphor"? Does this metaphor make sense to you? How is the United States like and unlike a lifeboat? Does the introduction of this metaphor show that Peter Singer is wrong to argue that we must give many of our supplies to other countries? Discuss.
3. What is the "tragedy of the commons"? What, according to Hardin, does it have to do with rich and poor countries? Do you agree with his application of the tragedy of the commons? Can you think of any examples in which common ownership does *not* result in neglect of the resource?
4. Should we allow people to immigrate to the United States? What do you think Hardin and Singer might say? Compare your argument with theirs.
5. How is letting people die by not providing them with famine relief morally different from murdering them? You might want to refer back to James Rachels' analysis of this distinction in Chapter 3 (see his "Active and Passive Euthanasia").
6. Is there any solution to the problem of overpopulation that does not involve letting people die?

 DIANA M. PEARCE

The Feminization of Poverty

According to Diana M. Pearce, two characteristics of women's poverty distinguish it from poverty experienced by men: children and labor market discrimination. Pearce coined the phrase the "feminization of poverty" to identify "the trend toward more and more of

Diana M. Pearce, First Annual Women's Policy Research Conference Proceedings, Washington, D.C.: Institute for Women's Policy Research, May 19, 1989, 147–152. Used by permission of the Institute for Women's Policy Research.

the burden of poverty being borne by women." In this article, Pearce evaluates a number of trends to determine if there is a continuing pattern whereby women bear more and more of the burden of poverty than men. She goes on to reveal three ways in which official poverty measures underestimate the extent and depth of women's poverty. She then examines the dynamics of women's poverty as they relate to macroeconomic changes in the economy, the labor market, and child rearing. Pearce concludes by outlining some new public policy priorities aimed at decreasing poverty among women.

Diana M. Pearce is a professor at the University of Washington's School of Social Work. This article was originally published in the *First Annual Women's Policy Research Conference Proceedings* (1989).

I. IS THERE STILL A FEMINIZATION OF POVERTY?

A. Defining the Feminization of Poverty

What is the "feminization of poverty"? As the term was first used in 1978, it described the trend toward more and more of the burden of poverty being borne by women. This can be measured by two different methods. One, which will be called the individual-base method, is simply to count all persons, or adults, who are poor by gender, and examine the changes over time in the proportion female. Thus wives and daughters in poor families with male householders are counted as well as women maintaining households alone. The other way, which will be called the household-base method, is to examine the number of people who are poor by the gender of the person(s) maintaining the household, i.e., the proportion of the poor in households which are maintained by women alone, and how that proportion changes over time. The household-base measure will be used here, for it has two distinct advantages: (1) it is consistent with the way poverty is actually measured, which is at the level of the household, not the individual, and (2) it more closely reflects the concept of the feminization of poverty, i.e., the idea that women have increasingly borne the burden of poverty alone.

B. The Trends

Over the last quarter of a century, the number of poor women-maintained families, particularly those with children, has more than doubled, increasing at a remarkably steady rate of roughly 100,000 families each year. There are now 3.6 million poor women-maintained families. The proportion of poor families maintained by women alone has risen from 23 to over 51% of all families. There has been a parallel growth of women-maintained families in each racial group: between 1959 and 1986, the proportion of poor white families maintained by women alone increased from 20 to 42%, and the proportion of poor black families from 30 to 75%. Likewise, the proportion of poor Hispanic families maintained by women alone increased from 45% in 1973 (the first year for which data was available) to 49% in 1986.

C. The Depth of Women's Poverty

The poverty of women-maintained families is greater, and more persistent, than the poverty experienced by married couples and their families. In 1984, about half of poor women-maintained families, but less than a third of all other poor families, had incomes below half the poverty line. The median deficit, i.e., the amount of money per family needed for them to reach the poverty level, was 25% greater for poor women-maintained families than for all other poor families. The only survey which has followed the same people year after year, the Panel Survey on Income Dynamics at the University of Michigan, found that about 60% of the persistently poor, i.e., people poor at least 8 out of 10 years, lived in woman-maintained families. With the same data set, Hill and Corcoran estimate that once poor, the likelihood of staying poor is ten times greater if one is in a woman-maintained family compared to a family with an adult male in it.[1]

Altogether, women-maintained households have experienced a steady decline in their economic status relative to that of married couples. The median income of women-maintained households, as a percentage of that of married couples, has steadily fallen from 70% in 1947 to 42% in 1987.[2] Even when the comparison is to married couples in which the wife is not working, there is a decline in the relative status of women-maintained families.

D. Is Poverty Underestimated?

Clear as these trends are, there are three ways in which these numbers *underestimate* the number of poor, and particularly underestimate the number of poor women-maintained families.

First, poor families who are doubled-up with other families, but are not the owners or renters of the unit which they are sharing, (since 1980) have not been in the count of poor families. Statistically speaking, these families, whom the Census Bureau calls sub-families, have thus been made invisible. Since these families are disproportionately women-maintained, these changes also underestimate the nature and extent of women's poverty.

Second, the method used since 1980 to calculate poverty thresholds creates systematically lower thresholds for single parent—compared to two-parent—families; since most single parent families are women-maintained, this leads to an underestimate of the number of poor families that seriously undercounts women's poverty.

Third, because the official annual poverty counts are based on a survey of households, they do not include the homeless. Women-maintained families are the most rapidly increasing group among the homeless. Thus excluding the homeless from the count of the poor underestimates poverty generally, and women's poverty especially.

II. THE DYNAMICS OF POVERTY: ARE THEY DIFFERENT FOR WOMEN?

To further examine the phenomenon of the "feminization of poverty," this paper will examine the nature of the feminization of poverty, why the number of poor women has increased, and the specific characteristics of women's poverty, including how women's poverty is related to the labor market and to child rearing.

A. What Is the Nature of the Feminization of Poverty?

How much of this trend towards the feminization of poverty is a function of "changing demographics"—the increase in the number of women-maintained households—how much is due to the pauperization (increase in poverty rates) of women, and how much to the depauperization (decrease in poverty rates) of other groups?

Basically, what has been happening are two opposite trends. First, "demographic changes" have increased the number of and proportion of the population who are in woman-maintained households, with a corresponding decrease in married-couple households. Second, there has been a "depauperization" of several groups that have historically experienced disproportionate rates of poverty. Many workers, who used to be labeled "the working poor," have been lifted out of poverty by postwar economic growth and are now economically secure enough to be seen as the working class or the middle class. Older Americans, whose poverty frequently occurred because of a health crisis or the lack of housing, and inadequate Social Security, have benefited from programs targeted to their needs: Medicare, elderly housing, and broadened and indexed Social Security benefits. As a result, the overall poverty rate for the elderly is actually less than that of the population as a whole.

It is important to understand the dynamics of women's poverty, including what it is not. The feminization of poverty is not the result of increased numbers of women suddenly becoming impoverished. Instead, it is due to a consistent, year after year, systematic increase in the number of poor women-maintained households, coupled with a systematic decrease in the number of other poor households, the elderly and male-present families.

B. Why Have Women Not Shared in the Poverty Reduction Experienced by Other Groups?

Why have women-maintained households not experienced the depauperization that has allowed other demographic groups to exit poverty? The answer to this question lies in the dynamics of poverty over the past quarter century. The most dramatic decrease in poverty occurred during the decade of the 1960's with most of the progress occurring among males (unrelated individuals) and male-present families. During the seventies and early eighties, a cyclical pattern appeared for married-couple and male-headed households: each recession resulted in the poverty population expanding rapidly with the influx of unemployed (disproportionately male) workers and their families, and during the recoveries that followed, these families left poverty relatively quickly. Even during and after the 1982 recession, which resulted in the highest unemployment levels in the last half-century, the increase and decrease in the numbers of families in poverty was much sharper among married-couple and male-headed families than among women-maintained families.

Women-maintained families do not experience, to the same extent, the sharp increase in poverty during a recession that is experienced by men and married couples, and their families, nor do they benefit when the economy is in recovery. This is reflected in the feminization of poverty index: for example, at the depths of the most recent recession, the "index" for families fell to 46%, meaning that 46% of the poor were in women-maintained families, but in the following two years it rose again, reaching 51.5% in 1987, its highest point ever. Similar patterns can be observed for the earlier, smaller, recessions in 1975 and 1980. Because the proportion of poor families which are women-maintained is higher at the end of each recession than it was before it began, the entire period of 1959 to 1987, the proportion of poor families who are women-maintained has risen.

C. The Specific Characteristics of Women's Poverty

1. *Women in the Labor Market*   While trends in women's poverty do not follow closely macroeconomic changes or cycles in the economy, that does not mean that the economy is not relevant to women's poverty. On the contrary, increasingly women's poverty is a direct result of the disadvantaged position women hold in the labor market, their structural position. Women experience discrimination not only in getting a job, but also once they have gotten one. Many poor women are employed women, i.e., they are poor in spite of their paid employment.

a. *Wages, Hours, and Benefits*   The nature of women's disadvantage in the labor market is to be found not just in higher unemployment rates, but in employment itself. Due to child-rearing responsibilities and the lack of affordable day care, women who maintain households alone find it extremely difficult to become full-time year-round workers, and even when they do, the new jobs created by the economy's expansion are often part-time and part-year. Job growth is clearly most rapid in such sectors as service and retail trade, sectors that are dominated by part-time, part-year jobs. In 1985, for example, one-third of the new jobs were part-time. Women workers, especially those who are newly entering or reentering the labor market, are likely to take a disproportionate share of these new jobs. Thus less than half of all women workers, and 40% of women who head households alone, work full-time year-round.

The disparity between part-time/seasonal jobs and "good" jobs in terms of non-wage fringe benefits is even greater than the differences in wages alone. In addition, their marginal labor force status is reinforced for many women by their lack of coverage under unemployment insurance programs. Altogether, the wages of full-time, year-round women workers are not improving significantly or consistently, while the proportion of women with poor paying, deadend, part-time and/or part-year jobs seems likely to increase.

2. *Women and Children*   An equally important dynamic of the feminization of poverty is the economic burden of children. Over the past two-plus decades, the proportion of poor women-maintained households that have children in them has risen from 80 to 90%. At the same time, divorce today occurs at younger ages of both mother and children, and an increased proportion of single mothers have never been married. As a consequence, single parents have greater needs, for example, younger children require more costly child care, and fewer resources with which to meet them: in general, shorter marriages, or no marriages at all, result in fewer resources, including subsequent child support, than do longer marriages.

In spite of these increasing economic burdens, neither private transfers nor public transfers adequately meet the costs of caring for children. Indeed, both types of income support, private and public, have *decreased* in recent years, exacerbating this dynamic of women's poverty. As for *private transfers,* only half of absent fathers are even *supposed* to pay child support, and less than half of those paid the full amount owed. Moreover, while the proportion of non-custodial parents, mostly fathers, who pay child support has remained virtually unchanged in recent years, the amount of support has actually decreased in constant dollars—about 12% between 1983 and 1985, and it averages only about $2200 annually (per family, not per child). Even if enforcement was thorough, however, and every penny owed were paid, it would do little to reduce poverty for the simple reason that the amounts of child support ordered are too low to raise most family incomes above the poverty line.

Since 1970, the real value of *public transfers,* in the form of welfare benefits, has decreased by about one-third. The 1981 Omnibus Budget Reconciliation Act also decreased both the number of persons eligible, and benefit levels, through changes in eligibility rules and benefit calculation formulas. And the 1988 Family Support Act further restricts the availability of income support by pushing welfare recipients into employment with only minimal support and training of the kind needed for women-maintained families to become not only self-sufficient, but no longer poor. Related programs providing subsidies to low-income families have also been cut significantly, particularly, low-income housing, but also child care, medical care, etc. Even non-welfare income support programs, such as unemployment insurance, are reaching fewer single parent families, and are lifting fewer of those out of poverty than was true before 1980.

3. *Older Women and Poverty* The nature of women's disadvantages, in the labor market, and as a result of child rearing, is such that it even contributes to the feminization of poverty among older women. While women over 65 have experienced decreased poverty *rates* in recent years, this is not likely to continue; moreover, all of the progress in poverty reduction among the elderly has happened among married couples and men. Most married women choose to receive Social Security benefits as wives, rather than in their own right as workers, because of their husbands' substantially higher earnings and thus higher Social Security benefits. As the proportion of women turning 65 who have not been married long enough to qualify for their ex-husbands' Social Security benefits increases, they are likely to have far less Social Security income.

Likewise, many divorced women, even those divorced near or during their husbands' retirement, receive little or no money from their ex-husbands' private pensions. Women's increased labor force participation still leaves them, because of their low wages, with very low Social Security benefits. Finally, women tend to outlive not only their husbands, but also their joint resources, as much or all of their savings are spent, and his pension often stops with his death. Until we develop policies to better protect women against these losses of income, increasing numbers of older women will spend their last years as impoverished widows.

III. THE IMPLICATION OF THE FEMINIZATION OF POVERTY PERSPECTIVE FOR UNDERSTANDING POVERTY: TOWARDS A NEW PUBLIC POLICY

Current public policy debate has begun to recognize the importance of some of the roots of women's poverty, but quite unevenly. In the area of child rear-

ing, the importance of child care, both the need to cover the costs, and issues of availability of safe and decent child care, are being at least debated. And for poor women, the creation of essentially an entitlement to child care in the Family Support Act of 1988 for those entering employment or education and training programs is significant for its implicit recognition of this need among poor women. At the same time, current debates, much less enacted legislation, do not address the inadequacy of income support for dependent children with absent or long-term unemployed parents. Without income support in the form of adequate AFDC benefits, or a public back-up child support for those children who have inadequate or no private child support, women will continue to be impoverished by the economic burdens of raising children alone.

In the area of employment disadvantage, it is clear that decreasing the incidence of working poverty among women requires addressing the inequalities women face in the labor market. Compared to the nascent recognition of needs created by child rearing, in the area of employment policy, there is virtually no recognition of the connections between women's labor force position and women's poverty. Thus the recent federal welfare reform mandates a range of education, training, and employment programs without a single reference to the occupational segregation, pay inequities, and other disadvantages women experience that were described above. Just as the War on Poverty saw anti-discrimination civil rights laws as integral to efforts to reduce black poverty, current employment policy must incorporate comparable anti-discrimination efforts if programs are going to effectively raise women's wages and reduce women's poverty. Moreover, efforts to portray the growth of part-time and seasonal employment as positive for women, on the theory that their "flexibility" facilitates balancing work and family obligations, obscures the ways in which these new jobs impoverish women and lock them into jobs that are deadend.

NOTES

1. Duncan et al., *Years of Poverty, Years of Plenty* (Ann Arbor, MI: Institute for Social Research, 1984).

2. *Money Income and Poverty Statistics in the United States: 1987,* U.S. Commerce, Bureau of the Census, March 1988. Figures for intervening years are: 56% in 1950, to 50% in 1960, to 48% in 1970, to 45% in 1980, to 44% in 1984.

DISCUSSION QUESTIONS

1. What does Pearce mean by the phrase "the feminization of poverty"? Does the evidence she provides convince you that poverty should be considered from the perspective of sex? Why or why not?
2. Amartya Sen, winner of the 1998 Nobel Prize in Economics, says that our moral thinking about poverty must involve some serious empirical investigation. Do you believe that moral thinking about the feminization of poverty deserves some serious empirical investigation? Why might someone disagree with you? How would you respond?
3. Do you think that the feminization of poverty is a relatively recent phenomenon? Why or why not?
4. What public policies does Pearce believe will help to slow down the feminization of poverty? What current public policies might help to slow down the feminization of poverty? Do some research, and provide a list of public policies in the last ten years that fit this description.
5. Pearce writes that "increasingly women's poverty is a direct result of the disadvantaged position women hold in the labor market, their structural position. Women experience discrimination not only in getting a job, but also once they have gotten one. Many poor women are employed women, i.e., they are poor in spite of their paid employment." Critically comment on this passage. What evidence does Pearce provide in support of it? Does this evidence convince you of the truth of this passage? Why or why not?

MARGARET B. WILKERSON AND JEWELL HANDY GRESHAM

The Racialization of Poverty

Margaret B. Wilkerson and Jewell Handy Gresham object to the way Diana Pearce uses the notion of the "feminization of poverty." According to Wilkerson and Gresham, the "feminization of poverty" is a "distortion that negates the role played by racial barriers to black employment, particularly among males." For them, any real consideration of the feminization of poverty must also take into account the *racialization* of poverty. The "impact of race, class and gender cannot be adequately examined by focusing on the status of women alone," say Wilkerson and Gresham; "it must also be viewed in the context of prescribed black and white women's roles in the labor marketplace vis-à-vis those of privileged males." Wilkerson and Gresham argue that by omitting an account of race, Pearce proposes a notion of the feminization of poverty that "unwittingly contributes" to the "insidious notion that households headed by black women are *destined* for poverty, not because of the absence of economic means but because of the absence of the male."

Jewell Handy Gresham is president of the Hansberry-Nemiroff Archival, Educational, and Cultural Fund. Dr. Margaret Wilkerson is director of Media, Arts, and Culture, the Ford Foundation.

Margaret B. Wilkerson and Jewell Handy Gresham, *The Nation, Special Issue* (24/31 July 1989). Reprinted by permission of the authors.

American policymakers have an uncanny ability to obfuscate and compartmentalize social problems—to recognize on the one hand that the United States has an unacceptably high level of unemployment, particularly among specific groups, and to recognize that we also have an incredibly high number of female-headed families, particularly within the same groups, but to avoid the cause-and-effect relationship between the two phenomena.

—Ruth Sidel,
Women and Children Last

The term "feminization of poverty," which was devised to describe the significant numbers of women and children living in poverty, is a distortion that negates the role played by racial barriers to black employment, particularly among males. The feminization of poverty is real, but the *racialization* of poverty is at its heart. To discuss one without the other is to play a mirror game with reality.

In *Women and Children Last: The Plight of Poor Women in Affluent America*, sociologist Ruth Sidel observes that in contemporary America, "welfare" has become a euphemism for Aid to Families with Dependent Children (A.F.D.C.). More, the term is now used to mask, barely, negative images of teeming black female fecundity—particularly among teenagers—and of feckless black males who abandon their children. The fact that it is specifically black unwed mothers who evoke this atavistic response shows that race, not gender, is the source of revulsion.

Currently, the most critical problem relating to the plight of black unwed mothers is the massive unemployment of the males who would otherwise be potential mates for them. Sidel ties her discussion of black male unemployment to a survey of black versus white incomes. In 1981, for example, 47 percent of black college graduates earned $20,000 to $40,000 a year, the income spread for the majority of white *high school* graduates. This is only one of many facts evidencing the degree of discrimination against blacks in the workplace.

Although the number of black men holding professional, technical, managerial and sales jobs has increased significantly, the number who are unemployed is "astronomical," Sidel observed. "It is estimated that approximately 45 percent of black men do not have jobs, including not only those officially classified by the Census Bureau but also those who are counted as 'discouraged and no longer looking for work.'" In addition, she wrote,

according to a statistician with the Children's Defense Fund, approximately 15–29 percent of

black men aged twenty to forty *could not be found by the Bureau in 1980*. They are presumed to have neither permanent residences nor jobs. If they are added to the number of unemployed, the number of black men without jobs can be estimated to be well over 50 percent. (Emphasis added.)

This level of unemployment is more than double the figure for all workers at the height of the Great Depression. William Julius Wilson, author of *The Truly Disadvantaged*, states that in one of the Chicago ghetto neighborhoods he studied, the ratio of employed black males to their impoverished female counterparts was 18 to 100.

Such a "shockingly high rate of male unemployment," Sidel points out, "has had a direct bearing on the dramatic rise in black female-headed families." Yet we still look for "the 'causes' of the rise in black-female families, debate whether the welfare system encourages their proliferation, blame the mothers for having babies outside of marriage—but largely ignore the impact of male unemployment on family life."

One of the most pernicious aspects of the white patriarchal definition of an acceptable household (one headed by a male who is able to provide for his family) is that the masses of black youth and men who are excluded from the opportunities and rewards of the economic system cannot possibly meet this requirement. Then both males and females of the subjugated class are castigated as being morally unfit because they have not held their reproductive functions in abeyance.

At the same time, there is the insidious notion that households headed by black women are *destined* for poverty, not because of the absence of economic means but because of the absence of the male. (Unwed mothers who happen to be affluent are sometimes dubbed "bachelor mothers" to distinguish them from this group.) Feminists who omit race and racism as a possible decisive variable in any analysis of American poverty—and most particularly the poverty of black women—unwittingly contribute to this notion. When sociologist Diana Pearce coined the term "feminization of poverty" in 1978, she had in mind "two characteristics of women's poverty that distinguish it from the poverty experienced by men: children and labor market discrimination."

But in view of the astronomical levels of black males who are excluded from the labor market, the plight of black children must be examined in light of the circumstances of both their mothers and fathers, even though the mothers are usually left with the responsibility of caring for the children after the fathers depart under economic duress.

"ALL THEY'LL DO IS HAVE MORE CHILDREN"

In her recent book *Regulating the Lives of Women: Social Welfare Policy from Colonial Times to the Present,* Mimi Abramovitz provides a comprehensive account of the welfare policies of this society from their beginnings in 1935, when the Social Security Act legitimized the idea of social insurance. The immediate predecessor of the act was a pension to widows with young children, limited almost entirely to white women. In the 1930s, Aid to Dependent Children (A.D.C.) was born in the provisions for a "means-tested" public assistance program for the impoverished elderly, blind adults and poor children with absent fathers.

With the passage of this program, Abramovitz notes, the state took direct responsibility for reproduction in female-headed households under certain conditions, foremost among them that the mothers stay at home to rear their children. While that patriarchal model was set up for some women, however, an opening was left to insure that an ample supply of low-paid female domestic and casual labor reached the market through provisions denying aid to "undeserving" women.

By race, black women fell collectively into the category of "the undeserving." By class, so did large numbers of white women. Some states drew up, Abramovitz noted, "employable mother" rules that disqualified able-bodied women with school-age children, especially black women, on the ground that they should work. In the late 1930s, one Southern public assistance field supervisor reported the following:

> The number of Negro cases is few due to the unanimous feeling on the part of the staff and board that there are more work opportunities for Negro women and to their intense desire not to interfere with local labor conditions. The attitude that they have always gotten along, and that "all they'll do is have more children" is definite. . . . There is hesitancy on the part of lay boards to advance too rapidly over the thinking of their own communities, which see no reason why the employable Negro mother should not continue her usual sketchy seasonal labor or indefinite domestic service rather than receive a public assistance grant.

This commonplace form of discrimination is only one example of the vicissitudes of the marketplace to which black women and children, like black men, have historically been subjected.

The A.D.C. program, which grew from 372,000 families in 1940 to 803,000 in 1960, declined temporarily during World War II and the Korean War. In 1962, it became Aid to Families with Dependent Children. In the face of its rapid expansion and a shift in the composition of the caseload from white widows to unwed mothers and women of color, A.D.C. was attacked for faltering in the task of regulating the lives of poor women by excluding the undeserving. With the entry of significant numbers of black women into the program, the attacks upon it became widespread and systematically racist.

The black women who are caught in oppressive circumstances can articulate better than anyone else the flavor of their predicament. Abramovitz quotes Johnnie Tillmon, welfare mother and a leader of the National Welfare Rights Organization in the 1960s and 1970s, who calls the relationship between A.F.D.C. mothers and the system a "supersexist marriage." Tillmon explains:

> You trade in "a" man for "The" man. But you can't divorce him if he treats you bad. He can divorce you of course, cut you off anytime he wants. But in that case "he" keeps the kids, not you. "The" man runs everything. In ordinary marriage, sex is supposed to be for your husband. On AFDC you're not supposed to have any sex at all. You give up control over your body. It's a condition of aid. . . . "The" man, the welfare system, controls your money. He tells you what to buy and what not to buy, where to buy it, and how much things cost. If things—rent, for instance—really cost more than he says they do, it's too bad for you.

Clearly, the impact of race, class and gender cannot be adequately examined by focusing on the status of women alone; it must also be viewed in the context of prescribed black and white women's roles in the labor marketplace vis-à-vis those of privileged males. It is interesting, for instance, to reflect on the significance of the polar extremes to which women, by race and class, are currently assigned. Felice Schwartz's article on "Management Women and the New Facts of Life," which caused such a furor when it appeared in the January-February issue of the *Harvard Business Review,* has little relevance to black women, whose presence in corporate management positions is negligible.

Schwartz recommended that a double-track system be set up to permit part-time work by women who wanted to spend time with their children (the so-called Mommy track) and full-time employment for "career primary" women who can be "worked like men." The corporate world's enthusiastic response to this proposal raises a question: Did it do so because the proposal offered desirable adjustments relating to the reproductive roles of women, or because it would lessen the economic competition coming from women of the corporate class and provide highly skilled female labor at a lower cost? Whatever the case, the issues affect only upper-class women, who can choose whether they work full- or part-time.

THE MOYNIHAN-ARMSTRONG "REFORM"

It is instructive to contrast Schwartz's plan with the welfare reform legislation enacted last fall for which New York Democratic Senator Daniel Patrick Moynihan and Republican Senator William Armstrong of Colorado took major public credit. Under this program, A.F.D.C. mothers, in keeping with Tillmon's description, will *not* be the ones making the decision as to whether they should remain at home with their children. Those who have children older than 3 *must* go forth as cheaply paid laborers unless they are under 19, in which case they are required to seek educational advancement, assuming the states chip in to fund such programs.

When one considers that a single Chicago housing project may hold as many as 20,000 largely jobless people packed into high-rise buildings of thirty or more stories, just how this program's proponents intend to insure adequate child care services for the poor mothers forced to leave their children is not clear, especially when day care facilities and personnel are unavailable even to large numbers of middle-class and upper-class mothers. And what means of transportation will these poor (and frequently inexperienced) mothers use when they pack themselves and their children off to babysitters? One wonders how many of the men who sit in the halls of Congress have ever played a parenting role in which they had the opportunity to engage in such tasks for even, let us say, one week.

For tens of thousands of the urban poor in housing projects, the length of time it takes for the elevators in their buildings merely to rise to their floors and descend again—assuming they work at all—can present a crisis. How far a mother and her child or children must travel after that—and by what means—before the youngsters can be deposited and mothers continue on their way may represent another; what arrangements can be made with the employer when the children are ill, yet another. What surcease will be available for the women themselves if they are ill, or harried, or weary beyond bearing? How can they summon up sufficient energy to help their school-age children with homework, assuming they have sufficient education to do so? And so on, endlessly.

Ponder just a fraction of the problems in populations in which babies, children, youth and adults die off at unconscionably high ratios from preventable or manageable diseases and conditions (and whose mothers, and fathers when they are present, must be particularly vigilant to guard their children against becoming casualties of the pervasive scourge of drugs, in psychologically and physically violent neighborhoods) and it becomes apparent why some "experts" and officials take refuge in abstract solutions, or none at all.

When one further reflects on where any jobs will come from, and—in the case of teen-age mothers ordered to finish high school—what miraculous educational services are contemplated, the picture for those deprived by race *and* class appears not brighter but potentially even more retrogressive.

In a chapter of her book entitled "Welfare," Sidel provides a picture of the intolerable treatment systematically accorded the nation's poor when applying for or receiving A.F.D.C. aid. In spite of the attempts of many caseworkers to preserve a sense of personal compassion, the weight of the system overwhelms them.

More than any other single factor, women on welfare report that the most damaging traumas they suffer are the humiliations daily meted out in welfare offices all over the country, which are designed to demean and punish them for being in need. Besides a barrage of examples drawn from A.F.D.C. mothers, Sidel quotes from an analysis of the working class, *The Hidden Injuries of Class,* by Richard Sennett and Jonathan Cobb.

"Dignity is as compelling a human need as food or sex," these men wrote, "and yet here is a society which casts the mass of its people into limbo, never satisfying their hunger for dignity." In describing the "plight of blue-collar workers who feel shamed and demeaned by their position in American society," the authors point out that these workers survive by keeping

> a certain distance from the problems of class and class consciousness, by separating themselves from their feelings when they are interacting with the world the same way as the poor attempt to protect themselves from the not-so-hidden injuries of poverty. They try to deal with the welfare bureaucracies with resignation and deadened emotions. They leave "the real me" somewhere else when they must cope with the intrusive questions, the unspoken (and all-too-often spoken) criticisms, the disregard for their humanness.

White blue-collar workers humiliated in such fashion may be able, in general, to hide behind a blanket of public anonymity, but black welfare recipients are seldom permitted even this refuge. Sidel quotes a black social worker in Atlanta, who describes the county offices that administer A.F.D.C. as "little nations" and the client population as "very fearful":

> They will use all of their resources rather than go to welfare. They're not going to take that ugliness, that humiliation. . . . Georgia will not give welfare to a two-parent family. These people are treated so badly that they would rather sell dope and steal instead.

The director of Family and Children Services in DeKalb County, Georgia, reports a dramatic increase over the past years in requests for emergency aid arising out of the state's "trimming the rolls." County workers may give emergency aid only once to a family. "When asked what a family did if it had received emergency aid once and was in dire need again, one worker replied dryly, 'Pray a lot.'"

Sidel recounts numerous tales of fortitude among welfare recipients, such as that of the mother of two children who took two buses to get her children to her grandmother's every day so that she could attend a community college. When she completed her work and, with the help of scholarships, went on to a four-year school, she could not tell her caseworker—because A.F.D.C. did not support students in four-year programs, only two-year or vocational schools. In such blatant fashion is revealed A.F.D.C.'s policy of keeping the poor poor.

The role of racism in the system is the traditional one of making racial and class exploitation easier. Dangerous precedents that will be harmful to the welfare of major segments of the society can be es-

tablished by first applying them only to blacks. One can gain some idea of how this works by examining the way the national political leadership treats the masses. An example is the targeting of black adolescents by top "centrist" echelons of the Democratic Party. On the one hand, teen-age mothers are projected as carriers of a particular strain of pathology against which drastic measures must be taken. (Only recently, Moynihan ascribed malignancy to the black "matriarchy"!) Concomitantly, black male teen-agers are propelled to the forefront of black criminality, which must be destroyed. This may be the first time in history that a nation has singled out a specific race of youths against whom to direct its frustration and fury.

SAM NUNN'S "NATIONAL SERVICE" SOLUTION

Writing in *The New York Times* on May 30, 1987, Frances Fox Piven and Barbara Ehrenreich argued that the welfare reform act will accomplish little more than creating a new form of "mass peonage." Some idea of what is in store for youthful black males and females bound into a single package for manipulation may be glimpsed in the legislation currently sponsored in the Senate by Sam Nunn. The ill-conceived proposal would eliminate all forms of Federal educational grants for higher education to poor students and replace them with a "Citizenship and National Service Act," which is, in effect, a "workfare" program. For two years of labor, young people would receive a stipend of $10,000 annually at the conclusion of their "service." If they volunteered for the military, their reward would be $12,000 per year. Virtually the only way that most of the poor could get into college would be through this "national service."

In combination, the two programs—welfare and national service—would create bureaucratic machinery for manipulating black young people. It would channel a pool of cheap black female labor, composed of welfare mothers, into the work force and harness the energies of their male counterparts through the national service plan. Disproportionate numbers of young black males would be drawn to the military by the added stipend, and thereby rendered disproportionately vulnerable to wartime death. (America has always found it easier to propel its black youths toward death than to educate them.)

One might also ask whether the stipends will help many deprived young people to enter college.

Not very much in the way of higher education can be purchased for $10,000 or $12,000, and the temptation would be great for black and white families of limited means to spend the money on a dozen needs having higher priority.

In the case of A.F.D.C. mothers, former Secretary of Labor Ray Marshall points out that 86 percent of all social welfare spending since the 1960s has gone to America's elderly, and only a small proportion to A.F.D.C. mothers or their offspring. The result has been that poverty among the elderly has declined almost by half, from more than 25 percent at the beginning of the War on Poverty to 14 percent in 1983. Just the opposite is true with regard to America's children, primarily blacks and others of color whose parents are poor. In a 1986 article in *Southern Changes* titled "The War Against the Poor," Robert Greenstein, director of the Washington-based Center on Budget and Policy Priorities, wrote:

> If you look at the statistics of American poverty today, one set—the figures for children's poverty—hits you over the head. Fifteen years ago the child poverty rate was between thirteen and fourteen percent. Last year it was over twenty-one percent. . . . And, while there has been a very slight recent reduction in the overall poverty rate during the past year, and in the overall child poverty rate, all the reduction in child poverty has occurred among white children. None of it has occurred among black or Hispanic children.
>
> The poverty rate for black children under the age of six now has reached just over fifty-one percent.

If one out of every two black children in this country is born poor, and the national leadership regards black adolescents as exemplars of pathology instead of promise, what must black Americans do? What must society do?

For one thing, we might begin by reviewing the attitudes of officials of the national government—of the Bush Administration and members of Congress of both political parties—toward the well-being of *all* members of the society. In particular, we should make certain that the political conditions are created and sustained that will encourage those who serve in positions of leadership to do so not by ignoring race, gender and class as determining variables affecting the lives of the people, but by developing infinitely more sophisticated means to address and redress what is wrong.

And we, who are most directly affected by race, class and gender, should advance our own knowledge accordingly.

Even, for example, if we were concerned simply with the reproductive roles, functions and rights of women, it would still be necessary to develop a keener awareness of the interrelated roles of race, gender and class oppression—including the institutionalized white-male-over-black-male oppression, which in this patriarchal (not matriarchal) society underpins everything else.

Black women must address the enormous problems within the black community, including black male sexism and rage, particularly the violence and, yes, the pathology of anger and frustration that is taken out against them and other members of the community. But we cannot turn our attention to any condition besetting black people without consideration of the terrible toll of the white racism and sexism which undergird and perpetuate an oppressive system.

Barbara Ommolade, a single-mother college counselor, activist and writer who has been on welfare, neatly and eloquently summed up the picture in "It's a Family Affair: The Real Lives of Black Single Mothers" (*Village Voice,* July 15, 1986):

> Today, the context of the struggle to have a black family is legal desegregation and superficial political gains for black people, along with high unemployment among black men, depressed wages for black women, and public denigration of poor people. The concept of a pathological underclass has become the rationale for continued racism and economic injustice; in attempting to separate racial from economic inequality and [in] blaming family pathology for black people's condition, current ideology obscures the system's inability to provide jobs, decent wages, and adequate public services for the black poor. And in a racist-patriarchal society, the effects of the system's weaknesses fall most heavily on black women and children. Just as black family life has always been a barometer of racial and economic injustice and at the same time a means of transcending and surviving those injustices, black families headed by women reflect the strength and the difficulty of black life in the 80's.

Black women know the critical problems of our communities, but we also know their strengths. We have to call on those strengths collectively from blacks now, but we also call on more. It is the obligation of all concerned Americans to join forces in seeking to remove the stigma from government assistance to citizens in need. And to make certain that channels exist for people who are temporarily down to recover their footing, thankful that a nurturing society exists for them and conscious of their responsibility to be nurturing too.

DISCUSSION QUESTIONS

1. What, according to Wilkerson and Gresham, is the problem with Diana Pearce's notion of the "feminization of poverty"? Do you agree with them? Why or why not?
2. Wilkerson and Gresham argue that, by omitting an account of race, Pearce's (and others') use of the notion of the feminization of poverty "unwittingly contributes" to the "insidious notion that households headed by black women are *destined* for poverty, not because of the absence of economic means but because of the absence of the male." What is their argument? How might Pearce respond to it?
3. What is the role of race, class, and gender in considerations of providing relief for the nation's poor? Defend your view in detail.
4. Peter Singer discusses our obligations to the poor without taking into account matters of race, class, and gender. Do you think this is a weakness in his account? Do you think considerations of race, class, and gender would change his account in any way? Explain.
5. Wilkerson and Gresham discuss some of the ways in which race and racism play a role in our policies and practices regarding the poor. What are they? If you can, examine some of this evidence in more detail by looking up additional materials on these policies and practices.
6. To what extent do you believe that our policies and practices regarding the poor of our nation are racist? Defend your view.

KAI NIELSEN

Radical Egalitarianism

Kai Nielsen argues for an equality of basic condition for everyone. For Nielsen, "everyone, as far as possible, should have equal life prospects, short of genetic engineering and the like and the rooting out any form of the family and the undermining of our basic freedoms." Furthermore, "classlessness is something we should all aim at if we are egalitarians," says Nielsen, for "it is only in such a classless society that the ideals of equality (the conception of equality as a very general goal to be achieved) can be realized." Nielsen maintains that his radical egalitarianism is a spelling out of Karl Marx's slogan, "From each according to his ability, to each according to his needs." If his principles of radical egalitarianism are correct, maintains Nielsen, then statist and capitalist societies should be regarded as defective in justice.

Kai Nielsen, *Equality and Liberty*. Rowan & Allanheld, 1985, 283–292, 302–306, 309. Reprinted with permission from Rowman & Littlefield.

Kai Nielsen is professor of philosophy at the University of Calgary and the author of many books, including *Contemporary Critiques of Religion* (1971), *Ethics Without God* (1973), *Scepticism* (1973), *Equality and Liberty: A Defense of Radical Egalitarianism* (1985), *Philosophy and Atheism: In Defense of Atheism* (1985), *God, Scepticism and Modernity* (1989), and *After the Demise of the Tradition: Rorty, Critical Theory, and the Fate of Philosophy* (1991). The following selection is from *Equality and Liberty*.

I

I have talked of equality as a right and of equality as a goal. And I have taken, as the principal thing, to be able to state what goal we are seeking when we say equality is a goal. When we are in a position actually to achieve that goal, then that same equality becomes a right. The goal we are seeking is an equality of basic condition for everyone. Let me say a bit what this is: everyone, as far as possible, should have equal life prospects, short of genetic engineering and the like and the rooting out any form of the family and the undermining of our basic freedoms. There should, where this is possible, be an equality of access to equal resources over each person's life as a whole, though this should be qualified by people's varying needs. Where psychiatrists are in short supply only people who are in need of psychiatric help should have equal access to such help. This equal access to resources should be such that it stands as a barrier to their being the sort of differences between people that allow some to be in a position to control and to exploit others; such equal access to resources should also stand as a barrier to one adult person having power over other adult persons that does not rest on the revocable consent on the part of the persons over whom he comes to have power. Where, because of some remaining scarcity in a society of considerable productive abundance, we cannot reasonably distribute resources equally, we should first, where considerations of desert are not at issue, distribute according to stringency of need, second according to the strength of unmanipulated preferences and third, and finally, by lottery. We should, in trying to attain equality of condition, aim at a condition of autonomy (the fuller and the more rational the better) for everyone and at a condition where everyone alike, to the fullest extent possible, has his or her needs and wants satisfied. The limitations on the satisfaction of people's wants should be only where that satisfaction is incompatible with everyone getting the same treatment. Where we have conflicting wants, such as where two persons want to marry the same person, the fair thing to do will vary with the circumstances. In the marriage case, freedom of choice is obviously the fair thing. But generally, what should be aimed at is having everyone have their wants satisfied as far as possible. To achieve equality of condition would be, as well, to achieve a condition where the necessary burdens of the society are equally shared, where to do so is reasonable, and where each person has an equal voice in deciding what these burdens shall be. Moreover, everyone, as much as possible, should be in a position—and should be equally in that position—to control his own life. The goals of egalitarianism are to achieve such equalities.

Minimally, classlessness is something we should all aim at if we are egalitarians. It is necessary for the stable achievement of equalities of the type discussed in the previous paragraph. Beyond that, we should also aim at a statusless society, though not at an undifferentiated society or a society which does not recognize merit. . . . It is only in such a classless, statusless society that the ideals of equality (the conception of equality as a very general goal to be achieved) can be realized. In aiming for a statusless society, we are aiming for a society which, while remaining a society of material abundance, is a society in which there are to be no extensive differences in life prospects between people because some have far greater income, power, authority or prestige than others. This is the *via negativia* of the egalitarian way. The *via positivia* is to produce social conditions, where there is generally material abundance, where well-being and satisfaction are not only maximized (the utilitarian thing) but, as well, a society where this condition, as far as it is achievable, is sought equally for all (the egalitarian thing). This is the underlying conception of the egalitarian commitment to equality of condition.

II

Robert Nozick asks "How do we decide how much equality is enough?" In the preceding section we gestured in the direction of an answer. I should now like to be somewhat more explicit. Too much equality, as we have been at pains to point out, would be to treat everyone identically, completely ignoring their differing needs. Various forms of "barracks equality" approximating that would also be too much. Too little equality would be to limit equality of condition, as did the old egalitarianism, to achieving equal legal and political rights, equal civil liberties, to equality of opportunity and to a redistribution of gross disparities in wealth sufficient to keep social peace, the rationale for the latter being that such gross inequalities if allowed to stand would threaten social stability. This Hobbesist stance indicates that the old egalitarianism proceeds in a very pragmatic manner. Against the old egalitarianism I would argue that we must at least aim at an equality of whole life prospects, where that is not read simply as the right to compete for scarce positions of advantage, but where there is to be brought into being the kind of equality of condition that would provide everyone equally, as far as possible, with the resources and the social conditions to satisfy their needs as fully as possible compatible with everyone else doing likewise. (Note that between people these needs will be partly the same but will still often be importantly different as well.) Ideally, as a kind of ideal limit for a society of wondrous abundance, a radical egalitarianism would go beyond that to a similar thing for wants. We should, that is, provide all people equally, as far as possible, with the resources and social conditions to satisfy their wants, as fully as possible compatible with everyone else doing likewise. (I recognize that there is a slide between wants and needs. As the wealth of a society increases and its structure changes, things that started out as wants tend to become needs, e.g., someone in the Falkland Islands might merely reasonably want an auto while someone in Los Angeles might not only want it but need it as well. But this does not collapse the distinction between wants and needs. There are things in any society people need, if they are to survive at all in anything like a commodious condition, whether they want them or not, e.g., they need food, shelter, security, companionship and the like. An egalitarian starts with basic needs, or at least with what are taken in the cultural environment in which a given person lives to be basic needs, and moves out to other needs and finally to wants as the productive power of the society increases.)

I qualified my above formulations with "as far as possible" and with "as fully as possible compatible with everyone else doing likewise." These are essential qualifications. Where, as in societies that we know, there are scarcities, even rather minimal scarcities, not everyone can have the resources or at least all the resources necessary to have their needs satisfied. Here we must first ensure that, again as far as possible, their basic needs are all satisfied and then we move on to other needs and finally to wants. But sometimes, to understate it, even in very affluent societies, everyone's needs cannot be met, or at least they cannot be equally met. In such circumstances we have to make some hard choices. I am thinking of a situation where there are not enough dialysis machines to go around so that everyone who needs one can have one. What then should we do? The thing to aim at, to try as far as possible to approximate, if only as a heuristic ideal, is the full and equal meeting of needs and wants of everyone. It is when we have that much equality that we have enough equality. But, of course, "ought implies can," and where we can't achieve it we can't achieve it. But where we reasonably can, we ought to do it. It is something that fairness requires.

The "reasonably can" is also an essential modification: we need situations of sufficient abundance so that we do not, in going for such an equality of condition, simply spread the misery around or spread very Spartan conditions around. Before we can rightly aim for the equality of condition I mentioned, we must first have the productive capacity and resource conditions to support the institutional means that would make possible the equal satisfaction of basic needs and the equal satisfaction of other needs and wants as well.

Such achievements will often not be possible; perhaps they will never be fully possible, for, no doubt, the physically handicapped will always be with us. Consider, for example, situations where our scarcities are such that we cannot, without causing considerable misery, create the institutions and mechanisms that would work to satisfy all needs, even all basic needs. Suppose we have the technology in place to develop all sorts of complicated life-sustaining machines all of which would predictably provide people with a quality of life that they, viewing the matter clearly, would rationally choose if they were simply choosing for themselves. But suppose, if we put such technologies in place, we will then not have the wherewithal to provide basic health care in outlying regions in the country or adequate educational services in such places. We should not, under those circumstances, put those technologies in place. But we should also recognize that where it becomes possible to put these technologies in place without sacrificing other more pressing needs, we should do so. The underlying egalitarian rationale is evident enough: produce the conditions for the most extensive satisfaction of needs for everyone. Where A's need and B's need are equally important (equally stringent) but cannot both be satisfied, satisfy A's need rather than B's if the satisfaction of A's need would be more fecund for the satisfaction of the needs of others than B's, or less undermining of the satisfaction of the needs of others than B's. (I do not mean to say that that is our only criterion of choice but it is the criterion most relevant for us here.) We should seek the satisfaction of the greatest compossible set of needs where the conditions for compossibility are (a) that everyone's needs be considered, (b) that everyone's needs be *equally* considered and where two sets of needs cannot both be satisfied, the more stringent set of needs shall first be satisfied. (Do not say we have no working criteria for what they are. If you need food to keep you from starvation or debilitating malnutrition and I need a vacation to relax after a spate of hard work, your need is plainly more stringent than mine. There would, of course, be all sorts of disputable cases, but there are also a host of perfectly determinate cases indicating that we have working criteria.) The underlying rationale is to seek compossible sets of needs so that we approach as far as possible as great a satisfaction of needs as possible for everyone.

This might, it could be said, produce a situation in which very few people got those things that they needed the most, or at least wanted the most. Remember Nozick with his need for the resources of Widner Library in an annex to his house. People, some might argue, with expensive tastes and extravagant needs, say a need for really good wine, would never, with a stress on such compossibilia, get things they are really keen about. Is that the kind of world we would reflectively want? Well, *if* their not getting them is the price we have to pay for everyone having their basic needs met, then it is a price we ought to pay. I am very fond of very good wines as well as fresh ripe mangos, but if the price of my having them is that people starve or suffer malnutrition in the Sahel, or indeed anywhere else, then plainly fairness, if not just plain human decency, requires that I forego them.

In talking about how much equality is enough, I have so far talked of the benefits that equality is meant to provide. But egalitarians also speak of an equal sharing of the necessary burdens of the society as well. Fairness requires a sharing of the burdens, and for a radical egalitarian this comes to an equal sharing of the burdens where people are equally capable of sharing them. Translated into the concrete this does *not* mean that a child or an old man or a pregnant woman are to be required to work in the mines or that they be required to collect garbage, but it would involve something like requiring every able bodied person, say from nineteen to twenty, to take his or her turn at a fair portion of the necessary unpleasant jobs in the world. In that way we all, where we are able to do it, would share equally in these burdens—in doing the things that none of us want to do but that we, if we are at all reasonable, recognize the necessity of having done. (There are all kinds of variations and complications concerning this—what do we do with the youthful wonder at the violin? But, that notwithstanding, the general idea is clear enough.) And, where we think this is reasonably feasible, it squares with our considered judgments about fairness.

I have given you, in effect appealing to my considered judgments but considered judgments I do not think are at all eccentric, a picture of what I would take to be enough equality, too little equality and not enough equality. But how can we know that my proportions are right? I do not think we can avoid or should indeed try to avoid an appeal to considered judgments here. But working with them there are some arguments we can appeal, to get them in wide reflective equilibrium. Suppose we go back to the formal principle of justice, namely that we must treat like cases alike. Because it does not tell us *what* are like cases, we cannot derive substantive criteria from it. But it may, indirectly, be of some help here. We all, if we are not utterly zany, want a life in which our needs are satisfied and in which we can live as we wish and do what we want to do. Though we differ in many ways, in our abilities, capacities for pleasure, [and] determination to keep on with a job, we do not differ about wanting our needs satisfied or being able to live as we wish. Thus, *ceterus paribus*, where questions of desert, entitlement and the like do not enter, it is only fair that all of us should have our needs equally considered and that we should, again *ceterus paribus*, all be able to do as we wish in a way that is compatible with others doing likewise. From the formal principle of justice and a few key facts about us, we can get to the claim that *ceterus paribus* we should go for this much equality. But this is the core content of a radical egalitarianism.

However, how do we know that *ceterus* is *paribus* here? What about our entitlements and deserts? Suppose I have built my house with my own hands, from materials I have purchased and on land that I have purchased and that I have lived in it for years and have carefully cared for it. The house is mine and I am entitled to keep it even if by dividing the house into two apartments greater and more equal satisfaction of need would obtain for everyone. Justice requires that such an entitlement be respected here. (Again, there is an implicit *ceterus paribus* clause. In extreme situations, say after a war with housing in extremely short supply, that entitlement could be rightly overridden.)

There is a response on the egalitarian's part similar to a response utilitarianism made to criticisms of a similar logical type made of utilitarians by pluralistic deontologists. One of the things that people in fact need, or at least reflectively firmly want, is to have such entitlements respected. Where they are routinely overridden to satisfy other needs or wants, we would *not* in fact have a society in which the needs of everyone are being maximally met. To the reply, but what if more needs for everyone were met by ignoring or overriding such entitlements, the radical egalitarian should respond that that is, given the way we are, a thoroughly hypothetical situation and that theories of morality cannot be expected to give guidance for all logically possible worlds but only for worlds which are reasonably like what our actual world is or plausibly could come to be. Setting this argument aside for the moment, even if it did turn out that the need satisfaction linked with having other things—things that involved the overriding of those entitlements—was sufficient to make it the case that more need satisfaction all around for *everyone* would be achieved by overriding those entitlements, then, for reasonable people who clearly saw that, these entitlements would not have the weight presently given to them. They either would not have the importance presently attached to them or the need for the additional living space would be so great that their being overridden would seem, everything considered, the lesser of two evils (as in the example of the postwar housing situation).

There are without doubt genuine entitlements and a theory of justice must take them seriously, but they are not absolute. If the need is great enough we can see the merit in overriding them, just as in law as well as morality the right of eminent domain is recognized. Finally, while I have talked of entitlements here, parallel arguments will go through for desert.

III

I want now to relate this articulation of what equality comes to my radically egalitarian principles of jus-

tice. My articulation of justice is a certain spelling out of the slogan proclaimed by Marx "From each according to his ability, to each according to his needs." The egalitarian conception of society argues for the desirability of bringing into existence a world, once the springs of social wealth flow freely, in which everyone's needs are as fully satisfied as possible and in which everyone gives according to his ability. Which means, among other things, that everyone, according to his ability, shares the burdens of society. There is an equal giving and equal responsibility here according to ability. It is here, with respect to giving according to ability and with respect to receiving according to need, that a complex equality of result, i.e., equality of condition, is being advocated by the radical egalitarian. What it comes to is this: each of us, where each is to count for one and none to count for more than one, is to give according to ability and receive according to need.

My radical egalitarian principles of justice read as follows:

1. Each person is to have an equal right to the most extensive total system of equal basic liberties and opportunities (including equal opportunities for meaningful work, for self-determination and political and economic participation) compatible with a similar treatment of all. (This principle gives expression to a commitment to attain and/or sustain equal moral autonomy and equal self-respect.)

2. After provisions are made for common social (community) values, for capital overhead to preserve the society's productive capacity, allowances made for differing unmanipulated needs and preferences, and due weight is given to the just entitlements of individuals, the income and wealth (the common stock of means) is to be so divided that each person will have a right to an equal share. The necessary burdens requisite to enhance human well-being are also to be equally shared, subject, of course, to limitations by differing abilities and differing situations. (Here I refer to different natural environments and the like and not to class position and the like.)

Here we are talking about equality as a right rather than about equality as a goal as has previously been the subject matter of equality in this chapter. These principles of egalitarianism spell out rights people have and duties they have under *conditions of very considerable productive abundance.* We have a right to certain basic liberties and opportunities and we have, subject to certain limitations spelled out in the second principle, a right to an equal share of the income and wealth in the world. We also have a duty, again subject to the qualifications mentioned in the principle, to do our equal share in shouldering the burdens necessary to protect us from ills and to enhance our well-being.

What is the relation between these rights and the ideal of equality of condition discussed earlier? That is a goal for which we can struggle now to bring about conditions which will some day make its achievement possible, while these rights only become rights when the goal is actually achievable. We have no such rights in slave, feudal or capitalist societies or such duties in those societies. In that important way they are not natural rights for they depend on certain social conditions and certain social structures (socialist ones) to be realizable. What we can say is that it is always desirable that socio-economic conditions come into being which would make it possible to achieve the goal of equality of condition so that these rights and duties I speak of could obtain. But that is a far cry from saying we have such rights and duties now.

It is a corollary of this, if these radical egalitarian principles of justice are correct, that capitalist societies (even capitalist welfare state societies such as Sweden) and statist societies such as the Soviet Union or the People's Republic of China cannot be just societies or at least they must be societies, structured as they are, which are defective in justice. (This is not to say that some of these societies are not juster than others. Sweden is juster than South Africa, Canada than the United States, and Cuba and Nicaragua than Honduras and Guatemala.) But none of these statist or capitalist societies can satisfy these radical egalitarian principles of justice, for equal liberty, equal opportunity, equal wealth or equal sharing of burdens are not at all possible in societies having their social structure. So we do not have such rights now but we can take it as a goal that we bring such a society into being with a commitment to an equality of condition in which we would have these rights and duties. Here we require first the massive development of productive power.

The connection between equality as a goal and equality as a right spelled out in these principles of justice is this. The equality of condition appealed to in equality as a goal would, if it were actually to obtain, have to contain the rights and duties enunci-ated in those principles. There could be no equal life prospects between all people or anything approximating an equal satisfaction of needs if there were not in place something like the system of equal basic liberties referred to in the first principle. Furthermore, without the rough equality of wealth referred to in the second principle, there would be disparities in power and self-direction in society which would render impossible an equality of life prospects or the social conditions required for an equal satisfaction of needs. And plainly, without a roughly equal sharing of burdens, there cannot be a situation where everyone has equal life prospects or has the chance equally to satisfy his needs. The principles of radical egalitarian justice are implicated in its conception of an ideally adequate equality of condition.

IV

The principles of radical egalitarian justice I have articulated are meant to apply globally and not just to particular societies. But it is certainly fair to say that not a few would worry that such principles of radical egalitarian justice, if applied globally, would force the people in wealthier sections of the world to a kind of financial hari-kari. There are millions of desperately impoverished people. Indeed, millions are starving or malnourished and things are not getting any better. People in the affluent societies cannot but worry about whether they face a bottomless pit. Many believe that meeting, even in the most minimal way, the needs of the impoverished is going to put an incredible burden on people—people of all classes—in the affluent societies. Indeed it will, if acted on non-evasively, bring about their impoverishment, and this is just too much to ask. Radical egalitarianism is forgetting Rawls' admonitions about "the strains of commitment"—the recognition that in any rational account of what is required of us, we must at least give a minimal healthy self-interest its due. We must construct our moral philosophy for human beings and not for saints. Human nature is less fixed than conservatives are wont to assume, but it is not so elastic that we can reasonably expect people to impoverish themselves to make the massive transfers between North and South—the industrialized world and the Third World—required to begin to approach a situation where even Rawls' principles would be in place on a global level, to say nothing of my radical egalitarian principles of justice.

The first thing to say in response to this is that my radical egalitarian principles are meant actually to guide practice, to directly determine what we are to do, only in a world of extensive abundance where, as Marx put it, the springs of social wealth flow freely. If such a world cannot be attained with the undermining of capitalism and the full putting into place, stabilizing, and developing of socialist relations of production, then such radical egalitarian principles can only remain as heuristic ideals against which to measure the distance of our travel in the direction of what would be a perfectly just society.

Aside from a small capitalist class, along with those elites most directly and profitably beholden to it (together a group constituting not more than 5 percent of the world's population), there would, in taking my radical egalitarian principles as heuristic guides, be no impoverishment of people in the affluent societies, if we moved in a radically more egalitarian way to start to achieve a global fairness. There would be massive transfers of wealth between North and South, but this could be done in stages so that, for the people in the affluent societies (capitalist elites apart), there need be no undermining of the quality of their lives. Even what were once capitalist elites would not be impoverished or reduced to some kind of bleak life though they would, the incidental Spartan types aside, find their life styles altered. But their health and general well-being, including their opportunities to do significant and innovative work, would, if anything, be enhanced. And while some of the sources of their enjoyment would be a thing of the past, there would still be a considerable range of enjoyments available to them sufficient to afford anyone a rich life that could be lived with verve and zest.

A fraction of what the United States spends on defense spending would take care of immediate problems of starvation and malnutrition for most of the world. For longer range problems such as bringing conditions of life in the Third World more in line with conditions of life in Sweden and Switzerland, what is necessary is the dismantling of the capitalist system and the creation of a socio-economic system with an underlying rationale directing it toward producing for needs—everyone's needs. With this altered productive mode, the irrationalities and waste of capitalist production would be cut. There would be no more built-in obsolescence, no more merely cosmetic changes in consumer durables, no more fashion roulette, no more useless products and the like. Moreover, the enormous expenditures that go into the war industry would be a thing of the past. There would be great transfers from North to South, but it would be from the North's capitalist fat and not from things people in the North really need. (There would, in other words, be no self-pauperization of people in the capitalist world.)...

V

It has been repeatedly argued that equality undermines liberty. Some would say that a society in which principles like my radical egalitarian principles were adopted, or even the liberal egalitarian principles of Rawls or Dworkin were adopted, would not be a free society. My arguments have been just the reverse. I have argued that it is only in an egalitarian society that full and extensive liberty is possible.

Perhaps the egalitarian and the anti-egalitarian are arguing at cross purposes? What we need to recognize, it has been argued, is that we have two kinds of rights both of which are important to freedom but to rather different freedoms and which are freedoms which not infrequently conflict. We have rights to *fair terms of cooperation* but we also have rights to *non-interference*. If a right of either kind is overridden our freedom is diminished. The reason why it might be thought that the egalitarian and the anti-egalitarian may be arguing at cross purposes is that the egalitarian is pointing to the fact that rights to fair terms of cooperation and their associated liberties require equality while the anti-egalitarian is pointing to the fact that rights to non-interference and their associated liberties conflict with equality. They focus on different liberties.

What I have said above may not be crystal clear, so let me explain. People have a right to fair terms of cooperation. In political terms this comes to the equal right of all to effective participation in government and, in more broadly social terms, and for a society of economic wealth, it means people having a right to a roughly equal distribution of the benefits and burdens of the basic social arrangements that affect their lives and for them to stand in such relations to each other such that no one has the power to dominate the life of another. By contrast, rights to non-interference come to the equal right of all to be left alone by the government and more broadly to live in a society in which people have a right peacefully to pursue their interests without interference.

The conflict between equality and liberty comes down to, very essentially, the conflicts we get in modern societies between rights to fair terms of co-operation and rights to non-interference. As Joseph Schumpeter saw and J. S. Mill before him, one could have a thoroughly democratic society (at least in conventional terms) in which rights to non-interference might still be extensively violated. A central anti-egalitarian claim is that we cannot have an egalitarian society in which the very precious liberties that go with the rights to non-interference would not be violated.

Socialism and egalitarianism plainly protect rights to fair terms of cooperation. Without the social (collective) ownership and control of the means of production, involving with this, in the initial stages of socialism at least, a workers' state, economic power will be concentrated in the hands of a few who will in turn, as a result, dominate effective participation in government. Some right-wing libertarians blind themselves to that reality, but it is about as evident as can be. Only an utter turning away from the facts of social life could lead to any doubts about this at all. But then this means that in a workers' state, if some people have capitalistic impulses, that they would have their rights peacefully to pursue their own interests interfered with. They might wish to invest, retain and bequeath in economic domains. In a workers' state these capitalist acts in many circumstances would have to be forbidden, but that would be a violation of an individual's right to non-interference and the fact, if it was a fact, that we by democratic vote, even with vast majorities, had made such capitalist acts illegal would still not make any difference because individuals' rights to non-interference would still be violated.

We are indeed driven, by egalitarian impulses, of a perfectly understandable sort, to accept interference with laissez-faire capitalism to protect non-subordination and non-domination of people by protecting the egalitarian right to fair terms of co-operation and the enhanced liberty that that brings. Still, as things stand, this leads inevitably to violations of the right to non-interference and this brings with it a diminution of liberty. There will be people with capitalist impulses and they will be interfered with. It is no good denying, it will be said, that egalitarianism and particularly socialism will not lead to interference with very precious individual liberties, namely with our right peacefully to pursue our interests without interference.

The proper response to this, as should be apparent from what I have argued throughout, is that to live in any society at all, capitalist, socialist or whatever, is to live in a world in which there will be some restriction or other on our rights peacefully to pursue our interests without interference. I can't lecture in Albanian or even in French in a standard philosophy class at the University of Calgary, I can't jog naked on most beaches, borrow a book from your library without your permission, fish in your trout pond without your permission, take your dog for a walk without your say so and the like. At least some of these things have been thought to be things which I might peacefully pursue in my own interests. Stopping me from doing them is plainly interfering with my peaceful pursuit of my own interests. And indeed it is an infringement on liberty, an interference with my doing what I may want to do.

However, for at least many of these activities, and particularly the ones having to do with property, even right-wing libertarians think that such interference is perfectly justified. But, justified or not, they still plainly constitute a restriction on our individual freedom. However, what we must also recognize is that there will always be some such restrictions on freedom in any society whatsoever, just in virtue of the fact that a normless society, without the restrictions that having norms imply, is a contradiction in terms. Many restrictions are hardly felt as restrictions, as in the attitudes of many people toward seat-belt legislation, but they are, all the same, plainly restrictions on our liberty. It is just that they are thought to be unproblematically justified.

To the question would a socialism with a radical egalitarianism restrict some liberties, including some liberties rooted in rights to non-interference, the answer is that it indeed would; but so would laissez-faire capitalism, aristocratic conceptions of justice, liberal conceptions or any social formations at all, with their associated conceptions of justice. The relevant question is which of these restrictions are justified.

The restrictions on liberty proferred by radical egalitarianism and socialism, I have argued, are justified for they, of the various alternatives, give us both the most extensive and the most abundant system of liberty possible in modern conditions with their thorough protection of the right to fair terms of cooperation. Radical egalitarianism will also, and this is central for us, protect our civil liberties and these liberties are, of course, our most basic liberties. These are the liberties which are the most vital for us to protect. What it will not do is to protect our unrestricted liberties to invest, retain and bequeath in the economic realm and it will not protect our unrestricted freedom to buy and sell. There is, however, no good reason to think that these restrictions are restrictions of anything like a basic liberty. Moreover, we are justified in restricting our freedom to buy and sell if such restrictions strengthen, rather than weaken, our total system of liberty. This is in this way justified, for only by such market restrictions can the rights of the vast majority of people to effective participation in government and an equal role in the control of their social lives be protected. I say this because if we let the market run free in this way, power will pass into the hands of a few who will control the lives of the many and determine the fundamental design of the society. The actual liberties that are curtailed in a radically egalitarian social order are inessential liberties whose restriction in contemporary circumstances enhances human well-being and indeed makes for a firmer entrenchment of basic liberties and for their greater extension globally. That is to say, we here restrict some liberty in order to attain more liberty and a more equally distributed pattern of liberty. More people will be able to do what they want and have a greater control over their own lives than in a capitalist world order with its at least implicit inegalitarian commitments.

However, some might say I still have not faced the most central objection to radical egalitarianism, namely its statism. (I would prefer to say its putative statism.) The picture is this. The egalitarian state must be in the redistribution business. It has to make, or make sure there is made, an equal relative contribution to the welfare of every citizen. But this in effect means that the socialist state or, for that matter, the welfare state, will be deeply interventionist in our personal lives. It will be in the business, as one right-winger emotively put it, of cutting one person down to size in order to bring about that person's equality with another person who was in a previously disadvantageous position. That is said to be morally objectionable and it would indeed be deeply morally objectionable in many circumstances. But it isn't in the circumstances in which the radical egalitarian presses for redistribution. (I am not speaking of what might be mere equalizing upwards.) The circumstances are these: Capitalist A gets his productive property confiscated so that he could no longer dominate and control the lives of proletarians B, C, D, E, F, and G. But what is wrong with it where this "cutting down to size"—in reality the confiscation of productive property or the taxation of the capitalist—involves no violation of A's civil liberties or the harming of his actual well-being (health, ability to work, to cultivate the arts, to have fruitful personal relations, to live in comfort and the like) and where B, C, D, E, F, and G will have their freedom and their well-being thoroughly enhanced if such confiscation or taxation occurs? Far from being morally objectionable, it is precisely the sort of state of affairs that people ought to favor. It certainly protects more liberties and more significant liberties than it undermines.

There is another familiar anti-egalitarian argument designed to establish the liberty-undermining qualities of egalitarianism. It is an argument we have touched upon in discussing meritocracy. It turns on the fact that in any society there will be both talents and handicaps. Where they exist, what do we want to do about maintaining equal distribution? Egalitarians, radical or otherwise, certainly do not want to penalize people for talent. That being so, then surely people should be allowed to retain the benefits of superior talent. But this in some circumstances will lead to significant inequalities in resources and in the meeting of needs. To sustain equality there will have to be an ongoing redistribution in the direction of the less talented and less fortunate. But this redistribution from the more to the less talented does plainly penalize the talented for their talent. That, it will be said, is something which is both unfair and an undermining of liberty.

The following, it has been argued, makes the above evident enough. If people have talents they will tend to want to use them. And if they use them they are very likely to come out ahead. Must not egalitarians say they ought not to be able to come out ahead no matter how well they use their talents and no matter how considerable these talents are? But that is intolerably restrictive and unfair.

The answer to the above anti-egalitarian argument is implicit in a number of things I have already said. But here let me confront this familiar argument directly. Part of the answer comes out in probing some of the ambiguities of "coming out ahead." Note, incidentally, that (1) not all reflective, morally sensitive people will be so concerned with that, and that (2) being very concerned with that is a mentality that capitalism inculcates. Be that as it may, to turn to the ambiguities, note that some take "coming out ahead" principally to mean "being paid well for the use of those talents" where "being paid well" is being paid sufficiently well so that it creates inequalities sufficient to disturb the preferred egalitarian patterns. (Without that, being paid well would give one no relative advantage.) But, as we have seen, "coming out ahead" need not take that form at all. Talents can be recognized and acknowledged in many ways. First, in just the respect and admiration of a fine employment of talents that would naturally come from people seeing them so displayed where these people were not twisted by envy; second, by having, because of these talents, interesting and secure work that their talents fit them for and they merit in virtue of those talents. Moreover, having more money is not going to matter much—for familiar marginal utility reasons—where what in capitalist societies would be called the welfare floors are already very high, this being made feasible by the great productive wealth of the society. Recall that in such a society of abundance everyone will be well off and secure. In such a society people are not going to be very concerned about being a little better off than someone else. The talented are in no way, in such a situation, robbed to help the untalented and handicapped or penalized for their talents. They are only prevented from amassing wealth (most particularly productive wealth), which would enable them to dominate the untalented and the handicapped and to control the social life of the world of which they are both a part. . . .

I think that the moral authority for abstract egalitarianism, for the belief that the interests of everyone matter and matter equally, comes from its being the case that it is *required by the moral point of view*. What I am predicting is that a person who has a good understanding of what morality is, has a good knowledge of the facts, is not ideologically mystified, takes an impartial point of view, and has an attitude of impartial caring, would, if not conceptually confused, come to accept the abstract egalitarian thesis. I see no way of arguing someone into such an egalitarianism who does not in this general way have a love of humankind. A hard-hearted Hobbesist is not reachable here. But given that a person has that love of humankind—that impartial and impersonal caring—together with the other qualities mentioned above, then, I predict, that that person would be an egalitarian at least to the extent of accepting the abstract egalitarian thesis. What I am claiming is that if these conditions were to obtain (if they ceased to be just counterfactuals), then there would be a consensus among moral agents about accepting the abstract egalitarian thesis. . . .

DISCUSSION QUESTIONS

1. Nielsen says that his radical egalitarian principles of justice are a spelling out of a line from Karl Marx: "From each according to his ability, to each according to his needs." What are those principles, and how do they spell out this line from Marx?
2. Nielsen discusses the distinction between "equality as a right" and "equality as a goal." What is the difference, according to Nielsen? Do you agree with him? How does Nielsen use this distinction in his argument for radical egalitarianism?
3. Some say that a society which adopted principles of justice like those based on Nielsen's radical egalitarianism would not be a free society. Nielsen says that "it is only in an egalitarian society that full and extensive liberty is possible." What sort of world does Nielsen have in mind? How does Nielsen defend this position? Do you agree with his defense? Do his detractors have a good argument? Explain.
4. What is the "right to fair terms of cooperation"? What is the "right to non-interference"? Do you agree that these are "rights"? What role do they play in Nielsen's radical egalitarianism?
5. Nielsen responds to a number of possible objections to radical egalitarianism. Which is the strongest objection? Critically evaluate Nielsen's response to it. Can you think of any objections to radical egalitarianism that Nielsen has not considered? What are they? How might Nielsen respond to them?
6. Do you agree with Nielsen's belief that every able-bodied person age nineteen to twenty be required to take his or her turn at a fair portion of the unpleasant jobs in the world? Defend your view against objections.
7. What do you think about Nielsen's critique of capitalism? What are his strongest points? His weakest ones? Why?

JOHN RAWLS

A Theory of Justice

John Rawls' theory of justice as fairness states that there are two principles of justice. The first principle involves equal basic liberties: each person has a right to the most extensive basic liberty that is compatible with the same liberty for others. The second principle concerns the arrangement of social and economic inequalities: inequalities of wealth are justified to the extent that they work out to the advantage of the disadvantaged. According to Rawls, these are the principles that free and rational persons would accept in a hypothetical original position in which a "veil of ignorance" hid from the contractors all the particular facts about themselves. Because contractors make their choices behind a veil of ignorance, it is appropriate for them to select that strategy whose worst possible outcome is superior to the worst possible outcome of any other strategy. According to Rawls, this would rule out utilitarianism as a rational choice because the maximum social benefit of that alternative is compatible with a benefit below the social minimum for some and perhaps then, given the veil of ignorance, for oneself. Justice as fairness, for Rawls, is the strategy whose worst possible outcome is superior to the worst possible outcome of any other strategy including utilitarianism.

John Rawls is a professor of philosophy at Harvard University and the author of *A Theory of Justice* (1971), *Political Liberalism* (1993), and *The Law of Peoples* (1999). He is one of the most respected liberal social and political philosophers in America today. The following selection is from *A Theory of Justice*.

THE ROLE OF JUSTICE

Justice is the first virtue of social institutions, as truth is of systems of thought. A theory however elegant and economical must be rejected or revised if it is untrue; likewise laws and institutions no matter how efficient and well-arranged must be reformed or abolished if they are unjust. Each person possesses an inviolability founded on justice that even the welfare of society as a whole cannot override. For this reason justice denies that the loss of freedom for some is made right by a greater good shared by others. It does not allow that the sacrifices imposed on a few are outweighed by the larger sum of advantages enjoyed by many. Therefore in a just society the liberties of equal citizenship are taken as settled; the rights secured by justice are not subject to political bargaining or to the calculus of social interests. The only thing that permits us to acquiesce

in an erroneous theory is the lack of a better one; analogously, an injustice is tolerable only when it is necessary to avoid an even greater injustice. Being first virtues of human activities, truth and justice are uncompromising.

These propositions seem to express our intuitive conviction of the primacy of justice. No doubt they are expressed too strongly. In any event I wish to inquire whether these contentions or others similar to them are sound, and if so how they can be accounted for. To this end it is necessary to work out a theory of justice in the light of which these assertions can be interpreted and assessed. I shall begin by considering the role of the principles of justice. Let us assume, to fix ideas, that a society is a more or less self-sufficient association of persons who in their relations to one another recognize certain rules of conduct as binding and who for the most part act in accordance with them. Suppose further that these rules specify a system of cooperation designed to advance the good of those taking part in it. Then, although a society is a cooperative venture for mutual advantage, it is typically marked by a conflict as well as by an identity of interests. There is an identity of interests since social cooperation makes possible a better life for all than any would have if each were to live solely by his own efforts. There is a conflict of interests since persons are not indifferent as to how the greater benefits produced by their collaboration are distributed, for in order to pursue their ends they each prefer a larger to a lesser share. A set of principles is required for choosing among the various social arrangements which determine this division of advantages and for underwriting an agreement on the proper distributive shares. These principles are the principles of social justice: they provide a way of assigning rights and duties in the basic institutions of society and they define the appropriate distribution of the benefits and burdens of social cooperation.

Now let us say that a society is well-ordered when it is not only designed to advance the good of its members but when it is also effectively regulated by a public conception of justice. That is, it is a society in which (1) everyone accepts and knows that the others accept the same principles of justice, and (2) the basic social institutions generally satisfy and are generally known to satisfy these principles. In this case while men may put forth excessive demands on one another, they nevertheless acknowledge a common point of view from which their claims may be adjudicated. If men's inclination to self-interest makes their vigilance against one another necessary, their public sense of justice makes their secure association together possible. Among individuals with disparate aims and purposes a shared conception of justice establishes the bonds of civic friendship; the general desire for justice limits the pursuit of other ends. One may think of a public conception of justice as constituting the fundamental charter of a well-ordered human association.

Existing societies are of course seldom well-ordered in this sense, for what is just and unjust is usually in dispute. Men disagree about which principles should define the basic terms of their association. Yet we may still say, despite this disagreement, that they each have a conception of justice. That is, they understand the need for, and they are prepared to affirm, a characteristic set of principles for assigning basic rights and duties and for determining what they take to be the proper distribution of the benefits and burdens of social cooperation.

Thus it seems natural to think of the concept of justice as distinct from the various conceptions of justice and as being specified by the role which these different sets of principles, these different conceptions, have in common. Those who hold different conceptions of justice can, then, still agree that institutions are just when no arbitrary distinctions are made between persons in the assigning of basic rights and duties and when the rules determine a proper balance between competing claims to the advantages of social life. Men can agree to this description of just institutions since the notions of an arbitrary distinction and of a proper balance, which are included in the concept of justice, are left open for each to interpret according to the principles of justice that he accepts. These principles single out which similarities and differences among persons are relevant in determining rights and duties and they specify which division of advantages is appropriate. Clearly this distinction between the concept and the various conceptions of justice settles no important questions. It simply helps to identify the role of the principles of social justice.

Some measure of agreement in conceptions of justice is, however, not the only prerequisite for a viable human community. There are other fundamental social problems, in particular those of coordination, efficiency, and stability. Thus the plans of individuals need to be fitted together so that their activities are compatible with one another and they can all be carried through without anyone's legitimate expectations being severely disappointed. Moreover, the execution of these plans should lead to the achievement of social ends in ways that are efficient and consistent with justice. And finally, the scheme of social cooperation must be stable: it must be more or less regularly complied with and its basic rules willingly acted upon; and when infractions occur, stabilizing forces should exist that prevent further violations and tend to restore the arrangement. Now it is evident that these three problems are connected with that of justice. In the absence of a certain measure of agreement on what is just and unjust, it is clearly more difficult for individuals to coordinate their plans efficiently in order to ensure that mutually beneficial arrangements are maintained. Distrust and resentment corrode the ties of civility, and suspicion and hostility tempt men to act in ways they would otherwise avoid. So while the distinctive role of conceptions of justice is to specify basic rights and duties and to determine the appropriate distributive shares, the way in which a conception does this is bound to affect the problems of efficiency, coordination, and stability. We cannot, in general, assess a conception of justice by its distributive role alone, however useful this role may be in identifying the concept of justice. We must take into account its wider connections; for even though justice has a certain priority, being the most important virtue of institutions, it is still true that, other things equal, one conception of justice is preferable to another when its broader consequences are more desirable. . . .

THE MAIN IDEA OF THE THEORY OF JUSTICE

My aim is to present a conception of justice which generalizes and carries to a higher level of abstraction the familiar theory of the social contract as found, say, in Locke, Rousseau, and Kant. In order to do this we are not to think of the original contract as one to enter a particular society or to set up a particular form of government. Rather, the guiding idea is that the principles of justice for the basic structure of society are the object of the original agreement. They are the principles that free and rational persons concerned to further their own interests would accept in an initial position of equality as defining the fundamental terms of their association. These principles are to regulate all further agreements; they specify the kinds of social cooperation that can be entered into and the forms of government that can be established. This way of regarding the principles of justice I shall call justice as fairness.

Thus we are to imagine that those who engage in social cooperation choose together, in one joint act, the principles which are to assign basic rights and duties and to determine the division of social benefits. Men are to decide in advance how they are to regulate their claims against one another and what is to be the foundation charter of their society. Just as each person must decide by rational reflection what constitutes his good, that is, the system of ends which it is rational for him to pursue, so a group of persons must decide once and for all what is to count among them as just and unjust. The choice which rational men would make in this hypothetical situation of equal liberty, assuming for the present that this choice problem has a solution, determines the principles of justice.

In justice as fairness the original position of equality corresponds to the state of nature in the traditional theory of the social contract. This original position is not, of course, thought of as an actual historical state of affairs, much less as a primitive condition of culture. It is understood as a purely hypothetical situation characterized so as to lead to a certain conception of justice. Among the essential features of this situation is that no one knows his place in society, his class position or social status, nor does anyone know his fortune in the distribution of natural assets and abilities, his intelligence, strength, and the like. I shall even assume that the parties do not know their conceptions of the good or their special psychological propensities. The principles of justice are chosen behind a veil of ignorance. This ensures that no one is advantaged or disadvantaged in the choice of principles by the outcome of natural chance or the contingency of social circumstances. Since all are similarly situated and no one is able to design principles to favor his particular condition, the principles of justice are the result of a fair agreement or bargain. For given the circumstances of the original position, the symmetry of everyone's relations to each other, this initial situation is fair between individuals as moral persons, that is, as rational beings with their own ends and capable, I shall assume, of a sense of justice. The original position is, one might say, the appropriate initial status quo, and thus the fundamental agreements reached in it are fair. This explains the propriety of the name "justice as fairness": it conveys the idea that the principles of justice are agreed to in an initial situation that is fair. The name does not mean that the concepts of justice and fairness are the same, any more than the phrase "poetry as metaphor" means that the concepts of poetry and metaphor are the same.

Justice as fairness begins, as I have said, with one of the most general of all choices which persons might make together, namely, with the choice of the first principles of a conception of justice which is to regulate all subsequent criticism and reform of institutions. Then, having chosen a conception of justice, we can suppose that they are to choose a constitution and a legislature to enact laws, and so on, all in accordance with the principles of justice initially agreed upon. Our social situation is just if it is such that by this sequence of hypothetical agreements we would have contracted into the general system of rules which defines it. Moreover, assuming that the original position does determine a set of principles (that is, that a particular conception of justice would be chosen), it will then be true that whenever social institutions satisfy these principles those engaged in them can say to one another that they are cooperating on terms to which they would agree if they were free and equal persons whose relations with respect to one another were fair. They could all view their arrangements as meeting the stipulations which they would acknowledge in an initial situation that embodies widely accepted and reasonable constraints on the choice of principles. The general recognition of this fact would provide the basis for a public acceptance of the corresponding principles of justice. No society can, of course, be a scheme of cooperation which men enter voluntarily in a literal sense; each person finds himself placed at birth in some particular position in some particular society, and the nature of this position materially affects his life prospects. Yet a society satisfying the principles of justice as fairness comes as close as a society can to being a voluntary scheme, for it meets the principles which free and equal persons would assent to under circumstances that are fair. In this sense its members are autonomous and the obligations they recognize self-imposed.

One feature of justice as fairness is to think of the parties in the initial situation as rational and mutually disinterested. This does not mean that the parties are egoists, that is, individuals with only certain kinds of interests, say in wealth, prestige, and domination. But they are conceived as not taking an interest in one another's interests. They are to presume that even their spiritual aims may be opposed, in the way that the aims of those of different religions may be opposed. Moreover, the concept of rationality must be interpreted as far as possible in the narrow sense, standard in economic theory, of taking the most effective means to given ends. I shall modify this concept to some extent, . . . but one must try to avoid introducing into it any controversial ethical elements. The initial situation must be characterized by stipulations that are widely accepted.

In working out the conception of justice as fairness, one main task clearly is to determine which principles of justice would be chosen in the original position. To do this we must describe this situation in some detail and formulate with care the problem of choice which it presents. . . . It may be observed, however, that once the principles of justice are thought of as arising from an original agreement in a situation of equality, it is an open question whether the principle of utility would be acknowledged. Offhand it hardly seems likely that persons who view themselves as equals, entitled to press their claims upon one another, would agree to a principle which may require lesser life prospects for some simply for the sake of a greater sum of advantages enjoyed by others. Since each desires to protect his interests, his capacity to advance his conception of the good, no one has a reason to acquiesce in an enduring loss for himself in order to bring about a greater net balance of satisfaction. In the absence of strong and lasting benevolent impulses, a rational man would not accept a basic structure merely because it maximized the algebraic sum of advantages irrespective of its permanent effects on his own basic rights and interests. Thus it seems that the principle of utility is incompatible with the conception of social cooperation among equals for mutual advantage. It appears to be inconsistent with the idea of reciprocity implicit in the notion of a well-ordered society. Or, at any rate, so I shall argue.

I shall maintain instead that the persons in the initial situation would choose two rather different principles: the first requires equality in the assignment of basic rights and duties, while the second holds that social and economic inequalities, for example inequalities of wealth and authority, are just only if they result in compensating benefits for everyone, and in particular for the least advantaged members of society. These principles rule out justifying institutions on the grounds that the hardships of some are offset by a greater good in the aggregate. It may be expedient but it is not just that some should have less in order that others may prosper. But there is no injustice in the greater benefits earned by a few provided that the situation of persons not so fortunate is thereby improved. The intuitive idea is that since everyone's well-being depends upon a scheme of cooperation without which no one could have a satisfactory life, the division of advantages should be such as to draw forth the willing cooperation of everyone taking part in it, including those less well situated. Yet this can be expected only if reasonable terms are proposed. The two principles mentioned seem to be a fair agreement on the basis of which those better endowed, or more fortunate in their social position, neither of which we can be said to deserve, could expect the willing cooperation of others when some workable scheme is a necessary condition of the welfare of all. Once we decide to look for a conception of justice that nullifies the accidents of natural endowment and the contingencies of social circumstance as counters in quest for political and economic advantage, we are led to these principles. They express the result of leaving aside those aspects of the social world that seem arbitrary from a moral point of view.

The problem of the choice of principles, however, is extremely difficult. I do not expect the answer I shall suggest to be convincing to everyone. It is, therefore, worth noting from the outset that justice as fairness, like other contract views, consists of two parts: (1) an interpretation of the initial situation and of the problem of choice posed there, and (2) a set of principles which, it is argued, would be agreed to. One may accept the first part of the theory (or some variant thereof), but not the other, and conversely. The concept of the initial contractual situation may seem reasonable although the particular principles proposed are rejected. . . .

THE ORIGINAL POSITION AND JUSTIFICATION

I have said that the original position is the appropriate initial status quo which ensures that the fundamental agreements reached in it are fair. This fact yields the name "justice as fairness." It is clear, then, that I want to say that one conception of justice is more reasonable than another, or justifiable with respect to it, if rational persons in the initial situation would choose its principles over those of the other for the role of justice. Conceptions of justice are to be ranked by their acceptability to persons so circumstanced. Understood in this way the question of justification is settled by working out a problem of deliberation: we have to ascertain which principles it would be rational to adopt given the contractual situation. This connects the theory of justice with the theory of rational choice.

If this view of the problem of justification is to succeed, we must, of course, describe in some detail the nature of this choice problem. A problem of rational decision has a definite answer only if we know the beliefs and interests of the parties, their relations with respect to one another, the alternatives between which they are to choose, the procedure whereby they make up their minds, and so on. As the circumstances are presented in different ways, correspondingly different principles are accepted. The concept of the original position, as I shall refer to it, is that of the most philosophically favored interpretation of this initial choice situation for the purposes of a theory of justice.

But how are we to decide what is the most favored interpretation? I assume, for one thing, that there is a broad measure of agreement that principles of justice should be chosen under certain conditions. To justify a particular description of the initial situation, one shows that it incorporates these commonly shared presumptions. One argues from widely accepted but weak premises to more specific conclusions. Each of the presumptions should by itself be natural and plausible; some of them may seem innocuous or even trivial. The aim of the contract approach is to establish that taken together they impose significant bounds on acceptable principles of justice. The ideal outcome would be that these conditions determine a unique set of principles; but I shall be satisfied if they suffice to rank the main traditional conceptions of social justice.

One should not be misled, then, by the somewhat unusual conditions which characterize the original position. The idea here is simply to make vivid to ourselves the restrictions that it seems reasonable to impose on arguments for principles of justice, and therefore on these principles themselves. Thus it seems reasonable and generally acceptable that no one should be advantaged or disadvantaged by natural fortune or social circumstances in the choice of principles. It also seems widely agreed that it should be impossible to tailor principles to the circumstances of one's own case. We should ensure further that particular inclinations and aspirations, and persons' conceptions of their good, do not affect the principles adopted. The aim is to rule out those principles that it would be rational to propose for acceptance, however little the chance of success, only if one knew certain things that are irrelevant from the standpoint of justice. For example, if a man knew that he was wealthy, he might find it rational to advance the principle that various taxes for welfare measures be counted unjust; if he knew that he was poor, he would most likely propose the contrary principle. To represent the desired restrictions, one imagines a situation in which everyone is deprived of this sort of information. One excludes the knowledge of those contingencies which sets men at odds and allows them to be guided by their prejudices. In this manner the veil of ignorance is arrived at in a natural way. This concept should cause no difficulty if we keep in mind the constraints on arguments that it is meant to express. At any time we can enter the original position, so to speak, simply by following a certain procedure, namely, by arguing for principles of justice in accordance with these restrictions.

It seems reasonable to suppose that the parties in the original position are equal. That is, all have the same rights in the procedure for choosing principles; each can make proposals, submit reasons for their acceptance, and so on. Obviously the purpose of these conditions is to represent equality between human beings as moral persons, as creatures having a conception of their good and capable of a sense of justice. The basis of equality is taken to be similarity in these two respects. Systems of ends are not ranked in value; and each man is presumed to have the requisite ability to understand and to act upon whatever principles are adopted. Together with the veil of ignorance, these conditions define the principles of justice as those which rational persons concerned to advance their interests would consent to as equals when none are known to be advantaged or disadvantaged by social and natural contingencies.

There is, however, another side to justifying a particular description of the original position. This is to see if the principles which would be chosen match our considered convictions of justice or extend them in an acceptable way. We can note whether applying these principles would lead us to make the same judgments about the basic structure of society which we now make intuitively and in which we have the greatest confidence; or whether, in cases where our present judgments are in doubt and given with hesitation, these principles offer a resolution which we can affirm on reflection. There are questions which we feel sure must be answered in a certain way. For example, we are confident that religious intolerance and racial discrimination are unjust. We think that we have examined these things with care and have reached what we believe is an impartial judgment not likely to be distorted by an excessive attention to our own interests. These convictions are provisional fixed points which we presume any conception of justice must fit. But we have much less assurance as to what is the correct distribution of wealth and authority. Here we may be looking for a way to remove our doubts. We can check an interpretation of the initial situation, then, by the capacity of its principles to accommodate our firmest convictions and to provide guidance where guidance is needed.

In searching for the most favored description of this situation we work from both ends. We begin by describing it so that it represents generally shared and preferably weak conditions. We then see if these conditions are strong enough to yield a significant set of principles. If not, we look for further premises equally reasonable. But if so, and these principles match our considered convictions of justice, then so far well and good. But presumably there will be discrepancies. In this case we have a choice. We can either modify the account of the initial situation or we can revise our existing judgments, for even the judgments we take provisionally as fixed points are liable to revision. By going back and forth, sometimes altering the conditions of the

contractual circumstances, at others withdrawing our judgments and conforming them to principle, I assume that eventually we shall find a description of the initial situation that both expresses reasonable conditions and yields principles which match our considered judgments duly pruned and adjusted. This state of affairs I refer to as reflective equilibrium. It is an equilibrium because at last our principles and judgments coincide; and it is reflective since we know to what principles our judgments conform and the premises of their derivation. At the moment, everything is in order. But this equilibrium is not necessarily stable. It is liable to be upset by further examination of the conditions which should be imposed on the contractual situation and by particular cases which may lead us to revise our judgments. Yet for the time being we have done what we can to render coherent and to justify our convictions of social justice. We have reached a conception of the original position.

I shall not, of course, actually work through this process. Still, we may think of the interpretation of the original position that I shall present as the result of such a hypothetical course of reflection. It represents the attempt to accommodate within one scheme both reasonable philosophical conditions on principles as well as our considered judgments of justice. In arriving at the favored interpretation of the initial situation there is no point at which an appeal is made to self-evidence in the traditional sense either of general conceptions or particular convictions. I do not claim for the principles of justice proposed that they are necessary truths or derivable from such truths. A conception of justice cannot be deduced from self-evident premises or conditions on principles; instead, its justification is a matter of the mutual support of many considerations, of everything fitting together into one coherent view.

A final comment. We shall want to say that certain principles of justice are justified because they would be agreed to in an initial situation of equality. I have emphasized that this original position is purely hypothetical. It is natural to ask why, if this agreement is never actually entered into, we should take any interest in these principles, moral or otherwise. The answer is that the conditions embodied in the description of the original position are ones that we do in fact accept. Or if we do not, then perhaps we can be persuaded to do so by philosophical reflection. Each aspect of the contractual situation can be given supporting grounds. Thus what we shall do is to collect together into one conception a number of conditions on principles that we are ready upon due consideration to recognize as reasonable. These constraints express what we are prepared to regard as limits on fair terms of social cooperation. One way to look at the idea of the original position, therefore, is to see it as an expository device which sums up the meaning of these conditions and helps us to extract their consequences. On the other hand, this conception is also an intuitive notion that suggests its own elaboration, so that led on by it we are drawn to define more clearly the standpoint from which we can best interpret moral relationships. We need a conception that enables us to envision our objective from afar: the intuitive notion of the original position is to do this for us. . . .

DISCUSSION QUESTIONS

1. What sorts of things could be expected from a Rawlsian society, as distinct from other ones?
2. What is the original position? What is its role in Rawls' doctrine of justice as fairness?
3. Would you rather be an industrialist or a day laborer in a Rawlsian society? Explain.
4. Rawls says that free and rational persons in the original position would reject the principle of utility. What is his argument? Do you agree with it? Why or why not?
5. Rawls says that it is not possible for free and rational persons in the original position to agree upon different principles other than those given by him. Do you agree? Why, for example, wouldn't contractors agree to an unequal distribution of wealth and income rather than an equal distribution? Why isn't an equal distribution of goods as rational as an unequal distribution of goods?
6. What is the veil of ignorance? What is its role in Rawls' theory of justice? Do you agree with the place it has in his theory of justice? Defend your view.
7. Compare and contrast Kai Nielsen and Rawls on the distribution of wealth and income. Who has the stronger arguments, and why?

 TIBOR R. MACHAN

The Nonexistence of Basic Welfare Rights

Tibor R. Machan defends a traditional libertarian position on welfare rights and the welfare state. People "have the right not to be killed, attacked, and deprived of their property—by persons in or outside of government," says Machan, but "these rights do not entitle one to receive from others the goods and resources necessary for preserving one's life." Machan argues that, since Lockean libertarianism is true, and "since the rights to welfare and equal opportunity require their violation, no one has these latter rights." For Machan, most of the world's poverty is the result of political oppression, not natural disaster or disease. This kind of political oppression is not experienced, says Machan, by "those who have the protection of even a seriously compromised document and system of protecting individual negative human rights, such as the U.S. Constitution." Therefore, the "first requirement for men and women to ameliorate

---

Tibor R. Machan, *Individuals and Their Rights*. Open Court Publishing, 1989, 100–110. Reprinted by permission of Open Court Publishing, a division of Carus Publishing Company, Peru, IL. Copyright © 1989 Open Court Publishing.

their hardship is to be free of other people's oppression, not to be free to take other people's belongings."

Tibor R. Machan is a Hoover Institution research fellow and distinguished fellow and professor in the Leatherby Center for Entrepreneurship and Business Ethics at the Argyros School of Business and Economics, Chapman University, in Orange, California. He is also professor emeritus in the Department of Philosophy at Auburn University. He has written and edited many books, including *Human Rights and Human Liberties* (1975), *Individuals and Their Rights* (1989), *Capitalism and Individualism* (1990), *Private Rights and Public Illusions* (1994), *Classical Individualism* (1999), and *Initiative: Human Agency and Society* (2000). The following selection is from *Individuals and Their Rights*.

James Sterba and others maintain that we all have the right to "receive the goods and resources necessary for preserving" ourselves. This is not what I have argued human beings have a right to. They have the right, rather, not to be killed, attacked, and deprived of their property—by persons in or outside of government. As Abraham Lincoln put it, "no man is good enough to govern another man, without that other's consent."

Sterba claims that various political outlooks would have to endorse these "rights." He sets out to show, in particular, that welfare rights follow from libertarian theory itself. Sterba wishes to show that *if* Lockean libertarianism is correct, then we all have rights to welfare and equal (economic) opportunity. What I wish to show is that since Lockean libertarianism—as developed in this work—is true, and since the rights to welfare and equal opportunity require their violation, no one has these latter rights. The reason some people, including Sterba, believe otherwise is that they have found some very rare instances in which some citizens could find themselves in circumstances that would require disregarding rights altogether. This would be in situations that cannot be characterized to be "where peace is possible." And every major libertarian thinker from Locke to the present has treated these kinds of cases.

Let us be clear about what Sterba sets out to show. It is that libertarians are philosophically unable to escape the welfare-statist implication of their commitment to negative liberty. This means that despite their belief that they are only supporting the enforceable right of every person not to be coerced by other persons, libertarians must accept, by the logic of their own position, that individuals also possess basic enforceable rights to being provided with various services from others. He holds, then, that basic negative rights imply basic positive rights.

To Lockean libertarians the ideal of liberty means that we all, individually, have the right not to

be constrained against our consent within our realm of authority—ourselves and our belongings. Sterba states that for such libertarians "Liberty is being unconstrained by persons from doing what one has a right to do." Sterba adds, somewhat misleadingly, that for Lockean libertarians "a right to life [is] a right not to be killed unjustly and a right to property [is] a right to acquire goods and resources either by initial acquisition or voluntary agreement."[1] Sterba does realize that these rights do not entitle one to receive from others the goods and resources necessary for preserving one's life.

A problem with this foundation of the Lockean libertarian view is that political justice—not the justice of Plato, which is best designated in our time as "perfect virtue"—for natural-rights theorists presupposes individual rights. One cannot then explain rights in terms of justice but must explain justice in terms of rights.

For a Lockean libertarian, to possess any basic right to receive the goods and resources necessary for preserving one's life conflicts with possessing the right not to be killed, assaulted, or stolen from. The latter are rights Lockean libertarians consider to be held by all individual human beings. Regularly to protect and maintain—that is, enforce—the former right would often require the violation of the latter. A's right to the food she has is incompatible with B's right to take this same food. Both the rights could not be fundamental in an integrated legal system. The situation of one's having rights to welfare, and so forth, and another's having rights to life, liberty, and property is thus theoretically intolerable and practically unfeasible. The point of a system of rights is the securing of mutually peaceful and consistent moral conduct on the part of human beings. As Rand observes,

> "Rights" are . . . the link between the moral code of a man and the legal code of a society,

between ethics and politics. *Individual rights are the means of subordinating society to moral law.*[2]

Sterba asks us—in another discussion of his views—to consider what he calls "a *typical* conflict situation between the rich and the poor." He says that in his situation "the rich, of course, have more than enough resources to satisfy their basic needs. By contrast, the poor lack the resources to meet their most basic needs even though *they have tried all the means available to them that libertarians regard as legitimate for acquiring such resources*"[3] (my emphasis).

The goal of a theory of rights would be defeated if rights were typically in conflict. Some bureaucratic group would have to keep applying its moral intuitions on numerous occasions when rights claims would *typically* conflict. A constitution is workable if it helps remove at least the largest proportion of such decisions from the realm of arbitrary (intuitive) choice and avail a society of men and women of objective guidelines that are reasonably integrated, not in relentless discord.

Most critics of libertarianism assume some doctrine of basic needs which they invoke to show that whenever basic needs are not satisfied for some people, while others have "resources" which are not basic needs for them, the former have just claims against the latter. (The language of resources of course loads the argument in the critic's favor since it suggests that these goods simply come into being and happen to be in the possession of some people, quite without rhyme or reason, arbitrarily [as John Rawls claims].)

This doctrine is full of difficulties. It lacks any foundation for why the needs of some persons must be claims upon the lives of others. And why are there such needs anyway—to what end are they needs, and whose ends are these and why are not the persons whose needs they are held responsible for supplying the needs? (Needs, as I have already observed, lack any force in moral argument without the prior justification of the purposes they serve or the goals they help to fulfill. A thief has a basic need of skills and powers that are clearly not justified if theft is morally unjustified. If, however, the justification of basic needs, such as food and other resources, presupposes the value of human life, and if the value of human life justifies, as I have argued earlier, the principle of the natural rights to life, liberty and property, then the attainment or fulfillment of the basic need for food may not involve the violation of these rights.)

Sterba claims that without guaranteeing welfare and equal-opportunity rights, Lockean libertarianism violates the most basic tenets of any morality, namely, that "ought" implies "can." The thrust of "'ought' implies 'can'" is that one ought to do that which one is free to do, that one is morally responsible only for those acts that one had the power either to choose to engage in or to choose not to engage in. (There is debate on just how this point must be phrased—in terms of the will being free or the person being free to will something. For our purposes, however, all that counts is that the person must have [had] a genuine option to do X or not to do X before it can be true that he or she ought to do X or ought to have done X.) If an innocent person is forced by the actions of another to forgo significant moral choices, then that innocent person is not free to act morally and thus his or her human dignity is violated.

This is not so different from the commonsense legal precept that if one is not sound of mind one cannot be criminally culpable. Only free agents, capable of choosing between right and wrong, are open to moral evaluation. This indeed is the reason that many so-called moral theories fail to be anything more than value theories. They omit from consideration the issue of self-determination. If either hard or soft determinism is true, morality is impossible, although values need not disappear.

If Sterba were correct about Lockean libertarianism typically contradicting "'ought' implies 'can,'" his argument would be decisive. (There are few arguments against this principle that I know of and they have not convinced me. They trade on rare circumstances when persons feel guilt for taking actions that had bad consequences even though they could not have avoided them.) It is because Karl Marx's and Herbert Spencer's systems typically, normally, indeed in every case, violate this principle that they are not bona fide moral systems. And quite a few others may be open to a similar charge.

Sterba offers his strongest argument when he observes that "'ought' implies 'can'" is violated "when the rich prevent the poor from taking what they require to satisfy their basic needs even though they have tried all the means available to them that libertarians regard as legitimate for acquiring such resources."[4]

Is Sterba right that such are—indeed, must be—typical conflict cases in a libertarian society? Are the rich and poor, even admitting that there is some simple division of people into such economic groups, in such hopeless conflict all the time? Even in the case of homeless people, many find help without having to resort to theft. The political factors contributing to the presence of helpless people in the United States and other Western liberal democracies are a hotly debated issue, even among utilitarians and welfare-state supporters. Sterba cannot make his argument for the typicality of such cases by reference to history alone. (Arguably, there are fewer helpless poor in near-libertarian, capitalist systems than anywhere else—why else would virtually everyone wish to live in these societies rather than those where welfare is guaranteed, indeed enforced? Not, at least originally, for their welfare-statist features. Arguably, too, the disturbing numbers of such people in these societies could be due, in part, to the lack of consistent protection of all the libertarian natural rights.)

Nonetheless, in a system that legally protects and preserves property rights there will be cases where a rich person prevents a poor person from taking what belongs to her (the rich person)—for example, a chicken that the poor person might use to feed herself. Since after such prevention the poor person might starve, Sterba asks the rhetorical question, "Have the rich, then, in contributing to this result, killed the poor, or simply let them die; and if they have killed the poor, have they done so unjustly?"[5] His answer is that they have. Sterba holds that a system that accords with the Lockean libertarian's idea that the rich person's preventive action is just "imposes an unreasonable sacrifice upon" the poor, one "that we could not blame them for trying to evade." Not permitting the poor to act to satisfy their basic needs is to undermine the precept that "'ought' implies 'can'" since, as Sterba claims, that precept means, for the poor, that they ought to satisfy their basic needs. This they must have the option to do if they ought to do it. . . .

When people defend their property, what are they doing? They are protecting themselves against the intrusive acts of some other person, acts that would normally deprive them of something to which they have a right, and the other has no right. As such, these acts of protectiveness make it possible for men and women in society to retain their own sphere of jurisdiction intact, protect their own "moral space." They refuse to have their human dignity violated. They want to be sovereigns and govern their own lives, including their own productive decisions and actions. Those who mount the attack, in turn, fail or refuse to refrain from encroaching upon the moral space of their victims. They are treating the victim's life and its productive results as though these were unowned resources for them to do with as they choose.

Now the argument that cuts against the above account is that on some occasions there can be people who, with no responsibility for their situation, are highly unlikely to survive without disregarding the rights of others and taking from them what they need. This is indeed possible. It is no less possible that there be cases in which someone is highly unlikely to survive without obtaining the services of a doctor who is at that moment spending time healing someone else, or in which there is a person who is highly unlikely to survive without obtaining one of the lungs of another person, who wants to keep both lungs so as to be able to run the New York City marathon effectively. And such cases could be multiplied indefinitely.

But are such cases typical? The argument that starts with this assumption about a society is already not comparable to the libertarianism that has emerged in the footsteps of Lockean natural-rights doctrine, including the version advanced in this book. That system is developed for a human community in which "peace is possible." Libertarian individual rights, which guide men and women in such an adequately hospitable environment to act without thwarting the flourishing of others, are thus suitable bases for the legal foundations for a human society. It is possible for people in the world to pursue their proper goals without thwarting a similar pursuit by others.

The underlying notion of society in such a theory rejects the description of human communities implicit in Sterba's picture. Sterba sees conflict as typically arising from some people producing and owning goods, while others having no alternative but to take these goods from the former in order to survive. But these are not the typical conflict situations even in what we today consider reasonably free human communities—most thieves and robbers are not destitute, nor are they incapable of doing something aside from taking other people's property in order to obtain their livelihood.

The typical conflict situation in society involves people who wish to take shortcuts to earning their living (and a lot more) by attacking others, not those who lack any other alternative to attacking others so as to reach that same goal. This may not be evident from all societies that team with human conflict—in the Middle East, or Central and South America, for example. But it must be remembered that these societies are far from being even near-libertarian. Even if the typical conflicts there involved the kind Sterba describes, that would not suffice to make his point. Only if it were true that in comparatively free countries the typical conflict involved the utterly destitute and helpless arrayed against the well-to-do, could his argument carry any conviction.

The Lockean libertarian has confidence in the willingness and capacity of *virtually all persons* to make headway in life in a free society. The very small minority of exceptional cases must be taken care of by voluntary social institutions, not by the government, which guards self-consistent individual rights.

The integrity of law would be seriously endangered if the government entered areas that required it to make very particular judgments and depart from serving the interest of the public as such. We have already noted that the idea of "satisfying basic needs" can involve the difficulty of distinguishing those whose actions are properly to be so characterized. Rich persons are indeed satisfying their basic needs as they protect and preserve their property rights. . . . Private property rights are necessary for a morally decent society.

The Lockean libertarian argues that private property rights are morally justified in part because they are the concrete requirement for delineating the sphere of jurisdiction of each person's moral authority, where her own judgment is decisive. This is a crucial basis for the right to property. And so is the contention that we live in a metaphysically hospitable universe wherein people normally need not suffer innocent misery and deprivation—so that such a condition is usually the result of negligence or the violation of Lockean rights, a violation that has made self-development and commerce impossible. If exceptional emergencies set the agenda for the law, the law itself will disintegrate. (A just legal system makes provision for coping with emergencies that are brought to the attention of the authorities, for example, by way of judicial discretion, without allowing such cases to determine the direction of the system. If legislators and judges don't uphold the integrity of the system, disintegration ensues. This can itself encourage the emergence of strong leaders, demagogues, who promise to do what the law has not been permitted to do, namely, satisfy people's sense of justice. Experience with them bodes ill for such a prospect.)

Normally persons do not "lack the opportunities and resources to satisfy their own basic needs." Even if we grant that some helpless, crippled, retarded, or destitute persons could offer nothing to anyone that would merit wages enabling them to carry on with their lives and perhaps even flourish, there is still the other possibility for most actual, known hard cases, that is, seeking help. I am not speaking here of the cases we know: people who drop out of school, get an unskilled job, marry and have kids, only to find that their personal choice of inadequate preparation for life leaves them relatively poorly off. "'Ought' implies 'can'" must not be treated ahistorically—some people's lack of current options results from their failure to exercise previous options prudently. I refer here to the "truly needy," to use a shop-worn but still useful phrase—those who have never been able to help themselves and are not now helpless from their own neglect. Are such people being treated *unjustly*, rather than at most uncharitably, ungenerously, indecently, pitilessly, or in some other respect immorally—by those who, knowing of the plight of such persons, resist forcible efforts to take from them enough to provide the ill-fated with what they truly need? Actually, if we tried to pry the needed goods or money from the well-to-do, we would not even learn if they would act generously. Charity, generosity, kindness, and acts of compassion presuppose that those well enough off are not coerced to provide help. These virtues cannot flourish, nor can the corresponding vices, of course, without a clearly identified and well-protected right to private property for all.

If we consider the situation as we are more likely to find it, namely, that desperate cases not caused by previous injustices (in the libertarian sense) are rare, then, contrary to what Sterba suggests, there is much that unfortunate persons can and should do in those plausible, non-emergency situations that can be considered typical. They need not resort to violating the private-property rights of those who are better off. The destitute can appeal for assistance both from the rich and from the many voluntary social service agencies which emerge from the widespread compassion of people who know about the mishaps that can at times strike perfectly decent people.

Consider, as a prototype of this situation on which we might model what concerns Sterba, that if one's car breaks down on a remote road, it would be unreasonable to expect one not to seek a phone or some other way of escaping one's unfortunate situation. So one ought to at least try to obtain the use of a phone.

But should one break into the home of a perfect stranger living nearby? Or ought one instead to request the use of the phone as a favor? "'Ought' implies 'can'" is surely fully satisfied here. Actual practice makes this quite evident. When someone is suffering from misfortune and there are plenty of others who are not, and the unfortunate person has no other avenue for obtaining help than to obtain it from others, it would not be unreasonable to expect, morally, that the poor seek such help as surely might be forthcoming. We have no justification for assuming that the rich are all callous, though this caricature is regularly painted by communists and by folklore. Supporting and gaining advantage from the institution of private property by no means implies that one lacks the virtue of generosity. The rich are no more immune to virtue than the poor are to vice. The contrary view is probably a legacy of the idea that only those concerned with spiritual or intellectual matters can be trusted to know virtue—those concerned with seeking material prosperity are too base.

The destitute typically have options other than to violate the rights of the well-off. "'Ought' implies 'can'" is satisfiable by the moral imperative that the poor ought to seek help, not loot. There is then no injustice in the rich preventing the poor from seeking such loot by violating the right to private property. "'Ought' implies 'can'" is fully satisfied if the poor can take the kind of action that could gain them the satisfaction of their basic needs, and this action could well be asking for help.

All along here I have been considering only the helplessly poor, who through no fault of their own, nor again through any rights violation by others, are destitute. I am taking the hard cases seriously, where violation of "'ought' implies 'can'" would appear to be most probable. But such cases are by no means typical. They are extremely rare. And even rarer are those cases in which all avenues regarded as legitimate from the libertarian point of view have been exhausted, including appealing for help.

The bulk of poverty in the world is not the result of natural disaster or disease. Rather, it is political oppression, whereby people throughout many of the world's countries are not legally permitted to look out for themselves in production and trade. The famines in Africa and India, the poverty in the same countries and in Central and Latin America, as well as in China, the Soviet Union, Poland, Rumania, and so forth, are not the result of lack of charity but of oppression. It is the kind that those who have the protection of even a seriously compromised document and system protecting individual negative human rights, such as the U.S. Constitution, do not experience. The first requirement for men and women to ameliorate their hardship is to be free of other people's oppression, not to be free to take other people's belongings.

Of course, it would be immoral if people failed to help out when this was clearly no sacrifice for them. But charity or generosity is not a categorical imperative, even for the rich. There are more basic moral principles that might require the rich to refuse to be charitable—for example, if they are using most of their wealth for the protection of freedom or a just society. Courage can be more important than charity or benevolence or compassion. But a discussion of the ranking of moral virtues would take us far afield. One reason that many critics of libertarianism find their own cases persuasive is that they think the libertarian can only subscribe to *political* principles or values. But this is mistaken.

There can be emergency cases in which there is no alternative available to disregarding the rights of others. But these are extremely rare, and not at all the sort invoked by critics such as Sterba. I have in mind the desert-island case found in ethics books where instantaneous action, with only one violent alternative, faces persons—the sort we know from the law books in which the issue is one of immediate life and death. These are not cases, to repeat the phrase quoted from Locke by H. L. A. Hart, "where peace is possible." They are discussed in the libertarian literature and considerable progress has been made in integrating them with the concerns of law and politics. Since we are here discussing law and politics, which are general systematic approaches to how we normally ought to live with one another in human communities, these emergency situations do not help us except as limiting cases. And not surprisingly many famous court cases illustrate just this point as they now and then confront these kinds of instances after they have come to light within the framework of civilized society. . . .

NOTES

1. James Sterba, "A Libertarian Justification for a Welfare State," *Social Theory and Practice*, 11 (Fall 1985): 295.

2. Ayn Rand, "Value and Rights," in *Readings in Introductory Analysis,* ed. John Hospers (Englewood Cliffs, NJ: Prentice-Hall, 1968), p. 382.

3. James Sterba, "The U.S. Constitution: A Fundamentally Flawed Document," in *Philosophical Reflections on the United States Constitution: A Collection of Bicentennial Essays,* ed. Christopher Gray (Lewiston, NY: Mellen, 1989), [n.p. provided].

4. Ibid.

5. Sterba, "A Libertarian Justification," pp. 295–296.

DISCUSSION QUESTIONS

1. Machan writes that "charity and generosity is not a categorical imperative, even for the rich." How does he defend this position? Do you agree with him? Why or why not?
2. What do you think about Machan's claim that the "first requirement for men and women to ameliorate their hardship is to be free of other people's oppression, not to be free to take other people's belongings"? How might James Sterba and/or Kai Nielsen respond to this claim? Whose argument is stronger, and why?
3. What is the difference between a "negative right" and a "positive right"? What role does this distinction play in Machan's argument?
4. Machan says that, "if Sterba were correct about Lockean libertarianism typically contradicting 'ought' implies 'can,' his argument would be decisive." Why does Machan believe that Sterba is incorrect about Lockean libertarianism typically contradicting "'ought' implies 'can'"? Do you agree with Machan's analysis of Sterba? Why or why not?
5. Do Machan's arguments convince you that we do not have the *right* to receive the goods and resources necessary for preserving ourselves? Why or why not? Try to anticipate criticisms of your view, and account for them in your defense of your position.

NANCY FRASER

Women, Welfare and the Politics of Need Interpretation

Nancy Fraser provides a feminist approach to welfare and poverty. Fraser asks us to consider the political costs of welfare and the kinds of roles men and women are assigned in the U.S. welfare system. She argues that the identities and needs which the U.S. social welfare system fashions for its recipients are interpreted identities and needs. "Moreover," says Fraser, "they are highly political interpretations which are in principle subject to dispute." Fraser believes that men and women do very different things and that women have needs very different from the ones assigned to them within the U.S. social welfare system. According to Fraser, that system views women as unpaid mothers and caregivers and men as breadwinners. In addition, the system defines women as dependent clients and men as rights-bearing beneficiaries. For Fraser, these roles assigned to women within the social welfare system reflect patriarchal norms and are consequently unfair to women. She suggests that we approach the U.S. social welfare system as a "judicial-administrative-therapeutic state apparatus" that translates political issues about the interpretation of people's needs into legal, administrative, and/or therapeutic matters.

Nancy Fraser is the Henry A. and Louise Loeb Professor of Politics and Philosophy at the New School for Social Research. She has written and edited a number of books, including *Unruly Practices: Power, Discourse, and Gender in Contemporary Social Theory* (1989), *Revaluing French Feminism: Critical Essays on Difference, Agency, and Culture* (coedited with

Nancy Fraser, *Unruly Practices: Power, Discourse, and Gender in Contemporary Social Theory*. University of Minnesota Press, 1989, 144–160. Reprinted by permission of the publisher.

Sandra Bartky, 1992), *Justice Interruptus: Critical Reflections on the "Postsocialist" Condition* (1997), and *Adding Insult to Injury: Social Justice and the Politics of Recognition* (2000). The following selection is from *Unruly Practices.*

Long before the emergence of welfare states, governments have defined legally secured arenas of societal action. In so doing, they have at the same time codified corresponding patterns of agency or social roles. Thus, early modern states defined an economic arena and the corresponding role of an economic person capable of entering into contracts. More or less at the same time, they codified the "private sphere" of the household and the role of household head with dependents. Somewhat later, governments were led to secure a sphere of political participation and the corresponding role of citizen with (limited) political rights. In each of these cases, the original and paradigmatic subject of the newly codified social role was male. Only secondarily and much later was it conceded that women, too, could occupy these subject-positions, without however entirely dispelling the association with masculinity.

Matters are different, however, with the contemporary welfare state. When this type of government defined a new arena of activity—call it "the social"—and a new societal role, the welfare client, it included women among its original and paradigmatic subjects. Today, in fact, women have become the principal subjects of the welfare state. On the one hand, they comprise the overwhelming majority both of program recipients and of paid social service workers. On the other hand, they are the wives, mothers and daughters whose unpaid activities and obligations are redefined as the welfare state increasingly oversees forms of caregiving. Since this beneficiary–social worker–caregiver nexus of roles is constitutive of the social-welfare arena, one might even call the latter as feminized terrain.

A brief statistical overview confirms women's greater involvement with and dependence on the U.S. social-welfare system. Consider first women's greater dependence as program clients and beneficiaries. In each of the major "means-tested" programs in the U.S., women and the children for whom they are responsible now comprise the overwhelming majority of clients. For example, more than 81% of households receiving Aid to Families with Dependent Children (AFDC) are headed by women; more than 60% of families receiving food stamps or Medicaid are headed by women; and 70% of all households in publicly owned or subsidized housing

are headed by women. High as they are, these figures actually underestimate the representation of women. As Barbara Nelson notes, in the androcentric reporting system, households counted as female-headed by definition contain no healthy adult men. But healthy adult women live in most households counted as male-headed. Such women may directly or indirectly receive benefits going to "male-headed" households, but they are invisible in the statistics, even though they usually do the work of securing and maintaining program eligibility.

Women also predominate in the major U.S. "age-tested" programs. For example, 61.6% of all adult beneficiaries of Social Security are women; and 64% of those covered by Medicare are women. In sum, because women as a group are significantly poorer than men—indeed they now comprise nearly two-thirds of all U.S. adults below the official poverty line—and because women tend to live longer than men, women depend more on the social-welfare system as clients and beneficiaries.

But this is not the whole story. Women also depend more on the social-welfare system as paid human service workers—a category of employment which includes education and health, as well as social work and services administration. In 1980, 70% of the 17.3 million paid jobs in this sector in the U.S. were held by women. This accounts for one-third of U.S. women's total paid employment and a full 80% of all professional jobs held by women. The figures for women of color are even higher than this average, since 37% of their total paid employment and 82.4% of their professional employment is in this sector. It is a distinctive feature of the U.S. social-welfare system, as opposed to, say, the British and Scandinavian systems, that only 3% of these jobs are in the form of direct federal government employment. The rest are in state and local government, in the "private non-profit" sector and in the "private" sector. But the more decentralized and privatized character of the U.S. system does not make paid welfare workers any less vulnerable in the face of federal program cuts. On the contrary, the level of federal social-welfare spending affects the level of human service employment in *all* sectors. State and local government jobs depend on federal and federally financed state and local government contracts; and private profit and non-profit jobs depend on federally financed transfer payments to individuals and households for the purchase of services like health care in the market. Thus, reductions in social spending mean the loss of jobs for women. Moreover, as Barbara Ehrenreich and Frances Fox Piven note, this loss is not compensated when spending is shifted to the military, since only 0.5% of the entire female paid workforce is employed in work on military contracts. In fact, one study they cite estimates that with each one billion dollar increase in military spending, 9500 jobs are lost to women.

Finally, women are subjects of and to the social-welfare system in their traditional capacity as unpaid caregivers. It is well known that the sexual division of labor assigns women primary responsibility for the care of those who cannot care for themselves. (I leave aside women's traditional obligations to provide personal services to adult males—husbands, fathers, grown sons, lovers—who can very well care for themselves.) Such responsibility includes child care, of course, but also care for sick and/or elderly relatives, often parents. For example, a 1975 British study cited by Hilary Land found that three times as many elderly people live with married daughters as with married sons, and that those without a close female relative were more likely to be institutionalized, irrespective of degree of infirmity. As unpaid caregivers, then, women are more directly affected than men by the level and character of government social services for children, the sick and the elderly.

As clients, paid human service workers and unpaid caregivers, then, women are the principal subjects of the social-welfare system. It is as if this branch of the state were in effect a "Bureau of Women's Affairs."

Of course, the welfare system does not deal with women on women's terms. On the contrary, it has its own characteristic ways of interpreting women's needs and positioning women as subjects. In order to understand these, we need to examine how gender norms and meanings are reflected in the structure of the U.S. social-welfare system.

This issue is quite complicated. On the one hand, nearly all U.S. social-welfare programs are officially gender neutral. Yet the system as a whole is a dual or two-tiered one; and it has an unmistakable gender subtext. There is one set of programs oriented to *individuals* and tied to participation in the paid workforce, for example, unemployment insurance and Social Security. These programs are de-

signed to supplement and compensate for the primary market in paid labor power. There is a second set of programs oriented to *households* and tied to combined household income, for example, AFDC, food stamps and Medicaid. These programs are designed to compensate for what are considered to be family failures, generally the absence of a male breadwinner.

What integrates the two sets of programs is a common core of assumptions, underlying both, concerning the sexual division of labor, domestic and nondomestic. It is assumed that families do or should contain one primary breadwinner who is male and one unpaid domestic worker (homemaker and mother) who is female. It is further assumed that when a woman undertakes paid work outside the home this is or should be in order to supplement the male breadwinner's wage and so it neither does nor ought override her primary housewifely and maternal responsibilities. It is assumed, in other words, that society is divided into two separate spheres of home and outside work and that these are women's and men's spheres respectively.

These assumptions are increasingly counterfactual. At present, fewer than 15% of U.S. families conform to the normative ideal of a domicile shared by a husband who is the sole breadwinner, a wife who is a full-time homemaker and their offspring.

Nonetheless, the separate spheres norms determine the structure of the social-welfare system. They determine that it contain a primary labor market–related subsystem and a family or household-related subsystem. Moreover, they determine that these subsystems be gender-linked, that the labor market–related system be implicitly "masculine" and the family-related system be implicitly "feminine." Consequently, the normative, ideal-typical recipient of primary labor market–oriented programs is a (white) male, while the normative, ideal-typical client of household-based programs is a female.

This gender subtext of the U.S. welfare system is confirmed when we take a second look at participation figures. Consider again the figures just cited for the "feminine" or family-based programs, which I earlier referred to as "means-tested" programs: more than 81% of households receiving AFDC are female-headed, as are more than 70% of those receiving housing assistance and more than 60% of those receiving Medicaid and food stamps. Now recall that these figures do not compare female vs. male individuals, but rather female- vs. male-headed *households*. They therefore confirm four things: (1) these programs have a distinctive administrative identity in that their recipients are not individualized but *familialized;* (2) they serve what are considered to be defective families, overwhelmingly families without a male breadwinner; (3) the ideal-typical (adult) client is female; and (4) she makes her claim for benefits on the basis of her status as an unpaid domestic worker, a homemaker and mother, not as a paid worker based in the labor market.

Now contrast this with the case of a typical labor market–based and thus "masculine" program, namely, unemployment insurance. Here the percentage of female claimants drops to 38%, a figure which contrasts female vs. male *individuals,* as opposed to households. As Diana Pearce notes, this drop reflects at least two different circumstances. First, and most straightforwardly, it reflects women's lower rate of participation in the paid workforce. Second, it reflects the fact that many women wageworkers are not eligible to participate in this program, for example, paid household service workers, part-time workers, pregnant workers and workers in the "irregular economy" such as prostitutes, babysitters and home typists. The exclusion of these predominantly female wage-workers testifies to the existence of a gender segmented labor market, divided into "primary" and "secondary" employment. It reflects the more general assumption that women's earnings are "merely supplementary," not on a par with those of the primary (male) breadwinner. Altogether, then, the figures tell us four things about programs like unemployment insurance: (1) they are administered in a way which *individualizes* rather than familializes recipients; (2) they are designed to compensate primary labor market effects, such as the temporary displacement of a primary breadwinner; (3) the ideal-typical recipient is male; and (4) he makes his claim on the basis of his identity as a paid worker, not as an unpaid domestic worker or parent.

One final example will round out the picture. The Social Security system of retirement insurance presents the interesting case of a hermaphrodite or androgyne. I shall soon show that this system has a number of characteristics of "masculine" programs in virtue of its link to participation in the paid workforce. However, it is also internally dualized and gendered, and thus stands as a microcosm of the entire dual-benefit welfare system. Consider that, while a majority—61.6%—of adult beneficiaries are female, only somewhat more than half of these—or 33.3% of all recipients—claim benefits on the basis of their own paid work records. The remaining female recipients claim benefits on the basis of their husbands' records, that is, as wives or unpaid domestic workers. By contrast, virtually no male recipients claim benefits as husbands. On the contrary, they claim benefits as paid workers, a labor market–located as opposed to family-located identity. So the Social Security system is hermaphroditic or androgynous; it is internally divided between family-based, "feminine" benefits, on the one hand, and labor market–based, "masculine" benefits, on the other hand. Thus, it too gets its structure from gender norms and assumptions.

So far, we have established the dualistic structure of the U.S. social-welfare system and the gender subtext of the dualism. Now, we can better tease out the system's implicit norms and tacit assumptions by examining its mode of operation. To see how welfare programs interpret women's needs, we should consider what benefits consist in. To see how programs position women as subjects, we should examine administrative practices. In general, we shall see that the "masculine" and "feminine" subsystems are not only separate but also unequal.

Consider that the "masculine" social-welfare programs are social insurance schemes. They include unemployment insurance, Social Security (retirement insurance), Medicare (age-tested health insurance) and Supplemental Social Security Insurance (disability insurance for those with paid work records). These programs are contributory; wage-workers and their employers pay into trust funds. They are administered on a national basis and benefit levels are uniform across the country. Though bureaucratically organized and administered, they require less, and less demeaning effort on the part of beneficiaries in qualifying and maintaining eligibility than do "feminine" programs. They are far less subject to intrusive controls and in most cases lack the dimension of surveillance. They also tend to require less of beneficiaries in the way of benefit-collection efforts, with the notable exception of unemployment insurance.

In sum, "masculine" social insurance schemes position recipients primarily as *rights-bearers.* The beneficiaries of these programs are in the main not stigmatized. Neither administrative practice nor popular discourse constitutes them as "on the dole." They are constituted rather as receiving what they deserve, what they, in "partnership" with their employers, have already paid in for, what they, therefore, have a *right* to. Moreover, these beneficiaries are also positioned as *purchasing consumers.* They receive cash as opposed to "in kind" benefits and so are positioned as having "the liberty to strike the best bargain they can in purchasing services of their choice on the open market." In sum, these beneficiaries are what C. B. MacPherson calls "possessive individuals." Proprietors of their own persons who have freely contracted to sell their labor-power, they become participants in social insurance schemes and, thence, paying consumers of human services. They therefore qualify as *social citizens* in virtually the fullest sense that term can acquire within the framework of a male-dominated capitalist society.

All this stands in stark contrast to the "feminine" sector of the U.S. social-welfare system. This sector consists in relief programs, such as AFDC, food stamps, Medicaid and public housing assistance. These programs are not contributory, but are financed out of general tax revenues, usually with one-third of the funds coming from the federal government and two-thirds coming from the states. They are not administered nationally but rather by the states. As a result, benefit levels vary dramatically, though they are everywhere inadequate, deliberately pegged below the official poverty line. The relief programs are notorious for the varieties of administrative humiliation they inflict upon clients. They require considerable work in qualifying and maintaining eligibility; and they have a heavy component of surveillance.

These programs do not in any meaningful sense position their subjects as rights-bearers. Far from being considered as having a right to what they receive, recipients are defined as "beneficiaries of governmental largesse" or "clients of public charity." In the androcentric-administrative framework, "welfare mothers" are considered not to work and so are sometimes required, that is to say coerced, to work off their benefits via "workfare." They thus become inmates of what Diana Pearce calls a "workhouse without walls." Indeed, the only sense in which the category of rights is relevant to these clients' situation is the somewhat dubious one according to which they are entitled to treatment governed by the standards of formal-bureaucratic procedural rationality. But if that right is construed as protection from administrative caprice, then even it is widely and routinely disregarded. Moreover, recipients of public relief are generally not positioned as purchasing consumers. A significant portion of their benefits is "in kind" and what cash they get comes already carved up and earmarked for specific, administratively designated purposes. These recipients are therefore essentially *clients*, a subject-position which carries far less power and dignity in capitalist societies than does the alternative position of purchaser. In these societies, to be a client in the sense relevant to relief recipients is to be an abject dependent. Indeed, this sense of the term carries connotations of a fall from autonomy, as when we speak, for example, of "the client-states of empires or superpowers." As clients, then, recipients of relief are *the negatives of possessive individuals*. Largely excluded from the market, both as workers and as consumers, claiming benefits not as individuals but as members of "failed" families, these recipients are effectively denied the trappings of social citizenship as the latter are defined within male-dominated capitalist societies.

Clearly, this system creates a double-bind for women raising children without a male breadwinner. By failing to offer them day care, job training, a job that pays a "family wage" or some combination of these, it constructs them exclusively as mothers. As a consequence, it interprets their needs as maternal needs and their sphere of activity as that of "the family." Now, according to the ideology of separate spheres, this should be an honorific social identity. Yet the system does not honor these women. On the contrary, instead of providing them a guaranteed income equivalent to a family wage as a matter of right, it stigmatizes, humiliates and harasses them. In effect, it decrees that these women must be, yet cannot be, normative mothers.

Moreover, the way in which the U.S. social-welfare system interprets "maternity" and "the family" is race- and culture-specific. The bias is made plain in Carol Stack's study, *All Our Kin*. Stack analyzes domestic arrangements of very poor Black welfare recipients in a midwestern city. Where ideologues see "the disorganization of the [sic] black family," she finds complex, highly organized kinship structures. These include kin-based networks of resource pooling and exchange which enable those in direst poverty to survive economically and communally. The networks organize delayed exchanges or "gifts," in Mauss' sense, of prepared meals, food stamps, cooking, shopping, groceries, furniture, sleeping space, cash (including wages and AFDC allowances), transportation, clothing, child care, even children. They span several physically distinct households and so transcend the principal administrative category which organizes relief programs. It is significant that Stack took great pains to conceal the identities of her subjects, even going so far as to disguise the identity of their city. The reason, though unstated, is obvious: these people would lose their benefits if program administrators learned that they did not utilize them within the confines and boundaries of a "household."

We can summarize the separate and unequal character of the two-tiered, gender-linked, race- and culture-biased U.S. social-welfare system in the following formulae: Participants in the "masculine" subsystem are positioned as *rights-bearing beneficiaries and purchasing consumers of services.* Participants in the "feminine" subsystem, on the other hand, are positioned as *dependent clients.*

DISCUSSION QUESTIONS

1. In an earlier article, Diana Pearce discussed the feminization of poverty. How is Pearce's discussion similar to and/or different from Fraser's analysis of women and welfare? What are the key differences? Similarities?
2. What does Fraser mean by the phrase "judicial-administrative-therapeutic state apparatus"? What is her interpretation of the U.S. social welfare system as a "judicial-administrative-therapeutic state apparatus"?
3. Why, according to Fraser, are women the principal subjects and workers in the welfare system? Do you agree with her analysis? Why or why not?
4. How, according to Fraser, do social welfare programs interpret women and their needs? Compare the treatment of men to the treatment of women. Critically evaluate Fraser's analysis.
5. Traditional (male-dominated) norms assume women are wives and mothers, and men are breadwinners. What is wrong with this according to Fraser? Do you agree with her criticism of these gender roles? Why or why not? Be specific.
6. Fraser says that women have needs that are not captured in a male-dominated capitalist society. What are they? Is she right? Explain.

 PETER MARIN

Helping and Hating the Homeless

Peter Marin says that questions concerning helping the homeless must be answered in two parts: (1) in relation to people who have been marginalized against their will and (2) in relation to those who have chosen their marginality. Marin argues that society owes men and women who have been marginalized against their will "whatever it takes for them to regain their places in the social order." For Marin, "those who are the inevitable casualties of modern industrial capitalism and the free-market system are entitled, *by right,* and by the simple virtue of their participation in that system, to whatever help they need." Regarding those who have chosen their marginality, Marin believes that we owe them "at least a place to exist, a way to exist." For Marin, this "may not be a *moral* obligation," but it is an "existential obligation." Marin also says that our basic desire with respect to the homeless people is simply to be rid of them. Most of the existing programs for the homeless do not address their needs and desires, but rather address our need to "rearrange the world cosmetically" to suit our own needs. Marin calls for programs that respect homeless people's rights to have different aspirations than our own and that take more account of homeless people's own understanding of themselves.

Peter Marin is a writer who has spent time on the streets and in the shelters of many American cities. He is the author of *Freedom and Its Discontents: Reflections on Four Decades of American Moral Experience* (1995).

The trouble begins with the word "homeless." It has become such an abstraction, and is applied to so many different kinds of people, with so many different histories and problems, that it is almost meaningless.

Homelessness, in itself, is nothing more than a condition visited upon men and women (and, increasingly, children) as the final stage of a variety of problems about which the word "homelessness" tells us almost nothing. Or, to put it another way, it is a catch basin into which pour all of the people disenfranchised or marginalized or scared off by processes beyond their control, those which lie close to the heart of American life. Here are the groups packed into the single category of "the homeless":

- Veterans, mainly from the war in Vietnam. In many American cities, vets make up close to 50 percent of all homeless males.

- The mentally ill. In some parts of the country, roughly a quarter of the homeless would, a couple of decades ago, have been institutionalized.

- The physically disabled or chronically ill, who do not receive any benefits or whose benefits do not enable them to afford permanent shelter.

- The elderly on fixed incomes whose funds are no longer sufficient for their needs.

- Men, women, and whole families pauperized by the loss of a job.

- Single parents, usually women, without the resources or skills to establish new lives.

- Runaway children, many of whom have been abused.

- Alcoholics and those in trouble with drugs (whose troubles often begin with one of the other conditions listed here).

- Immigrants, both legal and illegal, who often are not counted among the homeless because they constitute a "problem" in their own right.

- Traditional tramps, hobos, and transients, who have taken to the road or the streets for a variety of reasons and who prefer to be there.

You can quickly learn two things about the homeless from this list. First, you can learn that many of the homeless, before they were homeless, were people more or less like ourselves: members of the working or middle class. And you can learn that the world of the homeless has its roots in various policies, events, and ways of life for which some of us are responsible and from which some of us actually prosper.

We decide, as a people, to go to war, we ask our children to kill and to die, and the result, years later, is grown men homeless on the street.

We change, with the best intentions, the laws pertaining to the mentally ill and then, without intention, neglect to provide them with services; and the result, in our streets, drives some of us crazy with rage.

We cut taxes and prune budgets, we modernize industry and shift the balance of trade, and the result of all these actions and errors can be read, sleeping form by sleeping form, on our city streets.

The liberals cannot blame the conservatives. The conservatives cannot blame the liberals. Homelessness is the *sum total* of our dreams, policies, intentions, errors, omissions, cruelties, kindnesses, all of it recorded, in flesh, in the life of the streets.

You can also learn from this list one of the most important things there is to know about the homeless—that they can be roughly divided into two groups: those who have had homelessness forced upon them and want nothing more than to escape it; and those who have at least in part *chosen* it for themselves, and now accept, or in some cases, embrace it.

I understand how dangerous it is to introduce the idea of choice into a discussion of homelessness. It can all too easily be used to justify indifference or brutality toward the homeless, or to argue that they are only getting what they "deserve." And yet it seems to me that it is only by taking choice into account, in all of the intricacies of its various forms and expressions, that one can really understand certain kinds of homelessness.

The fact is, many of the homeless are not only hapless victims but voluntary exiles, "domestic refugees," people who have turned not against life itself but against *us*, our life, American life. Look for a moment at the vets. The price of returning to America was to forget what they had seen or learned in Vietnam, to "put it behind them." But some could not do that, and the stress of trying showed up as alcoholism, broken marriages, drug addiction, crime. And it showed up too as life on the street, which was for some vets a desperate choice made in the name of life—the best they could manage. It was a way of avoiding what might have occurred had they stayed where they were: suicide, or violence done to others.

We must learn to accept that there may indeed be people, and not only vets, who have seen so much of our world, or seen it so clearly, that to live in it becomes impossible. Here, for example, is the story of Alice, a homeless middle-aged woman in Los Angeles, where there are, perhaps, 50,000 homeless people. It was set down a few months ago by one of my students at the University of California, Santa Barbara, where I taught for a semester. I had encouraged them to go find the homeless and listen to their stories. And so, one day, when this student saw Alice foraging in a dumpster outside a McDonald's, he stopped and talked to her:

> She told me she had led a pretty normal life as she grew up and eventually went to college. From there she went on to Chicago to teach school. She was single and lived in a small apartment.
>
> One night, after she got off the train after school, a man began to follow her to her apartment building. When she got to her door she saw a knife and the man hovering behind her. She had no choice but to let him in. The man raped her.
>
> After that, things got steadily worse. She had a nervous breakdown. She went to a mental institution for three months, and when she went back to her apartment she found her belongings gone. The landlord had sold them to cover the rent she hadn't paid.
>
> She had no place to go and no job because the school had terminated her employment. She slipped into depression. She lived with friends until she could muster enough money for a ticket to Los Angeles. She said she no longer wanted to burden her friends, and that if she had to live outside, at least Los Angeles was warmer than Chicago.
>
> It is as if she began back then to take on the mentality of a street person. She resolved herself to homelessness. She's been out West since 1980, without a home or job. She seems happy, with her best friend being her cat. But the scars of memories still haunt her, and she is running from them, or should I say *him*.

This is, in essence, the same story one hears over and over again on the street. You begin with an ordinary life; then an event occurs—traumatic, catastrophic; smaller events follow, each one deepening the original wound; finally, homelessness becomes inevitable, or begins to *seem* inevitable to the person involved—the only way out of an intolerable situation. You are struck continually, hearing these stories, by something seemingly unique in American life, the absolute isolation involved. In what other culture would there be such an absence or failure of support from familial, social, or institutional sources? Even more disturbing is the fact that it is often our supposed sources of support—family, friends, government organizations—that have caused the problem in the first place.

Everything that happened to Alice—the rape, the loss of job and apartment, the breakdown—was part and parcel of a world gone radically wrong, a world, for Alice, no longer to be counted on, no longer worth living in. Her homelessness can be seen as flight, as failure of will or nerve, even, perhaps, as *disease*. But it can also be seen as a mute, furious refusal, a self-imposed exile far less appealing to the rest of us than ordinary life, but *better*, in Alice's terms.

We like to think, in America, that everything is redeemable, that everything broken can be magically made whole again, and that what has been "dirtied" can be cleansed. Recently I saw on television that one of the soaps had introduced the character of a homeless old woman. A woman in her thirties discovers that her long-lost mother has appeared in town, on the streets. After much searching the mother is located and identified and embraced; and then she is scrubbed and dressed in style, restored in a matter of days to her former upper-class habits and role.

A triumph—but one more likely to occur on television than in real life. Yes, many of those on the streets could be transformed, rehabilitated. But there are others whose lives have been irrevocably changed, damaged beyond repair, and who no longer want help, who no longer recognize the *need* for help, and whose experience in our world has made them want only to be left alone. How, for instance, would one restore Alice's life, or reshape it in a way that would satisfy *our* notion of what a life should be? What would it take to return her to the fold? How to erase the four years of homelessness, which have become as familiar to her, and as much a home, as her "normal" life once was? Whatever we think of the way in which she has resolved her difficulties, it constitutes a sad peace made with the world. Intruding ourselves upon it in the name of redemption is by no means as simple a task—or as justifiable a task—as one might think.

It is important to understand too that however disorderly and dirty and unmanageable the world of homeless men and women like Alice appears to us, it is not without its significance, and its rules and rituals. The homeless in our cities mark out for themselves particular neighborhoods, blocks, buildings, doorways. They impose on themselves often obsessively strict routines. They reduce their world to a small area, and thereby protect themselves from a world that might otherwise be too much to bear.

Pavlov, the Russian psychologist, once theorized that the two most fundamental reflexes in all animals, including humans, are those involving freedom and orientation. Grab any animal, he said, and it will immediately struggle to accomplish two things: to break free and to orient itself. And this is what one sees in so many of the homeless. Having been stripped of all other forms of connection, and of most kinds of social identity, they are left only with this: the raw stuff of nature, something encoded in the cells—the desire to be free, the need for familiar space. Perhaps this is why so many of them struggle so vehemently against us when we offer them aid. They are clinging to their freedom and their space, and they do not believe that this is what we, with our programs and our shelters, mean to allow them. . . .

It is important to . . . recognize the immensity of the changes that have occurred in the marginal world in the past twenty years. Whole sections of many cities—the Bowery in New York, the Tenderloin in San Francisco—were once ceded to the transient. In every skid-row area in America you could find what you needed to survive: hash houses, saloons offering free lunches, pawnshops, surplus-clothing stores, and, most important of all, cheap hotels and flop-houses and two-bit employment agencies specializing in the kinds of labor (seasonal, shape-up) transients have always done.

It was by no means a wonderful world. But it *was* a world. Its rituals were spelled out in ways most of the participants understood. In hobo jungles up and down the tracks, whatever there was to eat went into a common pot and was divided equally. Late at night, in empties criss-crossing the country, men would speak with a certain anonymous openness, as if the shared condition of transience created among them a kind of civility.

What most people in that world wanted was simply to be left alone. Some of them had been on the road for years, itinerant workers. Others were recuperating from wounds they could never quite explain. There were young men and a few women with nothing better to do, and older men who had no families or had lost their jobs or wives, or for whom the rigor and pressure of life had proved too demanding. The marginal world offered them a respite from the other world, a world grown too much for them.

But things have changed. There began to pour into the marginal world—slowly in the sixties, a bit faster in the seventies, and then faster still in the eighties—more and more people who neither belonged nor knew how to survive there. The sixties brought the counterculture and drugs; the streets filled with young dropouts. Changes in the law loosed upon the streets mentally ill men and women. Inflation took its toll, then recession. Working-class and even middle-class men and women—entire families—began to fall into a world they did not understand.

At the same time the transient world was being inundated by new inhabitants, its landscape, its economy, was shrinking radically. Jobs became harder to find. Modernization had something to do with it; machines took the place of men and women. And the influx of workers from Mexico and points farther south created a class of semipermanent workers who took the place of casual transient labor. More important, perhaps, was the fact that the forgotten parts of many cities began to attract attention. Downtown areas were redeveloped, reclaimed. The skid-row sections of smaller cities were turned into "old townes." The old hotels that once catered to transients were upgraded or torn down or became warehouses for welfare families—an arrangement far more profitable to the owners. The price of housing increased; evictions increased. The mentally ill, who once could afford to house themselves in cheap rooms, the alcoholics, who once would drink themselves to sleep at night in their cheap hotels, were out on the street—exposed to the weather and to danger, and also in plain and public view: "problems" to be dealt with.

Nor was it only cheap shelter that disappeared. It was also those "open" spaces that had once been available to those without other shelter. As property rose in value, the nooks and crannies in which the homeless had been able to hide became more visible. Doorways, alleys, abandoned buildings, vacant lots—these "holes" in the cityscape, these gaps in public consciousness, became *real estate.* The homeless, who had been there all the time, were overtaken by economic progress, and they became intruders.

You cannot help thinking, as you watch this process, of what happened in parts of Europe in the eighteenth and nineteenth centuries: the effects of the enclosure laws, which eliminated the "commons" in the countryside and drove the rural poor, now homeless, into the cities. The centuries-old tradition of common access and usage was swept away by the beginnings of industrialism; land became *privatized,* a commodity. At the same time, something occurred in the cultural psyche. The world itself, space itself, was subtly altered. It was no longer merely to be lived in; it was now to be owned. What was enclosed was not only the land. It was also *the flesh itself;* it was cut off from, denied access to, the physical world.

And one thinks too, when thinking of the homeless, of the American past, the settlement of the "new" world which occurred at precisely the same time that the commons disappeared. The dream of freedom and equality that brought men and women here had something to do with *space,* as if the wilderness itself conferred upon those arriving here a new beginning: the Eden that had been lost. Once God had sent Christ to redeem men; now he provided a new world. Men discovered, or believed, that this world, and perhaps time itself, had no edge, no limit. Space was a sign of God's magnanimity. It was a kind of grace.

Somehow, it is all this that is folded into the sad shapes of the homeless. In their mute presence one can sense, however faintly, the dreams of a world gone aglimmering, and the presence of our failed hopes. A kind of claim is made, silently, an ethic is proffered, or, if you will, a whole cosmology, one older than our own ideas of privilege and property. It is as if flesh itself were seeking, this one last time, the home in the world it has been denied.

Daily the city eddies around the homeless. The crowds flowing past leave a few feet, a gap. We do not touch the homeless world. Perhaps we cannot touch it. It remains separate even as the city surrounds it.

The homeless, simply because they are homeless, are strangers, alien—and therefore a threat. Their presence, in itself, comes to constitute a kind of violence; it deprives us of our sense of safety. Let me use myself as an example. I know, and respect, many of those now homeless on the streets of Santa Barbara. Twenty years ago, some of them would have been my companions and friends. And yet, these days, if I walk through the park near my home and see strangers bedding down for the night, my first reaction, if not fear, is a sense of annoyance and intrusion, of worry and alarm. I think of my teenage daughter, who often walks through the park, and then of my house, a hundred yards away, and I am tempted—only tempted, but tempted, still—to call the "proper" authorities to have the strangers moved on. Out of sight, out of mind.

Notice: I do not bring them food. I do not offer them shelter or a shower in the morning. I do not even stop to talk. Instead, I think: my daughter, my house, my privacy. What moves me is not the threat of *danger*—nothing as animal as that. Instead, there pops up inside of me, neatly in a row, a set of anxieties, ones you might arrange in a dollhouse living room and label: Family of bourgeois fears. The point is this: our response to the homeless is fed by a complex set of cultural attitudes, habits of thought, and fantasies and fears so familiar to us, so common, that they have become a *second* nature and might as well be instinctive, for all the control we have over them. And it is by no means easy to untangle this snarl of responses. What does seem clear is that the homeless embody all that bourgeois culture has for centuries tried to eradicate and destroy.

If you look to the history of Europe you find that homelessness first appears (or is first acknowledged) at the very same moment that bourgeois culture begins to appear. The same processes produced them both: the breakup of feudalism, the rise of commerce and cities, the combined triumphs of capitalism, industrialism, and individualism. The historian Fernand Braudel, in *The Wheels of Commerce,* describes, for instance, the armies of impoverished men and women who began to haunt Europe as far back as the eleventh century. And the makeup of these masses? Essentially the same then as it is now: the unfortunates, the throwaways, the misfits, the deviants. . . .

It is in the nineteenth century, in the Victorian era, that you can find the beginnings of our modern strategies for dealing with the homeless: the notion that they should be controlled and perhaps eliminated through "help." With the Victorians we begin to see the entangling of self-protection with social obligation, the strategy of masking self-interest and the urge to control as *moral duty*. Michel Foucault has spelled this out in his books on madness and punishment: the zeal with which the overseers of early bourgeois culture tried to purge, improve, and purify all of urban civilization—whether through schools and prisons, or, quite literally, with public baths and massive new water and sewage systems. Order, ordure—this is, in essence, the tension at the heart of bourgeois culture, and it was the singular genius of the Victorians to make it the main component of their medical, aesthetic, *and* moral systems. It was not a sense of justice or even empathy which called for charity or new attitudes toward the poor; it was *hygiene*. The very same attitudes appear in nineteenth-century America. Charles Loring Brace, in an essay on homeless and vagrant children written in 1876, described the treatment of delinquents in this way: "Many of their vices drop from them like the old and verminous clothing they left behind. . . . The entire change of circumstances seems to cleanse them of bad habits." Here you have it all: *vices, verminous clothing, cleansing them of bad habits*—the triple association of poverty with vice with dirt, an equation in which each term comes to stand for all of them.

These attitudes are with us still; that is the point. In our own century the person who has written most revealingly about such things is George Orwell, who tried to analyze his own middle-class attitudes toward the poor. . . .

To put it as bluntly as I can, for many of us the homeless are *shit*. And our policies toward them, our spontaneous sense of disgust and horror, our wish to be rid of them—all of this has hidden in it, close to its heart, our feelings about excrement. Even Marx, that most bourgeois of revolutionaries, described the deviant *lumpen* in *The Eighteenth Brumaire of Louis Bonaparte* as "scum, offal, refuse of all classes." These days, in puritanical Marxist nations, they are called "parasites"—a word, perhaps not incidentally, one also associates with human waste.

What I am getting at here is the *nature* of the desire to help the homeless—what is hidden behind it and why it so often does harm. Every government program, almost every private project, is geared as much to the needs of those giving help as it is to the needs of the homeless. Go to any government agency, or, for that matter, to most private charities, and you will find yourself enmeshed, at once, in a bureaucracy so tangled and oppressive, or confronted with so much moral arrogance and contempt, that you will be driven back out into the streets for relief.

Santa Barbara, where I live, is as good an example as any. There are three main shelters in the city—all of them private. Between them they provide fewer than a hundred beds a night for the homeless. Two of the three shelters are religious in nature: the Rescue Mission and the Salvation Army. In the mission, as in most places in the country, there are elaborate and stringent rules. Beds go first to those who have not been there for two months, and you can stay for only two nights in any two-month period. No shelter is given to those who are not sober. Even if you go to the mission only for a meal, you are required to listen to sermons and participate in prayer, and you are regularly proselytized—sometimes overtly, sometimes subtly. There are obligatory, regimented showers. You go to bed precisely at ten: lights out, no reading, no talking. After the lights go out you will find fifteen men in a room with double-decker bunks. As the night progresses the room grows stuffier and hotter. Men toss, turn, cough, and moan. In the morning you are awakened precisely at five forty-five. Then breakfast. At seven-thirty you are back on the street.

The town's newest shelter was opened almost a year ago by a consortium of local churches. Families and those who are employed have first call on the beds—a policy which excludes the congenitally homeless. Alcohol is not simply forbidden *in* the shelter; those with a history of alcoholism must sign a "contract" pledging to remain sober and chemical-free. Finally, in a paroxysm of therapeutic bullying, the shelter has added a new wrinkle: if you stay more than two days you are required to fill out and then discuss with a social worker a complex form listing what you perceive as your personal failings, goals, and strategies—all of this for men and women who simply want a place to lie down out of the rain!

It is these attitudes, in various forms and permutations, that you find repeated endlessly in America. We are moved either to "redeem" the homeless or to punish them. Perhaps there is nothing consciously hostile about it. Perhaps it is simply that as the machinery of bureaucracy cranks itself up to deal with these problems, attitudes assert themselves automatically. But whatever the case, the fact remains that almost every one of our strategies for helping the homeless is simply an attempt to re-arrange the world *cosmetically,* in terms of how it looks and smells to *us.* Compassion is little more than the passion for control.

The central question emerging from all this is, What does a society owe to its members in trouble, and *how* is that debt to be paid? It is a question which must be answered in two parts: first, in relation to the men and women who have been marginalized against their will, and then, in a slightly different way, in relation to those who have chosen (or accept or even prize) their marginality.

As for those who have been marginalized against their wills, I think the general answer is obvious: A society owes its members whatever it takes for them to regain their places in the social order. And when it comes to specific remedies, one need only read backward the various processes which have created homelessness and then figure out where help is likely to do the most good. But the real point here is not the specific remedies required—affordable housing, say—but the basis upon which they must be offered, the necessary underlying ethical notion we seem in this nation unable to grasp that those who are the inevitable casualties of modern industrial capitalism and the free-market system are entitled, *by right,* and by the simple virtue of their participation in that system, to whatever help they need. They are entitled to help to find and hold their places in the society whose social contract they have, in effect, signed and observed.

Look at that for just a moment: the notion of a contract. The majority of homeless Americans have kept, insofar as they could, to the terms of that contract. In any shelter these days you can find men and women who have worked ten, twenty, forty years, and whose lives have nonetheless come to nothing. These are people who cannot afford a place in the world they helped create. And in return? Is it life on the street they have earned? Or the cruel charity we so grudgingly grant them?

But those marginalized against their will are only half the problem. There remains, still, the question of whether we owe anything to those who are voluntarily marginal. What about them: the street people, the rebels, and the recalcitrants, those who have torn up their social contracts or returned them unsigned?

I was in Las Vegas last fall, and I went out to the Rescue Mission at the lower end of town, on the edge of the black ghetto, where I first stayed years ago on my way west. It was twilight, still hot; in the vacant lot next door to the mission 200 men were lining up for supper. A warm wind blew along the street lined with small houses and salvage yards, and in the distance I could see the desert's edge and the smudge of low hills in the fading light. There were elderly alcoholics in line, and derelicts, but mainly the men were the same sort I had seen here years ago: youngish, out of work, restless and talkative, the drifters and wanderers for whom the word "wanderlust" was invented.

At supper—long communal tables, thin gruel, stale sweet rolls, ice water—a huge black man in his twenties, fierce and muscular, sat across from me. "I'm from the Coast, man," he said. "Never been away from home before. Ain't sure I like it. Sure don't like *this* place. But I lost my job back home a couple of weeks ago and figured, why wait around for another. I thought I'd come out here, see me something of the world."

After supper, a squat Portuguese man in his mid-thirties, hunkered down against the mission wall, offered me a smoke and told me: "Been sleeping in my car, up the street, for a week. Had my own business back in Omaha. But I got bored, man. Sold everything, got a little dough, came out here. Thought I'd work construction. Let me tell you, this is one tough town."

In a world better than ours, I suppose, men (or women) like this might not exist. Conservatives seem to have no trouble imagining a society so well disciplined and moral that deviance of this kind would disappear. And leftists envision a world so just, so generous, that deviance would vanish along with inequity. But I suspect that there will always be something at work in some men and women to make them restless with the systems others devise for them, and to move them outward toward the edges of the world, where life is always riskier, less organized, and easier going.

Do we owe anything to these men and women, who reject our company and what we offer and yet nonetheless seem to demand *something* from us?

We owe them, I think, at least a place to exist, a way to exist. That may not be a *moral* obligation, in the sense that our obligation to the involuntarily marginal is clearly a moral one, but it is an obligation nevertheless, one you might call an existential obligation.

Of course, it may be that I think we owe these men something because I have liked men like them, and because I want their world to be there always, as a place to hide or rest. But there is more to it than that. I think we as a society need men like these. A society needs its margins as much as it needs art and literature. It needs holes and gaps, *breathing spaces,* let us say, into which men and women can escape and live, when necessary, in ways otherwise denied them. Margins guarantee to society a flexibility, an elasticity, and allow it to accommodate itself to the natures and needs of its members. When margins vanish, society becomes too rigid, too oppressive by far, and therefore inimical to life.

It is for such reasons that, in cultures like our own, marginal men and women take on a special significance. They are all we have left to remind us of the narrowness of the received truths we take for granted. "Beyond the pale," they somehow redefine the pale, or remind us, at least, that *something* is still out there, beyond the pale. They preserve, perhaps unconsciously, a dream that would otherwise cease to exist, the dream of having a place in the world, and of being *left alone.*

Quixotic? Infantile? Perhaps. But remember Pavlov and his reflexes coded in the flesh: animal, and therefore as if given by God. What we are talking about here is *freedom,* and with it, perhaps, an echo of the dream men brought, long ago, to wilderness America. I use the word "freedom" gingerly, in relation to lives like these: skewed, crippled, emptied of everything we associate with a full, or realized, freedom. But perhaps this is the condition into which freedom has fallen among us. Art has been "appreciated" out of existence; literature has become an extension of the university, replete with tenure and pensions; and as for politics, the ideologies which ring us round seem too silly or shrill by far to speak for life. What is left, then, is this mute and intransigent independence, this "waste" of life which refuses even interpretation, and which cannot be assimilated to any ideology, and which therefore can be put to no one's use. In its crippled innocence and the perfection of its superfluity it amounts, almost, to a rebellion against history, and that is no small thing.

Let me put it as simply as I can: what we see on the streets of our cities are two dramas, both of which cut to the troubled heart of the culture and demand from us a response we may not be able to make. There is the drama of those struggling to survive by regaining their place in the social order. And there is the drama of those struggling to survive outside of it.

The resolution of both struggles depends on a third drama occurring at the heart of the culture: the tension and contention between the magnanimity we owe to life and the darker tendings of the human psyche: our fear of strangeness, our hatred of deviance, our love of order and control. How we mediate by default or design between those contrary forces will determine not only the destinies of the homeless but also something crucial about the nation, and perhaps—let me say it—about our own souls.

DISCUSSION QUESTIONS

1. Why does Marin believe that people who have been marginalized against their will are *entitled* to whatever help they need? Do you agree with his argument? How would Tibor Machan respond to Marin's claim?
2. Marin distinguishes between people who have been marginalized against their will and people who have chosen their marginality. Is this a good distinction? Can you think of a counterexample that might challenge the soundness of this distinction?
3. What does Marin mean by an "existential obligation" to help those people who have chosen their marginality? Why isn't this merely a "moral obligation"? Do you agree with him? Why or why not?
4. Marin says that the attitudes of nonhomeless people toward homeless people violate their dignity. How does he defend this position? Evaluate his argument.
5. Marin calls for programs that respect homeless people's rights to have different aspirations. Should we respect homeless people's rights to have different aspirations? Why? Strengthen your argument by entertaining objections.
6. Compare and contrast proposed responses to Marin's position on helping the homeless from Kai Nielsen, Nancy Fraser, John Rawls, and Tibor Machan. Whose response is closest to your own? Explain.

MEDIA GALLERY

 ### "A MODEST PROPOSAL"

By Jonathan Swift

Complete essay: "A Modest Proposal, for Preventing the Children of Poor People in Ireland, from Being Burden to Their Parents or Country; And for Making Them Beneficial to the Public" is the full title of Swift's essay. Published in Dublin in October 1729, and reprinted seven times within a year, "A Modest Proposal" reveals the depths of Swift's disgust with the many foolish policies that were being proposed to improve the situation in Ireland. Swift uses satire in this essay to shock readers blind to the dire situation in Ireland into an awareness of the real miseries of the poor in his country. In a letter to the poet Alexander Pope shortly before the publication of the essay, Swift describes the state of Ireland at the time: "As to this country, there have been three terrible years' dearth of corn, and every place strewed with beggars; but dearths are common in better climates, and our evils here lie much deeper. Imagine a nation the two-thirds of whose revenues are spent out of it, and who are not permitted to trade with the other third, and where the pride of women will not suffer them to wear their own manufactures, even where they excel what come from abroad. This is the true state of Ireland in a very few words. These evils operate more every day, and the kingdom is absolutely undone, as I have been telling often in print these ten years past."

Jonathan Swift (1667–1745) was born and died in Dublin, but spent some many years in London. Swift, an Anglican, fled Dublin to escape Irish Catholic reaction to England's anti-Catholic revolution of 1688. His political and religious essays made him well known in his day, and until his death he was known as Dublin's foremost citizen. His most famous satires are *A Tale of a Tub* (1704), *Gulliver's Travels* (1726), and "A Modest Proposal" (1729). The following is the text of "A Modest Proposal."

It is a melancholy object to those who walk through this great town, or travel in the country, when they see the streets, the roads, and cabin doors crowded with beggars of the female sex, followed by three, four or six children, *all in rags,* and importuning every passenger for an alms. These mothers, instead of being able to work for their honest livelihood, are forced to employ all their time in strolling, to beg sustenance for their helpless infants, who, as they grow up, either turn thieves for want of work, or leave their dear native country to fight for the Pretender in Spain, or sell themselves to the Barbados.

I think it is agreed by all parties that this prodigious number of children in the arms, or on the backs, or at the heels of their mothers, and frequently of their fathers, is in the present deplorable state of the kingdom a very great additional grievance; and therefore whoever could find out a fair, cheap, and easy method of making these children sound and useful members of the commonwealth would deserve so well of the public as to have his statue set up for a preserver of the nation.

But my intention is very far from being confined to provide only for the children of professed beggars; it is of a much greater extent, and shall take in the whole number of infants at a certain age who are born of parents in effect as little able to support them as those who demand our charity in the streets.

As to my own part, having turned my thoughts, for many years, upon this important subject, and maturely weighed the several schemes of other projectors, I have always found them grossly mistaken in their computation. It is true a child, just dropped from its dam, may be supported by her milk for a solar year with little other nourishment, at most not above the value of two shillings, which the mother may certainly get, or the value in scraps, by her lawful occupation of begging: and it is exactly at one year old that I propose to provide for them, in such a manner as, instead of being a charge upon their parents, or the parish, or wanting food and raiment for the rest of their lives, they shall, on the contrary, contribute to the feeding and partly to the clothing of many thousands.

There is likewise another great advantage in my scheme, that it will prevent those voluntary abortions, and that horrid practice of women murdering their bastard children, alas, too frequent among us; sacrificing the poor innocent babes, I doubt, more to avoid the expense than the shame; which would move tears and pity in the most savage and inhuman breast.

The number of souls in Ireland being usually reckoned one million and a half, of these I calculate there may be about two hundred thousand couples whose wives are breeders; from which number I subtract thirty thousand couples who are able to maintain their own children, although I apprehend there cannot be so many under the present distresses of the kingdom; but this being granted, there will remain an hundred and seventy thousand breeders. I again subtract fifty thousand for those women who miscarry, or whose children die by accident or disease within the year. There only remain an hundred and twenty thousand children of poor parents, annually born: The question therefore is, how this number shall be reared, and provided for; which, as I have already said, under the present situation of affairs, is utterly impossible by all the methods hitherto proposed: for we can neither employ them in handicraft, or agriculture; we neither build houses (I mean in the country), nor cultivate land: they can very seldom pick up a livelihood by stealing until they arrive at six years old, except where they are of towardly parts; although, I confess they learn the rudiments much earlier, during which time they can however be properly looked upon only as *probationers;* as I have been informed by a principal gentleman in the County of Cavan, who protested to me that he never knew above one or two instances under the age of six, even in a part of the kingdom so renowned for the quickest proficiency in that art.

I am assured by our merchants that a boy or a girl, before twelve years old, is no saleable commodity, and even when they come to this age, they will not yield above three pounds, or three pounds and half a crown at most on the Exchange; which cannot turn to account either to the parents or kingdom, the charge of nutriment and rags having been at least four times that value.

I shall now therefore humbly propose my own thoughts, which I hope will not be liable to the least objection.

I have been assured by a very knowing American of my acquaintance in London, that a young healthy child well nursed is at a year old a most delicious, nourishing, and wholesome food, whether stewed, roasted, baked, or boiled; and I make no doubt that it will equally serve in a fricassee or a ragout.

I do therefore humbly offer it to public consideration, that of the hundred and twenty thousand children already computed, twenty thousand may be reserved for breed, whereof only one-fourth part to be males; which is more than we allow to sheep, black cattle, or swine; and my reason is that these children are seldom the fruits of marriage, a circumstance not much regarded by our savages, therefore one male will be sufficient to serve four females. That the remaining hundred thousand may at a year old be offered in sale to the persons of quality, and fortune, through the kingdom; always advising the mother to let them suck plentifully in the last month, so as to render them plump, and fat for a good table. A child will make two dishes at an entertainment for friends; and when the family dines alone, the fore- or hindquarter will make a reasonable dish, and seasoned with a little pepper or salt will be very good boiled on the fourth day, especially in winter.

I have reckoned upon a medium, that a child just born will weigh twelve pounds, and in a solar year if tolerably nursed increases to twenty-eight pounds.

I grant this food will be somewhat dear, and therefore very *proper for landlords,* who, as they have already devoured most of the parents, seem to have the best title to the children.

Infants' flesh will be in season throughout the year, but more plentiful in March, and a little before and after: for we are told by a grave author, an eminent French physician, that fish being a prolific diet, there are more children born in Roman Catholic countries about nine months after Lent than at any other season; therefore reckoning a year after Lent, the markets will be more glutted than usual, because the number of Popish infants is at least three to one in this kingdom; and therefore it will have one other collateral advantage by lessening the number of Papists among us.

I have already computed the charge of nursing a beggar's child (in which list I reckon all cottagers, laborers, and four-fifths of the farmers) to be about two shillings *per annum,* rags included; and I believe no gentleman would repine to give ten shillings for the carcass of a good fat child, which, as I have said, will make four dishes of excellent nutritive meat, when he hath only some particular friend or his own family to dine with him. Thus the squire will learn to be a good landlord, and grow popular among his tenants, the mother will have eight shillings net profit, and be fit for work until she produces another child.

Those who are more thrifty (*as I must confess the times require*) may flay the carcass; the skin of which, artificially dressed, will make admirable gloves for ladies, and summer boots for fine gentlemen.

As to our City of Dublin, shambles may be appointed for this purpose, in the most convenient parts of it; and butchers we may be assured will not be wanting, although I rather recommend buying the children alive, and dressing them hot from the knife, as we do roasting pigs.

A very worthy person, a true lover of his country, and whose virtues I highly esteem, was lately pleased, in discoursing on this matter, to offer a refinement upon my scheme. He said that many gentlemen of this kingdom, having of late destroyed their deer, he conceived that the want of venison might be well supplied by the bodies of young lads and maidens, not exceeding fourteen years of age, nor under twelve; so great a number of both sexes in every country being now ready to starve, for want of work and service: and these to be disposed of by their parents if alive, or otherwise by their nearest relations. But with due deference to so excellent a friend, and so deserving a patriot, I cannot be altogether in his sentiments. For as to the males, my American acquaintance assured me from frequent experience that their flesh was generally tough and lean, like that of our schoolboys, by continual exercise, and their taste disagreeable, and to fatten them would not answer the charge. Then as to the females, it would, I think with humble submission, be a loss to the public, because they soon would become breeders themselves: And besides, it is not improbable that some scrupulous people might be apt to censure such a practice (although indeed very unjustly) as a little bordering upon cruelty; which, I confess, hath always been with me the strongest objection against any project, how well soever intended.

But in order to justify my friend, he confessed that this expedient was put into his head by the famous Psalmanazar, a native of the island Formosa, who came from thence to London, above twenty years ago, and in conversation told my friend that in his country when any young person happened to be put to death, the executioner sold the carcass to persons of quality, as a prime dainty; and that, in his time, the body of a plump girl of fifteen, who was crucified for an attempt to poison the emperor, was sold to his Imperial Majesty's Prime Minister of State, and other great mandarins of the court, in joints from the gibbet, at four hundred crowns. Neither indeed can I deny that if the same use were made of several plump young girls in this town, who, without one single groat to their fortunes, cannot stir abroad without a chair, and appear at a playhouse, and assemblies in foreign fineries, which they never will pay for, the kingdom would not be the worse.

Some persons of a desponding spirit are in great concern about that vast number of poor people, who are aged, diseased, or maimed; and I have been desired to employ my thoughts what course may be taken to ease the nation of so grievous an encumbrance. But I am not in the least pain upon that matter, because it is very well known that they are every day dying, and rotting, by cold, and famine, and filth, and vermin, as fast as can be reasonably expected. And as to the younger laborers they are now in almost as hopeful a condition. They cannot get work, and consequently pine away for want of nourishment, to a degree, that if at any time they are accidentally hired to common labor, they have not strength to perform it; and thus the country and themselves are in a fair way of being soon delivered from the evils to come.

I have too long digressed, and therefore shall return to my subject. I think the advantages by the proposal which I have made are obvious and many, as well as of the highest importance.

For first, as I have already observed, it would greatly lessen the number of Papists, with whom we are yearly overrun, being the principal breeders of the nation, as well as our most dangerous enemies; and who stay at home on purpose with a design to deliver the kingdom to the Pretender; hoping to take their advantage by the absence of so many good Protestants, who have chosen rather to leave their country than stay at home, and pay tithes against their conscience to an idolatrous Episcopal curate.

Secondly, The poorer tenants will have something valuable of their own, which by law may be made liable to distress, and help to pay their landlord's rent, their corn and cattle being already seized, and *money a thing unknown.*

Thirdly, Whereas the maintenance of an hundred thousand children, from two years old, and upwards, cannot be computed at less than ten shillings apiece *per annum,* the nation's stock will be thereby increased fifty thousand pounds *per annum;* besides the profit of a new dish, introduced to the tables of all gentlemen of fortune in the kingdom, who have any refinement in taste; and the money will circulate among ourselves, the goods being entirely of our own growth and manufacture.

Fourthly, The constant breeders, besides the gain of eight shillings sterling *per annum,* by the sale of their children, will be rid of the charge of maintaining them after the first year.

Fifthly, This food would likewise bring great custom to taverns, where the vintners will certainly be so prudent as to procure the best receipts for dressing it to perfection, and consequently have their houses frequented by all the fine gentlemen, who justly value themselves upon their knowledge in good eating; and a skillful cook, who understands how to oblige his guests, will contrive to make it as expensive as they please.

Sixthly, This would be a great inducement to marriage, which all wise nations have either encouraged by rewards, or enforced by laws and penalties. It would increase the care and tenderness of mothers toward their children, when they were sure of a settlement for life, to the poor babes, provided in some sort by the public to their annual profit instead of expense. We should see an honest emulation among the married women, *which of them could bring the fattest child to the market.* Men would become as fond of their wives, during the time of their pregnancy, as they are now of their mares in foal, their cows in calf, or sows when they are ready to farrow; nor offer to beat or kick them (as it is too frequent a practice) for fear of a miscarriage.

Many other advantages might be enumerated. For instance, the addition of some thousand carcasses in our exportation of barreled beef; the propagation of swine's flesh, and improvement in the art of making good bacon, so much wanted among us by the great destruction of pigs, too frequent at our tables, and are no way comparable in taste or magnificence to a well-grown, fat yearling child, which roasted whole will make a considerable figure at a Lord Mayor's feast, or any other public entertainment. But this and many others I omit, being studious of brevity.

Supposing that one thousand families in this city would be constant customers for infants' flesh, besides others who might have it at merrymeetings, particularly at weddings and christenings, I compute that Dublin would take off annually about twenty thousand carcasses, and the rest of the kingdom (where probably they will be sold somewhat cheaper) the remaining eighty thousand.

I can think of no one objection that will possibly be raised against this proposal, unless it should be urged that the number of people will be thereby much lessened in the kingdom. This I freely own, and it was indeed one principal design in offering it to the world. I desire the reader will observe, that I calculate my remedy *for this one individual Kingdom of Ireland, and for no other that ever was, is, or, I think, ever can be upon earth.* Therefore let no man talk to me of other expedients: *Of taxing our absentees at five shillings a pound: Of using neither clothes, nor household furniture, except what is of our own growth and manufacture: Of utterly rejecting the materials and instruments that promote foreign luxury: Of curing the expensiveness of pride, vanity, idleness, and gaming in our women: Of introducing a vein of parsimony, prudence, and temperance: Of learning to love our Country, wherein we differ even from* LAPLANDERS, *and the inhabitants of* TOPINAMBOO: *Of quitting our animosities and factions, nor act any longer like the Jews, who were murdering one another at the very moment their city was taken: Of being a little cautious not to sell our country and consciences for nothing: Of teaching landlords to have at least one degree of mercy toward their tenants.* Lastly, *of putting a spirit of honesty, industry, and skill into our shopkeepers, who, if a resolution could now be taken to buy only our native goods, would immediately unite to cheat and exact upon us in the price, the measure, and the goodness; nor could ever yet be brought to make one fair proposal of just dealing, though often and earnestly invited to it.*

Therefore I repeat, let no man talk to me of these and the like expedients; until he hath at least a glimpse of hope that there will ever be some hearty and sincere attempt to put them in practice.

But as to myself, having been wearied out for many years with offering vain, idle, visionary thoughts, and at length utterly despairing of success, I fortunately fell upon this proposal, which as it is wholly new, so it hath something *solid* and *real,* of no expense and little trouble, full in our own power, and whereby we can incur no danger in *disobliging* ENGLAND. For this kind of commodity will not bear exportation, the flesh being of too tender a consistence to admit a long continuance in salt; *although perhaps I could name a country which would be glad to eat up our whole nation without it.*

After all I am not so violently bent upon my own opinion as to reject any offer, proposed by wise men, which shall be found equally innocent, cheap, easy, and effectual. But before something of that kind shall be advanced in contradiction to my scheme, and offering a better, I desire the author, or authors, will be pleased maturely to consider two points. First, as things now stand, how they will be able to find food and raiment for an hundred thousand useless mouths and backs. And secondly, there being a round million of creatures in human figure, throughout this kingdom, whose whole subsistence put into a common stock would leave them in debt two millions of pounds sterling; adding those, who are beggars by profession, to the bulk of farmers, cottagers, and laborers with their wives and children, who are beggars in effect; I desire those politicians, who dislike my overture, and may perhaps be so bold to attempt an answer, that they will first ask the parents of these mortals whether they would not at this day think it a great happiness to have been sold for food at a year old, in the manner I prescribe, and thereby have avoided such a perpetual scene of misfortunes as they have since gone through; by the oppression of landlords; the impossibility of paying rent without money or trade; the want of common sustenance, with neither house nor clothes to cover them from the inclemencies of the weather; and the most inevitable prospect of entailing the like, or greater miseries upon their breed forever.

I profess in the sincerity of my heart that I have not the least personal interest in endeavoring to promote this necessary work, having no other motive than the *public good of my country, by advancing our trade, providing for infants, relieving the poor, and giving some pleasure to the rich.* I have no children by which I can propose to get a single penny; the youngest being nine years old, and my wife past childbearing.

1. In "Helping and Hating the Homeless," Peter Marin argues that society owes men and women who have been marginalized against their will "whatever it takes for them to regain their places in the social order." Do you think that Swift believes the same thing? Explain.
2. In "Helping and Hating the Homeless," Peter Marin says that our basic desire with respect to homeless people is simply to be rid of them. Most of the programs for the homeless do not address their needs and desires, but rather address our need to "rearrange the world cosmetically" to suit our own needs. How similar to or different from Swift's position is Marin's? Explain.
3. In "The Feminization of Poverty," Diana Pearce argues that more and more of the burden of poverty is being borne by women. To what extent do you think that Swift would agree with Pearce that women sustain a disproportionate amount of the burden of poverty?
4. Analyze Swift's proposal to deal with poverty in Ireland from the perpsective of a developmentalist and a neo-Malthusian. Would either find the proposal as it is openly stated in the essay to be acceptable? Would either find the proposal to be objectionable? Explain.
5. Compare the proposal to deal with poverty made by Swift with the way in which poverty was dealt with in the film *Soylent Green* (discussed below). How are they similar to each other? How are they different? Which proposal is more powerful, and why?
6. Describe as best as you can the form of argument employed by Swift in this essay. Do you think that it is effective? What makes it effective or not effective? Use this form of argument to construct a "proposal" to deal with a contemporary social issue.

 ## "THE FREE VACATION HOUSE"

By Anzia Yezierska

Story summary: The narrator, a young immigrant mother with five children, is overworked, nervous, and exhausted. She accepts a "free vacation" at a country house run by the Social Betterment Society but is subject to a series of humiliations. She must answer personal questions about her family and her income before a group of strangers. She and the other mothers are treated with contempt, subjected to endless rules, and made to wear identification tags around their wrists. The house and grounds are beautiful, but the mothers and children must stay in the rear while visiting society ladies have tea on the front porch. "If the best part of the house what is comfortable is made up for a show for visitors," questions the narrator, "why ain't they keeping the whole business for a show for visitors? For why do they have to fool in worn-out mothers, to make them think they'll give them a rest? Do they need the worn-out mothers as part of the show? I guess that is it, already." The narrator returns joyfully home after two weeks, feeling renewed personal freedom in her cramped tenement apartment.

Anzia Yezierska (c. 1885–1970) and her family immigrated to the United States from Poland around the turn of the twentieth century. She lived in the Jewish ghetto on the Lower East Side of Manhattan and found time to take classes and write stories after long days working in the sweatshops. "The Free Vacation House" was written in 1920.

1. Social programs to aid the poor often come with humiliations similar to those described in Yezierska's story. Do you think that it is morally justifiable to treat the poor with contempt? To subject them to endless rules in order to receive what they need to live their lives in more comfort? Compare your view with Peter Marin's.

2. Yezierska uses violent imagery to describe the mother's discomfort in answering personal questions. "At every question I felt like she was stabbing a knife into my heart. . . . When she got through with me, my face was red like fire. I was burning with hurts and wounds." Why do you think that Yezierska chose this imagery? Why were these questions so painful?

3. The young mothers waiting at the charity offices are described as sitting with downcast eyes, "like guilty criminals." Why do these women feel guilty? What crimes have they committed? Should the poor be made to feel guilty for benefiting from social progams?

4. What do you think the narrator means when she refers to the mothers as being "part of the show"? Who is the audience for this show? Why would the audience attend such a show?

5. Do you think that sending poor women with children to the free vacation house can be defended as a feminist approach or response to poverty? Do you think Nancy Fraser would say that this is a good welfare program?

"JACK IN THE POT"

By Dorothy West

Story summary: Mrs. Edmunds and her husband have received government aid for the past two years. They live in a tiny three-room flat in an unheated tenement building. Mr. Edmunds goes out daily to look for work but is unsuccessful. When Mrs. Edmunds wins fifty-five dollars in a lottery, her first thought is to pay off her debts. The owner of the grocery market, to whom she is indebted, insinuates that the welfare investigator in charge of the Edmunds' case will be suspicious if she learns that the couple has funds in addition to their government checks. Defeated, Mrs. Edmunds makes a small purchase and does not settle her debt. She buys groceries at another store and makes her husband a good meal but does not tell him the true amount of her winnings. The investigator pays a visit, and the Edmunds are nervous that she will report their purchases to the central office. The Edmunds learn that their neighbor's baby has died of pneumonia and the father, Mr. Johnson, cannot afford to pay for the burial. Mr. Edmunds comments that if he had fifty dollars, he would give Mr. Johnson the money. Mrs. Edmunds disagrees: " 'As poor as you are,' she asked angrily, 'you'd give him that much money? That's easy to say when you haven't got it.' 'I look at it this way,' he said simply, 'I think how I'd feel in his shoes.' 'You got your own troubles,' she argued heatedly. 'The Johnson baby is better off dead. You'd be a fool to put fifty dollars in the ground. I'd spend my fifty dollars on the living.'" The next day, Mrs. Edmunds leaves the house early and goes to a downtown department store. She admires the luxurious goods and tries on some shoes but does not purchase them. She stops short when she sees the children's dresses. Mrs. Edmunds purchases a little white and gold baby dress and rushes home to present it to Mr. Johnson. He informs her that he could not find enough money for the baby's burial and so donated her body to science. Crushed, Mrs. Edmunds returns to her flat and hides the dress and the money under the mattress. "It was burial money. She could never use it for anything else."

Dorothy West (1907–1998) was born in Boston to a former slave who became a successful businessman. She attended Columbia University School of Journalism and later published two magazines and worked as a Harlem welfare investigator. West became a best-selling author in 1995 at the age of 88, when she published the story and essay collection *The Richer, the Poorer,* which included "Jack in the Pot."

1. In order to receive the government relief funds, the Edmunds must welcome the welfare investigator into their homes and disclose their spending habits. Is this an invasion of their right to privacy? Should the government supervise the lives of welfare re-

cipients in this way? If so, how closely? Defend your view from the perspective of one of the theories of distributive justice that you have studied.

2. When Mr. Edmunds is asked why he would give the money to Mr. Johnson even though his own means are meager, he responds, "I think how I'd feel in his shoes." How would a developmentalist respond to Mr. Edmunds' decision? Is his hypothetical gift a sacrifice of "comparable moral importance"?

3. Although she and her husband are in need of clothing, heat, and food, Mrs. Edmunds gives away many of the items she purchases. Why does she do this? Out of generosity? Fear of the "investigator"? Moral obligation? Does she spend her money wisely? Why or why not?

4. While arguing with her husband, Mrs. Edmunds insists that it is foolish to pay for a burial and "put money in the ground," that one should help living people instead. Yet in the end, Mrs. Edmunds refuses to use the money for anything but a burial. What made her change her mind? Is paying for the burial a waste of money? Is it morally questionable?

5. The market owner, Mr. Spiro, keeps Mrs. Edmunds in his debt by awakening her fear of the welfare investigator. Mrs. Edmunds leaves the store feeling "sick and ashamed, for she had turned tail in the moment that was to have been her triumph over tyranny." Are Mr. Spiro's business tactics tyrannical? Are they immoral? How can Mrs. Edmunds break her cycle of debt?

6. Mrs. Edmunds does not tell her husband the true amount of her winnings, and she hides the fact that Mr. Johnson has asked her for money for the funeral. "She lied again, as she had been lying steadily in the past twenty-four hours, as she had not lied before in all her life." Why does Mrs. Edmunds continue to lie? As part of a married couple who share resources, does she have a moral obligation to tell her husband about her winnings?

 SOYLENT GREEN

(USA, 1973) 1 hour 40 minutes
Directed by Richard Fleischer

Film summary: Police detective Thorn (Charlton Heston) lives with investigator Sol Roth (Edward G. Robinson) in a New York slum in the year 2022. Pollution, overpopulation, and environmental degradation have made living conditions unbearable. While a few individuals have become unbelievably wealthy, the majority of New York's 40 million residents live in poverty. Citizens are subject to curfews and food rations, and riots are a daily occurrence. Families sleep in the stairways of tenement houses, and vegetables and running water are unimaginable luxuries. Detective Thorn is sent to investigate the murder of William R. Simenson (Joseph Cotten). Simenson was a rich and influential board member of Soylent, a large food production and distribution company that controls the food supply for half the world. As Thorn learns more about the circumstances surrounding Simenson's death, he himself is nearly murdered, and the chief of detectives Hatcher (Brock Peters) closes the case. Meanwhile, Roth uncovers evidence that the main ingredient in Soylent's most popular product is not in fact plankton, but people. Horrified, Roth informs Thorn of Soylent's secret before taking his own life. Thorn secretly enters the Soylent manufacturing plant and witnesses the process. After a long chase through the city by a Soylent representative, Thorn is shot, but he manages to blurt out his discoveries to Hatcher before dying.

Soylent Green is based on the novel by Harry Harrison.

1. Did Soylent make the right decision in not telling its customers the actual contents of Soylent Green? What if people would not eat Soylent Green if they knew its contents, and eating it was the only way not to die of starvation?

2. Suppose the producers of Soylent Green said that they were producing it only because people have the right not to be hungry and no other food sources were available. Would their actions be morally justifiable? Discuss.

3. Developmentalists argue that, if we can help prevent something bad from happening to others, such as death from starvation or disease, without sacrificing anything of comparable moral worth, then we have a moral obligation to help. Do you think a developmentalist can support the distribution and production of Soylent Green as a response to overpopulation and potential starvation? Why or why not?

4. Analyze the distribution and production of Soylent Green as a response to overpopulation and potential starvation from a developmentalist and a neo-Malthusian perspective. Whose position do you favor, and why?

5. Do we have a fundamental right to know what is in our food? Do food producers have a moral obligation to tell us exactly what we are eating? Why or why not? Defend your view.

6. Amartya Sen has said that famine is not primarily caused by overpopulation. What do you think got these people into the situation of producing and consuming Soylent Green? Was it overpopulation or was it something else? What do you think is the best way to avoid getting into this type of situation?

 LIFEBOAT

(USA, 1944) 1 hour 38 minutes
Directed by Alfred Hitchcock

Film summary: Lifeboat is set against the background of World War II. When a passenger-carrying Allied freighter is torpedoed by a Nazi submarine, a group of survivors with little in common manage to end up in the same lifeboat. The passengers include a journalist, a ship steward, a leftist crew member, a young Red Cross nurse, a millionaire, a ship radio operator, a woman carrying her dead child, and a seaman with a badly injured leg. The Nazi sub also sank in the conflict, and a German emerges from the debris and climbs into the boat. The group discusses whether to let him stay, but when he saves the boat from capsizing and saves the life of the injured man with an emergency amputation, he begins to take command of the boat. After days in the boat with few rations, the survivors begin to quarrel among themselves. The German reveals his identity as a Nazi naval officer and determinedly rows the boat off course toward a German supply ship. He is the only survivor who has retained his strength, thanks to the water and rations he has secretly hoarded. When the injured seaman discovers the Nazi's flask of water, the German pushes him overboard and tells the others that it was suicide. The group soon becomes suspicious, and the steward discovers the hidden flask. The group gangs up on the Nazi, beating him to death and tossing his body overboard. As the German supply ship approaches, it is sunk by an Allied battleship, bringing the promise of rescue.

1. The Nazi naval officer is the only survivor who retains his strength, thanks to the water and rations he secretly hoards. Analyze the morality of his hoarding according to both the negative duties and the positive duties of the developmentalist line of argument. Can the Nazi officer's actions be justified according to the developmentalists?

2. How would a neo-Malthusian respond to the Nazi officer hoarding water and rations? Would the neo-Malthusian argue that it is morally justifiable? Compare the neo-Malthusian analysis with the developmentalist analysis. Which do you prefer, and why?

3. How would a radical egalitarian like Kai Nielsen respond to the Nazi officer hoarding water and rations? Can his actions be justified according to radical egalitarian principles of distributive justice?

4. How would John Rawls respond to the Nazi officer hoarding water and rations? Can his actions be justified according to Rawls' principles of distributive justice?
5. How would a traditional libertarian like Tibor Machan respond to the Nazi officer hoarding water and rations? Can his actions be justified according to traditional libertarian principles of distributive justice?
6. Which of the five analyses is the most appealing? Why? What are the strengths and weaknesses of the type of analysis you have chosen? If you were the Nazi officer, would you have shared or hoarded your water and rations? Defend your view.

 THE GRAPES OF WRATH

(USA, 1940) 1 hour 48 minutes
Directed by John Huston

Film summary: This adaptation of the novel by John Steinbeck chronicles the migration of Oklahoma farmers from the Dust Bowl to California during the Great Depression. Tom Joad (Henry Fonda) returns to his family farm in Oklahoma after four years in prison only to discover that his family has been forced by landowners to leave their land due to poor crop yields. Having heard promises of jobs and high wages, Tom and his family set off for California. On the road, the family struggles to find food to subsist, and the arduous trip costs Tom's two grandparents their lives. The surviving family members arrive in California but are forced to stay in migrant camps with hundreds of hungry neighbors. The Joads are confronted by angry locals who fear the loss of jobs and by dishonest labor contractors who have the support of the authorities. The Joads find a job picking peaches but later learn that they are strike-breakers and that their wages will soon be cut in half. Tom meets Casy (John Carradine), an ex-preacher and old family friend who has built a reputation as an agitator and labor organizer. When Casy is killed without provocation by the police, Tom is enraged and strikes back, killing an officer. Consequently, the entire family must run from the law. The Joads find happiness in a clean and orderly community-run campsite sponsored by the Department of Agriculture. Unfortunately, the authorities discover Tom's crime and his whereabouts, and he is forced to separate from his family to avoid prison.

1. When Casy encourages Tom to help him organize a strike on Keene Ranch, Tom replies that he doesn't believe that people will put their families in jeopardy for the good of the entire community of workers: "You think Pa's gonna give up his meat on account of some other fellas?" Would Peter Singer agree with Tom's reply to Casy? Does organizing a strike require Tom to sacrifice something of "comparable moral importance"? If so, what is it?
2. How do you think John Rawls would respond to Casy's request to help him organize a strike on Keene Ranch? Compare it with possible responses by Kai Nielsen and Tibor Machan, assuming that each of them were in Tom's position. Whose response do you favor, and why? What would you do if you were Tom?
3. Two gas attendants discuss the folly of the Joads' trip across the desert in their old truck. "They ain't human," says one attendant. "A human being wouldn't live the way they do. Human being couldn't stand to be so miserable." Do you think that describing the Joads as other than human helps the gas attendants to feel relief from any moral responsibility to help the poor? Explain.
4. Do you believe that wealthy individuals have a moral obligation to help out poor citizens like the Joads, who cannot find work that helps them feed their families and keep a roof over their heads? Why or why not?

5. When Tom first meets Casy, he asks the ex-preacher why he has fallen from the faith. Casy replies, "I ain't so sure of things. Maybe there ain't no sin and there ain't no virtue. There's just what people does. Some things folks do is nice and some ain't so nice. And that's all any man's got a right to say." What do you think of Casy's remarks?

6. Peter Marin says that questions concerning helping the homeless must be answered in two parts: first, in relation to people who have been marginalized against their will; and second, in relation to those who have chosen their marginality. Which best applies to the Joads? What, according to Marin, do we owe the Joads? Do you agree with Marin? Why or why not?

SUPPLEMENTARY READINGS

POVERTY AND WELFARE

Albelda, Randy, and Chris Tilly. *Glass Ceilings and Bottomless Pits: Women's Work, Women's Poverty.* Boston: South End Press, 1997.

Berrick, Jill Duerr. *Faces of Poverty: Portraits of Women and Children on Welfare.* New York: Oxford University Press, 1995.

Brandwein, Ruth A., ed. *Battered Women, Children, and Welfare Reform: The Ties That Bind.* Thousand Oaks, CA: Sage, 1999.

Connolly, Deborah R. *Homeless Mothers: Face to Face with Women and Poverty.* Minneapolis: University of Minnesota Press, 2000.

Daly, Mary E. *The Gender Division of Welfare: The Impact of the British and German Welfare.* New York: Cambridge University Press, 2000.

Dujon, Diane, and Ann Withorn, eds. *For Crying Out Loud: Women's Poverty in the United States.* Boston: South End Press, 1996.

Egendorf, Laura K. *Poverty: Opposing Viewpoints.* San Diego: Greenhaven Press, 1999.

Epstein, William M. *Welfare in America: How Social Science Fails the Poor.* Madison: University of Wisconsin Press, 1997.

Funiciello, Theresa. *Tyranny of Kindness: Dismantling the Welfare System to End Poverty in America.* New York: Atlantic Monthly Press, 1993.

Handler, Joel F., and Yeheskel Hasenfeld. *The Moral Construction of Poverty: Welfare Reform in America.* Newbury Park, CA: Sage, 1991.

Jayal, Niraja Gopal. *Democracy and the State: Welfare, Secularism, and Development in Contemporary India.* New York: Oxford University Press, 1999.

Jencks, Christopher. *Rethinking Social Policy: Race, Poverty, and the Underclass.* Cambridge, MA: Harvard University Press, 1992.

Jones, Chris, and Tony Novak. *Poverty, Welfare and the Disciplinary State.* New York: Routledge, 1999.

Lindenmeyr, Adele. *Poverty Is Not a Vice: Charity, Society, and the State in Imperial Russia.* Princeton, NJ: Princeton University Press, 1996.

Lord, Shirley A. *Social Welfare and the Feminization of Poverty.* New York: Garland, 1993.

Meyer, Harrington, ed. *Care Work: Gender, Labor, and Welfare States.* New York: Routledge, 2000.

Patterson, James T. *America's Struggle Against Poverty, 1900–1994.* Cambridge, MA: Harvard University Press, 1994.

Quadagno, Jill. *The Color of Welfare: How Racism Undermined the War on Poverty.* New York: Oxford University Press, 1994.

Schein, Virginia E. *Working from the Margins: Voices of Mothers in Poverty.* Ithaca, NY: ILR Press, 1995.

Schram, Sanford. *After Welfare: The Culture of Postindustrial Social Policy.* New York and London: New York University Press, 2000.

Tanner, Michael. *The End of Welfare: Fighting Poverty in the Civil Society.* Washington, DC: Cato Institute, 1996.

White, Julie Anne. *Democracy, Justice, and the Welfare State: Reconstructing Public Care.* University Park: Pennsylvania State University Press, 2000.

DISTRIBUTIVE JUSTICE

Barry, Brian. *The Liberal Theory of Justice.* London: Oxford University Press, 1973.

Buchanan, Allen. *Marx and Justice: The Radical Critique of Liberalism.* Totowa, NJ: Rowman & Allanheld, 1982.

Diamond, Irene. *Families, Politics, and Public Policy.* New York: Longman, 1983.

Fisk, Milton. *Ethics and Society: A Marxist Interpretation of Value.* New York: New York University Press, 1980.

Friedman, Milton. *Capitalism and Freedom.* Chicago: University of Chicago Press, 1962.

Gillespie, Ed, and Bob Schellhas. *The Contract with America: The Bold Plan by Rep. Newt Gingrich, Rep. Dick Armey and the House Republicans to Change the Nation.* New York: Random House, 1994.

Gutman, Amy. *Liberal Equality.* Cambridge: Cambridge University Press, 1980.

Harrington, Michael. *Socialism Past and Future.* New York: Arcade, 1989.

Hayek, F. A. *The Constitution of Liberty.* Chicago: University of Chicago Press, 1960.

Hegel, G. W. F. *Philosophy of Right,* trans. T. M. Knox. New York: Oxford University Press, 1962 (1821).

Hospers, John. *Libertarianism.* Los Angeles: Nash, 1971.

Machan, Tibor. *Individuals and Their Rights.* La Salle, IL: Open Court, 1989.

MacIntyre, Alasdair. *Whose Justice? Which Rationality?* Notre Dame, IN: Notre Dame University Press, 1988.

MacKinnon, Catharine. *Toward a Feminist Theory of the State.* Cambridge, MA: Harvard University Press, 1989.

Nielson, Kai. *Equality and Liberty.* Totowa, NJ: Rowman & Littlefield, 1985.

Nozick, Robert. *Anarchy, State and Utopia.* New York: Basic Books, 1974.

Okin, Susan. *Justice, Gender and the Family.* New York: Basic Books, 1989.

Peffer, R. G. *Marxism, Morality and Social Justice.* Princeton, NJ: Princeton University Press, 1990.

Rousseau, Jean-Jacques. *The Social Contract* (1762) and *Discourse on the Origin of Inequality* (1754).

Rawls, John. *A Theory of Justice.* Cambridge, MA: Harvard University Press, 1971.

Sandel, Michael. *Liberalism and the Limits of Justice.* Cambridge: Cambridge University Press, 1982.

Singer, Peter. *Practical Ethics.* Cambridge: Cambridge University Press, 1979.

Walzer, Michael. *Spheres of Justice.* New York: Basic Books, 1983.

Young, Iris. *Justice and the Politics of Difference.* Princeton, NJ: Princeton University Press, 1990.

FAMINE, WORLD HUNGER, AND POPULATION GROWTH

Aiken, William, and Hugh LaFollette, eds. *World Hunger and Morality.* Englewood Cliffs, NJ: Prentice-Hall, 1996.

Arthur, John. "Rights and Duty to Bring Aid." In *World Hunger and Morality,* ed. William Aiken and Hugh LaFollette. Englewood Cliffs, NJ: Prentice-Hall, 1996.

Brown, Peter, and Henry Shue, eds. *Food Policy.* New York: Free Press, 1977.

Eberstadt, Nick. "Myths of the Food Crisis." *The New York Review of Books* (19 Feb. 1976), pp. 32–37.

Harrison, G. A., ed. *Famine.* Oxford: Oxford University Press, 1988.

Hernandez, Donald. "Fertility Reduction Policies and Poverty in Third World Countries: Ethical Issues." *Journal of Applied Behavioral Science,* 20, 4 (1984).

Kahn, Herman. "The Confucian Ethic and Economic Growth." In *The Gap Between Rich and Poor*, ed. Mitchell A. Seligson. Boulder, CO: Westview Press, 1984.

Li, Lillian. "Famine and Famine Relief: Viewing Africa in the 1980s from China in the 1920s." In *Drought and Hunger in Africa*, ed. Michael A. Glantz. New York: Cambridge University Press, 1987.

Lucas, George, and Thomas Ogletree, eds. *Lifeboat Ethics.* New York: Harper & Row, 1976.

Malthus, Thomas. *Essay on the Principle of Population As It Affects the Future Improvement of Society.* London, 1798.

O'neill, Onora. *Faces of Hunger: An Essay on Poverty, Development and Justice.* London: Allen & Unwin, 1985.

Rachels, James. "Killing and Starving to Death." *Philosophy,* 54 (April 1979): 159–171.

Sen, Amartya. *Poverty and Famine.* London: Oxford University Press, 1981.

Simon, Julian L. *The Ultimate Resource.* Princeton, NJ: Princeton University Press, 1981.

10

Animal Rights and Environmental Ethics

Animal rights and environmental ethics are an important and controversial part of the contemporary social and political scene. Specific views on moral obligations to animals and the environment are connected to more general beliefs concerning the scope of morality. Animal rights and environmental ethics investigate our moral relationship to the biological kingdom.

Today, there is much debate as to whether humans (members of the species *Homo sapiens*) should be free to use animals (nonhuman members of the biological kingdom *animalia*) in any way they desire or whether our ethical practices should extend to animals. Animal ethics asks whether it is wrong to wear a fur coat, to harm animals in scientific research, or to raise animals for food even if we do not require these practices to live. Contemporary animal rights advocates reduce the moral difference between humans and (other) animals, whereas opponents work to widen it.

Parallels are often made between our treatment of animals and our treatment of other humans. Some animal rights advocates argue that *speciesism,* or discrimination based on species, is as morally objectionable as racism and sexism. In the case of speciesism, the interests of animals are less significant than the interests of humans. Most people who argue that we should treat animals of all species equally believe that being a member of one species rather than another is not a morally important difference. The differences between species, like the differences between races and sexes, are nothing more than a difference in genetic code, and so are not sufficient grounds for the human domination of animals.

The Judeo-Christian tradition seems to support speciesism. Humans, according to this tradition, are different from animals. Humans are created in the image of God and have immortal souls, whereas animals are not created in the image of God and do not have immortal souls. Rather, animals were placed on the earth to serve the needs of humans, which means humans have a right to dominate and discriminate against animals. As a result, animal rights advocates often turn to either utilitarian or rights-based arguments to support their positions, and not to the Judeo-Christian tradition.

According to a *utilitarian* argument for animal rights, the maximization of happiness is possible only if we stop using animals in research and refrain from eating animals and using them for clothing. The use of animals for research purposes is unnecessary; the consumption of animals is unessential for good health (and may even be bad for our health); and using clothing made from animals is gratuitous. But opponents have strong counterarguments for these claims. For example, using animals in research often expedites medical studies, which can save human lives. Therefore, the happiness brought about by new treatments discovered through animal research outweighs the unhappiness that would have resulted from not using animals in research.

Utilitarian proponents of animal rights often reinforce their arguments by pointing out that because most animals are sentient (have conscious experience) and can experience pain and pleasure, we have a moral obligation to maximize their happiness as well as our own. If we do not, we are guilty of speciesism. Opponents respond by saying that animals' sentience means only that we should refrain from making animals *suffer,* not that we should stop killing them for food, using them in research, or making clothing out of them.

According to the *rights-based* defense, animals have rights because they have interests. For example, if an animal has an interest in keeping its skin, then the loss of that skin is bad for the animal. Rights-based animal advocates thus argue that many of the rights of animals are violated when we use them for clothing, food, and research. One of the common objections to this line of argument is that to have rights one must also have duties. Since animals do not have duties, they cannot have rights. Others argue that even if animals have some rights they do not have a right to life. Beings have a right to life only if they understand the concept of the future. Thus, because animals do not understand what the future is, they do not have a right to life.

It should be noted that animals do not fare any better under either Kantianism or social contract theory. In the *Kantian* view, animals are different from humans because they are not autonomous and lack the capacity to reason about their actions. Therefore, they are not subject to moral law. Nevertheless, Kant believed that frivolous cruelty toward animals would indicate a depraved and immoral inclination. According to *social contract* theorists, we have moral obligations only to beings that enter into the social contract. Since animals cannot enter into such an agreement, we are not morally obligated to them. According to both the Kantian and the social contract view, morality is developed, maintained, and improved for humans and other possible beings that can enter into moral agreements. Therefore, we treat animals differently, not because they are not human, but because they cannot enter into moral agreements. Hence, the use of animals for food or research cannot be considered speciesism.

Animal rights advocates have two major criticisms of the Kantian and social contract views. First, they argue that our treatment of animals is based, not on the view that humans have better reasoning abilities, but on the view that the human species has a higher moral worth. In real life, we do not treat humans who lack the ability to enter into contracts (e.g., infants or people in comas) the same way we treat animals. Thus, we are inconsistent in our application of the Kantian and social contract positions. Second, animal rights advocates argue that the ability to enter into a contract should not be the criterion by which we determine whether we are morally obligated to a being.

Environmental ethics addresses a related moral matter. Whereas animal ethicists are concerned with our moral obligations to a *part* of the biological kingdom (*animalia*), environmental ethicists are concerned with our moral obligations to the *entire* biological kingdom. Environmental ethics advocates tend to reduce the moral differences between humans and *animalia;* opponents broaden it. Thus, the morality of decimating the rain forest, depleting the ozone, and polluting waterways depends to a great extent on our beliefs concerning our connection to the environment.

Just as parallels are often made between our treatment of animals and racism and sexism, parallels are also made between our treatment of the environment and racism and sexism. *Ecofeminists* link the exploitation of the environment with the domination of women. They find the roots of our need to destroy the environment in patriarchal concepts of reason and nature. Consequently, the resolution of current environmental crises is connected with the overcoming of patriarchal society. The ecofeminist approach to moral issues concerning the environment is far from the typical approach.

The most common approach to environmental ethics is the *anthropocentric* approach, in which issues are ranked according to the degree to which they relate to the needs and interests of humans. For example, if ozone depletion endangers our needs and interests, then it is morally objectionable. Our responses to environmental issues are thus connected to the fulfillment of our needs and desires. The focus of this approach to environmental ethics is the long-term good of the human species, not of the environment.

The *biocentric* approach to the environment directly challenges the anthropocentric approach. According to the biocentrist, humans must view themselves as part of a larger whole that includes all forms of life, including plants and animals. All life is inherently valuable, not just the lives of one species (*Homo sapiens*). Thus, it is our responsibility to preserve the environment, not because it serves our own needs and desires, but because we are part of a biotic community.

Finally, according to *environmental justice* advocates, no group of people should bear a disproportionate share of the impacts of environmental hazards. In the United States, the environmental justice movement arose out of concerns for public health dangers in low-income and minority communities. Evidence has shown that members of these communities are often exposed to a disproportionate level of health risks due to their proximity to industrial sites and waste dumps or to their exposure to toxic substances on the job. Environmental justice activists claim that people have a right to live in a clean, healthy environment regardless of race or economic circumstance. Thus, like environmental ethics and animal rights, environmental justice involves a consideration of the morality of our actions as members of a broader biological community.

 ALDO LEOPOLD

The Land Ethic

In this selection, Aldo Leopold points out that, while we have ethics dealing with relationships among individuals and ethics dealing with the relationship between individuals and society, there is no ethic dealing with the relationship between people and the land and animals. Says Leopold, "There is as yet no ethic dealing with man's relation to land and to the animals and plants which grow upon it." However, isolated thinkers throughout history have "asserted that the despoliation of land is not only inexpedient but wrong." Leopold believed that the emerging conservation movement of his day was the beginning of a societal affirmation of a land ethic that "enlarges the boundaries of the community to include soils, waters, plants, and animals, or collectively: the land."

Aldo Leopold (1887–1948) was a pioneer in the field of environmental ethics and wildlife conservation. He was the author of over 350 articles on science and wildlife management. His textbook *Game Management* (1937) is still in use today. The following selection is from his famous book *A Sand County Almanac* (1948).

When god-like Odysseus returned from the wars in Troy, he hanged all on one rope a dozen slave-girls of his household whom he suspected of misbehavior during his absence.

This hanging involved no question of propriety. The girls were property. The disposal of property was then, as now, a matter of expediency, not of right and wrong.

Concepts of right and wrong were not lacking from Odysseus' Greece: witness the fidelity of his wife through the long years before at last his black-prowed galleys clove the wine-dark seas for home. The ethical structure of that day covered wives, but had not yet been extended to human chattels. During the three thousand years which have since elapsed, ethical criteria have been extended to many fields of conduct, with corresponding shrinkages in those judged by expediency only.

THE ETHICAL SEQUENCE

This extension of ethics, so far studied only by philosophers, is actually a process in ecological evolution. Its sequences may be described in eco-logical as well as in philosophical terms. An ethic, ecologically, is a limitation on freedom of action in the struggle for existence. An ethic, philosophically, is a differentiation of social from anti-social conduct. These are two definitions of one thing. The thing has its origin in the tendency of interdependent individuals or groups to evolve modes of co-operation. The ecologist calls these symbioses. Politics and economics are advanced symbioses in which the original free-for-all competition has been replaced, in part, by co-operative mechanisms with an ethical content.

The complexity of co-operative mechanisms has increased with population density, and with the efficiency of tools. It was simpler, for example, to define the anti-social uses of sticks and stones in the days of the mastodons than of bullets and billboards in the age of motors.

The first ethics dealt with the relation between individuals; the Mosaic Decalogue [the Ten Commandments] is an example. Later accretions dealt with the relation between the individual and society. The Golden Rule tries to integrate the individual to society; democracy to integrate social organization to the individual.

There is as yet no ethic dealing with man's relation to land and to the animals and plants which grow upon it. Land, like Odysseus' slave-girls, is still property. The land-relation is still strictly economic, entailing privileges but not obligations.

The extension of ethics to this third element in human environment is, if I read the evidence correctly, an evolutionary possibility and an ecological necessity. It is the third step in a sequence. The first two have already been taken. Individual thinkers since the days of Ezekiel and Isaiah have asserted that the despoliation of land is not only inexpedient but wrong. Society, however, has not yet affirmed their belief. I regard the present conservation movement as the embryo of such an affirmation.

An ethic may be regarded as a mode of guidance for meeting ecological situations so new or intricate, or involving such deferred reactions, that the path of social expediency is not discernible to the average individual. Animal instincts are modes of guidance for the individual in meeting such situations. Ethics are possibly a kind of community instinct in-the-making.

THE COMMUNITY CONCEPT

All ethics so far evolved rest upon a single premise: that the individual is a member of a community of interdependent parts. His instincts prompt him to compete for his place in that community, but his ethics prompt him also to cooperate (perhaps in order that there may be a place to compete for).

The land ethic simply enlarges the boundaries of the community to include soils, waters, plants, and animals, or collectively: the land.

This sounds simple: do we not already sing our love for and obligation to the land of the free and the home of the brave? Yes, but just what and whom do we love? Certainly not the soil, which we are sending helter-skelter downriver. Certainly not the waters, which we assume have no function except to turn turbines, float barges, and carry off sewage. Certainly not the plants, of which we exterminate whole communities without batting an eye. Certainly not the animals, of which we have already extirpated many of the largest and most beautiful species. A land ethic of course cannot prevent the alteration, management, and use of these "resources," but it does affirm their right to continued existence, and, at least in spots, their continued existence in a natural state.

In short, a land ethic changes the role of *Homo sapiens* from conqueror of the land-community to plain member and citizen of it. It implies respect for his fellow-members, and also respect for the community as such.

In human history, we have learned (I hope) that the conqueror role is eventually self-defeating. Why? Because it is implicit in such a role that the conqueror knows, *ex cathedra,* just what makes the community clock tick, and just what and who is valuable, and what and who is worthless, in community life. It always turns out that he knows neither, and this is why his conquests eventually defeat themselves.

In the biotic community, a parallel situation exists. Abraham knew exactly what the land was for: it was to drip milk and honey into Abraham's mouth. At the present moment, the assurance with which we regard this assumption is inverse to the degree of our education.

The ordinary citizen today assumes that science knows what makes the community clock tick; the scientist is equally sure that he does not. He knows that the biotic mechanism is so complex that its workings may never be fully understood.

That man is, in fact, only a member of a biotic team is shown by an ecological interpretation of history. Many historical events, hitherto explained solely in terms of human enterprise, were actually biotic interactions between people and land. The characteristics of the land determined the facts quite as potently as the characteristics of the men who lived on it.

Consider, for example, the settlement of the Mississippi valley. In the years following the Revolution, three groups were contending for its control: the native Indian, the French and English traders, and the American settlers. Historians wonder what would have happened if the English at Detroit had thrown a little more weight into the Indian side of those tipsy scales which decided the outcome of the colonial migration into the cane-lands of Kentucky. It is time now to ponder the fact that the cane-lands, when subjected to the particular mixture of forces represented by the cow, plow, fire, and axe of the pioneer, became bluegrass. What if the plant succession inherent in this dark and bloody ground had, under the impact of these forces, given us some worthless sedge, shrub, or weed? Would Boone and Kenton have held out? Would there have been any overflow into Ohio, Indiana, Illinois, and Missouri? Any Louisiana Purchase? Any transcontinental union of new states? Any Civil War?

Kentucky was one sentence in the drama of history. We are commonly told what the human actors in this drama tried to do, but we are seldom told that their success, or the lack of it, hung in large degree on the reaction of particular soils to the impact of the particular forces exerted by their occupancy. In the case of Kentucky, we do not even know where the bluegrass came from—whether it is a native species, or a stowaway from Europe.

Contrast the cane-lands with what hindsight tells us about the Southwest, where the pioneers were equally brave, resourceful, and persevering. The impact of occupancy here brought no bluegrass, or other plant fitted to withstand the bumps and buffetings of hard use. This region, when grazed by livestock, reverted through a series of more and more worthless grasses, shrubs, and weeds to a condition of unstable equilibrium. Each recession of plant types bred erosion; each increment to erosion bred a further recession of plants. The result today is a progressive and mutual deterioration, not only of plants and soils, but of the animal community subsisting thereon. The early settlers did not expect this: on the ciénegas [marshes] of New Mexico some even cut ditches to hasten it. So subtle has been its progress that few residents of the region are aware of it. It is quite invisible to the tourist who finds this wrecked landscape colorful and charming (as indeed it is, but it bears scant resemblance to what it was in 1848). . . .

In short, the plant succession steered the course of history; the pioneer simply demonstrated, for good or ill, what successions inhered in the land. Is history taught in this spirit? It will be, once the concept of land as a community really penetrates our intellectual life.

THE ECOLOGICAL CONSCIENCE

Conservation is a state of harmony between men and land. Despite nearly a century of propaganda, conservation still proceeds at a snail's pace; progress still consists largely of letterhead pieties and convention oratory. On the back forty we still slip two steps backward for each forward stride.

The usual answer to this dilemma is "more conservation education." No one will debate this, but is it certain that only the *volume* of education needs stepping up? Is something lacking in the *content* as well?

It is difficult to give a fair summary of its content in brief form, but, as I understand it, the content is substantially this: obey the law, vote right, join some organizations, and practice what conservation is profitable on your own land; the government will do the rest.

Is not this formula too easy to accomplish anything worth-while? It defines no right or wrong, assigns no obligation, calls for no sacrifice, implies no change in the current philosophy of values. In respect of land-use, it urges only enlightened self-interest. Just how far will such education take us? . . .

No important change in ethics was ever accomplished without an internal change in our intellectual emphasis, loyalties, affections, and convictions. The proof that conservation has not yet touched these foundations of conduct lies in the fact that philosophy and religion have not yet heard of it. In our attempt to make conservation easy, we have made it trivial.

SUBSTITUTES FOR A LAND ETHIC

When the logic of history hungers for bread and we hand out a stone, we are at pains to explain how much the stone resembles bread. I now describe some of the stones which serve in lieu of a land ethic.

One basic weakness in a conservation system based wholly on economic motives is that most members of the land community have no economic value. Wildflowers and songbirds are examples. Of the 22,000 higher plants and animals native to Wisconsin, it is doubtful whether more than 5 percent can be sold, fed, eaten, or otherwise put to economic use. Yet these creatures are members of the biotic community, and if (as I believe) its stability depends on its integrity, they are entitled to continuance.

When one of these non-economic categories is threatened, and if we happen to love it, we invent subterfuges to give it economic importance. At the beginning of the century songbirds were supposed to be disappearing. Ornithologists jumped to the rescue with some distinctly shaky evidence to the effect that insects would eat us up if birds failed to control them. The evidence had to be economic in order to be valid.

It is painful to read these circumlocutions today. We have no land ethic yet, but we have at least drawn nearer the point of admitting that birds should continue as a matter of biotic right, regardless of the presence or absence of economic advantage to us.

A parallel situation exists in respect of predatory mammals, raptorial birds, and fish-eating birds. Time was when biologists somewhat overworked the evidence that these creatures preserve the health of game by killing weaklings, or that they control rodents for the farmer, or that they prey only on "worthless" species. Here again, the evidence had to be economic in order to be valid. It is only in recent years that we hear the more honest argument that predators are members of the community, and that no special interest has the right to exterminate them for the sake of a benefit, real or fancied, to itself. Unfortunately this enlightened view is still in the talk stage. In the field the extermination of predators goes merrily on: witness the impending erasure of the timber wolf by fiat of Congress, the Conservation Bureaus, and many state legislatures. . . .

When the private landowner is asked to perform some unprofitable act for the good of the community, he today assents only with outstretched palm. If the act costs him cash this is fair and proper, but when it costs only forethought, open-mindedness, or time, the issue is at least debatable. The overwhelming growth of land-use subsidies in recent years must be ascribed, in large part, to the government's own agencies for conservation education: the land bureaus, the agricultural colleges, and the extension services. As far as I can detect, no ethical obligation toward land is taught in these institutions.

To sum up: a system of conservation based solely on economic self-interest is hopelessly lopsided. It tends to ignore, and thus eventually to eliminate, many elements in the land community that lack commercial value, but that are (as far as we know) essential to its healthy functioning. It assumes, falsely, I think, that the economic parts of the biotic clock will function without the uneconomic parts. It tends to relegate to government many functions eventually too large, too complex, or too widely dispersed to be performed by government.

An ethical obligation on the part of the private owner is the only visible remedy for these situations. . . .

LAND HEALTH AND THE A-B CLEAVAGE

A land ethic, then, reflects the existence of an ecological conscience, and this in turn reflects a conviction of individual responsibility for the health of the land. Health is the capacity of the land for self-renewal. Conservation is our effort to understand and preserve this capacity.

Conservationists are notorious for their dissensions. Superficially these seem to add up to mere confusion, but a more careful scrutiny reveals a single plane of cleavage common to many specialized fields. In each field one group (A) regards the land as soil, and its function as commodity-production; another group (B) regards the land as a biota, and its function as something broader. How much broader is admittedly in a state of doubt and confusion.

In my own field, forestry, group A is quite content to grow trees like cabbages, with cellulose as the basic forest commodity. It feels no inhibition against violence; its ideology is agronomic. Group B, on the other hand, sees forestry as fundamentally different from agronomy because it employs natural species, and manages a natural environment rather than creating an artificial one. Group B prefers natural reproduction on principle. It worries on biotic as well as economic grounds about the loss of species like chestnut, and the threatened loss of the white pines. It worries about a whole series of secondary forest functions: wildlife, recreation, watersheds, wilderness areas. To my mind, Group B feels the stirrings of an ecological conscience.

In the wildlife field, a parallel cleavage exists. For Group A the basic commodities are sport and meat; the yardsticks of production are ciphers of take in pheasants and trout. Artificial propagation is acceptable as a permanent as well as a temporary recourse—if its unit costs permit. Group B, on the other hand, worries about a whole series of biotic side-issues. What is the cost in predators of producing a game crop? Should we have further recourse to exotics? How can management restore the shrinking species, like prairie grouse, already hopeless as shootable game? How can management restore the threatened rarities, like trumpeter swan and whooping crane? Can management principles be extended to wildflowers? Here again it is clear to me that we have the same A-B cleavage as in forestry. . . .

In all of these cleavages, we see repeated the same basic paradoxes: man the conqueror *versus* man the biotic citizen; science the sharpener of his sword *versus* science the searchlight on his universe; land the slave and servant *versus* land the collective organism. Robinson's injunction to Tristram may well be applied, at this juncture, to *Homo sapiens* as a species in geological time:

> Whether you will or not
> You are a King, Tristram, for you are one
> Of the time-tested few that leave the world,
> When they are gone, not the same place it was.
> Mark what you leave.

THE OUTLOOK

It is inconceivable to me that an ethical relation to land can exist without love, respect, and admiration for land, and a high regard for its value. By value, I of course mean something far broader than mere economic value; I mean value in the philosophical sense.

Perhaps the most serious obstacle impeding the evolution of a land ethic is the fact that our educational and economic system is headed away from, rather than toward, an intense consciousness of land. Your true modern is separated from the land by many middlemen, and by innumerable physical gadgets. He has no vital relation to it; to him it is the space between cities on which crops grow. Turn him loose for a day on the land, and if the spot does not happen to be a golf links or a "scenic" area, he is bored stiff. If crops could be raised by hydroponics instead of farming, it would suit him very well. Synthetic substitutes for wood, leather, wool, and other natural land products suit him better than the originals. In short, land is something he has "outgrown."

Almost equally serious as an obstacle to a land ethic is the attitude of the farmer for whom the land is still an adversary, or a taskmaster that keeps him in slavery. Theoretically, the mechanization of farming ought to cut the farmer's chains, but whether it really does is debatable.

One of the requisites for an ecological comprehension of land is an understanding of ecology, and this is by no means co-extensive with "education"; in fact, much higher education seems deliberately to avoid ecological concepts. An understanding of ecology does not necessarily originate in courses bearing ecological labels; it is quite as likely to be labeled geography, botany, agronomy, history, or economics. This is as it should be, but whatever the label, ecological training is scarce.

The case for a land ethic would appear hopeless but for the minority which is in obvious revolt against these "modern" trends.

The "key-log" which must be moved to release the evolutionary process for an ethic is simply this: quit thinking about decent land-use as solely an economic problem. Examine each question in terms of what is ethically and aesthetically right, as well as what is economically expedient. A thing is right when it tends to preserve the integrity, stability, and beauty of the biotic community. It is wrong when it tends otherwise.

It of course goes without saying that economic feasibility limits the tether of what can or cannot be done for land. It always has and it always will. The fallacy the economic determinists have tied around our collective neck, and which we now need to cast off, is the belief that economics determines *all* land-use. This is simply not true. An innumerable host of actions and attitudes, comprising perhaps the bulk of all land relations, is determined by the land-users' tastes and predilections, rather than by his purse. The bulk of all land relations hinges on investments of time, forethought, skill, and faith rather than on investments of cash. As a land-user thinketh, so is he.

I have purposely presented the land ethic as a product of social evolution because nothing so important as an ethic is ever "written." Only the most superficial student of history supposes that Moses "wrote" the Decalogue; it evolved in the minds of a thinking community, and Moses wrote a tentative summary of it for a "seminar." I say tentative because evolution never stops.

The evolution of a land ethic is an intellectual as well as emotional process. Conservation is paved with good intentions which prove to be futile, or even dangerous, because they are devoid of critical understanding either of the land, or of economic land-use. I think it is a truism that as the ethical frontier advances from the individual to the community, its intellectual content increases.

The mechanism of operation is the same for any ethic: social approbation for right actions: social disapproval for wrong actions.

By and large, our present problem is one of attitudes and implements. We are remodeling the Alhambra with a steam-shovel, and we are proud of our yardage. We shall hardly relinquish the shovel, which after all has many good points, but we are in need of gentler and more objective criteria for its successful use.

DISCUSSION QUESTIONS

1. What does Leopold mean by "biotic rights"? How are they similar to or different from the "human rights" discussed in Chapter 2? Do you believe that there are "biotic rights"? Why or why not?

2. Why does Leopold believe that "no special interest has the right to exterminate predators for the sake of a benefit, real or fancied, to itself"? How strong is his argument?

3. What, according to Leopold, are the weaknesses of a conservation system based wholly on economic motives? Do you agree with him?

4. What does Leopold mean when he says that "no important change in ethics was ever accomplished without an internal change in our intellectual emphasis, loyalties, affections and convictions"?
5. "All ethics so far evolved rest upon a single premise: that the individual is a member of a community of interdependent parts," says Leopold. How might some of the classical ethicists that you have read respond to this? Do you think they would agree? Discuss.
6. Leopold speaks of a shift from the Ten Commandments, to the Golden Rule, to democracy, which indicates that we have steadily expanded our sphere of sympathy to include a wider class of beings in the "moral community." Do you think that there has been such a logical progression in the history of ethics? Why or why not? Would you say that a similar shift has occurred this century from fighting racism and sexism to fighting speciesism and anthropocentrism? Defend your view.

 PETER S. WENZ

Ecology and Morality

Peter S. Wenz argues that we have *prima facie* obligations toward ecosystems. This position is known as *deep ecology*. In particular, Wenz says that we have an obligation to avoid destroying ecosystems, apart from any human benefits that their continued existence might provide. By *prima facie* obligations, Wenz means obligations that would exist in the absence of other, countervailing moral considerations. Wenz constructs two cases that are designed to illustrate his thesis.

Peter S. Wenz is a philosophy professor at the University of Illinois at Springfield and the author of *Environmental Justice* (1987), *Abortion Rights as Religious Freedom* (1992), *Faces of Environmental Racism* (coedited with Laura Westra, 1995), and *Nature's Keeper* (1996).

In the first section of this article I characterize good or healthy ecosystems. In the second I argue that we have a *prima facie* obligation to protect such ecosystems irrespective of all possible advantage to human beings.

GOOD ECOSYSTEMS

An ecosystem is what Aldo Leopold referred to as a "biotic pyramid." He describes it this way (1970, p. 252):

Plants absorb energy from the sun. This energy flows through a circuit called the biota, which may be represented by a pyramid consisting of layers. The bottom layer is the soil. A plant layer rests on the soil, an insect layer on the plants, a bird and rodent layer on the insects, and so on up through various animal groups to the apex layer, which consists of the large carnivores.

Proceeding upward, each successive layer decreases in numerical abundance. Thus, for every carnivore there are hundreds of his prey,

Peter Wenz, *Ethics and Animals.* Edited by Harlan B. Miller and William H. Williams, Humana Press, 1983, 185–191. Reprinted with permission from Humana Press.

thousands of their prey, millions of insects, uncountable plants.

The lines of dependency for food and other services are called food chains. Thus soil-oak-deer-Indian is a chain that has now largely converted to soil-corn-cow-farmer. Each species, including ourselves, is a link in many chains. The deer eats a hundred plants other than oak, and the cow a hundred plants other than corn. Both, then, are links in a hundred chains. The pyramid is a tangle of chains so complex as to seem disorderly, yet the stability of the system proves it to be a highly organized structure.[1]

It is so highly organized that Leopold and others write of it, at times, as if it were a single organism which could be in various stages of health or disease (p. 274):

Paleontology offers abundant evidence that wilderness maintained itself for immensely long periods; that its component species were rarely lost, neither did they get out of hand: that weather and water built soil as fast or faster than it was carried away. Wilderness, then, assumes unexpected importance as a laboratory for the study of land-health.

By contrast,

When soil loses fertility, or washes away faster than it forms, and when water systems exhibit abnormal floods and shortages, the land is sick (p. 272).

The disappearance of plant and animal species without visible cause, despite efforts to protect them, and the irruption of others as pests despite efforts to control them, must, in the absence of simpler explanations, be regarded as symptoms of sickness in the land organism (pp. 272–273).

In general, a healthy ecosystem consists of a great diversity of flora and fauna, as "the trend of evolution is to elaborate and diversify the biota" (p. 253). This flora and fauna is in a relatively stable balance, evolving slowly rather than changing rapidly, because its diversity enables it to respond to change in a flexible manner that retains the system's integrity. In all of these respects a healthy ecosystem is very much like a healthy plant or animal.

A description of one small part of one ecosystem will conclude this account of the nature of ecosys-

tems. It is Leopold's description of a river's sand bar in August (p. 55):

The work begins with a broad ribbon of silt brushed thinly on the sand of a reddening shore. As this dries slowly in the sun, goldfinches bathe in its pools, and deer, herons, killdeers, raccoons, and turtles cover it with a lacework of tracks. There is no telling, at this stage, whether anything further will happen.

But when I see the silt ribbon turning green with Eleocharis, I watch closely thereafter, for this is the sign that the river is in a painting mood. Almost overnight the Eleocharis becomes a thick turf, so lush and so dense that the meadow mice from the adjoining upland cannot resist the temptation. They move *en masse* to the green pasture, and apparently spend the nights rubbing their ribs in its velvety depths. A maze of neatly tended mouse-trails bespeaks their enthusiasm. The deer walk up and down in it, apparently just for the pleasure of feeling it underfoot. Even a stay-at-home mole has tunneled his way across the dry bar to the Eleocharis ribbon, where he can heave and hump the sod to his heart's content.

At this stage the seedlings of plants too numerous to count and too young to recognize spring to life from the damp warm sand under the green ribbon.

Three weeks later (pp. 55–56):

The Eleocharis sod, greener than ever, is now spangled with blue mimulus, pink dragonhead, and the milk-white blooms of Sagittaria. Here and there a cardinal flower thrusts a red spear skyward. At the head of the bar, purple ironweeds and pale pink joe-pyes stand tall against the wall of willows. And if you have come quietly and humbly, as you should to any spot that can be beautiful only once, you may surprise a fox-red deer, standing knee-high in the garden of his delight.

HUMAN OBLIGATIONS TO ECOSYSTEMS

Let us now consider whether or not we, you and I, have *prima facie* obligations towards ecosystems, in particular, the obligation to avoid destroying them, apart from any human advantage that might be gained by their continued existence. My argument consists in the elaboration of two examples, followed by appeals to the reader's intuition. The second, Case II, is designed to function as a counterexample to the claim that human beings have no obligations to preserve ecosystems except when doing so serves human interests or prevents the unnecessary suffering of other sentient beings.

Some clarifications are needed at the start. By "*prima facie* obligation" I mean an obligation that would exist in the absence of other, countervailing moral considerations. So I will construct cases in which such other considerations are designedly absent. A common consideration of this sort is the effect our actions have on intelligent beings, whether they be humans, extraterrestrials, or (should they be considered intelligent enough) apes and aquatic mammals. Accordingly, I will construct my cases so that the destruction of the environment affects none of these. Finally, the obligation in question is not to preserve ecosystems from any and every threat to their health and existence. Rather, the obligation for which I am contending is to protect ecosystems from oneself. The differences here may be important. A duty to protect the environment from any and every threat would have to rest on some principle concerning the duty to bring aid. Such principles concern positive duties, which are generally considered less stringent than negative duties. The duty to protect the environment from oneself, on the other hand, rests on a principle concerning the duty to do no harm, which is a negative duty. Those not convinced that we have a duty to bring aid may nevertheless find a *prima facie* duty not to harm the environment easy to accept.

Case I

Consider the following situation. Suppose that you are a pilot flying a bomber that is low on fuel. You must release your bombs over the ocean to reduce the weight of the plane. If the bombs land in the water they will not explode, but will, instead, deactivate harmlessly. If, on the other hand, any lands on the islands that dot this part of the ocean, it will explode. The islands contain no mineral or other resources of use to human beings, and are sufficiently isolated from one another and other parts of the world that an explosion on one will not affect the others, or any other part of the world. The bomb's explosion will not add to air pollution because it is

exceedingly "clean." However, each island contains an ecosystem, a biotic pyramid of the sort described by Aldo Leopold, within which there are rivers, sandbars, Eleocharis, meadow mice, cardinal flowers, blue mimulus, deer, and so forth, but no intelligent life. (Those who consider mice, deer, and other such animals so intelligent as to fall under some ban against killing intelligent life are free to suppose that in their wisdom, all such creatures have emigrated.) The bomb's explosion will ruin the ecosystem of the island on which it explodes, though it will not cause any animals to suffer. We may suppose that the islands are small enough and the bombs powerful enough that all animals, as well as plants, will be killed instantly, and therefore painlessly. The island will instantly be transformed from a wilderness garden to a bleakness like that on the surface of the moon.

Suppose that with some care and attention, but with no risk to yourself, anyone else or the plane, you could release your bombs so as to avoid hitting any of the islands. With equal care and attention you could be sure to hit at least one of the islands. Finally, without any care or attention to the matter, you might hit one of the islands and you might not. Assuming that you are in no need of target practice, and are aware of the situation as described, would you consider it a matter of moral indifference which of the three possible courses of action you took? Wouldn't you feel that you ought to take some care and pay some attention to insure that you avoid hitting any of the islands? Those who can honestly say that in the situation at hand they feel no more obligation to avoid hitting the islands than to hit them, who think that destroying the balanced pyramidal structure of a healthy ecosystem is morally indifferent, who care nothing for the island's floral displays and interactions between flora, fauna, soil, water, and sun need read no further. Such people do not share the intuition on which the argument in this paper rests.

I assume that few, if any, readers of the last paragraph accepted my invitation to stop reading. I would have phrased things differently if I thought they would. Many readers may nevertheless be skeptical of my intuitive demonstration that we feel a *prima facie* obligation to avoid destroying ecosystems. Even though no pain to sentient creatures is involved, nor the destruction of intelligent life nor pollution or other impairment of areas inhabited by human beings or other intelligent creatures, some readers may nevertheless explain their reluctance to destroy such an ecosystem by reference, ultimately, to human purposes. They can thereby avoid the inference I am promoting. They might point out that the islands' ecosystems may be useful to scientists who might someday want to study them. No matter that there are a great many such islands. The ecosystem of each is at least slightly different from the others, and therefore might provide some information of benefit to human beings that could not be gleaned elsewhere. Alternatively, though scientists are studying some, it might be to the benefit of humanity to establish Holiday Inns and Hilton Hotels on the others. Scientists have to relax too, and if the accommodations are suitable they will be more likely to enjoy the companionship of their families.

I believe that such explanations of our intuitive revulsion at the idea of needlessly destroying a healthy ecosystem are unhelpful evasions. They represent the squirming of one who intellectually believes ethics to concern only humans and other intelligent creatures, perhaps with a rider that one ought not to cause sentient creatures unnecessary suffering, with the reality of his or her own moral intuitions. The next case will make this clearer.

Case II

Suppose that human beings and all other intelligent creatures inhabiting the earth are becoming extinct. Imagine that this is the effect of some cosmic ray that causes extinction by preventing procreation. There is no possibility of survival through emigration to another planet, solar system or galaxy because the ray's presence is so widespread that no humans would survive the lengthy journey necessary to escape from its influence. There are many other species of extraterrestrial, intelligent creatures in the universe whom the cosmic ray does not affect. Nor does it affect any of the non-intelligent members of the earth's biotic community. So the earth's varied multitude of ecosystems could continue after the extinction of human beings. But their continuation would be of no use to any of the many species of intelligent extraterrestrials because the earth is for many reasons inhospitable to their forms of life, and contains no mineral or other resources of which they could make use.

Suppose that you are the last surviving human being. All other intelligent animals, if there were any, have already become extinct. Before they died, other humans had set hydrogen explosives all around the earth such that, were they to explode, all remaining plant and animal life on the earth would be instantly vaporized. No sentient creature would suffer, but the earth's varied multitude of ecosystems would be completely destroyed. The hydrogen explosives are all attached to a single timing mechanism, set to explode next year. Not wishing to die prematurely, you have located this timing device. You can set it ahead fifty or one hundred years, insuring that the explosion will not foreshorten your life, or you can, with only slightly greater effort, deactivate it so that it will never explode at all. Who would think it a matter of moral indifference which you did? It seems obvious that you ought to deactivate the explosives rather than postpone the time of the explosions.

How can one account for this "ought"? One suggestion is that our obligations are to intelligent life, and that the chances are improved and the time lessened for the evolution of intelligent life on earth by leaving the earth's remaining ecosystems intact. But this explanation is not convincing. First, it rests on assumptions about evolutionary developments under different earthly conditions that seem very plausible, but are by no means certain. More important, as the case was drawn, there are many species of intelligent extraterrestrials who are in no danger of either extinction or diminished numbers, and you know of their existence. It is therefore not at all certain that the obligations to intelligent life contained in our current ethical theories and moral intuitions would suggest, much less require, that we so act as to increase the probability of and decrease the time for the development of another species of intelligent life on earth. We do not now think it morally incumbent upon us to develop a form of intelligent life suited to live in those parts of the globe that, like Antarctica, are underpopulated by human beings. This is so because we do not adhere to a principle that we ought to so act as to insure the presence of intelligent life in as many earthly locations as possible. It is therefore doubtful that we adhere to the more extended principle that we ought to promote the development of as many different species of intelligent life as possible in as many different locations in the universe as possible. Such a problematic moral principle surely cannot account for our clear intuition that one obviously and certainly ought not to reset the explosives rather than deactivate them. It is more plausible to suppose that our current morality includes a *prima facie* obligation to refrain from destroying good ecosystems irrespective of both the interests of intelligent beings and the obligation not to cause sentient beings unnecessary suffering.

It is not necessary to say that ecosystems have rights. It is a commonplace in contemporary moral philosophy that not all obligations result from corresponding rights, for example, the obligation to be charitable. Instead, the obligation might follow from our concept of virtuous people as ones who do not destroy any existing things needlessly. Or perhaps we feel that one has a *prima facie* obligation not to destroy anything of esthetic value, and ecosystems are of esthetic value. Alternatively, the underlying obligation could be to avoid destroying anything that is good of its kind—so long as the kind in question does not make it something bad in itself—and many of the earth's ecosystems are good.

Our intuition might, on the other hand, be related more specifically to those characteristics that make good ecosystems good. Generally speaking, one ecosystem is better than another if it incorporates a greater diversity of life forms into a more integrated unity that is relatively stable, but not static. Its homeostasis allows for gradual evolution. The leading concepts, then, are diversity, unity, and a slightly less than complete homeostatic stability. These are, as a matter of empirical fact, positively related to one another in ecosystems. They may strike a sympathetic chord in human beings because they correspond symbolically to our personal, psychological need for a combination in our lives of both security and novelty. The stability and unity of a good ecosystem represents security. That the stability is cyclically homeostatic, rather than static, involves life forms rather than merely inorganic matter, and includes great diversity, corresponds to our desires for novelty and change. Of course, this is only speculation. It must be admitted that some human beings seem to so value security and stability as to prefer a purely static unity. Parmenides and the eastern religious thinkers who promote nothingness as a goal might consider the surface of the moon superior to that of the earth, and advocate allowing the earth's ecosystems to be vaporized under the conditions described in Case II.

My intuitions, however, and I assume those of most readers, favor ecosystems over static lifelessness and, perhaps for the same reason, good ecosystems over poorer ones. In any case, the above speculations concerning the psychological and logical derivations of these intuitions serve at most to help clarify their nature. Even the correct account of their origin would not necessarily constitute a justification. Rather than try to justify them, I will take them as a starting point for further discussion. So I take the cases elaborated above to establish that our current morality includes a *prima facie* obligation to avoid destroying good ecosystems, absent considerations of both animal torture and the well-being of intelligent creatures. . . .

NOTE

1. A. Leopold, *A Sand County Almanac, with Essays on Conservation from Round River* (New York: Ballantine Books, 1970).

DISCUSSION QUESTIONS

1. What is a "*prima facie* obligation"? What is the role of *prima facie* obligations in Wenz's argument for a deep ecology?
2. Wenz says that many readers will be skeptical of his intuitive demonstration that we have *prima facie* obligations to avoid destroying ecosystems. Are you skeptical? Why or why not?
3. Is Wenz successful in proving that ethics is not concerned solely with humans and other intelligent creatures? Explain.
4. Discuss the role of "moral intuition" in Wenz's argument. What role do moral intuitions play in your own beliefs about morality? Explain.
5. In the second case, Wenz says that "it seems obvious that you ought to deactivate the explosives rather than postpone the time of the explosion." Is this "obvious" to you? Explain why or why not.
6. In general, how do you feel about "deep ecology"? Do the arguments presented by Wenz persuade you to become an advocate of deep ecology? Or do you need more convincing? Explain.

WILLIAM F. BAXTER

People or Penguins

William F. Baxter argues against deep ecologies like that of Peter S. Wenz and for an anthropocentric perspective on the environment. There is no normative definition of the state of nature or the natural state, contends Baxter. Low pollution levels are only desirable if they contribute to human satisfaction. For Baxter, the ecosystem has no rights, and we ought only respect the balance of nature if it is of benefit to man. "My criteria are oriented to people, not penguins," says Baxter. "I have no interest in preserving penguins for their own sake." According to Baxter, the first and foremost step toward a solution to our environmental problems is a clear recognition that our objective is an optimal state of pollution. "Every man is entitled to his own preferred definition of Walden Pond," says Baxter, "but there is no definition that has any moral superiority over another, except by reference to the selfish needs of the human race." Damage to penguins, sugar pines, and geological marvels is in itself simply irrelevant.

William F. Baxter is William Benjamin Scott and Luna M. Scott Professor of Law at Stanford University and is the author of *People or Penguins: The Case for Optimal Pollution* (1974) and *The Political Economy of Antitrust* (coedited with Robert D. Tollison, 1980).

. . . My criteria are oriented to people, not penguins. Damage to penguins, or sugar pines, or geological marvels is, without more, simply irrelevant. One must go further, by my criteria, and say: Penguins are important because people enjoy seeing them walk about rocks; and furthermore, the well-being of people would be less impaired by halting use of DDT than by giving up penguins. In short, my observations about environmental problems will be people-oriented, as are my criteria. I have no interest in preserving penguins for their own sake.

It may be said by way of objection to this position, that it is very selfish of people to act as if each person represented one unit of importance and nothing else was of any importance. It is undeniably selfish. Nevertheless I think it is the only tenable starting place for analysis for several reasons. First, no other position corresponds to the way most people really think and act—i.e., corresponds to reality.

Second, this attitude does not portend any massive destruction of nonhuman flora and fauna, for people depend on them in many obvious ways, and they will be preserved because and to the degree that humans do depend on them.

Third, what is good for humans is, in many respects, good for penguins and pine trees—clean air for example. So that humans are, in these respects, surrogates for plant and animal life.

Fourth, I do not know how we could administer any other system. Our decisions are either private or collective. Insofar as Mr. Jones is free to act privately, he may give such preferences as he wishes to other forms of life: he may feed birds in winter and do with less himself, and he may even decline to resist an advancing polar bear on the ground that the bear's appetite is more important than those portions of himself that the bear may choose to eat. In short my basic premise does not rule out private altruism to competing life-forms. It does rule out, however, Mr. Jones' inclination to feed Mr. Smith to the bear, however hungry the bear, however despicable Mr. Smith.

Insofar as we act collectively on the other hand, only humans can be afforded an opportunity to participate in the collective decisions. Penguins cannot vote now and are unlikely subjects for the franchise—pine trees more unlikely still. Again each individual is free to cast his vote so as to benefit sugar pines if that is his inclination. But many of the more extreme assertions that one hears from some conservationists amount to tacit assertions that they are specially appointed representatives of sugar pines, and hence that their preferences should be weighted more heavily than the preferences of other humans who do not enjoy equal rapport with "nature." The simplistic assertion that agricultural use of DDT must stop at once because it is harmful to penguins is of that type.

Fifth, if polar bears or pine trees or penguins, like men, are to be regarded as ends rather than means, if they are to count in our calculus of social organization, someone must tell me how much each one counts, and someone must tell me how these life-forms are to be permitted to express their preferences, for I do not know either answer. If the answer is that certain people are to hold their proxies, then I want to know how those proxy-holders are to be selected: self-appointment does not seem workable to me.

Sixth, and by way of summary of all the foregoing, let me point out that the set of environmental issues under discussion—although they raise very complex technical questions of how to achieve any objective—ultimately raise a normative question: what *ought* we to do. Questions of *ought* are unique to the human mind and world—they are meaningless as applied to a nonhuman situation.

I reject the proposition that we *ought* to respect the "balance of nature" or to "preserve the environment" unless the reason for doing so, express or implied, is the benefit of man.

I reject the idea that there is a "right" or "morally correct" state of nature to which we should return. The word "nature" has no normative connotation. Was it "right" or "wrong" for the earth's crust to heave in contortion and create mountains and seas? Was it "right" for the first amphibian to crawl up out of the primordial ooze? Was it "wrong" for plants to reproduce themselves and alter the atmospheric composition in favor of oxygen? For animals to alter the atmosphere in favor of carbon dioxide both by breathing oxygen and eating plants? No answers can be given to these questions because they are meaningless questions.

All this may seem obvious to the point of being tedious, but much of the present controversy over environment and pollution rests on tacit normative assumptions about just such nonnormative phenomena: that it is "wrong" to impair penguins with DDT, but not to slaughter cattle for prime rib roasts. That it is wrong to kill stands of sugar pines with industrial fumes, but not to cut sugar pines and build housing for the poor. Every man is entitled to his own preferred definition of Walden Pond, but there is no definition that has any moral superiority over another, except by reference to the selfish needs of the human race.

From the fact that there is no normative definition of the natural state, it follows that there is no normative definition of clean air or pure water—hence no definition of polluted air—or of pollution—except by reference to the needs of man. The "right" composition of the atmosphere is one which has some dust in it and some lead in it and some hydrogen sulfide in it—just those amounts that attend a sensibly organized society thoughtfully and knowledgeably pursuing the greatest possible satisfaction for its human members.

The first and most fundamental step toward solution of our environmental problems is a clear recognition that our objective is not pure air or water but rather some optimal state of pollution. That step immediately suggests the question: How do we define and attain the level of pollution that will yield the maximum possible amount of human satisfaction?

Low levels of pollution contribute to human satisfaction but so do food and shelter and education and music. To attain ever lower levels of pollution, we must pay the cost of having less of these other things. I contrast that view of the cost of pollution control with the more popular statement that pollution control will "cost" very large numbers of dollars. The popular statement is true in some senses, false in others; sorting out the true and false senses is of some importance. The first step in that sorting process is to achieve a clear understanding of the difference between dollars and resources. Resources are the wealth of our nation; dollars are merely claim checks upon those resources. Resources are of vital importance; dollars are comparatively trivial.

Four categories of resources are sufficient for our purposes: At any given time a nation, or a planet if you prefer, has a stock of labor, of technological skill, of capital goods, and of natural resources (such as mineral deposits, timber, water, land, etc.). These resources can be used in various combinations to yield goods and services of all kinds—in some limited quantity. The quantity will be larger if they are combined efficiently, smaller if combined inefficiently. But in either event the resource stock is limited, the goods and services that they can be made to yield are limited; even the most efficient use of them will yield less than our population, in the aggregate, would like to have.

If one considers building a new dam, it is appropriate to say that it will be costly in the sense that it will require x hours of labor, y tons of steel and concrete, and z amount of capital goods. If these resources are devoted to the dam, then they cannot be used to build hospitals, fishing rods, schools, or electric can openers. That is the meaningful sense in which the dam is costly.

Quite apart from the very important question of how wisely we can combine our resources to produce goods and services, is the very different question of how they get distributed—who gets how many goods? Dollars constitute the claim checks which are distributed among people and which control their share of national output. Dollars are nearly valueless pieces of paper except to the extent that they do represent claim checks to some fraction of the output of goods and services. Viewed as claim checks, all the dollars outstanding during any period of time are worth, in the aggregate, the goods and services that are available to be claimed with them during that period—neither more nor less.

It is far easier to increase the supply of dollars than to increase the production of goods and services—printing dollars is easy. But printing more dollars doesn't help because each dollar then simply becomes a claim to fewer goods, i.e., becomes worth less.

The point is this: many people fall into error upon hearing the statement that the decision to build a dam, or to clean up a river, will cost $X million. It is regrettably easy to say: "It's only money. This is a wealthy country, and we have lots of money." But you cannot build a dam or clean a river with $X million— unless you also have a match, you can't even make a fire. One builds a dam or cleans a river by diverting labor and steel and trucks and factories from making one kind of goods to making another. The cost in dollars is merely a shorthand way of describing the extent of the diversion necessary. If we build a dam for $X million, then we must recognize that we will have $X million less housing and food and medical care and electric can openers as a result.

Similarly, the costs of controlling pollution are best expressed in terms of the other goods we will have to give up to do the job. This is not to say the job should not be done. Badly as we need more housing, more medical care, and more can openers, and more symphony orchestras, we could do with somewhat less of them, in my judgment at least, in exchange for somewhat cleaner air and rivers. But that is the nature of the trade-off, and analysis of the problem is advanced if that unpleasant reality is kept in mind. Once the trade-off relationship is clearly perceived, it is possible to state in a very general way what the optimal level of pollution is. I would state it as follows:

People enjoy watching penguins. They enjoy relatively clean air and smog-free vistas. Their health is improved by relatively clean water and air. Each of these benefits is a type of good or service. As a society we would be well advised to give up one washing machine if the resources that would have gone into that washing machine can yield greater human satisfaction when diverted into pollution control. We should give up one hospital if the resources thereby freed would yield more human satisfaction when devoted to elimination of noise in our cities. And so on, trade-off by trade-off, we should divert our productive capacities from the production of existing goods and services to the production of a cleaner, quieter, more pastoral nation up to—and no further than—the point at which we value more highly the next washing machine or hospital that we would have to do without than we value the next unit of environmental improvement that the diverted resources would create. . . .

DISCUSSION QUESTIONS

1. Baxter writes that "every man is entitled to his own preferred definition of Walden Pond, but there is no definition that has any moral superiority over another, except by reference to the selfish needs of the human race." What does this statement mean? Do you think that Aldo Leopold would agree with Baxter? What about Peter Wenz? Do you agree with Baxter? Explain.

2. How might Baxter respond to Wenz's deep ecology? In particular, how might Baxter respond to the two "cases" presented by Wenz?

3. Baxter argues that the "first and foremost step toward a solution to our environmental problems is a clear recognition that our objective is not pure air or water but rather some optimal state of pollution." What is his argument? Do you agree with it?

4. Critically evaluate the following statement from Baxter: "Low levels of pollution contribute to human satisfaction but so do food and shelter and education and music. To attain even lower levels of pollution, we must pay the cost of having less of these other things."
5. What is the role of economic value in Baxter's discussion of environmental ethics? Compare this role with the role of economic value in Leopold's environmental ethics. Whose position is stronger, and why?

K A R E N   J .   W A R R E N

Feminism and Ecology

In this article, Karen J. Warren argues that *ecological feminism* (or *eco-feminism*) is based on four claims: (1) there are important connections between the oppression of women and of nature; (2) understanding these connections is necessary to any adequate understanding of the oppression of women and of nature; (3) feminist theory and practice must include an ecological perspective; and (4) solutions to ecological problems must include a feminist perspective. Warren then shows why liberal feminism, traditional Marxist feminism, radical feminism, and socialist feminism—the four leading versions of feminism—are inadequate, incomplete, or problematic as theoretical foundations for ecological feminism. Consequently, argues Warren, if ecological feminism is to be taken seriously, then a *transformative feminism* is needed that will move beyond the four leading versions of feminism and will make an ecological feminist perspective central to feminist theory and practice.

Karen J. Warren is a philosophy professor at Macalester College in St. Paul, Minnesota, and is the editor of *Ecological Feminism* (1994), *Bringing Peace Home: Feminism, Violence and Nature* (with Duane L. Cady, 1996), and *Ecofeminism: Women, Culture, Nature* (1997).

The current feminist debate over ecology raises important and timely issues about the theoretical adequacy of the four leading versions of feminism—liberal feminism, traditional Marxist feminism, radical feminism, and socialist feminism. In this paper I present a minimal condition account of ecological feminism, or *eco-feminism*. I argue that if eco-feminism is true or at least plausible, then each of the four leading versions of feminism is inadequate, incomplete, or problematic as a theoretical grounding for eco-feminism. I conclude that, if eco-feminism is to be taken seriously, then a transformative feminism is needed that will move us beyond the four familiar feminist frameworks and make an eco-feminist perspective central to feminist theory and practice.

INTRODUCTION

In *New Woman/New Earth*, Rosemary Ruether writes:

> Women must see that there can be no
> liberation for them and no solution to the

Karen J. Warren, *Environmental Ethics*, vol. 9, no. 1 (spring 1987): 3–20. Reprinted by permission of the publisher and the author.

ecological crisis within a society whose fundamental model of relationship continues to be one of domination. They must unite the demands of the women's movement with those of the ecological movement to envision a radical reshaping of the basic socioeconomic relations and the underlying values of this society.[1]

According to Ruether, the women's movement and the ecology movement are intimately connected. The demands of both require "transforming that world-view which underlies domination and replacing it with an alternative value system."[2] Recent writings by feminists Elizabeth Dodson Gray, Susan Griffin, Mary Daly, Carolyn Merchant, Joan Griscom, Ynestra King, and Ariel Kay Salleh underscore Ruether's basic point: ecology is a feminist issue.[3]

Why is this so? Feminists who debate the ecology issue agree that there are important connections between the oppression of women and the oppression of nature,[4] but they disagree about both the nature of those connections and whether those connections are "potentially liberating or simply a rationale for the continued subordination of women."[5] Stated slightly differently, while many feminists agree that ecology is a feminist issue, they disagree about the nature and desirability of "ecological feminism," or *eco-feminism*.

This disagreement is to be expected. Just as there is not one version of feminism, there is not one version of eco-feminism. The varieties of eco-feminism reflect not only differences in the analysis of the woman/nature connection, but also differences on such fundamental issues as the nature of and solutions to women's oppression, the theory of human nature, and the conceptions of freedom, equality, and epistemology on which the various feminist theories depend.

In order to accommodate the varieties of eco-feminist perspectives, it is important to provide a minimal condition account of eco-feminism which captures the basic claims to which all eco-feminists are committed. As I use the term, *eco-feminism* is a position based on the following claims: (i) there are important connections between the oppression of women and the oppression of nature; (ii) understanding the nature of these connections is necessary to any adequate understanding of the oppression of women and the oppression of nature; (iii) feminist theory and practice must include an ecological perspective; and (iv) solutions to ecological problems must include a feminist perspective.[6]

Suppose that eco-feminism is true or at least plausible. To what extent do the four leading versions of feminism—liberal feminism, traditional Marxist feminism, radical feminism, and socialist feminism—capture or make a place for eco-feminism? To answer this question is to determine the extent to which the leading versions of feminism constitute an adequate theoretical grounding for eco-feminism.

My primary aim in this paper is to assess the adequacy of the four leading versions of feminism from the perspective of eco-feminism. I argue that while each may provide important insights into the oppression of women and nature, nonetheless, in its present form and taken by itself, each is inadequate, incomplete, or at least sufficiently problematic as a theoretical grounding for eco-feminism. I conclude by suggesting that if eco-feminism is to be taken seriously, then what is needed is a new one which moves us beyond the current debate over the four leading versions of feminism and makes an eco-feminist perspective central to feminist theory and practice.

Two qualifications on the scope of the paper are in order. First, eco-feminism is a relatively new movement. In some cases, the leading versions of feminism have not, in fact, articulated a position on ecology or on the nature of the connection between the oppression of women and the oppression of nature. As such, in some cases, the ecological implications attributed in this paper to a given feminist theory are only hypothetical: they are suppositions about what such feminist accounts *might* be like, given what is known of the more general tenets of those feminist positions, rather than accounts of viewpoints actually stated.

Second, I provide neither a defense of eco-feminism nor a defense of a "transformative feminism." Rather, on the assumption that eco-feminism is true or plausible, I attempt to clarify the extent to which the four leading versions of feminism are problematic as a theoretical basis for eco-feminism. The concluding discussion of a transformative feminism is intended mainly to be suggestive of possible directions to pursue which will both expand upon the insights of current feminisms and include eco-feminism as an integral aspect of feminist theory and practice.

ECO-FEMINISM AND PATRIARCHAL CONCEPTUAL FRAMEWORKS

Eco-feminists take as their central project the unpacking of the connections between the twin oppressions of women and nature. Central to this project is a critique of the sort of thinking which sanctions that oppression. One way to understand this critique is to talk about conceptual frameworks.

Underlying eco-feminism is the view that, whether we know it or not, each of us operates out of a socially constructed mind set or *conceptual framework,* i.e., a set of beliefs, values, attitudes, and assumptions which shape, reflect, and explain our view of ourselves and our world. A conceptual framework is influenced by such factors as sex-gender, race, class, age, sexual preference, religion, and nationality. A *patriarchal conceptual framework* is one which takes traditionally male-identified beliefs, values, attitudes, and assumptions as the only, or the standard, or the superior ones; it gives higher status or prestige to what has been traditionally identified as "male" than to what has been traditionally identified as "female."

A patriarchal conceptual framework is characterized by *value-hierarchical thinking.* In the words of eco-feminist Elizabeth Dodson Gray, such thinking "is a perception of diversity which is so organized by a spatial metaphor (Up-and-Down) that greater value is always attributed to that which is higher."[7] It puts men "up" and women "down," culture "up" and nature "down," minds "up" and bodies "down."

Such patriarchal value-hierarchical thinking gives rise to *a logic of domination,* i.e., a value-hierarchical way of thinking which explains, justifies, and maintains the subordination of an "inferior" group by a "superior" group on the grounds of the (alleged) inferiority or superiority of the respective group. By attributing greater value to that which is higher, the up-down organization of perceptions, mediated by a logic of domination, serves to legitimate inequality "when, in fact, prior to the metaphor of Up-Down one would have said only that there existed diversity."[8]

Eco-feminists assume that patriarchal value-hierarchical thinking supports the sort of "either-or" thinking which generates *normative dualisms,* i.e., thinking in which the disjunctive terms (or sides of the dualism) are seen as exclusive (rather than inclusive) and oppositional (rather than complementary), and where higher value or superiority is attributed to one disjunct (or, side of the dualism) than the other. It, thereby, conceptually separates as opposites aspects of reality that in fact are inseparable or complementary; e.g., it opposes human to nonhuman, mind to body, self to other, reason to emotion.[9]

According to eco-feminism, then, the connections between the oppression of women and the oppression of nature ultimately are *conceptual:* they are embedded in a patriarchal conceptual framework and reflect a logic of domination which functions to explain, justify, and maintain the subordination of both women and nature. Eco-feminism, therefore, encourages us to think ourselves out of "patriarchal conceptual traps,"[10] by *reconceptualizing* ourselves and our relation to the nonhuman natural world in nonpatriarchal ways.

What makes a critique of patriarchal conceptual frameworks distinctively "eco-feminist" has to do with the interconnections among the four minimal condition claims of eco-feminism. First, and most obviously, the critique is used to show that there are important connections between the oppression of women and the oppression of nature (condition [i]). Second, by understanding how a patriarchal conceptual framework sanctions the oppression of both women and nature (condition [ii]), eco-feminists are in a position to show why "naturism" (i.e., the domination of nature) ought to be included among the systems of oppression maintained by patriarchy. This opens the door for showing how, in Sheila Collins' words,

> Racism, sexism, class exploitation, and ecological destruction are four interlocking pillars upon which the structure of patriarchy rests.[11]

Third, the critique of patriarchal conceptual frameworks is grounded in familiar ecological principles: everything is interconnected with everything else; all parts of an ecosystem have equal value; there is no free lunch; "nature knows best"; healthy, balanced ecosystems must maintain diversity; there is unity in diversity.[12] This grounding is the basis for the uniquely eco-feminist position that an adequate feminist theory and practice embrace an ecological perspective (condition [iii]). Fourth, the critique goes two ways: not only must a proper feminist theory and practice reflect an ecological perspective (condition [iii]); the ecological movement must embrace a feminist perspective (condition [iv]). Otherwise, the ecological movement will fail to make the conceptual connections between the oppression of women and the oppression of nature (and to link these to other systems of oppression), and will risk utilizing strategies and implementing solutions which contribute to the continued subordination of women.

The stakes are high. If eco-feminism is correct, then a feminist debate over ecology is much deeper and more basic to both the feminist and ecology movements than traditional construals of feminism or ecology might have us believe. What is at stake is not only the success of the feminist and ecology movements, but the theoretical adequacy of feminism itself.

AN ECO-FEMINIST CRITIQUE OF THE FOUR LEADING VERSIONS OF FEMINISM

Feminism traditionally has been construed as the movement to end the oppression of women. All feminists agree that the oppression of women (i.e., the unequal and unjust status of women) exists, is wrong, and ought to be changed. But feminists disagree markedly about how to understand that oppression and how to bring about the necessary changes.

In her book *Feminist Politics and Human Nature,* Alison Jaggar offers an extensive analysis of the four leading versions of feminism and the key respects in which these theories differ. In what follows, I use Jaggar's analysis as the basis for my account of the eco-feminist critique of the leading versions of feminism.

Liberal Feminism

Liberal feminism emanates from the classical liberal tradition that idealizes a society in which autonomous individuals are provided maximal freedom to pursue their own interests. Liberal feminists trace the oppression of women to the lack of equal legal rights and unfair disadvantages in the public domain. Hence, the liberation of women requires the elimination of those legal and social constraints that prevent women from exercising their right to self-determination.

Liberal feminism endorses a highly individualistic conception of human nature. Humans are essentially separate, rational agents engaged in competition to maximize their own interests. The "mental" capacity to reason, i.e., the capacity to act in accordance with objective principles and to be consistent in the pursuit of ends, is what grounds the basic, essential, and equal dignity of all individuals. Basic human properties (e.g., rationality, autonomy, dignity) are ascribed to individuals independent of any historical or social context, and moral consideration is due humans on the basis of these distinctive human properties.

Because humans are conceived as essentially separate rational agents, a liberal feminist epistemology construes the attainment of knowledge as an individual project. The liberal feminist epistemological goal is to formulate value-neutral, intersubjectively verifi-

able, and universalizable rules that enable any rational agent to attain knowledge "under a veil of ignorance." Both genuine knowledge and "the moral point of view" express the impartial point of view of the rational, detached observer.

There are two sorts of ecological implications of liberal feminism. Both are generated within a liberal framework that applies traditional moral and legal categories to nonhumans. They are liberal feminist insofar as the ecological perspective is based on the same sorts of considerations that liberal feminists have appealed to traditionally in arguments for equal rights, equal opportunities, or fair consideration for women.

The first ecological implication draws the line of moral considerability at humans, separating humans from nonhumans and basing any claims to moral consideration for nonhumans either on the alleged rights or interests of humans, or on the consequences of such consideration for human well-being. Liberal feminists who do (or might) take this stance justify such practices as legal protection of endangered species, restrictions on the use of animals in laboratory research, or support for the appropriate technology, anti-nuclear, and peace movements on the grounds that they are mandated by consideration of the rights, interests, or well-being of present or future generations of humans (including women, mothers, and children).

The second extends the line of moral considerability to qualified nonhumans on the grounds that they, like women (or humans), are deserving of moral consideration in their own right: they are rational, sentient, interest carriers, or right holders.[13] According to this second sort of ecological stance, responsible environmental practices toward nonhumans are justified on the grounds that individual nonhumans share certain morally relevant characteristics with humans in virtue of which they are deserving of protection or moral consideration.

From an eco-feminist perspective, both sorts of ecological implications are inadequate or at least seriously problematic. First, both basically keep intact a patriarchal conceptual framework characterized by value-hierarchical thinking and oppositional normative dualisms: humans over and against nature, the "mind" (or "rational") over and against the "body" (or the "nonrational"). As such, although liberal feminist ecological concerns may expand the traditional ethical framework to include moral and legal consideration of qualified nonhumans, or even to include the instrumental value of ecosystemic well-being for human welfare, they will be unacceptable to eco-feminists.

Second, the extreme individualism of a liberal feminist ecological perspective conflicts with the eco-feminist emphasis on the independent value of the integrity, diversity, and stability of ecosystems, and on the ecological themes of interconnectedness, unity in diversity, and equal value to all parts of the human-nature system. It also conflicts with "ecological ethics" per se. Ecological ethics are holistic, not individualistic; they take the value and well-being of a species, community, or ecosystem, and not merely of particular individuals, let alone human individuals, as basic. For eco-feminists, an ecological ethics based on a "web-like" view of relationships among all life forms conflicts with the hierarchical rules and individual rights-based ethics of the liberal ethical tradition.

The eco-feminist critique of hierarchical rights- and rules-based ethical models reflects current feminist scholarship on ethics and moral reasoning. For example, in her recent book *In a Different Voice*, psychologist Carol Gilligan compares highly individualized and hierarchical rules- and rights-oriented ethics (embedded in the liberal tradition) with web-like and contextual ethics of care and reciprocal responsibility.[14] She argues that the two ethical orientations reflect important differences in moral reasoning between men and women, and on such basic issues as the conception of the self, morality, and conflict resolution. In her article "Moral Revolution," philosopher Kathryn Pyne Addelson argues that there is a bias in "our world view" by the near exclusion of women from the domain of intellectual pursuits, "a bias that requires a revolutionary change in ethics to remedy."[15] According to Addelson:

> It is a bias that allows moral problems to be defined from the top of various hierarchies of authority in such a way that the existence of the authority is concealed, and so the existence of alternative definitions that might challenge that authority and radically change our social organization is also concealed.[16]

Addelson's criticism of traditional ethics is at the same time a criticism of liberal feminism: the liberal feminist ethical tradition (what Addelson calls "the Judith Thomson tradition") assumes that defining moral problems from the top of the hierarchy is the "official" or "correct" or "legitimate" point of view;[17] it does not notice that "dominant-subordinate social structures are *creators* of inequality."[18] By contrast, what Addelson calls "the Jane tradition" uses the per-

ceptions and power of a subordinate group—women—"to eliminate dominant-subordinate structures through the creation of new social forms which do not have that structure."[19] The women of the Jane tradition, unlike those of the Thomson tradition, challenge the patriarchal conceptual framework which defines "our" worldview, how things "really are," and how things "ought to be," and which assumes the superiority of the hierarchical rules- and rights-approach to ethics.

Whatever else the strengths and weaknesses of the Gilligan and Addelson accounts of alternative ethical frameworks, their contributions to a discussion of eco-feminism are noteworthy. Each provides important reasons for being suspicious of approaches to feminism, ethics, or ecological concerns based on a patriarchal conceptual framework. To the extent that the ecological implications of liberal feminism do so, they perpetuate the sort of thinking and bias which, according to Gilligan and Addelson, fails to pay adequate attention to other values (e.g., care, friendship, reciprocity in relationships) and to the epistemological and moral point of view of a subordinate group in our society: women. The Gilligan and Addelson accounts thereby provide the sorts of reasons eco-feminists offer for rejecting a liberal feminist ecology.

Traditional Marxist Feminism

Traditional Marxist feminism views the oppression of women, like the oppression of workers, as a direct result of the institution of class society and, under capitalism, of private property. The specific oppression of women is due to the sexual division of labor whereby women are excluded from the public realm of production and occupy dependent economic positions in the traditional monogamous family. Thus, the liberation of women requires that the traditional family be dissolved as an economic (though not necessarily as a social) unit. As Engels states in a much quoted sentence, "The first condition of the liberation of the wife is to bring the whole female sex into public industry."[20] Since women's oppression is a class oppression, women's liberation will be a class movement accomplished together with male workers by overthrowing capitalism.

For traditional Marxist feminists (like traditional Marxists generally), the essential human activity is not pure thought or reason (as liberals assume) but conscious and productive activity—*praxis*. Praxis is conscious physical labor directed at transforming the material world to meet human needs. Humans are distinguished from nonhumans by their ability to consciously and purposefully transpose their environment to meet their material needs through the activity of praxis.[21]

Since human nature is developed historically and socially through praxis, human nature is not a fixed or immutable condition. Furthermore, since human nature is understood in terms of praxis, humans are only truly free when they engage in productive activity which extends beyond the satisfaction of basic survival needs. For traditional Marxist feminists, women will be free when they are economically independent and when their work expresses the full development of human productive activity (or praxis), rather than the coercion of economic necessity.

A Marxist feminist epistemology is a radical departure from that of liberal feminism. Since humans are viewed as necessarily existing in dialectical relationship with each other, knowledge is viewed as a social construction; it is part of the basic shared human activity of praxis. The development of knowledge is not an individual undertaking, and there is no value-neutral knowledge accessible to some impartial, detached observer. For traditional Marxist feminists, "all forms of knowledge are historically determined by the prevailing mode of production."[22]

In *Marx and Engels on Ecology,* Howard L. Parsons discusses four general sorts of ecological criticisms which have been raised against traditional Marxism:

> Marx, Engels, and Marxism, generally have been criticized for certain alleged positions on ecological matters: (1) they have pitted man against nature; (2) they have anthropocentrically denied the values of external nature; (3) they have overstressed the conflicts in nature and have understressed its harmony; and (4) they have denied basic human values.[23]

These criticisms rest on such Marxist claims as "nature is man's inorganic body," man is "the real conscious master of Nature," and "the purely natural material in which *no* human labor is objectified . . . has no value."[24] The alleged criticisms are that since such claims emphasize the use value of the natural world in the production of economic goods (e.g., food, clothing, shelter), the transformation of nature to meet human material needs in the essential human activity of praxis, and the domination, mastery, or control of nature "by man," Marxism is not a suitable basis for an ecological ethic.[25]

Whether traditional Marxism can overcome these objections is being rigorously debated; it is beyond the scope of this paper to discuss that issue here. Nonetheless, it is important to indicate what the particular challenges are for traditional Marxist feminism from an eco-feminist perspective.

First, given the primacy of class in the traditional Marxist feminist account of oppression and liberation, a Marxist feminist must reconcile traditional Marxist claims about nature with a political vision that does not pit men and women, as one class, over and against nature. Otherwise, the sort of patriarchal conceptual framework which traditionally has sanctioned the exploitation of nature will survive relatively unscathed, even if women get elevated to equal status with men (but against nature).

Second, traditional Marxists argue that environmental problems under capitalism will continue as long as the means of production (i.e., the raw materials, land, energy resources) and forces of production (i.e., the factories, machinery, skills) are used to support environmental research and development in the interest of expanding capital. Marxist feminists must show that a liberating or appropriate technology and science, based on ecological principles, could help protect and preserve, rather than exploit, nature.

Perhaps the most significant challenge to a plausible Marxist eco-feminism, however, lies in a third area of difficulty, viz., its general failure to take seriously gender as a constitutive category of social reality. This "gender blindness" in traditional Marxist analyses of women's oppression serves to distort, rather than clarify, the nature of women's oppression. Since eco-feminism assumes that the connections between the oppression of women and the oppression of nature have to do with sex-gender systems, a "gender blind" traditional Marxist feminism will be hard pressed to make visible those connections.

Radical Feminism

Radical feminism departs from both liberal feminism and traditional Marxist feminism by rooting women's oppression in reproductive biology and a sex-gender system. According to radical feminists, patriarchy (i.e., the systematic domination by men) oppresses women in sex-specific ways by defining women as beings whose primary functions are either to bear and raise children (i.e., to be mothers) or to satisfy male sexual desires (i.e., to be sex objects). Since the oppression of women is based on "male control of women's fertility and women's sexuality," the liberation of women is to "end male control of women's bodies" by dismantling patriarchy.[26] Women will be free when no longer bound by the constraints of compulsory heterosexuality and compulsory child-bearing and child-rearing roles.

Insofar as there is one radical feminist conception of human nature,[27] it is that humans are essentially embodied. We are not (as the Cartesian philosophical tradition might have us suppose) bodiless minds, i.e., "mental" or thinking beings whose essential nature exists independently from our own or others' physical, emotional, or sexual existence. By taking women's bodies, and, in particular, women's reproductive biology, as indispensable to women's nature, radical feminism brings child-bearing and child-rearing functions into the political arena. It makes women's sex politically significant. It is in this way that for the radical feminist, "the personal is (profoundly) political."

A radical feminist epistemology self-consciously explores strategies (e.g., consciousness-raising processes) to correct the distortions of patriarchal ideology. It emphasizes a variety of sources of reliable knowledge (e.g., intuition, feelings, spiritual or mystical experiences) and the integration of women's felt mystical/intuitive/spiritual experiences into feminist theory and epistemology. Challenging the traditional "political versus spiritual" dichotomy, many radical feminists support a "politics of women's spirituality" which makes a spiritual ingredient necessary to any adequate feminist political theory.[28]

Radical feminists have had the most to say about eco-feminism. Taking up the question "Are women closer to nature than men?" some radical feminists (e.g., so-called "nature feminists," Mary Daly, Susan Griffin, Starhawk) have answered "yes." They applaud the close connections between women and nature, and urge women to celebrate their bodies, rejoice in our place in the community of inanimate and animate beings, and seek symbols that can transform our spiritual consciousness so as to be more in tune with nature. Other radical feminists answer "no"; they criticize nature feminists for regressing to harmful patriarchal sex-role stereotyping which feeds the prejudice that women have specifically female or womanly interests in preventing pollution, nurturing animals, or saving the planet.[29]

Even though to date eco-feminism has tended to be associated with radical feminism, there are noteworthy worries about radical feminism from an eco-feminist perspective. First, since radical feminism generally pays little attention to the historical and material features of women's oppression (including the relevance of race, class, ethnic, and national background), it insufficiently articulates the extent to which women's oppression is grounded in concrete and diverse social structures. In this respect, it lacks the sort of theoretical leverage needed to reveal the interconnections between the oppression of nature and women, on the one hand, and other forms of oppression (e.g., racism, classism).

Second, it mystifies women's experiences to locate women closer to nature than men, just as it underplays important aspects of the oppression of women to deny the connection of women with nature, for the truth is that women, like men, are both connected to nature and separate from it, natural and cultural beings. Insofar as radical feminism comes down in favor of one side or the other of the nature-culture dualism—by locating women either on the nature or on the culture side—it mistakenly perpetuates the sort of oppositional, dualistic thinking for which patriarchal conceptual frameworks are criticized.

This last point raises a conceptual and methodological worry about radical feminism as a grounding of eco-feminist concerns; the worry has to do with framing the feminist debate over ecology in terms of the question "Are women closer to nature than men?"[30] In order for the question to be meaningfully raised, one must presuppose the legitimacy of the nature-culture dualism. The idea that one group of persons is, or is not, closer to nature than another group assumes the very nature-culture split that eco-feminism denies. As Joan Griscom puts it, "the question itself is flawed."[31] She argues:

> Since we are all part of nature, and since all of us, biology and culture alike, is part of nature, the question ultimately makes no sense.[32]

It is "unwitting complicity"[33] in the patriarchal mindset that accounts for the question being raised at all. Insofar as radical feminism engages in such complicity, its approach to the feminist debate over ecology is methodologically suspect and conceptually flawed.

Socialist Feminism

Socialist feminism attempts to integrate the insights of traditional Marxist feminism with those of radical feminism by making domination by class and by sex gender fundamental to women's oppression. The socialist feminist program applies the historical materialist method of traditional Marxism to issues of sex and gender made visible by radical feminists.[34] By widening the Marxist notions of praxis and production to include procreation and child rearing, socialist feminists argue that the economic system and sex-gender system are dialectically reinforced in historically specific ways.[35] Thus, for socialist feminists, the liberation of women requires the end of both capitalism and patriarchy.

The socialist feminist view of human nature is that humans are created historically and culturally through the dialectical interrelation of human biology, physical environment, and society.[36] Since contemporary society consists of groups of individuals defined by age, sex, class, race, nationality, and ethnic background, each of these is included in the conception of human nature. Differences between men and women are viewed as social constructions, not pre-social or biological givens. For the socialist feminist, even if human biology is in some sense determined, it is nonetheless also socially conditioned. As Jaggar puts it, "Biology is 'gendered' as well as sexed."[37] In this respect, according to Jaggar,

> The goal of socialist feminism is to abolish the social relations that constitute humans not only as workers and capitalists but also as women and men. . . . the ideal of socialist feminism is that women (and men) will disappear as socially constructed categories.[38]

Like traditional Marxist feminists, socialist feminists view knowledge as a social construction; like radical feminists, they claim that women, as a subordinate group, have a "special epistemological standpoint that makes possible a view of the world that is unavailable to capitalist or to working class men."[39] This "standpoint of women," as Jaggar calls it, is historical materialist as well as sex-gendered; it is constructed from and accounts for the felt experiences of women of different ages, classes, races, and ethnic and national backgrounds.[40]

Since socialist feminism is an attempt to wed the insights of traditional Marxist feminism and radical feminism, it might seem that it would provide the most promising theoretical framework for eco-feminist concerns. In fact, however, many socialist feminists have been quite guarded in their enthusiasm for ecological matters.[41] This is understandable. The Marxist side of their politics makes them suspicious of a radical feminist grounding of ecological concerns in women's spiritual or sex-gender-based connection with nature.

Some socialist feminists have attempted to make a place for eco-feminist concerns by interpreting the Marxist attitude of domination over nature as "the psychological result of a certain mode of organizing production."[42] They argue that what is needed are new modes of conceptualizing and organizing production which allow for both reproductive freedom for women and recognition of the independent value of nonhuman nature. From an eco-feminist perspective, such a reconceptualization of traditional Marxist views is necessary if women are not to be brought into public production with men over and against nature.

The attractiveness of socialist feminism from an eco-feminist perspective lies in its emphasis on the importance of factors in addition to sex gender and class for an understanding of the social construction of reality and the interconnections among various systems of oppression. But, as is, it is incomplete. From an eco-feminist perspective, insofar as socialist feminism does not explicitly address the systematic oppression of nature, it fails to give an account of one of the "four interlocking pillars upon which the structure of patriarchy rests"—sexism, racism, classism, *and* naturism.

TRANSFORMATIVE FEMINISM

So far I have argued that, from an eco-feminist perspective, there are good reasons to worry about the adequacy of each of the four leading versions of feminism as a theoretical grounding for eco-feminism. If this view is correct, what, then, is needed?

If one takes seriously eco-feminist claims about the nature and importance of the connections between the oppression of women and the oppression of nature, then I think what is needed is an integrative and transformative feminism, one that moves us beyond the current debate over the four leading versions of feminism and makes a responsible ecological perspective central to feminist theory and practice. In what follows, I offer a few suggestions about how such a transformative feminism might be developed.

First, a transformative feminism would expand upon the traditional conception of feminism as "the movement to end women's oppression" by recognizing and making explicit the interconnections between all systems of oppression. In this regard, a transformative feminism would be informed by the conception of feminism which has been advanced by many black feminists and Third World feminists articulating the needs and concerns of black women and women in development. These feminists have argued that because of the basic connections between sexist oppression and other forms of systematized oppression, feminism, properly understood, is a movement to end *all* forms of oppression.[43]

Socialist feminism has opened the door for such a transformative feminism by acknowledging the structural interconnections between sexism, racism, and classism; eco-feminism contributes insights about the important connections between the oppression of women and the oppression of nature. A transformative feminism would build on these insights to develop a more expansive and complete feminism, one which ties the liberation of women to the elimination of all systems of oppression.

Second, a transformative feminism must provide a central theoretical place for the diversity of women's experiences, even if this means abandoning the project of attempting to formulate one overarching feminist theory or one woman's voice.[44] This is in accordance with the basic goal of any theory. As Evelyn Fox Keller puts it:

> The essential goal of theory in general I take to be to represent our experience of the world in as comprehensive and inclusive a way as possible; in that effort we seek a maximal intersubjectivity.[45]

A transformative feminism would acknowledge the social construction of knowledge and conception of epistemology that takes seriously the felt experiences of women as a subordinate group—however different those experiences may be. As a related point, it would be a call to oppressed groups to collectively assert *for themselves* their felt experiences, needs, and distinctiveness. In this respect, it would reflect a commitment to what Iris Young calls "a politics of difference," viz., one that asserts the value and specificity of group difference in political theory and practice.[46]

Third, a transformative feminism would involve a rejection of a logic of domination and the patriarchal conceptual framework which gives rise to it. By showing how systems of oppression are rooted in this common conceptual framework, it would address the conceptual and structural interconnections among all forms of domination. In this way, it would encourage feminists concerned with ecology to join allegiance with those seeking to end oppression by race and class. Otherwise, feminist concerns over ecology would degenerate into a largely white middle-class movement. As Rosemary Ruether warns:

> The ethic of reconciliation with the earth has yet to break out of its snug corners of affluence and find meaningful cohesion with the revolution of insurgent people.[47]

The promise of a transformative feminism requires making connections with "the revolution of insurgent people."

Fourth, a transformative feminism would involve a rethinking of what it is to be human, especially as the conception of human nature becomes informed by a nonpatriarchal conception of the interconnections between human and nonhuman nature. This would involve a psychological restructuring of our attitudes and beliefs about ourselves and "our world" (including the nonhuman world), and a philosophical rethinking of the notion of the self such that we see ourselves as both comembers of an ecological community and yet different from other members of it.

Fifth, a transformative feminism would involve recasting traditional ethical concerns to make a central place for values (e.g., care, friendship, reciprocity in relationships, appropriate trust, diversity) underplayed or lost in traditional, particularly modern and contemporary, philosophical construals of ethics. It would include nonhierarchical models of morality and conflict resolution (e.g., consensual decision making and mediation) and involve a rethinking of the "moral point of view" in light of the social and historical context of human nature.

Sixth, a transformative feminism would involve challenging patriarchal bias in technology research and analysis and the use of appropriate science and technologies, i.e., those brought into the service of preserving, rather than destroying, the Earth.[48] Only then would the eco-feminist reconceptualization of the relationship between human and nonhuman nature come around full circle.

CONCLUSION

In this paper I have argued that from the perspective of eco-feminism, the four leading versions of feminism are inadequate, incomplete, or seriously problematic as a theoretical grounding of eco-feminist concerns. I have suggested that if eco-feminism is correct, then what is needed is a "transformative feminism." The adequacy of such a transformative feminism would depend on how accurately it captures and systematizes the points of view of women as oppressed persons, the insights of eco-feminism, and the interconnections between all systems of oppression.

When one describes a lake by looking down at it from above, or by only skimming across its surface, one gets a limited and partial view of the nature of the lake. It is only when one dives deep and looks at the lake from the bottom up that one sees the diversity and richness of the various life forms and processes that constitute the lake.

So, too, it is with feminist theorizing. It is only when we dive deep and conceptualize reality from the various points of view of women of different ages, races, ethnic and national backgrounds, however different those experiences may be, that our feminist theories will see the diversity and richness of those points of view. It is only when we dive deep and see the interconnections between various systems of oppression that our feminist theories will hold much water. A transformative feminism has the potential to make these connections. It has the potential for making the connections between feminism and ecology from the bottom up.

NOTES

1. Rosemary Radford Ruether, *New Woman/New Earth: Sexist Ideologies and Human Liberation* (New York: Seabury Press, 1975), p. 204.

2. Ibid.

3. Elizabeth Dodson Gray, *Green Paradise Lost* (Wellesley, MA: Roundtable Press, 1981), and *Patriarchy as a Conceptual Trap* (Wellesley, MA: Roundtable Press, 1982); Susan Griffin, *Women and Nature* (New York: Harper & Row, 1978); Mary Daly, *Gyn/Ecology: The Meta-Ethics of Radical Feminism* (Boston: Beacon Press, 1978); Carolyn Merchant, *The Death of Nature: Women, Ecology, and the Scientific Revolution* (New York: Harper & Row, 1983), and "Earthcare: Women and the Environmental Movement," *Environment,* 23 (1981): 2–13, 38–40; Joan L. Griscom, "On Healing the Nature/History Split in Feminist Thought," *Heresies #13: Feminism and Ecology,* 4 (1981): 4–9; Ynestra King, "Feminism and the Revolt of Nature," *Heresies #13: Feminism and Ecology,* 4 (1981): 12–16, and "The Eco-feminist Imperative," in *Reclaim the Earth: Women Speak Out for Life on Earth,* ed. Leonie Caldecott and Stephanie Leland (London: Women's Press, 1983), pp. 12–16, and "Toward an Ecological Feminism and a Feminist Ecology," in *Machina ex Dea: Feminist Perspectives on Technology,* ed. Joan Rothschild (New York: Pergamon Press, 1983), pp. 118–129; Ariel Kay Salleh, "Deeper Than Deep Ecology: The Eco-Feminist Connection," *Environmental Ethics,* 3 (1984): 339–345.

4. Although more traditional uses of the term *oppression* refer to domination or subordination of humans by humans, eco-feminists use the expression "oppression of nature" to refer to the domination or subordination of nonhuman nature by humans.

5. King, "Feminism and a Revolt of Nature," p. 12.

6. The minimal condition account given here does not, by itself, specify what counts as a "feminist perspective," an "ecological perspective," "feminist theory and practice," or "solutions to ecological problems." Nor does it specify whether a "science of ecology" must reflect a commitment to gender ideologies or in some sense be a "feminist science." Questions about the meaning, scope, and application of conditions (i) to (iv) are deliberately left open.

7. Gray, *Green Paradise Lost,* p. 20.

8. Ibid.

9. Alison M. Jaggar, *Feminist Politics and Human Nature* (Totowa, NJ: Rowman & Allanheld, 1983), p. 96. Joyce Trebilcot argues that "in feminism, there is a movement toward the elimination of all dualisms" because dualisms not only function evaluatively (to justify the "superior's" power over the "inferior") and epistemologically (they determine perceptions); they also function to determine in part the conception or meaning of the things related. Joyce Trebilcot, "Conceiving Women: Notes on the Logic of Feminism," in *Women and Values: Readings in Recent Feminist Philosophy,* ed. Marilyn Pearsall (Belmont, CA: Wadsworth, 1986), pp. 358–363.

10. Elizabeth Dodson Gray describes a "conceptual trap" as "a set of outmoded beliefs" and "a way of thinking that is like a room which—once inside—you cannot imagine a world outside." Gray, *Patriarchy as a Conceptual Trap,* pp. 16, 17.

11. Sheila D. Collins, *A Different Heaven and Earth* (Valley Forge, PA: Judson Press, 1974), p. 161. I take it that this account is compatible with there being other "pillars" on which patriarchal structures rest (e.g., "imperialism" in capitalist patriarchal structures).

12. See the discussions of eco-feminism given by King, "Toward an Ecological Feminism and a Feminist Ecology"; Don E. Marietta, Jr., "Environmentalism, Feminism, and the Future of American Society," *The Humanist,* 44 (1984): 15–18, 30; Merchant, "Earthcare: Women and the Environmental Movement."

13. For example, consider animal liberationism. According to Tom Regan's rights-based version of animal liberationism, individual nonhuman

animals have moral rights against humans which impose on us obligations to treat them in certain ways. Regan, *All That Dwell Therein: Essays on Animal Rights and Environmental Ethics* (Berkeley: University of California Press, 1982). According to Peter Singer's utilitarian-based version, our obligations to nonhuman animals are grounded in their capacity to feel pain and pleasure; failure to acknowledge that animals and other sentient nonhumans deserve moral consideration is just "speciesism," akin to racism, sexism, and classism, i.e., the view that humans are morally superior to animals. Singer, *Animal Liberation* (New York: New York Review/Random House, 1975). Both Regan's and Singer's versions of animal liberation extend traditional liberal ethical concerns to individual nonhumans on the basis of certain morally relevant characteristics they allegedly share with humans.

14. Carol Gilligan, *In a Different Voice* (Cambridge, MA: Harvard University Press, 1982).

15. Kathryn Pyne Addelson, "Moral Revolution," in *Women and Values*, p. 306.

16. Ibid., p. 307.

17. Ibid.

18. Ibid., p. 306.

19. Ibid.

20. Friedrich Engels, *The Origin of the Family, Private Property and the State* (New York: International Publishers, 1972), pp. 137–138.

21. For example, Marx writes, "Men can be distinguished from animals by consciousness, by religion or by anything else you like. They themselves begin to distinguish themselves from animals as soon as they begin to *produce* their means of subsistence, a step which is conditioned by their physical organization." Karl Marx and Friedrich Engels, *The German Ideology*, ed. with an introduction by C. J. Arthur (New York: International Publishers, 1970), p. 42.

22. Jaggar, *Feminist Politics and Human Nature*, p. 358.

23. *Marx and Engels on Ecology*, ed. Howard L. Parsons (Westport, CT: Greenwood Press, 1977), p. 35. Parsons defends Marx, Engels, and Marxism against each of these criticisms.

24. Ibid., pp. 133, 141, and 122.

25. For recent discussions of problems for an environmentally attractive interpretation of traditional Marxist doctrine, see Val Routley, "On Karl Marx as an Environmental Hero," *Environmental Ethics*, 3 (1981): 237–244; Hwa Yol Jung, "Marxism, Ecology, and Technology," *Environmental Ethics*, 5 (1983): 169–171; Charles Tolman, "Karl Marx, Alienation, and the Mastery of Nature," *Environmental Ethics*, 3 (1981): 63–74. For a defense of a Marxian ecological ethic, see Donald C. Lee, "On the Marxian View of the Relationship Between Man and Nature," *Environmental Ethics*, 2 (1980): 3–16, and "Toward a Marxian Ecological Ethic: A Response to Two Critics," *Environmental Ethics*, 4 (1982): 339–343; Parsons, *Marx and Engels on Ecology*.

26. Jaggar, *Feminist Politics and Human Nature*, p. 266.

27. Jaggar identifies four radical feminist conceptions of human nature. Ibid., pp. 11–12, 85–105.

28. See Charlene Spretnak, "Introduction," in *The Politics of Women's Spirituality*, ed. Charlene Spretnak (New York: Doubleday, 1982), p. xxx, n. 20.

29. For a discussion of these two radical feminist positions, see King, "Feminism and the Revolt of Nature."

30. Sherry B. Ortner was one of the first to address this question in her article, "Is Female to Male As Nature Is to Culture?" in *Woman, Culture, and Society*, ed. Michelle Rosaldo and Louise Lamphere (Stanford, CA: Stanford University Press, 1974), pp. 67–87.

31. Griscom, "On Healing the Nature/Culture Split in Feminist Thought," p. 9.

32. Ibid.

33. The phrase "unwitting complicity" is from King, "Feminism and the Revolt Against Nature," p. 15.

34. Jaggar, *Feminist Politics and Human Nature*, p. 124.

35. Ibid., p. 129.

36. Ibid., p. 125.

37. Ibid., p. 126.

38. Ibid., p. 132.

39. Ibid., p. 126.

40. According to Jaggar, a "standpoint" is "a position in society from which certain features of reality come into prominence and from which others are obscured" (ibid., p. 382). The "standpoint of women" is "that perspective which reveals women's true interests and this standpoint is reached only through scientific and political struggle. Those who construct the standpoint of women must begin from women's experience as

women describe it, but they must go beyond that experience theoretically and ultimately may require that women's experiences be redescribed" (ibid., p. 384).

41. For example, in her otherwise thorough treatment of socialist feminism in *Feminist Politics and Human Nature*, Alison Jaggar explicitly addresses the issue of the connection between socialist feminism and ecology in less than one full page (pp. 306–307). From an eco-feminist perspective, such a limited treatment of the feminism-ecology connection leaves the incorrect impression that ecology is not, or is not a very important, feminist issue. Furthermore, this (what might be called "ecology blindness") reinforces oppositional thinking which separates discussions of political philosophy from the life sciences (e.g., ecology) and discussions of human nature from non-human nature. From an eco-feminist perspective, it thereby reinforces the mistaken view that an adequate feminist political theory can be articulated without incorporation of an ecological perspective, and that an adequate theory of human nature can be articulated without essential reference to nonhuman nature.

42. Ibid., p. 306.

43. See, e.g., bell hooks, *Feminist Theory: From Margin to Center* (Boston: South End Press, 1984), pp. 17–31; "The Combahee River Collective Statement," in *Home Girls: A Black Feminist Anthology,* ed. Barbara Smith (New York: Kitchen Table Women of Color Press, 1983), p. 272; Gita Sen and Caren Gowen, *Development, Crisis and Alternative Visions: Third World Women's Perspectives* (New Delhi: DAWN, 1985), p. 13.

44. For an account of reasons to be wary of attempts to articulate "the women's voice," see Maria Lugones and Elizabeth V. Spelman, "Have We Got a Theory for You! Feminist Theory, Cultural Imperialism and the Woman's Voice," *Women's Studies International Forum,* 6 (1983): 573–581.

45. Evelyn Fox Keller, "Women, Science, and Popular Mythology," in *Machina ex Dea: Feminist Perspectives on Technology,* p. 134.

46. Iris Marion Young, "Elements of a Politics of Difference," read at the Second Annual North American Society for Social Philosophy, Colorado Springs, August 1985.

47. Rosemary Radford Ruether, "Mother Earth and the Megamachine," in *Woman-Spirit Rising: A Feminist Reader in Religion,* ed. Carol Christ and Judith Plaskow (San Francisco: Harper & Row, 1979), p. 51.

48. For a discussion of a variety of feminist perspectives on science and technology, see Rothschild, *Machina ex Dea;* see also Judy Smith, *Something Old, Something New, Something Borrowed, Something Due* (Missoula, MT: Women and Technology Network, 1980).

DISCUSSION QUESTIONS

1. What is "transformative feminism," and how is it different from other forms of feminism?

2. Why are liberal feminism, traditional Marxist feminism, radical feminism, and socialist feminism inadequate, incomplete, or problematic as theoretical foundations for eco-feminism? Which of the leading four versions of feminism comes the closest to supporting eco-feminism? Why?

3. How might William Baxter and Peter Wenz respond to eco-feminism? What are the similarities and differences between Wenz's deep ecology and Warren's eco-feminism? Between Baxter's anthropocentric perspective and Warren's eco-feminism?

4. Warren talks about the similarities between the oppression of nature and the oppression of women. Do you agree with her assessment? Why or why not?

5. Do you agree with Warren that there are interconnections between all forms of oppression? If so, why? If not, why not? Think specifically about the oppression of animals by humans and the oppression of humans based on race and religion.

6. How might Aldo Leopold respond to Warren's eco-feminism? What similarities and differences do you find between their views?

KARL GROSSMAN

Environmental Racism

Karl Grossman points out connections between race, poverty, and the environment. Grossman reports that "people of color have been the worst victim of environmental pollution for a long time." He cites a number of studies concluding that "communities of color are where most of America's places of poison are located." One study, for example, stated that "communities with the greatest number of commercial hazardous waste facilities had the highest composition of ethnic residents." The article concludes with a plea for us to be as "vigilant in attacking environmental racism as racism in health care, housing and schools."

Karl Grossman has specialized in investigative reporting on environmental and energy issues for thirty years. His books include *Cover Up: What You Are Not Supposed to Know About Nuclear Power* (1980), *The Poison Conspiracy* (1983), and *The Wrong Stuff: The Space Program's Nuclear Threat to Our Planet* (1997). He is a principal in EnviroVideo, a New York–based company that produces environmental documentary and news programming. He is also a professor of journalism at the State University of New York/College at Old Westbury. Among other citations, he has received the George Polk Award, the John Peter Zenger Award, and the James Aronson Award for journalism.

"We're sitting in a center of a donut surrounded by a hazardous waste incinerator that gives off PCB's, seven landfills that are constantly growing—they look like mountains," Hazel Johnson was saying. "There are chemical plants, a paint factory, two steel mills which give off odors, and lagoons filled with all kinds of contaminants that emit 30,000 tons of poison into the air each year. And there's a water reclamation district where they dry sludge out in the open. The smell is horrible, like bodies decomposing."

Mrs. Johnson was describing Atgeld Gardens, a housing project in which 10,000 people, nearly all African-Americans, reside on the Southeast Side of Chicago, surrounded on every side by sources of pollution.

The result: environmental diseases and death.

"We have lots of cancer, respiratory problems, birth deformities," Mrs. Johnson went on. "Just the other day, there were three cancer deaths. Then more. We've been having babies born with brain tumors. One baby was born with her brain protruding from her head. She's two now, blind and she can't walk. My daughter was five months pregnant. She took ultra-sound and the doctors found the baby had no behind, no head," said Mrs. Johnson, the mother of seven. "The baby had to be aborted."

Mrs. Johnson has no doubt that "the terrible health problems we have in our community are related to the pollution," the product of trying to live amid one of the most concentrated areas of environmental contamination in the U.S.

And she is clear about why her area gets dumped on: because it is largely inhabited by African-Americans and Hispanics. "In Chicago, everything is mostly dumped out in this area where we are. They figure that we're not going to come out and protest and disagree." But Mrs. Johnson has, for 10 years now, as the head of People for Community Recovery, been fighting back.

"Atgeld Gardens symbolizes environmental racism," the Rev. Benjamin Chavis, Jr., the noted civil rights leader and executive director of the United Church

Karl Grossman, *The Crisis*, vol. 98, no. 4 (April 1991): 14–17, 31–32. Jeffrey Di Leo wishes to thank The Crisis Publishing Co., Inc., the publisher of the magazine of the National Association for the Advancement of Colored People, for authorizing the use of this work.

of Christ's Commission for Racial Justice, declared. "The community is surrounded on all four sides by pollution and has one of the highest cancer rates in the nation. The public officials in Chicago are well aware of the circumstances that these people are forced to live in, yet, because of their race, the city has no priority in stopping this type of environmental injustice."

Rev. Chavis was the first to use the term "environmental racism" in 1987 with the release of what has become a landmark study by the commission, "Toxic Wastes and Race in the United States." It has taken several years for the import of the report, notes Rev. Chavis, to take hold.

But now that has well begun. There have been a series of important events, including a week-long tour by the Rev. Jesse Jackson, shortly before Earth Day 1990, of low-income minority communities struck by pollution. He stressed the "relationship between environment and empowerment" and declared it "a new day and a new way. No longer will corporations be allowed to use job blackmail to poison poor people be they black, brown, yellow, red, or white. We are demanding that all corporate poisoners sign agreements to stop the poisoning of our communities."

Rev. Jackson was accompanied by Dennis Hayes, a principal organizer of both the original Earth Day, in 1970, and last year's event, and John O'Connor, executive director of the National Toxics Campaign who emphasized that "for the environmental movement to be successful in saving the planet, it must include all races, ethnic groups, rich and poor, black and white, and young and old. When our movement to clean up the nation is truly a reflection of all people in the country, it is at that point that we will succeed in stopping the poisoning of America."

Issuing a report in 1990, at a National Minority Health Conference in Washington on environmental contamination, describing how "a marriage of the movement for social justice with environmentalism" was taking place was the Panos Institute. "Organizing for environmental justice among people of color has grown from a small group of activists in the 1970s to a movement involving thousands of people in neighborhoods throughout the U.S.," said Dana A. Alston, director of the Environment, Community Development and Race Project of Panos, an international group that works for "sustainable development." She added in the report, "We Speak for Ourselves: Social Justice, Race and Environment," that "communities of color have often taken a more holistic approach than the main-

stream environmental movement, integrating 'environmental' concerns into a broader agenda that emphasizes social, racial, and economic justice."

In Atlanta in 1990, at a conference on environmental problems in minority areas sponsored by the federal Agency for Toxic Substances and Disease Registry and others, attended by 300 community leaders, doctors and governmental officials, Dr. Aubrey F. Manley, deputy assistant secretary of the Department of Health and Human Services, stated, "Poor and minority organizations charged eight major national environmental groups with racism in their hiring practices and demanded that they substantially increase the number of people of color on their staffs." The environmental groups acknowledged the problem—"The truth is that environmental groups have done a miserable job of reaching out to minorities," said Frederick D. Krupp, executive director of the Environmental Defense Fund—and set up an Environmental Consortium for Minority Outreach.

And last year, too, the Commission for Racial Justice organized a workshop on racism and the environment for the Congressional Black Caucus whose members, unbeknownst to many, are rated as having among the best pro environmental voting records in Congress by the League of Conservation Voters, which scores Congressional representatives on their environmental records.

A key event to be held this year will be the first National Minority Environmental Leadership Summit in Washington, D.C., in October. "We want to bring together leaders of community groups, environmental groups, civil rights organizations and academic, scientific, governmental and corporate organizations to participate in this three-day corporate meeting," says Charles Lee, research director of the Commission for Racial Justice, which is organizing the gathering. "The purpose of this summit is to develop a comprehensive and tangible national agenda of action that will help reshape and redirect environmental policy-making in the United States to fully embrace the concerns of minority Americans."

People of color have been the worst victim of environmental pollution for a long time. Lee tells of the building of the Gauley Bridge in West Virginia in the 1930's: "Hundreds of African-American workers from the Deep South were brought in by the New Kanawha Power Company, a subsidiary of the Union Carbide Corporation, to dig the Hawks Nest tunnel. Over a two-year period, approximately 500 workers died and 1,500 were disabled from silicosis, a lung disease similar to Black Lung. Men literally dropped on their feet breathing air so thick with microscopic silica that they could not see more than a yard in front of them. Those who came out for air were beaten back into the tunnel with ax handles. At subsequent Congressional hearings, New Kanawha's contractor revealed, "I knew I was going to kill these niggers, but I didn't know it was going to be this soon."

Lee relates how "an undertaker was hired to bury dead workers in unmarked graves" and of his agreeing "to perform the service for an extremely low rate because the company assured him there would be a large number of deaths."

But it was not until recent years that this and other horror stories of environmental racism started to be examined in their systematic context.

It was in 1982 that residents of predominantly African-American Warren County, North Carolina, asked the Commission for Racial Justice for help in their protests against the siting of a dump for PCB's—the acronym for polychlorinated biphenyls, a carcinogen. In a campaign of civil disobedience that ensued, there were more than 500 arrests, including the commission's Rev. Chavis, Dr. Joseph Lowery of the Southern Christian Leadership Conference, and Congressman Walter Fauntroy of Washington.

It was during that effort that Rev. Chavis began considering the connection between the dumping in Warren County and the federal government's Savannah River nuclear facility, long a source of radioactive leaks and located in a heavily African-American area of South Carolina, and the "largest landfill in the nation" in the mainly black community of Emelle, Alabama. "We began to see evidence of a systematic pattern which led us to a national study," recounted Rev. Chavis.

That study—"Toxic Wastes and Race in the United States"—clearly shows what Rev. Chavis suspected: communities of color are where most of America's places of poison are located. In detail, the analysis looked at a cross-section of the thousands of U.S. "commercial hazardous water facilities" (defined by the U.S. Environmental Protection Agency as places licensed for "treating, storing or disposing of hazardous wastes") and "uncontrolled toxic waste sites" (defined by EPA as closed and abandoned sites), and correlated them with the ethnicity of the communities in which they are located.

Some of the study's major findings:

- "Race proved to be the most influential among variables tested in association with the location of commercial hazardous waste facilities. This represented a consistent national pattern."

- "Communities with the greatest number of commercial hazardous waste facilities had the highest composition of ethnic residents."

- "Although socio-economic status appeared to play an important role in the location of commercial hazardous waste facilities, race still proved to be more significant."

- "Three out of every five black and Hispanic Americans lived in communities with uncontrolled toxic waste sites."

- "Blacks were heavily over-represented in the populations of metropolitan areas with the largest number of uncontrolled toxic waste sites"—Memphis, St. Louis, Houston, Cleveland, Chicago, and Atlanta.

- "Approximately half of all Asian/Pacific Islanders and American Indians lived in communities with uncontrolled toxic waste sites."

The analysis called for change. "This report firmly concludes that hazardous wastes in black, Hispanic and other racial and ethnic communities should be made a priority issue at all levels of government. This issue is not currently at the forefront of the nation's attention. Therefore, concerned citizens and policymakers, who are cognizant of this growing national problem, must make this a priority concern."

It called for: the U.S. president "to issue an executive order mandating federal agencies to consider the impact of current policies and regulations on racial and ethnic communities"; state governments "to evaluate and make appropriate revisions in their criteria for the siting of new hazardous waste facilities to adequately take into account the racial and socio-economic characteristics of potential host communities"; the U.S. Conference of Mayors, the National Conference of Black Mayors and the National League of Cities "to convene a national conference to address these issues from a municipal perspective"; and civil rights and political organizations to gear up voter registration campaigns as a means to further empower racial and ethnic communities to effectively respond to hazardous wastes in racial and ethnic communities at the top of state and national legislative agendas."

Environmentalist Barry Commoner commented that the report showed the "functional relationship between poverty, racism and powerlessness and the chemical industry's assault on the environment."

It was in 1978 that sociologist Robert Bullard first began exploring environmental racism. He was asked by Linda McKeever Bullard, his wife, to conduct a study on the siting of municipal landfills and incinerators in Houston for a class-action lawsuit challenging a plan to site a new landfill in the "solid middle class," mostly African-American Houston neighborhood of Northwood Manor, notes Bullard. Just out of graduate school, a new professor at Texas Southern University, he found that from the 1920s to that time, all five of Houston's landfills and six out of eight of its incinerators were sited in black neighborhoods. That led to wider studies by Dr. Bullard on how "black communities, because of their economic and political vulnerability, have been routinely targeted for the siting of noxious facilities, locally unwanted land uses and environmental hazards."

He wrote several papers and, last year, his book, *Dumping in Dixie: Race, Class, and Environmental Quality,* came out. Black communities are consistently the ones getting dumped on "because of racism, plain and simple," says Dr. Bullard, now a professor at the University of California at Riverside.

Often it is a promise of "jobs, jobs, and jobs that are held out as a savior" for these communities although, in fact, "these are not labor-intensive industries." The companies involved, meanwhile, figure they can "minimize their investment" by avoiding the sort of lawsuit more likely to be brought by a white community faced with having a toxic dump, an incinerator, a paper mill, a slaughterhouse, a lead smelter, a pesticide plant, "you name it," said Dr. Bullard. Also, with planning and zoning boards commonly having "excluded people of color," the skids are further greased. And to top it off, "because of housing patterns and limited mobility, middle-income and lower-income blacks," unlike whites, often cannot "vote with their feet" and move out when a polluting facility arrives. "Targeting certain communities for poison is another form of discrimination," charged Dr. Bullard.

He tells in *Dumping in Dixie* of how African-Americans in Houston and Dallas; in Alsen, Louisiana; Institute, West Virginia; and Emelle, Alabama "have taken on corporate giants who would turn their areas into toxic wastelands." He is enthused by the existence of how "literally hundreds of environmental justice groups are made up of people of color."

One of the many organizations is the Gulf Coast Tenants Association. "We have not only the dumping here, but we get the upfront stuff; this is where much of the petrochemical industry is centered, and where they produce a lot of the stuff," says Darryl Malek-Wiley, the New Orleans–based group's director of research. "Cancer Alley is the nickname for this area," speaking of the 75-mile swath along the Mississippi from Baton Rouge to New Orleans. The group offers courses in environmental education and assists people to fight environmental hazards in their communities and block the siting of new ones. The placement of hazardous facilities in black communities in the South follows a pattern of subjugation going back "hundreds of years," notes Malek-Wiley, with "the industrial age" giving this a new translation. And, he says, it should be viewed in connection with the dumping of hazardous waste in Third World countries.

Up North, in the middle of America's biggest city, New York, Peggy Shepard has been challenging environmental racism as a leader of West Harlem Environmental Action (WHE ACT). Obnoxious, "exploitive" facilities placed in our area in recent years, she notes, have included a huge sewage treatment plant, a "marine transfer station" for garbage, and yet another bus storage depot. "We organized around a series of issues in our community that turned out to be all environmental [in] nature." WHE ACT has been "networking with organizations around" New York City and found that what had happened to West Harlem is typical of what has occurred to other African-American and Hispanic neighborhoods. "We get so used to the stereotype that what environmentalism means is wildlife and the preservation of open space. There had not been sufficient movement on urban environmental problems: incinerators, sewage treatment plants, factories polluting the air, devastating occupational exposure."

Sulalman Mahdi is southeast regional director of the Center for Environment, Commerce and Energy in Atlanta. "Our work involves educating the African-American community around the whole question of the environment. I am particularly interested in bridging the civil rights movement and the environmental justice movement," says Mahdi.

He became involved in the "green" movement while working in the campaign for reparations in land for African-Americans for the injustices committed against them. Living in southern Georgia, near Brunswick, "a papermill town and smelling the sulfur all the time" from the papermill lands, he concluded as he choked on the putrid air, that "we need to fight for environmental protection or the land we seek might not be of any real value once it's returned."

He takes the African-American perspective on nature right back to Africa, and indeed is writing a book on African ecology. The African approach to nature "is very similar to that of the Native Americans," says Mahdi. He speaks of the "founder of agriculture, the founder of botany," both ancient Egyptians. He sees a solid "relationship between our freedom struggle" and battling the environmental abuse subjected on African-Americans, what he terms "environmental genocide."

Genocide is also the word used by Lance Hughes of Native Americans for a Clean Environment. "As states and various municipalities have been closing down a lot of dumps because of public opposition, the companies have been descending on the reservations across the country," says Hughes. Indian reservations are seen as good dump sites by their firms because they are considered sovereign entities not subject to local or state environmental restrictions.

The group of which he is director was formed six years ago because of radioactive contamination caused by a twin set of nuclear production facilities run by Kerr-McGee in northeast Oklahoma amid a large concentration of Native Americans. One produces nuclear fuel for weaponry, the other for nuclear power plants. Further, some of the nuclear waste generated at them is put in fertilizer throughout the state, and also by Kerr-McGee on 10,000 acres surrounding the nuclear facilities.

"The hay and cattle from that land is sold on the open market," says Hughes. The Native Americans who live in the area have many "unusual cancers" and a high rate of birth defects from "genetic mutation. It gets pretty sad," says Hughes, "with babies born without eyes, babies born with brain cancers."

Wildlife is also born deformed. "We found a nine-legged frog and a two-headed fish. And there was a four-legged chicken." Hughes emphasizes that the subjugation of Native Americans "is still going on. The name of the game has been changed, but I would call it the same—genocide, because that is exactly what the result is."

The Southwest Organizing Project (SWOP) is a multi-ethnic, multi-issue organization which began a decade ago in a predominantly Chicano area of Albuquerque, New Mexico. "We have a municipal landfill, the largest pig farm in the city of Albuquerque, a dogfood plant, Texaco, Chevron, General Electric, a sewage plant," says Richard Moore, SWOP co-director. This, he said, is typical of Hispanic and African-American communities in the Southwest.

"Wherever you find working class, ethnic communities you find environmental injustice," says Moore, whose group has grown to fight environmental racism throughout New Mexico. "We have been organizing door-to-door, building strong organizations, going up against pretty major organizations." Non-partisan voter registration has been a key tool. The group was also the founding organization of the Southwest Network of Environmental and Economic Justice, which Moore co-chairs, that brings together people in seven Southwest states also on a multi-ethnic, multi-issue basis.

Moore was one of the signatories of the letter sent to eight major environmental organizations protesting their lack of minority representation (example: of the 315 staff members of the Audubon Society, only three were black).

Importantly, not scored in that letter were three prominent national environmental groups: Greenpeace, the National Toxics Campaign, and Earth Island Institute. In a breakthrough, in contradiction to the pattern elsewhere, the president of Earth Island Institute is an African-American.

Carl Anthony is not only president of Earth Island Institute, headquartered in San Francisco, but director of its Urban Habitat program. "We're very interested in issues at two ends of the spectrum: global warming, the ozone layer, depletion of global resources—and the negative environmental impacts on communities of poor people and people of color. In order to bring these two concerns together," says Anthony, "we have to develop a new kind of thrust and a new kind of leadership in communities of color to address the needs of our communities and also the larger urban community in making a transaction to more sustainable urban patterns." Urban Habitat is "basically a clearinghouse for a lot of people all over the country who want to work on these issues. And it helps alert people from our community to the issues that concern them: toxics, energy issues, air quality, water quality."

Anthony, an architect, says he has "always been aware of environmental issues." He is a designer of buildings and is a professor of architecture at the University of California at Berkeley where he is now teaching a new course for the school, Race, Poverty, and the Environment. He speaks with great pleasure of his involvement with Earth Island Institute, but is dubious about whether some of the other national environmental groups will become fully multi-ethnic. They have long taken an "elitist perspective. I doubt that Audubon, for instance, will ever make a big push in this direction."

Chicago's Hazel Johnson has worked closely with Greenpeace, the national environmental group most committed to direct action. "I have a very good working relationship with Greenpeace. It is more than an action group. I have gone with Greenpeace to many places and they have come out to assist us." She spoke of one recent demonstration carried on by her People for Community Recovery against yet one more incinerator planned for her community in which, with Greenpeace, "we chained ourselves to trucks."

"Unequivocally," says Lee, of the Commission for Racial Justice, "minority communities are the communities most at risk to environmental pollution." He paints in words the panorama of pollution. There is the heavy exposure to pesticides of Hispanic farmworkers, including those in Delano, California, where "there is an estimated 300,000 pesticide-related cancers among farm workers each year."

There are the effects of radioactive contamination on Native Americans, especially the Navajos, the nation's primary work force in the mining of uranium—who have extreme cancer rates as a result. "There is lead poisoning of children in urban areas—with an estimated 55 percent of the victims being African-Americans," says Lee. There is the mess in Puerto Rico, "one of the most heavily polluted areas in the world," with U.S. petrochemical and pharmaceutical companies long having discharged toxics on a massive scale. All the people in the island's town of La Ciudad Cristiana were forced to be relocated due to mercury poisoning. The terrible stories go on and on. Says Lee: "We still have a long way to go in truly addressing this issue."

"To understand the causes of these injustices, it is important to view them in a historical context," he notes. "Two threads of history help to explain the disproportionate impact of toxic pollution on racial and ethnic communities. The first is the long history of oppression and exploitation of African-Americans, Hispanic Americans, Asian-Americans, Pacific Islanders, and Native Americans. This has taken the form of genocide, chattel slavery, indentured servitude, and racial discrimination in employment, housing and practically all aspects of life in the United States. We suffer today from the remnant of this sordid history, as well as from new and institutionalized forms of racism. The other thread of history is the massive expansion of the petrochemical industry since World War II."

"Environmental racism is racial discrimination in environmental policy-making," says Rev. Chavis. "Wherever you find non-white people, that's where they want to dump stuff. And it's spreading all over the world. A lot of toxic chemicals have been going for dumping in the Pacific Islands, and Africa; it recently was revealed that Kenya has been allowing us to dump nuclear wastes." (The Organization of African Unity has denounced the dumping by the U.S. and European countries of hazardous waste in Africa as "toxic terrorism" and "a crime against Africa and the African people.")

"I think when we define the freedom movement, it now includes the environmental issues," says Rev. Chavis. "We now understand the insidious nature of racism. Fighting it does not just involve getting civil rights laws on the books. It goes beyond that. Racism has so permeated all facets of American society. We see the struggle against environmental racism as being an ongoing part of the civil rights and freedom movement in this country, something we are going to make part of our agenda, not a side issue but a primary issue. We must be just as vigilant in attacking environmental racism as racism in health care, housing, and schools."

DISCUSSION QUESTIONS

1. "Wherever you find non-white people, that's where they want to dump stuff," says Reverend Chavis in this article. Do you think that such a claim could be conclusively proved? If so, how? Does the evidence in this article convince you of the presence of environmental racism?

2. Assuming that the evidence in this article is conclusive, why do you think that environmental racism is so prevalent? What arguments do you think the polluters might use to justify their actions? Are they good ones?

3. Construct an argument against environmental racism, as well as possible objections to it.

4. What are the similarities and differences between environmental racism and racism concerning death penalty sentencing patterns? (See especially Amsterdam's article in Chapter 4.) Do you think that the Supreme Court would rule differently in cases con-

cerning alleged environmental racism than they did in cases concerning racist patterns in death penalty sentencing? Discuss.

5. Do you believe that environmental racism is as morally reprehensible as other forms of racism? Explain.

PETER SINGER

Animal Liberation

Peter Singer argues that prejudice toward the interests of members of one's own species and against the interests of members of other species is wrong. Singer calls prejudice of this kind *speciesism* (a term he owes to Richard Ryder) and argues that it is analogous to sexual and racial discrimination. If it is unjust to ignore the interests of women (sexism) and members of other races (racism), then it is also unjust to ignore the interests of members of other species (speciesism), particularly their interest in not suffering. According to Singer, all sentient beings are equal because all sentient beings have the ability to suffer. Therefore, we share with animals an interest in avoiding suffering, and each of our interests should be given equal consideration. His book *Animal Liberation* (1975), from which the following selection is taken, is one of the most influential books on the subject of animal rights. A biographical sketch of Peter Singer appears in Chapter 9.

ALL ANIMALS ARE EQUAL . . .

"Animal Liberation" may sound more like a parody of other liberation movements than a serious objective. The idea of "The Rights of Animals" actually was once used to parody the case for women's rights. When Mary Wollstonecraft, a forerunner of today's feminists, published her *Vindication of the Rights of Women* in 1792, her views were widely regarded as absurd, and before long an anonymous publication appeared entitled *A Vindication of the Rights of Brutes.* The author of this satirical work (now known to have been Thomas Taylor, a distinguished Cambridge philosopher) tried to refute Mary Wollstonecraft's arguments by showing that they could be carried one stage further. If the argument for equality was sound when applied to women, why should it not be applied to dogs, cats, and horses? The reasoning seemed to hold for these "brutes" too; yet to hold that brutes had rights was manifestly absurd; therefore the reasoning by which this conclusion had been reached must be unsound, and if unsound when applied to brutes, it must also be unsound when applied to women, since the very same arguments had been used in each case.

In order to explain the basis of the case for the equality of animals, it will be helpful to start with an examination of the case for the equality of women. Let us assume that we wish to defend the case for women's rights against the attack by Thomas Taylor. How should we reply?

One way in which we might reply is by saying that the case for equality between men and women cannot validly be extended to nonhuman animals. Women have a right to vote, for instance, because they are just as capable of making rational decisions about the future as men are; dogs, on the other hand, are incapable of understanding the significance of voting, so they cannot have the right to vote. There are many other obvious ways in which men and women resemble each other closely, while humans and animals differ greatly. So, it might be said, men and women are similar beings and should have similar rights, while humans and nonhumans are different and should not have equal rights.

The reasoning behind this reply to Taylor's analogy is correct up to a point, but it does not go far enough. There *are* important differences between humans and other animals, and these differences must give rise to *some* differences in the rights that each have. Recognizing this obvious fact, however, is no barrier to the case for extending the basic principle of equality to nonhuman animals. The differences that exist between men and women are equally undeniable, and the supporters of Women's Liberation are aware that these differences may give rise to different rights. Many feminists hold that women have the right to an abortion on request. It does not follow that since these same feminists are campaigning for equality between men and women they must support the right of men to have abortions too. Since a man cannot have an abortion, it is meaningless to talk of his right to have one. Since a dog can't vote, it is meaningless to talk of its right to vote. There is no reason why either Women's Liberation or Animal Liberation should get involved in such nonsense. The extension of the basic principle of equality from one group to another does not imply that we must treat both groups in exactly the same way, or grant exactly the same rights to both groups. Whether we should do so will depend on the nature of the members of the two groups. The basic principle of equality does not require equal or identical *treatment;* it requires equal *consideration.* Equal consideration for different beings may lead to different treatment and different rights.

So there is a different way of replying to Taylor's attempt to parody the case for women's rights, a way that does not deny the obvious differences between humans and nonhumans but goes more deeply into the question of equality and concludes by finding nothing absurd in the idea that the basic principle of equality applies to so-called "brutes." At this point such a conclusion may appear odd; but if we examine more deeply the basis on which our opposition to discrimination on grounds of race or sex ultimately rests, we will see that we would be on

shaky ground if we were to demand equality for blacks, women, and other groups of oppressed humans while denying equal consideration to nonhumans. To make this clear we need to see, first, exactly why racism and sexism are wrong.

When we say that all human beings, whatever their race, creed, or sex, are equal, what is it that we are asserting? Those who wish to defend hierarchical, inegalitarian societies have often pointed out that by whatever test we choose it simply is not true that all humans are created equal. Like it or not we must face the fact that humans come in different shapes and sizes; they come with different moral capacities, different intellectual abilities, different amounts of benevolent feeling and sensitivity to the needs of others, different abilities to communicate effectively, and different capacities to experience pleasure and pain. In short, if the demand for equality were based on the actual equality of all human beings, we would have to stop demanding equality.

Still, one might cling to the view that the demand for equality among human beings is based on the actual equality of the different races and sexes. Although, it may be said, humans differ as individuals there are no differences between the races and sexes *as such.* From the mere fact that a person is black or a woman we cannot infer anything about that person's intellectual or moral capacities. This, it may be said, is why racism and sexism are wrong. The white racist claims that whites are superior to blacks, but this is false—although there are differences among individuals, some blacks are superior to some whites in all of the capacities and abilities that could conceivably be relevant. The opponent of sexism would say the same: a person's sex is no guide to his or her abilities, and this is why it is unjustifiable to discriminate on the basis of sex.

The existence of individual variations that cut across the lines of race or sex, however, provides us with no defense at all against a more sophisticated opponent of equality, one who proposes that, say, the interests of all those with IQ scores below 100 be given less consideration than the interests of those with ratings over 100. Perhaps those scoring below the mark would, in this society, be made the slaves of those scoring higher. Would a hierarchical society of this sort really be so much better than one based on race or sex? I think not. But if we tie the moral principle of equality to the factual equality of the different races or sexes, taken as a whole, our opposition to racism and sexism does not provide us with any basis for objecting to this kind of inegalitarianism.

There is a second important reason why we ought not to base our opposition to racism and sexism on any kind of factual equality, even the limited kind that asserts that variations in capacities and abilities are spread evenly between the different races and sexes: we can have no absolute guarantee that these capacities and abilities really are distributed evenly, without regard to race or sex, among human beings. So far as actual abilities are concerned there do seem to be certain measurable differences between both races and sexes. These differences do not, of course, appear in each case, but only when averages are taken. More important still, we do not yet know how much of these differences is really due to the different genetic endowments of the different races and sexes, and how much is due to poor schools, poor housing, and other factors that are the result of past and continuing discrimination. Perhaps all of the important differences will eventually prove to be environmental rather than genetic. Anyone opposed to racism and sexism will certainly hope that this will be so, for it will make the task of ending discrimination a lot easier; nevertheless it would be dangerous to rest the case against racism and sexism on the belief that all significant differences are environmental in origin. The opponent of, say, racism who takes this line will be unable to avoid conceding that *if* differences in ability do after all prove to have some genetic connection with race, racism would in some way be defensible.

Fortunately there is no need to pin the case for equality to one particular outcome of a scientific investigation. The appropriate response to those who claim to have found evidence of genetically based differences in ability between the races or sexes is not to stick to the belief that the genetic explanation must be wrong, whatever evidence to the contrary may turn up: instead, we should make it quite clear that the claim to equality does not depend on intelligence, moral capacity, physical strength, or similar matters of fact. Equality is a moral idea, not an assertion of fact. There is no logically compelling reason for assuming that a factual difference in ability between two people justifies any difference in the amount of consideration we give to their needs and interests. *The principle of the equality of human beings is not a description of an alleged actual equality among humans: it is a prescription of how we should treat humans.*

Jeremy Bentham, the founder of the reforming utilitarian school of moral philosophy, incorporated the essential basis of moral equality into his system of ethics by means of the formula: "Each to count for one and none for more than one." In other words, the interests of every being affected by an action are to be taken into account and given the same weight as the like interests of any other being. A later utilitarian, Henry Sidgwick, put the point in this way: "The good of any one individual is of no more importance, from the point of view (if I may say so) of the Universe, than the good of any other." More recently the leading figures in contemporary moral philosophy have shown a great deal of agreement in specifying as a fundamental presupposition of their moral theories some similar requirement which operates so as to give everyone's interests equal consideration—although these writers generally cannot agree on how this requirement is best formulated.

It is an implication of this principle of equality that our concern for others and our readiness to consider their interests ought not to depend on what they are like or on what abilities they may possess. Precisely what this concern or consideration requires us to do may vary according to the characteristics of those affected by what we do: concern for the well-being of a child growing up in America would require that we teach him to read; concern for the well-being of a pig may require no more than that we leave him alone with other pigs in a place where there is adequate food and room to run freely. But the basic element—the taking into account of the interests of the being, whatever those interests may be—must, according to the principle of equality, be extended to all beings, black or white, masculine or feminine, human or nonhuman.

Thomas Jefferson, who was responsible for writing the principle of the equality of men into the American Declaration of Independence, saw this point. It led him to oppose slavery even though he was unable to free himself fully from his slaveholding background. He wrote in a letter to the author of a book that emphasized the notable intellectual achievements of Negroes in order to refute the then common view that they had limited intellectual capacities:

> Be assured that no person living wishes more sincerely than I do, to see a complete refutation of the doubts I have myself entertained and expressed on the grade of understanding allotted to them by nature, and to find that they are on a par with ourselves. . . . but whatever be their degree of talent it is no measure of their rights. Because Sir Isaac Newton was superior to others in understanding, he was not therefore lord of the property or person of others.

Similarly when in the 1850s the call for women's rights was raised in the United States a remarkable black feminist named Sojourner Truth made the same point in more robust terms at a feminist convention:

. . . they talk about this thing in the head; what do they call it? ["Intellect," whispered someone near by.] That's it. What's that got to do with women's rights or Negroes' rights? If my cup won't hold but a pint and yours holds a quart, wouldn't you be mean not to let me have my little half-measure full?

It is on this basis that the case against racism and the case against sexism must both ultimately rest; and it is in accordance with this principle that the attitude that we may call "speciesism," by analogy with racism, must also be condemned. Speciesism—the word is not an attractive one, but I can think of no better term—is a prejudice or attitude of bias toward the interests of members of one's own species and against those members of other species. It should be obvious that the fundamental objections to racism and sexism made by Thomas Jefferson and Sojourner Truth apply equally to speciesism. If possessing a higher degree of intelligence does not entitle one human to use another for his own ends, how can it entitle humans to exploit nonhumans for the same purpose?

Many philosophers and other writers have proposed the principle of equal consideration of interests, in some form or other, as a basic moral principle; but not many of them have recognized that this principle applies to members of other species as well as to our own. Jeremy Bentham was one of the few who did realize this. In a forward-looking passage written at a time when black slaves had been freed by the French but in the British dominions were still being treated in the way we now treat animals, Bentham wrote:

The day *may* come when the rest of the animal creation may acquire those rights which never could have been withholden from them but by the hand of tyranny. The French have already discovered that the blackness of the skin is no reason why a human being should be abandoned without redress to the caprice of a tormentor. It may one day come to be recognized that the number of the legs, the villosity of the skin, or the termination of the *os sacrum* are reasons equally insufficient for abandoning a sensitive being to the same fate. What else is it that should trace the insuperable line? Is it the faculty of reason, or perhaps the faculty of discourse? But a full-grown horse or dog is beyond comparison a more rational, as well as a more conversable animal, than an infant of a day or a week or even a month, old. But suppose they were otherwise, what would it avail? The question is not, Can they *reason?* nor Can they *talk?* but, Can they *suffer?*

In this passage Bentham points to the capacity for suffering as the vital characteristic that gives a being the right to equal consideration. The capacity for suffering—or more strictly, for suffering and/or enjoyment or happiness—is not just another characteristic like the capacity for language or higher mathematics. Bentham is not saying that those who try to mark "the insuperable line" that determines whether the interests of a being should be considered happen to have chosen the wrong characteristic. By saying that we must consider the interests of all beings with the capacity for suffering or enjoyment, Bentham does not arbitrarily exclude from consideration any interests at all—as those who draw the line with reference to the possession of reason or language do. The capacity for suffering and enjoyment is *a prerequisite for having interests at all,* a condition that must be satisfied before we can speak of interests in a meaningful way. It would be nonsense to say that it was not in the interests of a stone to be kicked along the road by a schoolboy. A stone does not have interests because it cannot suffer. Nothing that we can do to it could possibly make any difference to its welfare. A mouse, on the other hand, does have an interest in not being kicked along the road, because it will suffer if it is.

If a being suffers there can be no moral justification for refusing to take that suffering into consideration. No matter what the nature of the being, the principle of equality requires that its suffering be counted equally with the like suffering—in so far as rough comparisons can be made—of any other being. If a being is not capable of suffering, or of experiencing enjoyment or happiness, there is nothing to be taken into account. So the limit of sentience (using the term as a convenient if not strictly accurate shorthand for the capacity to suffer and/or experience enjoyment) is the only defensible boundary of concern for the interests of others. To mark this boundary by some other characteristic like intelligence or rationality would be to mark it in an arbitrary manner. Why not choose some other characteristic, like skin color?

The racist violates the principle of equality by giving greater weight to the interests of members of his own race when there is a clash between their interests and the interests of those of another race. The sexist violates the principle of equality by favoring the interests of his own sex. Similarly the speciesist allows the interests of his own species to override the greater interests of members of other species. The pattern is identical in each case.

Most human beings are speciesists. . . . [o]rdinary human beings, not a few exceptionally cruel or heartless humans, but the overwhelming majority of humans—take an active part in, acquiesce in, and allow their taxes to pay for practices that require the sacrifice of the most important interests of members of other species in order to promote the most trivial interests of our own species.

. . .

Animals can feel pain. As we saw earlier, there can be no moral justification for regarding the pain (or pleasure) that animals feel as less important than the same amount of pain (or pleasure) felt by humans. But what exactly does this mean, in practical terms? To prevent misunderstanding I shall spell out what I mean a little more fully.

If I give a horse a hard slap across its rump with my open hand, the horse may start, but it presumably feels little pain. Its skin is thick enough to protect it against a mere slap. If I slap a baby in the same way, however, the baby will cry and presumably does feel pain, for its skin is more sensitive. So it is worse to slap a baby than a horse, if both slaps are administered with equal force. But there must be some kind of blow—I don't know exactly what it would be, but perhaps a blow with a heavy stick—that would cause the horse as much pain as we cause a baby by slapping it with our hand. That is what I mean by "the same amount of pain," and if we consider it wrong to inflict that much pain on a baby for no good reason then we must, unless we are speciesists, consider it equally wrong to inflict the same amount of pain on a horse for no good reason.

There are other differences between humans and animals that cause other complications. Normal adult human beings have mental capacities which will, in certain circumstances, lead them to suffer more than animals would in the same circumstances. If, for instance, we decided to perform extremely painful or lethal scientific experiments on normal adult humans, kidnaped at random from public parks for this purpose, every adult who entered a park would become fearful that he would be kidnaped. The resultant terror would be a form of suf-

fering additional to the pain of the experiment. The same experiments performed on nonhuman animals would cause less suffering since the animals would not have the anticipatory dread of being kidnaped and experimented upon. This does not mean, of course, that it would be *right* to perform the experiment on animals, but only that there is a reason, which is *not* speciesist, for preferring to use animals rather than normal adult humans, if the experiment is to be done at all. It should be noted, however, that this same argument gives us a reason for preferring to use human infants—orphans perhaps—or retarded humans for experiments, rather than adults, since infants and retarded humans would also have no idea of what was going to happen to them. So far as this argument is concerned, nonhuman animals and infants and retarded humans are in the same category; and if we use this argument to justify experiments on nonhuman animals we have to ask ourselves whether we are also prepared to allow experiments on human infants and retarded adults; and if we make a distinction between animals and these humans, on what basis can we do it, other than a bare-faced—and morally indefensible—preference for members of our own species?

There are many areas in which the superior mental powers of normal adult humans make a difference: anticipation, more detailed memory, greater knowledge of what is happening, and so on. Yet these differences do not all point to greater suffering on the part of the normal human being. Sometimes an animal may suffer more because of his more limited understanding. If, for instance, we are taking prisoners in wartime we can explain to them that while they must submit to capture, search, and confinement they will not otherwise be harmed and will be set free at the conclusion of hostilities. If we capture a wild animal, however, we cannot explain that we are not threatening its life. A wild animal cannot distinguish an attempt to overpower and confine from an attempt to kill; the one causes as much terror as the other.

It may be objected that comparisons of the sufferings of different species are impossible to make, and that for this reason when the interests of animals and humans clash the principle of equality gives no guidance. It is probably true that comparisons of suffering between members of different species cannot be made precisely, but precision is not essential. Even if we were to prevent the infliction of suffering on animals only when it is quite certain that the interests of humans will not be affected to anything like the extent that animals are affected, we would be forced to make radical changes in our treatment of animals that would involve our diet, the farming methods we use, experimental procedures in many fields of science, our approach to wildlife and to hunting, trapping and the wearing of furs, and areas of entertainment like circuses, rodeos, and zoos. As a result, a vast amount of suffering would be avoided.

So far I have said a lot about the infliction of suffering on animals, but nothing about killing them. This omission has been deliberate. The application of the principle of equality to the infliction of suffering is, in theory at least, fairly straightforward. Pain and suffering are bad and should be prevented or minimized, irrespective of the race, sex, or species of the being that suffers. How bad a pain is depends on how intense it is and how long it lasts, but pains of the same intensity and duration are equally bad, whether felt by humans or animals.

The wrongness of killing a being is more complicated. I have kept, and shall continue to keep, the question of killing in the background because in the present state of human tyranny over other species the more simple, straightforward principle of equal consideration of pain or pleasure is a sufficient basis for identifying and protesting against all the major abuses of animals that humans practice. Nevertheless, it is necessary to say something about killing.

Just as most humans are speciesists in their readiness to cause pain to animals when they would not cause a similar pain to humans for the same reason, so most humans are speciesists in their readiness to kill other animals when they would not kill humans. We need to proceed more cautiously here, however, because people hold widely differing views about when it is legitimate to kill humans, as the continuing debates over abortion and euthanasia attest. Nor have moral philosophers been able to agree on exactly what it is that makes it wrong to kill humans, and under what circumstances killing a human being may be justifiable.

Let us consider first the view that it is always wrong to take an innocent human life. We may call this the "sanctity of life" view. People who take this view oppose abortion and euthanasia. They do not usually, however, oppose the killing of nonhumans—so perhaps it would be more accurate to describe this view as the "sanctity of *human* life" view.

The belief that human life, and only human life, is sacrosanct is a form of speciesism. To see this, consider the following example.

Assume that, as sometimes happens, an infant has been born with massive and irreparable brain damage. The damage is so severe that the infant can never be any more than a "human vegetable," unable to talk, recognize other people, act independently of others, or develop a sense of self-awareness. The parents of the infant, realizing that they cannot hope for any improvement in their child's condition and being in any case unwilling to spend, or ask the state to spend, the thousands of dollars that would be needed annually for proper care of the infant, ask the doctor to kill the infant painlessly.

Should the doctor do what the parents ask? Legally, he should not, and in this respect the law reflects the sanctity of life view. The life of every human being is sacred. Yet people who would say this about the infant do not object to the killing of nonhuman animals. How can they justify their different judgments? Adult chimpanzees, dogs, pigs, and many other species far surpass the brain-damaged infant in their ability to relate to others, act independently, be self-aware, and any other capacity that could reasonably be said to give value to life. With the most intensive care possible, there are retarded infants who can never achieve the intelligence level of a dog. Nor can we appeal to the concern of the infant's parents, since they themselves, in this imaginary example (and in some actual cases), do not want the infant kept alive.

The only thing that distinguishes the infant from the animal, in the eyes of those who claim it has a "right to life," is that it is, biologically, a member of the species Homo sapiens, whereas chimpanzees, dogs, and pigs are not. But to use *this* difference as the basis for granting a right to life to the infant and not to the other animals is, of course, pure speciesism. It is exactly the kind of arbitrary difference that the most crude and overt kind of racist uses in attempting to justify racial discrimination.

This does not mean that to avoid speciesism we must hold that it is as wrong to kill a dog as it is to kill a normal human being. The only position that is irredeemably speciesist is the one that tries to make the boundary of the right to life run exactly parallel to the boundary of our own species. Those who hold the sanctity of life view do this, because while distinguishing sharply between humans and other animals they allow no distinctions to be made within our own species, objecting to the killing of the severely retarded and the hopelessly senile as strongly as they object to the killing of normal adults.

To avoid speciesism we must allow that beings which are similar in all relevant respects have a similar right to life—and mere membership in our own biological species cannot be a morally relevant criterion for this right. Within these limits we could still hold that, for instance, it is worse to kill a normal adult human, with a capacity for self-awareness, and the ability to plan for the future and have meaningful relations with others, than it is to kill a mouse, which presumably does not share all of these characteristics; or we might appeal to the close family and other personal ties which humans have but mice do not have to the same degree; or we might think that it is the consequences for other humans, who will be put in fear of their own lives, that makes the crucial difference; or we might think it is some combination of these factors, or other factors altogether.

Whatever criteria we choose, however, we will have to admit that they do not follow precisely the boundary of our own species. We may legitimately hold that there are some features of certain beings which make their lives more valuable than those of other beings; but there will surely be some nonhuman animals whose lives, by any standards, are more valuable than the lives of some humans. A chimpanzee, dog, or pig, for instance, will have a higher degree of self-awareness and a greater capacity for meaningful relations with others than a severely retarded infant or someone in a state of advanced senility. So if we base the right to life on these characteristics we must grant these animals a right to life as good as, or better than, such retarded or senile humans.

Now this argument cuts both ways. It could be taken as showing that chimpanzees, dogs, and pigs, along with some other species, have a right to life and we commit a grave moral offense whenever we kill them, even when they are old and suffering and our intention is to put them out of their misery. Alternatively, one could take the argument as showing that the severely retarded and hopelessly senile have no right to life and may be killed for quite trivial reasons, as we now kill animals.

Since the focus [here] is on ethical questions concerning animals and not on the morality of euthanasia I shall not attempt to settle this issue finally. I think it is reasonably clear, though, that while both of the positions just described avoid speciesism, neither is entirely satisfactory. What we need is some middle position which would avoid speciesism but would not make the lives of the retarded and senile as cheap as the lives of pigs and dogs now are, nor make the lives of pigs and dogs so sacrosanct that we think it wrong to put them out of hopeless misery. What we must do is bring nonhuman animals within our sphere of moral concern and cease to treat their lives as expendable for whatever trivial purposes we

may have. At the same time, once we realize that the fact that a being is a member of our own species is not in itself enough to make it always wrong to kill that being, we may come to reconsider our policy of preserving human lives at all costs, even when there is no prospect of a meaningful life or of existence without terrible pain.

I conclude, then, that a rejection of speciesism does not imply that all lives are of equal worth. While self-awareness, intelligence, the capacity for meaningful relations with others, and so on are not relevant to the question of inflicting pain—since pain is pain, whatever other capacities, beyond the capacity to feel pain, the being may have—these capacities may be relevant to the question of taking life. It is not arbitrary to hold that the life of a self-aware being, capable of abstract thought, of planning for the future, of complex acts of communication, and so on, is more valuable than the life of a being without these capacities. To see the difference between the issues of inflicting pain and taking life, consider how we would choose within our own species. If we had to choose to save the life of a normal human or a mentally defective human, we would probably choose to save the life of the normal human; but if we had to choose between preventing pain in the normal human or the mental defective—imagine that both have received painful but superficial injuries, and we only have enough painkiller for one of them—it is not nearly so clear how we ought to choose. The same is true when we consider other species. The evil of pain is, in itself, unaffected by the other characteristics of the being that feels the pain; the value of life is affected by these other characteristics.

Normally this will mean that if we have to choose between the life of a human being and the life of another animal we would choose to save the life of the human; but there may be special cases in which the reverse holds true, because the human being in question does not have the capacities of a normal human being. So this view is not speciesist, although it may appear to be at first glance. The preference, in normal cases, for saving a human life over the life of an animal when a choice *has* to be made is a preference based on the characteristics that normal humans have, and not on the mere fact that they are members of our own species. This is why when we consider members of our own species who lack the characteristics of normal humans we can no longer say that their lives are always to be preferred to those of other animals. . . . In general, though, the question of when it is wrong to kill (painlessly) an animal is one to which we need give no precise answer. As long as we remember that we should give the same respect to the lives of animals as we give to the lives of those humans at a similar mental level, we shall not go far wrong.

In any case, the conclusions that are argued for [here] flow from the principle of minimizing suffering alone. The idea that it is also wrong to kill animals painlessly gives some of these conclusions additional support which is welcome, but strictly unnecessary. Interestingly enough, this is true even of the conclusion that we ought to become vegetarians, a conclusion which in the popular mind is generally based on some kind of absolute prohibition on killing.

DISCUSSION QUESTIONS

1. What is speciesism? Why does Singer believe that it is analogous to racism and sexism? Do you agree with his position? Explain.
2. Is killing an adult mouse as morally serious as killing an adult human? What do you think Singer might say? Why? Do you agree with him?
3. Why does Singer believe that all humans are equal? Do you agree with him? What is the connection between Singer's position and the philosophy of Jeremy Bentham?
4. Singer's article suggests that there are similarities between the civil rights movement and the animal rights movement. Do you agree with him? Do you think that members of the civil rights movement would be pleased to have their work connected with that of animal rights activists? Explain.
5. Does Singer believe that killing humans is wrong in the same way that killing animals is wrong? Critically evaluate his argument.
6. Compare Singer's position with the Universal Declaration of the Rights of Animals in the Media Gallery. Which of the principles would Singer support, and which would he oppose?

 BONNIE STEINBOCK

Speciesism and the Idea of Equality

Steinbock disagrees with Peter Singer and presents in this article a defense of speciesism. For Steinbock, humans have "morally relevant capacities" that nonhumans do not have. These morally relevant capacities include the ability to desire self-respect, to be morally responsible, and to reciprocate in ways that animals cannot. Steinbock claims that, while Singer is right to point out that nonhuman pain is deserving of moral consideration, she disagrees that it should be given equal moral consideration to human pain. For Steinbock, the morally relevant capacities, which are shared by humans but not by nonhumans, entitle humans to greater moral consideration.

Bonnie Steinbock is a professor of philosophy at the State University of New York at Albany and is the author of *Life Before Birth* (1992), *Killing and Letting Die* (coedited

Bonnie Steinbock, *Philosophy* 53, no. 204 (April 1978): 247–256. Reprinted with the permission of Cambridge University Press. Copyright © 1978 Cambridge University Press.

with Alastair Norcross, 2nd ed., 1994), *Ethical Issues in Modern Medicine* (coedited with John D. Arras, 4th ed., 1995), and *New Ethics for the Public's Health* (coedited with Dan E. Beauchamp, 1999).

Most of us believe that we are entitled to treat members of other species in ways which would be considered wrong if inflicted on members of our own species. We kill them for food, keep them confined, use them in painful experiments. The moral philosopher has to ask what relevant difference justifies this difference in treatment. A look at this question will lead us to re-examine the distinctions which we have assumed make a moral difference.

It has been suggested by Peter Singer[1] that our current attitudes are "speciesist," a word intended to make one think of "racist" or "sexist." The idea is that membership in a species is in itself not relevant to moral treatment, and that much of our behaviour and attitudes towards non-human animals is based simply on this irrelevant fact.

There is, however, an important difference between racism or sexism and "speciesism." We do not subject animals to different moral treatment simply because they have fur and feathers, but because they are in fact different from human beings in ways that could be morally relevant. It is false that women are incapable of being benefited by education, and therefore that claim cannot serve to justify preventing them from attending school. But this is not false of cows and dogs, even chimpanzees. Intelligence is thought to be a morally relevant capacity because of its relation to the capacity for moral responsibility.

What is Singer's response? He agrees that non-human animals lack certain capacities that human animals possess, and that this may justify different *treatment*. But it does not justify giving less consideration to their needs and interests. According to Singer, the moral mistake which the racist or sexist makes is not essentially the factual error of thinking that blacks or women are inferior to white men. For even if there were no factual error, even if it were true that blacks and women are less intelligent and responsible than whites and men, this would not justify giving less consideration to their needs and interests. It is important to note that the term "speciesism" is in one way like, and in another way unlike, the terms "racism" and "sexism." What the term "speciesism" has in common with these terms is the reference to focusing on a characteristic which is, in itself, irrelevant to moral treatment. And it is worth reminding us of this. But Singer's real aim is to bring us to a new understanding of the idea of equality. The question is, on what do claims to equality rest? The demand for *human* equality is a demand that the interests of all human beings be considered equally, unless there is a moral justification for not doing so. But why should the interests of all human beings be considered equally? In order to answer this question, we have to give some sense to the phrase "All men (human beings) are created equal." Human beings are manifestly *not* equal, differing greatly in intelligence, virtue and capacities. In virtue of what can the claim to equality be made?

It is Singer's contention that claims to equality do not rest on factual equality. Not only do human beings differ in their capacities, but it might even turn out that intelligence, the capacity for virtue, etc., are not distributed evenly among the races and sexes:

> The appropriate response to those who claim to have found evidence of genetically based differences in ability between the races or sexes is not to stick to the belief that the genetic explanation must be wrong, whatever evidence to the contrary may turn up; instead we should make it quite clear that the claim to equality does not depend on intelligence, moral capacity, physical strength, or similar matters of fact. Equality is a moral ideal, not a simple assertion of fact. There is no logically compelling reason for assuming that a factual difference in ability between two people justifies any difference in the amount of consideration we give to satisfying their needs and interests. The principle of equality of human beings is not a description of an alleged actual equality among humans: it is a prescription of how we should treat humans.[2]

In so far as the subject is human equality, Singer's view is supported by other philosophers. Bernard Williams, for example, is concerned to show that demands for equality cannot rest on factual equality among people, for no such equality exists.[3] The only respect in which all men are equal, according to Williams, is that they are all equally men. This seems to be a platitude, but Williams denies that it is trivial. Membership in the species *Homo sapiens* in itself has no special moral significance, but rather the fact that all men are human serves as a *reminder* that being human involves the possession of characteristics that are morally relevant. But on what characteristics does Williams focus? Aside from the desire for self-respect (which I will discuss later), Williams is not concerned with uniquely human capacities. Rather, he focuses on the capacity to feel pain and the capacity to feel affection. It is in virtue of these capacities, it seems, that the idea of equality is to be justified.

Apparently Richard Wasserstrom has the same idea as he sets out the racist's "logical and moral mistakes" in "Rights, Human Rights and Racial Discrimination."[4] The racist fails to acknowledge that the black person is as capable of suffering as the white person. According to Wasserstrom, the reason why a person is said to have a right not to be made to suffer acute physical pain is that we all do in fact value freedom from such pain. Therefore, if anyone has a right to be free from suffering acute physical pain, *everyone* has this right, for there is no possible basis of discrimination. Wasserstrom says, "For, if all persons do have equal capacities of these sorts and if the existence of these capacities is the reason for ascribing these rights to anyone, then all persons ought to have the right to claim equality of treatment in respect to the possession and exercise of these rights."[5] The basis of equality, for Wasserstrom as for Williams, lies not in some uniquely human capacity, but rather in the fact that all human beings are alike in their capacity to suffer. Writers on equality have focused on this capacity, I think, because it functions as some sort of lowest common denominator, so that whatever the other capacities of a human being, he is entitled to equal consideration because, like everyone else, he is capable of suffering.

If the capacity to suffer is the reason for ascribing a right to freedom from acute pain, or a right to well being, then it certainly looks as though these rights must be extended to animals as well. This is the conclusion Singer arrives at. The demand for human equality rests on the equal capacity of all human beings to suffer and to enjoy well being. But if this is the basis of the demand for equality, then this demand must include all beings which have an equal capacity to suffer and enjoy well being. That is why Singer places at the basis of the demand for equality, not intelligence or reason, but sentience. And equality will mean, not equality of treatment, but "equal consideration of interests." The equal consideration of interests will often mean quite different treatment, depending on the nature of the entity being considered. (It would be as absurd to talk of a dog's right to vote, Singer says, as to talk of a man's right to have an abortion.)

It might be thought that the issue of equality depends on a discussion of rights. According to this line of thought, animals do not merit equal consideration of interests because, unlike human beings, they do not, or cannot, have rights. But I am not going to discuss rights, important as the issue is. The fact that an entity does not have rights does not necessarily imply that its interests are going to count for less than the interests of entities which are right-bearers. According to the view of rights held by H. L. A. Hart and S. I. Benn, infants do not have rights, nor do the mentally defective, nor do the insane, in so far as they all lack certain minimal conceptual capabilities for having rights.[6] Yet it certainly does not seem that either Hart or Benn would agree that *therefore* their interests are to be counted for less, or that it is morally permissible to treat them in ways in which it would not be permissible to treat right-bearers. It seems to mean only that we must give different sorts of reasons for our obligations to take into consideration the interests of those who do not have rights.

We have reasons concerning the treatment of other people which are clearly independent of the notion of rights. We would say that it is wrong to punch someone because doing that infringes his rights. But we could also say that it is wrong because doing that hurts him, and that is, ordinarily, enough of a reason not to do it. Now this particular reason extends not only to human beings, but to all sentient creatures. One has a *prima facie* reason not to pull the cat's tail (whether or not the cat has rights) because it hurts the cat. And this is the only thing, normally, which is relevant in this case. The fact that the cat is not a "rational being," that it is not capable of moral responsibility, that it cannot make free choices or shape its life—all of these differences from us have nothing to do with the justifiability of pulling its tail. Does this show that rationality and the rest of it are irrelevant to moral treatment?

I hope to show that this is not the case. But first I want to point out that the issue is not one of cruelty to animals. We all agree that cruelty is wrong, whether perpetrated on a moral or non-moral, rational or non-rational agent. Cruelty is defined as the infliction of unnecessary pain or suffering. What is to count as necessary or unnecessary is determined, in part, by the nature of the end pursued.

Torturing an animal is cruel, because although the pain is logically necessary for the action to be torture, the end (deriving enjoyment from seeing the animal suffer) is monstrous. Allowing animals to suffer from neglect or for the sake of large profits may also be thought to be unnecessary and therefore cruel. But there may be some ends, which are very good (such as the advancement of medical knowledge), which can be accomplished by subjecting animals to pain in experiments. Although most people would agree that the pain inflicted on animals used in medical research ought to be kept to a minimum, they would consider pain that cannot be eliminated "necessary" and therefore not cruel. It would probably not be so regarded if the subjects were nonvoluntary human beings. Necessity, then, is defined in terms of human benefit, but this is just what is being called into question. The topic of cruelty to animals, while important from a practical viewpoint, because much of our present treatment of animals involves the infliction of suffering for no good reason, is not very interesting philosophically. What is philosophically interesting is whether we are justified in having different standards of necessity for human suffering and for animal suffering.

Singer says, quite rightly I think, "If a being suffers, there can be no moral justification for refusing to take that suffering into consideration."[7] But he thinks that the principle of equality requires that, no matter what the nature of the being, its suffering be counted equally with the like suffering of any other being. In other words, sentience does not simply provide us with reasons for acting; it is the *only* relevant consideration for equal consideration of interests. It is this view that I wish to challenge.

I want to challenge it partly because it has such counter-intuitive results. It means, for example, that feeding starving children before feeding starving dogs is just like a Catholic charity's feeding hungry Catholics before feeding hungry non-Catholics. It is simply a matter of taking care of one's own, something which is usually morally permissible. But whereas we would admire the Catholic agency which did not discriminate, but fed all children, first come, first served, we would feel quite differently about someone who had this policy for dogs and children. Nor is this, it seems to me, simply a matter of a sentimental preference for our own species. I might feel much more love for my dog than for a strange child—and yet I might feel morally obliged to feed the child before I fed my dog. If I gave in to the feelings of love and fed my dog and let the child go hungry, I would probably feel guilty. This is not to say that we can simply rely on such feelings. Huck Finn felt guilty at helping Jim escape, which he viewed as stealing from a woman who had never done him any harm. But while the existence of such feelings does not settle the morality of an issue, it is not clear to me that they can be explained away. In any event, their existence can serve as a motivation for trying to find a rational justification for considering human interests above non-human ones.

However, it does seem to me that this *requires* a justification. Until now, common sense (and academic philosophy) have seen no such need. Benn says, "No one claims equal consideration for all mammals—human beings count, mice do not, though it would not be easy to say *why* not. . . . Although we hesitate to inflict unnecessary pain on sentient creatures, such as mice or dogs, we are quite sure that we do not need to show good reasons for putting human interests before theirs."[8]

I think we do have to justify counting our interests more heavily than those of animals. But how? Singer is right, I think, to point out that it will not do to refer vaguely to the greater value of human life, to human worth and dignity:

> Faced with a situation in which they see a need for some basis for the moral gulf that is commonly thought to separate humans and animals, but can find no concrete difference that will do this without undermining the equality of humans, philosophers tend to waffle. They resort to high-sounding phrases like "the intrinsic dignity of the human individual." They talk of "the intrinsic worth of all men" as if men had some worth that other beings do not have or they say that human beings, and only human beings, are "ends in themselves," while "everything other than a person can only have value for a person." . . . Why should we not attribute "intrinsic dignity" or "intrinsic worth" to ourselves? Why should we not say that we are the only things in the universe that have intrinsic value? Our fellow human beings are unlikely to reject the accolades we so generously bestow upon them and those to whom we deny the honour are unable to object.[9]

Singer is right to be sceptical of terms like "intrinsic dignity" and "intrinsic worth." These phrases are no substitute for a moral argument. But they may point to one. In trying to understand what is meant by these phrases, we may find a difference or differences between human beings and non-human animals that will justify different treatment while not undermining claims for human equality. While we are not compelled to discriminate among people because of different capacities, if we can find a significant difference in capacities between human and non-human animals, this could serve to justify regarding human interests as primary. It is not arbitrary or smug, I think, to maintain that human beings have a different moral status from members of other species because of certain capacities which are characteristic of being human. We may not all be equal in these capacities, but all human beings possess them to some measure, and non-human animals do not. For example, human beings are normally held to be responsible for what they do. In recognizing that someone is responsible for his or her actions, you accord that person a respect which is reserved for those possessed of moral autonomy, or capable of achieving such autonomy. Secondly, human beings can be expected to reciprocate in a way that non-human animals cannot. Non-human animals cannot be motivated by altruistic or moral reasons; they cannot treat you fairly or unfairly. This does not rule out the possibility of an animal being motivated by sympathy or pity. It does rule out altruistic motivation in the sense of motivation due to the recognition that the needs and interests of others provide one with certain reasons for acting.[10] Human beings are capable of altruistic motivation in this sense. We are sometimes motivated simply by the recognition that someone else is in pain, and that pain is a bad thing, no matter who suffers it. It is this sort of reason that I claim cannot motivate an animal or any entity not possessed of fairly abstract concepts. (If some non-human animals do possess the requisite concepts—perhaps chimpanzees who have learned a language—they might well be capable of altruistic motivation.) This means that our moral dealings with animals are necessarily much more limited than our dealings with other human beings. If rats invade our houses, carrying disease and biting our children, we cannot reason with them, hoping to persuade them of the injustice they do us. We can only attempt to get rid of them. And it is this that makes it reasonable for us to accord them a separate and not equal moral status, even though their capacity to suffer provides us with some reason to kill them painlessly, if this can be done without too much sacrifice of human interests. Thirdly, as Williams points out, there is the "desire for self-respect": "a certain human desire to

be identified with what one is doing, to be able to realize purposes of one's own, and not to be the instrument of another's will unless one has willingly accepted such a role."[11] Some animals may have some form of this desire, and to the extent that they do, we ought to consider their interest in freedom and self-determination. (Such considerations might affect our attitudes toward zoos and circuses.) But the desire for self-respect *per se* requires the intellectual capacities of human beings, and this desire provides us with special reasons not to treat human beings in certain ways. It is an affront to the dignity of a human being to be a slave (even if a well-treated one); this cannot be true for a horse or a cow. To point this out is of course only to say that the justification for the treatment of an entity will depend on the sort of entity in question. In our treatment of other entities, we must consider the desire for autonomy, dignity and respect, but only where such a desire exists. Recognition of different desires and interests will often require different treatment, a point Singer himself makes.

But is the issue simply one of different desires and interests justifying and requiring different treatment? I would like to make a stronger claim, namely, that certain capacities, which seem to be unique to human beings, entitle their possessors to a privileged position in the moral community. Both rats and human beings dislike pain, and so we have a *prima facie* reason not to inflict pain on either. But if we can free human beings from crippling diseases, pain and death through experimentation which involves making animals suffer, and if this is the only way to achieve such results, then I think that such experimentation is justified because human lives are more valuable than animal lives. And this is because of certain capacities and abilities that normal human beings have which animals apparently do not, and which human beings cannot exercise if they are devastated by pain or disease.

My point is not that the lack of the sorts of capacities I have been discussing gives us a justification for treating animals just as we like, but rather that it is these differences between human beings and non-human animals which provide a rational basis for different moral treatment and consideration. Singer focuses on sentience alone as the basis of equality, but we can justify the belief that human beings have a moral worth that non-human animals do not, in virtue of specific capacities, and without resorting to "high-sounding phrases."

Singer thinks that intelligence, the capacity for moral responsibility, for virtue, etc., are irrelevant to equality, because we would not accept a hierarchy based on intelligence any more than one based on race. We do not think that those with greater capacities ought to have their interests weighed more heavily than those with lesser capacities, and this, he thinks, shows that differences in such capacities are irrelevant to equality. But it does not show this at all. Kevin Donaghy argues (rightly, I think) that what entitles us human beings to a privileged position in the moral community is a certain minimal level of intelligence, which is a prerequisite for morally relevant capacities.[12] The fact that we would reject a hierarchical society based on degree of intelligence does not show that a minimal level of intelligence cannot be used as a cut-off point, justifying giving greater consideration to the interests of those entities which meet this standard.

Interestingly enough, Singer concedes the rationality of valuing the lives of normal human beings over the lives of non-human animals.[13] We are not required to value equally the life of a normal human being and the life of an animal, he thinks, but only their suffering. But I doubt that the value of an entity's life can be separated from the value of its suffering in this way. If we value the lives of human beings more than the lives of animals, this is because we value certain capacities that human beings have and animals do not. But freedom from suffering is, in general, a minimal condition for exercising these capacities, for living a fully human life. So, valuing human life more involves regarding human interests as counting for more. That is why we regard human suffering as more deplorable than comparable animal suffering.

But there is one point of Singer's which I have not yet met. Some human beings (if only a very few) are less intelligent than some non-human animals. Some have less capacity for moral choice and responsibility. What status in the moral community are these members of our species to occupy? Are their interests to be considered equally with ours? Is experimenting on them permissible where such experiments are painful or injurious, but somehow necessary for human well being? If it is certain of our capacities which entitle us to a privileged position, it looks as if those lacking those capacities are not entitled to a privileged position. To think it is justifiable to experiment on an adult chimpanzee but not on a severely mentally incapacitated human being seems to be focusing on membership in a species where that has no moral relevance. (It is be-

ing "speciesist" in a perfectly reasonable use of the word.) How are we to meet this challenge?

Donaghy is untroubled by this objection. He says that it is fully in accord with his intuitions, that he regards the killing of a normally intelligent human being as far more serious than the killing of a person so severely limited that he lacked the intellectual capacities of an adult pig. But this parry really misses the point. The question is whether Donaghy thinks that the killing of a human being so severely limited that he lacked the intellectual capacities of an adult pig would be less serious than the killing of that pig. If superior intelligence is what justifies privileged status in the moral community, then the pig who is smarter than a human being ought to have superior moral status. And I doubt that this is fully in accord with Donaghy's intuitions.

I doubt that anyone will be able to come up with a concrete and morally relevant difference that would justify, say, using a chimpanzee in an experiment rather than a human being with less capacity for reasoning, moral responsibility, etc. Should we then experiment on the severely retarded? Utilitarian considerations aside (the difficulty of comparing intelligence between species, for example), we feel a special obligation to care for the handicapped members of our own species, who cannot survive in this world without such care. Non-human animals manage very well, despite their "lower intelligence" and lesser capacities; most of them do not require special care from us. This does not, of course, justify experimenting on them. However, to subject to experimentation those people who depend on us seems even worse than subjecting members of other species to it. In addition, when we consider the severely retarded, we think, "That could be me." It makes sense to think that one might have been born retarded, but not to think that one might have been born a monkey. And so, although one can imagine oneself in the monkey's place, one feels a closer identification with the severely retarded human being. Here we are getting away from such things as "morally relevant differences" and are talking about something much more difficult to articulate, namely, the role of feeling and sentiment in moral thinking. We would be *horrified* by the use of the retarded in medical research. But what are we to make of this horror? Has it moral significance or is it "mere" sentiment, of no more importance than the sentiment of whites against blacks? It is terribly difficult to know how to evaluate such feelings.[14] I am not going to say more about this, because I think that the treatment of severely incapacitated human beings does not pose an insurmountable objection to the privileged status principle. I am willing to admit that my horror at the thought of experiments being performed on severely mentally incapacitated human beings in cases in which I would find it justifiable and preferable to perform the same experiments on non-human animals (capable of similar suffering) may not be a moral emotion. But it is certainly not wrong of us to extend special care to members of our own species, motivated by feelings of sympathy, protectiveness, etc. If this is speciesism, it is stripped of its tone of moral condemnation. It is not racist to provide special care to members of your own race; it is racist to fall below your moral obligation to a person because of his or her race. I have been arguing that we are morally obliged to consider the interests of all sentient creatures, but not to consider those interests equally with human interests. Nevertheless, even this recognition will mean some radical changes in our attitude toward and treatment of other species.

NOTES

1. Peter Singer, *Animal Liberation* (a New York Review book, 1975).
2. Ibid., p. 5.
3. Bernard Williams, "The Idea of Equality," *Philosophy, Politics and Society* (2nd Series), ed. Laslett and Runciman (Blackwell, 1962), pp. 110–113, reprinted in *Moral Concepts,* ed. Feinberg (Oxford, 1970), pp. 153–171.
4. Richard Wasserstrom, "Rights, Human Rights, and Racial Discrimination," *Journal of Philosophy,* 61, 20 (1964), reprinted in *Human Rights,* ed. A. I. Melden (Wadsworth, 1970), pp. 96–110.
5. Ibid., p. 106.
6. H. L. A. Hart, "Are There Any Natural Rights?" *Philosophical Review,* 64 (1955), and S. I. Benn, "Abortion, Infanticide, and Respect for Persons," *The Problem of Abortion,* ed. Feinberg (Wadsworth, 1973), pp. 92–104.
7. Singer, *Animal Liberation,* p. 9.
8. Benn, "Equality, Moral and Social," *The Encyclopedia of Philosophy,* 3, p. 40.
9. Singer, *Animal Liberation,* pp. 266–267.
10. This conception of altruistic motivation comes from Thomas Nagel's *The Possibility of Altruism* (Oxford, 1970).
11. Williams, "The Idea of Equality," p. 157.
12. Kevin Donaghy, "Singer on Speciesism," *Philosophic Exchange* (Summer 1974).
13. Singer, *Animal Liberation,* p. 22.
14. We run into the same problem when discussing abortion. Of what significance are our feelings toward the unborn when discussing its status? Is it relevant or irrelevant that it looks like a human being?

DISCUSSION QUESTIONS

1. What, according to Steinbock, is the difference between speciesism, sexism, and racism? Do you agree with her? Is this a good criticism of Peter Singer's position? Explain.
2. Compare and contrast the basis for equality in Singer and Steinbock. Whose argument is better, and why?
3. Steinbock discusses a number of "morally relevant capacities" shared by humans that nonhumans do not have. Do you agree with her? Why?
4. What if someone, for some reason, does not have the "morally relevant capacities" discussed by Steinbock? What is this person's moral status? Does he or she have a lower moral status? Is it the same? Can an animal overtake the person in moral status? Critically examine Steinbock's position.
5. Do you believe that the interests of humans should be weighed more heavily than the interests of animals? Is this the case for all human interests, or just some? If so, which human interests, and why? Defend your view, and compare it to those of Singer and Steinbock.

IMMANUEL KANT

Our Duty to Animals

For Kant, humans are rational, which means that they are capable of thinking about the choices they face and selecting among them on the basis of reasons. Humans are also the authors of moral law, so that their obedience to duty is not an act of submission, but an act of *autonomy*. Animals, however, are not rational, nor are they the authors of moral law. Therefore, humans do not owe animals anything. Nevertheless, Kant argues, being kind to animals will help us to develop a good character and to be more considerate to our fellow humans. In his view, our duties to animals are basically indirect duties to other humans. A biographical sketch of Immanuel Kant appears in Chapter 1.

Baumgarten speaks of duties towards beings which are beneath us and beings which are above us. But so far as animals are concerned, we have no direct duties. Animals are not self-conscious and are there merely as a means to an end. That end is man. We can ask, "Why do animals exist?" But to ask, "Why does man exist?" is a meaningless question. *Our duties towards animals are merely indirect duties towards humanity.* Animal nature has analogies to human nature, and by doing our duties to animals in respect of manifestations of human nature, we indirectly do our duty towards humanity. Thus, if a dog has served his master long and faithfully, his service, on the analogy of human service, deserves reward, and when the dog has grown too old to serve, his master ought to keep him until he dies. Such action helps to support us in our duties towards human beings, where they are bounden duties. If then any acts of animals are analogous to human acts and spring from the same principles, we have duties towards the animals because thus we cultivate the corresponding duties towards human beings. If a man shoots his dog because the animal is no longer capable of service, he does not fail in his duty to the dog, for the dog cannot judge, but his *act is inhuman and damages in himself that humanity which it is his duty to show towards mankind.* If he is not to stifle his human feelings, he must practise kindness towards animals, for he who is cruel to animals becomes hard also in his dealing with men. We can judge the heart of a man by his treatment of animals. Hogarth depicts this in his engravings. He shows how cruelty grows and develops. He shows the child's cruelty to animals, pinching the tail of a dog or a cat; he then depicts the grown man in his cart running over a child; and lastly, the culmination of cruelty in murder. He thus brings home to us in a terrible fashion the rewards of cruelty, and this should be an impressive lesson to children. The more we come in contact with animals and observe their behaviour, the more we love them, for we see how great is their care for their young. It is then difficult for us to be cruel in thought even to a wolf. Leibnitz used a tiny worm for purposes of observation, and then carefully replaced it with its leaf on the tree so that it should not come to harm through any act of his. He would have been sorry—a natural feeling for a human man—to destroy such a creature for no reason. Tender feelings towards dumb animals develop humane feelings towards mankind. In England butchers and doctors do not sit on a jury because they are accustomed to the sight of death and hardened. Vivisectionists, who use living animals for their experiments, certainly act cruelly, although their aim is praiseworthy, and they can justify their cruelty, since animals must be regarded as man's

Immanuel Kant, *Lectures on Ethics.* Translated by Louis Infield, London: Methuen, 1932, 239–241.

instruments; but any such cruelty for sport cannot be justified. A master who turns out his ass or his dog because the animal can no longer earn its keep manifests a small mind. The Greeks' ideas in this respect were highminded, as can be seen from the fable of the ass and the bell of ingratitude. Our duties towards animals, then, are indirect duties towards mankind.

DISCUSSION QUESTIONS

1. Peter Singer believes that animals have rights, whereas Kant does not. Compare and contrast their views.
2. Both Singer and Kant come to similar conclusions about the ethical treatment of animals, but from two different sets of arguments. Whose argument is stronger, and why?
3. How would Bonnie Steinbock respond to Kant's claim that we have indirect duties toward animals? Do you agree with her? Explain.
4. Why doesn't Kant believe that we have a direct moral duty to be kind to animals? Evaluate his argument.
5. Kant uses a form of deontological argument to argue for the ethical treatment of animals. Can you construct a counterargument? Can you root it in the deontological moral tradition?
6. Does Kant believe that all animals are equal? Why or why not? How would Singer respond to Kant's argument?

MEDIA GALLERY

 ### "SHOOTING AN ELEPHANT"

By George Orwell

Essay summary: A British officer living in Burma is subjected to numerous anti-European pranks. The officer is finally presented with an opportunity to win the natives' respect when an elephant escapes and ravages the town, doing considerable damage to homes and property and trampling one man to death. Due to the loss of human life, the officer feels obligated to kill the elephant although it has calmed down and no longer poses a threat to the town. Under the watchful eyes of the townspeople, the officer follows the elephant to the marshy land where he finds it eating. The elephant looks as peaceful as a grazing cow, and the officer is reluctant to shoot it. But the pressure from the townspeople intensifies until the officer feels he has no choice. He explains: "The sole thought in my mind was that if anything went wrong those two thousand Burmans would see me pursued, caught, trampled on and reduced to a grinning corpse like that Indian up the hill. And if that happened it was quite probable that some of them would laugh. That would never do. There was only one alternative. I shoved the cartridges into the magazine and lay down on the road to get a better aim." The officer shoots again and again until he runs out of bullets, but the elephant will not die. Finally, the officer can no longer stand to watch the elephant suffer and leaves. He is later told that the animal clung to life for another half hour before it finally died. The shooting of the elephant is the subject of much talk around the town. Although the officer was justified legally for his actions, he still had a profound sense of guilt for what he had done—even though his actions appeased the natives. The officer explains, "I often wondered whether any of the others grasped that I had done it solely to avoid looking a fool."

The English novelist, essayist, and critic George Orwell (1903–1950) was born in India. "Shooting an Elephant" is based on his experiences as an officer in the Indian Imperial Police in Burma (now Myanmar). His most famous novels are *Animal Farm*

(1945) and *Nineteen Eighty-Four* (1949). "Shooting an Elephant" was published along with a number of other essays in a book of the same title in 1950.

1. What seems to you to be the best explanation as to why the officer does not want to kill the elephant? What do you think about this explanation? Could an animal rights advocate use this explanation as part of a pro–animal rights argument? If so, how? If not, why not?
2. What seems to you to be the best explanation as to why the officer kills the elephant? What does this explanation imply about morality? Can you challenge it? If so, how?
3. What seems to be Orwell's general claim about the moral status of animals? Do you agree with it? How does it compare to the positions on animal rights presented in this chapter?
4. What role do cultural differences play in our beliefs about the moral status of animals? Should animal rights advocates account for these cultural differences regarding animals? Why or why not?

"THE LEGEND OF ST. JULIAN THE HOSPITALER"

By Gustave Flaubert

Story summary: It is prophesized at his birth that Julian will someday become a great conqueror and a great saint. He has a normal childhood until one day he discovers that he enjoys killing animals. A mouse that he saw in church angers him to the point that he decides to kill it. He sprinkles some cake crumbs on the floor in front of the mouse's hole, and when the mouse emerges, he strikes it with a stick and kills it. Soon he becomes obsessed with killing animals. For years, his only excitement and passion in life is to kill animals, big and small. Flaubert describes Julian as coming home at night "covered with blood and mud, and reeking with the odor of wild beasts. He became like them." Julian aspires to be transformed into an animal. One night, he hears a voice that tells him he will eventually kill his parents. Frightened, he decides to stop killing animals. Julian then becomes a great conqueror. One of the rewards he receives for one of his greatest victories is the hand in marriage of an extremely beautiful and loving woman. Soon, however, he becomes bored and depressed and resumes hunting animals again. Much to his surprise, he discovers that a strange force is rendering his shots impotent. Suddenly, mysteriously, all the animals he has ever hunted form a circle around him. Terrified, he rushes home to his wife. What he does not know is that while he was away hunting, his parents came to visit and his wife gave his parents their bed. When he enters his bedroom and sees two bodies in it instead of one, he mistakes them for his wife and a lover and kills them. This tragic act changes his life. He becomes a saint who devotes his life to looking after the poor and the sick, and he even embraces a leper to give him warmth.

Gustave Flaubert (1821–1880) was a French novelist best known for *Madame Bovary* (1857). It took him five years to write this novel, and he was brought to trial (and acquitted) for its account of adultery. "The Legend of St. Julian the Hospitaler" was published along with two other stories in a book called *Three Tales (Trois contes)* in 1877. While most hold *Madame Bovary* to be his masterpiece, some contend that it is *Three Tales*.

1. Immanuel Kant argued that animals are not autonomous and therefore not subject to the same moral law as humans. Nevertheless, we should not kill them because doing so would lead us to become coarse in our dealings with humans. Based on the story of Julian, do you think that Flaubert would agree with Kant's position? Why or why not?
2. What seems to be Flaubert's position on the morality of killing animals? Do you agree with it?

3. In what way do you think the fact that Julian loved to kill animals contributed to the killing of his parents? Do you believe that committing acts of violence against animals can lead to acts of violence against people? Explain.

 ## BLOOD OF THE BEASTS

(France, 1949) 22 minutes
Directed by George Franju

Film summary: Consumers do not often consider how the steak in their neighborhood supermarket got there. Many people have never visited a slaughterhouse or seen animals slaughtered for meat. George Franju's documentary on a slaughterhouse outside of Paris is a brutally honest depiction of domestic animals being killed and processed for human consumption. The emphasis is on the routine of the process and the way killing animals is part of the everyday life of the slaughterhouse workers.

Blood of the Beasts is widely regarded as a masterpiece that changed the way in which documentary films are made. The film has also changed people's views on the consumption of meat.

1. Some people have changed their views about the morality of killing animals for food after viewing this documentary. Consequently, Franju's documentary raises important issues about the role of our emotional responses in reaching conclusions about morality. How important is it to see how animals are slaughtered before reaching a conclusion on the morality of killing animals for food? How does this affect our position on animal rights? Should it affect our position? Explain.
2. One of the more disturbing aspects of the film is how Franju juxtaposes scenes of a peaceful Parisian suburb with unflinching scenes of violence in the slaughterhouse. Why do you think he does this? Does this unfairly affect your position on animal rights?
3. Do you think that a depiction of how animals are slaughtered should be considered an argument regarding morality? Why or why not? Would your opinion differ if the documentary were about the Holocaust? Or abortion? Or rape?

 ## ALL THE LITTLE ANIMALS

(USA, 1999) 1 hour 52 minutes
Directed by Jeremy Thomas

Film summary: Twenty-four-year-old Bobby (Christian Bale) returns from his mother's funeral to be confronted by his stepfather (Daniel Benzali) over the young man's inheritance. The greedy businessman threatens to exploit the mental trauma Bobby incurred in a childhood automobile accident if he does not sign over his mother's properties. In fear of his stepfather, Bobby runs away from his home in London and hitchhikes to Cornwall. Bobby meets Mr. Sommers (John Hurt), a solitary man who travels the countryside burying dead animals. Sympathetic to Mr. Sommers' dedication to and love of animals, Bobby joins him in his work. The two men become good friends and spend the summer burying badgers, freeing moths, and feeding mice. Bobby becomes stronger without the mental stress of his stepfather's demands. When he is recognized by vacationers on the beach at Cornwall, Bobby becomes anxious that his stepfather will seek him out. He confesses his past to Sommers, who suggests that they visit the stepfather and seek an agreement. But the stepfather assaults Sommers and drives Bobby and his dying friend back to Sommers' cabin in Cornwall. He orders Bobby to dig two graves in the yard. On his deathbed, Sommers encourages Bobby to trick and kill his stepfather. Bobby manages to wound his stepfather and then lure him to a mine shaft, where the man plunges to his death. Bobby returns to bury his dear friend and then leaves for the countryside to continue his work.

1. Mr. Sommers tells Bobby that most people find rabbits to be pleasing and rats detestful, but "both are living creatures of equal value in nature's scheme." Why do you think that most people differentiate between rabbits and rats in this way? What is the justification? Do you think that it is a good one? If we substitute rabbits and mice for people, do you still feel the same way about the justification? Explain.
2. When Mr. Sommers accepts Bobby as an assistant and a companion, he makes the young man promise never to kill any living thing. Yet Sommers himself has suffocated his wife and encourages Bobby to kill his stepfather. People, according to Sommers, are "of no value at all." What do you think about Sommers' position? Compare it to the view that we should not kill people but that it is sometimes justifiable to kill animals.
3. When Bobby asks Mr. Sommers why he continues his work burying animals, the older man replies, "because I believe that they are life. Life equal to ourselves and not in some lesser, less valuable form." Do you agree with Sommers? Why or why not? How might Peter Singer respond to Sommers' belief? Explain.
4. Bobby witnesses an accident in which a truck driver who was purposely attempting to run over an animal in the road is himself killed in the crash. Mr. Sommers prevents Bobby from helping the dying man. "You're supposed to help people when there's been an accident," Bobby insists. "You only help good people. He killed this rabbit," replies Sommers. Is it ever possible for humans to disentitle themselves from moral consideration? Should we only help good humans as Sommers suggests? Why or why not? Should the moral interests of animals ever override the moral interests of humans? If so, when? If not, why not?

   GORILLAS IN THE MIST

(USA, 1988) 2 hours 10 minutes
Directed by Michael Apted

Film summary: Sigourney Weaver stars in this biography of Dian Fossey, a young American naturalist who lives among the mountain gorillas of Central Africa. Fossey is unprepared for the rigors of her research and of life in the Congo. But through her own determination and with the help of her assistant, Sembagare (John Omitrah Mituwi), Fossey makes contact with the gorilla population and survives confrontations with the local Batwa tribesmen. After long hours of observation and mimicry, Fossey gains the gorillas' trust and makes significant discoveries about the elusive animals. Her close relationship with the gorillas allows Bob Campbell (Bryan Brown), a National Geographic photographer, to capture rare footage of her interacting with the animals. As poachers become more aggressive in their pursuit of the gorillas, Fossey takes increasingly extreme measures to prevent the loss of more animals. She publicly confronts foreign animal traders, pretends to be a witch, burns the homes of Batwa whom she suspects of killing gorillas, and stages a mock execution of a Batwa poacher. Fossey's unfailing commitment to the protection of the mountain gorilla population may have cost her her life. The circumstances surrounding her murder remain a mystery.

1. Fossey's deep commitment to the gorilla population is clear. The film also depicts her shooting a dying deer to end its suffering and giving orders not to kill a pet chicken in camp. Yet Fossey also uses bags and gloves made of leather. Do you think that her position is inconsistent? Should animal rights activists like Fossey not use animal products? How would you describe her position on animal rights? How does it compare with Peter Singer's?

2. Fossey is enraged by the traps set in the jungle by Batwa poachers, but Bob reminds her of the Batwa's circumstances. "You can't put all the blame on the Batwa," Bob explains. "They've been feeding their families like this for generations. If you're going to blame anyone, blame the doctor in Miami. He's the one that hires the bloke that hires the Batwa. The Batwa get to feed their kids, the middleman gets a silk shirt, and the doctor gets a gorilla hand ashtray for his coffee table and a great big gorilla head for his wall." Do you believe that the Batwa's actions are morally justifiable? Do you believe that the Miami doctor's actions are morally justifiable? Explain. Does it make a difference that the Batwa feed their families through these actions whereas the doctor gets a gorilla hand ashtray for his coffee table?

3. In a confrontation with Van Vacten (Constantin Alexandrov), a European animal trader, Fossey accuses him of having "murdered" her favorite gorilla, Digit. She buries Digit in a grave in the traditional Batwa style. In what sense is killing a gorilla different from killing a human? If guilty, should Van Vacten be punished in the same way as someone who murders a human?

4. Fossey's tactics to protect the gorillas become increasingly aggressive. She is accused by Sembagare of having shot at tourists near the camp. "They're not going to turn this mountain into a goddamn zoo," she responds. Many zoos are actively involved in protecting and breeding endangered species. They also provide a means to increase awareness about distant populations of wild animals. Why do you think that Fossey objects to zoos? How does it relate to her beliefs about the moral status of animals? Do you agree with her?

5. The film's final scene shows Sembagare placing a circle of stones around the adjacent graves of Fossey and Digit. In the Batwa tradition, this circle unites the souls in death. What do Sembagare's actions tell us about his beliefs regarding the status of humans and animals? How much are our beliefs about the status of animals revealed in the different practices to which we subject them? Give some examples to support your claim.

  NEVER CRY WOLF

(USA, 1983) 1 hour 45 minutes
Directed by Carroll Ballard

Film summary: Biologist Tyler (Charles Martin Smith) is sent to the Arctic Circle to study the wolf and caribou populations. When he is dropped off in the middle of a barren, frozen landscape by Rosie (Brian Dennehy), a local pilot, the scientist begins to think the expedition was a mistake. In desperation, Tyler follows Ootek (Zachary Ittimangnaq), an Inuit who feeds and cares for him until he gets his bearings. As the weather warms, Tyler builds a camp and begins to research the wolves in earnest. Ootek and his adopted son Mike (Samson Jorah) take part in the study, and the men become close friends. Tyler comes to understand the wolves' habits and behaviors, and he even participates in a caribou hunt as a member of the pack. He returns from the hunt to find that George and Angie, his favorite wolves, have been killed by hunters who had hired Rosie as a guide. Enraged, Tyler takes aim at Rosie's plane as it takes off over the mountains. Tyler returns to his camp to find Mike, who knew the location of the wolves' den and had led the hunters to the site. The scientist remarks that "in the end there were no simple answers. No heroes, no villains. Only silence."

Never Cry Wolf was based on the autobiographical book by Farley Mowatt.

1. Tyler remarks, "I envy the wolves for how they experience the world. Their senses reveal a whole universe that we could never really know." Some argue that the rights of all sentient creatures should be protected. Do you agree with this line of argumentation? Does the "kind" of sentience matter more than the mere existence of sentience?

2. Mike tells Tyler, "To me, wolves mean money. It's a way of making a living. One wolf pelt is about $350. I've got to feed my family, my children." How might Aldo Leopold respond to this as a justification for killing wolves?

3. Tyler remarks, "This place doesn't belong to men, it belongs to the wolves." Should animals have rights to territories? Argue for your position, and respond to possible objections.

4. When Tyler confronts Mike about the missing wolves, Mike replies, "It's a question of how you survive. Survival of the fittest." Is it appropriate to apply tenets of Charles Darwin's theory of evolution to this situation? What are the consequences of applying social Darwinism to moral situations?

5. One of the hunters whom Rosie brings to the area remarks that the beautiful country has "limitless possibilities." They make plans to bring tourists and to bottle the hot springs water, which "won't cost a cent." How might Aldo Leopold respond? Is there a cost in removing natural resources? How might William F. Baxter respond? Whose arguments do you prefer, and why?

6. Aldo Leopold's land ethic expanded the idea of community to include soil, water, plants, and animals. Describe the community in *Never Cry Wolf*. How are the individuals interrelated? How do they depend upon one another?

7. Tyler approaches the wolves and their environment as if he were learning the customs of a new culture. He gives English names to some of his favorite wolves. How do you think the process of naming affects Tyler's view of the wolves?

 ERIN BROCKOVICH

(USA, 2000) 2 hours 12 minutes
Directed by Steven Soderbergh

Film summary: Erin Brockovich (Julia Roberts) is a young divorced mother of three living in Southern California. Desperate for work, she convinces Ed Masry (Albert Finney) to give her a job filing papers at his small law firm. Erin stumbles across files linking property sales and medical bills. She investigates matters further and learns that a plant owned by Pacific Gas and Electric, a $28-billion corporation, is contaminating groundwater in the adjacent town of Hinkley, California. The plant's improper storage of water containing a toxic chemical is linked to medical problems, including miscarriages and cancers, in the surrounding community. Erin is compelled by the people whom she meets in Hinkley and chooses to devote herself to their cause while her boyfriend George (Aaron Eckhart) cares for her children. At work, she battles prejudices due to her frank demeanor, limited education, and revealing wardrobe, but she comes to gain the trust and affection of her employer. Erin and Ed work long hours to build a case with over 600 plaintiffs and eventually uncover evidence proving the parent corporation's knowledge of the plant's illegal practices.

The film *Erin Brockovich* was based on a true story. The $333-million settlement awarded to the plaintiffs in the case of *Hinkley v. Pacific Gas and Electric* was the largest in a direct-action lawsuit in U.S. history.

1. Karl Grossman argues that people of color have been the worst victims of environmental pollution for a long time. The case of Pacific Gas and Electric presented in the film *Erin Brockovich* suggests that in addition to "environmental racism" there might be something like "environmental classism." Might this film be used as evidence to extend the connection Grossman establishes between racism and environmental injustice to classism and environmental injustice? Do you believe that "environmental classism" exists to at least the same degree as environmental racism?

2. Karen J. Warren argues that there are important connections between the oppression of nature and the oppression of women. Does the film *Erin Brockovich* make a case for Warren's thesis?

3. When Erin first meets George, she makes assumptions about him based on his biker clothing and current unemployment. Why does Erin judge George by his appearance when she herself struggles to avoid stereotyping based on her limited education and revealing wardrobe? Should she treat other people as she wishes them to treat her? Or is she doing the right thing by making assumptions about George based on his appearance?

4. One of the mothers in Hinkley tells Erin that, when she took her children to the hospital because of nosebleeds, the physicians called county services because they assumed the children were being abused. Is this a case of oppression based on class? If the mother was wealthy, do you think that she would have been treated the same way? Explain.

5. As Erin begins to spend more time at work, George comes to resent her absence and asks her to quit her job. Erin refuses, explaining, "All I've ever done is bend my life around what men decide they need." Is Erin insensitive to George's needs and the needs of her children, or is she doing the right thing by pursuing the opportunity presented to her by the class action lawsuit?

UNIVERSAL DECLARATION OF THE RIGHTS OF ANIMALS

The Universal Declaration of the Rights of Animals was adopted by the International League of the Rights of Animals and the affiliated leagues in London in September 1977. The declaration was solemnly proclaimed in Paris in October 1978 at UNESCO headquarters. Further information about this declaration is available from Ligue Française des Droits de l'Animal.

1. All animals are born with an equal claim on life and the same rights to existence.

2. All animals are entitled to respect. Man as an animal species shall not arrogate to himself the right to exterminate or inhumanely exploit other species. It is his duty to use his knowledge for the welfare of animals. All animals have the right to the attention, care, and protection of man.

3. No animals shall be ill-treated or be subject to cruel acts. If an animal has to be killed, this must be instantaneous and without distress.

4. All wild animals have the right to liberty in their natural environment, whether land, air, or water, and should be allowed to procreate. Deprivation of freedom, even for educational purposes, is an infringement of this right.

5. Animals of species living traditionally in a human environment have the right to live and grow at the rhythm and under the conditions of life and freedom peculiar to their species. Any interference by man with this rhythm or these conditions for purposes of gain is infringement of this right.

6. All companion animals have the right to complete their natural life span. Abandonment of an animal is a cruel and degrading act.

7. All working animals are entitled to a reasonable limitation of the duration and intensity of their work, to necessary nourishment, and to rest.

8. Animal experimentation involving physical or psychological suffering is incompatible with the rights of animals, whether it be for scientific, medical, commercial, or any other form of research. Replacement methods must be used and developed.

9. Where animals are used in the food industry they shall be reared, transported, lairaged, and killed without the infliction of suffering.

10. No animal shall be exploited for the amusement of man. Exhibitions and spectacles involving animals are incompatible with their dignity.

11. Any act involving the wanton killing of the animals is biocide, that is, a crime against life.
12. Any act involving the mass killing of wild animals is genocide, that is, a crime against the species. Pollution or destruction of the natural environment leads to genocide.
13. Dead animals shall be treated with respect. Scenes of violence involving animals shall be banned from cinema and television, except for human education.
14. Representatives of movements that defend animal rights should have an effective voice at all levels of government. The rights of animals, like human rights, should enjoy the protection of law.

1. According to item 13, "Dead animals shall be treated with respect. Scenes of violence involving animals shall be banned from cinema and television, except for human education." Do you agree with this? Critically discuss this item with reference to the films *Blood of the Beasts* and *All the Little Animals,* as well as other films that involve animals and violence.
2. Give a Kantian response to item 2. How does your own view compare with that of Kant and item 2? Explain.
3. Consider item 10 and its implications for zoos and circuses. Does this item imply that zoos and circuses are impermissible? Do you agree? Discuss.
4. How might Aldo Leopold respond to item 4? Compare your own view with his.
5. Many animal welfare organizations euthanize cats and dogs that are unwanted and encourage us to spay and neuter our own pets. Are these practices consistent with the Universal Declaration of the Rights of Animals? Why or why not? Do you agree?
6. Imagine that you are Peter Singer and you have just read the Universal Declaration of the Rights of Animals. What is your response to it? Which items do you find agreeable? Which, if any, do you find objectionable? Explain.

SUPPLEMENTARY READINGS

ENVIRONMENTAL ETHICS

Armstrong, Susan, and Richard Botzler. *Environmental Ethics.* New York: McGraw-Hill, 1993.

Attenfield, Robin. *Environmental Philosophy.* Aldershot: Avebury, 1994.

Callicott, J. Baird. *Beyond the Land Ethic: More Essays in Environmental Philosophy.* Albany: State University of New York Press, 1999.

De Silva, Padmasiri. *Environmental Philosophy and Ethics in Buddhism.* New York: St. Martin's Press, 1998.

Elliot, Robert, and Arran Gare, eds. *Environmental Philosophy.* New York: University of Queensland Press, 1983.

Gore, Al. *Earth in the Balance.* New York: Houghton Mifflin, 1992.

Hargrove, Eugene. *The Foundations of Environmental Ethics.* Englewood Cliffs, NJ: Prentice-Hall, 1988.

Kinsley, David R. *Ecology and Religion: Ecological Spirituality in Cross-Cultural Perspective.* Englewood Cliffs, NJ: Prentice-Hall, 1995.

Leopold, Aldo. *A Sand County Almanac.* New York: Oxford University Press, 1949.

Marrietta, Don. *For People and the Planet.* Philadelphia: Temple University Press, 1995.

McCloskey, H. J. *Ecological Ethics and Politics.* Totowa, NJ: Rowman & Littlefield, 1983.

Norton, Bryan. *Toward Unity Among Environmentalists.* New York: Oxford University Press, 1991.

Norton, Bryan, et al., eds. *Ethics on the Ark: Zoos, Animal Welfare, and Wildlife Conservation.* Washington, DC: Smithsonian Institution Press, 1995.

Oelschlaeger, Max, ed. *Postmodern Environmental Ethics.* Albany: State University of New York Press, 1995.

Plumwood, Val. *Feminism and the Mastery of Nature.* London: Routledge, 1993.

Pojman, Louis. *Environmental Ethics: Theory and Practice,* 3rd ed. Belmont, CA: Wadsworth, 2000.

Shrader-Frechette, Kristin S. *Environmental Ethics.* Pacific Grove, CA: Boxwood Press, 1981.

Sterba, James P. *Earth Ethics.* New York: Harper & Row, 1987.

Taylor, Paul. *Respect for Nature: A Theory of Environmental Ethics.* Princeton, NJ: Princeton University Press, 1986.

Warren, Karen J., ed. *Ecological Feminism.* New York: Routledge, 1994.

Westra, Laura, and Peter S. Wenz. *Faces of Environmental Racism: Confronting Issues of Global and Justice.* Lanham, MD: Rowman & Littlefield, 1995.

ANIMAL RIGHTS

Bekoff, Marc, and Carron A. Meaney, eds. *Encyclopedia of Animal Rights and Animal Welfare.* Westport, CT: Greenwood Press, 1998.

Carruthers, Peter. *The Animals Issue.* Cambridge: Cambridge University Press, 1992.

Clark, Stephen S. *Animals and Their Moral Standing.* New York: Routledge, 1997.

Dizard, Jan E. *Going Wild: Hunting, Animal Rights, and the Contested Meaning of Nature.* Amherst: University of Massachusetts Press, 1994.

Dombrowski, D. *The Philosophy of Vegetarianism.* Amherst: University of Massachusetts Press, 1994.

Donovan, Josephine, and Carol J. Adams. *Beyond Animal Rights: A Feminist Caring Ethic for the Treatment of Animals.* New York: Continuum, 2000.

Feinberg, Joel. *Rights, Justice and the Bounds of Liberty.* Princeton, NJ: Princeton University Press, 1980.

Frey, R. G. *Interests and Rights: The Case Against Animals.* Oxford: Oxford University Press, 1980.

Harnack, Andrew. *Animal Rights: Opposing Viewpoints.* San Diego: Greenhaven Press, 1996.

Hurley, Jennifer A. *Animal Rights.* San Diego: Greenhaven Press, 1999.

Leahy, Michael P. T. *Against Liberation: Putting Animals in Perspective.* New York: Routledge, 1994.

Midgley, Mary. *Animals and Why They Matter.* Athens: University of Georgia Press, 1984.

Rachels, James. *Created from Animals.* Oxford: Oxford University Press, 1990.

Regan, Tom. *The Case for Animal Rights.* Berkeley: University of California Press, 1984.

Regan, Tom, and Peter Singer, eds. *Animal Rights and Human Obligations,* 2nd ed. Englewood Cliffs, NJ: Prentice-Hall, 1989.

Rollin, Bernard. *The Unheeded Cry: Animal Consciousness, Animal Pain and Science.* Ames: Iowa State University Press, 1998.

Rowlands, Mark. *Animal Rights: A Philosophical Defense.* New York: St. Martin's Press, 1998.

Sechzer, Jeri. *The Role of Animals in Biomedical Research.* New York: New York Academy of Sciences, 1983.

Singer, Peter. *Animal Liberation,* 2nd ed. New York: New York Review, 1990.

———. *Ethics into Action: Henry Spira and the Animal Rights Movement.* Lanham, MD: Rowman & Littlefield, 1998.

Steeves, H. Peter, ed. *Animal Others: On Ethics, Ontology and Animal Life.* Albany: State University of New York Press, 1999.

Varner, Gary. *In Nature's Interests?: Interests, Animal Rights and Environmental Ethics.* New York: Oxford University Press, 1998.

Warren, Mary Anne. *Moral Status: Obligations to Persons and Other Living Things.* Oxford: Clarendon Press, 1997.

Glossary

abolitionist: In capital punishment debates, one who argues for the end of capital punishment. See *retentionist*.

abortion: The termination of a pregnancy.

acquaintance rape: Forcing a person one knows to submit to sexual intercourse.

active euthanasia: The act or practice of causing death by administering a lethal and humane treatment such as a drug overdose. See *euthanasia*.

actus reas: A legal term for the alleged criminal act of which the defendant stands accused in a court of law.

act utilitarianism: The view that the rightness or wrongness of an action is decided on a case-by-case basis according to the utilitarian principle. Compare with *rule utilitarianism*.

ad hominem: An argument or statement attacking the character of an alleged authority, rather than his or her argument or qualifications.

adultery: Sexual intercourse between a married person and someone other than the lawful spouse.

affirmative action: Refers to policies directed toward increasing the employment and educational opportunities of individuals or groups that either were previously not represented proportional to their percentage in the general population or were simply denied access to these opportunities. Though affirmative action policies are directed toward disabled or disadvantaged persons in general, they have been in practice most commonly aimed at providing employment and educational opportunities for women and racial minorities.

a fortiori: For a still stronger reason.

agent: A person who is capable of deliberate action or is in the process of acting.

altruism: The view that we should give moral consideration to others for their own sake and not for a self-interested reason. Compare with *egoism*.

androcentrism: The view that everything should be interpreted or viewed in terms of male or masculine values and experience.

androgyny: Having a combination of masculine and feminine gender or sex-role characteristics.

anthropocentrism: The view that everything should be interpreted or viewed in terms of human values and experience. Compare with *biocentrism*.

apostasy: The total abandonment of one's principles.

a posteriori: Designates a kind of knowledge that can be gained only from experience. Compare with *a priori*.

applied ethics: The attempt to explain and justify positions on specific moral problems such as abortion or capital punishment. Also called *applied normative ethics*.

a priori: Designates a kind of knowledge that is arrived at independent of experience. Compare with *a posteriori*.

aretaic: Virtuous. Based on the Greek word *areté*, meaning "virtue" or "excellence."

assimilation: The process whereby a person becomes part of a dominant culture by replacing the characteristics of his or her own subdominant group with the (major) characteristics of the dominant group.

autonomy: The power to determine one's own course in life. The act of self-government or self-direction.

bestiality: Sexual relations between a human and a nonhuman.

bias: A particular tendency, preference, or inclination that inhibits impartiality or unprejudiced consideration of a question.

bigotry: Intolerant attachment to a particular creed, opinion, or practice.

biocentrism: The view that humans must see themselves and interpret their world as part of a larger whole that includes all forms of life including plants and animals. Compare with *anthropocentrism*.

biota: The animal and plant life of a region.

biotic: Of or pertaining to life or to living organisms.

bourgeois: Middle class.

bisexual: A person who is sexually attracted to members of both sexes.

capitalism: An economic system characterized by a free market and open competition, in which goods are produced for profit, labor is performed for wages, and the means of production and distribution are privately owned. See also *laissez-faire capitalism*.

capital punishment: The death penalty. Punishment for a crime by taking the offender's life.

Cartesian dualism: Refers to René Descartes' (1596–1650) theory that reality is composed of two different substances that are distinct from one another: *res extensa* (thinking thing or mind) and *res cogitans* (extended thing or body).

categorical imperative: An unconditional command. For Immanuel Kant (1724–1804), this unconditional command can be formulated or expressed in several different ways. One version states that "I am never to act unless I am acting on a maxim that I can will to become a universal law." Another says to "act as if the maxims you choose to follow always become universal laws of nature." And yet another says to act so as "to treat humanity always also as an end and never merely as a means." Compare with *hypothetical imperative*.

censorship: Prohibition of the dissemination of words or pictures.

ceterus paribus: Other things being equal. Many times used to indicate that a claim may be false under other conditions or that there may be exceptions.

civil rights movement: Started in the late 1950s in the United States, this movement aimed at legal enforcement of rights guaranteed to African-Americans as citizens under the U.S. Constitution. While other groups such as the National Association for the Advancement of Colored People (NAACP), which was founded in 1910, and the National Urban League, which was founded in 1911, strove for similar ends, by the late 1950s they had come to be viewed by many as too slow and unsuited to overcome White resistance to change in the South.

compensation: A benefit granted to those who have experienced some type of harm or disadvantage.

consequentialism: The view that the morality of actions should be located in their nonmoral consequences. Examples of consequentialist general normative theories presented in this book include egoism and utilitarianism. Also called *teleological*.

conservatism: Beliefs and practices that in cultural and political contexts imply a resistance to change.

contraceptive: Any special device or drug used to intentionally prevent the fertilization of an ovum.

cooptation: To make use of for one's own purposes.

covert racism: When race is used as a sufficient ground for treating people differently, but is done so secretly.

critical race theory: Examines the economic, political, and legal systems of a country from the perspective of the role they play in maintaining injustice based on race.

cruel and unusual punishment: In *Furman v. Georgia* (1972), Justice William Brennan stated that for a punishment not to be cruel and unusual it "must not by its severity be degrading to human dignity," must not have been "inflicted in a wholly arbitrary fashion," must not be "clearly and totally rejected by society," and must not be unnecessarily severe.

cultural diversity: A general phrase used to refer to the presence of differences based in class, race, ethnicity, gender, sex, and sexuality. These differences may be manifested in individuals, groups of people, or the products of people.

date rape: Rape that occurs on or after a date. Date rape consists only of a part of acquaintance rape in general. See *acquaintance rape*.

deep ecology: The view in environmental ethics that we have *prima facie* obligations toward ecosystems.

deontological: Moral theories which maintain that the rightness or wrongness of an action depends on factors other than consequences. Examples presented in this book include divine command theory and the categorical imperative. Also called *nonconsequentialist*. Compare with *teleology* and *consequentialism*.

descriptive morality: The factual investigation of moral behavior without any element of approval or disapproval. An example is research on the moral customs of distant societies conducted by anthropologists. Descriptive morality is a type of nonnormative ethics. Compare with *prescriptive morality*.

developmentalism: The view that affluent countries such as the United States have a moral obligation to assist less economically fortunate countries stricken by famine or other life-threatening situations.

discrimination: Actions or choices that favor one group as opposed to another, based on their race, sex, sexuality, and/or ethnicity.

distributive justice: An area of philosophical inquiry centered around questions concerning the just distribution of benefits and burdens at both the national and international levels.

divine command theory: The view that we should always do the will of God. According to divine command theory, an act is right if it is commanded by God and wrong if it is forbidden by God.

ecofeminism: A type of feminism that links the exploitation of the environment with the domination of women. Ecofeminists locate the roots of our need to destroy the environment in patriarchal concepts of reason and nature.

ecosystem: A living system that includes the organisms of a natural community together with their environment.

egalitarianism: The view that all humans are equal and should be treated equally in terms of rights, liberties, respect, opportunities, and so on.

egoism: The view that we should consider only ourselves and that any consideration of others should be based on self-interest. Compare with *altruism*. See also *ethical egoism* and *psychological egoism*.

emotivism: The view that moral judgments express the emotional or affective state of the person making the moral judgment.

empiricism: The view that knowledge has its origins in and derives all of its content from experience.

ends, kingdom of: According to Immanuel Kant (1724–1804), the unity of all rational people under a universal moral law.

environmental ethics: Investigates our moral relationship to the biological kingdom and the independent/ absolute value of things such as the preservation of species and the protection of the wilderness.

Environmental ethics often challenges the notion that morality is only relative to the needs and desires of humans.

environmental justice: The view that no group of people should bear a disproportionate share of the impacts of environmental hazards.

Epicureans: A school of philosophy founded in ancient Greece by Epicurus (341–270 B.C.). The early Epicureans were hedonists, regarding pleasure as the highest good.

epistemic: Pertaining to knowledge.

epistemology: The branch of philosophy that studies the origins and nature of knowledge. Epistemic claims are about the nature of knowledge.

erotica: Sexually explicit, but not obscene, pictures or descriptions that are sexually interesting. Feminists many times further qualify the definition, calling erotica sexually explicit material that depicts sexuality in a mutually empowering manner. Compare with *pornography*. See also *obscene*.

ethical egoism: A normative view about how people *ought* to act. The ethical egoist believes that we have no obligation to do anything except what is in our own self-interest, that whatever we do in our own self-interest, regardless of its effect on others, is morally justified. Compare with *psychological egoism*. See also *egoism*.

ethical relativism: Any view that denies the existence of a single universally applicable moral standard.

ethical subjectivism: The view that moral judgments are simply assertions of opinion on the part of the person making the moral judgment.

ethics: Either moral philosophy or both morality and moral philosophy. See also *morality* and *moral philosophy*.

ethnocentrism: The view that one's own racial or ethnic group is superior to other racial or ethnic groups.

eudaimonia: For Aristotle, this word simply means "happiness." From the Greek *eu*, meaning "happy or harmonious," and *daimon*, meaning "individual spirit."

eudaimonistic utilitarianism: Moral theory claiming that what is morally right is whatever produces the greatest amount of happiness. This view was held by John Stuart Mill (1806–1873). Compare with *hedonistic utilitarianism*.

eugenics: Refers to the science of "improving" humankind through selective breeding. Often divided into positive eugenics, which encourages the reproduction of "superior" human beings, and negative eugenics, which attempts to prevent the procreation of those with "undesirable traits" through methods such as sexual sterilization. The term was coined in 1883 by Francis Galton, Charles Darwin's cousin.

euthanasia: The act or practice of painlessly putting to death (or of intentionally not preventing the death of) those who suffer from terminal conditions. Some choose to drop the requirement of a "terminal condition" when defining euthanasia.

exogamic: Refers to rules relating to marriage. Centers principally around the notions that marriage within a group is prohibited and that one should marry outside of one's group. However, the range and scope of this group varies from culture to culture.

extrinsic racism: According to Kwame Anthony Appiah, the view that races are morally significant because they are contingently connected with morally relevant properties.

false generalization: Occurs when one either applies a generalization that is usually true to an exceptional case or uses insufficient evidence or an isolated example as the basis for a widely general conclusion. The latter is often called a "hasty generalization" and the former a "sweeping generalization."

family planning: The use of contraception to limit fertility.

felony: A major crime, as distinguished from a minor one or a misdemeanor. Felonies include robbery, burglary, felonious assault, and murder.

feminism: There are many different definitions of feminism, and consequently many different feminisms. However, broadly conceived, feminism is a set of ideas connected with a social movement that advocates changing the political and legal rights of women. Many feminists work to establish equal opportunities for women in all areas of life and to secure the right of women to determine for themselves the kinds of lives and interests they will pursue. See Karen J. Warren's "Feminism and Ecology" in Chapter 10 for an account of five different types of feminism: radical, transformative, classical Marxist, liberal, and socialist.

free speech: Term used to designate forms of speech or, more generally, expression that are legally protected. In the United States, for example, debate concerning the scope of free speech has ranged from hate speech to flag burning. The question has been whether and to what extent these forms of expression are legally permissible as forms of free speech protected by the U.S. Constitution.

gay: A male homosexual.

gender: Refers to the differences between men and women that are cultural or societal in origin. Masculine and feminine are gen- erally used to refer to distinctions made on the basis of gender. Also called *sex role*. See *sex*.

Golden Mean: Refers to the concept of moderation, harmony, or balance that is utilized in many moral theories including Aristotle's virtue theory. For Aristotle (384–322 B.C.), courage, for example, is presented as a virtue that is a mean between the extremes of rashness (an excess) and cowardice (a deficiency). Also found in Confucian ethics in the claim that the harmonious life is the one which avoids excesses and deficiencies and that wisdom is to be found in both high places and low places and in the older people and in younger people. The term itself was coined by the first-century-B.C. Latin poet Horace (*Odes* 2.10.5).

Golden Rule: "Do unto others as you would have them do unto you." Versions of this rule are central to most religions and moral theories. Immanuel Kant's categorical imperative attempts to make this rule obligatory to rational persons.

greatest happiness principle: The view that what is morally right is whatever produces the greatest happiness for the greatest number. Associated with Jeremy Bentham (1748–1832) but first formulated by the English philosopher Francis Hutcheson (1694–1746) in 1725 in *An Inquiry into the Origins of Our Ideas of Beauty and Virtue* (iii.8).

hate speech: Offensive speech that is intended to insult and harm others on account of their race, ethnicity, gender, or sexuality.

hedonism: The view that pleasure is the only intrinsic value and is the proper end of all morally right action.

hedonistic utilitarianism: Moral theory that what is morally right is whatever produces the greatest amount of pleasure. This view was held by Jeremy Bentham. Compare with *eudaimonistic utilitarianism*.

hegemony: The dominance of one group, state, class, or set of ideas over others.

heterosexuality: Sexual feeling for a person or persons of the opposite sex.

heuristic: Something that encourages someone to discover for him- or herself.

Hobbesist: Refers to the social and political philosophy of Thomas Hobbes (1588–1679), who proposed that the state of nature is a "war of every man against every man" and that "the life of man is nasty, solitary, brutish and short" (*Leviathan*, ch. 13). The way out of the situation is the appointment of a sovereign with absolute power. According to Hobbes, we trade personal freedom for personal safety. People can contract together in order to bring themselves from a state of nature to a state of society.

holism: The view that the whole should be emphasized over its parts.

homosexuality: Sexual feeling for a person or persons of the same sex.

human rights: Entitlements that belong to each person by nature or by virtue of being human. Sometimes also called *natural rights*.

hypothetical imperative: A conditional command—for example, "If you want a better grade on the exam, then you'll have to study." Compare with *categorical imperative*.

ideology: Any system of beliefs or ways of thought that provide an account of how the world should be based on moral assumptions, economic interests, and/or social and political beliefs.

illocutionary act: Refers to something that is implied over and above the utterance of the statement or the act. Compare with *perlocutionary act*.

imperative: A command. See *categorical imperative* and *hypothetical imperative*.

imperfect duties: For Immanuel Kant (1724–1804), actions whose maxims *could* become universal laws of nature, but it is impossible for us to *will* that their maxims should be universal laws of nature since such a will would be in conflict with itself. Compare with *perfect duties*.

individual morality: Concerns how individuals should act in particular situations.

institutional racism: Formal practices and traditions in social organizations, or customs, that harm some racial groups or deny them the same opportunities as other racial groups.

instrumental value: Something that is valued as a means to some other end. Compare with *intrinsic value*.

intrinsic racism: According to Kwame Anthony Appiah, the view that races are morally significant because they are intrinsically morally significant.

intrinsic value: Something that is valuable in itself. Compare with *instrumental value*.

intuitionism: The view that moral values are intuitively apprehended or given. Also called *ethical intuitionism*.

involuntary euthanasia: When a person, despite severe suffering and faced with the prospect of a painful end, expresses the desire *not* to die but is killed or allowed to die anyway.

ipso facto: By the fact itself.

jus taliones: The right of retaliation. See *lex taliones*.

laissez-faire capitalism: A capitalist economic system marked by non-interventionism by the government into the workings of the markets. See also *capitalism*. Compare with *statism*.

land ethic: An ethic that enlarges the moral community to include the land, namely, soils, waters, plants, and animals. A land ethic is noteworthy because it extends the range of our moral community well beyond the relation among individuals and between individuals and society.

legal moralism: The view that governments may prohibit immoral acts even if they do not harm or offend anyone.

legal paternalism: The view that governments may prohibit acts in which someone may harm her- or himself.

lesbian: A female homosexual.

lex taliones: The law of retaliation, according to which deserved punishment is neither more nor less than the harm done in a crime and ideally mirrors the crime. Its best-known formulation is found in the Bible: "life for life, eye for eye, tooth for tooth . . . wound for wound . . ." (*Exodus* 21:22–25). Also referred to as *jus taliones*.

liberalism: A political ideology centered upon individuals possessing rights against the government, including the rights of equality of respect, freedom of expression and action, and freedom from religious and ideological constraint. Liberalism contends that individuals have the right to be protected from being harmed by others and to own property. Also, according to liberalism, a degree of economic and social inequality is acceptable. The least advantaged individuals have some positive right to be provided with some of the basic necessities of life, so long as it does not interfere too greatly with structure of the underlying capitalist economy. The historical figure most closely associated with liberalism is John Stuart Mill (1806–1873).

libertarianism: Refers to the belief that individuals have a fundamental right to liberty, that is, to be left alone and not to have the products of their labor taken from them. Libertarians do not believe that we have a right to life in the positive sense that others have a duty to provide us with goods to help us to live or even live well. The state exists mainly to protect individuals from harming one another and to enforce contracts. Accordingly, government programs to assist those without adequate food, shelter, or health care are generally not supported by libertarians. Libertarians trace the roots of their ideas back to John Locke (1632–1704) rather than John Stuart Mill (1806–1873). Also called *classical liberalism*.

matriarchal: Ruled by women.

maxim: For Immanuel Kant (1724–1804), a subjective rule that an individual uses in making a decision.

mens rea: Criminal intent, or the knowledge that one's act is criminal before or while committing the act.

metaethics: Investigates the meaning of ethical terms such as "right" and "wrong," "good" and "bad," as well as the procedures by which ethical claims are verified.

metaphysics: The branch of philosophy that studies the nature of reality. Metaphysical claims are claims about the nature of reality.

metatheory: The assumptions presupposed by any group of assertions. These might involve the concepts implied in the vocabulary used in the assertions or the rules of inference that allow derivations among assertions.

misogyny: Hatred of women.

modus operandi: Manner of working.

moral absolutism: The view that moral principles are absolute and hold for all people at all times and in all situations.

moral development: Refers to the acquisition, formation, and growth of beliefs about right and wrong, good and evil.

moral isolationism: The view that people should not be morally concerned with persons outside of their immediate group.

morality: The particular practices, precepts, and customs of people and cultures.

moral philosophy: Theoretical or philosophical reflection on morality in itself.

moral relativism: The view that there are no absolute moral principles. What is morally the right thing to do and what is morally the wrong thing to do depend on the time and place in which people live.

moral skepticism (*or* **skepticism**): Either the act of doubting all moral claims until they are proven or the view that moral knowledge is not possible.

multiculturalism: The view that the perspectives of women, minorities, and members of non-Western cultures are as equally valuable and valid as the perspectives of men, Whites, and members of Western culture(s).

mutatis mutandis: After making the necessary changes.

natural law theory: Any view that attempts to link the nature of human beings (or even the universe) with morality and the law. It is especially associated with Thomas Aquinas (1224–1274), who distinguishes four interrelated types of law: divine, natural, law of nations, and civil. For Aquinas, divine law is made known to us through revelation and reason. What we can discern of divine law (*jus divinum*) through our reason he calls natural law (*jus naturale*), and both the law of nations (*jus gentium*) and civil law (*jus civile*) are derived from natural law.

necessary condition: If x is a necessary condition of y, then y cannot be the case if x is not the case. Alternately, if not x, then not y. For example, being a plane-closed figure is a necessary condition of something being a triangle. Or, being a Ford Escort is not a necessary condition for being a car; there are many cars that are not Ford Escorts. See also *sufficient condition*.

negative duties: Duties that call on us to refrain from doing things—for example, the duty to refrain from harming other people. Compare with *positive duties*.

neo-Malthusian: The view that it is better to not help the poor and to allow some extreme poverty and death now in order to avoid more extreme poverty and death later. Derived from the work of Thomas Malthus (1766–1834), who wrote in his *Essay on the Principle of Population* (1797–1826) that checks in the rate of population growth are desirable. Malthus said that food production could only be increased in an arithmetical ratio, whereas population increase was potentially greater, in a geometrical ratio. We now know that population growth, at least in the short run, does not necessarily outrun resources. Nevertheless, many still cling to Malthusian beliefs, contending that overpopulation is the cause of world hunger. Compare with *developmentalism*.

nonconsequentialism: The view that the morality of an action depends on factors other than consequences. Examples presented in this book of nonconsequen-tialist moral theories include divine command theory and the categorical imperative. Also called *deontological*. Compare with *consequentialism*.

nonmoral: Refers to issues that lie outside the sphere of moral concern.

nonnormative ethics: Consists of the scientific or descriptive study of ethics, and metaethics. Scientific or descriptive study involves the factual investigation of moral behavior and is called descriptive morality. See also *metaethics* and *descriptive morality*. Compare with *normative ethics*.

nonvoluntary euthanasia: Refers to when a patient is incapable of requesting or indicating a desire for death or of forming judgments in the matter. Standard cases of nonvoluntary euthanasia occur when patients, for example, are comatose or senile and have left no legal document like a living will in which they state their preferences regarding extraordinary medical treatment.

normative ethics: The branch of ethics that makes judgments about obligation and value. Unlike nonnormative ethics, which is only concerned with issues such as the meaning of the terminology of ethics or the descriptive study of ethics, normative ethics is concerned with what is actually right or wrong. Compare with *nonnormative ethics*.

objective: That which has a public nature independent of the individual and his or her judgments about it. Compare with *subjective*.

obscene: The U.S. Supreme Court held that a work is obscene when (1) the average person, applying contemporary community standards, would find that the work, taken as a whole, appeals to the prurient interest and; (2) the work depicts or describes, in a patently offensive way, sexual conduct that is specifically defined by law and; (3) the work, taken as a whole, lacks serious literary, artistic, political or scientific value. See *pornography*.

ontology: A subdivision of metaphysics concerned with the nature of being and existence. An ontological problem is a problem concerning the nature of being.

oppression: The act of keeping down or weighing heavily upon the minds and spirits of others by cruel or unjust use of power or authority.

ordinance: A local law; a law passed by a legislative body of a city or township or other local government; a statute.

overt racism: The explicit and deliberate use of race as a sufficient ground for treating people differently.

ovum: An egg; the female reproductive cell.

paradigm: A set of shared beliefs through which an area of reality is interpreted.

passive euthanasia: The act or practice of letting a patient die by withholding or withdrawing all extraordinary equipment that may prolong life. An example of extraordinary equipment would be a respirator, iron lung, or radiation treatment.

patriarchy: A social system in which men dominate in all important areas of life, usually associated with their roles as fathers and husbands but extending to public life as well.

perfect duties: For Immanuel Kant (1724–1804), actions whose maxims can neither consistently be conceived nor willed by us to be universal laws of nature. Compare with *imperfect duties*.

performative acts: Refers to any act that is done as a part of saying something and/or that follows from what is said. See also *speech acts*.

perlocutionary act: Refers to an act that has a specific effect upon feelings, thoughts, or behavior. Compare with *illocutionary act*.

personhood: The necessary and sufficient conditions for being a person.

poena forensis: A penalty or punishment connected with or pertaining to courts of law. Compare with *poena naturalis*.

poena naturalis: A penalty or punishment instinctively felt to be right or fair, though not prescribed by any enactment or formal compact. Compare with *poena forensis*.

polyandry: The practice of having more than one husband at one time.

polygamy: The practice of having two or more spouses at one time, especially wives.

pornography: Sexually explicit material that is obscene. Feminists often further qualify the definition, calling pornography sexually explicit material that is degrading to women. Compare with *erotica*. See also *obscene*.

positive checks: Used in population growth theory to indicate the ways in which population growth is indirectly controlled or contained. Famine, disease, and war are examples of positive checks. Compare with *preventative checks*. See also *neo-Malthusian*.

positive duties: Duties that call on us to do something—for example, the duty to help those in harm's way. Compare with *negative duties*.

preferential treatment: A type of affirmative action in which qualified non-Whites and women are preferred over White males to whom they are equal in qualifications.

prescriptive morality: The study of moral behavior that makes judgments about obligation and value. Thus, unlike descriptive morality, which is only concerned with describing moral behavior, prescriptive morality is concerned with what is right or wrong. Compare with *descriptive morality*. See *normative ethics*.

preventative checks: Used in population growth theory to indicate the ways in which population growth is directly controlled or contained. Examples of preventative checks include premarital chastity, celibacy, and late marriage. Compare with *positive checks*. See also *neo-Malthusian*.

prima facie: At first view or appearance or on first consideration. The term is used to suggest that, while an inference can be made that appears to be valid, a complete investigation has yet to be done.

psychological egoism: The view that all people are selfish in everything they do. According to the psychological egoist, the only motive from which anyone ever acts is self-interest. Compare with *ethical egoism*.

quota system: A method of affirmative action whereby specific numbers of women and/or racial minorities are required to be admitted or employed even if their qualifications do not fully merit it.

racial discrimination: Actions or choices in favor of one racial group over another.

racialism: According to Kwame Anthony Appiah, the view that "there are heritable characteristics, possessed by members of our species, that allow us to divide them into a small set of races, in such a way that all the members of these races share certain traits and tendencies with each other that they do not share with members of any other race."

racial prejudice: According to Kwame Anthony Appiah, a tendency to assent to false propositions about races and "to do so even in the face of evidence and argument that should appropriately lead to giving those propositions up."

racism: Refers to the inability or refusal to recognize the rights, needs, dignity, or value of people of particular races or geographical origins.

racist: A practice, action, or belief that promotes, creates, or takes unfair advantage of any irrelevant or impertinent differences between races.

rape: The crime of forcing a person to submit to sexual intercourse.

reductio ad absurdum: Disproof of a principle or proposition by showing that it leads to an absurdity when followed to its logical conclusion.

rehabilitation: A process whereby criminals are assisted in order to restore or establish in them a socially acceptable set of behaviors and/or moral standards.

retentionist: In capital punishment debates, one who argues for capital punishment. See *abolitionist*.

retributionist: The view that a lawbreaker deserves to be punished. Punishment serves to give the lawbreaker what he or she deserves.

revenge retributionist: The view that the mere fact that a person has violated a law is sufficient justification for punishing that person.

reverse discrimination: When a group that previously practiced discrimination itself becomes the object of discrimination.

rule utilitarianism: The view that the utilitarian principle should be used to judge moral rules by examining the effects on overall happiness of rules. Compare with *act utilitarianism*.

sadomasochism: Obtaining pleasure from inflicting physical or psychological pain on others (sadism) and/or from receiving physical or psychological pain from others (masochism).

self-determination: Actions that are brought about by individual persons, and not by external forces or conditions.

sentient: Having sense perception or the capacity to feel.

sex: Refers to the differences between men and women that are biological in origin. "Male" and "female" are generally used to refer to distinctions made on the basis of sex. Also short for "sexual intercourse." See *gender* and *sex role*.

sex discrimination: Actions or choices that favor members of one sex over the other.

sexism: A practice, action, or belief which promotes, creates, or constitutes or takes unfair advantage of any impertinent or irrelevant differences between the sexes.

sex role: Refers to the differences between men and women that are cultural or social in origin. "Masculine" and "feminine" are generally used to refer to distinctions made on the basis of sex role. Also called *gender*.

sexual harassment: Unwanted sexual attention that makes a person feel uncomfortable or causes problems in school, the workplace, or social settings.

sexuality discrimination: Actions or choices in favor of one type of sexuality, such as heterosexuality, as opposed to another, such as homosexuality.

sexual morality: Concerns principles of right conduct in matters of sexual acts. Primary questions are the following: What sexual acts are morally permissible? With whom are they permissible?

sexual privacy: Refers to the alleged right of persons to pursue consensual sex acts and exercise sexualities free from criminal persecution.

sine qua non: An indispensable condition.

social contract theory: The view that the right to govern and make law and the duty to obey government and law arise from a contract, compact, or agreement either among the members of a society or between the state and the members of a society. Social contract theorists have used the social contract as an explanation for society, government, or both. While the social contract itself is usually postulated as an unwritten agreement rather than an actual historical event or document, the state and the members of a society are expected to act as if there were a written agreement. Some of its major proponents were Thomas Hobbes (1588–1679), who claimed that moral principles and obligations among people do *not* exist before the social contract and are created by it (see *Hobbesist*); John Locke (1632–1704), who claimed that moral principles and obligations among people *do* exist before the creation of the social contract and that the social contract should be altered if it does not uphold these principles; and Jean-Jacques Rousseau (1712–1778) in *The Social Contract* (1762). While social contract theory was overshadowed in the eighteenth century by utilitarianism, John Rawls is credited with reintroducing it to contemporary thought. Rawls argues that a particular contract hypothetically will be chosen by contractors within society from what he calls the "original position." See John Rawls, "A Theory of Justice," in Chapter 9.

socialization: Induction of persons into a culture's values, rules, and ways of operating.

social morality: Refers to how society ought to deal with morally important social issues.

sodomy: Any contact between the genitals of one person and the mouth or anus of another. Traditionally, however, the word has been used primarily to refer to male homosexuals and bestialists.

species: A taxonomic group of like individuals.

speciesism: Discrimination based on species; the refusal to respect the lives, dignity, rights, or needs of species other than the human species. Analogous to *racism* and *sexism*.

speech acts: Refers to any of a number of things done and affected in the act of speaking, including, but not limited to, persuading, altering another's opinion, describing, informing, and expressing thoughts or feelings. Contemporary speech act theorists like John Searle have developed complete philosophies of language on the basis of speech (and performative) acts. See also *performative acts*.

statism: The control and planning of a nation's economy by a centralized government. Compare with *laissez-faire capitalism* and *capitalism*.

statutory: Declared by an established rule, law, or formal regulation to be such, and hence, legally punishable. For example, statutory rape is the crime of having sexual intercourse with a girl below the established, legal age of consent.

stereotype: A fixed, often derogatory, notion or conception of a person, idea, or group, held by a number of people, and allowing for no individuality or critical judgment.

stigmatization: To characterize or mark as undesirable.

Stoics: Refers to a school of philosophy founded in ancient Greece by Zeno of Citium (c. 336–264 B.C.). Stoic moral philosophy is associated with the view that we all should calmly accept our place in the scheme of things, striving to attain *apatheia*, a form of psychic detachment from mental and physical disturbances. The main Stoic virtues are reason, courage, justice, and self-discipline. The major Stoics include Cicero (106–43 B.C.), Seneca (c. 4 B.C.–A.D. 65), Epictetus (c. A.D. 50–138), and Marcus Aurelius (c. A.D. 121–180).

subjective: That which is relative to the knower's own individual experiences, or that which has no objective reference outside of the contents of consciousness. Compare with *objective*.

subordination: Being placed under the power or authority of another.

sufficient condition: If x is a sufficient condition of y, then y will be the case if x is the case. Alternately, if x, then y. For example, being a plane-closed figure with three sides or three interior angles is a sufficient condition of something being a triangle. Or, being a Ford Escort is a sufficient condition for being a car, but it is not a necessary condition. See also *necessary condition*.

summum bonum: The highest good. Compare with *summum malum*.

summum malum: The highest bad or evil. Compare with *summum bonum*.

supererogatory: An act that is morally good but beyond what is morally required—for example, giving all your money to charity.

tao: According to Confucianism, the ideal way of life, as well as teaching about that way of life. Literally means "the way" or "the road" in Chinese.

teleology: The study of phenomena exhibiting order, design, purpose, ends, goals, tendencies, direction, aims, and ways they are achieved in the process of development. From the Greek *telos*, meaning "end" or "purpose," and *logos*, meaning "the study of." Teleological ethics views the consequences of a moral act to determine the act's worth or correctness.

terminus ad quem: The end to which.

transformative feminism: According to Karen Warren, a feminism that makes explicit interconnections between all forms of oppression, has a place for the diversity of women's experiences, rejects patriarchal conceptual frameworks, rethinks what it is to be human, and makes a place for values traditionally underemphasized in moral theory such as care and friendship. As such, a transformative feminism will move beyond the leading versions of feminism, and will make an ecological feminist perspective central to feminist theory and practice. See also *feminism*.

unintentional racism: An action, practice, or belief that has the effect of either exploiting or asserting irrelevant differences between the races.

uterus: The womb; a hollow, muscular organ in females in which the ovum is deposited and the embryo and fetus are developed.

utilitarianism: The view that what is morally right is whatever produces the greatest amount of pleasure (hedonistic utilitarianism) or happiness (eudaimonistic utilitarianism). See also *rule utilitarianism* and *act utilitarianism*.

utility, principle of: The view that one ought to do that which brings about the greatest happiness (pleasure) to the greatest number of people or to the community as a whole. Also called the *pleasure principle*.

viability: In human gestation, the point at which the fetus has developed sufficiently within the uterus to be able to live and continue normal development outside the uterus.

via negativia: The negative way.

via positivia: The positive way.

victimization: An act in which a person or persons suffer from a destructive, injurious, or adverse action or agency.

virtue theory: The view that the moral life should be concerned with cultivating a virtuous character rather than following rules of action.

voluntary euthanasia: The conscious and clear request for euthanasia by a person who is severely suffering and faced with the prospect of a painful end.

Weltanschauung: A worldview.